THE EUROPA
INTERNATIONAL
FOUNDATION
DIRECTORY 2015

THE EUROPA INTERNATIONAL FOUNDATION DIRECTORY 2015

Routledge
Taylor & Francis Group

LONDON AND NEW YORK

Twenty-fourth edition published 2015

by Routledge

2 Park Square, Milton Park, Abingdon, OX14 4RN, United Kingdom

and by Routledge

711 Third Avenue, New York, NY 10017

Routledge is an imprint of the Taylor & Francis Group, an informa business

First published 1974

ISBN 978-1-85743-776-8

ISSN 1366-8048

Typeset in Century Schoolbook 9/10 (essays), 8½/9 (directory)
by AMA DataSet Limited, Preston

Europa Commissioning Editor: Cathy Hartley
Editorial Assistant: Eleanor Simmons

Printed and bound in the United States of America by
Edwards Brothers Malloy on sustainably sourced paper

Foreword

Since it was first published in 1974 as *The International Foundation Directory*, this book has undergone many revisions. Now in its 24th edition, *The Europa International Foundation Directory* includes, as well as some 2,550 directory entries, a section of introductory essays, a bibliography and comprehensive indexes, and aims to provide a thorough and up-to-date overview of grantmaking civil society worldwide.

The distinction between foundations, trusts and foundation-type organizations and other non-governmental organizations (NGOs) is, to some extent, unclear; thus, since its 10th edition, the Directory has formally included grantmaking and non-grantmaking NGOs and similar civil society organizations. Hence, the Directory includes not only foundations and trusts (private, operating, grantmaking and corporate), but also charities and other NGOs, some of which make grants to organizations and individuals, while others carry out their own programmes and projects.

To gain entry to the publication, an organization must be international, or, where operating on a purely national basis, must be important enough to have a widespread impact; it must have charitable or public benefit status; and must have significant funds available, or make significant charitable donations, or run its own projects of importance (however, the Editors have no predetermined figure to establish inclusion, as the importance of an organization's funds is relative, depending on the wealth of the country in which it is located). The Editors have excluded foundations established purely for the benefit of a particular named hospital or school; moreover, governmental bodies may only be included if they are independent of political control. Community foundations are included where they are a major source of funding, or offer support to organizations working internationally.

The Directory contains introductory essays, a directory section and three indexes. The introductory section features essays examining the growing importance of community foundations, proposals for the building of charitable foundations through privatization, and foundations in Europe. The directory section is organized by country or territory, with entries arranged alphabetically under the appropriate heading: Foundation Centres and Co-ordinating Bodies, or Foundations, Trusts and Non-Profit Organizations. A bibliography is followed by three indexes: a full index of organizations; an index by main activity (where organizations are listed under headings including conservation and the environment, education, medicine and health, and social welfare); and an index by geographical area of activity, allowing the reader to find organizations active in, for example, South America, Central America and the Caribbean, Central and South-Eastern Europe, or South Asia.

The Editors and publishers of *The Europa International Foundation Directory* are greatly indebted to the many people who advised and helped with its compilation, and offer their sincere thanks. They gratefully acknowledge the assistance of those foundations, trusts, NGOs and other non-profit organizations that updated their entries to ensure accuracy, and would like to thank the governmental bodies and other national and international institutions, foundation centres and co-ordinating bodies that have helped provide information on foundations and NGOs in all parts of the world.

June 2015

Contents

CONTENTS

Abbreviations

AB	Alberta	e-mail	electronic mail
AC	Companion of the Order of Australia	Emer.	Emeritus
ACT	Australian Capital Territory	Eng.	Engineer
Admin	Administration	etc.	et cetera
Admin.	Administrative, Administrator	EU	European Union
AG	Aktiengesellschaft (Joint Stock Company)	eV	eingetragener Verein
a.i.	ad interim	Exec.	Executive
AIDS	Acquired Immune Deficiency Syndrome	f.	founded
al.	aleja (alley, avenue, Spanish)	Fax	facsimile
Amb.	Ambassador	FL	Florida
Apdo	Apartado (apartment, Spanish)	fmrly	formerly
approx.	approximately	Fr	Father
Apt	Apartment	FYR	former Yugoslav republic
AR	Arkansas	GA	Georgia
Assoc.	associate	Gdns	Gardens
Asst	assistant	Gen.	General
Aug.	August	GmbH	Gesellschaft mit beschränkter Haftung
Av.	Avenida (avenue, Portuguese)	h.c.	honoris causa (honorary)
Avda	Avenida (avenue, Spanish)	HE	His (Her) Excellency
Ave	Avenue	HH	His (Her) Highness
AZ	Arizona	HI	Hawaii
BC	British Columbia	HIV	Human immunodeficiency virus
Bldg	Building	HM	His (Her) Majesty
Blvd	Boulevard	Hon.	Honourable; honorary
BP	Boîte Postale	HRH	His (Her) Royal Highness
Bte	Boîte (P.O. Box)	IA	Iowa
bul.	bulvar (boulevard, Turkish)	ICT	Information and communication technology
CA	California	i.e.	id est (that is to say)
Cad.	Caddesi (street, Turkish)	IL	Illinois
CEO	Chief Executive Officer	IN	Indiana
Chair.	Chairman/woman, Chairmen/women	Inc	Incorporated
CIS	Commonwealth of Independent States	incl.	including
cnr	corner	Ing.	Engineer (German, Spanish)
CO	Colorado	Int.	International
Co	Company, County	Ir	Engineer (Dutch)
Col	Colonel	Izq.	Izquierda (left, Spanish)
Col.	Colonia	Jan.	January
COO	Chief Operating Officer	Jr	Junior
Corpn	Corporation	km	kilometre
CP	Case (Casa) Postale	Lic.	Licenciado (Spanish)
Cres.	Crescent	Lt	Lieutenant
CT	Connecticut	Ltd	Limited
Ct	Court	m.	million
Cttee	Committee	MA	Massachusetts
DC	District of Columbia	Maj.	Major
DE	Delaware	Man.	Manager, Managing
Dec.	December	MB	Manitoba
Dept	Department	MBA	Master of Business Administration
DF	Distrito Federal	MD	Maryland
Dir(s)	Director(s)	Mgr	Monseigneur, Monsignor
DNA	deoxyribonucleic acid	MI	Michigan
Dott.	Dottore	MN	Minnesota
Dr	Doctor	MO	Missouri
Dr.	Drive	Mons.	Monsignor
Drs	Doctorandus	MP	Member of Parliament
ECOSOC	Economic and Social Council (United Nations)	MS	Mississippi
Ed.	Editor	n.a.	not available
Edif.	Edificio (building, Spanish)	Nat.	National
Eds	Editors	NC	North Carolina

NGO	non-governmental organization		Rt Rev.	Right Reverend
NH	New Hampshire		s/n	sin número (no number, Spanish)
NJ	New Jersey		SA	South Australia
No(.)	Numéro, Número, Number		Sec.	Secretary
Nov.	November		Sec.-Gen.	Secretary-General
NSW	New South Wales		Sept.	September
NV	Naamloze Vennootschap		Sok.	Sokak (street, Turkish)
NW	North West		Sq.	Square
NY	New York		Sr	Senior
Of.	Oficina (Spanish)		St	Saint, Street
OH	Ohio		Str.	Strasse (street, German)
ON	Ontario		Treas.	Treasurer
On.	Honourable (Italian)		TX	Texas
PA	Pennsylvania		u./út	utca (street, Hungarian)
per.	pereulok (lane, alley, Russian)		UK	United Kingdom (of Great Britain and Northern Ireland)
Pl.	Place			
PLC	Public Limited Company		ul.	ulitsa (street, Polish, Russian)
POB	Post Office Box		UN	United Nations
PR	Public Relations		UNESCO	United Nations Educational, Scientific and Cultural Organization
Preb.	Prebendal, Prebendary			
Pres(.)	President, Presidents		UNHCR	United Nations High Commissioner for Refugees
Prof.	Professor			
Pty	Proprietary		UNICEF	United Nations Children's Fund
QC	Québec		US (A)	United States (of America)
Qld	Queensland		USSR	Union of Soviet Socialist Republics
qq.v.	quae vide (see—plural)		UT	Utah
q.v.	quod vide (see)		VA	Virginia
Rd	Road		Vic	Victoria
Rep.	Representative		vul.	vulitsa (street, Ukrainian)
Retd	Retired		WA	Washington (state), Western Australia
Rev.	Reverend		WHO	World Health Organization
RI	Rhode Island		WI	Wisconsin
Rm	Room		YMCA	Young Men's Christian Association
Rt Hon.	Right Honourable			

International Telephone Codes

The following codes should be added to the relevant telephone and fax numbers listed in the Directory. The code and number must be preceded by the International Dialling Code of the country from which you are calling.

Albania	355	Latvia	371
Algeria	213	Lebanon	961
Angola	244	Lesotho	266
Anguilla	1 264	Liechtenstein	423
Argentina	54	Lithuania	370
Armenia	374	Luxembourg	352
Australia	61	Macedonia (fmr Yugoslav republic)	389
Austria	43	Malawi	265
Azerbaijan	994	Malaysia	60
Bahamas	1 242	Malta	356
Bangladesh	880	Mexico	52
Barbados	1 246	Moldova	373
Belarus	375	Monaco	377
Belgium	32	Mongolia	976
Benin	229	Montenegro	382
Bermuda	1 441	Morocco	212
Bolivia	591	Mozambique	258
Bosnia and Herzegovina	387	Namibia	264
Botswana	267	Nepal	977
Brazil	55	Netherlands	31
Bulgaria	359	New Zealand	64
Burkina Faso	226	Nicaragua	505
Cambodia	855	Nigeria	234
Canada	1	Norway	47
Chile	56	Pakistan	92
China (People's Republic)	86	Palestinian Territories	970 or 972
Colombia	57	Panama	507
Costa Rica	506	Paraguay	595
Croatia	385	Peru	51
Curaçao	599	Philippines	63
Cyprus	357	Poland	48
Czech Republic	420	Portugal	351
Denmark	45	Puerto Rico	1 787
Dominican Republic	1 809	Qatar	974
Ecuador	593	Romania	40
Egypt	20	Russian Federation	7
El Salvador	503	Saint Lucia	1 758
Estonia	372	San Marino	378
Ethiopia	251	Saudi Arabia	966
Finland	358	Senegal	221
France	33	Serbia	381
Gambia	220	Singapore	65
Georgia	995	Slovakia	421
Germany	49	Slovenia	386
Ghana	233	South Africa	27
Greece	30	Spain	34
Guatemala	502	Sri Lanka	94
Haiti	509	Sweden	46
Honduras	504	Switzerland	41
Hong Kong	852	Taiwan	886
Hungary	36	Tajikistan	992
Iceland	354	Tanzania	255
India	91	Thailand	66
Indonesia	62	Timor-Leste	670
Iran	98	Turkey	90
Ireland	353	Uganda	256
Israel	972	Ukraine	380
Italy	39	United Arab Emirates	971
Jamaica	1 876	United Kingdom	44
Japan	81	United States of America	1
Jordan	962	Uruguay	598
Kazakhstan	7	Uzbekistan	998
Kenya	254	Vatican City	39
Korea (Republic)	82	Venezuela	58
Kosovo	381	Viet Nam	84
Kuwait	965	Zambia	260
Kyrgyzstan	996	Zimbabwe	263

Currencies and Exchange Rates

(as at 31 December 2014 unless otherwise indicated)

Country	Unit	Value (1,000 units)		
		£ sterling	US $	Euro €
Albania	lek	5.560	8.678	7.148
Algeria	dinar (AD)	7.289	11.376	9.370
Angola	kwanza	6.229	9.722	8.007
Anguilla	Eastern Caribbean dollar (EC $)	237.295	370.370	305.058
Argentina	new peso	75.288	117.509	96.787
Armenia	dram	1.349	2.105	1.734
Australia	Australian dollar ($A)	525.500	820.200	675.562
Austria	euro (€)	777.870	1,214.100	1,000.000
Azerbaijan	new manat	816.799	1,274.860	1,050.045
Bahamas	Bahamas dollar	640.697	1,000.000	823.655
Bangladesh *(28 November 2014)*	taka	8.148	12.829	10.277
Barbados	Barbados dollar	320.349	500.000	411.828
Belarus	rouble	0.054	0.084	0.070
Belgium	euro (€)	777.870	1,214.100	1,000.000
Benin	CFA franc	1.186	1.851	1.524
Bermuda	Bermuda dollar (B$)	640.697	1,000.000	823.655
Bolivia	boliviano	92.720	144.718	119.198
Bosnia and Herzegovina	convertible marka	397.719	620.759	511.292
Botswana	pula	67.338	105.102	86.568
Brazil	real	241.263	376.563	310.158
Bulgaria	lev	398.344	621.736	512.096
Burkina Faso	CFA franc	1.186	1.851	1.524
Cambodia *(28 November 2014)*	riel	0.156	0.246	0.197
Canada	Canadian dollar (C $)	552.373	862.143	710.109
Chile	peso	1.055	1.646	1.356
China (People's Republic)	yuan	104.706	163.425	134.606
Colombia	peso	0.268	0.418	0.344
Costa Rica	colón	1.188	1.854	1.527
Croatia	kuna	101.664	158.677	130.695
Curaçao	guilder (NA Fl.)	357.931	558.659	460.143
Cyprus	euro (€)	777.870	1,214.100	1,000.000
Czech Republic	koruna	28.059	43.794	36.071
Denmark	krone	104.665	163.361	134.553
Dominican Republic	peso	14.434	22.529	18.556
Ecuador	US dollar ($)	640.697	1,000.000	823.655
Egypt *(28 November 2014)*	Egyptian pound	88.899	139.972	112.130
El Salvador	colón	73.223	114.286	94.132
Estonia	euro (€)	777.870	1,214.100	1,000.000
Ethiopia *(30 August 2013)*	birr	49.247	53.278	55.352
Finland	euro (€)	777.870	1,214.100	1,000.000
France	euro (€)	777.870	1,214.100	1,000.000
Gambia *(28 November 2014)*	dalasi	14.295	22.507	18.030
Georgia	lari	343.795	536.596	441.970
Germany	euro (€)	777.870	1,214.100	1,000.000
Ghana	Ghana cedi	200.212	312.490	257.384
Greece	euro (€)	777.870	1,214.100	1,000.000
Guatemala	quetzal	84.353	131.658	108.441
Haiti	gourde	13.705	21.391	17.619
Honduras *(28 November 2014)*	lempira	29.643	46.674	37.390
Hong Kong	Hong Kong dollar (HK $)	82.612	128.941	106.203
Hungary	forint	2.472	3.859	3.179
Iceland	króna	5.049	7.880	6.491
India	Indian rupee	10.117	15.790	13.005
Indonesia	rupiah	0.052	0.080	0.066
Iran	rial	0.024	0.037	0.030
Ireland	euro (€)	777.870	1,214.100	1,000.000
Israel	new shekel	164.746	257.136	211.791
Italy	euro (€)	777.870	1,214.100	1,000.000
Jamaica	Jamaican dollar (J $)	5.601	8.742	7.200
Japan	yen	5.311	8.289	6.827
Jordan	dinar (JD)	902.390	1,408.451	1,160.078
Kazakhstan	tenge	3.514	5.484	4.517

Country	Unit	Value (1,000 units)		
		£ sterling	US $	Euro €
Kenya	Kenya shilling	7.072	11.038	9.091
Korea (Republic)	won	0.583	0.910	0.749
Kosovo	euro (€)	777.870	1,214.100	1,000.000
Kuwait	dinar (KD)	2,188.173	3,415.301	2,813.031
Kyrgyzstan	som	10.880	16.982	13.987
Latvia	euro (€)	777.870	1,214.100	1,000.000
Lebanon	Lebanese pound	0.425	0.663	0.546
Lesotho	loti	55.323	86.349	71.122
Liechtenstein	Swiss franc	647.758	1,011.020	832.732
Lithuania	litas	225.701	352.274	289.620
Luxembourg	euro (€)	777.870	1,214.100	1,000.000
Macedonia (fmr Yugoslav republic) *(28 November 2014)*	new denar	12.851	20.233	16.209
Malawi *(28 November 2014)*	kwacha	1.275	2.007	1.608
Malaysia	ringgit	183.318	286.123	235.667
Malta	euro (€)	777.870	1,214.100	1,000.000
Mexico	peso	43.532	67.944	55.962
Moldova	leu	41.030	64.040	52.747
Monaco	euro (€)	777.870	1,214.100	1,000.000
Mongolia	tögrög (tugrik)	0.340	0.530	0.437
Montenegro	euro (€)	777.870	1,214.100	1,000.000
Morocco	dirham	70.854	110.589	91.087
Mozambique	metical	19.068	29.762	24.514
Namibia	Namibian dollar (N $)	55.323	86.349	71.122
Nepal	Nepalese rupee	6.317	9.860	8.121
Netherlands	euro (€)	777.870	1,214.100	1,000.000
New Zealand	New Zealand dollar ($NZ)	501.602	782.900	644.840
Nicaragua	gold córdoba	24.088	37.596	30.966
Nigeria	naira	3.825	5.970	4.917
Norway	krone	86.231	134.590	110.855
Pakistan	Pakistani rupee	6.378	9.954	8.199
Palestinian Territories	n.a.	n.a.	n.a.	n.a.
Panama	balboa	640.697	1,000.000	823.655
Paraguay	guaraní	0.138	0.216	0.178
Peru *(31 October 2014)*	new sol	213.878	342.290	273.307
Philippines	peso	14.360	22.413	18.461
Poland	new złoty	182.681	285.128	234.847
Portugal	euro (€)	777.870	1,214.100	1,000.000
Puerto Rico	US dollar ($)	640.697	1,000.000	823.655
Qatar	Qatari riyal	176.016	274.725	226.279
Romania	new leu	173.781	271.238	223.407
Russian Federation	new rouble	11.388	17.775	14.641
Saint Lucia	Eastern Caribbean dollar (EC $)	237.295	370.370	305.058
San Marino	euro (€)	777.870	1,214.100	1,000.000
Saudi Arabia	Saudi riyal	170.853	266.667	219.641
Senegal	CFA franc	1.186	1.851	1.524
Serbia	Serbian dinar	6.441	10.054	8.281
Singapore	Singapore dollar (S $)	484.899	756.830	623.367
Slovakia	euro (€)	777.870	1,214.100	1,000.000
Slovenia	euro (€)	777.870	1,214.100	1,000.000
South Africa	rand	55.323	86.349	71.122
Spain	euro (€)	777.870	1,214.100	1,000.000
Sri Lanka	Sri Lanka rupee	4.889	7.631	6.285
Sweden	krona	82.814	129.256	106.462
Switzerland	Swiss franc	647.758	1,011.020	832.732
Taiwan	New Taiwan dollar (NT $)	20.200	31.528	25.968
Tajikistan	somoni	120.706	188.398	155.175
Tanzania *(30 September 2014)*	Tanzanian shilling	0.378	0.612	0.487
Thailand	baht	19.437	30.337	24.987
Timor-Leste	US dollar ($)	640.697	1,000.000	823.655
Turkey	new Turkish lira	276.049	430.858	354.879
Uganda	new Uganda shilling	0.231	0.361	0.297
Ukraine	hryvnya	40.631	63.417	52.234
United Arab Emirates	UAE dirham (AED)	174.458	272.294	224.276
United Kingdom	pound sterling (£)	1,000.000	1,560.800	1,285.561
United States of America	US dollar ($)	640.697	1,000.000	823.655
Uruguay	peso uruguayo	26.330	41.096	33.849
Uzbekistan	som	0.265	0.414	0.341

Country	Unit	Value (1,000 units)		
		£ sterling	US $	Euro €
Vatican City	euro (€)	777.870	1,214.100	1,000.000
Venezuela	bolívar fuerte	102.022	159.236	131.155
Viet Nam *(31 October 2014)*	new dông	0.029	0.047	0.038
Zambia *(28 November 2014)*	kwacha	100.738	158.611	127.062
Zimbabwe *(31 December 2008)*	Zimbabwe dollar (Z.$)	0.000	0.000	0.000

PART ONE

Introductory Essays

The Growing Global Importance of Community Foundations[1]

ELEANOR WOODWARD SACKS

Introduction

Community foundations reached a major milestone in 2014 when the world's first community foundation, the Cleveland Foundation of Cleveland, Ohio, celebrated its 100th anniversary. Another significant achievement for community foundations globally occurred in 2014—the 20th anniversary of the first community foundation formed in a post-communist country, the Banská Bystrica Healthy City Community Foundation in Slovakia, which was established in 1994, just five years after the fall of communism.[2] Although not the first community foundation formed outside the USA, the first community foundation in Central and Eastern Europe marked the take-off point for community foundations globally. From small beginnings in Cleveland, community foundations have now spread around the world and are becoming a global movement that is having a significant impact in the communities that they serve.

In the USA, community foundations have demonstrated impressive growth in asset size and impact, especially in the last 25 years. The number of community foundations actively making grants in the USA in 2015 was nearing 800[3]—at least 16 have assets of over US $1,000m. and one, the Silicon Valley Community Foundation, has assets of over $6,000m. Of the largest 100 grantmaking foundations of any type, 16 are community foundations.[4] In many areas they are the largest local foundations. Even where they are not, their local focus means that they are frequently the foundations with the largest local impact. The size and impact of US community foundations will continue to grow given that they are the only type of US grantmaking foundations that are required by law to raise funds continually to show public support, which they do from individuals, families, corporations and even other foundations. This surge in growth has occurred because they have learned how to attract and utilize the resources of living donors, rather than relying primarily on deferred forms of giving, such as legacies and charitable remainder trusts.

Even though asset size is often used as shorthand for impact in the USA, and the largest community foundations receive the most press attention, the US community foundations vary greatly in size and operate in vastly different circumstances, from large wealthy areas, to declining industrial cities that have lost their manufacturing base, to rural areas with small and ageing populations. The largest community foundations, those with assets ranging from US $50m. to $6,000m., account for only 28% of the total number; 'adolescent' or post-emerging community foundations (from $10m. to $49m.) represent about 32% of the total; and emerging community foundations (those with less than $10m. in assets) represent 40%. This number does not take into account the many thousands of so-called affiliate funds, which are component funds of the primary organizations and function as mini community foundations for smaller geographical areas.

The number of community foundations has more than doubled in the USA since the early 1990s. Even with this exceptional rate of growth, today there are more community foundations outside the USA than within, and the numbers worldwide continue to expand. A survey of community foundations carried out for the Community Foundation Atlas, which went online in 2014, identifies 1,837 community foundations in 68 countries and on all continents except Antarctica. Some 74% of these foundations have been formed in the last 25 years.[5] What accounts for this rapid development?

What are Community Foundations?

Individuals around the world and throughout time have demonstrated a charitable nature. They give of themselves willingly to promote the well-being of others and the betterment of their communities. Most acts of generosity or charity are offered informally, neighbour to neighbour, in times of crisis or out of a sense of religious duty. The act of giving back to one's community—by volunteering time and talents or by giving goods or money is called community philanthropy.

While community philanthropy may be informal and immediate in nature, it can also take a more structured form. Individuals can create community philanthropy organizations that collect, manage and distribute charitable resources. A community philanthropy organization provides a sustainable, longer-term approach to meeting community needs.

Community foundations are one of the most readily identifiable forms of structured community philanthropy. They bridge and combine community philanthropy with foundation philanthropy. Community foundations share several basic characteristics. They:

- are foundations that raise money in their communities and build a permanent resource to create vital communities by encouraging and supporting the local non-profit infrastructure;
- cover a defined geographic region and serve the needs of all the citizens in their region, regardless of race, religion or ethnic origin;
- have a board of local citizens who are responsible for maintaining the organization, and for identifying and funding communities priorities;
- are non-partisan and non-political, even though they may take political stands when the good of the community is at stake;

- operate in an open and accessible manner that is designed to build trust, which they do by reporting back to the community on a regular basis.

What do Community Foundations Do?

Community foundations in the USA were originally formed as a way to capture excess wealth and redistribute it in the form of grants to support the operations and missions of local charitable organizations. However, from the very beginning it was clear that there were a variety of ways that community foundations could build and support the local charitable infrastructure beyond their primary functions of resource development and grantmaking. Well before the Cleveland Foundation had accumulated enough money to make grants, its founder, Frederick Harris Goff, developed an innovative community leadership strategy, based on surveying community needs, to bring the foundation to the attention of the public and to identify and help solve community problems. The broader public roles that community foundations play make them powerful resources for their communities.

Teach and promote philanthropy. One of the chief roles of community foundations is to teach individuals and the community at large about the values of philanthropy and taking personal responsibility for improving their local areas. This role crosses cultural and state boundaries. Community foundations helped revive a culture of giving in Russia and other parts of Central and Eastern Europe, where before the fall of communism, the state was expected to provide all the basic needs of its citizens. It was precisely because community foundations make grants based on 'democratic principles, community co-operation, and traditions of legal and above board management of charitable money' that they could bring about real change in Russia's giving environment.[6]

Worlds apart, in the so-called Silicon Valley in the US state of California, many young millionaires and billionaires in the technology industry have money to donate but do not know how to give: they need to find the causes they care about and establish priorities for their giving. For many years the Silicon Valley Community Foundation (SVCF) has served as a mentor to these young entrepreneurs. The attention-grabbing gifts in 2012 and 2013 to the SVCF, totalling US $1,500m., from Facebook founder Mark Zuckerberg and his wife, Dr Priscilla Chan, were followed in 2014 by a $500m. gift from the high-tech camera company GoPro founders, Nicholas and Jill Woodman.[7] These represent only the latest donations from a large group of high-tech entrepreneurs who are using the community foundation to learn about and test out their philanthropy. These two extremes illustrate the many ways that community foundations can be effective in promoting philanthropy. All community foundations promote philanthropy, but how they do so may not be as obvious or dramatic.

Act as intermediary organizations. Community foundations do not, in most cases, provide services directly to individuals or operate programmes in the community. However, there are a number of exceptions to this general rule. The first is the awarding of scholarship funds to provide individuals with educational opportunity. In some countries—such as Germany—it is traditional for foundations to be operational, i.e. German community foundations routinely design, raise funding specifically for, and run their own programmes. In other areas, especially where the charitable infrastructure is weak, community foundations may also operate programmes. Even in areas where the charitable infrastructure is strong, community foundations may design programmes and work with partners to tackle larger issues that existing non-profit organizations are not designed or equipped to handle on their own.

Community leadership. As experts on the local non-profit infrastructure and on community needs, community foundations are in a position to convene key local decision-makers—including non-profit leaders, local and state government officials, the business community, and representatives of other foundations and funders—to develop a co-ordinated programme that will have greater impact.

One example of community leadership is the Vital Signs programme developed by Community Foundations of Canada. Vital Signs is an annual community survey that collects data on 'significant social and economic trends and assigns grades in areas critical to quality of life … Vital Signs reports promote awareness of community issues and are used by communities for social planning, by citizens and philanthropists to identify community needs and strengths, and by community foundations to inform their grantmaking and leadership activities'.[8] This highly successful programme has been adopted by community foundations outside of Canada, including in the USA and the United Kingdom.

Promote community development. It is difficult to know what Cleveland would be like today if it did not have the Cleveland Foundation with its focus on community development. The city was badly affected by structural changes in the US economy, and lost much of its manufacturing and industrial base. This caused its population to decline, as local citizens left the city to find work. Cleveland was the fifth largest city in the USA in 1920. By the early 2010s its population was one-half of what it was then. One of the elements of the Foundation's redevelopment strategy was the restoration of Cleveland's centrally located PlayhouseSquare in the city's theatre district. An article in the *New York Times* in April 2014 noted that this cultural attraction is anchoring the redevelopment of the downtown area and has had a multiplier effect: new shops, restaurants and apartment buildings are being built to cater for arts patrons who like the convenience of living close to the theatres. The number of individuals living in central Cleveland has doubled in the last 15 years.[9]

Community foundations have been identified as a means to effect community development in resource-poor areas, especially in the Global South. Community foundations have the ability to marshal external resources to address community needs in ways that are managed and controlled by local leaders who, sensitive to the needs of their communities, set the development agenda.[10] The Dalia Association, a community foundation for Palestinians,[11] was started as a means to encourage local people to take control of their community development and break a culture of dependency on external funders and external agendas. Palestinians 'are the largest per capita recipients of international aid, but they have no control and very little influence over how those resources are used on their behalf'. Dalia's mission is to advocate for 'Palestinian rights to self-determination in development'. Community foundations can be a driving force for community development. However, to be successful, external funders must be willing to step back and allow local leaders to take charge in order to create effective and sustainable development.

Increase the accountability and operating standards of non-profits. As grantmakers, community foundations have a responsibility to see that their funds are well spent. Community foundations have been active in setting and raising the operating standards of the non-profit organizations that they fund. This was especially the case in Russia and Central and Eastern Europe after the fall of communism, where non-profit organizations were being created anew and needed to learn the basics, such as how to write grant proposals and how to operate in open and accountable ways.

The early history of US community foundations showed the same pattern. The Permanent Charity Fund (Boston)—now The Boston Foundation[12]—had to teach local non-profit organizations how to account for their grant and endowment funds and operate in transparent ways, before they would offer them grants.

Focus resources in times of disaster. On the same day that the World Trade Center in New York City and the Pentagon in Washington, DC, were attacked, the New York Community Trust (NYCT) created a partnership with the United Way of New York City to establish The September 11th Fund.[13] It made its first grants 11 days later. By the time the Fund closed at the end of 2004 it had distributed over US $525m. to individuals, to other non-profit organizations and to businesses to help them rebuild the devastated areas of Manhattan.

On 25 April 2015 an earthquake with a magnitude of 7.8 on the Richter scale struck Nepal, followed shortly afterwards by a second, 7.3-magnitude earthquake, causing massive destruction. Vast areas of Nepal, including the capital, Kathmandu, were devastated. The death toll reached over 8,000 and significant tremors continued to plague the region. Tewa—Nepal Women's Fund,[14] a local community philanthropy organization—mobilized volunteers and co-ordinated relief work. Tewa's grantee partners operate in 65 out of 75 districts in Nepal, including the districts that were hardest hit by the earthquakes. Tewa's mission focuses primarily on the needs of women, girls and children, but they are using their local knowledge and skills to help rebuild their communities and create a better future for all Nepalis. Tewa has been working with grass-roots groups across Nepal for the past 20 years and is unique in that it encourages Nepali citizens to support its work, building up a network of 3,000 local donors.

Social justice. Most community foundations are general purpose, that is, they support a broad range of charitable interests and efforts in their communities, from the environment, education and the arts to social and economic needs. Where situations warrant, and the board and staff decide to take on the role, community foundations will focus more purposefully on issues of social justice. The most prominent community foundation to adopt this approach is the Community Foundation for Northern Ireland (CFNI).[15] CFNI is a leader in social justice grantmaking and in efforts to bring peace to divided societies around the globe. CFNI was established in 1979 as the Northern Ireland Voluntary Trust, with an initial grant of £500,000 from the British Government and the mission of bridging the sectarian divide in Northern Ireland through its grantmaking. Even during the worst of the sectarian violence, it kept the lines of communication open between the two sides of the conflict. It has made a successful transition from being the recipient of development funds from governments, foundations and aid agencies to being an active and successful fund-raiser in Northern Ireland and abroad. It changed its name in 2002 in recognition of its expanded role.

Community foundations are not static. They grow and evolve to meet changing situations and needs, and as assets increase. What was appropriate at one stage of development may no longer be appropriate at another. The solutions and methods community foundations use to address these needs also change.

No matter where they are located, community foundations are a reflection of the communities in which they operate, and of their times. They are human institutions and as such are an expression of the values of their founders, their boards and their donors. Ideally, the problems that community foundations identify and address through their grantmaking and programmes reflect the most pressing needs in their local areas. However, the ability to address these issues may be limited by the resources available to the community foundation and the vision and daring of its board and staff.

Community foundations globally have structural elements in common and operate in open and accountable ways. They have a number of roles and strategies that they can draw on to address community needs. There is, however, no formula, no 'right' way to be a community foundation. Community foundations will develop an agenda that best suits the communities they serve. The most important attribute that all community foundations share is their commitment to involving local people in decisions about how to change their communities for the better.

How and Why Community Foundations Spread Around the World

The community foundation concept spread quickly to all regions of the USA, reaching as far west as the Pacific territory of Hawaii in only two years (1916). The concept soon went international, crossing the border into Canada. A Canadian banker, who had prospered in his adopted city of Winnipeg, sent a representative to Cleveland to learn from Goff about the Cleveland Foundation. His approach resulted in the first community foundation being formed outside the USA, the Winnipeg Foundation (1921). By the time the first survey of North American community foundations was published in 1931, only 17 years after the formation of the Cleveland Foundation, 74 community foundations had been established.[16]

The concept gained wide acceptance due to the power of the idea and a strong national promotional effort led first by Goff himself, and after 1920 by the first community foundation support organization, the Committee on Community Trusts, established in 1920 by the Trust Company Division of the American Bankers Association to promote the concept to its members and the public at large. Without these efforts the growth in North America would have happened slowly, if at all.

Support organizations have played a crucial role in spreading the community foundation concept. They provide a central repository of knowledge about community foundation issues and best practices, as well as training and networking opportunities, so that lessons learned can be shared quickly. They work regionally and nationally to provide a supportive legal and political environment for philanthropy and to address issues of public policy. Support organizations can take many forms. They may be member associations that are formally or informally structured.

International funders and governmental aid agencies can also act as support organizations. Beyond making grants to help start community foundations, international funders support conferences, provide study tours to show what existing community foundations can do, and support the formation of national member-led support organizations. One of the most important things that international funders provide is validation for the community foundation concept.

The Great Depression, followed by the Second World War and its aftermath, slowed the growth of community foundations worldwide. Community foundations only began to expand across the Atlantic in the 1970s and 1980s, taking root first in the United Kingdom. There was real doubt at the time whether this North American invention could be adapted to vastly different charitable traditions and giving cultures. There was no certainty that the concept would take hold in the UK of the 1970s, with its strong social welfare programmes and lingering concerns about private benevolence derived from Victorian-era philanthropy and its focus on forms of social control. The fact that community foundations were able to succeed in the UK gave local and international funders the confidence that this form of community philanthropy could be translated outside its original context. The Charities Aid Foundation played a crucial role in the UK helping to spread the concept, and partnered with the Charles Stewart Mott Foundation to fund an early endowment challenge grant programme that raised interest in local communities.

A number of factors came together in the period from the 1980s to the mid-2000s to focus attention on community foundations as an effective means to strengthen and build communities.

- The top-down grant programmes developed by international foundations and funders were all too often not producing beneficial change at the local level. In many cases they were creating demonstrable harm, as development funds were diverted into the pockets of local leaders and their families, never reaching those in need. Foundations and funders came to the conclusion that for real change to occur at the local level it must be designed and directed by local communities from the bottom up. The efficacy of the community-driven approach was a core belief of the Charles Stewart Mott Foundation, a long-time supporter of community foundation initiatives in the USA and globally. The logic and success of this approach led other foundations and funders to adopt community-based and community-driven philanthropy as an effective way to bring about positive change at the local level.

- The sudden collapse of communism in the early 1990s in Russia and Central and Eastern Europe presented international foundations, funders and governmental aid agencies with a challenge quickly to develop ways to integrate the post-communist countries into Western political and economic systems. After initially focusing on the creation of structures and training programmes to support newly-forming capitalist economies and democratic governments, funders turned their attention to building civil society and a charitable infrastructure that would soften the hard edges of capitalism, and promote democratic action and individual responsibility. Community foundations, with their focus on local leadership, local resource development and local decision-making were well suited to these tasks.

- After the fall of communism, community foundations were identified by international foundations and funders as a way to rebuild a culture of philanthropy and citizenship in Russia and Central and Eastern Europe. Then, as international support for the political and economic transition in these countries began winding down, support for community foundations became part of the funders' long-term exit strategy.

- In Western democracies with large-scale social welfare programmes, there was a sense that they could no longer afford to spend large portions of their gross domestic product on meeting the social needs of their citizens. National governments began to cut back or privatize social programmes and looked to private philanthropy to fill the gaps.

- The effects of globalization led to greater integration of economies transnationally, causing severe economic dislocation within some countries and territories. At the same time, political power and responsibility for social programmes were being devolved more and more to local authorities, but the resources available did not meet needs.

- The end of the Cold War removed much of the impetus for large-scale governmental foreign aid programmes designed to ensure the loyalty of allies in the rivalry between East and West. Foreign aid budgets were reduced drastically, leaving many poor nations hard-pressed to provide for the needs of their people, and looking to find new ways to build and sustain resources locally.

- Community foundations were also seen as a way to support emerging democracies in other parts of the world, including Sub-Saharan Africa, Asia, Latin America and the Caribbean.

The growth of community foundations has been widespread, but uneven. Community foundations have been most successful, and most easily formed, in countries where there is excess wealth to be tapped and strong traditions of philanthropy. Outside the USA, the largest number of community foundations identified in the Community Foundation Atlas have been formed in Germany (375), the UK (65) and Canada (190). These four countries account for over 78% of community foundations worldwide. As a general rule, countries that have inherited traditions of English law have also been more receptive to the community foundation concept: Australia (33), India (21), New Zealand (23), South Africa (14). Mexico, which shares a border with the USA and maintains strong ties with its North American neighbour, also has a strong community foundation movement (27).

The intensive effort to build and support community foundations in post-Communist countries and emerging democracies was funded by large international foundations, including the Charles Stewart Mott Foundation, the Ford Foundation and the multiple in-country foundations funded by George Soros. Governmental aid agencies, such as USAID, also joined the effort, as did the World Bank. As these countries progressed and community foundations were established, direct support by international foundations and funders was phased out as they moved on to new priority areas.

International funders are no longer directly supporting the development of community foundations, although in some countries local foundations and funders continue to do so. Only two major initiatives remain: the Global Fund for Community Foundations,[17] a legacy organization with a focus on making small grants to community foundations and community philanthropy organizations to effect social change, primarily in the Global South; and the Global Alliance for Community Philanthropy (GACP),[18] a 'multi-donor and multi-stakeholder collaborative engaged in a series of joint research and learning activities aimed at advancing the practice of community philanthropy and at influencing international development actors to better understand, support and promote community philanthropy's role in achieving more lasting development outcomes'. The GACP, a five-year initiative housed within the Global Fund, is supported by five funders: the Aga Khan Foundation USA, the Charles Stewart Mott Foundation, the Ford Foundation, the Rockefeller Brothers Fund and USAID.

Even though they have now moved on, the efforts by international foundations and funders to help develop community foundations were effective. The Community Foundation Atlas reports that there are in 2015 162 community foundations in Central and Eastern Europe. Especially strong are the community foundation movements in Poland (26), Ukraine (25), Bulgaria (13), Romania (12), Slovakia (12) and Latvia (9). Perhaps most remarkable are the 48 community foundations that are currently operating in Russia.[19] It took a sustained effort on the part of CAF-Russia's redoubtable director, Olga Alexeeva, to find the right mix of attributes in order to adapt the community foundation concept to the Russian context.

In Western Europe, Germany has the strongest and most successful community foundation movement, with some 375 community foundations. The German community foundation movement is home grown. Reinhold Mohn, the owner of the international media conglomerate Bertlesmann AG, was an admirer of American philanthropy, and put the resources of the Bertelsmann Foundation, which owned the company, towards supporting the growth of community foundations in Germany. He was responsible for establishing the first German community foundation in Gütersloh in 1996. Most community foundations in Germany are operational, that is, they raise money for and operate programmes. They are relatively small, town- or city-based, and are run completely by volunteers. Only a few are professionally staffed, cover an area as large as a German state, and focus on endowment-building.

Italy also has a large number of community foundations (26), in part because its local community banks are sponsoring them, having a strong tradition of serving their communities.

Community foundations have not been established in Scandinavia, nor for the most part in countries that continue to maintain strong social welfare programmes. In such places they have not found their philanthropic niche, and the social case for developing them is weak.

It is very difficult for community foundations to operate in countries that have authoritarian regimes with tight political and economic control. To be effective, community foundations must have the space to act independently of the state. The Community Foundation Atlas lists two community foundations in China. Private organized philanthropy in China is on the rise,[20] but it is still unclear how community foundations will develop in that country.

In Asia, in addition to India, significant numbers of community foundations have been formed in Thailand (9) and the Republic of Korea (South Korea—5). Few community foundations exist in other parts of East and South Asia. The oldest community foundation in Asia, the Osaka Community Foundation in Japan, is a project of the local chamber of commerce. It was established in 1991 with technical assistance from the Cleveland Foundation.

In Africa, with the exception of South Africa, the number of community foundations is small, but numbers are increasing. The Kenya Community Development Foundation, a national community foundation, has been especially successful in raising endowment funds to fund its grantmaking. It was established in 1997 by a group of local professionals with the assistance of the Aga Khan and Ford foundations.

It is interesting to note that in a number of countries women academics have championed the formation of community foundations. The two community foundations in Egypt, the Community Foundation for South Sinai and Waqfayet-al-Maadi Community Foundation (Cairo), were both started by women academics, as was the community foundation for Palestine, the Dalia Association, and one of the three community foundations in Brazil.

Given their long history and widespread acceptance, it is remarkable that community foundations are not better known or understood. Community foundations are the least studied form of philanthropy, a field as a whole in need of scholarly attention. As a result, both within the USA and around the globe, the reasons for their foundation, where they fit into the overall landscape of philanthropy, their structures and their purposes are not apparent to the majority of people, even those who have a special interest in philanthropy: international funders, individual and corporate donors and academic researchers. It is to be hoped that this dearth of research will soon change. In 2014, in celebration of the 100th anniversary of the establishment of the first community foundation, the Charles Stewart Mott Foundation endowed a chair in Community Foundation Studies, the first of its kind, at the Indiana University Lilly Family School of Philanthropy.

Challenges for the 21st Century: Becoming a Global Movement

Community foundations have always been willing to share their experiences in order to make the movement stronger as a whole. In countries that are in close proximity, such as in Central and Eastern Europe, community foundations regularly conduct study tours across borders to increase learning. Some countries, such as Canada and the USA, welcome international participants to their national meetings.

Even though a few US community foundations have participated in international exchanges with community foundations in Europe and Latin America, the USA, for the most part, has been inward looking. As a result, its size and ways of operating do not resonate with new and emerging community foundations. This insularity is now changing, brought about by several new developments and advances in technology that offer new means of communicating.

- The 100th anniversary celebrations, with their focus on celebrating all community foundations, not just the Cleveland Foundation, and the launch of the Community Foundation Atlas, made US community foundations more aware of their sister organizations around the globe. The Atlas gives all community foundations a way to learn about and interact with community foundations in other parts of the world.

- The philanthropic interests of donors towards US community foundations are no longer strictly local; they often cross borders, especially in areas with large immigrant populations or businesses with international scope. While US community foundations will continue to focus primarily on local needs and local issues, many donors want to make charitable contributions to address international concerns. They can do this from their donor-advised funds and the Community Foundation Atlas provides them with an easy means to identify community foundations around the globe with whom they can work.

- Presentations by representatives from community foundations outside the USA at plenary and other sessions at the Fall Conference for Community Foundations in Cleveland, Ohio, in October 2014, reached a wide audience. For the first time a large number of US community foundations realized how creative and inspirational their international colleagues are in meeting the needs of their communities, and that learning can go both ways.

In December 2004, 10 years after the formation of the community foundation in Banská Bystrica, the first international meeting of 175 community foundation practitioners from around the world took place in Berlin, Germany. Community Foundations: Symposium on a Global Movement created a lot of excitement as representatives from all regions of the world met face-to-face and learned how much they had in common. The meeting was, however, ahead of its time: there was no way to follow up and continue the global conversation, as the technological infrastructure was weak in many parts of the world. Some 10 years on, the technology and interest in creating a truly global movement have progressed to the point where it is now possible to maintain ongoing contact. A second international meeting of community foundations is planned for Mexico in 2016.

Notes

1. Eleanor Woodward Sacks is writing a book about the history of the US community foundation movement. For more information about the development of community foundations in the USA, see her essay in the 2014 edition of *The Europa International Foundation Directory*, pp. 11–17. This essay for the 2015 edition of the Directory draws not only on the research conducted for her book, but also on the first five Community Foundation Global Status Reports she researched and wrote on the global growth of community foundations (2000–08) published by Worldwide Initiatives for Grantmaker Support (WINGS), and the two subsequent reports (2010 and 2012), available at wingsweb.org. The Community Foundation Atlas contains the most current information on the location and activities of community foundations globally. It was launched in 2014 as part of the 100th anniversary celebrations of community foundations. It uses a somewhat expanded definition of community foundations that includes some community philanthropy organizations, preferring to err on the side of inclusion. Some of these organizations may develop into community foundations, while others may not. Deciding what is and what is not a community foundation is more of an art than a science. See: http://communityfoundationatlas.org

2. Strecansky, Boris, 'Community foundations in Central and Eastern Europe 20 years on'. *Alliance Magazine*, (1 December 2014). Available at www.alliancemagazine.org/article/community-foundations-in-central-and-eastern-europe-20-years-on..

3. In October 2014 785 US community foundations were identified in the Foundation Center's master foundation database, a number arrived at in consultation with Foundation Center personnel. For the analysis of US community foundations, the number 785 will be used, rather than the 808 identified in the Community Foundation Atlas, which uses an expanded definition of

community foundations to include some community philanthropy organizations.

4. The list of Top 100 US Foundations by Asset Size is as of 9 May 2015: www.foundationcenter.org/findfunders/topfunders/top100assets.html. Assets of the largest US community foundations were updated in May 2015 using information provided on community foundation websites. On the local impact of community foundations, see, for example: *Key Facts on Georgia Foundations*, New York: Foundation Center, 2013, p. 2. The Community Foundation for Greater Atlanta is the region's second largest foundation, but its largest local grantmaker.

5. Data from the Community Foundation Atlas, http://communityfoundationatlas.org, accessed 15 May 2015.

6. Alexeeva, Olga. 'Community foundations in a country without a community', in *Alliance Magazine* (1 September 1998). Available at: www.alliancemagazine.org/en/content/community-foundations-a-country-without-a-community.

7. The Zuckerberg-Chan gifts are already having a major impact in the San Francisco area. In February 2015 they made a US \$75m. grant from their SVCF donor-advised fund to support the expansion of the publicly-funded San Francisco General Hospital and Trauma Center, the city's only safety-net provider of hospital care and only trauma center. See www.prnewswire.com/news-releases/mark-zuckerberg-and-priscilla-chan-give-75-million-to-support-san-francisco-general-hospital-and-trauma-center-300032048.html.

8. For more information on Vital Signs, see the Community Foundations of Canada website: www.cfc-fcc.ca/programs/vital-signs.html.

9. Piepenburg, Erik. 'Cleveland's Thriving Theater Hub Lures Residents', *New York Times*, 2 April 2014, p. B6.

10. Hodgson, Jenny. 'Tracking the growth of organized community philanthropy: Is it the missing piece in community development' in 2013 State of Civil Society Report, *Civicus*, ch. 24, pp. 237–243. Hodgson, Jenny, Barry Knight and Alison Mathie. 'The New Generation of Community Foundations', Global Fund for Community Foundations and Coady International Institute, March 2012. Knight, Barry and Andrew Milner. 'What does community philanthropy look like?' in *Case Studies on Community Philanthropy*, Vol. 1. Centris, 2014. These articles are available on the Global Fund for Community Foundations website: www.globalfundcommunityfoundations.org.

11. Dalia Association, www.dalia.ps.

12. The Boston Foundation: www.tbf.org.

13. More information about The September 11th Fund, including the Final Report, can be found on the NYCT. website: www.nycommunitytrust.org/AboutTheTrust/OurHistoryAwards/TheSeptember11thFund/tabid/622/Default.aspx.

14. See: www.tewa.org.np/site/index.php.

15. Community Foundation for Northern Ireland: www.communityfoundationni.org.

16. *Community Trusts in the United States and Canada*, Table VI, p. 20. Trust Company Division, American Bankers Association, New York, 1931.

17. www.globalfundcommunityfoundations.org.

18. www.globalfundcommunityfoundations.org/about-the-gacp.

19. Alexeeva, Olga, 'Community foundations in a country without a community'; Avrorina, L. 'Local Philanthropy of Federal Importance: community foundations in Russia,' CAF Russia, 2014. Available on the GFCF website: www.globalfundcommunityfoundations.org/information/local-philanthropy-of-federal-importance-community-foundatio.html. Olga Alexeeva died unexpectedly in London in July 2011. She had recently established the Philanthropy Bridge Foundation to teach Russian oligarchs and other newly rich individuals the importance of philanthropy. The Olga Aleexeva Memorial Prize awarded annually is for 'an individual who has demonstrated remarkable leadership, creativity and results in developing philanthropy for progressive social change in an emerging market country or countries'.

20. 'New Charitable Trust in China May Signal a New Era of Philanthropy', *Chronicle of Philanthropy* (25 April 2014). Available at: philanthropy.com/article/New-Charitable-Trust-in-China/222339.

Eleanor Woodward Sacks is a Visiting Scholar at the Indiana University Lilly Family School of Philanthropy, and is researching the history of US community foundations. She is a historian whose academic training focused on late 19th-century US business history. She has been active in the community foundation field for over 20 years as a practitioner, consultant and researcher, working at the local, national and international levels. Previously, she studied the growth of community foundations around the world and authored the first five *Community Foundation Global Status Reports* (2000–08) for Worldwide Initiatives for Grantmaker Support (WINGS). Eleanor Sacks' publications include: 'The Growing Importance of Community Foundations', in *The Europa International Foundation Directory 2014,* Routledge, Abingdon, UK, 2014 (this essay was adapted for use in the USA and published by the Indiana University Lilly Family School of Philanthropy. Available at: www.philanthropy.iupui.edu/research-by-category/the-growing-importance-of-community-foundations); 'Goff on the National Stage', an essay written for publication on the Cleveland Foundation's 100th anniversary website, available at www.issuu.com/clevelandfoundation/docs/cleveland-foundation-2013-goff-on-t; 'Frederick Harris Goff', in *International Encyclopedia of Civil Society*, edited by Helmut K. Anheier, Regina List and Stefan Toepler (Springer Science Business Media, New York, 2009); 'An International Perspective on the History, Development and Characteristics of Community Foundations', the opening chapter in *Building Philanthropic and Social Capital: The work of community foundations*, 2nd edition (Verlag Bertelsmann Stiftung, Gütersloh, 2008); and 'Frederick Harris Goff, Rockefeller Philanthropy and the Early History of U.S. Community Foundations', Rockefeller Archive Center (RAC) research report: 2009 (available at: www.rockarch.org/publications/resrep/sacks.pdf).

Philanthropication through Privatization: A Promising New Option for Building Charitable Foundations*

LESTER M. SALAMON

Introduction

On 30 July 1990 the Italian Parliament passed a law with monumental implications for the country's economic development and social progress. In one deft stroke, Italian lawmakers set in motion two remarkable developments that would make ancient practitioners of alchemy envious: first, the transformation of Italy's somewhat shaky banking system into a financial powerhouse whose tentacles now stretch into the farthest reaches of Europe; and second, the even more remarkable transformation of a charitable sector that lagged badly behind its European counterparts into the most well-endowed, well-heeled and generous such sector on a per head basis in all of Europe, and nearly the entire world.

To be sure, the legislators who passed this momentous piece of legislation may not have fully understood what they were setting in motion. For Law No. 218 of 1990, the Amato-Carli law, was a fairly arcane piece of legislation. Its stated purpose was to comply with European Union strictures to modernize a banking system dominated by two sets of institutions: first, a handful of public-law banks, some with origins stretching back to the 15th-century Franciscan tradition of pawnshop institutions;[1] and second, a network of 84 relatively small, regional savings banks, many with origins in the late 18th- and early 19th-century efforts to encourage habits of thrift among low- and middle-income people as exemplified by the Ersparniskasse created in 1778 in Hamburg, Germany, and the 1810 'trustee savings bank' first established in Dumfriesshire, Scotland, by minister Henry Duncan and later spread through Great Britain and the British Empire.

During the 1930s, however, both types of institutions had been swept up in the waves of nationalizations and government control unleashed by the Mussolini era and subsequent governments so that, by the 1980s, they found themselves caught in a difficult legal no-man's land—functioning partly as banks and partly as charitable institutions—and with their status a confusing mixture of public and private.

Under pressure to transform these institutions into regular joint-stock companies capable of raising capital in the international money markets, the Italian Parliament chose a novel course. First, it established powerful incentives for this collection of public-law and savings banks to transfer their banking functions to separate joint-stock companies. But instead of terminating the old savings banks and allowing outsiders to gain control of the new joint-stock banks, it left ownership of the new entities in the old institutions, which were still in possession of their traditional subsidiary charitable activities but were now the owners of 100% of a new set of joint-stock banking companies.

The rest, as they say, is history. The old banks, now awkwardly renamed 'conferring entities', began operating fundamentally as charitable foundations, but foundations in control of local banks. In this latter function, they proved—in most cases—to be very good stewards of their new joint-stock banking offspring. In rapid order, many of them agreed to merge these offspring in order to achieve necessary efficiencies. Thus, 13 of them came together to form what ultimately became Unicredit, now one of the largest European banking groups. Nineteen other of these new 'foundations of banking origin' (formerly 'conferring entities') decided to sell their newly formed, for-profit banks to existing for-profit banking companies. Thus, for example, the Fondazione Cariplo (Cariplo Foundation), the conferring entity that resulted from the transformation of the Cassa di Risparmio delle Provincie Lombarde into a for-profit bank, sold the resulting bank to Banco Ambrosiano Veneto, an existing, for-profit bank, for cash and stock. In the process it became the single largest owner of the resulting merged institution, renamed Banca Intesa. Later, the Compagnia di San Paolo, the conferring entity emerging from the transformation of one of the privatized public banks, the Istituto Bancario San Paolo di Torino, followed a similar course, selling its bank into the same Banca Intesa group, forming, along with some additional acquisitions, the Intesa Sanpaolo SpA, now the largest banking group in Italy and a major player on the European financial stage.[2]

Through these mergers and resulting efficiencies, the new bank offspring more than repaid their old savings-bank parents, increasing the value of their shares and also generating sizeable dividends. Along the way, a series of laws and regulations began to cut the umbilical cords linking the new banks to the old conferring entities—first, by banning the joint appointment of members to the boards of both entities; and second, by encouraging the conferring entities to divest themselves of their ownership positions in the new banks by selling portions of their bank stock and diversifying their holdings. Finally, on 23 December 1998 the Italian Parliament passed a further law, the Ciampi law, which completed the transformation of the conferring entities into full-fledged, endowed, private foundations, separated from their banks (except as minority shareholders), and fully empowered to act on their own authority to pursue public-benefit and economic development objectives with their much enhanced assets and earnings.[3] Thus was completed one of the most dramatic instances of a process I have termed 'Philanthropication

10

thru Privatization', or PtP—the creation of significant endowed charitable foundations out of the proceeds of the privatization of state-owned, or state-controlled, assets.

Ten years on from the passage of the Amato-Carli Law, therefore, Italy found itself not only with a substantially modernized private banking system, but also with a strong, new, private foundation community created almost magically out of a process of privatization, and pumping €1,700m. a year (US $2,200m.) into charitable endeavours. By 2010 these 'foundations of banking origin' (FBOs) boasted assets topping €50,000m. ($65,000m.). Even more amazingly, a number have taken their place among the largest such institutions in the world. Thus, the Cariplo Foundation, created out of the transformation of the Lombardy region savings bank, held assets in 2012, even after the 2008 financial crash, of $9,800m., putting its endowment on a par with that of the Ford Foundation, the second largest foundation in the USA. Compagnia di San Paolo, with assets of $8,600m. in 2011, ranks with the third and fourth largest foundations of the USA. The Rockefeller Foundation, one of the best known of the US institutions, is only one-third the size of these two new Italian institutions and lags behind two others—Fondazione Cassa di Risparmio di Torino (Fondazione CRT) and Fondazione Cassa di Risparmio di Verona Vicenza Belluno e Ancona (Fondazione Cariverona), each of which boasts assets well above the Rockefeller Foundation's $3,500m.[4]

Here, indeed, is an eye-opening model for the creation of charitable endowments in regions of the world that lack individual fortunes and the resulting charitable endowments that can grow out of them, but which have sizeable assets owned or controlled by government that are in the process of being privatized through any of a number of routes.

And with our eyes so opened, it becomes clear that the Italian experience does not stand alone. Indeed, what is most unusual about it is that it turns out to be not so unusual at all. To the contrary, even casual observation, informed by the Italian experience, reveals that this experience has counterparts in places far and wide—some of them virtual replicas of the transformation of the Italian savings banks and others more distant cousins, but with enough of a family resemblance to be recognizable as products of the same gene pool.

For example:

- In New Zealand in the 1980s a story virtually identical to that of the Italian foundations unfolded, with the transformation of another network of non-profit savings banks into stock companies and the vesting of ownership of the stock of the resulting banks in a network of 12 'community trusts', which now form the backbone of New Zealand's philanthropic community.
- Two decades earlier, in 1961, the German Government privatized the Volkswagen Company, sold 60% of the shares of the company to German citizens and dedicated the proceeds to a new foundation designed to promote German science. Called the VolkswagenStiftung (Volkswagen Foundation, though it has no relation to the Volkswagen Group), this foundation now boasts more than €2,500m. in assets and a long history of substantial grantmaking.[5]
- In the early 1990s, the Czech Republic set aside 1% of the shares of its sizeable privatization sales of major state-owned enterprises in a Czech Foundation Investment Fund, which ultimately distributed the resulting funds as endowments to 73 Czech foundations.
- In the late 1980s, the Koning Boudewijnstichting/Fondation Roi Baudouin (King Baudouin Foundation)

became the recipient of another type of 'privatization'—a contractually set stream of revenue generated by the Belgian National Lottery, an enterprise of the Belgian national Government.
- More recently, the conversion of a number of non-profit hospitals and health insurers in the USA into for-profit companies led almost overnight to the creation of nearly 200 so-called 'conversion foundations'.[6]
- More recently still, Austria's network of Sparkasse, or saving banks, was converted into stock companies in a pattern virtually identical to the developments in Italy and New Zealand, yielding the ERSTE Stiftung—Die ERSTE Österreichische SparCasse Privatstiftung (ERSTE Foundation) and more than 30 other foundations of banking origin in that country.

In short, it appears that, in a variety of circumstances, the privatization of state-owned or quasi-public assets has led to the establishment of often substantial charitable endowments. A kind of philanthropic alchemy has thus been under way in a significant number of areas through which the privatization of public or quasi-public assets has left behind not only a string of for-profit businesses, but also substantial deposits of charitable funding that has been used, in addition to other purposes, to help foster and support the civil society institutions without which democratic political systems and market-based economies cannot function.

Far from a mere historical curio, moreover, the PtP concept holds the promise of opening a new path to the creation of sizeable charitable endowments that offer win-win opportunities for communities, investors, governments and civil society institutions. If steps could be taken to channel into foundations even a small portion of the proceeds of the privatization transactions under way in developing and transition areas, not to mention in more developed countries where philanthropic assets are also frequently scarce, a fundamental transformation could be achieved in the philanthropic map of the world.

For example:

- If just 10% of the proceeds of Ukraine's sale of its Kryvorizhstal steel mill to Mittal Steel in 2005 could have been devoted to the strengthening of the country's embryonic community foundations or to the creation of a Ukrainian National Foundation, the result would have been €400m. (US $520m.) in charitable assets to help offset any ill effects of the privatization on workers and the surrounding communities, as well as creating a permanent source of resources to grow the country's nascent civil society sector.
- Similarly, if 10% of the sale in 2007 of 40% of the stock in Kenya's Safaricom mobile telephone network to the United Kingdom's Vodafone had been dedicated to buttressing the endowment of the Kenya Community Development Foundation, the result would have been a charitable institution with assets of over €50m. (US $65m.), 20 times larger than this institution's existing endowment. With just 5% of its assets, the resulting institution would be capable of generating €2.5m. in grants annually, more than five times larger than the €370,000 in grants that Vodafone currently contributes to the Safaricom Foundation.[7]
- If 10% of the US $5,500m. proceeds of the US Government's 2012 sale of a portion of its stake in the General Motors Corporation could have been reserved to finance a foundation dedicated to helping revitalize the city of Detroit, that city might be facing a far brighter future than it now does in the wake of its recent bankruptcy.

Such privatization deals are not just a thing of the past, moreover. Rumours about the death of privatization deserve the same reaction as the one that 19th-century American humourist Mark Twain offered upon reading news reports of his demise: 'The rumors of my death,' Twain told reporters, 'have been greatly exaggerated'. As it turns out, for better or worse, privatization remains very much alive and well across the globe. The two highest years of privatization transactions ever recorded, for example, occurred as recently as 2009 and 2010—and this using an extremely narrow definition of 'privatization'.[8] Furthermore, despite a partial cooling of such transactions as economic growth faltered in 2011, privatization activity picked up again in 2012, yielding the third highest year of privatization transactions in history,[9] and the latest reports suggest that no cooling has occurred more recently.

The PtP Project

To explore this phenomenon more systematically, I launched a 'Philanthropication thru Privatization' Project several years ago. With the aid of a network of 'discovery associates', we formulated a definition of the PtP concept, scoured the world to identify other examples of this phenomenon, conducted a series of case studies of PtP institutions, examined contemporary trends in privatization activity, and produced a report that was published by il Mulino, an Italian publishing company, entitled *Philanthropication thru Privatization: Building Permanent Endowments for the Common Good*.

This project has taken no position for or against privatization in its varied forms. Its one central concern has been to make sure that the interesting option of capturing in philanthropic endowments at least a portion of the proceeds of any privatization transactions that go forward is more seriously and explicitly considered whenever such transactions are under development. Underlying this concern is the conviction that the assets involved in privatization transactions are not ultimately 'the government's' assets, but 'the people's' assets, built up through the sweat, toil and resources of a country's citizens or belonging to the people as a birthright by virtue of their presence in the territory that they collectively occupy. A country's citizens, and particularly those living or working in close proximity to the assets in line for privatization, therefore deserve to receive some tangible benefit from any such transactions. For a variety of reasons, this can often best be achieved by vesting these proceeds into charitable endowments that can pursue a given objective over a long period instead of allowing them to be absorbed into state budgets. Properly done, this option has the advantage of usefully contributing to pluralism in the search for solutions to public problems; of bringing new resources and energies to the solution of public problems; and of helping to promote the independence and viability of civil society organizations, which have been found to be crucial for building the trust that is necessary for the operation of democratic governments and prosperous market economies. In the process, PtP can produce a new people-orientated form of privatization that overcomes what we will term the 'upside-down effects' of privatization—the tendency of privatization to impose significant early costs on the narrow groups of citizens directly affected by it while delivering whatever positive benefits it generates only over the long term and to widely dispersed populations.

With a new wave of privatization activity now under way, and efforts to generate charitable resources to support civil society and social purposes starved of funds, it is imperative that this option be better appreciated and understood. And that is precisely what the report summarized here seeks to accomplish.

Key Findings

More specifically, eight key findings have emerged from this investigation into the Philanthropication through Privatization phenomenon to date.

1. A Powerful New Concept

PtP is a powerful concept, providing a new analytical lens that brings into coherent view for the first time a long-overlooked but important set of transactions that hold the promise of changing the global philanthropic landscape and ushering in a new citizen-focused mode of privatization. More specifically, philanthropication can be defined as follows: 'Philanthropication involves the creation or expansion of a charitable or philanthropic endowment, a more or less permanent pool of assets dedicated to charitable or public-benefit purposes and under the control of a legal entity with a meaningful degree of autonomy from state authorities and from any for-profit company'. Thus, these transactions share three key features:

- an initial governmental or quasi-governmental asset;
- a process of divestiture that transfers ownership or control of all or a portion of this asset into one or more private charitable institutions; and
- a meaningfully autonomous private charitable institution that secures ownership or control of all or a portion of the proceeds of this transfer in the form of a permanent endowment or a quasi-permanent stream of resources that operates very much like an endowment.

PtP transactions vary considerably based on the type of initial assets involved. To date, five broad types of such transactions have been identified:[10]

- *Type I:* A *state-owned business* that is sold to an investor or transformed into a for-profit enterprise with the ownership of the assets or the proceeds of their sale transferred in whole or in part to a new or existing foundation (e.g., the sale of shares in the formerly state-owned Volkswagen auto and munitions firm and the transfer of 60% of the proceeds into the newly formed Volkswagen Foundation in Germany).
- *Type II:* Some *other publicly-owned asset*, such as a building, a cultural institution, or a public utility such as an airport, that is given to a non-profit foundation to manage (e.g., the conversion of Italy's public opera companies into foundations with rights in perpetuity to use their existing opera houses free of charge).
- *Type III:* A *stream of income resulting from government control of some asset that generates special-purpose income* that the government commits to share with a charitable foundation (e.g. the legal commitment of the Belgian National Lottery to devote a portion of its proceeds to the King Baudouin Foundation annually).
- *Type IV:* A *debt swap*, i.e. a foreign debt forgiveness transaction that requires the beneficiary government to place an equivalent amount of local currency into a charitable institution dedicated to some charitable or

public-benefit purpose (e.g. the German Government's forgiveness of repayment of the unpaid balance of a major loan it made to the Government of Poland on condition that Poland pay the equivalent amount in Polish currency into a Foundation for Polish-German Co-operation: Fundacja Współpracy Polsko-Niemieckiej/Stiftung für Deutsch-Polnische Zusammenarbeit).

- *Type V:* A *quasi-public or quasi-private organization*, i.e. a non-profit organization or mutual association that is converted into, or sold to, a for-profit firm with the assets resulting from the sale placed in whole or in part into a charitable endowment (e.g. the Italian bank conversions previously outlined).

2. An Enormous Engine of Social Wealth Creation

Once brought into focus with the help of the PtP concept, *Philanthropication thru Privatization* turns out to be far from just an abstract idea. It is already in operation. Indeed, some of the largest and most reputable foundations in the world—such as Germany's Volkswagen Foundation, Italy's foundations of banking origin, New Zealand's network of community trusts, Belgium's King Baudouin Foundation, and close to 200 health conversion foundations in the USA—have all resulted from, or been enlarged through, a PtP process.

More generally, our research has made clear that PtP is already an enormous engine of wealth creation. In particular, as detailed in Table 1:

- Close to 550 PtP foundations exist around the world, located in 22 countries, and holding nearly US $136,000m. in assets (€100,000m. at 2013 exchange rates).

TABLE 1 | Preliminary Tally of PtP Foundations, by Country

COUNTRY	FOUNDATIONS		ASSETS*	
	NUMBER	%	AMOUNT (US $ MILLIONS)	%
Austria	33	6.1%	$4,882.9	3.6%
Belgium	1	0.2%	$408.2	0.3%
Brazil	3	0.6%	$2,542.8	1.9%
Canada	1	0.2%	$53.0	0.0%
Czech Republic	74	13.6%	$413.5	0.3%
Germany	29	5.3%	$15,672.1	11.5%
Hungary	1	0.2%	N/A	N/A
Italy	103	18.9%	$72,021.9	53.1%
Japan	5	0.9%	$794.6	0.6%
Netherlands	1	0.2%	$497.8	0.4%
New Zealand	36	6.6%	$7,073.7	5.2%
Norway	4	0.7%	$6,227.7	4.6%
Poland	4	0.7%	$511.3	0.4%
Slovakia	2	0.4%	$24.7	0.0%
Sweden	35	6.4%	$1,478.8	1.1%
United Kingdom	9	1.7%	$3,170.7	2.3%
USA	199	36.5%	$19,988.5	14.7%
Other**	5	0.9%	N/A	N/A
TOTAL	**545**	**100.0%**	**$135,762.2**	**100.0%**

*Assets not available for some foundations

**Includes Bolivia, Chile, Morocco, Peru and Uruguay

Source: PtP Foundation Master List, Appendix A, Lester M. Salamon, *Philanthropication thru Privatization* (Milan, Italy: il Mulino, 2014).

- The most common type of PtP transactions are those involving the privatization of quasi-public institutions, but significant examples of all five types are evident.
- As is the case with foundations generally, most PtP foundations (54%) are small, with assets of less than $100m. each. However, 13% have assets in excess of US $3,000m. each, placing them among the largest foundations in the world. In fact, compared to the foundation universe in general, PtP foundations are more heavily weighted toward larger institutions, reflecting the enormous scale of the privatization transactions that have fuelled their growth.

3. Facilitating Factors

Philanthropication accompanies privatization where it is necessary, or useful, to do so. More specifically, this outcome seems to be most likely:

- Where privatization is proposed or under way;
- Where the assets involved have some unusual characteristic (e.g. contested or unclear ownership, unusual legal structure, or history of prior governmental subsidization);
- Where the legal environment facilitates philanthropication or discourages alternative uses of privatization proceeds;
- Where opposition to privatization has surfaced or is feared; and/or
- Where policy entrepreneurs or other advocates, including civil society, push for this outcome.

4. The Specific Structures of PtP Deals and Institutions Matter

- PtP deals that create endowments generally yield better financial results than those that establish a stream of revenue, even when the stream of revenue is secured over a period of time contractually or by law.
- PtP foundations can receive the proceeds of privatization transactions either in the form of cash (one-step deals) or in the form of shares of stock in a privatized company or other asset that they can later sell (two-step deals). Generally speaking, two-step deals yield larger charitable endowments than one-step deals. The experience of the ASB Community Trust (now Foundation North) in New Zealand is particularly revealing in this regard. The asset it received as the recipient of 100% of the shares of the Auckland Savings Bank (ASB) when it was privatized in 1988 was valued at NZ $100m. Within several years, the trust was approached by its savings bank with a request to consider a sale of a substantial portion of its shares to the Commonwealth Bank of Australia, which wanted to purchase the Auckland bank but insisted on majority ownership. Ultimately, the trust sold 75% of its shares in ASB for NZ $252m., a gain of 2.25 times what they were originally estimated to be worth and leaving the trust with a 25% share of a much larger institution. Several years later, the resulting CBA Bank approached the trust about acquiring its remaining 25% share, leading in 2000 to the sale of these remaining shares for NZ $560m. Within a little over a decade, the trust had thus parlayed its initial NZ $100m. endowment into an asset base approaching NZ $1,000m.
- PtP deals can be structured in ways that avoid any conflict between the establishment of PtP foundations and privatization's contribution to the reduction of government debt. The case of the Volkswagen Foundation is illustrative of this. This PtP foundation was created from its receipt of 60% of the proceeds of the sale of

the Volkswagen government corporation to private investors, many of them German citizens. But instead of immediately transferring the new Volkswagen Foundation's share of the cash generated by its sale of the Volkswagen Company, as originally agreed, the German federal Government insisted that the new foundation 'lend' these resources to the Federal Republic of Germany for a 20-year period, with the government paying the foundation 5% interest on its 'loan'. In this way, the Federal Republic was able to reduce its indebtedness and then pay back the foundation once its balance sheet had recovered sufficiently. This suggests a way for PtP to be reconciled with government debt relief.

5. Generally Impressive Operational Performance

With some notable exceptions, PtP foundations have adopted leading-edge techniques of foundation operations. Thus, they have generally established: governance arrangements that provide meaningful autonomy from governmental authorities and privatized companies; coherent mission statements and programmatic objectives; transparent reporting procedures that publicize programmes, sources, and uses of funds, governance arrangements, and conflict of interest policies; professionalized operations, featuring skilled experts in the fields in which the foundations work and in the management of foundation assets; and rationalized investment management.

6. Effective Programmatic Performance

Programmatically, PtP foundations have made significant contributions to their communities. Thus they have:

- generated substantial charitable contributions;
- strengthened civil society organizations;
- promoted regional development;
- supported a wide variety of objectives, though generally within an increasingly strategic sense of mission;
- generated important innovations; and
- modelled creative multi-stakeholder decision processes.

Of course, not all PtP foundations were equally effective, but the record overall is impressive.

7. A Promising Future

The future of PtP seems promising, for a number of reasons:

- The privatization surge of the 1990s hardly exhausted the supply of government-owned or -controlled assets. Significant assets are still available for privatization.
- Governments are under pressure to reduce debt and attract private investment.
- Because of its effects, privatization faces continued community hostility which PtP can help to resolve.
- PtP thus brings win-win benefits to investors, governments, communities, and civil society: *For investors, PtP brings:* Assurance of community support; consequent avoidance of costly delays in securing closure on deals; resulting advantages in the bidding process; early goodwill with employees, potential customers and suppliers; and positive international reputation. *For governments, PtP brings:* Investors eager to avoid uncertain investment climates; avoidance of community resistance; consequent avoidance of failed sales; guaranteed support for long-term priorities; new partners to share the burdens of addressing enduring problems; and improved international reputation for probity and social accountability. *For communities, PtP brings:* Solid promise of finally securing tangible, short-term as well as long-term benefits from privatization; opportunities to participate in community problem-solving; new resources for addressing community problems; and improved health, education, environment and infrastructure. *For civil society, PtP brings:* Liberation from sole dependence on external support; improved public image; broader promotion of charitable giving and philanthropy; improved channels for participation in governmental decision-making; and expanded resources with which to address community needs.

8. The Need for Standards and Guidelines

For PtP to deliver the benefits of which it is capable, however, great care must be taken in the design and operation of PtP foundations, as well as in the selection of privatization transactions to which it can appropriately be attached.

Features of privatization transactions that would make them potentially suitable for PtP applications include:

1. coherent and explicit legal and organizational structures for managing the transactions;

2. open and transparent procedures;

3. attention to market conditions likely to restrain competition and therefore create a need for regulation or other intervention; and

4. inclusion of a 'social package', a set of provisions committing investors to assist in mitigating any negative effects of privatization and to operate in an environmentally and socially responsible fashion.

Key features required in PtP foundations are: independent governance; professional management; transparency; strong accountability and conflict of interest provisions; representativeness; and meaningful and careful grantmaking activity.

Conclusion

The current efforts to build community foundations and other community-based philanthropic endowments in less-developed regions of the world hold enormous promise for unleashing new energies for social problem-solving. However, these efforts could end up generating deep frustration if meaningful sources of capital do not become available to sustain them. While some of this capital needs to come from local citizens and corporations, it seems clear that relying on these sources alone may well consign these fledgling institutions to a long path toward viability and effectiveness.

This is all the more frustrating in view of the fact that side-by-side with these efforts in many of these same countries, enormous privatization sales are being pursued with the potential of transferring billions of dollars of the peoples' assets into private hands and generating significant proceeds for governments in the process. But these efforts, too, are encountering challenges as citizen support for privatization has become increasingly problematic.

PtP offers a unique win-win solution to both of these challenges, allowing countries to benefit from needed investment while ensuring that significant shares of the resources resulting from such investments are permanently dedicated to improving the life-chances of citizens and strengthening indigenous civil society.

The existing PtP foundations examined here have, by their example, opened our eyes to the feasibility of just such an approach. By documenting the numerous past cases of such philanthropication through privatization, disseminating these experiences broadly, carefully generating materials showing how this option can be applied, and undertaking a series of pilot implementation efforts, it is our hope that the initiative described here, inspired by the experiences of the existing PtP foundations, will significantly increase the chances that this option for building independent charitable endowments will receive a reasonable hearing wherever privatization activity occurs in the future.

To be sure, there is nothing automatic about such an outcome. Convincing governments to part with even a fraction of the proceeds of privatization sales may be a difficult sales job. However, the privatization juggernaut has hit enough bumps in the road around the world to open the minds of even the most resistant governments to the need for new approaches, and the option of accompanying future sales with the creation of sizeable charitable endowments targeted towards the needs of local citizens could help assuage some of the hostility that privatization has engendered. This, at any rate, is the hope that this project is putting forward. With billions of privatization deals in play, and enormous problems confronting the very countries where many of these deals are proceeding, it surely seems a concept worth putting to the test.

Notes

1. Including, for example, the Banca Monte dei Paschi di Siena and the Compagnia di San Paolo di Torino.

2. In addition to the banks named here, the other institutions that came together to form the Intesa San Paolo SpA banking group included the Banca Commerciale Italiana and the Banco di Napoli.

3. Some of the smaller foundations, operating in small communities, were permitted to retain majority stakes in their 'conferred' banks.

4. US foundation assets drawn from foundation websites accessed 29 July 2013. Asset figures are as at 2011. These figures confirmed at foundationcenter.org (accessed 2 August 2013). Unless otherwise noted, throughout this report monetary values will be expressed in US dollars at exchange rates in effect as at 31 July 2013.

5. Data on Volkswagen Foundation assets as of 2013 available at volkswagenstiftung.de (accessed 28 July 2013). The actual transaction involved in the Volkswagen case was slightly more complicated than this. In the initial transaction, 60% of the shares of the new company were sold to the public and 20% each were given to the Federal Republic of Germany (FRG) and to the state of Lower Saxony where the Volkswagen plants were located. While the proceeds of the publicly-sold shares were dedicated to it, the new Volkswagen Foundation had to wait 20 years to receive them. Instead, the proceeds went to the FRG in the form of a loan and the FRG paid interest to the Foundation for the use of these funds. In addition, the Federal Republic ultimately sold its own shares and transferred most of these proceeds to the Foundation.

6. Grantmakers in Health, *A Profile of Foundations Created from Health Care Conversions,* (Grantmakers in Health, 2009), accessed 6 February 2010.

7. Vodafone contributions to Safaricom Foundation based on UK Vodafone Foundation accounts available from the UK Charity Commission. These records show that Vodafone contributed 43.8m. Kenyan shillings to Safaricom Foundation in the calendar year ending 31 March 2012.

8. William Megginson, 'Privatization Trends and Major Deals in 2012', in The PB Report 2012 (Milan: Fondazione Eni Enrico Mattei, 2013). Megginson defines privatization narrowly as the sale of state-owned enterprises or assets. The PtP project has identified three further forms of privatization, while other authors extend the definition well beyond this.

9. Ibid.

10. A sixth type involving the capture of some frozen assets resulting from governmental corruption, negligence penalties, or the death of wealthy individuals whose assets are not covered by a will has recently been added to the list. An example of a foundation resulting from the capture of frozen assets, in this case a penalty for infringement of anti-payoff laws, is the BOTA Foundation in Kazakhstan. (On this case, see: www.fcpablog.com/blog/2015/4/27/the-bota-foundation-explained-part-ten-lessons-from-bota.html.)

* This article draws heavily on *Philanthropication thru Privatization: Building Permanent Endowments for the Common Good* (Bologna: il Mulino, 2014). (For further information about the 'Philanthropication thru Privatization Project', visit www.p-t-p.org or contact Chelsea Newhouse at chelsea.newhouse@jhu.edu.)

Dr Lester M. Salamon is a professor at the Johns Hopkins University, director of the Johns Hopkins Center for Civil Society Studies, senior research professor at the Johns Hopkins School of Advanced International Studies Bologna Center, and scientific director of the International Laboratory for Nonprofit Sector Studies at Russia's Higher School of Economics. The former deputy associate director of the US Office of Management and Budget in the Office of the President, he is the author of numerous books and articles on the non-profit sector, the tools of government, and social welfare policy in the USA and around the world.

Foundations in Europe

VOLKER THEN AND KONSTANTIN KEHL

Introduction

The European foundation landscape is characterized by its variety of socio-political contexts, roles and operating styles.[1] In many countries such as Germany, Spain, Italy and France the traditional operating foundations originating from the Christian roots of philanthropy are still very numerous, and in some cases serve as substantial service providers in the public welfare system. Whereas private purpose foundations are most prominent in Austria, the Danish corporate foundations operate both for-profit enterprises and public-benefit activities in one legal entity. However, despite the differences, the strategies of foundations have in recent years benefited from common trends and issues which will have an impact on future philanthropy in Europe. After providing an overview of the substantial growth of foundations, we will address these rather new items on the strategic menu. We will argue that European foundation strategies should be viewed as the results of processes of stakeholder involvement, co-operation and coalition building, as long as foundations continue to grow in their role as private investors in the public good.

Growth Trend

Europe has never had more foundations than today. The foundation sector has experienced a substantial growth period in recent years. Data on European foundations are still far from satisfactory, but also, for the first time, the aggregate number of foundations, their annual budgets and total asset base have been targeted by substantial research efforts over the past few years. Starting from a first rough estimate which was included in the feasibility study of a European Foundations Statute for the European Commission in 2009,[2] and leading towards more recent efforts of the European Foundation Centre (EFC) in conjunction with DAFNE, the Donors and Foundations Network in Europe, we can draw a sketchy picture of a wealth of foundations in European countries.

The most recent available data suggest that the number of (public-benefit) foundations in Europe exceeds 130,000, their asset base approaches €450,000m., and annual expenditures exceed €53,000m.[3] This compares to a US total of 86,192 foundations, with an annual giving of close to US $52,000m. and total assets of more than $715,000m. (2012 data).[4] The most recent European figures compare to at least 110,000 European foundations estimated in 2009, i.e., the number has grown substantially and, at the same time, the data may have become more reliable through national associations of foundations reporting on a more exact basis.

However, at the same time the growth trend in numbers still leaves the observer with a lot of scope for interpretation, especially when it comes to the amount of assets and the annual spending of European foundations. A number of arguments need to be distinguished:

- The valuation of assets is still inconsistent owing to varying legal requirements in different European countries or European Union (EU) member states.
- The data on annual spending still remain to be validated due to pass-through funds from either public budgets or recipients of services (of operating foundations).
- The growth trend of the sector depends on the development of the political culture of the countries and shows a great degree of variation over the last 20 years.

With all due brevity of a reference article such as this, we would like to address each of the arguments in more detail. The currently available aggregation of foundation asset data included foundations valued using quite different measures, which range from fair market value of traded assets to nominal value of assets or any book value in between. As a result of a lack of legal standardization of valuation in major countries such as Germany, the asset data reported most likely grossly understate the actual value of total assets. This, in particular, applies to those foundations with majority holdings in substantial companies as part of their endowments.

The data on annual spending—again, the German case may serve as a point of reference, given its large share of the total—include different sources of income which are currently difficult to disentangle. They include funds provided to foundations from public budgets to support programmes or projects, as well as the revenue generated on the assets of the foundations and a share of revenue for services provided to beneficiaries in the market (or a regulated quasi-market). Again, this distortion is prevalent in Germany where large operating foundations play an important role in the provision of social welfare services in different regulated care markets (health, care for senior citizens, care for youth and care for disabled people). For their services, they receive fee income from either the social insurance systems or public budgets. As a result of this consideration, it is fairly obvious that a reported asset level of €70,000m. cannot result in an annual revenue stream of €17,000m. By contrast, the revenue level has to be explained by the above effects and only a minority share of the reported annual expenditure can be assumed to be revenue generated from the endowments or from cash donations (actual giving).

Finally, the growth trend of the past two decades in particular has been the result of a number of intersecting developments. First, the fall of the Berlin wall and the transformation towards market economies and democracy in Central and Eastern Europe has opened up a window of opportunity which, despite a still modest level of endowment assets, has led to the creation of thousands of new foundations in this part of Europe. Second, is the factor that there are a number of Western European countries, such as Spain, with emerging sectors as a consequence of still relatively young democratization. And finally, there is the overarching trend of the transfer of wealth to the next generation, which primarily represents the peace dividend of Europe after the Second World War and cohorts of (future) pensioners who are well-off in a way that is historically unique.

This has been complemented by political efforts in many European countries to improve the legal frameworks for foundations and thereby encourage the establishment of new foundations. A prime candidate in question could be France, with its fairly restrictive foundation law until substantial changes were made some 10 years ago.[5]

It is, however, worth noting that comparing EU foundation data to their US counterparts leads to a picture of comparatively thriving philanthropy on both sides of the Atlantic. Despite the smaller size of the population of the USA, giving levels are still higher than in many European countries, but at the same time they do not differ by dimensions and they are on the increase. It also needs to be added that US figures include the exceptional Bill & Melinda Gates Foundation, which holds more than US $37,000m. in assets and disburses some $3,200m. annually. The largest European foundation, the Wellcome Trust in the United Kingdom, is only somewhat more than one-half that size in terms of assets, and even less in terms of annual budget.[6] If we account for the relatively young foundation sector in many (Central and Eastern) European countries, the level of European foundation activity compares all the more favourably to the USA and indicates a growing relevance of foundations. However, it is worth assessing in more detail to what extent the growing size and relevance of the sector have given rise to growing expectations in European societies, not least in the aftermath of the financial crisis of recent years. We therefore focus in the following paragraphs on issues of effectiveness and impact, issues which have increasingly come to the attention of European foundation representatives (and policymakers) and are characterizing current debates.

Trend towards Impact

The growth of the foundation sector, and with it the current generation of donors, has given rise to increasing concern about the effectiveness of philanthropy (and, accordingly, its function in society). The professional strategies of foundations in recent years highlight these concerns and allow us to distinguish yet another historical phase in their development.

While scientific philanthropy in its US version had already emerged before the Second World War and had primarily been concerned with addressing the root causes of societal problems, more recent stages of foundation activities have, since the mid-1990s, been affected by the discussion surrounding strategic philanthropy. Arguably, the current debate on high-impact philanthropy is addressing the same concerns, but takes a somewhat different route of response. What remains common and pays tribute to the heritage of strategic philanthropy is the concern with societal problem solving. Yet, new insights have emerged concerning promising approaches to achieve this task.

This chapter only allows for a rather cursory examination of the key arguments of the debate, but we would like to concentrate on a set of highly relevant observations:

- The level of co-operation and network approaches among foundations has grown along with their quest for impact.

- The most successful high-impact programmes or projects have characteristics which are based on brokering resources additional to their own to very specific solutions of societal problems, starting from very well-defined and carved-out attitudes towards the issues.

- The interest in high impact has put the foundation as a whole on the radar screen, not just its programmatic or spending side. As a consequence (and also triggered by changes in the capital markets, which require higher returns to be based on strong levels of well-controlled risk-taking), approaches of mission- or programme-related investment as well as impact investing are increasingly being debated, albeit at a limited level of existing experience.

- As a consequence of cross-sectoral and cross-organizational strategies to address major societal issues, foundation strategies have become more 'political', in the sense of negotiated co-operation, cross-sectoral dissemination and social innovation strategies being required to accomplish foundation goals.

In the following sub-chapters we will take a closer look at each of these developments. It goes without saying that, with all the wealth of variations of European foundation cultures, these observations can only point at certain discourses that have recently become more prominent, without claiming to be representative of the foundation mainstream. The authors nevertheless make a case for the increasing relevance of such considerations vis-à-vis the legitimacy expectations of European societies with their growing levels of private investments in the public good.[7]

Networks and Co-operation for Impact

From recent case study-based research we have developed a number of insights.[8] As we know from the literature on social networks in general, many social and behavioural science questions can best be addressed by referring to their elements and environment 'as patterns or regularities in relationships among interacting units'[9]. Thus, in order to achieve any impact with regard to their mission at all, philanthropic organizations frequently have to resort to various levels of co-operation and work in such networks. Despite the variations, all situations do, however, start from a clear co-operation concept with a clear assessment of stakeholders that is highly relevant to the context of the programme or strategy. Against this background, organizations have developed ties and relationships with other organizations representing their different strategies of co-operation: for the pooling of resources and funding, for jointly implementing a shared theory of change on a programmatic level, for improving the advocacy impact in public policy contexts, or in general to strengthen the legitimacy base of their own operations. It is obvious that the approaches taken towards co-operation reflect the size of an organization and its own capacity to address the targets set out in its mission, but also the type of non-profit or social investment approach, the geographic scope of the organization and, finally, the welfare and policy regime in which it is operating.

Irrespective of the type of co-operation, we can, however, identify a number of preconditions which need to be met whenever a co-operation approach is targeted at effectiveness and impact:[10]

- A high degree of consensus on the problems to be solved and on the goals to be achieved must have been negotiated among the partners.
- The approach needs an evidence base concerning the problems addressed and progress made in the communities.
- The development of an awareness of the most relevant stakeholders for addressing the targeted problems.
- The development of a clear understanding of the complementarity of the roles of the organizations involved.
- The basis of the common approach on a clear theory of change (or an impact model).
- The development by the involved organizations of an interest in mutual learning processes.
- A high degree of trust and mutual respect in communication between the involved organizations.

These preconditions are met with due regard whenever organizations are operating on a clear strategic concept, which acknowledges that they may have to search for a substantial degree of leverage in investing their own resources in order to leave a mark, to have any strong impact on a major societal problem. Co-operation approaches will then not only address the challenge of a lack of overall resources at the disposal of the organization, but serve a whole list of different purposes:[11]

- Leveraging the potential and resources of different organizations with regard to one problem.
- Bridging the gaps between sectors in problem-solving.
- Bridging different organizational types and logics (in order to combine the strengths of different sectors).
- Deepening the community involvement and participation of citizens.
- Helping to disseminate or scale proven approaches.
- Sharing lessons learned or enabling learning processes.
- Strengthening the advocacy position and legitimacy of the approach chosen.

This systematic approach to co-operation pays off all the more if an organization is addressing major societal issues, so-called 'wicked problems'. These problems are not only characterized by a high degree of complexity, but also by contention with regard to the underlying values to be pursued and by unknown means–end relations. 'Hence, they are neither easy to understand nor easy to solve and often they cannot be solved at all. In particular, they elude comprehensive analysis, as well as strategically-planned, highly rational and linear modes of action'.[12]

Foundations are addressing major societal challenges and increasingly this implies that they take this avenue of a problem-orientated strategic approach. These strategies reflect the role of foundations as minority players for the public good, which need to reach arrangements with all the other players involved in the field, whether they are foundations, other non-profit bodies, private corporates or the state (other public agencies). Therefore, the problem-orientation as a strategic focus of foundations merits some more attention.

Problem-solving and Social Innovation

A clear consequence of a problem-orientated foundation strategy emerges to reduce complexity: organizations carve out well-defined specific niches of operations. They focus their perception of the social problem on a very specific aspect of the overall problem architecture and do not address the whole complex situation at the same time. This niching not only serves the purpose of reducing complexity, but also of matching needed resources to available means and resources of the organization. Over time the organization may be able to broaden the niche, learn from its experience in the more narrowly defined field, and bring in more stakeholders as compared to those involved at the beginning of the work.

These observations not only apply to a small number of carefully analysed cases of high-impact foundation work, but they emerge as the clear common denominator of foundation projects or programmes identified by independent evaluation studies as high-impact cases. At the Centre for Social Investment (CSI) at Heidelberg University, we distilled these analytical results from running research into such situations based on screening a larger number of candidates for high impact, which we identified by peer recommendation, and then included in the analysis only those whose high impact had been demonstrated by previous evaluation studies (of academic rigour). We then identified common characteristics of those cases and in conclusion came up with the above-mentioned basic observations.[13]

In looking at the analytical results of problem-solving philanthropy, we realize that foundations can choose from a menu of problem options and then need to adjust their interventions accordingly: from a very narrowly defined problem such as school absenteeism to the broadest possible approach of generally improving school achievement for disadvantaged migrant children, everything is possible. However, the broad problem definitions will be plagued by issues of prioritizing and allocating all too limited resources, even in situations of a large foundation budget which, compared to what the state spends on the same issues, may nevertheless represent a clear minority position. The resulting challenge will be 'how the tip of the tail can wag the dog'. The aggregate total of foundation education spending represents less than what the state can spend in a day or a few days (depending on the country of reference), and this only is one example of a general problem.[14]

Carving out specific aspects of larger problems by defining the strategic interventions very clearly in a theory of change not only reduces complexity and adapts the approach to available limited resources, but allows the foundation to 'reach a situation in which targeted evidence on the situation and its potential improvements can be collected'.[15] This evidence-gathering paves the way for learning processes which are one of the crucial purposes of co-operation in the first place. High-impact strategies necessarily reach beyond the boundaries of any particular organization, but also beyond the boundaries as originally perceived when a programme is started. Again, the bridging towards such additional stakeholders and efforts to attract them to a coalition of like-minded players is a core element of effective strategies.

It becomes obvious that high-impact strategies with a problem-solving focus have 'political' implications. They require co-operation and networks to be negotiated; they require normative consensus (or sufficient common ground) to be established among partners. They also call for connecting these strategies to social innovation and taking a closer look at the relationships between the sectors in such processes. While a prompt to establish an innovative approach in serving a public benefit purpose or resolving a societal problem can emerge from any sector in society, the discourses resulting from and supporting an innovative prompt are crucial for negotiating exactly those coalitions of like-minded stakeholders which share an interest in seeing a solution implemented and disseminated. It is these discourses in civil society that shape the mindsets and value systems of people which may result in a broader process of social change:

'If those solutions emerge from a market impulse, public debate in civil society and social movements paving the way for them have to address changing value systems of both customers and investors in order to allow for market differentiation of the social innovation. If state and public sector administration start an innovative impulse, they will equally have to rely on civil society preparing the ground for new advocacy coalitions of like-minded citizens and organizations joining forces to advocate for a policy change. And the same even applies for an impulse starting from the networks of local neighbourhoods and communities, which in turn will depend on civil society to see their approaches taken elsewhere in society and being replicated.'[16]

Failures by foundations to achieve effectiveness have frequently resulted from resource insufficiency. Foundations may be inclined to overestimate their role in these complex societal processes of change and as a consequence fail as a result of being over-ambitious. Studies on the roles of foundations in society repeatedly come across substitution illusions of foundations which are not aware of the gross lack of resources, even in aggregate, of all foundations in a country.[17] This scarcity of resources has been aggravated by recent developments in the capital markets which have (at least under certain legal conditions in continental Europe with civil and tax law regulations limiting the risk exposure of foundation endowments in their asset management policies) resulted in shrinking revenue from the asset base of the foundations. This may all the more prompt foundations to revisit their strategies and consider using all their assets and social impact investment strategies respectively. It may also prompt them to consider strategies of political advocacy as an alternative to actually funding the problem-solving directly. We explore these two options in the final paragraphs of this chapter.

Social Impact Investing

In recent years, a growing debate surrounding the use of the whole asset base of a foundation for the purposes laid out in its charter or mission has emerged. On the one hand, even in an environment with a legal pay-out requirement such as the USA, only 5% of the assets of a foundation are used annually; on the other, in a jurisdiction without a pay-out requirement, even less than this 5% is likely to be spent on the purposes. Given that the need for substantial leverage has been widely acknowledged in foundation strategy, using the invested assets of the foundation directly to pursue its mission is seen as an opportunity to broaden the asset base of the sector.

The impact investment discussion, however, also touches on the relationship between foundations and the public sector. It has already been mentioned that aspirations towards substituting for the public budget may overstrain

foundation resources, which lends more weight to a discussion of complementary roles. At the same time, the concept of social impact investing is a highly political concept, because it starts from the basic assumption that private investors can provide for innovative solutions to social problems and needs ahead of state capacity. In turn, the state can offer them some return on their investments using some part of the gains documented for the investment (be they costs avoided or additional value contributions made possible).

Social impact investments are, however, a distinct class of investment different from mainstream financial investments for private return. By definition, social impact investments are private assets combining a financial return orientation with a positive social and/or environmental impact. This blended value approach must not only be intended but also has to be documented. This implies an obligation to measure and communicate social impact and use it as a basis for future decision-making. Such an investment category is meant to bridge financial and social capital markets for the public benefit and to strengthen the social impact sector or market in order to work towards a more sustainable society.[18]

Any such investment is of particular interest to foundations if it can be aligned with the mission or programmatic interests of the foundation. Depending on the fields in which a foundation works, the potential for such business models based on social entrepreneurship may vary a great deal, but, in general, they can be regarded as feasible only in as much as they manage to create a sustainable business due to some sort of social innovation or niching in creating a hitherto non-existent market. However, due to market failure still prevailing in many of the public benefit fields (by definition, because otherwise the field would be served by for-profit players![19]), these business models may be highly hybrid in nature and include a substantial share of public subsidy or mixed funding from revenue for services, philanthropy and public support. Clients may play a role in the co-production of services which they need and non-monetary resources may be highly relevant for the sustainability of the business.

Most likely, these social impact investment markets will therefore be highly regulated quasi-markets, in which public regulation, public policy and the legitimacy of the solution for a societal problem play a crucial role. This implies that the market potential for such social impact investments very much depends on the welfare regime and its legal regulations in the respective countries. The strategic relevance for foundations may, therefore, be much higher in liberal market economies which favour competitive contracting solutions to provide public welfare, while being more challenging to establish in welfare regimes which give a legal entitlement to citizens and give them the freedom to choose from which provider to receive their services (albeit at a regulated price and frequently also at regulated quality standards). However, even in those strong welfare conditions, social impact investments can play a role as the research and development segment of non-profit service-providing sectors and can define their market niches as providers of social innovations.[20]

Both the Organisation for Economic Co-operation and Development (OECD), the G7 Social Impact Investment Task Force and the Global Impact Investing Network (GIIN) have identified a number of priority fields in which social impact investment has started to play a growing role internationally, albeit at greatly varying levels depending on the country in question. The most relevant fields identified on all priority lists are health, education and housing issues, followed by other social service fields such as ageing or fields such as environment, agriculture and energy in development contexts.[21]

From this brief glimpse at the potential of social impact investment for high-impact strategies of foundations, it follows that the remaining option of addressing the purposes of foundations by approaches of political advocacy is closely intertwined with the previous strategies: social impact investments combine in one way or another a relationship with the public sector and a private investment approach, and in doing so are dependent on the mechanisms of civil society in strengthening legitimacy. In our final sub-chapter, we will pay some attention to advocacy of foundations which can be seen as complementary to the other approaches aimed at high impact.

Political Advocacy

Foundations can play a major role as either funders of or proponents of political advocacy if they follow an operating strategy model. Their role as bridge builders between stakeholders has already been touched upon as critical for high impact strategies. One crucial way of building these bridges is that of a policy entrepreneur[22] driving and forging political discourse coalitions and advocacy coalitions.[23] This, above all, means shaping normative frames and problem perceptions which relevant stakeholders express in the respective discourses—or being a broker bridging different coalitions in order to reach a decent (political) solution.

If foundations play this role they are confronted with particularly high needs to secure the legitimacy of their involvement, because they cannot benefit from democratic legitimacy mechanisms as organizations that are inherently non-democratic (but rather independent and mission-driven). They have to demonstrate why it is useful for policymaking in a given field or for society as a whole to have them 'on board' in situations of societal negotiations between different values and interests. Moreover, as public benefit institutions their privileged status 'requires them to pay attention to public perceptions of their appropriate contributions to the public good'.[24]

We therefore suggest conceptualizing the legitimacy requirements of foundations in this situation and with strategic aspirations at political advocacy as indicated by the legitimacy triangle (see Figure 1). Generally, foundations can combine different levels of programmatic activity in order to meet the legitimacy requirements of a social investment, which are relevant on both input (motivation) as well as output (results for beneficiaries, impact) as well as process levels (civility).[25] They can strengthen their legitimacy base substantially by combining three levels of activities: their programmatic experience in funding or running practical projects with stakeholders in their field of interest, their co-operation with research and academia in order systematically to appraise the knowledge available for the field (and to put to fruitful use the potential to gather evidence as mentioned above), and their political skills to force co-operation and coalitions, i.e. advocacy work based on the other two. Both research on high-impact cases as well as research on European foundations with a strong interest in political advocacy shows that this approach is particularly promising to achieve goals of social change and social innovation. This is the case not only because of the described limitations in the relatively generous and highly regulated European welfare states, but also due to the complex democratic rules and routines both in countries with a high level of social cleavages (e.g.

Switzerland or the Netherlands) and in the Scandinavian societies with their deep-rooted political culture of consensus.[26]

Figure 1: Foundation Legitimacy Triangle

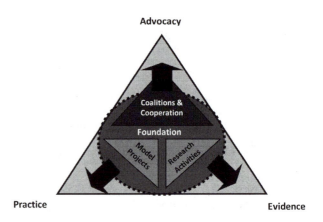

The level of practical project experience lends the foundation the credibility of first-hand experience with stakeholders in the field, the level of research and working with academic institutions assure the rigorous problem analysis and use of data to inform strategic learning and decision-making, and the advocacy level in turn benefits from both the claim of a rigorous expertise base and the practical rootedness in experience and stakeholder involvement. They therefore combine input and output legitimacy as described as generic categories of the democratic process in terms of both systems ('for the people') and social integration ('by the people').[27] A foundation which pursues this strategy can still not substitute for its lack of democratic governance, but it may be able to make a strong case as a policy entrepreneur convening a coalition of partners in civil society and beyond in public policy and the marketplace, or help to overcome conflicting values and interests.

Perspectives

Foundations are increasingly confronted with a need to put their concern for effectiveness centre-stage. Both the values of their donors and the expectations of society vis-à-vis a growing foundation sector lend this argument their combined weight. The strategies of foundations have in recent years benefitted from a great deal of rather new items on the menu to choose from. At the same time, recent research seems to suggest that foundation strategies should no longer be viewed in a merely instrumental way assuming that intervening at a single point in a complex societal system can really change the situation to the (desired) better. They should rather be viewed as negotiated, 'political' results of processes of stakeholder involvement, co-operation and coalition building, and resource brokering. In considering their overall role as a social investor—both in a narrow sense of providing capital and in the broad sense of working for the public good—foundations become an integral part of civil society. The wealth of traditions in different European countries has paved the way for this role, and foundations will continue to grow in their role as private investors in the public good.

Notes

1. Then, Volker, and Konstantin Kehl. 'Philanthropy in Europe', in Anheier, Helmut K. and Stefan Toepler (eds). *International Encyclopedia of Civil Society*, Springer, New York, 2010, pp. 1196–1201.

2. http://ec.europa.eu/internalmarket/company/docs/eufoundation/feasibilitystudy.en.pdf, pp. 18 ff.

3. See for DAFNE data report at www.dafne-online.eu, Survey on Public Benefit Foundations in Europe, www.dafne-online.eu/Documents/DAFNE%20data%2019%20Sept%202014%20rev2.docx.

4. 2012 Foundation Center data, see http://data.foundationcenter.org/#/foundations/all/nationwide/total/list/2012.

5. Hellio, François, 'Das Stiftungsrecht Frankreichs', Heft 11, Discussion Papers, Bucerius Law School, Hochschule für Rechtswissenschaft, Institut für Stiftungsrecht und das Recht der Non-Profit-Organisationen. See www.law-school.de/deutsch/lehre-forschung/institute-zentren/institut-fuer-stiftungsrecht/publikationen/#c2739.

6. www.wellcome.ac.uk/About-us/Publications/Annual-Report-and-Financial-Statements/index.htm.

7. Powell, Walter W., and Elizabeth S. Clemens (eds). *Private Action and the Public Good*, Yale University Press, 1998. Powell, Walter W., and Richard Steinberg. *The Nonprofit Sector. A Research Handbook*, 2nd Edition, Yale University Press, 2006. Then, Volker, and Konstantin Kehl. 'Soziale Investitionen, Ein konzeptioneller Entwurf', in Anheier, Helmut K., Andreas Schröer, and Volker Then (eds). *Soziale Investitionen*, VS, Wiesbaden, pp. 39–86, 2012. Kehl, Konstantin, and Volker Then. 'Social Investment, A Sociological Outline', Paper presented at ISTR's 10th International Conference on Democratization, Marketization, and the Third Sector 2012 in Siena, Italy, 2012.

8. Then, Volker, Thomas Scheuerle, and Ekkehard Thümler. 'Social Investment Bridge Builders, Cooperation for Impact'. Final Report, CSI Project Report, Heidelberg, 2014, p. 8.

9. Wasserman, Stanley, and Katherine Faust. *Social Network Analysis, Methods and Applications*, Cambridge University Press, 1994, p. 3.

10. Then et al. (2014), p. 9.

11. Ibid.

12. Ibid., p. 9; see also Rittel, Horst W. J., and Melvin M. Webber. *Dilemmas in a General Theory of Planning*, Policy Sciences, 4 (2), 1973, pp. 155–169.

13. Published in: Thümler, Ekkehard, Nicole Bögelein, Annelie Beller and Helmut K. Anheier (eds). *Philanthropy and Education, Strategies for Impact*, Palgrave MacMillan, Basingstoke, 2014.

14. Ibid.; see also for Germany in particular: Hertie School of Governance and Universität Heidelberg, CSI, Centrum für Soziale Investitionen. Positionierung und Beitrag deutscher Stiftungen, Erste Ergebnisse einer repräsentativen Umfrage, Briefing Paper 1, 2015, p. 3.

15. Then et al. (2014): p. 10.

16. Ibid., p. 16.

17. Most recently and as a first report of work in progress on German foundations: Hertie School of Governance and Universität Heidelberg, CSI, Centrum für Soziale Investitionen, 2015; see also: Anheier, Helmut K. and Diana Leat (eds). *Creative Philanthropy, Toward a New Philanthropy for the Twenty-First Century*, Routledge, Abingdon, 2006; Anheier, Helmut K. and Siobhan Daly. *The Politics of Foundations, A Comparative Analysis*, Routledge, Abingdon, 2006.

18. OECD (ed). *Social Impact Investment, Building the Evidence Base*, Paris 2015, see www.oecd.org/sti/ind/social-impact-investment.htm; and Bertelsmann Stiftung. *Social Impact Investing, Financing Social Change*, Final Report National Advisory Board of the Impact Investing Task Force, Germany, 2015, see www.bertelsmann-stiftung.de/fileadmin/files/user.upload/Final.Report.NAB.Germany.pdf.

19. Hansmann, Henry. 'Economic Theories of Nonprofit Organizations', in Powell, Walter W. (ed). *The Nonprofit Sector, A Research Handbook*, Yale University Press, 1987, pp. 27–42.

20. Bertelsmann Stiftung (2015), pp. 7–14.

21. OECD (2015), Figure 4.3., p. 46, based on the Social Impact Investment Task Force established by the G8 and GIIN website, www.thegiin.org/.

22. Kingdon, John W. *Agendas, Alternatives, and Public Policies*, 1995.

23. Wittrock, Björn, Peter Wagner, and Hellmut Wollmann. *Social Science and the Modern State, Knowledge, Institutions, and Societal Transformations*, Wissenschaftszentrum Berlin, 1987, p. 87-3; Jenkins-Smith, Hank C., Daniel Nohrstedt, Christopher M. Weible, and Paul A. Sabatier. 'Advocacy Coalition Framework: Foundations, Evolution, and Ongoing Research', in: Weible, Christopher M., and Paul A. Sabatier (eds). *Theories of the Policy Process*, 3rd Edition, Westview Press, Boulder, 2014, pp. 183–223.

24. Then, Volker, and Konstantin Kehl. 'Foundations, functions of', in Anheier, Helmut K., and Stefan Toepler (eds). *International Encyclopedia of Civil Society*, Springer, New York, 2010, pp. 695–699, here p. 695.

25. Then and Kehl (2012); Kehl and Then (2012).

26. Lijphart, Arend. *Patterns of Democracy, Government Forms and Performance in Thirty-six Countries*, Yale University Press, 1999.

27. Scharpf, Fritz W. *Governing in Europe, Effective and Democratic?*, Oxford University Press, 1999, p. 6.

Volker Then is the Managing Director of the Centre for Social Investment (CSI) at Heidelberg University. Previously, he worked at the Bertelsmann Foundation where he served as Director of Philanthropy and Foundations from 1999 to 2006, and built the philanthropy division of the Foundation. He earned his PhD in social history from the Free University of Berlin and has been a member of numerous boards and committees in philanthropy and civil society. He was a Senior Fellow of the Center for Civil Society, School of Public Affairs, UCLA, USA, and a member of the National Advisory Committee of New Ventures, the National Initiative to Promote the Growth of Philanthropy in the USA (Washington, DC, USA), the Legal and Tax Task Forces of the European Foundation Centre (EFC, Brussels). He served on the Governing Council (2000–06) and the International Committee (2000–06) of the EFC, the International Committee of the Council on Foundations in Washington, DC (2000–04), and was part of the Executive Session in Philanthropy of the Hauser Center for Nonprofit Organizations, Kennedy School of Government, Harvard University, USA (1999–2002). He has been a member of the boards of three German foundations for many years.

Konstantin Kehl is the director of the CSI Transfer and Advisory Services Department. In 2014 he defended his PhD on social investment care policies in Germany at the Faculty of Economics and Social Sciences, Heidelberg University. After receiving a Master's degree in Political Science and Sociology from Heidelberg University, he was a member of a project group analysing the socio-economic impact of multi-generation co-housing developments in Germany (2007–09). Since 2009 he has been the director of a research project on civic engagement. Beyond his research he has also been involved in the transfer, advisory and communication activities of the Centre. His research and advisory fields comprise social policy and political advocacy, civil society and foundations, and social impact analysis.

PART TWO

Directory

Albania

FOUNDATION CENTRE AND CO-ORDINATING BODY

Albanian Civil Society Foundation (Fondacioni Shqiptar i Shoqërisë Civile)

Established in 1995 to support the development of civil society, offering support to Albanian NGOs and encouraging public participation in decision-making.

Activities: Provides information, assistance and capacity building to NGOs and their staff through training and written materials. The Foundation maintains a database of NGOs in Albania, and supports community education and participation centres. Also focuses on Roma and marginalized groups.

Geographical Area of Activity: Albania.

Restrictions: No funding for individuals for social assistance or medical requirements, nor for political parties or foreign non-profit organizations operating in Albania.

Publications: Annual Report; directories of Albanian NGOs; newsletter (6 a year); study brochures on inter-ethnic understanding, project cycle management and logframe approach.

Finance: Donors include the EU Commission.

Principal Staff: Exec. Dir Pandeli Theodhori.

Address: Blvd Gjergj Fishta, Kulla 1, H1/7, Kati 6, Apt 26, Tirana; POB 1537, Tirana.

Telephone: (6) 82020482; **e-mail:** ptheodhori@acsf.org.al.

FOUNDATIONS, TRUSTS AND NON-PROFIT ORGANIZATIONS

Fondacioni Shqiptar per te Drejtat e Paaftesise (Albanian Disability Rights Foundation)

Initially established in 1994 as an Oxfam (q.v.) disability programme in Albania, and subsequently established as an independent local NGO in 1996. Aims to empower disabled people by improving their capacities to support their integration into society.

Activities: Assists people with disabilities, their families, disability NGOs, and professionals who work directly with the disabled. The Foundation works in the areas of information and documentation services; running a training and technical assistance centre; providing a counselling service; organizing lobbying initiatives; and awareness-raising.

Geographical Area of Activity: Albania.

Publications: Information brochures; monographs; *Challenge* magazine; Annual Report.

Governing Body: Arjana Haxhiu (Pres.).

Principal Staff: Exec. Dir Blerta Çani.

Address: Rr. Bogdani (ish-A. Z. Çajupi) pall. 15 kat i III (3), Tirana.

Telephone: (4) 269426; **Internet:** www.adrf.org.al; **e-mail:** adrf@albmail.com.

International Humanitarian Assistance—IHA

Established to provide humanitarian aid and assistance.

Activities: Operates in the fields of health, education and human rights. Health programmes include: basic preventative and curative services; maternal and child health care; training for midwives and traditional birth attendants; health education and training in the medical and managerial skills needed to serve local communities suffering from a breakdown in health services; information about HIV/AIDS, prevention of sexually transmitted diseases and opportunistic infections, as well as training for HIV/AIDS carers, distribution of appropriate informative materials, and public education; reproductive health care; nutrition services, including supplemental and therapeutic feeding programmes for populations affected by famine and shortages, particularly small children; microfinance community-based initiatives to help restore economic self-sufficiency and help finance local health programmes; and training courses for local health-care workers and community organizations to increase awareness of gender-based violence and establish treatment protocols. Education programmes include: support for education systems through public awareness, legislative lobbying and training programmes, and the development of partnerships with universities, policymakers and organizations that focus on helping students from developing countries to complete their public education; raising funds for humanitarian education programmes; increasing support for teacher quality programmes to recruit, train and retain highly qualified educators in developing countries and areas in need; and encouraging parents' involvement in their children's education. Also aims to promote peace and understanding throughout the world, through designing and implementing new initiatives that focus on ethical dilemmas in the field of human rights.

Geographical Area of Activity: Albania and international.

Publications: *Teens Sexually Transmitted Diseases and HIV/AIDS*; *Young Gay Men Talking*; *Euro-Atlantic Rift*; *Public Health Care Report for Albania 2002*; and other reports and publications.

Board: Alba Fishta (Chair.); Flora Bejko (Treas.).

Principal Staff: Law Programmes Dir Jorida Fishta.

Address: L.2 Rr. Shefqet Beja Nr. 823, Durres.

Telephone: (52) 25319; **Fax:** (52) 25319; **Internet:** www.iha-info.org.

Open Society Foundation for Albania—OSFA (Fondacioni Shoqeria e Hapur per Shqiperine)

Established in 1992 as an independent foundation, and part of the Soros foundations network, aiming to foster political and cultural pluralism, and to reform economic structures to encourage private enterprise and a market economy.

Activities: Operates mainly in the areas of economic reform, education (including a fellowship programme), information and youth, and strengthening public institutions, although grants are also made in the areas of the arts and culture, women's programmes, public health, ethnic minorities and civil society. Co-operates with other foundations in the Soros network on international programmes, and aims to assist with the integration of Albania into the European Union.

Geographical Area of Activity: Albania.

Finance: Total assets US $2,561,885, annual expenditure $3,215,725 (31 Dec. 2010).

Executive Board: Remzi Lani (Chair.).

Principal Staff: Exec. Andi Dobrushi.

Address: Rr. Qemal Stafa, pall. 120/2, Tirana.

Telephone: (4) 234621; **Fax:** (4) 235855; **Internet:** www.osfa.al; www.soros.al; **e-mail:** info@osfa.al.

Algeria

FOUNDATIONS, TRUSTS AND NON-PROFIT ORGANIZATIONS

African Youth Network for Sustainable Development (Réseau Africain de la Jeunesse pour le Développement Durable)

Established in 1997 to work towards sustainable development.

Activities: Operates in the field of the environment, particularly where it relates to children and young people, through networking and representation at international level at conferences and symposia. Also organizes media campaigns in Algeria and throughout Africa, volunteer programmes to support elderly people and environmental clean-up activities.

Geographical Area of Activity: Algeria and throughout Africa.

Publications: Electronic periodicals.

Principal Staff: Gen. Co-ordinator Réda Mehigueni.

Address: 22 rue Matiben, El-Mouradia, Algiers 16000.

Telephone: (61) 505-368; **Fax:** (21) 936-929; **e-mail:** redamgueni@yahoo.fr.

Angola

FOUNDATIONS, TRUSTS AND NON-PROFIT ORGANIZATIONS

Fundação Eduardo dos Santos—FESA (Eduardo dos Santos Foundation)

Established in 1996 by José Eduardo dos Santos.

Activities: Works in partnership with the Government in the fields of social welfare, culture, and science and technology. Projects include poverty alleviation, distributing food and clothing; building health centres and providing medical care; building schools and improving access to work and education; and promoting sports. Works with the Mundele Foundation, based in Canada, to implement the Community Development Program, focusing on science, education, health and agriculture.

Geographical Area of Activity: Angola.

Principal Staff: Pres. Dr Ismael Diogo da Silva; Exec. Vice-Pres. António Castelhano Maurício; Vice-Pres. Manuel Vicente; Gen. Man. Dr João de Deus Gomes Pereira.

Address: Edifício FESA/Fundação Eduardo dos Santos, Miramar, Luanda.

Telephone: 430315; **Internet:** www.fesa.og.ao; **e-mail:** info@fesa.ao.

Anguilla

FOUNDATIONS, TRUSTS AND NON-PROFIT ORGANIZATIONS

Anguilla Community Foundation

Established in 1999 with the support of the Social Security Development Fund.

Activities: Promotes local philanthropy. Manages seven funds: the General Endowment, a long-term fund that supports NGOs, projects and other initiatives; the Mouton Scholarship Fund, providing scholarships for general tertiary-level education abroad; the Anguilla College Scholarship Fund, providing scholarships for tertiary-level education abroad in the fields of information technology or medicine; the David Berglund Scholarship Fund, providing scholarships to study veterinary medicine and services; the David and Pauline Farmer Fund, providing services for senior citizens and homosexual young people; the Teacher Noonie Fund, focusing on early childhood development; the Lydia and Jeremiah Gumbs Fund, providing care for the mentally ill; and the Anguilla Cares Fund, which awards grants every 12–18 months based on community needs.

Geographical Area of Activity: Anguilla.

Finance: Total funds US $613,000, grants disbursed $556,000 (2013).

Board: Bonnie Richardson Lake (Chair.); Pamela Riley (Vice-Chair.); Seymour Hodge (Sec.); Carol Baines (Asst Sec.); Sally Randall (Treas.); Perin Bradley (Asst Treas.).

Address: POB 1097, The Valley AI2640.

Telephone: 4977209; **Internet:** www.acf.org.ai; **e-mail:** acf-accf@anguillanet.com.

Argentina

FOUNDATION CENTRE AND CO-ORDINATING BODY

Grupo de Fundaciones y Empresas (Group of Foundations and Businesses)

Established in 1995 to promote the development of foundations in Argentina.

Activities: Promotes the development of philanthropy; offers information to foundations about philanthropy in Argentina, including news on foundations' activities. The Group also maintains online databases on foundations and projects operated by not-for-profit organizations. Had 34 member organizations in 2013.

Geographical Area of Activity: Argentina.

Publications: Newsletter (monthly); *Proyectos Aprobados* (quarterly publication on projects funded by foundations).

Board of Directors: Constanza Gorleri (Pres.); Adolfo Navajas (Vice-Pres.); Cynthia Giolito (Treas.); Valeria Freylejer (Asst Treas.); Santos Lío (Sec.); Julia Díaz Ardaya (Asst Sec.).

Principal Staff: Exec. Dir Carolina Langan.

Address: Maipú 696, Piso 1B, C1006ACH Buenos Aires.

Telephone: (11) 5272-0513; **Fax:** (11) 5272-0513; **Internet:** www.gdfe.org.ar; **e-mail:** gdfe@gdfe.org.ar.

FOUNDATIONS, TRUSTS AND NON-PROFIT ORGANIZATIONS

Federación Argentina de Apoyo Familiar—FAAF (International Federation of Family Support)

Founded in 1986 by Dr Ana Mon to support families in need and to help children living on the streets.

Activities: Operates internationally in the field of social welfare. The Federation supports children, women and families in need through a network of day-care centres. Children are given education and training, including craft workshops and micro-enterprise training, and women are offered programmes in literacy, self-esteem and skills training, as well as support for drug and alcohol problems. Support is also offered to older family members.

Geographical Area of Activity: Mainly Argentina, but also Haiti, India, Mexico, Peru, South Africa, Uruguay and Venezuela.

Restrictions: No grants for individuals and only to organizations working in the area of social promotion among children and young people, women and families in need.

Publications: Various reports and publications.

Finance: Each National Federation has its own budget.

Board of Trustees: Dr Ana Mon (Pres.).

Address: Calle 33, No. 1078, 1900 La Plata.

Telephone: (221) 422-3734; **Fax:** (221) 422-3734; **Internet:** apoyofamiliar.org; **e-mail:** apoyo18familiar@gmail.com.

Fundación Acíndar (Acíndar Foundation)

Founded in 1962 by Arturo Acevedo, J. M. Aragón, J. E. Acevedo, A. F. A. Acevedo, M. Ezcurra, Rogelio A. Galarce, R. S. Pujals, J. José Ré, Thomas Jefferson Williams and C. A. Acevedo to provide social, cultural, educational and philanthropic assistance, and to promote scientific investigation and professional and technical training in Central and South America and the Caribbean.

Activities: Operates mainly in the areas of education, health, social welfare and the environment, including grants to hospitals, multimedia education projects and training schemes.

Geographical Area of Activity: Central and South America and the Caribbean.

Publications: Annual Report.

Administrative Council: Arturo T. Acevedo (Pres.).

Principal Staff: Exec. Dir Cecilia Barbón.

Address: Estanislas Zeballos 2739, 1643 Beccar, Buenos Aires.

Telephone: (11) 4719-8311; **Fax:** (11) 4719-8501; **Internet:** www.fundacionacindar.org.ar; **e-mail:** fundacion@acindar.com.ar.

Fundación Ambiente y Recursos Naturales—FARN (Environment and Natural Resources Foundation)

Founded in 1985 by Guillermo J. Cano to promote the conservation of natural resources and the environment, and sustainable development in South America.

Activities: Operates in the fields of agriculture, energy, conservation and forestry. The Foundation campaigns on environmental policy and law, public participation and the promotion of public debate. It also awards the annual Adriana Schiffrin Essay Prize on sustainable development. Maintains a library and database.

Geographical Area of Activity: South America (mainly Argentina).

Publications: Annual Report; *Suplemento de Derecho Ambiental* (quarterly, in Spanish); articles, reports, papers and other publications.

Finance: Annual income 2,032,072 pesos, expenditure 2,015,833 pesos (2012/13).

Board of Directors: Mariana Lomé (Pres.); Jorge Schiffrin (Vice-Pres.); Margarita Carlés (Sec.); Diego Luzuriaga (Treas.).

Principal Staff: Exec. Dir Andrés Nápoli; Deputy Exec. Dir Ana Di Pangracio.

Address: Tucumán 255, 6°A, 1049 Buenos Aires.

Telephone: (11) 4312-0788; **Fax:** (11) 4893-0718; **Internet:** www.farn.org.ar; **e-mail:** info@farn.org.ar.

Fundación Bariloche (Bariloche Foundation)

Founded in 1963 to improve the quality of life in Central and South America; to stimulate creative thinking in these regions; to conduct research and teaching programmes; and to offer activities of a similar type to leaders of social groups and to promote the exchange of ideas and information among them, as well as among scientists and intellectuals.

Activities: In 1978, as a result of changed socio-political conditions in Argentina, the Foundation changed its style of operation to become primarily a promotional rather than an executive institution for teaching and research. Since then, it has concentrated on four main fields of interest: energy economics and planning, with an emphasis on developing countries; environmental policy and sustainable development; quality of life; and philosophy. It assists with the planning of government programmes relating to these areas; promotes scientific meetings and the publication of a series of books in various languages to give worldwide diffusion to Central and South American intellectual activity; and maintains a library.

Geographical Area of Activity: Argentina.

Publications: *Boletín Bibliográfico* (2 a year); *Revista Desarrollo y Energía* (2 a year); *Revista Patagónica de Filosofía* (journal); *AEDH—Aspectos Económicos del Desarrollo Humano/Economic Aspects of Human Development; LAWM— Modelo Mundial Latinoamericano/The Latin American World Model;* books, periodicals, journals and papers.

Finance: Annual budget of Fundación Bariloche and its associated groups is approx. US $1.1m.

Board of Directors: Daniel Bouille (Pres.); Nicolás di Sbroiavacca (Vice-Pres.).

Principal Staff: Exec. Pres. Daniel Bouille.

Address: Sede Principal, Suiza 970, Casilla de Correo 138, 8400 San Carlos de Bariloche, Prov. de Río Negro.

Telephone: (29) 4446-2500; **Fax:** (29) 4446-1186; **Internet:** www.fundacionbariloche.org.ar; **e-mail:** fb@ fundacionbariloche.org.ar.

Fundación Bunge y Born (Bunge y Born Foundation)

Founded in 1963 by the Bunge group of companies to promote and facilitate studies and investigations that would benefit the community as a whole, through financial aid in the broad fields of social welfare, culture and science; and to award prizes to those who have best distinguished themselves in the field of scientific investigation.

Activities: Operates nationally in the fields of education, research, health and culture, chiefly through grants to institutions and the allocation of prizes and scholarships for research, or to attend conferences. The Foundation also provides emergency disaster aid and medical equipment.

Geographical Area of Activity: Argentina.

Publications: *Memoria* (Annual Report and financial statement); *Humor in Rural Argentine Schools*; *25 Years with Rural Argentine Schools*; *The Art of Juan Manuel Blanes*.

Finance: Receives contributions from the Bunge Group, private donations and bequests. Annual budget 10,132,366 pesos (2010).

Board of Directors: Jorge Born (Pres.); Alejandro de La Tour d'Auvergne (Vice-Pres.); Jenefer Féraud (Second Vice-Pres.); Alix Born (Third Vice-Pres.).

Principal Staff: Exec. Dir Ludovico Videla; Project Dir Asunción Zumárraga.

Address: 25 de Mayo 501, 6° piso, C1002ABK, 1002 Buenos Aires.

Telephone: (11) 4318-6600; **Fax:** (11) 4318-6610; **Internet:** www.fundacionbyb.org; **e-mail:** info@fundacionbyb.org.

Fundación Ecológica Universal—FEU (Universal Ecological Foundation)

Founded in 1990 to disseminate information and link fields of ecological information, and to promote sustainable development.

Activities: Operates in the field of conservation and the environment in Bolivia, Brazil, Chile, Mexico, Paraguay and Uruguay. Organizes environmental education projects in conjunction with schools, training workshops and conferences, and conducts research. Works in partnership with international organizations, and co-operates at government level for the dissemination of environmental policy information. A subsidiary, FEU-US, is registered in Alexandria, VA.

Geographical Area of Activity: Central and South America.

Publications: Reports and bulletins.

Board: Dr Gabriel Juricich (Founder-Pres.); Adrián Rosemberg (Treas.).

Principal Staff: Exec. Dir Angel Juricich.

Address: Avda Corrientes 1584, 4°, C1043ABA Buenos Aires.

Telephone: (11) 4373-1243; **Fax:** (11) 4373-0552.

Fundación para Estudio e Investigación de la Mujer—FEIM (Foundation for Women's Research and Studies)

Established in 1989 by Dr Mabel Bianco to promote the rights of women and the enhancement of their social and economic position in society.

Activities: Operates in Argentina in the area of women's rights, through providing services such as health care and health education (especially regarding AIDS and reproductive health); promotes the development of small enterprises; conducts research; and maintains a library. The Foundation also operates in the area of the environment, promoting recycling, solar energy and the development of environmental organizations in Argentina.

Geographical Area of Activity: Argentina.

Publications: *DeSidamos* (quarterly, in Spanish); *Safe Motherhood* (in Spanish); books and information on various health issues.

Finance: Annual budget approx. US $120,000.

Board of Directors: Dr Mabel Bianco (Pres.); Cecilia Correa (Sec.); Catalina Abifadel (Treas.).

Principal Staff: Admin. Daniel Aguirre.

Address: Paraná 135, 3° piso, Of. 13, C1017AAC Buenos Aires.

Telephone: (11) 4372-2763; **Internet:** www.feim.org.ar; **e-mail:** feim@feim.org.ar.

Fundación de Investigaciones Económicas Latino-americanas—FIEL (Foundation for Latin American Economic Research)

Founded in 1964 by the Chamber of Commerce of Argentina, the Stock Exchange of Buenos Aires, the Argentine Industrial Union and the Cattle Breeders' Association to analyse economic problems.

Activities: Operates in the field of economic affairs, by conducting research on business trends and structural problems of the Argentinian and Central and South American economies. The Foundation co-operates with similar Central and South American organizations. Maintains a library and database.

Geographical Area of Activity: Central and South America (mainly Argentina).

Publications: *FIEL News* (monthly); *Partes de Prensa* (monthly); *Indicadores de Coyuntura* (monthly); *Documentos de Trabajo* (quarterly); *Indicadores de Actividad y Precios* (monthly); surveys and studies.

Finance: Annual income 7,789,383 pesos, expenditure 10,554,584 pesos (31 Dec. 2013).

Board of Directors: Dr Juan Pedro Munro (Pres.); Juan C. Masjoan, Manuel Sacerdote, Vicor L. Savanti (Vice-Pres); Franco Livini (Sec.); Dr Mario E. Vázquez (Treas.); Dr Alberto Schuster (Asst Treas.).

Principal Staff: Dir and Chief Economist Juan Luis Bour.

Address: Córdoba 637, 4°, C1054AAF Buenos Aires.

Telephone: (11) 4314-1990; **Fax:** (11) 4314-8648; **Internet:** www.fiel.org; **e-mail:** postmaster@fiel.org.ar.

Fundación Mediterránea—IERAL (Mediterranean Foundation)

Founded in 1977 by a number of industrial concerns to promote national economic research and to contribute to a better understanding of and solution to Central and South American economic problems.

Activities: Sponsors a regional economic research institute, the Instituto de Estudios Económicos sobre la Realidad Argentina y Latinoamericana (IEERAL); organizes conferences and publishes the results of investigations.

Geographical Area of Activity: Central and South America.

Publications: *Revista Novedades*; reports and studies.

Board: Martín Amengual (Pres.); María Pía Astori (First Vice-Pres.); Sergio Oscar Roggio (Treas.).

Principal Staff: Gen. Man. José A. Santanoceto; Exec. Dir Myrian R. Martínez.

Address: Ituzaingó 1368, 5000 Córdoba.

Telephone: (351) 463-0000; **Internet:** www .fundmediterranea.org.ar; **e-mail:** info@fundmediterranea .org.ar.

Fundación Mujeres en Igualdad (Women in Equality Foundation)

Established in 1990 by Zita Montes de Oca to fight gender violence and discrimination, and to promote the social, economic, cultural and political development of women.

Activities: Supports women's empowerment, mainly in Argentina, with a focus on human rights, political and civil rights. The Foundation raises awareness about gender issues, such as human-trafficking prevention, through advocacy campaigns, networking, coalition building and training; and organizes international women's forums against corruption. Its project 'Organizing women against corruption' has been funded by UNIFEM/UNDEF.

Geographical Area of Activity: Mainly Argentina.

Publications: *Gender and Corruption* (2010); *Mujeres en Política* (magazine); handbooks, bulletins, brochures.

Board of Trustees: Silvia Carmen Ferraro (Pres.); Sonia Santoro (Vice-Pres.); Myrtha Schalom (Sec.); María Inés Rodríguez Aguilar (Treas.).

Principal Staff: Exec. Dir Monique Thiteux-Altschul.

Address: Urquiza 1835, 1602 Florida, Buenos Aires.

Telephone: (11) 4791-0821; **Fax:** (11) 4791-0821; **Internet:** www.mujeresenigualdad.org.ar; **e-mail:** mujeresenigualdad@infovia.com.ar; violencianunca@gmail .com.

Fundación Paz, Ecología y Arte—Fundación PEA (Foundation for Peace, Ecology and the Arts)

Established in 1997 for the promotion of peace throughout the world.

Activities: Promotes the peaceful resolution of war, and works towards world peace and a culture of peace through supporting ecology and the arts, and peace education.

Geographical Area of Activity: International.

Administrative Council: Nancy B. Ducuing de Martorelli (Pres.); Manuela D. Becerra (Sec.); Prof. Isabel Susana Guzzo (Treas.).

Principal Staff: Dir-Gen. Prof. Marcelo G. Martorelli.

Address: Córdoba 2069, 13°, Dpto A, 1120 Buenos Aires.

Telephone: (11) 4961-7941; **Fax:** (11) 4961-7941; **Internet:** www.fundacionpea.org; **e-mail:** contacto@fundacionpea .org.

Fundación Schcolnik (Schcolnik Foundation)

Founded in 1964 by Dr Enrique Schcolnik, Dr Manuel Schcolnik, José Schcolnik and Juan Schcolnik.

Activities: Operates nationally in the fields of education and social welfare, through self-conducted programmes, grants to individuals and institutions, scholarships, publications and lectures.

Geographical Area of Activity: Argentina.

Publications: List of schools and libraries assisted by the Schcolnik Foundation.

Board of Directors: Dr Enrique Schcolnik (Pres.); Dr Alejandro Carlos Piazza (Vice-Pres.); Dr Horacio della Rocca (Sec.); Jorge Acevedo (Treas.).

Address: Avda Jujuy 425, C1083AAE Buenos Aires.

Telephone: (11) 4931-0188; **Fax:** (11) 4956-1368; **Internet:** www.fundacionschcolnik.org.ar.

Fundación SES—Sustentabilidad, Educación, Solidaridad (SES Foundation—Sustainability, Education, Solidarity)

Established in 1999 to support disadvantaged young people, promote enhancement of the education system, and extend support to other NGOs undertaking similar activities.

Activities: Aims to promote educative strategies towards the social inclusion of disadvantaged adolescents; funds projects in schools and higher education establishments; and extends technological and financial assistance to other community organizations and NGOs operating in similar fields.

Geographical Area of Activity: Argentina.

Restrictions: No grants to individuals; grants only to partner organizations.

Publications: Report of innovative educational experiences; *Boletín* (electronic newsletter); *Construyendo con los Jóvenes Desde Organizaciones Comunitarias*; *Estrategias Educativas de Trabajo con Adolescentes y Jóvenes con Menos Oportunidades*; *Experiencias de Construyendo Vinculos*; *Herramientas para el trabajo con jóvenes*; *Prevención del fracaso escolar en el MERCOSUR—Las experiencias de las organizaciones de la sociedad civil*.

Administrative Council: Alberto C. Croce (Pres.); Alejandra E. Solla (Treas.); Luisa Cerar (Sec.).

Principal Staff: Exec. Dir Prof. Alberto C. Croce; Deputy Dir Prof. Alejandra E. Solla.

Address: San Martín 575, 6°A, C1004ABO Buenos Aires.

Telephone: (11) 5368-8370; **Internet:** www.fundses.org.ar; **e-mail:** info@fundses.org.ar.

Fundación Dr J. Roberto Villavicencio (Dr J. R. Villavicencio Foundation)

Established in 1982 by Dr Roberto L. Villavicencio and his family to promote teaching and research on medical sciences, and medical assistance to deprived people.

Activities: Operates in Rosario and its surrounding area in the fields of education, medicine and health, and science and technology. The Foundation carries out self-conducted programmes and research; awards grants to institutions and individuals, scholarships and fellowships and prizes; organizes conferences and training courses; and issues publications.

Geographical Area of Activity: Argentina (Rosario).

Publications: Annual Report; *Artículos de información médica*; *Trabajos de actualización médica*; *Trabajos científicos*; *Presentación de casos*.

Trustees: Susana Toncich (Pres.); Lisandro José Villavicencio (Vice-Pres.); Ivonne Villavicencio (Sec.); Roberto Villavicencio (Treas.).

Principal Staff: Dir Fernando Amelong; Exec. Sec. Claudia Miranda.

Address: Alvear 854, S2000QGB Rosario, Santa Fe.

Telephone: (341) 449-0152; **Fax:** (341) 449-0152; **Internet:** www.villavicencio.org.ar; **e-mail:** info@villavicencio.org.ar.

Instituto para la Integración de América Latina y el Caribe—BID-INTAL (Institute for Latin American and Caribbean Integration)

Founded in 1965 as a result of an agreement between the Inter-American Development Bank and the Government of Argentina to promote regional integration.

Activities: A unit of the Inter-American Development Bank. The Institute focuses mainly on trade issues; regional integration and co-operation; technical assistance, especially institutional strengthening and dialogue with civil society, including the private sector. It also contributes to the exchange of background knowledge in the areas of regional integration and physical infrastructure, and provides capacity building tools to governments of Latin America. Active in four principal areas: regional and national technical co-operation projects on integration; policy forums; integration forums; and the REDINT Integration Research Centres Network. The INTAL Documentation Center (CDI) identifies, compiles, organizes and disseminates information on integration, trade, infrastructure, development and related topics. It holds 40,000 documents, 11,500 books and 600 periodicals. A digitization process has begun for those publications made only on paper in the 1965–95 period to make their contents accessible online, in a full-text and open-access format, in a digital library model.

Geographical Area of Activity: North, Central and South America, Europe and the Asia-Pacific region.

Publications: *Integration and Trade* (2 a year, in English and Spanish); *Carta Mensual* (monthly); and *Sub-regional Integration Reports Series*; reports, periodicals, magazines and newsletters.

Principal Staff: Dir Gustavo Beliz.

Address: Calle Esmeralda 130, 11° y 16°, C1035ABD Buenos Aires.

Telephone: (11) 4323-2350; **Fax:** (11) 4323-2365; **Internet:** www.iadb.org/intal; **e-mail:** intal@iadb.org.

Instituto Torcuato di Tella (Torcuato di Tella Institute)

Founded in 1958 by the family of industrialist and philanthropist Torcuato di Tella to serve the community, promote education and intellectual activities in general, and scientific research in particular.

Activities: Operates nationally and internationally in the fields of economics, sociology, epistemology and methodology of the social sciences, political science, history and educational science. The Institute carries out self-conducted research; provides fellowships and scholarships; organizes conferences, courses, seminars and lectures; and issues publications. It creates, directs and administers research centres such as the Centro de Investigaciones Económicas and the Centro de Investigaciones Sociales; and also supports an associated centre, the Centro de Investigaciones en Ciencias de la Educación. It also holds training courses for graduate students, in economics, public policy and history, and maintains a library. Comprises the Fundación Torcuato di Tella (f. 1958).

Geographical Area of Activity: International.

Publications: Annual Report; books, working papers and articles in specialized journals.

Foundation Board of Directors: Luciano Nicolás Francisco di Tella (Pres.); Torcuato Salvador Francisco Nicolás di Tella (Vice-Pres.).

Principal Staff: Pres. (a.i.) Andrés Lautaro di Tella.

Address: Miñones 2159/77, 1° Piso, 1428 Buenos Aires.

Telephone: (11) 4783-8680; **Fax:** (11) 4783-3061; **Internet:** www.itdt.edu; **e-mail:** institutoditella@utdt.edu.

Armenia

FOUNDATION CENTRES AND CO-ORDINATING BODIES

Centre for the Development of Civil Society—CDCS

Established in 1988 during the period of 'perestroika' as the Ghevond Alishan Cultural Educational Association by a group of scholars from Yerevan State University and the Institute of Linguistics of the National Academy of Sciences of the Republic of Armenia. It was registered as an NGO when Armenia became independent of the USSR in 1991.

Activities: Promotes democracy and civil society. The Centre works in the fields of human rights and gender equality. It also provides training to NGOs; supports refugees and minority groups; and carries out research, which it disseminates through publications.

Geographical Area of Activity: Armenia.

Finance: Raises funds from grantmaking international development agencies and other donors. Activities are supported by individual or business donations.

Principal Staff: Exec. Dir Anahit Abrahamyan.

Address: 0025 Yerevan, 49 Nalbandian St, No. 7.

Telephone: (10) 56-05-44; **Fax:** (10) 58-56-77; **Internet:** www.cdcs.am; **e-mail:** info@cdcs.am.

NGO Centre—NGOC

Founded in 1997 to provide training and technical assistance on advocacy and public policy advocacy.

Activities: Supports NGOs aiming to influence decision-making bodies. Since 2001, the Centre has promoted social partnership, offering training and technical assistance to NGOs, representatives of national and local government, and establishing two social partnership mechanisms.

Geographical Area of Activity: Armenia.

Publications: *Armenian NGO News in Brief* (annual); *NGOC Gazette* (annual).

Board Members: Margarit Piliposyan (Pres.).

Principal Staff: Co-ordinator Arpine Hakobyan.

Address: Vanadzor, RA, Garegin Njdeh 9/2A.

Telephone: (917) 74-33-17; **Internet:** www.ngoc.am; **e-mail:** ngocenter@ngoc.am; ngoc.csd.ngo@gmail.com.

FOUNDATIONS, TRUSTS AND NON-PROFIT ORGANIZATIONS

AREGAK—Sun/Soleil

Established in 1996 (officially registered in 1998) to assist in the social development of orphaned Armenian children.

Activities: Operates in the fields of social welfare, education and health, offering assistance to needy orphan children and to the elderly, refugees and those living in poverty. Also offers training.

Geographical Area of Activity: Armenia.

Principal Staff: Pres. Varduhi Khatchikyan; Head of Programmes Lusine Vardanyan.

Address: 0009 Yerevan, 19A Koryun.

Telephone: (93) 28-73-61; **Internet:** vardanyan.am/aregak; www.childrensun.narod.ru; **e-mail:** aregaksun@yahoo.com.

Open Society Institute Assistance Foundation, Armenia—OSIAFA

Established in 1996; an independent foundation, part of the Soros foundations network.

Activities: Promotes reform in the fields of education, information and the media, social welfare, public health, law and human rights, ethnic minorities, and the arts and culture. The Foundation collaborates with other Armenian NGOs. It also operates on a regional level through the East-East programme.

Geographical Area of Activity: Armenia.

Publications: Annual Report; newsletter, reports, briefings.

Board of Directors: Armen Pirouzyan (Chair.).

Principal Staff: Exec. Dir Larisa Minasyan; Deputy Dir (Programmes) David Amiryan; Dir of Finance Kristina Danielyan.

Address: 375002 Yerevan, 7/1 Tumanyan St, 2nd cul-de-sac.

Telephone: (10) 53-38-62; **Fax:** (10) 53-67-58; **Internet:** www.osi.am; **e-mail:** info@osi.am.

Australia

FOUNDATION CENTRES AND CO-ORDINATING BODIES

CAF—Charities Aid Foundation Australia

Established in 1999; part of the CAF Global Alliance network of organizations.

Activities: Provides information and advisory services to charities.

Geographical Area of Activity: Australia and New Zealand.

Publications: *World Giving Index*; research and reports.

Finance: Total assets $A1,235,953, annual revenue $A1,506,313 (30 April 2013).

Board of Directors: Cynthia M. Nadai (Chair.).

Principal Staff: CEO Lisa Grinham.

Address: Suite 5, Level 5, 100 Walker St, North Sydney, NSW 2060; Locked Bag 962, North Sydney, NSW 2059.

Telephone: (2) 9929 9633; **Fax:** (2) 9929 9588; **Internet:** www.cafaustralia.org.au; **e-mail:** info@cafaustralia.org.au.

Philanthropy Australia

Established in 1975; formerly known as the Australian Association of Philanthropy.

Activities: Represents the philanthropic sector; promotes philanthropy by the community, business and government sectors; inspires and supports new philanthropists; increases the effectiveness of philanthropy through the provision of information, resources and networking opportunities; and promotes strong and transparent governance standards in the philanthropic sector.

Geographical Area of Activity: Australia.

Restrictions: A grantmaker support organization only; does not make grants itself.

Publications: *The Directory of Funders* (online only); *A Guide to Giving for Australians*; *Trustee Handbook*; *Private Ancillary Funds (PAF) Trustee Handbook*; *A Grantseeker's Guide to Trusts and Foundations*.

Finance: Total assets $A1,006,509, annual income $A2,595,918 (2014).

Council: Alan Schwartz (Pres.); David Ward (Treas.).

Principal Staff: CEO (a.i.) Chris Walsh (until Nov. 2015).

Address: Level 2, 55 Collins St, Melbourne, Vic 3000.

Telephone: (3) 9662 9299; **Fax:** (3) 9662 2655; **Internet:** www.philanthropy.org.au; **e-mail:** info@philanthropy.org.au.

FOUNDATIONS, TRUSTS AND NON-PROFIT ORGANIZATIONS

Activ Foundation

Established in 1951 by a group of parents to provide support services for people with intellectual disability and their families.

Activities: Provides accommodation, recreation, respite, employment, training and skills development to 2,300 people with a disability, and to their families. Employs some 1,070 people with a disability.

Geographical Area of Activity: Western Australia.

Publications: *Activ News* (quarterly newsletter); Annual Report.

Finance: Total assets $A51,347,000 (30 June 2014).

Board of Directors: Andrew Edwards (Chair.); Tina Thomas (Deputy Chair.).

Principal Staff: CEO Tony Vis.

Address: POB 446, Wembley, WA 6913; 327 Cambridge St, Wembley, WA 6014.

Telephone: (8) 9387 0555; **Fax:** (8) 9387 0599; **Internet:** www.activ.asn.au; **e-mail:** info@activ.asn.au.

AMP Foundation

Established in 1992 by the AMP Group, a financial services company, for general charitable purposes in the areas of capacity building and community involvement. Merged with the AXA Charitable Trust in 2011.

Activities: Invests in two key areas: Capacity Building and Community Involvement. The Capacity Building programmes focus on the education and employment of young people and the sustainability of the non-profit sector; the Community Involvement programmes focus on supporting the work of AMP employees and financial planners in the community, including an employee volunteering programme. Operates in long-term partnerships, not on a grantmaking basis.

Geographical Area of Activity: Australia, New Zealand.

Restrictions: No unsolicited applications for funding are accepted.

Publications: Annual Report.

Finance: Annual revenue $A7,230,608, expenditure A$3,681,337 (31 Dec. 2014).

Board of Directors: Richard Grellman (Chair.).

Principal Staff: Man. Helen Liondos.

Address: 33 Alfred St, Sydney, NSW 2000.

Telephone: (2) 9257 5334; **Fax:** (2) 9257 2864; **Internet:** www.amp.com.au/amp/in-the-community/amp-foundation; **e-mail:** amp_foundation@amp.com.au.

APACE Village First Electrification Group—APACE VFEG

Established in 1976 by Dr Robert Waddell and other senior academics from Sydney-based universities to promote renewable energy in rural communities in less-developed countries.

Activities: Operated in more than 150 rural communities in South and South-East Asia and the island states of the Pacific region, in the fields of aid to less-developed countries and environmental conservation. The Group provides technical assistance, research facilities, project design, and management and evaluation services in the areas of appropriate technology, micro-hydroelectricity and sustainable agriculture. Now involved only in support of existing hydro installations in the Pacific and the dissemination of information.

Geographical Area of Activity: Pacific and South-East Asia.

Restrictions: Not a donor organization.

Publications: Annual Report; *Village Power in Solomon Islands*; *Producing Power at the Local Level*; *Energia Newsletter on Gender and Energy in Oceania*; *Empowering the Poor: a radical path to peace?*; *Replanting the Banana Tree: a study in ecologically sustainable development*.

Trustees: Prof. Paul Bryce (Pres.).

Principal Staff: Admin. Officer Peter Vail.

Address: c/o UTS, POB 123, Broadway, NSW 2007.

Telephone: (2) 9514 2547; **Internet:** www.apace.uts.edu.au; **e-mail:** apacevfeg@gmail.com.

Apex Foundation

Founded in 1976 by the Association of Apex Clubs to improve the quality of life for young Australians with special needs.

Activities: Supports research and activities for social, economic and cultural programmes, working in collaboration with the Association of Apex Clubs. Managed 7 trusts in 2014.

Geographical Area of Activity: Australia.

Restrictions: Researchers may be of any nationality, but research must be undertaken in Australia.

Publications: Annual Report; *Apex in Action*.

Finance: Total assets $A690,125; annual amount distributed to trusts $A593,706 (30 June 2014).

Trustees: Stephen L. Bigarelli (Chair.); Phil Pregnell (Deputy Chair.); Mike Fitze (Sec.).

Principal Staff: Nat. Man. Noel Hadjimichael.

Address: Level 5, AON Tower, 201 Kent St, Sydney, NSW 2000.

Telephone: (2) 9253 7775; **Fax:** (2) 9253 7117; **Internet:** www.apexfoundation.org.au; **e-mail:** info@apexfoundation.org.au.

Arthritis Australia

Established in 1999 to provide information and support to people with arthritis and related conditions, and promote medical and scientific research in the field. Acts as the national secretariat for affiliated foundations throughout Australia.

Activities: Operates in Australia, the United Kingdom and the USA in the field of medicine and health, in particular arthritis research and education; provides assistance to the medical, scientific and allied health professions in the form of research grants, fellowships and scholarships.

Geographical Area of Activity: Australia, United Kingdom and USA.

Publications: Annual Report; books.

Finance: Total assets $A2,446,012; annual income $A3,490,949, expenditure $A3,326,957 (30 June 2013).

Board of Directors: Roger Mattar (Chair.); David Motteram (Deputy Chair.); Wayne Jarman (Treas.).

Principal Staff: Chief Exec. Ainslie Cahill.

Address: POB 550, Broadway NSW 2007; Level 2, 255 Broadway, Broadway NSW 2037.

Telephone: (2) 9518 4441; **Fax:** (2) 9518 4011; **Internet:** www.arthritisaustralia.com.au; **e-mail:** info@arthritisaustralia.com.au.

Arts Centre Melbourne Foundation

Comprises the Betty Amsden Arts Education Endowment for Children (f. 2009), which was established with an endowment of $A5m. from the philanthropist Betty Amsden; and the Kenneth Myer Asian Theatre Series Endowment Fund, also established with an endowment of $A5m.

Activities: Supports the work of the Victorian Arts Centre Trust.

Geographical Area of Activity: Australia.

Finance: Annual income $A73,077,000, expenditure $A70,117,000 (2014).

Board of Governors: Sandy Clark (Chair.).

Address: 100 St Kilda Rd, Melbourne, Vic 3004; POB 7585 St Kilda Rd, Vic 8004.

Telephone: (3) 9281 8000; **Fax:** (3) 9281 8282; **Internet:** artscentremelbourne.com.au.

Aussie Farmers Foundation

Established in 2010 to assist rural and regional communities in Australia.

Activities: Offers grants to organizations that improve the health and well-being of rural and regional communities in Australia.

Geographical Area of Activity: Australia.

Principal Staff: Commercial Man. Kate Palethorpe.

Address: 50–54 Clayton Rd, Clayton, Vic 3168; POB 309, Mount Waverley, Vic 3149.

Telephone: (3) 9015 9138; **Internet:** www.aussiefarmersfoundation.org.au; **e-mail:** info@aussiefarmersfoundation.org.au.

Australia-Japan Foundation

Founded in 1976 by the Australian Government as an independent statutory body to strengthen relations between Australia and Japan.

Activities: Operates in Australia and Japan under six main programmes: Reconstruction Initiative; Economics and Trade; Security, Regional and International Relations; Education and Science; Society and Culture; Communication, Information and Advocacy. Projects include a Japanese-language website and a public access Australian Resource Centre, as well as support for Australian community groups to gain access to a Japanese audience. The Sir Neil Currie Memorial Australian Studies Awards offer funding to Japanese postgraduate scholars and academics.

Geographical Area of Activity: Australia and Japan.

Publications: Annual Report; occasional papers; *Science Communication in Theory and Practice*; *Nourishing Terrains: Australian Aboriginal Views of Landscape and Wilderness*.

Finance: Total annual income $A1,000,000, expenditure $A928,045 (2011/12).

Advisory Board: Murray McLean (Chair.).

Address: RG Casey Bldg, John McEwen Cresc., Barton, ACT 0221; Australian Embassy, 2-1-14 Mita, Minato-Ku, Tokyo 108-8361, Japan.

Telephone: (2) 6261 3898 (Australia); (3) 5232-4063 (Japan); **Fax:** (2) 6261 2143 (Australia); (3) 5232-4064 (Japan); **Internet:** ajf.australia.or.jp; **e-mail:** ajf.australia@dfat.gov.au.

Australian Academy of the Humanities

Established in 1969 by the Australian Humanities Research Council to grant scholarships and further research in the field of humanities.

Activities: Aims to advance knowledge in the field of humanities, in particular archaeology; European languages and cultures; classical studies; history; the arts; Asian studies; English; linguistics; philosophy, religion and the history of ideas; and cultural and communication studies. Offers grants and awards, including the Crawford Medal, the McCredie Musicological Award, and the Ernst and Rosemarie Keller Award.

Geographical Area of Activity: Australia.

Restrictions: Maximum individual grant disbursed $A4,000.

Publications: *Humanities Australia* (journal); symposium papers; monographs; occasional papers; edited collections.

Finance: Annual income $A1,456,518, expenditure $A1,530,537 (30 June 2014).

Council: Prof. John Fitzgerald (Pres.); Prof. Peter Cryle (Vice-Pres and International Sec.); Prof. Elizabeth Minchin (Hon. Sec.); Prof. Richard Waterhouse (Hon. Treas.); Prof. Lesley Johnson (Immediate Past Pres.); Prof. Deirdre Coleman (Vice-Pres.).

Principal Staff: Exec. Dir Dr Christina Parolin.

Address: 3 Liversidge St, Acton, Canberra, ACT 2601; GPO Box 93, Canberra, ACT 2601.

Telephone: (2) 6125 9860; **Fax:** (2) 6248 6287; **Internet:** www.humanities.org.au; **e-mail:** enquiries@humanities.org.au.

Australian Academy of Technological Sciences and Engineering—ATSE

Established in 1976 as the Australian Academy of Technological Sciences. Renamed in 1987 to incorporate Engineering.

Activities: Facilitates a network of forums, working groups and advisory groups on a range of key issues. Disseminates information nationally through its STELR (Science and Technology Education Leveraging Relevance) Project. Also runs the *ATSE Clunies Ross Award* for the application of science and technology to benefit Australia economically, socially or environmentally.

Geographical Area of Activity: International.

Publications: Annual Report; *Focus* (magazine, 6 a year); Parliamentary Briefings; reports.

Finance: Annual revenue $A7,260,954, expenditure $A2,226,866 (30 June 2014).

Board of Directors: Dr Alan Finkel (Pres.); Prof. Peter Gray, Dr Susan Pond (Vice-Pres).

Principal Staff: CEO Dr Margaret Hartley.

Address: Level 1/1, Bowen Cresc., Melbourne, Vic 3004; POB 4055, Melbourne, Vic 3001.

Telephone: (3) 9864 0900; **Fax:** (3) 9864 0930; **Internet:** atse .org.au; **e-mail:** info@atse.org.au.

Australian Academy of Science

Founded in 1954 by Australian Fellows of the Royal Society of London, an independent body of Australia's research scientists.

Activities: Aims to foster excellence in Australian scientific research and education. Facilitates access to international scientific organizations and programmes; provides research grants and makes awards to overseas scientists; and supports research conferences to advance the application and development of science. Also maintains the Afolph Basser Library, which was established in 1962.

Geographical Area of Activity: Mainly Australia.

Publications: Annual Report; newsletters.

Finance: Total assets $A52,402,852; annual revenue $A13,729,524, expenditure $A11,199,213 (30 June 2014).

Executive Committee: Prof. Andrew Holmes (Pres.); Prof. Chennupati Jagadish (Sec. for Physical Sciences); Prof. Marilyn Renfree (Sec. for Biological Sciences); Prof. Leslie Field (Sec. for Science Policy); Prof. Pauline Ladiges (Sec. for Education and Public Awareness); Prof. Cheryl Praeger (Foreign Sec.); Dr Oliver Mayo (Treas.).

Principal Staff: Chief Exec. Dr Sue Meek.

Address: Ian Potter House Gordon St, Acton, ACT 2601; POB 783, Canberra, ACT 2601.

Telephone: (2) 6201 9400; **Fax:** (2) 6201 9494; **Internet:** www .science.org.au; **e-mail:** aas@science.org.au.

Australian-American Fulbright Commission

Founded in 1949 by the Governments of Australia and of the USA to further mutual understanding between the people of the two nations through educational and cultural exchanges.

Activities: Works in the field of education by operating the Fulbright Scholarship programme for Americans and Australians to undertake research, study or lecturing assignments in Australia or the USA respectively. Awards cover all academic disciplines and professions.

Geographical Area of Activity: USA and Australia.

Restrictions: Scholarships are open to Australian and US citizens only.

Publications: Annual Report; *The Fulbrighter* (newsletter).

Board of Directors: Tony Abbott, John Berry (Hon. Co-Chair.); Prof. Don DeBats (Chair.).

Principal Staff: Exec. Dir Dr Tangerine Holt.

Address: POB 9541, Deakin, ACT 2600.

Telephone: (2) 6260 4460; **Fax:** (2) 6260 4461; **Internet:** www .fulbright.com.au; **e-mail:** fulbright@fulbright.com.au.

Australian Cancer Research Foundation

Established in 1984 by Sir Peter Abeles and Lady Sonia McMahon.

Activities: Operates nationally in the field of cancer research. Provides funding for capital projects and equipment, research and seed grants. Raises funds through corporate sponsorship, donations, bequests and committee fund-raising activities.

Geographical Area of Activity: Australia.

Publications: Newsletter (annual).

Finance: Grants awarded $A4,690,000, annual income $A2,356,993 (31 Dec. 2013).

Board of Trustees: Tom S. Dery (Chair.).

Principal Staff: Chief Exec. Prof. Ian Brown.

Address: Suite 409, The Strand Arcade, 412 George St, Sydney, NSW 2000.

Telephone: (2) 9223 7833; **Fax:** (2) 9223 1800; **Internet:** www .acrf.com.au; **e-mail:** info@acrf.com.au.

Australian Communities Foundation

Established in 1997 as the Melbourne Community Foundation, but has since expanded to operate nationally and internationally.

Activities: Manages philanthropic investments on behalf of individuals, groups, companies and other organizations, pooling resources and using the funds to support projects that build healthy communities.

Geographical Area of Activity: Australia.

Finance: Annual revenue $A13,289,843, expenditure $A1,840,500 (30 June 2014).

Board of Directors: Sarah Hosking (Chair.); George Krithis (Sec.).

Principal Staff: Gen. Man. Andrea Heffernan.

Address: Fitzroy Town Hall, 201 Napier St, Fitzroy, Vic 3065; POB 1011, Collingwood, Vic 3066.

Telephone: (3) 9412 0412; **Internet:** communityfoundation .org.au; **e-mail:** admin@communityfoundation.org.au.

Australian Conservation Foundation

Founded in 1965 to promote the understanding and practice of conservation throughout Australia and its territories.

Activities: Operates in the field of conservation and the environment through campaigning, research, policy development, enterprises, membership services and promotion of public awareness. Has campaign offices in South Australia and New South Wales, and a national lobby office in Canberra.

Geographical Area of Activity: Australia and the Asia-Pacific region.

Restrictions: Not a grantmaking organization.

Publications: Annual Report; *Habitat* (6 a year); *Sustainability Report*; monthly online newsletter; reports, policy statements and discussion papers; financial report.

Finance: Annual income $A1,420,169, expenditure $A12,858,245 (30 June 2014).

Board: Geoffrey Cousins (Pres.); Irina Cattalina, Robert Fowler (Vice-Pres); Mary Latham (Treas.); Jon Anstey (Hon. Sec.).

Principal Staff: CEO Kelly O'Shanassy.

Address: 1st Floor, 60 Leicester St, Carlton, Vic 3053.

Telephone: (3) 9345 1111; **Fax:** (3) 9345 1166; **Internet:** www .acfonline.org.au; **e-mail:** acf@acfonline.org.au.

Australian Council for International Development

Founded in 1965 to provide for consultation and co-operation between member organizations concerning their work at home and abroad, with the federal and state governments, the UN and its specialized agencies, and in the field of overseas aid nationally and internationally; to bring the needs for, and the purposes and results of, overseas aid before member organizations, the Australian community and governments, and the UN and its agencies; to prepare and disseminate information on aid activities and issues of development, including refugee and migrant services; and to promote research into aid activities. Formerly known as the Australian Council for Overseas Aid—ACFOA.

Activities: Co-ordinates the activities of its numerous member organizations during international disasters or emergencies through the International Disaster Emergencies Committee, and has sub-committees co-ordinating activities in areas such as North-South relations, the Pacific, Indo-China and regional human rights. A development education programme co-ordinates the educational activities of member agencies, and informs and educates particular groups in the community that have a special opportunity to promote international development and co-operation, such as teachers, students and those engaged in voluntary aid administration. The Council holds specialized conferences and consultations and, in addition, promotes more stringent self-regulation by the aid sector, particularly through its development of a Code of Conduct for NGOs.

Geographical Area of Activity: International.

Publications: *ACFID Research in Development Series*; *ACFID-IHS Working Paper Series*; practice notes; research papers; position papers and analysis.

Finance: Annual revenue $A2,905,407, expenditure $A2,801,968 (30 June 2014).

Executive Committee: Sam Mostyn (Pres.); Nigel Spence, Ian Wishart, Julia Newton-Howes (Vice-Pres).

Principal Staff: Exec. Dir Marc Purcell.

Address: 14 Napier Cl., Deakin, ACT 2600; Private Bag 3, Deakin, ACT 2600.

Telephone: (2) 6285 1816; **Fax:** (2) 6285 1720; **Internet:** www .acfid.asn.au; **e-mail:** main@acfid.asn.au.

The Australian Elizabethan Theatre Trust

Founded in 1954 to promote independent drama, opera, ballet and the performing arts in general.

Activities: Sponsors national tours for Australian and overseas works. Conducts research, training courses and conferences, and awards prizes and grants within Australia. Also awards grants and scholarships for international programmes.

Geographical Area of Activity: Mainly Australia.

Publications: *Trust News* (6 a year).

Finance: Total assets $A7,576,689; annual revenue $A332,313 (31 Dec. 2014).

Board of Directors: Lloyd D. S. Waddy (Chair.); Brian R. Larking (Sec.).

Principal Staff: Gen. Man. Warwick D. Ross.

Address: POB 6064, North Sydney, NSW 2060; Level 1, Unit 5, 20 Young St, Neutral Bay, NSW 2089.

Telephone: (2) 9929 7449; **Fax:** (2) 9929 6964; **Internet:** thetrust.org.au; **e-mail:** reception@aett.com.au.

Australian Foundation for the Peoples of Asia and the Pacific—AFAP

Established in 1968, originally to co-ordinate philanthropic programmes in the Pacific region, now expanded to include Africa and Asia; formerly known as the Foundation for the Peoples of the South Pacific.

Activities: Supports the economic and social development of communities in Africa, Asia and the Pacific Islands, through grants to projects in the fields of health, education, rural development and the environment. Funded initiatives include HIV awareness, water and sanitation projects, literacy programmes, and training of health care workers. Funding is currently directed towards projects in Afghanistan, Cambodia, Timor-Leste, Fiji, India, Iran, Kazakhstan, Kenya, Kyrgyzstan, Laos, Malawi, Mozambique, Nepal, the Philippines, Papua New Guinea, Samoa, Sri Lanka, Tajikistan, Tonga, Turkmenistan, Uzbekistan, Viet Nam, Zambia and Zimbabwe. Also donates medical equipment and supplies.

Geographical Area of Activity: Africa, Asia and the Pacific.

Publications: Reports; newsletter.

Finance: Annual revenue $A8,836,600, expenditure $A8,682,629 (30 June 2014).

Board of Directors: John Rock (Chair.); Prof. Jock Harkness (Sec.).

Principal Staff: Exec. Dir Christine Murphy.

Address: POB 12, Crows Nest, NSW 1585; Suite 102, Level 1, 619 Pacific Highway, St Leonards, NSW 2065.

Telephone: (2) 9906 3792; **Fax:** (2) 9436 4637; **Internet:** www .afap.org; **e-mail:** info@afap.org.

Australian Institute of International Affairs

Founded in 1933 to stimulate interest in, and provide a forum for, the discussion of international affairs and foreign policy, both among its members and the general public. Provides a wide range of opportunities for the dissemination of information and the free exchange of views in this field; it does not itself hold or express any opinions.

Activities: Work covers international relations, economics, trade, strategic and defence studies, and international law, through research, publications, lectures, and national and international conferences. There are branches in all States and Territories.

Geographical Area of Activity: Australia.

Publications: *Australian Journal of International Affairs—(AJIA)* (journal, five issues a year); *Australia in World Affairs* (series); occasional papers and conference proceedings.

Finance: Total assets $A2,952,220 (30 June 2014).

National Executive Board: John McCarthy (Pres.); Zara Kimpton (Vice-Pres.); Dayle Redden (Treas.).

Principal Staff: Exec. Dir Melissa H. Conley Tyler.

Address: Stephen House, 32 Thesiger Ct, Deakin, ACT 2600.

Telephone: (2) 6282 2133; **Fax:** (2) 6285 2334; **Internet:** www .aiia.asn.au; **e-mail:** ceo@aiia.asn.au.

Australian Multicultural Foundation—AMF

Established in 1988 to foster commitment in Australians towards Australia.

Activities: Focuses on education, medicine and health, arts and humanities, law and human rights, and social welfare and studies. Works towards its objective by conducting research, organizing programmes, training courses, conferences, providing grants to institutions and issuing publications. Other significant activities include creating and promoting an awareness of different cultures through literacy programmes; improving cultural tolerance through improved community relations, social links and overseas links; and promoting the participation of Australians in organizations significant for community responsibility and citizenship.

Geographical Area of Activity: Australia, with ties to the People's Republic of China, Europe and the United Kingdom.

Restrictions: No grants to individuals or outside Australia.

Publications: Annual Report; newsletter; project reports; research and projects archive.

Finance: Total assets $A3,296,440, annual revenue $A315,750 (30 June 2014).

Board of Directors: Prof. Kwong Lee Dow (Chair.).

Principal Staff: Exec. Dir and Sec. Dr B. (Hass) Dellal.

Address: Level 1, 185 Faraday St, Carlton, Vic 3053; POB 538, Carlton South, Vic 3053.

Telephone: (3) 9347 6622; **Fax:** (3) 9347 2218; **Internet:** www .amf.net.au; **e-mail:** info@amf.net.au.

Australian Spinal Research Foundation

Established in 1976 to work towards the betterment of health of Australians through research on spinal health care.

Activities: Supports research on the causes, diagnosis, cure and prevention of spinal syndromes and diseases. Offers grants for research pertaining to the principles and practices of chiropractic care. The Dynamic Growth (DG) Congress, a fund-raising activity, is conducted annually by the Foundation on the Gold Coast in Queensland.

Geographical Area of Activity: Australia.

Restrictions: Priority is given to applicants from Australia.

Publications: Annual Report; newsletters; brochures.

Finance: Total assets $A986,009, annual revenue $A1,491,136 (30 June 2014).

Governors: Dr Martin Harvey (Pres.); Dr Angus Pyke (Deputy Pres.); Dr Nimrod Weiner (Treas.); Dr Mark Uren (Sec.).

Principal Staff: CEO Roley Cook.

Address: POB 1047, Springwood, Qld 4127; Suite 7, 3–9 University Dr., Springwood, Qld 4131.

Telephone: (7) 3808 4098; **Fax:** (7) 3808 8109; **Internet:** www.spinalresearch.com.au; **e-mail:** info@spinalresearch.com.au.

Australian Volunteers International

Founded in 1961, and previously known as the Overseas Service Bureau, to encourage the transference of technical expertise from Australia to people of the developing world, particularly countries of Africa, Asia and the Pacific.

Activities: Promotes exchanges between experts in international development; recruits, prepares and sends volunteers to work in less-developed countries, in partnership with local communities. The organization has placed approximately 6,000 Australian volunteers in more than 50 countries of Africa, Asia, the Pacific and Central and South America, and in Australian Aboriginal communities.

Geographical Area of Activity: Africa, Asia and the Pacific, and Central and South America.

Publications: *Australian Volunteers* (newsletter, 3 a year); Annual Report.

Finance: Annual revenue $A31,465,046, expenditure $A30,617,451 (30 June 2014).

Board of Directors: Kathy Townsend (Chair.); Jenny McGregor, Dr Peter Wilkins (Deputy Chair.); David Jones (Sec.).

Principal Staff: CEO Paul Bird.

Address: 71 Argyle St, POB 350, Fitzroy, Vic 3065.

Telephone: (3) 9279 1788; **Fax:** (3) 9419 4280; **Internet:** www.australianvolunteers.com; **e-mail:** info@australianvolunteers.com.

Baker IDI Heart & Diabetes Institute

Created in 2008 by the merger of the Baker IDI Heart Research Institute and the International Diabetes Institute (IDI).

Activities: Work extends from laboratory to wide-scale community studies, with a focus on the diagnosis, prevention and treatment of diabetes and cardiovascular diseas.

Geographical Area of Activity: Australia.

Publications: Annual Reports; *Perspectives Series* (1–2 a year); reports, fact sheets and other resources.

Finance: Annual revenue $A72,211,494, expenditure $A67,420,875 (31 Dec. 2013).

Board of Directors: Peter Scott (Chair.); Lindsay Maxstead (Treas.).

Principal Staff: Dir Prof. Garry Jennings.

Address: POB 6492, Melbourne, Vic 3004; 75 Commercial Rd, Melbourne, Vic 3004.

Telephone: (3) 8532 1111; **Fax:** (3) 8532 1100; **Internet:** www.bakeridi.edu.au; **e-mail:** reception@bakeridi.edu.au.

Jack Brockhoff Foundation—JBF

Established in 1979 by Sir Jack Brockhoff, Chair. and Man. Dir of Brockhoff Biscuits, to provide philanthropic support to organizations that aim to have a positive and enduring impact on the health and well-being of communities.

Activities: Grants funds to hospitals, research institutions, community groups, youth support and charitable organizations in Victoria. Funds are offered to assist those with disabilities, severely disadvantaged families, elderly people, children, people with debilitating diseases and unsheltered young people at risk. Particularly assists young people by providing opportunities to enable them to improve their circumstances and future livelihoods.

Geographical Area of Activity: Victoria, Australia only.

Restrictions: No funding for budget deficits, general operating expenses, core programmes funded from other sources, attendance at conferences and seminars, travel, bodies that are themselves grantmaking agencies, bequest programmes, contribution to the corpus of another trust, general fund-raising campaigns/annual appeals. The Foundation considers applications only from organizations endorsed by the Australian Taxation Office as a Deductible Gift Recipient and a Tax Concession Charity.

Publications: *Biscuits & Beyond* (Robert Murray, 2006).

Finance: Annual income $A8,080,323, expenditure $A313,726 (30 June 2014).

Board of Directors: Robert H. N. Symons (Chair.).

Principal Staff: Exec. Officer and Sec. Tanya Costello.

Address: Suite 501, 685 Burke Rd, Camberwell, Vic 3124.

Telephone: (3) 9006 1765; **Internet:** www.jackbrockhoff.org.au; **e-mail:** foundation@jackbrockhoff.org.au.

William Buckland Foundation

Established in 1964 by the will of William Buckland to benefit Australia and Australians.

Activities: One-half of the Foundation's income is used to fund public hospitals, benevolent institutions and societies in the state of Victoria, especially organizations for the benefit of children; the other half funds public scientific and educational institutions in Victoria.

Geographical Area of Activity: Australia.

Finance: Annual revenue $A6,909,856, expenditure $A795,766 (30 June 2014).

Board of Trustees: C. G. (Sandy) Clark (Chair.).

Address: c/o Equity Trustees, Philanthropy Services, Level 2, 575 Bourke St, Melbourne, Vic 3000; GPO Box 2307, Melbourne, Vic 3001.

Telephone: (3) 8623 5000; **Internet:** www.eqt.com.au/not-for-profit-organisations/confirmed-2015-programs/william-buckland-foundation.aspx; **e-mail:** charities@eqt.com.au.

Cancer Council Australia

Established in 1961, as the Australian Cancer Society, with the aim of preventing cancer, and the illnesses, disabilities and deaths caused by cancer.

Activities: Operates in the field of health and welfare. The Council and its eight member organizations, operating in each state and territory of Australia, work in partnership to undertake and fund cancer research, cancer prevention and control, and information and support services. Runs a telephone helpline.

Geographical Area of Activity: Australia.

Publications: Annual Report; *National Cancer Prevention Policy*; *Research Highlights*; *Cancer Forum*.

Finance: Annual expenditure A $9,346,934 (2013/14).

Board of Directors: Stephen Foster (Pres.); Jane Fenton (Vice-Pres.).

Principal Staff: CEO (a.i.) Catherine Sullivan.

Address: POB 4708, Sydney, NSW 2001; Level 14/477 Pitt Street, Sydney, NSW 2000.

Telephone: (2) 8063 4100; **Fax:** (2) 8063 4101; **Internet:** www.cancer.org.au; **e-mail:** info@cancer.org.au.

Children's Medical Research Institute

Established in 1958 to undertake and carry out paediatric research; to assess the findings of the research and disseminate such information to the medical field as well as those involved in childcare. Affiliated to the Children's Hospital Westmead and the University of Sydney.

Activities: Operates in the field of medical research. Grants funds to students carrying out research, in particular research into childhood diseases, especially cancer, genetic disorders, leukaemia and neurosciences, and to those using recombinant DNA technology. The Institute also offers grants for postdoctoral research to Australian residents, and fellowships to postgraduates from outside Australia.

Geographical Area of Activity: Australia.

Restrictions: Grants to students who are Australian residents and internationally to postgraduate students.

Publications: Annual Report; newsletters.

Finance: Annual revenue $A32,925,514, expenditure $A25,416,073 (31 Dec. 2014).

Board of Directors: Prof. Frank J. Martin (Pres.); Carolyn Forster (Vice-Pres.); Rod J. Atfield (Treas.).

Principal Staff: Dir Prof. Roger Reddel.

Address: Locked Bag 23, Wentworthville, NSW 2145; 214 Hawkesbury Rd, Westmead, NSW 2145.

Telephone: (2) 9687 2800; **Fax:** (2) 9687 2120; **Internet:** www .cmri.org.au; **e-mail:** info@cmri.org.au.

Winston Churchill Memorial Trust

Founded in 1965 to perpetuate and honour the memory of Sir Winston Churchill, who died that year, by the award of Memorial Fellowships, known as 'Churchill Fellowships'.

Activities: Awards Churchill Fellowships each year to Australian citizens to undertake an overseas investigative project of a kind not available in Australia. There are no prescribed qualifications, academic or otherwise, for the award of a Churchill Fellowship. Merit is the primary test, whether based on past achievements or on demonstrated ability for future achievement in any field. The value of an applicant's work to the community and the extent to which it will be enhanced by the applicant's overseas study project are also important criteria.

Geographical Area of Activity: Fellowships can be completed anywhere in the world.

Restrictions: Australian citizens only.

Publications: Annual Report.

Finance: Annual revenue $A10,754,072 (31 Jan. 2014).

Board of Directors: Elizabeth Alexander (Nat. Pres.); Margaret White (Nat. Chair.).

Principal Staff: CEO Paul Tys.

Address: POB 1536, Canberra, ACT 2601; Churchill House, 30 Balmain Cresc., Acton, ACT 2601.

Telephone: (2) 6247 8333; **Fax:** (2) 6249 8944; **Internet:** www .churchilltrust.com.au; **e-mail:** info@churchilltrust.com.au.

Clean Up the World Pty Ltd

Founded by Ian Kiernan in 1993 as a global outreach programme of Clean Up Australia to help communities make a positive impact on the health of their environment.

Activities: Operates internationally in the field of conservation and the environment, through supporting community-based environmental projects. Emphasizes simple activities, such as rubbish collection and removal, tree-planting, education initiatives such as schools-focused lectures and activities, worm-farming and composting. Clean Up events are currently held in 130 countries.

Geographical Area of Activity: International.

Restrictions: Acts as a sponsorship facilitator; no direct grants.

Publications: Fact sheets.

Finance: Total assets $A122,114, annual revenue $A1,343,484 (30 June 2014).

Board of Directors: Ian Kiernan (Chair.).

Principal Staff: Man. Dir Terrie-Ann Johnson.

Address: POB R725, Royal Exchange, NSW 1225; 193 Darlinghurst Rd, Darlinghurst NSW 2010.

Telephone: (2) 8197 3420; **Fax:** (2) 9251 6249; **Internet:** www .cleanuptheworld.org; **e-mail:** info@cleanuptheworld.org.

Collier Charitable Fund

Established in 1954 by the wills of three sisters, Alice, Annette and Edith Collier, to support charitable activities in Australia.

Activities: Operates in the fields of health, welfare and education through making grants to hospitals, institutions helping the sick and aged, for poverty relief, public education, to the Australian Red Cross, and for causes of significance in Australia.

Geographical Area of Activity: Australia.

Restrictions: Grants made within Australia only.

Publications: Annual Report.

Finance: Annual revenue $A13,849,000, expenditure $A568,000 (30 June 2014).

Trustees: Chris M. Beeny (Chair.).

Principal Staff: Sec. Geoff I. Linton.

Address: 570 Bourke St, Level 31, Melbourne, Vic 3000.

Telephone: (3) 9670 1647; **Fax:** (3) 9670 1647; **Internet:** www .colliercharitable.org; **e-mail:** glinton@colliercharitable.org.

Creative Partnerships Australia

Formed in 2012 by the merger of the Australia Business Arts Foundation—AbaF (f. 2000) and Artsupport Australia following the Mitchel Review of Private Sector Support for the Arts, which recommended a 'one-stop-shop' to promote and facilitate business, philanthropic and donor support for the arts.

Activities: Encourages and promotes private sector support for the arts and humanities in Australia and develops partnerships between the arts and business. Initiatives include Artsupport Australia, which assists the cultural sector, particularly small and medium-sized arts organizations and individual artists, to build capacity better to secure and manage philanthropic funding, and encourages and helps donors to find and connect with arts organizations and practitioners; and the Australia Cultural Fund, which channels corporate donations to arts practitioners and organizations.

Geographical Area of Activity: Australia.

Publications: *Partnerships News* (quarterly newsletter); *AbaF E-News* (online newsletter); *The Gold Book of Business Arts Partnerships*; *Business Arts Partnerships—a Guide to the Business Case Approach for the Cultural Sector*; *Connect* (magazine).

Finance: Annual revenue $A6,950,251, expenditure $A6,708,946 (30 June 2014).

Board of Directors: Carol Schwartz (Chair.); Sam Meers (Deputy Chair.).

Principal Staff: CEO Fiona Menzies; Exec. Dirs Emma Calverley, Matthew Morse.

Address: Level 2, 405 Collins St, Melbourne, Vic 3000.

Telephone: (3) 9616 0300; **Fax:** (3) 9614 2550; **Internet:** www .creativepartnershipsaustralia.org.au; **e-mail:** info@ creativepartnershipsaustralia.org.au.

Credit Union Foundation Australia—CUFA

Established in 1971 to support the development of credit unions in less-developed countries to assist in the empowerment of communities.

Activities: Operates in the field of aid to less-developed countries and economic affairs through supporting the development of credit unions in disadvantaged countries of South-East Asia and the Pacific. Also operates in Australia in community advocacy and education.

Geographical Area of Activity: Australia, South-East Asia and the Pacific.

Publications: Newsletters.

Finance: Annual revenue $A2,314,732, expenditure $A2,035,005 (30 June 2014).

Board of Directors: Margot Sweeny (Chair.).

Principal Staff: Chief Exec. Peter Mason.

Address: POB 1016, Sydney, NSW 2001; Suite 1, Level 11, 35 Clarence St, Sydney, NSW 2000.

Telephone: (2) 8299 9031; **Fax:** (2) 8299 9606; **Internet:** www .cufa.com.au; **e-mail:** info@cufa.com.au.

Vincent Fairfax Family Foundation

Established in 1962.

Activities: Operates in the areas of education, agriculture, Christianity and community well-being.

Geographical Area of Activity: Australia.

Finance: Grants distributed $A6,385,964 (2013–14); annual expenditure $A820,091 (2014).

Board of Directors: Tim Fairfax (Chair.).

Principal Staff: CEO Jenny Wheatley.

Address: GPO Box 1551, Sydney, NSW 2001.

Telephone: (2) 9291 2727; **Fax:** (2) 9251 7285; **Internet:** www .vfff.org.au; **e-mail:** foundation@vfff.org.au.

Foundation for National Parks and Wildlife

Established in 1970 by former lands minister Tom Lewis to preserve Australia's natural and cultural heritage.

Activities: Operates in the area of conservation of the environment through grants, projects and education.

Geographical Area of Activity: Australia.

Finance: Total assets $A5,875,092, annual expenditure $A917,070 (31 Dec. 2013).

Board of Directors: Garry Browne (Pres.); Fiona Archer (Treas. and Sec.).

Principal Staff: Chief Exec. Susanna Bradshaw.

Address: GPO Box 2666, Sydney, NSW 2001.

Telephone: (612) 9221 1949; **Internet:** www.fnpw.org.au; **e-mail:** fnpw@fnpw.org.au.

Foundation for Young Australians

Established in 2000 following the merger of the Queen's Trust for Young Australians and the Australian Youth Foundation; aims to create positive opportunities and outcomes for children and youth by leading the development of innovative strategies that enable young people to reach their potential and participate fully in society.

Activities: Some 50% of funding is spent on programmes to benefit disadvantaged young people in the fields of education, law and human rights, employment, health and mental health, housing and homelessness, and civic and youth participation. The remaining 50% is spent on programmes to develop leadership potential and promote the pursuit of excellence. The Foundation is an affiliated partner of the International Youth Foundation (USA, q.v.) and a member of the International Youth Foundation Global Network of Partners.

Geographical Area of Activity: Australia.

Restrictions: Funding is provided only to benefit young Australians.

Publications: Annual Report; *The Future Chasers* (2015); reports and evaluations.

Finance: Annual revenue $A7,749,687, expenditure $A10,815,970 (31 Dec. 2014).

Board of Directors: Robert Milliner (Chair.); Peter Williams (Treas.).

Principal Staff: CEO Jan Owen.

Address: POB 239, Melbourne, Vic 3001; 21–27 Somerset Pl., Melbourne, Vic 3000.

Telephone: (3) 9670 5436; **Fax:** (3) 9670 2272; **Internet:** www .fya.org.au; **e-mail:** info@fya.org.au.

John Grill Centre for Project Leadership

Established in 2012 with a donation of A$20m. by John Grill, a former extractives industry chief executive and alumnus of the University of Sydney.

Activities: Established to enhance leadership capability and provide executive education in leadership and governance; promotes links between industry and government in Australia and internationally; fosters research partnerships in relation to large-scale projects.

Geographical Area of Activity: Principally Australia.

Advisory Board: John Grill (Chair.).

Principal Staff: CEO Marc Vogts; Deputy CEO Prof. Suresh Cuganesan.

Address: Level 2, School of Information Technologies, Bldg J12, The University of Sydney, NSW 2006.

Telephone: (2) 9036 9704; **Internet:** sydney.edu.au/john-grill -centre; **e-mail:** johngrillcentre@sydney.edu.au.

The Fred Hollows Foundation

Established in 1992 by Gabi Hollows to continue the work of her husband, eye doctor Prof. Fred Hollows, in preventing unnecessary and avoidable blindness.

Activities: Operates worldwide in the field of medicine and health, providing funding, training and expertise to assist with the treatment of the cataract blind in developing countries; and working with local agencies to develop programmes to provide modern cataract surgery and support local health infrastructure relating to eye health in these countries. The Foundation is active in Australia, Africa, Asia and the Pacific and has links with various international blindness-prevention programmes, including Vision 2020: The Right to Sight. Maintains local programme offices in Australia, Cambodia, the People's Republic of China, New Zealand, Pakistan, South Africa and Viet Nam. Also has an office in London.

Geographical Area of Activity: Africa, Asia, the Pacific and Australia.

Restrictions: No grants or scholarships available.

Publications: *Sharing the Vision* (quarterly newsletter); *Strategic Framework: Seeing is Believing* (monthly electronic newsletter); Annual Report.

Finance: Annual income $A57,992,010, expenditure $58,627,578 (31 Dec. 2013).

Board of Directors: Les Fallick (Chair.); Ann Porcino (Deputy Chair.); Ram Neupane (Sec.).

Principal Staff: CEO Brian Doolan.

Address: Locked Bag 5021, Alexandria, NSW 2015; Level 2, 61 Dunning Ave, Rosebery, NSW 2018.

Telephone: (2) 8741 1900; **Fax:** (2) 8741 1999; **Internet:** www .hollows.org; **e-mail:** fhf@hollows.org.

Law and Justice Foundation of New South Wales

Founded in 1967.

Activities: Seeks to improve access to justice, particularly for socially and economically disadvantaged people. The Foundation conducts rigorous, independent research to inform policy development; contributes to the availability of understandable legal information; and supports organizations and projects that improve access to justice.

Geographical Area of Activity: Australia.

Restrictions: Grants only in New South Wales.

Publications: Annual Report; *e-Bulletin* (6 a year); electronic newsletters on Plain Language Law and JARA (Justice Access Research Alert).

Finance: Total assets $A5,176,805, annual revenue $A2,029,940 (30 June 2014).

Board of Governors: Paul Stein (Chair.).

Principal Staff: Dir Geoff Mulherin.

Address: POB 4264, Sydney, NSW 2001; Level 14, 130 Pitt St, Sydney, NSW 2000.

Telephone: (2) 8227 3200; **Fax:** (2) 9221 6280; **Internet:** www .lawfoundation.net.au; **e-mail:** lf@lawfoundation.net.au.

Lowy Institute for International Policy

Established in 2003 by Frank Lowy, Chair. and fmr CEO of Westfield Corpn, a retail shopping group.

Activities: Conducts research on international affairs; hosts speeches by leading figures and holds conferences; collaborates with think tanks and foundations worldwide to promote an Asia-Pacific perspective on world issues. Main programmes and projects include: East Asia; West Asia; Melanesia; G20 Studies Centre; International Security; The International Economy; Polling; Maritime Security in Indo-Pacific Asia; Nuclear Policy Centre; Nuclear Stability in Indo-Pacific Asia; and Perspectives on India. Runs the Lowy Institute-Rio Tinto China Fellowship and Distinguished International Fellowship programmes; and awards the annual Lowy Institute Media Award to Australian journalists writing on international policy issues.

Geographical Area of Activity: Worldwide.

Publications: Policy Briefs; Lowy Institute Papers; reports; polls; backgrounders; books.

Finance: Established with an endowment of A$30m.

Board of Directors: Frank Lowy (Chair.).

Principal Staff: Exec. Dir Dr Michael Fullilove.

Address: 31 Bligh St, Sydney, NSW 2000; POB H-159 Australia Sq., NSW 1215.

Telephone: (2) 8238 9000; **Internet:** www.lowyinstitute.org; **e-mail:** lowyinstitute@lowyinstitute.org.

Macquarie Group Foundation

Established in 1984 by the Macquarie Group.

Activities: Focuses on five main areas: the arts; education; the environment; welfare; and health. Also supports indigenous communities, and the philanthropic endeavours of Macquarie staff and businesses.

Geographical Area of Activity: International.

Publications: Annual Review; application guidelines.

Finance: Total disbursements $A24.7m. (2014).

Committee: Shemara Wikramanyake (Chair.).

Address: POB 4294, Sydney, NSW 1164; 50 Martin Pl., Sydney, NSW 2000.

Telephone: (2) 8232 3333; **Fax:** (2) 8232 0019; **Internet:** www .macquarie.com/foundation; **e-mail:** foundation@macquarie .com.

The Sir Robert Menzies Memorial Foundation

Founded in 1979 by the Sir Robert Menzies Memorial Trust using funds raised in memory of Sir Robert Menzies.

Activities: Provides funding for postgraduate scholarships in the discipline of law, engineering and the allied health sciences. Applicants must be Australian citizens. Also provides funds for three health research centres: the Menzies School of Health Research (Darwin); the Menzies Research Institute (Hobart); and the Menzies Centre for Health Policy (Canberra and Sydney).

Geographical Area of Activity: Australia.

Restrictions: Scholarship applicants must be Australian citizens.

Publications: Annual Report.

Finance: Annual revenue $A2,600,164, expenditure $A1,397,329 (31 Dec. 2014).

Board of Directors: Brian J. Doyle (Chair. and Sec.); Prof. Simon Maddocks (Deputy Chair.); Tony Connon (Treas.).

Principal Staff: CEO Sarah Hardy.

Address: Clarendon Terrace, 210 Clarendon St, East Melbourne, Vic 3002.

Telephone: (3) 9419 5699; **Fax:** (3) 9417 7049; **Internet:** menziesfoundation.org.au; **e-mail:** menzies@ menziesfoundation.org.au.

R. G. Menzies Scholarship Fund

Inaugurated in 1967 by prominent Australian alumni of Harvard to honour the Australian statesman and former Prime Minister.

Activities: Grants at least one annual award to talented Australians who have gained admission to a Harvard graduate school. Sponsored by The Harvard Club of Australia, The Menzies Foundation and The Australian National University.

Geographical Area of Activity: Australia and the USA.

Restrictions: Applicants must be Honours graduates (or equivalent) of an Australian university or other recognized Australian tertiary institution; be Australian citizens or have permanent residential status, and normally reside in Australia; intend to return to Australia after completing their studies or directly represent Australia overseas; have not previously undertaken a postgraduate degree course at a US university; and have not accepted another major scholarship. Applicants must also have either been accepted to Harvard graduate school, or be confident about meeting its admission requirements and deadlines.

Finance: Each academic year the selection Committee awards up two Menzies Scholarships, each worth US $60,000.

Selection Committee: Steph Neulinger (Sec.).

Address: Philanthropic Scholarships, Alumni Relations & Philanthropy, 28 Balmain Cresc., The Australian National University, Canberra, ACT 2601.

Telephone: (2) 6125 9521; **Fax:** (2) 6125 8524; **Internet:** philanthropy.anu.edu.au/philanthropy/scholarships/ menzies; **e-mail:** philanthropic.scholarships@anu.edu.au.

Murdoch Children's Research Institute

Established in 1960 as the Royal Children's Hospital Research Foundation; merged with the Murdoch Institute (established in 1984) in 2000.

Activities: Conducts, supports and promotes research to improve the health of children and adolescents. Operates in the field of medicine and health, nationally and internationally through carrying out and funding research in a number of themed areas, including bone disorders, addiction, cerebral palsy and chromosome abnormalities, each area encompassing biomedical and public health research and community education. All research is carried out at the Institute; however, the Institute maintains strong international links and encourages visits by overseas students.

Restrictions: No outside grants available.

Publications: Annual Report.

Finance: Annual revenue $A104,550,000, expenditure $A102,360,000 (31 Dec. 2013).

Board of Directors: Leigh Clifford (Chair.); Ian Miller (Deputy Chair.).

Principal Staff: Dir Prof. Kathryn North.

Address: Royal Children's Hospital, Flemington Rd, Parkville, Vic 3052.

Telephone: (3) 8341 6200; **Fax:** (3) 9348 1391; **Internet:** www .mcri.edu.au; **e-mail:** mcri@mcri.edu.au.

The Myer Foundation

Founded in 1959 by Kenneth B. Myer and S. Baillieu Myer to support programmes responding to community needs in areas not covered in the will of their father, businessman Sidney Myer, by which the Sidney Myer Fund (q.v.) was endowed.

Activities: Works nationally through self-conducted programmes and grants to institutions, particularly in the five following areas selected for specific focus: the arts and humanities, developing Australian and Aboriginal cultural identity; 'beyond Australia' projects, supporting Australian organizations that work in the Asia-Pacific region, and assisting refugees and asylum seekers; social justice, funding research and organizations in the field; water and the environment, empowering communities to engage actively in environmental protection, and improving water resources; and the development of Australian philanthropy. Also supports special projects, including the annual Sydney Myer Performing Arts Awards, collectively worth $A105,000, and research into the future needs of elderly people in Australia. The Foundation also manages the grant programme of the Sidney Myer Fund (q.v.).

Geographical Area of Activity: Australia and the Asia-Pacific region.

Restrictions: No support is given for medical research, scholarships, travel, film or video, nor to individuals.

Publications: Annual Report; *Aged Care: 2020 A Vision for Aged Care in Australia*; *Sidney Myer Centenary Celebration.*

Finance: Annual revenue $A4,972,554, expenditure $A1,180,356 (30 June 2014).

Board of Directors: Martyn Myer (Pres.); Emily Myer, Simon Herd, Anna Spraggett (Vice-Pres).

Principal Staff: CEO Leonard Vary.

Address: POB 21676, Little Lonsdale St, Melbourne, Vic 8011; 17 Bennetts Lane, Melbourne, Vic 3000.

Telephone: (3) 8672 5555; **Fax:** (3) 8672 5556; **Internet:** www.myerfoundation.org.au; **e-mail:** enquiries@myerfoundation.org.au.

Sidney Myer Fund

Founded in 1934 by the will of businessman Sidney Myer to support programmes that respond to community needs.

Activities: Operates nationally in all areas relating to community needs. Focuses on four programmes: Arts and Humanities; Education; Poverty and Disadvantage; and Sustainability and the Environment. Emphasis is placed on social development and innovation; in 2013 the Fund introduced Myer Innovation Fellowships, worth $A100,000. The Fund is managed by the Myer Foundation (q.v.).

Geographical Area of Activity: Australia.

Restrictions: No support is given for scholarships, travel, films or videos, nor for individuals.

Publications: Annual Report.

Finance: Total grants disbursed $A7,178,187 (2013/14).

Board of Trustees: Carrillo Gantner (Chair.).

Principal Staff: CEO Leonard Vary.

Address: 17 Bennetts Lane, Melbourne, Vic 3000; POB 21676, Little Lonsdale St, Melbourne, Vic 8011.

Telephone: (3) 8672 5555; **Fax:** (3) 8672 5556; **Internet:** www.myerfoundation.org.au; **e-mail:** admin@myerfoundation.org.au.

National Heart Foundation of Australia

Established in 1961 to support individuals and organizations pursuing efforts into the causes, diagnosis, cure and prevention of cardiac diseases so as to arrest the resulting disability and increased mortality rate in Australia; and to promote public awareness on treating and preventing cardiac diseases.

Geographical Area of Activity: Australia.

Finance: Total assets $A28,834,000, annual income $A7,246,000 (31 Dec. 2013).

Principal Staff: Chief Exec. Mary Barry.

Address: Level 12, 500 Collins St, Melbourne, Vic 3000.

Telephone: (3) 9329 8511; **Fax:** (3) 9321 1574; **Internet:** www.heartfoundation.org.au; **e-mail:** heartline@heartfoundation.org.au.

Oxfam Australia

Began in Melbourne in 1953 as a church-affiliated group, Food for Peace Campaign, sending weekly donations to a small health project in India. Food for Peace Campaign groups were later established throughout Victoria. Name changed in 1962 to Community Aid Abroad, reflecting an aim to assist communities more broadly. Became part of Oxfam International (q.v.) in 1995, changing its name to Oxfam Australia in 2005. Now a secular, independent, non-governmental, non-profit org.

Activities: Activities include: long-term development projects, helping poor communities in 19 countries in 2013, including Australia, create their own lasting solutions to poverty; responding to humanitarian emergencies and crises, then staying with communities over the longer term, helping them to rebuild their communities and livelihoods; campaigning for a just world without poverty, seeking to address the root causes of poverty and injustice; involving the Australian community through events such as Trailwalker; and Oxfam Australia Shops, which sell handicrafts and fair-trade goods, and support economic and social justice.

Geographical Area of Activity: Southern Africa, East Asia and South Asia.

Publications: *Oxfam News* (quarterly magazine); policy papers, reports and books.

Finance: Annual income $A91,087,653, expenditure $A89,165,097 (30 June 2014).

Board of Directors: Jane Hutchison (Chair.); Dr Ian Anderson (Deputy Chair.).

Principal Staff: Exec. Dir Dr Helen Szoke.

Address: 132 Leicester St, Level 3, Carlton, Vic 3053.

Telephone: (3) 9289 9444; **Fax:** (3) 9347 1983; **Internet:** www.oxfam.org.au; **e-mail:** enquire@oxfam.org.au.

OzChild

Established in 1993, through the merger of Family Action (f. 1851), Family Focus (f. 1893) and the National Children's Bureau of Australia (f. 1971), for the protection of children.

Activities: Operates primarily in Victoria in the areas of children's welfare, including the protection of children from abuse, disability, 'out of home' care, family support, youth pathways and educational support, with some national outreach services.

Geographical Area of Activity: Australia.

Publications: Annual Report; Newsletter.

Finance: Annual revenue $A18,644,353, expenditure A$19,312,394 (30 June 2014).

Board of Directors: Assoc. Prof. Erica Frydenberg (Pres.); David Impey, Helen Maxwell-Wright (Vice-Pres); Michael Wooten (Treas.).

Principal Staff: CEO Lisa Sturzenegger.

Address: POB 1312 South Melbourne, Vic 3205; Level 3, 150 Albert Rd, South Melbourne, Vic 3205.

Telephone: (3) 9695 2200; **Fax:** (3) 9695 0507; **Internet:** www.ozchild.org.au; **e-mail:** ozchild@ozchild.org.au.

Perpetual Foundation

Established in 1998 by Perpetual Trustees Australia, a trustee company operating throughout Australia.

Activities: Administers more than 550 charitable trusts and foundations operating in Australia. Income generated from the capital of these foundations is distributed annually to charitable organizations, in accordance with the wishes of the founders of the managed trusts, supporting initiatives in the areas of social and community welfare, education, medical and scientific research, arts and culture, and conservation and the environment.

Geographical Area of Activity: Australia.

Restrictions: No grants are made to individuals.

Finance: Annual disbursements of more than $A50m.; manages more than $A1,300m. in funds (31 Dec. 2013).

Board of Directors: Geoff Lloyd (Chair.); Glenda Charles (Sec.).

Principal Staff: Man. Dir and CEO Geoff Lloyd.

Address: POB 4172, Sydney, NSW 2001; Level 12, 123 Pitt St, Sydney, NSW 2000.

Telephone: (2) 9229 9633; **Fax:** (2) 8256 1471; **Internet:** www
.perpetual.com.au/philanthropy-the-perpetual-foundation
.aspx; **e-mail:** philanthropy@perpetual.com.au.

Ian Potter Foundation

Established in 1964.

Activities: Awards grants for general charitable purposes in the areas of the arts, community well-being, education, environment and conservation, health and disability, medical research and science. Also operates a travel grants programme that enables outstanding individuals to attend international conferences in their fields of growing expertise. Provides conference grants to support symposia and conferences of international status to be held within Australia. The Foundation established the Ian Potter Cultural Trust in 1993 to encourage and support the diversity and excellence of emerging Australian artists. The Trust offers grants to assist early career artists of exceptional talent to undertake professional development, usually overseas.

Geographical Area of Activity: Australia.

Restrictions: No grants to individuals (except through the Ian Potter Cultural Trust). Organizations must have approved tax status (DGR and TCC).

Publications: Annual Distribution Report; e-newsletter (3 a year).

Finance: Annual revenue $A37,708,034, expenditure $A16,515,506 (30 June 2014).

Board of Governors: Charles B. Goode (Chair.).

Principal Staff: CEO Janet Hirst.

Address: Level 3, 111 Collins St, Melbourne, Vic 3000.

Telephone: (3) 9650 3188; **Fax:** (3) 9650 7986; **Internet:** www
.ianpotter.org.au; www.ianpotterculturaltrust.org.au;
e-mail: admin@ianpotter.org.au.

Pratt Foundation

Established in 1978 by Richard Pratt, Chair. of Visy Industries, and his wife Jeanne to support charitable organizations.

Activities: Key areas of interest include family welfare, cancer care, performing arts, extreme poverty, mental health and social welfare.

Geographical Area of Activity: Worldwide.

Finance: Total assets $14,745, annual revenue $A3,159,765 (30 June 2014).

Board of Trustees: Heloise Waislitz (Chair.).

Principal Staff: Chief Exec. Sam Lipski.

Address: POB 5182, South Melbourne, Vic 3205; Level 11, 2 Southbank Blvd, South Melbourne, Vic 3006.

Telephone: (3) 9247 4798; **Fax:** (3) 9247 4798; **Internet:** www
.prattfoundation.com.au.

Clive and Vera Ramaciotti Foundations

Established in 1970 by Vera Ramaciotti to support biomedical research.

Activities: Operates in the field of biomedical resarch, in particular molecular biology, immunology and genetics, offering grants to research initiatives and biomedical institutions. In 2015 the Foundations awarded the Ramaciotti Biomedical Research Award, the Ramaciotti Medal for Excellence in Biomedical Research and the Ramaciotti Health Investment Grants.

Geographical Area of Activity: Australia.

Finance: The combined capital of the Foundations in 2012 was more than $A54m., managed by Perpetual Trustees.

Address: c/o Perpetual Trustee Co Ltd, GPO Box 4171, Sydney, NSW 2001.

Telephone: (2) 9229 9633; **Fax:** (2) 8256 1471; **Internet:** www
.perpetual.com.au/ramaciotti; **e-mail:** philanthropy@
perpetual.com.au.

Reichstein Foundation

Established in 1970 with the aim of facilitating structural change in society and community development.

Activities: Makes grants in priority areas of reducing inequality, social justice and the law, and environmental sustainability. The Foundation also organizes workshops aimed at raising awareness and understanding of social change philanthropy and tools for social change.

Geographical Area of Activity: Australia.

Restrictions: No grants for routine service or programme delivery; prioritizes supporting community organizations with a strong focus on advocacy and communications, and pursuing public policy reform at a systems level, including legislative, regulatory, funding, service and programme change, innovation in design, delivery and outcomes; only Australian not-for-profit organizations are eligible to apply.

Publications: *Jill's Blog.*

Board of Trustees: Jill Reichstein (Chair.).

Principal Staff: Exec. Officer John Spierings.

Address: 207 Queen St, Suite 207, Melbourne, Vic 3000.

Telephone: (3) 9614 0919; **Fax:** (3) 9614 1739; **Internet:** www
.reichstein.org.au; **e-mail:** info@reichstein.org.au.

R. E. Ross Trust

Founded in 1970 under the terms of the will of Roy Everard Ross, founder of Hillview Quarries.

Activities: Operates through awarding grants for projects in the fields of the arts, social welfare, health, nature conservation and the education of foreign students, through a teacher exchange programme, with particular regard to students from Timor-Leste and the South Pacific Islands. Makes several major grants each year and funds an annual travel scholarship awarded by the Royal Australasian College of Physicians. Grants are restricted to charitable organizations based within the State of Victoria.

Geographical Area of Activity: South-East Asia and the South Pacific, Australia.

Restrictions: Grants are made only in the Victoria area. Generally no funding for projects deemed to be the responsibility of government, general appeals, long-term support, travel expenses or conferences, or for projects too rigid in application to groups defined by religion or ethnic origin, social surveys or social research. No grants for individuals.

Publications: Annual Report and financial statement.

Finance: Total assets $A37,890,721, annual revenue $A5,001,882 (30 June 2013).

Board of Trustees: Eda Ritchie (Chair.).

Principal Staff: CEO Sylvia Admans.

Address: 7th Floor, 24 Albert Rd, South Melbourne, Vic 3205.

Telephone: (3) 9690 6255; **Fax:** (3) 9690 5497; **Internet:** www
.rosstrust.org.au; **e-mail:** information@rosstrust.org.au.

The Royal Australasian College of Physicians— RACP

Founded in 1938 to promote the study of the science and art of medicine; to encourage research in clinical science and the institutes of medicine; to bring together physicians for their common benefit and for scientific discussions and clinical demonstrations; and to disseminate knowledge of the principles and practice of medicine. Established the Research and Education Foundation in 1991 to increase funding to its medical research awards programme.

Activities: Presents the views of physicians and paediatricians on questions of medical importance to the Government and other bodies; it encourages continuing education for qualified physicians; conducts a training and examination programme for admission of trainees to Fellowship; makes grants for research and overseas study through its Research and Education Fund; provides lecturers for medical teaching in the Asia-Pacific region; maintains a library on the history of medicine; and publishes the results of research and study.

There are 70 Honorary Fellows and more than 9,000 Fellows and Trainees. Maintains a library of 30,000 volumes, including the Ford Collection. Awards more than 40 fellowships and awards annually, and the Eric Susman Prize for contributions to internal medicine.

Geographical Area of Activity: Asia-Pacific and Australia.

Publications: Annual Report; *Internal Medicine Journal*; *The Journal of Paediatrics and Child Health*; research reports; magazine.

Finance: Annual revenue $A4,589,070, expenditure $A2,519,078 (31 Dec. 2013).

Principal Staff: Interim CEO Linda Smith.

Address: RACP Foundation, 145 Macquarie St, Sydney, NSW 2000.

Telephone: (2) 9256 9679; **Fax:** (2) 9252 3310; **Internet:** www .racp.edu.au/page/foundation; **e-mail:** foundation@racp.edu .au.

Royal Flying Doctor Service of Australia—RFDS

Established in 1928 by the Very Rev. John Flynn as a charitable service to provide emergency medical care, primary health-care services and education assistance by air to people in remote areas of Australia.

Activities: Provides 24-hour emergency health services; primary health care clinics at remote sites; tele-health radio and telephone consultations; medical chests to be stored in isolated areas; inter-hospital transfers; and female health clinics. Currently operates from 21 bases throughout Australia.

Geographical Area of Activity: Australia.

Restrictions: Not a grantmaking organization.

Publications: Annual Report.

Finance: Total assets $A14,052,839, annual revenue $A67,001,202 (30 June 2014).

Board of Directors: Amanda Vanstone (Chair.); David Alley (Sec.).

Principal Staff: CEO Martin Laverty.

Address: Level 2, 10–12 Brisbane Ave, Barton, ACT 2600.

Telephone: (2) 6269 5500; **Fax:** (2) 9247 3351; **Internet:** www .flyingdoctor.org.au; **e-mail:** enquiries@rfdsno.com.

SpinalCure Australia

Established in 1994 by Joanna Knott and Stewart Yesner to find a cure for the paralysis caused by spinal cord injury. Formerly known as the Australasian Spinal Research Trust.

Activities: Funds and promotes research into curing spinal cord injury, fostering co-operation between all disciplines involved in central nervous system research, disseminating information about research progress, and co-operating with international efforts in the same field.

Geographical Area of Activity: Australia.

Publications: Annual Report; newsletters; e-newsletters.

Finance: Total assets $A1,715,831, annual income $A627,674 (30 June 2014).

Board of Directors: Joanna Knott (Chair.); Duncan Adams (Sec.).

Principal Staff: Exec. Dir Duncan Wallace.

Address: POB 908, Mona Vale, NSW 1660; Level 3, 100 William St, Woollomooloo, NSW 2011.

Telephone: (2) 9356 8321; **Fax:** (2) 9356 1135; **Internet:** www .spinalcure.org.au; **e-mail:** research@spinalcure.org.au.

TEAR Australia

Established in 1971 to support Christian non-profit organizations in less-developed countries involved in relief and development work.

Activities: Operates internationally in the field of aid to less-developed countries. Supports indigenous Christian development projects that aim for long-term, sustainable change in the life circumstances of communities living with poverty, in the fields of agriculture and livestock, fisheries and aquaculture, forestry, water resources, income generation, health, children's care and education, community organization, non-formal education, vocational training, and relief and rehabilitation. Also provides emergency relief assistance.

Geographical Area of Activity: Worldwide.

Publications: *Target Magazine* (2 a year); *TEAR News* (quarterly); Annual Report.

Finance: Total assets $A12,310,984, annual revenue $A17,039,647 (30 June 2014).

Board of Trustees: Anastasia Davy (Chair.); Brett Gresham (Vice-Chair.).

Principal Staff: Nat. Dir and Sec. Matthew Maury.

Address: POB 164, Blackburn, Vic 3130; 4 Solwood Lane, Blackburn, Vic 3130.

Telephone: (3) 9264 7000; **Fax:** (3) 9877 7944; **Internet:** www .tear.org.au; **e-mail:** info@tear.org.au.

The Paul Ramsay Foundation

Established in 2006 by entrepreneur Paul Ramsay, who died in 2013, leaving $A3,300m. to the Foundation in his will.

Geographical Area of Activity: Mainly Australia.

Finance: Total assets $A2,326,080, annual revenue $A119,349 (30 June 2014).

Board of Directors: Michael Siddle (Chair.).

Address: Level 9, 154 Pacific Highway, St Leonards, NSW 2065.

Telephone: (2) 9433 3444; **Internet:** www .paulramsayfoundation.org.au; **e-mail:** info@ paulramsayfoundation.org.au.

Union Aid Abroad—APHEDA

Established in 1984 by the ACTU (Australian Council of Trade Unions) as its humanitarian overseas aid agency.

Activities: Operates in 16 countries in the Asia Pacific, the Middle East, Southern Africa, South-East Asia and Cuba, in partnership with local communities and trade unions to promote skills development, better employment opportunities, education, sustainable agriculture, health care and workers' rights.

Geographical Area of Activity: Asia, Middle East, Southern Africa and Cuba.

Publications: *Solidarity Partnerships* (quarterly newsletter); Annual Report; monthly e-bulletin, reports and submissions.

Finance: Annual revenue $A9,681,175, expenditure $A8,466,382 (30 June 2014).

Management Committee: Angelo Gavrielatos (Chair.).

Principal Staff: Exec. Officer Kate Lee.

Address: Level 3, 377–383 Sussex St, Sydney, NSW 2000.

Telephone: (2) 9264 9343; **Fax:** (2) 9261 1118; **Internet:** www .unionaidabroad.org.au; **e-mail:** office@apheda.org.au.

Sylvia and Charles Viertel Charitable Foundation

Established in 1999 by the will of Charles Viertel to benefit organizations or institutions involved in medical research into diseases, and the alleviation of hardship of the aged and infirm. Money is also given to charities with low administrative expenses, and to three Queensland organizations: The Salvation Army (Queensland) Property Trust, Cancer Council Queensland and the Prevention of Blindness Foundation.

Activities: As well as long-term partnerships with three organizations, supports medical research, the disadvantaged, the homeless and the elderly. Has invested in young medical researchers, particularly through its medical research grant programmes. The Foundation's flagship programme is the Senior Medical Research Fellowships worth $A245,000 a year, for five years, helping outstanding researchers to establish a research career in Australia. Makes five annual Clinical Investigator awards of $A85,000.

Geographical Area of Activity: Australia.

Restrictions: Applicants must be medical or clinical graduates who have completed training normally to doctoral level.

Trustees: George Curphey (Chair.).

Principal Staff: Prof. Peter Leedman (Chair. of Medical Advisory Board).

Address: c/o Equity Trustees, Philanthropy Services, Level 2, 575 Bourke St, Melbourne, Vic 3000; GPO Box 2307, Melbourne, Vic 3001.

Telephone: (3) 8623 5000; **Internet:** viertel.org.au; **e-mail:** charitabletrusts@anz.com.

Walk Free Foundation

Established in 2013 by Andrew Forrest, founder of Fortescue Metals Group, and his wife Nicola to combat modern-day slavery; part of the Minderoo Foundation (f. 2013), which also comprises the Australian Children's Trust (f. 2001).

Activities: Activist organization combating slavery in countries and industries. Runs the Global Fund to End Slavery.

Geographical Area of Activity: International.

Publications: *Global Slavery Index* (annual).

Principal Staff: COO Josephine Wapakabulo Thomas; Exec. Dir of Global Research Fiona David.

Address: POB 3155, Broadway, Nedlands, WA 6009; 80 Birdwood Parade, Dalkeith, WA.

Telephone: (8) 6460 4949; **Internet:** www.walkfreefoundation.org.

Austria

FOUNDATION CENTRE AND CO-ORDINATING BODY

The World of NGOs

Founded in 1997 by Christiana Weidel and Christian Pichler-Stainern to promote and support the non-profit sector in Austria.

Activities: Operates nationally and internationally in the fields of education, law and human rights, social welfare and social studies, and the provision of information, through self-conducted programmes, research, conferences, training courses and publications.

Geographical Area of Activity: Austria and Europe.

Restrictions: No grants made.

Publications: Annual Report; annual brochure about the development of the Third Sector; and other publications.

Finance: Funded through membership fees, public funds and project finance.

Board of Directors: Christiana Weidel (Chair.); Dr Jürgen Nautz (Vice-Chair.).

Address: Nibelungengasse 7/7, 1010 Vienna.

Telephone: (676) 3359715; **Internet:** www.ngo.at; **e-mail:** office@ngo.at.

FOUNDATIONS, TRUSTS AND NON-PROFIT ORGANIZATIONS

Afro-Asiatisches Institut in Wien (Afro-Asian Institute in Vienna)

Founded in 1959 by Cardinal Dr Franz König, former Archbishop of Vienna, to provide a place for intercultural and interreligious dialogue.

Activities: Offers financial support for students of development countries in Africa and Asia, as well as other foreign students in Austria; it is a centre for encounter and adult education in development issues, intercultural topics and interreligious dialogue. Houses prayer rooms of three world religions—a Muslim prayer room, a Hindu temple and a Christian chapel—and invites people to meet representatives of these religions. In-house publishing company aa-infohouse publishes books in various fields by migrant authors in Austria.

Geographical Area of Activity: Africa, Asia, Central and South America, and Austria.

Publications: Newsletter, annual report, books.

Finance: Annual income €553,563, expenditure €621,256 (2013).

Supervisory Board: Josef Mayer (Chair.).

Principal Staff: Rector Christoph Matyssek.

Address: Türkenstr. 3, 1090 Vienna.

Telephone: (1) 3105145311; **Fax:** (1) 3105145312; **Internet:** www.aai-wien.at; **e-mail:** office@aai-wien.at.

AMINA—aktiv für Menschen in Not (AMINA—active for People in Need Austria)

Founded in 2003 as part of the AMURT international network. Present name adopted in 2011.

Activities: Works in the fields of emergency relief, sustainable development and co-operation. AMINA helps communities in need to develop survival strategies. Focuses on disadvantaged groups, including children, women, the aged, and sick and disabled people.

Geographical Area of Activity: Kenya, Niger, Mozambique, Senegal, Moldova, Georgia, Haiti.

Restrictions: Exclusively charitable.

Finance: Annual income €445,276 (2013).

Board of Directors: Sabrina Traar (Chair.); Michael K. Reiter (Treas.); Gertraud Hödl (Sec.).

Principal Staff: Project Officer (South and East) Gertraud Hödl; Office Man. Joachim Frank.

Address: Hütteldorferst. 253, 1140 Vienna.

Telephone: (1) 92916701; (699) 17073413; **Internet:** aktivfuermenschen.at; **e-mail:** info@aktivfuermenschen.at.

Ludwig Boltzmann Gesellschaft

Established in 1960; a non-profit association of 13 research institutes.

Activities: Institutes carry out research in thematic clusters: history; cardiovascular research; oncology; translational oncology; and rheumatology, balneology and rehabilitation. Most institutes are located in Vienna; outside Austria, institutes are located in Germany, Sweden and Switzerland.

Geographical Area of Activity: Europe.

Finance: Funded by annual grants from the Ministry of Science and Research (€3.6m.), Nationalstiftung für Forschung, Technologie und Entwicklung (€2.5m.) and Vienna City Council (€1.0m.).

Board: Josef Pröll (Pres.); Christoph Neumayer (Treas.); Dr Michael Stampfer (Sec.).

Principal Staff: Gen. Man. Claudia Lingner; Deputy Gen. Man. Marisa Radatz.

Address: Nußdorferstr. 64, 6th Floor, 1090 Vienna.

Telephone: (1) 5132750; **Fax:** (1) 5132310; **Internet:** www.lbg.ac.at; **e-mail:** office@lbg.ac.at.

Entwicklungshilfe-Klub (Aid for Development Club)

Established in 1973.

Activities: Supports community development initiatives in the developing world. Provides grants to small grassroots projects and work with partner organizations in Africa, Asia, Central and South America, Eastern Europe and North Africa.

Geographical Area of Activity: Africa, Asia, Central and South America, Eastern Europe and North Africa.

Publications: Annual Report.

Finance: Project finances €1,645,425 (2014).

Principal Staff: Dir Gabriele Tabatabai.

Address: Böcklinstr. 44, 1020 Vienna.

Telephone: (1) 7205150; **Fax:** (1) 7283793; **Internet:** www.eh-klub.at; **e-mail:** office@eh-klub.at.

ERSTE Stiftung—Die ERSTE Österreichische Spar-Casse Privatstiftung (ERSTE Foundation)

Established in 2003 (as a successor to a savings association originally established in 1819) to assist in social change in Central and South-Eastern Europe.

Activities: Supports social participation and civil-society engagement; disseminates knowledge of the history of the region since 1989. The Foundation develops its own projects within the framework of three programmes: Social Development, Culture and Europe. Makes the ERSTE Foundation

Award for Social Integration and Igor Zabel Award for Culture and Theory.

Geographical Area of Activity: Central and South-Eastern Europe.

Publications: Annual Reports; catalogues; books; series; studies; other publications.

Finance: Annual income €38,501,257, expenditure €9,482,778 (31 Dec. 2013).

Advisory Board: Doraja Eberle (Chair.).

Principal Staff: Man. Chair. Franz Karl Prüller; Deputy Man. Chair. Richard Wold.

Address: Friedrichstr. 10, 1010 Vienna.

Telephone: (501) 0015100; **Fax:** (501) 0011094; **Internet:** www.erstestiftung.org; **e-mail:** office@erstestiftung.org.

European Centre for Social Welfare Policy and Research

Established as the European Centre for Social Welfare Training and Research in 1974 in Vienna, based on an agreement between the UN and Austria. Subsequent agreements in 1978 and 1981 reconfirmed the European Centre as an autonomous, UN-affiliated intergovernmental organization. Present name adopted in 1989.

Activities: Provides expertise in the fields of welfare and social policy development in a broad sense, particularly in areas where multi- or interdisciplinary approaches, integrated policies and inter-sectoral action are required. Expertise includes issues of demographic development, work and employment, incomes, poverty and social exclusion, social security, migration and social integration, human security, care, health and well-being through the provision of public goods and personal services. The focus is on the interplay of socio-economic developments with institutions, public policies, monetary transfers and in-kind benefits, population needs and the balance of rights and obligations.

Geographical Area of Activity: Europe, USA, Canada and Israel.

Publications: Newletters; *Policy Briefs*; books; reports.

Board of Directors: Yury Fedotov (Chair.).

Principal Staff: Exec. Dir Prof. Dr Bernd Marin.

Address: Berggasse 17, 1090 Vienna.

Telephone: (1) 31945050; **Fax:** (1) 319450519; **Internet:** www.euro.centre.org; **e-mail:** ec@euro.centre.org.

European Institute of Progressive Cultural Policies

Founded in 2002 by Andrea Hummer and Raimund Minichbauer to promote the development of innovative cultural policies in the European Union and Central and Eastern Europe.

Activities: Encourages co-operation across Europe between arts organizations and cultural networks, carries out transnational research projects, organizes workshops, maintains a database of European art networks and issues publications.

Geographical Area of Activity: European Union and Central and Eastern Europe.

Publications: Publications in the field of art and culture and networking; *transversal* (e-journal).

Principal Staff: Chair. Monika Mokre.

Address: Gumpendorfer Str. 63в, 1060 Vienna.

Telephone: (1) 5856478; **Internet:** eipcp.net/institute; **e-mail:** contact@eipcp.net.

Fonds zur Förderung der Wissenschaftlichen Forschung—FWF (Austrian Science Fund)

Founded in 1967 with the aim of supporting scientific research.

Activities: Provides finance for basic research in all fields of science, including the humanities. Also responsible for assisting in the formulation and implementation of national science policy, for public relations work relating to science, and for the promotion of the internationalization (in particular Europeanization) of the scientific sector in Austria. Awards include

support for non-Austrian scientists working at Austrian science institutes and for Austrian postgraduate students wishing to carry out scientific research abroad.

Geographical Area of Activity: Austria.

Publications: Annual Report; *Info* (magazine in German); statistical publications.

Finance: Annual revenue €237,253,658, expenditure €237,253,658 (31 Dec. 2014).

Supervisory Board: Dieter Imboden (Chair.); Gerhard Grund (Deputy Chair.).

Principal Staff: Pres. Prof. Pascale Ehrenfreund; Man. Dir Dr Dorothea Sturn.

Address: Sensengasse 1, 1090 Vienna.

Telephone: (1) 5056740; **Fax:** (1) 5056739; **Internet:** www.fwf.ac.at; **e-mail:** office@fwf.ac.at.

International Institute for Applied Systems Analysis—IIASA

Founded in 1972 as a non-governmental interdisciplinary research institute by the Academies of Sciences or equivalent institutions in 12 countries in both East and West. Membership has since increased to 22 countries.

Activities: Researches global environmental, economic, technological and social change in the 21st century. Develops assessment and decision-support methodologies, global databases and analytical tools to study these issues. Concentrates efforts within three research themes: Energy and Climate Change; Food and Water; and Poverty and Equity. Awards a number of fellowships and scholarships.

Geographical Area of Activity: International.

Publications: Annual Report; *Options* (quarterly); Research Reports; *Interim Reports* (approx. 75 a year); and others.

Finance: Annual income €18,290,902, expenditure €18,290,902 (31 Dec. 2013).

Council: Prof. Don Saari (Chair.); Kirsten Broch Mathisen, Alexei Gvishiani (Vice-Chair.).

Principal Staff: Dir/CEO Prof. Pavel Kabat; Deputy Dir/Deputy CEO Prof. Nebojsa Nakicenovic.

Address: Schlossplatz 1, 2361 Laxenburg.

Telephone: (2) 2368070; **Fax:** (2) 23671313; **Internet:** www.iiasa.ac.at; **e-mail:** inf@iiasa.ac.at.

International Press Institute—IPI

Founded in 1950 in New York, USA, to promote and safeguard the freedom of the press.

Activities: Promotes the defence of freedom of expression, and protecting and strengthening the freedoms necessary for the purpose of collecting and disseminating news and carrying out journalistic activities anywhere in the world. As a network of editors, media executives and leading journalists from across the globe, the Institute's role is to raise awareness of the challenges that journalists face in the exercise of their profession, with a specific focus on those in breach of international principles regarding freedom of expression and media freedom; identifying ways to address such challenges through advocacy or dialogue with the authorities that are in charge of ensuring respect of press freedom guarantees and in close co-operation with local journalists; and encouraging journalists to be aware of the specific role that journalism can play in the democratic process and supporting it through their professional engagement.

Geographical Area of Activity: Worldwide.

Publications: *Use With Care—A Reporter's Glossary of Loaded Language in the Israeli–Palestine Conflict*; *Flags and Barriers—Essays on Reporting from Israel and Palestine*; *Reporter's Guide to the Millennium Development Goals: covering development commitments for 2015 and beyond*; *Out of Balance: Defamation Law in the European Union*; *Media and Money—Worldwide Economic Upheaval Changes the Shape of News*; *Brave News Worlds—Navigating the New Media Landscape*; *IPI World Press Freedom Review* (annually); *The Kosovo*

News and Propaganda War; *Caught in the Crossfire: The Iraq War and the Media (A Diary of Claims and Counterclaims)*; IPI Annual World Congress Reports.

Exec. Board: Galina Sidorova (Chair.); Monjurul Ahsan Bulbul, Ken MacQuarrie, John Yearwood (Vice-Chair.).

Principal Staff: Exec. Dir (a.i.) Barbara Trionfi.

Address: Spiegelgasse 2, 1010 Vienna.

Telephone: (1) 5129011; **Fax:** (1) 5129014; **Internet:** www .freemedia.at; **e-mail:** ipi@freemedia.at.

Bruno Kreisky Forum für internationalen Dialog
(Bruno Kreisky Forum for International Dialogue)

Aims to bring together politicians, academics, businesspeople and others from all over the world to create international dialogue.

Activities: Operates in five areas: the Middle East, Unemployment and the Global Economy, New Europe, North-South Dialogue and Human Rights. Conducts research projects, discussions, symposia, lectures and seminars. Maintains the Bruno Kreisky Archives, established the Bruno Kreisky Foundation for Outstanding Achievements in Human Rights, and awards the Bruno Kreisky European Scholarship.

Geographical Area of Activity: Austria.

Publications: Annual Report; newsletter; Dialogue Series; *Le rôle de la Social-Démocratie dans la Nouvelle Europe*; *From Cancún to Vienna. International Development in a New World*; *The Social Left: The Present and the Prospect*; and others.

Board of Directors: Franz Vranitzky (Hon. Pres.); Rudolf Scholten (Pres.); Max Kothbauer (Vice-Pres. and Dep. Treas.); Georg Lennkh (Treas.); Eva Nowotny (Sec.); Patricia Kahane (Deputy Sec.).

Principal Staff: Sec.-Gen. Gertraud Auer Borea d'Olmo.

Address: Armbrustergasse 15, 1190 Vienna.

Telephone: (1) 3188260; **Fax:** (1) 3188260-10; **Internet:** www .kreisky.org; **e-mail:** kreiskyforum@kreisky.org.

KulturKontakt Austria–KKA

Founded in 1989 to support cultural and art projects that are related both to the democratization processes in Central and Eastern Europe as well as European integration.

Activities: Promotes the development of the arts in, and collaborative activities between, Austria and countries in Eastern Europe. Activities include the sponsoring of individual artists, start-up funding for innovative initiatives, participation in infrastructure programmes, and pan-European co-operation programmes in the fine arts, film, media, literature, music, theatre and dance. Distributes awards including the Henkel CEE Art Award for experimental design, and the Henkel Young Artists' Award. Also promotes educational co-operation and sponsorship support for art projects. On behalf of the Austrian Federal Ministry of Education, Science and Culture, KulturKontakt maintains and supports an educational network of project offices in 11 Eastern European countries.

Geographical Area of Activity: Austria and Central, Eastern and South-Eastern Europe.

Publications: *KulturKontakt* (quarterly magazine).

Board: Hanspeter Huber (Chair.); Andrea Ecker (Vice-Chair.); Wolfgang Stelzmüller (Treas.).

Principal Staff: Dir Gerhard Kowař; Deputy Dir Monika Welz.

Address: Universitätsstr. 5, 1010 Vienna.

Telephone: (1) 52387650; **Fax:** (1) 523876520; **Internet:** www .kulturkontakt.or.at; **e-mail:** office@kulturkontakt.or.at.

mediacult—Internationales Forschungsinstitut für Medien, Kommunikation und Kulturelle Entwicklung (International Research Institute for Media, Communication and Cultural Development)

Founded in 1969, on the initiative of the International Music Council under the auspices of UNESCO, for research in the field of cultural development, with special reference to the audio-visual media.

Activities: Operates in the fields of the arts and humanities, and science and technology, especially in the areas of the digital technologies of production and distribution, and the globalization of culture and culture industries. Carries out research in three main areas: new communication technologies, art and culture; the global music market and music in Austria; and social policy and cultural development. Publishes the results of its research; advises on cultural policy; and holds congresses, symposia and workshops.

Geographical Area of Activity: International.

Publications: Books and research reports.

Finance: Regular subsidies are provided by the Austrian Government and the City of Vienna; in addition, the Institute receives donations and grants from other sources, and income is also derived from payment for research services.

Board of Directors: Prof. Raymond Weber (Pres.); Prof. Josef Trappel (Vice-Pres.); Prof. Roman Hummel (Treas.).

Principal Staff: Sec.-Gen. Prof. Dr Alfred Smudits.

Address: Ungargasse 14, 1030 Vienna.

Telephone: (1) 711553601; **Fax:** (1) 711553699; **Internet:** www .mediacult.at; **e-mail:** office@mediacult.at.

Österreichische Forschungsstiftung für Internationale Entwicklung—ÖFSE (Austrian Foundation for Development Research)

Founded in 1967 by the Afro-Asiatisches Institut in Wien (q.v.) and the Österreichischer Auslandsstudentendienst to support research in connection with developing countries.

Activities: Operates in the field of aid to less-developed countries, through grants to individuals and institutions, and issuing publications. Provides documentation and information on development aid and policy, developing countries and international development, particularly relating to Austria. Maintains a library of approximately 45,000 volumes, of which 30,000 are monographs and 10,000 periodicals, as well as 130 subscription magazines.

Publications: *Österreichische Entwicklungspolitik*; *ÖFSE-Forum*; *ÖFSE-Edition*; newsletter; publications on Austrian development politics and collaboration; country and statistical information.

Finance: Annual revenue €1,513,723, expenditure €1,508,241 (2011).

Trustees: Assoc. Prof. Andreas Novy (Chair.); Heinz Hödl (Deputy Chair.).

Principal Staff: Dir Werner Raza.

Address: Sensengasse 3, 1090 Vienna.

Telephone: (1) 3174010; **Fax:** (1) 3174010–150; **Internet:** www .oefse.at; **e-mail:** office@oefse.at.

Österreichische Gesellschaft für Außenpolitik und Internationale Beziehungen (Foreign Policy and United Nations Association of Austria—UNA-AUSTRIA)

Founded in 1945 to increase and widen interest in, and knowledge of, foreign policy, particularly Austrian foreign policy and the UN.

Activities: Operates internationally in the fields of foreign affairs and international relations, through international conferences, lectures, panel discussions and publications on foreign policy.

Geographical Area of Activity: Austria.

Publications: *Global View* (quarterly magazine); *Society* (magazine, 2 a year); *GAP-Journal* (annual); Newsletter; monographs.

Finance: Annual revenue €308,070, expenditure €307,803 (2011).

Principal Staff: Pres. Dr Wolfgang Schüssel; Sec.-Gen. Michael F. Pfeifer.

Address: Hofburg–Stallburg, Reitschulgasse 2/2. OG, 1010 Vienna.

Telephone: (1) 5354627; **Internet:** www.oegavn.org; **e-mail:** office@oegavn.org.

Österreichische Gesellschaft für Umwelt und Technik—ÖGUT (Austrian Society for Environment and Technology)

Established in 1985 to support communication and co-operation between its members.

Activities: Focuses on problems in the field of environment and technology, aiming for the avoidance or handling of environmental conflicts, strengthening the balance of interests between all relevant protagonists in environmental politics (especially environmental associations and organizations, businesses, interest groups and public administration), supporting Central and Eastern European countries in the solving of environmental problems, evaluating and developing the basic legal, social and economic conditions necessary for the implementation of environmental technologies, informing the public about possibilities and risks in the field of environmental technology, and tackling environmental and technological topics in the interests of its members. Works through supporting networking and communication between members, providing information, and promoting development and innovation in the environmental sphere. An annual award is given to projects presenting innovative ecological ideas, which serve ecological demands as well as economic aims. Makes the ÖGUT Environment Award.

Geographical Area of Activity: European Union and Central and Eastern Europe.

Publications: Newsletter; reports and research findings under the themes of: Power; Gender and Diversity; Green Investment; Innovative Building; Consumption and Quality of Life; Participation; Resources; Energy Contracting; Advanced Europe; CSR and Sustainability Reporting.

Board of Directors: Dr Rene Alfons Haiden (Pres.); Dr Elisabeth Freytag-Rigler, Christoph Haller, Reinhard Uhrig (Vice-Pres).

Principal Staff: Sec.-Gen. Monika Auer; Deputy Sec.-Gen. Inge Schrattenecker.

Address: Hollandstr. 10/46, 1020 Vienna.

Telephone: (1) 3156393; **Fax:** (1) 315639322; **Internet:** www.oegut.at; **e-mail:** office@oegut.at.

South East Europe Media Organisation—SEEMO (Südosteuropäische Medienorganisation)

Established in 2000 in Zagreb, Croatia, to promote and safeguard the freedom of the press in South-Eastern Europe, and as a leading media organization in the region.

Activities: Seeks to promote and safeguard press freedom, including freedom of access to news, freedom of transmission of news, freedom of publication of newspapers and freedom of expression. Its activities include fostering understanding between journalists and other media professionals; improving standards and practices; ensuring safety of journalists; and promoting co-operation. Programmes include a Media Aid Programme, Media Law Programme and a Media in Transition Programme. Through the SEEMO South-East Europe Media Foundation for Emergency Help, the Organisation offers support for projects in the region. It also awards the annual SEEMO Award for Better Understanding, a prize of €3,000 made to a journalist, editor or media executive in South-Eastern Europe who has promoted a climate of better understanding among peoples and worked towards ending minority problems, ethnic divisions, racism and xenophobia. Additional Awards are the CEI-SEEMO Award for investigative journalism (€5,000), the SEEMO Human Rights Award and the SEEMO Photo Human Rights Award. Also makes awards from the SEEMO Emergency Fund to provide direct help to journalists in need in South-Eastern Europe.

Geographical Area of Activity: South-Eastern and Central Europe.

Publications: *SEEMO Media Handbook* (annually, in English); *SEEMO Review*; *DeScripto* (quarterly journal); *SEEMO Investigative Journalism Handbook*; publications in local languages.

Principal Staff: Sec.-Gen. Oliver Vujovic.

Address: Stuwerstrasse 27B, 1020 Vienna.

Telephone: (1) 2297343; **Fax:** (1) 2297343; **Internet:** www.seemo.org; **e-mail:** info@seemo.org.

VIDC—Vienna Institute for International Dialogue and Co-operation (Wiener Institut für Internationalen Dialog und Zusammenarbeit)

Founded in 1987 as successor to the Vienna Institute for Development (founded in 1962 by Bruno Kreisky).

Activities: Aims to disseminate information on the cultural, social and economic life of the countries of Asia, Africa, and Central and South America to increase public awareness of the problems of economic development and international co-operation. Conducts research programmes, holds conferences, seminars and workshops on development policy and developing countries, and issues publications relating to international development. The Institute runs a cultural exchange programme with the countries of the South, and is the lead agency of a European-wide network of sports organizations concerned with anti-racism and anti-discrimination both within and outside sport. Members come from 20 countries.

Geographical Area of Activity: Worldwide.

Publications: Newsletter; studies on governance, the Occupied Palestinian Territories, gender and conflict, gender and land rights, women's rights and gender budgeting.

Advisory Board: Barbara Prammer (Pres.); Christa Esterházy (Vice-Pres.).

Principal Staff: Dir Walter Posch; Deputy Dir Franz Schmidjell.

Address: Möllwaldplatz 5/3, 1040 Vienna.

Telephone: (1) 7133594; **Fax:** (1) 713359473; **Internet:** www.vidc.org; **e-mail:** office@vidc.org.

Azerbaijan

FOUNDATIONS, TRUSTS AND NON-PROFIT ORGANIZATIONS

Heydar Aliyev Foundation

Established in 2004 in memory of former President Heydar Aliyev.

Activities: Operates in the areas of education, public health, the environment, science and technology, culture and sport.

Geographical Area of Activity: Azerbaijan.

Publications: *Ekhlagi-Nasiri* (2009); *Gala Archeological-Ethnographic Museum Complex* (2008); *Photoalbum 'Mir Jalal—100'* (2008); *Mugham Encyclopedia* (2008); *World of Uzeyir* (2008); *New Revivers of Mugham* (2008).

Trustees: Mehriban Arif gyzy Aliyeva (Pres.); Leyla Ilham gyzy Aliyeva (Vice-Pres.).

Principal Staff: Exec. Dir Anar Alekperov.

Address: 1000 Baku, Niyazi Str. 5.

Telephone: (12) 435-12-93; **Fax:** (12) 435-12-96; **Internet:** heydar-aliyev-foundation.org; **e-mail:** common@heydar-aliyev-foundation.org.

Open Society Institute—Assistance Foundation (Azerbaijan)

Established in 1999; an independent foundation, part of the Soros foundations network.

Activities: Promotes the development of an open society by supporting programmes in the fields of education, information and the media, women, the arts and culture, law and human rights, and public health. Encourages the creation and development of NGOs in Azerbaijan as well as developing community information centres in regional public libraries. In April 2014 the authorities froze the Foundation's bank account and seized its computers. Since then, limited work has been co-ordinated from the New York office of the Open Society Foundations (q.v.).

Geographical Area of Activity: Azerbaijan.

Address: 1110 Baku, Akademik Hasan Aliyev Str. 117A.

Telephone: (12) 564-34-65; **Fax:** (12) 564-34-66; **Internet:** www.opensocietyfoundations.org/about/programs/eurasia-program.

Bahamas

FOUNDATIONS, TRUSTS AND NON-PROFIT ORGANIZATIONS

TK Foundation

Established in 2002 to continue the work of J. Torben Karlshoe, founder of the Teekay Shipping Group.

Activities: Aims to advance knowledge of oceanography, marine biology, marine engineering, naval architecture, seamanship and other maritime sciences. Also aims to relieve poverty and promote the welfare of impoverished, sick or injured seamen. Current priorities are youth development, and maritime education and South Africa.

Geographical Area of Activity: Worldwide.

Restrictions: Makes grants only to registered non-profit organizations.

Finance: Annual grants awarded US $5.6m. (2014).

Board of Directors: Arthur F. Coady (Chair.).

Principal Staff: Man. Dir Susan Karlshoej; Administrator Esther Blair.

Address: c/o Teekay Corp., 1st Floor, Bayside House, Bayside Executive Park, West Bay St and Blake Rd, POB AP 59214, Nassau.

Telephone: (502) 8935; **Fax:** (502) 8840; **Internet:** www.thetkfoundation.com; **e-mail:** info@tkfoundation.bs.

Bangladesh

FOUNDATIONS, TRUSTS AND NON-PROFIT ORGANIZATIONS

Action in Development—AID

Founded in 1992 by Tarikul Islam Palash to promote development.

Activities: Operates in the fields of education, law and human rights, good governance, agriculture, community health care and social welfare through self-conducted programmes including the Disabled programme, Human Development programme and Income-Generating programme, and through conferences and seminars. Collaborates internationally with similar organizations. Has an office in Dhaka.

Geographical Area of Activity: Bangladesh.

Finance: Financed by the Bangladesh Government and by grants from the European Commission and SLF-Netherlands. Total assets 114,692,702 taka; annual income 38,182,908 taka, expenditure 38,182,908 taka (30 June 2013).

Executive Committee: Tarikul Islam Palash (Chair. and Chief Exec.); Israel Hossain Shanti (Vice-Chair.); Ehteshamul Haque Nutun (Gen. Sec.); Afrina Yasmen (Asst Gen. Sec.); Nurun Nahar Kusum (Treas.).

Principal Staff: Exec. Dir Aminul Islam Bakul.

Address: AID Complex, Shatbaria, POB #03, Jhenaidah 7300.

Telephone: (451) 6118890; **Fax:** (451) 61196; **Internet:** www .aid-bd.org; **e-mail:** info@aid-bd.org.

Bangladesh Freedom Foundation

Established in 1997 to make grants to not-for-profit organizations concerned with problems of fundamental freedoms of the citizens of Bangladesh, and to promote and strengthen indigenous philanthropy in Bangladesh.

Activities: Focuses on promoting secondary-level science education. The Foundation works in partnership with local NGOs.

Geographical Area of Activity: Bangladesh.

Restrictions: Not inviting new proposals.

Publications: Annual Report; *Science Newsletters*; research findings; reports.

Finance: Annual income 39,094,640 taka, expenditure 16,041,391 taka (31 Dec. 2012).

Board of Trustees: Syed Manzur Elahi (Chair.).

Principal Staff: Exec. Dir Sazzadur Rahman Chowdhury.

Address: Level 5, 6/5A Sir Syed Rd, Mohammadpur, Dhaka 1207.

Telephone: (2) 918511920; **Fax:** (2) 9131689; **Internet:** www .freedomfound.org; **e-mail:** info@freedomfound.org.

BRAC

Established in 1972 as the Bangladesh Rehabilitation Assistance Committee, originally as a relief organization; later renamed as the Bangladesh Rural Advancement Committee, and subsequently known as Building Resources Across Communities.

Activities: Works to relieve poverty and empower the poor. Operates in the field of development aid, mainly through microfinance, education and health services, especially targeting those not reached by government-administered programmes. Runs the BRAC University, BRAC Bank, craft shops and food projects. Has affiliate offices in the United Kingdom and the USA.

Geographical Area of Activity: Afghanistan, Bangladesh, Haiti, Liberia, Pakistan, the Philippines, Sierra Leone, South Sudan, Sri Lanka, Tanzania and Uganda.

Publications: Annual Report; reports and guidelines.

Finance: Annual income 49,088,848,100 taka, expenditure 42,531,112,430 taka (31 Dec. 2013).

Governing Body: Sir Fazle Hasan Abed (Chair. and Founder).

Principal Staff: Vice-Chair. and Interim Exec. Dir Dr Mushtaque Chowdhury.

Address: BRAC Centre, 75 Mohakhali, Dhaka 1212.

Telephone: (2) 9881265; **Fax:** (2) 8823542; **Internet:** www .brac.net; **e-mail:** info@brac.net.

Barbados

FOUNDATION CENTRE AND CO-ORDINATING BODY

Caribbean Policy Development Centre

Established in 1991; the leading umbrella body representing the major national and regional NGO networks in the Caribbean.

Activities: Represents Caribbean NGOs in both regional and international forums. The Centre's main areas of interest are sustainable development, trade liberalization, governance, and participation and capacity building.

Geographical Area of Activity: The Caribbean.

Publications: *Caribbean Beacon* (magazine); *Just Us* (magazine); research findings; reports; conference proceedings; manuals.

Board of Directors: Renwick Rose (Chair.).

Principal Staff: Exec. Co-ordinator Shantal Munro-Knight.

Address: POB 284, Bridgetown; Halsworth, Welches Rd, St Michael BB11000.

Telephone: 437-6055; **Fax:** 228-8657; **Internet:** www .cpdcngo.org; **e-mail:** cpdc@caribsurf.com.

FOUNDATIONS, TRUSTS AND NON-PROFIT ORGANIZATIONS

Barbados Entrepreneurship Foundation Inc

Established in 2010 to support business and promote Barbados as an entrepreneurial hub.

Activities: Aims to achieve a model of 'Growing Sustainable Entrepreneurship' supported by five 'Foundation Pillars': finance; government policy; education and skills; business mentorship; and business facilitation. Conducts research into best practices for each Pillar. Projects include the '$20 Challenge' microfinance initiative, which is aimed at schoolchildren; WiFi Barbados, to provide free Wi-Fi nationally; and an online Mentorship Forum.

Geographical Area of Activity: Barbados.

Board of Directors: Chris de Caires (Chair.).

Principal Staff: CEO Celeste Foster.

Address: Woodland Great House, St George BB19130.

Telephone: 621-2130; **Fax:** 621-0005; **Internet:** www .barbadosentrepreneurshipfoundation.org; **e-mail:** info@ barbadosentrepreneurshipfoundation.org.

Belarus

FOUNDATION CENTRES AND CO-ORDINATING BODIES

Assembly of Belarusian Pro-democratic Non-governmental Organizations

Established in 1997 by a group of Belarusian NGOs to facilitate their open and democratic development.

Activities: Represents the interests of NGOs in Belarus. The Assembly carries out annual monitoring, analysis and evaluation of the civil society legal framework; helps register and audit NGOs; disseminates information; maintains a database of more than 1,000 Belarusian civil leaders and NGOs; and facilitates regional and international co-operation of Belarusian NGOs. Comprises over 300 member organizations.

Geographical Area of Activity: Belarus.

Publications: *Creation of Non-Commercial Organizations in Belarus: Legal Acts* (2012, 2014); *Internet for Activists. Basics* (2012); *Legal Status of CSOs in Belarus: Review and Analytical Materials for 2011* (2012); *Perspectives of Development of the Law on Non-Commercial Organizations. Materials of Discussions in the Civil Society* (2011); *Freedom of Association in Belarus: Practice of International Defence. Decisions of the UN Committee on Human Rights* (2009).

Principal Staff: Chair. Siarhiej Mackievic.

Address: POB 196, 220036 Minsk.

Telephone: (29) 707-92-28; **Internet:** belngo.info/en; **e-mail:** international@belngo.info.

Support Centre for Associations and Foundations—SCAF

Founded in 1996; a member of the European Foundation Centre (q.v.) network of NGO resource centres under the EFC Orpheus Programme and a think tank focusing on education, peacebuilding and civil society development.

Activities: Acts as an education and information support centre and think tank for NGOs in Belarus. Maintains a database of Belarusian NGOs; provides advisory services and workshops for representatives of organizations, relating to grant management, proposal writing, leadership and staff development; promotes the exchange of knowledge and information between NGOs. Along with 27 other internationally known Belarusian organizations, SCAF is represented at the Public Advisory Council under the aegis of the Belarus Presidential Administration; civil society platform for strategy development in the areas of society, economy and politics.

Geographical Area of Activity: Belarus.

Publications: *Grantsmanship* (journal); *Belarus Civil Society: In Need of a Dialogue*; *The State of Civil Society in Belarus*; *Index on Civil Society in Belarus*; *Fundraising and Grantsmanship*; *Organizational Management and Development of NGOs*; *Partnership Building between NGOs and Local Government*; and others.

Principal Staff: Dir Dr Iouri Zagoumennov; Asst Dirs Tatiana Zagoumennova, Ihar Zahumionau.

Address: 16-425 Korolia St, 220004 Minsk.

Telephone: (29) 634-37-46; **Fax:** (17) 210-57-51; **Internet:** scaf.int.by; **e-mail:** scaf_belarus@yahoo.com.

United Way—Belarus/NGO Development Centre

Established in 1995 to provide an overview of NGOs in Belarus and assist in their development.

Activities: Operates as an information portal, disseminating information on the Belarusian third sector. The Centre promotes capacity building through collaboration, consultation and organizing training programmes. Maintains databases of Belarusian NGOs; offers legislative and NGO management services; monitors the Belarusian press; and provides online platform for searching for partners, volunteers and scholarships.

Geographical Area of Activity: Belarus.

Publications: Directories of Belarusian NGOs; legal handbooks on Belarus; directories of foundations; handbooks on NGO management; *Non-governmental organizations of Belarus: progress and achievenents* (monograph); *Third sector in Belarus: problems of formation and development* (research work).

Principal Staff: Exec. Dir Alicia Shybitskaya; Information Programmes Dir Svetlana Roussanova.

Address: 9 Masherov Ave, 220000 Minsk.

Telephone: (17) 295-10-96; **Fax:** (17) 295-10-96; **Internet:** www.ngo.by; **e-mail:** uwb@ngo.by.

FOUNDATIONS, TRUSTS AND NON-PROFIT ORGANIZATIONS

Belarusian Public Association 'For the Children of Chornobyl'

Established in 1990 by Prof. Dr Gennady V. Grushevoy and Prof. Dr Irina Grushevaya as a charitable fund to aid the victims of the Chornobyl (Chernobyl) disaster.

Activities: Operates in the fields of ecology, research into the consequences of the Chornobyl nuclear disaster, social and humanitarian aid, medical aid, rebuilding of community, cultural and educational exchanges, information, youth policy and alternative power supplies. Programmes include: the Medical Programme; Charitable Recuperation Programme (for the recuperation of mothers and children in families and rest homes abroad); Educational Programme (including funding postgraduate medical education or further training for Belarusian doctors, nurses and medical specialists abroad); Resettlement (encouraging partnership between regions, towns and institutions with institutions abroad, and construction and economic projects); Information and Cultural Programme (publishing, international congresses, seminars and conferences, cultural projects and exchanges); Youth Programmes (creation of regional youth centres and educational and international exchanges); and Social Programmes (including legal aid, assistance for 'street children', orphanages, 'weekend clubs' for elderly people, and social rehabilitation). The Association has established the Social Medical Consulting Centre. The Association collaborates with organizations and institutions in 26 countries and maintains local branches in more than 70 cities and districts in Belarus.

Geographical Area of Activity: International.

Publications: *DEMOS* (magazine); *World after Chernobyl*; *Chernobyl Digest.*

Finance: Financed through charitable donations and subscriptions.

Principal Staff: Contact Prof. Dr Irina Grushevaya.

Address: Kropotkina 97-115, 220123 Minsk.

Telephone: (17) 286-04-01; **Fax:** (17) 286-04-01; **e-mail:** gr.irina@mail.ru.

Belgium

FOUNDATION CENTRES AND CO-ORDINATING BODIES

Belgian Foundation Network

Established in 2004 by the Centre Européen pour Enfants Disparus et Sexuellement Exploités, Cera Holding, Fondation Belge de la Vocation, Fondation Bernheim, Fondation Charcot, Fondation Evens, Fondation Francqui, Fondation pour les Générations Futures, Fondation Roi Baudouin and Fortis Foundation Belgium, and administered by the Köning Boudewijnstichting/Fondation Roi Baudouin (q.v.).

Activities: Aims to make the Belgian foundations sector more transparent by creating a meeting forum where foundations can exchange good practices, as well as defending common interests of its members, informing the public and giving advice. Operates three main working parties: law and finance, communication and governance, through which the organization defends the interests of its members, provides information to the public and promotes transparency.

Geographical Area of Activity: Belgium.

Administrative Council: Johan Chiers (Pres.); Isabelle Bloem (Vice-Pres.); Lieven Vandeputte (Treas.); Dominique Allard (Sec.).

Principal Staff: Co-ordinator Diletta Brignoli.

Address: Correspondence address: pl. des Barricades 9, 1030 Brussels.

Telephone: (2) 214-01-31; **Internet:** www.reseaufondations.be; **e-mail:** info@reseaufondations.be.

European Foundation Centre—EFC

Established in 1989 by seven of Europe's leading foundations as an international membership association of foundations and corporate funders.

Activities: Develops and pursues activities in line with its four key objectives: creating an enabling legal and fiscal environment; documenting the foundation landscape; building the capacity of foundation professionals; and promoting collaboration among foundations, and between foundations and other actors. The Centre emphasizes transparency and best practice. Activities include: documenting and communicating information, such as on European philanthropy; maintaining knowledge resources on funders; capacity building through professional development; the International Fellowship Programme (IFP); network building through interest groups and fora; partnering with other grantmaker associations; and promoting a good legal and fiscal environment. Has more than 200 members.

Geographical Area of Activity: Europe and international.

Restrictions: Not a grantmaking organization.

Publications: *EFC Update De facto* (e-newsletter, 12 a year); *Effect Magazine* (2 a year); Annual Report; legal and fiscal publications; grantmaking guidelines; thematic studies; conference and meeting reports.

Finance: Annual income €6,241,292, expenditure €6,003,153 (2013).

Management Committee: Ewa Kulik-Bielinska (Chair.); Katherine Watson (Vice-Chair.); Göran Blomqvist (Treas.).

Principal Staff: CEO Gerry Salole.

Address: Philanthropy House, rue royale 94, 1000 Brussels.

Telephone: (2) 512-89-38; **Fax:** (2) 512-32-65; **Internet:** www.efc.be; **e-mail:** efc@efc.be.

EVPA—European Venture Philanthropy Association

Established in 2004; a membership association for organizations and individuals involved in venture philanthropy.

Activities: Promotes venture philanthropy and social investing through research publications and events. Member organizations include foundations and trusts, private equity firms, law firms and educational institutions. Has more than 190 members in 26 countries.

Geographical Area of Activity: Mainly Europe.

Publications: Newsletter; *European Venture Philanthropy Directory of Members*; *Praxis: European Venture Philanthropy in Practice*; *Establishing a Venture Philanthropy Fund in Europe*; *Distance Learning: Managing Investments Overseas*.

Board of Directors: Peter Oostlander (Chair.).

Principal Staff: CEO Kurt Peleman.

Address: rue Royale 94, 1000 Brussels.

Telephone: (2) 513-21-31; **Fax:** (2) 534-24-77; **Internet:** www.evpa.eu.com; **e-mail:** info@evpa.eu.com.

Fédération Européenne des Associations Nationales Travaillant avec les Sans-Abri—FEANTSA (European Federation of National Organisations Working with the Homeless)

Established in 1989; an umbrella body for not-for-profit organizations that participate in or contribute to the fight against homelessness in Europe.

Activities: Aims to prevent and alleviate the poverty and social exclusion of people threatened by or living with homelessness. Encourages and facilitates the co-operation of all those fighting homelessness in Europe. Has more than 130 member organizations among European Union member states. Engages with the European institutions, and national and regional governments, to promote the development and implementation of effective measures to fight homelessness; conducts and promotes research and data collection better to understand the nature, extent, causes of, and solutions for homelessness; facilitates the exchange of information, experience and good practice between member organizations and relevant stakeholders, to improve policies and practices addressing homelessness; and raises public awareness about the complexity of homelessness and the multi-dimensional nature of the problems faced by homeless people.

Geographical Area of Activity: Europe.

Publications: *Homeless in Europe* (magazine, 3 a year); *Flash* (monthly newsletter); *Health and Homelessness* (quarterly newsletter); *European Observatory on Homelessness*; national and international research reports; *European Journal on Homelessness* (2 a year); *Comparative Studies* (1 a year); briefings; policy statements; handbooks; toolkits; glossaries.

Finance: Total assets €419,509 (31 Dec. 2013).

Administrative Council: Mike Allen (Pres.); André Gachet, Stefano Galliani (Vice-Pres); Ian Tilling (Treas.); Péter Bakos (Sec.).

Principal Staff: Dir Freek Spinnewijn.

Address: chaussée de Louvain 194, 1210 Brussels.

Telephone: (2) 538-66-69; **Fax:** (2) 539-41-74; **Internet:** www.feantsa.org; **e-mail:** office@feantsa.org.

Network of European Foundations—NEF

Formerly known as the Association for Innovative Co-operation in Europe. Name changed in 2002.

Activities: Promotes co-operation between 12 member European foundations. Projects include: European Programme on Integration and Migration; Children and Violence; Evaluation Challenge Fund; European Fund for the Balkans; Tunisia Joint Fund; Without Violence; and New Pact for Europe. The Network produces publications on topics such as dementia, learning and democracy, religion and democracy, and philanthropy.

Publications: Annual Report; newletter (quarterly).

Finance: Total assets €3,311,731 (31 Dec. 2014).

Board of Directors: Luc Tayart de Borms (Chair.); Franz Karl Prüller (Vice-Chair.); Dominique Lemaistre (Treas.); Rui Esgaio (Sec.).

Principal Staff: Exec. Dir Peggy Saïller.

Address: Philanthropy House, rue Royale 94, 1000 Brussels.

Telephone: (2) 235-24-16; **Fax:** (2) 230-22-09; **Internet:** www .nef-europe.org; **e-mail:** info@nef-europe.org.

Pôle Européen des Fondations de l'Economie Sociale (European Network of Foundations for Social Economy)

Established in 1999 to link foundations working to bring about a process of social transformation within the European Union.

Activities: Key programmes are: integration of the children of immigrants, citizenship, interculturality and dialogue; and social entrepreneurship. In 2010, the Network launched the European Prize for Youth Employment in the Social Economy. Comprises nine member foundations.

Geographical Area of Activity: European Union.

Publications: White Paper on *Social Economy and Integration of First and Second Generation Immigrant Youth within European Society* (2003); White Paper on *Work for Integration* (2007); European guide on *Citizenship, Interculturality, Dialogue* (2009).

Board of Directors: José Rodrigo (Chair.); Pierre Guillot (Vice-Chair.); Marnic Speltdoorn (Treas.).

Principal Staff: Co-ordinator Sophie Chiha.

Address: rue Royale 151, 1210 Brussels.

Telephone: (2) 250-96-67; **Internet:** www.pefondes.eu; **e-mail:** pefondes@pv.be.

Union des Associations Internationales—UAI (Union of International Associations—UIA/Unie van de Internationale Verenigingen—UIV)

Founded 1907 as the Central Office of International Associations by Henri La Fontaine, Nobel Peace Prize winner in 1913, and Paul Otlet, Sec.-Gen.of the then International Institute of Bibliography, which subsequently became the International Federation for Information and Documentation (FID), and with which UIA activities were closely associated. Officially founded under patronage of the Belgian Government in 1908, and became a federation under its present name in 1910 at the First World Congress of International Organizations. Registered as an international association with scientific aims under the Belgian law of 25 October 1919.

Activities: Facilitates the evolution of the worldwide network of non-profit organizations; collects and disseminates information on these bodies and their inter-relationships; presents this information in both established and experimental ways to promote understanding of the role of non-profit organizations in global society; and promotes research on the legal and administrative problems common to these bodies. The Union maintains a database on more than 65,000 international organizations and more than 330,000 of their meetings. It also documents complementary information on international associations, including: biographies of their officers; logotypes and emblems; problems perceived and strategies adopted by international associations, and values and approaches that animate them.

Geographical Area of Activity: International.

Publications: *International Congress Calendar*; *Yearbook of International Organizations*; *Encyclopaedia of World Problems and Human Potential* (online); Open Yearbook and Open Calendar (online).

Finance: Budget €620,000 (2015).

Council and Bureau: Anne-Marie Boutin (Pres.); Tim Casswell, Marilyn Mehlmann, Cyril Ritchie (Vice-Pres); Ghislain Joseph (Treas.).

Principal Staff: Sec.-Gen. Jacques de Mévius.

Address: rue Washington 40, 1050 Brussels.

Telephone: (2) 640-18-08; **Fax:** (2) 643-61-99; **Internet:** www .uia.org; **e-mail:** uia@uia.be.

FOUNDATIONS, TRUSTS AND NON-PROFIT ORGANIZATIONS

Alamire Foundation

Founded in 1991 by the Catholic University of Leuven and Musica (the Flemish Early Music Centre) to stimulate research in the musical history of Belgium, southern Netherlands and northern France before 1800.

Activities: Organizes conferences and exhibitions, carries out research, publishes books, and has created a database of publications relevant to the Foundation's research.

Geographical Area of Activity: Europe and the USA.

Restrictions: Grants made to specific international research projects only.

Publications: *Journal of the Alamire Foundation*; facsimile editions, monographs, books, repertories and encyclopedias.

Finance: Receives funding from the Government of the Flemish region, from the University of Leuven and the Belgian National Lottery.

Board of Directors: Herman Vanden Berghe (Pres.); Herman Baeten (Treas.).

Principal Staff: Dir Bart Demuyt.

Address: K.U.Leuven/Onderzoekseenheid Musicologie, Centrale Bibliotheek, Mgr Ladeuzeplein 21, POB 5591, 3000 Leuven.

Telephone: (16) 32-87-50; **Fax:** (16) 32-87-49; **Internet:** www .alamirefoundation.org; **e-mail:** info@alamirefoundation.be.

ARGUS

Founded in 1970 as Stichting Leefmilieu (Environment Foundation); part of the KBC financial group. Present name adopted in 2002.

Activities: Promotes the environment and urban and rural sustainable development through providing information and awarding prizes. The foundation also acts as a forum, mostly via publications, on environmental problems and solutions; informs on environmental issues and is involved in educational programmes. Maintains a documentation centre and information databases.

Geographical Area of Activity: Europe.

Publications: Magazine, e-newsletters.

Board of Directors: Hubert David (Pres.); Karina De Beule (Vice-Pres.).

Principal Staff: Dir Helga Van der Veken.

Address: Eiermarkt 8 (onderaan KBC-Toren), 2000 Antwerp.

Telephone: (3) 202-90-70; **Fax:** (3) 202-90-88; **Internet:** www .argusmilieu.be; **e-mail:** info@argusmilieu.be.

ASMAE—Association de Coopération et d'Education aux Développements (Association for Development Co-operation and Education)

Established in 1981 to promote an equality of exchange between countries in the Northern and Southern hemispheres, in particular in the areas of action and education.

Activities: Operates in the fields of aid to less-developed countries and education, working in partnership with 67 local organizations to provide financial and material aid. Operates volunteer-exchange programmes for young people from Belgium to work in less-developed countries. Also promotes the establishment of links between partner associations for North–South and South–North co-operation.

Geographical Area of Activity: Mainly Egypt, Morocco, Senegal and Togo.

Restrictions: No grants for medical activities.

Publications: *Passerelles* (quarterly); *Les Cahiers asmae*; *Passe-Partout*; *Oops* (newspaper).

Board of Directors: Julie Rijpens (Pres.); Charles Albert de Radzitzky (Treas.); Nathalie Lambinet (Sec.).

Principal Staff: Co-ordinator Mathilde Serruys.

Address: pl. des Carabiniers 5, 1030 Brussels.

Telephone: (2) 742-03-01; **Fax:** (2) 742-03-13; **Internet:** www.asmae.org; **e-mail:** info@asmae.org.

Association Égyptologique Reine Elisabeth (Queen Elisabeth Egyptological Association)

Founded in 1923 by Jean Capart to promote studies in the fields of Egyptology and papyrology. Formerly known as Fondation Égyptologique Reine Elisabeth.

Activities: Operates nationally and internationally through research, conferences, lectures and publications; sponsors study trips to Egypt. Holds an extensive papyrus archive.

Geographical Area of Activity: International.

Publications: *Chronique d'Egypte* (2 a year); more than 100 books.

Board of Directors: Comte Arnoul D'Arschot Schoonhoven (Chair.).

Principal Staff: Sec.-Gen. Dr Luc Delvaux; Exec. Sec. Martine Gruselle.

Address: parc du Cinquantenaire 10, 1000 Brussels.

Telephone: (2) 741-73-64; **Fax:** (2) 733-77-35; **Internet:** www.aere-egke.be; **e-mail:** aere.egke@kmkg-mrah.be.

Association Internationale des Charités—AIC (International Association of Charities)

Founded by Saint Vincent de Paul in 1617, as Confraternity of Ladies of Charity. Re-established under Belgian law in 1986.

Activities: Operates internationally in the field of welfare. Works with member organizations to eliminate poverty and sustain the promotion and development of the underprivileged. Encourages voluntary work for, with, and of the poor. Develops various kinds of social work, mainly to fight poverty of women. Also support for drug addicts and alcoholics; care for the elderly and the sick; help to single mothers; assistance to the lonely; defence of human rights; and working towards a culture of solidarity, respect and peace. Runs literacy and other forms of educational workshops, provides technical training, as well as making loans to individuals in need. Comprises 53 member groups.

Geographical Area of Activity: International.

Restrictions: No grants available.

Publications: *Initiation to Associative Life*; *AIC Volunteers Today*; activity report; booklets.

Executive Board: Laurence de la Brosse (Int. Pres.); Alicia Duhne (Assoc. Pres.); Aliette Maredsous, Margaret Hanson (Vice-Pres); Elisabeth Gindre (Treas.).

Principal Staff: Sec.-Gen. Natalie Monteza.

Address: rampe des Ardennais 23, 1348 Louvain La Neuve.

Telephone: (10) 45-63-53; **Fax:** (10) 45-80-63; **Internet:** www.aic-international.org; **e-mail:** contact@aic-international.org.

Cera

Established in 1998 as the Cera Foundation, a division of Cera Holding, a co-operative financial group, following the merger of CERA Bank with Kreditbank and ABB Insurance. Present name adopted in 2004.

Activities: Supports projects that promote co-operative principles for the development of society and that are consistent with a pluralist view of society. Funding is provided within the areas of: poverty alleviation; medical and social aid; art and culture; agriculture, horticulture and the environment; and education, training and entrepreneurship. International operations are carried out by the affiliated Belgische Raiffeisenstichting.

Geographical Area of Activity: Belgium.

Restrictions: No funding for projects that receive substantial financial support from other financial institutions. No direct support for individuals, with the exception of art and culture grants, which requires prior selection by a small committee of experts; and there is no support for associations and enterprises where the submitted project has a commercial interest.

Publications: Annual Report; *To build our future together*; *Collection of the works of art of Cera*; *The marble smile of cosmos*.

Finance: Annual revenue €186,131,117, expenditure €38,891,774 (2013).

Executive Committee: Lode Morlion (Chair.).

Principal Staff: Gen. Man. Franky Depickere; Man. Luc Discry.

Address: Mgr. Ladeuzeplein 15, 3001 Leuven.

Telephone: (70) 69-52-42; **Fax:** (70) 69-52-41; **Internet:** www.cera.be; **e-mail:** info@cera.be.

Churches' Commission for Migrants in Europe (Commission des Eglises auprès des Migrants en Europe/Kommission der Kirchen für Migranten in Europa)

A network of churches and ecumenical groups in Europe established in 1964 to protect and defend the rights of migrants in Europe.

Activities: Operates in Europe in the area of human rights. The Commission raises awareness of migration problems in Europe and develops the role of religious organizations in solving these problems. It aims to defend the rights of migrants and asylum seekers in Europe, and lobbies various European institutions. It also conducts studies on problems relating to European migration policies and racial discrimination and anti-trafficking; and organizes seminars and conferences on migration and related legal issues. The Commission participates in a network of NGOs throughout Europe and has launched the Migration News Sheet and the Migration Policy Group. Includes churches and ecumenical councils from Austria, Belgium, Cyprus, the Czech Republic, Finland, France, Germany, Greece, Hungary, Ireland, Italy, the Netherlands, Norway, Romania, Slovakia, Spain, Sweden, Switzerland and the United Kingdom.

Geographical Area of Activity: Europe.

Publications: *Towards a Right of Permanent Residence for Long-Term Migrants*; *Combating Trafficking for forced Labour in Europe*; *Migrants' Experiences in Active Participation in Churches in Europe*; *Trafficking for Forced Labour in Europe: Emerging Challenges–Emerging Responses*; *Mapping migration–Mapping Churches responses*; newsletters; leaflets; workshop modules; guides; reports.

Finance: Annual budget €475,000 (2015).

Executive Committee: Prof. Dr Victoria Kamondji Johnston (Moderator); Elena Timoftciuc, Rev. Alfredo Abad (Vice-Moderators); Rev. Thorsten Leisser (Treas.).

Principal Staff: Gen. Sec. Doris Peschke; Exec. Sec. Dr Torsten Moritz.

Address: rue Joseph II 174, 1000 Brussels.

Telephone: (2) 234-68-00; **Fax:** (2) 231-14-13; **Internet:** www.ccme.be; ccme.ceceurope.org; **e-mail:** info@ccme.be.

CIDSE—Together for Global Justice

Established in 1967 (formerly known as International Co-operation for Development and Solidarity) to promote and provide aid to developing nations; to enable enhanced communication through information exchange, and co-ordination between Catholic development organizations in North

America and Europe; and to empower people in these countries through attainment of social, economic and political rights.

Activities: Operates in the field of aid to less-developed countries through advocating and campaigning for the reform of current policy-making. The organization promotes and facilitates the social justice agenda of its members and partners, targeting major events at European, North American and international level to influence policy-making and thereby improve the lives of the world's most vulnerable people. Advocacy priorities are: resources for development; food, agriculture and sustainable trade; climate justice; and business and human rights.

Geographical Area of Activity: International.

Restrictions: Not a grantmaking organization.

Publications: *Advocacy Newsletter* (quarterly, in English); Annual Report (in English and French), CIDSE Highlights (bi-monthly), EU News (monthly, in collaboration with Aprodev and Caritas Europa); policy papers.

Finance: Annual expediture €1,079,328 (2013).

Executive Committee: Heinz Hödl (Pres.); Bernard Pinaud (Vice-Pres.); Hilde Demoor (Treas.).

Principal Staff: Sec.-Gen. Bernd Nilles.

Address: rue Stévin 16, 1000 Brussels.

Telephone: (2) 230-77-22; **Fax:** (2) 230-70-82; **Internet:** www .cidse.org; **e-mail:** postmaster@cidse.org.

CONCAWE—Oil Companies' European Association for Environment, Health and Safety in Refining and Distribution

Founded in 1963 as the Oil Companies' International Study Group for Conservation of Clean Air and Water in Europe; a division of the European Petroleum Refiners Association. In 2013, it merged with EUROPIA, which represented the European oil refining and marketing industry.

Activities: Collects and disseminates scientific, technical and economic information on all aspects of environmental and health protection related to the petroleum-refining industry (including pollution control, safety advice for workers and customers, and legislation). The Association collects, exchanges and evaluates environmental and health data; initiates and evaluates research; assesses the consequences of proposed environmental legislation in terms of economic feasibility and cost/benefit; promotes co-operation between petroleum companies, industry and governments on all environmental issues concerning the oil-refining industry; and publishes reports and other information. Work areas comprise: industrial atmospheric emissions; water protection; packaging, labelling and safe handling of petroleum products; health protection; automotive fuels and vehicle emissions; oil-spill cleaning technology; pipeline integrity; and refinery safety management. Has 39 members in 19 Organisation for Economic Co-operation and Development (OECD) European countries and one associate member in Eastern Europe.

Geographical Area of Activity: Europe.

Publications: *CONCAWE Review* (2 a year); *CONCAWE Reports*.

Finance: Total assets €20,330,413 (31 Dec. 2013).

Board of Directors: Michel Bénézit (Chair.).

Principal Staff: Dir-Gen. Chris Beddoes.

Address: blvd du Souverain 165, 1160 Brussels.

Telephone: (2) 566-91-60; **Fax:** (2) 566-91-81; **Internet:** www .concawe.eu; **e-mail:** info@concawe.org.

Damien Foundation (Action Damien)

Founded in 1964 to promote the eradication of leprosy and tuberculosis in developing countries.

Activities: Operates in developing countries to provide specialist medical assistance, aiming to eradicate leprosy and tuberculosis, through long-term projects, research and international co-operation. The Foundation also supports field training and formal training in specialized institutions; operates charitable programmes; supports local people in developing countries both medically and morally; and maintains a library.

Geographical Area of Activity: Africa, America, Asia—Bangladesh, Burundi, the People's Republic of China, Comoros, the Democratic Republic of the Congo, Egypt, Guatemala, India, Laos, Nicaragua, Nigeria, Panama, Peru, Rwanda and Viet Nam.

Publications: *Perspectives* (quarterly, in Dutch and French); Annual Report.

Finance: Total assets €20,946,960 (2013).

Trustees: M. De Doncker (Pres.).

Principal Staff: Pres. Paul Jolie; Gen. Man. Koen Van Den Abeele.

Address: blvd Léopold II 263, 1081 Brussels.

Telephone: (2) 422-59-11; **Fax:** (2) 422-59-00; **Internet:** www .actiondamien.be; **e-mail:** info@actiondamien.be.

EGMONT—Institut Royal des Relations Internationales (Royal Institute of International Relations)

Founded in 1947 to further studies into foreign politics, international law and economics, in particular in relation to the foreign policies of Belgium, Luxembourg and the Netherlands. The Institute expresses no official opinion on national or international affairs.

Activities: Operates internationally through self-conducted programmes, including research projects, carried out on an international basis. The main research programmes are: Central Africa; European Affairs; Security and Global Governance; Youth and Europe; and Visitor Programmes. Also organizes national and international conferences and lectures, hosts working groups, and issues publications. Maintains a library.

Geographical Area of Activity: International.

Publications: *Studia Diplomatica* (quarterly, in English); *Egmont Papers*; publications on European affairs; conference notes; working papers.

Finance: Annual revenue €1,700,126, expenditure €1,698,143 (31 Dec. 2011).

Board of Directors: Étienne Davignon (Chair.); Dirk Achten (Vice-Chair.).

Principal Staff: Dir-Gen. Marc Otte; Exec. Dir Marina Cruysmans.

Address: rue des Petits Carmes 24A, 1000 Brussels; Postal address: rue des Petits Carmes 15, 1000 Brussels.

Telephone: (2) 223-41-14; **Fax:** (2) 223-41-16; **Internet:** www .egmontinstitute.be; **e-mail:** info@egmontinstitute.be.

EURODAD—European Network on Debt and Development

Established in 1994; a network of 48 NGOs from 19 European countries working on issues related to debt, development finance and poverty reduction.

Activities: Focuses on debt, effective aid, private finance, international financial institution reform and tax justice. The Network offers a platform for exploring issues, collecting intelligence and ideas, and undertaking collective advocacy. It promotes responsible financial principles and practices, and redesigning financial architecture. The main institutions targeted by the Network are European governments, the World Bank, IMF and OECD.

Geographical Area of Activity: International.

Publications: Annual Report, newsletter and other reports (available online).

Finance: Funded by EURODAD members, the European Commission and private foundations. Annual income €1,198,263, expenditure €1,067,911 (2013).

Board of Directors: Jenny Brown (Chair.); Antonio Gambini (Treas.).

Principal Staff: Dir Jesse Griffiths.

Address: rue d'Edimbourg 18–26, Mundo B Bldg (3rd Floor), 1050 Ixelles, Brussels.

Telephone: (2) 894-46-40; **Fax:** (2) 791-98-09; **Internet:** www.eurodad.org; **e-mail:** assistant@eurodad.org.

European Anti-Poverty Network—EAPN (Réseau européen des Associations de Lutte contre la Pauvreté et l'Exclusion Sociale)

Established in 1990; an independent coalition of national and international NGOs; aims to eliminate poverty and social exclusion in the member states of the European Union (EU).

Activities: Works in the countries of the EU and in Norway, combating poverty through campaigning for the issue to be dealt with by the institutions of the EU, promoting action against poverty and supporting existing campaigns against social exclusion; and providing advocacy services for people and groups affected by poverty. There are national secretariats in 29 European countries.

Geographical Area of Activity: Europe.

Publications: Annual Report; *Network News* (newsletter in Danish, Dutch, English, French, German, Hungarian, Italian and Spanish); *European Manual on the Management of the Structural Funds*; position papers and reports.

Finance: Total assets €1,013,437 (31 Dec. 2013).

Bureau: Sérgio Aires (Pres.).

Principal Staff: Dir Barbara Helfferich.

Address: sq. de Meeûs 18, 1050 Brussels.

Telephone: (2) 226-58-50; **Fax:** (2) 226-58-69; **Internet:** www.eapn.eu; **e-mail:** team@eapn.eu.

European Coalition for Just and Effective Drug Policies—ENCOD

Established in 1993 by 14 European NGOs to provide information on the causes of the international traffic in illegal drugs and the consequences of current anti-drugs policies. Formerly known as the European NGO Council Drugs Development.

Activities: Operates as a network of European NGOs and citizens concerned with the impact of current international drugs policies on the lives of the people who are most affected by this issue. Aims to improve understanding of the causes and effects of the drugs trade; contribute to the elaboration of just and effective drugs control policies; and to bring about greater consistency between drugs control efforts and economic and social policies. Facilitates co-ordination, information exchange and joint analysis among its members; carries out joint information campaigns aimed at the general public; and pursues joint advocacy activities, aimed at policy-makers and the media. Currently has 150 members.

Geographical Area of Activity: Europe.

Restrictions: Not a grantmaking organization.

Publications: Reports and articles.

Finance: Annual budget €60,000.

Principal Staff: Co-ordinator Joep Oomen.

Address: Haantjeslei 213, 2018 Antwerp.

Telephone: (0) 495-122644; **Internet:** www.encod.org; **e-mail:** office@encod.org.

European Environmental Bureau—EEB (Bureau Européen d'Environnement—BEE)

Established in 1974.

Activities: A federation of around 140 environmental citizens' organizations based in 31 countries across the enlarged European Union (EU) and beyond, which aims to protect the environment in Europe and to enable European citizens to play a part in its defence. The Bureau provides member organizations with information; produces reports; represents member organizations in relations with EU institutions; and organizes working groups and conferences. It works as an advocate for improved environmental and conservation protection policies, and co-ordinates workshops and seminars.

Geographical Area of Activity: Europe.

Restrictions: Not a grantmaking organization.

Publications: *Metamorphosis* (quarterly newsletter, also available online); *EU Environmental Policy Handbook*; conference reports; memoranda; position papers.

Executive Committee: Mikael Karlsson (Pres.); Axel Jansen (Treas.).

Principal Staff: Sec.-Gen. Jeremy Wates.

Address: blvd de Waterloo 34, 1000 Brussels.

Telephone: (2) 289-10-90; **Fax:** (2) 289-10-99; **Internet:** www.eeb.org; **e-mail:** eeb@eeb.org.

European Foundation for Management Development

Founded in 1971 to provide an international network of private and public organizations, educational institutions and individuals for promoting management development.

Activities: Organizes annual activities for particular sections of its membership, and an annual conference on a subject of current and prospective importance for all categories; initiates special studies, meetings, seminars, workshops and projects on selected topics; brings relevant issues in the field of management development and education to the attention of national or international representative bodies; sponsors professional associations in specific fields; and publishes or sponsors publications for its members. Has more than 800 member organizations, located in 81 countries. Members include major European business schools and management centres, and a large number of companies and consultancy organizations. The Foundation promotes the creation of national networks of members to facilitate the exchange of information on a national basis and the development of transnational activities, and co-operates with management development associations in Central and Eastern Europe, North, Central and South-East Asia and Africa. The Foundation administers management training programmes in the People's Republic of China, India, Algeria, the Russian Federation and the Commonwealth of Independent States.

Geographical Area of Activity: Worldwide.

Publications: *Global Focus* (magazine, 3 a year, in English and Chinese); *Bulletin* (newsletter, 3 a year); *Guide to the EC*; *Lobbying in the EU*; *European Directory on Executive Education*; Annual Report.

Finance: Total revenue €7,355,624, expenditure €7,355,624 (31 Dec. 2014).

Board Members: Alain Dominique Perrin (Pres.); Susan Cox (Vice-Pres.); Gerard van Schaik (Hon. Pres.).

Principal Staff: Dir-Gen. and CEO Eric Cornuel.

Address: rue Gachard 88, bte 3, 1050 Brussels.

Telephone: (2) 629-08-10; **Fax:** (2) 629-08-11; **Internet:** www.efmd.org; **e-mail:** info@efmd.org.

European Foundation for Quality Management—EFQM

Founded in 1988 by 14 of Europe's largest companies to promote management in Europe.

Activities: A non-profit membership foundation that shares information and methodologies to help its members—private and public organizations of every size and in many sectors—to implement strategies. There were 443 members in 2012.

Geographical Area of Activity: Worldwide.

Publications: Various print publications on management, training and similar issues.

Finance: Annual income €3,755,131, expenditure €3,477,369 (31 Dec. 2013).

Board of Directors: Andreas Wendt (Chair.).

Principal Staff: CEO Marc Amblard.

Address: ave des Olympiades 2, 5th Floor, 1140 Brussels.

Telephone: (2) 775-35-11; **Fax:** (2) 775-35-35; **Internet:** www.efqm.org; **e-mail:** info@efqm.org.

Eurostep—European Solidarity towards Equal Participation of People (Solidarité Européenne pour une Participation Égale des Peuples)

Established in 1990 as an association of NGOs involved in development. Seeks to influence development policies of national governments and of the European Union and other international organizations, and to improve the quality and effectiveness of development initiatives taken by NGOs.

Activities: A group of 18 development NGOs from 14 European countries, which seeks to lobby national governments and international organizations in areas such as the eradication of poverty, social development, trade and international trade agreements, and the quality of aid. Also aims to improve the quality and effectiveness of initiatives taken by NGOs in support of people-centred development. Issues numerous position papers on development issues.

Geographical Area of Activity: Europe.

Restrictions: No grants available.

Publications: Briefing papers; *Eurostep Weekly (e-bulletin).*

Principal Staff: Dir Simon Stocker.

Address: rue Stévin 115, 1000 Brussels.

Telephone: (2) 231-16-59; **Fax:** (2) 230-37-80; **Internet:** www.eurostep.org; **e-mail:** admin@eurostep.org.

Fondation pour l'Architecture (Foundation for Architecture)

Founded in 1986 by architect Philippe Rotthier; a private cultural institution which supports the interaction of different areas of contemporary design and promotes architectural excellence.

Activities: Operates internationally through self-conducted programmes. The Foundation has established a system of cultural and financial partnership between Belgian and foreign public authorities and private businesses, and also works closely with museums, galleries, publishers and cultural centres. Stages exhibitions, conferences and public events devoted to all aspects of the built environment—contemporary architecture, history, current affairs, urban planning and design. Maintains two exhibition halls and awards the Prix Philippe Rotthier every three years.

Geographical Area of Activity: International.

Publications: Numerous catalogues and reference books.

Board of Trustees: Maurice Culot (Pres.).

Principal Staff: Contact Bertille Amaudric.

Address: rue de l'Ermitage 55, 1050 Brussels.

Telephone: (2) 644-24-80; **Fax:** (2) 642-24-82; **Internet:** www.fondationpourlarchitecture.be; www.rotthierprize.be; **e-mail:** info@fondationpourlarchitecture.be.

Fondation Auschwitz–Mémoire d'Auschwitz (Auschwitz Foundation–Remembrance of Auschwitz)

Founded in 1980 by Amicale des Ex-Prisonniers Belge as a study and documentation centre to preserve the memory of the prisoners of Auschwitz.

Activities: Operates nationally and internationally in the fields of education, the arts, law and human rights, and holocaust studies, through self-conducted programmes, awarding prizes, conferences and issuing publications. The Foundation awards the annual Auschwitz Foundation Prize of €2,500 for an original and unpublished text that makes an important contribution to the political, economic, social or historical analysis of the world of the Nazi concentration camps and the processes leading to its creation. Established the Remembrance of Auschwitz Documentation Centre. Maintains a library of more than 10,000 vols.

Geographical Area of Activity: Europe.

Publications: *Bulletin Trimestriel de la Fondation Auschwitz/Driemaandelijks Tijdschrift*; *International Journal*; *Quarterly Bulletin*; *Sporen*; teaching materials.

Finance: Remembrance of Auschwitz total assets €430,004 (31 Dec. 2013).

Principal Staff: Pres. Henri Goldberg; Sec.-Gen. Claude Aronis; Exec. Dir Frédéric Crahay.

Address: rue des Tanneurs 65, 1000 Brussels.

Telephone: (2) 512-79-98; **Fax:** (2) 512-58-84; **Internet:** www.auschwitz.be; **e-mail:** info@auschwitz.be.

Fondation Bernheim (Bernheim Foundation)

Established in 1974 for general charitable purposes.

Activities: Operates in the fields of workforce development and civic integration. The Foundation awards grants and prizes, holds conferences and seminars, and issues publications. It also supports entrepreneurial initiatives and medical research, incl. chairs in entrepreneurial studies in Belgian universities.

Geographical Area of Activity: Belgium.

Publications: Information brochures; Annual Report.

Finance: Annual expenditure €1.95m. (30 April 2010).

Board of Directors: Françoise Thys-Clément (Pres.); Baron Raymond Vaxelaire (Vice-Pres. and Treas.); Baron Robert Tollet (Vice-Pres.); Jacques Dopchie (Hon. Pres.).

Principal Staff: Dir France de Kinder.

Address: rue des Bouchers 53, 1000 Brussels.

Telephone: (2) 213-14-99; **Fax:** (2) 213-14-95; **Internet:** www.fondationbernheim.be; **e-mail:** info@fondationbernheim.be.

Fondation Boghossian (Boghossian Foundation)

Established in 1992 by Robert Boghossian and his sons to support a better life for young people in Armenia and Lebanon.

Activities: Operates projects for young people in Armenia and Lebanon in the areas of welfare, education, art and culture, and medicine. Also offers the President of Armenia Prizes for young people in the arts and sciences. The Foundation awards the annual Boghossian Foundation Prize, awarding US $10,000 to three young Lebanese artists; the President of the Republic of Armenia Prize, worth $80,000, for achievements in science, the arts, literature and the developments of humanist values, and also a "Junior" Prize for young people's achievements in music, visual arts and literature; and the Award at the Fine Arts Academy of Antwerp.

Geographical Area of Activity: Armenia and Lebanon.

Advisory Committee: Jean Boghossian (Chair.); Albert Boghossian (Treas.).

Principal Staff: Gen. Man Diane Hennebert; Admin. Man. Benjamin Erarts.

Address: Villa Empain, ave Franklin Roosevelt 67, 1000 Brussels.

Telephone: (2) 627-52-30; **Fax:** (2) 537-43-24; **Internet:** www.fondationboghossian.com; **e-mail:** info@boghossianfoundation.be.

Fondation Evens Stichting (Evens Foundation)

Active since 1996; founded by late diamond trader and philanthropist Georges Evens.

Activities: Initiates, develops and supports projects that encourage citizens and ultimately nations to live together harmoniously in a diverse Europe. The Foundation promotes respect for diversity, both individual and collective, and works to strengthen people's physical, psychological and moral integrity. Has three main programmes: Peace Education, Media and European Citizenship. Awards biennial prizes in Peace Education, Media Education, and Arts and Science.

Geographical Area of Activity: European Union countries, particularly Belgium, France and Poland.

Restrictions: Does not support unsolicited applications.

Publications: Annual Report; booklets; learning materials; research reports; other publications.

Board of Directors: Corinne Evens (Co-Founder and Hon. Pres.); Luc Luyten (Chair.).

Address: Stoopstraat 1, 5th Floor, 2000 Antwerp.

Telephone: (3) 231-39-70; **Fax:** (3) 233-94-32; **Internet:** www
.evensfoundation.be; **e-mail:** antwerp@evensfoundation.be.

Fondation Francqui (Francqui Foundation)

Founded in 1932 by Emile Francqui and Herbert Hoover to promote the development of higher education and scientific
research in Belgium.

Activities: Operates in the field of higher education. Confers
the annual Prix Francqui on a Belgian under 50 years of age
who has made a notable advance in the fields of science, humanities or medicine. Also awards Francqui Professorships each
year, inviting two scholars from each Belgian university and
three foreign professors to teach in Belgium under the Foundation's auspices. Provides annual fellowships to selected young
Belgian academics to enable them to study abroad, mainly in
the USA.

Geographical Area of Activity: Belgium.

Restrictions: Grants available only to Belgian nationals.

Finance: Total assets €35,726,821 (31 Dec. 2014).

Board of Directors: Mark Eyskens (Chair.); Herman Baltha-
zar, Viscount Étienne Davignon (Vice-Chair.).

Principal Staff: Exec. Dir Prof. Dr Pierre van Moerbeke.

Address: rue d'Edmont 11, 1000 Brussels.

Telephone: (2) 539-33-94; **Fax:** (2) 537-29-21; **Internet:** www
.francquifoundation.be; **e-mail:** francquifoundation@skynet
.be.

Fondation Marcel Hicter (Marcel Hicter Foundation)

Established in 1980 to promote and carry out activities contributing to the socio-cultural development of the French community in Belgium, and to promote co-operation at a
European and international level in the area of culture.

Activities: Operates in the field of the arts and culture, formerly through organizing the European Diploma in Cultural
Project Management, which operates in three countries; training cultural managers from 36 countries; and managing, on
behalf of the Council of Europe, mobility grants for cultural
management experts and trainees. Also organizes conferences, carries out research and issues publications.

Geographical Area of Activity: Central, Eastern and Western Europe, the Russian Federation and Central Africa.

Publications: *Citoyens et Pouvoirs en Europe*; *Another brick in
the wall, A critical review of cultural management education in
Europe*; *Arts management in turbulent times: Adaptable quality
management*; *Survey on funding opportunities for international
cultural co-operation in and with South-eastern Europe*; *The
arts, politics and change. Participative cultural policymaking in
South-Eastern Europe*; guidance on heritage assessment.

Principal Staff: CEO Jean-Pierre Deru.

Address: Association Marcel Hicter pour la Démocratie Cul-
turelle, ave Maurice 1, 1050 Brussels.

Telephone: (2) 641-89-80; **Fax:** (2) 641-89-81; **Internet:** www
.fondation-hicter.org; **e-mail:** contact@fondation-hicter.org.

Fondation Fernand Lazard (Fernand Lazard Foundation)

Founded in 1949 and administered by representatives of seven
Belgian universities; promotes continuing education.

Activities: Makes awards to university students from the European Union (EU) member states for study in Belgium to fund
relocation costs and to finance study at universities or
research centres in Belgium and other EU countries. Planned
to make up to 50 awards of €25,000 each in 2015.

Geographical Area of Activity: Europe.

Board of Directors: Alain Siaens (Chair.); Pierre Lefebvre
(Vice-Chair.).

Principal Staff: CEO François Glansdorff; Sec.-Gen. Sophie
Castelein.

Address: ave de Merode 100, 1330 Rixensart.

Telephone: (2) 687-21-40; **Fax:** (2) 687-21-40; **Internet:** www
.redweb.be/lazard; **e-mail:** info@fernandlazard.com.

Fondation P&V

Established in 2000 by the company P&V Assurances to work
with young people.

Activities: Works with and for young people. The Foundation
makes an annual Citizenship Award to a person or organization for promoting openness, democracy, tolerance and inclusivity.

Geographical Area of Activity: International.

Board: Mark Elchardus (Chair.).

Principal Staff: Exec. Dir Marnic Speltdoorn.

Address: rue Royale 151, 1210 Brussels.

Telephone: (2) 250-91-24; **Fax:** (2) 250-91-45; **Internet:** www
.fondationpv.be; **e-mail:** fondation@pv.be.

**Fondation Paul-Henri Spaak—Stichting Paul-Henri
Spaak** (Paul-Henri Spaak Foundation)

Founded in 1973 by Vicomte Étienne Davignon, Fernand
Dehousse, Auguste Edmond De Schryver, André de Staercke,
Walter Ganshof van der Meersch, Marcel Grégoire, André Jau-
motte, Comte Georges Moens de Fernig, Jean Rey, Paul Smets
and Fernand Spaak to constitute a centre of thought and
action to prolong the European work of Paul-Henri Spaak, particularly in the field of the external relations of the European
Community (now the EU); and to promote any activity contributing to a better understanding of the European ideal and
associating new generations with the construction of Europe.

Activities: Established to operate nationally, internationally
and on a European level in the field of international relations
and economic affairs, through self-conducted programmes,
research, conferences and publications. Encourages education
and scientific research related to its aims, through creating
specialized professorships in EU external affairs to be occupied by distinguished foreigners; international fellowships
and scholarships; and the sponsoring of publications and diffusion of documentation and information. Organizes lectures
and seminars, as well as regional, national and international
congresses. Also awards a science prize.

Geographical Area of Activity: International.

Administrative Council: Vicomte Étienne Davignon (Pres.).

Principal Staff: Sec.-Gen. François Danis.

Address: ave George Bergmann 62, bte 4, 1050 Brussels.

Telephone: (2) 479-48-91; **Internet:** www.fondationspaak
.org; **e-mail:** fond.spaak@skynet.be.

Fonds InBev-Baillet Latour (InBev-Baillet Latour
Fund)

Created by Count Alfred de Baillet Latour in 1974.

Activities: Encourages human accomplishments in the scientific, educational or artistic fields, and awards prizes, research
grants, travel and gifts. Activities are in four fields: clinical
research, training, Belgian heritage and Olympic spirit.
Makes annual grants of approx. €3m.

Geographical Area of Activity: Worldwide.

Finance: Total assets €92,190,560 (31 Dec. 2013).

Board of Directors: Baron Jan Huyghebaert (Pres.).

Principal Staff: Gen. Sec. Alain De Waele.

Address: Brouwerijplein 1, 3000 Leuven.

Telephone: (16) 27-61-59; **Fax:** (16) 50-61-59; **Internet:** www
.inbevbailletlatour.com; **e-mail:** inge.raemaekers@inbev
.com.

Fonds National de la Recherche Scientifique—FNRS
(National Fund for Scientific Research)

Founded in 1928 by King Albert I to promote scientific
research in Belgium.

Activities: Provides subsidies each year to scientists or
research workers to enable them to continue their investigations, and awards about 800 grants annually to university
students in the field of science. Also provides more than 200
research posts of limited duration to qualified research

workers and supports the attendance at scientific meetings and conferences of Belgian researchers. Enables qualified research workers to undertake short visits abroad to familiarize themselves with new developments and techniques in scientific research. Awards prizes for achievement in the field of research. Also administers the Fund for Medical Scientific Research, the Fund for Fundamental Collective Research, the Inter-University Institute for Nuclear Sciences and the Industry and Agriculture Research Training Fund.

Geographical Area of Activity: Belgium.

Publications: Annual Report; *La Lettre du FNRS*; *Fnrsnews*; brochures; memoranda.

Finance: Annual revenue €175,680,180, expenditure €165,928,578 (31 Dec. 2012).

Board of Directors: Vincent Blondel (Chair.); Didier Viviers (Vice-Chair.).

Principal Staff: Sec.-Gen. Dr Véronique Halloin.

Address: rue d'Egmont 5, 1000 Brussels.

Telephone: (2) 504-92-11; **Fax:** (2) 504-92-92; **Internet:** www .frs-fnrs.be; **e-mail:** julie.dekemel@frs-fnrs.be.

Fonds Wetenschappelijk Onderzoek—Vlaanderen
(Research Foundation—Flanders)

Established in 1928 at the initiative of King Albert I to encourage and support fundamental scientific research.

Activities: Promotes and finances fundamental scientific research in the universities and in research institutions in Flanders (Belgium) in all fields of science, including medicine, technology, environmental studies, social sciences and the humanities, including law. Provides pre- and postdoctoral fellowships and grants for national and international research projects, contacts and co-operation.

Geographical Area of Activity: Flanders (Belgium).

Publications: *Founders of Knowledge: 80 years of FWO; FWO Excellence Prizes; FWO-nieuwsbrief*.

Finance: Annual budget €223.1m. (2014).

Board of Trustees: Prof. Rik Torfs (Pres.); Prof. Anne De Paepe (Vice-Pres.).

Principal Staff: Sec.-Gen. Elisabeth Monard.

Address: Egmontstraat 5, 1000 Brussels.

Telephone: (2) 512-91-10; **Fax:** (2) 512-58-90; **Internet:** www .fwo.be; **e-mail:** post@fwo.be.

GAIA—Groupe d'Action dans l'Intérêt des Animaux
(Global Action in the Interest of Animals)

Established in 1992 by Ann de Greef and Michel Vandenbosch.

Activities: Works for the cause of animal rights, through education, active campaigns, lobbying and the publication of informative materials. Promotes vegetarianism, campaigns against experimentation on animals for the production of cosmetics and for medical research and against maltreatment of animals in farming.

Geographical Area of Activity: Belgium.

Publications: *Animalibre*; *Vrijdier*; educational material.

Finance: Total assets €1,124,000 (31 Dec. 2014).

Board: Michel Vandenbosch (Chair.).

Principal Staff: Dir Ann De Greef.

Address: Galerie Ravenstein 27, 1000 Brussels.

Telephone: (2) 245-29-50; **Fax:** (2) 215-09-43; **Internet:** www .gaia.be; **e-mail:** info@gaia.be.

Îles de Paix (Islands of Peace)

Founded in 1965 by Father Dominique Pire to ameliorate conditions for people living in the Southern regions of the world through food security and infrastructure development; and to educate people in more developed countries about life in the Southern hemisphere.

Activities: Operates internationally in the field of aid to less-developed countries, through self-conducted programmes carried out with partner organizations in West Africa (including Benin, Burkina Faso, Mali, Niger and Togo) and South America (Bolivia and Ecuador). Also educates the public in Belgium about life in less-developed countries.

Geographical Area of Activity: West Africa and South America.

Publications: *Transitions* (quarterly); Annual Report; financial statements; reports and news-sheets.

Finance: Annual revenue €3,035,100, expenditure €3,824,953 (31 Dec. 2013).

Principal Staff: Sec.-Gen. Laurence Albert.

Address: rue du Marché 37, 4500 Huy.

Telephone: (85) 23-02-54; **Fax:** (85) 23-42-64; **Internet:** www .ilesdepaix.org; **e-mail:** info@ilesdepaix.org.

Institut Européen Interuniversitaire de l'Action Sociale—IEIAS

Founded in 1970 to provide the study of social welfare and to encourage a uniform social welfare policy for all European countries.

Activities: Finances and conducts research into methods of supplying the needs (physical and psychological) of individuals in society; assesses the effect of different methods; maintains a library of approximately 67,000 articles and publications and a database; organizes seminars and courses; and issues publications.

Geographical Area of Activity: Europe.

Publications: *COMM* (English and French, 3 a year); seminar papers and other publications.

Finance: Annual budget approx. US $400,000.

Board of Directors: Joseph Gillain (Chair.).

Principal Staff: CEO Dr Bernard Kennes.

Address: rue de la Bruyère 157, 6001 Marcinelle.

Telephone: (71) 44-72-11; **Fax:** (71) 47-27-44; **Internet:** www .hainaut.be/social/dgas/template/template.asp?page=ieias; **e-mail:** info@ieias.be.

International Yehudi Menuhin Foundation—IYMF

Founded by Yehudi Menuhin in 1991. Aims to remind political, cultural and educational institutions of the central role of art and creativity in the whole personal and societal development process.

Activities: Maintains a network of 11 national structures based in Europe and Israel. Activities concentrate on promoting the arts at school (MUS-E programme); arts on stage (multicultural concerts and international artist residencies); and arts and intercultural dialogue (ACE/Assembly of Culture of Europe). Also promotes music and the arts internationally; encourages exchanges and encounters between different cultures through organizing events; promotes the representation of those cultures that are under threat by organizing a forum (the Assembly of Cultures of Europe); and co-ordinates cultural projects initiated by Yehudi Menuhin, and disseminates them throughout the world.

Geographical Area of Activity: Worldwide.

Restrictions: Funds are dedicated only to the development of the Foundation's programmes and the training of MUS-E artists and co-ordinators.

Publications: Online newsletter; CDs; DVDs; books.

Finance: Total assets €100,087 (31 Dec. 2014).

Board of Administration: Enrique Barón Crespo (Pres.); Stefano Micossi (Treas.).

Principal Staff: Exec. Vice-Pres. Marianne Poncelet.

Address: blvd du Souverain 36, 1170 Brussels.

Telephone: (2) 673-35-04; **Fax:** (2) 672-52-99; **Internet:** www .menuhin-foundation.com; **e-mail:** marianne.poncelet@ menuhin-foundation.com.

Koning Boudewijnstichting/Fondation Roi Baudouin (King Baudouin Foundation)

Founded in 1976 as an independent public welfare institution to commemorate the 25th anniversary of King Baudouin's coronation, and 'to carry out initiatives to improve the life of the population, including measures of an economic, social, scientific and cultural nature'.

Activities: Operates in Belgium and internationally, supporting projects in the areas of justice, democracy and diversity. Current themes include: poverty and social justice; health heritage; social engagement; Africa and developing countries; philanthropy; democracy; developing talent; European engagement; and the German-speaking community. Awards the annual King Baudouin African Development Prize. Also organizes round tables, forums and seminars, works in partnership with governmental and non-governmental organizations, and issues publications.

Geographical Area of Activity: International.

Publications: Annual Report; *Zoom*; newsletter; reports and studies.

Finance: Receives a grant from the Belgian National Lottery. Annual revenue €120,468,744, expenditure €66,933,854 (31 Dec. 2014).

Board of Governors: Baroness Françoise Tulkens (Chair.); Baron Serge Brammertz, Luc Coene (Vice-Chair.).

Principal Staff: Man. Dir Luc Tayart de Borms.

Address: rue Bréderode 21, 1000 Brussels.

Telephone: (2) 511-18-40; **Fax:** (2) 511-52-21; **Internet:** www.kbs-frb.be; **e-mail:** info@kbs-frb.be.

Madariaga—College of Europe Foundation (Fondation Madariaga—Collège d'Europe)

Established in 1988 by former students of the College of Europe (f. 1949) to work towards prosperity, peace and solidarity through strengthening European union.

Activities: Focuses on two main programmes: Challenging Citizens and EU–China. The Foundation organizes events and projects within these programmes on: EU–China relations; economic and financial governance; European foreign policy and defence; natural resources, energy and the environment; and citizens, society and democracy.

Geographical Area of Activity: Europe.

Publications: Books, event reports and discussion papers.

Board of Directors: Javier Solana (Pres.); Jean Courtin (Treas.).

Principal Staff: Man. Dir Pierre Defraigne.

Address: ave de la Joyeuse Entrée 14, bte 2, 1040 Brussels.

Telephone: (2) 209-62-10; **Fax:** (2) 209-62-11; **Internet:** www.madariaga.org; **e-mail:** info@madariaga.org.

Open Society European Policy Institute

Established in 1997 as the representative office of the Open Society Foundations (qq.v.) to the European Union (EU) and West European partner countries.

Activities: Works to advocate open society values (transparency and rule of law, human rights and fundamental freedoms, and democratic principles) with regard to EU policies; also assists in collaboration between the Open Society Foundations network and the EU and other intergovernmental agencies.

Finance: Total assets €364,974 (31 Dec. 2010).

Principal Staff: Dir Heather Grabbe.

Address: rue du Trône 130, 1050 Brussels.

Telephone: (2) 505-46-46; **Fax:** (2) 502-46-46; **Internet:** www.osi-brussels.eu; **e-mail:** osi-brussels@osi-eu.org.

Oxfam-en-Belgique (Oxfam-in-Belgium)

Established in 1964 as Oxfam-Belgique and subsequrntly renamed Oxfam-Solidarité in 1996; part of the Oxfam confederation of organizations (qq.v.).

Activities: Works internationally to alleviate poverty. The organization focuses on seven main areas: food; inequality; climate; land grabbing; violence against women; conflicts and disasters; health; and civic participation.

Geographical Area of Activity: More than 90 countries worldwide.

Finance: Annual revenue €24,376,453, expenditure €25,645,631 (31 Dec. 2012).

Board of Directors: Guido Van Hecken (Chair.); Michel Gilson (Vice-Chair.); Joris Rycken (Sec.-Treas.).

Principal Staff: Exec. Dir Stefaan Declercq.

Address: rue des Quatre Vents 60, 1080 Brussels.

Telephone: (2) 501-67-00; **Internet:** www.oxfamsol.be; **e-mail:** oxfamsol@oxfamsol.be.

Pesticide Action Network Europe—PAN Europe

Established in 1983; a network of European environmental NGOs promoting a sustainable alternative to the use of pesticides; part of the PAN International network.

Activities: Works to protect people's health against the harms of pesticides in food and the environment, and biodiversity against the negative effects of industrial agriculture. The Network promotes alternatives to the use of pesticides, through pesticide reduction programmes, lobbying in Brussels and nationally. The Network issues publications and organizes conferences. Comprises 35 member NGOs from 25 countries, of which 22 are in the European Union.

Geographical Area of Activity: Europe.

Publications: Annual Report; reports; newsletters; briefings; fact sheets.

Principal Staff: Policy Adviser Henriette Christensen.

Address: rue de la Pépinière 1, 1000 Brussels.

Telephone: (2) 503-08-37; **Internet:** www.pan-europe.info; **e-mail:** coordinator@pan-europe.info.

Ruralité Environnement Développement—RED (Rurality Environment Development)

Founded in 1980 to encourage communication between those involved in rural development throughout Europe.

Activities: Organizes conferences and seminars in the fields of economic development, planning and cultural heritage in rural areas. The organization chairs and co-ordinates the European Countryside Movement, and is President of the Advisory Committee on Rural Development of the European Commission of the European Union. Has members in 15 countries.

Geographical Area of Activity: Europe.

Restrictions: No grants are made.

Publications: *RED Dossier* (2 a year); *Eurobrèves* (newsletter); seminar papers.

Board of Directors: Gérard Peltre (Pres.); Felipe González de Canales, Alfons Hausen, Istvan Bali (Vice-Pres); Alain Delchef (Treas.).

Principal Staff: Dir Patrice Collignon.

Address: rue des Potiers 304, 6717 Attert.

Telephone: (63) 23-04-90; **Fax:** (63) 23-04-99; **Internet:** www.ruraleurope.org; **e-mail:** infored@ruraleurope.org.

SELAVIP International—Service de Promotion de l'Habitation Populaire en Amérique Latine, Afrique et Asie (Latin American, African and Asian Social Housing Service)

Founded in 1976 by Fr Josse van der Rest in Belgium to help local urban communities, families and NGOs in cities of less-developed regions.

Activities: Focuses on providing shelter to the urban poor, and promoting and empowering organizations to initiate community-driven processes that will improve their shelter. The Service works with organizations such as NGOs, community-based organizations and social services to target very poor people in need of basic shelter (max. US $1,200 per unit). It insists on land title for the beneficiaries. Selavip International is a sister NGO of Fundación Selavip, Santiago de Chile.

Geographical Area of Activity: Africa, Asia, Latin America and the Caribbean.

Restrictions: Does not work in developed countries, with families or groups that are not in social emergency, or in rural areas.

Finance: Private donations from Fondation Caritative Van der Rest-Emsens, Liechtenstein.

Board of Directors: Jean-Paul van der Rest (Chair.).

Principal Staff: Sec.-Gen. Henri Thijssen.

Address: Blvd Brand Whitlock 66, 1200 Brussels.

Telephone: 475550075; **Internet:** www.selavip.be; **e-mail:** ht.selavip@gmail.com.

Service Civil International—SCI

Founded in 1920 by Pierre Ceresole to provide opportunities for men and women, young and old, irrespective of their race, nationality, creed or politics to join together in giving useful voluntary service to the community in a spirit of friendship and international understanding, with the aim of promoting peace, international understanding and solidarity, social justice, sustainable development and concern for the environment.

Activities: Offers a variety of volunteer opportunities to individuals, such as short, mid- and long-term projects, and also the opportunity to become active for a local branch or to participate in a seminar or training. The organization consists of 45 branches worldwide and a number of partner organizations.

Geographical Area of Activity: International.

Restrictions: Not a grantmaking organization.

Publications: Newsletter, Annual Report.

Finance: Total assets €251,373 (31 Dec. 2012).

International Executive Committee: Małgorzata (Gośka) Tur (Acting Pres.); Attanayake (Karu) Karunaratne (Acting Vice-Pres.); Katalin Somlai (Treas.).

Principal Staff: International Co-ordinator Sara Turra.

Address: Belgiëlei 37, 2018 Antwerp.

Telephone: (3) 266-57-27; **Fax:** (3) 232-03-44; **Internet:** www.sciint.org; **e-mail:** info@sciint.org.

Solidar

Established in 1948 as International Workers Aid.

Activities: A European network of 61 NGOs based in 25 countries, working to advance social justice in Europe and worldwide. The network voices the concerns of its member organizations to the European Union and international institutions across the policy sectors of social affairs, international co-operation and lifelong learning. In 2000 it launched the Silver Rose Awards for contributions to social justice and solidarity.

Geographical Area of Activity: Europe and worldwide.

Publications: *Weekly Round Up* (e-news bulletin); Activity Report; *60 years of SOLIDAR* book; Decent Work and Quality Jobs in Europe—series of case studies on different aspects and recommendations for EU decision-makers; Report on Global Social Protection; *Global Network Report on Decent Work and Millennium Development Goals; Decent Work Decent Life* (case studies), Collection of Good Practices: Decent working conditions: raising awareness among young people, Social Justice in MENA (case studies); *Building Learning Societies, EU 2020; Social Progress for a more inclusive Europe; TTIP: Main considerations.*

Board of Directors: Josef Weidenholzer (Pres.); Francisca Sauquillo (Vice-Pres.); Jean-Marc Roirant (Treas.).

Principal Staff: Sec.-Gen. Conny Reuter.

Address: rue du Commerce 22, 1000 Brussels.

Telephone: (2) 500-10-20; **Fax:** (2) 500-10-30; **Internet:** www.solidar.org; **e-mail:** solidar@solidar.org.

Universitaire Stichting (University Foundation)

Founded in 1920 to promote scientific progress.

Activities: Operates in the field of higher education, through grants to associations and individuals and for the publication of scientific works and periodicals. Participates in the awarding of the Emile Bernheim European Prizes and the Fernand Collin Prize for Law. The Foundation also maintains a university club with lecture room.

Geographical Area of Activity: Europe.

Publications: *Annual University Statistics for Belgium; Akkadica; Analecta Bollandiana; Annales d'histoire d'art et d'archéologie; Anthropologie et Préhistoire; Antiquité Classique; Augustiniana; Belgian Journal of Botany; Belgian Journal of English Language and Literature; Belgian Journal of Entomology; Belgian Journal of Linguistics; Belgian Journal of Zoology.*

Board of Directors: Prof. Jacques Willems (Pres.).

Principal Staff: Exec. Dir Eric de Keuleneer.

Address: rue d'Egmont 11, 1000 Brussels.

Telephone: (2) 545-04-00; **Fax:** (2) 513-64-11; **Internet:** www.universitairestichting.be; www.fondationuniversitaire.be; **e-mail:** fu.us@universityfoundation.be.

World Animal Handicap Foundation—WAHF

Founded in 1992 to care for disabled animals using adapted orthopaedic therapy.

Activities: Works with veterinary surgeons, pet clinics and hospitals, animal protection associations, pet owners and others to further its aims.

Geographical Area of Activity: International.

Publications: *WAHF News* (quarterly).

Finance: Funded by charities, gifts and membership fees.

Principal Staff: Chair. Comte Geoffroy de Beauffort; Sec. Michelle Mommer-Horikoshi.

Address: sq. Marie-Louise 40, bte 22, 1000 Brussels.

Telephone: (2) 230-76-46; **Internet:** wahf.over-blog.com; **e-mail:** asbl.wahf@telenet.be.

Benin

FOUNDATIONS, TRUSTS AND NON-PROFIT ORGANIZATIONS

Centre Pan-Africain de Prospective Sociale—Institut Albert Tévoèdjrè (CPPS-IAT) (Pan-African Centre for Social Prospects)

Founded in 1987 by Association Mondiale de Prospective Sociale. Present name adopted in 2012.

Activities: Undertakes research and training programmes linked to social and development issues; trains young professionals as future leaders in Africa in the areas of social policy, economics, communication, consumer protection, environmental protection and management; facilitates the exchange of business and technological information; and supports NGOs involved in development projects and programmes, and socio-economic projects. The Centre also helped found the African Humanitarian Initiative to assist refugees with food and medicines.

Geographical Area of Activity: Africa.

Publications: Annual Report; *Actes des Colloques et Séminaires.*

Board: Agon Valentin (Chair.).

Principal Staff: Exec. Dir Jacques Tévoèdjrè; Assoc. Dir Eric Tévoèdjrè.

Address: BP 1501, Porto Novo.

Telephone: 21-44-36; **Fax:** 21-44-36; **Internet:** www.cpps-iat.org; **e-mail:** cpps.iat@gmail.com.

Fondation de l'Entrepreneurship du Bénin (Enterprise Foundation of Benin)

Aims to help establish and promote new businesses and private companies in Benin.

Activities: Provides assistance and support to entrepreneurs (both nationals and foreigners) who wish to invest in Benin. Organizes seminars, offers advice on marketing and management skills and strategies, training, and the opportunity to contact other suppliers and potential customers around the world. Runs an annual entrepreneurial competition for young people, funded by the Benin National Lottery and the Canadian International Development Agency. Manages the Place du Québec socio-cultural centre.

Geographical Area of Activity: Benin.

Principal Staff: Dir Pierre Dovonou Lokossou.

Address: pl. du Québec, devant le Stade René Pleven, Akpakpa, 05 BP 337, Cotonou.

Telephone: 90-91-2001; **Fax:** 33-82-72; **e-mail:** fonda@intnet.bj.

Groupe d'Action pour la Justice et l'Egalité Sociale—GAJES (Action Group for Justice and Social Equality)

Founded in 1990; a pressure group dedicated to achieving equality for all women in society.

Activities: Operates in the field of social justice, primarily in the field of social justice for women. Programmes include education of girls in the Mono department; the development and support of parent-teacher associations; and the Unité Documentaire Femmes et Développement, a documentation centre providing information sources for women on sustainable development and empowerment.

Geographical Area of Activity: Benin.

Board of Directors: Marie-Odile Comlanvi-Hountondji (Chair.).

Principal Staff: Sec.-Gen. Gisèle Agboton Amoussou.

Address: Maison OKETOKOUN, 1er étage, face Église Protestante Béthanie, Quartier Misséssin, Akpakpa Centre, 04 BP 1102, Cadjèhoun.

Telephone: (229) 33-95-58; **e-mail:** ongajes_99@yahoo.com.

Bermuda

FOUNDATION CENTRE AND CO-ORDINATING BODY

Centre on Philanthropy

Established in 1991 to promote a philanthropic philosophy in the community and an attitude of giving, through information, seminars and dialogue with charities, the public, government and the business sector.

Activities: A resource and advocacy centre for Bermuda's charities and volunteers. The Centre promotes a philosophy of philanthropy in the community, through information, seminars and dialogue with its member charities, the public, the Government and the corporate sector. It provides information, training workshops and seminars for its members. Resources include databases of charities and volunteers, and a library of educational and reference materials.

Geographical Area of Activity: Bermuda.

Publications: Newsletter; guides for charities; town hall meeting; rotary speech (annually).

Finance: Annual revenue Bermuda $653,083, expenditure $814,137 (30 June 2014).

Board of Directors: Brian Madeiros (Chair.); Graham Pewter (Deputy Chair.).

Principal Staff: Exec. Dir Elaine Butterfield.

Address: POB HM 3217, Hamilton HM NX; Sterling House, 16 Wesley St, Hamilton.

Telephone: 236-7706; **Fax:** 236-7693; **Internet:** www.centreonphilanthropy.org; **e-mail:** info@centreonphilanthropy.org.

FOUNDATIONS, TRUSTS AND NON-PROFIT ORGANIZATIONS

Bermuda Community Foundation

Established in 2013, on the Initiative of Atlantic Philanthropies (q.v.), to fund non-profit organizations.

Activities: Current priority funding areas are: Youth Achievement and Community-based Education; Arts for All and Bermuda's Heritage; Caring Community Fund; Community Development; and Green and Blue Community. Manages community funds that are open to public contribution; the Community Grants Committee allocates a portion of these funds to emerging needs each year.

Geographical Area of Activity: Bermuda.

Board of Directors: Peter Durhager (Chair.).

Principal Staff: CEO and Man. Dir Myra Virgil.

Address: POB HM 11, Hamilton; Sterling House, Fourth Floor, 16 Wesley St, Hamilton.

Telephone: 294-4959; **Internet:** www.bermudacommunityfoundation.org; **e-mail:** info@bcf.bm.

International Charitable Fund of Bermuda—ICFB

Formed in 1994 and co-sponsored by the Centre on Philanthropy (q.v.) and PricewaterhouseCoopers (formerly Price Waterhouse) to promote and support the purposes and activities of not-for-profit charitable organizations in Bermuda through tax-deductible gifts from US taxpayers.

Activities: Makes grants to non-profit organizations in Bermuda operating exclusively for charitable, scientific or educational purposes.

Geographical Area of Activity: Bermuda.

Board of Trustees: David Lang (Pres. and Treas.); Mairi Redmond (Sec.).

Principal Staff: Contact Sally Hamilton.

Address: c/o Clarien Bank Private Banking, POB HM 1322, Hamilton HM FX.

Telephone: 294-5055; **Fax:** 294-3165; **Internet:** www.centreonphilanthropy.org/pages/icfb; **e-mail:** info@icfbermuda.org.

Bolivia

FOUNDATIONS, TRUSTS AND NON-PROFIT ORGANIZATIONS

Fundación Amigos de la Naturaleza (Friends of Nature Foundation)

Founded in 1988 by a small group of naturalists located in Santa Cruz for the conservation of biodiversity in Bolivia.

Activities: Aims to prevent environmental degredation and protect biodiversity in Bolivia and neighbouring countries. The Foundation runs self-conducted programmes, research, offering scholarships and fellowships, and conferences. Programme areas include: bio-commerce; climate change and environmental services; science; communication; and conservation.

Geographical Area of Activity: South America.

Publications: *Síntesis Ambiental* (policy brief); books on the environment, conservation, the flora and fauna of Bolivia, and for children.

Finance: Annual income US $2,417,731, expenditure $2,328,798 (2013).

Trustees: James M. Johnson (Pres.); Hermes Justiniano, José Luis Galvez (Vice-Pres).

Principal Staff: Exec. Dir Natalia Calderón.

Address: Km 7 1/2 Doble Via la Guardia, Casilla 2241, Santa Cruz de la Sierra.

Telephone: (3) 3556800; **Fax:** (3) 3547383; **Internet:** www.fan-bo.org; **e-mail:** fan@fan-bo.org.

Sembrar Sartawi (Sow Sartawi)

Established in 2009 following the merger of Fundación Sartawi (f. 1989) and Fundación Sembrar.

Activities: A financial development institution which promotes the inclusion of small-scale farmers in the financial system. Provides technical assistance to groups of people with little access to resources, with an emphasis on rural areas, facilitating economic initiatives and strengthening the artisan industry to increase job opportunities for women. Runs programmes relating to agricultural forestation in valleys and areas of the *altiplano*, micro-enterprises and providing easier access to credit for those in need.

Geographical Area of Activity: Bolivia.

Publications: Annual Report.

Finance: Total assets US $232,334,153 (31 Dec. 2013).

Board of Directors: Juan Despot Mitru (Chair.); María Elena Querejazu Vidovic (Vice-Pres.); Eduardo Ayllón Zamorano (Sec.); Miguel Zalles Denegri (Treas.).

Principal Staff: Man. Dir Marcelo Mallea Castillo.

Address: Calle Pedro Salazar, 509 Zona Sopocachi, La Paz.

Telephone: (2) 419252; **Fax:** (2) 415999; **Internet:** www.sembrarsartawi.org; **e-mail:** infoss@sembrarsartawi.org.

Bosnia and Herzegovina

FOUNDATIONS, TRUSTS AND NON-PROFIT ORGANIZATIONS

Open Society Fund—Bosnia-Herzegovina

Founded in 1992 to promote the values of an open society; an independent foundation, part of the Soros foundations network, which aims to foster political pluralism and reform economic structures to encourage private enterprise and a market economy.

Activities: Provides financial support to assist institutions working towards the development of an open society; funds educational programmes, including the printing of textbooks and initiating alternative educational programmes. The Fund also operates grant programmes within the fields of women's rights and empowerment; development of the Roma community; fighting corruption; and improving the public health system. Collaborates with other Soros foundations on various projects related to improving people's lives and building functional open societies.

Geographical Area of Activity: Bosnia and Herzegovina.

Publications: Reports.

Finance: Annual income US $2,320,054, expenditure $2,320,054 (31 Dec. 2014).

Board of Directors: Sevima Sali Terzic (Chair.).

Principal Staff: Exec. Dir Dobrila Govedarica; Financial Dir Nermana Karović.

Address: Marsala Tita 19/III, 71000 Sarajevo.

Telephone: (33) 444488; **Fax:** (33) 444488; **Internet:** www.osfbih.org.ba; **e-mail:** osf@osfbih.org.ba.

Botswana

FOUNDATION CENTRE AND CO-ORDINATING BODY

Botswana Council of Non-Governmental Organisations—BOCONGO

Established in 1995.

Activities: Facilitates the development of NGOs, and works to ensure their participation in the ongoing development process in Botswana; enables NGOs, the Government, the private sector and other development partners to network effectively, and promotes improved communication and the dissemination of information; and aims to take on a leading role in policy advocacy and lobbying to allow NGOs to work as a united body on issues of national interest.

Geographical Area of Activity: Botswana.

Publications: Programme reports (online); quarterly newsletters.

Executive Committee: Rev. Biggie Butale (Chair.).

Address: Bonokopila House, Plot 53957, Machel Dr., Gaborone; Private Bag 00418, Gaborone.

Telephone: 3911319; **Fax:** 3912935; **e-mail:** bocongo@bocongo.org.bw.

Brazil

FOUNDATION CENTRES AND CO-ORDINATING BODIES

GIFE—Grupo de Institutos, Fundações e Empresas (Group of Institutes, Foundations and Enterprises)

Established in 1995 as a membership organization representing companies and foundations in Brazil. Aims to improve and disseminate the concepts and practical means of using private funds for the good of the community.

Activities: Composed of institutes, foundations and corporations that are active within the third sector in Brazil. Provides member organizations with information, and a centre where they can exchange knowledge and experience through meetings, seminars, courses and forums. Establishes links between similar local and national organizations, aiming to create an environment to enable private businesses to invest in community development. Maintains a national reference centre, which contains materials on philanthropic knowledge and practices.

Geographical Area of Activity: Brazil.

Publications: *Censo GIFE* (biennial); others.

Finance: Annual income 2,933,076 reais, 3,133,820 reais (31 Dec. 2013).

Governing Board: Beatriz Gerdau Johannpeter (Pres.).

Principal Staff: Sec.-Gen. Andre Degenszajn.

Address: Av. Brigadeiro Faria Lima 2413, 1° andar, Conjunto 11, Jardim Paulistano, 01452-000 São Paulo, SP.

Telephone: (11) 3816-1209; **Fax:** (11) 3816-1209; **Internet:** www.gife.org.br; **e-mail:** redegife@gife.org.br.

Instituto para o Desenvolvimento do Investimento Social—IDIS (Institute for the Development of Social Investment)

Established in 1999; part of the CAF Global Alliance network of organizations.

Activities: Promotes social development through the structuring of social investment.

Geographical Area of Activity: Brazil.

Publications: *A Empresa na Comunidade: Um passo-a-passo para estimular sua participação social* ; *Comunidade: Foco de Filantropia e Investimento Social Privado*; *Desenvolvimento Comunitário Baseado em Talentos e Recursos Locais–ABCD*; *Fundos Patrimoniais–Criação e Gestão no Brasil*; *O papel da Filantropia no Desenvolvimento do Brasil*; *O Papel Transformador do Investimento Social Privado*; *Redes de Desenvolvimento Comunitário: Iniciativas para a transformação social*; *Repensando o Investimento Social: A importância do protagonismo comunitário*; *Tendências do Investimento Social Privado na América Latina* (also in Spanish and English).

Finance: Annual revenue 4.2m. reais (31 Dec. 2014).

Board of Directors: Henrique H. Ubrig (Pres.); Helio Nogueira Curz (Vice-Pres.).

Principal Staff: CEO Paula Jansco Fabiani.

Address: Rua Paes Leme 524, Caja 161, Pinheiros, 05424-904 São Paulo, SP.

Telephone: (11) 3037-8212; **Fax:** (11) 3031-9052; **Internet:** www.idis.org.br; **e-mail:** portalidis@idis.org.br.

Rede Iberoamericana de Fundações Civicas ou Comunitárias (Ibero-American Network of Community Foundations)

Established in 2013 by Fundación Bertelsmann (Spain); management subsequently transferred to the ICom—Instituto Comunitário Grande Florianópolis (f. 2005) community foundation.

Activities: Promotes and strengthens community foundations. In 2013 the Network assisted approx. 33,000 people directly and 1,950 organizations. Comprises 32 organizations from Brazil, Mexico, Portugal, Spain and Uruguay.

Geographical Area of Activity: Portugal, South America, Central America and the Caribbean, Spain.

Finance: Total community investments US $21.4m. (2013).

Principal Staff: Contact Cecília Mozzaquattro da Silva.

Address: c/o ICom, CAIS, Rua Lacerda Coutinho 100, Centro Florianópolis, SC.

Telephone: (48) 3222-5127; **Internet:** www.fciberoamerica .org; **e-mail:** cecilia@icomfloripa.org.br.

WINGS—Worldwide Initiatives for Grantmaker Support

Established in 2000 to support worldwide network between, and development of, associations of grantmaking organizations and to support organizations serving philanthropy.

Activities: Peer-learning events for members; regional meetings; global forum; knowledge generation and dissemination; e-library. Has 150 network participants in 56 countries.

Geographical Area of Activity: International.

Publications: *WINGS Dispatch* (monthly newsletter); case studies of grantmaker associations; *CF Global Status Report* (every 2 years); *Infrastructure in Focus*; *Community Foundation Atlas* (online).

Finance: Annual revenue US $648,641, expenditure $591,047 (31 Dec. 2013).

Board of Directors: Dr Atallah Kuttab (Chair.); Andre Degenszajn (Sec.); John Ulanga (Treas.).

Principal Staff: Exec. Dir Helena Monteiro.

Address: Av. 9 de Julho 5143, Conjunto 61, Jardim Paulistano, 01407-200 São Paulo, SP.

Telephone: (11) 3078-7299; **Internet:** www.wingsweb.org; **e-mail:** info@wingsweb.org.

FOUNDATIONS, TRUSTS AND NON-PROFIT ORGANIZATIONS

BrazilFoundation

Established in 2000 by Leona Forman.

Activities: Focuses on generating resources for projects that enable improvement of social and economic conditions of Brazilians. Operates in the fields of social welfare, culture, medicine and health, education and human rights, working in partnership with other charitable organizations. Maintains an office in New York, USA.

Geographical Area of Activity: Brazil.

Restrictions: Grants are made only in Brazil.

Publications: Annual Report; newsletter archives.

Finance: Annual revenue US $1,360,677, expenditure $1,259,267 (31 Dec. 2012).

Board of Directors: Leona Forman (Chair.); Roberta Mazzariol (Vice-Chair.); Marcello Hallake (Gen. Counsel); Will Landers (Treas.).

Principal Staff: Pres. and CEO Patricia Lobaccaro; Vice-Pres. Mônica de Roure.

Address: Av. Calógeras 15, 13° andar, 20030-070 Rio de Janeiro, RJ.

Telephone: (21) 2532-3029; **Fax:** (21) 2532-2998; **Internet:** www.brazilfoundation.org; **e-mail:** info@brazilfoundation.org.

Federação Democrática Internacional de Mulheres (Women's International Democratic Federation)

Founded in 1945 to prevent the recurrence of war and the resurgence of fascism for the sake of the well-being of women and children.

Activities: Defends women's rights in every area of life and every region of the world. Works for equal rights in society and in the workplace, and for women's rights to adequate health care and education. Also promotes world peace and democracy, and campaigns against racial inequality and discrimination. Organizes congresses. Has 126 affiliated organizations in 99 countries worldwide.

Geographical Area of Activity: International.

Publications: Bulletin.

Principal Staff: Nat. Co-ordinator Lúcia Rincón; Deputy Nat. Co-ordinator Vanja Andréa dos Santos.

Address: Rua Barão de Itapetininga 255, 9° andar, Sala 908, 01042-001 São Paulo, SP.

Telephone: (11) 3105-8216; **Internet:** www.ubmulheres.org.br/fdim; **e-mail:** ubm@ubmulheres.org.br.

Fundação Abrinq pelos Direitos da Criança e do Adolescente (Abrinq Foundation for the Rights of Children and Adolescents)

Established in 1990 to support the fundamental rights of children and adolescents.

Activities: Extends support to projects that work to defend the basic rights of children and young people; promotes inter-sector co-operation and offers technical assistance; and equips NGOs, government agencies and community groups with information and documentation.

Geographical Area of Activity: Brazil.

Publications: Annual Report; *A History of Action 1990–97*.

Finance: Annual income 24,064,683 reais, expenditure 23,695,212 reais (31 Dec. 2012).

Executive Board: Carlos Antonio Tilkian (Pres.); Synésio Batista da Costa (Vice-Pres.); Bento José Gonçalves Alcoforado (Sec.).

Principal Staff: Exec. Admin. Heloisa Helena Silva de Oliveira.

Address: Av. Santo Amaro 1386, 1° andar, Vila Nova Conceição, 04506-001 São Paulo, SP.

Telephone: (11) 3848-8799; **Internet:** www.fundabrinq.org.br; **e-mail:** doador@fundabrinq.org.br.

Fundação Armando Alvares Penteado—FAAP (Armando Alvares Penteado Foundation)

Founded in 1947 by Armando Alvares Penteado and Annie Alvares Penteado for exclusively pedagogical purposes.

Activities: Aims to contribute, through teaching and related activities, to Brazil's cultural expansion and integration into technology. The Foundation maintains a university, a museum of fine arts, and various centres and institutes. Courses are offered in science and technology, the arts and humanities, economics, business management and international relations. Awards scholarships.

Geographical Area of Activity: Brazil.

Publications: *Revista FAAP* (6 a year); *Revista de Economia e Relações Internacionais*; *Revista Qualimetria*; *Revista Gerente de Cidade*; other magazines; newsletter.

Board of Trustees: Celita Procopio de Carvalho (Pres.).

Principal Staff: Man. Dir Dr Antonio Bias Bueno Guillon.

Address: Rua Alagoas 903, Higienópolis, 01242-902 São Paulo, SP.

Telephone: (11) 3662-7159; **Fax:** (11) 3662-7103; **Internet:** www.faap.br; **e-mail:** rel.internacional@faap.br.

Fundação Aperam Acesita (Aperam Acesita Foundation)

Established in 1994 to promote sustainable social-educational, environmental and economic development.

Activities: Aims to improve the quality of life of local communities by contributing to integrated and sustainable development. Operates in the Vale do Aço and Timóteo areas, funding social and economic development projects, including educational, cultural, environmental and community programmes. Also runs a cultural centre, vocational training centre, the Institute of Stainless Steel and Oikós Environmental Education Centre.

Geographical Area of Activity: Brazil (Vale do Aço, Vale do Jequitinhonha).

Publications: Annual Report.

Principal Staff: Pres. Venilson Araújo Vitorino.

Address: Alameda 31 de Outubro 500, Centro CEP, 35180-014 Timóteo, MG.

Telephone: (31) 3849-7002; **Fax:** (31) 3849-7294; **Internet:** www.aperam.com/brasil/port/fundacao/; **e-mail:** inox.fundacao@aperam.com.

Fundação ArcelorMittal Brasil (ArcelorMittal Brasil Foundation)

Established in 1988 as the Fundação Belgo-Mineira to support cultural projects. Present name adopted in 2006.

Activities: Main focus is on children and adolescents. The Foundation works in the fields of education, culture and social inclusion, with specific projects directed at young entrepreneurs, health, the environment and improving living standards. Operates in more than 40 cities throughout Brazil.

Geographical Area of Activity: Brazil.

Publications: Newsletter.

Finance: Annual revenue 3,606,547 reais, expenditure 3,986,759 reais (31 Dec. 2013).

Board of Directors: Ricardo Garcia da Silva Carvalho (Chair.).

Principal Staff: Gen. Man. Leonardo Gloor.

Address: Av. Carandaí, 1115, 17th Floor, Funcionários, 30130-915 Belo Horizonte, MG.

Telephone: (31) 3219-1660; **Internet:** www.fundacaoarcelormittalbr.org.br; **e-mail:** fundacao@arcelormittal.com.br.

Fundação Banco do Brasil (Banco do Brasil Foundation)

Founded in 1985; dedicated to social community work in Brazil.

Activities: Promotes, assists and financially supports initiatives in urban and rural communities in five main areas: water; agro-ecology; agro-industry; solid waste; and education. Provides credit and technical support to other non-profit organizations and grassroots groups in Brazil, and promotes volunteerism and philanthropy. Awards a prize for social technology and maintains a database of social technologies.

Geographical Area of Activity: Brazil.

Publications: News articles; books; social and activities reports.

Finance: Annual income 207,393,000 reais, expenditure 223,626,000 reais (31 Dec. 2013).

Board of Directors: José Caetano de Andrade Minchillo (Chair.).

Principal Staff: Exec. Dirs Marcos Frade, Vagner Ribeiro.

Address: SCN Quadra 1, Bloco A, Edifício Number One, 10°
andar, 70711-900 Brasília, DF.
Telephone: (61) 3104-4600; **Fax:** (61) 3310-1966; **Internet:**
www.fbb.org.br; **e-mail:** fbb@fbb.org.br.

Fundação Gaia (Gaia Foundation)

Established in 1987 by environmentalist José A. Lutzenberger
to promote sustainable development.

Activities: Operates in the Brazilian state of Rio Grande do
Sul in the field of protection of the environment, by providing
advisory services, participating in conferences, offering training courses and issuing publications. Promotes sustainable
development, working with regenerative agriculture, environmental education, protection of biodiversity, conservation of
the cultural identity of minorities, and the use of 'soft' technologies.

Geographical Area of Activity: Brazil.

Restrictions: No grants available.

Publications: Annual Report; *Ecológica*; *Fruticultura*; *Sani-
dade Animal na Agroecologia*; *A Teoria da Trofobiose*; publications in English, German and other languages.

Finance: Financed by private donations, consultancies, projects, courses and sale of products.

Board of Directors: Lara Josette W. Lutzenberger (Pres.);
Franco A. Werlang (Vice-Pres.).

Address: Rincão Gaia, Pantano Grande, Rio Grande do Sul.

Telephone: (51) 9725-3685; **Fax:** (51) 9725-3686; **Internet:**
www.fgaia.org.br; **e-mail:** sede@fgaia.org.br.

Fundação Grupo Boticário de Proteção à Natureza
(Boticário Group Foundation)

Established in 1990 by Miguel G. Krigsner, founder of O Boticário, a cosmetics company, to conserve nature.

Activities: Protects natural areas and supports the projects
of other organizations. Raises awareness about and mobilizes
support for nature conservation. Through its nature preserves,
protects more than 11,000 hectares of natural Atlantic Forest
and Cerrado remnants, and surrounding areas. In addition,
encourages people to conserve natural areas, either via the
Oásis Project or by supporting other organizations' projects,
thereby protecting Brazilian biodiversity. Also promotes
events such as the Brazilian Congress on Protected Areas.
Created interactive Nature Station exhibitions, presenting
the beauty and importance of Brazilian nature to urban populations.

Geographical Area of Activity: Brazil.

Council: Miguel G. Krigsner (Pres.).

Principal Staff: Pres. Dir Artur N. Grynbaum; Exec. Dir
Maria de Lourdes Nunes.

Address: Gonçalves Dias 225, Batel, 80240-340 Curitiba, PR.

Telephone: (41) 3340-2636; **Fax:** (41) 3340-2635; **Internet:**
www.fundacaogrupoboticario.org.br; **e-mail:** contato@
fundacaogrupoboticario.org.br.

Fundação Iochpe

Established in 1989 by Iochpe-Maxion SA, a manufacturer of
vehicle parts.

Activities: Aims to promote the development of people's full
potential and improve the quality of life of the people and communities in which the founding company operates, including
funding not-for-profit organizations active in the areas of education, culture and social welfare, with a specific focus on the
education of at-risk children and young people. Also provides
information and documentation to not-for-profit organizations, grassroots groups, international organizations and government agencies, as well as technical assistance and training
for grassroots groups and other not-for-profit organizations.

Geographical Area of Activity: Argentina and Brazil.

Finance: Total assets 9,602,839 reais, annual income 4,991,645
reais (31 Dec. 2014).

Board of Trustees: Ivoncy Ioschpe (Chair.).

Principal Staff: Chief Exec. Evelyn Ioschpe; Gen. Co-ordinator Beth Callia.

Address: Al. Tietê 618, Casa 1, Cerqueira César, 01417-020 São
Paulo, SP.

Telephone: (11) 3060-8388; **Fax:** (11) 3060-8388; **Internet:**
www.fiochpe.org.br; **e-mail:** fundacao.iochpe@fiochpe.org
.br.

Fundação Roberto Marinho (Robert Marinho Foundation)

Established in 1977 by journalist Roberto Marinho to provide
quality education to Brazilians.

Activities: Undertakes activities on a national as well as an
international level, primarily focusing on the field of education, and several other areas, including national heritage,
and ecology and conservation. Operates in partnership with
other organizations focusing on similar issues to fund and execute projects such as literacy programmes for adults and children. Offers funds for music, dance and national museums;
awards annual prizes for young scientists; and devises ecological campaigns for environment protection.

Geographical Area of Activity: Brazil.

Board of Directors: José Roberto Marinho (Pres.).

Principal Staff: Sec.-Gen. Hugo Barreto.

Address: Rua Santa Alexandrina 336, 1° andar, Rio Com-
prido, 20261-232 Rio de Janeiro, RJ.

Telephone: (21) 2502-3233; **Internet:** www.frm.org.br;
e-mail: imprensa@frm.org.br.

**Fundação Museu do Homem Americano—FUMD-
HAM** (Foundation Museum of American Man)

Established in 1986 to encourage scientific research, ecology
conservation and sustainable development.

Activities: Operates nationally and internationally, with a
focus on supporting less-developed regions in Brazil; other
areas of focus are environment and conservation, sustainable
development studies, education, economic and international
affairs, science and technology, and medicine and health. Carries out self-conducted programmes, prizes, training courses
and conferences. Also protects Serra da Capivara National
Park and the Environmental Protection Area.

Geographical Area of Activity: Brazil.

Publications: Activity Report; *Fumdhamentos*; articles.

Principal Staff: CEO Niéde Guidon; Scientific Dir Maria
Gabriela Martin Ávila; Finance Dir Silvia Maranca.

Address: Centro Cultural Sérgio Motta s/n, Bairro Campes-
tre, 64770-000 São Raimundo Nonato, PI.

Telephone: (89) 3582-1612; **Fax:** (89) 3582-1293; **Internet:**
www.fumdham.org.br; **e-mail:** contato@fumdham.org.br.

Fundação Romi (Romi Foundation)

Established in 1957 in Santa Bárbara d'Oeste, São Paulo, to
promote educational and cultural development to ensure the
development of society.

Activities: Supports cultural, social and educational initiatives, such as computer training, to advance Brazilian development.

Geographical Area of Activity: Brazil.

Publications: *Conecte*.

Finance: Annual income 4,126,933 reais, expenditure
3,230,693 reais (31 Dec. 2014).

Principal Staff: Pres. Patrícia Romi Cervone; Vice-Pres.
Eugênio Guimarães Chiti.

Address: Av. Monte Castelo 1095, Jardim Primavera, 13450-
285 Santa Bárbara d'Oeste, SP.

Telephone: (19) 3455-1055; **Fax:** (19) 3455-1345; **Internet:**
www.fundacaoromi.org.br; **e-mail:** fundacaoromi@
fundacaoromi.org.br.

Fundação Maurício Sirotsky Sobrinho (Maurício Sirotsky Nephew Foundation)

Established in 1987 to defend the rights of children and young people.

Activities: Promotes sustainable self-development aimed at building citizenship and respecting fundamental social rights, with a particular focus on the defence of the rights of children and adolescents, primarily in the states of Rio Grande do Sul, Santa Catarina and Paraná. Also provides information resources to not-for-profit organizations.

Geographical Area of Activity: Brazil.

Publications: Articles.

Board of Trustees: Nelson P. Sirotsky (Chair.).

Principal Staff: Exec. Dir Lucia Ritzel.

Address: Avda Érico Veríssimo 400, 5° andar, 90160-180 Porto Alegre, RS.

Telephone: (51) 3218-6024; **Fax:** (51) 3218-6035; **Internet:** www.fmss.org.br; **e-mail:** fundacao@fmss.org.br.

Fundação SOS Mata Atlântica (Foundation for the Conservation of the Atlantic Rainforest)

Founded in 1986 to work towards the protection of the forests of Brazil's Atlantic region, the preservation of the communities inhabiting them and their cultural heritage, and the sustained development of these areas.

Activities: Operates in Brazil in the area of conservation and the environment.

Geographical Area of Activity: Brazil.

Publications: Newsletter.

Finance: Annual revenue 23,154,000 reais, expenditure 21,115,000 reais (31 Dec. 2013).

Board of Directors: Pedro Luiz Barreiros Passos (Pres.).

Principal Staff: Admin. and Finance Dir Marcia Hirota.

Address: Av. Paulista 2073, Conjunto 1318, Cd. Conjunto Nacional, Torre Horsa 1, 13° andar, Bela Vista, São Paulo, SP.

Telephone: (11) 3262-4088; **Internet:** www.sosmatatlantica .org.br; **e-mail:** info@sosma.org.br.

Fundação Hélio Augusto de Souza—Fundhas (Hélio Augusto de Souza Foundation)

Established in 1987 to assist children and young people.

Activities: Operates three basic programmes in education, welfare and training: the Child Programme, for children between the ages of six and 14 years; the Adolescent Programme, for young people aged 14–18 years; and the Supporting/Partnership Programmes. Currently assists around 5,000 children and young people through its programmes.

Geographical Area of Activity: São José dos Campos (Brazil).

Publications: *Notícias*.

Principal Staff: Pres. Vanda Siqueira.

Address: Rua Santarém 560, Parque Industrial, 12235-550 São José dos Campos, SP.

Telephone: (12) 3932-0533; **Fax:** (12) 3939-1180; **Internet:** www.fundhas.org.br; **e-mail:** imprensa@fundhas.org.br.

Fundação Maria Cecilia Souto Vidigal (Maria Cecilia Souto Vidigal Foundation)

Established in 1965 by Gastão Eduardo de Bueno Vidigal and Maria Cecília Souto Vidigal, following the death of their daughter, Maria Cecília, from leukemia.

Activities: Improved treatment and understanding of leukaemia led the founders of the organization to review its mission in 2001. It currently supports a number of programmes that focus on early childhood development.

Geographical Area of Activity: Brazil.

Publications: Activity Report; *Boletim FMCSV* (newsletter, 6 a year).

Finance: Annual revenue 23,420,000 reais, expenditure 53,818,000 reais (31 Dec. 2013).

Board of Trustees: Guilherme Vidigal Andrade Gonçalves.

Principal Staff: CEO Eduardo de Campos Queiroz; Admin. and Finance Man. Felipe Ferri.

Address: Rua Fidencio Ramos 195, CJ 42, Vila Olímpia, 04551-010 São Paulo, SP.

Telephone: (11) 3330-2888; **Fax:** (11) 3079-2746; **Internet:** www.fmcsv.org.br; **e-mail:** fmcsv@fmcsv.org.br.

GRUMIN—Grupo Mulher-Educação Indígena (Indigenous Women's Education Group)

Established in 1987 in north-east Brazil by Eliane Potiguara to aid native women's social, economic and political development by eradicating social discrimination and improving women's self-determination through seminars, conferences and vocational training.

Activities: Operates nationally through a wide network of offices. Finances several projects such as the creation of community gardens where landless families can grow food; organizes training courses to provide an insight into indigenous history and handicrafts; organizes vocational training, seminars and conferences for native women; and presents a forum to facilitate online debates.

Geographical Area of Activity: Brazil.

Publications: Journal; bulletin; and other publications.

Principal Staff: Gen. Co-ordinator Eliane Lima dos Santos (Eliane Potiguara).

Address: Daline Braga, Av. Heitor Beltrao 71, Sala 301, Tijuca, 20550-000 Rio de Janeiro, RJ.

Telephone: (21) 567-2675; **Fax:** (21) 567-2675; **Internet:** www .grumin.org.br; elianepotiguara.org.br/noticias/; **e-mail:** grumin@grumin.org.br.

Instituto Rio

Established in 2000 as a community foundation.

Activities: Brings together companies, civil society organizations and government initiatives to promote the development of the low-income Zona Oeste of Rio de Janeiro, and mobilize local resources. Provides financial and technical support and capacity building to community-based organizations; trains organization managers and community leaders in all aspects of strategic planning; promotes knowledge sharing, collaboration and social investment, taking into account local priorities. Initiatives include a Community University, Partner Network and Instituto Rio Network. Manages the Vera Pacheco Jordão Fund (f. 2005) for investment in social projects. In 2013 the Institute made the first Geraldo Pereira Jordan Awards for innovation in community development and private social investment.

Geographical Area of Activity: Zona Oeste, Rio de Janeiro.

Principal Staff: Exec. Dir Graciela Hopstein.

Address: Rua Voluntários da Pátria 45, Sala 1401, Botafogo, 22270-000 Rio de Janeiro, RJ.

Telephone: (21) 2259-1018; **Internet:** www.institutorio.org .br; **e-mail:** institutorio@institutorio.org.br.

Instituto Ayrton Senna (Ayrton Senna Institute)

Established in 1995 to commemorate late Brazilian racing-car driver Ayrton Senna and achieve his ideals: assisting child welfare and other welfare activities in the areas of education and health.

Activities: Activities focus nationally on: providing direct assistance to safeguard the rights of Brazilian adolescents and children, and advocating development activities that are of help to future generations; health and medicine, and education, supporting small-scale projects in the areas of education, poverty relief, health, nutrition, culture and sports; and anti-poverty programmes in support of 'street children' in Brazil. International activities carried out through the United Kingdom-based Ayrton Senna Foundation.

Geographical Area of Activity: Brazil.

Restrictions: Grants are not made to individuals.

Publications: *Educação em Cena*; books.

Finance: Receives 100% of the profits obtained from the licensing of the Senna brand and image, and is also financed through alliances with the Brazilian and multinational business community.

Board of Directors: Viviane Senna (Pres.).

Principal Staff: Pres. Viviane Senna.

Address: Rua Dr. Fernandes Coelho 85, 15º andar, Pinheiros, São Paulo, SP.

Telephone: (11) 2974-3000; **Fax:** (11) 2950-8007; **Internet:** www.senna.globo.com/institutoayrtonsenna; **e-mail:** ias@ias.org.br.

REDEH—Rede de Desenvolvimento Humano (Network for Human Development)

Established in 1990; works towards creating awareness among women on issues of health, education, environment, and sexual and reproductive rights.

Activities: A forum for women to exchange their views and voice their concerns in different forms, such as Fala Mulher (Speak Women), a daily one-hour radio broadcast. Conducts training programmes for activists; runs projects to contain desertification; and undertakes sustainable development initiatives, health and prevention initiatives, and programmes to better efforts undertaken to induct women in the local governing bodies in towns and cities.

Geographical Area of Activity: Brazil.

Publications: Numerous publications and videos.

Finance: Annual budget approx. 661,000 reais.

Principal Staff: Gen. Co-ordinator Thais Rodrigues Corral; Exec. Co-ordinator Maria Aparecida Schumaher.

Address: Rua Álvaro Alvim 21, 16º andar, Centro, 20031-010 Rio de Janeiro, RJ.

Telephone: (21) 2262-1704; **Fax:** (21) 2262-6454; **Internet:** www.redeh.org.br; www.mulher500.org.br; **e-mail:** redeh@redeh.org.br.

Bulgaria

FOUNDATION CENTRES AND CO-ORDINATING BODIES

Association of Community Foundations in Bulgaria

Established in 2005 by six community foundations with the support of USAID.

Activities: Lobbies on behalf of community foundations and promotes philanthropy more generally; develops partnerships between public foundations and corporate donors; and provides training and technical support to community foundations. Comprises 12 mem. foundations.

Geographical Area of Activity: Bulgaria.

Principal Staff: Chair. Ivan Karamanov; Exec. Dir Daniela Dimitrova.

Address: 6000 Stara Zagora, 14 Graf Ignatiev (Ground Floor).

Telephone: (42) 602-155; **Internet:** www.acfb-bg.org; **e-mail:** acfb@acfb-bg.org.

BCAF—Bulgarian Charities Aid Foundation

Founded by CAF—Charities Aid Foundation (q.v.) in 1995 to help design and build the framework for a robust voluntary sector in Bulgaria.

Activities: Manages seven charitable funds and runs grant-making programmes; promotes corporate giving, providing information to companies and helping them organize their giving schemes effectively; has developed Bulgaria's first payroll giving scheme; runs financial and legal management training courses; manages an emergency fund providing support for the medical treatment of children (up to the age of 18 years) from disadvantaged families; and awards scholarships.

Geographical Area of Activity: Bulgaria.

Publications: *Businesses and their Charitable Attitudes– research on corporate giving in Bulgaria*; *Financial Management, Legal and Tax Regulations of NGOs*; *Donations and Tax Relief*; *Corporate Social Responsibility–whys and hows in Bulgaria and worldwide*; *Partners Bulletin*; Annual Report.

Finance: Annual income 1,846,000 lev, expenditure 1,814,000 lev (31 Dec. 2012).

Board of Directors: Michael Boyadjiev (Chair.).

Principal Staff: Exec. Dir Elitsa Barakova.

Address: 1000 Sofia, Vitosha Blvd 65, 2nd Floor.

Telephone: (2) 981-19-01; **Fax:** (2) 987-15-74; **Internet:** www.bcaf.bg; **e-mail:** bcaf@bcaf.org.

Black Sea NGO Network—BSNN

Established in 1998, and registered in 1999, to operate as a regional association of NGOs from all Black Sea countries.

Activities: Aims to facilitate the free flow and exchange of information, resources and experience for the accomplishment of its aims of the protection and rehabilitation of the Black Sea, including the Azov Sea, and the sustainable development of the Black Sea countries, through increased participation of NGOs, governments, businesses and other institutions, as well as the general public. Operates through lobbying and advocacy for environmentally sound national legislation, for development and adoption of National Strategic Action Plans for rehabilitation and protection of the Black Sea environment, and for the appliance of international conventions in the Black Sea countries; encouraging sustainable practices in the Black Sea coastal area; raising environmental awareness for acute Black Sea environmental issues through environmental education and information; facilitating public participation in the decision-making processes concerning acute Black Sea environmental issues; promoting activities for solving Black Sea acute environmental problems and specific environmental issues; and building the capacity and self-sustainability of the Black Sea NGO community. Has more than 60 member organizations.

Geographical Area of Activity: Black Sea countries (Bulgaria, Georgia, Romania, the Russian Federation, Turkey and Ukraine).

Publications: Newsletter; topical items; regional directories on Bulgaria, Georgia, Romania, the Russian Federation, Turkey and Ukraine; numerous project publications.

Network Board: Prof. Dr Tanay Uyar (Chair.).

Principal Staff: Rep. Emma Gileva.

Address: 9000 Varna, POB 91; Varna, Dr L. Zamenhof St 2.

Telephone: (5) 261-58-56; **Fax:** (5) 260-20-47; **Internet:** www.bsnn.org; **e-mail:** bsnn@bsnn.org.

Bulgarian Donors' Forum

Established in 2003 to promote the development of civil society and the sustainable development of NGOs in Bulgaria.

Activities: Represents the interests of its members as well as aiming to build the financial sustainability of the Bulgarian non-profit sector, including encouraging new donors. Also carries out research, lobbies government and provides information and advice to members and NGOs. Has 47 members (incl. 16 foundations and 21 companies); membership is open to donor organizations that provide annual grants in excess of €5,000 and accept the Forum's Code of Ethics. Organizes annual Top Corporate Donor awards.

Geographical Area of Activity: Bulgaria.

Publications: *Developing local grantmaking in Bulgaria*.

Finance: Annual income 1,172,000 lev, expenditure 1,172,000 lev (31 Dec. 2013).

Principal Staff: Dir Krasimira Velichkova.

Address: 1124 Sofia, Leonardo da Vinci St 4в, 2nd Floor.

Telephone: (2) 951-59-78; **Fax:** (2) 951-59-78; **Internet:** www.dfbulgaria.org; **e-mail:** bkirilova@dfbulgaria.org.

FOUNDATIONS, TRUSTS AND NON-PROFIT ORGANIZATIONS

America for Bulgaria Foundation

Established in 2008 as successor to the Bulgarian-American Enterprise Fund (f. 1991).

Activities: Promotes the development of economic prosperity and democracy through free-market capitalism, legal justice and civic participation. Operates the Borgatti Scholarship Fund for Bulgarian students at the American University in Bulgaria.

Geographical Area of Activity: Bulgaria.

Publications: Newsletter.

Finance: Annual revenue US $4,742,723, expenditure $29,068,602 (31 Dec. 2012).

Board of Dirs: Gary E. MacDougal (Chair.).

Principal Staff: Exec. Dir Desislava Taliokova.

Address: 1000 Sofia, Malyovitsa St 6.

Telephone: (2) 806-38-00; **Fax:** (2) 843-51-23; **Internet:** www.americaforbulgaria.org; **e-mail:** applications@americaforbulgaria.org.

Bulgarian Fund for Women

Established in 2004 by the Gender Project for Bulgaria Foundation.

Activities: Provides financial and development support to NGOs for projects aiming to combat all forms of violence against women; to promote women's economic independence and to reduce poverty and unemployment; to encourage women's participation in public and political life for their promotion in decision-making positions; to achieve equal rights and equal opportunities for marginalized groups of women and those with different sexual orientation; and to facilitate women's access to information technology. Also seeks to improve the quality of services provided by trainers, consultants and facilitators who work with NGOs on gender equality, and participates in international networks of women's funds.

Geographical Area of Activity: Bulgaria.

Publications: *Identification of the Inner Gender Resources of the Roma Community for Enhancing their Integration with Bulgarian Society* (2007).

Finance: Annual income 82,000 lev, expenditure 82,000 lev (2011).

Board of Trustees: Stanimira Hadjimitova (Pres.).

Principal Staff: Chief Exec. Monica Pisankaneva.

Address: 1000 Sofia, Parchevich St 37в.

Telephone: (2) 986-47-10; **Fax:** (2) 981-56-04; **Internet:** www.bgfundforwomen.org; **e-mail:** gender@fastbg.net.

Creating Effective Grassroots Alternatives—CEGA

Established in 1995.

Activities: Promotes sustainable democratic development through providing support to disadvantaged minority groups and provides for their participation in the transformation of their communities. Provides funding and technical support to grassroots groups and organizations to increase their effectiveness and impact in resolving social problems; disseminates democratic practices that work and supports effective community-based initiatives; and engages in advocacy, coalition-building and public campaigns, based on lessons learned at the community level. Operates through two main programmes: Youth in Action and Initiative for Local Changes.

Geographical Area of Activity: Bulgaria.

Restrictions: No grants to individuals.

Publications: *Why Not* (newsletter).

Board of Directors: Lachezar Stoyanov (Chair.).

Principal Staff: Exec. Man. Roumyan Sechkov.

Address: 1000 Sofia, Kniaz Boris I St 85, 2nd Floor.

Telephone: (2) 988-36-39; **Fax:** (2) 988-96-96; **Internet:** www.cega.bg; **e-mail:** cega@cega.bg.

Evrika Foundation

Founded in 1990 to encourage and educate young people in the fields of science, economics, technology and management.

Activities: Operates nationally and internationally in the fields of economic and international affairs, education, medicine and health, and science and technology, through self-conducted programmes, grants to individuals and institutions, scholarships and fellowships, and conferences. The Foundation supports the education of talented young people; works towards implementing scientific and technological ideas and projects; provides equipment and material for creative work; encourages international co-operation in the fields of science, technology and management; disseminates information; organizes events; provides financial support for scientific research undertaken by talented young scholars; awards for innovative young farmers; and credit and loans to young inventors developing research and technological products and new products and services. In 2013/14 it awarded 41 scholarships to university and high-school students.

Geographical Area of Activity: Bulgaria.

Publications: Annual Report; *Computer*; *Do-it-Yourself*; *EVRIKA* (monthly bulletin); *Andromeda* (magazine); *Telescope*.

Finance: Annual budget 310,000 lev (2013).

Governing Council: Kiril Boyanov (Chair.); Vasil Velev, Georgi Ivanov, Jachko Ivanov (Vice-Chair.).

Principal Staff: Exec. Dir Boriana Kadmonova; Programme Dir Grigor Tzankov.

Address: 1000 Sofia, Patriarh Evtimii Blvd 1.

Telephone: (2) 981-51-81; **Fax:** (2) 981-54-83; **Internet:** www.evrika.org; **e-mail:** office@evrika.org.

Elizabeth Kostova Foundation for Creative Writing

Established in 2007 by US author Elizabeth Kostova.

Activities: Supports creative writing in Bulgaria, especially in the field of translation. The Foundation offers translation awards and fellowships for Bulgarian literary translators working from Bulgarian into English; organizes an international creative writing seminar; and runs a contest for contemporary Bulgarian writers and translators.

Geographical Area of Activity: Bulgaria and English-speaking countries.

Trustees: Julian Popov (Chair.).

Principal Staff: Man. Dir Milena Deleva.

Address: 1142 Sofia, Lyuben Karavelov St 15.

Telephone: (2) 988-81-88; **Fax:** (2) 988-81-88; **Internet:** ekf.bg; www.contemporarybulgarianwriters.com; **e-mail:** info@ekf.bg.

National Trust EcoFund

Established in 1995 to manage funds provided under debt-for-nature and debt-for-environment swaps, as well as funds provided under other types of agreements with international, foreign or Bulgarian sources aimed at environmental protection in Bulgaria.

Activities: Operates within the priority areas of pollution clearing, including hazardous waste and hazardous substances disposal; sources of drinking water or food contamination (by heavy metals, toxic organic compounds or other harmful chemicals); reduction of air pollution, including pollutants of health concern; clean water protection; and the protection of biodiversity, including the development of infrastructure in protected areas for species protection and habitat preservation, and biodiversity inventory and monitoring and sustainable utilization of components for creating social alternatives.

Geographical Area of Activity: Bulgaria.

Finance: Total assets 49,000 lev, annual expenditure 433,636 (31 Dec. 2014).

Board of Directors: Prof. Irena Georgieva (Chair.); Pavel Gudjerov, Naum Yakimov (Deputy Chair.).

Principal Staff: Exec. Dir Prof. Dimitar Nenkov.

Address: 1574 Sofia, Shipchenski Prohod Blvd 67в.

Telephone: (2) 973-36-37; **Fax:** (2) 973-38-18; **Internet:** www.ecofund-bg.org; **e-mail:** ecofund@ecofund-bg.org.

Open Society Institute—Sofia (Bulgaria)

Founded in 1990 as the Open Society Foundation to support education and culture and the development of Bulgarian society.

Activities: An independent foundation, part of the Open Society Foundations (q.v.) network, which aims to foster political and cultural pluralism and reform economic structures to encourage private enterprise and a market economy. Supports projects under the programme areas of economic integration and regional stability; public life and civil participation; democracy and rule of law; education policies; and public health. Initiatives include support for electoral reform and accession to the European Union. Also runs a nationwide network of 17 information centres offering consultation and funding advice.

Geographical Area of Activity: Bulgaria; some aid to Kosovo and Metohija.

Publications: *Wide Awake* (newsletter, 6 a year); fortnightly newsletter.

Finance: Annual revenue €1,702,000, expenditure €2,500,000 (2013).

Trustees: Nelly Ognyanova (Chair.).

Principal Staff: Exec. Dir George Stoytchev; Financial Dir Veliko Sherbanov.

Address: 1000 Sofia, Solunska St 56.

Telephone: (2) 930-66-19; **Fax:** (2) 951-63-48; **Internet:** www.osf.bg; **e-mail:** info@osf.bg.

Roma Lom Foundation

Established in 1996 with the aim of enhancing the social development and integration of the Roma community.

Activities: Aims to support the development of the Roma community in the areas of education, employment, social services, work with youth and women, crime prevention, sport, media, and agriculture, through encouraging participation of the Roma community in Foundation-initiated projects. The Foundation also established a Self-Help Bureau in 1996.

Geographical Area of Activity: Bulgaria.

Board Members: Nikolay Kirilov (Chair.).

Principal Staff: Programme Dir Assen Slavchev.

Address: 3600 Lom, Neofit Bozveli St 4.

Telephone: (9) 716-67-51; **Fax:** (9) 716-67-51; **Internet:** www.roma-lom.org; **e-mail:** roma-lom@roma-lom.org.

Saint Cyril and Saint Methodius International Foundation

Founded in 1982 as the Lyudmila Zhivkova International Foundation; dedicated to preserving and popularizing the spiritual heritage of St Cyril and St Methodius.

Activities: Aims to encourage cultural co-operation and the creative and educational development of young people, and to assist in the integration of Bulgaria into the 'New Europe' and the world. Operates internationally in the fields of the arts and humanities and cultural education; arranges cultural and educational exchanges; promotes cultural exchange, international understanding and the creative development of young people; awards prizes and scholarships; organizes conferences and exhibitions; supports publishing projects; organizes events and seminars; and maintains an art gallery.

Geographical Area of Activity: International.

Publications: Annual Report; brochure; financial report.

Executive Board: Prof. Dimo Platikanov (Pres.); Prof. Svetlin Russev, Boyko Vassilev, Dr Roumen Hristov, Prof. Alexander Fedotov (Vice-Pres).

Principal Staff: Chief Exec. Michael Tachev; Deputy Dir George Kuzmev.

Address: 1504 Sofia, Vassil Aprilov St 3; POB 12, 1504 Sofia.

Telephone: (2) 943-41-85; **Fax:** (2) 944-60-27; **Internet:** www.cmfnd.org; **e-mail:** cmfnd@cmfnd.org.

Trust for Social Achievement

Established to improve the educational and economic prospects of disadvantaged people in Bulgaria.

Activities: Supports efforts to increase the self-sufficiency and quality of life of the poor and, in particular, the Roma.

Geographical Area of Activity: Bulgaria.

Finance: Total assets 980,000 lev (31 Dec. 2012).

Principal Staff: CEO Sarah Perrine; CFO Veneta Ilieva.

Address: 1000 Sofia, Patriarch Evtimiy Blvd 64.

Telephone: (2) 424-66-80; **Fax:** (2) 348-92-51; **Internet:** socialachievement.org; **e-mail:** info@tsa-bulgaria.org.

Values Foundation

Founded in 1998 by Antonina Stoyanova to address the issue of sustainable development through culture.

Activities: Promotes and supports the development of Bulgarian science, education and culture. The Foundation is concerned with the integration of Bulgaria into Europe, while also preserving the cultural values and cultural diversity of the nation. Works to strengthen projects on social integration and communication. Also concentrates on secondary school and university education, awarding prizes and promoting exchanges. Collaborates with other Bulgarian organizations.

Geographical Area of Activity: Bulgaria.

Principal Staff: Project Man. Lilyana Panova.

Address: 1000 Sofia, POB 1302.

Telephone: (2) 988-12-04; **Internet:** www.values.bg; **e-mail:** eustory_bg@yahoo.com.

Burkina Faso

FOUNDATIONS, TRUSTS AND NON-PROFIT ORGANIZATIONS

Fédération Panafricaine des Cinéastes—FEPACI (Pan-African Federation of Film-makers)

Founded in 1969 by African film-makers for the development and promotion of African cinema.

Activities: Operates in all African countries (except Morocco because of disagreement over Western Sahara) to defend democracy in communications as a basic human right, through self-conducted programmes, conferences, training courses and publications. Members organize cinema festivals and campaigns, in conjunction with other organizations, for government funding for cultural organizations and the building of cultural economies throughout the continent.

Geographical Area of Activity: Africa and the African Diaspora.

Publications: *FEPACI-Infos* (quarterly); *Ecrans d'Afrique* (quarterly).

Finance: Membership fees and whichever Government that is hosting the Secretariat.

Principal Staff: Pres. Charles Mensah; Sec.-Gen. Bulane Hopa; Treas.-Gen. Albert Egbe.

Address: BP 2524, Ouagadougou 01.

Telephone: (223) 60572371; **Internet:** www.fepaci.org; **e-mail:** info@fepaci.org; fepacisg13@fepaci.org.

Fondation Jean-Paul II pour le Sahel (John Paul II Foundation for the Sahel)

Established in 1984 by Pope John Paul II, for the training of local leaders who place themselves at the service of their country, for the purpose of fighting desertification and its causes and the purpose of aiding victims of drought in the nine countries of the Sahel region.

Activities: Supports the professional training of local leaders to carry out micro-projects relating to agriculture, water and the environment.

Geographical Area of Activity: Sahelian region of Africa (Burkina Faso, Cabo Verde, Chad, Gambia, Guinea-Bissau, Mali, Mauritania, Niger and Senegal).

Restrictions: Grants made only within the nine Sahelian countries.

Finance: Receives donations from Catholics in Germany and Italy, through their Episcopal conferences. Total annual grants approx. US $3m.

Council of Administration: Jean-Pierre Bassène (Pres.).

Address: BP 4890, Ouagadougou 01; 106 blvd Tansoba Koyoudou, Ouagadougou.

Telephone: 50-36-53-14; **Fax:** 50-36-53-93; **Internet:** www.fondationjp2sahel.org; **e-mail:** contact@fondationjp2sahel.org.

Fondation Nationale pour le Développement et la Solidarité—FONADES (National Foundation for Solidarity and Development)

Established in 1973 to promote economic development designed to meet the needs of local populations and their capabilities.

Activities: Promotes sustainable economic development, through supporting locally administered development programmes. Types of projects include building anti-erosion structures to protect fragile areas; organization of local communities in the management and production of manure as a fertilizer; assisting in the production of seeds and tree-planting programmes; well-building in different villages; and the organization of micro-credit programmes among indigenous women to help them start commercial activities.

Geographical Area of Activity: Burkina Faso.

Publications: Annual Report; manuals.

Principal Staff: Dir Maurice Oudet.

Address: c/o SEDELAN, 01 BP 332, Koudougou.

Telephone: 50-36-10-79; **Internet:** www.abcburkina.net/fr/le-burkina-faso/de-a-a-z/307-fonades; **e-mail:** fonades@fasonet.bf.

Cambodia

FOUNDATION CENTRE AND CO-ORDINATING BODY

Co-operation Committee for Cambodia

Established in 1991; a professional association of NGOs in Cambodia, with a total of 136 member organizations in 2011.

Activities: Promotes the development of civil society in Cambodia.

Geographical Area of Activity: Cambodia.

Principal Staff: Exec. Dir Saroeun Soeung; Head of Operations Bunthong Khorn.

Address: POB 885, Phnom Penh; House 9–11, St 476, Sangkat Toul Tom Poung I, Chamkamorn.

Telephone: (23) 214152; **Fax:** (23) 216009; **Internet:** www.ccc-cambodia.org; **e-mail:** info@ccc-cambodia.org.

FOUNDATIONS, TRUSTS AND NON-PROFIT ORGANIZATIONS

Don Bosco Foundation of Cambodia—DBFC

Established in 1991 to support the development of young people in Cambodia.

Activities: Focuses on supporting education and training initiatives in Cambodia, with a particular emphasis on helping orphans and economically disadvantaged young people. Since its establishment, the DBFC has funded the construction of six technical schools in Phnom Penh, Sihanoukville, Battambang, Poipet and Kep. The DBFC also provides scholarships to young people aged 6–12 years, and organizes literacy projects through the Don Bosco Children Fund and Don Bosco Kep Children Fund; and runs a programme to help the social integration of young prisoners preparing for release.

Geographical Area of Activity: Cambodia.

Publications: Technical books for education (in Khmer language) about mechanic, automotive, welding, electricity, hotel management, secretarial, audiovisual edition, web development; *Don Bosco Sihanoukville 2007: Visit of HM Norodom Sihamoni*; Khmer Grammar for Spanish speakers.

Finance: International donations, from countries including the Netherlands, Italy, the USA, the United Kingdom and Germany.

Principal Staff: Country Rep. Fr Roel Soto.

Address: POB 47, Phum Chress, Khum Phnom Penh Thmey Russey Keo District, Phnom Penh; 67, St 315, Sangkat Boeng Kak 2, Tuol Kouk, Phnom Penh.

Telephone: (17) 354747; **Internet:** www.donboscokhmer.org; **e-mail:** management@donboscokhmer.org; donbosco1@camshin.net.

Friends-International

Established in 1994 as a local project to support marginalized urban children.

Activities: Creates and runs programmes to support vulnerable children. Maintains support offices in Indonesia, Laos and Thailand, and fund-raising offices in France, Germany, Switzerland and the USA.

Geographical Area of Activity: Cambodia, Egypt, Honduras, Indonesia, Laos, the Philippines, Thailand.

Publications: Annual Report; research findings; guide books.

Finance: Annual income US $2,925,680, expenditure $2,834,039 (31 Dec. 2014).

Board: Wilfried Schneider (Chair.); Len Coster (Treas.); Denis Marot (Sec.).

Principal Staff: Exec. Dir Sebastien Marot; Deputy Dir Kanchan Kapoor.

Address: POB 597, House 89B, St 103, Phnom Penh.

Telephone: (23) 986601; **Internet:** www.friends-international.org; **e-mail:** info@friends-international.org.

Canada

FOUNDATION CENTRES AND CO-ORDINATING BODIES

Canadian Co-operative Association

Established in 1987 by the merger of the Co-operative College of Canada and the Co-operative Union of Canada, as a co-ordinating organization for co-operatives in Canada. With the creation of a national apex organization (Co-operatives and Mutuals Canada—CMC), CCA became solely focused on international development in 2014.

Activities: Operates as a subsidiary of the national association of co-operatives and credit unions, Co-operatives and Mutuals Canada (CMC). Promotes individuals' economic, cultural and social growth; and establishes and grows co-operatives, credit unions and community-based organizations to reduce poverty, build sustainable livelihoods and improve civil society in less-developed countries. Climate resilience and gender are cross-cutting priorities in all programmes. The Association works closely with Canadian co-operatives and credit unions to channel their knowledge and experience to partner organizations and co-operatives abroad; and delivers programmes for the Co-operative Development Foundation of Canada (CDF), which helps communities fight poverty and create more secure lives through community-owned co-operatives. Operates in 18 countries worldwide.

Geographical Area of Activity: Africa, Asia, Eastern Europe, Latin America.

Publications: *International Development Digest* (1 a year); *International Dispatch* (monthly e-newsletter); Annual Report; research papers and reports; videos.

Finance: Funded by member dues for activities in Canada and by the Canadian International Development Agency (CIDA) and the affiliated Co-operative Development Foundation of Canada (CDF) for international development activities. Annual revenue C \$254,349, expenditure \$199,912 (31 March 2014).

Board of Directors: Patrice Pratt (Pres.).

Principal Staff: Exec. Dir Michael Casey.

Address: Co-operative House, 275 Bank St, Suite 400, Ottawa, ON K2P 2L6.

Telephone: (613) 238-6711; **Fax:** (613) 567-0658; **Internet:** www.coopscanada.coop; **e-mail:** international@coopscanada.coop.

Canadian Council for International Co-operation—CCIC/Conseil Canadien pour la Coopération Internationale—CCCI

Established in 1968; a coalition of more than 100 Canadian development organizations.

Activities: Conducts research, disseminates information, and co-ordinates the efforts of its members to work in the field of human development worldwide, to promote national and international policies which serve the public interest, and to build a social movement for global citizenship in Canada. In the international field, members of the Council aim to ensure that all people have the basic necessities for living: food, shelter, education, health and sanitation; other members actively campaign for human rights, fair trade and corporate social responsibility. The Council's International Co-operation Award recognizes organizations' innovative work to combat poverty.

Geographical Area of Activity: Canada.

Publications: *Corporate Social Responsibility/Engagement with the Private Sector*; *Ethics*; *Gender Issues and Diversity*.

Finance: Annual revenue C \$824,952, expenditure \$825,729 (31 March 2014).

Board of Directors: Jim Cornelius (Chair.).

Principal Staff: Pres. and CEO Julia Sánchez.

Address: 39 McArthur Ave, Ottawa, ON K1L 8L7.

Telephone: (613) 241-7007; **Fax:** (613) 241-5302; **Internet:** www.ccic.ca; **e-mail:** info@ccic.ca.

Community Foundations of Canada

Established in 1992 to act as the umbrella organization for community foundations in Canada.

Activities: Membership organization for community foundations in Canada. Facilitates partnerships between organizations and provides resources to promote effective grantmaking.

Geographical Area of Activity: Canada.

Finance: Annual revenue C \$2,126,436, expenditure \$1,862,608 (31 Dec. 2013).

Board of Directors: Rahul K. Bhardwaj (Chair.).

Principal Staff: Pres. Ian Bird; COO Andrew Chunilall.

Address: 75 Albert St, Suite 301, Ottawa, ON K1P 5E7.

Telephone: (613) 236-2664; **Fax:** (613) 236-1621; **Internet:** www.cfc-fcc.ca; **e-mail:** info@cfc-fcc.ca.

Imagine Canada

Established in 2005 following the merger of the Canadian Centre for Philanthropy and the Coalition of National Voluntary Organizations.

Activities: Assists Canadian charitable and voluntary organizations through research, public affairs, information products and professional development. The organization researches the charitable and voluntary sector and the environment in which they function; issues publications; and organizes conferences and seminars. It is involved in communicating with the Government, the media and the public on the voluntary sector, and informs its affiliates on proposed legislative and regulatory initiatives. Operates through a family of sub-sites, providing statistics and information on giving and volunteering; information on the non-profit sector in Canada; grants for research on volunteerism; and Imagine, which promotes corporate citizenship and community investment.

Geographical Area of Activity: Canada.

Publications: *Canadian Directory to Foundations and Grants*; *Building Foundation Partnerships*; *Portrait of Canada's Charities*; *Give and Take: a resource manual for Canadian Fundraisers*; *Connecting Companies to Communities*; *Promoting Corporate Citizenship*; *Charities and Not-for-Profits Fundraising Handbook*; *Front and Centre* (newspaper); Annual Report; publications on foundations and fundraising; pamphlets and special papers.

Finance: Annual revenue C \$4,005,088, expenditure \$4,061,541 (31 Dec. 2013).

Board of Directors: Stéphane Vaillancourt (Chair.).

Principal Staff: Pres. and CEO Bruce MacDonald.

Address: 65 St Clair Avenue East, Suite 700, Toronto, ON M4T 2Y3.

Telephone: (416) 597-2293; **Fax:** (416) 597-2294; **Internet:** www.imaginecanada.ca; **e-mail:** info@imaginecanada.ca.

FOUNDATIONS, TRUSTS AND NON-PROFIT ORGANIZATIONS

Aga Khan Foundation Canada

Established in 1980; part of the network of foundations established by HH Prince Karim Aga Khan, aiming to support social development projects in Africa and Asia to benefit the poor, regardless of race, religion or political affiliation.

Activities: Works to address the root causes of poverty: finding and sharing solutions which help improve the quality of life for poor communities. Programmes focus on four core areas: health, education, rural development and building the capacity of NGOs, with considerations for gender equity and protecting the environment integrated into every programme. Major initiatives include: the Pakistan-Canada Social Institutions Development Program; the Aga Khan Rural Support Program in Pakistan; the Tajikistan Institutional Support Program; the Coastal Rural Support Program in Mozambique; and the Non-Formal Education Program of the Bangladesh Rural Advancement Committee. Supports several school improvement projects carried out with Aga Khan Education Services and primary health care projects implemented with Aga Khan Health Services. Sectors receiving support include microfinance, the improvement of livelihoods and micro-enterprise development, as well as rural development, health and education.

Geographical Area of Activity: Canada, East Africa, and South and Central Asia.

Finance: Annual revenue C \$116,279,143, expenditure \$128,014,423 (31 Dec. 2013).

Board of Directors: Shah Karim Al Husseini Aga Khan, Amin Lalji (Chair.); Ameerally Kassim-Lakha (Vice-Chair.).

Principal Staff: CEO Khalil Z. Shariff.

Address: The Delegation of the Ismaili Imamat, 199 Sussex Dr., Ottawa, ON K1N 1K6.

Telephone: (613) 237-2532; **Fax:** (613) 567-2532; **Internet:** www.akfc.ca; **e-mail:** info@akfc.ca.

Alberta Innovates Health Solutions

Founded in 1980 as the Alberta Heritage Foundation for Medical Research, by an act of legislation to support biomedical and health research, principally in the province of Alberta. Present name adopted in 2009.

Activities: Supports biomedical and health research by offering awards based on international standards of excellence to researchers and researchers-in-training.

Geographical Area of Activity: Alberta, Canada and international.

Restrictions: Awards only for salary support, equipment costs, student support, renovation costs, construction costs and partnership initiatives.

Publications: Annual Report; *Apple Magazine*; *Health Solutions Magazine*; presentations; podcasts; reports; research papers.

Finance: Annual revenue C \$100,434,000, expenditure \$4,143,000 (31 March 2014).

Board of Directors: Robert A. Seidel (Chair.); Dr Raymond Rajotte (Vice-Chair.).

Principal Staff: CEO (a.i.) Dr Pamela Valentine.

Address: 10104 103 Ave, Suite 1500, Edmonton, AB T5J 4A7.

Telephone: (780) 423-5727; **Fax:** (780) 429-3509; **Internet:** www.aihealthsolutions.ca; **e-mail:** health@albertainnovates.ca.

The Alva Foundation

Established in 1965 to support Canadian not-for-profit organizations helping children at risk.

Activities: Helps Canadian children at risk, through funding organizations conducting research and/or developing services that address significant risk factors in early childhood development.

Geographical Area of Activity: Canada.

Restrictions: Grants will not be made to individuals, nor for emergency or deficit funding.

Finance: Annual revenue C \$1,125,561, expenditure \$278,997 (31 Dec. 2013).

Board of Directors: Graham F. Hallward (Pres.); Derek Fisher (Vice-Pres. and Treas.); Amanda Mathers (Sec.).

Address: c/o Graham Hallward, Chairman: Donations Committee, 199 Albertus Ave, Toronto, ON M4R 1J6.

Internet: www.alva.ca; **e-mail:** info@alva.ca.

Arctic Institute of North America—AINA (Institut Arctique de l'Amérique du Nord—IAAN)

Founded in 1945 by Act of Parliament in Canada; incorporated concurrently in the USA under the laws of the state of New York. The Canadian Corporation became an integral part of the University of Calgary in 1979.

Activities: Advances the study of Arctic and sub-Arctic conditions and problems; collects material on these regions and makes it available for scientific use; arranges for the publication of relevant material; maintains contact with organizations engaged in similar studies. The Institute works in the fields of the physical, natural and social sciences and the humanities. Although mainly concerned with the North, its interests also extend to Antarctica and to Alpine environments. Programmes investigating the ecology of the Arctic and the physiology of high altitude and expeditions are typical of its work. It also maintains a major library and an automated bibliographic database, the Arctic Science and Technology Information System (ASTIS). The Institute administers a small grants fund to assist student researchers on field projects, makes travel awards to enable researchers to travel to conferences, and awards scholarships.

Geographical Area of Activity: Canada, Alaska and Greenland.

Publications: Annual Report; *ARCTIC Journal* (quarterly); *Northern Lights* (book series); *Komatik* (book series); research papers, technical papers, monographs and other occasional publications.

Finance: Annual revenue revenue C \$1,110,473, expenditure \$1,114,972 (31 March 2012).

Board of Directors: Henry Sykes (Chair.); John Miller (Vice-Chair.).

Principal Staff: Exec. Dir Maribeth Murray.

Address: University of Calgary, 2500 University Dr. NW, Calgary, AB T2N 1N4.

Telephone: (403) 220-7515; **Fax:** (403) 282-4609; **Internet:** www.arctic.ucalgary.ca; **e-mail:** arctic@ucalgary.ca.

Asia Pacific Foundation of Canada

Founded in 1984 to enhance economic, social and cultural relations and networks between Canada and the countries of the Asia-Pacific Region.

Activities: Hosts the Asia-Pacific Economic Co-operation (APEC) Study Centre in Canada, which promotes collaborative research and disseminates information. The Foundation also acts as the secretariat for the Asia Pacific Business Network, the Pacific Economic Co-operation Council, the Pacific Basin Economic Council and the APEC Business Advisory Council. In partnership with the Federal Government, it is developing a network of Canadian Education Centres in Asian cities, including Seoul, Taipei, Kuala Lumpur, Jakarta, Bangkok, Singapore, Hong Kong and New Delhi. Maintains databases. Also has offices in Québec.

Geographical Area of Activity: Canada and the Asia-Pacific region.

Publications: *Canada/Asia Review*; *Canada Asia Commentary*; and other publications.

Finance: Annual revenue C $6,242,322, expenditure $6,533,952 (31 March 2013).

Board of Directors: John H. McArthur (Chair.).

Principal Staff: Pres. and CEO Stewart Beck.

Address: Suite 220, 890 West Pender St, Vancouver, BC V6C 1J9.

Telephone: (604) 684-5986; **Fax:** (604) 681-1370; **Internet:** www.asiapacific.ca; **e-mail:** info@asiapacific.ca.

Max Bell Foundation

Founded in 1965 by newspaper publisher George Maxwell Bell for general charitable purposes, particularly in the fields of health, medical education and veterinary sciences in Canada and the Asia-Pacific region.

Activities: Operates in Canada and the Asia-Pacific region through research and grants to institutions. The Foundation's main areas of focus are health and wellness, the environment and education.

Geographical Area of Activity: Canada and the Asia-Pacific region.

Publications: Programme Report.

Finance: Annual revenue C $2,182,784, expenditure $2,684,041 (31 Dec. 2013).

Board of Directors: Carolyn Hursh (Chair.); Ken Marra (Vice-Chair.).

Principal Staff: Pres. Dr David Elton; Vice-Pres. Allan Northcott.

Address: 1201 5th St SW, Suite 380, Calgary, AB T2R 0Y6.

Telephone: (403) 215-7310; **Fax:** (403) 215-7319; **Internet:** www.maxbell.org; **e-mail:** northcott@maxbell.org.

Samuel and Saidye Bronfman Family Foundation

Established in 1952 by the estate of Samuel Bronfman, who founded the Seagram brewery and distillery company, and family members to promote initiative and enterprise in Canada, and the development of new ideas and innovative projects aiming to find solutions to emerging problems in Canada.

Activities: Operates throughout Canada in the fields of the arts and humanities, conservation and the environment, education, human rights and social welfare, through grants to charitable organizations in Canada. The main funding priorities are: Urban Issues—supporting projects that unite urban conservation with community development, to protect and enhance community life inside city neighbourhoods; Futures—making grants for projects that exhibit potential for lasting national benefit; and Cultural Management Development—promoting, in particular, the concept of arts stabilization requiring multi-sector partnerships. Awards the C $25,000 Saidye Bronfman Award for craftwork and funds the Saidye Bronfman Centre for the Arts in Montréal and the Federation CJA of Montréal (formerly the Combined Jewish Appeal of Montréal).

Geographical Area of Activity: Canada.

Restrictions: Grants are currently restricted to existing commitments.

Publications: Brochure.

Finance: Annual revenue C $8,610 expenditure $35,707 (31 Dec. 2013).

Board of Directors: Phyllis Lambert (Hon. Pres.); Stephen R. Bronfman (Pres.); Glenn Hamilton-Browne (Treas.); Robert Vineberg (Sec.); Frederick Martel (Asst Treas.).

Principal Staff: Exec. Dir Nancy Rosenfeld.

Address: 1170 Peel St, Suite 800, Montréal, QC H3B 4P2.

Telephone: (514) 878-5268; **Fax:** (514) 878-5299.

The Canada Council for the Arts/Conseil des Arts du Canada

Created in 1957 by the Parliament of Canada as an independent agency providing grants and services to professional Canadian artists and arts organizations in dance, media, music, theatre, writing and publishing, visual and integrated arts.

Activities: Provides a wide range of grants, prizes and services to professional Canadian artists and arts organizations in accordance with its aims. The Council's Art Bank rents contemporary Canadian art to the public and private sectors in Canada. The Council maintains the secretariat for the Canadian Commission for UNESCO, administers the Killam Program of awards and prizes, and offers other awards. It operates the Public Lending Right Commission to administer payments to Canadian writers for their books held in Canadian libraries.

Geographical Area of Activity: Canada.

Publications: Annual Report.

Finance: Funded by and reports to Parliament through the Minister of Canadian Heritage; its annual appropriation from Parliament is supplemented by endowment income, donations and bequests. Annual revenue C $13,903,000, expenditure $189,092,000 (31 March 2013).

Board of Directors: Vacant (Chair.); Nathalie Bondil (Vice-Chair.).

Principal Staff: Dir and CEO Simon Brault; Sec.-Gen. for UNESCO Louise Filiatrault.

Address: 150 Elgin St, POB 1047, Ottawa, ON K1P 5V8.

Telephone: (613) 566-4414; **Fax:** (613) 566-4390; **Internet:** www.canadacouncil.ca; **e-mail:** info@canadacouncil.ca.

Canada Foundation for Innovation/Fondation Canadienne pour l'Innovation

Established in 1997 by the Federal Government to strengthen Canadian capability for research, ultimately contributing to economic growth and improvements in employment, health and the environment.

Activities: Invests in research infrastructure to encourage innovation in universities, colleges, hospitals and other non-profit institutions, including funding the acquisition of state-of-the-art equipment, buildings, laboratories, and databases required to conduct research. The Foundation promotes the training of young Canadians for research and other careers; attracts and retains able research workers; and works to ensure the best results in innovation by promoting sharing of information and resources among institutions. It also occasionally launches calls for proposals for international research projects.

Geographical Area of Activity: Canada and international.

Publications: Annual Report; other reports on activities.

Finance: Annual revenue and expenditure C $419,883,992 (31 March 2014).

Board of Directors: Kevin P. D. Smith (Chair.); Louise Proulx (Vice-Chair.).

Principal Staff: Pres. and CEO Gilles G. Patry.

Address: 230 Queen St, Suite 450, Ottawa, ON K1P 5E4.

Telephone: (613) 947-6496; **Fax:** (613) 943-0923; **Internet:** www.innovation.ca; **e-mail:** info@innovation.ca.

Canada Israel Cultural Foundation

Established in 1963 to promote intercultural exchange between Canada and Israel.

Activities: Operates in the field of the arts and humanities, organizing cultural, artistic, musical and social events, and support for Israeli performers to travel to Canada.

Geographical Area of Activity: Canada and Israel.

Finance: Annual revenue C $129,627, expenditure $172,528 (30 June 2014).

Board: Murray B. Koffler (Hon. Chair.); Ron Bresler (Nat. Pres.); Karen Green, Sara Riesman (Vice-Pres); Reesa Sud (Sec., Treas.).

Principal Staff: Exec. Dir Cheryl Wetstein; Assoc. Dir Janet Klugsberg.

Address: 4700 Bathurst St, 2nd Floor, Toronto, ON M2R 1W8.

Telephone: (416) 932-2260; **Fax:** (416) 398-5780; **Internet:** www.cicfweb.ca; **e-mail:** cicf@bellnet.ca.

Canada World Youth/Jeunesse Canada Monde

Founded in 1971 by Jacques Hébert.

Activities: Provides young people from Canada and overseas with an opportunity to participate in an educational international programme that helps foster informed and involved global citizens. The organization's core programme is the Youth Leaders in Action programme, where groups of 18 young people (nine Canadians and nine from overseas) from different cultures live with host families and work together on voluntary projects for six months (three in a Canadian community and three in a community abroad). The Global Learners programme is designed for educators, sending young people to an overseas community for a period of two weeks up to three months. Under the InterAction programme, young people may volunteer in an overseas host country for two to six weeks, in local projects dealing with health issues, eco-tourism or work with indigenous communities, while living with a host family.

Geographical Area of Activity: Africa, Asia, North, Central and South America and the Caribbean, and Central and Eastern Europe.

Publications: Annual Report; Newsletter (2 a year).

Finance: Annual revenue C $19,007,075, expenditure $18,922,637 (31 March 2014).

Board of Directors: Collin Robertson (Chair.); Marc LePage (Treas.).

Principal Staff: Pres. and CEO Rita S. Karakas.

Address: 2330 Notre-Dame St West, 3rd Floor, Montréal, QC H3J 1N4.

Telephone: (514) 931-3526; **Fax:** (514) 939-2621; **Internet:** www.cwy-jcm.org; www.canadaworldyouth.org; www.jeunessecanadamonde.org; **e-mail:** communication@cwy-jcm.org.

Canadian Cancer Society

Founded in 1938 to disseminate information about the early warning signs of cancer to the Canadian public; from 1947 it also funded research through its research partner, the National Cancer Institute of Canada, and more recently through the Canadian Cancer Society Research Institute.

Activities: A national, community-based organization of volunteers aiming to eradicate cancer and enhance the quality of life of people living with cancer. The Society operates nationally through funding and carrying out research on all types of cancer; providing comprehensive information about cancer care and treatment; giving support to people living with cancer; promoting healthy lifestyles and strategies for reducing cancer risk; and advocating public policy to prevent cancer and to help those living with it.

Geographical Area of Activity: Canada.

Publications: Annual Report; information on specific cancers, treatment, risk reduction, supportive care and tobacco control.

Finance: Annual revenue C $198,526,000, expenditure $153,992,000 (31 Jan. 2014).

Board of Directors: Stephen Bron (Chair.); Marc Généreux (Past Chair.).

Principal Staff: Pres. and CEO Pamela Fralick.

Address: 55 St Clair Ave West, Suite 300, Toronto, ON M4V 2Y7.

Telephone: (416) 961-7223; **Fax:** (416) 961-4189; **Internet:** www.cancer.ca; **e-mail:** ccs@cancer.ca.

Canadian Catholic Organization for Development and Peace

Established in 1967 to improve living and working conditions worldwide, support initiatives by people in less-developed countries to take control of their future, and to educate Canadians about North-South issues.

Activities: Supports local organizations in less-developed countries, in the fields of human rights, women's rights, community development, housing, education and employment opportunities, and agrarian reform. The Organization provides emergency relief for the victims of natural and man-made disasters, and humanitarian aid for those who need it. It educates Canadians about the causes of poverty and the alternatives to unjust social, political and economic systems; and offers support for democratization.

Geographical Area of Activity: Africa, Asia, Eastern and Western Europe, North, Central and South America, and the Middle East.

Publications: *Global Village Voice* (quarterly newsletter); Annual Report; general information leaflet.

Finance: Annual revenue C $46,013,966, expenditure $33,777,635 (31 Aug. 2014).

National Council: Ronald Breau (Pres.); Gilles Halley (Vice-Pres.); Ray Temmerman (Sec.); Wambui Kipusi (Treas.).

Principal Staff: Exec. Dir Michael Casey.

Address: 1425 René-Lévesque Blvd West, 3rd Floor, Montréal, QC H3G 1T7.

Telephone: (514) 257-8711; **Fax:** (514) 257-8497; **Internet:** www.devp.org; **e-mail:** info@devp.org.

Canadian Centre for International Studies and Co-operation/Centre d'Etude et de Coopération Internationale—CECI

Originally founded in 1958, the Centre was officially incorporated under its current name as a non-profit NGO in 1968, with the aim of fighting poverty and injustice in the developing world.

Activities: Works to strengthen the opportunities for development in disadvantaged communities around the world, operating in the fields of human rights and democracy, the environment, humanitarian aid, socio-economic rehabilitation, and supporting peace initiatives.

Geographical Area of Activity: Asia and the Far East, Africa, North, Central and South America and the Caribbean.

Publications: *Capacity Building: a Manual for NGOs and Field Workers*; Annual Report; other publications in French and Spanish.

Finance: Annual revenue C $43,259,883, expenditure $41,675,108 (31 March 2014).

Board of Directors: Robert Perreault (Chair.); Danielle Sauvage (Exec. Vice-Chair.); Veronique Duchesne (Treas.).

Principal Staff: Exec. Dir and Sec. Claudia Black.

Address: 3000 rue Omer-Lavallée, Montréal, QC H1Y 3R8.

Telephone: (514) 875-9911; **Fax:** (514) 875-6469; **Internet:** www.ceci.ca; **e-mail:** info@ceci.ca.

Canadian Crossroads International/Carrefour Canadien International—CCI

Established in 1960 as the Canadian Committee of Operations Crossroads, a counterpart to the US organization Operation Crossroads Africa, which was founded by Dr James H. Robinson in the 1950s; granted a charter as a separate organization in 1969.

Activities: Brings individuals, organizations and communities in Canada and the Global South together to reduce poverty, prevent the spread of HIV/AIDS and defend the rights of women. The organization helps people and organizations to collaborate across borders on pressing global issues; supports the development of international partnerships; and facilitates staff exchanges and volunteer placements. It helps community-based organizations find the skills, expertise and resources they need to strengthen their communities; and facilitates partnerships between organizations in West Africa, Southern Africa and the Andean region of South America with Canadian organizations working on similar issues.

Geographical Area of Activity: West Africa, Southern Africa, South America.

Restrictions: Programmes are available only to Canadian citizens and to volunteers from partner organizations.

Publications: Annual Report; *eBulletin* (monthly)*; Crossroads* (newsletter, 2 a year).

Finance: Annual revenue C $6,278,423, expenditure $6,162,700 (31 March 2014).

Board of Directors: Ian B. Anderson (Chair.); Susan Watts (Treas.).

Principal Staff: Acting Exec. Dir and Sec. Christine Campbell.

Address: 49 Bathurst St, Suite 201, Toronto, ON M5V 2P2.

Telephone: (416) 967-1611; **Fax:** (416) 967-9078; **Internet:** www.cintl.org; www.cciorg.ca; **e-mail:** info@cintl.org.

Canadian Executive Service Organization—CESO/Service d'Assistance Canadienne aux Organismes—SACO

Founded in 1967.

Activities: A non-profit volunteer-sending organization that works with clients in Canada, in Aboriginal and non-Aboriginal communities, and overseas in countries in the Americas, Africa, Asia and Eastern Europe. The Organization's mission is to build capacity in governance and economic development through the transfer of knowledge and skills by volunteer advisers, who work on short-term assignments to transfer their skills and knowledge.

Geographical Area of Activity: International.

Publications: Annual Report; *In Action!* (monthly newsletter); brochures.

Finance: Annual revenue C $8,133,308, expenditure $8,101,047 (31 March 2014).

Board of Directors: Peter Chiddy (Chair.); Martine Normand (Vice-Chair.).

Principal Staff: CEO and Pres. Wendy Harris.

Address: 700 Bay St, Suite 800, Box 328, Toronto, ON M5G 1Z6.

Telephone: (416) 961-2376; **Fax:** (416) 961-1096; **Internet:** www.ceso-saco.com; **e-mail:** information@ceso-saco.com.

Canadian Feed the Children

Established in 1986.

Activities: Aims to relieve the effects of hunger, poverty and suffering in Canada and around the world, and to help communities to achieve self-sufficiency successfully. The organization focuses on long-term solutions to poverty and hunger, and immediate aid to those who are suffering. It works nationally, running and supporting food supply and nutrition programmes in schools, community centres, refugee centres, women's shelters and subsidized housing projects; as well as supporting other programmes throughout the country that work to mitigate the effects of hunger and poverty. Internationally, the organization operates a number of programmes that work with communities to ensure that children have their basic needs fulfilled in terms of food, water, sanitation and education; train and support child-focused charities around the world; provide vegetable seeds to refugees and displaced families to provide them with a self-sufficient lifestyle; provide credit and training to families so that they can begin to break out of the poverty cycle; and provide emergency materials for communities and families in times of crisis.

Geographical Area of Activity: Bolivia, Ethiopia, Ghana, Haiti, Uganda.

Restrictions: Does not make grants.

Publications: Annual Report; newsletters.

Finance: Annual income C $7,078,332, expenditure $6,564,921 (31 Dec. 2013).

Board of Directors: Derek Briffett (Chair.); David Pell (Vice-Chair.).

Principal Staff: Exec. Dir Debra D. Kerby.

Address: 174 Bartley Dr., Toronto, ON M4A 1E1.

Telephone: (416) 757-1220; **Fax:** (416) 757-3318; **Internet:** www.canadianfeedthechildren.ca; **e-mail:** contact@canadianfeedthechildren.ca.

Canadian Foodgrains Bank

Established in 1983 to allow farmers in Canada to share their yield with hunger victims in less-developed countries, helping thereby to alleviate world hunger.

Activities: Operates in partnership with 13 Canadian churches. The Bank collects contributions in the form of money and agricultural produce including grains, to distribute them to hunger victims in developing countries. Other activities include: providing services and advice on food programming and related aspects; encouraging policy development; and educating people about hunger and food security.

Geographical Area of Activity: Less-developed countries.

Publications: Annual Report; *End Hunger; Myths About Hunger; Hungry Farmers; HIV/AIDS and Hunger; Bulletin Covers and Inserts.*

Finance: Annual revenue C $42,990,800, expenditure $43,456,118 (31 March 2014).

Board of Directors: Donald G. Peters (Chair.); Robert H. Granke (Vice-Chair.); Wayne de Jong (Treas.); Wendy Galloway (Sec.).

Principal Staff: Exec. Dir Jim Cornelius.

Address: POB 767, Winnipeg, MB R3C 2L4; 400-393 Portage Ave, Winnipeg, MB R3B 3H6.

Telephone: (204) 944-1993; **Fax:** (204) 943-2597; **Internet:** www.foodgrainsbank.ca; **e-mail:** cfgb@foodgrainsbank.ca.

Canadian Friends of the Hebrew University

Founded in 1944 to identify and maintain the interest of Canadian Jewish communities in Jewish and Hebrew studies, traditions and culture.

Activities: Operates nationally and internationally in the field of education, through speaker-orientated programmes, conferences, publications, and by awarding grants for study at the Hebrew University in Jerusalem.

Geographical Area of Activity: Canada.

Restrictions: Grants given only to students studying at the Hebrew University of Jerusalem.

Publications: Newsletter (monthly).

Finance: Annual revenue C $14,002,265, expenditure $13,785,588 (30 Sept. 2014).

Board of Directors: Murray Palay (Chair.); Ronald Appleby (Past Pres.); Ralph Halbert (Chair. Emeritus); Evelyn Bloomfield Schacter (Sec.).

Principal Staff: Nat. Dir, Pres. and CEO Rami Kleinmann; Assoc. Nat. Dir and Exec. Vice-Pres. Merle Goldman.

Address: 3080 Yonge St, Suite 5024, Toronto, ON M4N 3N1.

Telephone: (416) 485-8000; **Fax:** (416) 485-8565; **Internet:** www.cfhu.org; **e-mail:** info@cfhu.org.

Canadian Hunger Foundation

Founded in 1961 under the auspices of FAO to enable people in poor communities to attain sustainable, healthy livelihoods. Formerly known as the Canadian Hunger Foundation/Fondation Canadienne contre la Faim—Partners in Rural Development.

Activities: Works with NGOs in 38 countries in Africa, Asia, Central and South America and the Caribbean to strengthen the capacity of community-based organizations and support self-help projects. The Fouondation promotes policies that reduce poverty, and programmes that raise public understanding of development issues. Priorities are: subsistence food production and income generation; self-help initiatives—rural infrastructure and services; community-based organization building; NGO partners—institutional capacity development; long-term sustainability; participation of women; ecological practices; and Canadian development education. Projects focus on agriculture (food production and processing), water and sanitation, energy (alternative and renewable), nutrition and health, and capacity building and networking.

Geographical Area of Activity: Africa, Asia, Central and South America and the Caribbean.

Publications: Annual Report; technical papers; HIV/AIDS information; newsletter; e-bulletin.

Finance: Annual revenue C $13,548,645, expenditure $18,996,457 (31 March 2014).

Board of Directors: Nicole Goodfellow (Chair.).

Principal Staff: Pres. and CEO Stewart Hardacre.

Address: 323 Chapel St, Ottawa, ON K1N 7Z2.

Telephone: (613) 237-0180; **Fax:** (613) 237-5969; **Internet:** www.chf.ca; **e-mail:** info@chf-partners.ca.

Canadian International Council/Conseil International du Canada—CIC

Founded in 1928 as an independent, non-partisan organization with the aim of providing a nationwide forum for discussion and analysis of international affairs. Formerly known as the Canadian Institute of International Affairs.

Activities: Operates briefing missions, conferences, lectures, and a research and publications programme. Has 1,300 members in 16 brs across Canada.

Geographical Area of Activity: Mainly Canada.

Publications: Annual Report and financial statement; research reports; *International Journal* (quarterly); *International Security Series*; *International Insights*.

Finance: Annual revenue C $781,965, expenditure $1,123,331 (30 June 2014).

Board of Directors: Bill Graham (Chair.); Perrin Beatty (Vice-Chair.).

Principal Staff: Pres. Dr Jennifer A. Jeffs.

Address: 1 Devonshire Pl., Rm 064S, Toronto, ON M5S 3K7.

Telephone: (416) 946-7209; **Fax:** (416) 946-7319; **Internet:** www.opencanada.org; **e-mail:** info@opencanada.org.

Canadian Liver Foundation/Fondation Canadienne du Foie

Established in 1969 by a group of business leaders and doctors in response to the increasing rate of liver diseases to support education and research on the cause, diagnosis, treatment and prevention of all liver diseases.

Activities: Promotes liver health; educates the public about liver disease; supports patients and their families; and raises funds for research. The Foundation also provides studentships and operating grants to qualified individuals researching the causes, diagnosis, treatment and prevention of liver and biliary tract diseases.

Geographical Area of Activity: Canada.

Restrictions: Organizations must be registered in Canada.

Publications: Pamphlets and information sheets on all forms of liver disease; Annual Report.

Finance: Annual revenue C $4,869,439, expenditure $4,602,854 (31 Dec. 2013).

Board of Directors: Morris Sherman (Chair.); Kevork Peltekian (Past Chair.); Elliot M. Jacobson (Sec./Treas.).

Principal Staff: Pres. and COO Gary A. Fagan.

Address: Suite 801, 3100 Steeles Ave East, Markham, ON L3R 8T3.

Telephone: (416) 491-3353; **Fax:** (905) 752-1540; **Internet:** www.liver.ca; **e-mail:** clf@liver.ca.

Canadian Organization for Development through Education—CODE

Founded in 1959.

Activities: Encourages self-sufficiency through literacy in the developing world. The Organization supports literacy and education by distributing books from Canadian and US sources (usually new books from publishers) to countries in the developing world, primarily in Africa, but also to the Caribbean and the Pacific region. It also funds training of librarians, writers, illustrators and literacy workers.

Geographical Area of Activity: Mainly Africa and Guyana.

Publications: *NGOMA* (bi-annual newsletter); Annual Report.

Finance: Annual income C $4,621,795, expenditure $4,923,763 (31 March 2014).

Board of Directors: Timothy Hines (Chair.); Lynn Beauregard (Past Chair.); Jacque Bérubé (Treas.).

Principal Staff: Exec. Dir Scott Walter.

Address: 321 Chapel St, Ottawa, ON K1N 7Z2.

Telephone: (613) 232-3569; **Fax:** (613) 232-7435; **Internet:** www.codecan.org; **e-mail:** codehq@codecan.org.

Canadian Urban Institute (Institut Urbain du Canada)

Launched in 1990 by the Municipality of Metropolitan Toronto and the City of Toronto.

Activities: A not-for-profit organization focusing on improvement of urban life in Canada and abroad. The Institute works nationally and internationally to improve management and policy-making in urban areas, educating government, businesses and other significant institutions about urban issues. It conducts conferences and seminars; takes part in applied research and training; produces publications; and identifies emerging social and economic issues that can influence the urban sector in areas of social development, urban infrastructure, sustainability, housing, environment and economic development. The Institute presents the annual Brownie Awards in recognition of leadership, environmental sustainability and innovation; and the Urban Leadership Awards to individuals and organizations that have contributed to the urban environment.

Geographical Area of Activity: Canada and internationally.

Publications: *Smart Growth in North America: New Ways to Create Liveable Communities*; *The Urban Century* (quarterly newsletter); and other publications.

Finance: Annual revenue C $4,888,320. expenditure $0 (31 Dec. 2013).

Board of Directors: Marni Cappe (Chair.); Andréa Callà (Vice-Chair.).

Principal Staff: Pres. and CEO Peter Halsall.

Address: 30 St Patrick St, 5th Floor, Toronto, ON M5T 3A3.

Telephone: (416) 365-0816; **Fax:** (416) 365-0650; **Internet:** www.canurb.org; **e-mail:** cui@canurb.org.

Lucie and André Chagnon Foundation/Fondation Lucie et André Chagnon

Established in 2000 by André Chagnon, founder of telecommunications company Le Groupe Vidéotron.

Activities: Aims to contribute to the development and improvement of health through the prevention of poverty and disease, by intervening primarily with children and their parents; and to ensure that young people succeed in school, by taking notable action among those who live in poverty.

Geographical Area of Activity: Québec, Canada.

Restrictions: Not currently soliciting outside requests for project funding.

Publications: Factsheets; surveys; partner organizations' publications.

Finance: Annual revenue C $253,165,000, expenditure $84,126,000 (31 Dec. 2013).

Board of Directors: Claude Chagnon (Pres.).

Principal Staff: Pres. and CEO André Chagnon.

Address: 2001 McGill College Ave, Suite 1000, Montréal, QC H3A 1G1.

Telephone: (514) 380-2001; **Fax:** (514) 380-8434; **Internet:** www.fondationchagnon.org; **e-mail:** info@fondationchagnon.org.

Chastell Foundation

Established in 1987 for general charitable purposes.

Activities: Makes donations in the areas of social, educational and health services. In 2001, the Foundation established the Andrea and Charles Bronfman Ontario Graduate Scholarship to fund graduate students at McMaster University as part of an Ontario Graduate Scholarship in the Faculty of Humanities.

Geographical Area of Activity: Canada.

Restrictions: Moratorium on new funding because of fiscal constraints.

Finance: Annual revenue C $2,120,857, expenditure $2,022,612 (31 Dec. 2013).

Officers and Directors: Charles R. Bronfman (Pres.); Richard P. Doyle (Vice-Pres. and Treas.); Larry Fisher (Sec.).

Address: 1170 Peel St, 8th Floor, Montréal, QC H3B 4P2.

Telephone: (514) 878-5314; **Fax:** (514) 878-5299; **e-mail:** info@acbp.net.

Club 2/3

Founded in 1970 by students concerned about the poverty and injustice that affects around two-thirds of the world's population. Now a divison of Oxfam in Québec.

Activities: Works in the field of international development and international solidarity in co-operation with Oxfam Québec, through supporting projects, mostly concerned with drinking-water, education and training, initiated by partner organizations in 10 less-developed countries in Africa, Asia and Central and South America. The organization focuses, in particular, on young people between the ages of 12 and 17 years.

Geographical Area of Activity: Brazil, Burkina Faso, El Salvador, Haiti, Nepal, Paraguay, Peru, the Philippines, Senegal and Togo.

Publications: Project reports; Annual Report; *Courrier Sud* (quarterly).

Finance: Revenue C $152,557, expenditure $138,922 (31 March 2014).

Board of Directors: Jean-Guy Saint-Martin (Chair.); Lise Desmarais (Sec.); Donald Olds (Treas.).

Principal Staff: Exec. Dir Pierre Véronneau.

Address: 2330 rue Notre-Dame Ouest, Montréal, QC H3J 2Y2.

Telephone: (514) 937-1614; **Fax:** (514) 937-9452; **Internet:** oxfam.qc.ca/intervenants/mission-club2tiers; **e-mail:** ecoles@oxfam.qc.ca.

CNIB/INCA

Founded in 1918 as the Canadian National Institute for the Blind—CNIB.

Activities: Provides vital programmes and services, innovative consumer products, research, peer support and one of the world's largest libraries for the visually impaired. Focuses on protection and prevention, as well as on treatments and cures.

Geographical Area of Activity: Canada.

Publications: Annual Report; *Insight* (e-newsletter); *Vision* (newsletter, in French and English); research findings; other publications and resources.

Finance: Annual revenue C $81,891,000, expenditure $53,698,000 (31 March 2014).

Board of Directors: John Matheson (Chair.); Craig Oliver (Hon. Board Chair.); Jane Beaumont (Immediate Past Chair.).

Principal Staff: Pres. and CEO John M. Rafferty.

Address: 1929 Bayview Ave, Toronto, ON M4G 3E8.

Telephone: (416) 486-2500; **Fax:** (416) 480-7677; **Internet:** www.cnib.ca; **e-mail:** info@cnib.ca.

Coady International Institute

Founded in 1959 by the St Francis Xavier University to improve the lives of disadvantaged people by empowering them with knowledge and skills.

Activities: Offers diploma, certificate and graduate programmes that are driven by the immediacy of students' direct work on the ground. The Institute also works with partners throughout the world. It offers Canadian youth fellowships to promote community development.

Geographical Area of Activity: International.

Restrictions: An educational facility, not a grantmaking organization.

Publications: *From Clients to Citizens: Communities changing the course of their own development* (2009); *Reaching the Hard to Reach: A global comparative study on member owned microfinance in Ecuador & Mexico* (2008); 'ITC Choupal Fresh', in *Inclusive Value Chains in India*; occasional papers, journal articles and conference presentations (available online).

Finance: Annual revenue C $6,508,078, expenditure $6,508,078 (31 March 2014).

Advisory Board: Susan Crocker (Chair.).

Principal Staff: Co-Dirs Gord Cunningham, Shelagh Savage.

Address: St Francis Xavier University, POB 5000, Antigonish, NS B2G 2W5.

Telephone: (902) 867-3960; **Fax:** (902) 867-3907; **Internet:** www.coady.stfx.ca; **e-mail:** coady@stfx.ca.

Columbia Foundation

Established in 2000 by Working Enterprises, a group of companies owned by the labour movement, to invest in human and social capital for the benefit of all Canadians.

Activities: Funds innovative social research; develops and funds new scholarships that promote retraining and life-long learning; and promotes the inclusive involvement of citizens in decision making and community building.

Geographical Area of Activity: Canada.

Finance: Annual revenue C $0, expenditure $786,484 (31 May 2014).

Principal Staff: Exec. Dir Charley Beresford.

Address: POB 11171, Royal Centre, 2600-1055 West Georgia St, Vancouver, BC V6E 3R5.

Telephone: (604) 408-2500; **Fax:** (604) 408-2525; **Internet:** www.columbiainstitute.ca/about-us/columbia-foundation; **e-mail:** info@civicgovernance.ca.

CPAR—Canadian Physicians for Aid and Relief

Established in 1984 in response to famine and poor health conditions suffered by Ethiopian refugees in Sudan.

Activities: Aims to overcome poverty and build healthy communities for vulnerable people. CPAR supports community efforts to address the determinants of health by ensuring sustainable access to clean water and adequate food, improving hygiene and sanitation, and improving access to primary health care. It ensures the inclusion of components related to gender, people living with HIV and the environment in all of its programmes.

Geographical Area of Activity: Ethiopia, Malawi, Tanzania, Uganda.

Publications: Annual Report; Special Health Reports; newsletters.

Finance: Annual revenue C $2,677,449, expenditure $2,615,944 (31 March 2014).

Board of Directors: Andrew Williamson (Chair.); Bonnie McIlmoyl (Treas.).

Principal Staff: Exec. Dir Dusanka Pavlica.

Address: 1425 Bloor St West, Toronto, ON M6P 3L6.

Telephone: (416) 369-0865; **Fax:** (416) 369-0294; **Internet:** www.cpar.ca; **e-mail:** info@cpar.ca.

The CRB Foundation/La Fondation CRB

Founded in 1988 by Charles R. Bronfman to support major initiatives contributing to the enhancement of 'Canadianism' and to strengthening the unity of the Jewish people.

Activities: Operates at national and international levels through the Canadian heritage programme Historica; Project Involvement, a major educational reform programme running in Israel; and Birthright Israel, a programme that provides adults with their first living and learning experience in Israel. The Foundation currently prioritizes 'incubator' programmes in the areas of Jewish identity; relations between Israel and Jewish people worldwide; the quality of life in Israel, especially in the area of educational reform; general and Jewish strategic philanthropy; and building diverse networks of young Jewish people examining their identity, community and/or philanthropy.

Geographical Area of Activity: USA, Canada and Israel.

Restrictions: Does not support annual health, welfare or education campaigns; building campaigns or capital projects; equipment; general operating expenses; deficit funding or endowment funds; academic chairs or scholarship programmes.

Publications: Information booklet.

Finance: Annual revenue C $675,803, expenditure $1,685,149 (31 Dec. 2013).

Officers and Directors: Charles Bronfman (Chair.); Stephen Bronfman, Ellen Bronfman-Hauptman (Successor Co-Chair.); Richard Doyle (Sec.); Larry Fisher (Asst Sec.); Ann Dadson (Treas.); Glenn Hamilton-Browne (Controller).

Address: 1170 Peel St, 8th Floor, Montréal, QC H3B 4P2.

Telephone: (514) 878-5250; **Fax:** (514) 878-5299.

Cuso International

Established in 1961 to support alliances that work for global social justice, the elimination of poverty and international development.

Activities: Works to reduce poverty and inequality through the efforts of skilled volunteers. The organization places volunteers from North and South America in developing countries in Africa, Asia, the Caribbean and Latin America. Volunteers collaborate with local partners on health, education, environment, social justice and livelihoods projects, sharing knowledge and experience to create sustainable change.

Geographical Area of Activity: Asia and the Pacific, Africa, Central and South America and the Caribbean, Canada.

Publications: Annual Report; Annual Review; *CusoNews* (monthly newsletter); *Impact* (donor newsletter, 1–2 a year).

Finance: Annual revenue C $30,521,633, expenditure $32,256,592 (31 March 2014).

Board of Directors: Lloyd Axworthy (Chair.); Jamie Allison (Vice-Chair.); Dan Wright (Treas.).

Principal Staff: CEO Evelyne Guindon.

Address: 44 Eccles St, Suite 200, Ottawa, ON K1R 6S4.

Telephone: (613) 829-7445; **Fax:** (613) 829-7996; **Internet:** www.cusointernational.org; **e-mail:** questions@cusointernational.org.

Cystic Fibrosis Canada

Founded in 1960 as the Canadian Cystic Fibrosis Foundation, a non-profit voluntary health organization. Present name adopted in 2011.

Activities: Raises and allocates funds to promote public awareness of cystic fibrosis; conducts research into improved care and treatment; and seeks a cure or control for this disorder. The organization promotes research on cystic fibrosis in Canadian universities and hospitals; funds research grants and major research development programmes; and gives special grants for training and research to students, fellows, scholars and visiting scientists skilled in such areas as respirology, paediatrics and the behavioural sciences. Has more than 50 chapters throughout Canada.

Geographical Area of Activity: Canada.

Publications: Annual Report; *Candid Facts* (newsletter 2 a year, in English and French); *Circle of Friends* (newsletter, 2 a year, in English and French); *Report of the Canadian Cystic Fibrosis Patient Data Registry;* Annual Report; brochures and reports.

Finance: Annual revenue C $12,547,000, expenditure $9,920,000 (31 Jan. 2013).

Board of Directors: James Mountain (Chair.); Mitch LePage (Vice-Chair.).

Principal Staff: Pres. and CEO Norma Beauchamp.

Address: 2323 Yonge St, Suite 800, Toronto, ON M4P 2C9.

Telephone: (416) 485-9149; **Fax:** (416) 485-0960; **Internet:** www.cysticfibrosis.ca; **e-mail:** info@cysticfibrosis.ca.

Disabled People's International

Established in 1988; a network of national organizations or assemblies of disabled people, to promote human rights of disabled people through full participation, equalization of opportunity and development.

Activities: Promotes the human rights and economic and social integration of disabled persons; and works to develop and support organizations of disabled persons. There are currently 133 National Assemblies (member organizations), and five Regional Development Offices in Italy (Europe), Mauritania (Africa), Thailand (Asia/Pacific), Peru (Latin America) and Antigua and Barbuda (North America/Caribbean).

Geographical Area of Activity: International.

Publications: Position papers; newsletters.

Finance: Annual revenue C $219,003, expenditure $171,068 (31 March 2014).

Executive Council: Javed Abidi (Chair.); Henrietta Davis-Wray, Rachel Kachaje (Deputy Chair.); Samuel Kabue (Sec.); Wilfredo Guzman Jara (Treas.).

Principal Staff: Information Officer Kalle Konkkolla.

Address: 214 Montreal Rd, Suite 402, Ottawa, ON K1L 8L8.

Telephone: (613) 563-2091; **Fax:** (613) 563-3861; **Internet:** www.dpi.org; **e-mail:** secretariat.dpi@gmail.com.

Echo Foundation

Established in 1983 as EJLB Foundation to fund scientific research in all areas of neuroscience pertaining to mental illness, and to promote the protection of the environment. Present name adopted in 2012.

Activities: Operates in two main areas: Mental Health, with grants given to organizations in Montréal and Toronto that improve the quality of life of people suffering from mental health problems; and Environment, which focuses on Eastern Canada (Ontario, Québec and the Atlantic provinces) and prioritizes the protection of areas of ecological importance and the greening of urban areas, and supports the promotion of sustainable environmental practices.

Geographical Area of Activity: Canada, with limited international grantmaking.

Restrictions: Grants will be made for building funds, capital funds, endowment funds or equipment funds, laboratory renovations, but not for the applicant's salary or that of other faculty members who may be participating in the research project.

Finance: Annual revenue C $31,436,475, expenditure $4,642,821 (31 Dec. 2013).

Board of Directors: Robert Alain (Pres.); Ann Parsons, Katherine Lewis (Vice-Pres).

Principal Staff: Exec. Dir Kevin Leonard.

Address: 1350 Sherbrooke St West, Suite 1050, Montréal, QC H3G 1J1.

Telephone: (514) 843-5112; **Fax:** (514) 843-4080; **Internet:** www.echofoundation.ca; **e-mail:** general@echofoundation .ca.

Eldee Foundation

Founded in 1961 for the support of Canadian organizations and charitable institutions.

Activities: Operates nationally in the fields of medicine and health, the environment and Jewish causes in Canada and Israel. In particular, the Foundation is interested in medical research and hospital development where it pertains directly or indirectly to schizophrenia and mental illness; acquiring and preserving natural areas of significance to the urban landscape; and funding Canada-based environmental research.

Geographical Area of Activity: Canada and Israel.

Restrictions: No grants are made to individuals for awards, fellowships, scholarships, bursaries or research grants.

Finance: Annual revenue C $1,163,803, expenditure $1,768,001 (31 Dec. 2013).

Board: Harry J. F. Bloomfield (Pres.); Antonietta Ciarlone (Sec.); Linda Romanelli (Treas.).

Address: 1080 côte du Beaver Hill, Suite 1720, Montréal, QC H2Z 1S8.

Telephone: (514) 871-9261; **Fax:** (514) 397-0816; **Internet:** www.eldeefoundation.ca.

ETC Group—Action Group on Erosion, Technology and Concentration

Founded in 1985 as the Rural Advancement Foundation International and reformed as the ETC Group in 2001 to protect ecological diversity.

Activities: Addresses the socioeconomic and ecological issues surrounding new technologies that could have an impact on the world's poorest and most vulnerable. The Group investigates ecological erosion (including the erosion of cultures and human rights); the development of new technologies (especially agricultural, but also new technologies that work with genomics and matter); and monitors global governance issues, including corporate concentration and trade in technologies. It operates at the global political level, working closely with partner civil society organizations (CSOs) and social movements, especially in Africa, Asia and Latin America.

Geographical Area of Activity: Worldwide.

Restrictions: Not a grantmaking organization.

Publications: *Submission: ETC Group Submission to Rio+20– Tackling Technology: Three Proposals for Rio (2011); Earth Grab!–Geoengineering, biomass and climate-ready crops* (2011); *Road to Rio Countdown Map of Key Events* (2011); *The New Biomasters, Geopiracy: The case against Geoengineering, The Big Downturn? Nanogeopolitics (2010); Communiqué* (research journal published 4–6 times a year); *ETC Century: Erosion, Technological Transformation, and Corporate Concentration in the 21st Century* (2001); *The Seed Giants: Who Owns Whom?;* reports and financial statements; other specialist publications and occasional papers.

Finance: Annual revenue C $867,606, expenditure $872,333 (31 Aug. 2014).

Board of Directors: Tim Brodhead (Pres.), Michael Hansen (Sec.-Treas.).

Principal Staff: Exec. Dir Pat Mooney.

Address: 180 Metcalfe St, Suite 206, Ottawa, ON K2P 1P5.

Telephone: (613) 241-2267; **Fax:** (613) 241-2506; **Internet:** www.etcgroup.org; **e-mail:** etc@etcgroup.org.

Focus Humanitarian Assistance—FOCUS

Founded in 1994 by the Ismaili Muslim community in Europe and North America; a network of agencies providing emergency humanitarian assistance in less-developed countries. The organization is an affiliate of the Aga Khan foundations network (q.v.).

Activities: Operates in less-developed countries of Africa, and Central and Southern Asia, providing humanitarian assistance to areas stricken by natural disasters or by conflict. Maintains liaison offices in Afghanistan, the United Kingdom, India, Pakistan and the USA.

Geographical Area of Activity: Worldwide.

Publications: *FOCUS Global Newsletter.*

Finance: Annual revenue C $4,640,066, expenditure $3,275,199 (31 Dec. 2012).

Board of Directors: Samji Alnasir (Chair.); Farah Jivraj (Vice-Chair.).

Principal Staff: Global Co-ordinator Shakeel Hirji.

Address: 789 Don Mills Rd, Suite 201, Toronto, ON M3C 1T5.

Telephone: (416) 423-7988; **Fax:** (416) 423-4216; **Internet:** focus-canada.org; www.akdn.org/focus; **e-mail:** ficc@ focushumanitarian.org.

Fondation Marcelle et Jean Coutu (Marcelle et Jean Coutu Foundation)

Established in 1990 by the Groupe Jean Coutu pharmacy chain (f. 1969) to assist those in less-developed countries and the disadvantaged in Canada.

Activities: Operates in Canada, especially Québec, in the field of social welfare, in particular disadvantaged women and children, and drug abuse.

Geographical Area of Activity: Mainly Canada.

Finance: Annual revenue C $251,982,140, expenditure $9,352,979 (28 Feb. 2014).

Board of Directors: Marie-Josée Coutu (Chair.).

Address: 1374 Mont-Royal est, Bureau 101, Montréal, QC H2V 4P3.

Internet: corpo.jeancoutu.com; **e-mail:** hbisson@jeancoutu .com.

Fondation Armand-Frappier (Armand-Frappier Foundation)

Established in 1978 to support scholarship programmes and the purchase of scientific equipment, as well as the Institut Armand-Frappier, which aims to promote the pursuit of excellence and innovative research.

Activities: Operates in the fields of education and science and technology, offering scholarships to pre- and postdoctoral students studying at the Institut Armand-Frappier, and scholarships to students at Québec universities aiming to continue their studies at the Institut Armand-Frappier. The Foundation also awards Armand-Frappier prizes in the areas of Health, Innovation and Emerging Businesses in Québec working in relevant areas.

Geographical Area of Activity: Canada.

Publications: Annual Report.

Finance: Annual revenue C $2,552,670, expenditure $1,405,243 (30 April 2014).

Board of Directors: Clément Joly (Pres.); Luc Reny (Vice-Pres.); Louis-François Hogue (Sec.).

Principal Staff: Gen. Man. Muriel Amar.

Address: 531 blvd des Prairies, Ville de Laval, QC H7V 1B7.

Telephone: (450) 686-5360; **Fax:** (450) 686-5361; **Internet:** www.fondation-afrappier-inrs.ca; **e-mail:** fondation.armand -frappier@iaf.inrs.ca.

Fondation J-Louis Lévesque (J-Louis Lévesque Foundation)

Established in 1961 by businessman and philanthropist Jean-Louis Lévesque to promote the development of universities, research institutes and charitable organizations.

Activities: Operates in Québec, Ontario and the Atlantic Provinces of Canada in the fields of education, medical research and social welfare, through making grants for research and special projects.

Geographical Area of Activity: Canada.

Restrictions: All funds are currently committed.

Finance: Annual revenue C $8,959,619, expenditure $3,442,968 (31 Dec. 2013).

Board: Suzanne Lévesque (Pres.); Claude Dupont (Sec.).

Address: 2000 ave McGill College, Suite 2340, Montréal, QC H3A 3H3.

Telephone: (514) 849-8606; **Fax:** (514) 849-1983.

Fondation Baxter and Alma Ricard

Established in 1999 by Baxter and Alma Ricard, on the proceeds of their broadcast media holdings, to offer French Canadians living in a linguistic minority situation the opportunity to pursue graduate studies in the best schools in the world without having to go into debt.

Activities: Offers annual graduate and postgraduate scholarships to young French Canadians, for a period of up to three years. Candidates are evaluated on the basis of academic excellence, leadership, civic pride and their commitment to the community.

Geographical Area of Activity: Canada.

Finance: Annual revenue C $3,693,921, expenditure $1,749,231 (30 June 2014).

Board of Trustees: Paul Desmarais (Chair.); André Lacroix (Sec.).

Principal Staff: Exec. Dir Alain Landry.

Address: 225 rue Metcalfe, Suite 407, Ottawa, ON K2P 1P9.

Telephone: (613) 236-7065; **Fax:** (613) 236-3718; **Internet:** www.fondationricard.com; **e-mail:** fonricar@rogers.com.

Fondation Pierre Elliott Trudeau Foundation

Established in 2001 by the family of former Prime Minister of Canada Pierre Trudeau in his memory and endowed by the Government of Canada with the Advanced Research in the Humanities and Human Sciences Fund.

Activities: Awards doctoral scholarships and fellowships to encourage reflection and action in human rights and dignity, responsible citizenship, Canada's role in the world, and people and their environment.

Geographical Area of Activity: Canada.

Publications: Annual Report; *The Trudeau Foundation Papers*.

Finance: Annual revenue C $7,873,436, expenditure $5,319,996 (31 Aug. 2014).

Principal Staff: Pres. and CEO Morris Rosenburg; Exec. Dir Élise Comtois.

Address: 600-1980 Sherbrooke St West, Montreal, QC H3H 1E8.

Telephone: (514) 938-0001; **Fax:** (514) 938-0046; **Internet:** www.trudeaufoundation.ca; www.fondationtrudeau.ca; **e-mail:** tfinfo@trudeaufoundation.ca.

Foundation for International Training—FIT

Founded in 1976 to enhance self-reliance in developing countries by providing training.

Activities: Operates internationally in providing training and consultancy services and materials. The Foundation works with both private and public sectors, collaborating with local institutions; it concentrates on strengthening the capabilities of those who can then offer training to others. Its three main programme areas are: social development, economic development and environmental management.

Geographical Area of Activity: Worldwide.

Publications: Annual Report; training materials, and policy and background papers.

Finance: Annual revenue C $1,027,480, expenditure $1,250,174 (31 March 2013).

Board of Governors: Richard Beattie (Chair.).

Principal Staff: Exec. Dir Mirabelle Rodrigues.

Address: 7181 Woodbine Ave, Suite 110, Markham, ON L3R 1A3.

Telephone: (905) 305-8680; **Fax:** (905) 305-8681; **Internet:** www.ffit.org; **e-mail:** info@ffit.org.

Frontiers Foundation Inc/Fondation Frontière Inc

Established in 1968 by the Rev. Charles R. Catto to contribute to the relief of poverty by supporting tangible community development projects that have enduring significance. The Operation Beaver Program began in 1964; the Frontiers Foundation assumed responsibility for its administration in Canada in 1968 and overseas in 1969.

Activities: Operates through the Operation Beaver Program in Canada, Haiti and Bolivia in the areas of aid to less-developed countries, education and housing, through self-conducted programmes for community development, grants to individuals and institutions, training courses and publications.

Geographical Area of Activity: Canada, Bolivia and Haiti.

Publications: Annual Report; *Beaver Tales*; films, video documentaries, slides.

Finance: Annual revenue C $1,407,448, expenditure $1,353,146 (31 March 2014).

Board of Directors: Patrick Wilson (Chair.); Edwin D. Kolausok (Pres.); Suzanne Jones (Vice-Pres.); Robert Haggart (Sec.); Tejas Keahyap (Treas.).

Principal Staff: Exec. Dir Marco A. Guzman.

Address: 419 Coxwell Ave, Toronto, ON M4L 3B9.

Telephone: (416) 690-3930; **Fax:** (416) 690-3934; **Internet:** www.frontiersfoundation.ca; **e-mail:** frontiersfoundation@on.aibn.com.

Gairdner Foundation

Founded in 1957 by businessman and philanthropist James A. Gairdner for the recognition of individuals who have made outstanding contributions through research in the field of medical science.

Activities: Operates internationally in the fields of medicine, biomedical science and global health through awards to individuals.

Geographical Area of Activity: International.

Restrictions: Awards are made only on the basis of nominations and peer review.

Publications: News reports.

Finance: Annual revenue C $2,965,428, expenditure $2,180,979 (31 Dec. 2013).

Board of Directors: Lorne Tyrrell (Chair.).

Principal Staff: Pres. and Scientific Dir Dr John H. Dirks.

Address: 4 Devonshire Pl., Toronto, Ontario, M5S 2E1.

Telephone: (416) 596-9996; **Fax:** (416) 596-9992; **Internet:** www.gairdner.org/content/about-foundation; **e-mail:** thegairdner@gairdner.org.

Mahatma Gandhi Canadian Foundation for World Peace

Established in 1988.

Activities: Aims to share the beliefs and philosophies of Mahatma Gandhi to promote international understanding and world peace. The Foundation conducts and supports research and scholarship to promote Gandhian philosophy in a contemporary context, through supporting exchanges, lectureships and other academic posts; organizing conferences and lectures on the life and thoughts of Gandhi; and other educational projects.

Geographical Area of Activity: Canada.

Publications: *Declaration Towards a Global Ethic*; newsletter.

Finance: Annual revenue C $122,324, expenditure $102,160 (31 March 2014).

Board of Directors: Jitendra A. Shah (Chair.); Dr Prem Kharbanda (Vice-Chair.); Harchand Grewal (Treas.); Kim Mertick (Sec.); Prem Kalia (Past Chair.).

Principal Staff: Educational Co-ordinator Michelle Johnston.

Address: POB 60002, University of Alberta Postal Outlet, Edmonton, AB T6G 2S4.

Telephone: (780) 492-5504; **Fax:** (780) 492-0113; **Internet:** www.gandhifoundation.ca; **e-mail:** gandhifoundationcanada@gmail.com.

Globe Foundation of Canada—GLOBE

Founded in 1993 to promote the development of eco-business throughout the world.

Activities: A not-for-profit organization dedicated to finding practical business-orientated solutions to the world's environmental problems. The Foundation helps companies and individuals realize the value of economically viable environmental business opportunities through conferences and events, research and consulting, project management, communications and awards. It champions green initiatives and sustainable ventures.

Geographical Area of Activity: Canada, Asia and Eastern Europe.

Publications: *British Columbia's Green Economy: Securing the Workforce of Tomorrow.*

Finance: Annual budget approx. C $1.85m.

Board of Directors: Michael E. J. Phelps (Chair.).

Principal Staff: Pres. and CEO Dr John D. Wiebe.

Address: World Trade Center, 999 Canada Pl., Suite 404, Vancouver, BC V6C 3E1.

Telephone: (604) 695-5001; **Fax:** (604) 695-5019; **Internet:** www.globe.ca; **e-mail:** info@globe.ca.

Walter and Duncan Gordon Charitable Foundation

Established in 1965 by businessman and politician Walter L. Gordon, his wife Elizabeth, and brother, Duncan L. Gordon.

Activities: Operates in three main fields: the Canadian North (Northwest Territories, Nunavut and Yukon); Fresh Water Resources Protection (national), and Art Acquisitions (Ontario).

Geographical Area of Activity: Canada.

Restrictions: Does not offer scholarships, nor does it offer bursaries or make grants to individuals.

Publications: Annual Report; reports; e-books; fact sheets; infographics.

Finance: Annual revenue C $9,320,457, expenditure $3,147,298 (31 Dec. 2013).

Board of Trustees: Robert Pace (Chair.); Dr Janice Gross Stein (Vice-Chair.); Jonathan Wilkinson (Treas.).

Principal Staff: Pres. and CEO Dr Thomas S. Axworthy.

Address: 11 Church St, Suite 400, Toronto, ON M5E 1W1.

Telephone: (416) 601-4776; **Fax:** (416) 601-1689; **Internet:** www.gordonfoundation.ca; **e-mail:** info@gordonfn.org.

The Lotte and John Hecht Memorial Foundation

Established in 1962 by Lotte and John Hecht, owners of a sawmill and property investors, as the 1945 Foundation.

Activities: Operates in two main areas: research and support of alternative and complementary medicine, specifically for the treatment of cancer; and economic education that furthers the principles of free market, through offering grants to non-profit organizations.

Geographical Area of Activity: Canada.

Finance: Annual revenue C $22,170,543, expenditure $20,752,225 (31 Dec. 2013).

Board of Directors: Joan C. Hess (Chair.).

Principal Staff: Exec. Dir Angela Webster.

Address: 325 Howe St, Suite 502, Vancouver, BC V6C 1Z7.

Telephone: (604) 683-7575; **Fax:** (604) 683-7580; **Internet:** www.hecht.org/index.htm; **e-mail:** info@hecht.org.

HOPE International Development Agency—HOPE

Established in 1974.

Activities: Aims to support developing countries where environmental, economic or social circumstances have interfered with communities' abilities to sustain themselves. The Agency provides emergency aid, including clean water and sanitation, shelter, medicine and food; as well as more long-term solutions, such as technological and educational support, training in food production and nutrition, and health care and community development programmes. It aims to assist communities to learn the skills necessary to sustain themselves in the long term. Also maintains offices in Afghanistan, Australia, Cambodia, Ethiopia, Japan, Myanmar, New Zealand, the United Kingdom and the USA.

Geographical Area of Activity: International.

Publications: Annual Report.

Finance: Annual revenue C $21,713,772, expenditure $21,646,953 (31 Dec. 2013).

Principal Staff: Team Leader Brian Cannon.

Address: 214 Sixth St, New Westminster, BC V3L 3A2.

Telephone: (604) 525-5481; **Fax:** (604) 525-3471; **Internet:** www.hope-international.com; **e-mail:** hope@hope-international.com.

Horizons of Friendship

Established in 1973 by Tim Coughlan and Christine and David Stewart, with the aim of eliminating poverty in Mexico and Central America.

Activities: Works with people living with the effects of poverty in rural and urban communities. The organization runs development projects to provide clean water and sanitation, health care, housing and skills training. It has given humanitarian assistance to victims of war and political oppression, aided refugees in need of rehabilitation and provided aid to those affected by natural disasters.

Geographical Area of Activity: Mexico and Central America.

Publications: Newsletter; Annual Report.

Finance: Total revenue C $1,674,716, expenditure $1,619,837 (31 March 2013).

Board of Directors: Dr Paul Caldwell (Pres.); Dr Bill Moebius (Vice-Pres.); Rev. Timothy Coughlan (Hon. Pres.); Mike Dupuis (Sec.); Catherin Wenuck (Past Pres.).

Principal Staff: Exec. Dir Patricia Rebolledo Kloques.

Address: 50 Covert St, POB 402, Cobourg, ON K9A 4L1.

Telephone: (905) 372-5483; **Fax:** (905) 372-7095; **Internet:** www.horizons.ca; **e-mail:** info@horizons.ca.

Imperial Oil Foundation

Established in 1994 for general charitable purposes in Canada that are compatible with the company's business objectives and activities.

Activities: Operates nationally in the fields of arts and humanities, education, medicine and health, and social welfare (in particular community and social services and sport and recreation), through grants to Canadian charitable organizations for existing facilities and programmes.

Geographical Area of Activity: Canada.

Restrictions: No grants are made to individuals; grants are limited to communities in which the company has employees; no finance for research projects, fellowships or scholarships.

Finance: Annual revenue C $5,815,500, expenditure $6,265,000 (31 Dec. 2013).

Officers and Directors: David S. Sutherland (Chair.); Krystyna T. Hoeg (Vice-Chair.); Paul M. Masschelin (Treas.); Cathryn M. Walker (Sec.); Lorrie L. Hesch (Asst Sec.).

Principal Staff: Pres. Susan B. Swan.

Address: POB 2480, Station M, Calgary, AB T2P 3M9.

Telephone: (416) 968-4111; **Internet:** www.imperialoil.ca; **e-mail:** contact.imperial@esso.ca.

Institute of Cultural Affairs International

Established in 1977 as a global network of non-profit organizations to advance human development worldwide.

Activities: Operates in the fields of development, health, welfare and human rights, seeking to influence international development policies, and co-ordinating and supporting projects run by its member organizations. Programmes include: HIV and AIDS; Sustainable Agriculture; Forest Management; Global Youth Leadership; Youth Engagement; Ending Poverty; Women's Empowerment; and Peaceful Communities. Has member organizations in more than 30 countries.

Geographical Area of Activity: International.

Restrictions: Not a grantmaking organization.

Publications: Annual Report; *Winds and Waves* (magazine, 3 a year).

Finance: Annual revenue C $17,917, expenditure $1,990 (31 Dec. 2013).

Board of Directors: Martin Gilbraith (Pres.); Shankar Jadhav (Treas.); Staci Kentish (Sec.).

Address: c/o ICA Canada, 655 Queen St East, Toronto, ON M4M 1G4.

Telephone: (416) 691-2316; **Fax:** (416) 691-2491; **Internet:** www.ica-international.org; **e-mail:** icai@ica-international .org.

Inter Pares

Founded in 1975 by Timothy Brodhead and Ian Smiley to support the efforts of self-help groups in developing countries in gaining control over their lives, create economic alternatives and find sustainable solutions to poverty.

Activities: Supports local groups in 20 countries in Asia, Africa, Central America and the Caribbean to establish co-operatives and credit schemes; reclaim land for food production; promote reproductive rights; protect the environment; provide community-based health care, education and training; and organize women, farmers and urban poor to improve their lives. In Canada, Inter Pares promotes understanding of the causes of poverty and powerlessness, and encourages groups in Canada and developing countries to learn from and support each other in strategies for change. It works with local and regional organizations in Canada to support community development and social change.

Geographical Area of Activity: Africa, Asia, Central and South America, and Canada.

Publications: Annual Report; *Inter Pares Bulletin* (5 a year); occasional papers; reports.

Finance: Annual revenue C $6,442,575, expenditure $6,434,150 (31 Dec. 2014).

Board of Directors: Sari Tudiver (Vice-Chair.); Bill Van Iterson (Treas.).

Principal Staff: Exec. Dir Rita Morbia.

Address: 221 Laurier Ave East, Ottawa, ON K1N 6P1.

Telephone: (613) 563-4801; **Fax:** (613) 594-4704; **Internet:** www.interpares.ca; **e-mail:** info@interpares.ca.

International Development and Relief Foundation

Founded in 1984 by a group of Canadian Muslims aiming to empower the world's disadvantaged people.

Activities: Aims to empower the world's disadvantaged people of the world through emergency relief and participatory development programmes based on the Islamic principles of human dignity, self-reliance and social justice. The Foundation has successfully implemented relief and development projects in Asia, Africa, the Middle East, Eastern Europe and the Americas.

Geographical Area of Activity: International.

Publications: Annual report; *IDRF Reporter* (annually); newsletter.

Finance: Annual revenue C $3,647,000, expenditure $3,140,849 (30 June 2014).

Board of Directors: Zeib Jeeva (Chair.); Javed Akbar (Vice-Chair. and Treas.); Winston S. L. Kassim (Past Chair.).

Principal Staff: Gen. Sec. Nurhan Aycan.

Address: 908 The East Mall, 1st Floor, Toronto, ON M9B 6K2.

Telephone: (416) 497-0818; **Fax:** (416) 497-0686; **Internet:** www.idrf.com; **e-mail:** office@idrf.ca.

International Institute for Sustainable Development—IISD

Founded in 1990 to promote sustainable social and economic development worldwide and to promote innovation.

Activities: Collates and disseminates information on economic development; serves, in an advisory capacity, government agencies and national and international organizations involved in development work; devises business strategies and trade principles; and promotes community living and the creation of sustainable economies. The Institute also conducts research, produces educational materials and maintains a library. Maintains offices in Ottawa, Geneva and New York.

Geographical Area of Activity: Worldwide.

Publications: *IISD News*; Annual Report; various books, brochures and handbooks.

Finance: Annual revenue C $16,501,380, expenditure $16,939,298 (31 March 2014).

Board of Directors: Daniel J. Gagnier (Chair.).

Principal Staff: Pres. and CEO Scott Vaughan.

Address: 161 Portage Ave East, 6th Floor, Winnipeg, MB R3B 0Y4.

Telephone: (204) 958-7700; **Fax:** (204) 958-7710; **Internet:** www.iisd.org; **e-mail:** info@iisd.org.

Ivey Foundation

Established in 1947 by lawyer and businessman Richard G. Ivey and his son Richard M. Ivey, also a lawyer.

Activities: Supports three programmes: Conserving Canada's Forests, Strategic Opportunities and Director-Initiated.

Geographical Area of Activity: Canada.

Restrictions: No unsolicited applications.

Publications: Annual Report; programme brochures.

Finance: Annual revenue C $13,601,147, expenditure $1,035,923 (31 Dec. 2013).

Board of Directors: Rosamond A. Ivey (Chair.); Suzanne E. Ivey Cook (Vice-Chair.); Richard W. Ivey (Sec. and Treas.).

Principal Staff: Pres. Bruce Lourie.

Address: 11 Church St, Suite 400, Toronto, ON M5E 1W1.

Telephone: (416) 867-9229; **Fax:** (416) 601-1689; **Internet:** www.ivey.org; **e-mail:** info@ivey.org.

Laidlaw Foundation

Established in 1949 by W. C. Laidlaw, R. A. Laidlaw, R. W. L. Laidlaw and Dr R. G. N. Laidlaw; its was funded by the R Laidlaw Lumber Company, which was subsequently sold in 1972.

Activities: Operates in the fields of the arts and humanities, conservation and the environment, and social welfare. The Foundation's main programmes are: Contaminants and Child Health; Youth Arts; Youth Engagement, which promotes leadership and decision-making skills; and a pilot project, Inclusive Communities for Children, Youth and Families.

Geographical Area of Activity: Mainly Ontario, Canada.

Publications: Annual Report; information brochures; occasional papers.

Finance: Annual revenue C $9,774,002, expenditure $3,063,955 (31 Dec. 2013).

Board of Directors: John Fox (Pres.).

Principal Staff: Exec. Dir Jehad Aliweiwi.

Address: 365 Bloor St East, Suite 2000, Toronto, ON M4W 3L4.

Telephone: (416) 964-3614; **Fax:** (416) 975-1428; **Internet:** www.laidlawfdn.org; **e-mail:** info@laidlawfdn.org.

Daniel Langlois Foundation/Fondation Daniel Langlois

Established in 1997 by Daniel Langlois, founder of computer animation company SOFTIMAGE.

Activities: Seeks to bring art and science closer together by nurturing a critical awareness of technology's impact on people and the natural and cultural environments; and by promoting the exploration of aesthetics. The Foundation operates internationally in the fields of the arts, science, technology and the environment. It supports interdisciplinary research that encourages the co-operation of people from a variety of fields; funds projects by artists and scientists; makes the results of its research public; and encourages public exhibition of projects in galleries, museums and other public institutions. It also provides scholarships to individuals and organizations from less-developed countries, so that they can immerse themselves in technological contexts not usually available to them; and provides research grants to individual artists or scientists.

Geographical Area of Activity: International.

Restrictions: No grants to commercial projects.

Publications: Steina and Vasulka archives; *9 Evenings* archives, *Experiments in Art and Technology (E.A.T.)* archives, *Digital Snow* (DVD-Rom) by Michael Snow; *Latin American Electroacoustic Music Collection* (foreword by Ricardo Dal Farra); Documentation and Conservation of the Media Arts Heritage (DOCAM); Sonia Sheridan archives; Vera Frenkel 'Mapping a Practice'; *Towards an oral history of new media art* by Lizzie Muller.

Finance: Annual revenue C \$127,000, expenditure \$138.253 (31 Dec. 2013).

Board: Daniel Langlois (Chair.); Dominique Marchand (Sec.).

Principal Staff: Admin. Isabelle Gauthier.

Address: 3530 blvd St-Laurent, Suite 500, Montréal, QC H2X 2V1.

Internet: www.fondation-langlois.org; **e-mail:** info@fondation-langlois.org.

The Lawson Foundation

Established in 1956 by Ray Lawson, a buinessman and subsequently lieutenant-governor of Ontario, to enrich the quality of life of Canadians.

Activities: Aims to improve the quality of life of Canadians, with a particular focus on early childhood competencies and the strengthening of communities. The Foundation supports projects targeting young children, their families and care-givers, and the delivery of community-based, patient-centred health-care services.

Geographical Area of Activity: Canada.

Publications: Annual Report; *The Science of Early Child Development*; *The Motherisk Guide to Cancer in Pregnancy and Lactation*; *Parenting in the Beginning Years: Priorities for Investment*; *Parent Education*; *Toward the Development of a 'Know-How' Knowledge Diffusion and Utilization Model for Social and Health Programs*.

Finance: Annual revenue C \$18,295,825, expenditure \$6,133,210 (31 Dec. 2013).

Board of Directors: Richard E. Wood (Pres.); Susana K. Osler (Vice-Pres.); Edward Lawson (Sec.-Treas.).

Principal Staff: Exec. Dir Marcel Lauzière.

Address: 200 Queens Ave, Suite 511, London, ON N6A 1J3.

Telephone: (519) 667-5114; **Fax:** (519) 667-5118; **Internet:** www.lawson.ca; **e-mail:** mlauziere@lawson.ca.

Lifeforce Foundation

Founded in 1981 by Peter Hamilton as the first ecological organization to protect people, animals and the environment.

Activities: Promotes the harmonious co-existence of humans and animals. The Foundation operates internationally in the fields of human, animal and environmental problems, promoting vegetarianism and campaigning against factory farming, and animal experimentation and exploitation. It also conducts marine life programmes (education, conservation and research) to further the protection of marine habitats; develops public education programmes; compiles statistics; conducts symposia; provides educational packages and materials; and maintains a library and image gallery.

Geographical Area of Activity: International.

Restrictions: Not a grantmaking organization; seeks grants for its programmes.

Publications: Reports; field guides; guidelines.

Principal Staff: Dir Peter Hamilton.

Address: POB 3117, Main Post Office, Vancouver, BC V6B 3X6.

Telephone: (604) 649-5258; **Internet:** www.lifeforcefoundation.org; **e-mail:** lifeforcesociety@hotmail.com.

Light Up the World

Founded in 1997 to advance solid-state lighting technologies and renewable energy. Formally incorporated as an NGO in 2002. Merged with EnerGreen Foundation (f. 1994) in 2006.

Activities: Implements projects to provide 'off-grid' communities with sustainable energy and lighting using solar PV systems and LEDs. The organization trains local people to give them the necessary skills to install, maintain and repair renewable energy systems. Projects currently running in Costa Rica, Guatemala, Ecuador, Peru and Papua New Guinea.

Geographical Area of Activity: International.

Publications: Articles on renewable energy and the Millennium Development Goals; health impacts of fuel-based lighting; best practices for developing a solar home lighting market; promoting access to renewable energy; and using microfinance to expand access.

Finance: Annual revenue C \$487,082, expenditure \$489,339 (31 Dec. 2013).

Board of Directors: Michael Fark (Chair.); Alison White (Sec.); John Reid (Treas.).

Principal Staff: Programme Dir Christoph Schultz.

Address: 224 13 Ave SW, Calgary, AB T2R 0K2.

Telephone: (403) 266-5004; **Fax:** (403) 266-5433; **Internet:** www.lutw.org; **e-mail:** lutw@lutw.org.

The J. W. McConnell Family Foundation

Established in 1937 by industrialist and newspaper publisher J. W. McConnell.

Activities: Helps Canadians to build a more inclusive and sustainable society. Foundation programmes include: Arts and Social Inclusion; Child and Youth Mental Health; Cities for People; Engaging Youth; Indigenous-focused Philanthropy; Innoweave; Possible Canadas; RECODE; Social Innovation Fund; Social Finance; Social Innovation Generation; Sport for Development; and Sustainable Food Systems.

Geographical Area of Activity: Canada.

Restrictions: No grants for conferences, seminars, scholarships, fellowships, bursaries, research, nor to individuals nor to projects orientated towards Third World development.

Publications: Reports and other publications.

Finance: Annual revenue C \$29,453,120, expenditure \$20,544,832 (31 Dec. 2013).

Board of Directors: Josée Beauséjour (Sec.-Treas.).

Principal Staff: Pres. and CEO Stephen Huddart.

Address: Suite 1800, 1002 Sherbrooke St West, Montréal, QC H3A 3L6.

Telephone: (514) 288-2133; **Fax:** (514) 288-1479; **Internet:** www.mcconnellfoundation.ca; **e-mail:** information@ mcconnellfoundation.ca.

Macdonald Stewart Foundation

Established in 1967 by David Macdonald Stewart, owner of Macdonald Tobacco Inc., for general charitable purposes in the areas of the humanities, education and medicine.

Activities: Operates throughout Canada in the fields of the arts and humanities, in particular assisting museums, including the Stewart Museum; education, promoting new and innovative ideas; and medicine and health, supporting projects, short-term research and medical services.

Geographical Area of Activity: Canada.

Restrictions: Grants are not made to individuals. Projects supported must be Canadian or have Canadian content, and be carried out by registered charitable organizations.

Finance: Annual revenue C $8,568,924, expenditure $5,089,104 (31 Dec. 2013).

Officers and Directors: Liliane Stewart (Pres.).

Principal Staff: Exec. Dir Bruce D. Bolton.

Address: POB 1200, Stn A, Montréal, QC H3C 2Y9.

Telephone: (514) 284-0723; **Fax:** (514) 284-0123.

The McLean Foundation

Established in 1945 by James S. McLean, the owner of a meat packing company.

Activities: Supports projects showing promise of general social benefit, but which may initially lack broad public appeal, within the fields of the arts, education, conservation, health and social welfare.

Geographical Area of Activity: Canada.

Restrictions: Grants only to registered Canadian charities; no grants to individuals.

Finance: Annual revenue C $357,560, expenditure $474,024 (31 Dec. 2013).

Principal Staff: Pres. Paul S. McLean; Vice-Pres. Timothy C. Stewart; Sec. Ev McTaggart.

Address: 2 St Clair Ave West, Suite 1008, Toronto, ON M4V 1L5.

Telephone: (416) 964-6802; **Fax:** (416) 964-2804; **Internet:** mcleanfoundation.ca; **e-mail:** info@mcleanfoundation.ca.

The Ernest C. Manning Awards Foundation

Established in 1982 by David Mitchell, the CEO of Alberta Energy Co, and named after a former premier of Alberta.

Activities: Makes awards to resident Canadian citizens who have demonstrated recent innovative talent in developing and successfully marketing a new concept, process or procedure. Awards are made under the categories of the Principal Award, worth C $100,000; Award of Distinction, worth $25,000; Innovation Awards, two awards of $10,000 each; and the Young Canadian programme, which makes eight awards totalling a combined $20,000.

Geographical Area of Activity: Canada.

Publications: Newsletter.

Finance: Annual revenue C $685,687, expenditure $808,678 (31 Dec. 2013).

Board of Trustees: John K. Read (Chair.); Dr Jim A. McEwen (Vice-Chair.); David W. Kerr (Treas.).

Address: Alastair Ross Technology Centre, 3553 31st Street NW, Suite 267, Calgary, AB T2L 2K7.

Telephone: (403) 930-4332; **Fax:** (403) 930-4329; **Internet:** www.manningawards.ca; **e-mail:** info@manningawards.ca.

The MasterCard Foundation

Established in 2006.

Activities: Provides education, skills training and financial inclusion to catalyze prosperity in developing countries. The Foundation collaborates with partners in more than 45 countries to help people living in poverty to access opportunities to learn and prosper.

Geographical Area of Activity: Worldwide.

Finance: Annual revenue C $3,611,319,488, expenditure $190,623,406 (31 Dec. 2013).

Board of Directors: Lois Juliber (Chair.); Phillip L. Clay (Vice-Chair.); Paul M. Ostergard (Sec.-Treas.).

Principal Staff: Pres. and CEO Reeta Roy.

Address: 2 St Clair Ave East, Suite 301, Toronto, ON M4T 2T5.

Telephone: (416) 214-2857; **Internet:** www.mastercardfdn .org; **e-mail:** info@mastercardfdn.org.

Match International Centre

Established in 1976 to promote equal rights for women worldwide, through international solidarity.

Activities: Operates in the fields of gender equality, human rights and sustainable development, working with partner groups in Africa, Asia, South America and the Caribbean to improve conditions and quality of life for women. The Centre runs campaigns and awareness training, and carries out research on eliminating violence against women in Canada and abroad. It seeks to empower women in developing countries by giving them the opportunities to improve their lives and enhance their roles, through training, community work and networking initiatives.

Geographical Area of Activity: Canada, Africa, Asia, South America and the Caribbean.

Publications: Annual Report; reports.

Finance: Annual revenue C $483,621 expenditure $529,400 (31 March 2014).

Board of Directors: Joanna Kerr (Chair.); Nancy Gordon (Vice-Chair. and Sec.); Maxine Ifill (Treas.).

Principal Staff: Exec. Dir Jess Tomlin.

Address: 310-411 Roosevelt Ave, Ottawa, ON K2A 3X9.

Telephone: (613) 238-1312; **Fax:** (613) 238-6867; **Internet:** www.matchinternational.org; **e-mail:** info@ matchinternational.org.

The Maytree Foundation

Established in 1982 by Alan Broadbent, the Chair. and CEO of Avana Capital Corporation, and his wife Judy, a social worker by training, for social welfare purposes.

Activities: Committed to the reduction of poverty and inequality in Canada and to building strong civic communities. The Foundation identifies, supports and funds ideas, leaders and organizations with the capacity to achieve change and advance the common good. It makes grants to community leaders and to community organizations to support and sustain important solution-seeking efforts for community issues and problems, and the provision of scholarships to protected persons for post-secondary pursuits. The Foundation also supports and operates learning and leadership opportunities that empower communities to solve their problems; and funds convening and collaboration opportunities to bring together people with knowledge and differing perspectives to find effective solutions.

Geographical Area of Activity: Canada, primarily large urban areas.

Restrictions: No funding for deficit reduction, equipment purchases, building or renovation costs, capital campaigns or endowments, partisan political activities, religious activities, legal challenges, conferences or workshops.

Publications: Annual policy insights; programme brochures; policy and research papers.

Finance: Annual revenue C $3,306,305, expenditure $3,677,008 (30 Nov. 2013).

Board of Directors: Alan Broadbent (Chair.); Judy Broadbent (Vice-Chair.); Colin Robertson (Treas.); Vali Bennett (Sec.).

Principal Staff: Pres. Elizabeth McIsaac.

Address: 170 Bloor St West, Suite 804, Toronto, ON M5S 1T9.

Telephone: (416) 944-2627; **Fax:** (416) 944-8915; **Internet:** www.maytree.com; **e-mail:** info@maytree.com.

Medical Women's International Association—MWIA

Established in 1919 to assist communication between female doctors worldwide, encourage women into medicine, and overcome gender-related inequalities in the medical profession.

Activities: Operates in the field of medicine, encouraging women to enter the profession and to undertake postgraduate study, through regional and international scientific meetings and congresses, collaborating with the World Health Organization and running local health and women's projects. The Association also sponsors a scholarship programme for postgraduate education, open to its members. Comprises national associations in 43 countries, and individual members in a further 45 countries.

Geographical Area of Activity: Worldwide.

Publications: *Congress Report* (every 3 years); *Training Manual on Gender Mainstreaming in Health*; *Training Manual for Adolescent Sexuality*; newsletter; annual reports.

Executives: Prof. Kyung Ah Park (Pres.); Prof. Bettina Pleiderer (Pres.-elect); Dr Gail Beck (Treas.).

Principal Staff: Sec.-Gen. Dr Shelley Ross.

Address: 7555 Morley Dr., Burnaby, BC V5E 3Y2.

Telephone: (604) 522-1960; **Fax:** (604) 522-1960; **Internet:** www.mwia.net; **e-mail:** secretariat@mwia.net.

George Cedric Metcalf Charitable Foundation

Established in 1960 by George Cedric Metcalf, former Man. Dir of George Weston Ltd and Loblaw grocery companies, for general charitable purposes.

Activities: Operates in Canada and less-developed countries in three programme areas: the performing arts, the environment and community development initiatives.

Geographical Area of Activity: International (through Canadian organizations).

Restrictions: Grants available only to registered charitable organizations in Canada; no grants to individuals or for-profit organizations.

Publications: Annual Report.

Finance: Annual revenue C $20,036,799, expenditure $6,122,084 (31 Dec. 2013).

Board of Directors: Kirsten Hanson (Chair.); Johanna Metcalf (Vice-Chair.); Peter Hanson (Treas.).

Principal Staff: Pres. and CEO (a.i.) Robert Sirman.

Address: 38 Madison Ave, Toronto, ON M5R 2S1.

Telephone: (416) 926-0366; **Fax:** (416) 926-0370; **Internet:** www.metcalffoundation.com; **e-mail:** info@metcalffoundation.com.

Molson Coors Canada Donations Fund/Fonds de Bienfaisance Molson Coors Canada

Established in 1973 to channel the charitable giving for Molson, a brewing company and beer distributor.

Activities: Operates throughout Canada. Primary areas for funding consideration are: healthy communities (food banks, hunger programmes, community hospitals); active lifestyles (arenas, baseball diamonds, soccer pitches, etc.); skills development; and United Way chapters in select Canadian communities where Molson has a presence.

Geographical Area of Activity: Canada.

Restrictions: Grants made only to registered Canadian charities.

Publications: Annual Report.

Finance: Annual revenue C $710,000, expenditure $495,106 (31 Dec. 2013).

Board of Directors: Gavin Thompson (Chair.); William Fergus Devins, Kelly Brown (Vice-Chair.).

Principal Staff: Donations Officer Tonia Coletta.

Address: 33 Carlingview Dr., Etobicoke, ON M9W 5E4.

Telephone: (416) 679-1786; **Fax:** (416) 679-1494.

Molson Foundation

Established in 1958 by T. H. P. Molson, Hartland de Montarville Molson, E. H. Molson and S. T. Molson, whose family established the Molson brewery, to support innovative projects in the fields of the humanities, education, health and welfare, and social and national development; formerly known as the Molson Family Foundation.

Activities: Operates throughout Canada in the fields of health and welfare, education, social development, national development and the humanities, through grants to charitable organizations for special projects. The Foundation funds the Molson Prize for the Arts, comprising two prizes of C $50,000 each awarded annually to distinguished Canadians, in the fields of the arts and the social sciences and humanities, and administered by the Canada Council for the Arts (q.v.) and the Social Sciences and Humanities Research Council.

Geographical Area of Activity: Canada.

Restrictions: Grants are not made for conferences, seminars, publications, fellowships or scholarships. Only registered Canadian charities are eligible.

Publications: Annual Report.

Finance: Annual revenue C $93,556,058, expenditure $5,725,408 (30 Sept. 2014).

Board of Dirs: Andrew T. Molson (Pres.); Stephen T. Molson (Vice-Pres.); Michael R. McMaster (Sec.); Dominique Paliotti (Treas.).

Address: 1555 Notre Dame St East, Montréal, QC H2L 2R5.

Telephone: (514) 590-6335; **Fax:** (514) 599-5396.

The F. K. Morrow Foundation

Established in 1944.

Activities: Works to promote religion, education and charity for public welfare. The Foundation funds projects that promote the arts and culture; offers grants in the fields of education, special education, universities, native peoples culture, film and video, to Christian and religious institutions, libraries, hospitals, for community services, special needs groups, sports and recreation; and promotes science and environmental conservation.

Geographical Area of Activity: Mainly Canada.

Finance: Annual revenue C $10,642,889, expenditure $5,852,908 (30 Sept. 2014).

Board of Dirs: Joan Breech (Pres.).

Address: 101 Thorncliffe Park Dr., Toronto, ON M4H 1M2.

Telephone: (416) 467-2638; **Fax:** (416) 429-7921.

The Muttart Foundation

Founded in 1953 by Merrill and Gladys Muttart, businesspeople and philanthropists.

Activities: Supports the development of not-for-profit organizations in Canada, through grants for infrastructure development and capacity building. The Foundation also provides grants for technological development of not-for-profit organizations, community development, fellowships, training grants and bursaries, and a grant programme for young people that makes grants to not-for-profit organizations working with young people.

Geographical Area of Activity: Canada.

Restrictions: No unsolicited applications, apart from for the Bursary Program and Training Program.

Publications: Muttart Fellowship publications; Board Development Workbooks; surveys; evaluations; reports.

Finance: Annual revenue C $1,703,247, expenditure $3,206,807 (30 Nov. 2013).

Board: Dr Jeff Bisanz (Pres.); Malcolm Burrows (Vice-Pres.); W. Laird Hunter (Treas.).

Principal Staff: Exec. Dir Bob Wyatt; Asst Exec. Dir Dr Christopher Smith.

Address: 1150 Scotia Pl., 10060 Jasper Ave, Edmonton, AB T5J 3R8.

Telephone: (780) 425-9616; **Fax:** (780) 425-0282; **Internet:** www.muttart.org; **e-mail:** lbeairsto@muttart.org.

The Neptis Foundation

Established in 1998 following the division of the assets of the Richard and Jean Ivey Fund, founded in 1947, which were shared with the Salamander Foundation (q.v.).

Activities: Informs and improves policy- and decision-making on regional urban growth and management in Canada. The Foundation carries out and publicizes research, analysis and mapping on the design and function of national urban areas. Runs the Neptis Geoweb online mapping and statistics service.

Geographical Area of Activity: Canada.

Restrictions: No unsolicited requests for financial support for research.

Publications: Reports; analysis; briefing papers; books; posters.

Finance: Annual revenue C $880,993, expenditure $790,878 (31 Oct. 2013).

Board of Directors: Martha Shuttleworth (Founder and Pres.); Lorna McKay (Treas.); Zoe Coombes (Sec.).

Principal Staff: Exec. Dir Marcy L. Burchfield.

Address: 1240 Bay St, Suite 501, Toronto, ON M5R 2A7.

Telephone: (416) 972-9199; **Fax:** (416) 972-9198; **Internet:** www.neptis.org; **e-mail:** publications@neptis.org.

North-South Institute/Institut Nord-Sud

Founded in 1976; Canada's first independent, non-profit and non-partisan research institute, focusing on international development.

Activities: Provides research and analysis on foreign policy and international development issues for policy-makers, educators, business, the media and the general public; examines the role of the public and private sectors, and of civil society in Canada's relations with developing countries; supports global efforts to increase aid effectiveness; strengthens governance and accountability; prevents conflicts; promotes equitable trade and commercial relations; improves international financial systems and institutions; and enhances gender equality.

Geographical Area of Activity: Africa, Asia and the Americas.

Publications: Annual Report; *Canadian Development Report*; briefing papers.

Finance: Annual revenue C $1,989,031 expenditure $2,300,141 (31 Dec. 2013).

Executive Committee: Bruce H. Moore (Chair.); José Antonio Ocampo (Vice-Chair.); Julia D. Stewart (Sec.).

Address: 100 Argyle Ave, Suite 200, Ottawa, ON K2P 1B6.

Telephone: (613) 241-3535; **Fax:** (613) 241-7435; **Internet:** www.nsi-ins.ca; **e-mail:** nsi@nsi-ins.ca.

Operation Eyesight Universal/Action Universelle de la Vue

Founded in 1963 to promote the prevention of blindness and the restoration of sight to people in developing countries.

Activities: Works to eliminate avoidable blindness, with a focus on India, Ghana, Kenya and Zambia. The organization works in partnership with local medical professionals and community development teams, building resources for all people, especially the poor. It focuses on high-quality, comprehensive eye care, which ensures a sustainable service for entire communities, with long-lasting results.

Geographical Area of Activity: South Asia and Sub-Saharan Africa.

Publications: Annual Report; *SightLines* (newsletter, 3 a year).

Finance: Annual revenue C $4,606,729, expenditure $3,315,266 (31 Dec. 2013).

Board of Directors: Rob Olson (Chair.); Sophia Langois (Vice-Chair.); Dan Parlow (Past Chair.).

Principal Staff: Exec. Dir Brian Foster.

Address: 4 Parkdale Cres. NW, Calgary, AB T2N 3T8.

Telephone: (403) 283-6323; **Fax:** (403) 270-1899; **Internet:** www.operationeyesight.com; **e-mail:** info@operationeyesight.com.

Oxfam Canada

Established in 1967; part of the Oxfam confederation of organizations (qq.v.).

Activities: Supports long-term development, advocacy and emergency programmes in 28 countries worldwide, with core programmes in the Americas, East and Southern Africa, and South Asia.

Geographical Area of Activity: International.

Publications: Annual Report; reports; educational materials.

Finance: Annual revenue C $23,438,684, expenditure $23,159,975 (31 March 2013).

Trustees: Margaret Hancock (Chair.); Nidhi Tandon (Vice-Chair.); Lewis Auerbach (Treas.); Gerry Barr (Sec.).

Principal Staff: Exec. Dir Julie Delahanty.

Address: 39 McArthur Ave, Ottawa, ON K1L 8L7.

Telephone: (613) 237-5236; **Internet:** www.oxfam.ca; **e-mail:** info@oxfam.ca.

Oxfam-Québec

Established in 1973; part of the Oxfam confederation of organizations (qq.v.).

Activities: Operates in the areas of literacy and education; water and sanitation; the environment; women's economic development; disaster relief; health; food security; and civil society.

Geographical Area of Activity: Benin, Bolivia, Burkina Faso, Cambodia, Congo (Dem. Repub.), Dominican Republic, Haiti, Honduras, Jordan, Lebanon, Niger, Palestinian Territories, Peru, Sudan, Viet Nam.

Publications: Annual report; reports; studies; analysis; e-newsletters; educational materials.

Finance: Annual revenue C $33,931,833, expenditure $33,902,416 (31 March 2014).

Board of Directors: Jean-Guy Saint-Martin (Chair.); Julie Charbonneau, Michel Leguerrier (Vice-Chair.); Lise Desmarais (Sec.); Donald Olds (Treas.).

Principal Staff: Exec. Dir Denise Byrnes.

Address: 2330 rue Notre-Dame Ouest, Montréal, QC H3J 2Y2.

Internet: www.oxfam.qc.ca; **e-mail:** info@oxfam.qc.ca.

Pacific Peoples' Partnership

Founded in 1975 as the South Pacific Peoples' Foundation of Canada.

Activities: Promotes rights-based sustainable development initiatives that enable communities to harness their own creativity to address poverty, environmental degradation and loss of culture. The Partnership supports the aspirations of Pacific islanders for peace, justice, environmental sustainability and development; and aims to raise the profile of the Pacific island nations and territories internationally. It provides and supports educational programmes and print and audio-visual materials on Pacific island issues; encourages links between Canadian and Pacific island organizations working in similar areas, and between indigenous peoples in Canada and the Pacific; holds conferences and training courses; and provides direct and indirect support to projects in the Pacific.

Geographical Area of Activity: Canada and the Pacific islands.

Restrictions: Grants only to specific organizations.

Publications: *Tok Blong Pasifik* (quarterly); videos.

Finance: Annual revenue C $110,594, expenditure $108,948 (30 June 2014).

Board of Directors: Dr James Boutilier (Emeritus Pres.); Muavae (Mua) Va'a (Pres.); Kat Zimmer (Vice-Pres.); Andrea Clark (Treas.); Morgan Slavkin (Sec.).

Principal Staff: Exec. Dir April Ingham.

Address: 620 View St, Suite 407, Victoria, BC V8W 1J6.

Telephone: (250) 381-4131; **Fax:** (888) 812-7346; **Internet:** www.pacificpeoplespartnership.org; **e-mail:** info@ pacificpeoplespartnership.org.

Partnership Africa Canada—PAC

Established in 1986 with support from Canadian and African NGOs and the Canadian International Development Agency.

Activities: Operates in the field of sustainable human development in Africa, in partnership with NGOs in Canada.

Geographical Area of Activity: Africa.

Restrictions: No grants available.

Publications: Annual Report; *Diamond Watchlist*; research publications; briefing notes; programme publications; technical documents; manuals; legal texts; partner organizations' publications.

Finance: Annual revenue C $1,362,063, expenditure $1,367,755 (31 March 2013).

Board of Directors: Flora MacDonald (Hon. Pres.); Susan Côté-Freeman (Pres.); Baudouin Hamuli Kabarhuza (Vice-Pres.); Alex Neve (Treas.).

Principal Staff: Exec. Dir Bernard Taylor.

Address: 331 Cooper St, Suite 600, Ottawa, ON K2P 0G5.

Telephone: (613) 237-6768; **Fax:** (613) 237-6530; **Internet:** www.pacweb.org; **e-mail:** info@pacweb.org.

Presbyterian World Service and Development

Established in 1947; the development and relief agency of the Presbyterian Church in Canada.

Activities: Works to make positive changes in the world through partnerships supporting those affected by poverty, injustice, disease and disaster in Central America, Africa and Asia. Programmes focus on empowering communities to address poverty by providing nutrition through focusing on food security, health, livelihoods and agriculture training for farmers; literacy training human rights programming; refugee sponsorship and small business initiatives for women; education for vulnerable children; care and support for people living with and affected by HIV and AIDS; and clean-water wells and sanitation training for communities. The organization assists in overcoming natural disasters and emergencies through emergency relief efforts that meet physical and emotional needs, and helps refugees to Canada. It also works to educate and promote awareness of development issues within Canada.

Geographical Area of Activity: International.

Publications: PWSDevelopments (quarterly newsletter); PWS&D E-News (monthly e-newsletter); Annual Report.

Executive Committee: Lara Scholey (Convener).

Address: 50 Wynford Dr., Toronto, ON M3C 1J7.

Telephone: (416) 441-1111; **Fax:** (416) 441-2825; **Internet:** www .WeRespond.ca; **e-mail:** pwsd@presbyterian.ca.

Primate's World Relief and Development Fund

Established in 1959 by the General Synod of the Anglican Church of Canada as the official relief and development agency of the Anglican Church of Canada.

Activities: Committed to international development work. The Fund operates in the fields of justice, human rights and political advocacy (non-partisan), as well as community development and education. It helps local partners in developing countries to provide long-term solutions to the causes of suffering and disaster. It also provides emergency relief to victims of crisis, and to protect refugees. A percentage of funds is reserved for work with Canada's indigenous population for land claims, self-determination and aboriginal rights.

Geographical Area of Activity: International.

Publications: Annual Report; *Under the Sun* (three times a year).

Finance: Total revenue C $7,328,871, expenditure $7,402,306 (31 March 2013).

Board of Directors: Archbishop Fred Hiltz (Pres.); Maureen Lawrence (Vice-Pres.); Rev. Laura Marie Piotrowicz (Sec.); Dan Waterston (Treas.).

Principal Staff: Exec. Dir Adele Finney.

Address: 80 Hayden St, Toronto, ON M4Y 3G2.

Telephone: (416) 924-9192; **Fax:** (416) 924-3483; **Internet:** www.pwrdf.org; **e-mail:** pwrdf@pwrdf.org.

RBC Foundation

Established in 1993 by the Royal Bank of Canada for general charitable purposes. Formerly known as the Royal Bank of Canada Charitable Foundation.

Activities: Operates throughout Canada in the fields of education, health, arts and culture, social services and civic activities, through grants to organizations for programmes, projects, awards, fellowships and scholarships, operating funds, etc. RBC Financial Group is committed to contributing at least 1% of net income before tax.

Geographical Area of Activity: Canada.

Restrictions: Grants are not made for conferences or seminars, nor to individuals.

Publications: *Corporate Social Responsibility Report*.

Finance: Annual revenue C $59,862,486, expenditure $53,006,216 (31 Oct. 2013).

Board of Directors: Zabeen Hinji (Chair.).

Principal Staff: Exec. Dir Shari Austin.

Address: Royal Bank Plaza, South Tower, 9th Floor, Toronto, ON M5J 2J5.

Telephone: (416) 974-3113; **Fax:** (416) 974-0624; **Internet:** www.rbc.com/donations; **e-mail:** donations@rbc.com.

Richelieu International

Founded in 1944 by Horace Viau to promote the social and cultural needs of the francophone population of Canada. The Richelieu International Foundation was created in 1977.

Activities: Operates in the French-speaking regions of the world in the fields of the arts and humanities, education, and medicine and health, through self-conducted programmes, grants to individuals and institutions, scholarships and fellowships, and prizes.

Geographical Area of Activity: French-speaking communities in North America, Europe, Africa and the Caribbean.

Publications: *Le P'tit Bulletin* (online newsletter); and downloadable reports and information leaflets.

Finance: Annual revenue C $157,256, expenditure $71,592 (31 Dec. 2013).

Board of Directors: Patrice Forget (Chair.); Alain Breton (Vice-Chair.); Michelle Perreault (Treas.).

Principal Staff: International Pres. Claude Poirier.

Address: 1010 rue Polytek, Unité 25, Ottawa, ON K1J 9J1.

Telephone: (613) 742-6911; **Fax:** (613) 742-6916; **Internet:** www.richelieu.org/fondation; **e-mail:** international@ richelieu.org.

Rooftops Canada Foundation

Established in 1984 to support community housing projects in developing countries.

Activities: Provides technical assistance to community-based and co-operative housing organizations in less-developed countries; training and capacity building for NGOs; conducts educational programmes; and maintains a library.

Geographical Area of Activity: Africa, Asia, Central and South America, the Caribbean and Eastern Europe.

Restrictions: Grants only to community-based housing organizations.

Publications: *Program Report* (annually).

Finance: Annual revenue C $1,388,075, expenditure $1,396,262 (31 March 2014).

Board: Jo Ferris-Davies (Pres.); Céline Carrière (Vice-Pres.); Scott Jackson (Sec./Treas.).

Principal Staff: Exec. Dir Barry Pinsky.

Address: 720 Spadina Ave, Suite 313, Toronto, ON M5S 2T9.

Telephone: (416) 366-1445; **Fax:** (416) 366-3876; **Internet:** www.rooftops.ca; **e-mail:** info@rooftops.ca.

Salamander Foundation

Established in 1998 following the division of the assets of the Richard and Jean Ivey Fund (f. 1947), which were shared with the Neptis Foundation (q.v.).

Activities: Makes grants to Canadian registered charities within the fields of arts and culture and the environment, with particular emphasis on resource management, pollution, environmental degradation and their impacts on ecosystems and human health.

Geographical Area of Activity: Great Lakes–St Lawrence River Basins, east to the Atlantic. Regional issues in the Yukon, Northwest Territories and Nunavut.

Restrictions: No grants for annual appeals, capital campaigns, conferences or seminars, deficit financing, emergency funds, festivals, seed funding, bursaries, scholarships, individuals, sponsorship, public education or film projects.

Finance: Annual revenue C $1,514,849, expenditure $508,391 (31 Oct. 2013).

Board of Directors: Nan Shuttleworth (Pres.); Paul O. Gratias (Sec. Treas.).

Address: 180 Bloor St W, Suite 1201, Toronto, ON M5S 2V6.

Telephone: (416) 972-9200; **Fax:** (416) 972-9203; **Internet:** www.salamanderfoundation.org; **e-mail:** info@salamanderfoundation.org.

Shastri Indo-Canadian Institute

Founded in 1968 by the Governments of Canada and India to enhance mutual understanding between the two countries through academic activities and exchanges.

Activities: Operates internationally in the fields of development studies, the humanities and social sciences, management and law. The Institute offers fellowships for research and study, and language training in India, to junior and senior scholars in Canada. Its Library Programme acquires Indian documents and publications for scholarly use in Canada, and Canadian publications are presented to Indian institutions. The Institute also organizes international academic conferences; runs an educational resources programme for Canadian schools and a summer programme, when funding is available; co-ordinates a visiting lecturer programme for Canadian universities; and supports the growth of Canadian studies at Indian universities and of development studies at Canadian universities. Members of the Institute include 35 Canadian universities and 54 Indian universities.

Geographical Area of Activity: South Asia and Canada.

Restrictions: Grants only for Canadians or landed immigrants to go to India, or for Indians from India to go to Canada.

Publications: *Shastri News* (newsletter).

Finance: Annual revenue C $669,674, expenditure $717,311 (31 March 2014).

Executive Council: Dr Biju Abraham (Pres.); Dr Girish M. Shah (Vice-Pres.).

Principal Staff: Contact Mahmuda Aldeen.

Address: 1418 Education Tower, 2500 University Dr. NW, Calgary, AB T2N 1N4.

Telephone: (403) 220-3220; **Fax:** (403) 289-0100; **Internet:** www.sici.org; **e-mail:** sici@ucalgary.ca.

SickKids Foundation

Founded in 1972 by Duncan L. Gordon and John T. Law and others to provide funds for research, special programmes and public health education at the Hospital for Sick Children, Toronto, and throughout Canada.

Activities: Organizes educational and research programmes in two main areas: developing research skills, and knowledge generation and community action. The Foundation provides grants to Canadian institutions and individuals; awards fellowships and scholarships (including the Duncan L. Gordon Fellowships for postdoctoral study in child health, and the Visiting Scientists and Foreign Research Fellowship Program for researchers from Canada and abroad); and through its National Grants Program funds research, conferences, scholarships and fellowships nationally. It also runs a grants programme in youth and child home care and maintains a Research Institute .

Geographical Area of Activity: Canada.

Publications: Annual Report; *Planning for Kids* (newsletter, 2 a year).

Finance: Annual revenue C $2,419,130 , annual expenditure $2,983,342 (31 March 2014).

Board of Trustees: Kathleen Taylor (Chair.); Sonia A. Baxendale (Vice-Chair. and Treas.).

Principal Staff: Pres. and CEO Ted Garrard.

Address: The Hospital for Sick Children, 525 University Ave, Toronto, ON M5G 2L3.

Telephone: (416) 813-1500; **Fax:** (416) 813-5024; **Internet:** www.sickkidsfoundation.com; **e-mail:** public.affairs@sickkidsfoundation.com.

Steelworkers Humanity Fund

Established in 1985 by the United Steelworkers of America, a labour-based NGO, to support development, relief and social justice issues, nationally and internationally.

Activities: Four broad main areas of interest: project support, education, exchange, and policy and advocacy. The Fund is involved in social and development issues in Canada, setting up health clinics, credit unions, day-care centres and housing co-operatives for its members and others in the community. It works internationally in the fields of workers' rights, food self-sufficiency, structural adjustment and North-South relations, as well as providing emergency relief. An active member of NGO coalitions with policy and advocacy objectives worldwide.

Geographical Area of Activity: Africa, Central and South America and Canada.

Publications: *Global Solidarity Humanity Fund Bulletin*; *Our Union and the Environment*; *'The Global Class War'*; *Current Contract Summaries*; *Building Power*; *Steel Resource Publications*; *Securing Our Children's World*; *USW@Work*; *Contract Summaries*; *Archived Publications*; policy papers and fact sheets; newletter.

Finance: Annual revenue C $1,498,162, expenditure $1,556,013 (31 Dec. 2013).

Board of Directors: Ken G. Neumann (Pres.); Carolyn Egan (Vice-Pres.); Rob Healey (Sec.).

Address: 234 Eglinton Ave East, 8th Floor, Toronto, ON M4P 1K7.

Telephone: (416) 487-1571; **Fax:** (416) 482-5548; **Internet:** www.usw.ca/union/humanity; **e-mail:** humanityfund@usw.ca.

Joseph Tanenbaum Charitable Foundation

Established in 1967 by industrialist and philanthropist Joseph Tanenbaum for general charitable purposes.

Activities: Operates in the fields of aid to less-developed countries, the arts and humanities, education, health and welfare, and social welfare. The Foundation makes grants to organizations involved in the areas of education (including international education and community colleges), disabled children, international relief (including medical services), Jewish social services and medical research.

Geographical Area of Activity: International.

Restrictions: Grants are given primarily to Jewish organizations.

Finance: Annual revenue C $168,443, expenditure $0 (31 Jan. 2014).

Board of Directors: John Kaplan (Pres.).

Address: 1051 Tapscott Rd, Scarborough, ON M1X 1A1.

Telephone: (416) 298-0066; **Fax:** (416) 299-8008.

Terre Sans Frontières—TSF

Established in 1980 as Prodeva FIC by the Brothers of Christian Instruction; became Prodeva Tiers-Monde in 1986 and known as Terre Sans Frontières since 1994.

Activities: Operates in the field of sustainable development and self-sufficiency; works in partnership with associated organizations to conduct programmes for individuals in developing countries, especially in Africa, Haiti and Honduras. The organization provides grants and micro-credit to institutions, and also provides skilled volunteers. It also raises awareness among Canadians of development issues.

Geographical Area of Activity: Africa, Central America and the Caribbean.

Publications: Annual Report; newsletter.

Finance: Annual revenue C $7,343,288, expenditure $7,516,974 (31 March 2013).

Board of Trustees: Linda Bambonye (Pres.); Denis Majeau (Vice-Pres.); Judith Shumko (Sec.); Martine Gaudreault (Treas.).

Principal Staff: CEO Jean L. Fortin.

Address: 399 rue des Conseillers, Office 23, La Prairie, QC J5R 4H6.

Telephone: (450) 659-7717; **Fax:** (450) 659-2276; **Internet:** www.terresansfrontieres.ca; **e-mail:** tsf@terresansfrontieres.ca.

USC Canada

Established in 1945 as the Unitarian Service Committe by Dr Lotta Hirschmanova, a Czech refugee; an international development organization.

Activities: Operates in collaboration with local organizations in developing countries in the fields of water, health, income generation, training and education, savings and credit, the environment and food security. The organization's main programme is Seeds of Survival, a sustainable agriculture initiative that works to provide a long-term solution to hunger through the preservation, use and enhancement of farmers' indigenous seeds and traditional practices. The organization also works nationally in outreach and community projects, and education to improve awareness of global issues; and in 2013 launched the Bauta Family Initiative on Canadian Seed Security in partnership with Seeds of Diversity Canada. Maintains Seedmap.org, an online resource about seeds, biodiversity and food production. Has offices in Bangladesh, Nepal, Timor-Leste and Mali.

Geographical Area of Activity: Bangladesh, Bolivia, Burkina Faso, Canada, Cuba, Ethiopia, Honduras, Mali, Nepal, Senegal, Timor-Leste.

Publications: Annual Report; Newsletter; *Jottings*; educational materials.

Finance: Annual revenue C $5,293,760, expenditure $5,287,319 (30 April 2014).

Board of Directors: Kenton Lobe (Chair.); Abra Brynne, Dr Harriet Friedmann (Co-Vice-Chair.); Robert C. Kamp (Treas.); Troy Mitchell (Sec.).

Principal Staff: Exec. Dir Susan Walsh.

Address: 56 Sparks St, Suite 705, Ottawa, ON K1P 5B1.

Telephone: (613) 234-6827; **Fax:** (613) 234-6842; **Internet:** www.usc-canada.org; www.seedsecurity.ca; seedmap.org; **e-mail:** info@usc-canada.org.

Vancouver Foundation

Founded in 1943.

Activities: Canada's largest community foundation, which aims to make a lasting impact on communities in British Columbia through philanthropy and grants.

Geographical Area of Activity: Mainly British Columbia, Canada.

Publications: Annual Report; *Vancouver Foundation Magazine*; *Vital Signs*; surveys.

Finance: Annual revenue C $123,581,000, expenditure $12,967,000 (31 Dec. 2014).

Board of Directors: Gordon MacDougall (Chair.); Jason McLean (Vice-Chair.).

Principal Staff: Pres. and CEO Kevin McCort.

Address: 475 West Georgia St, Suite 200, Vancouver, BC V6B 4M9.

Telephone: (604) 688-2204; **Fax:** (604) 688-4170; **Internet:** www.vancouverfoundation.bc.ca; **e-mail:** info@vancouverfoundation.ca.

R. Howard Webster Foundation

Established in 1967 by investor R. Howard Webster to make grants to hospitals, universities and for general charitable purposes.

Activities: Operates throughout Canada in the fields of the arts and humanities, education, medicine and health, and social welfare, funding scholarships and fellowships.

Geographical Area of Activity: Canada.

Finance: Annual revenue C $9,495,314, expenditure $7,027,605 (31 Dec. 2013).

Board of Directors: Peter W. Webster (Chair.); Norman Webster (Vice-Chair.); Susan Lecouffe (Sec.-Treas.).

Principal Staff: Pres. Howard W. Davidson.

Address: 1155 René-Lévesque blvd ouest, Suite 2912, Montréal, QC H3B 2L5.

Telephone: (514) 866-2424; **Fax:** (514) 866-9918; **Internet:** www.rhowardwebsterfoundation.ca; **e-mail:** info@rhwfdn.ca.

World Accord

Established in 1980 to provide development assistance in less-developed countries.

Activities: Works in less-developed countries of Asia and Central America, in collaboration with partners in Canada and overseas, to improve the quality of life of individuals and communities in the developing world in the long term. The organization builds local institutional and human capacities and encourages participation in civil society. It funds educational self-help programmes to create a better future for disadvantaged people, and runs development education projects in Canada.

Geographical Area of Activity: Central America, Asia and Canada.

Publications: *Global Voice* (newsletter); Annual Report.

Finance: Annual revenue C $767,000, expenditure $737,447 (31 March 2014).

Board of Directors: Rosilyn Coulsoun-Teng (Pres.); Mary D. Pearson (Treas.).

Principal Staff: Exec. Dir David Barth.

Address: 1c 185 Frobisher Dr., Waterloo, ON N2V 2E6.

Telephone: (519) 747-2215; **Fax:** (519) 747-2644; **Internet:** www.worldaccord.org; **e-mail:** dbarth@worldaccord.org.

World Literacy of Canada—WLC

Founded in 1955 as a non-profit charitable organization.

Activities: Promotes adult literacy in Canada and abroad, raises public awareness, and funds community literacy development programmes in Southern Asia. The WLC operates internationally, aiming to improve general adult literacy worldwide and to improve social, cultural and economic conditions. In Canada, it has initiated presentations, forums and national tours; supported the formation of the Movement for Canadian Literacy; and provided resources for schools and literacy groups on effective and innovative strategies. Overseas, the WLC provides financial support for literacy programmes that integrate health, housing, vocational training, and credit and savings programmes; offers funding for teacher training, educational supplies and development of literary resources; and also arranges a variety of capacity-building programmes for human resource development at grassroots level. Has a particular focus on the literacy needs of poor women. Also maintains an office in India.

Geographical Area of Activity: Southern Asia and Canada.

Publications: WLC Engagement calender; *Askshar* (annual magazine); *The Kama Cookbook*; *Storytelling Soup*.

Finance: Annual revenue C $398,032, expenditure $491,475 (31 March 2014).

Board of Directors: Ken Setterington (Chair.); Virginia Bosomworth (Vice.-Chair.); Raluca Dobre (Sec.); Donna Inch (Treas.).

Principal Staff: Exec. Dir Jasmine Gill.

Address: 401 Richmond St West, Studio 236, Toronto, ON M5V 3A8.

Telephone: (416) 977-0008; **Fax:** (416) 977-1112; **Internet:** www.worldlit.ca; **e-mail:** info@worldlit.ca.

World University Service of Canada/Entraide Universitaire Mondiale du Canada

Founded in 1939 to involve Canadians in national and international social and academic development.

Activities: Operates nationally in development studies and education, and internationally in the fields of aid to less-developed countries, conservation, education, medicine, and science and technology, through self-conducted programmes, annual seminars and publications.

Geographical Area of Activity: International.

Publications: Annual Report; E-*Communiqué* (2 a year); *Fifty Years of Seminars*; general brochure; videos; fact sheets; project-related documents.

Finance: Annual revenue C $34,569,308, expenditure $33,872,453 (31 March 2014).

Board of Directors: Dr David Turpin (Chair.); Dr Don Wright (Vice-Chair.); Dr Amit Chakma (Past Chair.).

Principal Staff: Exec. Dir Chris Eaton.

Address: 1404 Scott St, Ottawa, ON K1Y 4M8.

Telephone: (613) 798-7477; **Fax:** (613) 798-0990; **Internet:** www.wusc.ca; **e-mail:** wusc@wusc.ca.

Chile

FOUNDATIONS, TRUSTS AND NON-PROFIT ORGANIZATIONS

Ciudad Viva

Established in 2000 by a group of 25 community-based organizations.

Activities: Promotes democratic, participatory and transparent urban planning; equity through improved public transport; recycling and 'green living'; cultural diversity and 'intangible heritage'. Carries out research and citizen mapping initiatives; maintains a community library with a focus on urbanism, sustainability, heritage, ecology, transportation and citizen participation; and hosts meetings and workshops.

Geographical Area of Activity: Chile.

Publications: *La Voz de la Chimba* (1–2 a year).

Board of Directors: Maria Elena Ducci (Pres.); Loreto Rojas (Vice-Pres.); Rodrigo Quijada (Sec.); Sofia Lopez (Treas.).

Principal Staff: Exec. Dir Magdalena Morel.

Address: Centro de Urbanismo Ciudadano, Dominica 14, al pie del Cerro San Cristóbal por Pío Nono, en pleno Barrio Bellavista, Santiago.

Internet: www.ciudadviva.cl; **e-mail:** info@ciudadviva.cl.

Educación 2020

Established in 2008 to promote quality and equality in education in Chile.

Activities: Works in three areas: education policy, active citizenship and the Center for Educational Leadership.

Geographical Area of Activity: Chile.

Finance: Annual income US $28,228,000, expenditure $5,881,000 (31 Dec. 2013).

Board of Directors: Mario Waissbluth (Chair.); Celia Alvariño (Vice-Chair.).

Principal Staff: Exec. Dir Mirentxu Anaya; Deputy Dir Patricia Schaulsohn.

Address: República 580, Santiago.

Telephone: (9) 9-513-545-99; **Internet:** www.educacion2020.cl; **e-mail:** contacto@educacion2020.cl.

Fundación Chile (Chile Foundation)

Established in 1976 by the Chilean Government and ITT Corporation of the USA.

Activities: Supports scientific and technological research and development, and the application of the scientific and technological advances made in the production and service areas. Aims to contribute to innovation and the use of technology to develop the Chilean economy, through support for projects in the fields of education, human capital, the environment, small business development, agribusiness, forestry and marine resources.

Geographical Area of Activity: Chile.

Restrictions: No grants to individuals.

Publications: *Lignum*; *Aqua* (trade magazines); monographs.

Finance: Total assets 40,022,917 pesos (31 Dec. 2013).

Board of Directors: Patricio Meller (Chair.).

Principal Staff: Gen. Man. Marcos Kulka Kuperman.

Address: Avda Parque Antonio Rabat Sur 6165, Vitacura, Santiago.

Telephone: (2) 222-400-300; **Fax:** (2) 242-6900; **Internet:** www.fundacionchile.com; **e-mail:** info@fundacionchile.cl.

Fundación para el Desarrollo Regional de Aysén (Regional Development Foundation of Aysén)

Established in 1976.

Activities: Aims to support integrated development activities for people with few resources in the Aysén region of Chile.

Geographical Area of Activity: Primarily the Aysén region of Chile.

Finance: Annual grants approx. US $500,000.

Board of Directors: Porfirio Alberto Díaz Reyes (Pres.); Francisco Cárcamo Uribe (Sec.).

Address: Pedro Dussen 360, Casilla 340, Coyhaique, XI Región de Aysén.

Telephone: (67) 23-11-27; **Fax:** (67) 23-20-50; **e-mail:** funda.aysen@gmail.com.

Fundación Educacional Súmate (Súmate Educational Foundation)

Founded in 1989 as Fundación Padre Álvaro Lavín to reintegrate excluded children and young people into the education system. Present name adopted in 2008.

Activities: Operates in the fields of education and employment.

Geographical Area of Activity: Chile.

Finance: Annual income 1,604,360,647 pesos, expenditure 1,667,916,093 pesos (2011).

Board of Directors: Emilio Sierpe Pavez (Chair.).

Principal Staff: Exec. Dir Liliana Cortés.

Address: Arica 3829, Estación Central, Santiago.

Telephone: (2) 779-7709; **Internet:** www.sumate.cl.

Fundación Invica (Invica Foundation)

Founded in 1959 to promote co-operation among housing projects; founded the Cooperativa Abierta de Vivienda—PROVICOOP in 1977 to operate in the area of housing.

Activities: Works in the fields of urban planning, housing finance, development assistance, co-operatives and community development; sponsors exhibitions; conducts research programmes and training courses; and operates a database.

Geographical Area of Activity: Chile.

Publications: *Boletín Construyendo*.

Board of Directors: Diego Vidal Sánchez (Pres.); Nicolas Parot Boragk (Vice-Pres.); Manuel Castillo Lea-Plaza (Sec.).

Principal Staff: Dir-Gen. Felipe Arteaga Manieu.

Address: Cienfuegos 67, Clasificador 900, Santiago.

Telephone: (2) 690-0400; **Fax:** (2) 696-7822; **Internet:** www.invica.cl; **e-mail:** casapropia@invica.cl.

Fundación Pablo Neruda (Pablo Neruda Foundation)

Established in 1986 to promote and cultivate the arts; named after the Chilean poet Pablo Neruda.

Activities: Operates in the fields of education and culture, offering scholarships and fellowships, awarding prizes, organizing conferences and cultural activities, and issuing publications. The Foundation maintains the Neruda library and archives in the Casa Museo La Chascona, incl. 5,000 vols from Neruda's personal collection. In 1987, it established the annual Pablo Neruda Award for poets aged under 40 years. In 2013, jointly with the Andrés Bello Archive at the Universidad de Chile, the Foundation created the Neruda Chair (Cátedra Neruda) to disseminate Neruda's work.

Geographical Area of Activity: Chile.

Publications: *Federico García Lorca*; *Neruda's Objects*; *Pablo Neruda's Houses*; *At the Table with Neruda*; *My Friend Pablo*; *Cuadernos*; *Nerudiana*; *Cuaderno*.

Board of Directors: Juan Agustín Figueroa Yávar (Pres.); Raúl Bulnes Calderón (Vice-Pres.).

Principal Staff: Exec. Dir Fernando Sáez García.

Address: Fernando Márquez de la Plata 0192, POB 6640152, Santiago.

Telephone: (2) 777-8741; **Fax:** (2) 737-8712; **Internet:** www .fundacionneruda.org; **e-mail:** info@fundacionneruda.org.

Red de Acción en Plaguicidas y sus Alternativas de América Latina—RAP-AL

Founded in 1983; sub-regional centre for the PAN International network.

Activities: Aims to reduce and eliminate the use of harmful pesticides, and promotes sustainable agriculture. The organization raises awareness about the effects of pesticide use in rural and urban areas; educates civil society about the impacts of conventional agriculture on health and the environment; carries out political and legal action to eradicate pesticides and use alternatives; publicizes the dangers of pesticides on health and the environment; and promotes research and studies on the impacts of pesticides on health and the environment.

Geographical Area of Activity: Central and South America.

Publications: Spanish translations of PAN publications.

Principal Staff: Co-ordinator María Elena Rozas.

Address: Alonso de Ovalle 1618, Oficina A, Santiago.

Telephone: (2) 699-7375; **Internet:** www.rap-al.org; **e-mail:** rap-al@terra.cl.

Red de Salud de las Mujeres Latinoamericanas y del Caribe (Latin American and Caribbean Women's Health Network—LACWHN)

Established in 1984, during the first Regional Women and Health meeting in Colombia, to promote women's health, women's civil and human rights, and women's citizenship through the cultural, political and social transformation of Central and South America and the Caribbean region.

Activities: Operates in Central and South America and the Caribbean, through linking regional organizations that work in the area of women's health to provide common objectives and strategies. Promotes health and rights for women of all ages throughout Central and South America and the Caribbean, particularly focusing on sexual and reproductive health rights. Incorporates human resource training, strengthens regional co-ordination among organizations and individuals working in this area, supports and organizes regional and international events, and runs international campaigns focused on priority issues in women's health. Also acts as an information network through its publications.

Geographical Area of Activity: Central and South America and the Caribbean.

Publications: *Boletín Especial*; Women's Health Journal (magazine, quarterly); *Women's Health Collection* (annually).

Principal Staff: Gen. Co-ordinator Sandra Castañeda Martínez.

Address: CP 6850892, Casilla 50610, Santiago 1, Santiago; Simón Bolívar 3798, Comuna de Nuñoa, Santiago.

Telephone: (2) 223-7077; **Fax:** (2) 223-1066; **Internet:** rsmlac .blogspot.co.uk; **e-mail:** comunicaciones@reddesalud.org.

The People's Republic of China

FOUNDATION CENTRES AND CO-ORDINATING BODIES

China Foundation Center

Established in 2010 to support foundations in China.

Activities: Provides information about foundations in China; maintains an online foundation database and an archive of information on China's foundation sector.

Geographical Area of Activity: People's Republic of China.

Board of Trustees: Yongguang Xu (Chair.).

Principal Staff: Exec. Pres. Gang Cheng; Exec. Vice-Pres. Ze Tao.

Address: Rm 216, Bldg A, Kelin Plaza, 107 Dongsi North Ave, Dongcheng District, Beijing 100007.

Telephone: (10) 65691231; **Fax:** (10) 65691231-612; **Internet:** www.foundationcenter.org.cn; **e-mail:** taoze@foundationcenter.org.cn.

NPI Initiative

Established in 2006; merged with China NPO Network in 2008. Formerly know as the Non-Profit Incubator.

Activities: Aims to advance the development of not-for-profit organizations in China, providing information and resources and acting as an information co-ordinator. Supports NGO capacity building, provides training in accountability, develops networks, carries out research, and issues publications.

Geographical Area of Activity: People's Republic of China.

Board of Directors: Yusheng Shang (Chair.).

Principal Staff: Founder and Dir Zhao Lv.

Address: 2F, Bldg A, No. 613, Eshan Rd, Pudong District, Shanghai 200127.

Telephone: (21) 51879851; **Fax:** (21) 58896986; **Internet:** www.npi.org.cn; **e-mail:** infosh@npi.org.cn.

FOUNDATIONS, TRUSTS AND NON-PROFIT ORGANIZATIONS

China Environmental Protection Foundation

Established in 1993 by Qu Geping to serve the cause of environmental conservation.

Activities: Operates in the area of conservation and the environment. Encourages the development of eco-friendly manufacturing by aiding in the development of eco-friendly products. Supports training, research, academic exchange and education in the field of environmental protection. Also sponsors eco-friendly businesses, organizations and individuals; issues publications; and implements environmental conservation projects.

Geographical Area of Activity: People's Republic of China.

Publications: Financial audit reports.

Finance: Total assets 139,590,000 yuan, annual income 54,420,000 yuan (2013).

Board of Directors: Qu Geping (Pres.); Wang Jirong, Xie Qihua, Wang Tao (Vice-Pres).

Principal Staff: Sec.-Gen. Li Wei; Deputy Sec.-Gen. Xu Gang.

Address: Environment Bldg, Rm 704, No. 16 Guang Qu Men Nei St, Chongwen District, Beijing 100062.

Telephone: (10) 67130419; **Fax:** (10) 67118190; **Internet:** www.cepf.org.cn; **e-mail:** pr@cepf.org.cn.

China Foundation for Poverty Alleviation—CFPA

Established in 1989 to help disadvantaged people improve their production conditions, upgrade their quality of life and promote sustainable development.

Activities: Programmes include the New Great Wall Project to support university students in need; the Maternal and Infant Health Project to help poor mothers and children and lower the maternal and infant death rate; the Microfinance Project, which has provided loans amounting to approx. 300m. yuan to more than 130,000 poor households since 1996; Project Angel to train hospital administrators and improve medical treatment and services; the Disaster Relief Project; the Integrated Project to improve infrastructure and quality of life in poor communities; Interaction for Poverty Alleviation and the Publicity Fund for Poverty Alleviation, to narrow the gap between rich and poor; and the China Poverty Eradication Awards.

Geographical Area of Activity: People's Republic of China.

Publications: Annual report.

Finance: Annual income 24,884,392 yuan, expenditure 41,770,350 yuan (Nov. 2013).

Board of Dirs: Duan Yingbi (Chair.); Daofeng Chen (Vice.-Chair.).

Principal Staff: Sec.-Gen. Liu Wenkui.

Address: South Bldg, 4th and 5th Floors, 36 Shuangyushu Xili, West Alley, Haidian District, Beijing 100086.

Telephone: (10) 82872688; **Fax:** (10) 62526268; **Internet:** www.fupin.org.cn; **e-mail:** fupin@fupin.org.cn.

China Soong Ching Ling Foundation (Children's Foundation of China)

Founded in 1982 as the Soong Ching Ling Foundation in memory of Soong Ching Ling (Madame Sun Yat-sen, 1893–1981), former Chinese Hon. Chair., to support the welfare, education and cultural advancement of Chinese children, and to promote international friendship and world peace. Present name adopted in 2005.

Activities: Operates in the areas of children's education, culture and welfare. Helped to set up and administer programmes with private sector partners to provide: financial assistance to college and university students; student scholarships; teacher training; libraries; the Soong Ching Ling Paediatrics Award for scientific achievement in paediatric medicine; maternal and infant health care and training; and disaster relief, schools reconstruction and child counselling following an earthquake in Sichuan province in 2008. Established a Children's Science and Technology Pavilion which provides activities for children; the Tianjin Bohai Children's World, an education and recreation centre; and the Huayin Music School. Sponsored the Red Apple Child Development Center in 2000, and promotes children's sports and exchanges. It awards various prizes, including a literary prize, given biennially, for children's literature in China, and the Children's Invention Prize; and sponsors an electric organ competition. Works in co-operation with the UN Children's Fund (UNICEF). Sister foundations have been established in Canada, Japan and the USA.

Geographical Area of Activity: People's Republic of China.

Publications: Books for children on a variety of subjects and documents about the life of Soong Ching Ling.

Finance: Total assets 323,138,196 yuan, annual income 196,348,145 yuan (2012).

Executive Council: Hu Qili (Chair.).

Principal Staff: Sec.-Gen. Li Ning; Deputy Secs-Gen. Li Xihui, Qiao Jian.

Address: A12/F Zhejiang Plaza, No. 26 Anzhen Xili, Chaoyang District, Beijing 100029.

Telephone: (10) 64450781; **Fax:** (10) 64450056; **Internet:** www .sclf.org; **e-mail:** csclf@sclf.org.

China Youth Development Foundation

Established in 1989 by the All-China Youth Federation.

Activities: Enlists the support of organizations in China and abroad to engage in development work with Chinese young people and children. Promotes the work, education, culture and social welfare of Chinese youth through projects and awarding prizes to outstanding young people; seeks to enhance relations between young people around the world with a view to safeguarding world peace. Main focus is Project Hope, a programme providing underprivileged children with improved educational opportunities, and financial aid to help children who do not attend school return to education. The programme funds the construction of Hope Schools in remote rural areas, with more than 8,890 schools built to date. Has established a Stars of Hope Award Fund to support Project Hope students in further studies and a Hope Primary School Teacher-Training Fund to allow teachers to sharpen their skills and expand their knowledge. Also operates a river and wetland protection programme. Conducts joint programmes with the company Nokia.

Geographical Area of Activity: People's Republic of China.

Publications: Annual Report; *Hope Journal*; *News of CYDF*; *The Project Hope Public Announcement* (annually).

Finance: Total assets 913,590,000 yuan, annual income 484,940,000 yuan (2013).

Board of Directors: He Junke (Chair.); Gu Xiaojin, Kang Xiaoguang (Vice-Chair.).

Principal Staff: Vice-Chair. and Sec.-Gen. Tu Meng.

Address: 51 Wangjing West Rd, Chaoyang District, Beijing 100102.

Telephone: (10) 64035547; **Fax:** (10) 64790600; **Internet:** www .cydf.org.cn; **e-mail:** info@cydf.org.cn.

Heren Philanthropic Foundation

Established in 2011 by Cao Dewang, Chair. and CEO of Fuyao Glass Industry Group Co Ltd.

Activities: Programmes include expanding access to education and medical services for vulnerable people; supporting infrastructure development and environmental protection; emergency disaster relief, and post-disaster recovery and reconstruction; social welfare and capacity building.

Geographical Area of Activity: People's Republic of China.

Finance: Initial funding: 3,550m. yuan.

Principal Staff: Chair. Cao Dewang; Vice-Chair. Cheng-Tiesheng; Sec.-Gen. Jenlin Ruihua.

Address: Fujian Fuyao Industrial Park II, Fuqing City 350301.

Telephone: (10) 82092066; **Fax:** (10) 82092066-808; **Internet:** www.hcf.org.cn; **e-mail:** heren@vip.163.com.

Jiangsu Yuanlin Charity Foundation

Established in 2012 by Ren Yuanlin, Pres. of Yangzijiang Shipbuilding Group.

Activities: Programmes focus on the health, welfare and tertiary education of the elderly. In 2012, the Foundation announced plans to build 8–10 universities for the elderly and 1–2 convalescence centres.

Geographical Area of Activity: People's Republic of China.

Finance: Initial funding 256.6m. yuan.

Principal Staff: Chair. Liu Jianguo; Pres. Lu Jiangping.

Address: 10 Jiyang Rd, Jiangyin City, Jiangsu Province, Wuxi City.

Telephone: (510) 86812600; **Fax:** (510) 86810300.

Minsheng Culture and Arts Foundation

Established in 2007 by China Minsheng Bank.

Activities: Organizes research and exchange programmes, and public events; provides training in arts and culture funding; linked with Minsheng Art Fund, which makes awards for contributions to Chinese contemporary art; Yuanhang Art Museum (f. 1991); Shanghai 21st Century Minsheng Art Museum (f. 2010); and Minsheng Contemporary Art Research Centre.

Geographical Area of Activity: Principally the People's Republic of China.

Finance: Initial funding: 2m. yuan.

Principal Staff: Chair. Diao Xuan; Pres. Shao Bo.

Address: Rm 1011, Yuanhuang Art Gallery, No. 9, Huizhong Rd, Asian Sports Village, Chaoyang, Beijing.

Telephone: (10) 57626053; **Fax:** (10) 57626052; **Internet:** www .minshengart.com; **e-mail:** info@minshengart.com.

New Huadu Foundation

Established in 2009 by Chen Fashu, Chair. of Fujian New Huadu Industrial Group Co.

Activities: Areas of interest include education, social welfare, poverty alleviation and disaster relief. Programmes include: the Sunshine (fmrly Spark) Programme, building 200 schools; Sunshine Action, providing scholarships to 100,000 college students; and the Blue Sky Project, offering vocational training to 200,000 college students. Also funds the New Huadu Business School, based in Fuzhou and Zurich (Switzerland).

Geographical Area of Activity: People's Republic of China, Switzerland.

Finance: Net assets 136.53m. yuan; annual income 120m. yuan, disbursements 112.96m. yuan (2012).

Principal Staff: Chair. Chen Fashu; Deputy Chair. Qiu Fei; Pres. Zhou Wengui; Exec. Dir Tang Jun.

Address: 28th Floor, North Huacheng Intl Bldg, No. 162, Wusi Rd, Fuzhou 350003.

Telephone: (591) 87832783; **Fax:** (591) 87987982; **Internet:** www.nhdfoundation.cn; **e-mail:** nqq77@sina.com.

Ningxia Yanbao Charity Foundation

Established in 2010 by Dang Yanbao, Pres. of Ningxia Baofeng Energy Group Co Ltd, and his wife Bian Haiyan.

Activities: Primary fields of interest are providing education, and community and rural health and welfare services for the elderly and disabled people. Also provides scholarships for college students and vocational learners; and has supported the building of primary schools and medical facilities in migrant communities. In 2011, the Foundation established a chain of 100 community supermarkets which operate as social enterprises, funding community social projects.

Geographical Area of Activity: Primarily Ningxia, People's Republic of China.

Finance: Initial endowment of 500m. yuan and a further 500m. yuan over the following ten years.

Principal Staff: Chair. Dang Yanbao.

Address: East Side, International Trade Bldg, Xingqing District, Yinchuan, Ningxia 750001.

Telephone: (951) 6075007; **Fax:** (951) 5616120; **Internet:** www .ybcf.cn; **e-mail:** xie_tengteng@126.com.

Shandong Oceanwide Foundation

Established in 2010 by Lu Zhiqiang, Chair. and CEO of China Oceanwide Holdings Group.

Activities: Main areas of interest are: social welfare and poverty alleviation; national arts and culture; environmental protection; rural development, including infrastructure, agricultural technology, education, health, culture and sports; and scientific research. Also contributes to disaster relief.

Geographical Area of Activity: China.

Finance: Total assets 200.05m. yuan, annual income 30.55m. yuan (2013).

Principal Staff: Pres. Lu Xiaoyun; Vice-Pres. Lu Zhiqiang.

Address: Minsheng Financial Center, Block C5, 28th Floor, Jianguomen Ave, Dongcheng District, Beijing 100005.

Telephone: (10) 85259794; **Fax:** (10) 85259393; **Internet:** www.oceanwidefoundation.org; **e-mail:** oceanwidef@163.com.

SOHO China Foundation

Established in 2005 by Zhang Xin, CEO of property development company SOHO China (f. 1995), and her husband Pan Shiyi, Chair. of SOHO China.

Activities: Programmes include: Teach for China (f. 2008), which trains university graduates from the USA and the People's Republic of China to teach at schools in Yunnan and Guangdong provinces; the Children's Virtues Project, promoting personal and communal responsibility in young children; the Bathroom Construction Campaign to improve school sanitation; and Futures Brightened through Helping Hands, which sponsors the university education of underprivileged students and encourages reciprocal volunteerism. In 2014, the Foundation set up the SOHO China Scholarships, with an endowment of US $100m., for Chinese students to study at universities abroad.

Geographical Area of Activity: Principally the People's Republic of China.

Principal Staff: Chair. Pan Shiyi; CEO Zhang Xin; Man. Annie Jin.

Address: c/o SOHO China Ltd, Chaowai SOHO, Bldg A, 11th Floor, 6в Chaowai St, Chaoyang District, Beijing 100020.

Telephone: (10) 58788327; **Internet:** www.sohochinafoundation.org; **e-mail:** jinyanni@sohochina.com.

Tencent Foundation

Established in 2007 by Tencent Inc. (f. 1998), an internet service provider.

Activities: Aims to use the internet and information communications and technology to the public benefit. Funds the construction of school buildings, dormitories and infrastructure, and provides teacher training, to improve education in disadvantaged areas; had funded the construction of 31 schools by 2009. Also raises awareness of welfare issues among university students; and runs the Tencent New Countryside Action public welfare programme in Guizhou and Yunnan. Other areas of interest include culture; environmental protection; economic development; disaster relief and reconstruction; and scientific research.

Geographical Area of Activity: People's Republic of China.

Finance: Initial funding 20m. yuan; total donations made since 2007 approx. 10,000m. yuan.

Principal Staff: Chair. Guo Kaitian; Pres. Zhai Hongxin.

Address: F5-10, FIYTA Mansion, Nanyidao, High-tech Park, Shenzhen, Guangdong.

Telephone: (755) 86013388; **Fax:** (755) 86013152; **Internet:** gongyi.qq.com/jjhgy/index.htm; **e-mail:** reagandou@tencent.com.

Yan Bao Hang Foundation

Established in 1991 by Gen. Zhang Xueliang, Ning En'cheng and the family of Yan Bao Hang, a wartime military intelligence officer and government official.

Activities: Programmes cover poverty alleviation and access to medicine in disadvantaged areas. Other fields of interest include culture, education, science and technology, social welfare and disaster relief.

Geographical Area of Activity: People's Republic of China.

Finance: Initial funding 2m. yuan.

Principal Staff: Chair. Huang Anqi; Pres. Yan Mingguang.

Address: Block H, 28th Floor, World Sq., No. 855, Pudong South Rd, Shanghai.

Telephone: (21) 64980193; **Fax:** (21) 64928348.

Colombia

FOUNDATIONS, TRUSTS AND NON-PROFIT ORGANIZATIONS

Centro Internacional de Agricultura Tropical—CIAT
(International Centre for Tropical Agriculture)

Established in 1967 by the Rockefeller Foundation and the Ford Foundation (qq.v.) to contribute to the alleviation of hunger and poverty in tropical developing countries by applying science to the generation of technology that will lead to lasting increases in agricultural output, while preserving the natural resource base.

Activities: Conducts research in five main areas: crop improvement; conservation of biological diversity; pest and disease management; soil quality and production systems; and land management. It carries out this work in collaboration with a wide range of national partner organizations. While concentrating mainly on tropical America (especially the Andean zone, the Amazon and Central America), the Centre also conducts projects in South-East Asia and Eastern, Central and Southern Africa. Scientists work on a global scale in crop improvement, and in research on soil quality. Focuses on three major agro-ecosystems of tropical America: forest margins, hillsides and savannahs.

Geographical Area of Activity: Central and South America, South-East Asia, and Eastern, Central and Southern Africa.

Publications: *Growing Affinities* (2 a year); *CIAT in Perspective* (annual report); *Pasturas Tropicales* (tropical pastures newsletter, 3 a year); Publications Catalogue; research reports; policy briefs; information briefs; brochures.

Finance: Annual revenue US $114,288,000, expenditure $111,841,000 (31 Dec. 2013).

Board of Trustees: Wanda Collins (Chair.); Geoffrey Hawtin (Vice-Chair.); María Fernanda Reyes (Sec.).

Principal Staff: Dir-Gen. Ruben G. Echeverría.

Address: Km 17, Recta Cai-Palmera, Apdo Aéreo 6713, Cali.

Telephone: (2) 4450000; **Fax:** (2) 4450073; **Internet:** www .ciat.cgiar.org; **e-mail:** ciat@cgiar.org.

Fundación Amanecer

Established in 1994 with the assistance of Ecopetrol S.A., BP, Total and Tempa. Since 2005, the Foundation has been an independent organization.

Activities: Works in the fields of human development, business development and environmental protection. The Foundation works to eradicate extreme poverty and hunger; promote gender equality and women's empowerment; and guarantee environmental sustainability. It provides grants and financial support, including loans, to not-for-profit organizations in Colombia; and also provides technical support in the field of agriculture and agricultural technology to co-operative enterprises and grassroots organizations.

Geographical Area of Activity: Colombia.

Finance: Annual grants approx. US $1m.

Principal Staff: Gen. Man. César Iván Velosa Poveda.

Address: Calle 24 No. 20A-27, Yopal, Casanare.

Telephone: (8) 6320500; **Internet:** www.amanecer.org.co.

Fundación Antonio Restrepo Barco

Established in 1986 by businessman and philanthropist Antonio Restrepo Barco to foster the educational, cultural and technical development of children and young people.

Activities: Supports projects in the fields of health, family, social participation and income improvement, and publishes books.

Geographical Area of Activity: Colombia.

Publications: Newsletter; reports.

Board of Directors: Oscar Echeverry (Chair.); Luis Hernán Pérez Páez (Vice-Chair.).

Principal Staff: Gen. Man. Marco Antonio Cruz Rincón.

Address: Carrera 7, No. 73-55, Piso 12, Bogotá.

Telephone: (2) 3121511; **Fax:** (2) 3121182; **Internet:** www .funrestrepobarco.org.co; **e-mail:** frb@funrestrepobarco.org .co.

Fundación Corona

Established in 1963 by the Echavarría Olózaga family, founders of Corona, an entrepreneurial organization mainly dedicated to the manufacture and commercialization of ceramic products.

Activities: Aims to contribute to social development by improving the management of social processes and through innovative programmes and projects that help the poorest members of the population have access to the benefits of development. Makes grants in the fields of health, education, the environment and the development of micro-enterprises at both local and national levels. Strategies comprise: development of management models useful to social organizations and groups, such as schools, hospitals, micro-enterprises and community organizations with the objective of working more efficiently (organizational effectiveness); development of knowledge in specific sectors and promotion of public debate in topics of interest to improve the design and development of public policies; promotion of citizenship participation to allow community problem solving and stimulate the follow-up and control of local governments; and development of programmes for the generation of job and income opportunities for the vulnerable population.

Geographical Area of Activity: Colombia.

Restrictions: Supports development projects only in Colombia.

Publications: Annual Report; *Intemperie* (2 a year); *Boletín Mensual* (monthly newsletter); briefing papers; reports.

Finance: Annual income 8,492,545,000 pesos, expenditure 5,458,087,000 pesos (31 Dec. 2013).

Board of Directors: Pedro Vargas Gallo (Pres.).

Principal Staff: Exec. Dir Ángela Escallón Emiliani.

Address: Calle 70, No. 7-30, Oficina 1001, 11001000, Bogotá.

Telephone: (1) 4000031; **Fax:** (1) 4010540; **Internet:** www .fundacioncorona.org.co; **e-mail:** fundacion@fcorona.org.

Fundación para la Educación Superior y el Desarrollo—Fedesarrollo (Foundation for Higher Education and Development)

Founded in 1970 by Manuel Carvajal Sinisterra, Rodrigo Botero Montoya and Alberto Vargas Martínez to promote cultural and scientific advancement and to stimulate research into Colombia's social, economic and political problems.

Activities: Operates nationally in the fields of social welfare and political science and administration, and nationally and internationally in the fields of economic affairs and international relations, through research, surveys, publications and lectures on an international level and through conferences and courses conducted in Colombia.

Geographical Area of Activity: Colombia.

Publications: *Tendencia Económica* (monthly); *Informe del Mercado Laboral* (monthly); *Informe del Mercado de Leasing*; *Coyuntura TIC*; *Prospectiva Económica* (3 a year); *Bitácora Semanal* (weekly); *Coyuntura Económica* (weekly); *Informe Mensual Macroeconómico* (monthly); books; working papers.

Principal Staff: Exec. Dir Leonardo Villar Gómez; Sec.-Gen. Marcela Pombo.

Address: Calle 78, No. 9-91, AA75064 Bogotá.

Telephone: (1) 3259777; **Fax:** (1) 3259770; **Internet:** www .fedesarrollo.org.co; **e-mail:** comercial@fedesarrollo.org.co.

Fundación Escuela Nueva (New School Foundation)

Established in 1987 by Vicky Colbert, Beryl Levinger and Óscar Mogollónto, creators of the Escuela Nueva pedagogical model, to ensure its quality and continuing development.

Activities: Promotes active, collaborative and personalized learning. The Foundation provides technical assistance, facilitates networking and partnerships, and carries out research and evaluations. It also maintains the Renueva virtual community.

Geographical Area of Activity: Central and South America, Timor-Leste, Viet Nam, Zambia.

Publications: Newsletter; learning guides; training manuals; research findings.

Principal Staff: Dir Vicky Colbert.

Address: Calle 39, No. 21-57, Bogotá.

Telephone: (1) 2452712; **Fax:** (1) 2452712-112; **Internet:** www .escuelanueva.org; **e-mail:** info@escuelanueva.org.

Fundación Hábitat Colombia—FHC (Colombian Habitat Foundation)

Established in 1991. Specializes in knowledge management on urban best practices, research, communication, technical assistance and co-operation for urban and regional development.

Activities: Operates in Colombia, promoting a better quality of life for urban dwellers in collaboration with the Government, the private sector and social organizations. Supports initiatives that encourage environmental development, the exchange of experience and information, and the establishment of strategic alliances, and that promote sustainability.

Geographical Area of Activity: Colombia.

Publications: *Hábitat Colombia* (magazine); *Intercambios/ Exchanges; Best Practices Transfer; Locals Demands/Offers Globals*.

Principal Staff: Dir Lucelena Betancur Salazar.

Address: Calle 127c, No. 6A-40, Bogotá.

Telephone: (1) 2163606; 3165284268; **Fax:** (1) 2163606; **Internet:** www.fundacionhabitatcolombia.org; **e-mail:** informacion@fundacionhabitatcolombia.org.

Fundación SERVIVIENDA (Housing Services Foundation)

Founded in 1972 by the Society of Jesus religious order to develop housing programmes for low-income families.

Activities: Produces, sells, finances and erects concrete prefabricated houses. As well in Colombia, the Foundation has worked in the Dominican Republic, Ecuador, Guatemala, Haiti, Honduras, Jamaica, Nicaragua, Peru and Venezuela.

Geographical Area of Activity: South America, Central America and the Caribbean.

Publications: Newsletter.

Finance: Annual revenue 32,675m. pesos (2013).

Board of Directors: Carlos Eduardo Correa Jaramillo (Chair.); Sandra Patricia Pérez (Sec.).

Principal Staff: Dir-Gen. María Margarita Ruíz Rodgers.

Address: Carrera 48, No. 95-15, Edificio Servivienda, Piso 6, Barrio La Castellana, Bogotá.

Telephone: (1) 2879666; **Fax:** (1) 2887605; **Internet:** www .servivienda.org.co; **e-mail:** info@servivienda.org.co.

Costa Rica

FOUNDATIONS, TRUSTS AND NON-PROFIT ORGANIZATIONS

DEMUCA—Fundación para el Desarrollo Local y el Fortalecimiento Municipal e Institucional de Centroamérica y el Caribe (Foundation for Local Development and the Municipal and Institutional Support of Central America and the Caribbean)

Founded in 1995.

Activities: Aims to strengthen the capacity of local governments in Central America and the Caribbean to promote human development. Promotes the exchange of experience and information, and international co-operation between Spain, Central America and the Caribbean to improve human development work in the latter two regions. Works to improve municipal finances, and raise the level of efficiency in grant-making and of basic public services in local governments, including clean water supplies and sanitation, rubbish disposal and public transport. Also provides general support for local and regional governments. Has offices in the Dominican Republic, El Salvador, Guatemala and Panama.

Geographical Area of Activity: Central America and the Caribbean.

Publications: Books; reports; research findings.

Principal Staff: Exec. Dir Mercedes Peñas Domingo.

Address: Apdo 697-1005, San José; Barrio Escalante, del Parque Francia 25m Sur, San José.

Telephone: 258-1813; **Fax:** 248-0297; **Internet:** www.demuca .org; **e-mail:** xdonato@demuca.org.

Fundación Acceso (Access Foundation)

Established in 1992 by Stephen Cox.

Activities: Provides training, technical assistance and institution-building services to organizations working towards sustainable development in Central and South America. The Foundation's main areas of interest are gender, rights, open knowledge and popular education.

Geographical Area of Activity: Central and South America.

Publications: Reports, booklets and directories.

Board of Directors: Susana García Perdomo (Chair.); Marcelo Gaete Astica (Sec.); José Montero Peña (Treas.).

Principal Staff: Co-ordinator Tanya Lockwood Fallas.

Address: Apdo 288-2050, San José; Sabanilla Montes de Oca, del AMPM de La Paulina 100m al norte y 150 al este, Urbanización Buenos Aires, Casa No. 23, San José.

Telephone: 2253-9860; **Fax:** 2280-6015; **Internet:** www .acceso.or.cr; **e-mail:** info@acceso.or.cr.

Fundación Arias para la Paz y el Progreso Humano (Arias Foundation for Peace and Human Progress)

Established in 1988 by Dr Oscar Arias Sánchez, former President of Costa Rica, to build just and peaceful societies in Central America.

Activities: Promotes democracy, gender equality, disarmament and demilitarization through self-conducted programmes, research, workshops, training courses and publications through three main centres: the Center for Human Progress, which carries out work on gender equality; the Center for Peace and Reconciliation, working in the field of demilitarization and conflict prevention; and the Center for Organized Participation, working in the field of civil society and democracy. Also administers the Museum of Peace.

Geographical Area of Activity: Central America.

Publications: Manuals; reports; research findings.

Finance: Annual budget approx. US $1m.

Board of Governors: Margarita Herdocia (Chair.).

Principal Staff: Exec. Dir Lina Barrantes Castegnaro.

Address: Costado suroeste de la Plaza de Democracia, sobre Avenida 2da, Apdo 8-6410-100, San José.

Telephone: 2222-9191; **Fax:** 2257-5011; **Internet:** www.arias .or.cr; **e-mail:** info@arias.or.cr.

Fundación para el Desarrollo de Base—FUNDEBASE (Foundation for Basic Development)

Founded in 1995 to offer alternative finance to NGOs and micro-enterprises in both rural and urban areas of the country.

Activities: Offers micro-credit under three programme areas: finance for micro-enterprise, finance for rural groups, and finance for NGOs.

Geographical Area of Activity: South and Central America.

Finance: Annual income 371,536,634 colones, expenditure 321,362,168 colones (31 Dec. 2013).

Principal Staff: Exec. Dir José Roberto Jiménez Barletta.

Address: Curridabat, Plaza del Sol, 125 metros al este, Edificio Galerías del Este, local #11, Curridabat, San José.

Telephone: 2234-8534; **Fax:** 2234-0393; **Internet:** www .fundebasecr.org; **e-mail:** fundeba@ice.co.cr.

Fundación para el Desarrollo Sostenible de la Pequeña y Mediana Empresa—FUNDES Internacional (Foundation for the Sustainable Development of Small and Medium-sized Enterprises—FUNDES International)

Founded in 1984 to develop the region's private sector.

Activities: Works with multinational companies and governments to improve the competitiveness of small and medium-sized enterprises. The Foundation conducts research into the sector. Its projects use complementary tools (training, business consulting, access to financing, and information technologies) and are based on the premise that businesses interact with other businesses and supporting organizations. Areas of intervention are: development at business level; value chain development; sectoral/territorial development; and improving the business environment. Has regional offices in Argentina, Bolivia, Chile, Colombia, Costa Rica, Ecuador, Guatemala, El Salvador, Mexico, Panama, Peru, Venezuela.

Geographical Area of Activity: South and Central America.

Principal Staff: CEO Elfid Torres; CFO Catalina Pacheco.

Address: Apdo 798-4005, San Antonio de Belén; La Asunción de Belén, Heredia, San Antonio de Belén.

Telephone: 2209-8300; **Fax:** 2209-8399; **Internet:** www .fundes.org; **e-mail:** internacional@fundes.org.

Fundación Integral Campesina—FINCA (Comprehensive Rural Foundation)

Founded in 1984 by Maria Marta Padilla.

Activities: Aims to aid rural communities by offering micro-credit for development projects. In 2011, the Foundation supported regional networks of 150 communal micro-credit organizations in Costa Rica.

Geographical Area of Activity: Costa Rica.

Finance: Total loans US $2.88m. (2011).

Principal Staff: Exec. Dir Luis Jiménez Padilla.

Address: 400m este y 15m norte del parqueo del Hotel San José Palacio, La Uruca, San José.

Telephone: 2520-2076; **Fax:** 2520-2075; **Internet:** www .fincacostarica.org; **e-mail:** info@fincacostarica.org.

Fundación Mujer (Women's Foundation)

Founded in 1988 to finance women in business.

Activities: Offers micro-finance to businesses run by women.

Geographical Area of Activity: Costa Rica.

Board of Directors: Gilberto Guzmán Saborío (Pres.); Priscila Devandas Artavia (Sec.); Jose Martinez Cruz (Treas.).

Principal Staff: Exec. Dir Licda Zobeida Moya Lacayo.

Address: Apdo Postal 770-2070, Montes de Oca; Barrio Betania, Mercedes, Montes de Oca, 200m norte y 50m este de la Escuela de Betania, San José.

Telephone: 2253-1661; **Fax:** 2253-1613; **Internet:** www .fundacionmujer.org; **e-mail:** funmujer@racsa.co.cr.

Fundación Unión y Desarrollo de Comunidades Campesinas (Foundation for the Unity and Development of Rural Communities)

Founded in 1990 as a CARE International project, becoming an independent foundation in 1993.

Activities: Community credit scheme for rural communities. The Foundation comprises 53 communal micro-credit organizations.

Geographical Area of Activity: Huetar Norte and Sarapiqui regions in Costa Rica.

Finance: Annual income 775,359,246 colones, expenditure 396,814,736 colones (31 Dec. 2013).

Principal Staff: Exec. Dir Carlos Rojas Hidalgo.

Address: 125m al este del Centro Comercial Plaza San Carlos, Ciudad Quesada, San Carlos.

Telephone: 2460-6035; **Fax:** 2460-0412; **Internet:** www .fundecoca.cr; **e-mail:** fundecoc@ice.co.cr.

Instituto Interamericano de Derechos Humanos— IIHR (Inter-American Institute of Human Rights)

Founded in 1980; dedicated to the promotion of, and investigation into, human rights in Central and South America.

Activities: Operates in the fields of education and human rights. Promotes human rights and social justice, and works to consolidate democracy through investigation, education, political mediation, technical assistance and the dissemination of relevant information through specialized publications. Organizes conferences, issues publications, and works with a number of other organizations and local governments. Maintains an online documentation centre. Hass offices in Colombia and Uruguay.

Geographical Area of Activity: Latin America.

Publications: *IIDH en las Américas* (newsletter); *Revista IIDH*; approx. 1,500 books; magazines; print, audiovisual and digital educational materials.

Board of Directors: Thomas Buergenthal, Pedro Nikken, Sonia Picado Sotela (Hon. Pres); Claudio Grossman (Pres.); Rodolfo Stavenhagen, Margaret Crahan (Vice-Pres).

Principal Staff: Exec. Dir José Thompson J.

Address: Apdo 10081-1000, San José; Avda 8, Calles 43-41, Casa No. 222, Barrio Los Yoses, Montes de Oca, San Pedro, San José.

Telephone: 234-0404; **Fax:** 234-0955; **Internet:** www.iidh.ed .cr; **e-mail:** instituto@iidh.ed.cr.

Red de Mujeres para el Desarrollo (Women's Development Network)

Established in 1998 as a strategic alliance among grassroots women's groups, NGOs, churches, development professionals, and international agencies, concerned for the economic development of excluded women in Central and South America and the Caribbean.

Activities: Operates in the field of women's rights by representing women at risk of exclusion in Central and South America and the Caribbean. Promotes communication and collaboration and the development and empowerment of women. Activities include publication of a quarterly newsletter; access to a database providing information on economic projects, bibliographic material and sources of financing and training; support for non-profit organizations searching for funding and training; and the formation of local support networks. Maintains offices in Brazil, Colombia, Curaçao, Dominica, Haiti, Honduras, Puerto Rico, Trinidad and Tobago, and the USA.

Geographical Area of Activity: Central and South America and the Caribbean, and the USA.

Publications: Newsletter (quarterly).

Principal Staff: Co-ordinators Noemi Barquero, Olga Parrado.

Address: Apdo 692-2070, Sabanilla, San José.

Telephone: 2253-9003; **Fax:** 2253-9128; **Internet:** www .redmujeres.org; **e-mail:** info@redmujeres.org.

Croatia

FOUNDATION CENTRES AND CO-ORDINATING BODIES

Association for Civil Society Development—SMART

Aims to strengthen and support the development of the non-profit sector in Croatia.

Activities: Promotes capacity building of civil society organizations in Croatia, through organizing training workshops, providing technical assistance and consultancy services to non-formal groups and non-profit organizations on the principles of strengthening, self-assistance, active involvement, maintenance of positive initiatives, stimulation of co-operation, mutual evaluation and respect of differences; carries out research, and funds capacity-building initiatives.

Geographical Area of Activity: Croatia.

Publications: Annual Report; *InfoSMART* (quarterly newsletter).

Finance: Annual income US $192,486 (31 Dec. 2012).

Principal Staff: Executive Team: Gordana Forcic, Sladjana Novota, Zvijezdana Schulz Vugrin.

Address: 51000 Rijeka, Blaza Polića 2/IV.

Telephone: (51) 332-750; **Fax:** (51) 330-792; **Internet:** www.smart.hr; **e-mail:** smart@smart.hr.

Centar za razvoj neprofitnih organizacija—CERANEO (Centre for Development of Non-profit Organizations)

Established in 1995; a think tank dedicated to collecting, analyzing and researching social policy problems, promoting development of civil society organizations and foundations in Croatia through debates, lobbying, organizing conferences and networking with similar organizations.

Activities: Analyzes drafts of laws or policy programmes on public policies; organizes debates (workshops, round tables, seminars, conferences) to influence decisions in Parliament; initiates changes of existing legislation and policies; builds bridges between academics, researchers, decision-makers in government and practitioners; and publishes results of projects and briefing articles in the media. Supports new initiatives and advocates a more important role for civil society. Researches civil society in Croatia; contributes to public debate about foundation law; offers resources to Croatian civil society orgs; and promotes the orgs to potential international donors.

Geographical Area of Activity: Croatia.

Publications: Newsletter, books, articles, translations, publications, research reports.

Governing Board: Dr Gojko Bezovan (Pres.); Dr Zdenko Babic (Vice-Pres.).

Principal Staff: Sec. Vesela Grabovac.

Address: 10000 Zagreb, Nazorova 51.

Telephone: (1) 4895-829; **Fax:** (1) 4812-384; **Internet:** www.ceraneo.hr; **e-mail:** petra@ceraneo.hr.

Nacionalne Zaklade za Razvoj Civilnoga Drustva (National Foundation for Civil Society Development)

Founded in 2003 to promote and support civil society development in Croatia.

Activities: Provides expert and financial support to innovative programmes that encourage the sustainability of the non-profit sector, inter-sector co-operation, civil initiatives, philanthropy, voluntary work and the improvement of democratic institutions in society. The Foundation aims to achieve active citizenship for the development of a modern, democratic and inclusive society in Croatia.

Geographical Area of Activity: Croatia.

Publications: Annual Report; e-newsletter (monthly); *Civilno društvo* (magazine); books; manuals; studies.

Finance: Annual income 46,933,066 kuna, expenditure 44,970,484 kuna (31 Dec. 2013).

Management Board: Vesna Vašiček (Pres.); Joško Klisović (Vice-Pres.).

Principal Staff: Dir Cvjetana Plavša-Matić.

Address: 10000 Zagreb, Štrigina 1A.

Telephone: (1) 2399-100; **Fax:** (1) 2399-111; **Internet:** zaklada.civilnodrustvo.hr; **e-mail:** zaklada@civilnodrustvo.hr.

FOUNDATIONS, TRUSTS AND NON-PROFIT ORGANIZATIONS

Budi aktivna, Budi emancipiran—BaBe (Be Active, Be Emancipated)

Founded in 1994 by Vesna Kesic and nine activists to promote women's human rights. Came out of the Center for Women War Victims.

Activities: Operates in the field of human rights, through advocacy and lobbying for the affirmation and implementation of women's rights and gender equality. The organization supports activities aimed at eliminating and protecting women from violence in the domestic and public spheres; promotes the right to freedom of choice and other reproductive rights, and adequate health care protection; and the right to equal and full participation in all areas of society. Its priorities and specific objectives change in response to the needs of women who are marginalized and discriminated against. Since 2008, its has created projects within three main programmes: gender equality; prevention and protection against gender-based violence; and human rights.

Geographical Area of Activity: Croatia and South-Eastern Europe.

Restrictions: Not a grantmaking organization.

Publications: Annual Report; books, documentaries, musical videos, social advertisements, installations, brochures, posters, leaflets.

Finance: Annual income 2,449,767 kuna, expenditure 2,675,157 kuna (2014).

Principal Staff: Pres. Sanja Sarnavka; Co-ordinator Zdravka Sadzakov.

Address: 10000 Zagreb, Human Rights House, Selska 112A.

Telephone: (1) 4663-666; **Fax:** (1) 4662-606; **Internet:** www.babe.hr; **e-mail:** babe@babe.hr.

Curaçao

FOUNDATIONS, TRUSTS AND NON-PROFIT ORGANIZATIONS

CARMABI Foundation

Established in 1955 as the Caribbean Marine Biological Institute. In 1996, it merged with the Stichting Nationale Parken—STINAPA (f. 1962).

Activities: Operates in the areas of conservation of the environment, and applied marine natural resource research. The Foundation conducts marine biological research and conservation research; manages nine protected areas; provides advice to local government; and carries out an education programme for schoolchildren. Visiting scientists from the Netherlands and the USA carry out research.

Geographical Area of Activity: Netherlands Dependencies.

Publications: *Caribbean Journal of Science* (journal); *Bina* (newsletter); Annual Report; research findings; scholarly publications.

Finance: Annual income 1,635,809 guilders, expenditure 1,971,972 guilders (2011).

Board: Peter Bongers (Chair.); Jeffrey Sybesma (Sec.); Alvin Francisco (Treas.).

Principal Staff: Dir Paul G. C. Stokkermans; Scientific Dir Dr Mark Vermeij.

Address: POB 2090, Piscaderabaai z/n, Willemstad.

Telephone: (9) 462-42-42; **Fax:** (9) 462-76-80; **Internet:** www.carmabi.org; **e-mail:** info@carmabi.org.

Cyprus

FOUNDATIONS, TRUSTS AND NON-PROFIT ORGANIZATIONS

Bank of Cyprus Cultural Foundation

Founded in 1994 by the Bank of Cyprus Group; promotes studies on Cyprus at a professional and scholarly level.

Activities: Maintains four major collections: coins, maps, rare historical documents and contemporary Cypriot art. Each collection is linked to a long-term project involving research, publications, lectures, seminars, educational programmes, and temporary and permanent exhibitions. All projects are aimed at extending the study of the history and culture of Cyprus as an island of the wider Hellenic world. The Foundation opened the Museum of the History of Cypriot Coinage in 1995, and the Museum of the Archaeological Collection of George and Nefeli Tziapra Rierides was inaugurated in 2002.

Geographical Area of Activity: Cyprus and Greece.

Publications: Newsletters; information brochures; monographs; multi-year report; publications catalogue/list. Publications programme includes publications in the following areas: Cypriot cartography; Cypriot coinage; archaeology and history of Cyprus; guides to archaeological and historical monuments; Cypriot literature; CDs and video publications.

Board of Directors: Prof. Vasiliki Kassianidou (Chair.).

Principal Staff: Dir Lefki Michaelidou; Curators Eleni Zapiti, Dr Ioanna Hadjicosti.

Address: POB 21995, 1515 Nicosia; 86–90 Phaneromenis St, 1011 Nicosia.

Telephone: (22) 128157; **Fax:** (22) 662898; **Internet:** www.boccf.org; **e-mail:** info@cultural.bankofcyprus.com.

Christos Stelios Ioannou Foundation

Established in 1983 by industrialist and philanthropist Stelios Ioannou and his wife Ellie Ioannou in memory of their son, Christos.

Activities: Operates in Cyprus in the field of medicine and health, and welfare. The Foundation promotes the treatment of people with mental disabilities as individuals, the development of their full potential, and the provision of opportunities for a fully active and fulfilling life within society. It seeks to increase public awareness and acceptance of mental disabilities, and provides support for people with such disabilities in a rehabilitation group for students and former students of the Foundation. It also provides accommodation services, and a variety of events and activities outside its basic services, incl. trips, foreign exchanges, music, dance and drama; and organizes staff training programmes. Maintains links with similar organizations throughout Europe.

Geographical Area of Activity: Cyprus.

Board of Directors: Christina Flourentzou Kakouri (Chair.); Aristoula Alexandrou (Sec.); Miranda Charalambous Prodromitou (Treas.).

Principal Staff: Dir Andreas R. Georgiou.

Address: POB 590, 1660 Nicosia; Megaron 2035, Nicosia.

Telephone: (22) 481666; **Fax:** (22) 485331; **Internet:** www.ioannoufoundation.org; **e-mail:** csjfound@spidernet.com.cy.

A. G. Leventis Foundation

Established in 1979 by the will of Anastasios G. Leventis to support artistic, cultural, educational and charitable activities in Greece, Cyprus and other areas.

Activities: Promotes and preserves Cyprus's cultural heritage, including supporting the establishment of new museums. Promotes environmental conservation; offers grants for study at the University of Cyprus and for postgraduate study abroad, especially in the fields of science and education; funds publications; and promotes social welfare.

Geographical Area of Activity: Greece, Cyprus, the Balkans, West Africa, Central and Western Europe.

Restrictions: No support for projects outside of the geographic focus.

Publications: Numerous publications in English, French and Greek on Cypriot and Greek art and civilization; archaeological reports and studies; Byzantine art; cartography; children's books; collections of essays; conference proceedings; coroplastic art of Cyprus; lecture series; proceedings of symposiums.

Governing Board: Anastasios P. Leventis (Chair.).

Principal Staff: Dir Prof. Dr Charalambos Bakirtzis.

Address: 40 Gladstonos St, POB 2543, 1095 Nicosia.

Telephone: (22) 667706; **Fax:** (22) 675002; **Internet:** www.leventisfoundation.org; **e-mail:** info@leventis.org.cy.

George and Thelma Paraskevaides Foundation

Founded in 1980 by George and Thelma Paraskevaides for medical, educational and cultural purposes.

Activities: Assists indigent Cypriots who need to go abroad for medical treatment, as well as making grants to medical institutions; awarding scholarships for higher studies abroad; and providing grants for cultural purposes in Cyprus (particularly conservation). The Foundation supports folk art and traditional architecture, and awards cultural and artistic grants. It also funds the Annual Prize for Journalism and Democracy awarded by the Organization for Security and Co-operation in Europe (OSCE).

Geographical Area of Activity: Cyprus.

Address: POB 2200, 1518 Nicosia; Paraskevaides Foundation Bldg, 36 Grivas Dighenis Ave, 1066 Nicosia.

Telephone: (22) 445367; **e-mail:** gnthparaskf@cytanet.com.cy.

Czech Republic

FOUNDATION CENTRES AND CO-ORDINATING BODIES

AGNES—Vzdělávací Organizace (Agency for the Non-profit Sector)

Established in 1998 to support the NGO sector in the Czech Republic.

Activities: Activities include training programmes for NGO staff; research and publishing on the NGO sector; and the promotion and development of NGOs in the Czech Republic. Aims to aid the development of NGOs across the country, increase bilateral activities, and foster international co-operation. Established the Jeleni Club in 2000 for NGOs' staff, clients, volunteers and supporters.

Geographical Area of Activity: Czech Republic.

Publications: *Non-profit Organizations and Influencing Public Policy; Philanthropy and Volunteerism in the Czech Republic*; textbooks; professional publications.

Principal Staff: Dir Jiri Jezek; Project Man. Irena Pekova.

Address: Jeleni 196/15, 118 00 Prague 1.

Telephone: 233350120; **Fax:** 233350120; **Internet:** www.agnes.cz; **e-mail:** agnes@agnes.cz.

Asociace komunitních nadací v České (Czech Association of Community Foundations)

Established in 2006.

Activities: Supports the development of community foundations. Comprises four mem. foundations and three 'support' orgs.

Geographical Area of Activity: Czech Republic.

Principal Staff: Chair. Tomáš Krejčí.

Address: Koněvova 1697/18, 400 01 Ústí nad Labem.

Telephone: 475211633; **Fax:** 475211633; **Internet:** akncr.cz; **e-mail:** akn@komunitninadace.cz.

Česká rada sociálních slueb—CRSS (Czech Council of Social Services)

Founded in 2011 as the successor to the Council of Humanitarian Associations, which was founded in 1990 as the Czechoslovak Council for Humanitarian Co-operation.

Activities: Work focuses on the elderly, disabled and homeless people, drug users, and abandoned and abused children. The Council provides a database of humanitarian organizations, training for members, and organizes seminars and workshops. Operates mainly in the Czech Republic, but has worked in Armenia and with organizations active internationally. Has around 180 member organizations.

Geographical Area of Activity: Mainly Czech Republic.

Publications: Monthly review; bulletin; newsletter; conference reports.

Principal Staff: Pres. Jaroslav Němec; Vice-Pres. Jiří Lodr.

Address: Ceskobratrská 9, 130 00 Prague 3.

Telephone: 222587455; **Fax:** 222960962; **Internet:** www.crss.cz; **e-mail:** kancelar@crss.cz.

Czech Donors Forum (Fórum dárců)

Established in 1995 as an association of grantmakers; became a registered civic association in 1997.

Activities: Operates as a support organization for grantmaking organizations in the Czech Republic, focusing on the cultivation and development of the foundation sector and philanthropy, strengthening the co-operation and development of the foundation and private sectors, and playing an infrastructural role. Main programmes are the Educational Training Programme, the Programme for the Development of Corporate Philanthropy and the 1% of tax designation project. Comprises 66 member organizations.

Geographical Area of Activity: Western, Central and Eastern Europe.

Restrictions: Not a grantmaking organization.

Publications: Newsletter (quarterly); *Directory of Foundations*; *The Economic Development of the Civil and Not-for-Profit Sector in the Czech Republic: Foundations and Assets*; *Foundations in the Czech Republic*; *Strategy for the Development of the Non-Profit Sector in the Czech Republic*; *Manual for Foundations without an Endowment*; *Cookbook* (manual for communication agencies); Annual Report.

Finance: Total assets 7,626,000 koruny (31 Dec. 2011).

Principal Staff: Exec. Dir Klára Šplíchalová.

Address: Palac Lucerna, 5 patro, Štěpánská 704/61, 110 00 Prague 1.

Telephone: 224216544; **Fax:** 224216544; **Internet:** www.donorsforum.cz; **e-mail:** donorsforum@donorsforum.cz.

Nadace Auxilia (Auxilia Foundation)

Founded in 1992 to provide information, training and co-ordination services to support the development of non-profit organizations in the Czech Republic. In 1998, the organization split into two: Auxilia Foundation (ICN Foundation until 2005), a grantmaking foundation that supports co-operation between NGOs, networking and partnership with public administration at regional level; and ICN—Information Centre for Non-profit Organizations (now Neziskovky.cz q.v.), providing information, training and co-ordination services to the Third Sector in the Czech Republic.

Activities: Offers educational training, consultancy, networking, publication services and support to the non-profit sector to support the development of non-profit activities.

Geographical Area of Activity: Czech Republic.

Restrictions: No grants are made to individuals; limited grants are made to state-run organizations.

Finance: Annual revenue 354,000 koruny, expenditure 111,000 koruny (2013).

Board of Directors: Lukáš Novák (Chair.); Marek Šedivý (Vice-Chair.).

Principal Staff: Sec. Hana Prchalová.

Address: Malé nám. 12, 110 00 Prague 1.

Telephone: 224239876; **Fax:** 224239875; **Internet:** www.auxilia.cz; **e-mail:** nadace@auxilia.cz.

Neziskovky.cz

Established in 1993 as ICN (Information Centre for Non-profit Organizations) Foundation. Present name adopted in 2005.

Activities: Aims to provide access to information on government regulations and training for organization personnel; to facilitate national and international co-operation; to encourage greater public involvement in the non-profit sector; and to influence government policy with regard to the development of the non-profit sector in the Czech Republic. The organization maintains a library and information centre, a database of financial resources for non-profits, and a database of non-profit organizations in the Czech Republic, comprising more than 2,600 entries. It also provides consultancy services to non-profit organizations; and information, educational and publishing services.

Geographical Area of Activity: Czech Republic.

Publications: *Svět neziskovek* ('NGO World', monthly e-newsletter); *GRANTIS—Non-Profit Sector Monthly* (monthly in Czech, annually in English); *Directory of Czech NGOs; Compendium of Financial Resources in the Czech Republic; Guide to the Law for Not-for-Profit Organizations;* Annual Report.

Finance: Annual revenue 5,029,000 koruny, expenditure 5,436,000 koruny (31 Dec. 2013).

Board of Directors: Lukáš Novák (Chair.); Soňa Nebeská (Vice-Chair.).

Principal Staff: Dir Věra Svobodová.

Address: Malé námesti 12, 110 00 Prague 1.

Telephone: 224239876; **Fax:** 224239875; **Internet:** www .neziskovky.cz; **e-mail:** nadace@neziskovky.cz.

PASOS—Policy Association for an Open Society

Established in 2004.

Activities: Supports civil society development in Central and Eastern Europe and Central Asia through: organizing conferences, seminars, workshops, etc.; supporting joint projects in public policy formulation; providing training in public policy; and disseminating information including publishing information. Has 50 member organizations in 28 countries.

Geographical Area of Activity: Central and Eastern Europe and Central Asia.

Publications: Annual Report; policy briefs; series of advocacy handbooks for civil society on understanding and influencing EU policy-making.

Finance: Annual income €473,068, expenditure €475,702 (2012).

Board of Directors: Andrew Cartright (Chair.); Piotr Kaźmierkiewicz (Deputy Chair.); Neža Kogovšek Šalamon (Treas.).

Principal Staff: Exec. Dir Jeff Lovitt.

Address: Tesnov 3, 110 00 Prague 1.

Telephone: (420) 22231644; **Fax:** (420) 22231644; **Internet:** www.pasos.org; **e-mail:** info@pasos.org.

FOUNDATIONS, TRUSTS AND NON-PROFIT ORGANIZATIONS

Česko-německý fond budoucnosti (Czech-German Fund for the Future)

Established in 1998, as an NGO based in the Czech Republic, by the Governments of the Czech Republic and Germany to compensate Czech victims of Nazism.

Activities: Operates in the field of social welfare, funding social projects for Czech survivors of atrocities committed during the country's occupation by German forces before and during the Second World War, including Jewish and Roma (Gypsy) people, Catholics, Jehovah's Witnesses, homosexuals and political prisoners. The Fund received €84m. between 1998 and 2002, with Germany contributing 84.3% of this amount. Of these funds, approximately €46m. of the Fund was expended on humanitarian aid to victims of National Socialist (Nazi) violence, while the remainder of approximately €38m. was designated for support of Czech-German projects focused on the future and for the work of the Czech-German discussion forum. In addition the Fund provides 10-month scholarships for Czech and German students in the fields of the humanities and social sciences who plan to work on a project with a Czech-German theme while studying in the partner country.

Geographical Area of Activity: Czech Republic.

Publications: Annual Report.

Finance: Annual income 119,508,000 koruny, expenditure 192,166,000 koruny (31 Dec. 2013).

Board of Directors: Kristina Larischová (Chair.); Albrecht Schläger (Deputy Chair.).

Principal Staff: Dir Dr Tomáš Jelinek.

Address: Zelezná 24, 110 00 Prague 71.

Telephone: 283850512; **Fax:** 283850503; **Internet:** www.fb .cz; www.fondbudoucnosti.cz; **e-mail:** info@fb.cz.

CINDI Foundation

Established in 1998 by the National Institute of Public Health (SZU).

Activities: Supports the Institute's CINDI (Countrywide Integrated Noncommunicable Diseases Intervention) Programme, which aims to promote preventative action in the field of public health, focusing on lifestyle and environmental risk factors. Funds conferences, meetings, educational activities, information dissemination and training, and fellowships. Maintains a library of approx. 90,000 items.

Geographical Area of Activity: Czech Republic.

Publications: *Acta hygienica, epidemiologica et microbiologica—AHEM* (journal, in Czech); *Central European Journal of Public Health* (journal, in English); *Czech Journal of Occupational Medicine* (quarterly journal); *Hygiena* (quarterly journal); *Bulletin of epidemiology and microbiology* (monthly); data and statistics.

Finance: Annual revenue 305,239,029 koruny, expenditure 315,994,897 koruny (31 Dec. 2012).

Principal Staff: Dir Jitka Sosnovcová.

Address: Státní Zdravotní Ústav, Šrobárova 48, 100 42 Prague 10.

Telephone: 267081111; **Fax:** 267311188; **Internet:** www.szu .cz/cindi; **e-mail:** zdravust@szu.cz.

Člověk v tísni (People in Need)

Established in 1992 by Jaromír Štětina and other journalists as Epicentrum, a humanitarian group raising money for Nagorno-Karabakh. It subsequently became part of the Lidové noviny foundation, which in 1994 merged with broadcaster České televize to become People in Need under the auspices of Czech Television.

Activities: Operates in the areas of human rights, relief and development assistance. The organization supports democratization processes and human rights protection. It also runs the annual One World human rights documentary film festival. Social integration programmes address poverty and social exclusion problems in the Czech Republic and Slovakia. Educational and informative programmes raise awareness on issues such as global problems and development co-operation, migration and multiculturalism among the public, the state administration and the media.

Geographical Area of Activity: International.

Publications: Annual Report.

Finance: Annual revenue €24,805,584, expenditure €24,755,771 (31 Dec. 2013).

Executive Board: Kristýna Taberyová (Pres.).

Principal Staff: Exec. Dir Šimon Pánek; Financial Dir Jan Kamenický.

Address: Šafaříkova 635/24, 120 00 Prague 2.

Telephone: 226200400; **Fax:** 226200401; **Internet:** www .clovekvtisni.cz; www.peopleinneed.cz; **e-mail:** mail@ clovekvtisni.cz.

Czech Music Fund Foundation (Nadacc Česky Hudebni Fond)

Founded in 1994 by the Czech Music Fund to support and encourage the development of Czech musical culture.

Activities: Provides grants and scholarships to talented Czech musicians; supports musical activities, such as competitions for composers and performers, workshops and music education; holds public composition competitions to stimulate new works. The Foundation has set up two beneficial institutions: the Music Information Centre; and the Czech Music

Fund, which runs an instrument hire service with branches throughout the Czech Republic, and hires out musical scores and parts from other institutions all over the world.

Geographical Area of Activity: Czech Republic.

Publications: Annual Report.

Finance: Annual income 16,386,000 koruny (31 Dec. 2013).

Board: Zdeněk Justoň (Chair.); Pavel Fiedler (Vice-Chair.).

Principal Staff: Dir Miroslav Drozd.

Address: Besední 3, 118 00 Prague 1.

Telephone: 257320008; **Fax:** 257312834; **Internet:** www.nchf .cz; **e-mail:** nadace@nchf.cz.

Hestia—The National Volunteer Centre

Established in 1993 to promote, develop and support volunteering.

Activities: Co-ordinates voluntary work in the Czech Republic. The Centre raises awareness of the voluntary opportunities available to the public, offers training programmes for volunteers, co-ordinators and organizations, and acts as an advice and information source for volunteers. Also helps supervise all existing regional voluntary centres throughout the Czech Republic, and organizes the national Five Ps/Pet P programme, a mentoring volunteer programme to help children who encounter social or health problems in life and need support.

Geographical Area of Activity: Czech Republic.

Publications: Books and articles on volunteer management.

Finance: Annual revenue 6,173,000 koruny, expenditure 5,720,000 koruny (2013).

Board: Dr Jiří Tošner (Chair.).

Principal Staff: Dir Dr Olga Sozanská.

Address: Na Poříčí 1041/12 (palác YMCA), 110 00 Prague 1.

Telephone: 224872075; **Fax:** 224872076; **Internet:** www.hest .cz; **e-mail:** info@hest.cz.

Nadace Českého Výtvarného Umění—NČVU (Czech Fine Art Foundation)

Established in 1994 as the successor to the Czech Fine Arts Fund. Present name adopted in 2008.

Activities: Aims to support artists and art projects through awarding grants as well as managing exhibition spaces in Prague. Provides support to the fine arts in the Czech Republic, through making grants to individuals and organizations and organizing and hosting exhibitions, including the biennial Salons, bringing together a group of artists and individual exhibitions. The Fund's exhibition spaces in Prague include the Mánes Exhibition Hall, the Gallery of Václav Spála and the Golden Lily Gallery. The Fund also owns the newly renovated recreational building the Staré Splavy 'farmhouse'. Established the Czech Architecture Fund (now known as the Czech Architecture Foundation) in 1997.

Geographical Area of Activity: Czech Republic.

Publications: Annual Report.

Finance: Annual giving 220,000 koruny (2013).

Principal Staff: Dir Dagmar Baběradová.

Address: Masarykovo nábřeí 250, 110 00 Prague 1.

Telephone: 224932938; **Fax:** 224930223; **Internet:** www.ncvu .eu; **e-mail:** baberadovad@seznam.cz.

Nadace Český literární fond—nčlf (Czech Literary Fund Foundation)

Founded in 1994 to promote literature in the Czech Republic; registered as a foundation in 1999.

Activities: Presents awards for prose, poetry, literary essays and literary research, including the Josef Hlavka Prize for an original piece of academic or specialist literature published in book form in the Czech Republic. The Foundation supports cultural organizations through subsidies in the fields of translation, film and television, theatre, science and journalism.

Geographical Area of Activity: Czech Republic.

Restrictions: Grants only to specific organizations in the Czech Republic.

Finance: Annual revenue 38,385,000, expenditure 41,235,000 koruny (31 Dec. 2012).

Board of Trustees: Dr Jan Lukeš (Chair.); Dr Dana Kalinová, Josef Kreuter, Jiří Novotný, Michal Novotný (Vice-Chair.).

Principal Staff: Dir Dr Ivo Purš; Deputy Dir Antonín Neumann.

Address: Pod Nuselskými schody 3, 120 00 Prague 2.

Telephone: 222560081; **Fax:** 222560083; **Internet:** www.nclf .cz; **e-mail:** nadace@nclf.cz.

Nadace Charty 77 (The Charta 77 Foundation)

Established in 1989 on the initiative of František Janouch, Karel Jan Schwarzenberg and George Soros; an autonomous branch of the Swedish Charta 77 Foundation.

Activities: Operates in the fields of education, law and human rights, medicine and health, and social welfare (especially for disabled citizens). Annual awards are the literary Jaroslav Seifert and Tom Stoppard prizes; the František Kriegel prize for civil courage; the Josef Vavrousek environmental prize; and the Václav Havel human rights prize.

Geographical Area of Activity: Czech Republic and Europe.

Publications: Annual Report.

Finance: Annual income 57,061,785 koruny, expenditure 76,598,424 koruny (2011).

Board of Trustees: František Janouch (Pres.); Evžen Hart (Vice-Pres.).

Principal Staff: Exec. Dir Boena Jirků.

Address: Melantrichova 5, 110 00 Prague 1.

Telephone: 224214452; **Fax:** 224213647; **Internet:** www .kontobariery.cz; **e-mail:** nadace77@bariery.cz.

Nadace Euronisa (Euronisa Foundation)

Founded in 1995 by the Moravian church in Liberec.

Activities: Operates in the fields of health and social welfare, culture and education. Provides support services to the elderly and the infirm; funds projects working to solve health and social problems such as drug abuse, AIDS, abandoned children and alcoholism. Operates mainly in the Czech area of the Neisse-Nisa-Nysa Euroregion.

Geographical Area of Activity: Czech Republic (mainly the Czech sectors of the Nisa Euroregion).

Restrictions: No grants to individuals.

Publications: Annual Report; newsletters.

Finance: Annual revenue 4,449,000 koruny, expenditure 4,279,000 koruny (2013).

Board: Miroslav Řehák (Chair.); Jaroslav Kašpar (Vice-Chair.).

Principal Staff: Dir Blanka Nedvědická; Grant Man. Jana Kovaříková.

Address: Rumjancevova 3, 460 01 Liberec 1.

Telephone: 485100218; **Fax:** 485102753; **Internet:** www .euronisa.cz; **e-mail:** nadace@euronisa.cz.

Nadace OF (Civic Forum Foundation)

Founded in 1990 by the Civic Forum to revive educational, cultural and humanist ideals in the Czech Republic.

Activities: Focuses on the protection and conservation of national cultural heritage through awareness-building and the promotion of partnerships between the business, non-profit and governmental sectors, with specific attention paid to neglected monuments. The Foundation operates through self-conducted projects, grants to organizations within the Czech Republic and conservation awards. It collaborates with international organizations on several projects. Maintains a cultural heritage database.

Geographical Area of Activity: Czech Republic.

Publications: Annual Report; newsletter (3 a year); *Children's Guide Book to Třeboň Chateau; Cultural Programme Information Sheet.*

Board of Directors: Dagmar Havlová (Chair.).

Address: Štěpánská 61, 110 00 Prague 1.

Telephone: 776575114; **Fax:** 605271540; **Internet:** www .nadaceof.cz; **e-mail:** info@nadaceof.cz.

Nadace Preciosa (Preciosa Foundation)

Founded in 1996 by the Preciosa company to raise funds to support non-profit and publicly beneficial activities in the Czech Republic.

Activities: Funds projects in the fields of health care, education, the arts and culture, science and research, sports, and humanitarian work. Projects are carried out mainly in the region of northern Bohemia, but some activities are carried out throughout the Czech Republic, often in co-operation with Prague-based organizations. The Foundation has set up seven funds, to support each operational area in which it works, including the Health Fund, the Ecology and Environment Fund, and the Education and Retraining Fund. These funds then distribute money to sponsor projects within that particular sphere.

Geographical Area of Activity: Czech Republic.

Finance: Total assets approx. 100,754,000 koruny (2012).

Board of Directors: Stanislav Kadlec (Chair.); Lucie Karlová (Vice-Chair.).

Principal Staff: Dir Ivo Schötta; Sec. Marcela Vojtíšková.

Address: Průmyslová 18, 466 67 Jablonec nad Nisou.

Telephone: 488115111; **Fax:** 488115761; **Internet:** www .nadace.preciosa.cz; **e-mail:** info@nadace.preciosa.cz.

Nadace Světový Étos (Global Ethic Foundation Czech Republic)

Established in 1993 by Karel Floss as an educational and ecological centre with the Global Ethic Foundation in Tübingen, Germany, and the Stiftung für Gesellschaftliche Lebensqualität in Basle, Switzerland, to promote human rights, health protection and public participation. Founded in 1999 in the Czech Republic.

Activities: Provides grants to NGOs in the Czech Republic carrying out educational activities, practical project implementation, exhibitions, heritage reconstruction, natural area protection, and for innovative approaches to sustainable rural development. Also provides consultancy services to NGOs and offers training.

Geographical Area of Activity: Czech Republic.

Finance: Annual revenue 1,739 koruny, expenditure 13,133 koruny (31 Dec. 2011).

Board of Directors: Dr Karel Floss (Chair.); Václav Frei, Dr Ivan Štampach (Vice-Chair.); Irena Flossová (Sec.).

Address: Centrum Prokopios, Černá 9, 115 55, Prague 1.

Telephone: 221988420; **Internet:** www.svetetos.cz; **e-mail:** nse.prokopios@gmail.com.

Nadace Táta a Máma (Dad and Mum Foundation)

Founded in 1997 by Tereza Maxová as the Tereza Maxová Foundation to address the social issues that lead to the abandonment of children, and to provide assistance to children's homes. Present name adopted in 2009.

Activities: Operates in the Czech Republic in the field of social welfare, specifically that of abandoned children. The Foundation works to prevent abandonment through education; provides assistance to adoptive families, thus shortening the time that children must stay in institutions; and raises public awareness of the plight of children who have been abandoned. It also provides material support to children's homes.

Geographical Area of Activity: Czech Republic.

Publications: Annual Report.

Finance: Annual revenue 397,000 koruny, expenditure 829,000 koruny (31 Dec. 2013).

Board: Dr František Francírek (Chair.).

Principal Staff: Admin. Kateřina Francírková.

Address: Klimentská 1246/1, 110 00 Prague 1.

Telephone: 226222050; **Fax:** 226222049; **Internet:** www .nadacetm.cz; **e-mail:** info@nadacetm.cz.

Open Society Fund Prague—OSF Prague

Founded in 1992 to support the building of civil society, the development of educational and cultural activities, and the promotion of intellectual co-operation between Central and Eastern European countries. The Fund is an independent foundation, part of the Open Society Foundations (q.v.) network.

Activities: Supports the development of civic society, education and culture, and law reform in the Czech Republic; co-operates with non-governmental and non-profit organizations; offers educational programmes; contributes to the promotion of intellectual co-operation between Central and Eastern European countries; issues publications; and supports other non-profit activities. The Fund offers three Romani Women's Fellowships for work in the field of women's rights.

Geographical Area of Activity: Czech Republic.

Restrictions: Fellowship applications are open to Romani women university graduates from Albania, Bulgaria, the Czech Republic, Hungary, Italy, the FYR Macedonia, Romania, Serbia, Slovakia, Spain and Turkey.

Publications: Annual Report; Newsletter (monthly, in Czech).

Finance: Annual budget approx. 30m.–35m. koruny.

Board of Trustees: Monika Ladmanová (Chair.).

Principal Staff: Exec. Dir Robert Basch; Financial Dir Zdenka Almerová.

Address: Hradecká 18, 130 00 Prague 3.

Telephone: 222540979; **Fax:** 222540978; **Internet:** www.osf .cz; **e-mail:** osf@osf.cz.

Slovak-Czech Women's Fund

Founded in 2004 by the Open Society Fund Prague and the Open Society Foundation Bratislava (qq.v.) to support the development of women in Slovakia and the Czech Republic.

Activities: Provides funding to NGOs and community organizations, targeting marginalized populations, including Roma women in Slovakia, young women who exceed the age for foster care in the Czech Republic and young women who can benefit from leadership skills. A sister office operates in Bratislava.

Geographical Area of Activity: Slovakia and the Czech Republic.

Finance: Annual revenue 2,552,000 koruny, expenditure 2,552,000 koruny (31 Dec. 2013).

Board of Directors: Markéta Hronková (Chair.).

Principal Staff: Exec. Dir Miroslava Bobáková.

Address: Bořivojova 105, 130 00 Prague 3.

Telephone: 222716823; **Fax:** 222716823; **Internet:** www .womensfund.cz; **e-mail:** bobakova@womensfund.sk.

VIA Foundation

Established in 1997 as the successor to the USA-based Foundation for a Civil Society's Prague office to promote and strengthen active public participation in democratic society in the Czech Republic.

Activities: Operates in the Czech Republic in the fields of community development, the development of philanthropy, and institutional support for NGOs. The Foundation makes grants to institutions, offers prizes (the Via Bona awards to philanthropic donors, businesses and individuals), organizes training courses and issues publications. Programmes include the Community Development Fund, the T-Mobile Fund, the Cultural Heritage Fund, Accelerator—The Academy of Social Enterpreneurship and many more. It co-operates with other organizations in Central and Eastern Europe.

Geographical Area of Activity: Czech Republic.

Publications: *Místo pro zivot* (A Place for Life, 1999); Annual Report; newsletter.

Finance: Annual revenue 33,448,623 koruny, expenditure 32,736,010 koruny (31 Dec. 2012).

Board of Directors: Lenka Mrázová (Chair.).

Principal Staff: Exec. Dir Jiří Bárta.

Address: Jelení 195/9, 118 00 Prague 1.

Telephone: 233113370; **Fax:** 233113380; **Internet:** www .nadacevia.cz; www.viafoundation.org; **e-mail:** via@ nadacevia.cz.

Výbor dobré vůle—Nadace Olgy Havlové (Committee of Good Will—Olga Havel Foundation)

Founded in 1990 by Olga Havel to alleviate suffering caused by disability and chronic illness, and to assist with social problems in society. Originally a clearing house for health-related aid from the West, but has now expanded to invest in public health and social assistance with long-term grants and projects.

Activities: Aims to raise awareness of the problems and challenges faced by people with disabilities and chronic illnesses, particularly in the areas of employment, education and housing; to provide organizational and financial support to humanitarian projects and for disaster relief; and to help create an integrated society. Programmes include: Salzburg Medical Cornell Seminars; Sasakawa Asthma Fund, established to address the growing problem of asthma-related diseases; Ordinary Life, supporting civic associations in their programmes for homeless, excluded communities and mothers in difficult situations; and the Education Fund, which awards scholarships to students with social problems and disabilities. The Sasakawa Asthma Fund operates in both the Czech Republic and Slovakia; the other programmes operate only in the Czech Republic. The Committee also distributes the annual Olga Havel Award to people who are engaged in helping others despite their own disability.

Geographical Area of Activity: Czech Republic.

Publications: Annual Report; books; *The Good News Magazine*.

Finance: Annual income 52,020 koruny, expenditure 48,297 koruny (2013).

Board of Directors: Dana Němcová (Pres.); Franziska Sternbergová (Vice-Pres.); Gabriela Bauer (Sec.).

Principal Staff: Dir Dr Milena Černá.

Address: POB 240, 111 21 Prague 1; Senováné náměstí č. 994/2, Prague 1.

Telephone: 224217331; **Fax:** 224217082; **Internet:** www.vdv .cz; www.sportprocharitu.cz; www.openmedicalclubcr.com; **e-mail:** vdv@vdv.cz.

Vzdělávací nadace Jana Husa (Jan Hus Educational Foundation)

Founded in 1990 by Miroslav Pospíil, Jana Kuchtová and Julie Tastná to support the development of higher education in the arts, humanities and law in the Czech Republic and Slovakia. Since 1993, the former branch office in Bratislava has operated as a sister foundation in Slovakia.

Activities: Operates in the Czech Republic in the fields of the development of education, and the development of civil society, through self-conducted programmes, training courses, grants to institutions and publication awards.

Geographical Area of Activity: Czech Republic and Slovakia.

Restrictions: Open only to applicants from the Czech Republic and Slovakia.

Publications: Annual Report; *Going Abroad to Study*; *The Velvet Philosophers*; *Granting—a Process of Grant-Giving in Foundations*; *Ethical Principles in Foundations*; *Work*; *The Management of Foundation Assets, a Way to Self-Sustainability of the Foundation Sector*.

Finance: Annual revenue 14,578,000 koruny, expenditure 11,859,000 koruny (31 Dec. 2013).

Board of Trustees: Jiří Müller (Chair.); D Krístina Korená, Dr Tomáš Holeček (Vice-Chair.).

Principal Staff: Exec. Dir Jana Švábová; Sec. Miroslava Rehulková.

Address: Cihlářská 15, 602 00 Brno.

Telephone: 549491049; **Fax:** 549491050; **Internet:** www.vnjh .cz; **e-mail:** jsvabova@vnjh.cz.

Denmark

FOUNDATIONS, TRUSTS AND NON-PROFIT ORGANIZATIONS

Aktion Børnehjælp (Action Child Aid)

Founded in 1965 to help children in need in India.

Activities: Provides funding to children's aid projects in India, as well as food, equipment and sponsorship.

Geographical Area of Activity: India.

Publications: Annual Report; *Aktion Børnehjælp Nyt* (3 a year); e-newsletter.

Board of Trustees: Rune Christoffer Dragsdahl (Chair.); Agnete Kofoed (Vice-Chair.).

Principal Staff: Sec. Klaus Iversen.

Address: Kontorfaellesskabet, Vermundsgade 38A, 2 th, 2100 Copenhagen Ø.

Telephone: 35-85-03-15; **Fax:** 35-85-03-15; **Internet:** www.aktionb.dk; **e-mail:** aktionb@mail.dk.

Alfred Benzons Fond (Alfred Benzon Foundation)

Founded by Dr Bøje Benzon in 1952 in memory of his paternal grandfather Alfred Nicolai Benzon, founder of the first pharmaceutical company in Denmark, to promote biomedical research.

Activities: Main activity is organizing the Benzon Symposia, which concentrate on medicine and pharmacy and related sciences. The Foundation also offers fellowships to Danish research scientists undertaking study at foreign institutions; and to a limited number of foreign scientists wishing to conduct their research in Denmark (applications for these must be forwarded by a Danish scientist). Grants are also made to the Copenhagen Zoological Garden.

Geographical Area of Activity: Denmark.

Restrictions: No grants to non-Danish individuals.

Publications: *The Alfred Benzon Foundation 1952–2002.*

Board of Trustees: Prof. Mads Bryde Andersen (Chair.); Prof. Povl Krogsgaard-Larsen, Prof. Niels Borregaard (Vice-Chair.).

Principal Staff: Admin Man. Leila Majdanac.

Address: c/o Copenhagen University, Faculty of Health and Medical Sciences, School of Pharmaceutical Sciences, Universitetsparken 2, 2100 Copenhagen.

Telephone: 22-97-87-52; **Internet:** www.benzon-foundation.dk; **e-mail:** mail@benzon-foundation.dk.

Carlsbergfondet (Carlsberg Foundation)

Founded in 1876 by Jacob Christian Jacobsen to contribute to the growth of science in Denmark; to continue and extend the work of the chemical-physiological Carlsberg Laboratory; and to set up and develop the Museum of National History at Frederiksborg Castle.

Activities: Operates in the fields of science and the arts and humanities. The Foundation carries out its activities through the New Carlsberg Foundation (f. 1902 by Carl Jacobsen) and four departments: Department A, the Carlsberg Laboratory, which studies science with a view to improvements in malting, brewing and fermentation; Department B awards grants to further the various natural sciences, together with mathematics, philosophy, history, linguistics and social sciences through self-conducted programmes, research, grants to institutions and individuals, fellowships, scholarships, publications and lectures; Department C supports the Museum of National History; and Department D, Tuborgfondet (the Tuborg Foundation, f. 1931, merged with the Carlsberg Foundation in 1991), which works for socially beneficial purposes. The New Carlsberg Foundation (q.v.) supports the visual arts and architecture, chiefly through the purchase of works for art galleries and public buildings.

Geographical Area of Activity: Denmark.

Publications: Annual Report; financial statement.

Board of Directors: Prof. Flemming Besenbacher (Chair.).

Principal Staff: Head of Secretariat Lene Kyhse Bisgaard.

Address: H. C. Andersen Blvd 35, 1553 Copenhagen V.

Telephone: 33-43-53-63; **Fax:** 33-43-53-64; **Internet:** www.carlsbergfondet.dk; **e-mail:** carlsbergfondet@carlsbergfondet.dk.

Danmark-Amerika Fondet & Fulbright Kommissionen (Denmark-America Foundation & Fulbright Commission)

Founded in 1914 to encourage understanding between the peoples of Denmark and the USA.

Activities: Encourages educational exchange between Denmark and the USA through the provision of grants to Danes; organizes programmes; assists Danish academics in finding appointments in US institutions of higher education; and awards prizes to Danish citizens. It works in conjunction with the Danish Fulbright Commission, sharing an administration and a secretariat.

Geographical Area of Activity: USA, Denmark.

Restrictions: Grants only to Danish citizens.

Publications: Reports (annually, in Danish).

Board of Directors: Jørgen Bardenfleth (Chair.); Peter Højland (Treas.).

Principal Staff: Exec. Dir Marie Mønsted.

Address: Nørregade 7A, 1165 Copenhagen K.

Telephone: 35-32-45-45; **Internet:** www.wemakeithappen.dk; **e-mail:** advising@daf-fulb.dk.

Danske Kulturinstitut (The Danish Cultural Institute)

Founded in 1940 (originally as Danske Selskab—The Danish Institute) to stimulate cultural relations between Denmark and other countries.

Activities: Promotes dialogue and understanding across cultural differences and national borders. The Institute's work encompasses art, culture and society, focusing on: co-creation; education and research; welfare; sustainability; and children and youth. It facilitates networks and strengthens collaboration between Danish and international artists, cultural institutions and the business community; and creates platforms for knowledge sharing, the exchange of ideas and experiences, and lasting cultural relations. Activities include concerts, exhibitions, conferences, field trips, theatre, film, dance, and, in some countries, Danish courses. Maintains international branches in Edinburgh, Brussels, Warsaw, Riga, St Petersburg, Beijing and Rio de Janeiro.

Geographical Area of Activity: Europe, EU, Estonia, Latvia, Lithuania, Poland, the United Kingdom, the People's Republic of China, the Russian Federation, Brazil.

Publications: *From the Golden Age to the Present Day; Flora Danica; Discover Denmark; Learning in Denmark; Songs from Denmark; Kierkegaard's Universe; Søren Kierkegaard; The Welfare Society in Transition; Danish Literature; Danish Painting and Sculpture.*

Finance: Receives a yearly grant from the Danish Ministry of Culture, which is supplemented by donations from foundations, business sponsors and local government organizations.

Board of Representatives: Michael Christiansen (Pres.); Anders Laursen (Acting Vice-Pres.).

Principal Staff: Sec.-Gen. Michael Metz Mørch.

Address: Vartov, Farvergade 27 L, 2nd Floor, 1463 Copenhagen K.

Telephone: 33-13-54-48; **Fax:** 33-15-10-91; **Internet:** www.dankultur.dk; **e-mail:** dankultur@dankultur.dk.

Egmont Fonden (Egmont Foundation)

Founded in 1920 in accordance with the wishes of Egmont Harald Petersen, printer to the Royal Danish Court, to operate the businesses established by him, so as to raise funds for charitable purposes.

Activities: Owns the Egmont Group, a Scandinavian media group. The Foundation's charitable activities are concentrated on initiatives that provide lasting improvements for children and young people. In the social welfare and health area, it prioritizes initiatives that seek to prevent or reduce marginalization of disadvantaged children. In the field of education and leisure, the Foundation concentrates on initiatives that address and develop curiosity, imagination and creativity, stimulating a broad range of learning and strengthening new ways of acquiring knowledge, and developing the communication skills of children and young people. Projects include modernization of the Danish National Museum; a children's art gallery in the Royal Museum of Fine Art; a science centre 'Experimentarium'; the establishment of the Children's Centre for Rehabilitation of Brain Injury; the 'Music as Medicine' Music Programme for Intensive Care and Recovery Patients; and the Centre for the Prevention of Congenital Malformations. Since 1992, the Foundation has been involved in the 'Democratization of Pre-school Education' project in co-operation with the Open Society Fund (q.v.) in Lithuania.

Geographical Area of Activity: Denmark.

Restrictions: No grants to individuals.

Publications: Annual Report.

Finance: Annual revenue 11,600m. Danish kroner (2014).

Trustees: Steen Riisgaard (Chair.); Lars-Johan Jarnheimer (Vice-Chair.).

Principal Staff: Dir Henriette Christiansen.

Address: Vognmagergade 9, 5th Floor, 1148 Copenhagen K.

Telephone: 33-91-36-44; **Internet:** www.egmontfonden.dk; **e-mail:** mail@egmontfonden.dk.

Foundation for Environmental Education—FEE

Founded in 1981 as the Foundation for Environmental Education in Europe to raise awareness of environmental issues and effect change through education, as a means of achieving sustainability. In 2001, became the Foundation for Environmental Education (FEE), with the addition of South Africa as the first non-European member country.

Activities: Co-ordinates international campaigns and creates awareness of environmental education. The Foundation's main programmes are: Blue Flag; Eco-Schools; Learning About Forests (LEAF); Young Reporters for the Environment; and Green Key. It also established the Global Forest Fund. Has members in 64 countries.

Geographical Area of Activity: Worldwide.

Publications: Newsletters; Annual Report.

Executive Board: Jan Eriksen (Pres.); Lesley Jones (Vice-Pres.); Michael Ierides (Treas.).

Principal Staff: CEO Daniel Schaffer.

Address: c/o The Danish Outdoor Council, Scandiagade 13, 2450 Copenhagen SV.

Telephone: 70-22-24-27; **Fax:** 33-79-01-79; **Internet:** www.fee-international.org; **e-mail:** info@fee-international.org.

Friluftsraadet (Danish Outdoor Council)

Founded in 1942.

Activities: Works in all areas of outdoor recreational facilities and conservation. Lobbies on relevant issues, including sustainable tourism and develops environmental education projects. Operates a small-grants programme for environmental work involving Danish organizations and indigenous organizations in Eastern and Southern Europe. Has more than 90 member organizations.

Geographical Area of Activity: Scandinavia, the Baltic region, and Eastern and Southern Europe.

Finance: Small grants available of up to 250,000 Danish kroner.

Board of Directors: Lars Mortensen (Chair.).

Principal Staff: Dir Jan Ejlsted; Deputy Dir Torbjørn Eriksen.

Address: Scandiagade 13, 2450 Copenhagen SV.

Telephone: 33-79-00-79; **Fax:** 33-79-01-79; **Internet:** www.friluftsraadet.dk; **e-mail:** fr@friluftsraadet.dk.

IBIS

Established in 1966 to provide assistance to people in developing countries.

Activities: Supports development and capacity-building projects in less-developed countries in Central and South America, and Africa; raises awareness in Denmark of problems suffered by people living in developing countries, including HIV and AIDS programmes; promotes ecologically sustainable growth; and campaigns for positive change in Denmark's foreign aid policy. IBIS supports 200 large- and small-scale projects in Ghana, Guatemala, Mozambique, Nicaragua, Liberia, Bolivia, Sierra Leone, South Sudan and Burkina Faso.

Geographical Area of Activity: Central and South America and Africa.

Publications: *IBIS Fokus;* Annual Report.

Finance: Income 277,335,000 Danish kroner, expenditure 279,217,000 Danish kroner (2013).

Trustees: Mette Müller (Chair.).

Principal Staff: Sec.-Gen. Vagn Berthelsen.

Address: Vesterbrogade 2B, 1620 Copenhagen V.

Telephone: 35-35-87-88; **Fax:** 35-35-06-96; **Internet:** www.ibis.dk; and www.ibis-global.org; **e-mail:** ibis@ibis.dk.

Institut for Menneskerettigheder (Danish Institute for Human Rights)

Founded in 1987.

Activities: Operates in the field of human rights, engaging in research and education, and disseminating information and documentation regionally, nationally and internationally. The Institute co-operates with other human rights organizations in Denmark and abroad. It established a student internship programme in collaboration with private companies and the Danish Industrialization Foundation for Developing Countries. Maintains a library.

Geographical Area of Activity: International.

Publications: Annual Report; review reports; research papers; e-resources.

Finance: Annual income 130,478 Danish kroner (2014).

Council: Ole Hartling (Chair.); Carsten Fenger (Vice-Chair.).

Principal Staff: Exec. Dir Jonas Christoffersen; Deputy Dirs Louise Holck, Eva Grambye.

Address: Wilders Plads 8K, 1403 Copenhagen K.

Telephone: 32-69-88-88; **Fax:** 32-69-88-00; **Internet:** humanrights.dk; menneskeret.dk; **e-mail:** info@humanrights.dk.

International Work Group for Indigenous Affairs—IWGIA

Established in 1968; aims to support and assist indigenous peoples around the world.

Activities: Operates in the field of human rights. The Group supports indigenous peoples' land rights, self-governance and independence, cultural integrity and the right to control their own futures. It works in collaboration with indigenous peoples' organizations; runs development projects all over the world (especially in Africa, Central and South America, Asia and the Pacific, and the Arctic); holds conferences; engages in research; and produces related publications and documentation, which it disseminates internationally. Worked on 60 projects in 25 countries in 2012.

Geographical Area of Activity: International.

Publications: *Indigenous Affairs* (periodical, 2 a year); *The Indigenous World* (annually); books (mainly in English and Spanish); briefing papers; handbooks; manuals; reports; videos.

Finance: Annual income 38,509,935 Danish kroner, expenditure 37,027,440 (2013).

Board of Directors: Frank Sejersen (Chair.); Jérémie Gilbert (Vice-Chair.).

Principal Staff: Exec. Dir Orla Bakdal.

Address: Classengade 11E, 2100 Copenhagen.

Telephone: 35-27-05-00; **Fax:** 35-27-05-07; **Internet:** www.iwgia.org; **e-mail:** iwgia@iwgia.org.

IUC-Europe Internationalt Uddanneless Center (IUC-Europe International Education Centre)

Founded in 1985 (reorganized in 1991) by Frits Korsgaard, Dr Jacob Christensen, Dr Tom Høyem, Dr Knud Overø, Bent le Févre and Ingolf Knudsen to promote international understanding and co-operation through a variety of interdisciplinary and intercultural programmes that emphasize experiential education.

Activities: Develops and implements numerous educational programmes, including study missions for students, teachers and business people to the capitals of the member states and the institutions of the European Union, and for North American students and teachers to Europe and European students and teachers to the USA; exchanges with Central, Eastern and Western Europe, Scandinavia and the Baltic republics; Holocaust study; and international conferences and seminars. The Centre's network includes affiliate offices in Hungary, Poland, Canada, the United Kingdom and the USA. It also has partners in most European countries and an International Board of Advisers.

Geographical Area of Activity: Western, Central and Eastern Europe, and North America.

Restrictions: Does not sponsor individuals, groups or programmes outside the IUC network.

Publications: Newsletter.

Board: Nina Nørgaard (Chair.); Rasmus Stobbe (Vice-Chair.).

Address: Hollændervænget 10, 2791 Dragør.

Telephone: 26-20-11-05; **Internet:** www.iuc-europe.dk; **e-mail:** iuc@iuc-europe.dk.

Lauritzen Fonden (Lauritzen Foundation)

Established in 1945 by two brothers, Ivar and Knud Lauritzen, and their sister, Anna Lønberg-Holm, to mark the 50th anniversary of Dampskibsselskabet Vesterhavet, the shipping company founded in 1895 by their father, Ditlev Lauritzen. Originally the J. L. Fondet, it was renamed in 2009 as the Lauritzen Fonden.

Activities: Makes large and small grants to institutions, associations and individuals over a broad spectrum of activities. The Foundation supports studies and projects of a technical, commercial or other nature in shipping, trade and industry, agriculture and other sectors; and the education or training of young people in Denmark and abroad. It promotes healthy and well-maintained workplaces and company housing, especially in the shipping sector. It also supports institutions, associations and people who work in and look after the interests of the shipping sector or that have an interest in other humanitarian institutions; and aids Foundation or Lauritzen Group employees and their families. The Foundation supports institutions, associations and people working to encourage awareness and esteem of Danish cultural activities, and Nordic and international relations of a purely humanitarian nature.

Geographical Area of Activity: Mainly Denmark.

Publications: Annual Report; prize essays.

Finance: Annual revenue 15,870,388 Danish kroner, expenditure 14,549,566 Danish kroner (31 Dec. 2014).

Board: Jens Ditlev Lauritzen (Chair.); Michael Fiorni (Vice-Chair.).

Principal Staff: Gen. Man. Inge Grønvold.

Address: Sankt Annæ Plads 28, 1291 Copenhagen K.

Telephone: 33-96-84-25; **Fax:** 33-96-84-35; **Internet:** www.lauritzenfonden.com; **e-mail:** lf@lauritzenfonden.com.

Lego Fonden (The Lego Foundation)

Established in 2009 with the aim of inspiring children through learning and play.

Activities: Donates Lego products worldwide; promotes children's education through new learning materials, research programmes and training of teachers in less-developed countries.

Geographical Area of Activity: International.

Restrictions: Does not provide financial support.

Finance: Annual income 1,817,916 Danish kroner, expenditure 84,000 (31 Dec. 2014).

Board of Directors: Kjeld Kirk Kristiansen (Chair.); Sofie Kirk Kiær Kristiansen, Thomas Kirk Kristiansen (Deputy Chair.).

Principal Staff: CEO Hanne Rasmussen.

Address: Koldingvej 2, 7190 Billund.

Internet: www.lego-fonden.dk; **e-mail:** legofoundation@lego.com.

Lundbeckfonden (Lundbeck Foundation)

Established in 1954 by Grete Lundbeck, whose late husband Hans founded pharmaceutical company H. Lundbeck A/S, to make grants for scientific research.

Activities: Operates in the field of science and technology through offering grants for research projects in the specific areas of health and natural sciences. Also offers the Nordic Research Award for a young scientist along with other awards. Makes grants to c. 600 researchers at Danish universities amounting to a total of between 400m. and 500m. Danish kroner annually.

Geographical Area of Activity: Mainly Denmark.

Finance: Annual revenue 29,904m. Danish kroner (31 Dec. 2014).

Board of Trustees: Jørgen Huno Rasmussen (Chair.); Steffen Kragh (Vice-Chair.).

Principal Staff: CEO Lene Skole.

Address: Scherfigsvej 7, 2100 Hellerup.

Telephone: 39-12-80-00; **Fax:** 39-12-80-08; **Internet:** www.lundbeckfonden.dk; **e-mail:** mail@lundbeckfonden.dk.

A. P. Møller og Hustru Chastine Mc-Kinney Møllers Fond til almene Formaal (The A. P. Møller and Chastine Mc-Kinney Møller Foundation)

Founded in 1953 by shipowner A. P. Møller and his wife Chastine Mc-Kinney Møller.

Activities: Supports Danish culture and heritage, Danish shipping and medical science. Grants are only occasionally made to non-Danish projects. Major institutions established with foundation funding include a new opera house in Copenhagen. The Foundation has set up a number of funds over its lifetime and in 2013 established holding company AP Moller Holding A/S.

Geographical Area of Activity: Denmark.

Restrictions: No grants are made to individuals. Applications not accepted by email.

Finance: Revenue approx. 900m. Danish kroner (2010–12).

Board of Directors: Ane Mærsk Mc-Kinney Uggla (Chair.); Peter Straarup (Vice-Chair.).

Principal Staff: Man. Henrik Tvarnø; Secs Mette Olufsen, Eva Mikkelsen.

Address: Esplanaden 50, 1098 Copenhagen K.

Telephone: 33-63-34-02; **Fax:** 33-63-34-10; **Internet:** www .apmollerfonde.dk; **e-mail:** mette.olufsen@maersk.com.

Otto Mønsteds Fond (Otto Mønsteds Foundation)

Founded in 1934 by Otto Mønsted, a margarine manufacturer, to further the development of Danish trade and industry, and, in particular, to assist in the education of young commercial workers and polytechnic students and graduates; to train teachers at commercial or technical universities; and to promote and sponsor plans or enterprises that might advance Danish commerce or industry.

Activities: Awards grants to teachers and students at commercial and technical universities for study and participation in congresses abroad.

Geographical Area of Activity: Denmark.

Publications: Annual Report.

Finance: Total assets 536,869,000 Danish kroner (2013).

Board of Directors: Prof. Knut Conradsen (Chair.).

Principal Staff: Dir Bent Larsen; Admin. Dir Bo Staernose; Admin. Annette Bergmann.

Address: Fondenes Hus, Otto Mønsteds Gade 1571, Copenhagen V.

Telephone: 21-27-45-04; **Internet:** www.ottomoensted.dk; **e-mail:** omf@omfonden.dk.

MS ActionAid Denmark

Established in 1944 as Fredsvenners Hjælpearbejde to promote solidarity and understanding through co-operation beyond geographical and cultural boundaries, and contribute to sustainable global development and fair distribution of resources. Adopted the name Mellemfolkeligt Samvirke (Danish Association for International Co-operation) in 1949.

Activities: Membership organization consisting of 65 institutional members and about 8,000 individuals. Carries out grassroots activism, political lobbying and provides development assistance. Maintains a searchable online database with information on partner organizations in the global South.

Geographical Area of Activity: International, including Kenya, Mozambique, Nepal, Southern Africa, Tanzania, Uganda, Zambia, Zimbabwe and Central America.

Publications: Annual Report; *Kontakt* (magazine).

Finance: Annual income 294,163,000 Danish kroner, expenditure 253,359,000 Danish kroner (2013).

Board: Helle Munk Ravnborg (Chair.); Dines Justesen (Vice-Chair.).

Principal Staff: Sec.-Gen. Frans Mikael Jansen.

Address: Fælledvej 12, 2200 Copenhagen N.

Telephone: 77-31-00-00; **Fax:** 77-31-01-01; **Internet:** www.ms .dk; **e-mail:** ms@ms.dk.

Nordisk Kulturfond (Nordic Culture Fund)

Founded in 1966 by the Nordic Council to encourage cultural co-operation in all its aspects by the Nordic countries (Denmark, Finland, Iceland, Norway and Sweden, including Greenland, Faroe Islands and Åland Islands).

Activities: Aims to further cultural co-operation between the Nordic countries. Concerned with a wide range of artistic and cultural areas, involving professionals and amateurs. Supports activities characterized by quality, vision, accessibility and variety, where both traditional and new ways of working can be developed. Contributions can be granted to conferences, concerts, tours, exhibitions and festivals, for example.

A project may be completed both within and outside the Nordic countries. Funds c. 250 projects each year; awarded grants amounting to approx. 29m. Danish kroner in 2013.

Geographical Area of Activity: Nordic countries and the rest of the world.

Restrictions: A project is considered 'Nordic' if a minimum of three Nordic countries or self-governing areas are involved, either as participants, organizers or as subject areas. Funding is not awarded for: activities already started before the Fund has made its decision; technical equipment; repairs; construction work; running expenses of institutions; production of records/CDs, computer games, feature films, short films, documentaries, TV drama or series; ordering of music compositions; translation of fiction or non-fiction literature; personal studies, further education, or research work; student exchange and school trips; or sports events.

Finance: Annual income 37,497,196 Danish kroner, expenditure 36,325,237 (2011).

Governing Board: Helgi Hjörvar (Chair.); Aðalsteinn Ásberg Sigurðsson (Vice-Chair.).

Principal Staff: Dir Benny Marcel.

Address: Ved Stranden 18, 1061 Copenhagen K.

Telephone: 33-96-02-42; **Internet:** www.nordiskkulturfond .org; **e-mail:** kulturfonden@norden.org.

Novo Nordisk Foundation

Founded in 1989 following the merger of the Novo Foundation (f. 1951), the Nordisk Insulinfond (Nordic Insulin Foundation, f. 1926) and the Nordisk Insulinlaboratorium (Nordic Insulin Laboratory).

Activities: Operates in the Nordic countries, supporting research in physiology, endocrinology, metabolism and other medical areas. It provides a base for the commercial and research activities conducted by the companies within the Novo Group, and supports various scientific, humanitarian and social programmes. Awards the Novo Nordisk Prize to a Danish scientist for a contribution in the field of medical science; and the Novozymes Prize for biotechnology research.

Geographical Area of Activity: Scandinavia.

Publications: Annual Report; *Novo Nordisk Foundation Magazine* (annual, in Danish and English).

Finance: Total assets 8,630m. Danish kroner (2014).

Trustees: Sten Scheibye (Chair.); Steen Riisgaard (Vice-Chair.).

Principal Staff: CEO Birgitte Nauntofte.

Address: Tuborg Havnevej 19, 2900 Hellerup.

Telephone: 35-27-66-00; **Fax:** 35-27-66-01; **Internet:** www .novonordiskfonden.dk; **e-mail:** nnfond@novo.dk.

Ny Carlsbergfondet (New Carlsberg Foundation)

Established in 1902 by Carl and Ottilia Jacobsen to promote the arts in Denmark. Part of the Carlsbergfondet (q.v.).

Activities: Operates in the field of the arts and culture, supporting the New Carlsberg Glypotek and other museums in Denmark, and promoting the study of art and art history through offering grants for travel and for publications on art. Offers the Carl Jacobsen Museologist Award, the New Carlsberg Foundation Travel Award and the Knud W. Jensen Award. In 2015, the Foundation awarded grants amounting to approx. 120m. Danish kroner.

Geographical Area of Activity: Denmark.

Restrictions: Applications for grants not accepted.

Finance: Annual income 207,638,000 Danish kroner, expenditure 24,575,000 (2013).

Board of Management: Karsten Ohrt (Chair.).

Address: Brolæggerstræde 5, 1211 Copenhagen K.

Telephone: 33-11-37-65; **Internet:** www.ny-carlsbergfondet .dk; **e-mail:** sekretariatet@nycarlsbergfondet.dk.

Plums Fond for Fred, Økologi og Bæredygtighed
(Plums Fund for Peace, Ecology and Sustainability)

Formed in 2013 by the merger of Fredsfonden (Danish Peace Foundation), which was founded in 1981 by Lise and Niels Munk Plum, and Plums Økologifond (Plums Ecology Fund), which was founded in 1988 by Lise Plum.

Activities: Works towards disarmament and peace and conflict resolution; promotes respect for human rights; supports the development of ecology and sustainability. Awards a Peace Prize worth between 50,000 and 100,000 Danish kroner to organizations or individuals for their contribution to human rights, peace and democracy.

Geographical Area of Activity: Mainly Denmark.

Restrictions: No scholarships.

Trustees: Knud Vilby (Chair.).

Principal Staff: Sec. Mille Rode.

Address: Dronningensgade 14, 1420 Copenhagen K.

Telephone: 32-95-44-17; **Fax:** 32-95-44-18; **Internet:** www .fredsfonden.dk; **e-mail:** info@fredsfonden.dk.

Realdania

Established in 2000 following a merger between three financial institutions—RealDanmark A/S, Danske Bank and Foreningen RealDanmark.

Activities: Supports projects that improve the built environment and quality of life for the common good. Currently involved in more than 600 projects. In 2013, it awarded grants ammounting to approx. €121m.

Geographical Area of Activity: Denmark.

Publications: Annual Report; Annual Magazine.

Finance: Annual income 3,085,500 Danish kroner, expenditure 2,153,800 Danish kroner (2014).

Supervisory Board: Michael Brockenhuus-Schack (Chair.); Carsten With Thygesen (Deputy Chair.).

Principal Staff: Chief Exec. Jesper Nygård; Exec. Dir Hans Peter Svendler.

Address: Jarmers Plads 2, 1551 Copenhagen V.

Telephone: 70-11-66-66; **Fax:** 32-88-52-99; **Internet:** www .realdania.dk; **e-mail:** realdania@realdania.dk.

Rockwool Fonden (Rockwool Foundation)

Founded in 1981 by the children of the late Gustav Kähler, founder of mineral wool manufacturer Rockwool, to support scientific, social and humanitarian goals, and contribute to the improvement of the environment and social development.

Activities: Programmes areas are: work and the wefare state; immigration and integration; the informal economy; national law; and families and children. The Foundation supports social and humanitarian projects carried out by small organizations or by individuals; practical self-help projects in the third world; and social capacity-building projects in Denmark.

Geographical Area of Activity: Denmark; some grants are made internationally, via Danish organizations.

Publications: Annual Report; books; newsletters; working papers.

Finance: Annual income 12,635,682 Danish kroner (2014).

Board: Lars Nørby Johansen (Chair.); Anders Eldrup (Deputy Chair.).

Principal Staff: Pres. Elin Schmidt.

Address: Kronprinsessegade 54, 2 tv, 1306 Copenhagen.

Telephone: 46-56-03-06; **Fax:** 46-59-10-92; **Internet:** www .rockwoolfonden.dk; **e-mail:** contact@rockwoolfoundation .org.

Sonnings-Fonden (Sonning Foundation)

Founded in 1949 by writer and editor C. J. Sonning to award a prize biennially for meritorious work in the promotion of European civilization.

Activities: Focuses on rehabilitation and restoration of historic buildings, and music research. Also awards The Sonning Prize, biennially, which amounts to 1m. Danish kroner; European universities have the right to propose candidates, and the winner is selected by a committee established by the Rector of the University of Copenhagen. Former prizewinners include Agnes Heller (2006), Renzo Piano (2008), Hans Magnus Enzensberger (2010), Orhan Pamuk (2012) and Michael Haneke (2014). In 2014, the Foundation awarded grants amounting to more than 1.5m. Danish kroner.

Geographical Area of Activity: Europe.

Restrictions: Does not fund the purchase of musical instruments or scholarships.

Publications: Books.

Sonning Prize Committee: Prof. Ralf Hemmingsen (Chair.); Dorrit Wivel (Sec.).

Principal Staff: Sr Exec. Advisor Charlotte Autzen.

Address: c/o DEAS A/S, Dirch Passer Allé 76, 2000 Frederiksberg.

Telephone: 39-46-62-54; **Internet:** sonning-fonden.ku.dk; **e-mail:** sonningpris@adm.ku.dk.

Léonie Sonnings Musikfond (Léonie Sonning Music Foundation)

Established in 1959.

Activities: Operates in the field of the arts and culture. The Foundation offers an annual prize of 600,000 Danish kroner to an internationally acknowledged composer, conductor, singer or musician. Prizewinners include Jordi Savall (2012), Sir Simon Rattle (2013), Martin Fröst (2014), Thomas Adès (2015) and Herbert Blomstedt (2016). Also offers grants to support young musicians, composers, conductors and singers in the Nordic countries.

Geographical Area of Activity: Worldwide.

Restrictions: Applications for grants not accepted.

Board of Directors: Esben Tange (Chair.); Torsten Hoffmeyer (Sec.).

Principal Staff: Sec. Bente Legarth.

Address: Advokatselskabet Horten, Philip Heymans Allé 7, 2900 Hellerup.

Telephone: 33-34-40-00; **Fax:** 33-34-40-01; **Internet:** www .sonningmusik.dk; **e-mail:** sekretariat@sonningmusik.dk.

Thomas B. Thriges Fond (Thomas B. Thrige Foundation)

Founded in 1934 by engineer and manufacturer Thomas B. Thrige to benefit Danish business, particularly industry and the trades.

Activities: Promotes scientific and educational projects that the Board of Trustees believe are of importance to the well-being of Danish business and industry. The Foundation provides grants to Danish universities and research institutes for specialized equipment, and finances study tours abroad for Danish researchers and participation in international conferences by Danish experts; it also gives grants to visiting professors from abroad.

Geographical Area of Activity: Denmark.

Restrictions: Does not fund study in Denmark.

Publications: Annual Report.

Finance: Annual income 8,706,000 Danish kroner, expenditure 2,908,000 Danish kroner (28 Feb. 2014).

Board of Directors: Niels Jacobsen (Chair.); Flemming H. Tomdrup (Vice-Chair.).

Address: c/o Terma A/S, Hovmarken 4, 8520 Lystrup.

Telephone: 39-61-50-30; **Fax:** 39-61-50-31; **Internet:** thrigesfond.wordpress.com; **e-mail:** sekretariatet@ thrigesfond.dk.

Folmer Wisti Fonden (Folmer Wisti Foundation)

Founded in 1974 by Folmer Wisti to contribute to international understanding and co-operation on issues of importance in daily life at local and regional level, the support of decentralization and regionalism, and the exchange of experience and ideas primarily in the fields of culture and general education.

Activities: Operates in Europe. The Foundation has sponsored the 'Europe of Regions' conferences on decentralization and regional autonomy; and supports activities of the Danske Kulturinstitut (q.v.). Institutions eligible for support must be independent of party politics, non-profit-making and non-governmental.

Geographical Area of Activity: Europe.

Restrictions: No grants to individual students.

Publications: *Industrial Life in Denmark, The Faroe Islands and Greenland*; *Danish Foundations*; *Regional Contact* (Vols 1–16, journal for the exchange of ideas and experiences in regionalism).

Principal Staff: Chair. Karsten Fledelius.

Address: Kristianiagade 4, 2 tv, 2100 København Ø.

Telephone: 45-86-13-36; **Fax:** 45-86-13-46.

Dominican Republic

FOUNDATION CENTRE AND CO-ORDINATING BODY

Solidarios—Consejo de Fundaciones Americanas de Desarrollo (Council of American Development Foundations)

Established in 1972 by representatives of national development foundations in Central and South American and Caribbean countries.

Activities: Provides technical assistance, training services and preferential loans to members carrying out social and economic development programmes in their own countries. Consists of 18 member organizations based in nine Central and South American countries.

Geographical Area of Activity: Central and South America and the Caribbean.

Publications: *Monthly newsletters; SOLIDARIOS Primera Mano* (quarterly); Annual Report.

Finance: Annual income US $154,229, expenditure $151,510 (31 Dec. 2014).

Executive Committee: Mercedes Canalda de Beras Goico (Pres.); Oscar Chicas (Vice-Pres.).

Principal Staff: Exec. Dir Alexia Valerio.

Address: Apdo 620, Calle 6, No. 10, Ensanche Paraíso, Santo Domingo.

Telephone: 549-5111; **Fax:** 544-0550; **Internet:** www.redsolidarios.org; **e-mail:** solidarios@claro.net.do.

FOUNDATIONS, TRUSTS AND NON-PROFIT ORGANIZATIONS

Fundación Dominicana de Desarrollo—FDD (Dominican Development Foundation)

Founded in 1962 to stimulate private sector participation in finding solutions to the basic problems encountered by the low-income sector, particularly those problems experienced in rural areas. Promotes the participation of individuals in the process of their own development.

Activities: Operates nationally in the fields of education, social welfare and economic affairs through research and capacity-building programmes. Also involved in funding environmental programmes and providing support to micro-enterprises.

Geographical Area of Activity: Dominican Republic.

Publications: Annual Report; *Notas de Desarrollo; Catálogo de Organizaciones Voluntarias de Acción Social.*

Finance: Total assets 270,424,851 Dominican pesos (31 Dec. 2013).

Board of Directors: Ernesto Armenteros Calac (Pres.); Lucille Houellemont (Vice-Pres.); Carolina Alorda (Sec.); Jaime Roca (Asst Sec.); Elías Juliá (Treas.); René M. Grullón F. (Asst Treas.).

Address: Calle Mercedes No. 4, Zona Colonial, Apdo 857, 10210 Santo Domingo.

Telephone: 338-8101; **Fax:** 686-0430; **Internet:** fdd.org.do; **e-mail:** info@fdd.org.do.

Fundación Solidaridad (Solidarity Foundation)

Established in 1991 to promote sustainable development in urban and rural communities, and to promote democracy.

Activities: Offers education, capacity-building and development services to non-profit enterprises in the Dominican Republic. Supports the structural development of community organizations, as well as co-ordinating networking activities between community organizations and the private sector, and providing information and resources. Also supports the development of democracy and youth education projects.

Geographical Area of Activity: Dominican Republic.

Publications: Newsletters; reports; guides; books.

Board of Directors: Denis Mota Álvarez (Pres.); Leandro Matínez (Sec.); Guillermina Peña (Treas.).

Principal Staff: Exec. Dir Juan Castillo.

Address: Avda Francia 40, Apdo 129-2, Santiago.

Telephone: 971-5400; **Fax:** 587-3656; **Internet:** www.solidaridad.org.do; **e-mail:** f.solidaridad@codetel.net.do; fsolidaridad@gmail.com.

Ecuador

FOUNDATION CENTRE AND CO-ORDINATING BODY

CERES—Ecuadorean Consortium for Social Responsibility

Established in 2002; an association of Ecuadorean private, independent organizations that aims to promote and develop social responsibility in Ecuador.

Activities: Aims to promote civil society in Ecuador by: promoting social responsibility; fostering dialogue between foundations and government agencies, the media and the private sector; and increasing the institutional capacity and skills of Ecuadorean foundations. Comprised 39 member organizations in 2013, including corporate, private and community foundations.

Geographical Area of Activity: Ecuador.

Publications: Annual Report; Newsletter (monthly); reports; studies; guides.

Board of Directors: Norberto Purtschert (Chair.); Vivianne Almeida (Vice-Chair.); Augusta Bustamante (Immediate Past Chair.).

Principal Staff: Exec. Dir Evangelina Gómez Durañona.

Address: Edif. World Trade Center, Torre A, Of. 1204, 12 Octubre y Luis Cordero, Quito.

Telephone: (2) 222-5883; **Fax:** (2) 252-5833; **Internet:** www.redceres.org; **e-mail:** comunicacion@redceres.org.

FOUNDATIONS, TRUSTS AND NON-PROFIT ORGANIZATIONS

EcoCiencia—Fundación Ecuatoriana de Estudios Ecologicos (Ecuadorean Foundation of Ecological Studies)

Founded in 1989 by Danilo Silva, Patricio Mena, Roberto Ulloa, Mario Garcia, Luis Suarez, Juan Manuel Carrión and Miguel Vazquez to promote wildlife and biodiversity conservation and environmental education.

Activities: Operates in the field of conservation and the environment, in particular the conservation of biodiversity, through research, environmental education, training programmes and natural resources management; maintains a GIS Laboratory, an Aquatic Ecology Laboratory and a Biodiversity Economics Department; runs a university scholarship programme for Ecuadorian students; current programmes include: Bioandes; Paramo Andino; Fortalecimiento a Gobiernos Locales (Strengthening of Local Governments); Ecosistemas del Cuaternario en el Parque Nacional Podocarpus (Quaternary Ecosystems in National Park Podocarpus); the platform Grupo Nacional de Trabajo en Páramos (National Páramo Working Group); and the Conservation Program for Endangered Species in Ecuador, among others.

Geographical Area of Activity: Ecuador.

Publications: Books on conservation and sustainable development, ethnobiology; technical reports and papers; maps; Páramo Series (dissemination of Grupo de Trabajo en Páramos sessions); educational materials.

Finance: Annual income US $570,346 (31 Dec. 2012).

Principal Staff: Pres. Rossana Manosalvas; Exec. Dir Fernando R. Rodríguez.

Address: Pasaje Estocolmo E2-166 y Avda Amazonas (Sector El Labrador), Quito.

Telephone: (2) 241-0781; **Fax:** (2) 241-0489; **Internet:** www.ecociencia.org; **e-mail:** direccion@ecociencia.org.

Fundación Alternativa para el Desarrollo (Alternative Foundation for Development)

Established in 1991 by Mónica Hernández de Phillips and Santiago Ribadeneira to promote alternatives for development.

Activities: Promotes small and micro-entrepreneurship by providing financial and non-financial sustainable services to foster local economic development. The Foundation works to improve the quality of life of vulnerable people, their families and communities. It specializes in micro-credit, training, technical assistance, entrepreneurship and local economic development through innovative projects in rural and urban areas. Beneficiaries are entrepreneurs, social enterprises, associations, migrants, artisans and peasants, as well as private organizations with social responsibility.

Geographical Area of Activity: Ecuador.

Publications: Annual Report.

Finance: Total assets US $24,089,860 (31 Dec. 2013).

Board of Directors: Eduardo Ventimilla Bueno (Pres.); Soledad Burbano Correa (Vice-Pres.).

Principal Staff: Exec. Dir Freddy Albarracín.

Address: Pablo Claudel N41-61 e Isla Floreana (Pinzón), Quito.

Telephone: (593) 2226-4580; **Fax:** (593) 2226-4500; **Internet:** www.fundacionalternativa.org.ec; **e-mail:** info@fundacionalternativa.org.ec.

Fundación Charles Darwin para las Islas Galápagos—FCD (Charles Darwin Foundation for the Galapagos Islands—CDF)

Founded in 1959 under the auspices of the Government of Ecuador, UNESCO and the World Conservation Union (IUCN, q.v.) to administer the Charles Darwin Research Station on the Galapagos Islands, and to provide facilities for research and conservation measures.

Activities: Operates internationally in the fields of science and the conservation of natural resources. The Charles Darwin Research Station, with its research vessel, *Beagle*, provides research facilities to visiting scientists of many nationalities, and undertakes conservation measures for the unique fauna, flora and habitat of the archipelago, including a breeding programme for tortoises and iguanas and the protection of endangered plants and animals. Supports the Galapagos National Park Service and assists in the management of a marine reserve. Also holds courses in field ecology, offers training to Ecuadorean university students, and publishes the results of research. Maintains a library of books, maps and photographs of the Galapagos Islands. Has fund-raising offices in the USA and Europe.

Geographical Area of Activity: Galapagos Islands, Ecuador.

Publications: *Noticias de Galápagos*; Annual Report; e-newsletter; and numerous specialist publications.

Finance: Annual revenue US $3,190,655, expenditure $3,419,705 (31 Dec. 2012).

Board of Directors: Prof. Dennis Geist (Pres.); Barbara West (Treas. and Sec.).

Principal Staff: Exec. Dir Swen Lorenz.

Address: Charles Darwin Research Station, Puerto Ayora, Santa Cruz Island, Galapagos; Juan González N35-26 y Juan Pablo Sanz, Edif. Vizcaya II, Torre Norte, Piso 5, Of. 5c, Quito.

Telephone: (5) 252-6146; **Fax:** (5) 252-6147; **Internet:** www.darwinfoundation.org; **e-mail:** cdrs@fcdarwin.org.cc.

Fundación Ecuatoriana de Desarrollo—FED (Ecuadorean Development Foundation)

Established in 1968 by Jorge Landivar Mantilla to improve the standard of living for the disadvantaged in Ecuador.

Activities: Operates in the fields of aid to less-developed countries, economic affairs and social welfare, through supporting business, economic and social development in microenterprise programmes, giving loans to individual borrowers, the majority of whom are women. The Foundation also offers training programmes. Has a branch in Tumbaco.

Geographical Area of Activity: Ecuador.

Publications: *Revista Emprendedores* (6 a year).

Principal Staff: Exec. Dir Dr César Augusto Alarcón Costta.

Address: Apdo Aéreo 17-01-2529, 9 de Octubre 1212 entre Colón y Orellana, Quito.

Telephone: (2) 547-864; **Fax:** (2) 509-084; **Internet:** fedfilialtumbaco.galeon.com; **e-mail:** fed@ecuanex.net.ec.

Fundación Eugenio Espejo (Eugenio Espejo Foundation)

Established in 1978 to work in social welfare and the development of civil society, particularly promoting development in rural and urban communities.

Activities: Supports small enterprises, education and training, special education, health and welfare. Also operates a private health clinic in southern Quito serving disadvantaged people, with plans for a network of similar clinics across Ecuador.

Geographical Area of Activity: Ecuador.

Principal Staff: Pres. Dr Francisco Huerta Montalvo; Exec. Dir Patricia Salvador de Dossman.

Address: Cdla Los Samanes, 2°, Mz. 204, Solar P21 entre Avda Francisco de Orellana y Calle Primera, Apdo 09014557, Guayaquil.

Telephone: (4) 221-0816; **Fax:** (4) 221-0813; **e-mail:** funespejo@live.com.

Fundación General Ecuatoriana (General Ecuadorean Foundation)

Established in 1980 to assist the disabled in areas such as education, health, housing and culture.

Activities: Operates nationally in the areas of education, medicine and health, and social welfare for disabled people, through conferences and training courses for mentally disabled young people.

Geographical Area of Activity: Ecuador.

Publications: Directory of institutes for people with mental disability, autism, cerebral palsy and Down's Syndrome; diagnostic of the occupational situation of disabled persons.

Board of Directors: Dr Esteban Pérez Arteta (Exec. Pres.).

Principal Staff: Exec. Dir Eduardo Acosta.

Address: Oficinas y Centro de Capacitación 'PRAM', Antonio Checa s/n y Atahualpa, Sector Selva Alegre, Sangolquí, Pichincha.

Telephone: (2) 208-7168; **Fax:** (2) 208-7313; **Internet:** www.fge.org.ec; **e-mail:** fge25@fge.org.ec.

Fundación Grupo Esquel—Ecuador (Esquel Group Foundation—Ecuador)

Established in 1990 to contribute to the sustainable human development of Ecuador, improve the quality of life of disadvantaged people and build a democratic society.

Activities: Operates through the following programmes: Children and Youth Development, which aims to improve the quality of life of children and young people; Sustainable Human Development, which aims to improve the quality of life of the rural and low-income urban populations of the coastal region, the highlands and the Amazon region; Economic and Social Community Development, which aims to improve the quality of life of low-income groups that have alternative business ideas but cannot access traditional financing sources; Social Responsibility, which promotes social responsibility through establishing the concept and value of citizenship, building solidarity and forming a new culture of dialogue; Civic Education, which works through training and the encouragement of civic education; and Community Development, which carries out socially orientated projects emerging from community initiatives and aims to strengthen small NGOs. Other foundations of the Group operate in Brazil and the USA.

Geographical Area of Activity: Ecuador.

Publications: Annual Report; *Esquela* (quarterly newsletter); *Con los sueños sobre la tierra*; *Responsabilidad Social: Una empresa de Todos*; *La Aventura de lo Alternativo*; *Publicaciones sobre Corrupción*; *Temas para una sociedad en crisis*; books; handbooks; working papers; monographs.

Finance: Annual revenue US $1,569,000, expenditure $1,818,000 (31 Dec. 2012).

Board of Directors: Pablo Better (Pres.); Walter Spurrier (Vice-Pres.).

Principal Staff: Exec. Pres. Boris Cornejo.

Address: Avda Colón E4-175 entre Amazonas y Foch, Edif. Torres de la Colón, Mezzanine Of. 12, Quito.

Telephone: (2) 252-0001; **Fax:** (2) 245-3777; **Internet:** www.esquel.org.ec; **e-mail:** comunicacion@esquel.org.ec.

GSFEPP—Grupo Social Fondo Ecuatoriano Populorum Progressio

Established in 1970 to promote the development of marginalized rural and urban groups.

Activities: Aims to support the development of marginalized groups in rural and urban areas of Ecuador, through the provision of grants and technical assistance, and by raising awareness. Target groups include children and young people, with grants made to projects in the fields of health, social services, development, civil and human rights, and conflict resolution.

Geographical Area of Activity: Ecuador.

Publications: Pamphlets; books.

Finance: Annual income US $12,950,958, expenditure $13,044,852 (31 Dec. 2013).

Principal Staff: Exec. Dir José Tonello Foscarini; Deputy Dir and Sec. Luis Hinojosa.

Address: Mallorca N24-275 y Avda La Coruña, La Floresta, Casilla 17-110-5202, Quito.

Telephone: (2) 252-0408; **Fax:** (2) 250-4978; **Internet:** www.fepp.org.ec; **e-mail:** edifepp@fepp.org.ec.

Egypt

FOUNDATIONS, TRUSTS AND NON-PROFIT ORGANIZATIONS

Arab Fund for Technical Assistance to African Countries—AFTAAC

Founded in 1974 (known until 1992 as the Arab Fund for Technical Assistance) to benefit African and Arab countries through the promotion of human resources development initiatives. The Fund is considered to be one of the organs of the League of Arab States but has an independent budget.

Activities: Provides technical assistance to African countries mainly through the dispatch of Arab experts and consultants, the financing and organizing of training programmes for African candidates in Arab and African countries, the granting of scholarships to African students to study at Arab universities and institutes, and the preparation of feasibility studies in the economic and scientific fields. AFTAAC co-operates with international, regional and national institutions sharing similar development goals in Africa.

Geographical Area of Activity: Africa.

Finance: Annual budget US $5m.

Board of Directors: Nabil Elaraby (Chair.).

Principal Staff: Dir-Gen. Amb. Abdelaziz Buhedma.

Address: 33 rue 14 Maadi, Cairo.

Telephone: (2) 3590322; **Fax:** (2) 3592099; **Internet:** www .lasportal.org; **e-mail:** aftaac@las.int.

Arab Office for Youth and Environment—AOYE

Established in 1978. Aims to encourage environmental protection.

Activities: Works to raise awareness, particularly among young people, of environmental issues and the need for sustainable development in Egypt. Co-operates with other environmental NGOs, the Government, and the UN to develop and carry out programmes and projects, and to educate young people to produce future leaders with an increased awareness of the need to protect the environment and natural resources, as well as collaborating to establish environmental networks. Founded the Arab Union for Youth and Environment in 1983 and is the Secretariat for the Arab Network for Environment and Development (RAED). Also participates in international conferences and networks.

Geographical Area of Activity: Egypt.

Publications: *Montada Elbiah* (RAED monthly newsletter).

Board: Dr Emad Adly (Pres.).

Address: POB 2, Maglei el-Shaab, Cairo; 3A Lel-Tameer Bldgs, Zahraa el-Maadi St, Maadi, Cairo.

Telephone: (2) 5161519; **Fax:** (2) 5162961; **Internet:** www.aoye .org; **e-mail:** aoye@link.net.

Arab Organization for Human Rights

Founded in 1983 to defend human rights.

Activities: Works to protect the human rights of those living in Arab countries, and to defend anyone whose rights have been violated. The Organization provides legal assistance and campaigns for people convicted without fair trial, as well as financial assistance to their families; supports improvements in conditions for prisoners of conscience; and fights for amnesty for people sentenced for political reasons. Has 22 branches in member Arab countries and in three European countries.

Geographical Area of Activity: Principally North Africa and the Middle East.

Publications: *Arab Manual for Human Rights* (2011); magazine; reports; studies; position papers.

Finance: Funded by members' dues and contributions.

Board of Trustees: Raji Sourani (Pres.); Hamid Fadlallah (Treas.).

Principal Staff: Sec.-Gen. Alaa Shalabi.

Address: 91 al-Marghany St, Apts 7–8, Heliopolis, Cairo 11341.

Telephone: (2) 4181396; **Fax:** (2) 4185346; **Internet:** www .aohr.net; **e-mail:** aohrarab@gmail.com.

Mohamed Shafik Gabr Foundation for Social Development

Established by Mohamed Shafik Gabr, Chair. and Man. Dir of the ARTOC Group for Investment and Development.

Activities: Areas of interest include: education, upgrading and equipping schools and libraries, and sponsoring initiatives in partnership with the American University in Cairo, Massachusetts Institute of Technology, Lee Kuan Yew School of Public Policy in Singapore, and other educational programmes; health, running a medical and social development centre in Mokattam, and mobile treatment centres; human trafficking; emergency aid; food; sports; culture; and women's issues.

Geographical Area of Activity: Egypt, with a particular focus on Mokattam, Mansouria and Greater Cairo.

Board of Trustees: Mohamed Shafik Gabr (Chair.); Jihan Shoukry (Vice-Chair.).

Address: Hassan al-Akbar St, Mokattam, Cairo 11571.

Telephone: (2) 26673322; **Fax:** (2) 25053222; **Internet:** www .msgabrfoundation.org; **e-mail:** info@msgabrfoundation.org.

Anna Lindh Euro-Mediterranean Foundation for Dialogue between Cultures

Established as a partnership between the European Union (EU) and its partners in the southern Mediterranean region, and launched at a conference in Barcelona, Spain, in 1995. The Foundation was the first common institution jointly established and financed by all the then 35 members of the Euro-Mediterranean Partnership, and aims to promote regional co-operation in the economic, social and cultural fields.

Activities: Operates in the fields of education, culture and media. As a network of national networks, the Foundation links more than 4,000 civil society organizations. It organizes the 'Sea of Words' Literary Competition; the Plural + Video Festival, a collaboration with the United Nations Alliance of Civilizations; the Mediterranean Journalist Award for reporting on cultural diversity; and, jointly with the Fondazione Mediterraneo, the Euro-Med Dialogue Award.

Geographical Area of Activity: The EU and southern Mediterranean countries.

Publications: Newsletter; reports; analysis.

Finance: Funded by the 43 member states of the Union for the Mediterranean and the European Commission.

Board of Governors: Abou Bakr Hefny (Chair.).

Principal Staff: Pres. Elisabeth Grigou; Exec. Dir Hatem Atallah.

Address: Bibliotheca Alexandrina, POB 732, el-Mansheia, Alexandria 21111.

Telephone: (3) 4820342; **Fax:** (3) 4820471; **Internet:** www .annalindhfoundation.org; www.euromedalex.org; **e-mail:** info@euromedalex.org.

Mansour Foundation for Development

Established in 2001 by the Mansour Family to manage the philanthropic activities of the Mansour Group.

Activities: High-priority areas of interests are education, health and capacity building; with a focus on young people, women and girls, children with special needs, and residents of informal settlements. Programmes include health; education; poverty alleviation; vocational training and employment; capacity building of vulnerable groups; and youth, entrepreneurship and volunteerism. Provides research and develop grants for social and business studies. Programmes assist c. 15,000 people annually.

Geographical Area of Activity: Egypt.

Principal Staff: Man. Dir Rania Hamoud.

Address: Zahraa El Maadi, Industrial Zone, POB 97, New Maadi, Cairo.

Telephone: (2) 27548360; **Fax:** (2) 27548385; **Internet:** mmd .mansourgroup.com/mansour-foundation; www .mansourgroup.com/csr; **e-mail:** info@mansourgroup.com.

Sawiris Foundation for Social Development

Established in 2001 by the Sawiris family.

Activities: Promotes social development through citizen empowerment and participation. Supports job creation by providing training, education and access to microcredit; and better health through improved infrastructure and access to basic services. Provides scholarships for study in Europe and abroad. The Foundation annually makes Sawiris Cultural Awards to Egyptian authors, screenwriters and playwrights. It has special consultative status with the United Nations Economic and Social Council (ECOSOC).

Geographical Area of Activity: Egypt.

Board of Trustees: Dr Mohamed Ibrahim Shaker (Chair.); Naquib Sawiris, Dr Ismail Serageldin (Vice-Chair.); Hazem Hassan (Hon. Treas.); Yousriya Loza Sawiris (Sec.-Gen.).

Principal Staff: Exec. Dir Prof. Dr Gannat El Samalouty.

Address: 10 El-Diwan St, Garden City, Cairo 11451.

Telephone: (2) 27927660; **Fax:** (2) 27927664; **Internet:** www .sawirisfoundation.org; **e-mail:** info@sawirisfoundation.org.

El Salvador

FOUNDATIONS, TRUSTS AND NON-PROFIT ORGANIZATIONS

Fundación de Capacitación y Asesoría en Microfinanzas—FUNDAMICRO (Foundation for the Qualification and Consultancy in Microfinance)

Founded in 1999 as part of a joint project by the European Union and Banco Multisectorial de Inversiones.

Activities: Provides specialist technical services for micro-enterprises.

Geographical Area of Activity: El Salvador and Central America.

Board of Directors: José Antonio Peñate (Pres.); Mercedes Llort (Vice-Pres.).

Principal Staff: Gen. Man. Jesus Peña.

Address: Calle Poniente 3856, 1°, Colonia Escalón, San Salvador.

Telephone: 2511-7100; **Fax:** 2265-2173; **Internet:** www.fundamicro.net; **e-mail:** fundamicro@fundamicro.net.

Fundación Nacional para el Desarrollo (National Foundation for Development)

Established in 1992; a research institution that formulates socio-economic policies, advocates and promotes development, with its target group being the most disadvantaged sectors of society.

Activities: Programmes include Macroeconomics and Development, Territorial Development, Violence Prevention and Transparency. The Foundation provides funding for development; integration and development; employment and growth; construction and development of territories; national public policies for territorial development; environmental management; and transparency.

Geographical Area of Activity: El Salvador and Central America.

Finance: Annual revenue US $2,898,449, expenditure $2,820,645 (31 Dec. 2014).

Board of Directors: Julio Ramírez Murcia (Pres.); Aida Carolina Quinteros Sosa (Vice-Pres.); David Amílcar Mena Rodríguez (Sec.); Carlo Giovanni Berti Lungo (Treas.).

Principal Staff: Exec. Dir Dr Roberto Rubio-Fabián.

Address: Calle Arturo Ambrogi No. 411 entre 103 y 105, Avda Norte, Col. Escalón, San Salvador.

Telephone: 2209-5300; **Fax:** 2263-0454; **Internet:** www.funde.org; **e-mail:** funde@funde.org.

Fundación Salvadoreña para el Desarrollo Económico y Social (El Salvador Foundation for Economic and Social Development)

Established in 1983; a think tank and research centre.

Activities: Studies economics, society, the environment and institutions to formulate and influence public policies. The aim is for social advancement through sustainable development.

Geographical Area of Activity: El Salvador.

Publications: Bulletins; numerous reports from the Research Centre, Development Centre, and the Economic and Legal Information System.

Board of Directors: Francisco R. R. de Sola (Pres.); Roberto Orellana Milla (Vice-Pres.); Claudia Umaña Araujo (Sec.); Pedro Luis Apóstolo (Asst Sec.); Freddie Frech (Treas.); Henry Yarhi (Asst Treas.).

Principal Staff: Exec. Dir José Ángel Quirós Noltenius.

Address: Edif. FUSADES, Apdo 01-278, Blvd y urbanización Santa Elena, Antiguo Cuscatlán, La Libertad.

Telephone: 2248-5600; **Fax:** 2278-3356; **Internet:** www.fusades.org; **e-mail:** fusades@fusades.org.

Estonia

FOUNDATION CENTRE AND CO-ORDINATING BODY

Eesti Mittetulundusühingute ja Sihtasutuste Liit (Network of Estonian Non-profit Organizations)

Established in 1991 by representatives of 26 Estonian foundations to promote co-operation between charitable, non-governmental and not-for-profit organizations. Previously known as the Estonian Foundation Center.

Activities: Operates nationally and internationally in the fields of education, international affairs, law and human rights, and information dissemination, through conducting research, organizing training courses and conferences, and issuing publications. Had 109 member NGOs and foundations in 2014.

Geographical Area of Activity: Estonia, Central and Eastern Europe.

Restrictions: Not a grantmaking organization.

Principal Staff: Exec. Dir Maris Jõgeva.

Address: Telliskivi Creative City, A3 Bldg, 3rd Floor, Telliskivi 60A, 10412 Tallinn.

Telephone: 664-5077; **Fax:** 664-5078; **Internet:** www.ngo.ee; **e-mail:** info@ngo.ee.

FOUNDATIONS, TRUSTS AND NON-PROFIT ORGANIZATIONS

Eestimaa Looduse Fond—ELF (Estonian Fund for Nature)

Established in 1991 to protect Estonia's biodiversity through the development, funding and implementation of nature conservation projects, to offer expertise in the formation of public policy, and to work towards increased public environmental awareness through education.

Activities: Operates in the fields of conservation and the environment, and education, through self-conducted programmes, research, conferences, training courses and publications. The Fund provides financial support for conservation and environmental projects such as scientific research, the application of practical conservation measures, and public information and education.

Geographical Area of Activity: Estonia.

Publications: *Naturewatch Baltic Report 2003*; *Baltic Forest Mapping: Keskkonna õigus (Environmental Justice)* (2003); *Keskkonnasõbra taskuraamat (Activist Handbook)* (2003); *Genetically modified organisms and their risks to the environment* (2006); *Overview Estonian forestry 2005–2008* (2009); *Environmental impacts of Forestry Drainage* (2009); Annual Report.

Finance: Annual revenue €845,000, expenditure €806,000 (2014).

Executive Committee: Silvia Lotman (Chair.); Tarmo Tüür (Vice-Chair.).

Address: PK 245, 51002 Tartu; Lai St 29, Tartu.

Telephone: 7428-443; **Fax:** 7428-166; **Internet:** www.elfond.ee; **e-mail:** elf@elfond.ee.

Open Estonia Foundation

Established in 1990, with the support of the philanthropist George Soros; a non-governmental, not-for-profit public benefit foundation affiliated with the Open Society Foundations network (q.v.).

Activities: Aims to build an open society in Estonia and other countries, with a focus on strengthening open governance, democracy and civil society; and reinforcing the principles of participatory democracy and equal opportunities in the democratic decision-making processes. Initiatives have ranged from school reforms to contemporary art and legal reforms. The Foundation helps shape and advocate public policies and actions that assure greater justice in society and promote fundamental rights. It also shares experiences with countries in democratic transition, and builds cross-border partnerships in the European Union and beyond.

Geographical Area of Activity: Estonia.

Publications: Annual Report; special reports.

Board of Directors: Ants Sild (Chair.).

Principal Staff: Exec. Dir Mall Hellam.

Address: Estonia Ave 5A, 10143 Tallinn.

Telephone: 631-5700; **Fax:** 631-3796; **Internet:** www.oef.org.ee; **e-mail:** info@oef.org.ee.

Sihtasutus Eesti Rahvuskultuuri Fond (Estonian National Culture Foundation)

Founded in 1991 to promote and preserve Estonian national culture.

Activities: Operates in the area of the arts and humanities. Offers scholarships and grants to individuals and projects dedicated to developing aspects of Estonian culture; presents Lifetime Achievement Awards to people who have made significant contributions to national culture; and works in co-operation with a number of institutions and individuals that support Estonian culture. Administers 150 special foundations.

Geographical Area of Activity: Estonia.

Finance: Total annual income €276,834, expenditure €190,902 (2014/15).

Council: Eri Klas (Chair.).

Principal Staff: Man. Dir Toivo Toomemets.

Address: A. Weizenbergi 20, A-13, 10150 Tallinn.

Telephone: 601-3428; **Fax:** 601-3429; **Internet:** www.erkf.ee; **e-mail:** post@erkf.ee.

Ethiopia

FOUNDATIONS, TRUSTS AND NON-PROFIT ORGANIZATIONS

Africa Humanitarian Action

Established in 1994 by Dr Dawit Zawde in response to the ethnic cleansing in Rwanda.

Activities: Offers humanitarian assistance to refugees, internally displaced persons and to local communities in Africa. Also carries out programmes on capacity building; HIV/AIDS prevention and health care; advocacy; sexual and gender-based violence; and disaster relief. Maintains a Europe office in Geneva, Switzerland, and an office in the USA; there are country offices in Burundi, Cameroon, Central African Republic, Democratic Republic of the Congo, Kenya, Liberia, Namibia, Rwanda, Somalia, South Sudan, Sudan, Uganda and Zambia.

Geographical Area of Activity: Sub-Saharan Africa.

Finance: Annual income US $12,380,474, expenditure $12,363,190 (2013).

Trustees: Dr Salim Ahmed Salim (Chair.); Dr Sheikh M. H. al-Ahmoudi (Co-Chair.); Asrat Betru (Treas.).

Principal Staff: Pres. Dr Dawit Zawde.

Address: Guinea-Conakry Rd, POB 110, Code 1250, Addis Ababa.

Telephone: (11) 551-3541; **Fax:** (11) 551-3851; **Internet:** www .africahumanitarian.org; **e-mail:** info@africahumanitarian .org.

Finland

FOUNDATION CENTRE AND CO-ORDINATING BODY

Säätiöiden ja rahastojen neuvottelukunta—SRNK (Council of Finnish Foundations)

Established in 1970 as an association of Finnish grantmaking foundations and associations.

Activities: Assists member foundations and associations in exchanging information and ideas; represents its members; advises members and grant seekers through its Foundation Service (Säätiöpalvelu), which also provides information on grants and foundations; and issues publications. Had 163 members in 2015.

Geographical Area of Activity: Finland.

Publications: Research findings; guidelines; reports; studies.

Finance: Annual grants disbursed by represented organizations €380m. (2013).

Board of Directors: Tuomo Lähdesmäki (Chair.); Stefan Mutanen (Vice-Chair.).

Principal Staff: Man. Dir Dr Liisa Suvikumpu; Co-ordinator Kai Kilpinen.

Address: Fredrikinkatu 61 A, 00100 Helsinki.

Telephone: (9) 6818949; **Internet:** www.saatiopalvelu.fi; **e-mail:** info@saatiopalvelu.fi.

FOUNDATIONS, TRUSTS AND NON-PROFIT ORGANIZATIONS

Baltic Sea Fund

Founded in 1989 by Anders Wiklöf to support activities for the protection of the Baltic Sea environment.

Activities: Grants scholarships, prizes and financial support for relevant scientific research, technology, published material and other activities in the Baltic Sea region. Aims to establish new economic relations between countries. The Fund awards the Baltic Sea Fund Prize, worth €20,000; the Lasse Wiklöf Prize, worth €10,000; and the Aland Prize, worth €3,000.

Geographical Area of Activity: The Baltic region.

Finance: Net assets €800,000 (2010).

Board of Trustees: Henrik Beckman (Chair.); Lotta Wickström-Johansson (Vice-Chair.).

Principal Staff: Chair. Peter Lindbäck.

Address: c/o Hotell Arkipelag, Strandgatan 35, 22100 Mariehamn.

Telephone: (18) 15270; **Internet:** www.ostersjofonden.org; **e-mail:** info@ostersjofonden.org.

Finnish Science Foundation for Economics and Technology—KAUTE

Founded in 1956 by Finnish business school and engineering graduate associations. Formerly known as the Foundation for Commercial and Technical Sciences.

Activities: Supports and promotes scientific research in economics and technology. The Foundation promotes the renewal of Finnish industry and business by allocating grants for studying, teaching and research. Member of the Council of Finnish Foundations. In 2014, it awarded grants amounting to €249,200.

Geographical Area of Activity: Finland.

Restrictions: Supports researchers in economics and technology who are Finnish citizens or permanent residents in Finland.

Principal Staff: Exec. Dir Jouni Lounasmaa.

Address: c/o Kordelin, Mariankatu 7 A 3, 00170 Helsinki.

Internet: www.kaute.fi; **e-mail:** info@kaute.fi.

Signe och Ane Gyllenbergs stiftelse (Signe and Ane Gyllenberg Foundation)

Established in 1948 to support medical and scientific research, especially in the area of psychosomatic illness, and research in the field of medicine following the ideas of Rudolf Steiner.

Activities: Operates internationally. The Foundation supports medical and scientific research, especially in the area of psychosomatic illness and blood disorders, through awarding grants; and organizes symposia on interdisciplinary themes. It also maintains the Villa Gyllenberg Art Museum in Helsinki. In 2014, the Foundation awarded grants amounting to €1.7m.

Geographical Area of Activity: International.

Restrictions: Grants are not given for research that involves painful experiments on animals.

Publications: *Acta Gyllenbergiana*.

Finance: Annual income €4,200,030, expenditure €1,414,179 (31 Dec. 2013).

Board of Directors: Prof. Per-Henrik Groop (Pres.); Magnus Bargum (Vice-Pres. and Treas.).

Principal Staff: Man. Dir and Sec. Jannica Fagerholm.

Address: Yrjönkatu 4 A 5, 00120 Helsinki.

Telephone: (9) 647390; **Fax:** (9) 607119; **Internet:** www.gyllenberg-foundation.fi; **e-mail:** stiftelsen@gyllenbergs.fi.

Helsingin Sanomain Säätiö (Helsingin Sanomat Foundation)

Formed in 2005 by the merger of the Helsingin Sanomat Centennial Foundation (f. 1990) and the Päivälehti Archive Foundation (f. 1984).

Activities: Aims to advance and support excellence in research as a means of insuring the broad base, independence and continuity of Finnish scientific work. The Foundation focuses on communications, the communications industry and futures research. It also promotes and supports freedom of expression, including research into the history of freedom of expression, and it fosters educational and cultural activities in Finland. In 2015, the Foundation established an annual Visual Journalism Award worth €10,000.

Geographical Area of Activity: Finland.

Finance: Annual income €2,780,540, expenditure €4,360,586 (31 Dec. 2014).

Board of Trustees: Kaius Niemi (Chair.); Prof. Matti Sintonen (Vice-Chair.); Ulla Koski (Sec.).

Principal Staff: Pres. Heleena Savela.

Address: POB 35, 00089 Sanoma; Sanoma House, Töölönlahdenkatu 2, 00100 Helsinki.

Telephone: (9) 1221; **Internet:** www.hssaatio.fi; **e-mail:** saatio@hssaatio.fi.

Yrjö Jahnssonin säätiö (Yrjö Jahnsson Foundation)

Founded in 1954 by lawyer Hilma Jahnsson in memory of her husband Yrjö Jahnsson, a professor of economics, to sponsor

Finnish research in economics and medicine, as well as to support Finnish educational and research institutes.

Activities: Operates nationally in the field of education, and internationally in economic affairs, and science and medicine, through grants to Finnish institutions and individuals, and fellowships and scholarships for Finnish citizens; and through international research, conferences, courses, publications and lectures. The Foundation presents the Yrjö Jahnsson Award in Economics to a young European economist who has significantly advanced the field of economics research. Member of the Foundations' Professor Pool, a joint temporary grant pool of 17 foundations.

Geographical Area of Activity: Finland and Europe.

Publications: Report of operations and financial statement.

Finance: Total assets €43,421,328 (31 Dec. 2014).

Board of Directors: Kimmo Kontula (Chair.); Antti Suvanto (Vice-Chair.).

Principal Staff: CEO Elli Dahl.

Address: Yrjönkatu 11 D 19, 00120 Helsinki.

Telephone: (9) 6869100; **Fax:** (9) 605002; **Internet:** www.yjs .fi; **e-mail:** toimisto@yjs.fi.

Sigrid Jusélius Säätiö (Sigrid Jusélius Foundation)

Founded in 1930 by the will of politician and industrialist Fritz Arthur Jusélius, in memory of his daughter Sigrid, to promote and support medical research, independently of language and nationality, with the aim of fighting diseases particularly harmful to humanity.

Activities: Operates in the fields of medicine, pharmacology, biochemistry and genetics. Supports research in those fields and awards grants to individuals and institutions. Organizes occasional symposia and workshops. Grants are made to medical research projects, conducted by senior researchers in Finland and to foreign nationals carrying out research in Finland, and can cover living costs, equipment, materials and consumables. In 2013, the Foundation awarded grants amounting to than more than €14m.

Geographical Area of Activity: Finland.

Restrictions: No direct grants for foreign medical research, or for studies or doctoral theses.

Publications: Annual Report (in Finnish and Swedish).

Finance: Annual income €19.8m. (2013).

Board: Leif Sevón (Chair.); Ann-Sofi Palin (Treas.).

Principal Staff: Man. Dir Christian Elfving.

Address: Aleksanterinkatu 48 B, 00100 Helsinki.

Telephone: (20) 7109083; **Fax:** (20) 7109089; **Internet:** www .sigridjuselius.fi; **e-mail:** info@sigridjuselius.fi.

Kansainvälinen solidaarisuussäätiö (International Solidarity Foundation)

Founded in 1970 to encourage co-operation between Finland and less-developed countries.

Activities: Through long-term projects in the partner countries, improves the living conditions of the poorest sectors of society, particularly women and children. The Foundation's main objective is to strengthen women's social, economic and political status and to provide the poorest people with opportunities for decent work. Operates in Finland, Nicaragua, Somalia and Uganda.

Geographical Area of Activity: International.

Publications: *Solidaarisuus* (magazine, 2 a year).

Finance: Annual budget approx. €2.8m. (2014).

Principal Staff: Exec. Dir Miia Nuikka; Deputy Exec. Dir Milla Mäkinen.

Address: Lintulahdenkatu 10, 00500 Helsinki.

Telephone: (10) 5012120; **Fax:** (9) 75997320; **Internet:** www .solidaarisuus.fi; **e-mail:** solidaarisuus@solidaarisuus.fi.

KIOS—Finnish NGO Foundation for Human Rights

Founded in 1998 by 11 Finnish NGOs working with human rights and development issues; aims to promote the awareness and realization of human rights in developing countries.

Activities: Funds the work of human rights organizations in developing countries. Typical projects that the Foundation supports focus on the prevention of human rights abuses; human rights awareness raising and education and advocacy or legal aid to victims of human rights abuses. It gives special consideration to projects promoting or protecting the rights of the most vulnerable groups, such as women, children, indigenous peoples, people with disabilities, sexual and gender minorities, human rights defenders and people living in extreme poverty.

Geographical Area of Activity: East Africa (Burundi, the Dem. Repub. of the Congo—The Kivus, Ethiopia, Kenya, Rwanda and Uganda) and South Asia (Afghanistan, Bangladesh, Nepal, Pakistan, Sri Lanka and Tibet).

Restrictions: No funding for individuals, international NGOs, or governmental bodies. Nor are projects targeted at development work, humanitarian aid, or socio-economic support for marginalized groups granted funding. No funding is granted for scholarships, fellowships, conference participation or travel.

Finance: Receives financial support for its activities from the Department for Development Policy at the Ministry for Foreign Affairs of Finland. Budget €1.8m. (2014).

Executive Board: Henna Hakkarainen (Chair.); Tuomas Laine (Vice-Chair.).

Principal Staff: Exec. Dir. Dr Ulla Anttila.

Address: Lintulahdenkatu 10, 00500 Helsinki.

Telephone: (40) 9527919; **Internet:** www.kios.fi; **e-mail:** kios@kios.fi.

Maj and Tor Nessling Foundation

Established in 1972 by Maj Nessling in memory of her husband Tor, former Managing Director of Suomen Autoteollisuus Ab (Finnish Motors Ltd), to promote Finnish science and culture, especially in the field of environmental protection.

Activities: Awards grants for scientific research projects in all areas of environmental protection; organizes and funds scientific symposia; supports dissemination of research findings. In 2015, the Foundation awarded grants amounting to €2.5m.

Geographical Area of Activity: Finland and the countries nearby.

Publications: Annual Report (in Finnish).

Finance: Total assets €67,187,589 (2014).

Governing Board: Dr Tellervo Kylä-Harakka-Ruonala (Chair.); Prof. Timo Kairesalo (Vice-Chair.).

Principal Staff: Office Man. Leena Pentikäinen.

Address: Fredrikinkatu 20 B 16, 00120 Helsinki, Finland.

Telephone: (9) 4342550; **Fax:** (9) 43425555; **Internet:** www .nessling.fi; **e-mail:** toimisto@nessling.fi.

Paavo Nurmen Säätiö (Paavo Nurmi Foundation)

Established in 1968 by Paavo Nurmen, an owner of a construction company, financier and former athlete, for the research and treatment of cardiovascular diseases.

Activities: Contributes to research into heart and vascular disease and promotes public welfare in Finland. The Foundation provides grants for post-doctoral research, and the acquisition of materials and equipment. It provides support to Estonian cardiologists for visiting research tenures in Finland, and to Finnish scientists for visits to foreign research institutions. It also presents the annual International Paavo Nurmi Foundation Award in recognition of outstanding work in the field of medical research; runs an annual symposia programme; and publishes research results. Co-founded the *Tiede 2000* (Science 2000) journal, which aims to make the latest research findings accessible to the public. In 2014, the Foundation awarded grants amounting to €150,000.

Geographical Area of Activity: Finland.

Board of Directors: Mika Nurmi (Chair.).

Address: POB 330, 00121 Helsinki; Vaniljgränden 6, 00990 Helsingfors.

Internet: www.paavonurmensaatio.fi; **e-mail:** petri .manninen@paavonurmensaatio.fi.

Paulon Säätiö (Paulo Foundation)

Founded in 1966 by the wills of restaurateurs Reka and Hulda Paulo and their daughter Marja, to support research in the fields of medicine and the economy, and to promote music and fine art.

Activities: Operates in the fields of the arts and humanities, economic affairs, medicine and health, and science and technology, nationally through research, grants to individuals and awarding prizes, and nationally and internationally through awarding scholarships and fellowships. The Foundation manages a number of trusts. It also organizes a researcher exchange programme with Sapporo Medical University in Japan; a biennial medical symposium; and is the main sponsor of The International Paulo Cello Competition, which is held every five years. In 2015, the Foundation awarded grants amounting to €637,000.

Geographical Area of Activity: Finland.

Restrictions: Grants and prizes are awarded to Finns and permanent residents of Finland.

Publications: *Why Finland is so Expensive* (1991).

Board of Directors: Timo Ritakallio (Chair. and CEO).

Principal Staff: Sec. Riita Kallavuo.

Address: Kappelitie 6 B, 1. krs, 02200 Espoo.

Telephone: (10) 2399290; **Fax:** (10) 2399293; **Internet:** www .paulo.fi; **e-mail:** toimisto@paulo.fi.

Suomen Kulttuurirahasto (Finnish Cultural Foundation)

Founded in 1939 by a national campaign to promote the development of cultural life in Finland.

Activities: Provides grants and scholarships for individuals, work groups and communities in the fields of arts and science. The Foundation operates primarily within Finland, but also internationally through travel and research grants; and also encourages large-scale, long-term projects, especially relating to Finnish culture, which require major support. Its own cultural activities include annual events and other special projects. The Mirjam Helin International Singing Competition, inaugurated in 1984, is held every five years is to support young, gifted singers. The Foundation hosts the Kirpilä Art Collection, a collection of Finnish art donated by Dr Juhani Kirpilä. Has established 17 regional funds to support cultural life throughout the country.

Geographical Area of Activity: Primarily Finland, with some international activity.

Publications: *Cultura* (series of publications); Annual Report; reports and brochures.

Finance: Current assets €1,450m. (20 March 2015).

Board of Trustees: Elina Ikonen (Chair); Riitta Pyykkö (Vice-Chair).

Principal Staff: Sec.-Gen. Antti Arjava.

Address: Bulevardi 5 A, 5 krs., POB 203, 00121 Helsinki.

Telephone: (9) 612810; **Fax:** (9) 640474; **Internet:** www.skr.fi/ en; **e-mail:** yleisinfo@skr.fi.

Svenska Kulturfonden (Foundation for Swedish Culture in Finland)

Founded in 1908 by the Svenska Folkpartiet to support educational institutions; associations, unions and institutions with cultural interests and purposes; individual scientific, literary and artistic activities; and other purposes serving Swedish culture in Finland.

Activities: Operates nationally in the fields of education, the arts and humanities, social studies, science and medicine, through grants to institutions and individuals, conferences and courses. Maintains an art collection comprising works by contemporary Finno-Swedish artists and operates regional grant offices.

Geographical Area of Activity: Finland.

Restrictions: Support is given only to projects serving Swedish culture in Finland.

Publications: Annual and conference reports; catalogues.

Finance: Budget approx. €33m.

Board of Directors: Stefan Wallin (Chair.); Christel Raunio (Vice-Chair.).

Principal Staff: Dir Leif Jakobsson.

Address: POB 439, 00101 Helsingfors.

Telephone: (9) 69307300; **Fax:** (9) 6949484; **Internet:** www .kulturfonden.fi; **e-mail:** kansliet@kulturfonden.fi.

Tekniikan Edistämissäätiö–Stiftelsen för teknikens främjande—TES (Finnish Foundation for Technology Promotion)

Founded in 1949 by 63 industrial or business institutions and persons to further technology in Finland by supporting relevant education and research, and generally to improve the conditions of technical activities in the various sectors of economic life, with special emphasis on essential tasks.

Activities: Operates nationally in the fields of technology, education, international relations and the conservation of natural resources. Programmes are carried out nationally, through research, grants to institutions, fellowships and scholarships, and nationally and internationally through grants to individuals, conferences, courses, publications and lectures. Awards are made chiefly to advanced technical students and in support of technical research, training and education.

Geographical Area of Activity: Finland.

Publications: Report of operations and financial statement.

Finance: Total grants approx. €700,000 (2013).

Principal Staff: Chair. Marjo Miettinen; Sec.-Gen. Kari Mäkinen.

Address: c/o Ministry of Employment and the Economy, POB 32, Aleksanterinkatu 4, 00023 Valtioneuvosto.

Telephone: (9) 16063722; **Fax:** (9) 16063705; **Internet:** www .tekniikanedistamissaatio.fi; **e-mail:** etunimi.sukunimi@ kolumbus.fi.

Väestöliitto (The Family Federation of Finland)

Founded in 1941.

Activities: Works in the fields of health and social welfare, carrying out advocacy work and conducting research. The Federation distributes information, and educational and publishing materials. It treats infertility, supports sexual health and people's responsible sexual well-being, as well as providing counselling.

Geographical Area of Activity: Finland, Africa (Malawi), Asia (Nepal) and Central Asia (Kazakhstan, Kyrgyzstan, Tajikistan, Uzbekistan and Turkmenistan).

Publications: Summary of the UNDPA *State of the World Population* report in Finnish; *Global SRHR News* (monthly newsletter); reports and educational materials; materials on family sexual and reproductive health, sexuality, and family and population policy; and on global development issues, especially sexual and reproductive health rights.

Board of Trustees: Maria Kaisa Aula (Chair.).

Principal Staff: Man. Dir Eija Koivuranta.

Address: POB 849, 00101 Helsinki; Kalevankatu 16, 00101 Helsinki.

Telephone: (9) 228050; **Fax:** (9) 6121211; **Internet:** www .vaestoliitto.fi; **e-mail:** eija.koivuranta@vaestoliitto.fi.

Wihurin kansainvälisten palkintojen rahasto
(Wihuri Foundation for International Prizes)

Founded in 1953 by Antti Wihuri to promote and sustain the cultural and economic development of society by distributing international prizes.

Activities: Presents the annual Wihuri Sibelius Award, for contributions to intellectual and economic development, and the Wihuri Sibelius Prize, awarded to internationally acclaimed composers; prizes are worth between €30,000 and €150,000 and are awarded at least every three years. The Foundation shares its administration with the Jenny ja Antti Wihurin Rahasto (q.v.).

Board of Directors: Simo Palokangas (Chair.); Erkki K. M. Leppävuori (Vice-Chair.).

Principal Staff: Exec. Dir Arto Mäenmaa.

Address: Kalliolinnantie 4, 00140 Helsinki.

Telephone: (9) 4542400; **Fax:** (9) 444590; **Internet:** www .wihurinrahasto.fi; **e-mail:** toimisto@wihurinrahasto.fi.

Jenny ja Antti Wihurin Rahasto (Jenny and Antti Wihuri Foundation)

Founded in 1942 by Antti Wihuri, a shipowner, and his wife Jenny to promote and sustain Finnish cultural and economic development.

Activities: In 1944, the Foundation established the Wihuri Research Institute for cardiovascular research. In 1953, it established the Wihuri Foundation for International Prizes (q.v.); and in 1957 the Foundation began collecting contemporary art, which became the basis of the Rovaniemi Art Museum (f. 1986). In 2014, the Foundation awarded grants amounting to €11m.

Geographical Area of Activity: Finland.

Restrictions: Grants are available to Finnish nationals.

Board of Directors: Simo Palokangas (Chair.); Erkki K. M. Leppävuori (Vice-Chair.).

Principal Staff: Exec. Dir Arto Mäenmaa.

Address: Kalliolinnantie 4, 00140 Helsinki.

Telephone: (9) 4542400; **Fax:** (9) 444590; **Internet:** www .wihurinrahasto.fi; **e-mail:** toimisto@wihurinrahasto.fi.

France

FOUNDATION CENTRES AND CO-ORDINATING BODIES

Centre Français des Fondations—CFF (French Foundation Centre)

Founded in 2002.

Activities: Promotes the development of foundations in France and their international representation. The Centre represents the interests of French foundations vis-à-vis public authorities whether national, European or international institutions. It advises individuals and corporations intending to create a foundation; is a source of information (database, research, studies and directories); and is a network of expertise, sharing and exchanging experiences. Comprised more than 200 member organizations in 2012.

Geographical Area of Activity: France and Europe.

Publications: E-newsletter.

Board of Directors: Francis Charhon (Pres.); Benoît Miribel, Catherine Monnier (Vice-Pres); Michèle Guyot-Roze (Sec.); François Martin (Treas.).

Principal Staff: CEO Béatrice de Durfort.

Address: 34 bis rue Vignon, 75009 Paris.

Telephone: 1-83-79-03-52; **Fax:** 1-44-21-31-01; **Internet:** www.centre-francais-fondations.org; **e-mail:** info@centre-francais-fondations.org.

Fédération des Agences Internationales pour le Développement—AIDE (Federation of International Agencies for International Development)

Founded in 1986 with the aim of helping developing countries to resolve their economic problems caused through increased industrialization. In 1998, formed the Federation of International Agencies for Development, represented in 18 countries and including 341 NGO members.

Activities: Operates educational programmes with an emphasis on self-help; provides training for industrial work; promotes agricultural projects; works towards improving the quality of life of people in developing countries by improving sanitation conditions, children's services and humanitarian aid; conducts research; organizes seminars and symposia; and operates a documentation centre and reference library. Holds General Consultative Status with the UN Economic and Social Council.

Geographical Area of Activity: International.

Publications: Annual Report; reports; conference proceedings.

Finance: Annual budget approx. US $4.6m.

Principal Staff: Pres. and CEO Abdelkbir el-Hakkaoui; Treas. Abdellatif Kerkeni; Sec. Ferdinand Lubanda.

Address: 29 rue Traversière, 75012 Paris.

Telephone: 1-40-19-91-51; **Fax:** 1-43-44-38-40; **Internet:** www.aide-federation.org; **e-mail:** international@aide-federation.org.

Fondation de France

Founded in 1969 with an initial endowment made by the Caisse des Dépôts et Consignations (Bank of Security Deposits) and 17 major French banks.

Activities: Fosters the practice of making charitable donations. The Foundation operates in three main areas: financial contributions to projects carried out by organizations acting in the fields of social welfare, scientific and medical research, culture and the environment; assistance to individuals or companies in the creation of a foundation under the aegis of the Fondation de France; and the development of associations, through helping them to raise funds. In 2012, it managed 715 individual foundations and maintained seven regional delegations.

Geographical Area of Activity: France and Europe.

Publications: Annual Report; newsletter; publications on social welfare, social work and philanthropy in France.

Finance: Annual revenue €311,974,722, expenditure €306,107,196 (2013).

Board of Directors: Philippe Lagayette (Chair.); Yves Sabouret, Bertrand Dufourcq (Hon. Chair.); Philippe Dupont (Treas.).

Principal Staff: CEO Francis Charhon.

Address: 40 ave Hoche, 75008 Paris.

Telephone: 1-44-21-31-00; **Fax:** 1-44-21-31-01; **Internet:** www.fondationdefrance.org; **e-mail:** fondation@fdf.org.

Réseau d'ONG Européennes sur l'Agro-alimentaire, le Commerce, l'Environnement et le Développement—RONGEAD (Network of European NGOs on Agriculture, Food, Trade and Development)

Founded in 1983 to support professional and non-governmental development organizations in Europe and less-developed countries.

Activities: Acts as a co-ordinating body for European NGOs, and NGOs and professional organizations in less-developed countries concerned with agriculture, food and trade issues in the developing world. The Network organizes an information exchange network and education programmes in Europe, and runs training seminars for local groups in developing countries.

Geographical Area of Activity: Europe, Africa, Pacific region, Caribbean, North America.

Publications: Articles, briefings, training and educational materials.

Finance: Annual revenue €1,144,904, expenditure €1,142,941 (31 Dec. 2013).

Board of Trustees: Maurice Perroux (Chair.); Joël Bonamy (Vice-Chair.); Marion Bayard (Treas.); Sylvie Pislar (Sec.).

Principal Staff: Dir Cédric Rabany.

Address: 29 rue Imbert-Colomès 69001 Lyon.

Telephone: 4-72-00-36-03; **Fax:** 4-72-00-35-98; **Internet:** www.rongead.org; **e-mail:** rongead@rongead.org.

FOUNDATIONS, TRUSTS AND NON-PROFIT ORGANIZATIONS

Académie Goncourt—Société des Gens de Lettres (Goncourt Academy— Literary Society)

Founded in 1896 by a legacy of Edmond de Goncourt, a writer and book publisher, to support literature, to give material assistance to particular writers and to strengthen the links between them.

Activities: Awards the annual Prix Goncourt for the best prose work of the year published in French, as well as scholarships in different fields of literature. The Academy has 10 members. Since 1973 the Academy has aimed to encourage francophone literature throughout the world and to support international cultural exchanges; it organizes conferences and lectures. Maintains an archive at Nancy, the birthplace of Edmond de Goncourt.

Geographical Area of Activity: France and francophone countries.

Principal Staff: Pres. Bernard Pivot; Sec.-Gen. Didier Decoin.

Address: c/o 8 rue de l'Abbaye, 75006 Paris.

Telephone: 1-40-46-88-11; **Internet:** www.academie -goncourt.fr.

Acting for Life

Established in 1981 as Groupe Développement. Present name adopted in 2009.

Activities: Operates in the field of aid to less-developed countries. The organization promotes local action in developing countries, supporting social and rural development projects; facilitates information exchange between development organizations; and campaigns for human rights and social justice for all, and against the sexual exploitation of women.

Geographical Area of Activity: Africa, Asia, the Middle East, and Central and South America.

Publications: Annual Report; *Transfaire* (newsletter).

Board of Directors: Jean-Cyril Spinetta (Hon. Pres.); René Lapautre (Pres.); Olivier Mondot (Treas.); Jean-Marie Joly (Sec.-Gen.).

Principal Staff: Exec. Dir Christophe Paquette.

Address: 1050 ave de l'Europe, Bâtiment 106, BP 07, 93352 Le Bourget Cedex.

Telephone: 1-49-34-83-13; **Fax:** 1-49-34-83-10; **Internet:** www.acting-for-life.com; **e-mail:** mmendes@acting-for-life .org.

Action contre la Faim (Action against Hunger)

Established in 1979 to combat hunger worldwide.

Activities: Operates emergency and post-emergency programmes to combat hunger; programmes include nutrition, health, water and food security, and agricultural development projects; sister organizations operate in Spain, the United Kingdom and the USA.

Geographical Area of Activity: International.

Publications: *Géopolitique de la Faim*; *Alimentation en eau*; *La Faim dans le Monde*; *Souffles du Monde*; *La Malnutrition en Situation de Crise*; newsletter (monthly).

Finance: Annual income €98,709,928, expenditure €99,453,127 (2013).

Board of Directors: Stéphanie Rivoal (Pres.); Madeleine Mukumabano (Vice-Chair.); Bertrand Brequeville (Treas.); Jérome Henry (Deputy Treas.); Thomas Ribemont (Sec.-Gen.); Lea Duhamel (Deputy Sec.-Gen.).

Principal Staff: CEO François Danel.

Address: 14–16 blvd Douaumont, CS 80060, 75854 Paris Cedex 17.

Telephone: 1-70-84-70-70; **Internet:** www .actioncontrelafaim.org; **e-mail:** info@actioncontrelafaim .org.

Action d'Urgence Internationale—AUI (International Emergency Action)

Founded in 1977 with the aim of co-ordinating organizations and volunteers to provide aid during times of natural disaster.

Activities: Operates in areas of natural disaster through prevention (training local populations), intervention (sending trained volunteers to carry out rescue and clearing tasks), and reconstruction (developing long-term reconstruction projects adjusted to local customs and needs).

Geographical Area of Activity: International.

Publications: *La Déferlante* (bulletin, 3 a year); Annual Report.

Principal Staff: Joint Pres and Chair. Christian Herbette, Fréderique Bonneaud.

Address: Les Terrasses de Montcalm, 1401 rue de Fontcouverte, 34070 Montpellier.

Telephone: 4-67-27-06-09; **Fax:** 4-67-27-03-59; **Internet:** www.aui-ong.org; **e-mail:** info@aui-ong.org.

Agriculteurs Français et Développement International—AFDI (French Agriculturalists and International Development)

Founded in 1975 to mobilize the French farming community and agricultural organizations to promote rural development in the countries of the South.

Activities: Promotes sustainable rural development throughout the world; supports farm workers internationally; arranges international exchanges; campaigns against the exploitation of agricultural workers; and works directly in rural areas of Africa, South America and Asia. Maintains representative offices throughout France and in Benin, Burkina Faso, Cameroon, Côte d'Ivoire, Madagascar, Mali and Senegal. Comprises 450 member organizations.

Geographical Area of Activity: Sub-Saharan Africa, Middle East, South America, Central America and the Caribbean, South-East Asia.

Publications: Annual Report.

Finance: Annual budget approx. €6m. (2015).

Board of Directors: Gérard Renouard (Pres.); Thomas Diemer, Claudine Faure (Vice-Pres); Thierry Chasles (Sec.-Gen.); Michel Renevier (Treas.).

Principal Staff: Dir Laure Hamdi.

Address: 11 rue de la Baume, 75008 Paris.

Telephone: 1-45-62-25-54; **Fax:** 1-42-89-58-16; **Internet:** www.afdi-opa.org; **e-mail:** contact@afdi-opa.org.

Agronomes et Vétérinaires sans Frontières—AVSF

Established in 1977 by Bertrand Naegelen, Jean-Marie Abbès and Jean-Marie Lechevallier, as the Centre International de Coopération pour le Développement Agricole (CICDA), to provide agricultural development aid. Merged with Vétérinaires sans Frontières in 2004.

Activities: Operates in the field of aid to less-developed countries, through supporting agricultural development, to improve the quality of life of people living in rural areas. Provides technical and financial support, exchange of knowledge and information, and training for land-workers; and funds local development projects and publications focusing on local aid. Operates within four core themes: improving agricultural production and sustainably managing natural resources; animal husbandry and health; adapting to climate change and natural disasters; and helping farmers' organizations gain access to local and international markets.

Geographical Area of Activity: Central and South America and the Caribbean, Sub-Saharan Africa, East and South-East Asia.

Restrictions: Grants only to specific countries and agricultural organizations.

Publications: Newsletter; *Revue Habbanae*; *Editions Ruralter* (technical manuals); *Collection Traverses*.

Finance: Annual income €13,804,220, expenditure €13,804,220 (2012).

Board of Directors: Claude Roger (Chair.); Juliette Soulabeille, Alexandre Martin (Vice-Pres.); Jean-Claude Cibert (Sec.-Gen.); Elisabeth Muller (Treas.); Charlène Nicolay (Asst Treas.).

Principal Staff: Dir-Gen. Frédéric Apollin.

Address: 45 bis ave de la Belle Gabrielle, 94736 Nogent-sur-Marne Cedex.

Telephone: 4-78-69-79-59; **Fax:** 4-78-69-79-56; **Internet:** www.avsf.org.

Alliance Israélite Universelle (Universal Jewish Alliance)

Founded in 1860 by Narcisse Leven, Charles Netter, Isidore Cahen, Eugène Manuel, Aristide Astruc and Jules Carvallo, to work for the emancipation and moral progress of Jewish people.

Activities: Operates internationally in the fields of education and religion through self-conducted programmes, publications and lectures. Maintains a network of schools in Belgium, Canada, France, Israel, Morocco and Spain, and a Hebrew teacher-training college in Casablanca, Morocco, the École Normale Hebraique. The Alliance holds a Jewish library of more than 120,000 volumes and runs the College des Etudes Juives and the Nadir publishing house. Through the Consultative Council of Jewish Organizations, the Alliance contributes to the defence of international human rights.

Geographical Area of Activity: International.

Publications: *Les Cahiers de l'Alliance*; *Les Cahiers du judaisme*; *Traces* collection; *The Basics*.

Governing Board: Marc Eisenberg (Pres.); Roger Benarrosh (Treas.).

Principal Staff: Dir-Gen. Jo Toledano.

Address: 45 rue La Bruyère, 75428 Paris Cedex 09.

Telephone: 1-53-32-88-55; **Fax:** 1-48-74-51-33; **Internet:** www.aiu.org; **e-mail:** info@aiu.org.

Aviation Sans Frontières—ASF (Aviation Without Borders)

Established in 1980 by André Gréard, Gérald Similowski and Alain Yout to make air transport available for humanitarian relief.

Activities: Operates in France and internationally, providing humanitarian relief through volunteer air services, transporting people in less-developed countries in need of medical aid, dispatching medical supplies and transporting medical personnel, offering emergency assistance following natural disasters, and assisting other NGOs in their activities; volunteers accompany children on flights to countries where they can be treated.

Geographical Area of Activity: International.

Publications: Bulletin (quarterly, in French).

Finance: Annual income €5,447,157 expenditure €5,447,157 (31 Dec. 2012).

Board of Directors: Primo Biason (Hon. Pres.); Pierre Lacorne (Chair.); André Fournerat (Vice-Pres.); Patrick Saumont (Sec.-Gen.); Henri Hurlin (Deputy Sec.-Gen.); Jean-Yves Gros (Treas.).

Address: Orly Fret 768, 94398 Orly Aérogares Cedex.

Telephone: 1-49-75-74-37; **Fax:** 1-49-75-74-33; **Internet:** www.asf-fr.org; **e-mail:** asfparis@asf-fr.org.

The Camargo Foundation

Founded in 1967 by Jerome Hill, a US film-maker and artist. In 2013, it merged with the Jerome Foundation (f. 1964).

Activities: Promotes the arts and education related to French and Francophone studies for scholars pursuing studies in the humanities and social sciences, as well as for composers, writers, and visual artists (painters, sculptors, photographers, film-makers, video artists and new media artists) pursuing creative projects. The Foundation organizes a fellowship and several partnership programmes. It also maintains a reference library and three art/music studios.

Geographical Area of Activity: France.

Board of Trustees: Charles Zelle (Chair.); Calogero Salvo (Vice-Chair.); Dr Gary Nan Tie (Treas.); Barbara Hunt McLanahan (Sec.).

Principal Staff: Pres. Cynthia A. Gehrig.

Address: 1 ave Jermini, 13260 Cassis.

Telephone: 4-42-01-11-57; **Fax:** 4-42-01-36-57; **Internet:** www.camargofoundation.org; **e-mail:** direction@camargofoundation.org.

Centre d'Études, de Documentation, d'Information et d'Action Sociales—CÉDIAS—Musée Social (Centre for Social Studies, Documentation, Information and Action)

Founded in 1963 by the merger of the Office Central des Oeuvres de Bienfaisance and the Musée Social, which was founded in 1894.

Activities: Operates nationally in the field of education, and nationally and internationally in the fields of social welfare and studies, economic affairs, law and other professions. The Centre organizes conferences, courses, publications and lectures; and maintains a library containing documentation compiled in France and abroad on subjects in the social field.

Geographical Area of Activity: France.

Publications: *Revue Vie Sociale* (quarterly); *Les implicites de la politique familiale*; postcards; reports and other publications; CDs and DVDs.

Board of Directors: Dr Pierre Charbonneau (Hon. Pres.); Simone Crapuchet (Hon. Vice-Pres.); Marc de Montalembert (Pres.); Edouard Secretan, Michel Laroque (Vice-Pres); Patrice Legrand (Treas.).

Principal Staff: Sec.-Gen. Christian Bazetoux; Deputy Sec.-Gen. Michel Dreyfus; Dir Jan-Yves Barreyre.

Address: 5 rue Las Cases, 75007 Paris.

Telephone: 1-45-51-66-10; **Fax:** 1-44-18-01-81; **Internet:** www.cedias.org; **e-mail:** cedias@cedias.org.

Centre Français de Droit Comparé (French Centre of Comparative Law)

Founded in 1951 to co-ordinate research and publication in the fields of international and comparative law within France; to co-ordinate libraries of comparative law and develop conformity of documentation in the field; to organize meetings on an international level; and to encourage exchange of scholars in the field.

Activities: Operates nationally and internationally in the field of international comparative law, through self-conducted programmes, research, conferences, courses, publications and lectures. The Centre awards prizes annually for theses in comparative law. It maintains a library of 50,000 vols and more than 700 periodical titles.

Geographical Area of Activity: International.

Publications: *La Lettre du CFDC* (newsletter, 3 a year); *Revue Internationale de Droit Comparé* (quarterly); series of monographs; *La présomption d'innocence en droit comparé*; *L'Europe des moyens de paiement à l'heure de l'euro et de l'internet*; *Les médiateurs en France et à l'étranger*.

Board of Directors: Prof. Jacques Robert (Chair.).

Principal Staff: Sec.-Gen. Didier Lamèthe; Deputy Sec.-Gen. Aliette Voinnesson.

Address: 28 rue Saint-Guillaume, 75007 Paris.

Telephone: 1-44-39-86-29; **Fax:** 1-44-39-86-28; **Internet:** www.centrefdc.org; **e-mail:** cfdc@legiscompare.com.

Centre International de Développement et de Recherche—CIDR (International Centre for Development and Research)

Established in 1961 to support less-developed countries.

Activities: Operates in the field of aid to less-developed countries, through providing assistance in areas such as agricultural development, health, community development, micro-enterprise and food security. Raises awareness of development issues in France and abroad.

Geographical Area of Activity: Africa, including Benin, Burkina Faso, Cameroon, Ghana, Madagascar, Mali, Tanzania, Togo.

Finance: Annual revenue € 7,130,200, expenditure €7,083,100 (31 Dec. 2013).

Board of Directors: Yannis Wendling (Pres.); Jacques de La Rocque (Treas.); Renée Chao-Béroff (Sec.).

Principal Staff: Chief Exec. Charles Ifrah; Dir of Admin. and Finance Gilles Ponsot.

Address: 17 rue de l'Hermitage, 60350 Autrêches.

Telephone: 3-44-42-71-40; **Fax:** 3-44-42-94-52; **Internet:** www.cidr.org.

Centre International de Recherche sur le Cancer—CIRC (International Agency for Research on Cancer—IARC)

Founded in 1965 as a self-governing body within the framework of the World Health Organization to generate and disseminate information useful for the primary prevention of cancer, through intra- and extra-mural activities.

Activities: Operates internationally in the field of medical research, through self-conducted programmes and collaboration with other agencies, as well as with national institutions and laboratories. Has developed programmes that represent an integrated approach to the identification of causative factors in human cancer, and of individuals and population groups at different risks of developing cancer. Topics of research include: studies on geographical incidence and time trends; determination of environmental and occupational hazards; site-orientated studies; childhood cancer; nutrition and cancer; genetics and cancer; mechanisms of carcinogenesis; and host susceptibility in chemical carcinogenesis. Studies for the improvement of data collection and of research methods are also conducted. Provides technical support in the form of computing services and statistical support, library and bibliographical services, banks of human biological material and common laboratory services. Research training fellowships and a visiting scientist award are awarded annually, and training courses on cancer epidemiology are held in various countries.

Geographical Area of Activity: Worldwide.

Publications: Biennial Report; *IARC Monographs on the Evaluation of Carcinogenic Risks to Humans*; *Directory of Ongoing Research in Cancer Epidemiology*; *Cancer Incidence in Five Continents*; *IARC Scientific Publications* (symposia proceedings, manuals, monographs); *Cancer Epidemiology*; *Social Inequalities and Cancer*.

Finance: Regular budget €40,424,491 (2014–15).

Governing Council: Prof. James F. Bishop (Chair.).

Principal Staff: Dir Dr Christopher Wild.

Address: 150 cours Albert-Thomas, 69372 Lyon Cedex 08.

Telephone: 4-72-73-84-85; **Fax:** 4-72-73-85-75; **Internet:** www.iarc.fr; **e-mail:** com@iarc.fr.

CIMADE—Service Oecuménique d'Entraide (Ecumenical Service for Mutual Help)

Founded in 1939 by French Protestant youth movements under the presidency of the Rev. Marc Boegner for work among refugees and immigrants.

Activities: Supports work among refugees and migrant workers in France, with emphasis on the defence of human rights. The organization also attempts to raise public awareness of these groups in France and the rest of Europe. Internationally, it works in partnership with 14 local organizations in Algeria, Mali, Mauritania, Morocco, Niger and Senegal, supporting projects in the field of human rights.

Geographical Area of Activity: Africa, Middle East and Europe.

Publications: Annual Reports about migration and detention centres; *Causes Communes* (quarterly journal).

Finance: Annual revenue €8.8m., expenditure €8.8m. (2013).

Advisory Council: Jacques Maury (Hon. Pres.); Geneviève Jacques (Pres.); Emmanuel de Bary (Vice-Pres.); Lionel Sautter (Treas.); Michel Rouanet (Sec.).

Address: 64 rue Clisson, 75013 Paris.

Telephone: 1-44-18-60-50; **Fax:** 1-45-56-08-59; **Internet:** www.lacimade.org; **e-mail:** infos@lacimade.org.

Cité Internationale des Arts

Initially conceived in 1937 by Eero Snellman, a Finnish artist, during a speech gave for the Exposition Universelle in Paris in 1937; the idea was taken up and developed by Mr and Mrs Félix Brunau with the support of the Ministry of Culture, the Ministry of Foreign Affairs, the City of Paris, and the Academy of Fine Arts, and the first building completed in 1965.

Activities: French and foreign operators underwrite 70% of the studios and designate resident-artists following their own application conditions (duration, scholarships, etc.); 30% are reserved for direct applications, subject to selection by two committees of professionals (one dedicated to the visual arts, the other to the music) that meet twice a year.

Geographical Area of Activity: International.

Principal Staff: CEO Jean-Yves Langlais.

Address: 18 rue de l'Hôtel de Ville, 75004 Paris Cedex 4.

Telephone: 1-42-78-71-72; **Fax:** 1-42-78-40-54; **Internet:** www.citedesartsparis.fr; **e-mail:** contact@citedesartsparis.fr.

Cité Internationale Universitaire de Paris (International University Centre of Paris)

Created during the inter-war period of the 1920s to restore France's international role in higher education, and promote exchanges and friendships between students and researchers from across the globe.

Activities: Accommodates 10,000 students and researchers each year within its 40 houses. Set in a 34-hectare park, it provides dedicated premises for international students.

Geographical Area of Activity: France.

Publications: Annual Report; Newsletter; Citescope cultural programme (monthly); periodicals.

Finance: Annual revenue €44,099,956, expenditure €41,939,006 (2013).

Board of Directors: Marcel Pochard (Pres.); François Weil, Marie-Hélène Bérard (Vice-Pres); Bernadette Petit (Sec.-Gen.); Patrice Henri (Treas.).

Principal Staff: CEO Carine Camby; Deputy CEO Eléna Menguy.

Address: 17 blvd Jourdan, 75014 Paris.

Telephone: 1-44-16-64-00; **Internet:** www.ciup.fr; **e-mail:** presse@ciup.fr.

Emmaüs International

Established internationally in 1971 (Emmaüs, f. 1949 by Abbé Pierre); an international movement promoting solidarity, combating the causes of exclusion and injustice.

Activities: Operates nationally and internationally in the areas of social welfare, development and conservation of the environment, assisting people with disabilities, those with addictions, ex-prisoners, refugees and other underprivileged people, through the creation of communities for marginalized people; promoting fair trade; developing networking between groups in less-developed countries; and supporting recycling activities. The international office acts as a liaison centre for 350 member organizations in 37 countries.

Geographical Area of Activity: International.

Publications: Annual Report; *Emmaus International Newsletter* (quarterly); *Tam-Tam* (6 a year); *Emmaus Express* (6 a year); reports; posters.

Finance: Annual income €4,501,000, expenditure €1,370,900 (2013).

Executive Committee: Jean Rousseau (Chair.); Simon Grainge, Moon Sharma (Vice-Chair.); Jean Karekezi (Sec.); Tânia Schubert Barbosa (Deputy Sec.); Gérard Racinne (Treas.).

Principal Staff: CEO Nathalie Péré-Marzano.

Address: 47 avenue de la Résistance, 93100 Montreuil.

Telephone: 1-41-58-25-50; **Fax:** 1-48-18-79-88; **Internet:** www.emmaus-international.org; **e-mail:** contact@emmaus-international.org.

Enfance et Partage (Children and Sharing)

Established in 1977.

Activities: Intervenes to protect child victims of neglect and physical, psychological and sexual abuse. Abroad, the organization helps tackle emergencies and invests in development programmes.

Geographical Area of Activity: France, Africa, South America and the Caribbean, and the Far East.

Restrictions: No public grants.

Publications: Annual Report; Newsletter; *Enfance et Partage* (quarterly).

Finance: Annual income €1,363,105, expenditure €3,125,333 (2013).

Board of Directors: Isabelle Guillemet (Chair.); Michel Maxant (Treas.).

Principal Staff: Sec.-Gen. Christiane Ruel; Deputy Sec. Béatrice Bailly.

Address: 96 rue Orfila, 75020 Paris.

Telephone: 1-55-25-65-65; **Fax:** 1-55-25-65-66; **Internet:** www.enfance-et-partage.org; **e-mail:** contacts@enfance-et -partage.org.

Enfance Réseau Monde—ERM (World Childhood Network)

Founded in 1981 as Enfants Réfugiés du Monde to rehabilitate refugees and homeless children in the developing world. Present name adopted in 2008.

Activities: Assists children in distress throughout the world, fulfilling their health care and educational needs. The Network extends psychological support to trauma victims and conducts training courses for local personnel.

Geographical Area of Activity: Africa, Asia, the Middle East, South-Eastern Europe and Central America.

Publications: Newsletter (quarterly); articles.

Principal Staff: Pres. Philippe Valls; Dir Nicole Dagnino.

Address: 35 blvd Pasteur, 75015 Paris.

Telephone: 6-34-49-61-38; **e-mail:** ermservices.asso@yahoo .fr.

Enfants du Mekong (Children of the Mekong)

Established in Laos in 1958 by René Péchard to assist children and families in South-East Asia.

Activities: Builds schools and medical centres and supports individual children and their families abroad. Nationally, the organization houses children from South-East Asia in France; and supports the French South-East Asian community. In 1990, it was awarded the French Prix des Droits de l'Homme (human rights prize).

Geographical Area of Activity: Cambodia, the People's Republic of China, France, Laos, Myanmar, the Philippines, Thailand and Viet Nam.

Publications: *Enfants du Mékong* (magazine, 6 a year).

Finance: Annual revenue €9,062,989, expenditure €8,809,700 (2012).

Board of Directors: François Foucart (Hon. Chair.); Christine Lotholary Nguyen (Chair.); Alain Deblock (Vice-Pres.); Didier Rochard (Sec.-Gen.); Hubert Paris (Deputy Sec.-Gen.); Tristan de Bodman (Treas.).

Principal Staff: CEO Yves Meaudre; Deputy CEO Antoine Filloux.

Address: 5 rue de la Comète, 92600 Asnières.

Telephone: 1-47-91-00-84; **Fax:** 1-47-33-40-44; **Internet:** www.enfantsdumekong.com; **e-mail:** contact@ enfantsdumekong.com.

Fédération Internationale des Ligues des Droits de L'Homme—FIDH (International Federation of Human Rights)

Established in 1922, as a non-profit NGO, to fight for international justice and defend human rights as contained in the Universal Declaration of Human Rights.

Activities: Priority areas are: human rights' defenders' freedom and capacity to act; universal human rights, particularly for women; promoting and protecting migrants' rights; ending impunity; and strengthening respect for human rights. The Federation organizes campaigns, lobbies internationally, co-ordinates a human rights network, provides information services, and works to protect people suffering from human rights abuse. Comprises 178 member organizations worldwide.

Geographical Area of Activity: Worldwide.

Publications: Annual Report; *La Lettre* (newsletter, 10 a year); *Mission Reports* (15 a year).

Finance: Annual revenue €6,144,424, expenditure €6,245,294 (2010).

International Board: Karim Lahidji (Pres.); Jean-François Plantin (Treas.).

Principal Staff: CEO Antoine Bernard; Exec. Dir Julianne Falloux.

Address: 17 passage de la Main d'Or, 75011 Paris.

Telephone: 1-43-55-25-18; **Fax:** 1-43-55-18-80; **Internet:** www.fidh.org.

Fondation Abbé Pierre pour le Logement des Défavorisés

Established in 1988 to assist homeless people; part of the Emmaüs network (q.v.).

Activities: Assists homeless people, offering counselling and support. Maintains regional offices in France.

Geographical Area of Activity: Mainly France; some international aid.

Publications: *Focus* (report series); *L'État du mal-logement*.

Finance: Annual revenue €45,028,000, expenditure €43,785,000 (30 Sept. 2013).

Board of Directors: Raymond Étienne (Chair.); Aminata Koné, Dominique Jeanningros (Vice-Chair.); Pierre Marcenac (Treas.); Laurent Demard (Sec.).

Principal Staff: CEO Christophe Robert; Deputy CEO Sonia Hurcet.

Address: 3–5 rue de Romainville, 75019 Paris.

Telephone: 1-55-56-37-00; **Internet:** www.fondation-abbe -pierre.fr; **e-mail:** contact@fondation-abbe-pierre.fr.

Fondation Agir Contre l'Exclusion—FACE (Campaign Against Exclusion Foundation)

Founded in 1993 on the initiative of Martine Aubry, deputy director of aluminium producer Péchiney, by 13 French companies, incl. Casino, Club Méditerranée, Crédit Lyonnais, Renault and Péchiney, in collaboration with local authorities and partners.

Activities: A network of enterprise clubs, created in partnership with local communities, contributing to the economic and social development of disadvantaged areas and encouraging social inclusion. The Foundation aims to reduce social exclusion in employment and local enterprise, through research and activities aimed locally and nationally. Enterprise centres in many different sectors, such as the environment, recreation, tourism, goods and services support local communities and rehabilitate training and employment facilities. The Foundation encourages the enterprises in its network to take diversity into account in their external affairs policy, human resources process and development.

Geographical Area of Activity: France.

Publications: Annual Report; *FACE.infos* (newsletter); *Les Journaux de Face*; *Temoignages*.

Finance: Annual revenue €2,070,834, expenditure €2,683,318 (31 Dec. 2012).

Governing Board: Gérard Mestrallet (Pres.); Pierre Mongin (Vice-Pres.); Philippe Aziz (Treas.); Jean-Jacques Rey (Sec.).

Principal Staff: CEO Vincent Baholet.

Address: 361 ave du Président Wilson, 93200 Saint-Denis La Plaine.

Telephone: 1-49-22-68-68; **Fax:** 1-42-23-77-94; **Internet:** www.fondationface.org; **e-mail:** secretariat@fondationface .org.

Fondation Auchan pour la Jeunesse (Auchan Foundation for Youth)

Established in 1996 by Auchan France retail group, under the aegis of the Fondation de France (q.v.).

Activities: Supports projects for young people in the fields of job creation, health and prevention, and community development. Priority is given to projects in close proximity to an Auchan hypermarket.

Geographical Area of Activity: France, particularly in areas of company operation.

Restrictions: Does not give money for sponsorship.

Publications: Annual Report.

Finance: Annual budget €1.5m.

Board of Directors: Vianney Mulliez (Chair.); Marie-Hélène Boidin-Dubrule (Vice-Chair.).

Principal Staff: CEO Alain Reners.

Address: Bâtiment Le Colibri, 200 rue de la Recherche, 59650 Villeneuve d'Ascq.

Telephone: 3-20-67-55-05; **Internet:** www.fondation-auchan .fr; **e-mail:** fondationauchan@auchan.fr.

Fondation de l'Avenir (Foundation of the Future)

Established in 1987 by the Mutualité Fonction Publique and the Association Française de Cautionnement Mutuel.

Activities: Operates nationally in the area of medicine and health, through supporting applied medical research into new surgical techniques, and training.

Geographical Area of Activity: France.

Publications: Newsletter (monthly).

Finance: Annual revenue €6,880,000, expenditure €5,489,000 (2014).

Board of Directors: Dominique Letourneau (Chair.); Jean-François Lemoine, Karim Ould-Kaci (Vice-Pres); Roland Masotta (Treas.); Myriam Reuter-Bourret (Sec.-Gen.).

Address: 255 rue Vaugirard, 75719 Paris Cedex 15.

Telephone: 1-40-43-23-80; **Fax:** 1-40-43-23-90; **Internet:** www.fondationdelavenir.org; **e-mail:** infocom@ fondationdelavenir.org.

Fondation Brigitte Bardot (Brigitte Bardot Foundation)

Established in 1986 for the protection of wild and domestic animals worldwide.

Activities: Operates in France and worldwide in the area of conservation and the environment, promoting the defence of the rights of wild and domestic animals. The Foundation also runs a retirement home for animals in Normandy, France.

Geographical Area of Activity: International.

Publications: *Info Journal.*

Finance: Annual revenue €13,807,561 (31 Dec. 2013).

Principal Staff: Pres. Brigitte Bardot.

Address: 28 rue Vineuse, 75116 Paris.

Telephone: 1-45-05-14-60; **Fax:** 1-45-05-14-80; **Internet:** www.fondationbrigittebardot.fr; **e-mail:** communication@ fondationbrigittebardot.fr.

Fondation Bettencourt Schueller (Bettencourt Schueller Foundation)

Founded in 1987 by Liliane Bettencourt, a businesswoman and heiress to the L'Oréal cosmetics company fortune, and her family to support projects in the humanitarian, cultural and medical fields.

Activities: Active in the fields of medical research, culture and social welfare. Devotes more than half of its budget to support medical research and health programmes including: the Young Researchers' Award, comprising up to 14 prizes of €21,000 annually to young researchers in life sciences for doctoral training courses abroad; the Liliane Bettencourt Life Sciences Award, awarded to a European researcher under 45 years of age, who is known in the scientific community and carrying out a particularly promising research project; and the Prix 'Coups d'Elan' pour la Recherche Française, awarded annually to two or three French laboratories engaged in biomedical research, each award worth €250,000. In the field of culture, the Foundation supports talented artists or craftsmen and the development of new projects of exceptional quality, as well as awarding the annual Prix Liliane Bettencourt pour le Chant Choral and the Prix Liliane Bettencourt pour l'Intelligence de la Main.

Geographical Area of Activity: France and developing countries.

Finance: Funds disbursed €30.4m. (2013).

Board of Trustees: Liliane Schueller Bettencourt (Hon. Pres.); Françoise Bettencourt Meyers (Pres.).

Principal Staff: CEO Olivier Brault; Sec.-Gen. Armand de Boissière.

Address: 27–29 rue des Poissonniers, 92522 Neuilly-sur-Seine Cedex.

Internet: www.fondationbs.org; **e-mail:** info@fondationbs .com.

Fondation Marcel Bleustein-Blanchet pour la Vocation (Marcel Bleustein-Blanchet Vocation Foundation)

Founded in 1960 by Marcel Bleustein-Blanchet, founder of the Publicis Groupe advertising and public relations company, to encourage young people to achieve their chosen vocation.

Activities: Gives financial and practical help to young people aged between 18 and 30 years. The Foundation awards 20 scholarships ('Bourses de la Vocation') annually to provide training for young French and European people in numerous branches of science, technology, medicine, the arts and sports. Two prizes, the Prix Littéraire de la Vocation and the Prix de Poésie, are awarded annually for literary work in the French language. 'Sister' foundations have been established in Belgium, Brazil, Israel, Spain and Switzerland.

Geographical Area of Activity: Europe.

Restrictions: No grants for pursuing religious or political vocations.

Finance: Annual revenue €1,172,318, expenditure €538,425 (31 Dec. 2011).

Board: Elisabeth Badinter (Chair.); Christine de Froment (Treas.).

Principal Staff: Permanent Representatives Anne de la Baume, Béatrice Netter-Leval, Nathalie Royer.

Address: 104 rue de Rennes, 75006 Paris.

Telephone: 1-53-63-25-90; **Fax:** 1-42-22-16-66; **Internet:** www.fondationvocation.org; **e-mail:** fondationpourlavocation@gmail.com.

Fondation BNP Paribas (BNP Paribas Foundation)

Established in 1984 to fund cultural and humanitarian projects, operating under the aegis of the Fondation de France (q.v.).

Activities: Works in the fields of culture, social welfare and the environment. The Foundation promotes the cultural wealth of museums, to encourage creative talent, to aid specialized medical research, and to support initiatives that promote education, social inclusion and overcoming disabilities. It also develops and guides BNP Paribas Group's corporate patronage policy. In 2014, the total amount the Foundation disbursed was €41m.

Geographical Area of Activity: Worldwide.

Publications: Annual Report; *Sustainable Development Report*; press releases.

Board of Directors: Michel Pébereau (Chair.).

Principal Staff: CEO Jean-Jacques Goron.

Address: 3 rue d'Antin, 75002 Paris.

Telephone: 1-42-98-12-34; **Fax:** 1-42-98-14-11; **Internet:** www .fondation.bnpparibas.com; mecenat.bnpparibas.com; **e-mail:** fondation@bnpparibas.com.

Fondation Caisses d'Epargne pour la Solidarité— FCES (Caisses d'Epargne Foundation for Social Solidarity)

Created in 2001 by the Groupe Caisse d'Epargne, with the aim of preventing social exclusion.

Activities: Operates nationally in the field of social welfare; in particular it manages nursing homes for elderly people, establishments for disabled people and sanitary establishments.

Geographical Area of Activity: France.

Publications: Annual Report.

Finance: Annual revenue €326,791,000, expenditure €326,050,000 (31 Dec. 2013).

Board of Directors: Astrid Boos (Chair.); Benoît Mercier, Jean-Paul Foucault (Vice-Chair.); Yves Hubert (Sec.).

Principal Staff: Sec.-Gen. Patrick Lambruschini.

Address: 11 rue de La Vanne, CS 20018, 92126 Montrouge.

Telephone: 1-58-07-16-60; **Internet:** www.fces.fr; **e-mail:** direction.generale@fces.fr.

Fondation Cartier pour l'Art Contemporain (Cartier Foundation for Contemporary Art)

Founded in 1984 by Alain Dominique Perrin to promote creative arts and to establish direct dialogue between artists and the general public.

Activities: Commissions works of art to exhibit at home and abroad; it collects and exhibits the works of young artists and stages exhibitions of its collection of contemporary art (it maintains a collection of more than 1,000 works of art by around 250 French and international artists). The Foundation commissions transitory or performance art for evening performances. The Foundation also organizes travelling exhibitions and promotes artistic exchange with foreign institutions, organizes conferences and issues publications.

Geographical Area of Activity: Asia, South America, Europe and the USA.

Publications: Artists' books and exhibition catalogues.

Finance: Financed by the Cartier Group.

Trustees: Alain Dominique Perrin (Pres.).

Principal Staff: Gen. Man. Hervé Chandès.

Address: 261 blvd Raspail, 75014 Paris.

Telephone: 1-42-18-56-50; **Fax:** 1-42-18-56-52; **Internet:** www.fondation.cartier.com; **e-mail:** info.reservation@ fondation.cartier.com.

Fondation Henri Cartier-Bresson (Henri Cartier-Bresson Foundation)

Established in 2003 to promote photography in general, as well as the work of Henri Cartier-Bresson.

Activities: Promotes the work of Henri Cartier-Bresson, through the establishment of a studio to house the photographer's works, books, films and designs; the studio is open to researchers. Every two years the Foundation awards the €35,000 HCB Award, launched in 2003. Also organizes films, screenings and exhibitions of Cartier-Bresson's work and the work of other photographers.

Geographical Area of Activity: Mainly Paris area.

Restrictions: No grants are made, apart from the HCB Award.

Publications: Newsletter; *Le Scrapbook d'Henri Cartier-Bresson* (exhibition catalogue); *Joan Colom—Les Gens du Raval* (exhibition catalogue); *Le silence intérieur d'une victime consentante* (exhibition catalogue); *Documentary and Anti-Graphic Photographs* (exhibition catalogue); *Les Choix d'Henri* (exhibition catalogue); *Walker Evans/Henri Cartier Bresson, photographier l'Amérique* (exhibition catalogue); *Robert Doisneau, Du metier à l'oeuvre* (exhibition catalogue); *Saul Leiter* (exhibition catalogue); *Jim Goldberg, Open See* (exhibition catalogue), *Harry Callahan, Variations* (exhibition catalogue).

Finance: Annual revenue €837,027, expenditure €772,779 (31 Aug. 2010).

Board of Directors: Kirsten van Riel (Chair.); Pierre Rochelois (Vice-Chair.); Julien Lauter (Sec.); Mélanie Cartier-Bresson (Asst Sec.); Christelle Grandin (Treas.).

Principal Staff: Dir Agnès Sire.

Address: 2 impasse Lebouis, 75014 Paris.

Telephone: 1-56-80-27-03; **Fax:** 1-56-80-27-01; **Internet:** www.henricartierbresson.org; **e-mail:** contact@ henricartierbresson.org.

Fondation Casip-Cojasor

Established in 1999 by the merger of the Comité d'Action Sociale Israélite de Paris—CASIP (f. 1809) and the Comité Juif d'Action Sociale et de Reconstruction—COJASOR (f. 1945); began its activities in 2000.

Activities: Aims to help children, the handicapped and the elderly, in particular members of the Jewish community. Foundation services include culturally sensitive social welfare and employment advice; legal guardianship services; distribution of donated new or used clothes; a kosher food delivery service; and a community centre for the elderly. It also provides access to a number of charitable funds.

Geographical Area of Activity: France.

Publications: Annual Report.

Finance: Annual revenue €41,235,000, expenditure €43,031,000 (2013).

Board of Directors: Eric de Rothschild (Pres.); Jean-Claude Picard, Henri Fiszer (Vice-Pres); Julien Roitman (Sec.-Gen.); Georges Amaraggi (Asst Sec.-Gen.); George Koltein (Treas.); Bernard Rechtman (Asst Treas.).

Principal Staff: Dir-Gen. Karêne Fredj.

Address: 8 rue Pali-Kao, 75020 Paris.

Telephone: 1-44-62-13-13; **Fax:** 1-44-62-13-14; **Internet:** www .casip-cojasor.fr; **e-mail:** fondation@casip-cojasor.fr.

Fondation Chirac (Chirac Foundation)

Established in 2007 by the former President of France, Jacques Chirac, to help build a peaceful international society.

Activities: Operates in the areas of development, health, safeguarding languages and cultures threatened with extinction and the environment, through its projects: access to medicines; access to water; combatting desertification; and support for endangered languages and cultures. The Foundation awards the Conflict Prevention Prize and Culture for Peace Prize.

Geographical Area of Activity: International.

Finance: Annual revenue €47,993,374, expenditure €46,569,368 (31 Dec. 2013).

Board of Directors: Jacques Chirac (Chair.); Claude Chirac (Vice-Chair.); Bernard Vatier (Vice-Pres. and Legal Adviser); Valérie Terranova (Sec.); Marie-Hélène Bérard (Treas.).

Address: 14 rue d'Anjou, 75008 Paris.

Telephone: 1-47-42-87-60; **Fax:** 1-47-42-87-78; **Internet:** www .fondationchirac.eu; **e-mail:** contact@fondationchirac.eu.

Fondation Le Corbusier—FLC (Le Corbusier Foundation)

Founded in 1968 according to the wish of Charles Edouard Jeanneret, known as 'Le Corbusier', to maintain a museum in the Villa La Roche in Paris displaying his works, and to encourage research in the spirit defined by his own written and architectural work.

Activities: Operates internationally in the field of the arts and humanities. Maintains a permanent exhibition in the Villa La Roche of Le Corbusier's works: furniture, paintings and sculptures. Loans original works for exhibitions. Advises and supervises the preservation of buildings designed by Le Corbusier. Maintains a library. Also awards research scholarships.

Geographical Area of Activity: France.

Publications: Annual Report; *informations* (newsletter); *Masilia*; conference proceedings; guidebooks.

Finance: Annual revenue €1,150,934, expenditure €1,492,940 (31 Dec. 2013).

Board of Directors: Antoine Picon (Chair.); Wanda Diebolt (Vice-Chair.); Christine Mengin (Sec.-Gen.); Martine Vittu (Treas.).

Principal Staff: Dir Michel Richard.

Address: 8–10 pl. du Docteur Blanche, 75016 Paris.

Telephone: 1-42-88-41-53; **Fax:** 1-42-88-33-17; **Internet:** www.fondationlecorbusier.fr; **e-mail:** info@fondationlecorbusier.fr.

Fondation de Coubertin (Coubertin Foundation)

Established in 1973 by Yvonne de Coubertin and Jean Bernard for the further training of young craft workers, and for the conservation of and research into craft techniques.

Activities: Operates in the area of education and training, offering courses of 11 months for some 30 young craft workers annually, from France or abroad, between the ages of 20 and 25 years. The Foundation offers general courses and courses in crafts such as joinery, decorative metal, fine-art foundry and stone masonry. It also organizes public concerts, and seminars for professionals. Maintains a library of around 3,000 vols.

Geographical Area of Activity: International.

Publications: Newsletter; *Le Compagnonnage de l'an 2000*; *Jean-Paul le Forézien Compagnon Menuisier du Devoir*; *Dodeigne*; *Etienne-Martin*; *Etienne Hajdu*; *Genèse d'une sculpture: Le monument à Michel Servet à Vienne*; *Jean Chauvin*; *Sculpture en taille directe en France de 1900 à 1950*; *Pierres et marbres de Joseph Bernard*; *Aux grands hommes*.

Principal Staff: Pres. Gilles de Navacelle.

Address: Domaine de Coubertin, 78470 Saint-Rémy les Chevreuse.

Telephone: 1-30-85-69-60; **Fax:** 1-30-85-69-69; **Internet:** www.coubertin.fr; **e-mail:** info@coubertin.fr.

Fondation Jean Dausset—Centre d'Étude du Polymorphisme Humain—CEPH

Founded in 1984 by Prof. Daniel Cohen and Prof. Jean Dausset to promote and conduct research into the human genome. Became the Fondation Jean Dausset in 1993.

Activities: Operates nationally and internationally in the fields of medicine and health, and science and technology, through self-conducted programmes, research and publications. It conducts genetic research and produced the first 'map' of the genetic constitution of human beings (genome map). Research is also carried out at its 'daughter' laboratory, Généthon, which is now an independent organization. The Centre maintains a database and the online Human BAC Library.

Publications: *A first generation physical map of the human genome*; *A YAC contig map of the human genome*.

Finance: The Centre was founded using a US $10m. bequest from a French art collector.

Board of Directors: Jean-Louis Mandel (Pres.); Bernard Bigot, Edgardo Carosella (Vice-Pres); Philippe Sudreau (Treas.); François Gros (Sec.).

Principal Staff: Admin. and Legal Dir Agnès Marcadet-Troton.

Address: 27 rue Juliette Dodu, 75010 Paris.

Telephone: 1-53-72-50-00; **Fax:** 1-53-72-51-28; **Internet:** www.cephb.fr; **e-mail:** agnes.marcadet@cephb.fr.

Fondation de Lourmarin Robert Laurent-Vibert (Foundation Robert Laurent-Vibert)

Founded in 1927 by the Académie des Sciences, Agriculture, Arts et Belles Lettres d'Aix, according to the will of Robert Laurent-Vibert, with the aim of promoting literature and the arts.

Activities: Provides grants in the field of the arts and humanities, and invites annually six to eight artists and scholars of French and other nationalities to spend one month as guests at the Castle of Lourmarin. Conducts seminars on the national and international aspects of education, social welfare, the arts and conservation. Programmes are also carried out through lectures, concerts, plays and exhibitions, including the 'Musiques d'été à Lourmarin' music festival. More recently, has widened its areas of interest to include the natural and social sciences, and collaborates in this field with the Académie des Sciences, Agriculture, Arts et Belles Lettres d'Aix.

Geographical Area of Activity: France.

Restrictions: Artists must be younger than 35 years of age.

Publications: Annual Report.

Principal Staff: Pres. Max Michelard; Curator Danièlle Antonelli; Man. Janet Mead.

Address: Château de Lourmarin, BP 23, 84160 Lourmarin.

Telephone: 4-90-68-15-23; **Fax:** 4-90-68-25-19; **Internet:** www.chateau-de-lourmarin.com; **e-mail:** contact@chateau-de-lourmarin.com.

Fondation Simone et Cino del Duca (Simone and Cino del Duca Foundation)

Founded in 1975 by Simone del Duca, the widow of publisher Cino del Duca, to support natural and cultural heritage, and to promote scientific research, especially biomedical research. Administered by the Institut de France.

Activities: Operates internationally in the fields of science and medicine, and the arts and humanities. The Foundation awards grants to organizations, and to French research workers wishing to study abroad and for foreign research workers to spend a period of time in a French laboratory. The Foundation awards four prizes each year: a science prize to encourage research, alternating between European and international winners, worth €275,000 (as well as three grants of €125,000); the Prix mondial del Duca, worth €200,000 for writing in the French language; an archaeology prize worth €150,000; and an arts prize worth €100,000. It also hosts conferences, seminars and other events organized by the Institut de France.

Geographical Area of Activity: Worldwide.

Restrictions: Grants are made exclusively to research workers whose scientific activity is in the following areas: the cardiovascular system (molecular and cellular biology, pathology, pharmacology and epidemiology), and the nervous system, behaviour and mental health (molecular and cellular biology, pathology, pharmacology and epidemiology), and are made to research workers who have obtained a doctorate before applying for the grant.

Publications: Annual Report.

Address: 10 rue Alfred-de-Vigny, 75008 Paris.

Telephone: 1-47-66-01-21; **Fax:** 1-46-22-45-02; **Internet:** www.institut-de-france.fr/institutions/prix-amp-fondations/fondations/fondation-simone-et-cino-del-d; **e-mail:** fondation-del-duca@institut-de-france.fr.

Fondation Énergies pour le Monde (Energies for the World Foundation)

Founded in 1990 by Alain Liebard, an architect, to assist developing countries by providing energy sources that do not damage the environment.

Activities: Operates internationally in the field of aid to less-developed countries, through self-conducted programmes.

Geographical Area of Activity: The Maghreb, Sub-Saharan Africa, Madagascar, Cambodia, Laos.

Publications: *Fondation Energies pour le Monde Infos* (2 a year); Brochure.

Board of Directors: Vincent Jacques le Seigneur (Chair.); Dominique Bidou (Sec.); Catherine Becquaert (Treas.).

Principal Staff: Dir Yves Maigne; Sec.-Gen. Sarah Holt.

Address: c/o Observ'ER, 146 rue de l'Université, 75007 Paris.

Telephone: 1-44-18-00-80; **Fax:** 1-44-18-00-36; **Internet:** www.energies-renouvelables.org/accueil-fondation.asp; **e-mail:** energiespourlemonde@energies-renouvelables.org.

Fondation Ensemble

Established in 2004 by Gérard Brémond and his wife Jacqueline Délia Brémond.

Activities: Works to alleviate poverty. The Foundation supports the activities of organizations that operate within its four intervention sectors: sustainable agriculture, biodiversity conservation, sustainable fishing and sustainable technologies.

Geographical Area of Activity: Cambodia, Ecuador, Laos, Mozambique, Peru.

Restrictions: Only funds projects that: fall within the Foundation's selection criteria; are driven by target populations' needs and make a lasting improvement to their living conditions; and take into account environmental conservation and rehabilitation.

Publications: Newsletters; technical sheets; Annual Report.

Board of Directors: Gérard Brémond (Pres.); Jacqueline Délia Brémond (Co-Chair.).

Principal Staff: Dir Olivier Braunsteffer; Sec.-Gen. Barry Windsor.

Address: 1 rue de Fleurus, 75006 Paris.

Telephone: (1) 45 51 18 82; **Internet:** www.fondationensemble .org; **e-mail:** contactfe@fondationensemble.org.

Fondation 'Entente Franco-Allemande' (Foundation for Franco-German Co-operation)

Established in 1981 to receive the funds offered by the German Government in settlement for the forced enrolment of French nationals in the German army during the Second World War and to distribute these funds to alleviate the social problems and uphold the human rights of these former soldiers, as well as to develop Franco-German co-operation through other projects.

Activities: Aims to develop Franco-German co-operation through funding projects in the fields of culture, science, sports, economics and social welfare. In 2012, the Foundation disbursed €137,601,608.

Geographical Area of Activity: France and Germany.

Board of Directors: Jean-Georges Mandon (Chair.); Pierre Rendler, Ulrich von Kirchbach (Vice-Chair.); Yves Muller (Sec.-Gen.); Marie-Paule Stintzi (Treas.).

Principal Staff: CEO Jacques Jola Sec.-Gen.

Address: 1 rue St-Léon, 67000 Strasbourg.

Telephone: 3-88-32-18-00; **Fax:** 3-88-22-48-14; **Internet:** www.fefa.fr; **e-mail:** info@fefa.fr.

Fondation d'Entreprise Air France (Air France Corporate Foundation)

Established in 1992 by the Air France Group.

Activities: Provides financial assistance to NGOs and associations' projects that help sick, disabled and vulnerable children and young people in France and in all the countries where Air France operates .

Geographical Area of Activity: International.

Publications: Press releases; fact sheets; news bulletins.

Board of Directors: Frédéric Gagey (Chair.).

Principal Staff: Dir-Gen. Cécile Vic; Asst Dir-Gen. Laurence Cuisance Kindraich.

Address: 45 rue de Paris, 95747 Roissy CDG Cedex.

Telephone: 1-41-56-57-27; **Fax:** 1-41-56-57-18; **Internet:** fondation.airfrance.com; **e-mail:** mail.fondationaf@ airfrance.fr.

Fondation d'Entreprise d'EDF (EDF Foundation)

Established in 1987 as Fondation Electricité de France.

Activities: Operates in France in the fields of social welfare, nature and culture. The Foundation has an exhibition area, Espace EDF Electra, in Paris for exhibitions of contemporary art, concerts, conferences, etc. It awards an annual medical research prize worth €45,000 and five post-doctoral research scholarships of €15,000 each. It also assisted in the restoration of, and supports the cultural activities of, the Villa Medici in Rome. Has regional delegations throughout France.

Geographical Area of Activity: International.

Restrictions: Individual artists are not supported.

Publications: Reports; catalogues; brochures.

Finance: Budget €40m. (2012–15).

Board of Directors: Jean-Bernard Lévy (Chair.).

Principal Staff: CEO Hugues Renson; Sec.-Gen. Emmanuelle Mercier.

Address: 9 ave Percier, 75008 Paris.

Telephone: 1-40-42-22-22; **Fax:** 1-40-42-48-62; **Internet:** fondation.edf.com; **e-mail:** fondation-edf@edf.fr.

Fondation d'Entreprise GDF Suez (GDF Suez Foundation)

Founded in 1992 as Fondation d'Entreprise Gaz de France to pursue charitable works related to society, the environment and cultural heritage. Present name adopted in 2012.

Activities: Operates nationally and internationally in the fields of the environment and social welfare, especially relating to young people. Also supports relief projects, sporting activities, literacy initiatives and employee volunteering.

Geographical Area of Activity: France and international, including Viet Nam.

Publications: Annual Report.

Finance: Funded solely by Gaz de France.

Board of Directors: Gérard Mestrallet (Chair.); Jean-François Cirelli, Valérie Bernis (Vice-Chair.).

Principal Staff: CEO Philippe Peyrat; Deputy CEO Valérie Vigouroux.

Address: 1 pl. Samuel de Champlain, Faubourg de l'Arche, 92930 La Défense Cedex.

Telephone: 1-56-65-55-98; **Internet:** www.fondation-gdfsuez .com; **e-mail:** fondation@gdfsuez.com.

Fondation d'Entreprise La Poste (Post Office Foundation)

Established in 1995 under the aegis of the Fondation de France (q.v.), principally to promote literature.

Activities: Operates nationally and in francophone countries in the area of the arts and culture, through financing festivals and literary prizes such as the Prix Wepler, promoting French songwriting through the Prix Timbres de Voix prize, and supporting publishing initiatives.

Geographical Area of Activity: France.

Publications: *Flori Lettre* (online newsletter).

Finance: Annual revenue €1,000,000, expenditure €878.512 (31 Dec. 2014).

Executive Committee: Philippe Wahl (Chair.).

Principal Staff: CEO Dominique Blanchecotte.

Address: 44 blvd de Vaugirard, Case Postale F603, 75757 Paris Cedex 15.

Telephone: 1-41-41-62-07; **Fax:** 1-41-41-62-60; **Internet:** www .fondationlaposte.org; **e-mail:** fondation.laposte@laposte.fr.

Fondation d'Entreprise Renault (Renault Foundation)

Established in 2001 to promote the French language and French and European culture worldwide.

Activities: Operates in the field of education, offering to fund a period of study in France for around 70 non-French postgraduate students each year. There are three postgraduate training programmes, located in Paris, Bordeaux and Strasbourg (Programme Renault, MBA IP Fondation Renault and Master ParisTech Fondation Renault). Also promotes collaboration between business and tertiary-level educational establishments in France and abroad.

Geographical Area of Activity: International.

Publications: Annual Report; Newsletter; *The Mediterranean Directory*.

Finance: Annual income €262,303,038, expenditure €288,001,662 (31 Dec. 2011).

Board of Directors: Carlos Ghosn (Chair.).

Principal Staff: Dir Claire Martin; Deputy Dir Sophie Chazelle.

Address: 13–15 quai Alphonse le Gallo, FQLG V 15140, 92513 Boulogne-Billancourt Cedex.

Telephone: 1-76-84-96-82; **Fax:** 1-76-84-25-00; **Internet:** www.fondation.renault.com; **e-mail:** fondation.renault@renault.com.

Fondation d'Entreprise VINCI pour la Cité (VINCI Corporate Foundation for the City)

Established in 2002 by the VINCI construction company to help disadvantaged people gain access to employment.

Activities: Grant programmes aim to help people who find themselves excluded to gain access to employment, and to encourage citizens' initiatives aimed at sustainable development and quality of life. The Foundation gives priority to projects developing social responsibility, or helping the socially excluded get back to work.

Geographical Area of Activity: France and several countries where the company operates in Western Europe (United Kingdom, Germany, Belgium, Czech Republic).

Restrictions: Projects from a country other than France must be submitted to the Foundation by a company employee.

Finance: Annual budget €2.5m.

Board of Directors: Xavier Huillard (Chair.).

Principal Staff: CEO Chantal Monvois.

Address: 12–14 rue Blériot, 92500 Rueil-Malmaison Cedex.

Telephone: 1-47-16-30-63; **Fax:** 1-47-16-49-45; **Internet:** www.fondation-vinci.com; **e-mail:** fondation@vinci.com.

Fondation Euris (Euris Foundation)

Founded in 2000 by Jean-Charles Naouri, Chairman of the company Euris, to promote the education of disadvantaged young French people.

Activities: Provides annual scholarships to French students from high schools classified as ZEP (Zones d'Education Prioritaire) and ZS (Zone Sensible) in need of financial support to acquire a university education. The Foundation has awarded scholarships to 538 students. Scholarships are granted for the first two years of university degree. Under the aegis of Fondation de France.

Geographical Area of Activity: France.

Board of Trustees: Jean-Charles Naouri (Chair.).

Principal Staff: Co-ordinator Edith Mikolajczak.

Address: 83 rue du Faubourg-Saint-Honoré, 75008 Paris.

Telephone: 1-44-71-14-70/90; **Fax:** 1-44-71-14-53; **e-mail:** fondationeuris@euris.fr.

Fondation Européenne de la Science (European Science Foundation)

Established in 1974 to provide a common platform for its member organizations to advance European research collaboration and explore new directions for research.

Activities: Promotes collaboration in research, the funding of research and science policy at the European level, and maintains close relations with other scientific institutions within and outside Europe. The Foundation is currently reducing its research programmes and developing new activities to serve scientists, including peer review and evaluation services.

Together with the former European Heads of Research Councils, it has established a strategic road map for the European Research Area and published the European Code of Conduct for Research Integrity and the European Peer Review Guide. Current membership comprises 66 research-funding and/or research-performing organizations and academies from 29 countries.

Geographical Area of Activity: Europe.

Publications: Annual Report (in English); Science Policy Briefings; Science Position Papers; other specialized publications, studies and reports.

Finance: Annual revenue €57,651,440, expenditure €57,998,715 (31 Dec. 2012).

Governing Council: Prof. Pär Omling (Pres.); Dr Véronique Halloin (Vice-Pres.).

Principal Staff: Chief Exec. Martin Hynes.

Address: 1 quai Lezay Marnésia, BP 90015, 67080 Strasbourg Cedex.

Telephone: 3-88-76-71-00; **Fax:** 3-88-37-05-32; **Internet:** www.esf.org; **e-mail:** communications@esf.org.

Fondation FARM—Fondation pour l'Agriculture et la Ruralité dans le Monde (FARM Foundation— Foundation for World Agriculture and Rural Life)

Established in 2006.

Activities: Carries out research to inform and influence policymakers. The Foundation operates in the fields of: agricultural policies and markets; value chain organization; agricultural financing and risk management; production systems; management of water for drinking, sanitation and agriculture; and training and advising agricultural producers. It carries out studies, publishing its findings and organizing events; builds pilot projects with local stakeholders; and provides training and education to build capacity and professionalize producer organizations.

Geographical Area of Activity: International.

Publications: Newsletter (6 a year); *Point de Vue*; reports; studies; working papers.

Finance: Annual income €1,086,220 (2012).

Board of Directors: René Carron (Chair.); Erik Orsenna (Vice-Chair.); Jean-Louis Blanc (Treas.); Jean-Paul Betbèze (Sec.).

Principal Staff: Dir Jean-Christophe Debar; Deputy Dir Fabienne Derrien.

Address: s/c Crédit Agricole SA, 12 pl. des Etats Unis, 92127 Montrouge Cedex; 72 rue Gabriel Péri, 92120 Montrouge.

Telephone: 1-57-72-07-19; **Internet:** www.fondation-farm.org; **e-mail:** contact@fondation-farm.org.

Fondation France-Israel (France-Israel Foundation)

Launched in 2005 by the French and Israeli Governments to reinforce links and relations between France and Israel at all levels.

Activities: Activities include combating anti-Semitism in France. Promotes the development of relations between the two countries through supporting educational, cultural, economic, scientific and technological projects.

Geographical Area of Activity: France and Israel.

Board of Directors: Nicole Guedj (Chair.); Anne-Marie Descôtes, Edouard Cukierman (Vice-Chair.); Alain Madar (Treas.); David Harari (Asst Treas.); Mikael Bensadoun (Sec.-Gen.); Claude Oliel (Asst Sec.-Gen.).

Address: BP 20024, 75008 Paris Cedex; 5 rue Alfred de Vigny, 75008 Paris.

Telephone: 1-82-28-95-85; **Fax:** 1-82-28-95-21; **Internet:** www.fondationfranceisrael.org; **e-mail:** info@fondationfranceisrael.org.

Fondation Franco-Japonaise Sasakawa (Franco-Japanese Sasakawa Foundation)

Founded in 1990 by the Sasakawa Foundation (Japan, q.v.) to promote cultural awareness and harmony between France and Japan.

Activities: Operates in France and Japan in the fields of the arts and humanities, education, and science and technology, by awarding scholarships, research grants and travel grants in several areas, including education, the teaching of French and Japanese, translation and publication of works, art, scientific research, promoting exchanges of people and of knowledge, journalism, exhibitions, etc. Also organizes conferences, operates self-conducted programmes and issues publications. In particular, aims to encourage projects dealing with contemporary rather than historical issues, and that favour the long-term development of Franco-Japanese relations.

Geographical Area of Activity: France and Japan.

Publications: Annual Report; Newsletter; *Cent Objets—Produits Artisanaux Traditionnels Japonais Commentés; Guide pour la promotion des objets d'artisanat traditionnel japonais*; cultural register of Japanese institutions located in France.

Finance: Annual budget €23,888,755 (2012).

Board of Directors: Yohei Sasakawa (Hon. Chair.); Shigeatsu Tominaga (Chair.); Jean-Bernard Ouvrieu (Vice-Chair.); Yves Rousset-Rouard (Sec.); Georges-Christian Chazot (Treas.); Masatoshi Watanabe (Asst Treas.).

Address: 27 rue du Cherche-Midi, 75006 Paris.

Telephone: 1-44-39-30-40; **Fax:** 1-44-39-30-45; **Internet:** www.ffjs.org; **e-mail:** siegeparis@ffjs.org.

Fondation Fyssen (Fyssen Foundation)

Established in 1979 by A. H. Fyssen, a businessman with an interest in all forms of scientific research into cognitive mechanisms, including thought and reasoning, that underlie animal and human behaviour, their biological and cultural bases, and phylogenetic and ontogenetic development.

Activities: Operates a research programme, awarding post-doctoral study grants and research grants, worth between €15,000 and €35,000, to French scientists going abroad and to foreign scientists wishing to work in French research centres. Organizes symposia and publishes research results, and awards an annual international scientific prize worth €60,000.

Geographical Area of Activity: Worldwide.

Restrictions: Grants are made only for a first post-doctorate, less than two years after a PhD thesis on 1 September of the year of application.

Publications: *Annales de la Fondation Fyssen*.

Board of Directors: Daniel Lallier (Chair.); Paul-Albertle Bâtonnie (Vice-Chair.); Jeanne-Marie Parly (Treas.).

Principal Staff: Man. Dir Geneviève Chertier.

Address: 194 rue de Rivoli, 75001 Paris.

Telephone: 1-42-97-53-16; **Fax:** 1-42-60-17-95; **Internet:** www.fondationfyssen.fr; **e-mail:** secretariat@fondationfyssen.fr.

Fondation Gan pour le Cinéma (Gan Foundation for the Cinema)

Established in 1987 to safeguard the cinematographic heritage and promote the production of full-length feature films by new cinematographers. One of two foundations belonging to Groupe Groupama, an insurance and finance company, along with Fondation Groupama pour la Santé.

Activities: Operates in France and internationally, including the People's Republic of China, Italy and Portugal, to promote cinema and the audiovisual arts through film restoration, supporting the work of new film-makers, offering financial assistance for the distribution of films, sponsoring French film festivals and awarding prizes. Also provides financial support to the Max Linder Panorama cinema in Paris.

Geographical Area of Activity: Mainly France.

Publications: Newsletter.

Principal Staff: Pres. Christian Collin; CEO Dominique Hoff.

Address: 4–8 cours Michelet, 92082 Paris La Défense Cedex.

Telephone: 1-70-94-25-16; **Internet:** www.fondation-gan.com.

Fondation Hugot du Collège de France (Hugot Foundation of the Collège of France)

Founded in 1979 by the Collège de France to foster scientific and cultural exchange.

Activities: Operates internationally in the fields of science and medicine, the arts and humanities, religious studies, international relations and the conservation of natural resources, through grants to institutions, research, conferences and publications, and by arranging for scholars from abroad to teach at the Collège de France. The Foundation organizes interdisciplinary academic conferences and seminars for members of the Collège de France faculty. It also awards the Fondation Hugot du Collège de France Prize.

Geographical Area of Activity: International.

Principal Staff: Dir and Chair. of the Board of Professors Serge Haroche.

Address: 11 rue Université, 75007 Paris.

Telephone: 1-42-96-04-22; **Internet:** www.college-de-france.fr; **e-mail:** message@college-de-france.fr.

Fondation Nicolas Hulot pour la Nature et l'Homme (Foundation Nicolas Hulot for Nature and Humankind)

Established in 1990 by Nicolas Hulot, a journalist and environmentalist, to protect the environment; a member of the International Union for Conservation of Nature and a non-governmental adviser to the Economic and Social Council of the UN.

Activities: Aims to encourage citizens to adopt eco-friendly habits on a daily basis; have an influence on the political and economic decision-makers and encourage them to take action; and to support projects in France and around the world. Also aims to bring about changes in daily behaviour to develop a new way of thinking and a culture based on sustainable development.

Geographical Area of Activity: France, Madagascar, Morocco, Romania, Senegal.

Finance: Annual revenue €3,779,963, expenditure €4,311,412 (31 Dec. 2012).

Board of Directors: Nicolas Hulot (Chair.); Geneviève Ferone Creuzet, Dominique Bourg (Vice-Chair.); André-Jean Guérin (Treas.).

Principal Staff: Man. Dir Cécile Ostria.

Address: 6 rue de l'Est, 92100 Boulogne-Billancourt.

Telephone: 1-41-22-10-70; **Fax:** 1-41-22-10-99; **Internet:** www.fnh.org; fondation-nicolas-hulot.org.

Fondation Internationale Léon Mba—Institut de Médecine et d'Epidémiologie Appliquée (International Foundation Léon Mba—Institute of Applied Medicine and Epidemiology)

Founded in 1967 by the Governments of France and Gabon, according to the wishes of Léon Mba, then President of Gabon, to promote, within the framework of the activities of the Hôpital Claude-Bernard, the progress of tropical medicine for the benefit of the populations of Black Africa.

Activities: Operates internationally in the fields of education, and science and medicine, through self-conducted programmes, research, grants to individuals, fellowships and scholarships, conferences, courses, publications and lectures. Organizes annual courses in tropical medicine and epidemiology, and related disciplines, conducted by a specialized staff of French and foreign professors.

Geographical Area of Activity: France, Africa.

Supervisory Board: Prof. Pierre-Marie Girard (Pres.).

Principal Staff: Man. Dir Prof. Jacques Le Bras.

Address: Faculté de Médecine Paris 7, Site Xavier Bichat, 16 rue Henri Huchard, 75018 Paris.

Telephone: 1-40-25-69-58; **Internet:** www.imea.fr; **e-mail:** imea@univ-paris-diderot.fr.

Fondation MACIF (MACIF Foundation)

Established in 1993 by MACIF, a non-profit insurance company, to support organizations working to improve the social economy in France and the rest of Europe.

Activities: Supports the creation of social economy initiatives, including co-operatives and mutual associations, which are independent of the state and not for personal profit. In 2014, the Foundation disbursed funds amounting to €2,743,854.

Geographical Area of Activity: France and Western Europe.

Finance: Annual revenue €3,409,500, expenditure €6,247,844 (2011).

Board of Directors: Catherine Le Gac (Chair.).

Principal Staff: Sec.-Gen. Cathy Rouy.

Address: 2–4 rue Pied-de-Fond, 79037 Niort, Cedex 9.

Telephone: 1-40-40-53-75; **Fax:** 1-40-40-35-14; **Internet:** www.fondation-macif.fr.

Fondation Marguerite et Aimé Maeght (Marguerite and Aimé Maeght Foundation)

Founded in 1964 by Aimé Maeght, an art collector and publisher, and his wife Marguerite to acquire, preserve and exhibit contemporary art.

Activities: Operates nationally and internationally in the field of modern art, through exhibitions, permanent collections, conferences and publications. The Foundation organizes exhibitions of contemporary art in its museum in Saint-Paul and exhibits its collections, incl. works by Braque, Giacometti, Kandinsky, Bonnard, Chagall, Calder, Miró, etc., abroad. It maintains a library of more than 30,000 vols, with documentation on various aspects of modern art, and a bookshop.

Geographical Area of Activity: Europe, the USA, Africa and Asia.

Publications: Catalogue and posters published to coincide with exhibitions.

Finance: Annual revenue €2,572,519, expenditure €2,612,713 (31 Dec. 2011).

Trustees: Adrien Maeght (Chair.).

Principal Staff: Dir Olivier Kaeppelin.

Address: 623 chemin des Gardettes, 06570 Saint-Paul-de-Vence.

Telephone: 4-93-32-81-63; **Fax:** 4-93-32-53-22; **Internet:** www.fondation-maeght.com; **e-mail:** contact@fondation-maeght.com.

Fondation MAIF (MAIF Foundation)

Established in 1989 by the Mutuelle Assurance des Instituteurs de France (mutual insurance company for primary school teachers) to promote technological improvements working towards an improved quality of life and an increase in safety.

Activities: Operates internationally in safety and risk prevention, promoting collaboration between local government, universities and research institutions, NGOs and industry, focusing on young people at risk and on traffic safety. The Foundation supports research, the establishment of a research institute and a database, offers prizes and research grants, issues publications and promotes conferences, meetings and the dissemination of information.

Geographical Area of Activity: International.

Publications: Annual report; newsletter.

Finance: Annual income €261,115,000, expenditure €592,912,000 (31 Dec. 2013).

Board of Directors: Christian Ponsolle (Chair.); Annick Couaillier (Sec.-Gen.); Alain Isambert (Treas.).

Principal Staff: Dir Marc Rigolot.

Address: Le Pavois, 50 ave Salvador Allende, 79000 Niort.

Telephone: 5-49-73-87-04; **Fax:** 5-49-73-87-03; **Internet:** www.fondation-maif.fr; **e-mail:** contact@fondation.maif.fr.

Fondation de la Maison de la Chimie (Chemistry Centre Foundation)

Founded in 1927 on the occasion of the centenary of the birth of Marcelin Berthelot, a chemist and politician, to contribute to the advancement of chemical science in the widest sense and the development of its applications, by promoting exchanges among scholars, technicians and industrialists of all countries.

Activities: Co-operates with other institutions in arranging scientific, cultural, professional and educational events. The Foundation makes a biennial award of €30,000 to recognize original work in chemistry of benefit to society, mankind or nature. Its Congress Centre provides lecture rooms, technical facilities and professional staff to French, foreign and international organizations to enable them to expand their mutual relations. It accommodates, on a permanent basis, institutions operating in the field of chemistry and provides accommodation for participants in the meetings and conferences that it sponsors.

Geographical Area of Activity: France.

Finance: Annuel revenue €10,783,405, expenditure €10,020,930 (31 Dec. 2013).

Board of Directors: Bernard Bigot (Chair.); Danièle Olivier, Jean-Bernard Borfiga (Vice-Chair.); Henri Dugert (Sec.); Henri Baquiast (Treas.).

Address: 28 rue Saint Dominique, 75007 Paris.

Telephone: 1-40-62-27-00; **Fax:** 1-40-62-95-21; **Internet:** www.maisondelachimie.com; **e-mail:** info@maisondelachimie.com.

Fondation Maison des Sciences de l'Homme—FMSH (Foundation House of the Social Sciences)

Founded in 1963 to promote the study of human societies.

Activities: Operates internationally in the fields of the humanities and social sciences, through research, publications, exchange of scientific information and a library (of 140,000 volumes and 1,800 current periodicals).

Geographical Area of Activity: International.

Publications: Newsletter (quarterly).

Finance: Annual revenue €15,519,755, expenditure €15,509,680 (31 Dec. 2012).

Board of Directors: Prof. Pierre Papon (Chair. a.i.); Yves Schemeil (Vice-Chair.); Maurice Garden (Sec.); Jean-Jacques Augier (Treas.).

Principal Staff: Dir Michel Wieviorka; Sec.-Gen. Nicolas Catzaras.

Address: 54 blvd Raspail, 75270 Paris Cedex 06.

Telephone: 1-49-54-20-30; **Fax:** 1-49-54-21-33; **Internet:** www.fmsh.fr; **e-mail:** andriap@msh-paris.fr.

Fondation Méditerranéenne d'Etudes Stratégiques—FMES (Mediterranean Foundation of Strategic Studies)

Established in 1990 to promote strategic studies in all areas of Mediterranean affairs.

Activities: Operates in the areas of education, scientific research and information, organizing conferences, seminars and international meetings, conducting research, organizing training, and publishing and disseminating information. Also participates in international networking activities.

Geographical Area of Activity: Mediterranean area.

Publications: Newsletter; *La revue méditerranéenne d'information stratégique*; *La revue d'information stratégique maritime; La revue d'information défense; La Collection Strademed;*

Memoires des Auditeurs des Sessions Méditerranénnes; conference proceedings.

Board of Directors: Admiral Jacques Lanxade (Chair.); Philippe Vitel, Gérard Masurel (Vice-Chair.); Jean Banivello (Treas.); Benoît le Masne de Chermont (Sec.-Gen.).

Principal Staff: CEO Alain de Lepinois; Sec.-Gen. Stéphane Brault.

Address: Maison des Technologies, pl. Georges Pompidou, 83000 Toulon.

Telephone: 4-94-05-55-55; **Fax:** 4-94-03-89-45; **Internet:** www.fmes-france.org; **e-mail:** info@fmes-france.org.

Fondation Mérieux (Mérieux Foundation)

Founded in 1967 by Dr Charles Merieux to promote research and education in biology, immunology, epidemiology and individual and collective prevention.

Activities: Operates nationally and internationally in the fields of medical and veterinary research, education, social welfare and aid to less-developed countries, through self-conducted programmes of research, grants to institutions and individuals, scholarships to overseas candidates, conferences and publications. The Foundation is closely involved with the Institut pour le Développement de l'Epidémiologie Appliquée (Annecy), the Association pour la Médecine Préventive (in conjunction with the Pasteur Foundation), and Bioforce (a training programme for polyvalent health auxiliaries).

Geographical Area of Activity: International.

Publications: *Collection fondation Mérieux.*

Finance: Annual income €7,075,000, expenditure €14,961,000 (2013).

Board of Directors: Alain Mérieux (Chair.); Sophie Mérieux (Sec.).

Principal Staff: Man. Dir Benoît Miribel; Sec.-Gen. Emmauel de Guibert.

Address: 17 rue Bourgelat, 69002 Lyon.

Telephone: 4-72-40-79-79; **Fax:** 4-72-40-79-50; **Internet:** www.fondation-merieux.org; **e-mail:** fondation.lyon@fondation-merieux.org.

Fondation Mondiale Recherche et Prévention SIDA (World Foundation for AIDS Research and Prevention)

Established in 1993 by Luc Montagnier and Federico Mayor, the UNESCO Dir-Gen., to assist in efforts to combat AIDS and to mobilize the private sector. Also known as the Fondation Mondiale pour la Recherche contre le SIDA—World Foundation for AIDS Research. Japan office established in 1998.

Activities: Operates internationally, in close co-operation with UNESCO, in the area of AIDS research and prevention, to promote global awareness and humanitarian concern; to develop research by opening four research centres in Europe, Africa, Asia and the USA; to help developing countries acquire indigenous capacities in building national AIDS programmes (including preventative education and assistance to AIDS orphans); and to promote networking among scientists and the twinning of universities within developing countries and between developed and developing countries.

Geographical Area of Activity: International.

Principal Staff: Pres. Prof. Luc Montagnier.

Address: c/o UNESCO, 1 rue Miollis, 75732 Paris Cedex 15.

Telephone: 1-45-68-38-41; **Fax:** 1-42-73-37-45; **Internet:** montagnier.org/-world-foundation-aids-research-and -prevention; **e-mail:** fondation.sida@unesco.org.

Fondation Marc de Montalembert (Marc de Montalembert Foundation)

Established in 1994 in memory of Marc de Montalembert; operates under the aegis of the Fondation de France (q.v.).

Activities: Aims to provide opportunities to young people from Mediterranean countries to experience other cultures in the fields of literature, architecture, music, photography and singing, and through the organization of discussion forums on themes relating to peace and tolerance among Mediterranean countries. The Foundation maintains a dialogue centre in Rhodes, Greece. It awards scholarships of €7,000 for projects on Mediterranean cultures or artistic crafts and trades. In partnership with the Institut National d'Histoire de l'Art, it also awards the annual Marc de Montalembert Prize, worth €8,000, for research in Mediterranean history of art.

Geographical Area of Activity: Mediterranean countries.

Address: c/o Fondation de France, 40 ave Hoche, 75008 Paris.

Internet: www.fondationmdm.com; **e-mail:** montalembert@fondationmdm.com.

Fondation Nationale pour l'Enseignement de la Gestion des Entreprises (French National Foundation for Management Education)

Founded in 1968 by the Conseil National du Patronat Français, the Assemblée Permanente des Chambres de Commerce et d'Industrie and the state to promote management education in France.

Activities: Operates nationally and internationally in the field of management education, in five basic areas: promotion of stronger ties between education and industry; training and improvement of management teachers; updating of the curricula of management training institutions; development of management institutions; and promotion of French management education abroad. The Foundation operates through research, grants both to institutions and individuals, scholarships, conferences, courses, seminars and publications.

Geographical Area of Activity: International.

Publications: *Lettre FNEGE* (newsletter, 6 a year).

Finance: Financed by French public authorities and businesses.

Board of Directors: Jean-Marie Descarpentries (Hon. Chair.); Michel Bon (Chair.).

Principal Staff: CEO Pierre-Louis Dubois; Exec. Dir Valérie Fourcade.

Address: 2 ave Hoche, 75008 Paris.

Telephone: 1-44-29-93-60; **Fax:** 1-47-54-05-99; **Internet:** www.fnege.org; **e-mail:** info@fnege.fr.

Fondation Nationale des Sciences Politiques—SciencesPo (National Foundation for Political Sciences)

Founded in 1945 by government ordinance to succeed the École Libre des Sciences Politiques (founded in 1872), to foster the progress and diffusion of the political, economic and social sciences in France and abroad.

Activities: Operates internationally in the fields of political, economic and social sciences, and international relations, through research, teaching, publications and documentation services. Conducts research into: international relations; political life in France; economic activity; social affairs; contemporary European history; economic conditions; American studies; and social change. Documentation services comprise a social science library of more than 620,000 books and 6,000 periodicals, and compiling and keeping a documentation centre maintaining around 16,000 press-cuttings files since 1945. The Foundation also administers the Institut d'Études Politiques de Paris, assists the research and documentation activities of the Institutes of Political Studies at Grenoble and Bordeaux, and owns publisher Presses de Sciences Po.

Geographical Area of Activity: France.

Publications: *Revue française de science politique* (6 a year, jointly with the Association Française de Science Politique); *Critique Internationale* (quarterly); *Raisons Politique* (quarterly); *Revue économique* (6 a year); *Vingtième Siècle—Histoire* (quarterly); *Revue de l'OFCE* (quarterly); books and research monographs in the social sciences and history published by the Presses de Sciences Po.

Finance: Annual revenue €154,891,234, expenditure €153,163,585 (31 Dec. 2013).

Board of Directors: Jean-Claude Casanova (Chair.).

Principal Staff: Dir Frédéric Mion; Deputy Dir Michel Gardette; Sec.-Gen. Charline Avenel.

Address: 27 rue Saint-Guillaume, 75007 Paris Cedex 07.

Telephone: 1-45-49-50-50; **Fax:** 1-42-22-31-26; **Internet:** www.sciences-po.fr.

Fondation Orange (Orange Foundation)

Established in 1987 as Fondation d'Entreprise France Telecom. Present name adopted in 2007.

Activities: Operates in France and internationally in the fields of health and disability, education and culture, and also international emergencies. Orange subsidiaries have established local foundations to carry out philanthropic activities in Armenia, Botswana, Cameroon, Côte d'Ivoire, Guinea, Mauritius, Madagascar, Mali, Moldavia, Niger, Poland, Romania, Senegal, Slovakia.

Geographical Area of Activity: France and international.

Publications: Annual Report.

Finance: Annual revenue €10,079,190, expenditure €9,443,693 (31 Dec. 2013).

Board of Directors: Stéphane Richard (Chair.); Christine Albanel (Vice-Chair.).

Principal Staff: Sec.-Gen. Brigitte Audy.

Address: 78 rue Olivier-de-Serres, 75505 Paris Cedex 15.

Telephone: 1-44-44-22-22; **Fax:** 1-44-44-00-96; **Internet:** www.fondationorange.com; **e-mail:** fondation.orange@orange.com.

Fondation du Patrimoine (Heritage Foundation)

Established in 1996 to protect threatened heritage sites not protected by the state.

Activities: Acts as an umbrella organization, bringing together private and corporate funders to protect heritage sites in France, including unprotected heritage, natural or landscaped areas of interest, and architectural sites; and funding the restoration of buildings not covered by state subsidies.

Geographical Area of Activity: France.

Publications: *Patrimoines en devenir* (2 a year).

Finance: Annual revenue €36,950,000, expenditure €36,890,000 (2013).

Board of Directors: Charles de Croisset (Chair.); Édouard de Royere (Hon. Chair.); Bertrand de Feydeau, Dominique Léger (Vice-Chair.); Loïc Armand (Treas.); Bernard de La Rochefoucauld (Sec.).

Principal Staff: Man. Dir François-Xavier Bieuville.

Address: 23–25 rue Charles Fourier, 75013 Paris.

Telephone: 1-53-67-76-00; **Fax:** 1-40-70-11-70; **Internet:** www.fondation-patrimoine.com; **e-mail:** info@fondation-patrimoine.com.

Fondation Claude Pompidou (Claude Pompidou Foundation)

Established in 1970 at the instigation of Claude Pompidou, wife of the former President of France Georges Pompidou, to help children with disabilities, elderly people and people in hospital.

Activities: Supports projects helping children with disabilities, elderly people and people in hospital, as well as establishing residential homes and centres. Other current Foundation projects include an initiative to help elderly hospitalized people return home. Awards the Claude Pompidou Prize, worth €100,000, for research into Alzheimer's disease.

Geographical Area of Activity: France.

Publications: Newsletter.

Finance: Annual revenue €6,947,758, expenditure €6,947,758 (31 Dec. 2013).

Board of Directors: Bernadette Chirac (Chair.); Josselin de Rohan (Sec.); Bernard Esambert (Treas.).

Principal Staff: CEO Richard Hutin.

Address: 42 rue de Louvre, 75001 Paris.

Telephone: 1-40-13-75-00; **Fax:** 1-40-13-75-19; **Internet:** www.fondationclaudepompidou.fr; **e-mail:** direction.fcp@club-internet.fr.

Fondation 'Pour la Science'—Centre International de Synthèse (Foundation for International Scientific Co-ordination)

Founded in 1924 by Henri Berr to encourage links between different scientific disciplines, and to develop and co-ordinate research and contacts among experts and researchers.

Activities: The Centre holds international conferences for scientists of different disciplines, and issues scientific publications.

Geographical Area of Activity: France.

Publications: *Revue de Synthèse; Revue d'Histoire des Sciences; Semaines de Synthèse; L'Evolution de l'Humanité* (series).

Principal Staff: Dir Éric Brian.

Address: Ecole Normale Supérieure, 45 rue d'Ulm, 75005 Paris.

Telephone: 1-55-42-83-11; **Fax:** 1-55-42-83-19; **Internet:** revue-de-synthese.eu; **e-mail:** revuedesynthese@ens.fr.

Fondation pour la Recherche Médicale (Foundation for Medical Research)

Founded in 1947 by 13 researchers to promote all forms of scientific medical research, in particular research connected with the basic biological sciences related to medicine, and to co-ordinate these endeavours.

Activities: Operates exclusively in the field of medicine and the biological sciences nationally and internationally; and awards grants to individuals and institutions, especially in France, through grants to young researchers and to laboratories. The Foundation subsidizes study abroad and assists the purchase of scientific equipment. It also publishes *Recherche & Santé* (mainly for its donors), organizes conferences, lectures and exhibitions, and maintains regional committees. Major annual awards include the Rosen Prize for Cancer Research, and other prizes for research in molecular biology, endocrinology, immunology, infectiology, clinical investigation, neurobiology, nephrology and cancer. Awards special prizes in the field of scientific communication.

Geographical Area of Activity: France.

Publications: Annual Report; *E-Lettre* (newsletter); *Recherche & Santé* (quarterly).

Finance: Annual revenue €55,957,261, expenditure €55,957,261 (31 Dec. 2014).

Supervisory Committee: Jacques Bouriez (Pres.).

Principal Staff: Pres. Denis Le Squer.

Address: 54 rue de Varenne, 75335 Paris Cedex 07.

Telephone: 1-44-39-75-75; **Fax:** 1-44-39-75-86; **Internet:** www.frm.org; **e-mail:** infos@frm.org.

Fondation pour la Recherche Stratégique (Foundation for Strategic Research)

Established in 1993 as the Fondation pour les Études de Défense (FED) to conduct research in the field of defence and international security studies; later merged with the Centre de Recherches et d'Études sur les Stratégies et les Technologies (CREST).

Activities: Conducts research in the fields of defence and security, and strategic and international issues, in three main areas: defence policies, technological and security issues, and regional issues. The Foundation organizes public events and closed seminars to foster debate on defence and security in France and abroad.

Geographical Area of Activity: Worldwide.

Publications: *Notes de la FRS; Recherches & Documents* (annual collection); *Défense&Industries* (quarterly magazine); books, reports and occasional papers (in French and English).

Finance: Annual revenue €4,398,653, expenditure €4,398,653 (31 Dec. 2014).

Board of Directors: Bruno Racine (Chair.); Benoît d'Aboville (Vice-Chair.); Bernard Zeller (Treas.).

Principal Staff: Dir Camille Grand; Deputy Dirs Yves Boyer, Jean-François Daguzan; Sec.-Gen. Alexandre Houdayer.

Address: 4 bis rue des Patures, 75016 Paris.

Telephone: 1-43-13-77-77; **Fax:** 1-43-13-77-78; **Internet:** www .frstrategie.org; **e-mail:** a.houdayer@frstrategie.org.

Fondation Ripaille (Ripaille Foundation)

Founded in 1976 by Elizabeth Necker-Engel to promote the use of the Château de Ripaille, ancient residence of Duke Amédée VIII of Savoy, as a centre for study, meditation, work, training and cultural exchange in ecology, and human and physical geography; and the conscientious development of resources and the environment, particularly in the most underprivileged areas and countries.

Activities: Works to preserve the environmental and cultural heritage of Ripaille, and promote culture more generally. The Foundation organizes exchanges between the institutions and associations concerned at regional, national and international levels. It also organizes colloquia, seminars and congresses, exhibitions, tours and conferences; and holds cultural, artistic, historical or scientific events or meetings.

Geographical Area of Activity: International.

Principal Staff: Pres. Louis Necker.

Address: Château de Ripaille, 74200 Thonon-les-Bains.

Telephone: 4-50-26-64-44; **Fax:** 4-50-26-54-74; **Internet:** www.ripaille.fr/fondation.php; **e-mail:** fondation@ripaille .fr.

Fondation Sanofi Espoir (Sanofi Espoir Foundation)

Established in 2010 by the Sanofi Group, a health care provider.

Activities: Operates in less-developed countries in the areas of medicine and health, including support for midwives and the provision of medicines and vaccines, and humanitarian disaster assistance, through grants to partner organizations for programmes and projects. In 2013, the Foundation funded 58 development programmes in 41 countries.

Geographical Area of Activity: Central and South America, Africa, East, South and South-East Asia.

Finance: Annual revenue €2,558,489, expenditure €1,592,135 (31 Dec. 2010).

Principal Staff: Pres. Jean-François Dehecq; CEO Caty Forget.

Address: 262 blvd St Germain, 75007 Paris.

Telephone: 1-53-77-91-38; **Internet:** fondation-sanofi-espoir .com; **e-mail:** fondationsanofiespoir@sanofi.com.

Fondation Scelles (Scelles Foundation)

Established in 1993 by Jean and Jeanne Scelles to campaign against all forms of sexual exploitation and assist the victims of sexual violence.

Activities: Operates nationally and internationally in the field of human rights in three areas: collecting information for the Centre of International Research and Documentation on Sexual Exploitation (CRIDES) database; giving grants to organizations assisting victims of sexual violence; and providing information to the public and the media on prostitution, sexual exploitation and people trafficking. The Foundation awards annual prizes, each worth €1,500, for best oral argument, photograph, 'slam' poem, article, indictment and online documentary; additional awards of €500 per category are made to the winners of an online public vote.

Geographical Area of Activity: Worldwide.

Publications: Annual Report; newsletter; reports; books.

Finance: Annual revenue €446,632, expenditure €385,883 (31 Dec. 2010).

Board of Directors: Yves Charpenel (Chair.); Yves Scelles, Philippe Scelles (Vice-Chair.).

Principal Staff: Sec.-Gen. Stéphane Jacquot.

Address: 14 rue Mondétour, 75001 Paris.

Telephone: 1-40-26-04-45; **Fax:** 1-40-26-04-58; **Internet:** www.fondationscelles.org; **e-mail:** fondationscelles@ wanadoo.fr.

Fondation Schneider Electric (Schneider Electric Foundation)

Established in 1998 by Schneider Electric SA, an energy supplier, under the aegis of the Fondation de France (q.v.) to help the development of young people. Formerly known as Fondation Schneider Electric pour l'Insertion des Jeunes.

Activities: Main programmes focus on access to energy, fuel poverty and sustainable development. The Foundation supports projects that provide sustainable and practical training; help young people to find work, primarily in the energy sector; and sustainable development education. It also assists emergency operations following natural disasters. Active in 75 countries in 2012.

Geographical Area of Activity: Worldwide.

Executive Committee: Henri Lachmann (Chair.).

Principal Staff: CEO Gilles Vermot Desroches.

Address: c/o Schneider Electric SA, 35 rue Joseph Monier, 92500 Rueil Malmaison.

Telephone: 1-41-29-70-00; **Fax:** 1-41-29-71-00; **Internet:** www2.schneider-electric.com/sites/corporate/fr/groupe/ fondation/fondation-schneider-electric.page; **e-mail:** fr -fondation@schneider-electric.com.

Fondation Robert Schuman (Robert Schuman Foundation)

Founded in 1991 after the fall of the Berlin Wall; a reference research centre.

Activities: Promotes the construction of Europe and European ideals and values. The Foundation produces high-level studies on European policies. It organizes and participates in European and international meetings and conferences; and develops research programmes in co-operation with university centres and think tanks.

Geographical Area of Activity: Europe.

Publications: *La Lettre de la Fondation Robert Schuman* (weekly electronic newsletter); *Notes de la Fondation Robert Schuman* (hard copy); *Observatoire des Elections en Europe* (electronic publication); *The State of the Union, Schuman Report on Europe* (annual); *The European Opinion* (annual); *EUscope* (digital app).

Finance: Annual revenue €2,097,750, expenditure €2,097,750 (31 Dec. 2012).

Board of Directors: Jean-Dominique Giuliani (Chair.).

Principal Staff: CEO Pascale Joannin.

Address: 29 blvd Raspail, 75007 Paris.

Telephone: 1-53-63-83-00; **Fax:** 1-53-63-83-01; **Internet:** www.robert-schuman.eu/en/robert-schuman-foundation; **e-mail:** info@robert-schuman.eu.

Fondation René Seydoux pour le Monde Méditerranéen (René Seydoux Foundation for the Mediterranean World)

Founded in 1978 by Geneviève René Seydoux, the widow of director of the Schlumberger mining and mineral exploration company René Seydoux, to promote her husband's belief that Mediterranean countries share a common culture, and that dialogue between all peoples is vital.

Activities: Aims to help unite countries on both sides of the Mediterranean by organizing, encouraging and facilitating actions that bring people together. The Foundation supports several partnership projects with other independent organizations working towards the same goal. It collects information on the Mediterranean and it manages a database of organizations and journals in this field. It also offers advice and support to those developing cultural projects. Member of NGO network Euromed Platform—EUPA (f. 2003).

Geographical Area of Activity: European and Mediterranean countries.

Publications: *Mediterranean Directory* (online database).

Board: Jérôme Seydoux (Chair.).

Principal Staff: CEO Giovanna Tanzarella.

Address: 21 rue du Sommerard, 75005 Paris.

Telephone: 1-53-10-24-34; **Fax:** 1-53-10-87-12; **Internet:** www.fondation-seydoux.org; **e-mail:** fondation-seydoux@fondation-seydoux.org.

Fondation Singer-Polignac (Singer-Polignac Foundation)

Founded in 1928 by Princess Edmond de Polignac (née Singer) to promote science, literature, art and general culture in France.

Activities: Operates in the fields of science, the arts, humanities and the conservation of natural resources, awarding grants, scholarships and prizes to individuals and institutions in France. The Foundation also publishes reports on works undertaken under its auspices and organizes lectures, conferences and concerts.

Geographical Area of Activity: France.

Publications: Letters.

Board of Directors: Yves Pouliquen (Chair.); André Miquel (Vice-Chair.); Michael Zink (Sec.-Gen.).

Address: 43 ave Georges Mandel, 75116 Paris.

Telephone: 1-47-27-38-66; **Fax:** 1-53-70-99-60; **Internet:** www.singer-polignac.org; **e-mail:** infos@singer-polignac.org.

Fondation Teilhard de Chardin (Teilhard de Chardin Foundation)

Founded in 1964 by Jeanne Mortier to preserve and disseminate the writings of Pierre Teilhard de Chardin, a philosopher and Jesuit priest.

Activities: Operates internationally in those fields covered by the thoughts of Teilhard de Chardin, especially religion and science, philosophy and education, but also social welfare and studies, humanities and international relations. The Association des Amis de P. Teilhard de Chardin, under the Foundation, runs study centres internationally, which organize meetings, publications, courses and lectures.

Geographical Area of Activity: International.

Publications: Annual Report; the complete works of Teilhard de Chardin (in progress); *Teilhard Aujourd'hui.*

Board of Directors: Prof. Henry de Lumley (Pres.); Maurice Ernst (Treas.).

Principal Staff: Contact Marie-Isabelle de Montfort.

Address: Bibliothèque Centrale du Muséum National d'Histoire Naturelle, 38 rue Geoffroy-Saint-Hilaire, 75005 Paris.

Telephone: 1-43-31-18-55; **Fax:** 1-43-31-01-15; **Internet:** www.teilhard.fr; **e-mail:** teilhard@mnhn.fr.

Fondation Total (Total Foundation)

Founded in 1992 by TOTAL, an international oil and gas company.

Activities: Supports projects nationally and internationally in the fields of community support and humanitarian aid; health; culture and heritage; and the environment and biodiversity.

Geographical Area of Activity: International.

Publications: Annual Report; *Le corail et les récifs coralliens* (book); *La France Marine* (book); *Ecological maps of the French coast* (maps); leaflets.

Finance: Minimum annual budget €10m. (2013–17).

Board of Directors: Yves-Louis Darricarrère (Chair.); Jean-François Minster (Vice-Chair.).

Principal Staff: CEO Catherine Ferrant.

Address: 2 pl. Jean Millier, La Défense 6, 92400 Courbevoie.

Internet: fondation.total.com; **e-mail:** fondation.total@total.com.

Fondation 30 Millions d'Amis (30 Million Friends Foundation)

Established in 1982 as the Association de Défense des Animaux de Compagnie by Jean-Pierre Hutin to promote respect for and protection of animals. Present name adopted in 1995.

Activities: Operates nationally and internationally to protect animals. Makes grants to centres for abandoned animals, provides food supplies and veterinary support for the treatment, vaccination and sterilization of animals. Campaigns against experimentation on animals, and for the protection of animals close to extinction. Runs an online animal adoption service and database of animal protection organizations.

Geographical Area of Activity: International.

Publications: Newsletter; magazine.

Finance: Annual revenue €12,997,240, expenditure €8,420,235 (30 Sept. 2012).

Principal Staff: Pres. Réha Kutlu-Hutin.

Address: 40 cours Albert 1er, 75402 Paris Cedex 08.

Telephone: 1-56-59-04-44; **Fax:** 1-58-56-33-55; **Internet:** www.30millionsdamis.fr.

Fonds Européen pour la Jeunesse—FEJ (European Youth Foundation—EYF)

Founded in 1972 by the Council of Europe to provide financial support to international youth activities undertaken by non-governmental youth organizations and networks.

Activities: Provides financial support for youth activities at international, regional, national and local levels promoting peace, understanding and respect in accordance with the values of the Council of Europe. The Foundation finances activities dealing with themes such as human rights education and education for democratic citizenship, peacebuilding and conflict transformation, intercultural dialogue, social exclusion, discrimination and xenophobia, young people's autonomy, and empowerment of vulnerable groups.

Geographical Area of Activity: 47 member European countries (European Cultural Convention), Belarus, Holy See, Kazakhstan.

Restrictions: No grants to individuals.

Publications: Newsletter.

Finance: Finance provided by the 47 member states of the Council of Europe. Annual budget c. €3m.

Principal Staff: Foundation Head Jean-Claude Lazaro.

Address: 30 rue Pierre de Coubertin, 67000 Strasbourg.

Telephone: 3-88-41-20-19; **Fax:** 3-90-21-49-64; **Internet:** eyf.coe.int; www.coe.int/web/european-youth-foundation; **e-mail:** eyf@coe.int.

Forum International de l'Innovation Sociale—FIIS (International Forum for Social Innovation—IFSI)

Founded in 1976 to promote social innovation and institutional transformation in private and public institutions.

Activities: Encourages meetings, studies and exchange of information, and the implementation of projects; disseminates information; organizes workshops and seminars; organizes international working conferences on institutional transformation; and maintains an information centre on social innovation projects.

Geographical Area of Activity: International.

Publications: *FIIS-IFSI Annual Agenda*; books.

Board of Directors: Louise Edberg (Chair.); David Gutmann (Vice-Chair.); Sylvie Toral (Sec.-Gen.); Leonardo Veneziani (Treas.).

Address: 60 rue de Bellechasse, 75007 Paris.

Telephone: 1-45-41-39-49; **Fax:** 1-45-41-39-42; **Internet:** www.ifsi-fiis-conferences.com; **e-mail:** ifsi.fiis@wanadoo.fr.

France Amérique Latine—FAL (Latin America France)

Established in 1970 to support and provide aid to Central and South America.

Activities: Works to protect the cultural heritage of and support the people of Central and South America. Defends human rights by condemning violations of the rights of indigenous peoples and children within the region, and fighting discrimination regarding the image of the region throughout the rest of the world by holding conferences, debates, exhibitions and exchanges. Works to improve literacy and education, health care and sanitation, and provides emergency aid in Central and South America.

Geographical Area of Activity: Central and South America, France.

Publications: Newsletter; *FALMag* (quarterly); *One Culture*.

Management Committee: Sophie Thonon (Exec. Chair.); Jean-Marie Hericher, Franck Gaudichaud (Chair.); Fabien Cohen (Sec.-Gen.); Michel Forgeon (Treas.).

Principal Staff: Man. Dir Sarah Pick.

Address: 37 blvd Saint-Jacques, 75014 Paris.

Telephone: 1-45-88-22-74; **Fax:** 1-45-65-20-87; **Internet:** www.franceameriquelatine.org; **e-mail:** falnationale@franceameriquelatine.fr.

France-Libertés Fondation Danielle Mitterrand (Danielle Mitterrand France-Liberty Foundation)

Founded in 1986 by Danielle Mitterrand, the widow of President of France François Mitterrand, to improve living standards for the less affluent in society, and to protect their human rights.

Activities: Operates internationally in the fields of human rights, the environment, racial discrimination, apartheid, AIDS, poverty and hunger. The Foundation supports numerous projects including the construction of housing for 'street children' and orphans in Peru, providing humanitarian aid for landless people in Brazil and equipment for a clinic working to prevent deafness in children in Senegal; it works to combat the marginalization of the disabled in Mauritania, organizes an AIDS information campaign and provides disposable syringes in Africa, and runs several education programmes in Cambodia and Bangladesh.

Geographical Area of Activity: International.

Publications: Annual Report; newsletter; *Olivier Unchained* (article).

Finance: Annual budget €1,113,963 (2012).

Board of Directors: Gilbert Mitterrand (Chair.); Claude Vercoutere (Vice-Chair.); Alain Souvreneau (Treas.); Michel Joli (Sec.-Gen.).

Principal Staff: Dir Emmanuel Poilâne.

Address: 22 rue de Milan, 75009 Paris.

Telephone: 1-53-25-10-40; **Fax:** 1-48-74-01-26; **Internet:** www.france-libertes.fr; **e-mail:** contact@france-libertes.fr.

France Nature Environnement

Established in 1968 to co-ordinate environmental protection and conservation nationally and internationally.

Activities: Disseminates information on the state of the environment in the areas of scientific research, the conservation of fauna and flora, and the protection of biodiversity. The organization operates as a national federation of around 3,000 associations for the protection of nature and the environment, concerned with biodiversity, agriculture, forestry, water, industrial production cycles, power, waste, development, transport and health.

Geographical Area of Activity: International.

Publications: Newsletter; *Lettre du Hérisson*; *La Lettre Eau*; *La Lettre des Sylves*; *La Voie du Loup*; *Le Blaireau et l'homme*; *Mettons les toxiques hors la loi*; *Les emballages utiles et inutiles*;

Dès aujourd'hui moins d'ordures pour les générations futures; *Faites une fleur à votre environnement*; *Changement climatique: la nature menacée en France?*.

Finance: Annual income €3,731,596, expenditure €3,515,693 (31 Dec. 2013).

Board of Directors: Denez L'Hostis (Chair.); Michel Dubromel, Jean-David Abel, Serge Urbano (Vice-Chair.); Raymond Léost (Treas.); Marc Saumureau (Asst Treas.).

Principal Staff: Nat. Secs José Cambou, Florence Denier-Pasquier.

Address: 81–83 blvd Port-Royal, 75013 Paris.

Telephone: 1-44-08-02-50; **Internet:** www.fne.asso.fr; **e-mail:** information@fne-asso.fr.

Frères des Hommes—FDH

Created in 1965; an organization for international solidarity, working in the area of global development.

Activities: Supports development projects that have been initiated and implemented by local populations in Africa, Asia, Latin America and the Caribbean to build long-term solutions to world poverty. The organization intervenes mainly in favour of community-supported farming, community-based economy and civil democracy. In France, it raises public awareness about the international aspects of sustainable development.

Geographical Area of Activity: Africa, Asia, Latin America and the Caribbean.

Restrictions: Grants made only in partnership with specific organizations.

Publications: *Agir*; *Témoignages et Dossiers* (quarterly); *Résonances* (newsletter).

Finance: Annual revenue €2,064,812, expenditure €2,064,812 (31 Dec. 2013).

Board of Directors: Luc Michelon (Chair.); Anne-Marie Auvergne (Vice-Chair.); Marie-Jeanne Letulle (Sec.-Gen.); Daniel Grenapin (Asst Sec.-Gen.); Guy Chevreau (Treas.); Claude Perseval (Asst Treas.).

Principal Staff: Dir Yves Altazin.

Address: 2 rue de Savoie, 75006 Paris.

Telephone: 1-55-42-62-62; **Fax:** 1-43-29-99-77; **Internet:** www.fdh.org; **e-mail:** fdh@fdh.org.

Handicap International

Founded in 1982 to support people with disabilities and war victims, using local resources. In 2014, established the Fondation Vivre Debout under the aegis of l'Université de Lyon to help disabled or vulnerable people affected by conflict, natural disasters or health emergencies, or chronic poverty.

Activities: Operates internationally in 59 countries. The organization supports programmes to meet the needs and defend the rights of people with disabilities. In countries affected by poverty, disasters and conflicts, it implements prevention, emergency relief and mine action projects, and provides long-term development support. Co-founder of the International Campaign to Ban Landmines and Co-Winner of the 1997 Nobel Peace Prize. It has consultative status with the UN Economic and Social Council (ECOSOC). National sections operate in Belgium, Canada, France, Germany, Luxembourg, Switzerland, the United Kingdom and the USA.

Geographical Area of Activity: Worldwide.

Publications: Newsletter (quarterly); Annual Report; technical publications; videos.

Finance: Annual income €126,327,100, expenditure €127,122,000 (31 Dec. 2013).

Principal Staff: Chair. Jacques Tassi; Exec. Dir Jean-Baptiste Richardier.

Address: 138 ave des Frères Lumière, 69008 Lyon.

Telephone: 4-78-69-79-79; **Fax:** 4-78-69-79-94; **Internet:** www.handicap-international.org; **e-mail:** contact@handicap-international.org.

Institut Océanographique—Fondation Albert 1er, Prince de Monaco (Oceanographic Institute—Albert 1st, Prince of Monaco Foundation)

Established in 1906 by Albert I, Prince of Monaco for the study and teaching of oceanographic science, and for knowledge of marine science to be transmitted to as many people as possible.

Activities: Comprises two institutions: the Institut Océanographique in Paris (also the headquarters of the Foundation); and the Musée Océanographique in Monaco. Supports exhibitions and maintains libraries at both centres.

Geographical Area of Activity: France and Monaco.

Publications: Books on marine science.

Board of Directors: HRH Prince Albert II; (Hon. Chair.); Michel Petit (Chair.); Pierre Bordry (Vice-Chair.); Gérard Riou (Sec.-Treas.).

Principal Staff: Man. Dir Robert Calcagno.

Address: 195 rue Saint-Jacques, 75005 Paris.

Telephone: 1-44-32-10-70; **Fax:** 1-40-51-73-16; **Internet:** www.institut-ocean.org; **e-mail:** institut@oceano.org.

Institut Pasteur (Pasteur Institute)

Founded in 1886 by Louis Pasteur and incorporated as a foundation in 1887 to promote research into infectious and parasitic diseases, including their prevention and treatment, and into immunity from disease; to further the study of microorganisms, incl. their role in natural processes, both normal and pathological, and the reactions they provoke; to further the study and teaching of all aspects of microbiology, as well as the training of scientific and technical staff in view of the growth of study into basic and applied microbiology; and to study all the theoretical and practical problems connected with microbiology and immunology or, more generally, with basic and applied biology.

Activities: Operates essentially in the field of microbiology and its related disciplines, through research, teaching, prevention and diagnosis of infectious and parasitic diseases. The Institute maintains a large library at its headquarters and operates through 21 branches throughout the world. The work of several of its laboratories has been recognized as of great importance by the World Health Organization and they have accordingly been granted the status of regional, national or international centres. The Institute has its own medical centre providing international vaccinations as well as specialized consultations (including allergies, tropical diseases and HIV).

Geographical Area of Activity: Worldwide.

Publications: Annual Report; *Research in Microbiology* (10 a year); *Lettre de l'Institut Pasteur* (quarterly); *Annales de l'Institut Pasteur: Actualités* (quarterly); *Microbes and Infection* (15 a year); *Collections des Laboratoires de Références et d'expertise* (11-title series of technical publications).

Finance: Annual revenue €55,257,000, expenditure €81,770,000 (31 Dec. 2013).

Board of Directors: Rose-Marie Van Lerberghe (Chair.); Bernard Guirkinger, Laurent Degos (Vice-Chair.); Sophie Mantel (Treas.); Alain Jacquier (Sec.).

Principal Staff: CEO Prof. Christian Bréchot.

Address: 25–28 rue du Docteur Roux, 75724 Paris Cedex 15.

Telephone: 1-45-68-80-00; **Fax:** 1-43-06-98-35; **Internet:** www.pasteur.fr; **e-mail:** info@pasteur.fr.

Institut Pasteur de Lille (Pasteur Institute of Lille)

Founded in 1899 by the City of Lille for biological and medical research, training and analysis.

Activities: The four main areas are biological research (developing vaccinations against diseases caused by parasites, particularly tropical diseases; molecular oncology); public health, including providing information; training; and medical analysis and toxicology. Awards are available for French and non-French researchers.

Geographical Area of Activity: France.

Publications: *Signes de Vie* (magazine); newsletter; books.

Finance: Annual revenue €30,377,022, expenditure €28,789,350 (2013).

Board of Directors: Martine Aubry (Pres.); Jacques Richir (Vice-Chair.).

Principal Staff: Man. Dir Prof. Patrick Berche; Sec.-Gen. Eric Diers.

Address: 1 rue du Professeur Calmette, BP 245, 59019 Lille Cedex.

Telephone: 3-20-87-78-00; **Fax:** 3-20-87-79-06; **Internet:** www.pasteur-lille.fr; **e-mail:** webmaster@pasteur-lille.fr.

International Union for Health Promotion and Education—IUHPE

Founded in 1951 as an independent global association of professionals and organizations committed to worldwide health promotion and education.

Activities: Promotes global health and contributes to the achievement of equity in health, through advocacy, professional development, networking, partnership building and strengthening capacity. The Union has members in more than 90 countries, and works through seven decentralized regional offices (in Africa, Europe, North America, the northern part of the Western Pacific, the South-West Pacific, Central and South America, and South-East Asia). It works closely with international organizations such as the World Health Organization, UNESCO and the UN Children's Fund (UNICEF) to influence and facilitate the development of health promotion strategies and projects. It organizes a World Conference on Health Promotion and Health Education every three years, and also regional conferences, seminars and workshops.

Geographical Area of Activity: Worldwide.

Restrictions: Not a grantmaking organization.

Publications: Annual Report; *Global Health Promotion* (quarterly, in English, French and Spanish); *Health Education Research* (the official IUHPE research journal); *Health Promotion International* (an official IUHPE journal); research reports; e-newsletter; conference reports, academic research, studies and information manuals.

Finance: Annual income €745,166, expenditure €756,606 (2013).

Executive Board: Michael Sparks (Pres.); David McQueen (Immediate Past Pres.).

Principal Staff: Exec. Dir Marie-Claude Lamarre.

Address: 42 blvd de la Libération, 93203 St-Denis Cedex.

Telephone: 1-48-13-71-20; **Fax:** 1-48-09-17-67; **Internet:** www.iuhpe.org; **e-mail:** iuhpe@iuhpe.org.

Médecins du Monde International (Doctors of the World International)

Established in 1980.

Activities: Aims to promote international solidarity through providing emergency health care and medical support internationally. Operates in the field of medicine and health, sending voluntary doctors and other medical staff into areas of crisis and disaster to administer emergency aid and to provide necessary medical support. Also works to develop new approaches to health care in developing countries based on the principles of dignity and respect, works to improve standards and accessibility of public health facilities in less-developed regions, and promotes human rights and social justice.

Geographical Area of Activity: Worldwide.

Publications: *Médecins du Monde* (journal); newsletters; *Revue humanitaire*; reports; documentary films; bulletins.

Finance: Annual revenue €67,419,134, expenditure €67,620,306 (31 Dec. 2013).

Board of Directors: Dr Thierry Brigaud (Chair.); Dr Françoise Sivignon, Luc Jarrigue (Vice-Chair.); Margarita Gonzalez (Sec-Gen.); Gérard Pascal (Asst Sec.-Gen.); Christophe Adam (Treas.); Dr Gérard Pascal.

Address: 62 rue Marcadet, 75018 Paris.

Telephone: 1-44-92-15-15; **Fax:** 1-44-92-14-55; **Internet:** www .medecinsdumonde.org; **e-mail:** infomdm@ medecinsdumonde.net.

Mouvement International ATD Quart-Monde (International Movement ATD Fourth World)

Founded in 1957 by Father Joseph Wresinksi as Aide à Toute Détresse (ATD). Since 2009, ATD has stood for All Together in Dignity.

Activities: Aims to eliminate extreme poverty and exclusion all over the world, and is open to people of all religious or political convictions. Operates in Europe, Africa, North, Central and South America, and Asia in the fields of human rights and social development. The organization runs education and training programmes in the areas of nursery schools, family centres, literacy and basic skills training; regular Fourth World University gatherings and artistic and cultural programmes with children and young people are undertaken by members of ATD's Volunteer Corps. The organization raises awareness about poverty, carries out research into poverty in partnership with the people affected, and works to combat these problems. Holds consultative status with the UN Economic and Social Council (ECOSOC), the UN Children's Fund (UNICEF), the International Labour Organization and the Council of Europe.

Geographical Area of Activity: Europe, Africa, North, Central and South America, and Asia.

Publications: Newsletter; *Artisans of Democracy*; *The Human Face of Poverty*; *Talk With Us, Not At Us*; *This is How We Live: Listening to the Poorest Families*; and other publications.

Finance: Annual income €225,252, expenditure €225,252 (2011).

Board of Directors: Cassam Uteem (Pres.); Janet Nelson (Vice-Pres.); Paul Maréchal (Treas.); Dominique Foubert (Vice-Treas.).

Principal Staff: Dir-Gen. Isabelle Pypaert Perrin.

Address: 12 rue Pasteur, 95480 Pierrelaye.

Telephone: 1-34-30-46-10; **Fax:** 1-34-30-46-21; **Internet:** www.atd-fourthworld.org; **e-mail:** information@atd -fourthworld.asso.org.

Office International de l'Eau (International Office for Water)

Established in 1991 to promote improved and integrated water management throughout the world.

Activities: Operates internationally in the areas of water conservation, basin management and environmental protection. The Office is the world secretariat of the International Network of Basin Organizations (INBO) and other institutions involved in water resources management and protection. It also holds international conferences, training courses, exhibitions and symposia; produces water-related publications; manages water data; and is in charge of the French National Water Training Center.

Geographical Area of Activity: Worldwide.

Publications: *Information Eaux*; *INBO Newsletter*; *IOWater* international; news.

Finance: Annual revenue €16,907,000, expenditure €16,688,000 (2013).

Directors: Pierre Roussel (Pres.).

Principal Staff: CEO Jean-Francois Donzier.

Address: 21 rue de Madrid, 75008 Paris.

Telephone: 1-44-90-88-60; **Fax:** 1-40-08-01-45; **Internet:** www.oieau.fr; www.iowater.org; www.inbo-news.org; **e-mail:** dg@oieau.fr.

Organisation Panafricaine de Lutte pour la Santé—OPALS (Pan-African Organization for Health)

Founded in 1988 as Organisation Panafricaine de Lutte Contre le SIDA (Pan-African Organization for AIDS Prevention) to provide an information service and training for medical practitioners and scientists involved in trying to prevent the spread of AIDS, and caring for AIDS patients. Present name adopted in 2011.

Activities: Aims to improve the quality of life of sick people by providing access to comprehensive medical care and upholding their rights in society. The organization supports existing public health systems.

Geographical Area of Activity: Africa and Europe.

Finance: Annual income €869,278, expenditure €853,604 (31 Dec. 2012).

Board of Directors: Prof. Marc Gentilini (Chair.); Prof. Dominique Richard-Lenoble (Sec.-Gen.); Jacques Vaysse (Treas.).

Principal Staff: Exec. and Medical Dir Dr Claude Moncorgé.

Address: 8 rue Maria Helena Vieira da Silva, CS 11417, 75993 Paris Cedex 14; 15–21 rue de l'Ecole de Médecine, 75006 Paris.

Fax: 1-42-21-04-35; **Internet:** www.opals.asso.fr; **e-mail:** contact@opals.asso.fr.

Oxfam France

Oxfam France, created under the name Agir ici (Act here) in 1988, is a non-profit organization registered and based in France that works on the causes of poverty and injustice through advocacy and citizen mobilization campaigns. Part of the Oxfam confederation of organizations (qq.v.).

Activities: Activities include campaigning, advocacy and mobilization comprising: high-level research and advocacy targeting economic and political decision-makers, towards respect of fundamental human rights; information and mobilization of the general public, through opinion campaigns, by highlighting the causes of global inequalities and by giving each citizen opportunities to act against injustice; and proposal of concrete recommendations, such as new public policies or regulations, budget priorities and policies, signature of international agreements or the adoption of fair commercial rules.

Geographical Area of Activity: International.

Finance: Annual income €3,682,281, expenditure €3,682,281 (2013–14).

Board of Directors: Lisa Dacosta (Chair.); Lora Verheecke (Vice-Chair.); Christopher Chermont (Treas.); Johanne Ruyssen (Asst Treas.); Vincent Truelle (Sec.).

Principal Staff: Man. Dir Claire Fehrenbach.

Address: 104 rue Oberkampf, 75011 Paris.

Telephone: 1-56-98-24-40; **Fax:** 1-56-98-24-09; **Internet:** www.oxfamfrance.org; **e-mail:** info@oxfamfrance.org.

Partage (Share)

Established in 1973, as Comité de Soutien aux Orphelins du Viêtnam, by Pierre Marchand to help orphans of the Viet Nam war; registered in 1976 as Partage avec les Enfants du Tiers-Monde, renamed Partage in 1998.

Activities: Operates nationally and internationally in the fields of aid to less-developed countries, education, health and social welfare. It assists individual sponsors in helping children to access all that is vital for their development: food and shelter, care, clothing and education.

Geographical Area of Activity: Benin, Bosnia and Herzegovina, Brazil, Burkina Faso, Cambodia, Comoros, Ecuador, Egypt, Ethiopia, France, Haïti, Honduras, India, Lebanon, Madagascar, Nepal, Palestinian Territories, Romania, Thailand, Viet Nam.

Publications: Annual Report; news magazine (quarterly); newsletter (monthly).

Finance: Annual income €8,931,444, expenditure €8,931,444 (2013).

Bord of Directors: Pascal Ponty (Chair.); Christian Renoux (Vice-Chair.); Alain Gayet (Treas.); Danièle Chagnon (Sec.).

Principal Staff: Dir Erik Jorgensen.

Address: 40 rue Vivenel, 60203 Compiègne.

Telephone: 3-44-20-92-92; **Fax:** 3-44-20-94-95; **Internet:** www.partage.org; **e-mail:** info@partage.org.

Patrimoine Mondial (World Heritage)

Established in 1972 by the Convention Concerning the Protection of the World Cultural and Natural Heritage to protect world cultural and natural heritage.

Activities: Assists in identifying and preserving World Heritage sites through providing international assistance in five specific areas: preparatory assistance; promotion and education, technical co-operation; emergency assistance; and training.

Geographical Area of Activity: International.

Publications: *World Heritage Review* (quarterly magazine); *World Heritage Newsletter* (2 a month); books, manuals and reports.

Finance: The organization receives its income essentially from compulsory contributions from states party to the Convention (amounting to 1% of their UNESCO dues) and from voluntary contributions: 1% of 2015 contributions US $1,296,891.

Governing Committee: Prof. Maria Böhmer (Chair.).

Principal Staff: Dir Kishore Rao.

Address: c/o UNESCO, 7 pl. de Fontenoy, 75352 Paris 07 SP.

Telephone: 1-45-68-15-71; **Fax:** 1-45-68-55-70; **Internet:** whc.unesco.org; **e-mail:** wh-info@unesco.org.

Première Urgence—Aide Médicale Internationale

Formed in 2011 by the merger of Première Urgence, which was founded in 1992, and Aide Médicale Internationale (f. 1979) to meet the needs of victims of humanitarian crises.

Activities: Works in the fields of: health; nutrition; food security; construction and rehabilitation; water, sanitation and hygiene; and economic recovery. The organization operates more than 150 projects in 18 countries.

Geographical Area of Activity: Africa, the Middle East, Asia, the Caribbean and the South Caucasus.

Publications: Reports.

Finance: Annual income €42,215,000, expenditure €42,280,000 (31 Dec. 2012).

Board of Directors: Vincent Basquin (Chair.); Philippe Augoyard (Vice-Chair.); Guillaume Huon de Kermedec, Ernst van der Linden (Secs); Jérôme Spiesse (Asst Sec.); Jean-Philippe Horen (Treas.).

Principal Staff: Man. Dir Thierry Mauricet.

Address: 2 rue Auguste Thomas, 92600 Asnières-sur-Seine.

Telephone: 1-46-36-04-04; **Fax:** 1-46-36-66-10; **Internet:** www.pu-ami.org; **e-mail:** contact@pu-ami.org.

Santé Sud (Southern Health)

Founded in 1984 to improve the quality of care provided to people living in underprivileged areas, by supporting its partners in their efforts to take their development into their own hands.

Activities: Operates in the field of assistance to less-developed countries, through long-term projects that provide financial, technical and material aid, especially in the area of health care. The organization co-operates with local grassroots organizations. Maintains offices in Madagascar, Mali, Mongolia and Tunisia.

Geographical Area of Activity: Africa, Asia and the Middle East.

Publications: *Santé Sud Infos* (quarterly newsletter); reviews; articles; films.

Finance: Budget €3.3m.

Steering Committee: Paul Benos (Chair.); Pascal Faucher (Treas.).

Principal Staff: Dir Nicole Hanssen.

Address: 200 blvd National, le Gyptis Bt N, 13003 Marseille.

Telephone: (4) 91-95-63-45; **Fax:** (4) 91-95-68-05; **Internet:** www.santesud.org; **e-mail:** contact@santesud.org.

Schlumberger Foundation

Established in 1956 to generate conditions that result in more women pursuing scientific disciplines.

Activities: Operates in the field of education, in recognition of the role of education in realizing people's potential, and of the link between science, technology and socio-economic development. The Foundation focuses on strengthening university faculties and mitigating obstacles faced by women scientists through its Faculty for the Future programme, which offers fellowships to women from developing and emerging economies preparing for PhD or postdoctoral study in the physical sciences, engineering or related disciplines to pursue study at top universities abroad. Grant recipients are selected for their leadership capabilities as well as their scientific talents, and they are expected to return to their home countries to continue their academic careers and inspire other young women.

Geographical Area of Activity: Worldwide.

Restrictions: Does not accept unsolicited grant requests.

Publications: Conference proceedings; DVDs.

Board of Directors: Gerard Martellozo (Chair.); Roseline Chapel (Pres. and Treas.).

Address: 42 rue Saint Dominique, 75007 Paris.

Internet: www.slb.com/about/foundation.aspx; **e-mail:** foundation@paris.sl.slb.com.

Secours Catholique—Caritas de France (Catholic Help—Caritas France)

Founded in 1946 by Mgr Jean Rodhain as part of Caritas Internationalis (q.v.) with the aim of helping poor people throughout the world.

Activities: Provides aid to developing countries and operates its own programmes in the fields of education, human rights, health care and social welfare. The organization provides grants to institutions and finances scholarships and fellowships, and also publishes annual statistical surveys of the extent of poverty in France.

Geographical Area of Activity: Worldwide.

Publications: *Messages* (monthly); *Paix et réconciliation*; reports.

Finance: Annual revenue €131,442,105, expenditure €135,140,762 (31 Dec. 2013).

Board of Directors: Joël Thoraval, François Soulage (Hon. Chair.); Véronique Fayet (Chair.); Claire Escaffre, Pierre Colmant (Vice-Chair.); Claudine Berland (Sec.); Claude Marchal (Treas.).

Principal Staff: Sec.-Gen. Bernard Thibaud.

Address: 106 rue du Bac, 75341 Paris Cedex 7.

Telephone: 1-45-49-73-00; **Fax:** 1-45-49-94-50; **Internet:** www.secours-catholique.asso.fr; **e-mail:** info@secours-catholique.org.

Service d'Entraide et de Liaison—SEL (Mutual Aid and Liaison Service)

Established in 1980 by the French Evangelical Alliance, a Christian (Protestant) organization.

Activities: Operates internationally in the field of aid to less-developed countries through local partners. The Service raises public awareness about poverty and aid to developing countries; and provides aid and assistance in developing countries, particularly to children. It supports child sponsorship programmes and development projects in the areas of health, nutrition, agriculture, micro-credit, water, sanitation and other social concerns; and offers emergency relief to areas in crisis.

Geographical Area of Activity: Worldwide through local partners (with a focus on French-speaking African countries and Madagascar).

Publications: *SEL–Informations* (periodical).

Finance: Annual income €5,670,291, expenditure €5,670,291 (31 March 2014).

Board of Directors: Claude Grandjean (Chair.).

Principal Staff: Dir-Gen. Patrick Guiborat.

Address: 157 rue des Blains, 92220 Bagneux.

Telephone: 1-45-36-41-51; **Fax:** 1-46-16-20-86; **Internet:** www.selfrance.org; **e-mail:** info@selfrance.org.

Solidarité (Solidarity)

Founded in 1980.

Activities: Aims to reduce unemployment in rural areas and to improve the quality of life of people living in developing countries. The organization promotes sustainable rural development in Africa, Central and South America, and Asia, supporting local organizations financially, technically or physically to carry out development projects to encourage and enable rural people to become more independent. It creates small industries by using local resources; carries out research into suitable technologies; promotes improved medical and sanitary systems, and environmental awareness. The organization focuses in particular on the development and empowerment of women and children, and tribal peoples' rights. It also disseminates information about the projects, runs training courses and liaises with local and international NGOs.

Geographical Area of Activity: Africa, Central and South America, Asia and Europe.

Publications: Annual Report; *Solidarité* (quarterly magazine); newsletter (monthly).

Finance: Annual budget €154,727 (2010).

Governing Board: Francine Cueille; Marie-Hélène Delon; Mathieu de Maupeou.

Principal Staff: Exec. Dir Clotilde Bato.

Address: 20 rue de Rochechouart, 75009 Paris.

Telephone: 1-48-78-33-26; **Fax:** 5-61-13-66-95; **Internet:** www.solidarite.asso.fr; **e-mail:** contact@solidarite.asso.fr.

The Gambia

FOUNDATION CENTRE AND CO-ORDINATING BODY

Association of Non-Governmental Organizations in The Gambia—TANGO

Established in 1983.

Activities: Co-ordinates activities of member organizations to ensure that resources are used efficiently to further social development in The Gambia. The Association has five working groups: Gender and Poverty; Climate, Agriculture and Environment; Education and Life Skills; Youth, Child, Health and Population; Human Rights and Governance. It is an information forum and a meeting place for NGOs to exchange information, knowledge and expertise. It also co-ordinates the National Poverty Alleviation Programme and works on voter education programmes to increase female participation in elections and to raise agricultural concerns.

Geographical Area of Activity: The Gambia.

Publications: Reports.

Board Members: Yankuba Dibba (Chair.); Jainaba Nyang-Njie (Vice-Chair.); Sandang B. Bojang (Treas.).

Principal Staff: Exec. Dir and Sec. Ousman M. S. Yabo.

Address: c/o Fajara 'M' Section, PMB 392, Serekunda.

Telephone: 390525; **Fax:** 390521; **Internet:** www.tangogambia.org; **e-mail:** info@tangogambia.org.

FOUNDATIONS, TRUSTS AND NON-PROFIT ORGANIZATIONS

Foundation for Research on Women's Health, Productivity and the Environment—BAFROW

Established in 1991 by nine individuals to assist in and contribute to the development of a conceptual framework on gender and development, and to facilitate dialogue on empowerment, focusing on major factors significant to the development and sustainability of women and female children.

Activities: Operates in the fields of conservation and the environment, economic affairs, education, and medicine and health, nationally through self-conducted programmes, conferences and training courses, and internationally through research. Projects include research into genital mutilation, and a series of public education campaigns to end its practice, as well as the promotion of access to schooling for girls and research into the implications of polygamy for women. The Foundation works in association with other international organizations, including the American Jewish World Service (q.v.). It maintains libraries in Banjul and Mandinabaeach containing approx. 400 vols in English and local languages.

Geographical Area of Activity: Mainly The Gambia.

Publications: *The Well Woman* (newsletter); *The ASGP Girls' Newsletter* (newsletter); *Baaty Ndow-Yi*; training curricula and educational materials.

Principal Staff: Exec. Dir Fatou Waggeh; Clinical Dir Hassan Azadeh.

Address: POB 2854, Kanifing, Serrekunda; 214 Tafsir Demba Mbye St, Tobacco Rd Estate, Banjul.

Telephone: 4225270; **Fax:** 4226739; **e-mail:** bafrow@gamtel.gm.

Georgia

FOUNDATION CENTRES AND CO-ORDINATING BODIES

Center for Training and Consultancy

Established in 1999.

Activities: Provides support to non-profit organizations in Georgia, for the institutional development of the not-for-profit sector. The Center offers training and consultancy services in institutional development, capacity building and strategic planning, and provides support through its resource centre. Promotes co-operation between Georgian NGOs and organizations from other Eastern and Western European countries. It is a regional partner of the Management for Development Foundation based in the Netherlands; and has an office in Azerbaijan, with links to Armenia and Kyrgyzstan.

Geographical Area of Activity: Armenia, Azerbaijan, Georgia and Kyrgyzstan.

Publications: *Directory of non-government organizations of Tbilisi working on public policy* (2005); *European Institute of Public Administration* (2005); *The Role in System Education in Civil Integration of Ethnic Minorities: The vision of interested bodies in civil and governmental sectors* (2005); *Basic Competances for life-long learning European framework* (2006); *An Assessment of Georgian Civil Society* (2006); *European Studies* (series, 2006); Annual Report.

Finance: Total assets 4,355,911 laris (2010).

Principal Staff: Exec. Dir Irina Khantadze; Financial Man. Julia Shendrikova.

Address: 0177 Tbilisi, 5 Otar Chkheidze Str.

Telephone: (32) 20-67-74; **Internet:** www.ctc.org.ge; **e-mail:** ctc@ctc.org.ge.

Georgian Evaluation Association

Founded in 2008 by Nino Saakashvili as the successor to Horizonti Foundationi for the Third Sector, which supported the development of a civil society in Georgia.

Activities: A membership organization that operates in the field of evaluation. The Association supports the development of democratic governance; carries out monitoring and evaluation activities; and organizes conferences, workshops and seminars. Projects include Empowering Marginalized and Ethnic Minority Citizens for Participation in Local Government Decision Making and Monitoring Activities.

Geographical Area of Activity: Georgia, countries of the former USSR.

Finance: Funded by the US Agency for International Aid (USAID), other international and local organizations and by private donations.

Principal Staff: Pres. Nino Saakashvili.

Address: 0171 Tbilisi, 2 Dolidze Str.

Telephone: (32) 2-36-51-56; **Fax:** (32) 2-36-74-94; **Internet:** www.evaluation.org.ge; **e-mail:** gea@evaluation.org.ge.

FOUNDATIONS, TRUSTS AND NON-PROFIT ORGANIZATIONS

Caucasus Institute for Peace, Democracy and Development—CIPDD

Established in 1992 as an independent policy research organization.

Activities: Primary areas of research are regional security, state building, democratization and civil integration. The Institute's main activities include public policy research, publishing research results, and organizing debates and round-table discussions. It also hosts an online discussion forum and services for journalists and researchers.

Geographical Area of Activity: Mainly Georgia, but co-operates with organizations in the South Caucasus and Black Sea regions.

Publications: Annual Report; periodicals; policy briefs and reports; discussion papers.

Finance: Annual budget US $394,997 (2014).

Board: Giga Zedania (Chair.).

Principal Staff: Chair. Ghia Nodia; Exec. Dir Avtandil Jokhadze.

Address: POB 101, 0108 Tbilisi; 0154 Tbilisi, 72 Tsereteli Ave, 2nd Floor.

Telephone: (32) 35-51-54; **Fax:** (32) 35-57-54; **Internet:** www.cipdd.org; **e-mail:** info@cipdd.org.

Civil Society Development Center

Established in 2010 in support of education and leadership opportunities for women and girls.

Activities: Promotes women's rights, leadership and gender equality. The Center also helps to improve women's health care and increase women's economic independence. It focuses on women from conflict zones, internally displaced people, and other vulnerable groups, including unemployed mothers and those with disabled children, victims of violence and the homeless.

Geographical Area of Activity: Georgia.

Principal Staff: Exec. Dir Nino Todua.

Address: 0102 Tbilisi, King Tamar Ave 18.

Telephone: 570-10-01-39; **Internet:** csdc-itv.ge; csdc.gol.ge; **e-mail:** csdc-itv@gmail.com.

OSGF—Open Society Georgia Foundation

Established in 1994; an independent foundation, part of the Open Society Foundations (q.v.) network, which aims to foster political and cultural pluralism and reform economic structures to encourage private enterprise and a market economy.

Activities: Programmes include: Human Rights and Good Governance; Civil Society Support; Media; Public Health; and Academic Fellowship. The Foundation supports 26 national and regional programmes. It also supports other NGOs in Georgia, as well as regional projects in collaboration with the Soros foundations of Armenia and Azerbaijan.

Geographical Area of Activity: Georgia.

Publications: Annual Report; reports; studies; assessments; guidelines.

Finance: Annual expenditure US $4,758,350 (2012).

Executive Board: Giorgi Chkheidze (Chair.).

Principal Staff: Exec. Dir Keti Khutsishvili; Deputy Exec. Dir Hatia Jinjikhadze.

Address: 0108 Tbilisi, 10 Chovelidze Str.

Telephone: (32) 25-04-63; **Fax:** (32) 29-10-52; **Internet:** www.osgf.ge; **e-mail:** osgf@osgf.ge.

People's Harmonious Development Society

Founded in 1996.

Activities: Works for and with people on issues of human rights and sustainable development, through education, training and research. The organization conducts research on migration issues and people-trafficking, environmental security, and disseminates results through seminars, training, conferences and mass-media campaigns.

Geographical Area of Activity: Worldwide, particularly in the South Caucasus and Black Sea regions.

Publications: Training manuals; research materials; booklets.

Finance: Support from European Union and others.

Principal Staff: Chair. and Programme Co-ordinator Tsovinar Nazarova.

Address: Tbilisi, Zubalashvili Str. 31.

Telephone: (32) 18-21-82; **Fax:** (32) 22-23-47; **Internet:** www .phds.ge; **e-mail:** phds@phds.ge.

Germany

FOUNDATION CENTRES AND CO-ORDINATING BODIES

Bundesverband Deutscher Stiftungen eV (Association of German Foundations)

Founded in 1948 to represent the interests of German foundations.

Activities: Provides information about German foundations; publishes directories, books, reports, brochures and leaflets; organizes conferences, exhibitions and training for foundation staff. The Association maintains a database with more than 21,000 entries for foundations, and works internationally with similar national and international organizations.

Geographical Area of Activity: Germany.

Restrictions: Does not make grants.

Publications: *Verzeichnis Deutscher Stiftungen*; *StiftungsRatgeber*; *StiftungsReport*; *Stiftungsfokus*; *StiftungsWelt* (quarterly magazine).

Board of Directors: Prof. Dr Michael Göring (Chair.); Prof. Dr Joachim Rogall (Deputy Chair.).

Principal Staff: Sec.-Gen. Prof. Dr Hans Fleisch; Deputy Sec.-Gen. Birgit Radow.

Address: Mauerstr. 93, Haus Deutscher Stiftungen, 10117 Berlin.

Telephone: (30) 897947-0; **Fax:** (30) 897947-11; **Internet:** www .stiftungen.org; **e-mail:** post@stiftungen.org.

Initiative Bürgerstiftungen (Community Foundations Initiative)

Established in 2001 to support new community foundations and professionalize existing ones, and to promote and offer a platform for all community foundations in Germany.

Activities: Promotes the development of community foundations in Germany, through mentoring, coaching, and providing consultancy and advice to community foundations; an annual grants programme to support operating costs for selected community foundations; a travel fund for community foundation practitioners; regional meetings, seminars and workshops; information and communication; and research, including an annual survey of the community foundation sector in Germany.

Geographical Area of Activity: Germany.

Publications: Electronic newsletter (monthly); information resources; books.

Board of Directors: Prof. Dr Michael Goering (Chair.).

Principal Staff: Acting Dir Ulrike Reichart.

Address: c/o Bundesverband Deutscher Stiftungen, Haus Deutscher Stiftungen, Mauerstr. 93, 10117 Berlin.

Telephone: (30) 897947-90; **Fax:** (30) 897947-91; **Internet:** www.buergerstiftungen.org; **e-mail:** sebastian.buehner@ stiftungen.org.

Maecenata Stiftung (Maecenata Foundation)

Established in 2010 as an umbrella organization that incorporated the Maecenata Institute (f. 1997) and transnational giving charity Maecenata International (f. 2002).

Activities: Operates in the field of research into civil society and philanthropy, through collecting and publishing information on foundations and other third-sector organizations; maintaining a database on around 18,000 German foundations and trusts; carrying out research; academic teaching; organizing conferences; and promoting research in the field through academic exchange. The Foundation acts as a policy think tank in the fields of civil society, civic engagement and philanthropy. Its Transnational Giving programme is the German partner to the Transnational Giving Europe Network (TGE). It facilitates cross-border giving worldwide by enabling donors to obtain a tax-deductible receipt in their country of residence.

Geographical Area of Activity: Germany, Europe and worldwide.

Restrictions: Does not accept unsolicited applications.

Publications: *Maecenata Schriften* (10 vols to date); *Opuscula series*; *Maecenata Notizen* (3 a year); Europe Bottom-Up series (e-publication).

Finance: Voluntary donations, grants.

Council: Christian Petry (Chair.).

Principal Staff: Contacts Dr Rupert Graf Strachwitz, Dr Felix Weber.

Address: Adalbertstrasse 108, 80798 München; Linienstrasse 139, 10115 Berlin.

Telephone: (30) 2838 7909; **Fax:** (30) 28387910; **Internet:** www.maecenata.eu; **e-mail:** mst@maecenata.eu.

Stifterverband für die Deutsche Wissenschaft eV (Donors' Association for the Promotion of Sciences and Humanities)

Founded in 1920 and re-established in 1949 by 61 national industrial and commercial organizations to support the sciences and humanities in research and teaching, as well as the rising scientific and technical generation; and to undertake measures that might be helpful in bringing support to science and technology.

Activities: Operates nationally in the fields of education, the arts and humanities, and nationally and internationally in the fields of science, medicine and international relations, through self-conducted programmes. The Association has around 3,000 members, comprising companies, associations and individuals making donations on an annual basis. Administers more than 600 trusts and foundations (German Foundation Centre).

Geographical Area of Activity: Germany and international.

Publications: Annual Report; *Wirtschaft und Wissenschaft* (quarterly); *Forschung & Entwicklung* (annually); *Materialien aus dem Stiftungszentrum*; *Materialien zur Wissenschaftsstatistik*; *Beiträge zu Statistiken über Forschung und Entwicklung*; *Schriftenreihe zum Stiftungswesen*.

Finance: Annual income €34,721,975, expenditure €34.721.975 (2013).

Board of Trustees: Prof. Dr Andreas Barner (Pres.); Kurt Bock, Dr Nikolaus von Bomhard (Vice-Pres.).

Principal Staff: Sec.-Gen. Andreas Schlüter; Deputy Sec.-Gen. Volker Meyer-Guckel.

Address: Barkhovenallee 1, 45239 Essen.

Telephone: (201) 84010; **Fax:** (201) 8401301; **Internet:** www .stifterverband.de; **e-mail:** mail@stifterverband.de.

FOUNDATIONS, TRUSTS AND NON-PROFIT ORGANIZATIONS

Konrad-Adenauer-Stiftung eV—KAS (Konrad Adenauer Foundation)

Founded in 1964, emerging from the Society for Christian Democratic Education (f. 1956), and named after the first Chancellor of the Federal Republic, Konrad Adenauer. The Foundation is guided by the same principles that inspired Adenauer's work.

Activities: Operates in the field of the humanities, development and international relations, through: granting scholarships to gifted individuals; organizing public events; and supporting projects in the field of international understanding (approx. 200 projects and programmes are organized in more than 100 countries). The Foundation offers political education and research for political projects; researches the history of Christian Democracy; supports and encourages European unification, operates a think tank on domestic policy and the social market economy, international understanding and co-operation on development policy. It has two education centres and 21 education institutes.

Geographical Area of Activity: Worldwide.

Publications: Annual Report; *KAS International* (3 a year); Country Reports series; conference, seminar and event proceedings; *Facts & Findings*; *KAS Auslandsinformationen* (periodical); books.

Finance: Annual income €139,880,000, expenditure €139,880,000 (31 Dec. 2014).

Board of Trustees: Prof. Dr Roman Herzog (Chair.).

Principal Staff: Chair. Dr Hans-Gert Poettering; Vice-Chair. Prof. Dr Norbert Lammert, Prof. Dr. Beate Neuss, Hildigund Neubert; Sec.-Gen. Michael Thielen; Treas. Dr Franz Schoser.

Address: Klingelhöferstr. 23, 10785 Berlin.

Telephone: (30) 269960; **Internet:** www.kas.de; **e-mail:** zentrale-berlin@kas.de.

Aid to the Church in Need—ACN

Founded in 1947 by Fr Werenfried van Straaten to promote Christianity and support and provide pastoral relief to Catholics in need; a Pontifical Foundation.

Activities: Operates in around 144 less-developed countries of Africa, Asia, Central and South America and the Caribbean, and Eastern Europe, through providing grants towards church-building and transport funds, for students, seminarians, novices and clergy, and in the area of the press, radio and religious literature; it also supports persecuted, oppressed and poor Catholics, Russian Orthodox, and refugees, regardless of religion. National offices operate in 16 countries in Europe, North and South America and Australia.

Geographical Area of Activity: International.

Publications: *Fifty Years of the Church in Need*; and other publications.

Finance: Annual income €89,250,883, expenditure €90,049,480 (2013).

Trustees: Cardinal Mauro Piacenza (Pres.).

Principal Staff: Exec. Pres. Baron Johannes Heereman von Zuydtwyck.

Address: Postfach 1209, 61452 Königstein im Taunus; Bischof-Kindermann-Str. 23, 61462 Königstein im Taunus.

Telephone: (6174) 2910; **Fax:** (6174) 3423; **Internet:** www.acn-intl.org; **e-mail:** projects@acn-intl.org.

Allianz Kulturstiftung (Allianz Cultural Foundation)

Established in 2000 by the former Allianz AG, now Allianz SE, for the promotion of culture, especially with regard to young people, and European integration with an emphasis on Eastern and South-Eastern Europe, and the Mediterranean.

Activities: Operates in Europe in its broadest sense, primarily supporting multinational and intercultural co-operation projects that promote European integration with a lasting influence. Innovativeness and European dynamism are essential criteria for selecting the projects, as well as outstanding artistic and academic quality or a special relevance to European cultural history.

Geographical Area of Activity: Europe.

Restrictions: No grants to individuals.

Publications: Publications on the Foundation.

Finance: Initial capital €50m.

Board of Trustees: Dr Werner Zedelius (Chair.); Prof. Dr Christina Weiss (Assoc. Chair.).

Principal Staff: Man. Dir Michael M. Thoss.

Address: Pariser Platz 6A, 10117 Berlin.

Telephone: (30) 20915731-30; **Fax:** (30) 20915731-40; **Internet:** www.allianz-kulturstiftung.de; **e-mail:** kulturstiftung@allianz.de.

Allianz Umweltstiftung (Allianz Foundation for Sustainability)

Established in 1990 by Allianz Versicherung, an insurance company, to work towards ensuring a safe future.

Activities: Operates in Germany in the field of environmental conservation, focusing on the protection and development of the countryside, land planning and sustainable development. The Foundation supports innovative and inspirational projects. It also sponsors the Benediktbeurer Talks, a forum for debating environmental protection issues.

Geographical Area of Activity: Germany.

Publications: *10 Jahre Allianz Umweltstiftung*; various project reports; video.

Finance: Assets €50m.

Board of Trustees: Prof. Dieter Stolte (Chair.); Dr Werner Zedelius (Vice-Chair.).

Principal Staff: Chair. Dr Lutz Spandau.

Address: Pariser Platz 6, 10117 Berlin.

Telephone: (30) 20671595-50; **Fax:** (30) 20671595-60; **Internet:** www.allianz-umweltstiftung.de; **e-mail:** info@allianz-umweltstiftung.de.

Arbeiterwohlfahrt Bundesverband eV—AWO (Federal Association of Social Welfare Organizations)

Founded in 1919, the organization aims to improve the social welfare of those in need in Germany, particularly the young and the sick.

Activities: Organizes and finances social welfare programmes in Germany, incl. the operation of sheltered accommodation, day centres and counselling centres; runs training courses for social workers; operates educational programmes for adults; and co-operates with other social welfare organizations at both national and international levels, including development, aid and disaster relief projects in Eastern Europe, Asia, and Central and South America.

Geographical Area of Activity: Mainly Germany, some work carried out internationally.

Publications: *Theorie und Praxis* (monthly); *Sozialprism* (monthly); directory; yearbook; monographs and handbooks.

Finance: Total assets €34,404,217 (31 Dec. 2013).

Board of Directors: Wolfgang Stadler (Chair.).

Principal Staff: Pres. Wilhelm Schmidt.

Address: Heinrich-Albertz-Haus, Blücherstr. 62–63, 10961 Berlin.

Telephone: (30) 26309-0; **Fax:** (30) 32599; **Internet:** www.awo.org; **e-mail:** info@awo.org.

ASKO Europa-Stiftung (ASKO Europe Foundation)

Established in 1990 by ASKO Deutsche Kaufhaus AG, a retail company, to promote academic research and education, especially in the area of European integration on a federal basis. In 1996, when ASKO Deutsche Kaufhaus AG merged with METRO AG, the Foundation became an independent entity.

Activities: Promotes study in the area of European integration. The Foundation gives special emphasis to Franco-German relations and their significance for the European integration process. It is committed to the development of the European region spanning Saarland, Lorraine and Luxembourg.

Geographical Area of Activity: Europe.

Restrictions: No scholarships to individuals.

Publications: Denkart Europa; activity reports; discussion report; AES-News; *Dialogue in dialogue*; newsletter.

Board of Trustees: Arno Krause (Hon. Chair.); Klaus-Peter Beck (Chair.); Rudolf Schäfer (Vice-Chair.).

Principal Staff: Sec. Barbara Dony.

Address: Pestelstr. 2, 66119 Saarbrücken.

Telephone: (681) 92674-0; **Fax:** (681) 92674-99; **Internet:** www.asko-europa-stiftung.de; **e-mail:** info@asko-europa-stiftung.de.

Aventis Foundation

Established in 1996 by Hoechst AG, a life sciences company, and formerly known as the Hoechst Foundation, for the promotion of projects in the areas of culture, civil society and science. Present name adopted in 2000.

Activities: Operates internationally, promoting projects in areas such as the fine arts, civil society and science, through making grants to organizations. Special funds operate in the field of education, offering grants to gifted students in need, and for scientific research.

Geographical Area of Activity: International.

Restrictions: Individual scholarship applications not accepted.

Publications: Annual Report; newsletter.

Finance: Total assets €58,812,787 (2014).

Board of Trustees: Prof. Dr Günther Wess (Chair.).

Principal Staff: Chair. Dieter Kohl; Man. Dir Eugen Müller.

Address: Industriepark Höchst, Bldg F 821, 65926 Frankfurt am Main.

Telephone: (69) 3057256; **Fax:** (69) 30580554; **Internet:** www.aventis-foundation.org; **e-mail:** eugen.mueller@aventis-foundation.org.

Professor Otto Beisheim-Stiftung (Professor Otto Beisheim Foundation)

Founded by Prof. Otto Beisheim in 1976.

Activities: Promotes education, entrepreneurship and culture, particularly in Germany, through funding symposia and colloquia, donating art exhibits and funding chairs in entrepreneurship at German universities. Also established the Otto Beisheim Graduate School of Management in Vallendar, Germany. Promotes the use of new technologies, including funding the first Swiss Internet House.

Geographical Area of Activity: Germany and Europe.

Principal Staff: Chair. Dr Fredy Raas.

Address: c/o Metro, Helene Wessel Bogen 39, 80939 Munich.

Telephone: (351) 46333138; **Fax:** (351) 46337176; **e-mail:** beisheim-stiftung@mailbox.tu-dresden.de.

Otto-Benecke-Stiftung eV (Otto Benecke Foundation)

Founded in 1965 by the Verband Deutscher Studentenschaften (Association of German Student Bodies) to provide assistance for refugee students and students from developing countries.

Activities: Operates internationally in the field of education, by providing a counselling and scholarship programme enabling students from less-developed countries (particularly refugees from Southern Africa) to study at universities, polytechnics and vocational schools in Germany and less-developed countries; it also runs a programme for training in manual and industrial occupations in African countries of asylum. International conferences are held, in collaboration with other organizations, on basic questions concerning the right to asylum.

Geographical Area of Activity: International.

Restrictions: Grants are made only to immigrants, refugees and asylum seekers.

Publications: Annual Report; *Die Nationalstaaten und die internationale Migration* series; conference proceedings.

Finance: Total expenditure approx. €37m.

Board of Trustees: Eberhard Diepgen (Chair.).

Principal Staff: Chair. Dr Lothar Theodor Lemper; Deputy Chair. Wolfgang Roth.

Address: Kennedyallee 105–107, 53175 Bonn.

Telephone: (228) 81630; **Fax:** (228) 8163300; **Internet:** www.obs-ev.de; **e-mail:** post@obs-ev.de.

Berghof Stiftung für Konfliktforschung GmbH (Berghof Foundation for Conflict Research)

Founded in 1971 by Prof. Dr Georg Zundel, deriving its name from the Berghof Estate, the home of the founder, with an aim to perform research in peace-related conflict studies.

Activities: Works in the areas of conflict reserach, peace support and peace education. Supports research in constructive conflict management and significant issues in ethics and natural sciences. Maintains the Berghof Centre for Constructive Conflict Management in Berlin. Also awards the annual Hans Götzelmann Prize in conflict studies and the Georg Zundel Scholarship.

Geographical Area of Activity: Europe, Germany, Sri Lanka.

Restrictions: Grants restricted to Western, Southern, Central and Eastern Europe, for a three-year period of support only. Currently offering only the Grant for Innovation in Conflict Transformation.

Publications: *Berghof Papers*; *Berghof Handbook for Conflict Transformation*; reports and other publications.

Finance: Annual revenue €4,617,000, expenditure €4,617,000 (2013).

Board of Trustees: Johannes Zundel (Chair.).

Principal Staff: Exec Dirs Prof. Dr Hans J. Giessmann, Sandra Pfahler.

Address: Altensteinstr. 48A, 14195 Berlin.

Telephone: (30) 844154-0; **Fax:** (30) 844154-99; **Internet:** www.berghof-foundation.org; **e-mail:** info@berghof-foundation.org.

Bertelsmann Stiftung (Bertelsmann Foundation)

Founded in 1977 by Reinhard Mohn to support projects in education, economic and social issues, democracy and civil society, international co-operation and health.

Activities: Operates two core programmes: 'Helping people' and 'Strengthening society'. Additional programmes provide tools and findings as strategic resources for the main project teams. The Foundation awards the Reinhard Mohn Prize annually for innovative and exemplary solutions in areas of pressing social concern. Offices in Washington, DC, and Brussels are dedicated to promoting knowledge transfer and creating new local networks as the basis of an international framework.

Geographical Area of Activity: Germany, Europe and USA.

Restrictions: Operating foundation; no grants on application.

Publications: Annual Report; newsletter (3–4 a year); e-books; *Shaping Globalizaton* (2012); *Rethinking National Identity in the Age of Migration* (2012); *Megatrends in Global Interaction* (2012); *Transformation Index BTI 2012*; *Inspiring Democracy* (2013); *Corporate Responsibility in Europe*.

Finance: Annual income €126,066,700 expenditure €50,570,000 (2014).

Board of Trustees: Prof. Dr Werner J. Bauer (Chair.).

Principal Staff: CEO Aart de Geus; Deputy CEO Liz Mohn.

Address: Carl-Bertelsmann-Str. 256, 33311 Gütersloh.

Telephone: (5241) 810; **Fax:** (5241) 8181999; **Internet:** www
.bertelsmann-stiftung.de; **e-mail:** info@bertelsmann
-stiftung.de.

Bischöfliches Hilfswerk Misereor eV (German Catholic Bishops' Organization for Development Co-operation)

Founded in 1958 by the Catholic Church in the Federal Republic of Germany with the aim of combating world hunger and injustice.

Activities: Promotes long-term solutions to the problems of developing countries by organizing and financing education and training programmes that emphasize self-help.

Geographical Area of Activity: International.

Publications: Annual Report; pamphlets.

Finance: Annual income €179.3m., expenditure €177.8m. (2013).

Principal Staff: Dir-Gen. Primin Spiegel; Man. Dirs Dr Martin Bröckelmann-Simon, Thomas Antkowiak.

Address: POB 101545, 52015 Aachen; Mozartstr. 9, 52064 Aachen.

Telephone: (241) 4420; **Fax:** (241) 442188; **Internet:** www
.misereor.org; **e-mail:** info@misereor.de.

BMW Stiftung Herbert Quandt (BMW Foundation Herbert Quandt)

Founded in 1970 by BMW AG, a motor vehicle manufacturer, on the 60th birthday of industrialist Herbert Quandt, to foster international dialogue.

Activities: Seeks to foster national and international dialogue and mutual understanding between business, politics and society. Organizes a range of events bringing together leaders of industry and society, which aim to demonstrate the importance of co-operation between social institutions to ensure industrial nations have stable and successful economies. International events are often organized in co-operation with other partners.

Geographical Area of Activity: International.

Restrictions: Unsolicited applications are not accepted: no scholarships or any other kind of financial support are provided.

Publications: Texts of lectures and conference documentation.

Finance: Initial endowment of €50m.; annual income €4.6m. (2011).

Trustees: Dr Michael Schaeffer (Chair.).

Principal Staff: Exec. Dir Markus Hipp.

Address: Reinhardtstr. 58, 10117 Berlin.

Telephone: (30) 33963500; **Fax:** (30) 33963530; **Internet:** www.bmw-stiftung.de; **e-mail:** info@bmw-stiftung.de.

Boehringer Ingelheim Fonds–Stiftung für medizinische Grundlagenforschung (Foundation for Basic Research in Biomedicine)

Established in 1983 by the companies C. H. Boehringer Sohn and Boehringer Ingelheim International as an independent non-profit organization for the exclusive and direct promotion of basic research in biomedicine.

Activities: Operates internationally and focuses on four activities: PhD fellowships for pre-doctoral fellows working on projects in basic biomedical research; MD fellowships for medical students carrying out experimental research; travel grants for pre- and post-doctoral researchers who wish to learn new methods by visiting other laboratories or taking practical courses; and twice a year the Foundation invites leading researchers from different sub-disciplines to three-day International Titisee Conferences to discuss trends and new lines of research in the life sciences.

Geographical Area of Activity: Europe and overseas (supports Europeans in Europe and overseas; scientists from overseas working in Europe).

Restrictions: No grants to scientific institutions; no grants for the payment of staff or for overheads, equipment or materials.

Publications: *B.I.F.—FUTURA* (three times a year).

Finance: Annual budget €4,880,000 (2012).

Board of Directors: Prof. Andreas Barner (Chair.); Prof. U. Benjamin Kaupp (Deputy Chair.).

Principal Staff: Man. Dir Dr Claudia Walther.

Address: Schusterstr. 46–48, 55116 Mainz.

Telephone: (6131) 27508-0; **Fax:** (6131) 27508-11; **Internet:** www.bifonds.de; **e-mail:** secretariat@bifonds.de.

Heinrich-Böll-Stiftung (Heinrich Böll Foundation)

Established in 1987 and associated with the German Green Party, to promote political education in the areas of ecology, solidarity, democracy, arms control and sexual equality; and preserve the works and thoughts of the writer Heinrich Böll.

Activities: Operates nationally and internationally in the fields of the arts and humanities, conservation and the environment, international affairs, economic sustainability, and law and human rights; co-operates with NGOs working in 60 countries. The Foundation runs a fellowship study programme open to students and postgraduates in all fields and of all nationalities; and also founded the Feminist Institute and the Green Academy. It has 28 offices in Europe, North America, South America, Africa, Asia and the Middle East.

Geographical Area of Activity: International.

Publications: Annual Report; newsletter.

Finance: Annual income €54,908,647, expenditure €52,951,647 (31 Dec. 2014).

Board of Directors: Ralf Fücks, Barbara Unmüssig (Chair.).

Principal Staff: CEO Dr Livia Cotta.

Address: Schumannstr. 8, 10117 Berlin-Mitte.

Telephone: (30) 28534-0; **Fax:** (30) 28534-109; **Internet:** www
.boell.de; **e-mail:** info@boell.de.

Robert-Bosch-Stiftung GmbH (Robert Bosch Foundation)

Founded in 1964 by the Bosch organization to embody the philanthropic and social endeavours of its founder, Robert Bosch (1861–1942).

Activities: Supports and promotes public health, international relations (especially with France, the USA, Central and Eastern Europe, and Turkey), education, civic society, arts and culture, the humanities, and social and natural sciences. The Foundation develops innovative programmes, competitions and prizes, and supports promising pilot projects within these objectives. In Stuttgart, it runs three public health and research facilities: the Robert Bosch Hospital, the Dr Margarete Fischer-Bosch Institute for Clinical Pharmacology and the Institute for the History of Medicine. It also an office in Berlin.

Geographical Area of Activity: Europe, Turkey, Japan, India, USA, People's Republic of China.

Restrictions: Grants given only in defined areas of interest and for limited periods.

Publications: Annual Report; magazine.

Finance: Annual income €99,674,000, expenditure €84,090,000 (2014).

Board of Trustees: Dr Kurt W. Liedtke (Chair.).

Principal Staff: Exec. Dirs Dr Ingrid Hamm, Prof. Dr Joachim Rogall.

Address: POB 100628, 70005 Stuttgart; Heidehofstr. 31, 70184 Stuttgart.

Telephone: (711) 46084-0; **Fax:** (711) 46084-1094; **Internet:** www.bosch-stiftung.de; **e-mail:** info@bosch-stiftung.de.

Bundeskanzler-Willy-Brandt-Stiftung (Federal Chancellor Willy Brandt Foundation)

Established in 1994 by the German Bundestag to further the aims of the former Chancellor Willy Brandt.

Activities: Aims to contribute to an understanding of the history of the 20th century, and of the development of the Federal Republic of Germany. The Foundation promotes the ideals of Willy Brandt in the areas of the peace, freedom and unity of the German people; the safeguarding of democracy; and understanding and reconciliation between nations. It operates in the areas of the arts and humanities, education, international affairs, law and human rights, and social welfare, nationally and internationally, through self-conducted programmes, research, conferences, training courses and publications. It also maintains two permanent exhibitions in Berlin and Luebeck; and awards the biennial Willy Brandt Prize for Contemporary History.

Geographical Area of Activity: International.

Restrictions: No grants. Conducts only its own projects. Provides external financial support only to college students and rising young scholars, through awarding the Willy Brandt Prize for the Advancement of Rising Young Scholars and granting internships to students of political science and/or modern history.

Publications: Newsletter; *Edition Willy Brandt—Berliner Ausgabe; Willy-Brandt-Dokumente; Willy-Brandt-Studien; Schriftenreihe der Bundeskanzler-Willy-Brandt-Stiftung.*

Finance: Annual expenditure €1,550,000 (2014).

Board of Trustees: Dr Wolfgang Thierse (Chair.); Dr Jürgen Burckhardt (Vice-Chair.).

Principal Staff: Chair. Karsten Brenner; Man. Dir Dr Wolfram Hoppenstedt; Deputy Man. Dir Dr Bernd Rother.

Address: Unter den Linden 62–68, 10117 Berlin.

Telephone: (30) 787707-0; **Fax:** (30) 787707-50; **Internet:** www.willy-brandt.de; **e-mail:** info@willy-brandt.de.

Brot für die Welt (Bread for the World)

Founded in 1959 by Protestant churches in Germany to help people living in need and misery.

Activities: Operates more than 700 self-help projects each year in around 80 developing countries, including countries of Central and South America, Africa and South-East Asia, in collaboration with partner organizations. Projects operate in the areas of education, advice and practical assistance, health and welfare, and emergency relief.

Geographical Area of Activity: Developing countries in Central and South America, Africa, South-East Asia and the Far East; Germany.

Restrictions: Does not conduct own projects in the countries of the Southern hemisphere, but supports local partners in their work.

Finance: Total income €271.8m., expenditure €271.8m. (2014).

Principal Staff: Dir Cornelia Füllkrug-Weitzel.

Address: Caroline-Michaelis-str.1, 10115 Berlin.

Telephone: (711) 2159-0; **Internet:** www.brot-fuer-die-welt.de; **e-mail:** kontakt@brot-fuer-die-welt.de.

CBM

Founded in 1908 by Pastor Ernst Jakob Christoffel and formerly known as Christoffel Blindenmission, CBM is an international Christian disability and inclusive development organization, committed to improving the quality of life of persons with disabilities in the poorest countries of the world.

Activities: Works with people with disabilities, their families, local partner organizations, alliance partners including UN agencies, global organizations, and disabled persons' organizations. The organization is involved with 'VISION 2020: the Right to Sight', a global initiative with the World Health Organization and the International Agency for the Prevention of Blindness (IAPB). It also collaborates with international organizations. Ten CBM member associations (in Australia, Canada, Germany, Ireland, Italy, Kenya, New Zealand, Switzerland, the United Kingdom and the USA) support a joint programme of work. The organization has supported more than 700 projects in 73 countries in Africa, Asia and Central and South America.

Geographical Area of Activity: Worldwide.

Publications: Annual Reports.

Finance: Annual programme expenditure approx. €63.8m. (2014).

Supervisory Board: Marion Mills (Chair.).

Principal Staff: Pres. Dave McComiskey; Vice-Pres Markus Hesse, Matthias Späth.

Address: Nibelungenstr. 124, 64625 Bensheim.

Telephone: (6251) 131131; **Fax:** (6251) 131165; **Internet:** www.cbm.org; **e-mail:** contact@cbm.org.

Sergiu-Celibidache-Stiftung (Sergiu Celibidache Foundation)

Founded in 1999 by Serge Ioan and Joana Celibidache.

Activities: Aims to promote the musical work of Sergiu Celibidache, through documentation, continuation and discussion of his music through seminars and publications. Activities include supporting young musicians, organizing master classes, discussions, and conducting courses and concerts. The Foundation has also organized Sergiu Celibidache Festivals.

Geographical Area of Activity: International.

Publications: Books; CDs.

Principal Staff: Pres. Serge Celebidachi; Dir Mark Mast.

Address: Bäckerstr. 46, 81241 Munich.

Telephone: (89) 120220320; **Fax:** (89) 120220322; **Internet:** www.celibidache.net; **e-mail:** info@celibidache.net.

Daimler und Benz Stiftung (Daimler and Benz Foundation)

Founded in 1986 by Daimler-Benz AG (now Daimler AG), a motor vehicle manufacturer, to support research relating to the inter-relationships between people, the environment and technology.

Activities: Provides funds for research undertaken by groups working on special topics within the frame of defined research programmes; research activities are co-ordinated and the results published. Grants are also awarded to individuals and institutions.

Geographical Area of Activity: Germany and international.

Publications: Annual Reports; *Bertha Benz Lectures* series; additional and recent publications are on the website.

Finance: Total assets €130,715,734 (31 Dec. 2013).

Board of Trustees: Prof. Dr Thomas Weber (Chair.).

Principal Staff: Exec. Chair. Dr Eckard Minx; Man. Dir Dr Jörg Klein.

Address: Dr Carl-Benz-Platz 2, 68526 Ladenburg.

Telephone: (6203) 10920; **Fax:** (6203) 10925; **Internet:** www.daimler-benz-stiftung.de; **e-mail:** info@daimler-benz-stiftung.de.

Deutsch-Russischer Austausch eV—DRA (German-Russian Exchange)

Established in 1992 to assist the democratic process of Russia through co-operative projects.

Activities: Operates in Germany, Russia, Ukraine and Belarus through local activities in large cities, including St Petersburg and Berlin. The organization provides support to citizens' initiatives, human rights organizations and non-governmental social organizations, as well as running programmes in the fields of continuing education and exchange initiatives as well as facilitating the search for contacts with Western partners.

Geographical Area of Activity: Germany, Belarus, Ukraine and the Russian Federation.

Publications: German and Russian newsletter.

Principal Staff: Exec. Dir Stefan Melle.

Address: Badstr. 44, 13357 Berlin.

Telephone: (30) 4466800; **Fax:** (30) 44668010; **Internet:** www .austausch.org; **e-mail:** info@austausch.org.

Deutsche AIDS-Stiftung (German AIDS Foundation)

Established in 1987 to help HIV-positive individuals. Also supports projects to assist those affected and has received more than 70,000 project proposals. Has provided assistance to individuals and funded projects to the value of almost €30m.

Activities: Main spheres of activity include financial assistance and improved care for the HIV-affected, and promotion of the Foundation's objectives; and assisting best-practice projects in Sub-Saharan Africa. It awards an annual Media Prize, worth €15,000, and an additional prize for students and young journalists, worth €3,000.

Geographical Area of Activity: Germany and Sub-Saharan Africa.

Publications: Annual Report; electronic newsletter; additional material for events; *Stiftung konkret*; and other publications.

Finance: Annual income €300,527, expenditure €254,313 (31 Dec. 2013).

Supervisory Board: Reinhold Schulte (Chair.); Dr Ute Canaris, Dr Volkmar Schön (Vice-Chair.).

Principal Staff: CEO Prof. Dr Elisabeth Pott; Exec. Dir Dr Ulrich Heide.

Address: Münsterstr. 18, 53111 Bonn.

Telephone: (228) 604690; **Fax:** (228) 6046969; **Internet:** www .aids-stiftung.de; **e-mail:** info@aids-stiftung.de.

Deutsche Bank Stiftung (Deutsche Bank Foundation)

Established in 2005 following the merger of Alfred Herrhausen Stiftung Hilfe zur Selbsthilfe, which was founded in 1986, and Deutsche Bank Kulturstiftung.

Activities: Spheres of activity include the humanities, social welfare and economic affairs. Aims to assist people in attaining self-reliance in social spheres through self-conducted programmes. Provides grants to individuals, as well as to projects that help achieve the Foundation's goals.

Geographical Area of Activity: Germany and Europe.

Publications: Annual Report (in German and English).

Finance: Total assets €141,881,000, annual income €4,750,000 (2014).

Board of Directors: Dr Clemens Börsig (Chair.); Michael Münch (Deputy Chair.).

Principal Staff: Man. Dir Jörg Eduard Krumsiek.

Address: Postkorb 46Z02A, 60262 Frankfurt; Börsenplatz 5, 60313 Frankfurt.

Telephone: (69) 91034999; **Fax:** (69) 91038371; **Internet:** www .deutsche-bank-stiftung.de; **e-mail:** office.dbstiftung@db .com.

Deutsche Bundesstiftung Umwelt—DBU (German Federal Foundation for the Environment)

Established in 1990 by the German Government for research, development and innovation in the field of the environment.

Activities: Encourages research, development and innovation in the field of environmentally- and health-friendly products, especially by small and medium-sized companies; promotes the exchange of information on the environment between the scientific and business communities; and aims to safeguard national natural and cultural heritage from environmental damage. The Foundation also awards an annual environmental prize worth €500,000.

Geographical Area of Activity: Germany, with occasional grants to other countries in Central and Eastern European countries and beyond.

Restrictions: No grants to state organizations.

Publications: See website.

Finance: Annual income €134,203,397, expenditure €13,624,320 (31 Dec. 2013).

Board of Trustees: Rita Schwarzelühr-Sutter (Chair.); Undine Kurth (Vice-Chair.).

Principal Staff: Sec.-Gen. Dr Heinrich Bottermann.

Address: Postfach 1705, 49007; An der Bornau 2, 49090 Osnabrück.

Telephone: (541) 9633-0; **Fax:** (541) 9633-190; **Internet:** www .dbu.de; **e-mail:** info@dbu.de.

Deutsche Gesellschaft für Auswärtige Politik—DGAP (German Council on Foreign Relations)

Founded in 1955; a national foreign-policy network and independent, non-partisan and non-profit organization.

Activities: Aims to improve the understanding of German foreign policy and international relations. The Council promotes research in these areas and provides documentation regarding problems of international relations. It operates in the field of international relations through research and advises decision-makers in politics, business and society. Operations include a research institute, documentation, conferences and study groups, courses, publications and lectures. It also maintains a research library specializing in foreign affairs.

Geographical Area of Activity: Europe, USA, the Russian Federation, Eurasia and the People's Republic of China.

Publications: *Jahrbuch Internationale Politik* (annually); *Internationale Politik* (bimonthly); *Internationale Politik* (global edition, bimonthly).

Finance: The DGAP is funded by the German Federal Foreign Office, private corporations, foundations and others, as well as through the financial support of its more than 2,000 members. Total assets €8,007,605 (2013).

Board: Dr Arend Oetker (Pres.); Dr Harald Kindermann (Sec.-Gen.); Dr Tessen von Heydebreck (Treas.).

Principal Staff: Dir of Research Institute Dr Eberhard Sandschneider.

Address: Rauchstr. 17–18, 10787 Berlin.

Telephone: (30) 2542310; **Fax:** (30) 25423116; **Internet:** www .dgap.org; **e-mail:** info@dgap.org.

Deutsche Gesellschaft für Internationale Zusammenarbeit—GIZ (German Society for International Co-operation)

Formed in 2011 by the merger of the Internationale Weiterbildung und Entwicklung (Capacity Building International) and the Deutsche Entwicklungsdienst (German Development Service).

Activities: Supports the German Government internationally in the fields of sustainable development and education.

Geographical Area of Activity: International.

Publications: Annual Report; corporate reports; information brochures; project evaluations; specialist publications.

Finance: Total assets €1,217.3m, annual turnover €1,945.2m (31 Dec. 2013).

Supervisory Board: Dr Friedrich Kitschelt (Chair.).

Principal Staff: CEO Tanja Gönner; Deputy CEO Christoph Beier.

Address: Friedrich-Ebert-Allee 40, 53113 Bonn.

Telephone: (228) 44600; **Fax:** (228) 44601766; **Internet:** www .giz.de; **e-mail:** info@giz.de.

Deutsche Krebshilfe eV (German Cancer Aid)

Founded in 1974 by Dr Mildred Scheel, Dr Helmut Geiger, D. Kühn, Bechtold Freiherr von Massenbach, F. L. Müller, Prof.

Hermann Schardt, Heinz Schmidt and Martin Virchow to support the welfare of cancer patients, and to fight against cancer.

Activities: Operates in the fields of education, research and medicine and health, nationally through research and training courses, and nationally and internationally through self-conducted programmes and conferences. The organization makes grants to institutions to support research into cancer diagnosis, therapy, after-care and self-help, organizes and supports medical education projects, further education courses and information events; and provides advice, help and financial support to people suffering from cancer. It also administers the Stiftung Deutsche KinderKrebshilfe and Dr Mildred Scheel Stiftung für Krebforschung.

Geographical Area of Activity: Germany.

Publications: Annual Report; booklets on cancer; videos; CD-ROM; newsletter and other publications.

Finance: Annual income €76,326,532 (2013).

Board of Trustees: Hans-Peter Krämer (Chair.).

Principal Staff: Pres. Dr Fritz Pleitgen; CEO Gerd Nettekoven.

Address: Buschstr. 32, 53113 Bonn.

Telephone: (228) 72990-0; **Fax:** (228) 72990-11; **Internet:** www.krebshilfe.de; **e-mail:** deutsche@krebshilfe.de.

Deutsche Nationalstiftung (German National Trust)

Established in 1993 by former Chancellor Helmut Schmidt and a group of his friends, including Herman J. Abs, Gerd Bucerius, Kurt Körber and Michael Otto, to bring to the public consciousness the mutual relationship between science, art and literature, law, politics and commerce, and to influence the values of the nation with respect to domestic and international concerns so as to contribute to the common good; to promote and strengthen the process of German unity and promote German cultural identity within a European cultural mosaic; and to comment on the pressing questions facing Germany at present and in the future.

Activities: Organizes annual meetings to consider urgent problems and discuss questions of national and European relevance; bestows an annual National Prize of approximately €75,000; organizes forums; and publishes theses on issues affecting Germany and Europe.

Geographical Area of Activity: Germany and European Union countries.

Publications: Annual Report; conference proceedings.

Board of Trustees: Dr Manfred Bischoff (Chair.).

Principal Staff: Chair. Prof. Dr Richard Schröder; Exec. Dir Dirk Reimers.

Address: Feldbrunnenstr. 56, 20148 Hamburg.

Telephone: (40) 413367-53; **Fax:** (40) 413367-55; **Internet:** www.nationalstiftung.de; **e-mail:** info@nationalstiftung.de.

Deutsche Orient-Stiftung (German Orient Foundation)

Established in 1960 by the German Near and Middle East Association (NUMOV) to promote relations between Germany and the 'lands of the Orient'; comprises the German Orient-Institute (Deutsches Orient-Institut—DOI), the oldest private scientific institute in Germany.

Activities: Operates in the fields of science, culture, general knowledge and modern history, promoting dialogue between Germany and the countries of the Middle East. The Foundation carries out research into local political and social developments in the Middle East.

Geographical Area of Activity: Germany and the Middle East.

Restrictions: Does not make grants to individuals.

Publications: *ORIENT* (magazine); *DOI-Kurzanalysen;* studies.

Board of Trustees: Michelle Müntefering (Chair.); Prof. Dr. Mathias Rohe (Vice-Chair.).

Principal Staff: CEO Dr Gerald Bumharter; Deputy CEOs Helene Rang, Henry Hasselbarth, Dr Michael Lüders; Dir of the DOI Dr Gunter Mulack.

Address: Kronenstr. 1, 10117 Berlin.

Telephone: (30) 2064100; **Fax:** (30) 20641010; **Internet:** www.deutsche-orient-stiftung.de; **e-mail:** doi@deutsches-orient-institut.de.

Deutsche Stiftung für Internationale Rechtliche Zusammenarbeit eV (German Foundation for International Legal Co-operation)

Established in 1992 as a non-profit-making association at the initiative of the then Federal Minister of Justice Dr Klaus Kinkel. In the early years, the work of the Foundation was largely promoted within the framework of the TRANSFORM consultation programme, and after this additionally by the Stability Pact for South-Eastern Europe, and primarily from the budget of the Federal Ministry of Justice.

Activities: Supports partner states on behalf or the German Federal Government in reforming their legal systems and judiciary. In providing legislative consultation, the Foundation undertakes discussions with experts, draft expert reports and assists in drawing up draft bills; promotes the implementation of reform statutes, in particular through basic and further training of judges, public prosecutors, attorneys, notaries, academics and young lawyers, including within the framework of the European Union (EU)'s IPA and ENPI programmes; arranges seminars, workshops, lecture events and symposia in the partner states, as well as working visits, training periods and guest visits, primarily to Germany but also to other EU states; focus on German and European law, supplemented by a cross-border exchange of experience.

Geographical Area of Activity: Bulgaria, the Czech Republic, Hungary, Poland, Romania and the Slovak Republic, the countries of the former USSR (Azerbaijan, Belarus, Estonia, Georgia, Latvia, Lithuania, the Russian Federation, Ukraine), and the partner states of the Stability Pact for South-Eastern Europe (Albania, Bosnia and Herzegovina, Croatia, Kosovo, the former Yugoslav republic of Macedonia, Moldova, Montenegro, Serbia). Also carries out projects with Algeria, Iraq, Jordan, Lebanon, Saudi Arabia, Syria, Turkey, Tunisia, Uzbekistan, Kazakhstan and Viet Nam, as well as with states in Latin America.

Restrictions: No unsolicited applications for grants are accepted.

Publications: Annual Report; *WiRO - Wirtschaft und Recht in Osteuropa* (monthly).

Finance: Funded by the German Federal Government and the EU.

Board of Trustees: Dr Jörg Freiherr Frank von Fürstenwerth (Chair.); Dr Bernhard Dombek, Christian Lange (Vice-Chair.).

Principal Staff: Dir Dirk Mirow; Deputy Dir Dr Stefan Hülshörster.

Address: POB 200409, 53134 Bonn; Ubierstr. 92, 53173 Bonn.

Telephone: (228) 9555-0; **Fax:** (228) 9555-100; **Internet:** www.irz.de; **e-mail:** info@irz.de.

Deutsche Stiftung Weltbevölkerung—DSW (German Foundation for World Population)

Established in 1991 by Dirk Rossmann and Erhard Schreiber, a development co-operation organization working at international level, focusing on demographic development and reproductive health.

Activities: Promotes development, especially in the areas of family planning, prevention of HIV and AIDS, and population studies in Ethiopia, Kenya and Uganda. The Foundation carries out development projects with local non-profit organizations, carries out information and advocacy campaigns in Germany and Europe, and awards a limited number of fellowships. It has country offices in Ethiopia, Kenya, Tanzania and Uganda and a Liaison Office in Brussels.

Geographical Area of Activity: Ethiopia, Kenya, Tanzania, Uganda.

Publications: Annual Report; *DSW Update* (monthly); *The Guide to European Population Assistance*; *Tips and Tricks: How to Apply for the European Commission's Budget Lines for Sustainable Development;* reports; fact sheets; newsletters; statistical reports; posters.

Finance: Total assets €7,854,996 (31 Dec 2013).

Board of Trustees: Elmar Bingel (Chair.).

Principal Staff: Exec. Dir Renate Bähr.

Address: Göttinger Chaussee 115, 30459 Hanover.

Telephone: (511) 943730; **Fax:** (511) 9437373; **Internet:** www.weltbevoelkerung.de; **e-mail:** hannover@dsw.org.

Deutsche Telekom Stiftung (Deutsche Telekom Foundation)

Established in 1993 to further education in science and technology in Germany.

Activities: Operates in Germany in the field of education, specifically in the areas of natural science, technology and mathematics, through funding projects in all sectors of education, including pre-schools, primary and secondary schools, and universities. Also offers prizes for innovation in new technology.

Geographical Area of Activity: Germany.

Restrictions: Does not accept unsolicited applications for grants.

Finance: Annual income €12,898,635, expenditure €8,991,430 (31 Dec. 2013).

Board of Trustees: Timothy Höttges (Chair.); Dr Hans-Jürgen Schinzler (Deputy Chair.).

Principal Staff: Chair. Prof. Dr Wolfgang Schuster; Dir Dr Ekkehard Winter.

Address: POB 2000, 53105 Bonn; Grauerheindorfer Str. 153, 53117 Bonn.

Telephone: (228) 18192001; **Internet:** www.telekom-stiftung.de; **e-mail:** stiftung@telekom.de.

Deutscher Akademischer Austauschdienst—DAAD (German Academic Exchange Service)

Founded in 1925 (re-established in 1950), the DAAD is a joint organization of institutions of higher education that aims to promote academic exchanges between Germany and other countries.

Activities: Awards long- and short-term scholarships in all fields of study to foreign students and young research workers, including 'sur place' scholarships tenable at some universities in developing countries, and to students from European countries for university summer vacation and language courses. The Service has bilateral agreements with German and foreign institutions and promotes student exchange in connection with specific research projects. It supports a programme of exchanges of university teachers for short-term teaching and research visits on a reciprocal basis.

Geographical Area of Activity: International.

Publications: Annual Report; newsletter.

Finance: Annual income €410,295,840, expenditure €387,076,275 (2013).

Board of Trustees: Prof. Dr Margret Wintermantel (Chair.); Prof. Dr Joybrato Mukherjee (Vice-Chair.).

Principal Staff: Chair. Prof. Dr Margret Wintermantel; Vice-Chair. Prof. Dr Joybrato Mukherjee; Sec.-Gen. Dr Dorothea Rüland.

Address: POB 200404, 53134 Bonn; Kennedyallee 50, 53175 Bonn.

Telephone: (228) 882-0; **Fax:** (228) 882-444; **Internet:** www.daad.de; **e-mail:** postmaster@daad.de.

Deutsches Institut für Internationale Pädagogische Forschung (German Institute for International Educational Research)

Incorporated in 1951 as a foundation under public law to support international and intercultural comparative and historical educational research as well as educational planning.

Activities: Consists of five units, focusing on two themes: educational information and history of education, and the quality of education. The Educational Information Centre comprises the office of the German Educational Server, the Information System for Education, Information and Documentation, and the Frankfurt Research Library, including the Frankfurt Teacher Library. The Centre for History of Education incorporates the Bibliothek für Bildungsgeschichtliche Forschung (Library for Research on Educational History) in Berlin and the Research Office, Berlin. Other units are the Centre for Educational Quality and Evaluation, the Centre for Financing and Planning in Education, and the Centre for Education and Culture. The Institute also collaborates with universities and educational research institutes in Germany and abroad.

Geographical Area of Activity: Germany.

Restrictions: Applications for grants are not accepted.

Publications: *DIPF informiert* (2 a year); Biennial Report.

Board of Trustees: Dr E. Jürgen Zöllner (Chair.); Anja Steinhofer-Adam (Vice.-Chair.).

Principal Staff: Exec. Dir Dr Marcus Hasselhorn; Deputy Exec. Dir Prof. Dr Marc Rittberger; Man Dir Susanne Boomkamp-Dahmen.

Address: Schlossstr. 29, 60486 Frankfurt am Main.

Telephone: (69) 24708-0; **Fax:** (69) 24708-444; **Internet:** www.dipf.de; **e-mail:** onlineredaktion@dipf.de.

Deutsches Rheuma-Forschungszentrum Berlin (German Rheumatism Research Centre Berlin)

Founded in 1988 by the City of Berlin and Immanuel Hospital to promote research into rheumatic diseases.

Activities: Operates in the fields of medicine and health, and science and technology, nationally and internationally through self-conducted programmes and research, and internationally through conferences, training courses and publications.

Geographical Area of Activity: Mainly Germany.

Publications: Annual scientific report.

Finance: Financed by the City of Berlin and other sources; annual expenditure approx. €3m.

Board of Trustees: Traudl Herrhausen (Chair.).

Principal Staff: Scientific Dir Prof. Dr Andreas Radbruch; Deputy Scientific Dir Prof. Dr Angela Zink; Business Dir Petra Starke.

Address: Charitéplatz 1, 10117 Berlin.

Telephone: (30) 28460-0; **Fax:** (30) 28460-111; **Internet:** www.drfz.de; **e-mail:** info@drfz.de.

Dräger-Stiftung (Dräger Foundation)

Established in 1974 by Dr Heinrich Dräger as a non-profit foundation for the promotion of science and research in the fields of economic and social order.

Activities: Operates nationally and internationally in the fields of economic and social affairs, international affairs, and medicine and health, through self-conducted programmes, conferences and publications; national (regional) activities in the areas of conservation and the environment.

Geographical Area of Activity: Europe and USA.

Restrictions: No grants are made to individuals; no postgraduate scholarships.

Publications: *Edition 'Zukunft', Series* (Vols 1–17, 1980–2001); *Conference Documentations Malente Symposia* (2001–2008).

Finance: Total assets approx. €6.1m.

Principal Staff: Dirs Stefan Dräger, Claudia Dräger.

Address: Moislinger Allee 53–55, 23558 Lübeck.

Telephone: (451) 8822151; **Fax:** (451) 8823050; **Internet:** www
.draeger-stiftung.de; **e-mail:** draeger-stiftung@draeger.com.

Friedrich-Ebert-Stiftung eV (Friedrich Ebert Foundation)

Founded in 1925 as a political legacy of Friedrich Ebert, the
first President of the Weimar Republic, and re-established
after the Second World War, to further the democratic education of the German people, and international co-operation
towards democracy.

Activities: Operates internationally through developing its
own projects in the field of aid to less-developed countries,
and nationally and internationally in the fields of education,
the arts and humanities, social welfare and studies, economic
affairs and international relations, through self-conducted
programmes, research, fellowships, scholarships, conferences,
courses, publications and lectures. The Foundation has offices
in Bonn and Berlin, four academies and 13 regional offices in
Germany, as well as maintaining its own representations in 70
countries of Africa, Asia, the Middle East, and Central and
South America, and offices in 33 countries of Western Europe,
Central and South-Eastern Europe, the CIS countries and the
USA and Japan. It maintains a specialized library of approximately 700,000 volumes on the German and international
labour movement, the archive of social democracy, which is
the largest collection of documents on the history of the labour
movement in Germany.

Geographical Area of Activity: Africa, Asia, CIS countries,
Central and South-Eastern Europe, Central and South America, Japan, Middle East, USA, Western Europe.

Restrictions: Does not provide financial assistance of any
sort.

Publications: Annual Report; publications on economic policy, labour and social research, technology and society, social
and contemporary history, and foreign policy research (nearly
600 titles a year in German, in addition to approx. 500 worldwide); political reviews: *Neue Gesellschaft/Frankfurter Hefte*;
International Politics and Society, Nueva Sociedad.

Finance: Annual income €152,577,657, expenditure
€132,063,660 (31 Dec. 2012).

Board of Trustees: Ingrid Matthäus-Maier (Chair.).

Principal Staff: Chair. Kurt Beck; Vice-Chair. Hannelore
Kraft, Michael Sommer; Exec. Dir Dr Roland Schmidt.

Address: Godesberger Allee 149, 53175 Bonn.

Telephone: (228) 883-0; **Fax:** (228) 833-9207; **Internet:** www
.fes.de; **e-mail:** presse@fes.de.

Erinnerung, Verantwortung und Zukunft (Remembrance, Responsibility and the Future)

Established in 2000 by an Act of the German Federal Government and German companies to mark their historical and
moral responsibility for the forced labour perpetrated under
the National Socialist regime, particularly during the Second
World War, through assisting former forced labourers and
other victims of the Nazis, and keeping alive the memories of
the Holocaust to prevent a resurgence of a totalitarian system.
More than 6,500 German companies had contributed to the
fund by the end of 2001.

Activities: Operates through partner organizations in countries of Western, Central and Eastern Europe, Israel and the
USA to make payments to former forced labourers who were
detained in a concentration camp or ghetto and were subjected
to forced labour, or who were deported from their native country to the German Reich or countries occupied by the German
Reich (apart from Austria) and who were subjected to forced
labour and harsh living conditions. Those affected by other
injustices from the period (e.g. personal injury or loss of property) may also apply for compensation. A Remembrance and
Future Fund fosters international understanding, social justice, remembrance and future-orientated projects, and promotes projects in the interest of the heirs of those who did not
survive the National Socialist regime. Grants are currently
directed primarily to projects in the interests of the victims

and their heirs, as well as work with witnesses. Future grant
programmes will focus on projects that promote youth
exchange, reconciliation, international understanding,
respect of human rights and social justice.

Geographical Area of Activity: International.

Restrictions: No funding for institutions.

Finance: The capital fund is financed by German companies
(the Foundation Initiative of German Industry) and the German Federal Government; initial capital approx. €5,200m.
The Remembrance and the Future Fund had an initial endowment of approx. €350m. Total assets €458m. (31 Dec. 2013);
annual income €6.83m. (2013).

Board of Trustees: Dr. Jörg Freiherr Frank von Fürstenwerth (Chair.).

Principal Staff: Chair. Dr Michael Jansen; Vice-Chair.
Günter Saathoff.

Address: Lindenstr. 20–25, 10969 Berlin.

Telephone: (30) 259297-0; **Fax:** (30) 259297-11; **Internet:** www
.stiftung-evz.de; **e-mail:** info@stiftung-evz.de.

EuroNatur

Established in 1987 as the Stiftung Europäisches Naturerbe by
German environmental organizations for nature and environmental protection.

Activities: Operates in Europe in the fields of conservation
and the environment and environmental policies on an international level, through self-conducted programmes, grants to
NGOs and other institutions, conferences, training courses
and issuing publications. Awards the 'EuroNatur Environmental Award' (unendowed) and 'European Stork Village' prize.

Geographical Area of Activity: Europe.

Restrictions: Grants only for measures supporting self-conducted programmes.

Publications: *Euronatur* (quarterly journal); newsletter
(bimonthly); papers on scientific and environmental issues.

Finance: Total assets €4,583,000; annual expenditure
€2,791,000 (2013).

Board: Christel Schroeder (Chair.); Prof. Dr Sven Olaf Hoffmann (Vice-Chair.).

Principal Staff: Exec. Dir Gabriel Schwaderer.

Address: Konstanzerstr. 22, 78315 Radolfzell.

Telephone: (7732) 92720; **Fax:** (7732) 927222; **Internet:** www
.euronatur.org; **e-mail:** info@euronatur.org.

Europäische Rechtsakademie—ERA (Academy of European Law)

Established in 1992 on the initiative of the European Parliament by the governments of Luxembourg and the Rhineland-
Palatinate, the City of Trier and the Association for the Promotion of the Academy.

Activities: Provides legal training and a forum for debate for
lawyers throughout Europe. Activities include the organization of conferences, seminars, language courses, e-learning
courses and the implementation of legal training projects, as
well as publishing activities and the rental of congress facilities. The Academy runs a scholarship programme to enable
lawyers from new and future European Union member states
to attend its training courses in Trier.

Geographical Area of Activity: Austria, Bulgaria, Croatia,
Cyprus, the Czech Republic, Finland, France, Germany,
Greece, Hungary, Ireland, Italy, Luxembourg, Malta, the Neth-
erlands, Poland, Portugal, Romania, Slovakia, Slovenia,
Spain, Sweden, the United Kingdom.

Restrictions: Unsolicited applications for grants outside the
framework of the Peter Caesar Scholarship Programme are
not accepted.

Publications: Annual Report; *ERA Forum* (quarterly review
of European law, published in co-operation with Springer);
books.

Finance: Annual income €8.1m., expenditure €8.0m. (2013).

Board of Trustees: Dr Pauliine Koskelo (Chair.); Prof. Josef Azizi, Dr Péter Köves (Deputy Chair.).

Principal Staff: Chair. Pavel Svoboda; Dir Wolfgang Heusel.

Address: Metzer Allee 4, 54295 Trier.

Telephone: (651) 937370; **Fax:** (651) 93737773; **Internet:** www .era.int; **e-mail:** info@era.int.

European Youth For Action—EYFA

Founded in 1986 as an activist network to encourage young people to work towards the prevention of environmental pollution and the decimation of forests.

Activities: Works in Europe in the fields of conservation and the environment, through promoting sustainable ways of living and working, non-violent campaigns against ecologically and socially unsustainable systems, cultural activism and alternative media. The organization helps other groups with their fund-raising, as well as providing financial services, including bookkeeping assistance and the legal status to receive funds on behalf of other organizations. It focuses particularly on youth-initiated activities and projects; and organizes training and workshops on campaigning and social change. Has partner organizations in 18 European countries.

Geographical Area of Activity: Europe.

Publications: *Green Pepper;* newsletter; online resources and toolkits.

Finance: Receives funding from various organizations, including the European Union.

Principal Staff: Rep. Shannon Stephens.

Address: New Yorck im Bethanien, Mariannenplatz 2A, 10997 Berlin.

Telephone: (0) 3061740102; **Fax:** (0) 15210105373; **Internet:** www.eyfa.org; **e-mail:** eyfa@eyfa.org.

Evangelisches Studienwerk eV (Protestant Study Foundation)

Founded in 1948 by several Protestant Churches to bring together and promote Protestant students of any faculty; to provide for their advanced training and to give advice, also beyond the limits of their studies, regarding their evangelical responsibilities in their profession, community and society. The organization is now supported by all Protestant Churches in Germany.

Activities: Operates nationally in the fields of religion, education and research, social welfare and studies, economic affairs, science and medicine, the arts and humanities, law and other professions, through self-conducted programmes, grants to individuals, fellowships, scholarships, seminars, conferences, courses and advisory services. Support is given to German Protestant university students and graduates in Germany and in other European Union countries.

Geographical Area of Activity: Europe.

Publications: *Villigst Profile; Oriens Christianus: History and Presence of Middle East Christianity; Individuality in Russia and Germany; The Uneasiness in the 'Third generation': Reflections of the Holocaust, Antisemitism and National Socialism; Challenge Development: Newer contributions for theoretical and practice-oriented development research.*

Board of Directors: Bishop Dr Johannes Friedrich (Chair.).

Principal Staff: CEO Albert Henz.

Address: Iserlohner Str. 25, 58239 Schwerte.

Telephone: (2304) 755196; **Fax:** (2304) 755250; **Internet:** www .evstudienwerk.de; **e-mail:** info@evstudienwerk.de.

filia.die frauenstiftung (filia—the Women's Foundation)

Established in 2001 to promote women playing a decisive role in all areas of society.

Activities: Works on behalf of women who are discriminated against, not only because of their gender, but also because of the colour of their skin, their origins or sexual orientation. The Foundation provides grants to women's NGOs, community and grassroots organizations in Central and Eastern Europe (50% of budget), Germany (20%), the Global South (20%) and for rapid response (10%). Grants are dedicated to projects in the focal areas of participation and freedom from violence for women and girls.

Geographical Area of Activity: Central and Eastern Europe, Germany and the Global South.

Restrictions: Does not accept unsolicited applications from Central Eastern Europe and the Global South; does not fund individuals; does not award scholarships.

Publications: Annual Report; *filianews* (e-newsletter).

Finance: Total grants disbursed €157,000 (2014).

Principal Staff: Exec. Dir Sonja Schelper.

Address: Alte Königstr. 18, 22767 Hamburg.

Telephone: (40) 38038199-0; **Fax:** (40) 380381999; **Internet:** www.filia-frauenstiftung.de; **e-mail:** info@filia -frauenstiftung.de.

F. C. Flick-Stiftung gegen Fremdenfeindlichkeit, Rassismus und Intoleranz (F. C. Flick Foundation against Xenophobia, Racism and Intolerance)

Established in 2001 by Dr Friedrich Christian Flick to fight against xenophobia, intolerance and racism and to encourage international open-mindedness.

Activities: Supports projects that focus on developing ways of combating xenophobia, racism and intolerance, in the focus areas of culture, sport and young people, aged between five and 15 years. The Foundation focuses on work with children and young people in the eastern states of Germany, supporting existing projects, youth exchanges with Eastern Europe, assisting initiatives linking artistic ideas with political and contemporary enlightenment and promoting sport projects. Long-term projects include the German-Polish student exchange programme, Kopernikus; the Lindenstrasse Workshop for Youth in Potsdam; and the Rosa Luxemburg Elementary School in Potsdam.

Geographical Area of Activity: Germany.

Publications: Annual Report; funding guidelines.

Board of Trustees: Dr Friedrich Christian Flick (Chair.).

Principal Staff: Exec. Dir Susanne Krause-Hinrichs.

Address: Am Neuen Markt 8, 14467 Potsdam.

Telephone: (331) 2007770; **Fax:** (331) 2007771; **Internet:** www .stiftung-toleranz.de; **e-mail:** info@stiftung-toleranz.de.

Forschungsgesellschaft für das Weltflüchtlingsproblem—AWR (Association for the Study of the World Refugee Problem)

Founded in 1951 to promote, examine and co-ordinate the scientific study of refugee problems to give competent organs throughout the world the scientific basis to solve these problems; in 1961, it merged with the European Association for the Study of Refugee Problems.

Activities: Operates internationally as an independent association in which scholars from all fields of knowledge co-operate with experts from national and international organizations to investigate refugee problems and provide theoretical bases of possible solutions. The field of study has also been extended to the problems of migrant workers. The Association is a consultative body of the UN and the Council of Europe. National sections exist in most Western European countries, connected by the International General Assembly; there are observers in many other countries. The scientific investigations are carried out by international committees of experts, each dealing with a particular aspect such as population and health, international refugees, cultural questions, legal questions, sociology, economic integration, housing and employment. Their findings are co-ordinated by the International Curatorium. The results of the Association's comparative research work are communicated to specialists from countries with refugee problems and, often with recommendations, to governments and the appropriate organizations. Congresses are held annually; there are members in 21 countries.

Geographical Area of Activity: International.

Publications: *AWR-Bulletin* (quarterly); reports are published regularly in four languages.

Board of Trustees: Prof. Dr Andrzej Sakson (Chair.); Prof. Dr Peter Van Krieken, Lê Quyên Ngô Đính (Vice-Chair.); Prof. Dr Sibylle Wollenschläger (Treas.).

Principal Staff: Sec.-Gen. Prof. Dr Markus Babo.

Address: POB 1241, 97201 Höchberg.

Telephone: (931) 3511486; **Internet:** www.awr-int.de; **e-mail:** sibylle.wollenschlaeger@fhws.de.

Frankfurter Stiftung für Deutsch-Italienische Studien (Frankfurt Foundation for German-Italian Studies)

Established in 1992 by the Deutsch-Italienische Vereinigung eV for the promotion of international understanding through the cultivation of academic, cultural and human relations between Germany and Italy.

Activities: Operates in the fields of the arts and humanities and education, nationally and internationally through self-conducted programmes and publications and funding of other publications, and nationally through conferences.

Geographical Area of Activity: Europe.

Publications: *Italienisch* (magazine of Italian language and literature).

Board of Directors: Dietrich Herbst (Hon. Chair.); Salvatore A. Sanna (Chair.); Konrad von Bethman (Vice-Chair.).

Address: Arndtstr. 12, 60325 Frankfurt am Main.

Telephone: (69) 746752; **Fax:** (69) 7411453; **Internet:** www.div-web.de; **e-mail:** stiftung@div-web.de.

Freudenberg Stiftung (Freudenberg Foundation)

Founded in 1984 to support the cause of peace and helping the needy.

Activities: Operates nationally, principally in the fields of education and social welfare, which are promoted through self-conducted programmes, grants to institutions, training courses and prizes. The Foundation also supports young people at risk, the mentally-challenged, and cultural minorities, favouring social, economic or cultural projects that help surmount disadvantage and exclusion, and strengthen democracy. It functions at grassroots level; allows inter-organizational co-operation and promotes self-help, as well as managing other foundations.

Geographical Area of Activity: Germany.

Restrictions: No grants are made to individuals, for scholarships, research or construction.

Publications: Reports.

Finance: Returns on company capital are used to advance science, education and humanities, and to promote peace.

Board of Trustees: Dr Dorothee Freudenberg (Chair.).

Principal Staff: Exec. Dirs Dr Pia Gerber, Sascha Wenzel.

Address: Freudenbergstr. 2, 69469 Weinheim.

Telephone: (6201) 49944330; **Fax:** (6201) 49944350; **Internet:** www.freudenbergstiftung.de; **e-mail:** info@freudenbergstiftung.de.

Friedensdorf International (Peace Village International)

Established in 1967 as a citizens' initiative to provide assistance to children in areas of war and crisis and to campaign for peace.

Activities: Operates worldwide in the areas of medicine, health and social welfare. Children are brought to Europe for short-term medical care and rehabilitation, although projects for the improvement of medical care have also been established in the native countries of the children, and where possible children are treated there. The organization also promotes peace and carries out educational work, including the Peace Village Bildungswerk educational centre, which promotes peace.

Geographical Area of Activity: International.

Publications: *Peace Village Report* (2 a year).

Finance: Annual income €6,957,308, expenditure €7,105,282 (31 Dec. 2013).

Board of Directors: Dr Susanne Grünewald (Chair.); Stefan Hennig (Deputy Chair.); Klaus Wieprecht (Treas.); Annegret Hübbers-Brechtmann (Sec.).

Principal Staff: Dir Thomas Jacobs; Deputy Dirs Kevin Dahlbruch, Wolfgang Mertens.

Address: POB Postfach 140162, 46131 Oberhausen; Lanterstr. 21, 46539 Dinslaken.

Telephone: (2064) 4974; **Fax:** (2064) 4974; **Internet:** www.friedensdorf.de; **e-mail:** info@friedensdorf.de.

Gemeinnützige Hertie-Stiftung (Hertie Foundation)

Established in 1974 by Georg Karg as a charity for the promotion of science and education.

Activities: Operates in the fields of pre-school and school, higher education, neurosciences as well as the compatibility of job and family. The Foundation supports democracy training, acquisition of new knowledge about neuroscience, European integration, and work-family balance.

Geographical Area of Activity: Germany and the rest of Europe.

Restrictions: Preference is given to projects that are innovative, with a broad span of application.

Finance: Annual income €33,934,000, expenditure €23,800,000 (31 Dec. 2013).

Board of Directors: Dr Frank-J. Weise (Chair.); Bernd Knobloch (Vice-Chair.).

Principal Staff: Man. Dir John-Philip Hammersen.

Address: Grüneburgweg 105, 60323 Frankfurt am Main.

Telephone: (69) 6607560; **Fax:** (69) 660756999; **Internet:** www.ghst.de; **e-mail:** info@ghst.de.

GIGA—German Institute of Global and Area Studies (Leibniz-Institut für Globale und Regionale Studien)

Founded in 1964 for research and documentation on political, economic and social developments in overseas countries, especially in the countries of Africa, Asia, Latin America and the Middle East. Known as the Deutsches Übersee-Institut until 2005.

Activities: Examines the issues and challenges facing Africa, Asia, Latin America and the Middle East and also new developments in North–South and South–South relationships. The Institute supports the advancement of junior researchers; provides consultation services to media, the Government and civil-society organizations; and makes information available to the public through its Information Centre.

Restrictions: Applications for grants are not accepted.

Publications: Publishes four academic open access journals: *Africa Spectrum, Journal of Current Chinese Affairs, Journal of Politics in Latin America, Journal of Current Southeast Asian Affairs* (all available online); GIGA Working Papers; *GIGA Focus.*

Finance: Annual revenue €10,600,546, expenditure €10,600,546 (31 Dec. 2013).

Board of Trustees: Dr Horst-Michael Pelikahn (Chair.); Katrin aus dem Siepen (Vice-Chair.).

Principal Staff: Pres. Prof. Dr Amrita Narlikar; Vice-Pres. Prof. Dr Detlef Nolte.

Address: Neuer Jungfernstieg 21, 20354 Hamburg.

Telephone: (40) 42825593; **Fax:** (40) 42825547; **Internet:** www.giga-hamburg.de; **e-mail:** info@giga-hamburg.de.

Goethe-Institut Inter Nationes

Founded in 1951 to promote the German language abroad and foster international cultural relations.

Activities: Operates internationally in the fields of the arts and humanities, international relations, language teaching and information brokerage, through self-conducted programmes, partnership programmes, grants to institutions and individuals, fellowships, scholarships, conferences, courses, publications and lectures. The Institute is particularly concerned with the teaching and promotion of the German language abroad and provides professional assistance to foreign teachers of German and students of German philology, and for the development and improvement of teaching methods and materials. It also provides information abroad about the cultural life of Germany and co-operates with cultural organizations abroad. Has 16 branches in Germany and 126 abroad in 77 countries.

Geographical Area of Activity: Worldwide.

Publications: Annual Report; *Goethe Institut Aktuell*; *Markt; Legal Principles*; newsletters; and other publications.

Finance: Annual income €351,001,000 expenditure €350,496,000 (2013).

Board of Trustees: Prof. Dr Klaus-Dieter Lehmann (Chair.).

Principal Staff: Sec.-Gen. Johannes Ebert; Business Dir Bruno Gross.

Address: Dachauerstr. 122, 80637 Munich.

Telephone: (89) 159210; **Fax:** (89) 15921450; **Internet:** www .goethe.de; **e-mail:** info@goethe.de.

Haniel-Stiftung (Haniel Foundation)

Founded in 1988 by Franz Haniel & Cie GmbH to encourage the European business community to support humanitarian causes, to promote the image of business in educational establishments, and to further the development of management techniques and training.

Activities: Promotes achievement and making entrepreneurial decisions in a socially responsible manner. The Foundation strengthens entrepreneurs' commitment to public welfare; promotes the entrepreneurial image in society; and supports the training and further education of young leaders on nationally and internationally.

Geographical Area of Activity: International, especially Europe.

Publications: Project and conference reports; Annual reports; *Stippvisite*.

Finance: Net assets €45m.; annual grant expenditure approx. €2m. (2014).

Board of Trustees: Franz M. Haniel (Chair.); Christoph Böninger (Deputy Chair.).

Principal Staff: Exec. Dir Dr Rupert Antes.

Address: Franz-Haniel-Platz 1, 47119 Duisburg.

Telephone: (203) 806367/368; **Fax:** (203) 806720; **Internet:** www.haniel-stiftung.de; **e-mail:** stiftung@haniel.de.

H. W. und J. Hector-Stiftung (H. W. and J. Hector Foundation)

Established in 1995 by Hans-Werner Hector.

Activities: Promotes medical research, especially in the areas of cancer and AIDS, as well as art and historical preservation.

Geographical Area of Activity: Europe.

Finance: Annual expenditure approx. €1m.

Board of Trustees: Hans-Werner Hector (Chair.).

Principal Staff: Contact Dr Ernstlothar Keiper.

Address: Elisabethstr. 9, 68165 Mannheim.

Telephone: (621) 410980; **Fax:** (621) 4109858; **Internet:** www .hector-stiftung.de; **e-mail:** info@hector-stiftung.de.

Minna-James-Heineman-Stiftung (Minna James Heineman Foundation)

Founded in 1928 (to provide care for elderly Jewish women in Hanover) and re-established in 1951 by Dannie N. Heineman for the promotion of scientific research, education and international co-operation; and for the support of charitable institutions. The Foundation is administered by the Stifterverband für die Deutsche Wissenschaft (q.v.).

Activities: Makes grants to scientific institutions in Germany, the USA and Israel, in particular the Max-Planck-Gesellschaft (q.v.), the Weizmann Institute of Science (Israel) and the Heineman Medical Research Centre (USA), preferably for research in the life sciences. The Dannie Heineman Award, worth €30,000, is conferred biennially by the Academy of Sciences at Göttingen for an outstanding work, mainly in the field of natural and life sciences. Dannie Heineman scholarships are awarded to students and doctoral students. The Foundation also presents the James Heineman Research Award, worth €60,000.

Geographical Area of Activity: Germany, Israel and the USA.

Publications: *People Can No Longer Escape People.*

Finance: Assets approx. €5m.

Board of Directors: Anders Bergendahl (Chair.); Dr Lorenz C. Stech (Sec.); Dr Agnes Gautier (Treas.).

Principal Staff: Gen. Man. Rainer Lüdtke.

Address: c/o Deutsches Stiftungszentrum (DSZ), Barkhovenallee 1, 45239 Essen.

Telephone: (201) 8401154; **Fax:** (201) 8401255; **Internet:** www .heinemanstiftung.org; **e-mail:** matthias.germeroth@ stifterverband.de.

Gerda Henkel Stiftung (Gerda Henkel Foundation)

Founded in 1976 by Lisa Maskell in memory of her mother Gerda Henkel as a private, non-profit, grantmaking organization dedicated to foster research in the humanities.

Activities: Focuses on the support of academic projects and PhD fellowships, primarily in the fields of history, art history, archaeology and history of Islam. The Foundation supports research projects by national and international scholars as well as academic conferences on clearly defined, humanities-based topics; awards research and doctoral scholarships to national and international scholars; supporting measures in the field of historic preservation based on scholarly grounds; undertakes and supports all measures that serve the purposes of the Foundation; and implements measures to raise public awareness of the above-mentioned objectives. It focuses particularly on the advancement of young scholars. When awarding scholarships, special consideration is given to research projects that provide young scholars with the opportunity to be involved in research and to improve their professional qualifications.

Geographical Area of Activity: International.

Restrictions: Only supports research projects with a clearly defined scope and time frame. Priority is given to research projects that are outstanding because of the nature of their results and which promise to make the greatest use of the funds available.

Publications: Annual Report; lecture series.

Finance: Total assets €168,074,341 (31 Dec. 2014).

Board of Trustees: Julia Schulz-Dornburg (Chair.); Prof. Dr Hans-Joachim Gehrke (Vice-Chair.).

Principal Staff: Chair. Dr Michael Hanssler.

Address: Malkastenstr. 15, 40211 Düsseldorf.

Telephone: (211) 9365240; **Fax:** (211) 93652444; **Internet:** www.gerda-henkel-stiftung.de; **e-mail:** info@gerda-henkel -stiftung.de.

Hirschfeld-Eddy-Stiftung (Hirschfeld-Eddy Foundation)

Established in 2007 to uphold the rights of homosexual, bisexual and transgender people worldwide.

Activities: Encourages respect for the human rights of homosexual, bisexual and transgender people, actively supporting human rights defenders and working to remove prejudice.

Geographical Area of Activity: Worldwide.

Foundation Council: Günter Dworek (Chair.); Dr Christian Peters (Vice-Chair.).

Principal Staff: Treas. Uta Kehr.

Address: Postfach 040165, 10061 Berlin; Almstadtstr. 7, 10119 Berlin.

Telephone: (30) 78954778; **Fax:** (30) 78954779; **Internet:** www.hirschfeld-eddy-stiftung.de; **e-mail:** info@hirschfeld-eddy-stiftung.de.

Dietmar-Hopp-Stiftung (Dietmar Hopp Foundation)

Established in 1995 by Dietmar Hopp, a founder member of the computer software company SAP AG.

Activities: Operates nationally and internationally in the fields of sport, education, social affairs and medical research. The Foundation makes grants to to charities working in these areas.

Geographical Area of Activity: Mainly the metropolitan Rhein-Neckar region.

Finance: The Foundation holds more than 15% of SAP AG shares. Since 1995, the Foundation has disbursed more than €410m.

Principal Staff: CEO Dietmar Hopp.

Address: Raiffeisenstr. 51, 68789 St Leon-Rot.

Telephone: (6227) 8608560; **Fax:** (6227) 8608591; **Internet:** www.dietmar-hopp-stiftung.de; **e-mail:** info@dietmar-hopp-stiftung.de.

Alexander von Humboldt Stiftung (Alexander von Humboldt Foundation)

Established in 1860 as a private foundation in memory of the naturalist Alexander von Humboldt, and re-established as a public foundation under private law in 1925 and again in 1953.

Activities: Promotes academic co-operation between scientists and scholars from abroad and from Germany. The Foundation maintains a network of more than 23,000 Humboldtians from all disciplines in more than 130 countries worldwide, including Nobel Prize winners. Annually awards more than 800 research fellowships and awards for scientists and scholars from abroad to work on a research project with a host and collaborative partner in Germany. Scientists and scholars from Germany can carry out a research project abroad as a guest of one of the alumni of the foundation. Programmes include the Humboldt Research Fellowship (for postdoctoral and experienced researchers); the Georg Forster Research Fellowship (for postdoctoral and experienced researchers from developing countries); the Feodor Lynen Research Fellowship (for postdoctoral and experienced researchers in Germany going abroad); the Humboldt Research Award (for foreign researchers at the peak of their academic career); the Alexander von Humboldt Professorship (for internationally recognized cutting-edge researchers); the Sofja Kovalevskaja Award (for outstanding junior researchers); and the Friedrich Wilhelm Bessel Research Award (for internationally renowned scientists and scholars).

Geographical Area of Activity: Worldwide.

Publications: Annual Report; newsletter; *Bibliographia Humboldtiana* (online); *Humboldt Kosmos* (magazine); *Profile and Services* (brochure); *Alexander von Humboldt Professorship* (brochure); *EURAXESS Germany—National Co-ordination Point at the Alexander von Humboldt Foundation* (flyer).

Finance: Annual expenditure €110,472,600 (2014).

Board of Trustees: Prof. Dr Helmut Schwarz (Pres.); Prof. Dr Peter Strohschneider (Vice-Pres.).

Principal Staff: Sec.-Gen. Dr Enno Aufderheide; Deputy Sec.-Gen. Thomas Hesse.

Address: Jean-Paul-Str. 12, 53173 Bonn.

Telephone: (228) 833-0; **Fax:** (228) 833-199; **Internet:** www.avh.de; www.humboldt-foundation.de; **e-mail:** info@avh.de.

Indienhilfe eV (India Assistance)

Established in 1980.

Activities: Operates in the areas of sustainable agriculture, environment, health, women's self-help groups, education (formal and informal), promotion of fair trade, education for sustainability and intercultural dialogue between Bengal and Bavaria (school partnerships, town twinning between Chatra near Kolkata and Herrsching near Munich). The organization offers financial assistance to Indian partner NGOs for projects aimed at improving the situation of children (access to education, reduction of infant mortality, proper nutrition, protection from exploitation and abuse, and combating child labour in hazardous jobs).

Geographical Area of Activity: West Bengal, India.

Restrictions: Operates in co-operation with NGOs and organizations in India with which it already has a partnership.

Publications: Annual Report; brochures; books; magazines.

Finance: Annual revenue €395,011, expenditure €403,865 (31 Dec. 2013).

Board of Directors: Elisabeth Kreuz (Chair.); Dr Dirk Provoost (Sec.); Martha Stumbaum (Treas.).

Address: Luitpoldstr. 20, 82211 Herrsching.

Telephone: (8152) 1231; **Fax:** (8152) 48278; **Internet:** www.indienhilfe-herrsching.de; **e-mail:** info@indienhilfe-herrsching.de.

Initiative und Leistung, Stiftung der Nassauischen Sparkasse für Kultur, Sport und Gesellschaft (Initiative and Achievement, Foundation of the Nassauische Sparkasse for Culture, Sport and Society)

Established in 1989 by the Nassauische Sparkasse savings bank.

Activities: Operates in the areas of culture and the arts, sport, conservation and the environment, health care and the support of young people.

Geographical Area of Activity: Germany.

Publications: Newsletter.

Finance: Total assets €10,621m. (31 Dec. 2013).

Board of Trustees: Sven Greich (Chair.); Achim Schwickert (Vice-Chair.).

Principal Staff: Chair. Stephan Ziegler; Vice-Chair. Burkhard Albers; Man. Dir Jutta Dedio.

Address: Naspa Stiftung 'Initiative und Leistung', Jutta Dedio, Geschäftsführerin, Rheinstr. 42–46, 65185 Wiesbaden.

Telephone: (611) 36406601; **Fax:** (611) 36406609; **Internet:** www.naspa-stiftung.de; **e-mail:** naspa-stiftung@naspa.de.

Institut für Agrarentwicklung in Mittel- und Osteuropa—IAMO (Institute for Agricultural Development in Central and Eastern Europe)

Established in 1994 by the Federal State of Saxony-Anhalt as a public foundation; a non-affiliated research institute to promote knowledge and research in the field of international agricultural development.

Activities: Supports basic and applied research in international agricultural development, especially in the former communist countries of Central and Eastern Europe, with projects in the areas of studying the economic and social implications of changing agricultural processes, providing advice to those involved in changing agricultural systems, and training for new academics; shares research findings through publications, conferences and international co-operation. The Institute maintains a library containing approximately 18,000 publications.

Geographical Area of Activity: Central and Eastern Europe.

Restrictions: Unsolicited applications are not accepted.

Publications: Annual Report; *IAMO Newsletter*; *IAMO Policy Briefs*; *IAMO Discussion Papers*; *IAMO Studies*; *Monographien*; magazines; series of studies.

Board of Trustees: Thomas Reitmann (Chair.); Friedrich Wacker (Vice-Chair.).

Address: Theodor-Lieser-Str. 2, 06120 Halle/Saale.

Telephone: (345) 2928-325; **Fax:** (345) 2928-199; **Internet:** www.iamo.de; **e-mail:** iamo@iamo.de.

INTEGRATA—Stiftung für Humane Nutzung der Informationstechnologie (INTEGRATA Foundation)

Founded in 1999 by Prof. Dr Wolfgang Heilmann.

Activities: Aims to sponsor and implement research, and fund longer-term projects and academic institutions engaged in the pursuit of the humane use of information technology in the fields of work, education, health, art and culture, in particular in working and professional life. The Foundation awards the annual Wolfgang Heilmann-Preis in recognition of work in the social uses of information technology.

Geographical Area of Activity: International.

Publications: Newsletter; *Thesis and Objectives on the Management of Tele-Processes.*

Finance: Initial endowment €1m.

Board of Trustees: Prof. Dr Wolfgang Heilmann (Hon. Chair.); Dr Frank Schönthaler (Chair.); Rolf Pfeiffer (Vice-Chair.).

Address: Vor dem Kreuzberg 28, 72070 Tübingen.

Telephone: (1727) 400482; **Internet:** www.integrata-stiftung .de; **e-mail:** info@integrata-stiftung.de.

International Arctic Science Committee—IASC

Founded in 1990; a membership oganization comprising national science organizations covering all fields of Arctic research.

Activities: Aims to encourage and facilitate co-operation in all aspects of Arctic research, in all countries engaged in Arctic research and in all areas of the Arctic region. Acts as an information and communication forum for the Arctic science community, with 22 member countries. Promotes Arctic research and develops research projects that necessitate international and multi-disciplinary co-operation.

Geographical Area of Activity: Arctic countries.

Publications: *IASC Bulletin; IASC-Progress* (newsletter).

Executive Committee: Susan Barr (Pres.); Huigen Yang, Naja Mikkelsen, Larry Hinzman, Vladimir Pavlenko (Vice-Pres).

Principal Staff: Exec. Sec. Dr Volker Rachold.

Address: Telegrafenberg A43, 14473 Potsdam.

Telephone: (331) 2882214; **Fax:** (331) 2882215; **Internet:** www .iasc.info; **e-mail:** iasc@iasc.info.

International Environmental Foundation of the Kommunale Umwelt-AktioN UAN—IntEF-UAN

Established in 2001 by the Kommunale Umwelt-AktioN UAN.

Activities: Promotes environmental protection activities in Germany and in other European countries, in particular the promotion of international waste-water partnerships.

Geographical Area of Activity: Germany and Europe.

Restrictions: Grants only to communities that take part in international waste-water partnerships.

Publications: Comprehensive manuals; informative materials.

Board of Trustees: Dr Marco Trips (Chair.); Uwe-Peter Lestin (Vice-Chair.).

Principal Staff: Chair. Dir Joachim Vollmer; Deputy Chair. Dirs Wilfried Luhnen; Exec. Dir Katrin Flasche.

Address: Arnswaldtstr. 28, 30159 Hannover.

Telephone: (511) 3028560; **Fax:** (511) 3028556; **Internet:** www .umweltaktion.de; **e-mail:** info@uan.de.

International Society for Human Rights—ISHR

Established in 1972 to uphold the UN Universal Declaration of Human Rights.

Activities: Operates worldwide in the field of law and human rights. National sections operate in 24 countries, with working groups in an additional four countries. Projects include strengthening civil society in Central and Eastern Europe and the countries of the former USSR, promoting the International Criminal Court, and providing democracy and human rights training to the Ukrainian military. Holds consultative status with the Council of Europe, consultative status (Roster) with ECOSOC and associated status with the UN Dept of Public Information. Has more than 30,000 members.

Geographical Area of Activity: Worldwide.

Restrictions: No grants available directly, except through co-financed international projects.

International Board: Prof. Dr Thomas Schirrmacher (Pres.); Henriette Baronin Payrebrune de Saint Sêve (Treas.); Dr Haydee Marin, Dr Liubov Nemcinova, Patrice Renault-Sablonière, Dr Andrey Sukhorukov, Prof. Dr Marat Zakhidov.

Principal Staff: Sec.-Gen. Michel Baumann.

Address: International Secretariat, c/o German Section, Borsigalle 9, 60388 Frankfurt am Main.

Telephone: (69) 420108-0; **Fax:** (69) 420108-33; **Internet:** www.ishr.org; **e-mail:** info@ishr.org.

Internationale Bachakademie Stuttgart (Stuttgart International Bach Academy)

Established in 1981 by the Stuttgarter Konzertvereinigung eV for the development and management of a research and further education institute for German and foreign music researchers and musicians to carry out research into the theoretical and practical interpretation of the works of Johann Sebastian Bach.

Activities: Operates in the field of music through co-ordinating international research into Bach, and co-operating in the promotion of Bach's music. Organizes conferences and seminars, concerts and exhibitions in Germany and abroad. Organizes the Music Fest Stuttgart. Maintains a specialized library and documentation centre.

Geographical Area of Activity: International.

Restrictions: Unsolicited applications are not accepted.

Publications: Newsletter; *Series of the Stuttgart International Bach Academy; Forum Bachakademie* (both in German).

Board of Trustees: Dr Manfred Gentz (Chair.).

Principal Staff: Chair. Prof. Dr Berthold Leibinger; Treas. Peter M. Haid; Academy Dir Prof. Hans-Christoph Rademann; Dir Gernot Rehrl.

Address: Johann-Sebastian-Bach-Platz, 70178 Stuttgart.

Telephone: (711) 61921-0; **Fax:** (711) 61921-23; **Internet:** www .bachakademie.de; **e-mail:** office@bachakademie.de.

Internationale Jugendbibliothek (International Youth Library Foundation)

Established in 1996.

Activities: Main fields of activity include arts and humanities, education and international affairs. The Foundation operates nationally, providing training courses and issuing publications, and internationally, granting scholarships and fellowships. Other activities include: creating awareness among adults and educationists on the importance of books for children and youngsters by providing information to organizations involved in composing children's literature and their distribution; contributing to advanced training of the personnel involved; advising illustrators, publishers, writers, translators, etc.; extending support to organizations with similar objectives in Germany and abroad; promoting inter-cultural and international understanding through acquisition and distribution of children's literature from Germany and abroad; and furthering research on international literature for children, particularly within the scope of the International Youth Library, which has an estimated 530,000-volume collection. The Foundation also offers study fellowships.

Geographical Area of Activity: International.

Restrictions: Applications for grants are not accepted; grants are made only to professionals working in the area of children's and youth literature.

Publications: *IJB Report* (2 a year); *The White Ravens* (annually); books; *Children Between Worlds; Children's Books from Canada; Cold World; Hello, dear Enemy; Young and Old;*

Paddington, Pu und Baloo; *Pinocchio*; *Waterworlds in books for children and pictures made by children*; *Ivan Gantschev*; *From Robinson to Lummerland.*

Finance: Annual income €2,457,184, expenditure €2,377,536 (2014).

Board of Trustees: Dr Freiherr Dominik von König (Chair.); Dr Rolf Griebel (Deputy Chair.).

Principal Staff: Chair. Nikolaus Turner.

Address: Schloss Blutenburg, 81247 Munich.

Telephone: (89) 891211-0; **Fax:** (89) 8117553; **Internet:** www.ijb.de; **e-mail:** info@ijb.de.

Internationale Stiftung zur Förderung von Kultur und Zivilisation (International Foundation for Culture and Civilization)

Established in 1995 by Erich Fischer.

Activities: Supports cultural and humanitarian projects in Germany and internationally, principally musical activities, including festivals, and partnerships with Amnesty International (q.v.).

Geographical Area of Activity: Germany and international.

Publications: Newsletter report.

Board: Jürgen Dorn (Chair.); Eva Köhler (Deputy Chair.).

Principal Staff: Project Man. Gabriele Mantaj.

Address: Dr Carl von Linde Str. 9, 81479 Munich.

Telephone: (89) 5404118-0; **Fax:** (89) 5404118-19; **Internet:** www.internationalestiftung.de; **e-mail:** contact@kulturstiftungmuenchen.de.

Japanisch-Deutsches Zentrum Berlin (Japanese-German Centre Berlin)

Founded in 1985 to promote and strengthen Japanese-German and international co-operation in the fields of science and culture.

Activities: Organizes academic conferences, seminars and workshops on a wide range of topics, and joint exhibitions and concerts of German, Japanese and international artists. The Centre offers Japanese language courses, manages the German side of the German-Japanese Forum and co-ordinates several programmes for German-Japanese Peoples Exchange. It maintains a library of more than 10,000 vols.

Geographical Area of Activity: Germany and Japan, Europe, Asia and North America.

Restrictions: Unsolicited applications are not accepted.

Publications: *jdzb echo* (quarterly newsletter); documents and proceedings of the Centre's events; Directory of German-Japanese Co-operation.

Finance: Annual expenditure approx. €2.3m. (2010).

Board of Trustees: Prof. Dr Bernhard Scheuble (Chair.); Akira Kojima (Vice-Chair.).

Principal Staff: Chair. Yûshû Takashima; Vice-Chair. Matthias Nass; Sec.-Gen. Dr Friederike Bosse; Deputy Sec.-Gen. Masaru Sakato.

Address: Saargemünder Str. 2, 14195 Berlin.

Telephone: (30) 839070; **Fax:** (30) 83907220; **Internet:** www.jdzb.de; **e-mail:** jdzb@jdzb.de.

Klassik Stiftung Weimar (Foundation of Weimar Classics)

Founded in 1991 (becoming an independent foundation in 1994); the legal successor to the former non-independent National Research and Memorial Centre of Classical German Literature in Weimar, to preserve and expand the sites and collections of classical German literature in Weimar; to make them available to the public; to encourage the communication, research and dissemination of this cultural heritage; and to maintain the sites and collections of the former National Research and Memorial Centre, as well as the collections of 19th- and 20th-century works. Formerly known as the Stiftung Weimarer Klassik; merged with the Kunstsammlungen zu Weimar in 2003.

Activities: Maintains the Goethe National Museum, the Schiller House, the Palace Museum, the Bauhaus Museum, the New Museum, Belvedere Palace, and 18 other literary museums, palaces and memorials, the Duchess Anna Amalia Library, the Goethe-Schiller Archives, five parks in and around Weimar, and several other properties. The Foundation carries out research, organizes exhibitions and events, issues numerous publications and holds conferences.

Geographical Area of Activity: Europe and USA.

Restrictions: Applications for grants are not accepted.

Publications: *Johann Wolfgang Goethe: Geschichte des Hauses*; *Bestandsübersicht*; *Inventare des Goethe- und Schiller-Archivs*; *Erschienene Publikationen*; *Reineke Fuchs*; *Goethe-Briefrepertorium*; *Goethe Autographensammlung*; *Goethes Tagebücher*; *Nietzsche*; *Büchner*.

Finance: Financed by the Federal Government, the State of Thuringia and the City of Weimar.

Board of Trustees: Prof. Dr Benjamin-Immanuel Hoff (Chair.).

Principal Staff: Pres. Hellmut Seemann.

Address: Burgplatz 4, 99423 Weimar.

Telephone: (3643) 545401; **Fax:** (3643) 419816; **Internet:** www.klassik-stiftung.de; **e-mail:** poststelle@klassik-stiftung.de.

Körber-Stiftung (Körber Foundation)

Founded in 1959 by the entrepreneur Kurt A. Körber in Hamburg-Bergedorf, the Foundation runs national and international projects and events.

Activities: Works in the fields of international affairs, education, science, civil society and youth culture. The Foundation offers people the opportunity to participate actively, and provides them with ideas and initiative.

Geographical Area of Activity: Worldwide.

Restrictions: Finances and runs its own projects. Does not make grants to individuals.

Publications: *Reflexion und Initiative* (report, 2 a year); information brochure; annual list; books; newsletter.

Finance: Total assets €526m. (2015).

Board of Trustees: Christian Wriedt (Chair.); Werner Redeker (Vice-Chair.); **Foundation Council:** Dr Klaus Wehmeier (Chair.); Dr Sabine Bergmann-Pohl (Vice-Chair.).

Principal Staff: Chair. Dr Lothar Dittmer.

Address: Kehrwieder 12, 20457 Hamburg.

Telephone: (40) 808192-0; **Fax:** (40) 808192-300; **Internet:** www.koerber-stiftung.de; **e-mail:** info@koerber-stiftung.de.

Else Kröner-Fresenius-Stiftung (Else Kröner-Fresenius Foundation)

Established in 1983 by Else Kröner to extend support to medical and scientific research.

Activities: Focuses on medicine, health and science and technology by providing grants for research projects, in particular novel research in nutritional medicine, clinical research, infections and dialysis. The Foundation also finances humanitarian and educational initiatives, especially if they are conducive to development.

Geographical Area of Activity: International.

Restrictions: Basic research is not funded.

Publications: Annual reports.

Finance: Total grants disbursed €31,310,000 (2014).

Board of Directors: Dr Dieter Schenk (Chair.); Dr Karl Schneider (Vice-Chair.).

Address: POB 1852, 61288 Bad Homburg; Am Pilgerrain 15, 61352 Bad Homburg.

Telephone: (6172) 8975-0; **Fax:** (6172) 8975-15; **Internet:** www.ekfs.eu; **e-mail:** kontakt@ekfs.de.

Alfried Krupp von Bohlen und Halbach-Stiftung
(Alfried Krupp von Bohlen und Halbach Foundation)

Founded in 1967 by Dr Alfried Krupp von Bohlen und Halbach for philanthropic aims of benefit to the community.

Activities: Operates nationally and internationally through support of Foundation projects in the fields of scientific research and teaching (including the fostering of young scientific talent); education and training; health services; sport; and literature, music and the fine arts. The Foundation offers grants and fellowships (incl. an Internship Programme for students of Stanford University, CA, USA to train in Germany, and a China Studies Programme for German students to spend a year of study in the People's Republic of China). It also awards an annual environmental prize.

Geographical Area of Activity: International.

Finance: Total assets €1,100m. (31 Dec. 2013).

Board of Trustees: Prof. Dr Ursula Gather (Chair.); Prof. Dr Reimar Lüst (Deputy Chair.).

Address: POB 23 02 45, 45070 Essen; Hügel 15, 45133 Essen.

Telephone: (201) 188-1; **Fax:** (201) 412587; **Internet:** www .krupp-stiftung.de; **e-mail:** info@krupp-stiftung.de.

Karl-Kübel-Stiftung für Kind und Familie (Karl Kübel Foundation for Child and Family)

Founded in 1972 by Karl Kübel to support family-orientated programmes.

Activities: Operates nationally and internationally, mainly in German-speaking countries, Kosovo and Metohija, India and the Philippines, through self-conducted programmes, grants to institutions, prizes, training courses, publications and the implementation of development projects. The Foundation's four main programmes are: the Karl Kübel Award and the support of family-centred self-help activities; family-centred housing projects; education through the Foundation's institutes in Germany and India; and supporting development projects and training development personnel. It also provides humanitarian relief.

Geographical Area of Activity: Germany, Kosovo and Metohija, India and the Philippines.

Publications: Annual Report; *newsletter; Against Trafficking of Children and Women in Commercial Sexual Exploitation.*

Finance: Total assets €94,053,774; annual income €15,278,540, expenditure €5,808,809 (31 Dec. 2013).

Foundation Council: Matthias Wilkes (Chair.); Dr Klaus-Volker Schutz, Dr Kerstin Humberg (Vice-Chair.).

Principal Staff: Dirs Daniela Kobelt Neuhaus, Ralf Tepel, Michael Böhmer.

Address: POB 1563, 64605 Bensheim; Darmstädter Str. 100 64625 Bensheim.

Telephone: (6251) 7005-0; **Fax:** (6251) 7005-55; **Internet:** www.kkstiftung.de; **e-mail:** info@kkstiftung.de.

Kulturstiftung der Länder—KSL (Cultural Foundation of the German Länder)

Established in 1988 to promote and preserve national art and culture.

Activities: Operates nationally and internationally in the field of the arts, promoting and preserving cultural heritage of national importance.

Geographical Area of Activity: Germany.

Publications: *Patrimonia, Arsprototo.*

Finance: Annual expenditure €9.7m. (2010).

Board of Trustees: Dr Heribald Närger (Chair.); Prof Dr Rolf-E. Breuer, Dr. Werner Müller, Prof. Dr Klaus-Dieter Lehmann (Vice-Chair.).

Principal Staff: Sec.-Gen. Isabel Pfeiffer-Poensgen; Deputy Sec.-Gen. Prof. Dr Frank Druffner.

Address: Lützowpl. 9, 10785 Berlin.

Telephone: (30) 8936350; **Fax:** (30) 8914251; **Internet:** www .kulturstiftung.de; **e-mail:** kontakt@kulturstiftung.de.

Lateinamerika-Zentrum eV—LAZ (Latin America Centre)

Established in 1961 by Prof. Hermann M. Görgen to help alleviate suffering in Latin America.

Activities: Operates in Central and South America, mainly in Brazil, supporting local organizations that develop projects to suit local needs. Projects include schooling and training for disadvantaged children and young people; combating the abandonment of the countryside; promotion of women; basic health care; protection of the environment; and the promotion and protection of indigenous peoples. Also publishes books on the politics of development, and hosts exhibitions and workshops.

Geographical Area of Activity: Central and South America, with an emphasis on Brazil.

Restrictions: Operates in collaboration with local partner organizations. No grants to individuals.

Publications: Annual Report; *Tópicos* (German/Brazilian pamphlets); leaflets; brochures.

Finance: Annual income €570,463, expenditure €111,560 (2012).

Board: Astrid Prange de Oliveira (Chair.); Dr Hans Thomas, Dr Claudio Zettel (Vice-Chair.).

Address: Dr Werner-Schuster-Haus, Kaiserstr. 201, 53113 Bonn.

Telephone: (228) 210788; **Fax:** (228) 241658; **Internet:** www .lateinamerikazentrum.de; **e-mail:** info@ lateinamerikazentrum.de.

The Ronald S. Lauder Foundation

Founded in 1987 by Ronald S. Lauder for the support of Central and Eastern Europe and the former USSR to promote Jewish education, and for the preservation of Jewish monuments and buildings.

Activities: Operates primarily in Central and Eastern Europe, in Austria, Belarus, Bulgaria, the Czech Republic, Estonia, Germany, Hungary, Latvia, Lithuania, Moldova, Poland, Romania, the Russian Federation, Slovakia and Ukraine, making grants in the areas of Jewish welfare, religion, cultural programmes, conservation and education. Also supports a non-sectarian international student exchange.

Geographical Area of Activity: Central and Eastern Europe, and the former USSR.

Restrictions: No applications for grants accepted.

Publications: Information brochure; newsletter.

Trustees: Ronald S. Lauder (Chair. and Pres.); David Gerson (Treas.).

Principal Staff: Exec. Vice-Pres. and CEO Joshua I. Spinner; COO Nataly Fischman.

Address: Rykestrasse 53, 10405 Berlin.

Telephone: (30) 440131610; **Fax:** (30) 440131619; **Internet:** lauderfoundation.com; **e-mail:** info@lauderfoundation.com.

Rosa-Luxemburg-Stiftung (Rosa Luxemburg Foundation)

Established in 1991 for the promotion of political education (associated with the Social Democratic Party—SPD), knowledge and research, culture and the arts, and international understanding.

Activities: Operates in the fields of the arts and humanities, economic affairs, education, international affairs, and law and human rights, through promoting research; publications; awarding scholarships and the annual Rosa Luxemburg Prize; maintaining archives and a library; and national and international projects, in particular in countries of Africa, Asia, and Central and South America. Maintains regional offices in the Russian Federation, Brazil, Poland and South Africa.

Geographical Area of Activity: International, in particular Central and Eastern Europe and the Russian Federation, Africa, Asia, and Central and South America.

Publications: Annual Report; *Utopie kreativ* (magazine); reports; books.

Finance: Annual invoice €43,279,718, expenditure €43,037,737 (31 Dec. 2012).

Board of Directors: Dr Dagmar Enkelmann (Chair.); Dr Thomas Händel, Dr Sabine Reiner (Vice-Chair.).

Principal Staff: Exec. Dir Dr Florian Weis.

Address: Franz-Mehring-Platz 1, 10243 Berlin.

Telephone: (30) 44310221; **Fax:** (30) 44310222; **Internet:** www.rosalux.de; **e-mail:** info@rosalux.de.

medica mondiale e.V.

Established in 2004 by Monika Hauser to support women and girls in areas of conflict and natural disasters.

Activities: Operates in the areas of human rights, and medicine and health, to assist women and girls in areas of crisis.

Geographical Area of Activity: Areas of conflict and natural disasters, incl. Africa, Central and South America, the Middle East and South Asia.

Finance: Annual income €5,330,830, expenditure €5,367,406 (31 Dec. 2013).

Principal Staff: Exec. Dirs Christiane Overkamp, Dr Monika Hauser.

Address: Hülchrather Str. 4, 50670 Cologne.

Telephone: (221) 9318980; **Fax:** (221) 9318981; **Internet:** www.medicamondiale.org; **e-mail:** mbauer@medicamondiale.org.

Medico International

Established in 1968 to send medical supplies to countries in need.

Activities: Operates worldwide, in particular in less-developed countries or in countries where emergency relief is necessary, in the field of medicine and health, offering medicines and medical equipment, medical personnel, ambulances and other equipment. The organization runs campaigns against landmines, and various projects in the areas of asylum, rehabilitation, AIDS, human rights and basic health care. Long-term projects have been instituted in Central and South America, North, Central and Southern Africa, the Middle and Far East, and Central Asia (Kurdistan).

Geographical Area of Activity: International.

Publications: Newsletter; *medico-Reports*; posters; leaflets.

Finance: Annual income €10,513,143, expenditure €12,252,258 (2013).

Board of Directors: Brigitte Kühn (Chair.); Prof. Dr Alexander Wittkowsky, Dr Anne Blum (Vice-Chair.).

Principal Staff: Exec. Dir Thomas Gebauer.

Address: Burgstr. 106, 60389 Frankfurt am Main.

Telephone: (69) 944380; **Fax:** (69) 436002; **Internet:** www.medico.de; **e-mail:** info@medico.de.

Messerschmitt-Stiftung (Messerschmitt Foundation)

Established in 1976 by Prof. Willy Messerschmitt.

Activities: Works in the fields of conservation of heritage, and science and technology; promotes science and research, especially in the area of aero- and space technology; also promotes the conservation of German art and cultural memorials nationally and internationally. The Foundation owns several historically important Messerschmitt aircraft.

Geographical Area of Activity: Europe.

Finance: Annual expenditure approx. €11m.

Board of Trustees: Prof. Gero Madelung (Chair.).

Principal Staff: Chair. Dr Hans Heinrich von Srbik.

Address: Pienzenauerstr. 17, 81679 Munich.

Telephone: (89) 981830; **Fax:** (89) 98290126; **Internet:** www.flugmuseum-messerschmitt.de/page1/index.html.

Morat-Institut für Kunst und Kunstwissenschaft (Morat Institute for Art and Science)

Founded in 1983 as the Morat-Instituts für Kunst und Kunstwissenschaft by Franz Morat, Charlotte A. Morat, Franz Armin Morat. Present name adopted in 1984 following merger with the Heinrich-Heine-Stiftung für Philosophie und Kritische Wissenschaft, founded in 1972 by Charlotte A. Morat to promote philosophy and critical theory in research and teaching; to promote pure theory in the classical tradition; and to improve social relations through constructive criticism.

Activities: Houses a graphic arts collection, masks and sculptures from Burkina Faso, and Renaissance medals. The Institute operates nationally and internationally in the field of the arts and humanities, by providing grants to individuals, fellowships and scholarships to promote philosophy and critical knowledge, and research. Has a library of c. 50,000 vols.

Geographical Area of Activity: Germany and international.

Principal Staff: Man. Eva-Maria Morat.

Address: Lörracher Str. 31, 79115 Freiburg im Breisgau.

Telephone: (761) 4765916; **Fax:** (761) 42117; **Internet:** www.morat-institut.de; **e-mail:** info@morat-institut.de.

Munich Re Foundation/Münchener Rück Stiftung

Established in 2005 to support innovative solutions to the challenges faced by people worldwide in areas such as population growth, globalization, diminishing natural resources, pollution and climate change.

Activities: Operates in four principal fields: knowledge accumulation and implementation, through which it supports education and training, funds a chair at the United Nations University, supports publishing projects, etc.; clarification and dissemination of information, such as brochures, training programmes and exhibitions; networking; and direct help and support for disaster relief and local projects.

Geographical Area of Activity: International.

Board of Trustees: Dr Hans-Jürgen Schinzler (Chair.).

Principal Staff: Chair. Thomas Loster; Vice-Chair. Dirk Reinhard.

Address: POB 80791, Munich; Königinstr. 107, 80802 Munich.

Telephone: (89) 38918888; **Fax:** (89) 389178888; **Internet:** www.munichre-foundation.org; **e-mail:** info@munichre-foundation.org.

Friedrich-Naumann-Stiftung (Friedrich Naumann Foundation)

Founded in 1958 by Dr Theodor Heuss, former President of the Federal Republic of Germany, to promote a liberal foundation for political and civic education, improve dialogue between Eastern and Western industrial countries, and developed and developing countries, and give advisory and vocational assistance to developing countries.

Activities: Operates nationally and internationally, primarily in the field of civic education, but also in the areas of aid to less-developed countries, economic and international affairs, and law and human rights, through self-conducted programmes, research, scholarships and fellowships, prizes, conferences, training courses and publications. In developing countries, assistance is given to co-operative associations, training institutes for journalism and organizations in the field of adult education. The Foundation has projects in around 45 countries and maintains offices in approximately 47 countries outside Germany.

Geographical Area of Activity: International.

Publications: Annual Report; *liberal* (quarterly); *Classical author of liberty*; *Philosopher of liberty*; *Arguments of liberty*; *Concepts of Liberty*; occasional papers; *Political principles*; *Tasks and activities*; *Friedrich Naumann*.

Finance: Annual income €48,392,544, expenditure €48,590,788 (31 Dec. 2012).

Board of Trustees: Walter Scheel (Hon. Chair.); Dr Jürgen Morlok (Chair.); Ludwig Theodor Heuss, Liane Knüppel (Vice-Chair.).

Principal Staff: Chair. Dr Wolfgang Gerhardt; Vice-Chair. Prof. Karl-Heinz Paqué; CEO Steffen Saebisch; Treas. Manfred Richter.

Address: Karl-Marx-Str. 2, 14482 Potsdam-Babelsberg.

Telephone: (331) 70190; **Fax:** (331) 7019188; **Internet:** www.freiheit.org; **e-mail:** info@freiheit.org.

Niedersächsische Sparkassenstiftung (Lower Saxony Savings Bank Foundation)

Established in 1984 by the Niedersächsischer Sparkassen und Giroverband savings bank.

Activities: Operates in the Federal State of Lower Saxony in the field of the arts, with an emphasis on fine art, music, conservation of monuments and museums. Supports projects undertaken by other organizations, carries out its own activities, awards prizes and scholarships, and maintains an art collection. awards the €45,000 Museum Prize every two years. Works closely with the VGH Foundation (f. 2000), which promotes science and culture; and supervises hbs-kulturfonds (f. 1998), which awards the hbs Musuem Prize and hbs Critics Award, each worth €5,000, every two years.

Geographical Area of Activity: The Federal State of Lower Saxony, Germany.

Restrictions: Grants are made only to organizations in Lower Saxony.

Finance: Total assets approx. €24m. (2014).

Trustees: Kai-Uwe Bielefeld (Pres., Board of Trustees); Thomas Mang (Pres. of Board).

Principal Staff: Man. Dir Dr Sabine Schormann; Deputy Man. Dir Michael Heinrich Schormann.

Address: Schiffgraben 6–8, 30159 Hannover.

Telephone: (511) 3603489; **Fax:** (511) 3603684; **Internet:** www.nsks.de/nsks; **e-mail:** sparkassenstiftung@svn.de.

Novartis-Stiftung für therapeutische Forschung (Novartis Foundation for Therapeutical Research)

Established in 1969 by Sandoz AG Nuremberg to further therapeutical research, and to carry out other research in the field of medicine.

Activities: Operates in the field of medical research; organizes inter-disciplinary symposia. The Foundation awards the annual Novartis Prize, worth €10,000, for pharmaceutical research.

Geographical Area of Activity: Germany.

Restrictions: Grants up to approx. €150,000 made in the areas of the heart/circulation, anti-coagulation, dermatology, immunology, haematology, oncology, stem cell research, endocrinology, pulmonary diseases and neurology.

Publications: *Ecomed*; *'ME-TOO'-preparations*; *Bases of the Measurement of Quality of Life* (book).

Finance: Foundation capital approx. €11.5m.

Principal Staff: CEO Andreas Kreiss.

Address: Roonstr. 25, 90429 Nuremberg.

Telephone: (911) 27312796; **Fax:** (911) 27312056; **Internet:** www.novartis.de/forschung_entwicklung/stiftung_fuer_therap_forschung/index.shtml; **e-mail:** andreas.kreiss@novartis.com.

Michael-Otto-Stiftung für Umweltschutz (Michael Otto Foundation for Environmental Protection)

Established in 1993 by Dr Michael Otto.

Activities: Develops strategies and supports projects for future-orientated initiatives in the conservation of nature and the environment through funding, education and dialogue. The Foundation aims to direct and motivate initiatives to conserve the environment for future generations. It provides funding for innovative environmental projects, financing major nature conservation projects, and helping young people to implement their own 'Aqua Projects'. Its current focus is on the protection of flowing water and sustainable treatment of rivers and streams. The Foundation has set up academic chairs such as 'The Economics of Climate Change' (Berlin Technical University), and supports research and educational institutions. In early 2010, the Foundation launched its own educational project, 'Aqua Agents', aimed at primary schools in Hamburg. Alongside its educational and funding work, the Foundation mediates between different interest groups, initiating dialogue between influential players from business, nature conservation, government and academia. Its goal is to work with policy-makers to develop pragmatic solutions for current environmental issues.

Geographical Area of Activity: Mainly Germany and Eastern Europe.

Publications: Proceedings of the annual Hamburg Nature Conservation Forum.

Board of Trustees: Dr Michael Otto (Chair.).

Principal Staff: Exec. Dir Dr Johannes Merck.

Address: Werner-Otto-Str. 1–7, 22179 Hamburg.

Telephone: (40) 64617723; **Fax:** (40) 64647723; **Internet:** www.michaelottostiftung.de; **e-mail:** info@michaelottostiftung.org.

Oxfam Deutschland e.V.

Established in 1995; part of the Oxfam confederation of organizations (qq.v.).

Activities: Operates in the areas of relief, development and poverty alleviation in Africa and South Asia. The organization campaigns for rights to sustainable livelihoods, access to health care and education, security, representation, and personal choice.

Geographical Area of Activity: Africa and South Asia.

Publications: Annual Report.

Finance: Annual income €8,507,822, expenditure €8,148,093 (2013).

Board of Directors: Dr Matthias von Bismark-Osten (Chair.); Babette Neumann (Vice-Chair.); Ralf Südhoff (Treas.).

Principal Staff: Man. Dir Marion Leiser.

Address: Am Köllnischen Park 1, 10179 Berlin.

Telephone: (30) 453069-0; **Fax:** (30) 453069-401; **Internet:** www.oxfam.de; **e-mail:** info@oxfam.de.

Max-Planck-Gesellschaft zur Förderung der Wissenschaften eV (Max Planck Society for the Advancement of Science)

Founded in 1948 to succeed the Kaiser-Wilhelm-Gesellschaft (f. 1911) with the object of promoting basic research in the sciences.

Activities: Operates nationally and internationally in the fields of science, medicine, social sciences and humanities, and law and other professions. Maintains international relations through self-conducted projects, research, conferences, prizes, publications and lectures. Basic research, particularly in the fields of biology, medicine, chemistry, physics and the humanities, is carried out in 83 institutes and research facilities belonging to the Society, with the aim of complementing research conducted at universities. The Society presents the annual Max Planck Research Award to two internationally renowned scientists, one working in Germany and one abroad.

Geographical Area of Activity: International, centered in Germany.

Restrictions: Not a funding organization.

Publications: *Max-Planck-Forschung* (research journal in German); *Max Planck Research* (research journal in English); information booklets; *Research perspectives 2000, 2005 and 2010*.

Finance: Annual income €1,940.5m., expenditure €1,818.5m. (2013).

Principal Staff: Pres. Martin Stratmann; Vice-Pres Angela D. Friederici, Bill S. Hansson, Ferdi Schüth; Treas. Ralph P. Thomas.

Address: Hofgartenstr. 8, 80539 Munich.

Telephone: (89) 21080; **Fax:** (89) 21081111; **Internet:** www .mpg.de; **e-mail:** post@gv.mpg.de.

Prix Jeunesse Foundation

Established in 1964 by the Government of Bavaria, the City of Munich and Bayerischer Rundfunk to improve the quality of television worldwide for young people, deepen understanding, promote communication between nations and increase programme exchange.

Activities: Operates internationally in the field of children's and youth television, awarding the Prix Jeunesse International Prizes for children's and youth television programmes, organizing conferences, training courses and issuing publications. Maintains a video library covering more than four decades of children's and youth television and organizes the Prix Jeunesse International Festival every two years.

Geographical Area of Activity: International.

Publications: *WATCHwords Online* (newsletter, 3 a year).

Finance: Financed by annual contributions from its founders.

Principal Staff: Man. Dir Dr Maya Goetz; Co-ordinator Kirsten Schneid.

Address: c/o Bayerischer Rundfunk, Rudfunkpl. 1, 80335 Munich.

Telephone: (89) 590042058; **Fax:** (89) 59003053; **Internet:** www.prixjeunesse.de; **e-mail:** info@prixjeunesse.de.

Johanna-Quandt-Stiftung (Johanna Quandt Foundation)

Founded in 1995 by Johanna Quandt.

Activities: Aims to promote the importance of private entrepreneurship as a contributor to economic development in the public and the media. The Foundation awards the Herbert Quandt Media Prize, worth €50,000.

Geographical Area of Activity: Germany.

Finance: Annual income €70,214, expenditure €47,588 (31 Dec. 2012).

Board of Trustees: Johanna Quandt (Chair.); Stefan Quandt (Vice-Chair.).

Principal Staff: Dirs Dr Jörg Appelhans, Dr Johannes Fritz.

Address: Günther-Quandt-Haus, Seedammweg 55, 61352 Bad Homburg v.d. Hohe.

Telephone: (6172) 404342; **Fax:** (6172) 404420; **Internet:** www .johanna-quandt-stiftung.de; **e-mail:** info@johanna-quandt -stiftung.de.

Werner-Reimers-Stiftung (Werner Reimers Foundation)

Founded in 1963 by Werner Reimers to contribute towards explaining the development of human society and its institutions, to analyse its present problems, to recognize tendencies of its further development and to open for it ways into the future.

Activities: Operates nationally and internationally in the fields of social welfare and studies, the physical and social sciences, medicine and the humanities. Interdisciplinary study groups organized by the Foundation form the focal point of its activities. The groups devote several years to the study of well-defined problems, meet regularly to exchange information and publish the results of their work. Meetings take place at the Foundation's conference centre and the Foundation provides travelling expenses and accommodation.

Restrictions: Does not award scholarships.

Publications: Report of operations.

Finance: Annual expenditure approx. €700,000.

Trustees: Ruth Wagner (Chair.); Werner Knopp (Hon. Chair.).

Principal Staff: Pres. Dr Albrecht Graf von Kalnein.

Address: Am Wingertsberg 4, 61348 Bad Homburg.

Telephone: (6172) 24058; **Fax:** (6172) 21408; **Internet:** www .reimers-stiftung.de; **e-mail:** info@reimers-stiftung.de.

Hedwig und Robert Samuel-Stiftung (Hedwig and Robert Samuel Foundation)

Established in 1932 to support education, primarily in Central America and Asia.

Activities: Aims to provide occupational qualifications for the poor, focusing on children and teenagers to improve their quality of life in the future. The Foundation runs projects in Costa Rica, Cuba, Germany, India, Nicaragua and Thailand.

Geographical Area of Activity: Central America and Asia.

Publications: Newsletter.

Finance: Funded through the Foundation's own capital, donations and co-financing.

Board of Directors: Martin Barth (Chair.).

Address: Königsallee 14, 40212 Düsseldorf.

Telephone: (211) 1386666; **Fax:** (211) 1386611; **Internet:** www .samuel.de; **e-mail:** info@samuel.de.

Wilhelm-Sander-Stiftung (Wilhelm Sander Foundation)

Founded in 1974 to support medical research.

Activities: Operates in the field of medicine and health, through sponsoring medical research and supporting the fight against ill health, especially cancer, by means of grants to institutions and individuals.

Geographical Area of Activity: Germany and Switzerland.

Publications: Report of operations and financial statement.

Board of Trustees: Dr Jörg Koppenhöfer (Pres.); Prof. Dr Udo Löhrs (Vice-Pres.).

Principal Staff: Exec. Dirs Bernhard Knappe, Ulrich Reuter.

Address: Goethestr. 74, 80336 Munich.

Telephone: (89) 5441870; **Fax:** (89) 54418720; **Internet:** www .wilhelm-sander-stiftung.de; **e-mail:** info@sanst.de.

Save Our Future Umweltstiftung—SOF (Save Our Future Environmental Foundation)

Founded in 1989 by Jürgen Oppermann to create environmental awareness and encourage environmental protection.

Activities: Operates nationally and internationally in the field of environmental education and sustainability, mainly through projects in education for children, pre-school children and young people. The Foundation develops model projects such as 'richtig Leben', an agenda of 21 climate protection projects for kindergartens, providing play activities for children, as well as training for educators, as well as building up an Internet-communication system for environmental education activities in Hamburg. It has established the first two mobile environmental education vehicles as a model for the People's Republic of China, in collaboration with Friends of Nature Beijing and the Shanghai Education Centre. It also organizes environmental round tables for young people in Germany, carried out a Sport and Environment campaign and established a Chair for water economy and water supply at the Technical University of Hamburg.

Geographical Area of Activity: International, mainly Germany and the People's Republic of China.

Restrictions: Only supports its own projects.

Publications: *S.O.F.-Newsletter* (1–2 a year); *Die Sonne und ihre Kinder* (children's publication); *Umweltschutz im Sportverein—Ein Praxisleitfaden* (video and brochures).

Finance: Total assets approx. €5m.

Foundation Council: Jürgen Oppermann (Chair.); Johannes Lorenzen (Vice-Chair.).

Principal Staff: Chair. Dr Jörg von Bargen; Deputy Chair. Sabine Gabler; Man. Dir Ralf Thielebein-Pohl; Deputy Man. Dir Meike Wunderlich.

Address: Friesenweg 1, 22763 Hamburg.

Telephone: (40) 240600; **Fax:** (40) 240640; **Internet:** www
.save-our-future.de; **e-mail:** info@save-our-future.de.

Ernst-Schering-Stiftung (Ernst Schering Foundation)

Established in 2002 by Schering AG, Berlin; an independent,
non-profit foundation, to promote science and the arts.

Activities: Promotes science, with a focus on the natural
sciences, and the arts, with a focus on the contemporary visual
and performing arts, including dance and music; the scientific
and cultural education of children and young people; and dialogue between science and society. Gives particular emphasis
to projects in frontier areas, especially at the interface of art
and science. This is also the focus of the Foundation's project
space, where it puts on shows by young, experimental artists
as well as lectures and workshops, thus serving as a platform
for interdisciplinary dialogue among science, culture and
society.

Geographical Area of Activity: Germany and international.

Publications: Image Brochure; exhibition catalogues; publications of scientific symposia; others; e-newsletter (monthly).

Finance: Initial endowment of €35m.

Council: Prof. Dr Stefan H. E. Kaufmann (Chair.); Dr Hubertus Erlen (Deputy Chair.).

Principal Staff: Exec. Dir of Science Dr Sonja Kießling;
Exec. Dir of Arts and Culture Heike Catherina Mertens.

Address: Unter den Linden 32–34, 10117 Berlin.

Telephone: (30) 206229-65; **Fax:** (30) 206229-61; **Internet:**
www.scheringstiftung.de; **e-mail:** info@scheringstiftung.de.

Eberhard-Schöck-Stiftung (Eberhard Schöck Foundation)

Established in 1992 by Eberhard Schöck to promote the building trade in the former communist countries of Central and
Eastern Europe.

Activities: Operates internationally in Eastern and Central
Europe in the areas of aid, economic affairs and education,
through self-conducted programmes, grants, scholarships
and fellowships, conferences, training courses and publications. The Foundation runs practical programmes to train
young building workers from the former communist countries
of Europe to become self-employed builders in their own countries; it thus aims to contribute to stability and the principles
of democracy and the market economy. It also runs practical
programmes to train vocational teachers and managers of
small and medium-sized enterprises in the building trade.
The Foundation awards two prizes: the Schöck Building Innovation Prize and the German Language Cultural Prize (in co-
operation with the Dortmund Verein Deutsche Sprache). Since
1998 the Foundation has run pilot projects to modernize vocational training in the Russian Federation, Ukraine and, since
2010, in Moldova.

Geographical Area of Activity: Central and Eastern Europe.

Restrictions: Grants are made only within the Foundation's
own projects.

Publications: Annual Report; conference documentation;
and commemorative publication.

Finance: Total disbursements €2.9m. (2011/12).

Board of Directors: Eberhard Schöck (Chair.); Dr Jürgen D.
Wickert (Deputy Chair.).

Principal Staff: Man. Dir Peter Möller.

Address: Vimbucher Str. 2, 76534 Baden-Baden.

Telephone: (7223) 967-371; **Fax:** (7223) 967-373; **Internet:**
www.eberhard-schoeck-stiftung.de; **e-mail:** kontakt@
eberhard-schoeck-stiftung.de.

Schwarzkopf-Stiftung Junges Europa (Schwarzkopf
Foundation Young Europe)

Founded in 1971 as the Heinz-Schwarzkopf Foundation to promote political awareness and social responsibility in young

people aged 16–28 years, thus building on and strengthening
European integration.

Activities: Operates across Europe in the fields of international relations, culture, political and economic affairs,
science and education, through international youth conferences and travel scholarships. The Foundation organizes lectures, seminars and debates, as well as visits to embassies
and exhibitions. It annually presents the Young European of
the Year prize and Schwarzkopf Europe Award, as well as travel grants. It is also the international umbrella organization of
the European Youth Parliament.

Geographical Area of Activity: Western, Central and Eastern Europe.

Publications: Travel reports on areas of Europe, with an
emphasis on young people.

Board of Directors: Dr André Schmitz-Schwarzkopf
(Chair.).

Principal Staff: Dir European Youth Parliament Krista
Simberg.

Address: Sophienstr. 28–29, 10178 Berlin.

Telephone: (30) 28095146; **Fax:** (30) 28095150; **Internet:** www
.schwarzkopf-stiftung.de; **e-mail:** info@schwarzkopf
-stiftung.de.

Schweisfurth-Stiftung (Schweisfurth Foundation)

Founded in 1985 by entrepreneur Karl Ludwig Schweisfurth as
an 'ideas business'.

Activities: Promotes innovative approaches, visions and concrete models relating to the future of agriculture, science, education and society. The Foundation works towards identifying
environmentally friendly methods of agriculture and the
improvement of the living standards of livestock. Other focal
points are heightened food safety, the safeguarding of food
quality, innovative means of organic food processing and
novel marketing methods. The Foundation also proposes new
forms of education and training in the artisanal aspects of
food processing. It works closely with government agencies in
these areas, and has published guidelines for sustainable agriculture and food production.

Geographical Area of Activity: Germany, Europe and the
People's Republic of China.

Restrictions: Runs its own projects; no funds or scholarships
are given.

Publications: Newsletter; books; leaflets.

Board of Trustees: Karl Ludwig Schweisfurth (Hon. Chair.);
Josef Jacobi (Chair.); Anna Schweisfurth (Vice-Chair.).

Principal Staff: Chair. Prof. Dr Franz-Theo Gottwald; Sec.
Christa Thomas.

Address: Südliches Schlossrondell 1, 80638 Munich.

Telephone: (89) 1795951-0; **Fax:** (89) 179595-19; **Internet:**
www.schweisfurth-stiftung.de; **e-mail:** info@schweisfurth
.de.

Hanns-Seidel-Stiftung eV (Hanns Seidel Foundation)

Founded in 1967 to promote the democratic and civic development of the German people on a Christian basis; to foster the
academic sector; to foster international attitudes and understanding between peoples; and to promote the process of European unification.

Activities: Operates nationally in the fields of the arts and
humanities and education; internationally it works in the
fields of education, international affairs, health and social welfare, through promoting self-sufficiency and individual initiatives, and through scholarships, travel grants, conferences and
publications. The Foundation works through the following
departments: Academy for Politics and Current Affairs; Institute for Political Education; Institute for International Co-
operation; and Scholarship Organization. It has three liaison
offices and more than 50 project offices.

Geographical Area of Activity: International.

Publications: Infobrief; Annual Report; Political Studies.

Finance: Annual income €59,246,174, expenditure €59,246,174 (31 Dec. 2013).

Board of Directors: Prof. Ursula Männle (Chair.); Alois Glück, Markus Ferber (Vice-Chair.); Dr Ingo Friedrich (Treas.); Michael Glos (Sec.).

Principal Staff: CEO Dr Peter Witterauf.

Address: Lazarettstr. 33, 80636 Munich.

Telephone: (89) 1258-0; **Fax:** (89) 1258-356; **Internet:** www.hss.de; **e-mail:** info@hss.de.

Software AG Foundation

Established in 1992 by Peter M. Schnell and Software AG.

Activities: Provides funding and technical support to non-profit organizations operating in the areas of education, support for young people, care for people with disabilities, science and research, and environmental protection.

Geographical Area of Activity: Europe and Brazil.

Finance: Total assets €418,392,000 (31 Dec. 2013).

Board of Trustees: Hans Ramann, Horst Kinzinger (Chair.).

Principal Staff: Chair. Dr Peter M. Schnell; Exec. Dirs Prof. Dr Horst Philipp Bauer, Achim Grenz, Helmut Habermehl, Markus Ziener.

Address: Am Eichwäldchen 6, 64297 Darmstadt.

Telephone: (6151) 916650; **Fax:** (6151) 91665129; **Internet:** www.software-ag-stiftung.de; **e-mail:** stiftung@sagst.de.

Sparkassen-Kulturstiftung Hessen-Thüringen
(Hesse and Thuringia Savings Banks Cultural Foundation)

Established in 1989 by the Sparkassen- und Giroverband Hessen-Thüringen savings banks for the promotion of culture and the arts in the Federal States of Hesse and Thuringia.

Activities: Operates in Hesse and Thuringia in the fields of the arts and humanities, and conservation and the environment, through conservation of cultural heritage, research, and care for the environment; and in the fields of health and welfare, in particular with relation to young people, the aged, and public health care.

Geographical Area of Activity: Hesse and Thuringia, Germany.

Finance: Total assets €112,973.2m. (2013).

Principal Staff: Pres. Stefan Reuss; CEO Gerhard Grandke.

Address: Alte Rothofstr. 9, 60313 Frankfurt.

Telephone: (69) 2175-0; **Fax:** (69) 2175-595; **Internet:** www.sparkassen-finanzgruppe-ht.de; **e-mail:** sgvht@sgvht.de.

Sparkassenstiftung für internationale Kooperation eV (Savings Banks Foundation for International Co-operation)

Established in 1992 for the promotion of economic and social development in developing and transition countries and areas.

Activities: Operates internationally, especially in Central and Eastern Europe, Central America, Asia and Africa, in the field of aid to developing countries, supporting retail banks and microfinance institutions through providing technical assistance in the areas of internal organization, human resource development and product development (especially lending to micro- and small entrepreneurs and attracting deposits).

Geographical Area of Activity: International, especially Central and Eastern Europe, Central America, Asia and Africa.

Restrictions: Unsolicited applications for grants are not accepted.

Publications: Annual Report.

Finance: Total assets €1,112m. (2013).

Board of Trustees: Georg Fahrenschon (Chair.); Michael Breuer (Vice-Chair.).

Principal Staff: CEO Heinrich Haasis; Deputy CEO Dr Hans-Ulrich Schneider.

Address: Simrockstr. 4, 53113 Bonn.

Telephone: (228) 9703-0; **Fax:** (228) 9703-613; **Internet:** www.sbfic.de; **e-mail:** office@sparkassenstiftung.de.

Friede Springer Herz Stiftung (Friede Springer Heart Foundation)

Founded in 2004 to aid research into cardiac and vascular diseases.

Activities: Supports publications in professioal journals and other media, organizes scientific seminars and lectures, and supports non-profit institutions.

Board of Trustees: Prof. Dr Roland Hetzer (Chair.); Prof. Dr Steffen Behrens (Vice-Chair.).

Principal Staff: CEO Dr Erik Lindner.

Address: Pacelliallee 55, 14195 Berlin.

Telephone: (30) 259172204; **Fax:** (30) 259172202; **Internet:** www.friede-springer-herz-stiftung.de; **e-mail:** info@friede-springer-herz-stiftung.de.

Axel-Springer-Stiftung (Axel Springer Foundation)

Founded in 1953 by publisher Axel Springer to support scholarly and philanthropic activities within the country and abroad.

Activities: Supports all branches of learning through grants for research work; publications (printing of PhD theses, especially about German-Jewish history, the Third Reich, history of the media, international relations); conferences; and courses of further education. The Foundation supports poor elderly journalists and actors in need as a result of sickness; youth welfare; and restoration of religious buildings. It also encourages good relations between Germany and Israel by supporting youth and student exchanges.

Geographical Area of Activity: Germany, Eastern Europe and Israel.

Publications: Foundation anniversary booklet, 2012.

Board of Directors: Friede Springer (Chair.).

Principal Staff: Exec. Dir Dr Erik Lindner.

Address: Pacelliallee 55, 14195 Berlin.

Telephone: (30) 8441-4100; **Fax:** (30) 8441-41099; **Internet:** www.axelspringerstiftung.de; **e-mail:** mail@axelspringerstiftung.de.

Friede Springer Stiftung (Friede Springer Foundation)

Founded in 2011 as an organization independent of politics and religion to promote and support philanthropic goals on an economic, spiritual and cultural basis.

Activities: Supports scientific, artistic and cultural projects, meetings and symposia in scientific, artistic, cultural and educational areas; funds scholarships and endowments; and promotes scientific publications and research projects.

Geographical Area of Activity: Germany.

Finance: Initial endowment €80m. (2011).

Board of Trustees: Dr Eric Schweitzer (Chair.); Marianne Birthler (Vice-Chair.).

Principal Staff: CEO Friede Springer; Deputy CEO Karin Arnold.

Address: Pacelliallee 55, 14195 Berlin.

Telephone: (30) 8441410-0; **Fax:** (30) 8441410-99; **Internet:** www.friedespringerstiftung.de; **e-mail:** mail@friedespringerstiftung.de.

Stiftung CAESAR (Centre of Advanced European Studies and Research)

Established in 1995 by the German Government and the Federal State of North-Rhine-Westphalia to support science and research.

Activities: Operates nationally and internationally in the fields of education, science and technology, through self-conducted programmes and training courses. Operates the CAESAR Centre. Current research priorities are: nanotechnology/

materials science; coupling of biological and electronic systems; ergonomics in communications; molecular sensory systems; and behaviour and brain organization. Maintains a library.

Geographical Area of Activity: International.

Restrictions: No grants are made.

Publications: *Smart Materials*; *Proceedings of the First Caesarium* (1999); annual reports; research materials and publications.

Finance: Annual income €14,359,907, expenditure €12,995,637 (2013).

Board of Trustees: Prof. Dr Martin Stratmann (Chair.).

Principal Staff: Man. Dir Prof. Dr Ulrich Benjamin Kaupp; Dir Dr Jason Kerr; Admin. Dir Gertrud Bilski.

Address: Ludwig-Erhard-Allee 2, 53175 Bonn.

Telephone: (228) 9656-0; **Fax:** (228) 9656-111; **Internet:** www.caesar.de; **e-mail:** office@caesar.de.

Stiftung Entwicklung und Frieden—SEF (Development and Peace Foundation)

Established in 1986 by the Federal States of North Rhine-Westphalia, Berlin, Brandenburg and Saxony on the initiative of the former Chancellor of the Federal Republic of Germany (Bundesrepublik Deutschland) Willy Brandt.

Activities: A cross-party, not-for-profit organization, which argues for a new political order in a world marked by globalization. The Foundation's work is based on three principles: global responsibility, cross-party and cross-cultural dialogue, and an interdisciplinary approach to understanding interdependencies. It carries out its work through conferences, including symposia, expert workshops and dialogues, and publications.

Geographical Area of Activity: Germany and international.

Restrictions: Does not make grants.

Publications: Annual Report; *Global Trends* (biennially); *Series ONE WORLD*; *SEF Policy Papers*; *SEF News* (3 a year, in German and English); *World Politics*; *UN Peacekeeping Operations in Africa*; *Una mirada desde América Latina*.

Finance: Annual income €459,720, expenditure €424,546 (31 Dec. 2013).

Board of Trustees: Hannelore Kraft (Chair.); Michael Müller, Stanislaw Tillich, Dr Dietmar Woidke (Vice-Chair.).

Principal Staff: Exec. Dir Karin Kortmann; Deputy Exec. Dirs Dr Gerd Harms, Prof. Dr Robert Kappel; Treas. Klaus Brückner.

Address: Dechenstr. 2, 53115 Bonn.

Telephone: (228) 95925-0; **Fax:** (228) 95925-99; **Internet:** www.sef-bonn.org; **e-mail:** sef@sef-bonn.org.

Stiftung Ettersberg

Established in 2002 on the initiative of the Spanish author and Buchenwald survivor Jorge Semprún.

Activities: Concerned with comparative research into European dictatorships in the 20th century, focusing on the reasons for their emergence, the form they took and the ways in which they were overcome. The Foundation hosts international symposia and academic seminars, the results of which are presented in a series of publications and periodicals. It also conducts academic research into the Socialist dictatorship in East Germany, using its results to further the teaching of political history in schools and other contexts. In 2012, the Foundation took over the establishment and running of the Memorial and Study Centre Andreasstraße in the former Stasi remand prison in Erfurt.

Geographical Area of Activity: Germany.

Publications: Results of international symposia and academic seminars are presented in a series of publications and periodicals.

Executive Board: Dr Jörg Ganzenmüller (Chair.).

Principal Staff: Man. Dir Michael Siegel.

Address: Jenaer Str. 4, 99425 Weimar.

Telephone: (3643) 49750; **Fax:** (3643) 497522; **Internet:** www.stiftung-ettersberg.de; **e-mail:** weimar@stiftung-ettersberg.de.

Stiftung zur Förderung der Hochschulrektorenkonferenz (Foundation for the Promotion of the German Rectors' Conference)

Founded in 1965 by Prof. Dr Julius Speer, Prof. Dr Rudolf Sieverts, Prof. Dr Helmut Witte, Prof. Dr Gerhard Kielwein and Prof. Dr Hans Leussink to provide personnel and appropriate facilities for the accomplishment of the tasks of the Conference of Rectors of higher/further education institutes in Germany.

Activities: Operates within the spheres of activity of the German Rectors' Conference, a voluntary association of universities and other institutions of higher education, which aims to find a common solution to problems of higher education, and publicizes those problems; makes recommendations to the appropriate authorities; aims to promote co-operation among state, scientific and academic bodies, etc.; provides information services to member institutions and all other interested parties; and generally concerns itself with developments in higher education. Staff put at the disposal of the conference by the Foundation are mainly active in the field of education, nationally and internationally, and in the fields of social welfare and studies and international relations. Programmes are carried out through conferences, courses, publications and reports. Awards a biennial Corporate Communications Prize, worth €25,000, in conjunction with ZEIT, a publishing company, and the Robert-Bosch-Stiftung GmbH (q.v.).

Geographical Area of Activity: Mainly Germany.

Publications: Annual Report; statements.

Executive Board: Prof. Dr Horst Hippler (Pres.).

Principal Staff: Sec.-Gen. Dr Thomas Kathöfer.

Address: Ahrstr. 39, 53175 Bonn.

Telephone: (228) 887-0; **Fax:** (228) 887-110; **Internet:** www.hrk.de; **e-mail:** post@hrk.de.

Stiftung Jugend forscht e. V. (Foundation for Youth Research)

Founded in 1965 by Henri Nannen to promote competitions for young scientists under the age of 21 years to encourage the research work of students, trainees and other young people.

Activities: Organizes competitions in Germany; also makes grants, and awards scholarships and fellowships.

Geographical Area of Activity: Germany.

Restrictions: Applications for grants are not accepted.

Publications: Annual Report; commemorative volumes and brochures concerning the competitions; *Jugend forscht*; *Schüler experimentieren*.

Finance: Annual revenue €2,132,508, expenditure €2,132,508 (31 Dec. 2013).

Principal Staff: Dir Dr Sven Baszio; Deputy Dir Dr Nico P. Kock.

Address: Baumwall 5, 20459 Hamburg.

Telephone: (40) 374709-0; **Fax:** (40) 374709-99; **Internet:** www.jugend-forscht.de; **e-mail:** info@jugend-forscht.de.

Stiftung für Kinder (Foundation for Children)

Established in 1986 to help children in less-developed countries learn and experience new forms of living together after their basic needs have been met, and to set an example of sharing in developed countries.

Activities: Operates in Germany and the Philippines in the areas of development aid, education, law and human rights, and medicine and health, through research, grants to organizations and individuals, and issuing publications. The Foundation's main concern is to use its resources for the elimination of misery, to overcome social, economic, political and cultural domination and power structures through co-operation with project partners on a reciprocal basis. It maintains a database of more than 6,000 German child-related foundations and associations.

Geographical Area of Activity: Germany and the Philippines.

Restrictions: Grants are not normally made to individuals.

Publications: *Children—War and Persecution: Proceedings of the Congress, Hamburg, Sept. 26–29 1993* (in Romanian, 2001); *Documents of the European Forum for Child Welfare*; *Focus Philippines* (journal); *Eliminating Racist Discrimination in Germany* (from the UN Committee on the Elimination of All Forms of Racial Discrimination, 2008).

Principal Staff: Exec. Dir Ekkehard Arnsperger.

Address: c/o RA. Ekkehard Arnsperger, Schwaighofstr. 14, 79100 Freiburg im Breisgau.

Telephone: (761) 71015; **Fax:** (761) 77306; **Internet:** www.stiftung-fuer-kinder.org; **e-mail:** stiftung.fuer.kinder@t-online.de.

Stiftung Kinder in Afrika (Children in Africa Foundation)

Founded in 1984 by Horst W. Zillmer to grant aid and assistance to children in Africa.

Activities: Operates in Africa in the fields of education, and medicine and health, through grants to individuals and institutions. Projects since 1985 have taken place in Burkina Faso, Cameroon, Equatorial Guinea, Ghana, Kenya, Madagascar, Morocco, Mozambique, Namibia, South Africa, Sudan, Tanzania, Togo and Zambia.

Geographical Area of Activity: Sub-Saharan Africa.

Trustees: Horst W. Zillmer (Chair.); Dr Hans-Dieter Höhnk (Vice.-Chair.).

Address: Holsteiner Str. 12c, 21465 Reinbek.

Telephone: (40) 7221105; **Fax:** (40) 7221105; **Internet:** www.kinder-in-afrika.de; **e-mail:** info@kinder-in-afrika.de.

Stiftung Lesen (Foundation for Reading)

Established in 1988 to promote reading.

Activities: Operates in the fields of the arts and humanities, and education for young people and adults, promoting the reading of books, newspapers and magazines; supporting a reading and oral culture; and supporting research into reading, communication and the media.

Restrictions: Applications for grants are not accepted.

Publications: Annual Report; studies; e-books.

Finance: Total assets €9,137,051 (31 Dec. 2013).

Board of Trustees: Prof. Dr Markus Schächter (Chair.); Prof. Dr Barbara Ischinger, Sylvia Löhrmann (Vice-Chair.).

Principal Staff: CEO Dr Jörg F. Maas; Man. Dir Dr Joerg Pfuhl; Deputy Man. Dir Barbara Schleihagen.

Address: Römerwall 40, 55131 Mainz.

Telephone: (6131) 28890-20; **Fax:** (6131) 230333; **Internet:** www.stiftunglesen.de; **e-mail:** mail@stiftunglesen.de.

Stiftung Nord-Süd-Brücken (North-South-Bridge Foundation)

Established in 1994 to assist development in less-developed cuntries, and to promote an understanding of the necessity of co-operation in development and international understanding.

Activities: Promotes partnerships for development projects in less-developed regions, informing the public about the necessity of co-operation in development, especially through promoting tolerance and international understanding. The Foundation supports only NGOs based in the former German Democratic Republic (East Germany) and East Berlin.

Geographical Area of Activity: Asia, Africa and Latin America.

Finance: Total assets €18,635,480 (31 Dec. 2013).

Board of Trustees: Kerstin Wippel (Chair.); Arndt von Massenbach, Jessica Weiss (Vice-Chair.).

Principal Staff: CEO Reinhard Hermie; Deputy CEOs Michael Kreuzberg, Christiane Schulte.

Address: Greifswalder Str. 33A, 10405 Berlin.

Telephone: (30) 42851385; **Fax:** (30) 42851386; **Internet:** www.nord-sued-bruecken.de; **e-mail:** info@nord-sued-bruecken.de.

Stiftung Ökologie & Landbau (Ecology and Agriculture Foundation)

Founded in 1962 by Karl Werner Kieffer, CEO of manufacturing company G. M. Pfaff AG, to promote scientific research into the cultivation of agricultural produce with a view towards saving natural resources, preserving the ecological equilibrium and producing high-quality foodstuffs free of noxious substances.

Activities: Operates through the encouragement and support of the ecological schools of thought developing in agricultural science and practice; the co-ordination of exchange of knowledge and experience; support for active initiatives in training practice and science; and the organization of meetings and other events.

Geographical Area of Activity: Western Europe.

Restrictions: Does not award grants.

Publications: *Ökologie & Landbau*; *Ökologische Konzepte* (series); *SÖL-Sonderausgaben* (series); report on operations and activities.

Finance: Annual revenue and expenditure approx. €500,000.

Board of Trustees: Dagi Kieffer (Chair.); Edda Knief (Vice-Chair.).

Principal Staff: Chief Exec. Uli Zerger.

Address: Weinstr. Süd 51, Postfach 1516, 67089 Bad Dürkheim.

Telephone: (6322) 989700; **Fax:** (6322) 989701; **Internet:** www.soel.de; **e-mail:** info@soel.de.

Stiftung Weltethos (Global Ethic Foundation)

Established in 1995 by Count K. K. von der Groeben for inter-cultural and inter-religious research, education and encounter, for the dissemination of the idea of a global ethic, with the basic conviction that there can be no peace among nations without peace between religions; that there can be no peace among religions without dialogue between religions; and that there can be no dialogue between religions without research into the foundations of religions.

Activities: Operates nationally and internationally in the areas of the humanities, inter-cultural and inter-religious dialogue, education, international affairs, and human rights, through self-conducted programmes, research, lectures, conferences, training courses and publications. A small research team engages in long-term work to further a global ethic, and the Foundation also supports wider initiatives and projects. The basis of the Foundation's programme is the Declaration toward a Global Ethic endorsed by the Parliament of the World's Religions in 1993 (i.e. a commitment to a culture of non-violence and respect for life, to a culture of solidarity and a just economic order, to a culture of tolerance and a life of truthfulness, and to a culture of equal rights and partnership between men and women).

Geographical Area of Activity: International.

Publications: *Global Responsibility: In Search of a New World Ethic*; *Yes to a Global Ethic*; *A Global Ethic for Global Politics and Economics*; *A Global Ethic and Global Responsibilities*; fact sheets.

Principal Staff: CEO Eberhard Stilz; Sec.-Gen. Dr Stephan Schlensog.

Address: Waldhäuser Str. 23, 72076 Tübingen.

Telephone: (7071) 62646; **Fax:** (7071) 610140; **Internet:** www.global-ethic.org; **e-mail:** office@global-ethic.org.

Stiftung West-Östliche Begegnungen (Foundation for East-West Encounters)

Established in 1994 to promote contacts between the peoples of Germany and of the countries of the former USSR for understanding, friendship, good international neighbourhood and peace.

Activities: Provides grants for echange projects among young people, active citizens, schools and municipalities in fields including culture, history, peace, social activities, inclusion, environment, sustainable development, civic engagement, etc. The Foundation carries out its own projects in co-operation with civil society and other partners on town twinning and NGO networking.

Geographical Area of Activity: Germany with Armenia, Azerbaijan, Belarus, Estonia, Georgia, Kazakhstan, Kyrgyzstan, Latvia, Lithuania, Moldova, the Russian Federation, Tajikistan, Turkmenistan, Ukraine, Uzbekistan.

Restrictions: Grants only to German institutions (e.g. registered NGOs, schools, municipalities, institutes, etc.). No grants to individuals, foundations.

Publications: Activity Report; financial statement; information brochures.

Finance: Annual expenditure approx. €450,000.

Board of Trustees: Prof. Dr Hans-Peter Füssel (Chair.); Fritz Tangerman (Vice-Chair.).

Principal Staff: Chair. Dr Helmut Domke; Man. Dir Monika Tharann.

Address: Mauerstr. 93, 10117 Berlin.

Telephone: (30) 2044840; **Fax:** (30) 20647646; **Internet:** www.stiftung-woeb.de; **e-mail:** info@stiftung-woeb.de.

Stiftung Wissenschaft und Politik—Deutsches Institut für internationale Politik und Sicherheit—SWP (German Institute for International and Security Affairs)

Founded in 1962; an independent research centre that advises the German Parliament and the German Federal Government on all matters relevant to German foreign and security policy.

Activities: Organized into eight research units, currently consisting of approximately 60 researchers. The Institute organizes conferences and workshops. It also maintains a library of approx. 85,000 volumes and a computerized information system with c. 900,000 bibliographical references in international relations and area studies.

Geographical Area of Activity: Germany.

Restrictions: Does not make grants or offer scholarships.

Publications: *Internationale Politik und Sich*; *SWP-Aktuell*; *SWP-Zeitschriftenschauen*; *Kurzgesagt*; *Aktuelle Materialien zur Internationalen Politik*; *SWP-View*; research papers and newsletter.

Finance: Mainly funded by the Federal Chancellery; institutional funding €11.7m. (2013).

Board of Trustees: Prof. Dr Hans-Peter Keitel (Pres.); Peter Altmaier (Deputy Pres.).

Principal Staff: Dir Prof. Dr. Volker Perthes; Deputy Dir Christoph Geisler.

Address: POB 31 13 19, 10643 Berlin; Ludwigkirchplatz 3–4, 10719 Berlin.

Telephone: (30) 88007-0; **Fax:** (30) 88007-100; **Internet:** www.swp-berlin.org; **e-mail:** swp@swp-berlin.org.

Stiftungsfonds Deutsche Bank im Stifterverband für die Deutsche Wissenschaft (Deutsche Bank Endowment Fund at the Donors' Association for the Promotion of Sciences and Humanities)

Established in 1970 by Deutsche Bank AG for the promotion of science and research.

Activities: Operates in the field of science and technology, mainly through funding programmes at universities and other institutions.

Geographical Area of Activity: Europe.

Publications: Study courses.

Finance: Total endowment approx. €10m.

Principal Staff: Dirs Jürgen Fitschen, Prof. Dr Andreas Schlüter.

Address: c/o Stifterverband für die Deutsche Wissenschaft eV, Barkhovenallee 1, 45239 Essen.

Telephone: (201) 8401-0; **Fax:** (201) 8401-301; **Internet:** www.stiftungsfonds-deutsche-bank.de; **e-mail:** andreas.schlueter@stifterverband.de.

Studienstiftung des deutschen Volkes (German National Academic Foundation)

Refounded in 1948 to give grants and scholarships to particularly gifted students and to aid them in their university studies.

Activities: Operates in the fields of science and medicine, the arts and humanities, law and other professions, through grants to individuals. Scholars may participate in summer schools arranged by the Foundation, receive special research grants or special tuition at any German and many foreign universities. Awards around 2,000 scholarships each year.

Geographical Area of Activity: Germany.

Publications: Annual Report.

Finance: Annual revenue €79,220,862, expenditure approx. €79,220,862 (2013).

Board of Trustees: Prof. Dr Dr h.c. Erika Fischer-Lichte (Chair.); Prof. Dr Michael Boutros, Prof. Dr Johannes Masing (Vice-Chair.).

Principal Staff: Pres. Prof. Dr Reinhard Zimmermann; Vice-Pres. Prof. Dr Stefan Matuschek; Sec.-Gen. Dr Annette Julius.

Address: Ahrstr. 41, 53175 Bonn.

Telephone: (228) 820960; **Fax:** (228) 82096103; **Internet:** www.studienstiftung.de; **e-mail:** info@studienstiftung.de.

Südost-Institut—Stiftung für wissenschaftliche Südosteuropaforschung (South-East Institute—Foundation for Academic Research into South-Eastern Europe)

Founded in 1930 by the German Government to carry out research into the history, societies and politics of South-Eastern Europe.

Activities: Operates nationally and internationally in the fields of the history and current affairs of South-Eastern Europe, through research, conferences and publications; hosts guest researchers; public research library of approx. 130,000 items.

Geographical Area of Activity: Europe.

Restrictions: No grants are made.

Publications: Journals: *Südost-Forschungen* (history); *Südosteuropa* (current affairs); Series: *Südosteuropäische Arbeiten*; *Südosteuropa Bibliographie – Ergänzungsbände*.

Finance: Annual income €3,180,329, expenditure €2,985,186 (2014).

Foundation Council: Prof. Dr Udo Hebel (Chair.); Dr Georg Brun (Deputy Chair.).

Principal Staff: Man. Dir Prof. Dr Ulf Brunnbauer; Dir Prof. Dr Jürgen Jerger.

Address: Landshuter Str. 4, 93047 Regensburg.

Telephone: (941) 9435410; **Fax:** (941) 9435427; **Internet:** www.suedost-institut.de; www.ios-regensburg.de; **e-mail:** info@ios-regensburg.de.

Fritz Thyssen Stiftung (Fritz Thyssen Foundation)

Founded in 1959 by Amélie Thyssen and her daughter, Anita Countess Zichy-Thyssen, to promote research and scholarships in universities and research institutes, particularly in Germany. Special consideration is given to the rising generation of scientists and scholars.

Activities: Supports particular research projects of limited duration, mainly in basic research in the humanities; international relations; state, economy and society; and medicine.

Geographical Area of Activity: Mainly Germany.

Publications: Annual Report; *The Establishment the Fritz Thyssen Foundation*; *Historia Scientiarum*; *Tradition and Tasks of National and Private Science Promotion*; *Thyssen Lectures*; *THESEUS European Leadership in Challenging Times-Academia & Politics in Dialogue*.

Finance: Annual income €32,188,172, expenditure €19,630,290 (2012).

Board of Trustees: Werner Wenning (Chair.); Prof. Dr Utz-Hellmuth Felcht, Erwin Staudt (Vice-Chair.).

Principal Staff: Exec. Dir Dr Frank Suder.

Address: Apostelnkloster 13–15, 50672 Cologne.

Telephone: (221) 2774960; **Fax:** (221) 27749629; **Internet:** www.fritz-thyssen-stiftung.de; **e-mail:** fts@fritz-thyssen-stiftung.de.

Alfred Toepfer Stiftung F.V.S. (Alfred Toepfer Foundation F.V.S.)

Founded in 1931 by Dr Alfred Toepfer to promote European unity and understanding between nations. Formerly known as Stiftung F.V.S.

Activities: Operates in Europe in the fields of the arts, science, humanities, young people, European relations and the conservation of natural resources, through self-conducted programmes, scholarships, grants to institutions and the awarding of prizes. Four awards are made annually for achievements in the field of European relations. The Foundation also operates an extensive scholarship programme for students from Central and Eastern Europe.

Geographical Area of Activity: Europe.

Publications: Annual Report and a variety of books on the Foundation's history and prizes; *Jahrbuch Alfred Toepfer Stiftung F.V.S.* (year book); articles, essays, speeches.

Finance: Annual income €4,511,860, expenditure €2,426,234 (30 June 2013).

Foundation Supervisory Council: Prof. Dr Jürgen Schlaeger (Chair.); Marlehn Thieme (Vice-Chair.).

Principal Staff: Chair. Ansgar Wimmer.

Address: Georgplatz 10, 20099 Hamburg.

Telephone: (40) 33402-10; **Fax:** (40) 335860; **Internet:** www.toepfer-fvs.de; **e-mail:** benecke@toepfer-fvs.de.

Transparency International—TI

Established in 1993 to combat corruption at national and international level.

Activities: Anti-corruption organization operating in more than 90 countries worldwide, through national chapters that work in collaboration with relevant players from civil society organizations, government, business and the media to promote transparency in elections, in public administration, in procurement and in business. The organization is involved in regional as well as national programmes. It also uses advocacy campaigns to lobby governments to implement anti-corruption reforms.

Geographical Area of Activity: International.

Publications: Annual Report; *Corruption Perceptions Index* (annual); *Global Corruption Report*; working papers; *Policy Positions*; *Progress Reports*.

Finance: Annual income €26,850,094, expenditure €26,714,222 (31 Dec. 2014).

Board of Directors: José Carlos Ugaz (Chair.); Elena A. Panfilova (Vice-Chair.).

Principal Staff: Man. Dir Cobus de Swardt; Deputy Man. Dir Miklos Marschall.

Address: Alt-Moabit 96, 10559 Berlin.

Telephone: (30) 3438200; **Fax:** (30) 34703912; **Internet:** www.transparency.org; **e-mail:** ti@transparency.org.

Klaus Tschira Stiftung GmbH (Klaus Tschira Foundation)

Established in 1995 by Dr Klaus Tschira, co-founder of software company SAP AG.

Activities: Operates in the fields of promoting the natural sciences, mathematics and computer science, working with children from pre-school age, in school and extracurricular activities, and with young scientists, supporting research projects and helping them to improve their communication skills. The Foundation spends 51% of its annual budget on its own projects, particularly the European Media Laboratory, founded by Klaus Tschira in 1997. It invites applications for funding of projects that are in line with the central concerns of the Foundation.

Geographical Area of Activity: International.

Restrictions: Grants not normally made to individuals.

Finance: Capital consists of approx. 11.5% of shares in SAP AG.

Principal Staff: Man. Partner Dr Klaus Tschira; Man. Dir Beate Spiegel.

Address: Villa Bosch, Schloss-Wolfsbrunnenweg 33, 69118 Heidelberg.

Telephone: (6221) 533101; **Fax:** (6221) 533199; **Internet:** www.kts.villa-bosch.de; **e-mail:** stiftungsbuero@klaus-tschira-stiftung.de.

Kurt-Tucholsky-Stiftung (Kurt Tucholsky Foundation)

Founded 1969 by Mary Gerold-Tucholsky to promote international communication and understanding.

Activities: Promotes international student exchanges through scholarships in the fields of German studies, journalism, sociology or political sciences, awarding scholarships to German students to study abroad, and to foreign students to study in Germany for one year. The Foundation also administers the Tucholsky literary legacy at the German literature archives in Marbach am Neckar; and awards the Tucholsky Prize, worth €3,000.

Geographical Area of Activity: International.

Publications: Newsletter; *Rundbrief* (2–3 a year); conference proceedings.

Principal Staff: First Chair. Dr Ian King; Second Chair. Henriette Harder; Sec. Klaus Neumann; Treas. Bernd Brüntrup.

Address: Besselstraße 21/II, 32427 Minden.

Telephone: (571) 8375440; **Fax:** (571) 8375449; **Internet:** www.tucholsky-gesellschaft.de; **e-mail:** info@tucholsky-gesellschaft.de.

Vodafone Stiftung Deutschland (Vodafone Foundation Germany)

One of the largest company foundations in Germany.

Activities: Operates in the fields of education, social welfare, medicine and health, and culture and the arts.

Geographical Area of Activity: Germany.

Restrictions: No new projects are currently being taken on for funding.

Publications: Newsletter.

Advisory Council: Thomas Ellerbeck (Chair.).

Principal Staff: Man. Dirs Thomas Holtmanns, Dr Mark Speich.

Address: Ferdinand-Braun-Platz 1, 40549 Dusseldorf.

Telephone: (211) 5335579; **Fax:** (211) 5331898; **Internet:** www.vodafone-stiftung.de; **e-mail:** info@vodafone-stiftung.de.

VolkswagenStiftung (Volkswagen Foundation)

Founded in 1961 by the Federal Republic of Germany and the State of Lower Saxony for the promotion of science, technology and the humanities in research and university teaching.

Activities: Operates nationally and internationally, through grants for specific purposes to academic and technical institutions engaged in research and teaching. The Foundation is free to support any area of science, as well as the humanities, but has limited its funding programme to a range of specific fields; special programmes operate for Sub-Saharan Africa and Central Asia/the Caucasus.

Geographical Area of Activity: International.

Restrictions: In the case of applications from abroad, co-operation with German research workers or scholars is usually essential.

Publications: Annual Report; *Crossing Borders* (information in English); *Impulse für die Wissenschaft*; brochures.

Finance: Total grants expenditure since 1962 approx. €4,200m.; total assets €2,900m. (2013).

Board of Trustees: Dr Gabriele Heinen-Kljajić (Chair.); Dr Georg Schütte, Prof. Dr Stefan Treue (Vice-Chair.).

Principal Staff: Sec.-Gen. Dr Wilhelm Krull.

Address: Kastanienallee 35, 30519 Hannover.

Telephone: (511) 8381-0; **Fax:** (511) 8381-344; **Internet:** www.volkswagenstiftung.de; **e-mail:** info@volkswagenstiftung.de.

WasserStiftung (Water Foundation)

Established in 2000 by Ernst Frost and Henner Lang to support those in regions with too little, or polluted, drinking water, helping them to help themselves.

Activities: Operates in the areas of development aid, health and welfare, and environmental conservation. Supports water projects in Afghanistan, Bolivia, Chile, Eritrea, Ethiopia and the Palestinian Territories. Awards the Hundertwasser Prize, worth €5,000, which recognizes contributions to the sustainable use of water resources and water supply to remote communities.

Geographical Area of Activity: Afghanistan, Bolivia, Chile, Eritrea, Ethiopia and Palestinian Territories.

Board of Directors: Ernst Frost (Chair.).

Address: Lechnerstr. 23, 82067 Ebenhausen.

Telephone: (8178) 998418; **Fax:** (8178) 998419; **Internet:** www.wasserstiftung.de; **e-mail:** wasserstiftung@t-online.de.

Max Weber Stiftung (Max Weber Foundation)

Established in 2002 as the Deutsche Geisteswissenschaftliche Institute im Ausland—DGIA. Present name adopted in 2012.

Activities: Promotes research, particularly in the fields of history, cultural studies, economics and the social sciences, in selected countries; and mutual understanding between Germany and these countries. The Foundation is an umbrella organization comprising various institutes worldwide, which carry out research and promote co-operation between scholars and institutions within their own spheres by means of publications and academic conferences, providing academic information and advice, facilitating contacts between scholars, supporting the future generation of scholars, as well as setting up and maintaining libraries and collections of other media.

Geographical Area of Activity: International.

Publications: *Weltwiet vor Ort* (magazine); series of monographs; journals; bulletins.

Finance: Annual expenditure €36,148,898 (2012).

Board of Trustees: Dr Heinz Duchhardt (Chair.).

Principal Staff: Exec. Dir Dr Harald Rosenbach; Deputy Exec. Dir Dr Bernhard Roscher.

Address: Rheinallee 6, 53173 Bonn.

Telephone: (228) 37786-0; **Fax:** (228) 37786-19; **Internet:** www.maxweberstiftung.de; **e-mail:** info@maxweberstiftung.de.

Dr Rainer Wild-Stiftung—Stiftung für gesunde Ernährung (Dr Rainer Wild Foundation for Healthy Nutrition)

Established in 1991 by Dr Rainer Wild, and accorded full legal status by the governing council of Karlsruhe in 1993, to organize actively, on an international basis, scientific research, public education, occupational training and scientific and cultural events aimed at advancing the area of healthy human nutrition.

Activities: Operates in the fields of nutritional education, consumer behaviour, food and culture, food sensory science; through networking, conventions and awarding prizes. Target groups are food scientists, nutritionists, dieticians, social scientists and educationalists. It hosts conventions, publishes books and journals, awards the Dr Rainer Wild Prize for outstanding accomplishments in the field of healthy nutrition, initiates research projects and provides scholarships to young scientists.

Geographical Area of Activity: International.

Restrictions: No grants are made to individuals or organizations.

Publications: Annual Report; *Healthy Nutrition* (book series)*; Mitteilungen* (journal)*;* textbooks; articles; lectures.

Finance: Annual budget €750,000 (2014).

Principal Staff: Chair. Prof. Dr Rainer Wild; Deputy Chair. Prof. Dr Harald Schaumburg; Man. Dir Dr Gesa Schönberger.

Address: Mittelgewannweg 10, 69123 Heidelberg.

Telephone: (6221) 7511-200; **Fax:** (6221) 7511-240; **Internet:** www.gesunde-ernaehrung.org; **e-mail:** info@gesunde-ernaehrung.org.

Carl-Zeiss-Stiftung (Carl-Zeiss Foundation)

Founded in 1889 by Dr Ernst Abbe with the following objectives: to develop the precision technical industry, at the Optical Works and the Glass Works, Jena; to fulfil higher social obligations than individual owners could permanently guarantee towards all the employees to improve their situation with regard to their personal and economic rights; outside the works, to promote the general interests of the branches of precision technical industry as mentioned above, to participate in organizations and measures designed for the public good of the working population in Jena and its immediate neighbourhood; and to promote study in natural and mathematical sciences in research as well as teaching. After the expropriation of the Carl-Zeiss-Stiftung in 1948, the legal seat of the Foundation was transferred to the Federal Republic of Germany (Bundesrepublik Deutschland).

Activities: Runs the two companies Carl Zeiss AG, Oberkochen and SCHOTT AG, Mainz. As well as these commercial ventures, the Foundation supports research in the field of science and technology. It operates through self-conducted programmes; and supports young scientists and research projects at selected German universities.

Geographical Area of Activity: Germany.

Restrictions: Religious or political institutions are not supported.

Publications: Annual Report.

Board of Trustees: Dr Dieter Kurz (Chair.).

Principal Staff: Man. Dir Dr Klaus Herberger; Deputy Man. Dir Dennys Klein.

Address: Ministerium für Wissenschaft, Forschung und Kunst Baden-Württemberg, Königstr. 46, 70173 Stuttgart.

Telephone: (711) 2793253; **Internet:** www.carl-zeiss-stiftung.de; **e-mail:** klaus.herberger@mwk.bwl.de.

ZEIT-Stiftung Ebelin und Gerd Bucerius (Ebelin and Gerd Bucerius ZEIT Foundation)

Established in 1971 by Gerd Bucerius, founder of weekly newspaper *Die Zeit* (f. 1946).

Activities: Operates in three areas: science and scholarships (including innovation in higher education, scholarship in the field of history, and research); education and training (including press and journalism, dialogue in society, development of the Hamburg secondary-school system); and art and culture (including literature, art and museums, cultural heritage, and music and theatre), through research centres, scholarships and prizes. The Foundation also established the Bucerius Law School (f. 2000) and the Bucerius Art Forum (f. 2002).

Geographical Area of Activity: Germany, Central, Eastern and Western Europe, and Israel.

Publications: Report (biennially); newsletter; variety of brochures.

Finance: Total assets €772.9m. (2014).

Principal Staff: CEO and Chair. Prof. Dr Michael Göring.

Address: Feldbrunnenstr. 56, 20148 Hamburg.

Telephone: (40) 413366; **Fax:** (40) 41336700; **Internet:** www.zeit-stiftung.de; **e-mail:** zeit-stiftung@zeit-stiftung.de.

Ghana

FOUNDATIONS, TRUSTS AND NON-PROFIT ORGANIZATIONS

African Women's Development Fund—AWDF

Established in 2000 by Bisi Adeleye-Fayemi, Hilda Tadria and Joana Foster to support organizations promoting women's rights in Africa.

Activities: Finances sub-regional, regional, local and national organizations that empower women; extends technical support to projects on women's development; and disseminates information on the work of organizations that benefit African women. The Fund has six programmes: Women's Human Rights; Economic Empowerment and Livelihoods; Governance, Peace and Security; Health and Reproductive Rights; HIV/AIDS; and Arts, Culture and Sports. Since 2001, it has disbursed US $17m. in grants to 800 women's organizations in 42 countries.

Geographical Area of Activity: Africa.

Publications: Annual Report.

Executive Board: Dr Hilda M. Tadria (Chair.); Bisi Adeleye-Fayemi (Pres.).

Principal Staff: CEO Theo Sowa.

Address: PMB CT 89 Cantonments, Accra; Plot Number 78, AWDF House, Ambassadorial Enclave, East Legon, Accra.

Telephone: (30) 2521257; **Internet:** www.awdf.org; **e-mail:** awdf@adwf.org.

The Bridge Foundation—TBF

Established in 1996 by Ray Quarcoo to support the development of disadvantaged children living in distressed non-formal urban settlements and rural communities.

Activities: Operates in the fields of social welfare and education for disadvantaged children, through sports and literacy programmes, and vocational training initiatives. The Foundation runs a youth development resource centre to promote and channel the talents and energies of disadvantaged young people. It also operates sports clubs and runs literacy programmes for out-of-school children, particularly homeless street children living in deprived urban areas.

Geographical Area of Activity: Ghana.

Restrictions: Partners only European and American NGOs working with children in West Africa.

Board of Trustees: E. Ray Quarcoo (Pres.).

Address: The Bridge Boxing Gym, Aviation Rd Extension, Roman Ridge, POB 13463, Accra.

Telephone: (8) 9553020; **Internet:** bridgefoundationghana .org; **e-mail:** info@bridgefoundationghana.org.

Volunteer Partnerships for West Africa

Established in 2007 by Hayford Siaw to improve opportunities for people in underprivileged communities in the areas of education, health, sanitation and sustainable development.

Activities: Runs projects in the areas of education; eradication of child labour; human rights; sustainable development; poverty reduction through skills building; and combating the spread of diseases, including malaria, HIV/AIDS, tuberculosis and Buruli ulcers. The organization runs the Street Libraries project.

Geographical Area of Activity: Ghana.

Principal Staff: Exec. Dir Hayford Siaw.

Address: POB OF 75, Ofankor, Accra; H/No. 6, Wulomo St, Pokuase ACP Rridge, Pokuase, Accra.

Telephone: (30) 2937040; **Fax:** (30) 2928245; **Internet:** www .vpwa.org; **e-mail:** info@vpwa.org.

Greece

FOUNDATIONS, TRUSTS AND NON-PROFIT ORGANIZATIONS

Bodossaki Foundation

Founded in 1972 by Prodromos Bodossakis Athanassiades to promote education, health care and the environment.

Activities: Operates nationally in the fields of conservation and the environment, education, medicine and health, and civil society. The Foundation runs self-conducted programmes, and awards grants to institutions and individuals, scholarships, fellowships and prizes. Greek citizens are also eligible to apply for the Bodossaki Graduate Scholarships at Oxford University, United Kingdom (in science), London School of Economics, Hellenic Observatory, United Kingdom (in economics), and Tufts University, Fletcher School of Law and Diplomacy, USA (in economics).

Geographical Area of Activity: Mainly Greece.

Restrictions: Benefits are restricted to persons of Greek origin.

Publications: Information brochures; co-publishing of special editions; electronic/online information; newsletters; reports.

Finance: Total assets €142,084,238, annual expenditure €30,172,910 (2014).

Board of Directors: Dimitris Vlastos (Pres.); Ioannis Detsis (Vice-Pres.); Prof. Dr Theodoros Theodorou (Associate Vice-Pres.).

Principal Staff: Sec. Ioannis Mathioudakis.

Address: 5 Vassilissis Georgiou II, 106 74 Athens.

Telephone: (21) 03237973; **Fax:** (21) 03237976; **Internet:** www .bodossaki.gr; **e-mail:** info@bodossaki.gr.

The J. F. Costopoulos Foundation

Established in 1979 by endowment of the late Spyros and Eurydice Costopoulos, for the promotion of Greek culture and civilization in Greece and internationally.

Activities: Aims to support the promotion of Hellenic culture, through the funding of scientific, educational and cultural activities. The Foundation focuses on the fields of cultural heritage and tradition; society; science and research; education and studies; and arts. It funds museums; libraries; holy dioceses and churches; public welfare societies; associations and unions; foundations and schools; research projects, seminars and conferences; studies; Chairs of Greek studies abroad; archaeological excavations and publications; theatre and dance companies; musical productions; and visual arts projects.

Geographical Area of Activity: Mainly Greece and Europe; some activity in the USA.

Restrictions: Activities supported focus on the promotion of Hellenic culture, and are non-profit and for public benefit. This forms part of the Foundation's policy to subsidize important initiatives that would not be otherwise funded. Priority is given to Greek researchers or researchers of Greek origin. The Board of Trustees has temporarily suspended the provision of financial support for doctoral and postdoctoral programmes and consequent publications. In the field of holy dioceses and churches, grants are given for the restoration of Byzantine monuments but not contemporary churches. In the field of films, grants are given mainly for short films and documentaries.

Publications: Annual Report; Anniversary Report (1979–2009); catalogues of visual arts exhibitions organized by the Foundation.

Finance: Annual income €3,531,344, expenditure €3,436,984 (2014).

Trustees: Yannis S. Costopoulos (Chair.); Anastasia S. Costopoulos (Vice-Chair. and Sec.); Demetrios P. Mantzounis (Treas.).

Principal Staff: Dir Hector P. Verykios.

Address: 9 Ploutarchou St, 106 75 Athens.

Telephone: (21) 07293503; **Fax:** (21) 07293508; **Internet:** www .costopoulosfoundation.org; **e-mail:** info@ costopoulosfoundation.org.

ELEPAP—Rehabilitation for the Disabled

Established in 1937; formerly known as the Hellenic Society for Disabled Children.

Activities: Operates nationally in the fields of medicine, social welfare and education. Maintains six centres in Greece, which provide rehabilitation for disabled children up to the age of 16 years through physical, occupational and speech therapy and computer training. The centres also provide vocational training for people with disabilities aged between 15 and 30 years. Conferences and lectures are organized for medical staff to follow recent developments in their fields. Also extended to parents. In 2008, a Neuropsychological Rehabilitation Programme was implemented for people with brain injuries, in co-operation with the Rusk Institute of Rehabilitation Medicine of New York Medical Center and a donation from Eurobank EFG.

Geographical Area of Activity: Greece and Europe.

Restrictions: No grants outside Greece.

Publications: Report of operations and financial statement.

Finance: Total revenue €7,685,540, expenditure €6,940,514 (31 Dec. 2013).

Principal Staff: Pres. Marianna A. Moschou.

Address: 16 Kononos St, 116 34 Athens.

Telephone: (21) 07228360; **Fax:** (21) 07228380; **Internet:** www .elepap.gr; **e-mail:** adminath1@elepap.gr.

Foundation of the Hellenic World

Established in 1993 by Lazaros D. Efaimoglou and his family.

Activities: Aims to raise awareness of the importance of Hellenic culture and history throughout the world. The Foundation runs a cultural centre, 'Hellenic Cosmos', which holds exhibitions, educational programmes and an Internet café providing access to the Foundation's online projects. It participates in a number of technological and historical projects, a genealogy programme, made available to the public through cultural events, and produces publications, films, documentaries and DVDs.

Geographical Area of Activity: Mainly Greece.

Publications: Annual Report; *Olympia: A Journey to Four Dimensions* (2004); *History of Perge Political and Ecclesiastical* (2004); *Tales of Olympic Games: A unique exhibition*; *Ancient Athens* (2003); *Is there an answer to everything: a journey to the world of Greek mathematics* (2004); *Plato's Rhapsody and Homer's Music: the Poetics of the Panathenaic Festival in Classical Athens* (2002); *Greek Ritual Poetics* (2004); *Towards a Ritual Poetics* (2003).

Finance: Established with an initial endowment of €1.2m.

Board of Trustees: Lazaros D. Efraimoglou (Pres.); Elias G. Klis, Ourania L. Efraimoglou (Vice-Pres); Marina M. Efraimoglou (Sec.); Sophia Kounenaki-Efaimoglou (Treas.).

Principal Staff: Man. Dir Dimitris Efraimoglou; Gen. Man. Theoklitos Dragonas.

Address: 38 Poulopoulou St, 118 51 Athens.

Telephone: (21) 22545000; **Fax:** (21) 22543838; **Internet:** www.ime.gr/fhw; **e-mail:** info@fhw.gr.

Foundation of Youth and Lifelong Learning—INEDIVIM

Established in 2011 by the merger of the Institute of Adult Continuing Education (IDEKE) and the Youth Institute of the National Youth Foundation (EIN; f. 1947). INEDIVIM; a non-profit private legal entity, with financial and operational autonomy, overseen by the Ministry of Education.

Activities: Promotes Lifelong Learning through various programmes. The Foundation runs adult education courses, congresses, lectures and publications; and also youth programmes. The EU co-funds many programmes.

Geographical Area of Activity: Greece.

Publications: Reports of operations, press bulletins, books and educational material.

Board: Philip Lentzas (Pres.); Evangelia Kaloudi (Vice-Pres.).

Principal Staff: CEO Manouris Panagotis.

Address: 417 Acharnon St and Kokkinaki St, 111 43, Athens.

Telephone: (213) 1314406; **Fax:** (213) 1314407; **Internet:** www.inedivim.gr; **e-mail:** tm-dimosiotitas@inedivim.gr.

Hellenic Foundation for Culture

Established in 1992.

Activities: Promotes Greek language and culture through developing and implementing exhibitions, concerts, lectures, dramas and other major cultural events in Greece and in other countries, as well as organizing events devoted to Greek culture that promote Greek artists and writers abroad, including cultural months and weeks, anniversary celebrations, film festivals and concerts. The Foundation plans and co-ordinates the participation and representation of Greece in international cultural events, and participates in international cultural networks. It also collaborates with museums, universities, cultural centres and organizations, in Greece and abroad, to plan and develop cultural programmes; and has branches and offices in Europe, North Africa, Australia and the USA.

Geographical Area of Activity: Europe, Middle East, the USA, Australia.

Restrictions: Institutions applying for sponsorship must come within the scope of the Foundation's interests and offer guarantees of quality.

Publications: Bulletin (2 a year); brochures; exhibition catalogues; newsletter.

Executive Board: Christodoulos K. Yiallouridis (Pres.); Panayiotis Makris (Vice-Pres.); Nikos Koukis (Treas.).

Address: 50 Stratigou Kallari, 154 52 Palaio Psychico, Athens.

Telephone: (21) 06776540; **Fax:** (21) 06725826; **Internet:** www.hfc.gr; **e-mail:** hfc-centre@hfc.gr.

Hellenic Foundation for European and Foreign Policy—ELIAMEP

Established in 1988 as an independent, policy-orientated, non-profit research and training institute for the study of European integration, transatlantic relations as well as the Mediterranean, South-Eastern Europe, the Black Sea and other regions of particular interest to Greece.

Activities: Operates in Europe, South-Eastern Europe, the Black Sea region and the Mediterranean Middle East in the area of international affairs, through self-conducted programmes, research, scholarships and fellowships, conferences, training courses and publications.

Geographical Area of Activity: Europe, South-Eastern Europe, the Black Sea region, the Mediterranean and the Middle East.

Publications: *Journal of South-East European and Black Sea Studies*; ELIAMEP Thesis; books; policy papers; working papers.

Finance: Total assets €993,383 (31 Dec. 2012).

Board of Directors: Prof. Loukas Tsoukalis (Pres.); Thanos Veremis (Vice-Pres.); Eleni Papakonstantinou (Sec.-Gen.); Panagis Vourloumis (Treas.).

Principal Staff: Dir-Gen. Thanos Dokos; Deputy Dir Elizabeth Phocas.

Address: 49 Vasilissis Sofias Ave, 106 76 Athens.

Telephone: (21) 07257110; **Fax:** (21) 07257114; **Internet:** www.eliamep.gr; **e-mail:** eliamep@eliamep.gr.

Kokkalis Foundation

Established in 1998 to honour the vision of Socrates Kokkalis, an international business leader in information technology and telecommunications, and his father Petros Kokkalis, an eminent surgeon and professor of medicine at the University of Athens.

Activities: Promotes a peaceful, democratic and prosperous South-Eastern Europe through the development of public, cultural and scientific life in the region. The Foundation fosters education in South-Eastern Europe through the Kokkalis fellowship programme at Harvard University, USA, and education programmes organized in strategic collaboration with Harvard University, AIT and Carnegie Mellon University. It organizes a research and publications programme, with emphasis on the fields of innovation and entrepreneurship; medicine and medical research; social policies; geopolitics and international relations; sports and athletics. Supports public dialogue through public fora and an event series. Runs a sponsorship programme in the areas of education and human capital; medical research and human development; culture and athletics. It also promotes the development of South-Eastern Europe through the creation of human networks for regional co-operation and effective democratic governance.

Geographical Area of Activity: South-Eastern Europe, Western Europe, USA and international.

Publications: Research publications and studies (in English and Greek) in the areas of innovation and entrepreneurship, medicine and medical research, social policies, geopolitics and international relations, sports and athletics; monographs; newsletters; information brochures; electronic/online information.

Board of Directors: Socrates P. Kokkalis (Chair.); Petros S. Kokkalis (Vice-Chair.); Eleni S. Kokkali (Treas. and Sec.).

Address: 2 Adrianiou St, 115 25 Athens.

Telephone: (213) 0004901-2; **Fax:** (213) 0004905; **Internet:** www.kokkalisfoundation.gr; **e-mail:** kf@kokkalisfoundation.gr.

Lambrakis Foundation

Established in 1991 by Christos D. Lambrakis to promote the introduction of technological innovations in the Greek education system; the dissemination of Greek and European cultural heritage through the use of new technologies; and research into social and environmental issues and regional development within the framework of the European Union (EU). Formerly known as the Lambrakis Research Foundation.

Activities: Operates in Greece and countries of the EU in the areas of education, the arts and humanities, science and technology, and conservation of the environment, by undertaking studies, projects and awareness activities and addressing the increasing needs for human resources policies and human capital development, through self-conducted programmes, research, scholarships, conferences, training courses and publications (books, videos and CD-ROM multimedia publications on ancient and Byzantine history, astronomy, biology and chemistry). The Foundation awards Manolis Andronikos scholarships for archaeologists wishing to pursue postgraduate studies in archaeological computing; and the Christos Lambrakis Prize to recognize exceptional work in addressing social inequality. It has a specialist website addressed to schools in Greece, offering educational and cultural material in digital form, suggestions for using modern technological tools and educational software in schools, as well as information on current educational issues in Greece and the rest of the world.

Geographical Area of Activity: Europe.

Restrictions: Grants only to specific organizations.

Publications: *Teaching Greek as a Second (Foreign) Language*; *Teachers Training on ICT*; *ICT Policies in School Education, in Europe and the World*; electronic multimedia publications; educational videos with accompanying printed material; conference proceedings.

Board of Directors: Manuel Savidis (Pres.); Demetrios Savidis (Vice-Pres.); Lena Savidis (Treas.).

Principal Staff: Gen. Dir Manuel Savidis.

Address: 3 Anagnostopoulou St, 106 73 Athens.

Telephone: (21) 03626150; **Fax:** (21) 03390119; **Internet:** www.lrf.gr; **e-mail:** info@lrf.gr.

A. G. Leventis Foundation

Established in 1979 to preserve the cultural heritage of Greece and Cyprus.

Activities: Operates in a number of areas in Cyprus and Greece as well as internationally, protecting and promoting the cultural heritage of Cyprus and Greece; working to preserve the environment; granting scholarships for postgraduate study abroad and at the University of Cyprus (particularly in the fields of education and science); financing publications; working in the field of social welfare; and funding agricultural and technical education in West Africa. Has branch foundations in Cyprus (the Anastasios G. Leventis Foundation, q.v.) and Nigeria.

Geographical Area of Activity: West Africa, Cyprus, Greece, Europe.

Publications: *The A. G. Leventis Collection: 19th and 20th Century Greek Paintings*; *The A. G. Leventis Foundation and the Cultural Heritage of Cyprus*; *Ancient Cypriot Art in Berlin*; *Ancient Cypriot Art in Copenhagen*; catalogues and other publications on the arts and culture.

Governing Board: Anastasios (Tasso) P. Leventis (Chair.).

Address: 9 Fragoklissias St, 151 25 Maroussi.

Telephone: (21) 06165232; **Fax:** (21) 06165235; **Internet:** www.leventisfoundation.org; **e-mail:** foundation@leventis.net.

Marangopoulos Foundation for Human Rights

Established in 1977 by the bequest of George M. Marangopoulos, President of the Supreme Administrative Court of Greece.

Activities: Promotes human rights, focusing on the advancement of human rights education, through organizing courses, lectures, seminars, symposia and conferences in Greece and representing Greece in similar events abroad. Awards scholarships, provides financial support and sponsorship for specialized studies in human rights, particularly for young scholars and human rights activists, funds research and awards prizes. Also lobbies governments and public authorities on general human rights issues, as well as specific instances of human rights violations. Provides free legal aid to people whose fundamental rights have allegedly been violated, and the dispatch or funding of fact-finding missions in Greece and abroad. Disseminates information and maintains a library open to the public, containing collections of case-law, series of the major human rights periodicals, specialized books and other relevant material, mainly in Greek, English, French, Italian and German.

Geographical Area of Activity: Greece.

Publications: *1st Anniversary of the Universal Declaration of Human Rights: Poverty, a Challenge to Human Rights* (2010); *Trafficking in Human Beings* (2010); *Le genocide révisité-* *Genocide Revisited* (2010); *Criminology in the Face of Contemporary Challenges* (2011); *Human Dignity: The functional use of its regulatory scope in legal reasoning* (2012); *Corruption and how to address it* (2013); *Liberté et sécurité: les mesures antiterroristes et la Convention européenne des droits de l'homme* (2014); *Welfare State and Public Health Policies. Innovative national actions for social solidarity* (2014); *L'évolution de la notion du réfugié* (2014); *TAIPED: An instrument for the 'sell-off' of public property and for the abolition of the national sovereignty of Greece* (2014, 2015); *The impact of the financial crisis on children* (2015); *Civil partnership of same-sex couples: The need for adaptation of the Greek legal order* (2015).

Governing Board: Alice Yotopoulos-Marangopoulos (Pres.); Gerasimos Arsenis (Vice-Pres.); Sotiris Mousouris (Sec.-Gen.).

Principal Staff: Dir Prof. S.-H. Aktypis.

Address: 1 Lycavittou St, 106 72 Athens.

Telephone: (21) 03637455; **Fax:** (21) 03622454; **Internet:** www.mfhr.gr; **e-mail:** info@mfhr.gr.

National Bank of Greece Cultural Foundation

Established in 1966 by the National Bank of Greece to support fine art, humanities and sciences in Greece.

Activities: Houses a collection of works of art and organizes exhibitions; manages three cultural centres in Athens; maintains an archive of maps and a paper conservation laboratory; organizes seminars; and issues publications that cannot be published commercially.

Geographical Area of Activity: Greece.

Publications: Numerous publications in the fields of history, archaeology, anthropology, classical studies, art theory, law, philosophy, etc.

Board of Directors: Georgios P. Zanias (Chair.); E. A. Zachariadou (Vice-Chair.); Savvas Kontaratos (Gen. Sec.); Michalis A. Tiverios (Treas.).

Principal Staff: Dir Dionysis Kapsalis.

Address: 13 Thoukydidou St, 105 58 Athens.

Telephone: (21) 03221335; **Fax:** (21) 03245089; **Internet:** www.miet.gr; **e-mail:** mietekd@otenet.gr.

Stavros Niarchos Foundation

Established in 1996 as an international philanthropic organization to make grants to non-profit organizations, in support of education, health and medicine, social welfare, and arts and culture.

Activities: Operates worldwide in the areas of arts and culture, education, health and medicine, and social welfare. The Foundation also supports projects within Greece and worldwide that promote and/or maintain Greek heritage and culture. In January 2012, it announced a three-year programme committing €100m. of funds to projects aimed at easing the adverse effects of the socio-economic crisis in Greece; and in 2013 a further €100m. to address youth unemployment. The Foundation has offices in Athens, Monte Carlo and New York. A new cultural centre in Athens was expected to be completed in 2016.

Geographical Area of Activity: Worldwide.

Restrictions: No grants are made to individuals.

Finance: Total grants disbursed US $1,590m. (1996–2015).

Board of Directors: Philip Niarchos, Spyros Niarchos, Andreas C. Dracopoulos (Co-Pres.).

Principal Staff: COO Vasili Tsamis; CFO Christina Lambropoulou.

Address: 86A Vasilissis Sofias Ave, 115 28 Athens.

Telephone: (21) 08778300; **Fax:** (21) 06838304; **Internet:** www.snf.org; **e-mail:** info@snf.org.

Alexander S. Onassis Public Benefit Foundation

Established in 1975 according to the will of Aristotle Onassis, as a public benefit foundation with numerous cultural and public benefit projects. The main purpose of the Foundation's activities is to promote Hellenic culture in Greece and abroad.

Activities: Operates in the fields of education, medicine, social welfare, the arts and humanities. The Foundation's areas of activities include: scholarship programmes for postgraduate and doctoral studies in Greece or abroad, and for foreigners for research and postgraduate studies in Greece; the promotion of Greek culture and Greek studies abroad through subsidized programmes in the USA, Canada, South America, Europe and Asia; the donation of teaching material and technical equipment to primary and secondary schools for children with special needs, and to Greek communities abroad; the funding of the annual Onassis Foundation Science Lecture Series, in association with the Foundation for Research and Technology in Heraklion, Crete, given on the applied sciences by Nobel Prize winners and other acclaimed scientists from Greece and elsewhere; and the awarding of the Onassis International Prizes. The Onassis Prize in Shipping, Trade and Finance, in co-operation with the City of London and Cass Business School of the City University London, is awarded biennially to recognize the lifetime achievement of an academic of international stature, rotating between shipping, trade and finance. The Onassis Prize in Law and Humanities, in collaboration with the French Institute, is awarded biennially in rotation to academics, thinkers or distinguished personalities. The prize in law is awarded to an individual who has contributed to improved understanding between states and cultures and to the protection of human rights, while the prize in humanities is bestowed on those who have concentrated their studies on Greek culture and the promotion of Greek cultural heritage in the fields of archaeology, history and literature. The Foundation has established the affiliated Alexander S. Onassis Public Benefit Foundation in the USA to promote Greek culture. It sponsors seminar and lecture programmes of visiting professors to universities in the USA, Canada and South America, and organizes diverse cultural events in New York. The events are based on Classical, Byzantine and contemporary Greek culture and include exhibitions of archaeology, contemporary art and sculpture, lectures, concerts and drama. The Foundation has also constructed the Onassis House of Arts and Letters, a cultural centre to encourage the development of modern Greek culture, as well as promoting it outside Greece, and to provide Greek artists with a fully equipped venue from which to present their work.

Geographical Area of Activity: International.

Publications: Brochure; newsletter of the Onassis Foundation Scholars' Association; catalogues of the exhibitions at the Onassis Cultural Center, New York.

Finance: Sole beneficiary of an endowment bequeathed to it by Aristotle Onassis.

Board of Directors: Anthony S. Papadimitriou (Pres. and Treas.); Ioannis P. Ioannidis (Vice-Pres.); Marianna Moschou (Sec.); Paul I. Ioannidis (Hon. Vice-Pres.).

Principal Staff: Dir Effie Tsiotsiou.

Address: 56 Amalias Ave, 105 58 Athens.

Telephone: (21) 03713000; **Fax:** (21) 03713013; **Internet:** www .onassis.gr; **e-mail:** contact@onassis.gr.

State Scholarships Foundation

Founded in 1951 to grant scholarships to foreigners for postgraduate or postdoctoral studies in Greece.

Activities: Offers scholarships annually for postgraduate and postdoctoral studies in Greece to nationals of any other country worldwide and to non-Greek nationals of Greek origin. The Foundation awards scholarships to teachers or researchers (foreigners or foreign nationals of Greek origin) working in Greek centres of studies abroad for further education in language, literature, philosophy, history and art. Scholarships are provided for postgraduate doctoral studies; for postdoctoral research; for further education in Greek language, literature, philosophy, history and art for professors of Greek language in foreign universities; for further study in fine arts; and for collection of research data for applicants who are conducting doctoral studies in their country.

Geographical Area of Activity: International.

Board of Directors: Prof. Effie K. Badra (Pres.); Elrini Cheila (Vice-Pres.).

Address: 41 Ethnikis Antistaseos Ave, 142 34 Nea Ionia, Athens.

Telephone: (21) 03726300; **Fax:** (21) 03221863; **Internet:** www .iky.gr; **e-mail:** iky@hol.gr.

Swedish Institute at Athens

Founded in 1946 by King Gustaf VI Adolf and others to promote the study of the ancient culture of Greece and to stimulate and support cultural exchange between Sweden and Greece and to further education.

Activities: Operates internationally in the fields of the arts and humanities (mainly archaeology) and Greek-Swedish relations, through research, conferences, courses, publications and lectures. The Institute maintains a database and archive on Swedish archaeological research in Greece.

Geographical Area of Activity: Greece.

Restrictions: Grants only to students at Swedish universities.

Publications: *Skrifter utgivna av Svenska institutet i Athen* (monographs); collections of articles in *Opuscula Atheniensia*.

Principal Staff: Dir Dr Arto Penttinen; Asst Dir Dr Monica Nilsson; Sec. Eleni Gultidou.

Address: 9 Mitseon, 117 42 Athens; Stiftelsen Svenska institutet i Athen, Skeppargatan 8, 114 52 Stockholm, Sweden.

Telephone: (21) 09232102; **Fax:** (21) 09220925; **Internet:** www .sia.gr; **e-mail:** swedinst@sia.gr.

Guatemala

FOUNDATION CENTRE AND CO-ORDINATING BODY

Consejo de Fundaciones Privadas de Guatemala— CFPG (Council of Private Foundations of Guatemala)

Founded in 1996 as one association to represent the many foundations that seek social improvements in Guatemala.

Activities: Aims to facilitate and co-ordinate organizations in Guatemala whose aims comprise social development, economic development and industrial development. Its members include private foundations and governmental organizations.

Geographical Area of Activity: Guatemala.

Publications: *Conceptos Básicos de la RSE*; *Alianzas RSE*; *Empresas Privadas de RSE, los Indicadores Ethos de Responsabilidad Social de la Empresa*.

Principal Staff: Exec. Dir Miguel Antonio Gaitan Pellecer.

Address: 6ª Av. 7-39, Zona 10, Of. 301, Edif. Las Brisas, 01010 Guatemala City.

Telephone: (2) 2277-5131; **Fax:** (2) 2277-5132; **e-mail:** administracion@fundazucar.org.

FOUNDATIONS, TRUSTS AND NON-PROFIT ORGANIZATIONS

Fundación de Asesoría Financiera a Instituciones de Desarrollo y Servicio Social—FAFIDESS (Foundation for the Financial Assessment of Social Service and Development Institutions)

Established in 1986 by members of the Rotary Club of Guatemala City.

Activities: Aims to support the economic and social development of Guatemala by offering sustainable microfinance, technical advice and support to small and medium-sized enterprises, particularly those run by women.

Geographical Area of Activity: Guatemala.

Board of Directors: José Francisco Monroy Galindo (Pres.); Leonel Fernando González Cifuentes (Vice-Pres.); Arturo Melville Aguirre (Sec.); Eduardo Sebastian Aballi Coto (Treas.).

Principal Staff: Exec. Dir Reynold O. Walter.

Address: 5A Avda 16-68, Zona 10, 01010 Guatemala City.

Telephone: (2) 311-5800; **Fax:** (2) 311-5807; **Internet:** www .fafidess.org; **e-mail:** fafidess@fafidess.org.

Fundación de Asistencia para la Pequeña Empresa (Foundation for the Assistance of the Small Business)

Founded in 1986.

Activities: Provides holistic business and personal development services beyond financial resources. Under the motto 'Healthy Women = Healthy Business', encourages the development of micro- to small-sized businesses through microcredit services, business training and health resources, including free health consultations.

Geographical Area of Activity: Guatemala.

Finance: Total assets US $1.3m. (2013).

Board of Directors: Carlos Spiegler (Pres.); Gustavo Martinez (Vice-Pres.).

Principal Staff: Exec. Dir Manuel García Marroquín.

Address: 2 Avda 3-16, Residenciales Santa Mónica, Zona 2 de Mixco, Guatemala City.

Telephone: (2) 2250-7800; **Fax:** (2) 2250-7820; **Internet:** www .fundacionfape.org; **e-mail:** fape@c.net.gt.

Fundación para el Desarrollo—FUNDAP (Development Foundation)

Established in 1982 by a group of business people to develop the western part of Guatemala by supporting small businesses.

Activities: Aims to develop the low-income areas of western Guatemala through innovative projects that improve the quality of life of those communities.

Geographical Area of Activity: Guatemala.

Publications: Annual Report.

Finance: Annual expenditure 185,552 quetzals (2013).

Board of Directors: Francisco Roberto Gutiérrez Martínez (Chair.); Jacobo L. Cabassa Oliver (Vice-Chair.); Jorge A. Gándara Gaborit (Sec.); Julio R. Bagur Cifuentes (Treas.).

Principal Staff: Exec. Dir Jorge A. Gándara Gaborit.

Address: 17 Avda 4-25, Zona 3, Quetzaltenango.

Telephone: (7) 767-4538; **Fax:** (7) 767-5831; **Internet:** www .fundap.com.gt; **e-mail:** info@fundap.com.gt; central@ fundap.com.gt.

Fundación Esperanza de los Niños (Hope for the Children Foundation—Childhope)

Founded in 1988 in Guatemala to provide information about the problems of 'street children'—homeless young people living and working in the streets—and previously known as the Childhope International Foundation. Now a network of independent regional and national ChildHope (q.v.) groups operating in the United Kingdom and Europe, Asia and Central and South America.

Activities: Operates in the fields of human rights and social welfare, with the aim of upholding the Convention on the Rights of Children, which the Government of Guatemala ratified in 1990. The Foundation operates programmes in the areas of mental health, children's rights, and research into various issues including child labour and violence against children.

Geographical Area of Activity: Guatemala.

Publications: Newsletter; *Cuentos de mi Comunidad*; *Contemos Cuentos*; *Guía Básica para la Elaboración de un Plan de Desarrollo Municipal*; *Los Jóvenes del Quiché Opinamos Qué ..*; *Diagnóstico de la Situación Actual de los Niños que viven en la Calle*; *El Trabajo Infantil y el Trabajo Infantil de Alto Riesgo*.

Principal Staff: Dir Lucas Ventura.

Address: 4A 2-84, Sector B-5, Ciudad San Cristóbal, Zona 8 de Mixco, Guatemala City.

Telephone: (502) 2472-5125; **Fax:** (502) 2472-5125; **Internet:** childhopeguate.wix.com/childhope-guatemala; **e-mail:** childhopegua@yahoo.com.

Fundación Génesis Empresarial (Génesis Empresarial Foundation)

Founded in 1988 as a non-governmental, non-profit private development organization.

Activities: Promotes the social and economic strengthening and development of micro-enterprises and small businesses, as well as communal banks in urban, marginal and rural areas of Guatemala; provides credit, training and advice. The Foundation also helps poor rural communities to improve dwellings and introduce basic services. It has 59 branches throughout Guatemala.

Geographical Area of Activity: Guatemala.

Publications: *ACCION International Annual Reports; Génesis Annual Report, Mix Market Profile.*

Finance: Total assets US $92.3m. (2013).

Board of Directors: Salvador Ortega (Chair.).

Principal Staff: Gen. Man. Carlos Enrique Herrera Castillo.

Address: 13 Calle 5-51, Zona 9, Guatemala City.

Telephone: (502) 2383-9000; **Fax:** (502) 2334-4474; **Internet:** www.genesisempresarial.com; **e-mail:** genesis@genesisempresarial.com.

Fundación Rigoberta Menchú Tum

Established in 1992 as the Fundación Vicente Menchú to work towards peace, justice and democracy, especially for indigenous peoples. Renamed in 1995 following the award of the Nobel Peace Prize to Rigoberta Menchú Tum, an activist for indigenous peoples' rights.

Activities: Operates in the area of human rights, especially with regard to indigenous peoples, supporting education, community development and citizen participation.

Geographical Area of Activity: Guatemala and Mexico.

Principal Staff: Pres. Dr Rigoberta Menchú Tum.

Address: Avda Simeón Cañas 4-04, Zona 2, Guatemala City.

Telephone: (502) 2230-2431; **Fax:** (502) 2221-3999; **Internet:** www.frmt.org; **e-mail:** guatemala@frmt.org.

Fundación MICROS—Fundación para el Desarrollo de la Microempresa (Microenterprise Development Foundation)

Founded 1987.

Activities: Helps poor communities to sustain themselves through micro-enterprise, by providing advice, training and financing, through the granting of credit on an individual basis.

Geographical Area of Activity: Guatemala.

Principal Staff: Exec. Dir Otto Mauricio González Molina.

Address: 20 Calle 6-37, Zona 11, Col. Mariscal, Guatemala City.

Telephone: (502) 2473-1579; **Fax:** (502) 2473-1579; **Internet:** www.fundacionmicros.org; **e-mail:** fundacionmicros@gmail.com.

PRODESSA—Proyecto de Desarrollo Santiago (Santiago Development Project)

Established in 1989 to promote development in rural communities in Guatemala and to help build a just and multicultural society.

Activities: Operates programmes in the fields of education, the environment and development, providing loans, grants and technical assistance. The Project works with organizations to exercise the rights of the Maya people.

Geographical Area of Activity: Guatemala.

Publications: Bulletin; educational materials; research papers.

Finance: Annual grants expenditure approx. US $1m.

Board of Directors: Oscar Azmitia Barranco (Chair.); Cecilio Herrera (Treas.); Francisco Velásquez (Sec.).

Principal Staff: Dirs Federico Roncal Martínez, Edgar García Tax.

Address: Km 15, Carretera Roosevelt, Zona 7, Mixco, Apdo 13-B, 19103 Guatemala City.

Telephone: (2) 435-3911; **Fax:** (2) 435-3913; **Internet:** www.prodessa.net; **e-mail:** gestion@prodessa.net.

Haiti

FOUNDATIONS, TRUSTS AND NON-PROFIT ORGANIZATIONS

Fondation Connaissance et Liberté (Haiti)—FOKAL (Foundation for Knowledge and Liberty)

Established in 1995 to promote the development of open society in Haiti; an independent foundation, part of the Open Society Foundations (q.v.) network.

Activities: Operates in the fields of education, culture and strengthening of civil-society organizations, especially land-workers' and women's organizations. The Foundation runs programmes promoting debate, libraries, the Internet, early childhood education, local production and water facilities in rural areas. It also promotes the rule of law and provides technical and financial support to the judiciary. Through the community library project, the Foundation supports 17 community libraries, as well as providing training in library management, finance and computers. In 2007, FOKAL signed a contract with the Government of Haiti for the creation and management of the urban Martissant Park project, which includes a botanical garden specializing in traditional medicinal plants, a memorial garden to the victims of the 2010 earthquake, and a cultural centre and Monique Calixte Library. In 2012, work began to establish the Institute for Environmental Skills and Research at the park.

Geographical Area of Activity: Haiti.

Publications: *Nouvèl FOKAL* (weekly newsletter); *Beyond Mountains More Mountains.*

Finance: Total expenditure US $4.2m. (2010).

Board of Trustees: Michèle D. Pierre-Louis (Pres.); Danièle Magloire (Chair.); Nicole Magloire (Vice-Chair.).

Principal Staff: Exec. Dir Lorraine Mangonès.

Address: 143 ave Christophe, BP 2720, Port-au-Prince.

Telephone: 2813-1694; **Fax:** 2510-9814; **Internet:** www.fokal.org; www.parcdemartissant.org; www.fokal-usa.org; **e-mail:** jvangelis@fokal.org.

Fondation pour le Développement Economique et Social—FODES-5 (Foundation for Economic and Social Development)

Established in 1998 to promote economic, social and cultural development.

Activities: Helps local people to develop economic strategies and social services to improve their quality of life. The Foundation runs four main programmes: health, agriculture, education and natural resources. It works in communities in four departments: Petit-Goâve (Ouest), Aquin (Sud), Côtes de Fer (Sud-Est) and Miragoâne (Nippes). It also has a co-ordination office in Port-au-Prince. Has more than 7,000 members.

Geographical Area of Activity: Haiti.

Board of Directors: François Merisma (Chair.).

Principal Staff: Gen. Co-ordinator Alfred Etienne.

Address: Delmas 31, Prolongée, rue Roux 20; POB 13380 Delmas, HT 6120.

Telephone: (509) 3701-6509; **Internet:** www.fodes5.org; **e-mail:** info@fodes5.org.

Honduras

FOUNDATIONS, TRUSTS AND NON-PROFIT ORGANIZATIONS

Fundación BANHCAFE—FUNBANHCAFE (BANH-CAFE Foundation)

Established in 1985; an initiative of Banco Hondureño del Café (BANHCAFE) and the Ministry of Home Affairs and Justice, to aid the development of coffee-producing communities in Honduras.

Activities: Aims to develop social, cultural, economic and environmental elements of coffee-producing communities, through non-profit organizations in the local area.

Geographical Area of Activity: Honduras.

Publications: Guides; strategic reports; manuals; reports on different agricultural products.

Board of Directors: Miguel Alfonso Fernández Rápalo (Pres.); Guillermo Sagastume Perdomo (Sec.).

Principal Staff: Exec. Dir Arnold Sabillón Ortega.

Address: Colonia Rubén Dario, Avda Las Minitas, Calle Cervantes 319, Apdo 3814, Tegucigalpa.

Telephone: 239-5211; **Fax:** 239-9171; **Internet:** funbanhcafe .hn; **e-mail:** direccion@funbanhcafe.hn.

Fundación para la Inversión y Desarrollo de Exportaciones—FIDE (Foundation for the Investment and Development of Exports)

Established in 1984 to promote investment in Honduras, support export development and work closely with the Government and other private organizations to promote and design new legislation aimed at improving the country's business environment.

Activities: Promotes sustainable development in Honduras through strengthening investment and export by seeking to improve the international competitiveness of the country and its business sector. The Foundation runs a series of programmes and activities to offer investors and business owners, both local and foreign, a wide range of services to develop new exports or expand existing ones, forge strategic alliances and take advantage of emerging business opportunities.

Geographical Area of Activity: Honduras.

Publications: Annual Report; *Export Directory*; promotional brochures.

Board of Directors: Leonel Z. Bendeck (Pres.); Ramón Medina Luna (Vice-Pres.); Fernando Ceballos (Treas.).

Principal Staff: Exec. Pres. and Sec. Vilma Sierra de Fonseca.

Address: Colonia La Estancia, costado sur/este de Plaza Marte, final del Blvd Morazán, Apdo 2029, Tegucigalpa.

Telephone: 221-6304; **Fax:** 221-6318; **Internet:** www .hondurasinfo.hn; www.hondurassiexporta.hn; **e-mail:** dpe@fidehonduras.com.

Fundación Nacional para el Desarrollo de Honduras—FUNADEH (National Foundation for the Development of Honduras)

Founded in 1983.

Activities: Aims to provide community development through education and training, and through microfinance.

Geographical Area of Activity: Honduras.

Board of Directors: María Teresa Bográn de Quezada (Pres.); José Manuel Pineda Silva (Vice-Pres.); Martha Moncada de Valenzuela (Sec.); Mirian Andino de Rivera (Treas.).

Address: Colonia El Pedregal B-31, 3ª, Blvd Las Torres San Pedro Sula, Tegucigalpa.

Telephone: 2556-0809; **Fax:** 2280-9905; **Internet:** www .funadeh.org; **e-mail:** yomecapacito@funadeh.org.

Hong Kong

FOUNDATIONS, TRUSTS AND NON-PROFIT ORGANIZATIONS

Croucher Foundation

Founded in 1979 to promote education, learning and research in the areas of natural science, technology and medicine.

Activities: Operates a scholarship and fellowship scheme for individual applicants who wish to pursue doctoral or postdoctoral research outside Hong Kong. The Foundation also makes grants to institutions: it offers senior research fellowships to universities in Hong Kong to promote research; contributes to international scientific conferences held in Hong Kong; supports advanced study institutes; funds international exchanges between scientific institutions in Hong Kong and other countries; and provides funds for a scheme to enable scientists in mainland China to undertake attachments at Hong Kong institutions. It also offers Innovation Awards to exceptionally talented scientists; supports Summer Schools in local universities; and co-sponsors Clinical Assistant Professorships with the two medical schools in Hong Kong.

Geographical Area of Activity: Hong Kong.

Restrictions: Individual fellowships and scholarships scheme for overseas studies limited to permanent Hong Kong residents.

Trustees: Prof. Tak Wah Mak (Chair.).

Principal Staff: Dir David Foster.

Address: Suite 501, 9 Queens Rd Central, Hong Kong.

Telephone: 27366337; **Fax:** 27300742; **Internet:** www.croucher.org.hk; **e-mail:** cfadmin@croucher.org.hk.

HER Fund

Established in 2004 to promote the development of women's rights in Hong Kong through fund-raising, grantmaking and gender educational activities.

Activities: Operates in the fields of education and fund-raising. Makes small grants to women and girls' rights projects, and promotes the development of philanthropy that recognizes the status of women. Funding is directed towards projects and rights initiatives, with particular attention paid to economic justice, grassroots women's initiatives and the rights of young girls. The Fund also supports women's efforts to instigate social change.

Geographical Area of Activity: Hong Kong.

Publications: Research reports; Annual Report; *HER Voice* (newsletter and e-news).

Finance: Annual income HK $1,977,209, expenditure $1,451,154 (31 March 2014).

Executive Committee: Mary Ann King (Chair.); Fong Man-ying (Vice-Chair.); Brigit Fung Pui-kee (Hon. Sec.); Fly Lam Ying-hing (Hon. Treas.).

Principal Staff: Exec. Dir Linda To Kit-lai.

Address: Flat A, 1st Floor, Fa Yuen St, Prince Edward, Kowloon.

Telephone: 27941100; **Fax:** 23967488; **Internet:** www.herfund.org.hk; **e-mail:** info@herfund.org.hk.

Hong Kong Society for the Blind

Established in 1956 to investigate blindness and advance the science of ophthalmology.

Activities: Operates in South-East Asia, conducting and supporting research in ophthalmology, through grants to institutions and individuals; and assists in the training of all kinds of ophthalmic and multidisciplinary staff. The Society places special emphasis on cataract operations, the prevention of blindness and services that will benefit the blind directly. It also organizes conferences and co-operates with governmental and other organizations working for the prevention and cure of blindness; and is a member of the Vision 2020 Right to Sight campaign.

Geographical Area of Activity: South-East Asia.

Publications: Annual Report; training manuals.

Finance: Annual income HK $201,522,568, expenditure $202,403,107 (2013/14).

Council: Nancy Law Tak Yin (Chair.); Michael Szeto Chak Wah (Vice-Chair.); Patrick Ng Wing Hang (Hon. Treas.).

Principal Staff: Exec. Dir Maureen Tam Ching Yi.

Address: East Wing, 248 Nam Cheong St, Samshuipo, Kowloon.

Telephone: 27788332; **Fax:** 27881336; **Internet:** www.hksb.org.hk; **e-mail:** enquiry@hksb.org.hk.

Li Ka-shing Foundation

Established in 1980 by Li Ka-shing to provide support in the fields of education, medical care and research, and poverty relief, and to nurture a culture of giving.

Activities: Operates in the fields of education, and medicine and health through grants and sponsorships. The Foundation's most notable project is the founding and continuing development of Shantou University in mainland China to engineer reforms in the higher education sector. The Foundation also makes significant contributions to medical research at leading institutions worldwide, particularly in the area of cancer research. In mainland China, the Foundation has pioneered a number of innovative programmes to improve rural health care and to provide free hospice care services. Operates in 19 countries.

Geographical Area of Activity: International.

Publications: *Sphere* bulletin.

Finance: Grants, sponsorships and commitments of HK $14,500m. to date.

Board of Directors: Sir Ka-shing Li (Chair.).

Address: Cheung Kong Center, 7th Floor, 2 Queen's Rd Central, Hong Kong.

Telephone: 21288888; **Internet:** www.lksf.org; **e-mail:** general@lksf.org.

Oxfam Hong Kong

Established in 1976. Part of the Oxfam confederation of organizations (qq.v.).

Activities: Operates in Southern Africa, and South and South-East Asia, offering assistance in emergencies and natural disasters, advocacy and development education, and development programmes.

Geographical Area of Activity: Southern Africa, South and South-East Asia.

Finance: Revenue HK $255,936,000, expenditure $245,067,000 (31 March 2013).

Executive Committee: Dr Lo Chi Kin (Chair.); Prof. Emily Chan, May Tan (Vice-Chair.); Josephine Chesterton (Treas.).

Address: 17th Floor China United Centre, 28 Marble Rd, North Point, Hong Kong.

Telephone: 25202525; **Fax:** 25276307; **Internet:** www.oxfam.org.hk; **e-mail:** info@oxfam.org.hk.

Tai Hung Fai Charitable Foundation

Established in 2005 by Edwin Leong Siu-hung, Chair. of Tai Hung Fai Enterprise Co Ltd (f. 1977), a property development company.

Activities: Programmes include health screening and monitoring for the elderly, and community health care for people with dementia. Sponsors university scholarships and professorships.

Geographical Area of Activity: Principally Hong Kong.

Address: c/o Tai Hung Fai Enterprises, Far East Finance Centre, 16 Harcourt Rd, Wan Chai.

Telephone: 25292110; **Fax:** 25275855.

Hungary

FOUNDATION CENTRES AND CO-ORDINATING BODIES

Autonómia Alapítvány (Autonómia Foundation)

Founded in 1990 to promote the development of civil society and the not-for-profit sector in Hungary. Formerly known as the Hungarian Foundation for Self-Reliance.

Activities: Aims to improve employment opportunities for Roma people by providing assistance to develop their civil organizations.

Geographical Area of Activity: Hungary, Bulgaria, Romania, Serbia, Slovakia.

Publications: Annual Report.

Finance: Financed mainly on an individual project basis by the European Union. Total assets 132,117,000 forint (2013).

Board of Trustees: Anna Csongor (Chair.); **Supervisory Board:** István Boros (Chair.).

Principal Staff: Exec. Dir András Nun.

Address: 1137 Budapest, Pozsonyi útca 14, II/9.

Telephone: (1) 237-6020; **Fax:** (1) 237-6029; **Internet:** www.autonomia.hu; **e-mail:** autonomia@autonomia.hu.

Nonprofit Információs és Oktató Központ Alapítvány—NIOK (Non-Profit Information and Training Centre Foundation)

Established in 1994 by the Nonprofit Research Association to promote the development of civil society in Hungary.

Activities: Promotes the development of the third sector in Hungary, through the provision of capacity-building services to NGOs, and by supporting NGOs. The Foundation campaigns on behalf of Hungarian NGOs, including organizing the 1% Campaign ('Give your 1% to a civil society organization'), promoting philanthropic giving in Hungary, and social dialogue. It also maintains a Civil Service Centre, a library and a database of more than 12,000 Hungarian NGOs.

Geographical Area of Activity: Hungary.

Publications: Annual Report; *Citizen's Votes for Nonprofit Activities in Hungary*; *International Fund-Raising Techniques*; *Effective Management for Voluntary Organizations and Community Groups*.

Finance: Total assets 159,617,000 forint (2013).

Board of Trustees: Jellen Kornél (Chair.).

Principal Staff: Dir Balázs Gerencsér.

Address: 1122 Budapest, Maros útca 23–25. mfszt. 2.

Telephone: (1) 315-3151; **Fax:** (1) 315-3366; **Internet:** www.niok.hu; **e-mail:** contact@niok.hu.

FOUNDATIONS, TRUSTS AND NON-PROFIT ORGANIZATIONS

Carpathian Foundation

Founded in 1994 by the Institute for East–West Studies to support projects to improve the quality of life and the community in rural areas of the Carpathian mountains, through integrated community development.

Activities: A cross-border regional foundation that provides grants and technical assistance to NGOs and local governments, focusing primarily on interregional, economic development and transfrontier activities. The Foundation encourages the development of public/private/NGO partnerships, including cross-border and inter-ethnic approaches to promote regional and community development and to help prevent conflicts. It promotes good relations, social stability and economic progress in the border regions of Hungary, Poland, Romania, Slovakia and Ukraine; and provides financial and technical assistance to projects that will result in tangible benefits to the communities on both sides of national borders, and will improve the quality of life of the people in the cities and small towns of the Carpathian Mountains.

Geographical Area of Activity: The Carpathian region, bordering areas of Hungary, Poland, Romania, Slovakia and Ukraine. In Slovakia the Foundation concentrates its activities on the Košice and Presov regions situated in Eastern Slovakia.

Restrictions: No grants for investment activities, nor to businesses, state organizations or churches.

Publications: Annual Report; *Research and Analysis of Community Economic Development in the Carpathian Euroregion*; *The Potential of Regional Co-operation in Overcoming Social Marginality Within the Hungarian–Romanian–Ukrainian Border Area*.

Finance: Total grants disbursed approx. US $15m. (2010).

Board of Directors: Sándor Köles (Chair.).

Principal Staff: Exec. Dir Boglárka Bata.

Address: 3300 Eger, Mekcsey útca 1.

Telephone: (36) 516-750; **Fax:** (36) 516-751; **Internet:** www.carpathianfoundation.org; **e-mail:** cfhu@cfoundation.org.

Czegei Wass Alapítvány (Czegei Wass Foundation)

Established in 1996 by the five sons of the late Albert Wass de Czege, the noted Transylvanian-Hungarian novelist, to provide economic and humanitarian aid to that region.

Activities: Promotes economic and social development, primarily in small villages of the Transylvanian area of Hungary, in a variety of areas. Support is given for the repair and maintenance of school buildings and churches; sponsorship of Scout troops; provision of agricultural equipment; the establishment of orphanages for homeless children; provision of scholarships for high-school graduates to attend college; financial assistant for creation of local businesses; and emergency relief to families in need. Maintains sister foundations in Romania and the USA.

Geographical Area of Activity: Hungary.

Board of Directors: Vid Wass de Czege (Chair.); Geza Wass de Czege (Treas.).

Principal Staff: Pres. Simó József.

Address: 1112 Budapest, Brasso útca 6A.

Telephone: (1) 319-3540.

DemNet

Established in 1996 by Herbert Ascherman to assist in the development of civil society.

Activities: Supports civil society development through its programmes in Hungary, the Western Balkans and 'Arab Spring' countries of the Middle East.

Geographical Area of Activity: Hungary, Western Balkans and countries of the Middle East.

Publications: Annual Report; newsletters; reports.

Finance: Annual revenue 66,849,000 forint, expenditure 63,533,000 forint (2013).

Board of Trustees: Thomas Donovan (Chair.).

Principal Staff: Exec. Dir and Sec. Péter Pálvölgyi.

Address: 1052 Budapest, Apáczai Csere János u. 1 IV/40.

Telephone: (1) 411-0410; **Internet:** www.demnet.hu; **e-mail:** info@demnet.org.hu.

Demokratikus Átalakulásért Intézet (International Centre for Democratic Transition—ICDT)

Established in 2005.

Activities: Collects and shares information on countries that have experienced recent democratic transition. The Centre aims to facilitate the smooth and peaceful process of democratic transition on the basis of participatory principles. It records the political, economic, legal, cultural and civil societal aspects of transformation, and the socio-cultural context of regions and countries where the process takes place. Also promotes interregional co-operation between governments and civil societies of neighbouring countries to enable democratic transition and to ensure regional stability; it provides assistance and learning opportunities to new and fragile democracies, concentrating on practical elements of democracy, such as elections and freedom of speech; and it strengthens the involvement of marginalized groups, such as ethnic minorities, women and similar social groups in both the transition process and the functioning of democracy.

Geographical Area of Activity: North Africa, the Middle East, Latin America, Asia, Central, Eastern and South-Eastern Europe.

Publications: *Development of Democracy in the Visegrád Countries after the Democratic Transformation* (2015); *Democratic Attitudes in Ukraine* (2015); *Strengthening Civil Society Through Community Development in Ribnita* (2014); *Afghanistan after ISAF Policy Paper* (2012); *Democracy in Central Europe* (2011); *Project Final Study Analyzing the Visegrad Experience* (2011); *5 years of Promoting Democratic Transition Worldwide* (2011); *The Hungarian Transition* (2011).

Executive Board: Sonja Licht (Chair.).

Principal Staff: Pres. Prof. Dr István Gyarmati; CEO László Várkonyi.

Address: 1022 Budapest, Árvácska u. 12.

Telephone: (1) 438-0820; **Fax:** (1) 438-0821; **Internet:** www .icdt.hu; **e-mail:** info@icdt.hu.

Europako Rromano Čačimasko Centro—ERRC (European Roma Rights Centre)

Established in 1996 to increase awareness on issues of human rights of Roma people.

Activities: Operates internationally, extending legal support in cases of human rights to Roma people, and carrying out research into human rights. The Centre disseminates legal findings and issues publications; advocates Roma rights; maintains a documentation centre consisting of legal material; awards scholarships to Roma students pursuing law and public administration studies; and offers internships for Roma people to study human rights law.

Geographical Area of Activity: Europe.

Publications: *Roma Rights Quarterly* (quarterly newsletter); *Knowing Your Rights and Fighting for Them: A Guide for Romani Activists* (2004); thematic and country reports; fact sheets; position papers; Romani language translations; pamphlets.

Board of Directors: Robert A. Kushen (Chair.).

Principal Staff: Exec. Dir András Ujlaky.

Address: 1077 Budapest, Wesselényi útca 16.

Telephone: (1) 413-2200; **Fax:** (1) 413-2201; **Internet:** www .errc.org; **e-mail:** office@errc.org.

Magyar Ökumenikus Segélyszervezet (Hungarian Interchurch Aid—HIA)

Established in 1991 by a multi-faith coalition.

Activities: Provides international aid and emergency relief in Central and Eastern Europe and Africa; helps refugees and displaced people; supports programmes relating to social welfare issues in Hungary through a network of 17 social institutions with 100 staff members, in particular focusing on finding solutions for families facing crisis situations, drug addicts, endangered and disadvantaged children and homeless people. The organization also operates a home nursing service for sick people and promotes the integration of Roma minorities.

Geographical Area of Activity: Africa, Central and Eastern Europe.

Publications: Annual Report; newsletter; *HIA activity in Uzbekistan.*

Finance: Annual revenue 1,760.2m. forint, expenditure 1,465.7m. forint (2013).

Principal Staff: Pres. and Dir Rev. László Lehel.

Address: 1116 Budapest, Tomaj u. 4.

Telephone: (1) 208-4932; **Fax:** (1) 208-4934; **Internet:** www .segelyszervezet.hu; **e-mail:** segelyszervezet@segelyszervezet .hu.

Open Society Institute–Budapest

Established in 1993; part of the Open Society Foundations (q.v.) network.

Activities: Programmes include Education Support, Global Drug Policy, Information, International Higher Education and Public Health. Coordinates the following Open Society Foundations initiatives: Support Human Rights; Program on Independent Journalism; Open Society Justice; Roma Initiatives; and the Think Tank Fund.

Geographical Area of Activity: Central and Eastern Europe.

Principal Staff: Exec. Dir Katalin E. Koncz.

Address: 1051 Budapest, Oktober 6 u. 12.

Telephone: (1) 882-3100; **Fax:** (1) 882-3101.

Regional Environmental Center for Central and Eastern Europe—REC

Established in 1990; legally based on a charter signed by the governments of 30 countries and the European Commission.

Activities: Assists in solving environmental problems. The Center fulfils this mission by promoting co-operation among governments, NGOs, businesses and other environmental stakeholders, and by supporting the free exchange of information and public participation in environmental decision-making. It has its head office in Szentendre, Hungary, and country offices and field offices in 17 beneficiary countries: Albania, Bosnia and Herzegovina, Bulgaria, Croatia, the Czech Republic, Estonia, Hungary, Latvia, Lithuania, the former Yugoslav republic of Macedonia, Montenegro, Poland, Romania, Serbia, Slovakia, Slovenia and Turkey. The Center actively participates in key global, regional and local processes and contributes to environmental and sustainability solutions within and beyond its country office network, transferring transitional knowledge and experience to countries and regions.

Geographical Area of Activity: Central and Eastern Europe.

Publications: *Developing a Priority Environmental Investment Programme for South Eastern Europe; Assessing Environmental Law Drafting Needs in South Eastern Europe; Developing and Implementing Integrated National Pollutant Release and Transfer Registers; Investing in the Local Environment: Assisting Municipalities in South Eastern Europe to Access Environmental Financing;* and others.

Finance: Annual revenue €12,656,000, expenditure €12,850,000 (31 Dec. 2012).

Board of Directors: Andrzej Kassenberg (Chair.).

Principal Staff: Exec. Dir Marta Szigeti Bonifert; Deputy Exec. Dirs Radoje Lausevic, Zoltan Erdelyi.

Address: 2000 Szentendre, Ady Endre út 9–11.

Telephone: (26) 504-000; **Fax:** (26) 311-294; **Internet:** www .rec.org; **e-mail:** mbonifert@rec.org.

Iceland

FOUNDATIONS, TRUSTS AND NON-PROFIT ORGANIZATIONS

Mannréttindaskrifstofa Íslands (Icelandic Human Rights Centre)

Established in 1994 by the Bishops Office of the Lutheran Church, the Icelandic Red Cross Society, Icelandic Church Aid, the Icelandic Section of Amnesty International, the Office for Gender Equality, the National Federation for the Aid of the Disabled, Save the Children in Iceland, the Women's Rights Association and Association of '78, and the United Nations Development Fund for Women (UNIFEM) in Iceland.

Activities: Aims to promote human rights by creating awareness and acquiring information on issues of human rights in Iceland and abroad; works towards disseminating information on human rights issues and making such information accessible to general public through organizing seminars on issues of human rights and imparting education on human rights; promotes research and legal reforms in the sphere of human rights issues, and has been responsible for the establishment of a specialized library on human rights in Iceland; and issues comments on bills of law, and equips treaty bodies working on human rights issues in Iceland with pertinent information.

Geographical Area of Activity: Iceland.

Publications: Research Reports; *The Human Rights Reference Handbook*; *Universal and Regional Human Rights Protection: Cases and Commentaries*; *Human Rights Instruments* and *Human Rights Ideas, Concepts and Fora*; *Réttarstaða fatalaðra*; *Nordic Journal of Human Rights*; *Yearbook of Human Rights in Development*; *Ragnarsbók: a tribute to Supreme Court Attorney Ragnar Aðalsteinsson, an avid advocate for human rights*; brochures on *CEDAW, The UN Declaration on Human Rights, on National Human Rights Institutions*.

Board of Trustees: Bjarni Jónsson (Chair.); Ugla Stefanía Jónsdóttir (Vice-Chair.); Hugrún Hjaltadóttir (Treas.).

Principal Staff: Dir Margrét Steinarsdóttir.

Address: Túngata 14, 101 Reykjavík.

Telephone: 552-2720; **Fax:** 552-2721; **Internet:** www.humanrights.is; **e-mail:** info@humanrights.is.

West-Nordic Foundation

Founded in 1986 following an agreement signed by the Governments of Denmark, Finland, Iceland, Norway and Sweden, along with the autonomous governments of the Faroe Islands and Greenland to provide funding for small and medium-sized business enterprises in the Faroe Islands, Greenland and Iceland; and to encourage industrial and technical co-operation between Nordic countries.

Activities: Makes loans to businesses in the Faroe Islands and Greenland, financing new and existing fishing businesses, expanding the Greenland tourist industry as well as developing co-operative projects to include the participation of Icelandic businesses.

Geographical Area of Activity: The Faroe Islands, Greenland and Iceland.

Finance: Annual income 2,939,130 Danish kroner, expenditure 2,878,323 Danish kroner (31 Dec. 2012).

Principal Staff: Man. Dir Sverri Hansen.

Address: POB 8096, 128 Reykjavík; Sigtúni 42, 105 Reykjavik.

Telephone: 530-2100; **Fax:** 530-2109; **Internet:** www.vestnorden.is; **e-mail:** vestnorden@vestnorden.is.

India

FOUNDATION CENTRES AND CO-ORDINATING BODIES

Association of Voluntary Agencies for Rural Development—AVARD

Established in 1958; a network of organizations, to strengthen voluntary action and capacity building of Indian NGOs.

Activities: Works in the fields of conservation and the environment, economic affairs, education, law and human rights, international affairs, medicine and health, science and technology, social welfare, and self-governance and empowerment of the disadvantaged, through research, conferences, workshops, seminars and projects (particularly in the areas of poverty reduction, food security, women's empowerment and self-governance).

Geographical Area of Activity: India.

Restrictions: Works in association with other NGOs; is not a funding agency.

Publications: *Voluntary Action* (6 a year); planning studies.

Finance: Annual revenue and expenditure Rs 6m.

Executive Committee: P. M. Tripathi (Pres.); Narayan Bhai (Vice-Pres.); Bharat Bhushan (Treas.).

Principal Staff: Gen. Sec. Dr. B. Mishra.

Address: 5 (FF) Institutional Area, Deen Dayal Upadhyay Marg, New Delhi 110 002.

Telephone: (11) 23234690; 23236782; **Fax:** (11) 23232501; **Internet:** www.avard.in; **e-mail:** avard@bol.net.in.

CAF India

Established in 1998; part of the CAF Global Alliance network of organizations.

Activities: Provides support to corporate organizations, individuals and charities to ensure greater impact of their philanthropic investments. The organization has a regional office in Bangalore.

Geographical Area of Activity: India.

Publications: Annual Report; Newsletter (1–2 a year); *World Giving Index*; reports.

Finance: Annual income Rs 200,364,553, expenditure Rs 194,960,144 (31 March 2014).

Principal Staff: CEO Meenakshi Batra; Dir Avijeet Kumar.

Address: Plot/Site No. 2, First Floor, Sector C (OFC Pocket), Nelson Mandela Marg, Vasant Kunj, New Delhi 110 070.

Telephone: (11) 29233392; **Fax:** (11) 29233396; **Internet:** www.cafindia.org; **e-mail:** contact@cafindia.org.

Centre for Advancement of Philanthropy—CAP

Founded in 1986 to provide philanthropic organizations with information, advice and assistance in the areas of charity law, taxation, investments, financial planning, management, good governance and resources.

Activities: Organizes training courses, seminars, conferences and workshops. The Centre provides consultancy services, conducts research, and publishes books and journals. It set up the Bombay Community Public Trust (f. 1991), which is now run independently. Has around 500 members, including corporate bodies, grantmaking foundations, NGOs and professionals involved in the field of philanthropy.

Geographical Area of Activity: India.

Publications: Annual Report; *Management of Philanthropic Organizations*; *Art of Fundraising*; *Merchants of Philanthropy*; *FAQ*; *Profile 500*; *Philanthropy* (quarterly newsletter); and other publications.

Finance: Funded by grants from local foundations and companies and membership fees. Annual income Rs 4,465,253, expenditure 3,558,210 (31 March 2014).

Board of Directors: Rati Forbes (Chair.).

Principal Staff: CEO Noshir H. Dadrawala; COO Meher Gandevia-Billimoria.

Address: Mulla House, 4th Floor, 51 M. G. Rd, Flora Fountain, Mumbai 400 001.

Telephone: (22) 22846534; **Fax:** (22) 22029945; **Internet:** www.capindia.in; **e-mail:** connect@capindia.in.

Centre for Civil Society

Established in 1997; an independent, non-profit, research and educational organization aiming to improve the quality of life for all citizens of India by reviving and reinvigorating civil society.

Geographical Area of Activity: India.

Publications: Annual Report; brochures; newsletters; books (in Hindi and English).

Finance: Total assets Rs 24,576,313 (31 March 2012).

Board of Trustees: Luis Miranda (Chair.).

Principal Staff: Pres. and Exec. Dir Dr Parth J. Shah.

Address: A-69 Hauz Khas Enclave, New Delhi 110 016.

Telephone: (11) 26521882; **Fax:** (11) 26512347; **Internet:** www.ccs.in; **e-mail:** ccs@ccs.in.

Dasra

Established in 1999 by Deval Sanghavi and Neera Nundy to assist in the development of the non-profit sector in India.

Activities: Provides support and capacity building to non-profit organizations through its Social Impact Program. The organization oversees the Indian Philanthropy Forum. It has offices in the United Kingdom and the USA.

Geographical Area of Activity: India.

Publications: Annual Report.

Finance: Annual income Rs 154,560,969, expenditure Rs 142,157,891 (31 March 2014).

Board: Tarun Jotwani (Chair.).

Address: M.R. Co-op Housing Society, 1st Floor, Bldg No. J/18, opp. Raheja College of Arts and Commerce, Relief Rd, off Juhu Tara Rd, Juhu, Santa Cruz (West), Mumbai 400 054.

Telephone: (22) 61200400; **Internet:** www.dasra.org; **e-mail:** info@dasra.org.

IndianNGOs.com Pvt Ltd

Founded in 2009 by Sanjay Bapat.

Activities: Provides Internet-based information, data and analysis on global social, environmental, economic and developmental issues. The organization hosts a solutions exchange and partnership-promotion platform, where free space is offered to NGOs across the world to share volunteering and donation opportunities.

Geographical Area of Activity: Worldwide.

Publications: Online portals.

Address: c/o Corporate Sustainability & Reputation Consulting, Devendra Apartments, next to Sahayog Mandir, Ghantali, Naupada, Thane 400 602.

Telephone: (91) 9769473599; **Fax:** (22) 25412571; **Internet:** www.indianngos.com/aboutus.asp; **e-mail:** rohini@IndianNGOs.com.

Sampradaan Indian Centre for Philanthropy

Founded in 1996 as a national support organization to promote the development of the non-profit sector, particularly the philanthropy sector, in India.

Activities: Fosters co-operation between the state, corporations and civil society; encourages networking between donors and between donors and NGOs; and carries out advocacy in support of philanthropy. The Centre organizes conferences, seminars and workshops; carrying out research and providing documentation; conducting campaigns; offering advice and supporting the third sector; institution building, establishment of local funds and foundations; and maintaining a resource centre.

Geographical Area of Activity: India.

Publications: *Sampradaan* (newsletter, 6 a year); *Directory of Indian Donor Organisations*; occasional papers, monographs, information leaflets and case studies; publications on social development, resource mobilization, fund-raising and leadership.

Governing Council: Jyoti Sagar (Pres.); Dr Mrithyunjay Athreya (Chief Mentor).

Principal Staff: Exec. Dir Dr Pradeepta Kumar Nayak.

Address: C-8/8704, Vasant Kunj, New Delhi 110 019.

Telephone: (11) 46594572; **Fax:** (11) 46594573; **e-mail:** info@sampradaan.org; sicp.philanthropy@gmail.com.

Voluntary Action Network India—VANI

Established in 1990 as a platform for research, advocacy, capacity building and information exchange on issues relating to voluntarism and voluntary agencies.

Activities: An umbrella body that provides advocacy for the development sector at a national level. The Network provides co-ordination and action to support and promote the voluntary sector in India. It comprises 20 federations and around 5,000 NGOs across the country.

Geographical Area of Activity: India.

Publications: Annual Report; *E-VANI* (newsletter, in Hindi and English); reports.

Finance: Annual income Rs 18,285,000, expenditure Rs 13,966,314 (31 March 2014).

Working Committee: Jayant Kumar (Chair.); Farida Vahedi (Co-Chair.); K. Shivakumar (Treas.).

Principal Staff: CEO Harsh Jaitli.

Address: BB-5, First Floor, Greater Kailash Enclave-II, New Delhi 110 048.

Telephone: (11) 29226632; **Fax:** (11) 414355535; **Internet:** www.vaniindia.org; **e-mail:** info@vaniindia.org.

FOUNDATIONS, TRUSTS AND NON-PROFIT ORGANIZATIONS

African-Asian Rural Development Organization—AARDO

Founded in 1962 in Cairo, Egypt, to act as a catalyst to restructure the economy of the rural populations of Africa and Asia, and to explore opportunities for promoting welfare and eradicating malnutrition, disease, illiteracy and poverty among rural people in Africa and Asia. Formerly known as the Afro-Asian Rural Reconstruction Organization.

Activities: Conducts collaborative research on development issues; gives financial assistance for development projects and disseminates information; organizes international conferences and seminars; facilitates pilot projects; and awards more than 200 individual training fellowships at nine institutes in India, Taiwan, Bangladesh, Republic of Korea, Malaysia, Nigeria, Zambia and Egypt. Membership comprises 15 African and 14 Asian countries, and the Institute of Rural Development (Kenya).

Geographical Area of Activity: Africa and Asia.

Publications: Annual Report; *African-Asian Journal of Rural Development* (2 a year); *AARDO Newsletter* (2 a year, in Arabic and English); workshop and seminar reports.

Finance: Receives annual membership contributions from member countries. Annual income US $680,650 (2014).

Principal Staff: Sec.-Gen. Wassfi Hassan El-Sreihin; Asst Sec.-Gen. Dr Manoj Nardeosingh.

Address: 2 State Guest Houses Complex, Chanakyapuri, New Delhi 110 021.

Telephone: (11) 26877783; **Fax:** (11) 24672045; **Internet:** www.aardo.org; **e-mail:** aardohq@aardo.org.

All India Disaster Mitigation Institute

Established in 1995 to work towards promoting disaster risk mitigation and adaptation to climate change.

Activities: Operates in a variety of areas of disaster management including risk reduction, knowledge management, innovations in disaster response and recovery, and policy advocacy covering 42 cities and 52 districts in India. The Institute's focus is on promoting community based disaster risk reduction through capacity building; facilitating exchange and synergy of risk reduction strategies; providing targeted relief to disaster-affected communities; and supporting human security through shelter, livelihood, water and food projects, protecting and promoting rights of disaster-affected victims, especially women, children, dalits and minorities.

Geographical Area of Activity: India and South Asia.

Restrictions: Supported efforts must reduce risks.

Publications: *Vipada Nivaran* (in Hindi); *Afat Nivaran* (in Gujarati); newsletters; online news; reports, surveys and studies.

Finance: Annual income Rs 7,952,490, expenditure Rs 7,952,490 (31 March 2014).

Trustees: Arvind Krishnaswamy (Chair.); Mihir R. Bhatt (Man. Trustee).

Principal Staff: Co-ordinators Vanadana Chauhan, Vishal Pathak.

Address: 411 Sakar Five, near Old Natraj Cinema, Mithakhadi Railway Crossing, Ashram Rd, Ahmedabad 380 009, Gujarat.

Telephone: (79) 26582962; **Fax:** (79) 26582962; **Internet:** www.aidmi.org; www.southasiadisasters.net; **e-mail:** bestteam@aidmi.org.

Ambuja Cement Foundation—ACF

Established in 1993 by Narotam Sekhsaria, founder of Ambuja Cements Ltd, and Suresh Neotia, the company's Chair. Emeritus, to engage with the rural communities in and around Ambuja Cements Ltd manufacturing locations.

Activities: Aims to make people in India both productive and prosperous and to improve their quality of life, by managing human and natural resources for sustainable development; through technical and financial support; and by serving as a catalyst for appropriate planning, implementation and post-implementation care. Operates in the areas of livelihoods (agricultural and skill-based), natural resource management (water and energy), human development (health, education, women's empowerment and training), and rural infrastructure. Also provides disaster relief and long-term reconstruction support.

Geographical Area of Activity: India.

Publications: Annual Report; *The story of an NGO Network, Kutch Nav Nirman Abhiyan; A Year of People Centred Development; Enriching Experience: A step forward by women farmers to sustain traditional agriculture wisdom; Salinity Prevention* *and Mitigation Initiative: agriculture and water resource development in salinity ingress affected coastal areas; Integrated Development of the village Valadar through Wasteland Development Initiative: managing Common Property Resources through community participation; Health Services at Rural Doorsteps: Creating a cadre of village health functionaries; Village Education Committees: Recharging School Education Systems; Water Resource Management in Junagadh: Transforming Lives* (all in English); a number of publications in Gujarati.

Finance: Annual income, Rs 629,337,000 expenditure Rs 629,337,000 (2013–14).

Board of Directors: Narotam Sekhsaria (Chair.); Suresh Neotia (Chair. Emeritus).

Principal Staff: CEO Pearl Tiwari.

Address: 1st Floor, Elegant Business Park, MIDC Cross Rd 'B', off Andheri Kurla Rd, Andheri (East), Mumbai 400 059.

Telephone: (22) 66167000; **Fax:** (22) 30827794; **Internet:** www.ambujacementfoundation.org; **e-mail:** admin.acf@ambujacement.com.

Angaja Foundation

Founded in 1998 to help improve the lives of underprivileged people.

Activities: Works to protect children's rights, with a focus on: promoting creative non-formal education for children living in slum areas; increasing school admissions for children in need; improving government schools; providing health check-ups for children from slum areas; and health education for adult men and women and adolescents living in slum areas. The Foundation runs training workshops for judges, public prosecutors of the lower courts, police, doctors, NGOs and the media on child rape, child sexual abuse, crimes against women and street children. It also runs a Child Sexual Abuse and Child Rape Programme, which provides counselling, legal, financial and educational services.

Geographical Area of Activity: Delhi, India.

Restrictions: No grants made.

Publications: Annual Report; *Child Rape and Child Sexual Abuse—Sensitization for Lawyers, Police, Doctors and NGOs* (workshop report).

Finance: Funding from ActionAid (q.v.) and Siddartha's Intent. Annual revenue Rs 3m., annual expenditure Rs 2m.

Principal Staff: Gen. Sec. Raka Sinha Bal; Admin. and Accounts Officer C. V. Daniel.

Address: D 298 (Basement), Defence Colony, New Delhi, India 110 024.

Telephone: (11) 41643401; **Fax:** (11) 224617414; **Internet:** angaja.org; **e-mail:** angajafoundation@gmail.com.

Asian Development Research Institute—ADRI

Established in 1991 by a group of social scientists in the eastern Indian state of Bihar.

Activities: Active in the fields of development and social science research, in the Bihar region and internationally, particularly concentrating on promoting literacy development and education. Also active in the area of cultural regeneration, including documenting Bihar's folk art tradition. The Institute has established two financially independent research centres, in Ranchi and New Delhi, and works in collaboration with foreign universities and development organizations. It also holds conferences and the annual ADRI Foundation Lecture.

Geographical Area of Activity: Mainly India.

Board of Directors: Prof. Muchkund Dubey (Chair.); Dr Sunita Lall (Treas.).

Principal Staff: Dr Prabhat P. Ghosh.

Address: BSIDC Colony, off Boring Patliputra Rd, Patna 800 013.

Telephone: (612) 2267773; **Fax:** (612) 2267102; **Internet:** www.adriindia.org; **e-mail:** prabhat.ghosh@adriindia.org.

Asian Institute for Rural Development

Established in 1976 by Dr A. T. Ariyaratne, Dr K. C. Naik, M.V. Rajasekharan and others to undertake scientific research, training and field action in the area of rural development.

Activities: Operates in Asia and Africa in the fields of conservation and the environment, science and technology, and social welfare, through promoting networking among NGOs, running training programmes and field projects, carrying out research, working to develop public policy and issuing publications. Founding member of the Asian NGO Coalition for Agrarian Reform and Rural Development.

Geographical Area of Activity: Asia and Africa.

Restrictions: Does not make grants.

Publications: *AIRD News.*

Board of Trustees: Dr A. T. Ariyaratne (Patron); M.V. Rajasekharan (Chair.); Neetha Ariyaratne, Prof. Govind Ram Agarwal (Vice-Chair.).

Principal Staff: Exec. Dir and Co-ordinator Sandhya Pradeep Kumar.

Address: 17 Katriguppa Main Rd, BSK 3rd Stage, nr Vidyapeeta Circle, Bangalore 85.

Telephone: (80) 226692218; **Internet:** airdindia.org; **e-mail:** asiancarebgl@vsnl.net.

AWHRC—Asian Women's Human Rights Council

Established in 1990 to foster solidarity among women's groups in the Asia region and to promote a feminist and critical perspective on human rights, including focusing on violence against women.

Activities: Pursues human rights for women in Asia through campaigns, lobbying, organizing workshops and conferences, networking, participating in regional and international meetings, conducting fact-finding missions, Women in Black protest actions, and organizing Courts of Women public hearings, as well as through issuing publications and producing and disseminating audio-visual material. The secretariat rotates between the Philippines and India every five years.

Geographical Area of Activity: Asia.

Publications: *Asia Womenews* (newsletter, 2 a year); *Quilt* (journal); *War and Crimes on Asian Women*; and other publications.

Finance: Funding from foundations and international funding agencies.

Principal Staff: Regional Co-ordinator Corinne Kumar.

Address: c/o Vimochana, 33/1-9 Thyagaraj Layout, Jaibharathnagar, M S Nagar Post, Bangalore 560 033.

Telephone: (80) 25492782; **e-mail:** vimochana79@gmail.com.

The Bridge Foundation

Established in 1984 by Dr Vinay Samuel to work with the economically disadvantaged in their struggle to attain economic security and social justice with dignity and self-worth. Affiliated with Opportunity International (q.v.).

Activities: Operates in Southern India in the field of microenterprise development, extending credit to people too poor to borrow from the traditional banking system, through self-conducted programmes and training courses. Loans are made to individuals and to groups from village communities wishing to acquire skills or equipment, and the Foundation offers training in basic accounting and group leadership. The Foundation is particularly interested in assisting marginalized women in rural areas, encouraging them to form self-help groups.

Geographical Area of Activity: Southern India.

Publications: Annual Report; newsletter.

Finance: Net assets approx. Rs 20,203,153.

Board of Trustees: Rev. Dr Vinay K. Samuel (Chair.).

Principal Staff: Dir Albin Pinto.

Address: 139 Infantry Rd, 1st Floor, Bangalore 560 001.

Telephone: (80) 25581869; **Fax:** (80) 25466485; **Internet:** www.bridgefoundation.org.in; **e-mail:** tbfindia@vsnl.com.

Chandana Art Foundation International

Established in 1999 by K. Venkatesh; a charitable trust, to preserve and promote the art and cultural heritage of India, in particular aiming to foster an intellectual and artistic environment for children, women and disabled people and socially and economically disadvantaged people.

Activities: Promotes various forms of art, including traditional and folk art, puppetry, photography and tribal art, through research and documentation, education, exhibitions, workshops, scholarships, competitions, and cultural exchange programmes. The Foundation runs programmes for the visually impaired and physically challenged, especially women and children.

Geographical Area of Activity: India, Germany, Republic of Korea, United Arab Emirates, USA.

Principal Staff: Man. Trustee K. Venkatesh.

Address: No. 784, 10th Main, II Block, BSK I Stage, Bangalore 560 050.

Telephone: (80) 22424820; **Internet:** www.chandanaartfoundation.in; **e-mail:** chandanaartfoundation@gmail.com.

Chemtech Foundation

Established in 1975; an industry association promoting creating platforms for business interactions and strategic alliances.

Activities: Focuses on innovations in technology across various sectors: chemicals and processing; oil and gas; refining; engineering; procurement and construction; automation and process control; pharmaceuticals biotechnology; water; shipping and maritime; power and infrastructure; and design.

Geographical Area of Activity: India.

Publications: *Chemical Engineering World, Offshore World, Pharma Bio World, Shipping Marine & Ports World, Chemical Product Finder* (magazines).

Advisory Board: Jasu Shah (Chair.); Maulik Jasubhai (Vice-Chair.).

Address: 26 Maker Chambers VI, Nariman Point, Mumbai 400 021.

Telephone: (22) 40373737; **Fax:** (22) 22870502; **Internet:** www.chemtech-online.com.

Concern India Foundation

Founded in 1991.

Activities: Supports NGOs across India in the areas of education, health and community development. Through financial and non-financial support to over 270 programmes, the Foundation helps destitute children, young people, differently-abled people, women and the aged. It has offices in Mumbai, Delhi, Bengaluru, Chennai, Hyderabad, Kolkata and Pune.

Geographical Area of Activity: India.

Publications: Annual Report.

Finance: Total assets Rs 213,200m. (31 March 2014).

Board of Trustees: Ardeshir B. K. Dubash (Chair. and Man. Trustee).

Principal Staff: CEO Kavita Shah.

Address: Ador House, 3rd Floor, 6 K. Dubash Marg, Mumbai 400 001.

Telephone: (22) 22029708; **Fax:** (22) 22818128; **Internet:** www.concernindiafoundation.org; **e-mail:** concern@concernindia.org.

Dalit Foundation

Established in 2003.

Activities: Works on behalf of Dalits (Scheduled Castes or 'Untouchables'), who account for more than 200m. people in India. Promotes equal rights and the elimination of caste discrimination; supports individuals, community-based organizations and networks; builds capacity and leadership through its Young Professionals Programme and Professionals Programme; and awards small grants and fellowships; also runs the Dalit Arts and Culture Programme. The Foundation is a founder member of the UK-based Foundations for Peace Network.

Geographical Area of Activity: India.

Board: Martin Macwan (Chair.).

Principal Staff: Exec. Dir Santosh K. Samal.

Address: Dalit Foundation, C-58, Basement, South Extension-II, New Delhi 110 049.

Telephone: (11) 26265071; **Fax:** (11) 26265072; **Internet:** www.dalitfoundation.org; **e-mail:** programmes@dalitfoundation.org.

Dignity, Education, Vision International—DEVI

Established in 1992 by Dr Sunita Gandhi to promote education and development in India.

Activities: Provides education for the poor in India and encourages self-help through learning and development. Particular focus on empowering poor women from both rural and urban areas.

Geographical Area of Activity: India.

Principal Staff: Convenor Dr Sunita Gandhi.

Address: C/o Global Classroom Pvt Ltd, 10 G Station Rd, Lucknow 226 001.

Telephone: (923) 5620013; **Internet:** www.globaleducation.org/devi.htm; **e-mail:** sunitag@ims.is.

Environmental Protection Research Foundation

Founded in 1981 by Dr B. Subba Rao, Dr S. V. Ranade and Prof. J. M. Gadgil to promote research in the field of environmental engineering.

Activities: Operates in the fields of conservation and the environment. The Foundation helps companies, pollution control boards, local bodies and governmental agencies carry out effective implementation of pollution control programmes. It also runs development activities in agro-based industries, environmental degradation and watershed management.

Geographical Area of Activity: India.

Publications: *Souvenirs*; laboratory manuals.

Council of Management: Dr B. Subba Rao (Pres.); Dr S. V. Ranade (Vice-Pres.).

Address: c/o Dnyandeep Foundation, Arundhati, nr MSEB, Vishrambag, Sangli 416 415.

Telephone: (233) 2301857; **e-mail:** bssubbarao@yahoo.com.

Foundation of Occupational Development—FOOD

Established in 1979 by Ms Rajeswari S. and Loyola Joseph with the objective of implementing welfare programmes and carrying out research on social development.

Activities: Fosters sustainable development among rural and urban poor communities through participatory social development and welfare programmes in the fields of water and sanitation, job creation, health, energy conservation, ICTs and capacity building for women's networks.

Geographical Area of Activity: India.

Finance: Total assets approx. Rs 8.5m.

Principal Staff: Exec. Dir Loyola Joseph.

Address: Bharathiar Complex, C-Block, 1st Floor, 100 Feet Rd, Vadapalani, Chennai 600 026.

Telephone: (44) 24848201; **Fax:** (44) 24838826; **Internet:** www.foodindia.org.in; **e-mail:** food@foodindia.org.in.

Foundation for Revitalization of Local Health Traditions—FRLHT

Established in 1991.

Activities: Operates in the field of health care by encouraging the use of traditional medicine as part of public health programmes. Maintains medicinal plant database and promotes their conservation. The Foundation is committed to international co-operation in the field of complementary medicine. Engages in trans-disciplinary research, education and training in the use of medicinal plants and traditional health care. Set up the Institute of Trans-disciplinary Health Sciences and Technology in 2014.

Geographical Area of Activity: India.

Restrictions: Research grants only.

Publications: *Challenging Indian Medical Heritage* (2004); books on conservation of medicinal plants; *Amruth* (traditional health care magazine, 6 a year); educational material, such as CD-ROMs and posters; *Ksemakutuhalam* (medicinal plant guide).

Finance: Total assets Rs 833,683,524; annual expenditure Rs 177,115,159 (March 2013).

Board of Trustees: Sam G. Pitroda (Chair.); R. Jayachandran (Treas.).

Principal Staff: Dir Padma Venkat.

Address: 74/2, Jarakbande Kaval, Post Attur, Via Yelahanka, Bangalore 560 106.

Telephone: (80) 28568000; **Fax:** (80) 28568007; **Internet:** ihstuniversity.org; **e-mail:** info@frlht.org.

Foundation for Social Transformation

Established in 2008.

Activities: Strengthens civil society and builds capacity; lobbies for participatory, inclusive, transparent and accountable government. Programmes include Empowerment of Women in conflict-prone areas of north-east India and Youth for Social Action.

Geographical Area of Activity: North-east India (the states of Arunachal Pradesh, Assam, Manipur, Meghalaya, Mizoram, Nagaland and Tripura).

Restrictions: Not currently awarding grants or fellowships.

Finance: Annual income and expenditure Rs 644,000 (31 March 2014).

Principal Staff: Exec. Dir Gayatri Buragohain.

Address: J. N. Borooah Lane, Jorpukhuri, Guwahati 781 001, Assam.

Telephone: (361) 2733696; **Internet:** www.fstindia.org; **e-mail:** fstnortheast@gmail.com.

Rajiv Gandhi Foundation

Established in 1991 by Sonia Gandhi to promote the ideals of her late husband Rajiv Gandhi.

Activities: Operates in the areas of: natural resource management; libraries and education; health; welfare of the disabled; women and children's development; applied science and technology in rural areas; and the promotion of grassroots democracy through local self-government. The Foundation's largest programmes include the establishment of village libraries throughout India; implementing schemes for rainwater harvesting and environmental regeneration in rural India through its own corps of volunteers; supporting the education of child victims of terrorism; projects for the economic and educational empowerment of women; and AIDS control and awareness campaigns. These are implemented through self-conducted programmes, grants to institutions, scholarships, research, conferences, and publications. The attached Rajiv Gandhi Institute for Contemporary Studies is a centre for interdisciplinary studies, including economic and legal reform, social issues and international relations; it also conducts seminars and workshops, and issues publications. Following a tsunami in late 2004, the Foundation announced plans to support all children in India orphaned by the disaster.

Geographical Area of Activity: India.

Publications: Annual Report; *Challenges of Globalization*; *Economic Reforms for the Poor*; *Salvaging the WTO's Future: Doha and Beyond*; *Reinventing the Public Sector*; *District Level Deprivation in the New Millennium*.

Finance: Annual income Rs 137,191,442, expenditure Rs 146,003,197 (31 March 2014).

Board of Trustees: Sonia Gandhi (Chair.); Priyanka Gandhi Vadra (Exec. Trustee).

Address: Jawahar Bhawan, Dr Rajendra Prasad Rd, New Delhi 110 001.

Telephone: (11) 23755117; **Fax:** (11) 23755119; **Internet:** www.rgfindia.com; **e-mail:** info@rgfindia.org.

Gandhi Peace Foundation

Founded in 1958 to promote the beliefs and practices of Mohandas Karamchand Gandhi; registered in 1964.

Activities: Works towards fostering and maintaining peaceful, happy and harmonious social relations. The Foundation encourages the principles of truth and non-violence in national and international affairs, and promotes the teaching of the practices of Gandhi. It is also active in environmental affairs, including forest preservation and support for environmental activists. Awards the annual Pranavanand Peace Award.

Geographical Area of Activity: India.

Publications: *Gandhi Marg* (quarterly in English, 6 a year in Hindi); several books.

Finance: Funded by the Gandhi Memorial Trust. Annual budget approx. Rs 47,790,500.

Trustees: Radha Bhatt (Chair.); Shri P. M. Tripathi (Treas.).

Principal Staff: Gen. Sec. Shri Surendra Kumar.

Address: 221–23 Deen Dayal, Upadhyaya Marg, New Delhi 110 002.

Telephone: (11) 23237491; **Fax:** (11) 23236734; **Internet:** gandhibookhouse.com/aboutus.php; **e-mail:** gpf18@rediffmail.com; gpfsecretary@gmail.com.

IIEE—Indian Institute of Ecology and Environment

Established in 1999; a not-for-profit autonomous institution decreed as a public charitable trust.

Activities: Focuses on environmental protection, sustainable development, disaster mitigation, study of meteorological phenomena, population control, energy and resource management, and other issues pertaining to environment and ecology. The Institute carries out consultancy, research and training, and issues several publications on research results.

Geographical Area of Activity: India.

Publications: *International Encyclopaedia of Ecology and Environment*; *Encyclopaedia of International Environmental Laws*; *Concise Encyclopaedia of Indian Environment*; *Global Environmental Education: World Ecology and Environment Directory;* and other publications.

Principal Staff: Pres. Prof. Dr Priya Ranjan Trivedi.

Address: A-15, Paryavaran Complex, Maidangarhi Rd, New Delhi 110 030.

Telephone: (11) 29535053; **Fax:** (11) 29533514; **Internet:** www.ecology.edu; **e-mail:** ecology@ecology.edu.

Indian Council for Child Welfare

Established in 1952 to promote development services for children in India.

Activities: Promotes development services for children, particularly focusing on welfare and education. The Council runs educational programmes, childcare centres and creches for young children; operates childcare and education centres; disseminates information throughout India, enhancing awareness of children's needs; acts as an advocate for children's rights and benefits; funds training centres; and organizes seminars, conferences and workshops on issues relating to child development. It also maintains a library. There are 31 State or Union Territory Councils throughout India.

Geographical Area of Activity: India.

Board of Trustees: Gita Siddhartha (Pres.); Kasturi Mahapatra, Chandra Devi Thanikachalam (Vice-Pres); T. Phanbuh

(Vice-Pres. and Sec.-Gen.); Nivedita Hazarika (Joint Sec.); Asha Gupta (Treas.); Bharat S. Naik (Asst Treas.).

Principal Staff: Contact Sunita Gadgil.

Address: 4 Deen Dayal Upadhayay Marg, New Delhi 110 002.

Telephone: (11) 23236616; **Internet:** www.iccw.in; **e-mail:** iccw.delhi@gmail.com.

Indian Council for Cultural Relations

Founded in 1950 to establish and strengthen cultural relations between India and other countries.

Activities: Operates nationally and internationally through the reciprocal development of studies in Indian and foreign universities; awards scholarships and fellowships; exchanges cultural material with libraries and museums abroad; and promotes of exchange visits of cultural delegations, scholars and artists. The Council organizes the Azad Memorial Lectures, international seminars, symposia and conferences; establishes chairs and centres of Indian studies abroad; looks after the welfare of foreign students in India; compiles select bibliographies and publishes books and journals in English, French, Spanish and Arabic. It also administers the Jawaharlal Nehru Award for international understanding, instituted by the Government of India in 1964. The Council has 20 regional offices and 35 cultural centres worldwide.

Geographical Area of Activity: International.

Publications: *Indian Horizons* (periodic, in English); *Gagananchal* (6 a year, in Hindi); *Thaqafat-ul-Hind* (quarterly, in Arabic); *Papeles de la India* (2 a year, in Spanish); *Rencontre avec l'Inde* (2 a year, in French); books on diplomacy, language and literature, and the arts, with a particular focus on Indian culture, philosophy and mythology, music, dance, theatre, and translations of Sanskrit classics.

Finance: Annual income Rs 1,580,048,820, expenditure Rs 2,426,869,000 (2012/13).

Governing Body: Prof. Lokesh Chandra (Pres.); Shri Lalit Mansingh, Dr S. N. Pathan (Vice-Pres).

Principal Staff: Dir-Gen. Shri Satish C. Mehta.

Address: Azad Bhavan, Indraprastha Estate, New Delhi 110 002.

Telephone: (11) 23379309; **Fax:** (11) 23378639; **Internet:** iccr.gov.in; **e-mail:** dg.iccr@nic.in.

Indian Council of Social Science Research—ICSSR

Founded in 1969 by the Government of India as an autonomous organization to promote and co-ordinate research in social sciences.

Activities: Funds research projects in social sciences proposed by scholars, and sponsors projects on its own initiative (e.g. research on the North-Eastern region of India, women's studies and entrepreneurship). The Council conducts surveys of research in the social sciences and publishes them periodically; awards research fellowships, contingency grants and grants for study and publications; gives financial support for conferences and seminars; and organizes or supports training courses in research methodology. It provides guidance and consultancy services in data-processing, and has a documentation centre that provides information support to social scientists; collaborates in research and exchange programmes with a number of countries; and evaluates research proposals submitted by foreign nationals intending to undertake research in India. It also part-finances 27 other research institutes and has six regional offices throughout the country.

Geographical Area of Activity: India.

Publications: Annual Report; *ICSSR Journal of Abstracts and Reviews: Economics* (2 a year); *ICSSR Journal of Abstracts and Reviews: Geography* (2 a year); *ICSSR Journal of Abstracts and Reviews: Political Science* (2 a year); *ICSSR Newsletter* (quarterly); *ICSSR Research Abstracts* (quarterly); *Indian Psychological Abstracts and Reviews* (2 a year); NASSDOC research information series; ICSSR surveys of research; and various other publications of research reports, monographs, national and international seminar proceedings.

Finance: Total expenditure Rs 524,384,000 (2009–10).

Council: Prof. Sukhadeo Thorat (Chair.).

Principal Staff: Member Sec. Ramesh Dadhich.

Address: Aruna Asaf Ali Marg, JNU Institutional Area, New Delhi 110 067.

Telephone: (11) 26741849; **Fax:** (11) 26749836; **Internet:** www.icssr.org; **e-mail:** info@icssr.org.

Indian National Trust for Art and Cultural Heritage—INTACH

Established in 1984 for the conservation and promotion of Indian heritage: architectural, natural, cultural and environmental.

Activities: Supports the preservation of man-made and natural heritage of India, including places of archaeological, historical, artistic and scientific value. The Trust also promotes public awareness of cultural issues and preservation of Indian heritage and acts as a pressure group when necessary. It works through eight divisions: Art Conservation; Heritage Education and Communication Services; Architectural Heritage; Natural Heritage; Cultural Affairs; Intangible Heritage; Heritage Tourism; and Chapters. There are 140 Chapters across India and three Chapters in Belgium, the United Kingdom and the USA. The INTACH UK Trust offers scholarships and funding for British nationals to carry out research on India, and exchanges for young architects and planners in association with the Charles Wallace India Trust and the British Council (qq.v.).

Geographical Area of Activity: Belgium, India, United Kingdom, USA.

Publications: Annual Report; *Virasat* (quarterly newsletter); *Young INTACH* (newsletter); environmental series; studies in ecology and sustainable development; science in public policy series; INTACH Southern Western Ghats environment series; documentation on heritage properties; and other series.

Finance: Annual income Rs 82,666,255, expenditure 56,984,927 (31 March 2014).

Executive Committee: Maj.-Gen. L. K. Gupta (Chair.); Tasneem Mehta (Vice-Chair.).

Principal Staff: Mem. Sec. Dr C. T. Misra.

Address: 71 Lodi Estate, New Delhi 110 003.

Telephone: (11) 24631818; **Fax:** (11) 24611290; **Internet:** www.intach.org; **e-mail:** intach@intach.org.

Inlaks Shivdasani Foundation

Founded in 1976 by Indoo Shivdasani to give education and medical assistance, mainly in India.

Activities: Main activity is awarding scholarships in any subject to exceptionally talented Indians for study or research at any reputed university or institution. In the United Kingdom, the Foundation has joint scholarships with the Royal College of Art, Imperial College London, the School of Oriental and Asian Studies, and the London Academy of Music and Dramatic Art in; and in Italy, with UNIDEE, Fondazione Pistoletto. The Foundation assists young Indians through Take-Off Grants in India, which aim to develop individual talent, and offers Inlaks Fine Arts Awards to help artists under 35 years of age in India to develop their talent. It also runs a fellowship programme and special projects.

Geographical Area of Activity: International.

Restrictions: Candidates for scholarships abroad must have been accepted for a course before applying for a scholarship, and must be under 30 years of age.

Publications: Annual Report.

Board of Trustees: Lakshmi Shivdasani (Chair.).

Principal Staff: Asst Krishna Kumar; Admin. Amita Malkani.

Address: POB 2108, Delhi 110 007; c/o ICGEB (International Centre for Genetic Engineering and Biotechnology), Aruna Asaf Ali Marg, New Delhi 110 067.

Telephone: (11) 26741260; **Fax:** (11) 27667965; **Internet:** www .inlaksfoundation.org; **e-mail:** info@inlaksfoundation.org.

International Foundation for Human Development—IFHD

Founded in 1993 to improve quality of life through development.

Activities: Promotes self-help, self-employment and long-term development programmes in collaboration with other national and international organizations. Works to improve education systems, and offers a number of scholarships and grants for students; promotes volunteerism and social justice; and runs a documentation centre and library with reference to development studies and voluntary service. The Foundation runs conferences and workshops; and co-operates with NGOs in Asia and the Pacific, Africa and the Middle East.

Geographical Area of Activity: Africa, Asia and the Middle East.

Publications: *Asia Pacific Link*; Annual Report.

Trustees: Dr Chelikani Rao (Chair.).

Principal Staff: Sec. P. Rajeswara Rao.

Address: Balaji Residency 106, 12-13–705/10/A&B, Gokulnagar, Tarnaka, Hyderabad 500 017.

Telephone: (40) 55214993; **Fax:** (40) 27154118; **e-mail:** ifhd@sify.com.

iPartner India

Established in 2008 by Bina Rani.

Activities: Co-ordinates philanthropic giving from within India and abroad to a network of 42 partner organizations in 16 states in India; educates donors, and ensures the effective and transparent use of funds. Main fields of interest are children, education, health and livelihoods, and climate change. Has offices in India and the UK.

Geographical Area of Activity: India.

Principal Staff: Chief Exec. Bina Rani; Country Dir Sumitra Mishra.

Address: c/o PCVC, 4/203 Kaushalya Park, Haus Khas, New Delhi 110 016.

Telephone: (11) 26528916; **Internet:** www.ipartnerindia.org; **e-mail:** info@ipartnerindia.org.

Nand and Jeet Khemka Foundation

Established in 2005.

Activities: Seeks to develop multi-stakeholder, strategic, long-term initiatives in four main areas: social entrepreneurship; leadership and ethics; climate change; and governance and accountability. The Foundation jointly administers the Action to Improve Public Scheme Access and Delivery—AIPAD project in Bihar with the European Union.

Geographical Area of Activity: Mainly in India.

Restrictions: No unsolicited grant proposals.

Publications: *Jan Samvad* (newsletter, 6 a year); handbooks; podcasts; reports.

Trustees: Uday Nabha Khemka (Man. Trustee and CEO); Don Mohanlal (Vice-Chair.).

Principal Staff: COO Debadideb Datta.

Address: Khemka House, 1st Floor, 11 Community Centre, Saket, New Delhi 110 017.

Telephone: (11) 46034800; **Fax:** (11) 46034823; **Internet:** khemkafoundation.in; **e-mail:** info@khemkafoundation.net.

Naandi Foundation—A New Beginning

Established in 1998 by four businesses—Dr Reddy's Laboratories Ltd, Global Trust Bank, Satyam Computer Services Ltd and the Nagarjuna Group of companies—and a state government as a unique non-profit autonomous development organization.

Activities: Supports development initiatives in the fields of children's rights, the sustainable livelihood of marginal and small farmers, and safe drinking water, through working directly with communities in partnership with the Government and civil society organizations.

Geographical Area of Activity: Nine states in India: Andhra Pradesh, Madhya Pradesh, Chhattisgarh, Nagaland, Rajasthan, Punjab, Haryana, Andaman and Nicobar Islands.

Publications: Annual Report.

Finance: Annual income Rs 929,625,198, expenditure Rs 925,686,567 (31 March 2012).

Board of Trustees: Dr K. Anji Reddy (Chair.).

Principal Staff: CEO Manoj Kumar.

Address: 502 Trendset Towers, Rd No. 2, Banjara Hills, Hyderabad 500 034.

Telephone: (40) 23556491; **Fax:** (40) 23556537; **Internet:** www .naandi.org; **e-mail:** info@naandi.org.

National Institute for Sustainable Development—NISD

Established in 1992 by Prakash Palande; a non-profit, secular, voluntary organization.

Activities: Works to improve the lives of the rural poor, especially *bidi* (cigarette) workers and people displaced by irrigation projects. Current project activities are concentrated in the rural areas of Ahmednagar and Pune districts in Maharashtra state. Works to improve the quality of life of *bidi* rollers and people affected by the Pimpalgoan Joge and Dimbhe irrigation projects. The Institute implements programmes such as organizing a strong network of self-help groups, youth and children groups. It also runs programmes including pre-school centres, training for teachers, youth development, and support to schoolchildren to encourage attendance at school. The Institute assists with building houses, toilets and other hygiene and sanitation facilities; and has started a programme on reproduction, children's health, rights and protection, HIV awareness, and youth development. It also undertakes land-levelling and land development activities for tribal and marginal farmers and supports them to create small income-generating activities so that they can earn/supplement their income.

Geographical Area of Activity: India, Pune and Ahmednagar districts of Maharashtra state.

Restrictions: Does not award grants.

Finance: Supported by the Government and by national and international funding organizations. Annual budget Rs 10m.

Trustees: Prakash J. Palande (Pres.); Dr Chandrashekhar Divekar (Sec.).

Principal Staff: Exec. Dir Prakash J. Palande.

Address: C-6/84, Shanti Rakshak Society, Yerwada, Pune.

Telephone: (20) 26688207; **e-mail:** nisdpune@nisd.org.in.

NFI—National Foundation for India

Established in 1992 under the aegis of Ford Foundation, USA (q.v.) to fund and provide grants in support of social development.

Activities: Focuses on gender equity, child and health issues pertaining to adolescent reproduction, urban environment, urban management, poverty, illiteracy, health and hygiene, and communication-building between communities. The Foundation funds initiatives involving children and youngsters; awards annual media fellowships in recognition of young journalists working on issues of development; and recognizes NGOs through good governance awards to encourage efficacious multi-sectoral partnership between the corporate sector, the state and civil society.

Geographical Area of Activity: India.

Restrictions: No grants to groups and organizations affiliated to political or religious organizations.

Publications: *Status of the Girl Child in India*; *Accountablility and Decentralization in Urban Governance*; *Women's Empowerment: Role of Women's Universities and Women's Studies Centre*; *Assignment—Giving Voices to the Unheard*; and booklets.

Finance: Annual income Rs 8,344m., expenditure Rs 8,987m. (31 March 2014).

Board of Trustees: Deep Joshi (Chair.).

Principal Staff: Exec. Dir Amitabh Behar.

Address: India Habitat Centre, Core 4A, Upper Ground Floor, Lodhi Rd, New Delhi 110 003.

Telephone: (11) 24641864; **Fax:** (11) 24641867; **Internet:** nfi .org.in; **e-mail:** info@nfi.org.in.

Nirnaya

Established in 1998 by Mini Nair, Uma Maheshwari and Indira Jena to empower marginalized women in rural and urban regions.

Activities: Aims to develop the position of women in India. The organization assists in the formation of self-help groups promoting social and economic empowerment; encourages entrepreneurship and other means of subsistence; works to improve women's skills base; extends support to organizations working to promote literacy and education among women and girls; and supports individual efforts, as well as organizations run by women.

Geographical Area of Activity: India.

Restrictions: Funds are provided only to women who are working in India.

Board of Trustees: Indira Jena (Man. Trustee).

Principal Staff: CEO B. Girija Devi; Asst Dir Nilima R. Jones.

Address: Flat No. 11, Deepthi Apartments, S. P. Rd, Secunderabad 500 003.

Telephone: (40) 27805089; **Fax:** (40) 27717305; **Internet:** www .nirnaya.org; **e-mail:** info@nirnaya.org.

Oxfam India

Established in 2008 by a merger of Oxfam affiliates that had been working in India since 1951. Became a fully affiliated member of the Oxfam confederation of organizations (qq.v.) in 2011.

Activities: Operates in India in the areas of poverty reduction, humanitarian relief, gender justice and economic justice. Maintains a number of offices in India.

Geographical Area of Activity: India.

Finance: Annual income Rs 680m., expenditure Rs 681m. (31 March 2014).

Governing Board: Kiran Karnik (Chair.); Mridula Bajaj (Vice-Chair.).

Principal Staff: Chief Exec. Nisha Agrawal.

Address: Shriram Bharatiya Kala, 4th and 5th Floors, 1 Copernicus Marg, Kendra, New Delhi 110 001.

Telephone: (11) 4653 8000; **Fax:** (11) 4653 8099; **Internet:** www.oxfamindia.org; **e-mail:** delhi@oxfamindia.org.

Pratham Education Foundation

Established in 1994, and formerly known as the Pratham Mumbai Education Initiative Trust, to provide literacy programmes to children in India.

Activities: Operates literacy programmes throughout India. The Foundation has established the Pratham Institute for Literacy, Education and Vocational Training and also runs the Pratham Council for Vulnerable Children, an outreach programme that is active in eight states. Sister organizations operate in the United Kingdom and the USA.

Geographical Area of Activity: India.

Publications: Annual Report; *Annual Status of Education Report* ; newsletter; reports.

Finance: Annual revenue Rs 927,075,113, expenditure Rs 917,278,195 (31 March 2014).

Board of Directors: Ajay G. Piramal (Chair.).

Principal Staff: Pres. and CEO Madhav Chavan.

Address: YB Chavan Centre, 4th Floor, Gen. J. Bhosale Marg, Nariman Point, Mumbai 400 021.

Telephone: (22) 22819561; **Fax:** (22) 22819563; **Internet:** www .pratham.org; www.pcvc.org; www.prathaminstitute.org; **e-mail:** info@pratham.org.

Azim Premji Foundation

Established in 2001 by Azim Premji, Chair. of the Wipro Corporation.

Activities: Aims to develop elementary education for all children in India, through funding training, development of the education system and innovative utilization of technology, creating models to promote orientated learning, building capacity through local planning processes, and effectively using research, academic, advocacy and communication tools to augment these efforts.

Geographical Area of Activity: India.

Publications: *Learning Curve* (newsletter); *Milestones* (newsletter); *Kindle* (newsletter, 6 a year); *Language Learning and Teaching* (2 a year); *At right Angles* (2–3 a year); Field Newsletters; position papers; reserach studies; books; reports; papers and articles; CDs; online teaching and learning resources.

Board of Trustees: Azim Premji (Chair.).

Principal Staff: Chief Exec. Dileep Ranjekar.

Address: 134 Doddakannelli, next to Wipro Corporate Office, Sarjapur Rd, Bangalore 560 035.

Telephone: (80) 55144900; **Fax:** (80) 55144903; **Internet:** www .azimpremjifoundation.org; **e-mail:** info@ azimpremjifoundation.org.

C. P. Ramaswami Aiyar Foundation

Established in 1966 in remembrance of the work of statesman and educationist Dr C. P. Ramaswami Aiyar.

Activities: Funds projects and institutions to advance Indian community development, incl. the C. P. Ramaswami Aiyar Institute of Indological Research, which carries out research, and holds seminars, courses and lectures on subjects relating to Indian culture and society; the C. P. Art Centre, an exhibition centre, which displays the work of Indian artists and holds workshops and demonstrations; and the Saraswathi Kendra Centre for Children, which provides aid for children suffering from behavioural and learning difficulties. Works in association with the Indian Government through the C. P. R. Environmental Education Centre, established in 1989 to promote environmental awareness, produce and disseminate basic educational and reference material on environment and to support environmental education projects. The Foundation maintains a library of more than 20,000 titles on Indian philosophy, religions, history, law, the arts and the environment.

Geographical Area of Activity: India.

Publications: Reports and Prospects.

Council of Management: Dr Sarojini Varadappan (Pres.); V. K. Rajamani (Vice-Pres.); M. Bargavi Devendra (Hon. Sec.); K. Krishnan (Hon. Treas.).

Principal Staff: Hon. Dir Dr Nanditha Krishna.

Address: 1 Eldams Rd, Alwarpet, Chennai 600 018.

Telephone: (44) 24341778; **Fax:** (44) 24341022; **Internet:** cprfoundation.org; **e-mail:** cprafoundation@gmail.com; cpraf@vsnl.com.

Ryan Foundation International

Founded in 1982 to promote the use of appropriate technologies in rural areas, and to provide safe water for those without it, through the use of renewable energy and minimal investment.

Activities: Organizes training programmes for government organizations and NGOs from all over the world, and income-generating programmes for women in rural areas; disseminates information; conducts research; and promotes community development organizations and co-operatives. The Foundation's main area of interest is a sea-water distillation programme that uses solar energy and reflectors. It also conducts research into plants that grow well in sea water and looks at ways of exploiting their potential.

Geographical Area of Activity: International.

Publications: *Better Life Technologies for the Poor* (3 vols); *RYFO Handout*; *RYFO Income Generation Series*; *Drought Trees for Dry Villages*; *Water Management in Homes and Villages*; *How to Convert Sea Water into Drinking Water*; *Survival by Sea Water*; *Sea water canals*; *Sea water for cooking*; *Water a basic human right*; and other publications.

Finance: Funded by founders' endowment, publication sales, membership fees, consultation fees and donations. Annual revenue Rs 500,000.

Principal Staff: Pres. Dr Felix Ryan; Man. Trustee A. Veethoose.

Address: 15 West Mada St, Srinagar Colony, Saidapet, Chennai 600 015.

Telephone: (44) 22351993; **Internet:** www.felixryanh2o.com; **e-mail:** info@felixryanh2o.com.

Sabera Foundation India

Created in 1999 by Spanish singer Nacho Cano to support development projects in India, with a particular emphasis on women.

Activities: Focuses on helping destitute and street children, and those with disabilities. Runs the Kalitala Girls' Home and Home for Disabled Persons.

Geographical Area of Activity: India.

Publications: Annual Report; Bulletin (monthly).

Finance: Annual income Rs 11,326,355, expenditure Rs 11,326,355 (2011/12).

Governing Body: Arnab Ranjan Ghosh (Pres.); Abhjit Dey (Vice-Pres.); Manas Chandra Das (Sec.); Basudev Mondal (Asst Sec.); Amit Auddy (Treas.).

Address: Dey's Estate, Vill-Gazipur, P. O. Kangaberria, P. S. Bishnupur, 24 Parganas South 743 503, West Bengal.

Telephone: (33) 4957186; **Internet:** sabera-foundation.org; **e-mail:** info@sabera-foundation.org.

M. S. Swaminathan Research Foundation—MSSRF

Founded in 1988 by Prof. M. S. Swaminathan, Prof. V. L. Chopra, Dr V. K. Ramachandran and Mina Swaminathan to support research and training in the application of modern science and technology, and to apply contemporary development experience to the problems of ecologically sustainable agricultural production and the distribution and consumption of agricultural commodities; to ensure a reasonable standard of living; and to secure the livelihood of poor people in rural areas.

Activities: Operates in the fields of rural development and science and technology through research, conferences, publications and training courses. The Foundation collaborates with individuals and other institutions to achieve its aims and objectives. Programmes include the Every Child a Scientist project, Coastal Systems Research, Information Village Research Project, Farmers' Rights Information Service, and Eco-Technology and Eco-Jobs. Also operates four field centres across India.

Geographical Area of Activity: India.

Restrictions: Not a grantmaking organization.

Publications: Annual Report; newsletter; numerous books.

Finance: Annual income Rs 11,288.5m., expenditure Rs 11,288.5m. (2013/14).

Trustees: Dr Madhura S. Swaminathan (Chair.).

Principal Staff: Exec. Dir Dr Ajay K. Parida.

Address: 3rd Cross St, Institutional Area, Taramani, Chennai 600 113.

Telephone: (44) 22541229; **Fax:** (44) 22541319; **Internet:** mssrf .org; **e-mail:** swami@mssrf.res.in.

Lady Tata Memorial Trust—LTMT

Founded in 1932 by Sir Dorabji Jamsetji Tata to encourage and advance original research in medical science, in relation to the diseases of the blood, especially leukaemia, and related diseases.

Activities: Operates in the fields of science and medicine: 80% of the Trust's annual income is allocated to international awards for study and research into leukaemia, with special reference to leukaemogenic viruses, the epidemiology, pathogenesis and immunology of leukaemia; 20% is allocated to Indian nationals working in India for scientific investigation into the alleviation of human suffering from the disease. International awards are made on the recommendation of a Scientific Advisory Committee, based in London, United Kingdom.

Geographical Area of Activity: International.

Finance: Annual income US $61,810,000, expenditure $61,810,000 (2010–11).

Board of Trustees: Ratan N. Tata (Chair.).

Address: Bombay House, 24 Homi Mody St, Fort, Mumbai 400 001.

Telephone: (22) 66658282; **Fax:** (22) 22826092; **Internet:** www.dorabjitatatrust.org; **e-mail:** sdtt@sdtatatrust.com.

Sir Dorabji Tata Trust

Founded in 1932 by Sir Dorabji Jamsetji Tata to relieve distress, and advance learning, especially research work in connection with medical and industrial problems; provision of scholarships in any branch of science or the arts; and to give aid to charitable institutions.

Activities: Operates nationally in the fields of the management of natural resources, livelihood, education, health, and social development initiatives, covering community development, human rights, family welfare, the physically and mentally challenged, civil society, art and culture, and relief. Projects are carried out through self-conducted programmes, research, grants to national institutions, grants to individuals, fellowships and scholarships. The Trust has established pioneering institutions in India, including the Tata Institute of Social Sciences (1936), the Tata Memorial Hospital (for cancer, 1941), the Tata Institute of Fundamental Research (1945, now known as the National Centre for Nuclear Science and Mathematics) and the National Centre for the Performing Arts (1966). In association with the UN, the Trust started the first Demographic Research Institute in 1956 (now the International Institute for Population Studies, Mumbai). The Trust established the National Institute for Advanced Studies, Bangalore, in 1988, the J. R. D. Tata Centre for Ecotechnology, Chennai, in 1998 and the Sir Dorabji Tata Centre for Research in Tropical Diseases, Bangalore, in 2000.

Geographical Area of Activity: India.

Restrictions: Currently funding only projects within India because of exchange restrictions.

Publications: Annual Report; Strategy Papers.

Finance: Annual income US $57,010,000, expenditure $57,010,000 (31 March 2013).

Board of Trustees: Ratan N. Tata (Chair.).

Principal Staff: Sec. and Chief Accountant Rukshana Savaksha.

Address: Bombay House, 24 Homi Mody St, Fort, Mumbai 400 001.

Telephone: (22) 66658282; **Fax:** (22) 22045427; **Internet:** www.dorabjitatatrust.org; **e-mail:** sdtt@sdtatatrust.com.

Vanarai

Founded in 1986 by Mohan Dharia to promote use of natural resources and sustainable development throughout India.

Activities: Implements sustainable development initiatives in villages in co-operation with villagers, schools, co-operatives, community leaders, etc. The organization promotes the greening of rural and urban areas through tree-planting schemes run in co-operation with other organizations. Programmes include: training for farmers in integrated rural development, watershed management, new agricultural techniques, improved seeds, cattle breeding, nurseries, harvesting technologies, etc.; wasteland development, including lobbying local and central governments; the empowerment of women and young people; sanitation and energy; and the Latur Project, which promotes integrated rural development in 21 villages in the Latur district—this project is implemented in conjunction with the central Government and local governments, and is partially funded by the Sir Dorabji Tata Trust (q.v.).

Geographical Area of Activity: India.

Publications: *Vanarai* (magazine, monthly, in Marathi); booklets; videos; slides.

Board of Trustees: Shri Ravindra Dharia (Pres.).

Principal Staff: Sec. Shri Shriram Gomarkar.

Address: 498 Aditya Residency, Parvati, nr Mitramandal Chowk, Pune 411 009.

Telephone: (20) 24440351; **Fax:** (20) 24445299; **Internet:** www.vanarai.org; **e-mail:** info@vanarai.org; vanaraitrust@gmail.com.

M. Venkatarangaiya Foundation

Established in 1981 in memory of Prof. Mamidipudi Venkatarangaiya.

Activities: Aims to abolish child labour through campaigning for a universal education system in India, enrolling children at school and providing support, and running summer camps and extra courses. The Foundation works to empower women through action on issues such as livelihood and natural resource management. It was involved in the implementation of the RTE Act 2009 through empowerment of local elected bodies. Has an office in the USA.

Geographical Area of Activity: Andhra Pradesh.

Board of Trustees: Dr M. Krishnamurthi (Chair. and Managing Trustee); M. Ravindra Vikram (Sec.).

Principal Staff: Nat. Convener R. Venkat Reddy.

Address: 201 Narayan Apartments, West Maredpally, Secunderabad 500 026.

Telephone: (40) 27801320; **Fax:** (40) 27808808; **Internet:** www.mvfindia.in; **e-mail:** mvfindia@gmail.com.

World Teacher Trust

Founded in 1971 by Dr Ekkirala E. Krishnamacharya to promote health and hygiene; to establish and maintain hospitals and clinics; to distribute free medicines to the public; to promote homeopathic medicine; to establish and maintain educational institutions; and to organize seminars and conferences.

Activities: Promotes family life, human rights, social harmony, education, and health and welfare.

Geographical Area of Activity: North and South America, Europe and India.

Restrictions: Does not support financial schemes, only those related to human values.

Publications: *Paracelsus Health and Healing* (magaznie); *Vaisakh* (newsletter); numerous books, articles, leaflets and pamphlets.

Managing Council: Dr K. Parvathi Kumar (Global Chair.); Dr K. S. Sastry (Chair.); Sri A. L. N. Rao (Vice-Chair.); Sri B. R. K. Raju (Sec.); Sri U. C. H. B. Varma (Treas.).

Address: 15-7-1 Angels Enclave, Krishna Nagar, Visakhapatham 530 002.

Telephone: 2509154; **Internet:** www.worldteachertrust.org; **e-mail:** theworld_teachertrust@hotmail.com.

Indonesia

FOUNDATION CENTRE AND CO-ORDINATING BODY

International NGO Forum on Indonesian Development—INFID

Established in 1985 to give a voice to the concerns of the people represented by NGOs involved in Indonesia and to facilitate communication between NGOs inside and outside Indonesia.

Activities: Network of more than 100 NGOs from Indonesia, member countries of the Consultative Group for Indonesia and international organizations with a commitment to Indonesia. The Forum works to alleviate poverty in Indonesia by addressing its root causes. It acts as an advocate for the creation and implementation of new policies relating to development aid, investment and trade to ensure that they are in the interests of the underprivileged and are based on principles of peace and justice. It also creates an environment in which democracy can develop and be strengthened, particularly placing an emphasis on human rights. Member organizations assemble twice a year, and the INFID Conference is held biennially. Has a liaison office in Belgium.

Geographical Area of Activity: International.

Publications: Books; leaflets; conference proceedings; fact sheets.

Steering Committee: J. Danang Widoyoko (Chair.); Antarini Pratiwi Arna (Vice-Chair.); Farah Sofa (Treas.).

Principal Staff: Exec. Dir Sugeng Bahagijo.

Address: Jl. Jatipadang Raya Kav 3 No. 105, Pasar Minu, Jakarta 12540.

Telephone: (21) 7819734; **Fax:** (21) 78844703; **Internet:** www .infid.org; **e-mail:** infid@infid.org; infid@live.com.

FOUNDATIONS, TRUSTS AND NON-PROFIT ORGANIZATIONS

ASEAN Foundation

Established in 1997 at the Association of Southeast Asian Nations' (ASEAN) 30th Anniversary Summit to help bring about shared prosperity and a sustainable future to the countries of ASEAN (Brunei, Cambodia, Indonesia, Laos, Malaysia, Myanmar, the Philippines, Singapore, Thailand and Viet Nam).

Activities: Operates in the fields of social and economic development, and poverty reduction, promoting access to information and communication technologies in particular to disadvantaged groups, young people, women, the disabled and rural communities. The Foundation also promotes awareness of ASEAN, and volunteer exchanges for young people.

Geographical Area of Activity: ASEAN countries.

Publications: Annual Report; *the ASEAN beat* (magazine); *Gazette*; fact sheets; curricula; handbooks.

Finance: Annual revenue US $506,621, expenditure $1,129,542 (31 Dec. 2013).

Board of Trustees: Rahmat Pramono (Chair.); Latsamy Keomany (Vice-Chair.).

Principal Staff: Exec. Dir Elaine Tan.

Address: Jl. Sam Ratulangi No. 2, Menteng, Jakarta 10350.

Telephone: (21) 31924828; **Fax:** (21) 31926078; **Internet:** www .aseanfoundation.org; **e-mail:** secretariat@aseanfoundation .org.

Tahir Foundation

Established by Dato Sri Tahir, Chair. and CEO of Mayapada Group.

Activities: Main areas of activity are education, providing scholarships to universities in Indonesia and computers to disadvantaged students; health care, funding hospitals and health programmes; and research into legal reforms. In 2014, it established the Indonesa Health Fund, in co-operation with the Bill & Melinda Gates Foundation (q.v.), to address issues such as HIV/AIDS, malaria, tuberculosis and polio, child mortality and family planning.

Geographical Area of Activity: Principally Indonesia.

Principal Staff: Chair. Dato Sri Tahir.

Address: Mayapada Tower, Jl. Jendral Sudirman Kav 28, Karet Setiabudi, Jakarta Selatan, Jakarta.

Telephone: (21) 5213059; **Internet:** www.tahirfoundation.or .id.

WALHI—Wahana Lingkungan Hidup Indonesia (Indonesian Forum for the Environment—Friends of the Earth Indonesia)

Established in 1980 to pursue justice, social equity, control of people over resources management, and fair governance. Part of the Friends of the Earth network (q.v.).

Activities: Operates in the areas of conservation of natural resources, and civil and human rights, through advocacy, community empowerment, assisting community development and self-organization, and networking. In 2011, the Forum comprised 479 member organizations and 156 individual members in 28 provinces.

Geographical Area of Activity: Indonesia.

Restrictions: Grants made only to member organizations.

Publications: *Tanah Air* (quarterly magazine); *Simpul Jaringan* (monthly magazine); *Walhi Updates* (electronic newsletter, 2 a month).

National Council: Dada Surdaja (Chair.).

Principal Staff: Exec. Dir Abetnego Tarigan.

Address: Jl. Tegal Parang Utara No. 14, Jakarta 12790.

Telephone: (21) 79193363; **Fax:** (21) 7941673; **Internet:** www .walhi.or.id; **e-mail:** informasi@walhi.or.id.

Yayasan Dian Desa (Light of the Village Foundation)

Founded in 1972 to improve the welfare of rural communities by making use of effective and efficient technologies.

Activities: Aims to improve the welfare of rural communities in Indonesia, through acting as a catalyst, introducing new ideas, which are then implemented and popularized by village communities. Provides guidance, support and training to help people help themselves. The Foundation is active in the fields of water and sanitation, renewable energy, agriculture and aquaculture, small industry and micro-finance. It has branch offices in East Nusa Tenggara and Bali.

Geographical Area of Activity: Indonesia.

Publications: *The Kotakatikotakita Urban Bulletin*; *ASAP* (magazine); *SODIS* (magazine).

Principal Staff: Exec. Dir Anton Soedjarwo.

Address: Jl. Kaliurang Km 7, Gg Jurug Sari IV/19, POB 19, Yogyakarta.

Telephone: (27) 4885247; **Fax:** (27) 4885423; **Internet:** diandesa.org; **e-mail:** secretariat.yogya@diandesa.org; diandesa.yk@gmail.com.

Yayasan Insan Sembada (Insan Sembada Foundation)

Founded in 1974 to promote national self-reliance and sustainable development. Formerly known as Yayasan Indonesia Sejahtera.

Activities: Operates through supporting development activities in Indonesia in the fields of education and training, institution building, community development and publications, and providing public information. The Foundation runs training courses, provides technical assistance to NGOs, carries out research and collaborates with other organizations. It also provides emergency and disaster relief.

Geographical Area of Activity: Indonesia.

Publications: *Vibro* (newsletter); *Bergetar* (bulletin); books.

Board of Trustees: Joseph Gustama (Pres.).

Principal Staff: Chair. Muki Reksoprojo; Sec. Fitrianti Roby; Treas. Lanny Hendrata.

Address: Jalan Kramat Lontar H-IIA, RT.004 RW.007, Jakarta 10430.

Telephone: (21) 3902973; **Fax:** (21) 31926914; **Internet:** www.yis.or.id; **e-mail:** insan.sembada@yahoo.co.id.

Yayasan Keanekaragaman Hayati Indonesia— KEHATI (Indonesia Biodiversity Foundation)

Founded in 1994 to promote biological diversity conservation and the sustainable use of natural resources, and to empower local communities.

Activities: Promotes biodiversity and the conservation of natural resources in local communities, through grants to projects in the fields of education and training, organizational development, environmental conservation, community development and research. The Foundation also runs training courses and workshops, publishes information for public use, lobbies government and provides technical assistance to NGOs.

Geographical Area of Activity: Indonesia.

Publications: Annual Report; *Warta KEHATI* (newsletter); fact sheets.

Finance: Annual revenue 140,383,552,161 rupiah, expenditure 105,205,251,903 rupiah (31 Dec. 2013).

Governing Board: Ismid Hadad (Chair.); **Executive Board:** Suzy Hutomo (Chair.).

Principal Staff: Exec. Dir Mohamed Senang Sembiring.

Address: Jl. Bangka VIII No. 3B, Pela Mampang, Jakarta 12720.

Telephone: (21) 7183185; **Fax:** (21) 7193161; **Internet:** www.kehati.or.id; **e-mail:** kehati@kehati.or.id.

Yayasan Pengembangan Masyarakat Desa— YADESA (Foundation of Village Community Development)

Established in 1987 to run activities in the fields of education and training, home industry, rural development, co-operation, guidance and counselling.

Activities: Operates within the above areas, providing funding and technical support to NGOs, generating resources, organizing co-operatives and running micro-credit activities, and channelling funding distributed by international NGOs.

Geographical Area of Activity: South-East Asia, Indonesia.

Restrictions: No grants to individuals.

Publications: Publications on micro-credit and development issues.

Board of Trustees: Abdul Gani Nurdin (Chair.) Dr Martunis Yahya (Vice-Chair.); Dr Syarwan Ahmad (Sec.); M. Daud Yoesoef (Treas.).

Principal Staff: Man. Dir Dr Martunis Yahya.

Address: Jl. T. Nyak Arief 33A, Pasar Lamnyong 2311, POB 137.

Telephone: (651) 7400911; **Fax:** (651) 7552127; **e-mail:** yadesa@eudoramil.com.

Yayasan Tifa (Tifa Foundation—Indonesia)

Established in 2012; part of the Open Society Foundations (q.v.) network.

Activities: Promotes democratic development in Indonesia based on the rule of law, good governance and support for the rights of all citizens, including women, minority groups and marginalized populations. Focuses its activities on human rights and access to justice; equality and citizenship; civil society and democracy; local governance; and information and media.

Geographical Area of Activity: Indonesia.

Finance: Annual income US $5,956,285, expenditure $5,947,447 (31 Dec. 2012).

Board of Directors: Rizal Malik (Chair.).

Address: Graha Mustika Ratu, 5th Floor, #505, Jln. Jend. Gatot Subroto kav. 74–75, Jakarta 12870.

Telephone: (21) 83790611; **Fax:** (21) 83783648; **Internet:** www.tifafoundation.org; **e-mail:** public@tifafoundation.org.

Iran

FOUNDATIONS, TRUSTS AND NON-PROFIT ORGANIZATIONS

Islamic Thought Foundation

Founded in 1983 to promote Islam internationally and to introduce Islamic teachings to all people of the world.

Activities: Operates in the fields of development studies, the arts and humanities, conservation, economic affairs, education, international affairs, human rights, medicine and health, science and technology, and social welfare. Publishes magazines in various languages.

Geographical Area of Activity: Iran.

Publications: *Echo of Islam*; *Mahjubah*; *Sauti ya Ummah*; *Message del'Islam*; *Al-Tahira-Ashra-Al-Wahda*; *Sakon Musulurci*; *ZamZam* (all monthly); and numerous books, including *A Jug of Love*; *Abdullah—Ibn Saba & Other Myths*; *Velaa and Vilayat*; *Imam Ali AS's Letter*; *Wahabiya in Mizan*; *The Role of Divine Assistance in Human Life*; *Ethical Aspects of Power in Islam*; *Sexual Ethics in Islam and the West*; *The Glory of Martyrdom*; *Footprint of Blood*; *Everlasting Life*; *The Collector of Felicities*; *Imam Ali AS's Hadiths*; *Equality*; *The Marriage Portion of Blood*; *Midnight Call to Prayer*; *Islamic Morals in Wav*; *The Answered Prayer*; *Juibar and Zulfa*; *The Cancelled Immunity*; *Hatam's Son*; *In Rustam's Court*; *The Possessors of the Elephant*; *The Candle of the Dawn*; *India Bird on the Branch of Art of Iran*; *Poetry in Pre-Islamic Iran*; *Angular Kufic*; *Migration to Habasheh*; *Night but the Light*; *Religious Instructions for Young People*; *Message of Imam Khomeini RA on the Occasion of Hajj (1408–1988)*; *Spirit of Monotheism*; *The Enchanted Necklace*; *When He Comes*; *The Tale of Two Palm Trees*.

Principal Staff: Man. Dir Prof. Mehdi Goljan; Editor-in-Chief Shaqayeqh Qandehari.

Address: 766 Valiy-e Asr Ave, POB 14155-3899, Teheran 14155.

Telephone: (21) 88897662-5; **Fax:** (21) 88902725; **Internet:** www.itf.org.ir; **e-mail:** info@itf.org.ir.

Ireland

FOUNDATION CENTRES AND CO-ORDINATING BODIES

Dóchas

Established in 1993 as a co-ordinating body for development NGOs in Ireland, following the merger between CONGOOD, which represented the common interests of Irish development NGOs since 1974, and the Irish National Assembly.

Activities: Promotes co-operation between development organizations in Ireland to increase the efficiency and effectiveness of programmes carried out in less-developed countries. The organization disseminates information and research findings to its 44 members and promotes development education, as well as providing a forum for member agencies to meet together.

Geographical Area of Activity: Ireland.

Restrictions: Not a funding agency.

Publications: Annual Report; *DOCHAS Wednesday News* (weekly e-mail news bulletin).

Finance: Annual income €396,738, expenditure €402,740 (31 Dec. 2014).

Board: Sharan Kelly (Chair.); Olive Towey (Vice-Chair.).

Principal Staff: Dir Hans Zomer.

Address: 1–2 Baggot Ct, Lower Baggot St, Dublin 2.

Telephone: (1) 4053801; **Fax:** (1) 4053802; **Internet:** www .dochas.ie; **e-mail:** anna@dochas.ie.

Philanthropy Ireland

Established in 1998 as the Funders' Forum; present name adopted in 2004.

Activities: Aims to increase the level of philanthropy in Ireland and to expand the community of engaged donors who are regular, strategic, long-term contributors to good causes. Supports quality research on giving, advocating for tax and policies that encourage philanthropy; and provides membership services.

Geographical Area of Activity: Ireland.

Publications: Annual Report; *Philanthropy Scope* (journal, 2 a year); Guide to Effective Giving (2010); Guide to Setting up a Foundation in Ireland (2008); Guide to Giving (2007).

Finance: Annual income €797,200, expenditure €749,495 (31 Dec. 2012).

Board of Directors: Maurice A. Healy (Chair.).

Principal Staff: Exec. Dir Seamus Mulconry.

Address: 85 Merrion Sq. South, Dublin 2.

Telephone: (1) 6768751; **Internet:** www.philanthropy.ie; **e-mail:** info@philanthropy.ie.

FOUNDATIONS, TRUSTS AND NON-PROFIT ORGANIZATIONS

The Barretstown Camp Fund Ltd

Launched in 1994 by the US actor Paul Newman following the success of his first Hole In The Wall Camp in Connecticut, USA, which is a camp for children who have life-threatening conditions and serious illnesses.

Activities: Gives European children suffering from life-threatening illnesses, such as cancer or other serious illnesses, an opportunity to enjoy 'serious fun'. The organization runs a medically endorsed programme of therapeutic recreation presents children with 'challenge by choice' and helps to rebuild self-esteem and confidence. It also organizes sibling camps, recognizing the negative impact that childhood cancer has on siblings' lives. Special autumn and spring family camps are also organized for the children, as well as their carers and families; programmes are also included for bereaved families.

Geographical Area of Activity: Europe.

Publications: Annual Review; *Barrestown Family Newsletter*.

Finance: Annual income €4,557,136, expenditure €5,222,765 (2013).

Board of Directors: Maurice Pratt (Chair.).

Principal Staff: CEO Dee Ahearn.

Address: Barretstown Castle, Ballymore Eustace, Co Kildare.

Telephone: (45) 864115; **Fax:** (45) 864197; **Internet:** www .barretstown.org; **e-mail:** info@barretstown.org.

Bóthar

Established in 1991 by a group of farmers, businesspeople and community and church leaders under the chairmanship of the late T. J. Maher. Aims to help families in need to overcome hunger and malnutrition in a sustainable manner through the use of livestock in development aid.

Activities: Operates internationally in the field of aid to less-developed countries. Establishes livestock development projects for families in need, providing a sustainable solution to the problems of poverty and hunger. Each family receives a farm animal or animals, such as a dairy cow, a dairy goat, a flock of laying hens or three hives of bees, as well as the training and support necessary to establish a micro-farming enterprise. Nutrition is improved by the consumption of the resulting produce and income is generated by the sale of the surplus produce. Recipients pass on a gift of offspring, similar to that which they receive, to other families chosen by the community. Maintains four additional offices in Ireland and Northern Ireland.

Geographical Area of Activity: Africa, South America, Asia and Eastern Europe.

Publications: *The Bó Vine* (quarterly newsletter).

Finance: Total assets €1,047,710, annual income €6,372,238 (30 June 2013).

Board: Harry Lawlor (Chair.); Sinead Baggott (Vice-Chair.); Jim Quigley (Treas.).

Principal Staff: CEO David Moloney.

Address: Old Clare St, Limerick.

Telephone: (61) 414142; **Fax:** (61) 315833; **Internet:** www .bothar.ie; **e-mail:** info@bothar.ie.

Concern Worldwide

Established in 1968.

Activities: Operates in the fields of development aid, emergency relief, and advocacy and development education, working to alleviate the effects of severe poverty in the developing world, particularly in Africa and Asia. Projects involving volunteers include improving health care and sanitation, and providing clean water, food, shelter and education. Also works to eliminate poverty through advocacy, and funds development education on issues such as third-world debt, human rights, fair trade and refugees. The organization has offices in Belfast, Glasgow and London, and an affiliate in the USA.

Geographical Area of Activity: Worldwide.

Publications: Newsletter; Annual Review.

Finance: Annual income €145,455,000, expenditure €138,042,000 (31 Dec. 2014).

Board of Trustees: Chris Elliot (Chair.); **Council:** Tom Shipsey (Chair.); Siobhan Toale (Sec.).

Principal Staff: CEO Dominic MacSorely; Deputy CEO and COO Jim Hynes.

Address: 52–55 Lower Camden St, Dublin 2.

Telephone: (1) 4177700; **Fax:** (1) 4757362; **Internet:** www .concern.net; **e-mail:** info@concern.net.

European Foundation for the Improvement of Living and Working Conditions

Founded in 1975 by the Council of Ministers of the European Community (now the European Union—EU) to contribute to the formulation of policies that would improve living and working conditions in member states.

Activities: Operates in the member states of the EU in the field of social issues, by conducting research and publishing the results. The Foundation provides the EU with a scientific basis against which medium- and long-term policies for the improvement of social and work-related matters can be developed. In particular, it carries out research in the following areas: employment and competitiveness; industrial relations and the workplace; and living conditions and quality of life.

Geographical Area of Activity: Europe (member states of the European Union and candidate countries).

Restrictions: Does not make grants.

Publications: Annual Report; *Eurofound News* (newsletter); *Eurofound Yearbook*; research reports and infosheets; information brochures and booklets; electronic publications online.

Finance: Annual revenue €20,770,591, expenditure €20,853,659 (2013).

Governing Board: Herman Fonck (Chair.); Aviana Bulgarelli, Stefania Rossi, Armindo Silva (Vice-Chair.).

Principal Staff: Dir Juan Menéndez-Valdes; Deputy Dir Erika Mezger.

Address: Wyattville Rd, Loughlinstown, Dublin 18.

Telephone: (1) 2043100; **Fax:** (1) 2826456; **Internet:** www .eurofound.europa.eu; **e-mail:** information@eurofound .europa.eu.

GOAL

Founded in 1977 by Irish sports journalist John O'Shea to relieve suffering in the developing world caused by war, disaster and catastrophe regardless of race, religion or nationality.

Activities: Operates in 12 countries of Africa, Asia, Central America, in the areas of aid to less-developed countries, nursery and primary education, medicine and health, and social welfare, through direct implementation of relief and development projects, and grants to missionary and indigenous organizations. The organization runs programmes that provide rehabilitation, emergency aid, housing, health care, clean water and education to those who need it, as well as a number of projects working with 'street children' around the world. It also runs training programmes for local people in less-developed countries to help precipitate long-term improvements. Also maintains offices in the United Kingdom and the USA.

Geographical Area of Activity: Worldwide.

Publications: Newsletter.

Finance: Annual income €65,432,649, expenditure €63,701,510 (31 Dec. 2013).

Trustees: Pat O'Mahony (Chair.); James H. Casey (Sec.).

Principal Staff: CEO Barry Andrews.

Address: POB 19, Dun Laoghaire, Co Dublin; 12–13 Cumberland St, Dun Laoghaire, Co Dublin.

Telephone: (1) 2809779; **Fax:** (1) 2809215; **Internet:** www.goal .ie; **e-mail:** info@goal.ie.

Gorta-Self Help Africa

Established in 1965 by the Department of Agriculture. Formerly known as Gorta—Freedom from Hunger Council of Ireland. Present name adopted following the merger in 2014 with Self Help Africa.

Activities: Co-operates with local NGOs to support development projects in Sub-Saharan Africa. The organization works to combat hunger through long-term projects encouraging self-sufficiency, emphasising the importance of local resources and training local people so that they can manage their own projects. It raises funds through public events and by running charity shops throughout Ireland; and also hosts the annual World Food Day Conference. Maintains offices in Ireland, United Kingdom and USA, as well as in programme countries throughout Sub-Saharan Africa.

Geographical Area of Activity: Sub-Saharan Africa.

Publications: Newsletter, Annual Report/Review.

Board: Tom Kitt (Chair.).

Principal Staff: CEO Ray Jordan.

Address: Kingsbridge House, Parkgate Street, Dublin 2.

Telephone: (1) 677 8880; **Fax:** (1) 677 8880; **Internet:** www .gorta.org; **e-mail:** info@gorta.org.

Katharine Howard Foundation

Founded in 1979 by Katharine Howard.

Activities: Operates through the provision of small grants to community organizations across the 32 counties of Ireland. The Foundation places special emphasis on helping disadvantaged people, the elderly, young people, refugees and asylum seekers, and people with disabilities, provided that these projects are community-based and involve the targeted group in their design and management.

Geographical Area of Activity: Ireland.

Restrictions: Grant schemes are run on a limited basis.

Publications: *Young Men on the Margins: Suicidal Behaviour amongst Young Men*; *The Whitaker Committee Report 20 Years On, Lessons Learned or Lessons Forgotten?*; *Community Matters No. 5: Tallaght West Small Grants Programme* (in partnership with Atlantic Philanthropies); *Community Matters No. 6: Parent & Toddler Group Initiative 2006–2008* (in partnership with the Office of the Minister for Children and Youth Affairs); newsletters; interim reports.

Finance: Annual income €326,022, expenditure €191,478 (2013).

Trustees: David Kingston (Chair.).

Principal Staff: Development Dir Dr Noelle Spring.

Address: 10–12 Hogan Pl., Dublin 2.

Telephone: (1) 6618963; **Fax:** (1) 4531862; **Internet:** www.khf .ie; **e-mail:** info@khf.ie.

International Fund for Ireland

Founded in 1986 by the Governments of Ireland and the United Kingdom to promote economic and social advance and to encourage contact, dialogue and reconciliation between nationalists and unionists throughout the island of Ireland.

Activities: Operates in Northern Ireland and the six border counties of the Republic of Ireland. The Fund's programmes are: the Business Enterprise Programme, which promotes the development of local businesses through training schemes, marketing, business accommodation and revolving loan funds; the Rural Development Programme, which promotes the regeneration of disadvantaged rural areas; the Community Leadership Programme, which provides the resources and support necessary to initiate community-led development programmes; the Community Bridges Programme, which is designed to bring people from different communities to work together on joint projects for mutual benefit, while encouraging the participants to address issues of difference and division; the Wider Horizons Programme, which promotes improved relations between communities in Northern Ireland and on a cross-border basis through training and work experience schemes for young people abroad; the Key Programme, which works to develop the personal and entrepreneurial skills of young people while facilitating contact and dialogue; the Newradiane Programme, a pilot programme aimed at helping local companies undertake product and process development projects in partnership with a company located in the USA, Canada, Australia and New Zealand or in a European Union member state; and the Tourism Programme, which encourages economic regeneration by stimulating private sector investment in the provision and upgrading of tourist accommodation and amenities and by supporting tourism marketing and human resource development initiatives. Maintains an office in Belfast.

Geographical Area of Activity: Northern Ireland and the border counties of the Republic of Ireland.

Publications: Annual Report; Accounts.

Finance: Annual income €761,000, expenditure €7,605,000 (30 Sept. 2013).

Governing Board: Dr Adrian Johnston (Chair.).

Address: POB 2000, Dublin 2.

Telephone: (1) 4082130; **Fax:** (1) 4705407; **Internet:** www.internationalfundforireland.com.

Irish Youth Foundation

Established in 1985 as an independent development trust to support projects and programmes making a positive difference in the lives of marginalized and socially excluded children and young people.

Activities: Operates in Ireland and the United Kingdom in the area of children and young people between the ages of five and 20 years, through research, grants to voluntary and community groups, and in partnership with statutory and state agencies. Supports projects tackling problems of poverty, unemployment, drugs, alcohol abuse, crime, violence and vandalism; AIDS preventative programmes that promote personal growth and development; and facilities and amenities for education and recreation. Promotes standards of excellence in service providers and in programmes, and seeks to identify, strengthen and expand existing programmes for Irish children and young people. There are Boards of Trustees in the United Kingdom and the USA, where the Foundation raises funds. Works in partnership with the International Youth Foundation (q.v.).

Geographical Area of Activity: Ireland and United Kingdom.

Publications: Annual Report; various papers and studies on youth and children's sector issues.

Board: Ursula Murphy (Chair.).

Principal Staff: Dir of Development Niall McLoughlin.

Address: DogPatch, Unit 1 The CHQ Bldg, Custom House Quay Dublin 1.

Telephone: (1) 6766535; **Fax:** (1) 6769893; **Internet:** www.iyf.ie; **e-mail:** info@iyf.ie.

Oxfam Ireland

Founded in 1998; part of the Oxfam confederation of organizations (qq.v.).

Activities: Works in less-developed countries of Africa in the areas of sustainable livelihood, emergency relief, campaigning, equal rights and status, and fair trade. Its head offices are located in Dublin and Belfast; maintains an office in Tanzania.

Geographical Area of Activity: Congo (Dem. Repub.), Kenya, Malawi, Rwanda, South Africa, Sudan, Tanzania, Uganda, Zimbabwe.

Finance: Annual income €17,730,000, expenditure €19,500,000 (31 March 2014).

Board of Directors: Henrietta Campbell (Chair.); Paul Shovlin (Treas.); Hugh Walker (Sec.).

Principal Staff: CEO Jim Clarken.

Address: Portview House, 4 Thorncastle St, Dublin 4.

Telephone: (1) 6727662; **Fax:** (1) 6727680; **Internet:** www.oxfamireland.org; **e-mail:** info@oxfamireland.org.

Plan Ireland

Founded in 1937 during the Spanish Civil War; established in Ireland in 2003.

Activities: Carries out welfare activities for children. Works with regional partners on long-term projects in the fields of education, health, habitat, building relationships and livelihood; handles anti-child-trafficking projects, support programmes for orphans and susceptible children, assistance programmes for street children, and child media projects; sponsors a child through its Sponsor a Child programme; promotes and protects child rights; also focuses on promoting awareness on HIV/AIDS and its prevention, and birth registration. The organization is active in 46 developing countries.

Geographical Area of Activity: Africa, South America, Asia and Europe.

Publications: Annual Report.

Finance: Annual income €12,240,120, expenditure €12,352,948 (30 June 2014).

Board of Trustees: Geraldine Kelly (Chair.); Brian Lehane (Sec.).

Principal Staff: Chief Exec. David Dalton.

Address: 126 Lower Baggot St, Dublin 2.

Telephone: (1) 6599601; **Fax:** (1) 6599602; **Internet:** plan.ie; **e-mail:** info@plan.ie.

RIA—Royal Irish Academy

Founded in 1785 for the promotion of study in the sciences, humanities and social sciences.

Activities: Involved in the development of many academic and scientific disciplines in Ireland; provides key policy advice, as well as fostering international academic links including membership of the International Council of Scientific Unions. The Academy operates in the fields of the humanities and sciences through research programmes, a library, publications, conferences and around 30 Charlemont grants each year.

Geographical Area of Activity: Ireland.

Publications: *The Proceedings of the RIA*—three sections (mathematical and physical sciences; biology and environmental sciences; archaeology, Celtic studies, history, linguistics and literature); *Ériu* (Irish philology and literature); *Irish Journal of Earth Sciences; Irish Studies in International Affairs;* conference proceedings; books on Irish archaeology, history, folklore, science and arts.

Finance: Annual income €4,291,451, expenditure €3,641,883 (31 Dec. 2013).

Council: Mary E. Daly (Pres.); Roger Downer (Sr Vice-Pres.); Prof. John McGilp (Treas.); Eugene Kennedy (Sec.).

Principal Staff: Exec. Sec. Laura Mahoney.

Address: 19 Dawson St, Dublin 2.

Telephone: (1) 6762570; **Fax:** (1) 6762346; **Internet:** www.ria.ie; **e-mail:** webmaster@ria.ie.

Self Help Africa

Established in 2008 by the merger of Self Help Development International and Harvest Help, which were both founded in 1984, following the famine in Ethiopia, to provide long-term development solutions to the challenges facing communities in Africa.

Activities: Implements integrated rural development programmes. The organization employs no expatriate staff, and implements sustainable development programmes that promote self-sufficiency and seek to build the capacity of local communities. The primary focus of work is on improving agricultural productivity and farm household incomes, improving access to social services such as health and education, together with measures that are designed to combat deteriorating natural resources, gender inequality and HIV/AIDS. The organization operates in Benin, Burkina Faso, Ethiopia, Ghana, Kenya, Malawi, Togo, Uganda and Zambia.

Geographical Area of Activity: Sub-Saharan Africa.

Publications: Annual Report; newsletter (annual).

Finance: Annual income €13,136,645, expenditure €12,790,628 (31 Dec. 2013).

Board of Directors: Tom Kitt (Chair.); John Whelan (Sec.).

Principal Staff: Chief Exec. Ray Jordan.

Address: Kingsbridge House, 17–22 Parkgate St, Dublin 8.

Telephone: (1) 6778880; **Internet:** www.selfhelpafrica.org; **e-mail:** info@selfhelpafrica.org.

Trócaire—Catholic Agency for World Development

Established in 1973 by the Catholic Bishops of Ireland to provide funding to developing countries in need, and to raise awareness in Ireland of development issues.

Activities: Aims to relieve the suffering of people in need around the world, including those suffering the effects of poverty, conflict and oppression, through projects, grants, publications and conferences. The Agency supports programmes in a number of areas, including food security, education, health, human rights, community development of agriculture and microfinance. It funds emergency relief in man-made and natural disaster areas, engaging in food assistance, construction of new homes and providing emergency water, clothing and medical supplies. It also works to raise awareness within Ireland of development issues and problems suffered by people in other parts of the world.

Geographical Area of Activity: Africa, Latin America, Asia, Middle East and Europe.

Restrictions: No grants to individuals.

Publications: Annual Report; *Trócaire Development Review*; *Trócaire World*; *Campaigns Update* .

Finance: Annual income €61,143,000, expenditure €66,500,000 (28 Feb. 2014).

Board of Trustees: Bishop William Crean (Chair.).

Principal Staff: Exec. Dir Dir Éamonn Meehan.

Address: Maynooth, Co Kildare.

Telephone: (1) 6293333; **Fax:** (1) 6290661; **Internet:** www.trocaire.org; **e-mail:** webmaster@trocaire.ie.

Vita

Founded in 1989 as Refugee Trust International.

Activities: Aims to bring an end to extreme poverty and reduce the vulnerability of poor people in Africa by building sustainable livelihoods. The organization works to bring about lasting positive change in the living conditions of poor and marginalized people in Ethiopia, Eritrea and Kenya, by developing and supporting income generation activities. Goals include eradicating extreme poverty and hunger; promoting gender equality; reducing child mortality; combating HIV/AIDS, malaria and other diseases; and creating a global partnership for development.

Geographical Area of Activity: Africa.

Publications: Annual Report.

Finance: Annual income €2,642,371, expenditure €2,594,406 (31 Dec. 2013).

Board of Directors: Seamus Crosse (Chair.); John Wallace (Sec.).

Principal Staff: CEO John Weakliam.

Address: Equity House, 16–17 Upper Ormond Quay, Dublin 7.

Telephone: (1) 8734303; **Fax:** (1) 8734325; **Internet:** www.vita.ie; **e-mail:** info@vita.ie.

Women's Aid

Founded in 1974; a feminist, service-based political and campaigning voluntary organization.

Activities: Aims to eliminate violence against women through effecting political, cultural and social change. Responds to some 12,000 calls annually. Services include a national telephone helpline; a one-to-one support service from a centrally located service and five outreach clinics; and a court accompaniment service for women accessing the legal system. Also provides an Arts Programme for women and children living in refugee accommodation in Dublin. Works with community groups countrywide on the issue of violence against women. Provides training on the issue of domestic violence to a range of voluntary and statutory agencies and service providers, including health professionals, refuge workers, An Garda Síochána, community and social services, and community groups. Provides research, statistics and vital information to the media and public. Influences policy and lobbies for improved legislation.

Geographical Area of Activity: Ireland.

Publications: *Vision Action Change: Feminist Principles and Practice of Working on Violence Against Women* (2002); *Responding to Violence Against Women With Disabilities* (2003); *Child Custody and Access in the Context of Domestic Violence: Women's Experiences and the Response of the Legal System* (2003); *Women's Aid National Freephone Helpline Statistics* (annual).

Finance: Net assets €1,362,863 (31 Dec. 2012).

Board of Directors: Ursula Regan (Chair.).

Principal Staff: Dir Margaret Martin.

Address: 5 Wilton Pl., Dublin 2.

Telephone: (1) 6788858; **Fax:** (1) 6788915; **Internet:** www.womensaid.ie; **e-mail:** info@womensaid.ie.

World Mercy Fund (Ireland) Ltd

Established in 1969 by Fr Thomas Rooney to fund health-care projects in Africa.

Activities: Works internationally to improve health care facilities and support community development in less-developed countries, establishing clinics and hospitals and providing clean water and basic education. The Fund financially supports small community development projects. Has branches in Austria, Germany, Italy, Switzerland and the USA.

Geographical Area of Activity: International.

Publications: Annual Report; regional reports.

Board of Directors: Ute Harms (Pres.); Fr Michael Reynolds (Vice-Pres.); David O'Brien (Sec.).

Address: 5 Stokes Rd, rear of 7 Main St, Dundrum Rd, Dublin 14.

Telephone: (1) 2961360; **Fax:** (1) 2961372; **Internet:** www.worldmercyfund.ie; **e-mail:** info@worldmercyfund.ie.

Israel

FOUNDATIONS, TRUSTS AND NON-PROFIT ORGANIZATIONS

Lady Davis Fellowship Trust

Founded in 1973 in the name of the late Lady Davis of Montréal, Canada, to make the cultural heritage of ancient and modern Israel, and its achievements in development, state-building, scholarship, science and education, widely available and known to people from both technologically advanced and evolving societies; and to advance the interests of international scholarship and of higher education in Israel.

Activities: Operates through providing fellowships to visiting professors, postdoctoral researchers and doctoral students at the Hebrew University of Jerusalem and at the Technion—Israel Institute of Technology in Haifa. Since its establishment the Trust has supported more than 1,400 scholars, who have spent between three months and one year at these institutions. The fellowship programme is open to scholars of any age, from any region and in any field of study.

Geographical Area of Activity: International.

Publications: Report of operations; newsletter.

Principal Staff: Gen. Sec. Prof. Esty Shohami; Exec. Sec. M. Mark Sopher; Sec. Debbie Yakobian.

Address: Hebrew University, Givat Ram, Jerusalem 91904.

Telephone: (2) 6512306; **Fax:** (2) 5663848; **Internet:** ldft.huji.ac.il; **e-mail:** ld.fellows@mail.huji.ac.il.

Joseph S. and Caroline Gruss Life Monument Fund

Established in 1968 by Joseph S. Gruss to help former members of the Israel Defense Forces to integrate into civilian society.

Activities: Provides scholarships to former service personnel, as well as providing assistance to projects that further their personal development in the fields of education and employment. The TELEM programme is aimed specifically at Ethiopian ex-service personnel. The Fund runs Centers for Young Adults in 32 cities that offer education, employment and cultural services. Since its inception, the Fund has disbursed approx. 391m. shekels in scholarships.

Geographical Area of Activity: Israel.

Finance: Receives interest from the Life Monument Fund.

Board of Trustees: Dr Ayala Procaccia (Chair.).

Principal Staff: Exec. Dir Naomi Freund.

Address: 2 Beitar St, Jerusalem 93386.

Telephone: (2) 5617176; **Fax:** (2) 5660549; **Internet:** www.gruss.org.il; **e-mail:** gruss@gruss.org.il.

Guttman Center for Surveys

Founded in 1947 by Prof. Louis Guttman and others to plan and carry out research projects in the fields of social psychology, sociology, psychology and related disciplines; to supply government offices and other public and private institutions with research material and advice in these areas; to co-operate with organizations in Israel and abroad that are engaged in these fields and in related fields; and to raise the level of research in Israel in these areas and to maintain its professional standards. Became part of the Israel Democracy Institute in 1999.

Activities: Carries out research projects initiated by its own staff and conducts research commissioned by government departments, public and academic institutions in Israel and abroad, and by private commercial and industrial organizations in a wide variety of theoretical and applied fields of social science. Projects include methodological and theoretical research; a continuing survey of social problem indicators; research on political attitudes, conflict resolution, demographic problems, the mass media, cultural activities, immigration and emigration, health and the quality of life; and market research. The Center puts the use of its technical equipment and facilities at the disposal of other research organizations and provides advisory technical services.

Geographical Area of Activity: Israel.

Publications: Annual research report; Israeli democracy index; a portrait of Israeli jewry; occasional brochures in English, books, research papers and reports.

Finance: Budget US $385,000 (2012).

Principal Staff: Dir Prof. Tamar Hermann.

Address: c/o The Israel Democracy Institute, 4 Pinsker St, Jerusalem 91046.

Telephone: (2) 5300888; **Fax:** (2) 5300837; **Internet:** en.idi.org.il/tools-and-data/guttman-center-for-surveys/about-the-guttman-center/; **e-mail:** info@idi.org.il.

Jerusalem Foundation

Founded in 1966 by former Mayor of Jerusalem Teddy Kollek.

Activities: Aims to strengthen and enrich Jerusalem's cultural life and communities. Capital projects include community centres, sports facilities and parks, libraries, theatres, museums, schools, neighbourhood and community facilities, and educational centres. The Foundation also funds social and educational activities for the benefits of all the city's residents.

Geographical Area of Activity: Jerusalem.

Publications: Annual Report; brochures.

Finance: Annual income US $34.9m., expenditure $32.8m. (2014).

Board of Directors: Nir Barkat (Hon. Chair.); Sallai Meridor (Int. Chair.); David Brodet (Chair.); Ruth Cheshin (Pres. Emeritus).

Principal Staff: Dir-Gen. Daniel Mimran; Vice-Pres. Alan Freeman.

Address: 11 Rivka St, POB 10185, Jerusalem 91101.

Telephone: (2) 6751711; **Fax:** (2) 6734462; **Internet:** www.jerusalemfoundation.org; **e-mail:** info@jerusalem-foundation.org.

Jewish Agency for Israel Allocations Program

Founded in 1986 by the Jewish Agency for Israel.

Activities: Aims to improve the quality of life in Israel by supporting innovative and creative social and environmental projects implemented by NGOs. The Agency funds projects that promote the strengthening of Jewish identity, mutual respect and unity of the Jewish people, within the fields of education and social welfare.

Geographical Area of Activity: Israel.

Restrictions: Funds only NGOs in Israel.

Publications: *Mapping Programs*; Annual Report.

Finance: Annual revenue US $449,153,000, expenditure $441,163,000 (31 Dec. 2012).

Board of Governors: Charles (Chuck) Horowitz Ratner (Chair.).

Principal Staff: Exec. Chair. Natan Sharansky; Deputy Exec. Chair. Rany Trainin (a.i.); Dir-Gen. Alan D. Hoffmann.

Address: 48 King George St, POB 92, Jerusalem 99000.

Telephone: (2) 6202727; **Fax:** (2) 6204116; **Internet:** www.jewishagency.org; www.jafi.org.il.

KIEDF—Koret Israel Economic Development Funds

Established in 1994 to promote the deployment of philanthropy in the private sector to stimulate economic development and job creation via support to small businesses.

Activities: Operates revolving loan funds offered through commercial banks, providing bank guarantees and subsidizing interest rates to small business borrowers, offering micro-enterprise lending to home-based businesses, and operating a loan facility for not-for-profit organizations. Since its inception, the organization has provided loans equivalent to US \$225m. to more than 8,500 small and micro-businesses.

Geographical Area of Activity: Israel.

Restrictions: Operates solely through granting loans.

Publications: Annual Report.

Board of Directors: Tal Keinan (Chair.); Brig.-Gen. (Res.) Eival Gilady (Immediate Past Pres.); Dr Michael Reiner (Sec.).

Principal Staff: Man. Dir Carl. H. Kaplan.

Address: 35 Shaul Hamelech St, POB 33406, Tel-Aviv 61333.

Telephone: (3) 6916827; **Fax:** (3) 6950029; **Internet:** www .kiedf.org; **e-mail:** cskcon@arbafin.com.

Van Leer Jerusalem Institute

Established in 1959 by the late Polly van Leer to provide a platform for studying cultural, social and educational issues, as well as to voice a wide range of opinions existing on these subjects in Israel.

Activities: Focuses on research and practical activities in the fields of social policies, education and Jewish-Arab coexistence; projects are considered that offer lessons of universal value, including their repercussions on Israeli society. The Institute initiates discussions and debates on key social and cultural topics through workshops, lectures and conferences.

Geographical Area of Activity: Israel.

Restrictions: The Institute does not make grants.

Publications: Annual Review; books; journals; research reports and position papers; newsletter.

Finance: Annual budget 23,917,736 shekels (2012).

Board of Trustees: Tom de Swaan (Chair.).

Principal Staff: Dir Prof. Gabriel Motzkin; COO Shimon Alon.

Address: POB 4070, Jerusalem 9104001; 43 Jabotinsky St, Jerusalem 9214116.

Telephone: (2) 5605222; **Fax:** (2) 5619293; **Internet:** www .vanleer.org.il; **e-mail:** vanleer@vanleer.org.il.

Peres Center for Peace

Established in 1996 by Nobel Peace Laureate Shimon Peres, with the aim of furthering his vision in which people of the Middle East region work together to build peace through socio-economic co-operation, science and research activities and people-to-people interaction.

Activities: Focuses on common Arab and Israeli economic and social interests, with particular emphasis on Palestinian-Israeli relations. The Center develops peace-building projects to address these interests, through partnerships with regional and international players. Core programmes are medicine and health care, business and environment and peace education.

Geographical Area of Activity: Middle East.

Publications: *Peace in Progress* (newsletter); e-bulletins (monthly); newsletter (2 a year); research and position papers.

Board of Directors: Chemi Peres (Chair.); Uri Savir (Hon. Pres.).

Principal Staff: Dir-Gen. Efrat Duvdevani; Deputy Dir-Gen. Orly Nabel.

Address: The Peres Peace House, 132 Kedem St, Tel-Aviv-Jaffa 62745.

Telephone: (3) 5680680; **Fax:** (3) 5627265; **Internet:** www .peres-center.org; **e-mail:** info@peres-center.org.

Arthur Rubinstein International Music Society

Founded in 1980 by Jan Jacob Bistritzky in tribute to the artistry of Arthur Rubinstein (1887–1982) and to maintain his spiritual and artistic heritage in the art of the piano.

Activities: Organizes and finances the Arthur Rubinstein International Piano Master Competition; runs masterclasses, worldwide concert series, film shows and memorial festivals.

Geographical Area of Activity: International.

Publications: Newsletter.

Board of Trustees: Adv. P. Gad Naschitz (Chair.).

Principal Staff: Artistic Dir Idith Zvi; Exec. Producer Shuly Haberman.

Address: 12 Huberman St, Tel-Aviv 64075.

Telephone: (3) 6856684; **Fax:** (3) 6854924; **Internet:** www .arims.org.il; **e-mail:** competition@arims.org.il.

Henrietta Szold Institute—National Institute for Research in the Behavioural Sciences

Founded in 1941 by Henrietta Szold to undertake research in human behaviour, policy evaluation and experimentation, with special emphasis on children and youth.

Activities: Conducts research and experiments in the fields of education, psychometrics, sociology and psychology; operates an information retrieval centre for Israeli research in the social sciences; provides a measurement and evaluation service for the Israeli education system; organizes workshops and training courses; and maintains databases for researchers.

Geographical Area of Activity: Israel.

Publications: *Megamot* (quarterly); research reports; bibiliographies; monographs; literature reviews and publications.

Finance: Annual budget approx. 25m. shekels.

Exec. Committee: Eliezer Shmueli (Chair.).

Principal Staff: Dir Dr Rachel Zorman.

Address: 9 Colombia St, Jerusalem 96583.

Telephone: (2) 6494444; **Fax:** (2) 6437698; **Internet:** www .szold.org.il; **e-mail:** szold@szold.org.il.

United States-Israel Educational Foundation— USIEF

Founded in 1956 to administer the Fulbright Program between the USA and Israel.

Activities: Enables outstanding Israeli and American scholars and students to pursue research, lectures and study at leading institutes of higher learning in the USA and Israel.

Geographical Area of Activity: USA and Israel.

Restrictions: No grants to institutions or organizations.

Publications: *Alumni Newsletter.*

Finance: Financed by the Governments of the USA and Israel. Annual budget approx. US \$1.6m.

Board of Directors: Dan Vilenski (Chair.); Daniel B. Shapiro (Hon. Chair.).

Principal Staff: Exec. Dir Dr Anat Lapidot-Firilla; Deputy Dir Judy Stavsky.

Address: 1 Ben Yehuda St, POB 26160, Tel-Aviv 61261.

Telephone: (3) 5172392; **Fax:** (3) 5162016; **Internet:** www .fulbright.org.il; **e-mail:** info@fulbright.org.il.

Italy

FOUNDATION CENTRE AND CO-ORDINATING BODY

Associazione di Fondazioni e di Casse di Risparmio Spa—ACRI (Association of Italian Foundations and Savings Banks)

Established in 1912 to represent and support the development of Italian savings banks and, since 1990, Italian banking foundations.

Activities: Provides support to Italian banking foundations and savings banks, representing their interests in Italy and abroad. The Association maintains and develops the relations with other non-profit organizations and foundation networks. It comprises 129 members.

Geographical Area of Activity: Italy.

Publications: Annual Report; *Il Risparmio* (monthly magazine); *Fondazioni* (magazine, 6 a year); reports; studies.

Finance: Annual income €1,488.2m., expenditure €884.8m. (2013).

Board of Directors: Giuseppe Guzzetti (Chair.); Dr Vincenzo Marini Marini, Dr Luca Remmert, Prof. Umberto Tombari (Vice-Chair.).

Principal Staff: Gen. Man. Giorgio Righetti; Deputy Gen. Man. Dr Alessandro del Castello.

Address: Via del Corso 262, 00186 Rome.

Telephone: (06) 681841; **Fax:** (06) 68184269; **Internet:** www .acri.it; **e-mail:** area.comunicazione@acri.it.

FOUNDATIONS, TRUSTS AND NON-PROFIT ORGANIZATIONS

Accademia Musicale Chigiana

Founded in 1932 by Count Guido Chigi Saracini to provide courses in advanced musical studies.

Activities: Operates internationally in the fields of education and the arts and humanities, through publications and courses, and scholarships and fellowships organized on an international basis. The Academy has a library of around 75,000 vols.

Geographical Area of Activity: International.

Publications: *Chigiana* (annual magazine); music recordings; *Quaderni dell'Accademia Musicale Chigiana*; *Numeri Unici delle 'Settimane Musicali Senesi'*.

Board of Directors: Marcello Clarich (Pres); Vittorio Carnesecchi (Vice-Pres.).

Principal Staff: Man. Dir Angelo Armiento; Artistic Consultant Nicola.

Address: Via di Città 89, 53100 Siena.

Telephone: (0577) 22091; **Fax:** (0577) 288124; **Internet:** www .chigiana.it; **e-mail:** accademia.chigiana@chigiana.it.

Biblioteca dell'Accademia Nazionale dei Lincei (Library of the National Academy of Lincei)

Founded in 1924 by Leone Caetani di Sermoneta, Prince of Teano, and formerly known as the Fondazione Leone Caetani, to promote knowledge of the ancient and contemporary Muslim world and Islamic culture, by means of conferences, lectures and publications.

Activities: Has organized a series of conferences on the Muslim world. The Library maintains a specialized collection of 23,000 volumes, 350 manuscripts (Arabic, Persian and Ethiopian) and 350 periodicals on Arab-Islamic classical civilization, which constitutes the Oriental Section of the Biblioteca dell'Accademia Nazionale dei Lincei e Corsiniana.

Geographical Area of Activity: Italy.

Publications: *Giuseppe Montalenti*; *Biotecnologie e Produzione Vegetale*; *Norberto Bobbio*; *Allosteric Proteins*.

Finance: Annual income €8,528,568, expenditure €9,654,765 (2010).

President's Council: Lamberto Maffei (Pres.); Prof. Alberto Quadrio Curzio (Vice-Pres.).

Principal Staff: Dir-Gen. and Sec. Dr Ada Baccari; Dir of the Library Dr Marco Guardo.

Address: Palazzo Corsini, Via della Lungara 10, 00165 Rome.

Telephone: (06) 680271; **Fax:** (06) 6893616; **Internet:** www .lincei.it; **e-mail:** segreteria@lincei.it.

CENSIS—Fondazione Centro Studi Investimenti Sociali (Foundation Centre for the Study of Social Investment)

Established in 1964 as a research institute; became a foundation in 1973.

Activities: Operates in the fields of the arts and culture, economic affairs, social welfare, employment and the environment. The Centre provides training and advice, and engages in research commissioned by exterior groups and institutions, including the European Union, chambers of commerce and private businesses. It publishes an annual report on the social situation in Italy.

Geographical Area of Activity: Italy and Europe.

Restrictions: No grants available.

Publications: Annual Report; *La rivista del CENSIS* (monthly); *Rapporto sulla situazione sociale del Paese* (annual); *Italy Today*; *Duemila*; *Censis—Materiali di Ricerca*; *Forum per la Ricerca Biomedica (FBM)*; *Europa*.

Finance: Funding from contracts. Annual budget US $5m.

Board of Directors: Giuseppe de Rita (Chair.).

Principal Staff: Sec.-Gen. Giuseppe Roma.

Address: Piazza di Novella 2, 00199 Rome.

Telephone: (06) 860911; **Fax:** (06) 86211367; **Internet:** www .censis.it; **e-mail:** censis@censis.it.

Centro di Cultura e Civiltà Contadina (Rural Culture and Civilization Centre)

Founded in 1955 by the Giorgio Cini Foundation (q.v.) to promote and facilitate activities and initiatives contributing to the arts and sciences.

Activities: Awards scholarships and organizes meetings, national and international conferences, lectures and advanced international courses in the field of culture. The Centre administers the School of San Giorgio for the Study of Venetian Civilization, which comprises five institutes: the Institute of the History of Art; the Institute of the History of Society and the State; the Institute of Letters, Theatre and Opera; the Institute of Music; and the Venice and the East Institute. Also organizes exhibitions, concerts and theatrical performances and sponsors the publication of studies on Venetian art and civilization. The International Library (f. 1961) specializes in studies of agricultural and rural culture and comprises 50,000 vols.

Geographical Area of Activity: Italy.

Publications: *La Vigna* (quarterly bulletin); publications on culture and traditions.

Board of Directors: Mario Bagnara (Chair.); Luigino Curti (Vice-Chair.).

Principal Staff: Sec.-Gen. Massimo Carta.

Address: Palazzo Brusarosco Zaccaria, contrà Porta Santa Croce 3, 36100 Venice.

Telephone: (0444) 543000; **Fax:** (0444) 321167; **Internet:** www.lavigna.it; **e-mail:** info@lavigna.it.

Centro Studi e Ricerca Sociale Fondazione Emanuela Zancan (Emanuela Zancan Foundation Centre for Social Studies and Research)

Founded in 1964; works in the field of research, in particular educational, social and health services.

Activities: Operates nationally and internationally in the fields of education, health and social welfare and studies, through self-conducted programmes, research, conferences, publications and lectures. The Centre works in collaboration with other institutions as well as with foreign experts.

Geographical Area of Activity: International.

Publications: *Studi Zancan* (journal, 2 a month); *La valutazione di efficacia nei servizi alle persone; La continuità assistenziale nei rapporti tra ospedale e territorio; La valutazione di efficacia degli interventi con le persone anziane; Solidarietà; Improving outcomes for children and families; Rapporto su povertà ed esclusione sociale; La valutazione di impatto della progettazione sociale del volontariato; Le risposte domiciliari; Forme di convivenza; Disabilità, famiglia e servizi; L'integrazione sociosanitaria;* and others.

Principal Staff: Dir Dr Tiziano Vecchiato.

Address: Via Vescovado 66, 35141 Padova.

Telephone: (028) 663800; **Fax:** (049) 663013; **Internet:** www.fondazionezancan.it; **e-mail:** fz@fondazionezancan.it.

Compagnia di San Paolo

Established in 1563 as a brotherhood to help the poor and fight usury; now an independent grantmaking foundation.

Activities: Aims to foster civic, cultural and economic development. The organization operates in the following areas in particular: scientific, economic and legal research; education; the arts and humanities; preservation of cultural heritage and activities, and of environmental assets; and health and welfare. The following permanent bodies also come under the remit of the organization's institutional activities: the Istituto Superiore Mario Boella, which operates in the field of information and communication technologies, in co-operation with Turin Polytechnic; the Consorzio Collegio Carlo Alberto, for setting up a Centre for Advanced Training in Finance and Economics, also in association with Turin University; the Ufficio Pio, which operates in co-operation with a strong network of volunteers and acts as a crisis centre for people most in need and gives training-as-you-study grants for the vocational training of socially-at-risk young people; and the Educatorio Duchessa Isabella, which during 2001 became the Fondazione per la Scuola (the Foundation for Schools) with the aim of becoming a centre for education able to support self-governing schools. Also maintains a searchable grants database.

Geographical Area of Activity: Worldwide.

Restrictions: Operates exclusively to the benefit of non-profit-making organizations. No grants are made to individuals.

Publications: Annual Report; newsletter (3 a year); *Quaderni della Compagnia; Quaderni dell'Archivio Storico* (monograph series, in Italian); reports; studies and research.

Finance: Total assets €6,346.481,236, annual income €272,187,145 (2013).

Management Committee: Luca Remmert (Chair.); Marco Mezzalama (Vice-Pres.).

Principal Staff: Sec.-Gen. Piero Gastaldo.

Address: Corso Vittorio Emanuele II 75, 10128 Turin.

Telephone: (011) 5596911; **Fax:** (011) 5596976; **Internet:** www.compagniadisanpaolo.it; www.compagnia.torino.it; **e-mail:** info@compagnia.torino.it.

Cooperazione Internazionale—COOPI (International Co-operation)

Founded in 1965 by Vincenzo Barbieri; an independent and lay NGO legally recognized by the Italian Ministry of Foreign Affairs.

Activities: Campaigns against poverty. The organization works in the following main areas: agriculture, education, health, water and sanitation, socio-economic services, humanitarian assistance, governance, civil society and human rights. It assists populations struck by natural disasters and promotes their civil, economic and social development; carries out development projects and emergency interventions abroad; and in Italy has been working towards eliminating the cause of the economic gap between emerging countries of the southern hemisphere and those of the north.

Geographical Area of Activity: Sub-Saharan Africa; Central and South-Eastern Europe; Middle East and North Africa; South America, Central America and the Caribbean.

Publications: Annual Report; newsletter; brochure.

Finance: Annual income €41,093,480, expenditure €41,451,530 (2013).

Board of Directors: Claudio Ceravolo (Chair.); Carla Ricci (Vice-Chair.).

Principal Staff: Dir Ennio Miccoli.

Address: Via De Lemene 50, 20151 Milan.

Telephone: (02) 3085057; **Fax:** (02) 33403570; **Internet:** www.coopi.org; **e-mail:** coopi@coopi.org.

EMERGENCY

Established in 1994 by Italian surgeon Gino Strada.

Activities: Provides medical and surgical care to the victims of war, through the provision of medical and technical personnel. The organization constructs and rehabilitates health clinics and hospitals, supports educational institutions and distributes medical and first aid supplies. It currently operates relief projects in Afghanistan, Cambodia, Iraq and Sierra Leone, and has supported humanitarian activities in Algeria, Chechnya, Eritrea and Rwanda. It also organizes cultural activities designed to promote awareness about development and humanitarian needs.

Geographical Area of Activity: Worldwide.

Publications: *Magazine* (quarterly); newsletter.

Finance: Annual income €31,225,759, expenditure €2,167,598 (2013).

Executive Board: Cecilia Strada (Pres.); Alessandrao Bertani (Vice-Pres.); Patrizia Bragalini (Treas. and Sec.).

Principal Staff: Exec. Dir Gino Strada.

Address: Via Gerolamo Vida 11, 20127 Milan.

Telephone: (02) 863161; **Fax:** (02) 86316336; **Internet:** www.emergency.it; **e-mail:** info@emergency.it.

Eni Foundation

Established in 2006 to apply business efficiency criteria to philanthropy.

Activities: Aims to protect the rights of children and the elderly through social initiatives that encourage their overall well-being and development.

Geographical Area of Activity: Worldwide.

Publications: Annual Report.

Finance: Annual income €242,017 expenditure €2,409,209 (31 Dec. 2013).

Board of Directors: Claudio Descalzi (Chair.); Raffaella Leone (Vice-Chair.).

Principal Staff: Sec.-Gen. Filipo Uberti.

Address: Piazzale Enrico Mattei 1, 00144 Rome.

Telephone: (06) 59824108; **Fax:** (06) 59822106; **Internet:** www
.eni.it/enifoundation/eng-home.shtml;   **e-mail:**
enifoundation@eni.it.

Ente Cassa di Risparmio di Firenze (Florence Savings Bank Foundation)

Founded in 1992 to promote social and economic development and to continue the tradition of Cassa di Risparmio di Firenze (a fund established in 1829 to encourage saving among poorer people and to promote socio-economic development through the distribution of banking profits).

Activities: Supports the arts and humanities, scientific research and technological innovation, medicine and health, social welfare and restoration projects, through self-conducted programmes and grants in Tuscany. The Foundation also administers three smaller foundations.

Geographical Area of Activity: Italy.

Publications: *I Fatti* (magazine); *OmA* (magazine); newsletter; electronic/online information; grants list.

Finance: Total assets €1,507,002,884, annual expenditure €7,100,359 (31 Dec. 2012).

Board of Directors: Umberto Tombari (Chair.); Prof. Pierluigi Rosi Ferrini (Vice-Chair.).

Principal Staff: Gen. Man. Gabriele Gori.

Address: Via Bufalini 6, 50122 Florence.

Telephone: (055) 5384001; **Fax:** (055) 5384873; **Internet:** www.entecarifirenze.it; **e-mail:** info@entecarifirenze.it.

European Training Foundation—ETF

Established in 1990 by the Council of Ministers of the European Community (now the European Union—EU); began its activities in 1995.

Activities: An EU agency and centre of expertise that supports vocational education and training reform in third countries (partner countries) in the context of the EU external relations programme. The Foundation also provides technical assistance to the European Commission for the implementation of the Tempus programme in the field of higher education. Provides expertise in the areas of human resources, vocational training reform policies, skills development for enterprises, management and entrepreneurial training, and active labour market policies. Supports the European Commission's project cycle and contributes to the development and design of country strategy papers and indicative and action programmes, including country analyses; sector analyses; analyses of needs and feasibility studies; training needs assessment methodologies; key indicators and benchmarking; impact assessment, evaluation and peer reviews; and examples of good practice. Since 2009, the Foundation has worked worldwide in the area of human capital development.

Geographical Area of Activity: Worldwide.

Restrictions: Not a training provider, nor a provider of financial assistance for individual students.

Publications: Annual Activity Report; *Live & Learn*; *Albania Stabilisation and Association report—European Commission; Adult learning strategy papers and action plans; Assessment and certification of vocational training in Kosovo*; yearbook; reports; periodicals.

Finance: Annual revenue €22,004,049, expenditure €22,005,753 (31 Dec. 2013).

Governing Board: Michel Servoz (Chair.).

Principal Staff: Dir Madlen Serban.

Address: Villa Gualino, Viale Settimio Severo 65, 10133 Turin.

Telephone: (011) 6302222; **Fax:** (011) 6302200; **Internet:** www.etf.europa.eu; **e-mail:** info@etf.europa.eu.

FEEM—Fondazione ENI Enrico Mattei (Enrico Mattei Eni Foundation)

Established in 1989.

Activities: Aims to improve the quality of decision-making in public and private spheres through research. The Foundation maintains an international and multidisciplinary network of researchers working on several innovative programmes, by providing and promoting training in specialized areas of research; by disseminating research results through a wide range of outreach activities; and by delivering directly to policy-makers via participation in various institutional fora. It conducts research on a wide range of economic, environmental and energy issues; and fosters awareness of the interaction between businesses and the environment, the economy and energy scenarios, corporate responsibility and social conflict, and cultural responsibility.

Geographical Area of Activity: International.

Publications: Annual Report; working papers series '*Note di Lavoro*'; policy briefs; books; *Equilibri* (journal); *FEEM News* (digital newsletter, 2 a month).

Finance: Annual revenue €7,692,669, expenditure €7,548,059 (31 Dec. 2013).

Board of Directors: Emma Marcegaglia (Chair.).

Principal Staff: Exec. Dir Sabina Ratti.

Address: Palazzo delle Stelline, Corso Magenta 63, 20123 Milan.

Telephone: (02) 52036934; **Fax:** (02) 52036946; **Internet:** www.feem.it; **e-mail:** letter@feem.it.

Fondation Emile Chanoux—Institut d'Etudes Fédéralistes et Régionalistes (Emile Chanoux Foundation—Institute for Federalist and Regionalist Studies)

Established in 1995; a university-level institute for the study and defence of federalism and regionalism, including linguistic minorities.

Activities: Operates in the fields of economic affairs, education, international affairs, law and human rights, and social welfare and social studies, through research, awarding prizes, grants to individuals, conferences, training courses and publications. The Foundation maintains a library of around 4,000 items (books, magazines, CDs, DVDs).

Geographical Area of Activity: Europe.

Publications: *On parle de nous* (bulletin); *L'Ordre nouveau; Une Vallée d'Aoste bilingue dans une Europe plurilingue; Contre l'Etat totalitaire; Tra baita e bunker.*

Finance: Annual revenue approx. €150,000.

Board of Directors: Alessandro Celi (Chair.); Nicolas Schmitt (Vice-Chair.).

Principal Staff: Sec.-Gen. and Dir Étienne Andrione.

Address: 26 rue Guido Rey, 11100 Aoste.

Telephone: (0165) 40777; **Fax:** (0165) 234819; **Internet:** www.fondchanoux.org; **e-mail:** info@fondchanoux.org.

Fondazione 1563 per l'Arte e la Cultura (1563 Foundation for the Arts and Culture)

Founded in 1985; an initiative of the Istituto Bancario San Paolo di Torino, to promote the arts and science; formerly known as the Fondazione San Paolo di Torino, and established by the Compagnia di San Paolo (q.v.).

Activities: Operates in the fields of arts and culture, through grants for the performing arts, exhibitions and restoration projects. The Foundation works in association with the Compagni di San Paolo, with programmes focusing on the safeguarding, enrichment and enhancement of artistic heritage. The Foundation also focuses on training and research projects in the fields of history, art and restoration, as well as implementing new models for managing and enhancing museums and cultural heritage, through a number of different initiatives.

Geographical Area of Activity: Italy and Europe.

Publications: Information brochures; books on art.

Finance: Annual income €2,656,761, expenditure €2,300,581 (31 Dec. 2014).

Board of Directors: Rosaria Cigliano (Chair.); Michela Di Macco (Vice-Chair.).

Principal Staff: Sec.-Gen. Marco Demarie.

Address: Vigna di Madama Reale, Strada San Vito Revigliasco 65, 10133 Turin.

Telephone: (011) 6603573; **Fax:** (011) 6603855; **Internet:** www .fondazione1563.it; **e-mail:** info@fondazione1563.it.

Fondazione Giovanni Agnelli (Giovanni Agnelli Foundation)

Founded in 1966 by Fiat SpA and the Istituto Finanziario Industriale on the 100th anniversary of Senator Giovanni Agnelli's birth to carry out research in social, cultural, political and economic problems in Italy and elsewhere.

Activities: Aims to spread knowledge of the conditions on which Italy's progress in economic, scientific, social and cultural fields depends, as well as supporting research. Research focuses on education (schools, universities, adult training systems and lifelong learning) as an asset for economic and social growth. The Foundation also offers a limited number of scholarships in various research fields.

Geographical Area of Activity: Italy.

Finance: Annual budget €3,234,845 (2013).

Board of Directors: Maria Sole Agnelli Teodorani-Fabbri (Chair.); John P. Elkann (Vice-Chair.).

Principal Staff: Dir Andrea Gavosto.

Address: Via Nizza 250, 10126 Turin.

Telephone: (011) 6500500; **Fax:** (011) 6500012; **Internet:** www .fga.it; www.fondazione-agnelli.it; **e-mail:** fondazione -agnelli@fga.it; segreteria@fga.it.

Fondazione Ambrosiana Paolo VI (Ambrosiana Paolo VI Foundation)

Founded 1976 to promote research into religion.

Activities: Funds research, conferences and studies primarily in the fields of faith and religion, including a collection of studies on the religious history of Ireland.

Geographical Area of Activity: Europe.

Publications: *Quaderni della Gazzada*; *Storia religiosa della Lombardia*; *Europa ricerche*.

Principal Staff: Pres. Luigi Stucchi; Dir Prof. Eros Monti; Sec.-Gen. Luciano Vaccaro.

Address: Villa Cagnola, 21045 Gazzada Schianno.

Telephone: (0332) 462104; **Fax:** (0332) 463463; **Internet:** www .villacagnola.it/it/varese-villa-cagnola/fondazione -ambrosiana-paolo-vi; **e-mail:** fapgazzada@tin.it.

Fondazione per l'Arte (Foundation for the Arts)

Established in 2011 to encourage and promote the arts and culture.

Activities: Aims to promote the city of Rome nationally and internationally as a centre of artistic production and cultural exchange. The Foundation organizes exhibitions, talks and other events.

Geographical Area of Activity: International.

Publications: Catalogues; monographs.

Board of Directors: Ilaria Bozzi (Chair.).

Address: Via del Mandrione 105, 00181 Rome.

Internet: www.fondazioneperlarte.org; www.fxarte.org; **e-mail:** info@fondazioneperlarte.org.

Fondazione Lelio e Lisli Basso Issoco—Sezione Internazionale (Lelio and Lisli Basso Issoco Foundation—International Section)

Founded in 2005 following the merger of the Fondazione Lelio e Lisli Basso-Issoco (f. 1974) and the Fondazione Internazionale Lelio Basso per il Diritto e la Liberazione dei Popoli.

Activities: Operates in the fields of the environment, development studies and human rights. Promotes information exchange between politicians, academics and lawyers concerned with human rights issues; offers grants to individuals for research; operates training courses and workshops; and organizes seminars and conferences.

Geographical Area of Activity: Worldwide.

Publications: Newsletter (quarterly); numerous publications on human rights issues.

Finance: Financed by private funds.

Principal Staff: Man. Linda Bimbi.

Address: Via della Dogana Vecchia 5, 00186 Rome.

Telephone: (06) 066877774; **Fax:** (06) 066877774; **Internet:** www.internazionaleleliobasso.it; **e-mail:** filb@iol.it.

Fondazione Benetton Studi Ricerche (Benetton Foundation for Study and Research)

Founded in 1981; adopted present name in 1987.

Activities: Operates nationally and internationally through self-conducted programmes, research, prizes, conferences, training courses and publications, with the general aim of improving the knowledge, protection and promotion of the natural and built heritage. Research activities focus on the knowledge and stewardship of landscapes, with special reference to Europe and the Mediterranean basin. A secondary branch of research concerns the history of games and sports. The Foundation awards the annual International Carlo Scarpa Prize for Gardens to promote the conservation of sites that are particularly rich in natural and historical values. It has a documentation centre, open to the public, with a library, archives, and map and image collections.

Geographical Area of Activity: Mainly Europe.

Restrictions: No grants or sponsorship.

Publications: *Bollettino* (irregular); annual booklet on Premio Internazionale Carlo Scarpa per il Giardino; *Ludica* (annual review of games and sport); *Studi veneti*.

Board of Directors: Luciano Benetton (Chair.); Gilberto Benetton (Vice-Chair.).

Principal Staff: Dir. Marco Tamaro.

Address: Via Cornarotta 7–9, 31100 Treviso.

Telephone: (0422) 5121; **Fax:** (0422) 579483; **Internet:** www .fbsr.it; **e-mail:** fbsr@fbsr.it.

Fondazione Ugo Bordoni (Ugo Bordoni Foundation)

Founded in 1952 by Cesare Albanese, Albino Antinori, Felice Calvanese, Antonio Carrelli, Romolo De Caterini, Andrea Ferrara-Toniolo, Alberto Fornò, Vittorio Gori, Ernesto Lensi, Algeri Marino, Enrico Medi, Michele Paris, Giuseppe Spataro and Scipione Treves to facilitate and promote research and scientific studies applicable to the postal system, telecommunications and electronics; and to facilitate initiatives to further technical-scientific development in the same field. The Foundation was reconstituted in 2000.

Activities: Operates in the fields of electronics and communications, through research and publications, mainly in co-operation with the Istituto Superiore delle Comunicazioni e delle Tecnologie dell' Informazione (Advanced Institute for Communications and Information Technology). The Foundation collaborates with national and international bodies.

Geographical Area of Activity: Italy.

Publications: Annual Report; magazines; conference proceedings; books.

Finance: Annual income €11,983,774, expenditure €13,081,890 (31 Dec. 2013).

Board of Directors: Alessandro Luciano (Chair. and Interim Gen. Man.).

Principal Staff: Deputy Gen. Man. Mario Frullone.

Address: Viale del Policlinico 147, 00161 Rome.

Telephone: (06) 54801; **Fax:** (06) 54804400; **Internet:** www .fub.it; **e-mail:** info@fub.it.

Fondazione Cariplo (Cariplo Foundation)

Established in 1991 as part of the reorganization process resulting from the implementation of the Amato-Carli Act for the rationalization and privatization of Italian banks, with a mission to continue the philanthropic activities previously carried out by the Cassa di Risparmio delle Provincie Lombarde (Savings Bank of the Lombard Provinces, founded in 1823).

Activities: Aims to foster the growth of the local economy, culture and civil society; to help social and civil organizations better serve their community; to anticipate emerging needs, try new solutions or attempt to respond to problems more effectively and in a less costly fashion; and to disseminate successful solutions.

Geographical Area of Activity: Italy.

Restrictions: No grants to individuals; trade union or patronage organizations; political parties and trade associations.

Publications: Annual Report; newsletter; monographs; conference reports; financial statements.

Finance: Total assets €8,049.7m. (31 Dec. 2014).

Board of Directors: Giuseppe Guzzetti (Chair.); Carlo Sangalli, Enoc Mariella (Vice-Chair.).

Principal Staff: Sec.-Gen. Sergio Urbani.

Address: Via Manin 23, 20121 Milan.

Telephone: (02) 62391; **Fax:** (02) 623928202; **Internet:** www .fondazionecariplo.it; **e-mail:** comunicazione@ fondazionecariplo.it.

Fondazione Cassa di Risparmio di Padova e Rovigo
(Foundation Cassa di Risparmio di Padova e Rovigo)

Established in 1991 as the continuation of Cassa di Risparmio di Padova e Rovigo, which was founded in 1822 to support economic development of local communities.

Activities: Works to promote quality of life and sustainable development in the regions of Padova and Rovigo in Italy. The Foundation promotes an open, co-operative community aiming at innovation. It supports and plans projects in the fields of scientific research; education; art and cultural activities; health and the environment; assistance and protection of minorities; and other sectors (sport, civil protection, food safety, quality agriculture).

Geographical Area of Activity: Italian provinces of Padova and Rovigo.

Restrictions: No grants are made to individuals, profit-seeking organizations, parties, political movements, trade unions or charitable institutions and trade associations.

Publications: Annual Report; information brochures.

Finance: Total assets €2,268.9m. (31 Dec. 2014).

Board of Directors: Antonio Finotti (Chair.); Marina Bastianello, Sandro Fioravanti (Vice-Chair.).

Principal Staff: Sec.-Gen. Roberto Saro.

Address: Piazza Duomo 15, 35141 Padova.

Telephone: (049) 8234800; **Fax:** (049) 657335; **Internet:** www .fondazionecariparo.it; **e-mail:** info@fondazionecariparo.it.

Fondazione Cassa di Risparmio di Torino (Turin Savings Bank Foundation)

Established following the Amato law in 1991.

Activities: Operates principally, but not exclusively, in the regions of Piemonte and Valle d'Aosta in Italy, promoting the economic and social development of those regions. The Foundation awards grants in the fields of: scientific research, education, art, culture and conservation of artistic heritage, health, assistance to socially-disadvantaged groups, and the general social and economic development of the regions.

Geographical Area of Activity: Mainly the regions of Piemonte and Valle d'Aosta, Italy.

Restrictions: No grants are made to individuals.

Publications: Annual Report; brochure; books; monographs; press releases; online magazine.

Finance: Total assets, €2,842.8m., annual income €104,665,713 (31 Dec. 2014).

Board of Directors: Antonio Maria Marocco (Chair.); Fulvio Gianaria, Anna Chiara Invernizzi (Vice-Chair.).

Principal Staff: Sec.-Gen. Massimo Lapucci.

Address: Via XX Settembre 31, 10121 Turin.

Telephone: (011) 5065100; **Fax:** (011) 5065580; **Internet:** www .fondazionecrt.it; **e-mail:** info@fondazionecrt.it.

Fondazione Cassa di Risparmio di Verona Vicenza Belluno e Ancona—Fondazione Cariverona

Originated with the Cassa di Verona bank in 1825; became a private non-profit institution in 2000.

Activities: Offers grants to organizations working in scientific research, education, the arts and humanities, the environment, health care and social welfare.

Geographical Area of Activity: Italy.

Publications: Specialist publications on subjects including the city and history, nature and the environment, churches and art, and art in villas and palaces; exhibition catalogues.

Finance: Total assets €3,392.7m. (31 Dec. 2014).

Board of Directors: Paolo Biasi (Chair.); Giovanni Sala, Silvano Spiller (Vice-Pres.).

Principal Staff: Gen. Man. Fausto Sinagra.

Address: Via A. Forti 3A, 37121 Verona.

Telephone: (045) 8057311; **Internet:** www .fondazionecariverona.org; **e-mail:** segreteria@ fondazionecariverona.org.

Fondazione Giorgio Cini (Giorgio Cini Foundation)

Founded in 1951 by Count Vittorio Cini in memory of his son Giorgio. The island of San Giorgio Maggiore, Venice, was entrusted to the Foundation for the purpose of restoring the area's historic buildings and supporting the development of social, cultural and artistic institutions in this area.

Activities: Operates through eight advanced-study institutes: the Institute for the History of Art; the Institute for the History of the Venetian State and Society; the Institute for Music; the Institute for Literature and Theatre; the Venice and the East Institute; the Venice and Europe Institute; the Intercultural Institute of Comparative Music Studies; and an institute devoted to the study and illustration of the works of Antonio Vivaldi. The institutes each have their own director, possess a library, undertake research, organize study-encounters and seminars, and promote publications, concerts and artistic exhibitions. The Foundation works nationally and internationally organizing postgraduate courses, conferences and seminars on topics of historic, scientific, social or cultural interest.

Geographical Area of Activity: Italy.

Publications: Newsletter; art catalogues; periodicals; essays.

Principal Staff: Pres. Prof. Giovanni Bazoli; Sec.-Gen. Pasquale Gagliardi.

Address: Palazzo Cini, Dorsoduro (San Vio) 864, 30123 Venice.

Telephone: (041) 2710230; **Fax:** (041) 5205842; **Internet:** www .cini.it; **e-mail:** fondazionegiorgiocini@pec.it.

Fondazione CittàItalia (CittàItalia Foundation)

Established in 2003 by Mecenate 90 Association, banking foundations and several art cities to address and support the cause of arts and restore cultural and artistic heritage.

Activities: Creates, promotes and spreads art and culture symbolic of Italian cultural heritage, as well as artistic, historic and monumental works. Extends support to art through awareness- and fund-raising campaigns aimed to protect, conserve and recover cultural heritage. Designs and implements projects to restore, recover and enhance Italy's artistic and cultural heritage as a step towards protection of heritage.

Geographical Area of Activity: Italy.

Publications: Newsletter.

Finance: Annual income €197,084, expenditure €195,624 (31 Dec. 2011).

Board of Directors: Prof. Giuseppe De Rita (Chair.); Dr Alain Elkann (Past Chair.).

Principal Staff: Sec.-Gen. Dr Ledo Prato.

Address: Corso Vittorio Emanuele II 21, 00186 Rome.

Telephone: (06) 36006206; **Fax:** (06) 3208396; **Internet:** www
.fondazionecittaitalia.it; **e-mail:** fondazione@
fondazionecittaitalia.it.

Fondazione Rodolfo Debenedetti—FRDB (Foundation Rodolfo Debenedetti)

Established in 1998 by Carlo de Benedetti.

Activities: Promotes applied and policy-orientated research on the following main topics: the reform of public pension systems in light of demographic trends and the transformation of capital markets and of the political economy limits of the reforms; the causes of European unemployment, its social costs and the political feasibility of strategies aimed at liberalizing European Union (EU) labour markets; the harmonization and co-ordination of social and immigration policies in the EU as a precondition for effective labour mobility across EU countries; and the dynamics of poverty and inequalities and the role played in this respect by the welfare systems. The Foundation also organizes conferences and maintains a public documentation centre on social policy reforms and EU labour markets.

Geographical Area of Activity: Europe.

Publications: *Note Rapide* (online newsletter); conference proceeds.

Board: Carlo de Benedetti (Pres.).

Principal Staff: Co-ordinator Paolo Pinotti.

Address: Via Roentgen 1, Room 5.C1-11, 20136 Milan.

Telephone: (02) 58363341; **Fax:** (02) 58363309; **Internet:** www.frdb.org; **e-mail:** info@frdb.org.

Fondazione Giordano Dell'Amore (Giordano Dell'Amore Foundation)

Founded in 1977 as Finafrica Foundation by Cassa di Risparmio delle Province Lombarde bank; a member of RITMI—the Italian microfinance network—and of Comitato Nazionale Italiano Permanente per il Microcredito, it is associated with the European Microfinance Network and the European Microfinance Platform.

Activities: Aims to activate and catalyze the skills and resources of Italian agents to develop projects and methods of intervention in the microfinance sector, in industrialized and developing countries, in compliance with consolidated best practice. The Foundation aims to contribute significantly to the development and innovation of the microfinance sector. It also sponsors the annual Microfinance Best Practices Awards.

Geographical Area of Activity: Worldwide.

Board of Directors: Federico Manzoni (Chair.).

Principal Staff: Sec.-Gen. Maria Cristina Negro.

Address: Via Andegari 18, 20121 Milan.

Telephone: (2) 89012767; **Fax:** (2) 98652653; **Internet:** www.fgda.org; **e-mail:** info@fgda.org.

Fondazione Angelo Della Riccia (Angelo Della Riccia Foundation)

Founded in 1939 by Angelo Della Riccia to encourage, support and reward Italian students of micro-physics; and to promote research in nuclear, atomic and molecular physics, including collective and cosmic radiation.

Activities: Awards prizes and scholarships for researchers resident in Italy. The Foundation supports research in microphysics. Fellowships are given by the Italian and the Swiss Foundation.

Geographical Area of Activity: Italy and Switzerland.

Finance: Grants available in 2015/16: €210,000.

Principal Staff: Pres. Prof. Roberto Casalbuoni; CEO Dr Vieri Chiariotti.

Address: Casella Postale 38, 50123 Florence.

Telephone: (05) 5212836; **Internet:** theory.fi.infn.it/
casalbuoni/dellariccia; **e-mail:** dellariccia@fi.infn.it.

Fondazione Guido Donegani (Guido Donegani Foundation)

Founded in 1951 by Guido Donegani to further the study of chemistry in Italy; the Foundation is managed by the Accademia Nazionale dei Lincei (q.v.).

Activities: Operates internationally in the field of science. The Foundation awards study grants to Italian and foreign students and graduates in the field of chemistry, and has created special prizes for Italian scientists and technicians who have made an outstanding contribution towards the investigation or solution of problems in chemistry. It has also established courses of higher education and grants for research and experiment in the field of chemistry.

Geographical Area of Activity: Europe.

Publications: A series of publications regarding the activities of the Foundation, published by the Accademia Nazionale dei Lincei.

Finance: Source of finance is income from property and investments. Annual revenue approx. €77,000, expenditure approx. €72,000.

Board of Directors: Lamberto Maffei (Chair.); Marco Fortis (Vice-Chair.).

Principal Staff: Sec. Ada Baccari.

Address: c/o Accademia Nazionale dei Lincei, Via della Lungara 10, 00165 Rome.

Telephone: (06) 6838831; **Fax:** (06) 6893616; **e-mail:** ufficio
.premi@lincei.it.

Fondazione Luigi Einaudi (Luigi Einaudi Foundation)

Founded in 1964 by the family of Luigi Einaudi, former President of Italy, with the help of local financial institutions and the Italian Government, to train young scholars in economics and political and historical studies, and to maintain a library in the social sciences open to all scholars.

Activities: Maintains the Luigi Einaudi Library, which currently contains more than 230,000 vols and 2,700 periodicals; awards fellowships and research grants, organizes seminars and conferences, and sponsors publications in the fields of economics, politics and history. The Foundation also operates internationally, collaborating with the Colegio de México in Mexico and Cornell University in the USA; carrying out research into the effect of property on agricultural productivity in Europe and Central and South America; as well as developing projects dealing with regional integration, conflict resolution, comparative models of employment and social policy, and contemporary political thought.

Geographical Area of Activity: Mainly Italy.

Publications: *Annali della Fondazione Luigi Einaudi*; *Scrittori italiani di politica, economia e storia* (collection of classics); *Studi* (collection of monographs).

Board of Directors: Prof. Enrico Filippi (Chair.); Dr Emanuele Bellavia (Sec.).

Address: Palazzo d'Azeglio, Via Principe Amedeo 34, 10123 Turin.

Telephone: (011) 835656; **Fax:** (011) 8179093; **Internet:** www
.fondazioneeinaudi.it; **e-mail:** segreteria@
fondazioneeinaudi.it.

Fondazione Giangiacomo Feltrinelli (Giangiacomo Feltrinelli Foundation)

Established in 1949 to collect, preserve and make available to scholars and interested members of the public diverse materials documenting the history of ideas, in particular those related to the development of the international labour and socialist movements.

Activities: Makes available for consultation library and archival holdings consisting of some 200,000 books, extensive newspaper and periodical collections, and more than 1m. primary source materials. The Foundation also promotes scholarly research initiatives, organizes seminars, conferences and exhibitions exploring both historical and contemporary subjects, and produces a range of printed and online publications. A long-term digitization project is under way to enable online access to reproductions of thousands of the most significant materials in the holdings.

Geographical Area of Activity: Italy.

Restrictions: Does not make grants.

Publications: *Movimento Operaio*; *Annali* (annual series featuring original research by international scholars within the fields of modern social history and historiography); *Biblioteca Europea* (collection of anastatic reprints of significant 17th- to 19th-century works); *Quaderni*; catalogues and other library finding aids (both printed and online) to the principal thematic sections and archives; an online eBook collection of hard-to-find texts held at the Foundation.

Board of Directors: Carlo Feltrinelli (Chair.); Salvatore Veca (Hon. Chair.).

Principal Staff: Sec.-Gen. Massimiliano Tarantino.

Address: Via Gian Domenico Romagnosi 3, 20121 Milan.

Telephone: (02) 874175; **Fax:** (02) 86461855; **Internet:** www.fondazionefeltrinelli.it; **e-mail:** segreteria@fondazionefeltrinelli.it.

Fondazione Piera, Pietro e Giovanni Ferrero (Piera, Pietro and Giovanni Ferrero Foundation)

Established in 1983 by Michele Ferrero for the welfare of pensioners of Ferrero companies, and to make grants for cultural activities and medical research.

Activities: Operates nationally, carrying out cultural activities in Alba, including conferences and publications; funding and organizing activities for Ferrero pensioners; and supporting medical research, especially in relation to the aged.

Geographical Area of Activity: Italy.

Publications: *Filodiretto* (magazine); and other publications.

Board of Directors: Maria Franca Ferrero (Chair.).

Principal Staff: Dir Dr Mario Strola.

Address: Via Vivaro 49, 12051 Alba.

Telephone: (0173) 295259; **Fax:** (0173) 363274; **Internet:** www.fondazioneferrero.it; **e-mail:** info@fondazioneferrero.it.

Fondazione Edoardo Garrone

Established in 2004 to support and implement new models and instruments of social and cultural management.

Activities: Supports and promotes art and culture; social integration and development; education; sustainable cultural development of the province of Siracusa, Sicily. The Foundation is in the process of creating a centre of excellence and a school for international studies in tourism economics in Siracusa, Sicily.

Geographical Area of Activity: Italy.

Publications: Newsletter.

Board of Directors: Alessandro Garrone (Chair.); Carla Garrone Mondini (Vice-Chair.).

Principal Staff: Sec.-Gen. Francesca Campora.

Address: Via San Luca 2, 16124 Genova.

Telephone: (010) 8681530; **Fax:** (010) 8681539; **Internet:** www.fondazionegarrone.it; **e-mail:** info@fondazionegarrone.it.

Fondazione Internazionale Menarini (Menarini International Foundation)

Founded in 1976 to promote research and knowledge in the fields of biology, pharmacology and medicine but also, though more implicitly, of economic and human sciences.

Activities: Promotes biomedical and economic and human sciences research, primarily through the organization of conferences and symposia. The Foundation also produces art and scientific publications.

Geographical Area of Activity: Italy.

Publications: *Minuti Menarini* (monthly journal).

Principal Staff: Pres. Sergio Gorini.

Address: Edificio L, Strada 6, Centro Direzionale Milanofiori, 20089 Rozzano, Milan.

Telephone: (02) 55308110; **Fax:** (02) 55305739; **Internet:** www.fondazione-menarini.it; **e-mail:** milan@fondazione-menarini.it.

Fondazione ISMU—Iniziative e Studi sulla Multietnicità (ISMU Foundation—Initiatives and Studies on Multi-ethnicity)

Established in 1991.

Activities: Promotes internationalism and multiculturalism, particularly within Europe; and study and research, especially in the field of immigration issues. The Foundation holds seminars and produces publications promoting multi-ethnicity; funds training and maintains a document archive consisting of national and international informative material.

Geographical Area of Activity: Mainly Europe.

Publications: *ISMU informa* (newsletter); *Multicultural Policies and Modes of Citizenship;* annual report.

Board of Directors: Mariella Enoc (Chair.).

Principal Staff: Sec.-Gen. Vincenzo Cesareo.

Address: Via Copernico 1, 20125 Milan.

Telephone: (02) 6787791; **Fax:** (02) 66877979; **Internet:** www.ismu.org; **e-mail:** ismu@ismu.org.

Fondazione per l'Istituto Svizzero di Roma (Foundation for the Swiss Institute of Rome)

Founded in 1947 to provide an opportunity for young Swiss scholars and artists to pursue their activities in the 'classical' environment of Rome.

Activities: Operates internationally in the field of the arts and humanities. The Foundation organizes regular events in the artistic and scholarly fields to contribute to mutual understanding and to deepen further intellectual and artistic relations between Switzerland and Italy. It has a Resource Centre with a library of 40,000 vols. Has branch offices in Milan and Venice.

Geographical Area of Activity: International, with a special focus on Swiss-Italian relations.

Publications: Annual Report; *Bibliotheca Helvetica Romana*; and others.

Finance: Funded by the Swiss Confederation, Pro Helvetia, BSI, the Swiss National Foundation and others. Annual income 3,339,409 Swiss francs, expenditure 3,337,844 Swiss francs (2013).

Governing Board: Charles Kleiber (Chair.).

Principal Staff: Dir Prof. Dr Michele Luminati.

Address: Istituto Svizzero di Roma, Via Ludovisi 48, 00187 Rome.

Telephone: (06) 420421; **Fax:** (06) 42042420; **Internet:** www.istitutosvizzero.it; **e-mail:** direzione@istitutosvizzero.it.

Fondazione Italcementi Cavaliere del Lavoro Carlo Presenti (Italcementi Carlo Presenti Foundation)

Established in 2004 by Italcementi and Italmobiliare, in honour of industrialist Carlo Presenti.

Activities: Promotes education and scientific research, and sustainable economic and social development of enterprises. The Foundation also undertakes humanitarian projects, helping those affected by natural disasters and in similar emergency situations.

Geographical Area of Activity: Worldwide.

Publications: Brochure.

Board of Directors: Giovanni Giavazzi (Chair.); Giampiero Pesenti (Vice-Chair.).

Address: Via Gabriele Camozzi 124, 24121 Bergamo.

Telephone: (035) 219774; **Fax:** (035) 210509; **Internet:** www.fondazioneitalcementi.it; **e-mail:** info@fondazioneitalcementi.it.

Fondazione Ing. Carlo M. Lerici—FL (Ing. Carlo M. Lerici Foundation)

Founded in 1947 by Carlo Maurilio Lerici to promote, develop and co-ordinate initiatives and activities concerned with archaeological prospecting both within Italy and abroad. Fondazione Ing. Carlo M. Lerici is a founder member of the European Consortium for Asian Field Study (ECAF).

Activities: Carries out archaeological prospecting campaigns in Italy and abroad, including experimental surveys independently and in collaboration with other institutions. Conducts research for the development of new instruments and of new methods of treatment, interpretation and representation of surveying results. Operates its own archaeological researches and restoration of monuments in Laos, Viet Nam, Myanmar and Brazil.

Geographical Area of Activity: Italy, Asia and South America.

Restrictions: Does not make grants.

Publications: Occasional reports on specific research; *Prospezioni Archeologiche* (in Italian and English); monographic volumes and reviews of geophysical prospecting and archaeology; *Filtering Optimisation and Modelling of Geophysical Given in Archaeological Prospecting.*

Governing Board: Prof. Giulio Ballio (Chair.).

Principal Staff: Dir Mauro Cucarzi.

Address: Politecnico di Milano, Via Vittorio Veneto 108, 00187 Rome.

Telephone: (06) 4880083; **Fax:** (06) 4827085; **Internet:** www .lerici.polimi.it; **e-mail:** folerici@tin.it.

Fondazione Giovanni Lorenzini (Giovanni Lorenzini Foundation)

Established in 1969 as a non-profit scientific organization by presidential decree.

Activities: Consists of two not-for-profit scientific organizations, one based in Milan, established in 1969, and the second in Houston, USA, established in 1984. Both are committed to international scientific exchange and education in basic and medical research. The Foundation aims to transfer the most recent developments and results in experimental science to clinical and applied research to be used for both individual patients and for the community as a whole. It organizes international conferences and promotes public educational campaigns mainly focused on the prevention of cardiovascular disease and on women's health.

Geographical Area of Activity: International.

Publications: Brochure; position papers; guidelines; conference proceedings; websites; CD-ROMs; e-newsletters.

Board of Governors: Rodolfo Paoletti (Hon. Pres.); Sergio Pecorelli (Pres.); Andrea Peracino (Vice-Pres.).

Principal Staff: Sec-Gen. and CEO Emanuela Folco.

Address: Viale Piave 35, 20129 Milan.

Telephone: (02) 29006267; **Fax:** (02) 29007018; **Internet:** www.lorenzinifoundation.org; **e-mail:** info@ lorenzinifoundation.org.

Fondazione Salvatore Maugeri—Clinica del Lavoro e della Riabilitazione (Salvatore Maugeri Foundation—Occupational Health and Rehabilitation Clinic)

Founded in 1965 as the Fondazione Pro Clinica del Lavoro di Pavia by Prof. Salvatore Maugeri for health-care assistance and medical research in occupational health. Present name adopted in 1995. In 2013, it merged with the Fondazione Europea Riabilitazione e Sport.

Activities: Supports clinics and institutes of occupational medicine that carry out research of international significance in the field of occupational diseases. The Foundation also supports five medical centres for cardio-respiratory and neurological rehabilitation. In total, it comprises 13 scientific institutes and three environmental health centres.

Geographical Area of Activity: Italy.

Publications: Brochure.

Board of Directors: Walter Brugger (Chair.).

Address: Via Salvatore Maugeri 4, 27100 Pavia.

Telephone: (0382) 592504; **Fax:** (0382) 592576; **Internet:** www .fsm.it; **e-mail:** segreteria.presidenza@fsm.it.

Fondazione Nazionale Carlo Collodi (Carlo Collodi National Foundation)

Founded in 1952 for the diffusion of the works of Carlo Lorenzini (Collodi), particularly 'The Adventures of Pinocchio'; for the collection and exhibition of national and international publications regarding Carlo Collodi and his works; for the promotion of children's literature and establishment of a centre for the study of children's literature; and for the conservation and enlargement of the Monumental Park of Pinocchio in the village of Collodi.

Activities: Operates nationally through self-conducted programmes and grants to individuals, and nationally and internationally through conferences, courses, publications and lectures. The Foundation maintains a library of more than 6,000 works by and about Collodi, including translations; the Monumental Park of Pinocchio; and the International Study Centre for Young People's Literature. Awards the Rolando Anzilotti prize for a critical or historical monograph on children's or young people's literature.

Geographical Area of Activity: Worldwide.

Publications: *Quaderni della Fondazione Nazionale Carlo Collodi*; *Le Avventure di Pinocchio Official*; research papers; conference proceedings.

Trustees: Prof. Dr Vincenzo Cappelletti (Chair.); Dr Pier Francesco Bernacchi (Sec.).

Principal Staff: Man. Daniele Narducci.

Address: Villa Arcangeli, Via Benvenuto Pasquinelli 6, 51014 Collodi.

Telephone: (057) 2429613; **Fax:** (057) 2429614; **Internet:** www .pinocchio.it/fondazione-carlo-collodi-c3/fondazione -nazionale-carlo-collodi-837.html; www.biblio; **e-mail:** fondazione@pinocchio.it.

Fondazione Adriano Olivetti (Adriano Olivetti Foundation)

Founded in 1962 by Maria Luisa Lizier Galardi, Dino Olivetti, Magda Olivetti Jaksic, Roberto Olivetti and Silvia Olivetti Marxer.

Activities: Promotes, develops and co-ordinates research on: constitutional and federalist studies; the international organization of economic structures; city planning; local government; labour problems; the sociology of co-operation; cultural services and social work; and studies aimed at increasing knowledge of the conditions that affect social progress. The Foundation operates nationally and internationally, through self-conducted programmes, grants, research and publications. Works in four main areas: Institutional and Public Policies; Processes of Economic and Social Development; Cultural and Social Policies; and Art, Architecture and Urban Studies.

Geographical Area of Activity: Europe and USA.

Publications: Annuall Report; *Esiste un Diritto di Ingerenza? L'Europa di fronte alla guerra*; *MoltepliCittà;* archive; annual report; and numerous other publications.

Board of Directors: Laura Olivetti (Chair.); Davide Olivetti (Vice-Chair.).

Principal Staff: Sec.-Gen. Melina Decaro.

Address: Via Guiseppe Zanardelli 34, 00186 Rome.

Telephone: (06) 6877054; **Fax:** (06) 6896193; **Internet:** www .fondazioneadrianolivetti.it; **e-mail:** info@ fondazioneadrianolivetti.it; fondazioneadrianolivetti@pec.it.

Fondazione Giulio Pastore—FGP (Giulio Pastore Foundation)

Founded in 1971 by the Associazioni Cristiane Lavoratori Italiani, Confederazione Italiana Sindacati dei Lavoratori,

Democrazia Cristiana, Prof. Mario Romani, Prof. Vincenzo Saba, Vincenzo Scotti, Don Pierfranco Pastore and Idolo Marcone to promote research and study concerning the problems of labour and the trade union experience of workers, both as a single relevant discipline and in interdisciplinary terms; and to promote the diffusion and application of the results.

Activities: Operates in the fields of education, social welfare and studies, and economic affairs, nationally through self-conducted programmes, and nationally and internationally through research, grants to individuals, fellowships, scholarships, conferences, courses, publications and lectures.

Geographical Area of Activity: Worldwide.

Publications: *Annali* (annual report of operations); yearbooks; *Lavoro e Sindacato* (6 a year); *Quaderni della Fondazione Giulio Pastore 01*; *Quaderni della Fondazione Giulio Pastore 02*; *Quaderni della Fondazione Giulio Pastore 03*; *Quaderni della Fondazione Giulio Pastore 04*; *Quaderni della Fondazione Giulio Pastore 05*.

Board of Directors: Aldo Carera (Pres.); Pierciro Galeone (Vice-Pres.).

Principal Staff: Sec.-Gen. Prof. Gustavo De Santis.

Address: Via del Viminale 43, 00184 Rome.

Telephone: (06) 83960192; **Fax:** (06) 81172707; **Internet:** www.fondazionepastore.it; **e-mail:** info@fondazionepastore.it.

Fondazione Alessio Pezcoller (Alessio Pezcoller Foundation)

Founded in 1980 by Prof. Alessio Pezcoller to promote biomedical research.

Activities: Operates nationally and internationally in the fields of medicine and health, by awarding prizes: the Pezcoller Foundation-AACR International Award for Cancer Research, worth €75,000 and presented annually to a scientist who has made a major scientific discovery in the field of cancer, and the Pezcoller Foundation-ECCO Recognition for Contribution to Oncology, worth €30,000 and presented biennially to an individual for his or her unique contribution to oncology, and for the dedication of his or her professional life to cancer. The Foundation organizes an annual symposium promoting interaction between international scientists working in basic oncological sciences, and a series of educational meetings for local medical doctors.

Geographical Area of Activity: International.

Restrictions: No grants to individuals.

Publications: *The Pezcoller Foundation Journal* (2 a year).

Board of Directors: Davide Bassi (Chair.); Gios Bernardi (Hon. Chair.).

Address: Via Dordi 8, 38122 Trento.

Telephone: (0461) 980250; **Fax:** (0461) 980350; **Internet:** www.pezcoller.it; **e-mail:** pezcoller@pezcoller.it.

Fondazione Prada (Prada Foundation)

Established in 1993 by Miuccia Prada and Patrizio Bertelli.

Activities: Curates exhibitions and organizes cultural symposia; also produces visual art exhibitions. The Foundation maintains a collection of catalogues, monographs and artists' books.

Geographical Area of Activity: Italy and Europe.

Publications: Catalogues; books on architecture; conference proceedings.

Board of Trustees: Miuccia Prada, Patrizio Bertelli (Co-Chair.).

Principal Staff: Artistic Dir Germano Celant.

Address: Largo Isarco 2, 20139 Milan.

Telephone: (02) 56662611; **Internet:** www.fondazioneprada.org; **e-mail:** info@fondazioneprada.org.

Fondazione Querini Stampalia (Querini Stampalia Foundation)

Founded in 1869 by Count Giovanni Querini to support university studies in Venice and Padua, and to promote the diffusion of culture through library and museum services, and cultural activities, particularly in and around Venice.

Activities: Operates in the field of the arts and humanities, through seminars and conferences, training courses, concerts and publications. The Foundation maintains a library of 350,000 vols and a museum.

Geographical Area of Activity: Italy.

Publications: Newsletter; numerous historical and cultural publications.

Finance: Annual income €3,371,000, expenditure €3,395,000 (2013).

Trustees: Marino Cortese (Pres.); Antonio Foscari (Vice-Pres.); Lucia Marina Broccato (Sec.).

Principal Staff: Dir Marigusta Lazzari.

Address: Santa Maria Formosa, Castello 5252, 30122 Venice.

Telephone: (041) 2711411; **Fax:** (041) 2711445; **Internet:** www.querinistampalia.it; **e-mail:** fondazione@querinistampalia.org.

Fondazione Ricci Onlus (Ricci Foundation)

Established in 1990 by da Giovanni Mario Ricci; a non-profit corporation aiming to promote initiatives of a social and humanitarian nature, and to encourage the restoration and protection of the environmental, cultural and historical heritage of the middle and upper valley of the Serchio river.

Activities: Operates in the fields of the arts and humanities, and conservation and the environment, through self-conducted programmes, conferences and publications. The Foundation aims to acquire an art collection to exhibit to the public.

Geographical Area of Activity: Italia.

Publications: Annual Report; books.

Board of Directors: Dr Cristiana Ricci (Chair.); Dr Rolando Notini (Vice-Chair.); Daniela Papi, Antonio Ricci (Co-Treas.).

Principal Staff: Pres. Ettore Ricci.

Address: Via Roma 20, 55051 Barga, Lucca.

Telephone: (0583) 724357; **Fax:** (0583) 724921; **Internet:** www.fondazionericcionlus.it; **e-mail:** fondricci@iol.it.

Fondazione Roma (Rome Foundation)

Established in 1836 as the Cassa di Risparmio di Roma.

Activities: Aims to provide social benefit and to promote economic development in the fields of health, fine arts and cultural heritage, education, scientific research, aid to the underprivileged, and also to support activities in the voluntary service sector. The Foundation runs its own programmes and co-operates on initiatives proposed by non-profit organizations in the areas of health, fine arts and cultural heritage, education, scientific research, and aid to the underprivileged. It funds hospitals and health centres; operates an exhibition space and has established a youth orchestra; supports a Master's Course in International Studies on Philanthropy; sponsors the Centre for the Dissemination of the Results of Agricultural Research—CEDRA; and operates through the Fondazione Italiana per il Volontariato (f. 1991) and the Fondazione Europa Occupazione: Impresa e Solidarietà (f. 1995). The former promotes, encourages and supports voluntary service, and the latter fosters occupational opportunities, through training activities for young people, the disabled and the socially disadvantaged.

Geographical Area of Activity: Italy, with focus on the province of Rome and the region of Lazio.

Restrictions: No funding for profit-making organizations, individuals and enterprises.

Publications: *NFR Notiziario Fondazione Roma* (quarterly magazine); TTR series (conference proceedings); *Una* *tradizione culturale. Storia, Ambienti e Collezioni della Fondazione Roma* (2008); newsletter.

Finance: Total assets €1,891.6m. (2014).

Board of Directors: Prof. Emmanuele F. M. Emanuele (Chair.); Serafino Gatti (Vice-Chair.).

Principal Staff: CEO Franco Parasassi.

Address: Palazzo Sciarra, Via Marco Minghetti 17, 00187 Rome.

Telephone: (06) 6976450; **Fax:** (06) 697645300; **Internet:** www.fondazioneroma.it; **e-mail:** info@fondazioneroma.it.

Fondazione Romaeuropa (Romaeuropa Foundation)

Founded in 1990 to promote the arts between European countries.

Activities: Non-profit organization that administers and promotes the Romaeuropa Festival for contemporary culture.

Geographical Area of Activity: Italy.

Publications: Newsletter.

Finance: Annual income €3,590,128, expenditure €3,476,148 (31 Dec. 2013).

Board of Directors: Monique Veaute (Chair.); Giovanni Pieraccini (Hon. Chair.).

Principal Staff: Artistic and Man. Dir Fabrizio Grifasi.

Address: Via dei Magazzini Generali 20A, 00154 Rome.

Telephone: (06) 45553000; **Fax:** (06) 45553005; **Internet:** www.romaeuropa.net; **e-mail:** romaeuropa@romaeuropa .net; fondazioneromaeuropa@pec.romaeuropa.net.

Fondazione RUI (RUI Foundation)

Founded in 1959 by university teachers, professional workers and parents concerned with studying and resolving problems facing young people.

Activities: Promotes the further training of university students and intellectuals, and cultural activities for young people; awards scholarships to Italian and foreign students, collaborating with national and international organizations to these ends. The Foundation operates nationally in the field of the arts and humanities, and nationally and internationally in the fields of education, social welfare and studies. It is also active in the fields of international relations and aid to less-developed countries. Programmes are carried out internationally through self-conducted projects, and nationally and internationally through research, fellowships and scholarships, conferences, courses, publications and lectures. Has an office in Rome.

Geographical Area of Activity: Europe.

Publications: *Fondazione Rui* (magazine); *Universitas* (magazine); guides on higher education in Italy.

Principal Staff: Pres. Prof. Vincenzo Lorenzelli; Gen. Man. Antonio Chiveri.

Address: Via Domenichino 16, 20149 Milan.

Telephone: (02) 48010813; **Fax:** (02) 4819286; **Internet:** www .fondazionerui.it; **e-mail:** sede.milano@fondazionerui.it.

Fondazione di Studi di Storia dell'Arte 'Roberto Longhi' (Roberto Longhi Foundation for the Study of the History of Art)

Founded in 1971 by Prof. Roberto Longhi to promote and develop the study of the history of art among young Italian and foreign students.

Activities: Operates internationally in the field of the arts and humanities, through research and study courses. A number of grants, fellowships and prizes are available to both Italian and non-Italian students studying at the Foundation's own institute. The Foundation maintains a library of 35,000 art publications and 60,000 photographs of Italian art, and also a collection of pictures of some 200 important artists.

Geographical Area of Activity: International.

Publications: *Proporzioni* (art magazine); *Annali della Fondazione Roberto Longhi* (art magazine); catalogues.

Board of Trustees: Mina Gregori (Pres.).

Principal Staff: Scientific Dir Maria Cristina Bandera.

Address: Via Benedetto Fortini 30, 50125 Florence.

Telephone: (055) 6580794; **Fax:** (055) 6580794; **Internet:** www.fondazionelonghi.it; **e-mail:** longhi@fondazionelonghi .it.

Fondazione Terzo Pilastro—Italia e Mediterraneo

Founded in 2007 as the Fondazione Roma—Terzo Settore by the merger of the Fondazione Italiana per il Volontariato—FIVOL (f. 1991) and the Fondazione Europa Occupazione—Impresa e Solidarietà (f. 1995); an initiative of the Fondazione Roma (q.v.). Present name adopted in 2014 following its merger with the Fondazione Roma-Mediterraneo (f. 2008).

Activities: Works in the fields of health; education and training; art and culture; scientific research; support for vulnerable groups; and job-creation schemes. The Foundation promotes and supports social enterprise and voluntary work. It also manages the Fondazione Miglioranzi, which supports those who occasionally need financial assistance. Has representative offices in Catania, Cosenza, Naples and Palermo, and abroad in Rabat, Morocco, and Valencia, Spain.

Geographical Area of Activity: Italy.

Publications: Brochure; books.

Principal Staff: Sec.-Gen. Prof. Alessandra Taccone.

Address: Palazzo Sciarra, Via Marco Minghetti 17, 00187 Rome.

Telephone: (06) 97625591; **Fax:** (06) 98380693; **Internet:** www.fondazioneroma-terzosettore.it; **e-mail:** fondazione@ fondazioneroma-terzosettore.it.

Fondazione Umana Mente (Umana Mente Foundation)

Established in 2001 by Allianz Group S.p.A. to support disadvantaged people.

Activities: Aims to provide valid and effective solutions for people with social and behavioural problems. The Foundation's activities are focused mainly on children with social and behavioural problems or people affected by congenital mental disabilities, by supporting and financing projects promoted by non-profit organizations throughout Italy. It offers financial and managerial support to non-profit organizations through a structured operating model based on an evaluation process and continuous monitoring of supported projects.

Geographical Area of Activity: Italy.

Publications: *Polinrete: Il lavoro in rete tra servizi per persone disabili* (2007); *Sestante: un'esperienza di counselling per il benessere dei minori*; *Attivare risorse nelle periferie: Guida alla promozione di interventi nei quartieri difficili di alcune città italiane* (2009).

Finance: Total assets €1,013,348 (31 Dec. 2013).

Board of Directors: Maurizio Devescovi (Chair.); Paola Di Lieto (Vice-Chair.).

Principal Staff: Gen. Sec. Nicola Corti.

Address: Corso Italia 23, 20122 Milan.

Telephone: (02) 72162669; **Fax:** (02) 72162793; **Internet:** www .umana-mente.it; **e-mail:** info@umana-mente.it.

Fondazione Unipolis

Established in 2007 by Unipol Gruppo Financiario as successor to the Fondazione Cesarm (f. 1989), which was formerly known as the Centro Europeo di Ricerca dell'Economia Sociale e dell'Assicurazione per iniziativa dell'allora Unipol Assicurazioni.

Activities: Operates through grants to non-profit organizations in the areas of the arts and culture, social welfare and research.

Finance: Annual income €1,316,335, expenditure €1,337,445 (2013).

Board of Directors: Pierluigi Stefanini (Chair.).

Principal Staff: Man. Dir Walter Dondi.

Address: Via Stalingrado 53, 40128 Bologna.

Telephone: (051) 6437601; **Fax:** 051 6437600; **Internet:** www
.fondazioneunipolis.org; **e-mail:** info@fondazioneunipolis
.org.

Fondazione di Venezia (Venice Foundation)

Established in 1992 by the Cassa di Risparmio di Venezia.

Activities: Active in the areas of education, training, scientific research, conservation and culture, through its own programmes and projects, direct grants and co-operation with other organizations.

Geographical Area of Activity: Mainly Venice, Italy.

Publications: Annual Report; newsletter; conference reports; exhibition catalogues; studies.

Finance: Total assets €346,506,003 (31 Dec. 2013).

Board of Directors: Giuliano Segre (Pres.); Giampietro Brunello (Vice-Pres.).

Principal Staff: Dir Fabio Achilli; Sec.-Gen. Gianpaolo Fortunati.

Address: Dorsoduro 3488/U, 30123 Venice.

Telephone: (041) 2201211; **Fax:** (041) 2201219; **Internet:** www
.fondazionedivenezia.org; **e-mail:** segretaria@
fondazionedivenezia.org.

Fondo per l'Ambiente Italiano—FAI (Fund for the Italian Environment)

Founded in 1975 to increase awareness of environmental protection and the preservation of Italy's cultural heritage.

Activities: Operates nationally, acquiring historically, culturally or environmentally valuable sites and opening them to the public, and also running educational conferences and exhibitions.

Geographical Area of Activity: Italy.

Publications: Annual Report; newsletter.

Finance: Annual income €15,942,569, expenditure €16,133,933 (31 Dec. 2012).

Trustees: Giulia Maria Mozzoni Crespi (Hon. Chair.); Andrea Carandini (Chair.); Marco Magnifico (Exec. Vice-Pres.).

Principal Staff: Dir-Gen. Angelo Maramai.

Address: La Cavallerizza, Via Carlo Foldi 2, 20135 Milan.

Telephone: (02) 467615248; **Fax:** (02) 48193631; **Internet:** www.fondoambiente.it; **e-mail:** a.ughi@fondoambiente.it.

Institute for Scientific Interchange Foundation—ISI

Established in 1983 to promote international co-operation in scientific research.

Activities: Operates internationally in the field of science and technology, through funding scientific programmes, and recruiting scientists to lecture and carry out research to encourage and support science. The Institute is particularly interested in the study of complex systems and the field of complexity science. Other fields of research are: data science; computational social science; citizen science and smart cities; computational epidemiology and public health; collective phenomena in physics and materials science; quantum science and mathematics of networks; and mathematics and foundation of complex systems.

Geographical Area of Activity: International.

Finance: Total assets €3,844,393 (31 Dec. 2013).

Board of Trustees: Mario Rasetti (Chair.).

Principal Staff: COO Tiziana Bertoletti.

Address: Via Alassio 11c, 10126 Turin.

Telephone: (011) 6603090; **Fax:** (011) 6600049; **Internet:** www.isi.it; **e-mail:** isi@isi.it.

International Balzan Prize Foundation

Founded in 1956 by Angela Lina Balzan to honour the memory of her father, Eugenio Balzan, a famous Italian journalist, who died in 1953. The Foundation acts jointly through two foundations, the International Balzan Foundation-Fund under Swiss jurisdiction, and the International Balzan Foundation-Prize under Italian jurisdiction.

Activities: Awards the Balzan Prizes. Four prizes are awarded annually: two within the humanities, and two within the sciences on subjects chosen each year. In 2015, prizes were awarded in the areas of history of European art (1300–1700); economic history; oceanography; and astroparticle physics. The 2012 prizes were worth 750,000 Swiss francs each and one-half of this amount had to be used for research projects involving young scholars and scientists. The Foundation also awards the Balzan Prize for Humanity, Peace and Fraternity among Peoples every three years. The General Prize Committee, responsible for the selection of the candidates, is made up of about 20 European academics and scientists. The candidates are submitted by universities and learned societies from all over the world, following an invitation by the Chairman of the Balzan General Prize Committee to presidents of academies and universities, and other similar institutions, to submit nominations for the awards.

Geographical Area of Activity: Worldwide.

Restrictions: Personal applications not accepted.

Publications: Newsletter; Balzan Prizes (information on the Prizewinners and the Foundation, annually, in English, French, German and Italian); *Balzan Prizes Interdisciplinary Forum* (includes Prizewinners' research projects, annually); *The Annual Balzan Lecture* (annual); *The Balzan Prizewinners' Research Projects: An Overview* (2 a year) .

Board: Enrico Decleva (Chair.); Alberto Quadrio Curzio (Vice-Chair.).

Principal Staff: Sec.-Gen. Suzanne Werder.

Address: Piazzetta Umberto Giordano 4, 20122 Milan.

Telephone: (02) 76002212; **Fax:** (02) 76009457; **Internet:** www
.balzan.org; **e-mail:** balzan@balzan.it.

International Development Law Organization—IDLO (Organisation Internationale de Droit du Développement—OIDD)

Founded in 1983 by L. Michael Hager, Gilles Blanchi and William Loris.

Activities: Enables governments and empowers people to reform laws and strengthen institutions to promote peace, justice, sustainable development and economic opportunity. The Organization works in a range of fields, including peace and institution building, and assisting economic recovery in countries emerging from conflict and striving towards democracy. It comprises a network of more than 2,500 experts and 47 alumni associations and has worked in more than 170 countries. Has a branch office in The Hague, the Netherlands, and observer status at the UN.

Geographical Area of Activity: International.

Publications: Guides; guidelines; reports; toolkits.

Finance: Governments, multilateral development organizations, foundations and private companies contribute towards the Organization's budget, programme and fellowship requirements. Annual revenue €25,379,069, expenditure €24,802,905 (31 Dec. 2013).

Principal Staff: Dir-Gen. Irene Khan.

Address: Viale Vaticano 106, 00165 Rome.

Telephone: (06) 40403200; **Fax:** (06) 40403232; **Internet:** www.idlo.int; **e-mail:** idlo@idlo.int.

International Fund for Agricultural Development—IFAD

Founded in 1977; a specialized agency of the UN, to improve food production in developed countries and to assist developing countries in establishing productive farming methods and better standards of nutrition.

Activities: Works with poor rural people to enable them to grow and sell more food, increase their incomes and determine the direction of their own lives. Since 1978, the organization has invested more than US $16,300m. in grants and low-interest loans to developing countries. Operates as a partnership of 176 member countries.

Geographical Area of Activity: Asia, Central and South America and the Caribbean, the Middle East and North Africa, and Sub-Saharan Africa.

Publications: *IFAD Annual Report* (in Arabic, English, French and Spanish); also publishes books, electronic newsletters and thematic publications.

Finance: Total assets US $8,228,429,000; annual operating expenditure $171,379,000 (2014).

Principal Staff: Pres. Kanayo F. Nwanze.

Address: Via Paolo di Dono 44, 00142 Rome.

Telephone: (06) 54591; **Fax:** (06) 5043463; **Internet:** www .ifad.org; **e-mail:** ifad@ifad.org.

Istituto Affari Internazionali—IAI (Institute of International Affairs)

Founded in 1965 by Altiero Spinelli to promote the study of international relations, in particular Europe's position in world affairs.

Activities: Promotes research, often in collaboration with research institutes of other countries, and belongs to a number of international networks of research centres. The Institute organizes national and international conferences in international relations. Its main fields of interest are: Italian integration and international competition; the evolution of European integration and European policy; new issues in the security and defence field; transatlantic relations; international relations (particularly with the countries on the southern shore of the Mediterranean); and relations between Europe and Asia. Has an extensive library containing more than 27,000 publications in book and periodical form, in the major European languages, on international relations, especially of a politico-cultural nature.

Geographical Area of Activity: International.

Publications: *The International Spectator* (quarterly English language review); *IAI Research Papers* (series, irregular); *Quaderni IAI* (series, irregular); *AffarInternazionali* (webzine); numerous books and pamphlets, some in collaboration with other publishers.

Board of Trustees: Carlo Azeglio Ciampi (Hon. Pres.); Ferdinando Nelli Feroci (Pres.); Gianni Bonvicini, Vincenzo Camporini, Fabrizio Saccomanni (Vice-Pres).

Principal Staff: Dir Ettore Greco; Deputy Dir Nathalie Tocci.

Address: Via Angelo Brunetti 9, 00186 Rome.

Telephone: (06) 3224360; **Fax:** (06) 3224363; **Internet:** www .iai.it; **e-mail:** iai@iai.it.

Istituto Auxologico Italiano (Italian Institute for Auxology)

Founded in 1958, in 1963 it became a scientific institute for biomedical research focusing on the treatment of diseases that undermine physical and psychological development. In 1972, it was recognized by the Ministries of Health and for Universities and Scientific and Technological Research as a Scientific Institute for Research and Care.

Activities: Operates in the area of medicine and health, and in particular endocrinology and metabolism, cardiovascular disease and neuroscience. The Institute comprises the Istituto Scientifico San Michele (Milan), the Istituto Scientifico San Luca (Milan) and the Istituto Scientifico San Giuseppe (Verbania). Its diagnostic and clinical activities are supported by the continuous research activity of several experimental laboratories.

Geographical Area of Activity: Mainly Italy.

Publications: Annual Report; *Acta Medica Auxologica* (scientific review).

Principal Staff: Pres. Prof. Giovanni Ancarani.

Address: Via Ariosto 13, 20145 Milan.

Telephone: (02) 582111; **Fax:** (02) 58211480; **Internet:** www .auxologico.it; **e-mail:** info@auxologico.it.

Istituto Carlo Cattaneo (Carlo Cattaneo Institute)

Founded in 1965 by a group of academic scientific publishers; granted foundation status in 1986.

Activities: Aims to promote democratic values through the dissemination of research findings on politics and social science. The Institute conducts research, studies and activities relating to culture and education, particularly in the fields of social and political science. Spreads knowledge of Italian society, especially regarding its political system.

Geographical Area of Activity: Italy.

Publications: *Polis. Ricerche e studi su società e politica in Italia* (journal); *Politica in Italia/Italian Politics* (annually); *Ricerche e studi dell-Istituto Cattaneo*; *Stranieri in Italia; Elezioni, Governi, democrazia; Cultura in Italia; Misure e Materiali di Ricerca dell'Istituto Cattaneo*.

Executive Board: Francesco Vella (Chair.).

Principal Staff: Dir Stefania Profeti.

Address: Via Santo Stefano 11, 40125 Bologna.

Telephone: (051) 239766; **Fax:** (051) 262959; **Internet:** www .cattaneo.org; **e-mail:** istitutocattaneo@cattaneo.org.

Istituto di Ricerche Farmacologiche Mario Negri (Mario Negri Pharmacological Research Institute)

Founded in 1961 by the will of Mario Negri to promote technical and scientific research in pharmacology and in the biomedical sciences, and to prevent and cure human and animal diseases.

Activities: Operates nationally and internationally in the fields of education, science and medicine, through self-conducted biomedical research programmes, research fellowships, scholarships, conferences, courses, publications and lectures. Research institutes are also situated in Bergamo and in Ranica (Bergamo) and Santa Maria Imbaro (Chieti), and the friends of the Institute established the Mario Negri Institute Foundation (f. 1973) in New York.

Geographical Area of Activity: International.

Restrictions: The Institute does not apply for patents.

Publications: *Negri News* (monthly); *Research and Practice* (6 a year); scientific reports; books; journals.

Board of Directors: Dr Paolo Martelli (Chair.); Dr Mario Russo (Deputy Chair.); Dr Federico Guasti (Sec.).

Principal Staff: Dir Prof. Silvio Garattini.

Address: Via Giuseppe La Masa 19, 20156 Milan.

Telephone: (02) 390141; **Fax:** (02) 3546277; **Internet:** www .marionegri.it; negribergamo.marionegri.it; **e-mail:** mnegri@marionegri.it.

Istituto Luigi Sturzo (Luigi Sturzo Institute)

Founded in 1951 by a committee in honour of Luigi Sturzo to promote the social sciences, in particular sociology, in Italy and abroad.

Activities: Operates in the fields of history and the social sciences, through research, conferences and discussions, scholarships and publications. The Institute awards prizes to Italian and foreign scholars. It also maintains a library.

Publications: Annual Report; *Sociologia* (3 a year); scientific studies.

Board of Directors: Nicola Antonetti (Chair.); Andrea Bixio (Vice-Chair.).

Principal Staff: Sec.-Gen. Giovanni Dessi.

Address: Palazzo Baldassini, Via delle Coppelle 35, 00186 Rome.

Telephone: (06) 6840421; **Fax:** (06) 68404244; **Internet:** www .sturzo.it; **e-mail:** info.segretariogenerale@sturzo.it.

Lama Gangchen World Peace Foundation

Founded in 1992 by T. Y. S. Lama Gangchen to develop a culture of peace, through non-formal education and funding projects in support of UN humanitarian programmes; has special UN Economic and Social Council (ECOSOC) status.

Activities: Works on international humanitarian projects and promotes world peace in the fields of the arts and humanities, conservation and the environment, non-formal education, and medicine and health, and provides aid to less-developed countries. The Foundation also runs cultural exchanges and promotes inter-religious dialogue.

Geographical Area of Activity: Europe, Asia and South America.

Restrictions: Grants only to specific organizations.

Publications: *Peace Times Quarterly*; books.

Principal Staff: CEO and UN Representative Isthar D. Adler.

Address: Via Zara 20, Albagnano di Bée.

Telephone: (0335) 6140584; **Fax:** (0323) 569608; **Internet:** www.lgpt.net; **e-mail:** lgwpf@lgpt.net.

Mani Tese (Outstretched Hands)

Founded in 1964 to raise public awareness about the problems of developing countries and financing development projects.

Activities: Operates self-conducted programmes, in conjunction with local partners in the areas of education, agriculture, infrastructure development, humanitarian aid and preventive health programmes. The organization also runs training courses in development studies; lobbies and campaigns on related issues; organizes conferences; and maintains a reference library of approx. 20,000 publications.

Geographical Area of Activity: Africa, Asia, and Central and South America.

Publications: Newsletter; *Mani Tese* (monthly newspaper); books, educational materials, audio-visual aids, pamphlets and brochures.

Finance: Annual revenue €4,218,467, expenditure €4,209,635 (31 Dec. 2013).

Board of Directors: Valerio Bini (Chair.); Fiorella Lazzari (Vice-Chair.).

Address: Piazzale Gambara 7–9, 20146 Milan.

Telephone: (02) 4075165; **Fax:** (02) 4046890; **Internet:** www.manitese.it; **e-mail:** manitese@manitese.it.

Oxfam Italia

Established in 1970 as Ucodep; became part of the Oxfam confederation of organizations (qq.v.) in 2010.

Activities: Works to improve livelihoods and promotes long-term sustainable development; provides international disaster relief and post-disaster reconstruction; runs education and information campaigns; and lobbies politicians. Comprises Cooperativa Oxfam Italia Intercultura and Cooperativa Oxfam Italia Commercio Equo.

Geographical Area of Activity: Albania, Bosnia Herzegovina, Brazil, Burkina Faso, Cambodia, Congo (Democratic Repub.), Dominican Repub., Ecuador, El Salvador, Guatemala, Haiti, Honduras, Italy, Lebanon, Morocco, Palestinian Territories, the Philippines, Senegal, Sri Lanka, South Africa, Tunisia.

Finance: Total assets €9,437,932 (31 March 2014).

Principal Staff: Man. Dir Roberto Barbieri.

Address: Via Concino Concini 19, 52100 Arezzo.

Telephone: (575) 182481; **Fax:** (575) 1824872; **Internet:** www.oxfamitalia.org.

SID—Society for International Development

Established in 1957.

Activities: A global network concerned with development that is participative, pluralistic and sustainable. The Society comprises approx. 3,000 individual members, local chapters and institutional members, as well as partner institutions from a variety of fields, in more than 100 countries. It supports development innovation at all levels; encourages and facilitates the creation of a sense of community among individuals and organizations committed to social justice at local, national, regional and international levels; and promotes dialogue, understanding and co-operation for social and economic development that furthers the well-being of all peoples. Activities focus on five areas: sustainable livelihoods; democratic approaches to national governance; women's empowerment; international relations and global governance; and strengthening civil society in post-conflict situations. Projects are implemented at global, national and local level, and include networking and advocacy, cross-sectoral dialogues, research, publications and online debates. Also maintains an office in Nairobi, Kenya.

Geographical Area of Activity: International.

Publications: *Development* (quarterly journal); annual reports, programme reports and other publications.

Governing Council: Juma V. Mwapachu (Pres.); Jean Gilson (Vice-Pres.); René Grotenhuis (Treas.).

Principal Staff: Man. Dir Stefano Prato; Deputy Man. Dir Arthur Muliro.

Address: Via Ardeatina 802, 00178 Rome.

Telephone: (06) 4872172; **Fax:** (06) 4872170; **Internet:** www.sidint.net; **e-mail:** info@sidint.org.

Svenska Institutet i Rom/Istituto Svedese di Studi Classici a Roma (Swedish Institute in Rome)

Founded in 1926 by Crown Prince Gustaf Adolf and others to further, within the framework of Swedish cultural activity, the knowledge of classical culture in the Mediterranean area; to act as a medium for Swedish humanist research and education primarily in the field of classical antiquity and history of art and architecture.

Activities: Operates internationally in the fields of archaeology and art sciences, through excavations, research, fellowships, scholarships, conferences, courses, publications and lectures. The Institute maintains a library of approx. 70,000 vols and also has an archaeological laboratory.

Geographical Area of Activity: International.

Publications: *Skrifter utgivna av Svenska Institutet i Rom; Opuscula: Annual of the Swedish Institutes at Athens and Rome; Suecoromana: Studia artis historiae Instituti Romani Regni Sueciae.*

Principal Staff: Dir Dr Kristian Göransson; Vice-Dir Dr Martin Olin.

Address: Via Omero 14, Valle Giulia, 00197 Rome.

Telephone: (06) 3201596; **Fax:** (06) 3230265; **Internet:** www.isvroma.it; **e-mail:** info@isvroma.org.

UniCredit Foundation—Unidea

Established in 2003 by UniCredito Italiano to operate in the areas of development and co-operation through humanitarian intervention.

Activities: Operates in less-developed countries and in countries of Central and South-Eastern Europe that need to develop to join the European Union, in the fields of medicine and health, education, and conservation and the environment, through the creation and management of projects.

Geographical Area of Activity: Developing countries and Central and South-Eastern Europe.

Finance: Total assets €9,252,272; annual revenue €4,116,795 (31 Dec. 2013).

Board of Directors: Maurizio Carrara (Chair.); Maria Cristina Molinari, Paolo Cornetta (Vice-Chair.).

Principal Staff: Gen. Man. Anna Pace.

Address: Via San Protaso 3, 20121 Milan.

Telephone: (02) 88623071; **Fax:** (02) 88623937; **Internet:** www.unicreditfoundation.org; **e-mail:** info@unicreditfoundation.org.

Jamaica

FOUNDATIONS, TRUSTS AND NON-PROFIT ORGANIZATIONS

Culture, Health, Arts, Sports and Education Fund—CHASE

Established in 2003 to administer, manage and distribute monetary contributions from the Jamaican lottery companies.

Activities: Operates in four principal areas in Jamaica: sports development; early childhood education; health; and arts and culture. The Fund also administers the annual Courtney Walsh Award, worth US $500,000, given in recognition of exemplary qualities in male or female Jamaican nationals between 18 to 40 years of age who have represented Jamaica at senior level in the field of sports.

Geographical Area of Activity: Jamaica.

Publications: Annual Report.

Finance: Annual income US $1,328,832, expenditure $1,012,690 (31 March 2012).

Board of Directors: Dr Carlton E. Davis (Chair.); Tasha Manley (Sec.).

Principal Staff: CEO W. Billy Heaven.

Address: 52–60 Grenada Cresc., Kingston 5.

Telephone: 908-4134; **Fax:** 908-4139; **Internet:** www.chase.org.jm; **e-mail:** chase12@cwjamaica.com.

Environmental Foundation of Jamaica

Established in 1993 under a formal agreement between the Governments of Jamaica and the USA as an independent foundation.

Activities: Promotes, implements and funds activities that conserve the natural resources and the environment of Jamaica, and address child welfare and development.

Geographical Area of Activity: Jamaica.

Publications: Annual Report; public lecture booklets (annually); brochures.

Finance: Uses the proceeds from a debt-swap arrangement. Net current funds US $134,747,000 (31 July 2013).

Board of Directors: Prof. Dale Webber (Chair.); Stephen Hodges (Vice-Chair.); Albert Walker (Treas.); Richard Troupe (Sec.).

Principal Staff: CEO Karen McDonald Gayle.

Address: 1B Norwood Ave, Kingston 5.

Telephone: 960-6744; **Fax:** 920-8999; **Internet:** www.efj.org.jm; **e-mail:** support@efj.org.jm.

Sandals Foundation

Established in 2009 as the philanthropic arm of Sandals Resorts International.

Activities: Supports sustainable projects in education, conservation of the environment and community development.

Geographical Area of Activity: Caribbean.

Publications: Annual Report.

Finance: Annual income US $12,314,930, expenditure $11,241,043 (31 March 2013).

Board of Directors: Adam Stewart (Pres.).

Principal Staff: Dir of Programmes Heidi Clarke.

Address: 5 Kent Ave, Montego Bay.

Internet: www.sandalsfoundation.org; **e-mail:** foundation@grp.sandals.com.

Japan

FOUNDATION CENTRES AND CO-ORDINATING BODIES

JANIC—Japanese NGO Center for International Co-operation

Established in 1987 to foster closer relations among Japanese NGOs working in international co-operation; to provide services for the development of NGOs; to encourage networking between domestic and international NGOs and related organizations; to encourage dialogue between NGOs and other sectors of society; to deepen Japanese public understanding of and support for the activities of NGOs; and to conduct research on NGOs and international co-operation.

Activities: Runs courses and training programmes; carries out research; hosts meetings; offers advisory services; conducts lobbying and networking activities aimed at the Japanese Government and business; promotes educational activities, including the 'Global Citizenship Education Caravan' held throughout Japan; and issues publications. Maintains a library and database on NGOs. The Center comprises 96 member organizations.

Geographical Area of Activity: Japan.

Restrictions: Does not make grants.

Publications: Annual Report; *Directory of Japanese NGOs Concerned with International Co-operation*; *NGO Correspondence: Global Citizens* (newsletter in Japanese, 10 a year); *Kokoro* (quarterly newsletter, in English); *Directory of Non-governmental Organizations in Japan 1994*; *Creating Together a New Partnership—NGO Support Schemes Contributing to People's Self-Reliance*; other publications on NGOs; conference and symposia reports.

Finance: Annual revenue ¥185,694,889, expenditure ¥175,761,088 (31 March 2014).

Board of Trustees: Masaaki Ohashi (Chair.); Kazuo Tsurumi, Hiroshi Taniyama, Akiko Mera (Vice-Chair.).

Principal Staff: Sec.-Gen. Masashi Yamaguchi.

Address: Avaco Bldg, 2-3-18 Nishiwaseda, 5th Floor, Shinjuku-ku, Tokyo 169-0051.

Telephone: (3) 5292-2911; **Fax:** (3) 5292-2912; **Internet:** www.janic.org; **e-mail:** global-citizen@janic.org.

Japan Association of Charitable Organizations—JACO

Established in 1972 by Masao Watanabe to represent the charity sector in Japan.

Activities: Offers information, advice and support to the charity sector in Japan. The Association represents around 1,500 organizations. Major activities include: consulting services, training programmes, public relations and publications, exchange of information, study and research, and advocacy.

Geographical Area of Activity: Japan.

Publications: *Koueki Houjin* (monthly magazine, in Japanese); books on management, commentaries on accounting standards, tax theories and practice, glossary of technical terms.

Finance: Annual revenue ¥217,170,000, expenditure ¥229,690,000 (31 March 2012).

Board of Directors: Tatsuo Ohta (Pres. and CEO).

Principal Staff: Exec. Dir and Sec.-Gen. Toshihiro Kanazawa; Exec. Dir Katuji Suzuki.

Address: 2-27-15 Hon-komagome, Bunkyo-ku, Tokyo 113-0021.

Telephone: (3) 3945-1017; **Fax:** (3) 3945-1267; **Internet:** www.kohokyo.or.jp; **e-mail:** shiraishi@kohokyo.or.jp.

Japan Foundation Center

Founded in 1985 to disseminate information on foundations in Japan, provide assistance to member foundations, and publicize the role and activities of grantmaking foundations.

Activities: Compiles and publishes information on the activities of grantmaking foundations in Japan; conducts research and publishes the results; maintains a library of publications relating to Japanese and overseas foundations; and sponsors seminars, lectures and symposia.

Geographical Area of Activity: Japan.

Restrictions: No direct grantmaking to individuals or organizations.

Publications: *JFC Views* (in Japanese); *Directory of Grantmaking Foundations* (Japanese and English); *Summary of Current Grant Awards* (in Japanese); *Guide to Private Grant Sources* (in Japanese).

Finance: Total net assets ¥464,154,373 (31 March 2014).

Principal Staff: Pres. Yamaoka Yoshinori; Sec.-Gen and Exec. Dir Akira Tanaka.

Address: 1-26-9 Shinjuku, Believe Shinjuku Bldg, 4th Floor, Tokyo 160-0022.

Telephone: (3) 3350-1857; **Fax:** (3) 3350-1858; **Internet:** www.jfc.or.jp; **e-mail:** pref@jfc.or.jp.

JEN

Established in 1994 as Japan Emergency NGOs, a network of Japanese relief organizations operating internationally to give emergency relief.

Activities: Operates internationally in the fields of assistance to less-developed countries, especially in the area of disaster relief. The organization works with local people, promoting self-reliance, with a focus on peoples and regions that receive little attention. Projects cover emergency supplies, reconstruction and rehabilitation, education, health and social welfare. The organization had 434 members in 2010.

Geographical Area of Activity: Afghanistan, Iraq, Haiti, Japan (Tohoku), Jordan, Pakistan, South Sudan, Sri Lanka.

Publications: Annual Report; newsletter.

Finance: Annual income ¥1,080.9m., expenditure ¥1,197.1m. (31 Dec. 2013).

Trustees: Kenji Yoshida, Yukiko Kuroda (Co-Pres); Takeshi Hayasaka (Vice-Pres.).

Principal Staff: Sec.-Gen. Keiko Kiyama.

Address: 2-16, Agebacho, Daini Tobundo Bldg, 7th Floor, Shinjuku-ku, Tokyo 162-0824.

Telephone: (3) 5225-9352; **Fax:** (3) 5225-9357; **Internet:** www.jen-npo.org; **e-mail:** info@jen-npo.org.

FOUNDATIONS, TRUSTS AND NON-PROFIT ORGANIZATIONS

Asahi Glass Foundation

Established in 1933 as the Asahi Foundation for Chemical Industry Promotion, by the Asahi Glass Company Ltd; present name adopted in 1990.

Activities: Funds for research and commendation programmes aimed at contributing to solving the major issues facing mankind. Research grants are made in the fields of life sciences, information sciences, the environment, energy, humanity and the global environment. The Foundation also provides funding for overseas research at Chulalongkorn University, Thailand, and the Institut Teknologi Bandung, Indonesia. As part of its commendation programmes, since 1992 the Foundation has presented the Blue Planet Prize, an international annual award given in recognition of individuals and organizations that have made major contributions to solving global environmental problems. Each year two recipients are chosen from a list of candidates put forward by nominators from Japan and overseas; each winner receives a certificate of merit, a commemorative trophy, and a supplementary award of ¥50m.

Geographical Area of Activity: International.

Restrictions: Research grants generally made to university researchers in Japan.

Publications: Annual Report; *Conditions for Survival* (in Chinese, Japanese and Korean), *Results of the Questionnaire on Environmental Problems* and *The Survival of Humankind* (annually); *af News* (newsletter, 2 a year); *Blue Planet Prize Commemorative Lectures* (annually); Annual Report; research reports; brochure (updated annually).

Finance: Annual income ¥907,757,966, expenditure ¥777,570,377 (28 Feb. 2014).

Board of Directors and Councillors: Tetsuji Tanaka (Chair.).

Principal Staff: CEO Kunihiko Adachi Sec.-Gen. Tetsuro Yasuda; Deputy Sec.-Gen. Koji Kogawa.

Address: 2nd Floor, Science Plaza, 5-3 Yonbancho, Chiyoda-ku, Tokyo 102-0081.

Telephone: (3) 5275-0620; **Fax:** (3) 5275-0871; **Internet:** www.af-info.or.jp; **e-mail:** post@af-info.or.jp.

Asahi Group Arts Foundation (Asahi Biiru Geijutsu Bunka Zaidan)

Founded in 1989 by Asahi Breweries Ltd to contribute to the enhancement of Japanese culture by awarding grants for artistic and cultural activities, including fine arts and music, and by extending financial support for international exchange in artistic and cultural activities.

Activities: Grants-in-aid are made towards fine arts exhibitions and music concerts in Japan, sponsorship and scholarships are awarded to foreign students studying the arts at higher education institutions in Japan, and scholarships are awarded to Japanese students studying the arts abroad (sponsorship is only provided for exhibitions and concerts organized in Japan on their return). The Foundation also awards prizes and manages the Asahi Beer Oyamazaki Villa Museum of Art in Kyoto Oyamazaki.

Geographical Area of Activity: Japan.

Restrictions: Grants are given only for events held in Japan.

Publications: *Guide to the Foundation; Mécénat* (quarterly newsletter).

Board of Directors: Naoki Izumiya (Chair.).

Principal Staff: Man. Takeda Yoshinobu.

Address: 23-1 Azumabashi 1-chome, Sumida-ku, Tokyo 130-8602.

Telephone: (3) 5608-5202; **Fax:** (3) 5608-5152; **Internet:** www.asahigroup-foundation.com.

Asia Africa International Voluntary Foundation—AIV

Founded in 1989.

Activities: Operates in the fields of aid to less-developed countries, education, and medicine and health, through the provision of technical and financial assistance to encourage appropriate and sustainable development in less-developed countries. The Foundation promotes co-operation between Japan and developing countries. Its current activities focus on education and NGO support in India and Uganda.

Geographical Area of Activity: Asia and Africa.

Publications: Activity Report; *Tsubosaka Tsubokokoro-kai* (newsletter).

Finance: Annual revenue ¥7,642,695 (2013).

Board of Directors: Shoshu Hiraoka (Chair./Pres.); Tokiwa Katsunori (Vice-Pres.).

Address: 3 Tsubosaka Takatori-cho, Takaichi-gun, Nara 635-0102.

Telephone: (7) 4452-3172; **Fax:** (7) 4452-3835; **Internet:** www.aivjapan.org; **e-mail:** aivjapan@hotmail.com.

Asia Crime Prevention Foundation—ACPF

Founded in 1982 by Atsushi Nagashima to promote effective measures for the prevention of crime and for the treatment of offenders in the Asian, Pacific, African, and Central and South American regions.

Activities: Organizes lectures on crime prevention and the treatment of offenders; carries out research; provides grants to institutions and individuals for relevant study programmes. The Foundation has members in 93 countries, and has general consultative status with the UN. It has nine offices in Japan and international offices in Bangladesh, the People's Republic of China, Fiji, India, Indonesia, Kenya, the Republic of Korea, Malaysia, Mongolia, Nepal, Pakistan, the Philippines, the Solomon Islands, Sri Lanka, Thailand, Tonga and Uganda.

Geographical Area of Activity: International.

Publications: *ACPF Today*; newsletter.

Finance: The Foundation is financed by interest on capital, membership fees and donations from public and private sources. Total assets ¥87,012,312 (31 March 2014).

Board of Directors: Taichi Sakaiya (Chair.).

Principal Staff: Pres. Masaharu Hino; Vice-Pres. Kunihiro Matsuo; Sec.-Gen. Kunihiro Horiuchi.

Address: ACPF Secretariat, 1-26, Harumi-cho, Fuchu-shi, Tokyo 183-0057.

Telephone: (4) 2334-6639; **Fax:** (4) 2334-3461; **Internet:** www.acpf.org; **e-mail:** info@acpf.org.

Asia/Pacific Cultural Centre for UNESCO—ACCU

Founded in 1971 to promote mutual understanding and cultural co-operation among peoples in the Asia-Pacific region through the implementation of various programmes in the fields of culture, book development and literacy promotion.

Activities: Operates regionally in Asia and the Pacific in the fields of culture, book development and literacy, through joint programmes of UNESCO member states in the region for production of low-priced quality books for children, materials such as posters, booklets and video cassettes for literates in rural areas, audio-visual materials; training of cultural and book personnel in the region; publications (see below); special programmes (annual photography contest and travelling exhibition, biennial Noma Concours for illustrators of children's picture books in developing countries); Asia/Pacific Programme for Regional Co-operation in Protection of Cultural Heritage and the International Exchange Programme for the Promotion of International Co-operation and Mutual Understanding; and maintenance of the ACCU Library, with emphasis on children's books and school textbooks from Asian countries, as well as UNESCO publications.

Geographical Area of Activity: Asia and the Pacific.

Restrictions: UNESCO member states in Asia-Pacific region.

Publications: *Asian/Pacific Book Development (ABD)* (quarterly); reference materials; meeting reports; brochure.

Finance: Total assets ¥213,908,835 (31 March 2014).

Board of Directors: Fujio Cho (CEO and Chair.).

Principal Staff: Exec. Dir Tetsuo Tamura.

Address: Japan Publishers Bldg, 6 Fukuromachi, Shinjuku-ku, Tokyo 162-8484.

Telephone: (3) 3269-4435; **Fax:** (3) 3269-4510; **Internet:** www.accu.or.jp; **e-mail:** general@accu.or.jp.

Asian Community Trust—ACT

Founded in 1979 to promote social and economic development in Asian communities, and mutual understanding between people in Japan and in neighbouring Asian countries, by assisting activities that contribute to development. Since 2005, the Asian Community Centre 21 (ACC21) has acted as the Trust steering committee and secretariat.

Activities: Provides financial assistance to institutions in South-East and South Asia for specific activities in rural development, education and youth development, health, environment and conservation, and the institutional development of NGOs. The Trust also administers a number of semi-independent trust funds and runs two resource desks in Indonesia and the Philippines. In 2011, the Trust contributed to relief work and funding in the aftermath of the Tohoku earthquake and tsunami in Japan in March.

Geographical Area of Activity: South-East Asia and South Asia.

Publications: Annual Report; *ACT Now* (2 a year).

Finance: Annual revenue ¥78,180,000, expenditure ¥56,500,000 (31 March 2013).

Principal Staff: Chair. Satoshi Mitsuru; Exec. Dir Michio Ito.

Address: Asian Community Center 21, ABK Bldg, 2-12-13 Hon-komagome, Bunkyo-ku, Tokyo 113-8642.

Telephone: (3) 3945-2615; **Fax:** (3) 3945-2692; **Internet:** www.acc21.org/act; **e-mail:** act-info@acc21.org.

Asian Health Institute—AHI

Established in 1980 by Dr Hiromi Kawahara, a member of the Japan Christian Medical Doctors' Association, to promote accessible and affordable health care for marginalized people in Asia through human resource development among NGOs throughout Asia.

Activities: Encourages the formation and maintenance of effective community health care organizations through training. The Institute funds courses to enhance the leadership skills of community-based health workers to develop their own organizations, and work to combat curable diseases in less-developed parts of Asia.

Geographical Area of Activity: Asia.

Restrictions: No grants to individuals or to organizations.

Publications: Annual Report; *Asian Health Institute* (newsletter, 3–4 a year); *Children of Asia* (newsletter for children, 1–2 a year).

Finance: Funded by membership fees and donations. Annual revenue ¥64,831,708, expenditure ¥60,365,386 (2013).

Board of Directors: Michitaro Nakamura (Chair.).

Principal Staff: Gen. Sec. Kagumi Hayashi.

Address: 987-30, Namsan-cho, Komenoki, Minamiyama, Nisshin, Aichi, 470-0111.

Telephone: (561) 73-1950; **Fax:** (561) 73-1990; **Internet:** www.ahi-japan.jp; **e-mail:** info@ahi-japan.jp.

Bridge Asia Japan—BAJ

Established in 1993 as Indochina Co-operation Centre Japan to undertake projects in Myanmar and Viet Nam. Present name adopted in 1994.

Activities: Operates in the areas of aid to less-developed countries, and conservation and the environment, in Myanmar and Viet Nam, through self-conducted projects, especially to assist vulnerable people, including refugees, disabled people, and women and children. Projects include supporting education and school construction, water and sanitation, afforestation and training. Nationally, the organization supports exchanges and study tours, and issues publications. Has offices in Myanmar and Viet Nam.

Geographical Area of Activity: Myanmar and Viet Nam.

Publications: Annual Report; *BAJ Newsletter* (2 a month).

Finance: Receives funding from donations, grants, public funding and membership fees. Annual revenue ¥351,649,436, expenditure ¥354,274,325 (31 Dec. 2013).

Principal Staff: Pres. Etsuko Nemoto.

Address: Shintoshin Mansion Rm 303, 3-48-21 Honmachi, Shibuya-ku, Tokyo 151-0071.

Telephone: (3) 3372-9777; **Fax:** (3) 5351-2395; **Internet:** www.baj-npo.org; **e-mail:** info@baj-npo.org.

Defense of Green Earth Foundation—DGEF

Founded in 1982 to promote the protection of the environment.

Activities: Supports projects to protect the environment, including afforestation projects, the protection of the Oze swamp, and attempts to reduce desertification; sponsors environmental research and surveys; aims to increase awareness of environmental issues.

Geographical Area of Activity: Japan, Tanzania, People's Republic of China.

Publications: *Green Earth* (quarterly newspaper); *Environmental Issues Research Report* (annually).

Finance: Annual revenue ¥33,961,000, expenditure ¥40,033,000 (31 March 2013).

Principal Staff: Chair. Oishi Mashamitsu.

Address: 2-6-16 Shinkawa, Chuo-ku, Tokyo 104-0033.

Telephone: (3) 3297-5505; **Fax:** (3) 3297-5507; **Internet:** green-earth-japan.net; **e-mail:** defense@green.email.ne.jp.

GEA—Global Environmental Action

Established in 1991 to promote sustainable development and help solve global environmental problems.

Activities: Operates internationally in the field of conservation and the environment, through organizing conferences and disseminating the results of conferences. Initiatives include an information resource for environmental NGOs in developing countries. In 2003, the organization launched the Virtual Globe Project, which supports NGOs that are engaged in environmental conservation activities.

Geographical Area of Activity: International.

Advisory Committee: Toshiki Kaifu (Chair.).

Principal Staff: Chair. Juro Saito; Deputy Chair. Mikio Aoki; Dir-Gen. Wakako Hironaka.

Address: 404c Tokyo Sakurada Bldg, 1-1-3 Nishishinbashi, Minato-ku, Tokyo 105-0003.

Telephone: (3) 3503-7484; **Fax:** (3) 3503-6953; **Internet:** www.gea.or.jp; **e-mail:** gea@gea.or.jp.

Global Voluntary Service—GVS

Established in 1992 by Teiko Inabata to foster volunteer activity in developing nations, for the improvement of living conditions, expertise and for the protection of the environment.

Activities: Operates in less-developed countries in the areas of rural and agricultural development, education, training, medical assistance, environmental protection and welfare for underprivileged women. The organization does this through developmental education, medical missions, health programmes, vocational training, information provision, exchange of personnel, collaboration with other NGOs, exhibitions, study tours, work camps and seminars. Maintains an office in Tokyo and overseas offices in Manila.

Geographical Area of Activity: Japan and less-developed countries, in particular the Democratic Republic of the Congo, Kenya, Lebanon and the Philippines.

Publications: Annual Report; brochures and audio-visual materials.

Principal Staff: Pres. Teiko Inabata; Man. Dir Seizo Inabata.

Address: 12–6 Funato-cho, Ashiya City, Hyogo 659-0093.

Telephone: (7) 9734-0078; **Fax:** (7) 9734-1061; **Internet:** www.gvs.jp; **e-mail:** gvs@cc.mbn.or.jp.

The Hitachi Scholarship Foundation

Set up in 1984 under the aegis of electrical goods manufacturer Hitachi Ltd to promote cultural, academic and educational exchange between Japan and the South-East Asian countries.

Activities: Aims to develop human resources in South-East Asian universities to advance education, co-operation and collaboration among the universities in Japan and South-East Asia. The Foundation also aims to develop a co-operative network among university personnel in Japan and South-East Asian countries and better cultural understanding. It supports and finances promising research in Japan carried out by successful young faculty members and graduates from universities of Singapore, Indonesia, Malaysia, Thailand and the Philippines. Awards scholarships, fellowships and grants.

Geographical Area of Activity: South-East Asia.

Restrictions: No grants to individuals.

Finance: Annual revenue ¥92,770,840, expenditure ¥126,656,000 (31 March 2014).

Board of Trustees: Masahide Tanigaki (Chair.).

Principal Staff: Representative Dir Tanigaki Katsuhide.

Address: Marunouchi Center Bldg, 12th Floor, 1-6-1, Marunouchi, Chiyoda-ku, Tokyo 100-8220.

Telephone: (3) 3257-0853; **Fax:** (3) 3257-0854; **Internet:** www.hitachi-zaidan.org/global/scholarship; **e-mail:** scholarship@hdg.hitachi.co.jp.

Honda Foundation

Founded in 1977 by Soichiro Honda to support the development of environmentally-friendly technology.

Activities: Supports annual international symposia, seminars and workshops at which experts from all countries gather to discuss scientific and technological problems inherent in modern civilization with a view to creating a better society. Awards the annual Honda Prize of ¥10m. to an individual or organization, irrespective of nationality, for a distinguished achievement in 'eco-technology'. Launched the YES Award programme in Viet Nam in 2006 to foster students who are helping to develop science and eco-technology for the future; the programme was subsequently extended to India, Cambodia, Laos and Myanmar.

Geographical Area of Activity: International.

Publications: Annual Report.

Finance: Total assets ¥5,673m. (31 March 2014).

Board of Directors: Hiroto Ishida (Pres.); Kunio Nakajima (Vice-Pres.).

Principal Staff: Man. Dir Masataka Yamamoto.

Address: 2nd Floor, Honda Yaesu Bldg, 6-20 Yaesu 2-chome, Chuo-ku, Tokyo 104-0028.

Telephone: (3) 3274-5125; **Fax:** (3) 3274-5103; **Internet:** www.hondafoundation.jp; **e-mail:** h_info@hondafoundation.jp.

Hoso Bunka Foundation, Inc—HBF

Founded in 1974 by the Japan Broadcasting Corpn—NHK to contribute to the advancement of broadcasting and the dissemination of culture through broadcasting.

Activities: Provides financial assistance for research in broadcasting technology; for the development of receiving equipment; for international co-operation in broadcasting; and for legal, socio-economic and cultural studies related to broadcasting. The Foundation awards the annual HBF Prizes for outstanding domestic television and radio programmes and for broadcasting technology development.

Geographical Area of Activity: International.

Restrictions: Grants only to professional projects related to broadcasting culture.

Publications: *HBF* (annually, in Japanese); Annual Research Report (in Japanese); activity report (3 a year, in Japanese); activity report in English available on website.

Finance: Annual revenue ¥349,347,099, expenditure ¥237,019,370 (31 March 2014).

Board of Directors: Prof. Hiroshi Shiono (Pres.).

Principal Staff: Gen. Man. Dir Toshiki Sakimoto.

Address: Kyodo Bldg, 5th Floor, 41-1 Udagawa-cho, Shibuya-ku, Tokyo 150-0042.

Telephone: (3) 3464-3131; **Fax:** (3) 3770-7239; **Internet:** www.hbf.or.jp; **e-mail:** inform@hbf.or.jp.

IATSS—International Association of Traffic and Safety Sciences

Founded in 1974 by Soichiro Honda and Takeo Fujisawa to develop the transportation system.

Activities: Operates nationally and internationally in conducting research; collecting and applying data; sponsoring domestic and international conferences and meetings; publishing the results of research; and giving annual IATSS Dissertation, Literature and Achievement Awards to (respectively) the author of the best paper appearing in the *IATSS Review and IATSS Research*, for outstanding literary works concerning the realization of an ideal mobile society, and to the individual and organization making the most useful contribution to mobile society. The IATSS Forum provides the opportunity for young people from the countries of South-East Asia to learn together.

Geographical Area of Activity: International.

Publications: *IATSS Forum Reviews and Reports* (2 a year); *IATSS Research* (2 a year, in English); *IATSS Review* (quarterly, in Japanese); *Statistics-Road Accidents Japan* (abridged edn, annually, in English).

Principal Staff: Chair. Yasuhei Oguchi; Vice-Chair. Hiroshi Oyama; Man. Dir Hiroshi Ishizuki; Exec. Dir Kaji Sumitaka.

Address: 2-6-20, Yaesu, Chuo-ku, Tokyo 104-0028.

Telephone: (3) 3273-7884; **Fax:** (3) 3272-7054; **Internet:** www.iatss.or.jp; **e-mail:** mail@iatss.or.jp.

Institute of Developing Economies/Japan External Trade Organization—IDE-JETRO

Established in 1958 for basic and comprehensive research on economic and related affairs in developing countries to contribute to the improvement of economic co-operation and trade relations between Japan and these countries; reorganized in 1960 as a semi-governmental body. In 1998, the Institute merged with the Japan External Trade Organization (JETRO), an Incorporated Administrative Agency under the supervision of the Ministry of Economy, Trade and Industry.

Activities: Operates in Asia, the Middle East, Africa and Latin America with various regional organizations. The Institute conducts its own research projects on about 50 topics annually, covering various aspects of development, economic co-operation and statistical analysis; research is carried out by the Institute's own staff, with the co-operation of outside experts. It also runs a Joint Research Programme for joint studies with scholars in developing countries, and a Visiting Research Fellows Programme, under which foreign researchers or experts are invited to work at the Institute. Every year about 150 researchers are sent overseas for up to 30 days to conduct field surveys, and 34 research staff are sent abroad for two years. The Institute also collects and compiles statistical data, and maintains a library. Makes awards in recognition of outstanding publications. It holds international symposia, and conducts about 50 seminars and lectures a year in various parts of Japan to inform the public on development issues.

Geographical Area of Activity: Asia, Middle East, Central Asia, Africa and Latin America.

Publications: Annual Report; *The Developing Economies* (quarterly, in English); *Ajia Keizai* (Asian Economies, monthly); *Ajiken warudo torendo* (Asian World Trends, monthly); *Yearbook of Asian Affairs* (in Japanese); *The Contemporary Middle East* (in Japanese); *Latin America Report* (2 a year, in Japanese); *Africa Report* (2 a year, in Japanese); *Development Perspective Series;* occasional papers, symposium proceedings, statistical data, bibliographies and research reports.

Finance: Annual income ¥3,206.9m., expenditure ¥3,206.9m. (2014).

Principal Staff: Pres. Takashi Shiraishi.

Address: 3-2-2 Wakaba, Mihama-ku, Chiba-shi, Chiba 261-8545.

Telephone: (4) 3299-9500; **Fax:** (4) 3299-9724; **Internet:** www.ide.go.jp; **e-mail:** info@ide.go.jp.

The Institute of Energy Economics, Japan—IEEJ

Founded in 1966 by the energy industry to conduct research and studies that will contribute towards the framing of Japan's energy policy and towards the business activities of the energy industries, through an extensive collection of information and data on the world energy situation and the energy policy in major countries, and through their objective and positive analysis.

Activities: Operates nationally and internationally in the fields of economic affairs, the conservation of natural resources and climate change, through self-conducted programmes, research, conferences, courses, publications and lectures. Current projects include a long- and mid-term forecast of the demand and supply of energy in Japan; an analysis of the flow of the world's and Asia's crude petroleum and natural gas market, and an evaluation of crude petroleum and natural gas in the Japanese market; an analysis of energy-related technologies, including nuclear, renewable energy and clean coal technology; and an analysis of the relationship between economic activity and energy. A number of researchers are sent abroad each year to obtain first-hand information on energy and the environment, or to attend international conferences; several others are also sent to research institutes abroad under exchange programmes. The Institute established the affiliated Oil Information Centre in 1981, the Asia Pacific Energy Resource Centre in 1996 and the Green Energy Certification Centre in 2008, all of which carry out research into energy and environmental issues.

Geographical Area of Activity: Japan.

Publications: *IEEJ Energy Journal* (quarterly, in English); *EDMC Handbook of Energy & Economic Statistics in Japan*; *EDMC Energy Trend* (monthly, in Japanese); *Energy Economics* (6 a year, in Japanese).

Finance: Annual revenue ¥2,803,407,165, expenditure ¥2,853,939,815 (31 March 2012).

Principal Staff: Chair. and CEO Masakazu Toyoda; Sr Man. Dir and COO Tsuyoshi Otani.

Address: Inui Bldg, Kachidoki, 10th and 11th Floors, 13-1, Kachidoki 1-chome, Chuo-ku, Tokyo 104-0054.

Telephone: (3) 5547-0211; **Fax:** (3) 5547-0223; **Internet:** eneken.ieej.or.jp/en.

International Development Center of Japan

Founded in 1971 by Toshiwo Doko and Saburo Okita to assist the advancement of the economic growth of developing countries by promoting Japanese development co-operation, and by contributing to the efforts of national and international organizations.

Activities: Organizes development training programmes (some of which are open to participants from developing nations) in, for example, development economics, project analysis, project leaders' training and language and cultural orientation. The Center conducts basic research on problems of economic development, and undertakes research and surveys commissioned by other organizations. It sponsors international conferences, accepts overseas research associates, and sends Japanese scholars (five or six a year) abroad for study connected with development problems.

Geographical Area of Activity: International.

Publications: Annual Report; *IDC Forum* (2 a year); regular series of working papers; occasional publications.

Finance: Annual revenue ¥1,651,222,000, expenditure ¥1,630,427,000 (31 March 2010).

Board of Directors: Masaji Shinagawa (Chair.).

Principal Staff: Pres. Masaoki Takeuchi.

Address: Shinagawa Crystal Square 12th Floor, 1-6-41 Konan, Minato-ku, Tokyo 108-0075.

Telephone: (3) 6718-5931; **Fax:** (3) 6718-1651; **Internet:** www.idcj.or.jp; **e-mail:** general_dep@idcj.or.jp.

International Lake Environment Committee Foundation

Founded in 1986 by the Shiga Prefectural Government to promote the environmentally sound management of the world's lakes and reservoirs; given legal status in 1987.

Activities: Operates nationally and internationally in the fields of aid to less-developed countries and conservation and the environment, through self-conducted programmes, research, conferences, training courses and publications. The Foundation's major activities include collecting and organizing data on the condition of lakes throughout the world; organizing training seminars and workshops on development issues and lake environment conservation in developing countries; promoting lake environment management; and providing support for the UN Environment Programme's International Environmental Technology Centre. Also maintains a database surveying the condition of the world's lakes and awards the annual Biwako Prize for Ecology.

Geographical Area of Activity: International.

Publications: *ILEC Newsletter* (3 a year, in Japanese and English); *Lakes and Reservoirs: Research and Management* (quarterly journal); surveys and guidelines on lake management and workshop reports; *Lake Basin Management Initiative*; *World Lake Vision*.

Principal Staff: Dir-Gen. Hironori Hamanaka; Deputy Dir-Gen. Masahisa Nakamura; Sec.-Gen. Shigekazu Ichiki.

Address: 1091 Oroshimo-cho, Kusatsu-shi, Shiga 525-0001.

Telephone: (7) 7568-4567; **Fax:** (7) 7568-4568; **Internet:** www.ilec.or.jp; **e-mail:** infoilec@ilec.or.jp.

The International Movement against All Forms of Discrimination and Racism—IMADR

An international, not-for-profit NGO founded in 1988 by the Burakumin in Japan, one of Japan's largest minority groups, to serve the cause of human rights through elimination of racism and discrimination, establishing international solidarity among minorities subjected to discrimination, and enhancing the international human rights system.

Activities: Focuses on eliminating discrimination based on both race and gender. Activities include developing grassroots movements; building links between minority groups to promote solidarity and support; and building awareness of the adverse effects of discrimination on society through participation in and organization of regional, local and international events. The organization also carries out research to assist national and international advocacy against discrimination; partners with academic institutions and NGOs to sponsor joint action/research projects on exploitative migration and trafficking of women and children; promotes networking among minority groups through the Internet and publications; conducts campaigns advocating against discrimination; and addresses discrimination issues at major world conferences and UN meetings. IMADR has regional committees and partners in Europe, North, Central and South America, and Asia, and maintains a UN liaison office in Geneva, Switzerland.

Geographical Area of Activity: Worldwide.

Restrictions: Grants only to specific organizations that are in partnership with IMADR.

Publications: *Connect* (quarterly newsletter); *Peoples for Human Rights* (journal); *ICERD: A Guide for NGOs*.

Board of Directors: Nimalka Fernando (Pres.); Bernadette Hétier, Kinhide Mushakoji, Mario Jorge Yutzis (Vice-Pres).

Principal Staff: Sec.-Gen. Yuriko Hara; Under-Sec.-Gen. Megumi Komori.

Address: 6th Floor, 1-7-1, Irifune, Chuo-ku, Tokyo 104-0042.

Telephone: (3) 6280-3100; **Fax:** (3) 6280-3102; **Internet:** www
.imadr.org; **e-mail:** imadr@imadr.org.

Ishizaka Foundation

Founded in 1976 to further mutual understanding and friendship between Japan and other countries by cultural and educational interchange.

Activities: Provides scholarships for Japanese undergraduate and graduate students to study abroad, and for foreign (Asian) students enrolled at Japanese universities. The Foundation also sponsors lectures and symposia that contribute to international cultural and educational interchange, and disseminates the proceedings.

Geographical Area of Activity: Brunei, Cambodia, Indonesia, Japan, Laos, Malaysia, Myanmar, Philippines, Singapore, Thailand and Viet Nam.

Finance: Annual revenue ¥51,043,275, expenditure ¥66,473,379 (31 March 2014).

Principal Staff: Pres. Junichi Fujikawa; Exec. Dir Masakazu Kubota.

Address: c/o Keidanren, 1-3-2 Otemachi, Chiyoda-ku, Tokyo 100-8188.

Telephone: (3) 6741-0162; **Fax:** (3) 5255-6233; **Internet:** www
.keidanren.or.jp/japanese/profile/ishizaka/; **e-mail:** kyoikuzaidan@keidanren.or.jp.

Iwatani Naoji Foundation

Founded in 1973 by Naoji Iwatani, President of Iwatani & Co, Ltd, to improve national welfare and promote international mutual understanding by providing assistance for research, development and international exchange in the fields of science and technology.

Activities: Operates nationally through providing grants for research and development projects in science and technology that will result in the improvement of the national welfare, and through giving recognition to those whose work in these fields will make a lasting contribution to Japan. The Foundation also promotes the international exchange of information in science and technology. It presents the annual Iwatani Naoji Memorial Prize for research into gas and energy; and the Iwatani International Scholarships, which are awarded to foreign students from East or South-East Asian countries for postgraduate study in natural science and technology.

Geographical Area of Activity: Grants for East and South-East Asian students (mainly from Japan).

Publications: Annual Report; *Kenkyu Hokokusho* (report on the research results funded by the Foundation, annually, in Japanese).

Finance: Net assets ¥11,285,890,856 (31 Dec. 2013).

Councillors: Fumio Kitamura (Chair.).

Principal Staff: Pres. Saeki Naotaka; Exec. Dir Yukio Komatsu.

Address: 3rd Floor, Building 5, 13-4, Hatchobori 2-chome, Chuo-ku, Tokyo 104-0032.

Telephone: (3) 3552-9960; **Fax:** (3) 3552-9961; **Internet:** www
.iwatani-foundation.or.jp; **e-mail:** information@iwatani
-foundation.or.jp.

Japan Economic Research Institute Inc—JERI

Founded in 1962 to promote the overall development of Japan's economy and to contribute to interchange between nations in economic research and to the making of economic policy at industrial, national and international levels.

Activities: Operates nationally and internationally in the fields of economic affairs and management, including urban and regional development, social infrastructure, energy and industry, through research, international co-operation and dissemination of material. Economic research is carried out by research committees involving experts from industry, government agencies and the academic world. The resulting reports, as well as other up-to-date information on national and international economics, are distributed to members of the Institute and other organizations. Other activities include the organization of conferences, lectures and seminars, as well as playing an advisory role in private finance initiative (PFI) projects.

Geographical Area of Activity: International.

Finance: Total assets ¥1,569m. (31 March 2013).

Principal Staff: Pres. Takashi Ando.

Address: Shin Otemachi Bldg, 3rd Floor, 2-2-1 Otemachi, Chiyoda-ku, Tokyo 100-0004.

Telephone: (3) 6214-4600; **Fax:** (3) 6214-4601; **Internet:** www
.jeri.co.jp; **e-mail:** info@jeri.co.jp.

The Japan Foundation

Founded in 1972 to further international mutual understanding through the promotion of cultural exchange; reorganized in 2003.

Activities: Operates internationally by offering fellowships to overseas scholars, enabling them to conduct research in Japan. Dissertation fellowships are offered to scholars in the social sciences and humanities, and professional fellowships to scholars engaged in studies on Japanese society and culture. Visiting professorships abroad are offered to Japanese professors, enabling them to teach in institutions overseas or to take part in research or conferences connected with Japan. The Foundation promotes Japanese language studies abroad and produces, collects and distributes materials that introduce Japanese culture abroad. It provides funding for cultural exhibitions and the performing arts, organizes lectures and seminars, and supports arts-related and media exchanges (including Special Programs for Japan-Europe Cultural Exchange). The Japan Foundation Information Center, which is based at the Foundation's headquarters in Tokyo, incorporates a library. The Japan Foundation Centre for Global Partnership was established in 1991 to promote relations between Japan and the USA through intellectual exchange and the promotion of mutual understanding. The Foundation maintains overseas offices in Australasia, North, Central and South America, Asia, Africa and Europe, and Japanese Language Centers/Centres for Global Partnership in Australia, Brazil, Indonesia, the Republic of Korea, Malaysia, Thailand, the United Kingdom and the USA; information may also be obtained from Japanese diplomatic missions.

Geographical Area of Activity: Worldwide.

Publications: Annual Report; *Japanese Book News* (quarterly); *Wochi Kochi* (online, 6 a year); *CGP Newsletter* (quarterly); bibliographical series; *Nihongo Kyoiku Tsushin* (journal, online); *Asia Center News* (quarterly); *Japanese-Language Education around the World* (journal); *Bunka Jigyo Tsushin* (newsletter).

Finance: Annual revenue ¥37,563.5m., expenditure ¥16,570.5m. (31 March 2014).

Governing Board: Hiroyasu Ando (Pres.); Eiji Taguchi (Exec. Vice-Pres.).

Principal Staff: Exec. Dir Suzuko Nishihara.

Address: 4-4-1 Yotsuya, Shinjuku-ku, Tokyo 160-0004.

Telephone: (3) 5369-6075; **Fax:** (3) 5369-6044; **Internet:** www
.jpf.go.jp; **e-mail:** jf-toiawase@jpf.go.jp.

Japan Foundation Center for Economic Research— JCER

Founded in 1963 to conduct studies and research on various problems of government finance, money and credit, economy, industry, management and other related subjects at home and abroad; and to promote mutual study and training of its members with the aim of contributing to the economic growth of Japan.

Activities: Conducts research on Japan's economy with particular emphasis on economic forecasting; organizes joint economic research; and undertakes research projects on a contractual basis. The Center sponsors economic study courses, seminars, lectures and symposia, and provides training for junior businesspeople in advanced economics and research. It publishes the results of its research projects and operates a specialized library of 37,500 vols, 861 periodicals and 1,280 statistical sources. At the international level, the Center conducts joint research on specific problems with foreign institutions, organizes lectures and seminars for foreign economists, and sponsors an annual conference to which leading economists from both advanced and developing countries are invited. Study facilities are made available to a limited number of foreign researchers, particularly from Asia. Has approx. 300 institutional members.

Geographical Area of Activity: International.

Publications: Annual Report and financial statement; *Bulletin* (monthly); *Short-term Economic Forecast Series* (quarterly); *International Conference Series*; *Japan Financial Report* (2 a year, in Japanese); *Asia Research Report* (annually, in English); *China Research Report* (annually, in English); *Asian Economic Policy Review* (2 a year, in English).

Board of Directors: Ryoki Sugita (Chair.).

Principal Staff: Pres. Kazumasa Iwata.

Address: NIKKEI Inc. Bldg, 11th Floor, 1-3-7 Otemachi, Chiyoda-ku, Tokyo 100-8066.

Telephone: (3) 6256-7710; **Fax:** (3) 6256-7924; **Internet:** www .jcer.or.jp.

The Japan Foundation Center for Global Partnership—CGP

Established in 1991 inside the Japan Foundation; an independent administrative institution, to promote collaboration between Japan and the USA with the goal of fulfilling shared global responsibilities and contributing to improvements in the world's welfare, and to enhance dialogue and interchange between Japanese and US citizens on a wide range of issues, thereby strengthening mutual understanding and improving bilateral relations.

Activities: Makes institutional grants in three programme areas: intellectual exchange, grassroots exchange and education. In addition, the Center operates the Abe Fellowship for scholars and researchers of the humanities and social sciences, and the NPO Fellowship for mid-career staff members working in Japan's non-profit sector.

Geographical Area of Activity: Japan and the USA.

Restrictions: Supports only projects from Japan or the USA.

Publications: Annual Report (in Japanese and English); newsletter; *NewsOnline*; symposia reports; field surveys; conference papers.

Finance: Funded by investment income and other sources.

Advisory Committee: Kazuo Ogoura (Pres.).

Principal Staff: Dir-Gen. Junichi Chano.

Address: 4-4-1 Yotsuya, Shinjuku-ku, Tokyo 160-0004.

Telephone: (3) 5369-6072; **Fax:** (3) 5369-6042; **Internet:** www .cgp.org; **e-mail:** info@cgp.org.

Japan Heart Foundation

Founded in 1970 to contribute to the improvement of national welfare by providing financial aid for research on heart and blood vessel diseases by educating the public about heart disease prevention, and by co-operating with counterpart organizations in foreign countries.

Activities: Operates nationally and in South-East Asia through providing grants to individuals, groups and research institutes engaged in research into heart and blood vessel diseases and providing finance for the publication of research findings; and internationally through maintaining contact and exchanging information with foreign institutions with similar interests.

Geographical Area of Activity: International, mainly South-East Asia and Japan.

Publications: *Kenko Heart* (monthly).

Finance: Annual revenue ¥1,952,078,579, expenditure ¥1,922,835,040 (31 March 2012).

Principal Staff: Chair. Takuji Shidachi; Vice-Chair. Dr Tsuneaki Sugimoto; Pres. Yoshio Yazaki.

Address: Dai-ichi Mutual Life Insurance Building, 4th Floor, 2-7-1 Nishi-Shinjuku, Shinjuku-ku, Tokyo 163-0704.

Telephone: (3) 3201-0810; **Fax:** (3) 3213-3920; **Internet:** www .jhf.or.jp; **e-mail:** info@jhf.or.jp.

Japan International Volunteer Center—JVC

Established in 1980, originally to assist refugees from Indochina, now an international NGO supporting development.

Activities: Currently operates in nine countries of Asia, Africa and the Middle East (Afghanistan, Cambodia, Palestinian Territories, Iraq, Sudan, Laos, the Democratic People's Republic of Korea, South Africa and Thailand), as well as in Japan, in the fields of aid to less-developed countries, education and agricultural development, through projects in collaboration with local people; also involved in disaster relief operations in Africa and Asia.

Geographical Area of Activity: Africa, Asia and the Middle East.

Finance: Annual revenue ¥387,904,651, expenditure ¥376,515,725 (31 March 2013).

Board of Directors: Hiroshi Taniyama (Pres.); Atsuko Isoda (Vice-Pres.).

Principal Staff: Sec.-Gen. Takatoshi Hasebe.

Address: Creative One Akihabara Bldg, 6th Floor, 5-3-4 Ueno, Taito-ku, Tokyo 110-8605.

Telephone: (3) 3834-2388; **Fax:** (3) 3835-0519; **Internet:** www .ngo-jvc.net; **e-mail:** info@ngo-jvc.net.

Japan Society for the Promotion of Science—JSPS

Founded in 1932 through an endowment granted by Emperor Showa; re-established in 1967 by the Japanese Government to contribute to the advancement of science.

Activities: Operates nationally through providing research fellowships and giving grants for joint research activities among Japanese scientists belonging to different institutions; promoting joint research by industrial concerns and universities; providing information services; publishing scientific works and producing films; and organizing lectures. The Society awards the International Prize for Biology annually to a person judged to have made outstanding scientific achievements in the field of biology. The Society operates internationally in providing research fellowships for overseas scientists, and grants to Japanese scientists for travel abroad; it supports international joint research projects, international research workshops and seminars. It also administers a number of bilateral programmes for scientific co-operation and exchange with various foreign academic institutions. It has overseas liaison offices in the People's Republic of China, Egypt, France, Germany, Kenya, Sweden, Thailand, the United Kingdom and the USA.

Geographical Area of Activity: International.

Publications: *JSPS Brochure*; *JSPS Quarterly*; *Gakujutsu Geppo (Japanese Science Monthly)* (magazine); *Life in Japan for Foreign Researchers*; information resources; scientific publications.

Finance: Approx. 99.8% of funds are provided by the Japanese Government, the rest by private sources. Annual revenue ¥203,329,502,268, expenditure ¥203,110,694,816 (31 March 2012).

Principal Staff: Pres. Dr Yuichiro Anzai; Exec. Dirs Makoto Asashima, Jumpei Watanabe.

Address: Kojimachi Business Center Bldg, 5-3-1 Kojimachi, Chiyoda-ku, Tokyo 102-0083.

Telephone: (3) 3263-1722; **Fax:** (3) 3221-2470; **Internet:** www .jsps.go.jp; **e-mail:** enquire@jsps.org.

JCIE—Japan Center for International Exchange

Founded in 1970 by Tadashi Yamamoto to promote Japan's role in international affairs.

Activities: Operates internationally, specifically in the USA, Europe and the Asia-Pacific region. The Center sponsors exchange and study programmes, conducts comparative studies of public policy in Japan and the USA, organizes seminars and conferences, conducts research into all areas of policy development and international relations, examines relations between Japan and the Association of South-East Asian Nations (ASEAN), and encourages philanthropic works through the Asian Community Trust (q.v.). New initiatives include Global ThinkNet, the basis of the Center's research programmes, and CivilNet, a programme to strengthen civil society and philanthropy. In addition, the Center administers a donor-advised fund on behalf of Levi Strauss & Co.

Geographical Area of Activity: USA, Europe and the Asia-Pacific region.

Publications: Annual Report; *Civil Society Monitor* (annual newsletter); *GrassNet* (online magazine); *Pacific Asia 2022: Sketching Futures of a Region*; *Asian Reflections on a New World after 9–11*; *A Gender Agenda: Asia-Europe Dialogue*; *JCIE Papers Series*; *Major Power Relations in Northeast Asia*; *Guidance for Governance*; *Asia Pacific Security Outlook 2005*; *The Third Force: the Rise of Transnational Civil Society*; *Governance and Civil Society in a Global Age*; *New Perspectives on US-Japan Relations*; *Philanthropy and Reconciliation*; *East Asian Regional Response to HIV/AIDS, Tuberculosis, and Malaria*; *Fighting a Rising Tide*; *ASEM in its Tenth Year*; *New Challenges, New Approaches: Regional Security Cooperation in East Asia*; *A Pacific Nation: Perspectives on the US Role in an East Asia Community*; *Report on the New Shimoda Conference: Revitalizing Japan-US Strategic Partnership for a Changing World*; *Reinvigorating US-Japan Policy Dialogue and Study*.

Board of Directors: Kunitake Ando (Hon. Chair.); Hideko Katsumata (Exec. Dir and COO); Satoko Itoh, Toshihiro Menju (Man. Dirs and Chief Programme Officers).

Principal Staff: Pres. and CEO Akio Okawara.

Address: 4-9-17 Minami Azabu, Minato-ku, Tokyo 106-0047.

Telephone: (3) 3446-7781; **Fax:** (3) 3443-7580; **Internet:** www.jcie.or.jp; **e-mail:** admin@jcie.or.jp.

JIIA—Japan Institute of International Affairs
(Nihon Kokusai Mondai Kenkyusho)

Founded in 1959 by Shigeru Yoshida, the late Prime Minister, as a national institution authorized by the Ministry of Foreign Affairs to promote studies on international affairs and foreign policy; to encourage new thinking on major foreign policy issues; to give information on international affairs and foreign policy to its members; to promote wider public understanding of international affairs and foreign policy issues; to provide a forum for discussion on these subjects; and to exchange information with institutions abroad.

Activities: Operates in the field of international affairs mainly through research and publications, and through international conferences and seminars. Studies are conducted on the former USSR and Eastern European countries (by the Center for Soviet Studies, established within the Institute in 1984), arms control and disarmament, international organizations, South-East Asia and the People's Republic of China. The Center for Asia-Pacific Studies (f. 1987), conducts research relating to Japan's Asia-Pacific neighbours. Research at the Center for American Studies (f. 1989), concentrates on US current affairs. In 1993, two centres were established: the European Studies Center, which conducts research on Western Europe and the Middle East, and the Global Issue Section, which is responsible for research on human rights, nuclear proliferation, the UN and environmental issues. The Center for the Promotion of Disarmament and Non-Proliferation was established in 1996. The Institute maintains a library of 6,200 books and more than 600 periodicals, and an online database of organizations working for conflict prevention in the Asia-Pacific region. It has around 150 corporate members and 800 individual members.

Geographical Area of Activity: Japan.

Publications: *Kokusai Mondai* (International Affairs) (monthly, in Japanese); *Shoten (Focus)* (newsletter, 10 times a year); books; policy reports; brochure.

Finance: Primary funding sources are public and private research contracts, corporate and individual membership fees, donations and publication sales. Annual revenue ¥697,206,000, expenditure ¥703,440,000 (31 March 2014).

Board of Trustees: Taizo Nishimuro (Chair.); Shigemitsu Miki, Akishige Okada, Yukio Satoh (Vice-Chair.).

Principal Staff: Pres. and Dir-Gen. Yoshiji Nogami; Exec. Dir Tetsuo Takagi.

Address: Toranomon Mitsui Bldg, 3rd Floor, 3-8-1 Kasumigaseki, Chiyoda-ku, Tokyo 100-0013.

Telephone: (3) 3503-7261; **Fax:** (3) 3503-7292; **Internet:** www.jiia.or.jp; **e-mail:** jiiajojho@jiia.or.jp.

Kajima Foundation

Established in 1976 to promote research in science and to encourage international co-operation in science.

Activities: Provides grants to students, who are selected by their university or educational institution, to undertake research, especially in the fields of science and technology; finances visits by overseas researchers as well as long-term (spanning one year) and short-term (spanning three months) studies abroad for Japanese researchers; supports international scientific conferences held in Japan, and joint co-operative research carried out by Japanese and foreign scholars. In 2009, the Foundation provided an overall ¥57m. to a total of 46 projects (including 12 international academic conferences held in Japan).

Geographical Area of Activity: Mainly Japan.

Publications: Annual Report.

Finance: Annual revenue ¥96,835,891, expenditure ¥89,727,908 (31 March 2014).

Principal Staff: Pres. and CEO Kashima Shoichi.

Address: Kajima KI Bldg, 6-5-30 Akasaka, Minato-ku, Tokyo 107-8502.

Telephone: (3) 3584-7418; **Fax:** (3) 5561-2016; **Internet:** www.kajima-f.or.jp; **e-mail:** kajima-gakuzai@ml.kajima.com.

KDDI Foundation

Established in 2009 by the merger of the International Communications Foundation (f. 1988) and KDDI Engineering and Consulting, Inc.

Activities: Aims to contribute to a peaceful, healthy global society using profits from information and communications technology to achieve social, economic and cultural progress. Operates internationally in the area of information, communications and technology, by supporting a range of projects relating to international telecommunications, including grants for research and conferences, social support and cultural activities, and educational programmes. Fellowships are also available for foreign students.

Geographical Area of Activity: Worldwide.

Finance: Annual revenue ¥261,916,649, expenditure ¥256,757,445 (31 March 2014).

Principal Staff: Pres. Yutaka Yasuda.

Address: Garden Air Tower, 3-10-10, Iidabashi, Chiyoda-ku, Tokyo 102-8460.

Fax: (3) 5978-1050; **Internet:** www.kddi-foundation.or.jp; **e-mail:** office@kddi-foundation.or.jp.

Maison Franco-Japonaise

Founded in 1924 by Paul Claudel and Eiichi Shibusawa for the development of French and Japanese cultural and scientific research activities and exchanges.

Activities: Conducts simultaneous studies of the French and Japanese cultures, organizes collections and exhibitions of study materials, meetings and conferences and publishes works relating to these studies. The foundation operates research exchanges between France and Japan.

Geographical Area of Activity: France, Japan and Asia.

Publications: Annual Report; *Ebisu*; *Nichifutsu Bunka*; monographs on diverse subjects; brochure.

Finance: Activities are funded by private Japanese sources and by the French Ministry of Foreign Affairs. Annual budget: revenue ¥160,293,000, expenditure ¥228,717,000 (2015/16).

Board of Directors: Yoïchi Higuchi (Hon. Chair.); Koichiro Matsuura (Chair.); Isao Hirota, Hisao Ikegami (Vice-Chair.).

Principal Staff: Dir Christophe Marquet.

Address: 3-9-25 Ebisu Shibuya-ku, Tokyo 150-0013.

Telephone: (3) 5424-1141; **Fax:** (3) 5424-1200; **Internet:** www .mfjtokyo.or.jp; **e-mail:** bjmfj@mfjtokyo.or.jp.

The Matsumae International Foundation

Established in 1979 by Dr Shigeyoshi Matsumae to make a real contribution to permanent peace worldwide, by deepening the understanding of Japan; and establishing links with other countries through inviting to Japan young research workers of outstanding character, without regard to sex, race, religion, ideology or nationality.

Activities: Operates worldwide in the fields of medicine and health and science and technology, through offering grants to individuals, and scholarships and fellowships, tenable for three to six months. The Foundation prioritizes fields of study in the areas of natural science, engineering and medicine.

Geographical Area of Activity: International.

Restrictions: Non-Japanese applicants must have a doctorate degree, be under 49 years old, have not been to Japan previously and have established professions or positions in their home country.

Publications: *Fellowship Announcement*; *Newsletter*; *Fellowship Directory*; *Fellowship Research Report*.

Board of Directors: Dr Hirohisa Uchida (Chair.).

Address: 4-14-46 Kamiogi, Suginami-ku, Tokyo 167-0043.

Telephone: (3) 3301-7600; **Fax:** (3) 3301-7601; **Internet:** www .mars.dti.ne.jp/mif; **e-mail:** contact2mif@mist.dti.ne.jp.

Moriya Foundation

Founded in 1982 by Kimio Moriya to provide scholarships.

Activities: Offers two-year scholarships to students from Asia who are in postgraduate courses at designated universities in Tokyo, Japan. The designated universities choose and recommend candidates to the Foundation every April. Fields of study are limited to geography, history, education and related cultural sciences.

Geographical Area of Activity: Asia.

Finance: Annual revenue ¥14,016,756, expenditure ¥14,080,833 (31 March 2014).

Principal Staff: Sec. Junichi Takahashi.

Address: c/o Teikoku-Shoin Co Ltd, 3-29 Kanda Jimbo-cho, Chiyoda-ku, Tokyo 101-0051.

Telephone: (3) 3263-7952; **Fax:** (3) 3262-7770; **e-mail:** somu@ teikokushoin.co.jp.

Naito Foundation

Founded in 1969 by Toyoji Naito to extend financial aid to researchers engaged in basic studies on the life sciences, particularly medical, biological, chemical and pharmaceutical studies for the prevention and treatment of human diseases.

Activities: Operates nationally in the fields of education, science and medicine. The Foundation supports researchers in universities and public institutions, Japanese researchers who wish to study abroad and domestic research institutions. It sponsors educational visits to Japan by foreign research workers and supports the publication of reading materials in the life sciences; and arranges exhibitions for the promotion of studies and research in the life sciences, particularly pharmacy. Also awards prizes in recognition of outstanding contributions to the advancement of the life sciences.

Geographical Area of Activity: Mainly Japan.

Publications: Report of operations and financial statement; various books; newsletter.

Finance: Annual revenue ¥708,858,486, expenditure ¥667,496,517 (31 March 2014).

Principal Staff: Pres. Haruo Naito; Exec. Dir Hiroyuki Mitsui.

Address: NKD Bldg, 8th Floor, 3-42-6 Hongo, Bunkyo-ku, Tokyo 113-0033.

Telephone: (3) 3813-3005; **Fax:** (3) 3811-2917; **Internet:** www .naito-f.or.jp; **e-mail:** naitofound@naito-f.or.jp.

Nippon Foundation

Founded in 1962 by Ryoichi Sasakawa for general philanthropic purposes; initially focused on the maritime and shipping sectors.

Activities: Operates nationally in supporting the development of shipbuilding technology, the prevention of marine disasters, and promotion of physical training and social welfare. The Foundation also provides international humanitarian assistance, particularly through the agencies of the UN, such as for programmes conducted by the World Health Organization, the UN High Commissioner for Refugees (UNHCR), the UN Children's Fund (UNICEF) and the UN Environment Programme (UNEP). It also supports the treatment of leprosy in a number of countries (through the Sasakawa Memorial Health Foundation); training in shipbuilding technology in developing countries; and activities aimed at strengthening links between Japan and the USA, the United Kingdom and Scandinavia. In Africa, the Foundation is conducting a project aimed at solving the food-shortage crisis through improved agricultural methods, and in Asia and Central and South America it supports agricultural, crop-research and training programmes. The Foundation has also established various other national and international foundations.

Geographical Area of Activity: International.

Finance: The Foundation draws the funds required to finance its many projects from the proceeds of Japanese motorboat racing. Annual revenue ¥28,746,751,704, expenditure ¥26,753,457,004 (31 March 2012).

Board of Trustees: Yohei Sasakawa (Chair.).

Principal Staff: Pres. Takejyu Ogata.

Address: The Nippon Zaidan Bldg, 1-2-2 Akasaka, Minato-ku, Tokyo 107-8404.

Telephone: (3) 6229-5111; **Fax:** (3) 6229-5110; **Internet:** www .nippon-foundation.or.jp; **e-mail:** cc@ps.nippon-foundation .or.jp.

Niwano Peace Foundation

Established in 1978 to work towards the attainment of world peace and the betterment of culture through promotion of research and other constructive actions, based on religious spirit and serving to promote world peace, in such fields as culture, thought, education and science.

Activities: Offers annual grants for activities on religion, ethics and peace; sponsors symposia and lectures throughout Japan. The Foundation supports counterparts in South Asia in improving human well-being by alleviating poverty in the region; and awards the Niwano Peace Prize annually to an organization or individual contributing to the cause of peace through promotion of inter-religious tolerance.

Geographical Area of Activity: International.

Finance: Annual revenue ¥139,236,524, expenditure ¥111,387,284 (31 March 2014).

Principal Staff: Hon. Chair. Nichiko Niwano; Chair. Hiroshi Niwano; Exec. Dir Yoichi Noguchi.

Address: Shamvilla Catherina 5th Floor, 1-16-9 Shinjuku, Shinjuku-ku, Tokyo 160-0022.

Telephone: (3) 3226-4371; **Fax:** (3) 3226-1835; **Internet:** www .npf.or.jp; **e-mail:** info@npf.or.jp.

OISCA International

Established in 1961 by Dr Yonosuke Nakano to carry out development and reforestation projects in less-developed countries.

Activities: Operates internationally, with an emphasis on the Asia-Pacific region, in the areas of aid to less-developed countries, and conservation and the environment, through sending volunteers to assist indigenous organizations to carry out projects such as tree-planting, the development of agriculture, and the Children's Forest Programme. The organization co-operates with local NGOs and indigenous populations and holds consultative status with the UN Economic and Social Committee (ECOSOC). It has four training centres in Japan. Affiliated organizations exist in more than 100 countries worldwide.

Geographical Area of Activity: Worldwide, but mainly in Asia-Pacific region.

Publications: Annual Report.

Finance: Annual revenue US $7,635,967, expenditure $7,635,967 (31 March 2014).

Administrative Board: Dr Yoshiko Y. Nakano (Pres.); Toshihiro Nakano (Exec. Vice-Pres.); Etsuko Nakano (Vice-Pres.).

Principal Staff: Sec.-Gen. Yasuaki Nagaishi; Deputy Sec.-Gen. Fumio Kitsuki; Asst Sec.-Gen. Aravind Babu.

Address: 17-5 Izumi 2-chome, Suginami-ku, Tokyo 168-0063.

Telephone: (3) 3322-5161; **Fax:** (3) 3324-7111; **Internet:** www .oisca.org; **e-mail:** oisca@oisca.org.

Osaka Community Foundation

Established in 1991.

Activities: Areas of interest include: medical research; education and scholarships; arts and culture; intercultural activities; overseas development aid; environmental protection; community development; disaster relief; and social welfare. Administers the Osaka Community Fund (f. 2006).

Geographical Area of Activity: Principally Osaka and neighbouring areas.

Finance: Annual funds ¥279,915,505 (2013); grants awarded ¥78,181,168 (April 2014).

Board of Directors: Tsutomu Miyagi (Pres.).

Principal Staff: Exec. Dir Yoshiaki Sakaue; Sec.-Gen. Eiichiro Katsuyama.

Address: 2-8 Hommachibashi, Chuo-Ku, Osaka 540-0029.

Telephone: (6) 6944-6260; **Fax:** (6) 6944-6261; **Internet:** www .osaka-community.or.jp; **e-mail:** info@osaka-community.or .jp.

Oxfam Japan

Established in 2003; part of the Oxfam confederation of organizations (qq.v.).

Activities: Raises awareness of global issues among the Japanese population and lobbies the Japanese Government; supports Oxfam poverty-alleviation and disaster-relief initiatives worldwide; runs a Youth Program; organizes lectures, workshops and other events.

Geographical Area of Activity: Worldwide.

Principal Staff: Exec. Dir Akiko Mera.

Address: 7F Creative One, Akihabara 5-3-4, Ueno Taito-ku, Tokyo 110-0005.

Telephone: (3) 3834-1556; **Fax:** (3) 3834-1025; **Internet:** www .oxfam.jp; **e-mail:** oxfaminfo@oxfam.jp.

Peace Winds Japan—PWJ

Established in 1996 to assist people internationally who are victims of political circumstances, conflict, poverty or natural disasters; a non-political, non-religious organization.

Activities: Operates internationally, assisting those in need in collaboration with local organizations, offering emergency relief, medical assistance, scholarships, social services, promoting equal rights for women, and supporting education, agriculture, and housing and sanitation. Projects operate in many countries, including Afghanistan, Timor-Leste, Indonesia, Iran, Iraq, Kosovo and Metohija, Liberia, Mongolia, Sudan and Sierra Leone. Nationally, the organization promotes its work through symposia and lectures, and through fair trade activities. Operates in the USA as Peace Winds America (f. 2009).

Geographical Area of Activity: International.

Publications: Annual Report; newsletter.

Finance: Total revenue ¥2,500,370,115, expenditure ¥2,500,370,115 (31 Jan. 2014).

Principal Staff: CEO Kensuke Onishi.

Address: 2nd Floor, 1161-2, Hiroshima Chikada, Jinsekikogen, Jinseki District, Yubinbango, Hiroshima 720-1622.

Telephone: (3) 5213-4070; **Fax:** (3) 3556-5771; **Internet:** www .peace-winds.org; **e-mail:** meet@peace-winds.org.

The PHD Foundation—Peace, Health and Human Development Foundation

Established in 1981 by Dr Noboru Iwamura.

Activities: Aims to promote activities that would help bring about peace and health through human development among people in Asia and the South Pacific. The Foundation promotes the sharing of values, knowledge and skills to improve the quality of life of those living in poverty in Asia and the South Pacific. It runs training programmes in Japan to provide long-term solutions for people suffering the effects of poverty, as well as follow-up programmes to consolidate technical and leadership skills. It also aims to build stronger links between the Japanese people and their less-wealthy neighbours.

Geographical Area of Activity: Asia and the South Pacific.

Publications: *Irebun Nepal* (study tour reports, 1983); *Kobe Hatsu Asia* (1986); *Asia No Kusanone Kokusaikoryu* (1993); *PHD Letter* (quarterly newsletter); project reports and other publications.

Finance: Financed by membership fees, private contributions, income from publications sales, etc.; Total assets ¥323,666,127, annual revenue ¥41,920,000, expenditure ¥42,020,000 (31 March 2012).

Principal Staff: Pres. Yuji Mizuno; Sec.-Gen. Takuro Sakanishi; Treas. Inoue Riko.

Address: 601 Yamate Towers, 4-2-12 Yamamoto-dori, Chuo-ku, Kobe-shi, Hyogo 650-0003.

Telephone: (78) 414-7750; **Fax:** (78) 414-7611; **Internet:** www .phd-kobe.org; **e-mail:** info@phd-kobe.org.

Refugees International Japan—RIJ

Established in 1979 to assist in the restoration of the physical well-being and dignity of refugees throughout the world.

Activities: Raises funds to assist refugees who have lost everything as a result of war and conflict. The organization funds projects for emergency situations, provides assistance to meet basic survival needs, supports pilot schemes and distributes grants for training and education. Countries and regions supported over the past 30 years include Burma (Myanmar), Cambodia, the Caucasus, Congo, Ethiopia, Guinea, Kenya, Palestinian Territories, Sierra Leone, Sri Lanka, Sudan, Tanzania, Thailand and Timor-Leste.

Geographical Area of Activity: International.

Publications: Annual Review; regular e-newsletters to members.

Finance: Funded through donations, membership and annual fund-raising events and activities. Annual revenue ¥29,521,491, expenditure ¥15,776,286 (30 Nov. 2013).

Board of Directors: Shigeya Kato (Chair.); Simon Black (Chair.).

Principal Staff: Pres. and CEO Jane Best; Treas. Tomoko Yoshida.

Address: c/o Showa Shell Sekiyu K. K. Daiba Frontier Bldg, 12th Floor, 2-3-2 Daiba, Minato-ku, Tokyo 135-8074.

Telephone: (3) 5500-3093; **Fax:** (3) 5500-3094; **Internet:** www .refugeesinternationaljapan.org; **e-mail:** enquiries@ refugeesinternationaljapan.org.

Rohm Music Foundation

Established in 1991 for the promotion of music in Japan and throughout the world.

Activities: Operates in the field of the arts and humanities, through supporting young Japanese musicians, organizing international music exchange activities, offering grants for music research, awarding scholarships, disseminating information and carrying out research. The Foundation organizes the Kyoto International Music Students' Festival for the promotion of young musicians from around the world.

Geographical Area of Activity: Japan.

Finance: Annual income ¥291,717,293, expenditure ¥739,375,313 (31 March 2014).

Principal Staff: Chair. Ken Sato; Man. Dir Hiroshi Watanabe; Sec.-Gen. Susumu Taniguchi.

Address: 1 Nishinakamizu-cho, Saiin, Ukiyo-ku, Kyoto 615-0044.

Telephone: (75) 311-7710; **Fax:** (75) 311-0089; **Internet:** www.rohm.com/rmf/index.html.

Rotary Yoneyama Memorial Foundation, Inc

Founded in 1967; an endeavour by Rotarians in Japan to promote international relations by granting scholarships to foreigners aspiring to study or pursue research at Japanese higher education institutions (including universities, junior colleges, colleges of technology and specialized training colleges).

Activities: Supported by 90,000 Rotarians. The Foundation functions at an international level, focusing on education. It grants scholarships and fellowships to foreign students.

Geographical Area of Activity: Worldwide.

Restrictions: Stipulations for grants include the enrolment of the applicant in the designated Japanese college or university as an undergraduate or graduate on a full-time basis.

Finance: Annual revenue ¥138,927m., expenditure ¥138,927m. (30 June 2012).

Board of Trustees: Kazuhiko Ozawa (Chair.).

Principal Staff: Sec.-Gen. Hiroyasu Sakashita.

Address: Kokuryu-Shibakoen Bldg, 3rd Floor, 2-6-15, Shibakoen, Minato-ku, Tokyo 105-0011.

Telephone: (3) 3434-8681; **Fax:** (3) 3578-8281; **Internet:** www.rotary-yoneyama.or.jp; **e-mail:** mail@rotary-yoneyama.or.jp.

The Saison Foundation

Established in 1987 by Seiji Tsutsumi to carry out activities conducive to the stimulation of creativity among individuals or organizations engaged in the arts, especially contemporary Japanese theatre and dance, and to expedite international cultural exchanges.

Activities: Operates nationally and internationally in the field of the performing arts. The Foundation has two main grant programmes: Direct Support to Artists, which supports the activities and projects by individual artists (e.g. playwrights, directors, choreographers) as well as their sabbatical (overseas travel/vacation) projects; and Partnership Programmes, which support individuals and organizations as partners working to improve the infrastructure of contemporary performing arts in Japan or to enhance international artistic exchange. The Foundation also allows grantees to use its Morishita Studio in Tokyo.

Geographical Area of Activity: Worldwide.

Publications: Annual Report; *Viewpoint* (quarterly newsletter).

Finance: Total assets ¥9,444,929,684; annual revenue ¥408,295,341, expenditure ¥378,792,417 (31 March 2011).

Principal Staff: Pres. Isamu Ito; Vice-Pres. Asako Tsutsumi; Man. Dir Masao Katayama.

Address: Toka Bldg, 8th Floor, 16-1, Ginza, 1-chome, Chuo-ku, Tokyo 104-0061.

Telephone: (3) 3535-5566; **Fax:** (3) 3535-5565; **Internet:** www.saison.or.jp; **e-mail:** foundation@saison.or.jp.

Sanaburi Foundation

Established in 2011 under the auspices of the Sendai Miyagi NPO Center in response to the earthquake, tsunami and nuclear power plant accident that affected the Tohoku region in March of that year.

Activities: A community foundation that disburses general and capital grants for reconstruction and community development in disaster-affected areas. Manages the Japan Society Tohoku Earthquake Relief Fund (Rose Fund), which had raised approx. £620,000 in donations in the United Kingdom by Sept. 2011, to support relief activities in the medium to long term in Iwate, Miyagi and Fukushima Prefectures. Also collaborates with Save the Children Japan in the Sanaburi Foundation Kodomo Hagukumi Fund (Fund for Foster Children), awarding grants for the protection, education and participation of children in community reconstruction.

Geographical Area of Activity: Tohoku region.

Board of Directors: Seiichi Ohtaki (Chair.); Mitsutoshi Sasaki (Vice-Chair.).

Principal Staff: Sr Man. Dir Yuji Suzuki.

Address: Sakura-Omachi Building, 3rd Floor, 1-2-23 Omachi Aoba-Ward, Sendai, Miyagi Prefecture 980-0804.

Telephone: (22) 748-7283; **Fax:** (22) 748-7284; **Internet:** www.sanaburifund.org; **e-mail:** info@sanaburifund.org.

Sasakawa Peace Foundation—SPF

Founded in 1986.

Activities: Seeks to contribute to general human welfare and the substantial development of the international community, and thereby to world peace, through programmes promoting international communication, understanding and co-operation. Functions at an international level organizing programmes and issuing grants to institutions. Activities include: developing human resources; undertaking research and surveys; organizing international forums and conferences; conducting other activities to strengthen international understanding and co-operation; and publishing information in support of the Foundation's objectives.

Geographical Area of Activity: Worldwide.

Restrictions: No grants are made to individuals or business corporations.

Publications: Annual Report; newsletter; brochures; survey reports; conference transcripts/minutes; books.

Finance: Annual income ¥2,181.2m., expenditure ¥1,679.6m. (31 March 2013).

Board of Trustees: Jiro Hanyu (Chair.); Nobuo Tanaka (Pres.).

Principal Staff: Exec. Dir Akinori Sugai.

Address: Nippon Foundation Bldg, 4th Floor, 1-2-2, Akasaka, Minato-ku, Tokyo 107-8523.

Telephone: (3) 6229-5400; **Fax:** (3) 6229-5470; **Internet:** www.spf.org; **e-mail:** spfpr@spf.or.jp.

Tokyu Foundation for Foreign Students

Established in 1975 by the Tokyu Corporation and other companies to promote international exchanges; to promote communication between students, and between students and the Japanese people; and to foster the development of international goodwill between Japan and other Asia-Pacific countries to contribute to international co-operation and cultural exchange.

Activities: Offers up to 30 scholarships a year to non-Japanese postgraduate students from the Asia-Pacific region to enable them to study in Japan. Scholarships are normally awarded for up to two years.

Geographical Area of Activity: Asia and Pacific areas.

Restrictions: Scholarships for doctoral degrees are available only to those aged under 34 years old; scholarships for Master's degrees are available only to those aged under 29.

Finance: Annual revenue ¥107,837,238, expenditure ¥106,809,266 (31 March 2014).

Principal Staff: Chair. Shoichiro Nagayama.

Address: 1-16-14 Shibuya, Shibuya-ku, Shibuya Subway Bldg 5th Floor, Tokyo 150-0002.

Telephone: (3) 6418-3099; **Fax:** (3) 5458-1696; **Internet:** www .tokyu-f.jp; **e-mail:** info@tokyu-f.jp.

Toshiba International Foundation—TIFO

Founded in 1989 by the Toshiba Corpn to promote international exchange activities and a better understanding of Japan.

Activities: Operates in the fields of the arts and humanities, education, international affairs and science and technology, through its own international programmes and the provision of grants to institutions. The Foundation also awards scholarships to overseas nationals to promote international understanding of Japan.

Geographical Area of Activity: Worldwide.

Publications: *Japan's Role in the 1990s*; *Proceedings of Toshiba International Foundation Symposium*; *TIFO News*.

Finance: Total assets ¥4,231,108,802 (31 March 2014).

Board of Trustees: Taizo Nishimuro (Chair.); Shigeji Ueshima, Shinji Fukukawa (Vice-Chair.).

Principal Staff: Pres. Makoto Shirai.

Address: 3rd Floor, Toshiba Bldg, 1-1 Shibaura 1-chome, Minato-ku, Tokyo 105-8001.

Telephone: (3) 3457-2733; **Fax:** (3) 3457-4389; **Internet:** www .toshibafoundation.com; **e-mail:** tifo@toshiba.co.jp.

Totto Foundation

Established in 1981 as a social welfare corporation by actress and television presenter Tetsuko Kuroyanagi.

Activities: Helps disabled people worldwide and lobbies for their equal rights. Manages the vocational Totto Cultural Institute (f. 1987) and Japanese Theatre for the Deaf. Provides sign language training for volunteer workers.

Geographical Area of Activity: Principally Japan.

Finance: Annual income ¥66,879,000, expenditure ¥70,511,000 (31 March 2013).

Principal Staff: Chair. Tetsuko Kuroyanagi.

Address: 141-0033 Shinagawa-ku, 2-2-16 Nishishinagawa, Tokyo.

Telephone: (3) 3779-0233; **Fax:** (3) 3779-0206; **Internet:** www .totto.or.jp/tottofoundation.html; **e-mail:** totto.swc@tokyo .email.ne.jp.

The Toyota Foundation

Founded in 1974 by Toyota Motor Corpn to contribute towards creating a human-orientated society by providing grants for research and projects related to the human and natural environments, social welfare, education, culture and other fields.

Activities: Grant programmes include: the Asian Neighbors Programme, which supports practical projects in Asia; the Research Grant Programme, which supports research reflecting original thinking and with broad social significance; and the Grant Programme for Community Activities in Japan. The Foundation sets 'realizing a sustainable society' and 'community revitalization and coexistence' as common goals of these programmes.

Geographical Area of Activity: Mainly Japan and Asian countries.

Restrictions: In general, the Foundation does not approve grants for capital investment, plant or equipment; endowments; museum or library acquisitions; annual budgets of organizations or institutions, or of established programmes; propaganda or lobbying activities; religious activities; nor for unsponsored individuals.

Publications: *The Toyota Foundation Occasional Report* (annually); *JOINT* (3 a year).

Finance: Annual revenue ¥697,538,000, expenditure ¥702,573,000 (31 March 2013).

Principal Staff: Chair. Hiroshi Okuda; Pres. Atsuko Toyama; Man. Dir Hiroshi Ito; Hon. Chair. Tatsuro Toyoda.

Address: Shinjuku Mitsui Bldg, 37th Floor, 2-1-1 Nishi Shinjuku, Shinjuku-ku, Tokyo 163-0437.

Telephone: (3) 3344-1701; **Fax:** (3) 3342-6911; **Internet:** www .toyotafound.or.jp; **e-mail:** admin@toyotafound.or.jp.

Jordan

FOUNDATIONS, TRUSTS AND NON-PROFIT ORGANIZATIONS

King Hussein Foundation—KHF

Established by Royal Decree in 1999 as a national and international NGO dedicated to the humanitarian vision of the late King Hussein of Jordan.

Activities: Operates nationally and internationally in the fields of peace and democracy, sustainable community development, education and leadership, the environment and health. The Foundation has established a number of institutes in Jordan: the Jubilee Institute (teacher training), the Information and Research Centre, the National Centre for Culture and the Performing Arts, the National Music Conservatory and the Institute for Family Health. In 2001, the Foundation launched the King Hussein Foundation International (KHFI) in Washington, DC, USA, to raise endowment funds for the Foundation. KHFI programmes include the King Hussein Leadership Prize and the Media and Humanity Program.

Geographical Area of Activity: Jordan and the USA.

Publications: Newsletter (quarterly).

Board: HM Queen Noor al-Hussein (Chair.).

Principal Staff: Exec. Dir Hana Mitra Shahin.

Address: POB 926687, Amman 11110.

Telephone: (6) 5607460; **Fax:** (6) 5606994; **Internet:** www.kinghusseinfoundation.org; **e-mail:** khf-nhf@khf.org.jo.

JOHUD—Jordanian Hashemite Fund for Human Development

Established in 1977 to advance comprehensive and sustainable human development through the enhanced participation of Jordanian people.

Activities: Through its network of 50 community development centres, the Fund focuses on developing a model of integrated development activities, through support for projects working in a range of areas, including: economic empowerment; women's rights; political participation; youth engagement; creative information and communications technology for development; early childhood development and disability; sustainable livelihoods; good governance and local development; and health and well-being.

Geographical Area of Activity: Jordan.

Publications: *Humanity* (quarterly newsletter); *Jordan National Human Development Report*.

Board of Trustees: HRH Princess Basma bint Talal (Chair.); Waleed Asfour (Deputy Chair.).

Principal Staff: Exec. Dir Farah al-Daghistani.

Address: 127 Madina St, Amman; POB 5118, Amman 11183.

Telephone: (6) 5560741; **Fax:** (6) 5515950; **Internet:** www.johud.org.jo; **e-mail:** info@johud.org.jo.

Jordan River Foundation

Established in 1995 by HM Queen Rania al-Abdullah to empower local community members, help to combat poverty and ensure sustainable development.

Activities: Aims to promote the development of Jordanian society through sustainable social, economic and cultural programmes. It works to protect the rights and needs of children, and to empower individuals and communities; projects include the Community Empowerment Programme, the Child Safety Programme and the Capacity Building and Business Development Programme.

Geographical Area of Activity: Jordan.

Publications: Annual Report; *Jordan in Bloom – Wildflowers of the Holy Land*; *Crossing the River Jordan*; *Historical Trees of Jordan*; newsletter; *Paths to Success* (Jordan River Foundation Success Stories).

Finance: Annual revenue 13,016,876 Jordanian dinars, expenditure 12,901,021 Jordanian dinars (2013).

Board of Trustees: HM Queen Rania al-Abdullah (Chair.); Amin Khlifat (Vice-Chair.).

Principal Staff: Dir-Gen. Ghaleb al-Qudah.

Address: POB 2943, Abdoun, Amman 11181.

Telephone: (6) 5933211; **Fax:** (6) 5933210; **Internet:** www.jordanriver.jo; **e-mail:** info@jrf.org.jo.

Noor al-Hussein Foundation—NHF

Established by Royal Decree in 1985 to initiate and support projects nationally and internationally in the fields of integrated community development, microfinance, child and family health, women and enterprise development. Operates as an independent entity under the umbrella of the King Hussein Foundation (q.v.).

Activities: Works to create a lasting, positive impact on the lives of disadvantaged people in Jordan and the Middle East through projects that promote self-help and participation in decision-making and project management. The Foundation initiated and owns the Jordan Micro Credit Company, Tamweelcom, now a financially independent company, to disburse loans to low-income entrepreneurs to enable them to set up micro-enterprises or expand existing ones. The Foundation also provides comprehensive health-care services for children and families, and refugees through its Institute for Family Health. The Community Development Programme provides capacity building, business development services, loans and grants to establish income-generating projects, as well as the creation of job opportunities at the grassroots level, assisting in reducing poverty and unemployment.

Geographical Area of Activity: Jordan.

Board: HM Queen Noor al-Hussein (Chair.).

Principal Staff: Exec. Dir Hana Mitra Shahin.

Address: POB 926687, Amman 11110.

Telephone: (6) 5607460; **Fax:** (6) 5606994; **Internet:** www.nooralhusseinfoundation.org; **e-mail:** khf-nhf@khf.org.jo.

Scientific Foundation of Hisham Adeeb Hijjawi

Established in 1981 by Hisham Hijjawi to support education in the field of technical and applied sciences.

Activities: Operates in Jordan and the Palestinian Territories in the field of education, and in particular in the area of research in technical and applied sciences at universities and colleges; also supports scientific conferences and workshops, funds the purchase of scientific equipment, and makes three awards annually for research projects in the applied sciences. The Foundation funds a technical college in the Palestinian Territories. It also operates in the field of social welfare and is a founding member of the Welfare Association, providing development assistance in human resource development, institutional building and the promotion of culture and identity for Palestinians, in the Palestinian Territories and elsewhere.

Geographical Area of Activity: Jordan and the Palestinian Territories.

Finance: Funded by investment portfolio of founder, the late Hisham Hijjawi.

Board of Directors: Ayman Hisham Hijjawi (Chair.); Jaafar Hisham Hijjawi (Vice-Chair.).

Principal Staff: Exec. Dir Naser Aloul.

Address: 190 Zhran St, POB 1944, Amman 11821.

Telephone: (6) 5500999; **Fax:** (6) 5500998; **Internet:** www .hijjawi.org; **e-mail:** loamman@najah.edu.

Abdul Hameed Shoman Foundation

A non-profit cultural institution established in 1978 by the Arab Bank PLC, to embody and perpetuate the legacy of the Bank's founder, the late Abdul Hameed Shoman; to support and enhance scientific research and Arab humanistic creativity; to build bridges of dialogue and cultural communication; and to collect and disseminate general knowledge by all feasible means.

Activities: Awards annual prizes in 12 fields to 'Young Arab Researchers' whose works demonstrate exceptional scientific value. The Foundation also grants prizes biennially to teachers in Jordanian preparatory and secondary schools who demonstrate original approaches to the teaching of science; and grants annual prizes for children's literature. In 1986, the Foundation established the Abdul Hameed Shoman Public Library, and the Abdul Hameed Shoman Cultural Forum, which hosts lectures made by prominent Jordanian or Arab lecturers, and tackles important public issues; and the Dialogue of the Month, where prominent intellectuals present their viewpoints and opinions, as well as organizing seminars and workshops. In 1989, the Forum established a cinema, which offers weekly screenings of modern and classical films. In 1999, the Foundation established the Abdul Hameed Shoman Fund for the Support and Encouragement of Scientific Research, which funds research at Jordanian universities.

Geographical Area of Activity: Jordan.

Publications: Proceedings from lectures, seminars and workshops; numerous works in Arabic and English.

Finance: Endowment based on 3% of net annual profits of the Arab Bank PLC.

Board of Directors: Sabih Taher Masri (Chair.); Prof. Basem Ali al-Imam (Sec.).

Principal Staff: CEO Valentina Qussisiya.

Address: POB 940255, Amman 11194.

Telephone: (6) 4633627; **Fax:** (6) 4633565; **Internet:** www .shoman.org; **e-mail:** ahsf@shoman.org.jo.

Kazakhstan

FOUNDATIONS, TRUSTS AND NON-PROFIT ORGANIZATIONS

Soros Foundation—Kazakhstan

Founded in 1995; an independent foundation, part of the Open Society Foundations (q.v.) network, which aims to foster political and cultural pluralism and reform economic structures to encourage free enterprise and a market economy.

Activities: Operates in the fields of economic affairs, health and statistics, law and juvenile justice, media and information, and civil society. The Foundation provides support for innovative projects focused on budget and extractive industries transparency at all levels, supports Kazakhstan's NGOs and the independent mass media, economic and law reform projects, including policy-making, dissemination of information and exchange of expertise.

Geographical Area of Activity: Kazakhstan.

Publications: Annual Report; policy papers; books.

Finance: Total funds allocated 651,817,980 tenge (2013).

Board of Trustees: Nargis Kassenova Umirserikovna (Chair.).

Principal Staff: Chair. Exec. Council Anton Artemeyev; Deputy Chair. Exec. Council Irina V. Koshkina.

Address: 050000 Almaty, ul. Zheltoksan 111A-9.

Telephone: (727) 2503811; **Fax:** (727) 2503814; **Internet:** www.soros.kz; **e-mail:** sfk@soros.kz.

Kenya

FOUNDATION CENTRES AND CO-ORDINATING BODIES

Allavida—Alliances for Voluntary Initiatives and Development

Founded in 2001 by the merger of Charity Know How and Alliance magazine, both of which were formerly part of CAF—Charities Aid Foundation (q.v.).

Activities: Allavida works in Africa mobilizing financial resources, building local grantmaking and grant management capacity, enhancing skills in community organizations for local development, encouraging local philanthropy, and facilitating learning in and between organizations. Concentrates on five key themes: organizational development, individual learning, grantmaking, promoting philanthropy, and influencing. Operates small grants programmes, training programmes, provides consultancy support, and carries out research and development activities in the areas of capacity building of non-profit organizations and the development of local and regional philanthropy. Set up the Kenya Social Investment Exchange (KSIX).

Geographical Area of Activity: East Africa.

Publications: *An Introduction to the Non-Profit Sector in Kenya*; *An Introduction to the Non-Profit Sector in Uganda*; *An Introduction to the Non-Profit Sector in Tanzania*; *Philanthropy in East Africa*; *In Trust for Tomorrow*; *Promoting Philanthropy in Kenya—The Case for Tax Law Reform*; *One Woman at a Time*; *A Legacy of Giving*; *East Africa Grant makers & Grants Programmes Directory*; *For the good of the Kingdom – A history of the Kabaka Foundation*; *Social Investment in Kenya*; *Allavida* (newsletter); Annual Report.

Finance: Funded by a variety of trusts and foundations.

Principal Staff: Chief Exec. Justus Macharia.

Address: 3rd Floor, Rattansi Educational Trust Building, Koinange St, POB 10434-00100, Nairobi.

Telephone: (20) 310526; **Fax:** (20) 310525; **Internet:** www.allavida.org; **e-mail:** info@allavida.or.ke.

East African Association of Grantmakers

Incorporated in 2003 to develop a culture of local philanthropy to improve the lives of the people of East Africa.

Activities: Aims to develop local philanthropy in East Africa, through demonstrating and promoting philanthropy in East Africa as an integral strategy for permanent wealth-creation for social development. The Association promotes ethical grantmaking practices as a tool for development; supports members with learning and capacity-building opportunities for effective asset development, management, governance and grantmaking; strengthens the individual and collective voice of member organizations; and enters into dialogue with governments, the private sector and civil society partners in an effort to influence policy. It also organizes conferences and seminars.

Geographical Area of Activity: East Africa.

Publications: Annual Report; newsletter.

Board of Directors: Tom Were (Chair.); Olive Luena (Vice-Chair.).

Principal Staff: CEO and Sec. Nicanor Sabula.

Address: Rattansi Educational Trust Bldg, 1st Floor, Koinange St, POB 49626-00100, Nairobi.

Telephone: (20) 315773; **Fax:** (20) 2244470; **Internet:** www.eaag.org; **e-mail:** info@eaag.org.

ELCI—Environment Liaison Centre International

Established in 1974. Aims to ensure good communication between NGOs and local communities, and increase the capacity of environmental organizations.

Activities: Works internationally as a networking body between organizations and communities, and between NGOs and international organizations to improve co-operation between these groups and the effectiveness of the environmental work carried out. The Centre aims to strengthen NGOs by providing information and training workers in communication skills, and project and resource management. It has more than 850 member organizations.

Geographical Area of Activity: International.

Publications: *Ecoforum* (quarterly magazine); *ELCI News*; *Lake Victoria Report*.

Board of Directors: Cyril Ritchie (Chair.); Rajen Awotar (Treas.).

Principal Staff: Exec. Dir Kennedy Orwa.

Address: POB 72461-00200, Nairobi; ELCI International Secretariat, The International Center for Insect Physiology and Ecology (ICIPE), Duduville, Kasarani.

Telephone: (20) 8566172; **Fax:** (20) 8566175; **Internet:** www.elci.org; **e-mail:** info@elci.org.

Ufadhili Trust

Established in 2000.

Activities: Acts as a resource for the non-profit sector in Kenya and East Africa to facilitate strategic and effective partnerships between business, non-profit organizations, individuals and governments towards sustainable development. The Trust maintains a resource centre; provides technical assistance to East African foundations; operates community development pilot projects; and lobbies on issues relating to the legal and fiscal status of NGOs and foundations. Has advisory boards in Uganda and Tanzania.

Geographical Area of Activity: East Africa.

Publications: *Corporate Concern* (quarterly newsletter); reports.

Board of Trustees: John H. Mramba (Chair.).

Principal Staff: Exec. Dir Mumo Kivuitu.

Address: Rattansi Educational Trust Bldg, 1st Floor, Koinange St, POB 14041-00100, Nairobi.

Telephone: (20) 343061; **Fax:** (20) 343067; **Internet:** www.ufadhilitrust.org; **e-mail:** info@ufadhilitrust.org.

FOUNDATIONS, TRUSTS AND NON-PROFIT ORGANIZATIONS

ACORD—Agency for Co-operation and Research in Development

Founded in 1976 as a consortium of international agencies with headquarters in the North to empower its members with operational capacity to tackle poverty issues ensuant to droughts in Sub-Saharan Africa; became Africa-led in 2006.

Activities: Promotes aid and social welfare through grants and research into long-term development. The Agency undertakes programmes based around five core themes: conflict prevention and peacebuilding; strengthening civil society; women's rights; HIV/AIDS; and livelihoods within a global programme to promote social activism. Maintains offices in

London, United Kingdom, and country offices throughout Africa.

Geographical Area of Activity: Africa.

Publications: Annual Report; ACORD policies; reports; newsletter.

Finance: Annual income £1,877,000, expenditure £1,838,000 (31 Dec. 2013).

Board of Trustees: Sylli Gandega (Chair.).

Principal Staff: Exec. Dir and Company Sec. Ousainou Ngum.

Address: ACK Garden Annex, 4th Floor, 1st Ngong Ave, First Floor, Wing C, POB 61216-00200, Nairobi.

Telephone: (20) 2721172; **Fax:** (20) 2721166; **Internet:** www .acordinternational.org; **e-mail:** info@acordinternational .org.

The African Agricultural Technology Foundation—AATF

A non-profit organization established in 2002.

Activities: Aims to facilitate and promote public-private partnerships for the access and delivery of appropriate proprietary agricultural technologies for use by resource-poor smallholder farmers in Sub-Saharan Africa. The Foundation provides advice and expertise in the area of agricultural technologies, working towards food security and poverty reduction.

Geographical Area of Activity: Sub-Saharan Africa.

Publications: Annual Report; newsletters; project briefs; policy briefs.

Finance: Annual income US $20,010,886, annual expenditure $19,437,422 (31 Dec. 2013).

Board of Trustees: Idah Sithole-Niang (Chair.); Stanford F. Blade (Vice-Chair.).

Principal Staff: Exec. Dir Denis Tumwesigye Kyetere.

Address: POB 30709-00100, Nairobi.

Telephone: (20) 4223700; **Fax:** (20) 4223701; **Internet:** www .aatf-africa.org; **e-mail:** aatf@aatf-africa.org.

AMREF Health Africa

Established in 1957 to provide health-care services in East Africa; originally known as the Flying Doctors Service of East Africa and subsequently as the African Medical and Research Foundation. Present name adopted in 2014.

Activities: Operates in Africa in the fields of aid to less-developed countries, and medicine and health, through five main projects: Child and Adolescent Health and Development; Sexual and Reproductive Health; Clinical Services and Emergency Response; Health Policy and Systems Reform; and Environmental Health. The Foundation runs a Flying Doctor Service in East Africa, which carries out emergency medical evacuations. It maintains country offices in Kenya, South Africa, Tanzania and Uganda, and field offices in Ethiopia, Mozambique, Rwanda, Somalia and Sudan. It also has offices in European countries, the USA and Canada. The Foundation won the 1999 Conrad Hilton Humanitarian Award and the 2005 Gates Award for Global Health.

Geographical Area of Activity: Africa.

Publications: Annual Report; books and manuals on health care; reports (technical and medical); *AMREF News* (quarterly newspaper).

Finance: Annual income US $93,302,000, expenditure $91,660,000 (30 Sept. 2013).

Board of Directors: Omar Issa (Chair.).

Principal Staff: CEO Dr Lennie Bazira Igbodipe-Kyomuhangi (a.i.).

Address: Wilson Airport, Langata Rd, POB 27691-00506, Nairobi.

Telephone: (20) 6993000; **Fax:** (20) 609518; **Internet:** www .amref.org; **e-mail:** info@amrefhq.org.

Chandaria Foundation

Established in 1956 by the Chandaria Family.

Activities: Has funded hospital facilities in Nairobi and Mombassa, and a network of 15 rural clinics; and also established the Mabati Medical Centre (f. 2000) and Mabati Technical Training Institute (f. 2004), a vocational training centre. In Nairobi, the Foundation supports the Chandaria School of Business at the United States International University and the Chandaria Business Innovation and Incubation Centre at Kenyatta University (f. 2013); and provides scholarships to more than 100 secondary school and university students each year.

Geographical Area of Activity: Kenya.

Principal Staff: Chair. Manu Chandaria.

Address: Parklands, Limuru Rd, 1st and 2nd Ave, POB 50826, Nairobi.

Telephone: (20) 3742081; **Fax:** (20) 3741271; **e-mail:** ckl@ cpmcraft.com.

EABL Foundation

Established in 2005 by East African Breweries Limited to lead community investment efforts.

Activities: A corporate community development foundation operating in East Africa with an emphasis on water, environment and education. Offers scholarships to universities in East Africa to students in need for study in the areas of business, information technology, engineering and food science.

Geographical Area of Activity: East Africa.

Publications: Newsletter; reports.

Principal Staff: Man. Keith Obure.

Address: Office of the Dir of Corporate Affairs, East African Breweries Ltd, POB 30161-00100, Nairobi.

Internet: www.eablfoundation.com.

KCDF—Kenya Community Development Foundation

Established in 1997 to mobilize resources effectively to build permanent funds for grantmaking in the area of community development.

Activities: Active in the area of grantmaking to community-based and civil society organizations, and NGOs working with communities in need at grassroots level in community capacity building and endowment fund building (in areas including food security, gender equality, youth development and educational scholarships) as a basis for building permanent assets for sustainable community development.

Geographical Area of Activity: Kenya.

Restrictions: Grants only to community-based, civil society organizations and NGOs working mainly with communities in need.

Publications: Annual Report; *Endowment Challenge Booklet*; booklets on local philanthropy.

Finance: Net assets Ks. 620,518,053 (30 Sept. 2013).

Board of Trustees: Isaac Wanjohi (Chair.); **Board of Directors:** Atia Yahya (Chair.).

Principal Staff: CEO Janet Mawiyoo.

Address: Morning Side Office Park, 4th Floor, Ngong Rd (just after the Nakumatt Prestige Plaza), POB 10501-00100, Nairobi.

Telephone: (20) 3540239; **Fax:** (20) 8067440; **Internet:** www .kcdf.or.ke; **e-mail:** info@kcdf.or.ke.

Zarina & Naushad Merali Foundation

Established by Naushad Merali, Exec. Chair. of Sameer Group, a business conglomerate, and his wife Zarina.

Activities: Has funded the construction of medical facilities. Also provides bursaries to orphans and disadvantaged students.

Geographical Area of Activity: Kenya.

Address: c/o Sameer Group, 49 Riverside Dr., POB 55358-00200 Nairobi.

Telephone: (204) 204000; **Fax:** (204) 4441492; **Internet:** info@sameer-group.co.ke; **e-mail:** info@sameer-group.co.ke.

Open Society Initiative for Eastern Africa—OSIEA

Established in 2004; part of the Open Society Foundations (q.v.) network.

Activities: Priority areas are citizen participation and human rights; supports legal reforms, and access to rights and information. Promotes equality and justice; and supports marginalized and victimized people, including the disabled.

Geographical Area of Activity: Kenya, South Sudan, Sudan, Tanzania, Uganda.

Publications: Reports and other publications.

Principal Staff: Exec. Dir Mburu Gitu.

Address: ACS Plaza, Lenana Rd, Nairobi.

Telephone: (20) 387-7508; **Fax:** (20) 386-0201; **Internet:** www.osiea.org; **e-mail:** info@osiea.org.

Safaricom Foundation

Established in 2003 by Safaricom Ltd (now owned by Vodafone) to help build communities in Kenya.

Activities: Operates in the areas of education, the environment, health and welfare, the arts and humanities, and disaster relief. Since its inception, it has disbursed approx US $21m.

Geographical Area of Activity: Kenya.

Board of Trustees: Joseph Ogutu.

Principal Staff: Head of Corporate Responsibility Sanda Ojiambo; Principal Operations Officer Eunice Kibathi.

Address: Safaricom House, POB 66827-00800, Westlands, Nairobi.

Internet: safaricomfoundation.org; **e-mail:** thefoundation@safaricom.co.ke.

The Republic of Korea

FOUNDATIONS, TRUSTS AND NON-PROFIT ORGANIZATIONS

Arts Council Korea

Founded in 1973 as the Korean Culture and Arts Foundation to promote Korean culture and art and to encourage their development; became Arts Council Korea in 2005.

Activities: Promotes Korean culture abroad and encourages international cultural exchange; awards fellowships; finances research into aspects of Korean culture through institutions in the Republic of Korea and in other countries; runs courses; maintains a library. Nationally, invests in Korean artistic and cultural infrastructures.

Geographical Area of Activity: Worldwide.

Publications: *Promotion of Arts and Culture* (monthly); *Almanac of Culture and Arts* (annually); financial statements.

Council: Young Bin Kwon (Chair.).

Address: 640 Bitgaram-ro, Naju-si, Jeollanam-do 520-350.

Telephone: (61) 900-2100; **Fax:** (61) 900-2366; **Internet:** www.arko.or.kr; **e-mail:** arko@arko.or.kr.

The Beautiful Foundation (Areumdaun Jaedan)

Established in 2000.

Activities: Aims to create a world filled with 'affluent beauty' in which extremes of wealth and poverty are eradicated. The Foundation holds an annual international symposium entitled 'Giving Korea'. It hosts the Center on Philanthropy, which conducts research on philanthropy and corporate social responsibility.

Geographical Area of Activity: Republic of Korea.

Publications: *Giving Korea* (conference proceedings); books on philanthropy.

Finance: Total assets 68,287,113,735 Korean won (31 Dec. 2013).

Board of Directors: Ye Jong Suk (Chair.).

Address: 6 Jahamun-ro 19-gil, Jongno-gu, Seoul 110-260.

Telephone: (2) 766-1004; **Fax:** (2) 6930-4598; **Internet:** www.beautifulfund.org; **e-mail:** research@beautifulfund.org.

ChildFund Korea

Founded in 1948 as a non-governmental social welfare organization aiming to improve the lives of less-privileged children. Renamed Korea Children's Foundation in 1979 and Korea Welfare Foundation in 1994. Present name adopted in 2008.

Activities: Helps needy children, with programmes to prevent child abuse, support severely ill children, protect children in local society, and prevent child loss. The organization also runs a foster family programme.

Geographical Area of Activity: East and South-East Asia, South Asia, South America and Africa.

Publications: *Danbee* (newsletter, 6 a year); *Apple Tree* (monthly magazine); books.

Finance: Annual income 129,649,458 Korean won, expenditure 129,649,458 Korean won (2012).

Principal Staff: Pres. Lee Je-Hoon.

Address: 95 Mugyo-dong, ChildFund Bldg, 11th Floor, Jung-Gu, Seoul 100-170.

Telephone: (2) 775-9121; **Fax:** (2) 756-4256; **Internet:** eng.childfund.or.kr; **e-mail:** kwf@kwf.or.kr.

Good Neighbors International

Established in 1991, as Good Neighbors, Inc Korea, to provide humanitarian aid to people in developing countries and Korea. Re-established in 1996 as Good Neighbors International.

Activities: Operates humanitarian and development projects throughout the world, providing relief for the suffering, and funding long-term development projects in poor communities. The organization focuses particularly on teaching young people to be self-sufficient as a lasting solution to poverty and hunger. It was involved in the Rwandan refugee crisis, providing medical teams and setting up schools in refugee camps. It also played a role in relief operations in Haiti following an earthquake in 2010. Activities supported include child abuse prevention and counselling centres, training in vocational skills, dam construction and well drilling, soup kitchens, dairy farms, latrine construction, refugee medical teams, rural community development and agricultural training for young people and women. Maintains some 23 field offices worldwide.

Geographical Area of Activity: Asia, Africa and Central and South America and the Caribbean.

Publications: Annual Report; *Partnership* (newsletter, 6 a year); *Good Neighbours* (magazine).

Finance: Receives funding from membership dues, the Government and gifts-in-kind.

Principal Staff: Pres. Lee Il-Ha; Sec.-Gen. Yang Jin-ok.

Address: 101-4 Cheongpa-dong 2ga, Yongsan-gu, Seoul 140-132.

Telephone: (2) 6717-4000; **Fax:** (2) 6717-4293; **Internet:** www.goodneighbors.kr; **e-mail:** gni@gni.kr.

IACD—Institute of Asian Culture and Development

Established in 1983.

Activities: Offers long-term assistance mainly to developing countries in Asia in the areas of education and training, community development and medical services in its endeavour to build peaceful and fair communities. The Institute participates in founding and managing educational institutions; sends experts to oversee social and economic development projects; provides medical relief services; organizes academic, sports and cultural exchange programmes; hosts international academic conferences; provides training opportunities and scholarships; operates welfare programmes for children, women and the disabled; provides international peace volunteers; provides business/investment consultancy services.

Geographical Area of Activity: Asia, Central Asia and Middle East and North Africa.

Publications: *International Journal of Central Asian Studies*.

Board of Directors: Sung-sam Kang (Chair.).

Principal Staff: Sec.-Gen. Sung-han Kang.

Address: POB 180, Seoul 100-601.

Telephone: (7) 077-349410; **Internet:** www.iacd.or.kr; **e-mail:** iacd@chol.com.

The Korea Foundation

Established in 1991 to promote understanding of the Republic of Korea worldwide, and to enhance international goodwill and friendship through international exchange programmes.

Activities: Operates internationally to promote Korean studies overseas, cultural exchange activities, and exchange and publication programmes, through grants to individuals and institutions, sponsorship of international forums, awarding scholarships and fellowships, and supporting overseas organizations, including museums and art galleries, and international conferences. Maintains six overseas offices (two in the USA, and one in the People's Republic of China, the Russian Federation, Germany and Viet Nam, respectively).

Geographical Area of Activity: Worldwide.

Publications: Annual Report; *Koreana* (quarterly, in Arabic, German, English, French, Chinese, Russian, Spanish and Japanese); *Korea Focus* (monthly web magazine, in English); newsletter (quarterly, in English and Korean).

Finance: Total assets 160,302m. Korean won (2013).

Board of Directors: Dr Yu Hyun-Seok (Pres.); Zeon Nam-Jin, Yoon Keum-Jin (Exec. Vice-Pres.).

Address: Diplomatic Center Bldg, 10th Floor, 2558 Nambusunhwanno, Seocho-gu, Seoul 137-863.

Telephone: (2) 2046-8500; **Fax:** (2) 3463-6076; **Internet:** www .kf.or.kr; **e-mail:** webmaster@kf.or.kr.

Seoam Scholarship Foundation

Established in 1989 by the Taeyoung Group.

Activities: Aims to improve education and to contribute to the education of students who will go on to have a positive effect on the development of the Republic of Korea. Provides scholarships to promising secondary school and university students in various fields. Established the Seoam Library; engages in fund-raising activities; and supports a number of activities. Also awards the Seoam Scholarship Education Prize.

Geographical Area of Activity: Republic of Korea.

Principal Staff: Dir Yoon Se-Young; Gen-Sec. Hong Seong-wook.

Address: 58-1 Deungchon-dong, 157-030 Seoul.

Telephone: (2) 2113-5352; **Fax:** (2) 3661-1585; **Internet:** foundation.sbs.co.kr.

Kosovo

FOUNDATIONS, TRUSTS AND NON-PROFIT ORGANIZATIONS

Kosovar Civil Society Foundation

Established in 1998 to assist in the development of civil society.

Activities: Provides information on European integration. Launched 'Democratic Society Promotion' project in 2011.

Geographical Area of Activity: Kosovo.

Publications: Various research documents and manuals.

Finance: Annual revenue €590,931, expenditure €575,067 (31 Dec. 2013).

Board Members: Xheraldina Vula (Pres.).

Principal Staff: Exec. Dir Venera Hajrullahu.

Address: 10000 Prishtina, Fazli Grajqevci 4A.

Telephone: (38) 248643; **Fax:** (38) 248636; **Internet:** www.kcsfoundation.org; **e-mail:** office@kcsfoundation.org.

Kosovo Foundation for Open Society—KFOS

Established in 1999; an independent foundation, formerly the Prishtina office of the Fund for an Open Society—Yugoslavia; part of the Open Society Foundations (q.v.) network, which aims to foster political and cultural pluralism and reform economic structures to encourage free enterprise and a market economy.

Activities: Operates in the areas of humanitarian aid to refugees, as well as supporting small-scale projects in the fields of education, culture and the arts, information and the media, democratic institutions and human rights. Internationally, the Foundation co-operates with the East-East programme, collaborating regionally on democracy programmes. Other programmes cover the areas of Civil Society, European Integration, and Minorities and Roma.

Geographical Area of Activity: Kosovo and Metohija.

Publications: Annual Report; *European Magazine*; reports; books.

Finance: Annual income €3,208,706, expenditure €3,073,272 (2010).

Board: Robert Muharremi (Chair.).

Principal Staff: Exec. Dir Luan Shllaku; Finance Dir Dukagjin Hyseni.

Address: Prishtina, Ulpiana, Imzot Nike Prela Vila 13.

Telephone: (38) 542157; **Fax:** (38) 542157; **Internet:** kfos.org; **e-mail:** info@kfos.org.

Kuwait

FOUNDATIONS, TRUSTS AND NON-PROFIT ORGANIZATIONS

IOMS—Islamic Organization for Medical Sciences

Founded in 1984 to raise awareness of Islamic medicinal practices.

Activities: Promotes Islamic methods of treatment for physical and psychological afflictions; supports research carried out by Muslim physicians, especially studies to find common ground between traditional Islamic medicine and modern medicine, and to find alternatives to drugs prohibited by Islam; provides health centres for Muslims in need around the world; publishes Islamic scientific and medical journals; and holds seminars and international conferences. Awards the Islamic Organization for Medical Sciences Prize, worth 6,000 Kuwaiti dinars, every two years.

Geographical Area of Activity: Mainly North African and Middle Eastern countries.

Publications: *The Law of Herbal Drugs*; *The Islamic Guide to Medical Jurisprudence*; *Topics in Islamic Medicine*; *Islamic Perspectives in Obstetrics and Gynaecology*; conference proceedings.

Finance: Funded by Government of Kuwait and donations; annual budget more than US $1m.

Principal Staff: Pres. Dr Abdul Rahman al-Awadi; Sec.-Gen. Ali al-Saif.

Address: c/o Kuwait Foundation for the Advancement of Science, Sharq, Ahmad Al Jaber St, POB 25263, 13113 Safat, Kuwait City.

Telephone: 4834984; **Fax:** 4840083.

Kuwait Awqaf Public Foundation

Established in 1993 as a *waqf*, or community fund, to support private sector organizations in the promotion and development of society.

Activities: Operates nationally in the areas of religion and culture, the environment, community development, health and social welfare, science and technology, and Islamic co-operation.

Geographical Area of Activity: Kuwait.

Publications: *Journal of Endowments* (online).

Principal Staff: Sec.-Gen. Abdul Mohsen Abdullah al-Kharafi.

Address: Sharq, Dasman Complex, Block 6, Al-Manqaf St, POB 482, 13005 Safat, Kuwait City.

Telephone: 1804777; **Fax:** 22532670; **Internet:** www.awqaf.org.kw.

Kuwait Foundation for the Advancement of Sciences—KFAS

Established in 1976 by HH Sheikh Jaber al-Ahmad al-Sabah; a private, non-profit scientific organization.

Activities: Supports pure and applied research of national importance in all disciplines and promotes collaborative studies and deliberations with scientists internationally through conferences and symposia. Annual prizes are awarded for meritorious contributions by scientists and researchers in Kuwait and other Arab and Islamic countries. The Foundation awards scholarships and fellowships to Kuwaiti nationals. Established the Scientific Center, the Dasman Diabetes Institute and the Sabah Al-Ahmad Center for Giftedness and Creativity, and hosts the Kuwaiti branch of the Arab School for Science and Technology.

Geographical Area of Activity: Mainly Kuwait.

Publications: *Atlas of the State of Kuwait from Satellite Images*; *Majallat Al-Oloom* (monthly, Arabic language edition of Scientific American); *Majallat Al-Oloom* (monthly magazine); *Al-Taqaddum Al-Ilmi Magazine* (quarterly); and others.

Finance: Funded by public Kuwaiti corporations (1% of their annual profits) and by other organizations and individuals. Annual revenue 3,751m. Kuwaiti dinars, expenditure 3,258m. Kuwaiti dinars (2012).

Board of Directors: HH The Amir Sheikh Sabah al-Ahmed al-Jaber al-Sabah (Chair.); Suleiman A. al-Awadi (Sec.).

Principal Staff: Dir-Gen. Dr Adnan A. Shihab-Eldin.

Address: Sharq, Ahmad Al Jaber St, POB 25263, 13113 Safat, Kuwait City.

Telephone: 22278100; **Fax:** 22270421; **Internet:** www.kfas.org; **e-mail:** info@kfas.org.kw.

Kuwait Institute for Scientific Research—KISR

Founded in 1967 by the Arabian Oil Company Ltd (Japan) to promote and conduct applied scientific research related to national industrial development and environmental protection.

Activities: Conducts research in environmental science, earth science, food and water resources, engineering, petroleum, petrochemicals, urban development, infrastructure services and techno-economics; also researches ways of using technology to help people with special needs. The Institute provides documentation and information services, and training schemes for scientific research workers.

Geographical Area of Activity: Kuwait.

Publications: Annual Reports; *Science and Technology Magazine*; *Environmental Characteristics and the Natural Resources of Kuwait*; *The Effects of Insecticides on the Human and the Environment*; *New Technologies for Soil Reclamation and Desert Greenery*; *Plankton of the Arabian Gulf*; and others.

Principal Staff: Dir-Gen. Dr Naji Mohamed al-Mutairi.

Address: POB 24885, 13109 Safat, Kuwait City.

Telephone: 24836100; **Fax:** 24830643; **Internet:** www.kisr.edu.kw; **e-mail:** public_relations@kisr.edu.kw.

Zakat House

Founded in 1982 with the aim of implementing the Islamic practice of *zakat* (giving a fixed proportion of one's wealth to charity), and collecting and distributing *zakat* by implementing the appropriate technology and management.

Activities: Funds numerous Islamic humanitarian programmes in Kuwait and abroad. Zakat House's major project is an orphan sponsorship programme, which supports more than 17,000 orphans, mainly in Asia. It also supports a number of other charitable projects, aiming to alleviate suffering and improve the quality of life for people worldwide; and organizes symposia.

Geographical Area of Activity: Mainly Asia.

Board of Directors: Yacoub Abdul Mohsen Yacoub Abdul Rahman al-Sanea (Chair.); Sherida Abdullah Saad al-Maousherji (Vice-Chair.).

Principal Staff: Dir-Gen. Ibrahim al-Saleh.

Address: Salmiya Qater St, Block 6, POB 23865, 13099 Safat, Kuwait City.

Telephone: 2241911; **Fax:** 2241888; **Internet:** www.zakathouse.org.kw; **e-mail:** info@zakathouse.org.kw.

Kyrgyzstan

FOUNDATIONS, TRUSTS AND NON-PROFIT ORGANIZATIONS

Soros Foundation—Kyrgyzstan

Founded in 1993 to promote open society; part of the Open Society Foundations (q.v.) network, which aims to foster the development of open societies around the world, particularly in the post-communist countries.

Activities: Promotes the development of an open society in Kyrgyzstan. The Foundation operates in the fields of civil society, legal reform, education, mass media, budget transparency, public health, development of youth initiatives, and other areas.

Geographical Area of Activity: Kyrgyzstan.

Publications: Annual Report; books.

Finance: Annual budget US $4,903,837 (2013).

Advisory Board: Ulan Shabynov (Chair.).

Principal Staff: Exec. Dir Shamil Ibragimov.

Address: Bishkek 720040, ul. Logvinenko 55A.

Telephone: (312) 66-34-75; **Fax:** (312) 66-34-48; **Internet:** www.soros.kg; **e-mail:** office@soros.kg.

Latvia

FOUNDATIONS, TRUSTS AND NON-PROFIT ORGANIZATIONS

Foundation for an Open Society DOTS

Founded in 1992, as Soros Foundation Latvia, to promote the development of open society. Present name adopted in 2014.

Activities: Works in the fields of democracy, social economy and social entrepreneurship, and inclusive society. Since its inception, the Foundation has supported the establishment of organizations, including the Centre for Public Policy—PROVIDUS, the Latvian Centre for Contemporary Art, Civic Alliance of Latvia, Education Development Centre, Latvian Judicial Training Centre, Society for Transparency—TI (Delna), Riga Graduate School of Law, Public Service Language Centre, and several community foundations.

Geographical Area of Activity: Latvia.

Publications: Newsletter.

Finance: Total expenditure €1,070,538 (2013).

Board of Directors: Ivars Ijabs (Chair.).

Principal Staff: Exec. Dir Ieva Morica.

Address: Alberta iela 13, 1010 Riga.

Telephone: 6703-9241; **Fax:** 6703-9242; **Internet:** www.fondsdots.lv; **e-mail:** dots@fondsdots.lv.

Latvijas Bērnu fonds (Latvia Children's Fund)

Founded in 1988 to protect children's rights in Latvia. Since 1991, it has been the official representative of the Christian Children's Fund International in Latvia. In 2003, the Fund became a member of the UN Children's Fund (UNICEF) regional network for children in Central Europe, Eastern Europe, Russia and the Baltic States.

Activities: Activities come under four programmes: Family, Orphans, Health, and Development-Sport-Culture-Talent. Projects are developed within these programmes to provide practical support to groups of children and individual children who have no parents, who are in crisis situations or are severely ill, as well as talented children who lack assets for the development of their talent. Currently, the Fund's main activities are: implementation of the projects financed by the European Union and other funds; organization of summer camps for children with special needs; treatment of severely ill children, support for low-income large families; grants for large families, grants for high-school students from large families and for orphans; grants for winners of the competition 'Talent for Latvia' from children's music schools; support of rehabilitation and crisis centres; organization of the Christmas charity campaign 'Don't Pass By!' and charity concert; and the collection and distribution of humanitarian aid.

Geographical Area of Activity: Latvia.

Board: Andris Bērziнš (Pres.); Vaira Vucāne (Vice-Pres.).

Address: Brīvības Ave 310-75, 1006 Rīga.

Telephone: 6754-2072; **Fax:** 6754-1814; **Internet:** www.lbf.lv; **e-mail:** bernufonds@latnet.lv.

Lebanon

FOUNDATION CENTRE AND CO-ORDINATING BODY

ANND—Arab NGO Network for Development

Established in 1997; a network of NGOs operating in 11 countries of the Middle East.

Activities: Aims to strengthen the role of civil society, enhance the values of democracy, respect for human rights and sustainable development. The Network advocates more sound and effective socio-economic reforms in the region. It organizes conferences, workshops and seminars.

Geographical Area of Activity: Middle East.

Publications: Annual Report; monthly newsletter (online, in Arabic and English); papers and conference reports.

Finance: Total income US $1,271,338, total expenditure $1,184,155 (31 Dec. 2012).

Principal Staff: Exec. Dir Ziad Abdel Samad.

Address: Wata Museitbeh, Boustani St, Quantz II Blgd, 4th Floor, POB 5792/14, Mazraa, 1105-2070 Beirut.

Telephone: (1) 319366; **Fax:** (1) 815636; **Internet:** www.annd .org; **e-mail:** annd@annd.org.

FOUNDATIONS, TRUSTS AND NON-PROFIT ORGANIZATIONS

Arab Image Foundation (Fondation Arabe pour l'Image)

Established in 1997 to preserve and promote the photographic heritage in the Middle East, North Africa and the Arab Diaspora.

Activities: Dedicated to the collection, preservation, and study of photography and other related visual material from the Middle East, North Africa and the Arab Diaspora. The Foundation holds a collection of more than 600,000 photographs dating from the mid-19th century to the present day. Since its inception, the Foundation has produced 15 exhibitions and eight publications in partnership with international museums, galleries, and cultural institutions. In addition, it organizes and participates in local and regional events related to the study of photography and its preservation.

Geographical Area of Activity: Middle East and North Africa.

Publications: *Histoires Intimes: 1900–1960*; *Portraits du Caire*; *The Vehicle*; *Mapping Sitting: On Portraiture and Photography*; *Hashem el-Madani, Studio Practices*; *Hashem el-Madani, Promenades*.

Board of Directors: Akram Zaatari (Pres.); Yasmine Eid-Sabbagh (Vice-Pres.); Vartan Avakian (Treas.); Zeina Arida (Sec.).

Principal Staff: Dir Rima Mokaiesh; Deputy Dir Reem Akl; Acting Collection Man. Charbel Saad.

Address: Zoghbi Bldg, 4th Floor, 337 Gouraud St, Gemmayzeh (opp. Byblos Bank), Beirut.

Telephone: (1) 569373; **Fax:** (1) 569374; **Internet:** www.fai.org .lb; **e-mail:** info@fai.org.lb.

Arab Thought Foundation

Established in 2000.

Activities: Offers the Arab Creativity Award, for achievement in a variety of fields; the Most Valuable Arabic Book Award; and the Entrepreneurship Award for pioneering work; the Innovator Award for creative work in science, knowledge and culture; and the Talent Award, which recognizes academic, intellectual, technological or artistic achievement, and leadership from a young age. The Foundation undertakes educational projects and youth programmes, and organizes the annual Fikr Conference. In 2010, it established the ATF Research and Studies Center, comprising a research unit and a translation unit; and also hosts a Media Center, which collaborates with Arab media.

Geographical Area of Activity: Middle East.

Publications: *Ofoq* (e-newsletter); *One Civilization* book series.

Board of Trustees: HH Prince Khalid bin Faisal bin Abdul Aziz al-Saud (Pres.).

Principal Staff: Chair. HH Prince Bandar bin Khalid al-Faisal Bin Abdul Aziz; Gen. Man. Henri Awit; Deputy Secs-Gen. Dr Mounira el-Nahed, Hamad bin Abdallah al-Ammari.

Address: Al-Maarad St, behind al-Oumary Mosque, Arab Thought Foundation Bldg, Down Town, POB 524-11, Beirut.

Telephone: (1) 997100; **Fax:** (1) 997101; **Internet:** www .arabthought.org; **e-mail:** info@arabthought.org.

Rafik Hariri Foundation

Founded in 1979 by former Prime Minister of Lebanon Rafik Hariri as the Islamic Institute for Culture and Higher Education to promote education as a means of development for children and young people.

Activities: Operates in the fields of education, arts and humanities, and health care, through language programmes designed to enable students to attend university. The Foundation grants loans and scholarships to students, and provides support for academic institutions affected by conflict in the Middle East. It offers career guidance and support for educational organizations and programmes; promotes Lebanese heritage through the renovation and care of old buildings; and fosters relations with international organizations. The Foundation also supports five schools, two of which are in Sidon and the others in Beirut, and the Hariri Canadian University (f. 1999).

Geographical Area of Activity: Lebanon and other countries of the Middle East.

Publications: *Lebanon: Its History and Heritage*; *Lebanon at Present: Its Needs for Development*; *The Arabs*; *Islam in Western Europe*; *Islam and the Moslems in the World*; *The Generations of Hariri Foundation*; *The Educational Evaluation Process*; *Proceedings: Seminar on the Teaching of the Arts in Universities and Higher Institutes*; *Sidon: The Old City*; *Dialogue on Coexistence Among All Denominations and Religions: The Lebanese Model*; *Civic Education and the Rights of Citizens*.

Board of Trustees: Nazek Rafik Hariri (Pres.).

Principal Staff: Dir-Gen. Salwa Siniora Baassiri.

Address: POB 13/5171, Chouran, Beirut 1102-2020; Rafik Hariri Foundation Bldg, Adnan Hakim St, Bir Hasan Area, Beirut.

Telephone: (1) 1853055; **Fax:** (1) 1853006; **Internet:** www.rhf .org.lb; **e-mail:** rhf@rafichariri-foundation.org.

Institute for Palestine Studies, Publishing and Research Organization—IPS

Founded in 1963 by Najla Abou Izzedin, Maurice Gemayel, Said Himadeh, Burhan Dajani, Edmond Rabbath, Constantine Zurayk, Fuad Sarrouf, Nabih Amin Faris, Wadad Cortas and

Walid Khalidi to encourage research into all aspects of the Palestine problem.

Activities: Specializes in research, documentation, analysis and publication on Palestinian affairs and the Arab–Israeli conflict, and possible ways of arriving at a peaceful resolution. The Institute publishes books, occasional papers and documentary collections in Arabic, English and French. It also conducts occasional seminars. The Beirut office houses the IPS Information and Documentation Center, which includes the largest library specializing in Palestinian affairs, the Arab–Israeli conflict, Judaica and Zionism. Maintains offices in Beirut, Jerusalem, Paris and Washington, DC.

Geographical Area of Activity: Middle East.

Publications: *Journal of Palestine Studies* (quarterly, in English); *Jerusalem Quarterly* (in English); *Majallat al-Dirasat al-Filistiniyah* (quarterly, in Arabic); Hawliyyat al-Quds (in Arabic); *IPS Papers*; monographs.

Board of Trustees: Tarek Mitri (Chair.); Basel Aql (Deputy Chair.); Mazen Dajani (Treas.); Walid Khalidi (Sec.).

Principal Staff: Gen. Dir Mahmoud Soueid; Dir Mona Nsouli.

Address: Nsouli-Verdun St, POB 11-7164, 1107-2230 Beirut.

Telephone: (1) 804959; **Fax:** (1) 814193; **Internet:** www.palestine-studies.org; **e-mail:** ipsbrt@palestine-studies.org.

René Moawad Foundation

Established in 1990, in memory of President René Moawad, to promote social, economic and rural development, and to assist in the development of civil society in Lebanon.

Activities: Works in the fields of human rights, education, health and welfare, economic affairs and agriculture, in particular to assist disadvantaged people. The Foundation operates the Agricultural Centre of the North, centres for working young people, and medical and business development centres.

Geographical Area of Activity: Lebanon.

Finance: Annual budget approx. US $4m.

Principal Staff: Pres. Nayla René Moawad; Gen. Man. Nabil Moawad.

Address: BP 468, Hazmieh; 844 rue Alfred Naccache, Achrafieh, Beirut.

Telephone: (1) 613367; **Fax:** (1) 613370; **Internet:** www.rmf.org.lb; **e-mail:** rmf@rmf.org.lb.

Lesotho

FOUNDATION CENTRE AND CO-ORDINATING BODY

Lesotho Council of Non-Governmental Organisations

Established in 1990 to provide support services to the NGO community in Lesotho.

Activities: Operates through networking and leadership training and development, providing information, capacity building, co-ordination, advocacy and representation when dealing with the Government and the international community.

Geographical Area of Activity: Lesotho.

Publications: Annual Report; project reports.

Board of Directors: Mampho Thulo (Pres.); Ntsoaki Khosi (Vice-Pres.); Lehlohonolo Chefa (Treas.).

Principal Staff: Exec. Dir Seabata Motsamai.

Address: House No. 544, Hoohlo Extension, Private Bag A445, Maseru 100.

Telephone: 22317205; **Fax:** 22310412; **Internet:** www.lcn.org.ls; **e-mail:** admin@lcn.org.ls.

Liechtenstein

FOUNDATIONS, TRUSTS AND NON-PROFIT ORGANIZATIONS

International Music and Art Foundation

Established in 1988 to promote art and cultural activities.

Activities: Aims to preserve, facilitate the study of, and disseminate information on art and culture.

Geographical Area of Activity: International.

Restrictions: Does not make grants to individuals, only to recognized and established organizations in the performing arts such as: opera companies, symphony orchestras, chamber music ensembles, ballet and theatre companies, etc.; for architectural restorations and for the conservation of art; to museums; and for research and publication on the history of art. Average grant approx. 33,000 Swiss francs.

Finance: Total assets 44,289,425 Swiss francs (31 Dec. 2014).

Board: Brigitte Feger; Walter Feilchenfeldt; Kurt Kimmel.

Address: Heiligkreuz 40, POB 39, 9490 Vaduz.

Internet: www.imaf.li; **e-mail:** trustees@imaf.li.

Kulturstiftung Liechtenstein (Liechtenstein Foundation for Culture)

Established in 2008.

Activities: Promotes artistic activities of all kinds through the support of projects and training.

Geographical Area of Activity: Liechtenstein.

Publications: Annual Report.

Finance: Annual income 2,923,527 Swiss francs, expenditure 2,923,527 Swiss francs (31 Dec. 2013).

Board of Trustees: Prof. Dr Winfried J. Huppmann (Chair.); Cornelia Kolb-Wieczorek (Vice-Chair.).

Principal Staff: Man. Dir Elisabeth Stöckler.

Address: St Florinsgasse 3, 9490 Vaduz.

Telephone: 2366087; **Fax:** 2366084; **Internet:** www.kulturstiftung.li; **e-mail:** info@kulturstiftung.li.

Lithuania

FOUNDATION CENTRE AND CO-ORDINATING BODY

NGO Information and Support Centre—NISC

Founded by the Open Society Fund—Lithuania in 1995 to develop the NGO sector in Lithuania.

Activities: Sponsored by the UN Development Programme. The Centre operates in the fields of information dissemination, consultancy, training and support for NGOs and their development. It promotes co-operation between NGOs and other institutions and provides information on the legal constitution of NGOs in Lithuania. It also maintains an online database of funding sources for Lithuanian NGOs and a library of more than 1,000 publications.

Geographical Area of Activity: Lithuania.

Publications: *Partnership among NGOs and local governments*; *The Third Sector* (occasional newsletter); and other research publications.

Finance: Annual income 569,105 litas, expenditure 470,807 litas (2011).

Board: Ričardas Diržys (Chair.).

Principal Staff: Dir Martinas Zaltauskas; Project Man. Olga Zuravliova.

Address: 01122 Vilnius, Odminių g. 12.

Telephone: (5) 2618782; **Fax:** (5) 2126045; **Internet:** www.nisc.lt; www.3sektorius.lt; **e-mail:** info@nisc.lt.

FOUNDATIONS, TRUSTS AND NON-PROFIT ORGANIZATIONS

Lietuvos vaikų fondas (Lithuanian Children's Fund)

Founded in 1988 to protect the interests of children in Lithuania.

Activities: Operates nationally, providing financial support to foster families, for housing and scholarships to gifted students. The Fund runs literacy and other educational programmes, as well as funding activities that aim to improve access to social, economic and health-care services for Roma people. It also co-operates with NGOs in Belarus and organizes study trips.

Geographical Area of Activity: Lithuania.

Finance: Partly financed by the European Union and the European Social Fund.

Principal Staff: Dir Romualda Navikaitė.

Address: 06118 Vilnius, Laisvės pr. 125.

Telephone: (2) 628836; **Fax:** (2) 627180; **Internet:** www.lvf.lt; **e-mail:** info@lvf.lt.

Pilietinės Atsakomybės Fondas (Civic Responsibility Foundation)

Established in 2006 to strengthen civic responsibility by fostering philanthropy and empowering the people of Lithuania.

Activities: Works through capacity building to advance democracy, voluntary activity and awareness of NGOs, especially community-based activities.

Geographical Area of Activity: Lithuania.

Restrictions: No support to organizations that foment hatred, discrimination, inequality, social exclusion, violence, are established by public institutions or dependent on public authorities, or are of a political or religious nature.

Principal Staff: Dir Birute Jatautaite.

Address: 01108 Vilnius, J. Basanaviciaus St 15-14.

Telephone: (6) 9978044; **Internet:** www.paf.lt; **e-mail:** info@paf.lt.

Luxembourg

FOUNDATIONS, TRUSTS AND NON-PROFIT ORGANIZATIONS

Action Solidarité Tiers Monde—ASTM (Third World Solidarity Action)

Established in 1969 to support the political, economic and social emancipation of the people of the developing world and to address the global economic issues affecting this emancipation.

Activities: Works in partnership with indigenous organizations in less-developed countries in the areas of education and sustainable development, concentrating on access to land, commercialization of agricultural production, microcredit, and health and women's rights. The organization also provides information on the cultures of the developing world, generates support for cultural activities and develops cultural exchanges, initially through a programme linking Luxembourg with Algeria, India and Senegal.

Geographical Area of Activity: Africa, Asia, Central and South America and the Middle East.

Publications: *Brennpunkt Drëtt Welt* (newsletter); reports and brochures.

Finance: Financed by private donations and state subsidies.

Board of Directors: Richard Graf (Chair.); Monique Langevin (Vice-Chair.); Pierre Schmit (Treas.).

Principal Staff: Co-ordinator and Sec. Nicole Etikwa Ikuku.

Address: 55 ave de la Liberté, 1931 Luxembourg.

Telephone: 40-04-27; **Fax:** 40-04-27-27; **Internet:** www.astm .lu; **e-mail:** astm@astm.lu.

European Federation for Street Children—EFSC

Founded in 1995 in Amsterdam; a network of European and other organizations.

Activities: Works to improve living conditions for street children and provide better opportunities for them by addressing the causes of their homelessness and poverty. The Federation raises public awareness of homeless children and of their rights and needs; promotes strategies to eliminate this phenomenon; and lobbies on behalf of homeless children. It also seeks financial and technical support for member organizations; and facilitates the exchange of information through workshops and conferences.

Geographical Area of Activity: Worldwide.

Publications: Annual Report; newsletter.

Finance: Annual income €44,290, expenditure €114,038 (2011).

Principal Staff: Dir Reinhold Müller.

Address: 15 route d'Esch, 1470 Luxembourg.

Telephone: 27-44-51; **Fax:** 27-44-51-70; **Internet:** www.efsc -eu.org; **e-mail:** info@efsc-eu.org.

Fondation Follereau Luxembourg—FFL (Follereau Foundation Luxembourg)

Established in 1966 by Raoul Follereau to promote international solidarity and combat leprosy.

Activities: Operates mainly in Africa in the fields of aid to less-developed countries, medicine and health, and social welfare. The Foundation's main projects aim to combat leprosy, Buruli ulcer and tuberculosis, and assist those who have been cured of these diseases. It helps underprivileged children through the Follereau-Children project and aims to increase awareness in Luxembourg of these issues. It also collaborates with other organizations and members of the International Federation of Anti Leprosy Associations.

Geographical Area of Activity: Mainly Africa.

Publications: Annual Report; *Solidarité Follereau* (newsletter).

Finance: Annual income €3,878,190, expenditure €3,741,106 (2013).

Board of Directors: Jean Hilger (Pres.); Jos Hilger (Hon. Pres.); Emile Rossler (Vice-Pres.).

Principal Staff: Dir Christophe Wantz.

Address: 151 ave du Dix Septembre, 2551 Luxembourg.

Telephone: 44-66-06-1; **Fax:** 44-66-06-60; **Internet:** www.ffl .lu; **e-mail:** info@ffl.lu.

International Association for the Exchange of Students for Technical Experience—IAESTE

Founded in 1948 by James Newby to provide students at institutions of higher education with technical experience abroad relative to their studies in the broadest sense, and to promote international understanding and goodwill among students of all nations.

Activities: Arranges the exchange of training places among its 93 members and co-operating institutions in 86 countries worldwide, mainly for students of engineering and technology, but also for students of agriculture, applied arts, commerce, languages and science, enabling them to spend two–18 months gaining experience abroad as trainees of industrial and other organizations.

Geographical Area of Activity: International.

Restrictions: Does not make grants.

Publications: Annual Report; Activity Report; newsletters.

Finance: Funded by member subscriptions.

Principal Staff: Pres. Bernard Baeyens.

Address: 51 rue Albert I, First Floor, 1117 Luxembourg.

Telephone: (8) 2709428; **Fax:** (8) 2709428; **Internet:** www .iaeste.org; **e-mail:** info@iaeste.org.

Unity Foundation

Established in 1980.

Activities: Runs two core programmes: Community Schools, working to build the capacity of individuals and communities to care for children's educational needs, providing pre-primary, primary and secondary schooling for children; and Preparation for Social Action, which uses education as a tool for development and targets high-school-aged children in rural areas.

Geographical Area of Activity: Africa, Asia, and Central and South America.

Publications: Annual Report; newsletter.

Finance: Annual project expenditure €521,773 (2013).

Administrative Council: Fernand Schaber (Pres.); Abbas Rafii (Vice-Pres.); Claude Wiltgen (Treas.).

Principal Staff: Office Man. Thomas Hueck.

Address: 17 allée Léopold Goebel, 1635 Luxembourg.

Telephone: 25-26-20; **Internet:** www.unityfoundation.lu; **e-mail:** info@unityfoundation.lu.

The former Yugoslav republic of Macedonia

FOUNDATION CENTRES AND CO-ORDINATING BODIES

Association for Democratic Initiatives—ADI

Established in 1994 to build a civil society in Macedonia.

Activities: Promotes the development of civil society in Macedonia, through conducting voter education activities and a range of other civic initiatives throughout the country; currently operating in 32 towns and villages. The Association runs programmes in the fields of human rights, refugees, youth, election monitoring and the media, including a Civic and Voter Education Programme; Election Monitoring Programme; Civic Education Programme; Promotion of Inter-Ethnic Co-operation and Intercultural Learning Programme; Local Government Programme; Youth Programme; and Human Rights Programme. It has set up three NGO Resource Centres, in Gostivar, Stip and Tetovo, which offer individuals and organizations interested in developing civic initiatives advice and technical support. It is also a member of numerous national and international networks and NGO coalitions and is a founding member of the Steering Committee of the Balkan Human Rights Network—BHRN (q.v.). Has Country Offices in Prishtina, Kosovo and Metohija, Sarajevo, Bosnia and Herzegovina, Tirana, Albania, and New York, USA.

Geographical Area of Activity: the former Yugoslav republic of Macedonia.

Publications: Annual Report; *RETURN* (periodical); *Social integration of refugees and stateless people in Macedonia*; *Conflict and the Media*; *Arms in Macedonia*; publications in the areas of human rights, refugees and migrants, democracy and civil society, and education and youth.

Board: Shpend Imeri (Pres.).

Principal Staff: Exec. Dir Albert Musliu.

Address: Bul. Braka Ginovski 61, 3rd Entrance, 3rd Floor, 1230 Gostivar.

Telephone: (42) 221100; **Fax:** (42) 221102; **Internet:** www.adi.org.mk; www.adi.imeri.biz; **e-mail:** adi@adi.org.mk.

Macedonian Centre for International Co-operation—MCIC

Established in 1993.

Activities: Provides funding to organizations active in the fields of civic society, peace, human rights, education, arts and culture, democratization, health, economics, refugees and returnees, water and sanitation, and tolerance. The Centre supports activities carried out by NGOs, principally in Macedonia, including: the promotion of education of young people, especially in rural and suburban areas, as well as among different nationalities; emergency assistance; civil society and democracy development; and cultural understanding and tolerance. It also began operating in Kosovo in 1999. The Centre is the founder and manager of the Macedonian Enterprise Development Foundation—MEDF, which provides loans for small and micro-enterprises.

Geographical Area of Activity: the former Yugoslav republic of Macedonia, Kosovo and Metohija.

Publications: *NGO-Bulletin*; *NGO-Address Book*; *Ten Years of MCIC*; Annual Report.

Finance: Annual revenue 61,405,000 denars, expenditure 60,363,000 denars (31 Dec. 2013).

Governance Board: Sulejmani Rizvan (Chair.); Gabriela Micevska (Vice-Chair.).

Principal Staff: First Exec. Dir Alexander Krzalovski; Exec. Dir Dimce Mitreski.

Address: Ul. Nikola Parapunov bb, POB 55, 1060 Skopje.

Telephone: (2) 3065381; **Fax:** (2) 3065298; **Internet:** www.mcms.org.mk; **e-mail:** mcms@mcms.org.mk.

FOUNDATIONS, TRUSTS AND NON-PROFIT ORGANIZATIONS

Foundation Open Society Macedonia—FOSIM

Founded in 1992 (previously known as the Open Society Fund of Macedonia) to support the development of Macedonia as an independent and democratic state respectful of multi-ethnic cultural traditions, and to encourage the development of Western standards in the country; an independent foundation, part of the Open Society Foundations (q.v.) network.

Activities: Operates in the fields of education, information and the media, publishing, Roma people and ethnic minorities, youth and women's programmes, public health, law and criminal justice, the arts and culture, civil society and economic reform. Supported initiatives to assist refugees from Kosovo in 1999. Advocates the speedy accession of Macedonia to the European Union. Finances and operates the Soros International House—Skopje, the Soros Centre for Contemporary Arts, the SOS Centre (which provides counselling to teenagers), the Civil Society Resource Centre and Student Resource Centres.

Geographical Area of Activity: the former Yugoslav republic of Macedonia.

Publications: Annual Report and other publications.

Finance: Overall budget 319,784,116 denars (2013).

Executive Board: Maja Bojadzievska (Chair.).

Principal Staff: Exec. Dir Vladimir Milcin.

Address: Bul. Jane Sandanski 111, POB 378, 1000 Skopje.

Telephone: (2) 2444488; **Fax:** (2) 2444499; **Internet:** www.soros.org.mk; **e-mail:** osi@soros.org.mk.

Malawi

FOUNDATIONS, TRUSTS AND NON-PROFIT ORGANIZATIONS

Tea Research Foundation of Central Africa

Founded in 1966 to conduct research into Central African tea and coffee production.

Activities: Conducts research into aspects of tea and coffee production in southern and central Africa, with an emphasis on plant breeding, plant propagation and crop management. The Foundation maintains two research stations in Malawi and one on-farm research centre in Chipinge, Zimbabwe. It runs a training programme for tea estate workers and managers.

Geographical Area of Activity: Malawi, Zimbabwe, Mozambique and Zambia.

Publications: Annual Report; newsletter (2 a year); *Tea Planter's Handbook*; *Coffee Manual for Malawi, Clonal Catalogue, Code of Practice Handbook on the use of Pesticides in Tea in Malawi and Zimbabwe.*

Finance: Funded by members; budget approx. US $800,000 (2011).

Board of Management: Sam E. Magombedze (Chair.).

Principal Staff: Dir Dr Albert Changaya; Chief Research Scientist Dr H. E. N. Nyirenda.

Address: POB 51, Mulanje, Malawi.

Telephone: (1) 467250; **Fax:** (1) 467209; **Internet:** www.trfca .net; **e-mail:** trfdirector@trfca.org.

Malaysia

FOUNDATIONS, TRUSTS AND NON-PROFIT ORGANIZATIONS

Azman Hashim Foundation

Established in 1991 by Tan Sri Azman Hashim, founder and Exec. Chair. of Ambank Group, and his wife Tunku Arishah Tunku Maamor.

Activities: Awards scholarships and study grants. The Foundation has funded the construction of faculty and sports facilities, including at the International Islamic University of Malaysia, Universiti Sains Malaysia, Penang, and University of Malaya.

Geographical Area of Activity: Malaysia.

Finance: The founders pledged US $300m. to the Foundation.

Principal Staff: Chair. Tan Sri Azman Hashim.

Address: c/o Amcorp Group Berhad, 2-01 Amcorp Tower, 18 Persiaran Barat, 46050 Petaling Jaya, Selangor.

Telephone: 79662300; **Fax:** 79662525; **Internet:** www .amcorp.com.my/html/corporate_social_responsibilities.aspx.

Pesticide Action Network Asia and the Pacific—PAN AP

Established in 1992; the co-ordinating regional branch of the PAN International network, which aims to promote sustainable agricultural methods without the need for pesticides.

Activities: Co-ordinates agricultural programmes and projects in the Asia-Pacific region, particularly focusing on sustainable, pesticide-free farming methods, the empowerment of women and peasants in agriculture, and food security. The Network disseminates information and organizes campaigns, workshops and conferences, training and practical field work. It comprises 103 organizations.

Geographical Area of Activity: the Asia-Pacific region.

Publications: Annual Report; *Pesticide Monitor* (quarterly newsletter); books; booklets; fact sheets; monographs.

Principal Staff: Exec. Dir Sarojeni V. Rengam; Admin. and Finance Dir Rosmah Ismail.

Address: POB 1170, 10850 Penang.

Telephone: (4) 6560381; **Fax:** (4) 6583960; **Internet:** www .panap.net; **e-mail:** panap@panap.net.

Third World Network—TWN

Founded in 1984; a non-profit international network of organizations and individuals.

Activities: Carries out research on cultural, social, environmental and economic issues affecting less-developed countries and regions. The Network organizes seminars and articulates the interests of developing countries at international conferences. Maintains offices in Ghana, India, Switzerland and Uruguay, and affiliated organizations in Africa, Asia, the Far East, and Central and South America.

Geographical Area of Activity: Asia, Africa, Latin America, Western Europe.

Publications: *Third World Resurgence* (magazine, monthly); *Third World Economics* (magazine, 2 a month); *SUNS bulletin* (bulletin, daily); *TWN Features Service* (media service, 3 a week); books on environment, technology, economics and trade issues.

Finance: Funded by magazine subscription fees and sale of publications.

Principal Staff: Co-Dirs Chee Yoke Ling, T. Rajamoorthy.

Address: 131 Jalan Macalister, 10400 Penang.

Telephone: (4) 2266728; **Fax:** (4) 2264505; **Internet:** www.twn .my; **e-mail:** twnet@po.jaring.my.

Women's Aid Organisation—WAO (Pertubuhan Pertolongan Wanita)

Established in 1982 to promote women's rights in Malaysia, originally through the provision of women's refuges.

Activities: Works as an advocate for women suffering domestic violence in Malaysia by monitoring the implementation of laws to protect them. Lends support to women suffering violence by helping them with legal advocacy and loans, and giving refuge to them and their children. Also raises awareness of the problem through research, conferences and disseminating information.

Geographical Area of Activity: Malaysia.

Publications: *Inroads* (quarterly newsletter); Annual Report.

Finance: Total annual expenditure approx. 1m. ringgit Malaysia.

Executive Committee: Mok Chuang Lian (Pres.); Vivienne Lee (Vice-Pres.); Chin Oy Sim (Sec.); Carol Chin (Treas.).

Principal Staff: Exec. Dir Ivy N. Josiah.

Address: POB 493, Jalan Sultan, 46760 Petaling Jaya, Selangor Darul Ehsan.

Telephone: (3) 79575636; **Fax:** (3) 79563237; **Internet:** www .wao.org.my; **e-mail:** womensaidorg@gmail.com.

The WorldFish Center

Established in 1973; an initiative of the Rockefeller Foundation (q.v.), and previously known as the International Center for Living Aquatic Resources Management (ICLARM). In 1975, it became a small programme of the University of Hawaii and was incorporated in Manila in 1977. It became a member of the Consultative Group on International Agricultural Research (CGIAR) in 1992.

Activities: Conducts research on all aspects of fisheries and other living aquatic resources. The Center's main areas of research are: improving productivity; protecting the environment; improving policies; saving biodiversity and strengthening national programmes. It operates through research, conferences, publications, scholarships and awarding prizes. The Naga Award is given annually to a nominated scientific paper or book by an author from a developing country in any area of fisheries science. The Center has project offices in Bangladesh, Cambodia, Egypt, the Philippines, the Solomon Islands and Zambia; and conducts research projects with collaborators in 50 countries and with 39 regional and international organizations.

Geographical Area of Activity: Asia, Africa and the Pacific.

Publications: Annual Report; *NAGA* (quarterly); conference proceedings, reviews, studies, technical reports, education and software series.

Finance: Annual revenue US $41,116,000, expenditure $40,320,000 (31 Dec. 2014).

Board of Trustees: Dr Beth Woods (Chair.).

Principal Staff: Dir-Gen. Dr Stephen J. Hall; Deputy Dir-Gen. Dr Patrick Dugan.

Address: POB 500, GPO 10670, Penang; Jalan Batu Maung, Batu Maung, 11960 Bayan Lepas, Penang.

Telephone: (4) 6261606; **Fax:** (4) 6265530; **Internet:** www .worldfishcenter.org; **e-mail:** worldfishcenter@cgiar.org.

Malta

FOUNDATION CENTRE AND CO-ORDINATING BODY

Solidarity Overseas Service Malta—SOS Malta

Established in 1991; aims to help people in times of crisis and empower them by providing support services and opportunities to implement development and change in their country to ensure a better quality of life.

Activities: Operates internationally through encouraging advocacy on behalf of social causes, research and training, promoting models of good care and practice, volunteering and sustainable development. The organization maintains the Malta Resource Centre for Civil Society NGOs.

Geographical Area of Activity: International.

Publications: *SOS Malta Final Reports; SOS Malta Activity Reports; Handbook—INTI; The Structural Funds Training Technical Assistance Programme for NGOs and Civil Society Organisations (2007); Attaining the Millennium Development Goals: The need for increased international cooperation; Malta's Overseas Development Priorities;* Annual Report.

Board: Philip Calleja (Dir); Lilian Miceli Farrugia (Chair.); Francis Frendo (Treas.).

Principal Staff: CEO and Sec. Claudia Taylor-East.

Address: 10 Triq il-Ward, Santa Venera SVR 1640.

Telephone: 21244123; **Fax:** 21224742; **Internet:** www.sosmalta.org; **e-mail:** info@sosmalta.org.

FOUNDATIONS, TRUSTS AND NON-PROFIT ORGANIZATIONS

Fondazzjoni Patrimonju Malti (Maltese Heritage Foundation)

Established in 1992 by a small group of Maltese cultural heritage enthusiasts with the backing of government.

Activities: Activities aim to advance and enrich the understanding of Maltese cultural heritage through exhibitions that display artefacts from private collections and public and non-profit institutions and organizations, which would otherwise not be accessible to the public. The Foundation has restored the Palazzo Falson in the medieval city of Mdina. This 13th-century palazzo, together with all its extensive collections, has been open to the public as a state-of-the-art Historic House Museum since 2007.

Geographical Area of Activity: Malta.

Publications: *Treasures of Malta* (3 a year); various publications about Melitensia.

Principal Staff: CEO Michael Lowell.

Address: 63 Old Mint St, Valletta VLT 1518.

Telephone: 21231515; **Fax:** 21250118; **Internet:** www.patrimonju.org; **e-mail:** info@patrimonju.org.

Strickland Foundation

Established in 1979 by newspaper owner and politician Mabel Strickland to promote cultural heritage and human rights in Malta.

Activities: Promotes Maltese cultural heritage through organizing and hosting seminars and conferences, supporting awards for Maltese journalists through the Malta-EU Information Centre, and funding publications, including *The Mediterranean Journal of Human Rights*, which is published by the University of Malta. In 2013, the Foundation launched an annual writing competition offering a prize of €5,000.

Geographical Area of Activity: Malta.

Council: Ronlad Agius (Chair.); Peter Portelli (Exec. Sec.).

Principal Staff: CEO Victor Aquilina.

Address: Villa Parisio 36, Mabel Strickland St, Lija.

Telephone: 21435890; **e-mail:** admin@thestricklandfoundation.com.

Mexico

FOUNDATION CENTRES AND CO-ORDINATING BODIES

Asociación Latinoamericana de Organizaciones de Promoción al Desarrollo—ALOP (Latin American Association of Development Organizations)

Established in 1979 by 11 Central and South American organizations.

Activities: Works to develop communication and co-operation between members. The Association promotes the rights of native peoples affected by development projects; supports the use of appropriate technology in development projects; and collates and distributes information on projects worldwide. It also awards prizes, and organizes conferences and training courses.

Geographical Area of Activity: Central and South America and the Caribbean.

Publications: *El Mercosur ciudadano: Retos para una nueva institucionalidad; Mito y Realidad de la Ayuda Externa: América Latina; La negociación del Acuerdo de Asociación Centroamérica y la Unión Europea: Balance y Alternativas;* newsletter.

Finance: Annual income US $36,620,390, expenditure $30,936,180 (31 Dec. 2013).

Executive Committee: Oscar Azmitia (Chair.).

Principal Staff: Exec. Sec. Jorge Balbis Pérez.

Address: Chilpancingo 148, Despacho 506, Col. Roma Sur, 06760 México, DF.

Telephone: (55) 5273-3400; **Fax:** (55) 5273-3449; **Internet:** www.alop.org.mx; **e-mail:** info@alop.org.mx.

Centro Mexicano para la Filantropía—CEMEFI (Mexican Centre for Philanthropy)

Founded in 1988 to obtain and disseminate information on organizations and groups committed to philanthropic activities; to establish communications between associations involved in philanthropic activities; and to promote relations with philanthropic organizations worldwide.

Activities: Operates through self-conducted programmes, research, conferences, training courses and publications to promote philanthropy. The Centre lobbies the Government on fiscal and legal issues and represents the Mexican third sector at the international level. It comprises 341 member foundations, associations, companies and individuals.

Geographical Area of Activity: Mexico.

Publications: Annual Report; *Directorio de Instituciones Filantrópicas; Mexican Civil Society Index; Vision con Futuro* (newsletter); *Cemefi Informa* (newsletter); guides to strengthening the internal organs of government and on legal aspects for non-profit organizations; publications on philanthropy, civil society, business social responsibility, fund procurement and volunteering.

Finance: Total assets US $103,050,397 (31 Dec. 2014).

Board of Directors: Mercedes C. Aragonés y Ruipérez (Pres.); Jorge Aguilar Valenzuela (Treas.); Mario González Cos Garciadiego (Sec.).

Principal Staff: Exec. Pres. Jorge V. Villalobos Grzybowicz.

Address: Cerrada de Salvador Alvarado 7, Col. Escandón, 1800 México, DF.

Telephone: (55) 5276-8530; **Fax:** (55) 5515-5448; **Internet:** www.cemefi.org; **e-mail:** cemefi@cemefi.org.

Comunalia—Alianza de Fundaciones Comunitarias de México (Mexico Community Foundations Network)

Established in 2009.

Activities: Aims to strengthen community foundations. Comprises 16 mem. foundations. In 2011, the Network provided financial and other support to 830 civil society orgs and 228 community groups.

Geographical Area of Activity: Principally Mexico.

Publications: Annual Report.

Finance: Total assets US $123,053,000 (31 Dec. 2013).

Board of Directors: David Pérez Rulfo Torres (Pres.); Sec. Juan Carlos Ruiz Campillo (Sec.); Diana Elisa Chávarri Cazaurang (Treas.).

Principal Staff: Exec. Dir Laura J. Trejo.

Address: México, DF.

Telephone: (55) 1952-9270; **Internet:** www.comunalia.org .mx; **e-mail:** info@comunalia.org.mx.

FOUNDATIONS, TRUSTS AND NON-PROFIT ORGANIZATIONS

Centro Internacional de Mejoramiento de Maíz y Trigo—CIMMYT (The International Maize and Wheat Improvement Center)

Founded in 1966 by the Government of Mexico and the Rockefeller Foundation (q.v.); an international, non-profit, agricultural research and training centre.

Activities: Operates internationally through self-conducted programmes, research, fellowships, scholarships, conferences, courses, publications and lectures. The Center supports the development and distribution worldwide of higher-yielding maize and wheat with in-built genetic resistance to diseases and insects; the conservation and distribution of maize and wheat genetic resources; research on natural resource management in maize- and wheat-based cropping systems; documentation of new knowledge in the area of wheat and maize; development of more effective research methods; training; and technical consultation.

Geographical Area of Activity: Worldwide.

Publications: CIMMYT Annual Report; *Literature Update on Wheat, Barley and Triticale;* newsletter.

Finance: Funding comes from overseas development assistance agencies.

Board of Trustees: Dr John Snape (Chair.); Dr Pedro Brajcich Gallegos (Vice-Chair.).

Principal Staff: Dir-Gen. Dr Thomas A. Lumpkin.

Address: Apdo 6-641, 06600 México, DF.

Telephone: (55) 5804-2004; **Fax:** (55) 5804-7558; **Internet:** www.cimmyt.org; **e-mail:** cimmyt@cgiar.org.

Fundación Miguel Alemán AC (Miguel Alemán Foundation)

Founded in 1984 by Miguel Alemán Valdés to promote and support humanitarian activities, tourism development, health and ecological issues, and technological advances in agriculture.

Activities: Operates nationally in the fields of conservation and the environment, gender equality, agricultural productivity, tourism, the arts and humanities, economic affairs, education, international affairs, medicine and health, science and technology, and social welfare, through self-conducted programmes, research, grants to institutions, prizes, conferences, training courses and publications.

Geographical Area of Activity: Mexico.

Publications: *Inform* (annually); several other publications.

Finance: Annual income US $14,294,016, expenditure $18,710,830 (31 Dec. 2011).

Executive Committee: Miguel Alemán Velazco (Pres.); Beatriz Alemán de Girón (Treas.); Francisco Javier Mondragón (Sec.).

Principal Staff: Gen. Man. Dr Alejandro Carrillo Castro.

Address: Rubén Darío 187, Col. Chapultepec Morales, 11570 México, DF.

Telephone: (55) 1946-2200; **Fax:** (55) 1946-2211; **Internet:** www.miguelaleman.org; **e-mail:** info@miguelaleman.org; fundacionmiguelaleman@fma.com.mx.

Fundación Ethos

Established in 2008; a think tank to analyse themes relevant to development in Mexico and Latin America.

Activities: Produces case studies on tax reporting and management, and poverty alleviation policies in Latin America. The Foundation works with federal ministries to evaluate government programmes and improve their effectiveness. It has developed programmes to fight poverty, improve public finance and tax collection, and make direct spending programmes more efficient.

Geographical Area of Activity: Mexico.

Publications: Various publications and analysis on public finance, poverty, and gender and competitiveness.

Finance: Funded by donors.

Principal Staff: Gen. Man. José Luis Chicoma.

Address: Enrique Rebsamen 1108 Col. del Valle, 03100 Mexico, DF.

Telephone: (55) 5335-0460; **Internet:** www.ethos.org.mx; **e-mail:** info@ethos.org.mx.

Fundación Teletón México

Established in 1998.

Activities: Funds 21 rehabilitation centres for children with disabilities and cancer. The Foundation set up the Fondo de Apoyo a Instituciones Teletón—FAI to support other organizations that support people with disabilities. Since its inception, FAI has disbursed 162,668,034 pesos to 486 organizations. In 2000, in collaboration with the Universidad Autónoma del Estado de México the Foundation set up the Instituto Teletón de Estudios Superiores en Rehabilitación, which specialized in training rehabilitation professionals in occupational and physical therapy, and expanded to become the Universidad Teletón in 2013.

Geographical Area of Activity: Mexico.

Principal Staff: Pres. Dr Fernando Landeros Verdugo; Dir of FAI Alejandro Oceguera.

Address: Av. Gustavo Baz No. 219, Col. San Pedro Barrientos, 54010 Tlalnepantla.

Telephone: 5321-2223; **Fax:** 5321-2001; **Internet:** www.teleton.org; **e-mail:** internet@teleton.org.mx.

Oxfam Mexico

Founded in 1996 as Fundación Vamos and later renamed as Rostros y Voces; became part of the Oxfam confederation of organizations (qq.v.) in 2008.

Activities: Operates in the areas of humanitarian assistance, climate change, migration, and health and education.

Geographical Area of Activity: South America, Central America, the Caribbean and Africa.

Finance: Annual income 25,607,953 pesos, expenditure 32,549,707 pesos (31 Dec. 2013).

Board of Directors: Jesús Cantú Escalante (Chair.).

Principal Staff: Exec. Dir Consuelo López Zuriaga; Dir of Finance Mirian Reyna.

Address: Alabama 105 Col. Nápoles, Del. Benito Juárez, 03810 México, DF.

Telephone: (55) 5687-3002; **Internet:** www.oxfammexico.org; **e-mail:** contacto@oxfammexico.org.

Moldova

FOUNDATION CENTRES AND CO-ORDINATING BODIES

National Assistance and Information Centre for NGOs in Moldova—CONTACT (Centrul Național de Asistență și Informare a Organizațiilor Neguvernamentale din Republica Moldova)

Established in 1995, at the initiative of the Soros Foundation—Moldova (q.v.).

Activities: Promotes the development of civil society in Moldova, principally through its NGO Development Department, which aims to respond to the needs of the developing non-governmental sector in Moldova, particularly in rural areas, through provision of a broad spectrum of services for NGOs, including information, training, consultancy and technical assistance and an online database. Provides additional help through a support network of NGOs, which lobbies government and serves to develop dialogue between the non-governmental sector and state institutions, and promotes information exchange.

Geographical Area of Activity: Moldova.

Publications: *Study: Community Participation and Development in the Republic Moldova*; *The White Book II*; *Non-Governmental Organizations in the Republic of Moldova: Their evolution and future* (1998); *Catalogue of Non-Governmental Organizations from the Republic of Moldova* (1998).

Finance: Total assets 3,303,933 lei (31 Dec. 2014).

Board: Arcadie Barbarosie, Igor Nedera, Aliona Niculita, Adrian Evtuhovici.

Principal Staff: Exec. Dir Serghei Neicovcen.

Address: Bucuresti str. 83, 2012 Chișinău.

Telephone: (22) 233946; **Fax:** (22) 233948; **Internet:** www.contact.md; **e-mail:** info@contact.md; centrulcontact@gmail.com.

NGO Rural and Social Initiative

Established in 2000 to consolidate democracy in Moldova through the development of civil society, poverty alleviation and specific services for vulnerable categories of people.

Activities: Operates in the fields of project management. The Initiative provides expertise to authorities to develop specific projects/programmes, and capacity building for rural grassroots civil society organizations in human rights, democracy and community development.

Geographical Area of Activity: Moldova.

Publications: *Dialog* (bulletin); *Work Participative Methods in the Community*; guide for public servants, posters and booklets, leaflets and other publications.

Finance: Annual budget approx. US $190,000.

Principal Staff: Exec. Dir Maria Brodesco.

Address: str. Decebal 9, 6811, Bardar, Ialoveni.

Telephone: 9471568; **Fax:** 26837361; **Internet:** www.ngorural.org; **e-mail:** office@ngorural.org; mariabrodesco@yahoo.com.

Resource Centre for the Human Rights Nongovernmental Organizations of Moldova—CReDO

Established in 1999 to promote the development of civil society in Moldova; an initiative of three Moldovan human rights NGOs (the League for Defence of Human Rights of Moldova, the Moldovan Helsinki Committee for Human Rights and the Independent Society for Education and Human Rights), with financial and technical support from CordAid (the Netherlands) and the Netherlands Helsinki Committee.

Activities: Helps community groups and NGOs working in Moldova in support of human rights to strengthen organizational and institutional capacities. The Centre provides policy analysis, advocacy, training and consultancy services.

Geographical Area of Activity: Moldova.

Publications: Annual Report; policy analyses.

Principal Staff: Exec. Dir Serghei Ostaf.

Address: str. Alexandru Hasdeu 95A, 2005 Chișinău.

Telephone: (22) 212816; **Fax:** (22) 225257; **Internet:** www.credo.md; **e-mail:** credo@credo.md.

FOUNDATIONS, TRUSTS AND NON-PROFIT ORGANIZATIONS

Soros Foundation—Moldova

Established in 1992 to promote the development of open society; part of the Open Society Foundations (q.v.) network, which aims to foster political and cultural pluralism and reform the economy so as to encourage free enterprise and a market economy.

Activities: Principal areas of concern are: supporting independent media by providing training and access to information; civil society, promoting human rights and the rights of ethnic minorities; and providing grants for NGOs and training for NGO workers through the contact centres for NGOs. The Foundation also works in the areas of public administration and good governance, law and criminal justice, public health and European integration.

Geographical Area of Activity: Moldova.

Publications: Annual Report; newsletter (monthly).

Finance: Annual expenditure US $6,397,494 (2014).

National Board: Stela Bivol (Chair.).

Principal Staff: Exec. Dir Victor Ursu; Dep. Dir Varvara Colibaba; Financial Dir Elena Vacarciuc.

Address: Bulgara str. 32, 2001 Chișinău.

Telephone: (22) 270031; **Fax:** (22) 270507; **Internet:** www.soros.md; **e-mail:** foundation@soros.md.

Monaco

FOUNDATIONS, TRUSTS AND NON-PROFIT ORGANIZATIONS

AMADE Mondiale—Association Mondiale des Amis de l'Enfance (World Association of Children's Friends)

Founded in 1963 by Princess Grace of Monaco, the Association strives to contribute to the well-being of the world's most vulnerable children.

Activities: Works to provide access to education and health care for all children worldwide, promotes the defence of children's essential rights and raises public awareness of children's place in society. The Association is the umbrella body for a network of local organizations in Belgium, Burundi, Chile, Italy, Monaco and the Netherlands.

Geographical Area of Activity: Europe, Asia, South America and Africa.

Publications: Annual Report; newsletter.

Finance: Funds disbursed €677,710 (2013).

Board of Directors: HRH The Princess of Hanover (Chair.); Jean-Claude Michel (Vice-Chair.); Jean-Paul Samba (Treas.).

Principal Staff: Sec.-Gen. Jérôme Froissart; Man. Pieter Bogaardt.

Address: 4 rue des Iris, 98000 Monaco.

Telephone: 97-70-52-60; **Fax:** 97-70-52-72; **Internet:** www.amade-mondiale.org; **e-mail:** info@amade-mondiale.org.

Francis Bacon MB Art Foundation

Established in 2014 by Majid Boustany for research into the life and works of the artist Francis Bacon.

Activities: Organizes exhibitions and seminars; offers grants for scholarly research into the life and works of Francis Bacon, and to emerging artists working in the area of figurative imagery.

Geographical Area of Activity: Monaco.

Principal Staff: Founder Majid Boustany.

Address: Villa Elise, 21 blvd d'Italie, 98000 Monaco.

Telephone: 93-30-30-33; **Internet:** www.mbartfoundation.com; **e-mail:** info@mbartfoundation.com.

Fondation Prince Albert II de Monaco

Established in 2006.

Activities: Aims to protect the environment and to encourage sustainable development. Programmes cover three main issues: limiting climate change; safeguarding biodiversity; and managing water resources and preventing desertification. Maintains overseas branches in Canada, France, Germany, Italy, Singapore, Switzerland, the United Kingdom and the USA.

Geographical Area of Activity: Worldwide (with particular emphasis on the Arctic and Antarctic, the Mediterranean and the least-developed countries of the world).

Publications: Annual Report; brochures and bulletins.

Finance: Funds disbursed €22.1m. (2012).

Board of Directors: HSH Prince Albert II (Pres.); Bernard Fautrier (Vice-Pres. and CEO); Sébastien Lubert (Treas.).

Principal Staff: Exec. Dir Olivier Wenden; Sec.-Gen. Pascal Granero.

Address: Villa Girasole, 16 blvd de Suisse, 98000 Monaco.

Telephone: 98-98-44-44; **Fax:** 98-98-44-45; **Internet:** www.fpa2.com; **e-mail:** contact@fpa2.mc.

Fondation Prince Pierre de Monaco

Established in 1966 by Prince Rainier III in memory of his father, Prince Pierre.

Activities: Promotes contemporary creativity through awarding prizes, which include: the Prince Pierre Literary Prize, recognizing the achievements of a young francophone writer; the annual Discovery Grant and High School Students Favorite Choice, both for a young author's first work of fiction in French; the Musical Composition Prize; the Young Musicians Favorite Choice; and the International Prize for Contemporary Art.

Geographical Area of Activity: Monaco and international.

Board of Directors: HRH The Princess of Hanover (Chair.); Carole Laugier (Treas.) .

Principal Staff: Sec.-Gen. Jean-Charles Curau; Deputy Sec.-Gen. Françoise Gamerdinger.

Address: 4 blvd des Moulins, 98000 Monaco.

Telephone: 98-98-85-15; **Fax:** 93-50-66-94; **Internet:** www.fondationprincepierre.mc; **e-mail:** communication@fondationprincepierre.mc.

Fondation Princesse Grace

Founded in 1964 to carry out general charitable activities.

Activities: Main activities are supporting children in hospital, modernizing hospitals in developing countries and providing financial aid for medical research. Projects include: the Boutiques du Rocher, which supports local craftspeople, the Université Médicale Virtuelle de Monaco (an online educational facility for paediatric medicine), the Académie de Danse, which funds training for talented young dancers, and the Princess Grace Irish Library. The Foundation also contributes to humanitarian projects related to children's health care, including some international work, and to cultural activities, providing scholarships to students of the arts. The Princess Grace Foundation—USA operates independently in the USA.

Geographical Area of Activity: Mainly Monaco and France.

Restrictions: No grants directly to students or children.

Board of Trustees: HRH Caroline Princess of Hanover (Pres.); HSH Prince Albert (Vice-Pres.); Jean-Claude Riey (Sec.-Treas.).

Principal Staff: Exec. Dir Caroline O'Connor.

Address: 9 rue Princesse Marie de Lorraine, BP 520, 98015 Monte Carlo.

Telephone: 97-70-86-86; **Fax:** 97-70-79-99; **Internet:** www.fondation-psse-grace.mc; **e-mail:** fpg@monaco.mc.

Princess Charlene of Monaco Foundation

Established in 2012 to promote sports in order to assist in the education and development of children.

Activities: Operates in three main areas: educational projects on water safety; supporting excellence in young athletes; and supporting sports projects in communities.

Board: HSH Princess Charlene (Pres.); HSH Prince Albert II (Vice-Pres.); Agnès Falco (Gen. Sec.); Lady Cristina Green (Treas.).

Principal Staff: Man. Jean-Marie Véran.

Address: Les Jardins d'Apolline, 1 promenade Honoré II, BP 1, 98001 Monaco.

Telephone: 98-98-99-99; **Internet:** www.fondationprincessecharlene.mc; **e-mail:** contact@fondationprincessecharlene.mc.

Mongolia

FOUNDATION CENTRE AND CO-ORDINATING BODY

Mongolian Women's Fund—MONES

Established in 2000 to support public projects by women's NGOs and grassroots women's groups, as well as female-led NGOs and civic groups working towards women's human rights.

Activities: Raises funds and provides financial support to women's organizations and groups that are committed to issues such as gender-based discrimination and violence; increasing the income capacity of women; increasing women's participation in civic life; and the capacity building of women's organizations and groups.

Geographical Area of Activity: Mongolia.

Restrictions: No support for religious or political activities.

Finance: Total annual disbursements 21.4m. tugriks (2013).

Board of Trustees: Sharav Tsevelmaa (Chair.).

Principal Staff: Exec. Dir Erdenechimeg Badrakh.

Address: No. 305, Bldg 48, Small Ring Rd, Sukhbaatar District, Ulaanbaatar; POB 280, Ulaanbaatar 210646A.

Telephone: (11) 77119991; **Fax:** (11) 77119991; **Internet:** www.mones.org.mn; **e-mail:** info@mones.org.mn.

FOUNDATIONS, TRUSTS AND NON-PROFIT ORGANIZATIONS

Open Society Forum (Mongolia)

Established in 1996 as the Mongolian Foundation for Open Society—MFOS to promote the development of open society in Mongolia; an independent foundation, part of the Open Society Foundations (q.v.) network. Present name adopted in 2005.

Activities: Operates in the areas of education, information and the media, arts and culture, civil society, law and criminal justice, public health, economic development, women and youth. The Forum also runs an extensive scholarship programme and an online grants database.

Geographical Area of Activity: Mongolia.

Publications: Annual Report; *Freedom in the world 2007: Freedom stagnation amid pushback against democracy*; *Conceptions of Democracy*; *Social Protection Index for Committed Poverty Reduction*; *Politbarometer*.

Board of Directors: Purevjav Tsenguun (Chair.).

Principal Staff: Exec. Dir Perenlei Erdenejargal.

Address: Silk Rd Bldg, Jamiyan Gun St 5/1, Sukhbaatar District, Ulaanbaatar 48.

Telephone: (11) 313207; **Fax:** (11) 324857; **Internet:** www.forum.mn/en/; **e-mail:** osf@forum.mn.

Zorig Foundation

Established in 1998 in memory of the late Sanjaasürengiin Zorig.

Activities: Aims to advance the formation of democratic society and support political reforms in Mongolia. The Foundation focuses on three areas: good governance, community development, and youth and education. It promotes good governance and democracy through organizing workshops, conferences, lectures and seminars in areas such as anti-corruption and free media. It also provides scholarships for students from families with low incomes; organizes year-long leadership programmes to help young professionals, and high-school and university students; and supports families and communities through a variety of projects.

Geographical Area of Activity: Mongolia.

Publications: *Zorig's Smile* (1999); *Corruption and ways to fight against it* (collection of seminar presentations, 2000); *Good Governance* (records from the international conference, 2001); *Corruption is not forever* (collection of best essays and posters, 2003); *The immense efforts of the journalists who drove the impeachment of the President* (booklet, 2004); *Implementation of National Anti Corruption Program* (monitoring report, 2004); *On Democracy* (translated Mongolian edn, 2004); *My Constitution, My Freedom* (explanatory comic book for children, 2005); *Monitoring Report of the Customs Office* (2006); *Anti Corruption* (compilation, 2007); *The Resource Curse* (2007); *Migrants' handbook* (2008); *State Scholarship Monitoring Report* (booklet, 2008); *Together with Migrants* (guidelines, 2012).

Finance: Annual revenue US $387,536, expenditure $376,118 (2014).

Board of Directors: Dr Oyun Sanjaasürengiin (Chair.).

Principal Staff: Exec. Dir Tsolmon Bayaraa.

Address: Central Post Office, POB 357, Ulaanbaatar; Peace Ave 17, Sukhbaatar District, Ulaanbaatar.

Telephone: (11) 315444; **Fax:** (11) 315444; **Internet:** zorigfoundation.org; zorigsan.mn; **e-mail:** admin@zorigfoundation.org.

Montenegro

FOUNDATION CENTRE AND CO-ORDINATING BODY

Centre for the Development of Non-governmental Organizations (Centar za Razvoj Nevladinih Organiza-cija—CRNVO)

Established in 1999 to provide support to development of NGOs in Montenegro and contribute to the creation of a favourable environment for citizens' participation in public policy issues and civil society development.

Activities: Aims to build capacity of NGOs, improve co-operation between the state, NGOs and the commercial sector, increase understanding of the importance of the role that NGOs play in society, and contribute to the development of democracy, the rule of law and human rights. The Centre provides training and technical assistance to NGOs, acts as a policy advocate to government, organizes discussion meetings between donors and NGOs, and trains NGO leaders in policy advocacy and human rights issues.

Geographical Area of Activity: Montenegro.

Publications: *Tax and Financial Guidebook for NGOs; Learning Through Work; Co-operation Between State and NGOs; Strategic Planning; Volunteers; Grassroots Fundraising; Report on the Readiness of Serbia and Montenegro to Negotiate on a Stabilization and Association Agreement with the European Union; Basic Terms of Non-Governmental Sector; Citizen* (newsletter).

Finance: Annual income €200,543,000, expenditure €191,650,000 (31 Dec. 2014).

Principal Staff: Exec. Dir Ana Novaković; Deputy Exec. Dir Marina Vuković.

Address: 20000 Podgorica, Dalmatinska St 78.

Telephone: (81) 20219120; **Fax:** (81) 20219121; **Internet:** www.crnvo.me; **e-mail:** crnvo@crnvo.me.

Morocco

FOUNDATIONS, TRUSTS AND NON-PROFIT ORGANIZATIONS

Fondation Addoha (Addoha Foundation)

Established in 2011 by Anas Sefrioui, Chair. of Groupe Addoha, a property development company.

Activities: Funds educational and vocational youth training programmes, and provides university scholarships. Runs two training centres in Aïn Aouda and Fès, and plans to open others in Tangiers, Marrakech and Casablanca; the centres aim to train 5,000 young people in building trades between 2012 and 2016.

Geographical Area of Activity: Morocco.

Principal Staff: Chair. Anas Sefrioui.

Address: c/o Groupe Addoha, Km 7, Route de Rabat (Ain Sebaa), Casablanca.

Telephone: (52) 2679900; **Fax:** (52) 2351763; **Internet:** www .fondationaddoha.org; **e-mail:** contact@groupeaddoha.com.

Fondation BMCE Bank (BMCE Bank Foundation)

Established in 1995 by Othman Benjelloun, Chair. and CEO of BMCE Bank Group.

Activities: Main areas of interest are education for disadvantaged children in rural areas, through the Medersat.com schools programme and in co-operation with the Ministry of National Education, Higher Education, Training and Scientific Research; and conservation of the environment.

Geographical Area of Activity: Morocco.

Principal Staff: Chair. Dr Leila Mezian Benjelloun; Gen. Sec. Wafaa Chafi Fathi.

Address: Zénith Millénium, Imm. 2 bis, BP 89, 4th Floor, Lot. Attaoufik, Sidi Mâarouf, Casablanca.

Telephone: (52) 2977505; **Fax:** (52) 2972421; **Internet:** www .fondationbmce.org.

Fondation Miloud Chaabi (Miloud Chaabi Foundation)

Established in 1965 by Miloud Chaabi, Chair. of YNNA Holding.

Activities: Main areas of interest are development and education; provides scholarships for students to study in Morocco and abroad; and has funded the construction of university facilities in Morocco, incl. the Al Qalam Institute in Agadir (f. 1995), Essaouira Higher Institute of Technology (f. 2005) and Indiana State University of Morocco in Casablanca (f. 2008).

Geographical Area of Activity: Morocco.

Restrictions: Provides grants to projects in the areas of health, education, social welfare, the arts, sport and the environment.

Address: c/o Groupe Chaabi, 233 blvd Mohammed V, 20000 Casablanca.

Internet: www.ynna.ma/fmc.

Fondation Orient-Occident (Orient-Occident Foundation)

Established in 1994 by Yasmine Filali.

Activities: Aims to contribute to enhancing dialogue between cultures and promoting mutual understanding. Has established socio-educational and professional training centres in seven centres in Morocco. Operates programmes for Moroccan and immigrant young people in the areas of educational reinforcement, psychological counselling, vocational training, solidarity economy and human rights.

Geographical Area of Activity: Morocco.

Publications: Newsletter.

Finance: Financed by the Government, European Union grants and a number of private sponsors.

Board of Directors: Yasmine Filali (Founding Chair. and CEO); Abdou Filali-Ansary, Patrick Guerrand-Hermès (Vice-Chair.); Saïd Lamrani (Treas.).

Principal Staff: Dir and Sec.-Gen. Rachid Badouli.

Address: ave des FAR, Commune de Yacoub el Mansour, BP 3210, Massira, Rabat.

Telephone: (53) 7793637; **Fax:** (53) 7291543; **Internet:** fondation.orient-occident.org; **e-mail:** reseaufoo@gmail .com.

Fondation du Roi Abdul-Aziz al-Saoud pour les Etudes Islamiques et les Sciences Humaines (King Abdul-Aziz al-Saoud Foundation for Islamic Study and the Humanities)

Established in 1985 to offer library and database services to researchers working in the field of Islamic culture and in the humanities.

Activities: Maintains a research library of approximately 380,000 monographs and 2,793 periodicals, mainly in Arabic, English and French. The Foundation also maintains three databases: the Ibn Rushd database of more than 78,000 bibliographical references, with information on the Maghreb, Western European and West African Islamic communities; the Fahras database of approximately 58,000 references, with information covering the rest of the Arab world and general Islamic research; and the Mawsu'a database of more than 241,000 entries containing bibliographical information on the human and social sciences, regarding their methodological and theoretical aspects. There is also a multimedia service. In addition, the Foundation organizes international conferences and seminars in collaboration with other research and documentation institutions.

Geographical Area of Activity: Morocco.

Publications: *Études maghrébines; Ethique et entreprises: perspectives maghrébines* (books); *Le droit international privé dans les pays maghrébins; La Méditerranée en question: conflits et interdépendance; Renouveau de la pensée islamique; Renouveau des études sur l'Islam et le Monde arabe; Droit et environnement social;* newsletter (twice a year).

Principal Staff: Deputy Dir Mohamed-Sghir Janjar.

Address: BP 12585, Casablanca 20052; rue du Corail, Ain Diab, Anfa, Casablanca 20050.

Telephone: (52) 2391027; **Fax:** (52) 2391031; **Internet:** www .fondation.org.ma; **e-mail:** secretariat@fondation.org.ma.

Mozambique

FOUNDATIONS, TRUSTS AND NON-PROFIT ORGANIZATIONS

FDC—Fundação para o Desenvolvimento da Comunidade (Community Development Foundation)

Established in 1994 by Graça Machel, wife of President of South Africa Nelson Mandela and a former Minister of Education in Mozambique, to bring health care, education, economic development, access to technology and peace to the African continent. Originally constituted in 1990 as the Association for the Development of the Community.

Activities: Promotes economic development, health care and related programmes in disadvantaged communities in Mozambique and other parts of Africa, aiming to increase human and financial resources for development at the community level. Priority is given to education, health, water and training projects, which develop human potential, generate income, and put in place necessary infrastructure. The Foundation has financed the construction of hospitals and schools, and skills training, and has provided micro-credit funds. Also acts as an advocate in the areas of land tenure, promotes a landmine ban, supports education for girls, and works in the areas of external debt and development issues.

Geographical Area of Activity: Mozambique and Africa.

Publications: Newsletter, manuals and reports.

Administrative Council: Graça Simbine Machel (Chair.).

Principal Staff: Exec. Dir Narciso Matos; Dir of Programmes Jacinto Uqueio; Dir of Admin. and Finance Eunica Zunguza.

Address: Av. 25 de Setembro, Edificio Times Square, 2º–3º andar, Bloco 2, CP 4206, Maputo.

Telephone: (21) 355300; **Fax:** (21) 355355; **Internet:** www.fdc.org.mz; **e-mail:** info@fdc.org.mz.

Namibia

FOUNDATIONS, TRUSTS AND NON-PROFIT ORGANIZATIONS

DRFN—Desert Research Foundation of Namibia

Established in 1990. Incorporates the Desert Ecological Research Unit, which was founded by Dr Charles Koch in 1963 to promote ecological education and research training.

Activities: Works to further understanding and competence appropriately to manage arid environments for sustainable development. The Foundation collaborates in all sectors involved in management and use of natural resources, concentrating on the agriculture, water and energy sectors, with government, commercial, non-governmental and community-based organizations. It functions at a number of levels: involving communities in participatory learning to develop sustainable management practices; engaging managers and policy-makers in dialogue to improve the policy and regulatory framework for sustainable development; building a body of knowledge to improve understanding of arid and semi-arid lands; building the capacity and commitment to manage natural resources sustainably. The Foundation is a co-partner, together with the Ministry of Environment and Tourism, in guiding the Gobabeb Training and Research Centre in the Namib Desert, on the banks of the ephemeral Kuiseb River. It also undertakes commercial environmental work through its consulting arm, Environmental Evaluation Associates of Namibia (Pty) Ltd.

Geographical Area of Activity: Southern Africa, particularly Namibia.

Publications: Annual Report; *Age and dynamics of linear dunes in the Namib Desert; Dynamics of flood water infiltration and ground water recharge in hyperarid desert; Ecophysiology of atmospheric moisture in the Namib Desert; Community-driven local level monitoring: recording environmental change to support multi-level decision-making in Namibia; Water points and their influence on grazing resources in central northern Namibia; Recovery of lichen-dominated soil crusts in a hyper-arid desert; Infection of the cones and seeds of Welwitschia mirabilis by Aspergillus niger var. phoenicis in the Namib-Naukluft Park.*

Finance: Funded by grants, donations and a trust fund. Implements donor funds. Annual budget approx. N $10m.

Board of Trustees: Roy Miller (Chair.); Penny T. Akwenye (Vice-Chair.).

Principal Staff: Exec. Dir Viviane Kinyaga.

Address: POB 20232, Windhoek; 7 Rossini St, Windhoek West.

Telephone: (61) 377500; **Fax:** (61) 230172; **Internet:** www.drfn.org.na; **e-mail:** drfn@drfn.org.na.

Gobabeb Training and Research Centre

Established in 1962 as the Namib Desert Research Station to carry out research on desert climate, ecology, geology and geomorphology of the desert landscape.

Activities: Offers training at all levels to Namibian institutions and environmental groups, and conducts long-term ecological research, and, through the Gobabeb Environmental Observatories Network, is linked worldwide. Since 1990, the Centre has been a Southern African Development Community (SADC) Centre of Excellence, promoting sustainable lifestyles and practices through wise management of natural resources within Namibia and the SADC region, with an emphasis on desertification, land degradation and sustainable natural resource management.

Geographical Area of Activity: Namibia and southern Africa.

Publications: *Gobabeb Times* (newsletter); *Management of alluvial aquifers in two Southern African ephemeral rivers; The impacts of an invasive species and hydrological change in an aquifer-dependent ecosystem; Home range and seasonal movements of* Giraffa camelopardalis angolensis *in the northern Namib Desert;* and others.

Finance: Annual budget N $10m.

Board of Trustees: Simeon Negumbo (Chair.); Penny T. Akwenye (Deputy Chair.).

Principal Staff: Exec. Dir Gillian Maggs-Kölling.

Address: POB 953, Walvis Bay.

Telephone: (64) 694199; **Fax:** (64) 694197; **Internet:** www.gobabebtrc.org; www.gobabeb.org; **e-mail:** gobabeb@gobabeb.org.

Rössing Foundation

Established in 1978 by Rössing Uranium Ltd, Namibia and Rio Tinto Zinc, London (United Kingdom) to promote research and education in Namibia.

Activities: Carries out community development projects, mainly in the Erongo region, focusing on education, health, poverty alleviation, innovation, the environment and enterprise development. Under its Education Programme, the Foundation provides resources for primary- and secondary-school pupils and teachers. It has built three English language centres and maintains libraries, maths and science centres. Under its Outreach Programme, the Foundation supports school leadership and management. It also runs the Arandis Sustainable Development Plan and Erongo Micro Credit Initiative.

Geographical Area of Activity: Southern Africa.

Finance: Funded almost entirely by Rössing Uranium Ltd. Total expenditure N $285,850 (2011).

Board of Directors: Rehabeam R. Hoveka (Chair.).

Principal Staff: Dir Job Tjiho.

Address: Private Bag 13214, Windhoek; 360 Sam Nujoma St, Klein Windhoek, Windhoek.

Telephone: (61) 211721; **Fax:** (61) 233637; **Internet:** rossingfoundation.com; **e-mail:** jtjiho@rossing.com.na.

Nepal

FOUNDATIONS, TRUSTS AND NON-PROFIT ORGANIZATIONS

Asia-Pacific Mountain Network—APMN

Established in 1995; a network of organizations and individuals concerned with sustainable mountain development in the Asia-Pacific region; managed by the International Centre for Integrated Mountain Development (ICIMOD). Functions as the Asia-Pacific node of the Mountain Forum.

Activities: Operates in the area of conservation and development in mountainous areas of the Asia-Pacific region, promoting the idea of a sustainable ecosystem in these areas. The Network disseminates information on this subject, encouraging information exchange among members; works on capacity building, especially relating to technological advances and electronic communications; acts as an advocate for improved legislation in the field of sustainable mountain development; and supports the alleviation of poverty among mountain populations. New initiatives include grassroots outreach activities targeting young people and the development of a subsidiary office in Central Asia.

Geographical Area of Activity: Asia-Pacific region.

Publications: *Asia Pacific Mountain Courier* (2 a year); *Tough Terrain: Media Reports on Mountain Issues;* occasional reports and briefs.

Principal Staff: Man. Tek Jung Mahat.

Address: c/o ICIMOD, Khumaltar, Khumaltar Patan (Lalitpur) 44700; POB 3226, Kathmandu.

Telephone: (1) 5003222; **Fax:** (1) 5003277; **Internet:** www .icimod.org/apmn; www.mtnforum.org; **e-mail:** apmn@ mtnforum.org.

Himalayan Light Foundation—HLF

Established in 1997 by Adam Friedensohn (Lama Rangbar Nyimai Özer) to support the use of environmentally friendly energy technology to improve the quality of life of people living in remote Himalayan communities.

Activities: Operates in the fields of conservation and the environment, education and social welfare, through self-conducted programmes, research and dissemination of information. The Foundation has four main programmes: emergency relief for Helambu (Yolmo), Upper Sankhu and Kartike, areas affected by the April 2015 earthquakes; using Solar Power Ozone Water Treatment Systems (SPOWTS) to provide safe drinking water in earthquake-affected areas; the Heritage Renewal Initiative, in collaboration with the Bodhivastu Foundation, to repair and restore sites of cultural significance at Boudhanath Stupa, Swayambunath Temple and Sankhu Vajrayogini Temples; and the Solar Sisters Renewable Energy Relief Corps, installing solar lighting systems in community-owned buildings. HLF USA has an office in Poughquag, New York.

Geographical Area of Activity: Nepal and South Asia.

Publications: *The Solar Siblings Manual; The Solar Sisters and Home Employment and Lighting Package Manual; Charged Newsletter.*

Board of Directors: Sapana Shakya (Pres.); Sarita Pradhan (Vice-Pres.); Shanti Laxmi Shakya (Treas.); Bhim Bahadur Mahara (Sec.).

Principal Staff: Prog. Man. Yadav Raj Gurung.

Address: POB 12191, Dhumbarai (Peepalbot), Kathmandu.

Telephone: (1) 4425393; **Fax:** (1) 4412924; **Internet:** www.hlf .org.np; **e-mail:** info@hlf.org.np.

INHURED International—International Institute for Human Rights, Environment and Development

Founded in 1991 to defend human rights in the Asia-Pacific region, particularly in South Asia.

Activities: Works to advance human rights and gender equality and to promote democracy in Asia, by strengthening existing human rights bodies; monitoring international institutions for signs of human and environmental rights abuses; observing elections; funding training; co-ordinating international conferences and workshops; and disseminating information. The Institute offers internship and fellowship programmes for international and university students and scholars in the areas of human rights, environment, development and the democratization process. It also promotes environmental conservation.

Geographical Area of Activity: Asia-Pacific region.

Finance: Funded by membership fees, donations, sale of publications and grants.

Board: Dr Gopal Krishna Siwakoti (Pres.); Hemant Raj Dahal (Vice-Pres.); B.P. Adhikari (Sec.-Gen.); Rekha Rana (Sec.); Deepika Naidu (Treas.).

Principal Staff: Exec. Dir Shreejana Pokhrel.

Address: Ceasefire House, Jhamsikhel, Lalitpur 2; POB 12684, Kathmandu.

Telephone: (1) 5520054; **Fax:** (1) 5520042; **Internet:** www .inhuredinternational.org; **e-mail:** inhured@ntc.net.np; info@inhuredinternational.org.

Tewa

Established in 1996 by Rita Thapa to promote the advancement of women through grantmaking to women's groups in Nepal.

Activities: Operates in three principal areas: grantmaking, fund-raising and training of fund-raising volunteers. The organization launched a community children's programme in 2007 and the Tewa Model Adaptation Initiative in 2008.

Geographical Area of Activity: Nepal.

Publications: *Tewa Times* (annual report); newsletter.

Finance: Annual income NRs 53,428,228, expenditure NRs 54,550,557 (15 July 2012).

Executive Board: Sadhana Shrestha (Chair.); Chhaya Jha (Vice-Chair.); Amita Adhikary (Gen. Sec.); Rama Laxmi Shrestha (Treas.).

Principal Staff: Exec. Dir Astha Thapa Pandé; Development Dir Deepak Dewan.

Address: Dhapakhel Rd, Laltipur; POB 11, Lalitpur.

Telephone: (1) 5572654; **Fax:** (1) 5572659; **Internet:** www .tewa.org.np; **e-mail:** info@tewa.org.np.

Netherlands

FOUNDATION CENTRES AND CO-ORDINATING BODIES

The Hague Club

Established in 1971; an informal association of individuals.

Activities: Facilitates discussion and co-operation between chief executives of important foundations in Europe and prominent persons involved with foundations. Membership is restricted to the chief executives of selected foundations in Europe (and one foundation from Israel), and so-called Corresponding Members from different parts of the world. The members convene once a year. A Steering Committee, elected for a period of two years, conducts day-to-day affairs. The members of the Club are the Chief Executives of: Fundação Calouste Gulbenkian; Fondation Roi Baudouin; Bernard van Leer Foundation; European Cultural Foundation; Ramón Areces Fundación; Nuffield Foundation; Finnish Cultural Foundation; Fritz-Thyssen-Stiftung; Bodossaki Foundation; Jenny and Antti Wihuri Foundation; Volkswagen-Stiftung; Leverhulme Trust; Oranje Fonds (formerly the Juliana Welzijn Fonds); Robert-Bosch-Stiftung GmbH; Novartis Foundation; Fondazione Adriano Olivetti; Bank of Sweden Tercentenary Foundation; Prince Bernhard Cultural Foundation; Compagnia di San Paolo; ZEIT-Stiftung Ebelin und Gerd Bucerius; Fundación Instituto de Empresa; Institusjonen Fitt ord; Nobel Foundation; the Wellcome Trust; Zuger Kulturstiftung Landis & Cyr (qq.v.), and the Velux Foundation. The Corresponding Members are the Chief Executives of: Consiglio Italiano per le Scienze Sociali, Italy; the Council on Foundations, USA; Fundacão Roberto Marinho, Brazil; Japan Center for International Exchange, Japan; the Myer Foundation, Australia; the Jacobs Foundation, Switzerland; and the Van Leer Group Foundation, Netherlands.

Geographical Area of Activity: Mainly Europe.

Restrictions: Does not make grants.

Principal Staff: Treas. Ronald C. van der Giessen.

Address: Postbus 90, 3500 AB Utrecht; Maliebaan 18, 3581 CP Utrecht.

Vereniging van Fondsen in Nederland—FIN (Association of Foundations in the Netherlands)

Established in 1988; members are private foundations established in the Netherlands.

Activities: Promotes the interests of its approx. 300 member foundations and helps them to function in the most effective way by: organizing meetings, workshops and symposia for its members; providing information concerning foundations operating in the Netherlands; maintaining contact with public authorities, social organizations and the media; and providing advice on matters of management and donations policy. The Association also promotes the establishment of new foundations and the exchange of information between members.

Geographical Area of Activity: Netherlands.

Publications: Newsletter; *Fondsenboek*; *Fondsendisk* (annually); informative publications including *Het besturen van een fonds* (*Managing a Foundation*) and *Fiscaliteit* (*Tax Law*).

Finance: Financed by subscriptions from its members.

Board: Dr M. C. E. (Rien) van Gendt (Chair.); E.Y. Beelaerts van Blokland-van Schaijk (Vice-Chair.); Jennifer Van Vliet (Treas.).

Principal Staff: Dir H. (Rick) Wagenvoort.

Address: Jan van Nassaustraat 102, 2596 BW The Hague.

Telephone: (70) 3262753; **Fax:** (70) 3262229; **Internet:** www .verenigingvanfondsen.nl; **e-mail:** info@ verenigingvanfondsen.nl.

FOUNDATIONS, TRUSTS AND NON-PROFIT ORGANIZATIONS

ActionAid

Established in 1997 as the Nederlands instituut voor Zuidelijk Afrika (NiZA) following the merger of the Eduardo Mondlane Foundation, the Anti-Apartheid Movement Netherlands and the Dutch Committee on Southern Africa. Present name adopted in 2012.

Activities: Operates in the Netherlands, Southern Africa and the European Union member states. The organization focuses on the themes of land and food, fair mining and tax evasion. It organizes campaigns, conferences, lectures, including the Mandela Lecture, debates and exchange programmes to stimulate mutual contact between Southern Africa and the Netherlands; and aims to influence Dutch and European policy towards Southern Africa through lobbying. It also issues publications and disseminates information; and maintains a library and information and resource centre.

Geographical Area of Activity: Netherlands, Southern Africa and European Union member states.

Publications: Annual Report; e-newsletter; reports; conference proceedings.

Finance: Annual income €3,078,356, annual expenditure €2,532,194 (2014).

Board: Ingrid Roestenburg Morgan (Chair.); Venda Sykora (Treas.).

Principal Staff: Exec. Dir Ruud van den Hurk.

Address: POB 10707, 1001 ES Amsterdam; Stadhouderskade 60, Amsterdam.

Telephone: (20) 5206210; **Fax:** (20) 5206249; **Internet:** www .niza.nl; **e-mail:** info@actionaid.nl.

Adessium Foundation

Established in 2005 by the van Vliet family.

Activities: Funds initiatives that benefit people and society; and projects promoting sustainable exploitation, production and certification of natural resources.

Geographical Area of Activity: Worldwide, social initiatives mainly in the Netherlands.

Restrictions: Projects must have a scientific basis; self-sustaining capacity; a focus on innovative and practical solutions; aim for structural and sustainable change; and have visible and quantifiable results. Does not accept unsolicited project proposals.

Finance: Total expenditure €16,031,000 (2013).

Board of Directors: Rogier D. van Vliet (Chair.).

Principal Staff: Man. Dir Pieter M. Stemerding; Dir of Progs Rogier van der Weerd.

Address: POB 76, 2810 AB Reeuwijk.

Telephone: (182) 646100; **Fax:** (182) 646199; **Internet:** www .adessium.org; **e-mail:** info@adessium.org.

Eduard Van Beinum Stichting (Eduard Van Beinum Foundation)

Founded in 1960 by harpist Phia Berghout for the stimulation of musical life in general and particularly the promotion of the artistic and social interests of musicians, all in the broadest sense.

Activities: Operates nationally and internationally in the arts; provides sums annually for commissions in the field of contemporary classical music, including operatic works.

Geographical Area of Activity: International.

Publications: *Eduard van Beinum Over zijn leven en werk*; *Eduard van Beinum 1900–1959, Musicus Tussen Musici.*

Governing Board: Floris A. W. Bannier (Pres.); Yvonne van Baarle (Sec.).

Principal Staff: Man. Aleida Hamel.

Address: Postbus 327, 1200 AH Hilversum; Tafelbergweg 6, 1251 AE Laren.

Telephone: (35) 6245788; **Internet:** www .eduardvanbeinumstichting.nl; **e-mail:** info@ eduardvanbeinumstichting.nl.

Evert Willem Beth Foundation

Founded in 1978 under the terms of the will of Cornelia P. C. Beth-Pastoor to promote interest in logic, the philosophy of the exact sciences, and research into the foundations of the sciences.

Activities: Operates nationally and internationally in education and the humanities, through publications, teaching and organizing symposia. The Foundation conducts research in logic, the origins and philosophy of the exact sciences, and any philosophical activity that is conceptually connected with these subjects. It also funds an endowed chair of study and research and scientific gatherings. Regular series of E. W. Beth Lectures are given by philosophers and scientists of international repute.

Finance: Annual income €40,568, expenditure €27,752 (2014).

Board of Management: Prof. Dr Frank J. M. M. Veltman (Chair.); Prof. Dr Albert Visser (Sec.).

Address: Royal Netherlands Academy of Arts and Sciences, Postbus 19121, 1000 GC Amsterdam.

Telephone: (20) 5510782; **Internet:** www.knaw.nl/beth; **e-mail:** bernadette.peeters@bureau.knaw.nl.

Canon Foundation in Europe

Founded in 1987 by Canon Europa NV to facilitate mutual understanding and the development of scientific expertise, in particular between Europe and Japan.

Activities: Offers up to 15 Research Fellowships every year to individuals in all fields of interest, in order for Europeans to carry out research in Japan, and to enable Japanese people to carry out research in Europe.

Geographical Area of Activity: Europe and Japan.

Publications: *Bulletin* (annually).

Board of Directors: Paul Kers (Chair.); Willem R. van Gulik (Treas. and Sec.).

Principal Staff: Exec. Chair. Claire Guédron Pike; Exec. Vice-Chair. Andrew Fisher.

Address: Bovenkerkerweg 59, 1185 XB Amstelveen; POB 2262, 1180 EG Amstelveen.

Telephone: (20) 5458934; **Fax:** (20) 7128934; **Internet:** www .canonfoundation.org; **e-mail:** foundation@canon-europe .com.

Carnegie-Stichting, Watelerfonds (Carnegie Foundation, Wateler Fund)

Founded in 1927 by J. G. D. Wateler for the awarding of an annual peace prize.

Activities: Awards the Wateler Peace Prize biennially to the person or institution having rendered the most valuable service in the cause of peace, or having contributed to finding the means of preventing war. The prize is given alternately to a person of Dutch and foreign nationality; in 2014 it was awarded to Lakhdar Brahimi, the UN special envoy to Syria.

Geographical Area of Activity: International.

Publications: *The Peace Palace* (annual); *The Trusteeship of an Ideal.*

Trustees: Dr Bernard R. Bot (Chair.).

Principal Staff: Gen. Dir Erik de Baedts (from 1 July 2015).

Address: Carnegieplein 2, 2517 KJ The Hague.

Telephone: (70) 3024242; **Fax:** (70) 3024234; **Internet:** www .vredespaleis.nl; **e-mail:** reception@carnegie-stichting.nl.

EP-Nuffic

Formed in 2015 by the merger of the European Platform and the Netherlands Organization for International Co-operation in Higher Education—NUFFIC (f. 1952).

Activities: Operates nationally and internationally in the field of education. The organization's main activity areas are development co-operation, internationalization of education from primary to higher levels, international recognition and certification.

Geographical Area of Activity: Worldwide.

Finance: Funded by the Ministries of Foreign Affairs and of Education, Culture and Science of the Netherlands, and the European Commission.

Board of Trustees: Arie Nieuwenhuijzen Kruseman (Chair.).

Principal Staff: Dir-Gen. Freddy Weima.

Address: POB 29777, 2502 LT The Hague; Kortenaerkade 11, 2518 AX The Hague.

Telephone: (70) 4260260; **Fax:** (70) 4260399; **Internet:** www .epnuffic.nl; **e-mail:** info@epnuffic.nl.

Europa Nostra (Pan-European Federation for Cultural Heritage)

Established in 1963 in response to the threat to Venice caused by rising floodwaters.

Activities: An umbrella network of heritage organizations that act at local, regional, national or European levels. The Federation aims to increase public awareness of cultural heritage; to campaign at local, national and international levels for the preservation and rescue of Europe's endangered heritage; to highlight the multiple benefits that cultural heritage provides for society; and to make cultural heritage a priority for public policy both at European and national levels. Comprises more than 400 member and associate organizations. In 2002, the European Union (EU) selected the Federation to run the EU Prize for Cultural Heritage/Europa Nostra Awards, which promote exemplary restorations and initiatives of the many facets of Europe's cultural heritage in various categories, including the restoration of monuments and buildings; urban and rural landscape rehabilitation; archaeological site interpretation; care for art collections; research and education; and dedicated service to heritage conservation. Annually awards up to six monetary awards of €10,000 to the top laureates in the various categories.

Geographical Area of Activity: Europe (greater Europe as defined by the Council of Europe).

Restrictions: Member organizations must be approved by the Council. Europa Nostra has no funding available for restorations, etc.

Publications: Annual Report; electronic newsletter; *European Cultural Heritage Review* (including themed *Dossiers issues,* annually); issues dedicated to the laureates of the EU Prize for Cultural Heritage/Europa Nostra Awards (annually); *Scientific Bulletin* (annually).

Finance: Annual income €1,240,579, expenditure €1,165,949 (2013).

Board: Plácido Domingo (Pres.); Denis de Kergorlay (Exec. Pres.); John Sell (Exec. Vice-Pres.); Truze Lodder (Treas.).

Principal Staff: Sec.-Gen. Sneška Quaedvlieg-Mihailović.

Address: Lange Voorhout 35, 2514 EC The Hague.

Telephone: (70) 3024050; **Fax:** (70) 3617865; **Internet:** www.europanostra.org; **e-mail:** info@europanostra.org.

European Climate Foundation

Established in 2008 to promote climate and energy policies that greatly reduce Europe's greenhouse gas emissions and help Europe play a strong international leadership role in mitigating climate change.

Activities: Aims to develop and implement climate and energy policies to reduce Europe's global greenhouse gas emissions through five priority programmes: Energy Efficiency; Climate Diplomacy; Low-Carbon Power Generation; Transportation; and EU Climate Policies. Maintains offices in Berlin and Brussels.

Geographical Area of Activity: European Union.

Restrictions: Does not accept unsolicited proposals.

Publications: Newsletter.

Finance: Total grants disbursed €15.3m. (2013).

Supervisory Board: Caio Koch-Wesser (Chair.); John McCall MacBain, Susan Bell (Vice-Chair.).

Principal Staff: CEO Dr Johannes Meier.

Address: Riviervismarkt 5, 2513 AM The Hague.

Telephone: (70) 7119600; **Fax:** (70) 7119601; **Internet:** www.europeanclimate.org; **e-mail:** info@europeanclimate.org.

European Cultural Foundation—ECF (Fondation Européenne de la Culture/Europese Culturele Stichting)

Founded in 1954 in Geneva as an NGO; supported by Dutch charity lotteries and private sources to promote cross-cultural co-operation on a multilateral European level.

Activities: Initiates and manages its own programmes and projects, and gives grants to other bodies for European-level cultural activities. The Foundation aims to be a catalyst of cultural expression and interaction that makes the diverse societies of Europe more open and inclusive. It supports high-quality artistic activities and cultural co-operation across different countries, borders and boundaries, targeting those places believed to be in most need of support and with a special commitment to young people.

Geographical Area of Activity: Europe.

Restrictions: ECF programmes are initiated, developed and run in partnership with other organizations. Grants are made only to non-profit organizations for a cultural co-operation project; grants are made only in Europe. All pertinent information on the different programmes and grants schemes can be found on the ECF website.

Publications: Annual Report; e-zine.

Finance: Annual income €6,107,326, expenditure €4,777,517 (2013).

Board: HRH Princess Laurentien of the Netherlands (Pres.); Görgün Taner (Chair.); Rien van Gendt (Dep. Chair.); Arent A. Foch (Treas.).

Principal Staff: Dir and Exec. Sec. Katherine Watson.

Address: Jan van Goyenkade 5, 1075 HN Amsterdam.

Telephone: (20) 5733868; **Fax:** (20) 6752231; **Internet:** www.culturalfoundation.eu; www.eurocult.org; **e-mail:** ask@culturalfoundation.eu.

Eurotransplant International Foundation

Founded in 1967 to facilitate the exchange of human organs to save lives.

Activities: Supports co-operation between transplant centres, donor hospitals, tissue typing laboratories and national authorities; aims to maximize the outcome of organ transplants and minimize the risks by making the best possible match between donor organ and transplant candidate; assists in the organization of organ transplants; works to ensure an optimal use of available donor organs in Austria, Belgium, Croatia, Germany, Luxembourg, the Netherlands, and Slovenia. The Foundation provides finance for programmes intended to improve the system whereby human organs may be transplanted. Maintains a database of patients.

Geographical Area of Activity: Europe.

Publications: Annual Report; *Eurotransplant Newsletter*; articles and brochures.

Finance: Annual income €10,183,000, expenditure €10,797,000 (31 Dec. 2013).

Board of Management: Dr Bruno Meiser (Pres.); L. van Hattum (Sec.).

Principal Staff: Gen. Dir Dr Peter Branger; Medical Dir Dr Undine Samuel.

Address: Plesmanlaan 100, 2332 CB Leiden; POB 2304, 2301 CH Leiden.

Telephone: (71) 5795700; **Fax:** (71) 5790057; **Internet:** www.eurotransplant.org.

De Faunabescherming (Wildlife Protection)

Founded in 1975 to work toward scientific and ethical wildlife management.

Activities: Operates nationally in the field of conservation and wildlife management; issues publications, legal procedures, actions.

Geographical Area of Activity: Netherlands.

Publications: *Argus* (quarterly); online newsletter.

Principal Staff: Pres. Harm H. Niesen; Sec. A.P. de Jong.

Address: Amsteldijk Noord 135, 1183 TJ Amstelveen.

Telephone: (20) 6410798; **Fax:** (20) 6473700; **Internet:** www.faunabescherming.nl; **e-mail:** info@faunabescherming.nl.

FEMCONSULT (Consultants on Gender and Development)

Founded in 1985 as a non-profit organization; a multidisciplinary group of professionals applying a gender perspective in programmes and projects in developing countries.

Activities: Offers technical expertise with a focus on gender-based constraints and opportunities for the development of programmes and projects aimed at the reduction of poverty. In particular, promotes the participation of women in development programmes; implements projects in developing countries focusing on women, in areas such as agriculture and rural development, education and communication; democracy and good governance; human resources development; nutrition and food aid; natural resources and the environment; small businesses; and public and reproductive health. Also offers a range of consultancy services concerning development programmes and projects, including participatory planning; project identification and appraisal; pre-investment studies; project design, planning, management, monitoring and evaluation; institutional strengthening and training; social, poverty and gender assessment studies; and preparation of tender documents.

Geographical Area of Activity: International.

Publications: *FEMCONSULT* (newsletter, in English); *Project Report*; *Skills Bank* (2 a year, in Dutch and English); *Symposium Report*.

Principal Staff: Man. Dir Angélique Verweij; Deputy Dir and Sr Adviser Kitty Bentvelsen.

Address: Nassaulaan 5, 2514 JS The Hague.

Telephone: (70) 3655744; **Fax:** (70) 3623100; **Internet:** www.femconsult.org; **e-mail:** info@femconsult.org.

FONDAD—Forum on Debt and Development

Independent policy research centre and forum for international discussion established in the Netherlands in 1987.

Activities: Supported by a worldwide network of experts. The Forum provides policy-orientated research on a range of North-South issues, with particular emphasis on international financial issues. Through research, seminars and publications, it aims to provide factual background information and practical strategies for policy-makers and other interested groups in industrial, developing and transition countries.

Geographical Area of Activity: International.

Restrictions: No grants are available.

Publications: *Global Imbalances and Developing Countries: Remedies for a Failing International Financial System; Global Imbalances and the US Debt Problem: Should Developing Countries Support the US Dollar?; Africa in the World Economy: The National, Regional and International Challenges; Protecting the Poor: Global Financial Institutions and the Vulnerability of Low-Income Countries.*

Principal Staff: Dir Jan Joost Teunissen.

Address: Nieuwendammerdijk 421, 1023 BM Amsterdam.

Telephone: (20) 6371954; **Fax:** (20) 6371954; **Internet:** www.fondad.org; **e-mail:** jj.teunissen@fondad.org.

Foundation for Democracy and Media

Established in 2003 as the successor to Foundation Het Parool (f. 1944) to influence public opinion in the Netherlands and elsewhere in favour of democratic ideas, and to support the surviving relatives of the deceased staff of the Het Parool newspaper illegally published during the German occupation of the Netherlands in the Second World War.

Activities: Offers support in the form of subsidies, loans and investment to those promoting the Foundation's ideals, including support to institutions organizing debates and lectures, for publications, exhibitions, etc.

Geographical Area of Activity: Europe.

Finance: Total funds disbursed €1,051,000 (2012).

Administrative Board: Wim van Norden (Hon. Chair.); Alex F. M. Brenninkmeijer (Chair.); Judith Brandsma (Treas.); Adriaan N. Stoop (Sec.).

Principal Staff: Dir Nienke Venema.

Address: De Lairessestraat 129-hs, 1075 HJ Amsterdam.

Telephone: (20) 5300300; **Internet:** stdem.org; **e-mail:** info@stdem.org.

Anne Frank Stichting (Anne Frank Foundation)

Founded in 1957 to preserve the Anne Frank House and to propagate the ideals left to the world in Anne Frank's diary; and to fight against prejudice and discrimination in the world.

Activities: Operates nationally and internationally in the fields of education and international relations. The Foundation runs a museum in the house where Anne Frank and her family lived in hiding, providing visitors with information on the developments and events of the Second World War, and regular exhibitions on contemporary subjects, such as its Free2choose programme, about fundamental rights that clash with the safeguarding of the democratic rule of law. The education department organizes study programmes in collaboration with teachers. The Foundation also maintains archives, develops educational material on the Second World War for schools, and investigates neo-Nazi groups.

Geographical Area of Activity: Netherlands and international.

Publications: Annual Report; newsletter; numerous reports and books.

Finance: Total assets €5,302,315 (31 Dec. 2014).

Supervisory Board: Wim Kok (Chair.); Prof. Dr Ernst M. Hirsch Ballin (Vice-Chair.); N. G. Ketting (Treas.).

Principal Staff: Exec. Dir Ronald Leopold; Man. Dir Garance Reus-Deelder.

Address: Postbus 730, 1000 AS Amsterdam.

Telephone: (20) 5567100; **Fax:** (20) 6207999; **Internet:** www.annefrank.org; **e-mail:** press@annefrank.nl.

Friends of the Earth International

Established in 1971; a federation of environmental organizations and groups.

Activities: Campaigns on environmental and social issues; challenges the current model of economic and corporate globalization; and promotes the creation of environmentally sustainable and socially just societies. The organization operates internationally in the area of the environment, by campaigning on issues such as genetically-modified crops, climate change, trade and sustainability, human rights and natural resources. It also issues publications on sustainable use of the environment. The International Secretariat supports its member network, by raising funds, co-ordinating campaigns, organizing workshops, disseminating information and maintaining databases. There are currently 75 member organizations.

Geographical Area of Activity: International.

Publications: Annual Report; electronic bulletins.

Finance: Annual income €1,860,371, expenditure €1,809,571 (31 Dec. 2013).

Executive Committee: Jagoda Munić (Chair.); Karin Nansen (Vice-Chair.); Hemantha Withanage (Treas.).

Principal Staff: International Co-ordinator Dave Hirsch.

Address: POB 19199, 1000 GD Amsterdam.

Telephone: (20) 6221369; **Fax:** (20) 6392181; **Internet:** www.foei.org; **e-mail:** foei@foei.org.

Health Action International

Founded in 1981.

Activities: An international network of more than 200 health, consumer and development groups operating in more than 70 countries. The organization works to increase access to essential medicines and improve their rational use through research excellence and evidence-based advocacy.

Geographical Area of Activity: Africa, Asia and the Pacific, Europe, and North, Central and South America.

Publications: Reports; briefing papers; press releases; fact sheets.

Finance: Total income €1,365,674, expenditure €1,193,833 (2014).

Board: Atze J. Sybrandy (Chair.); Prem C. John (Deputy Chair.); Paul T. Lindgreen (Treas.).

Principal Staff: Exec. Dir Dr Tim Reed; Financial Dir Philip Meerloo.

Address: Overtoom 60/II, 1054 HK Amsterdam.

Telephone: (20) 4124523; **Fax:** (20) 6855002; **Internet:** www.haiglobal.org; www.haieurope.org; **e-mail:** info@haiglobal.org; info@haieurope.org.

Heineken Prizes (Heineken Prijzen)

Established in 1963 by Heineken's Bierbrouwerij Maatschappij NV to promote science and culture.

Activities: Comprising awards made by the Alfred Heineken Fondsen Foundation, Dr H. P. Heineken Foundation, Dr A. H. Heineken Stichting voor de Kunst, Dr A. H. Heineken Foundation for Medicine, Dr A. H. Heineken Foundation for History, Dr A. H. Heineken Foundation for Environmental Sciences and C. L. de Carvalho-Heineken Foundation for Cognitive Science. The Royal Netherlands Academy of Arts and Sciences (KNAW) appoints expert committees and an independent jury of members of the Academy to choose the prizewinners. Five international science prizes are awarded every two years and are worth US $200,000: the Dr H. P. Heineken Prize for Biochemistry and Biophysics (f. 1963); Dr A. H. Heineken Prize for Art (f. 1988); Dr A. H. Heineken Prize for Medicine (f. 1989); Dr A. H. Heineken Prize for History (f. 1990); Dr A. H. Heineken Prize for Environmental Sciences (f. 1990); and the C. L. de Carvalho-Heineken Prize for Cognitive Science (f. 2006; formerly the Dr A.H. Heineken Prize for Cognitive Science). In addition, the Academy presents the Dr A. H. Heineken Prize for Art, which is worth $50,000, to a Dutch artist living and working in the Netherlands. It also presents the Heineken Young Scientists Awards, each worth $10,000, to young researchers working the same fields as the main prizes for Dutch organizations.

Geographical Area of Activity: International.

Restrictions: Not currently accepting nominations.

Principal Staff: Chair. Charlene L. de Carvalho-Heineken.

Address: c/o KNAW, POB 19121, 1000 GC Amsterdam.

Telephone: (20) 5510700; **Internet:** www.knaw.nl/en/awards/prijzen/heinekenprijzen; **e-mail:** hp@knaw.nl.

Humanistisch Instituut voor Ontwikkelings Samenwerking—HIVOS (Humanistic Institute for Co-operation with Developing Countries)

Founded in 1968; a development organization working towards emancipation, democratization and the alleviation of poverty in developing countries.

Activities: Operates two main programmes: the Open Society, with a focus on freedom of expression, transparency and accountability, women's empowerment, and sexual rights and diversity; and the Green Society, with a focus on renewable energy and sustainable food. The Institute currently supports more than 700 organizations in Africa, Asia and Central and South America, as well as organizations in the Netherlands; it aimed to reduce this number by half by 2016.

Geographical Area of Activity: Africa, Asia, Central and South America, South and South-East Europe, the Middle East and the Netherlands.

Restrictions: Grants made only in specific countries.

Publications: Annual Review; *Hivos International* (newsletter).

Finance: Annual income €135,888,000, expenditure €132,708,000 (31 Dec. 2013).

Supervisory Council: Jan E. de Groot (Chair.); A. van Gorsel (Vice-Chair.).

Principal Staff: Exec. Dir Edwin Huizing; Dir of Programmes and Projects Ben Witjes.

Address: Raamweg 16, 2596 HL The Hague; POB 85565, 2508 CG The Hague.

Telephone: (70) 3765500; **Fax:** (70) 3624600; **Internet:** www.hivos.nl; **e-mail:** info@hivos.nl.

IKEA Foundation

Established in 1982, originally to work in the areas of architecture and interior design; since 2009, the Foundation has worked to improve opportunities for children and young people in less-developed countries.

Activities: Operates to support children in four main project areas: a place to call home; a healthy start in life; a quality education; and a sustainable family income. As part of the its partnership with the Office of the UN High Commissioner for Refugees (UNHCR), it was announced in 2011 that the Foundation was to give US $62m. over three years to the UNHCR, for the assistance of refugees from Somalia in Kenya.

Geographical Area of Activity: International, with a focus on the Caribbean (Haiti), South and South-East Asia (particularly India) and Africa.

Publications: Annual Report.

Finance: Annual income €103,946,606, expenditure €103,946,606 (2013).

Principal Staff: CEO Per Heggenes; Programme Dirs Vandana Verma, Elizabeth McKeon.

Address: Postbus 11134, 2301 EC Leiden; Crown Business Centre, Schipholweg 103, 2316 XC Leiden.

Internet: ikeafoundation.org; **e-mail:** info@ikeafoundation.org.

Institute of Social Studies—ISS (International Institute of Social Studies)

Founded in 1952; part of Erasmus University Rotterdam since 2009.

Activities: An international university institute focusing on research and education in the area of development studies and international co-operation.

Geographical Area of Activity: All continents, focusing on developing countries and countries in transition.

Publications: *Development and Change* (quarterly); *Development Issues* (magazine, once a year); Annual Report; study programme; research reports; books; newsletters.

Finance: Total income €16.9m. (2014).

Advisory Board: Prof. Hans van Ginkel (Chair.).

Principal Staff: Rector Prof. Dr Leo de Haan; Exec. Sec. Linda Johnson.

Address: POB 29776, 2502 LT The Hague; Kortenaerkade 12, 2518 AX The Hague.

Telephone: (70) 4260460; **Fax:** (70) 4260799; **Internet:** www.iss.nl; **e-mail:** information@iss.nl.

Internationaal Instituut voor Sociale Geschiedenis—IISG (International Institute of Social History—IISH)

Founded in 1935 by Dr N. W. Posthumus and the Central Workers' Insurance Company to preserve and make available for study material of importance for social history, especially in the field of socialism and the international labour movement; an institute of the Royal Netherlands Academy of Arts and Sciences (KNAW).

Activities: Operates internationally in the field of social history, through the maintenance of a library and archives, and the publication of monographs, reviews and source material. Acquisitions include the archives of many socialist organizations and trade unions, and original documents, books, letters, pamphlets, posters, photographs, etc., relating to political events and leading Marxist, anarchist and socialist figures of the 19th and 20th centuries.

Geographical Area of Activity: International.

Publications: Annual Report; *International Review of Social History* (3 a year); *Sources for a History of the German and Austrian Working-class Movements* (series); *Studies in Social History* (series); *Contributions to the History of Labour and Society* (series); *Archives Michael Bakounine* (series); *Household Strategies for Survival, 1600–2000: Fission, Faction and Co-operation*; books; journals and various other publications.

Finance: Subsidized by an annual grant from the Netherlands Ministry of Education and Science, and by contributions from various institutions and organizations. Annual income €8,036,352, expenditure €8,036,352 (2014).

Governing Board: Hans M. van de Kar (Chair.).

Principal Staff: Gen. Dir Henk Wals; Exec. Sec. Monique Kruithof.

Address: POB 2169, 1000 CD Amsterdam; Cruquiusweg 31, 1019 AT Amsterdam.

Telephone: (20) 6685866; **Fax:** (20) 6654181; **Internet:** www.iisg.nl; **e-mail:** info@iisg.nl.

International Penal and Penitentiary Foundation—IPPF (Fondation Internationale Pénale et Pénitentiaire—FIPP)

Founded in 1951 as successor to the Commission Internationale Pénale et Pénitentiaire.

Activities: Promotes study in the fields of crime prevention, criminal procedure law and penitentiary law relating to detention and imprisonment, and treatment of offenders, especially by scientific research, publications and teaching. The Foundation has consultative status with the UN Commission on Crime Prevention and Criminal Justice, the UN Economic and Social Council (ECOSOC) and the Council of Europe.

Geographical Area of Activity: International.

Publications: Books on relevant topics (in English and French); report of operations; reports of sessions and meetings (in English and French).

Executive Committee: Phillip Rapoza (Pres.); Prof. Dr Piet Hein van Kempen (Sec.-Gen.); Dr Manon Jendly (Treas.).

Address: c/o Prof. Dr Piet Hein van Kempen, Radboud University of Nijmegen, BP 9049, 6500 KK Nijmegen.

Telephone: (24) 3615538; **Fax:** (24) 3616145; **Internet:** fondationinternationalepenaleetpenitentiaire.org; **e-mail:** info@internationalpenalandpenitentiaryfoundation.org.

Koninklijke Hollandsche Maatschappij der Wetenschappen (Royal Holland Society of Sciences and Humanities)

Founded in 1752 by seven leading citizens of Haarlem for the promotion of science.

Activities: Operates nationally in the field of science through grants to institutions and individuals, conferences and courses, publications and lectures. The Society awards annual prizes and subsidies for research and publication of scientific work. It has 350 directors and more than 400 members.

Geographical Area of Activity: Netherlands.

Publications: *Oeuvres complètes de Christiaan Huygens*; *Martinus of Marum, Life and Work*; *Geleerden en Leken*; *The Future of the Sciences and Humanities*; *Mappae Mundi*; *Haarlemse Voordrachten*; *Jan Brouwer Conferences*.

Finance: Manages several funds: funds: the Pieter Langerhuizen Son Lambert Fund, the Fund Van der Knaap, the Dr W. J. E. Base Fund, the Van De Zeeuw Dishoeckstraat Fund, the Jan Brouwer Fund and the Saal van Zwanenberg Foundation.

Board: Dr Marlies L. L. E. Veldhuijzen van Zanten-Hyllner (Chair.); A. A. Röell (Treas.); Prof. A. Soeteman (Sec.).

Address: Spaarne 17, 2011 CD Haarlem; POB 9698, 2003 LR Haarlem.

Telephone: (23) 5321773; **Internet:** www.khmw.nl; **e-mail:** secretaris@khmw.nl.

KWF Kankerbestrijding (Dutch Cancer Society)

Founded in 1949 by Queen Wilhelmina.

Activities: Operates nationally in the field of cancer control, through subsidizing programmes at major specialized cancer hospitals, and providing grants for projects on fundamental, epidemiological, clinical and psychosocial cancer research, research on methods for cancer prevention, fellowships, scholarships, conferences, courses and publications. The Society promotes international scientific co-operation. It also runs a cancer information centre, a free telephone helpline, publishes information brochures for patients and the general public, and subsidizes national support groups for cancer patients. It is a member of the International Union Against Cancer.

Geographical Area of Activity: Netherlands, its dependencies and former colonies.

Restrictions: There are limited funds for financial support of individual cancer patients.

Publications: Annual Report and financial statement; *Current Cancer Research in the Netherlands* (annually); *KWF Journal* (11 a year); *Kracht* (quarterly); progress reports and brochures.

Finance: Funding is provided by individual and corporate donations, legacies and various lotteries. Annual income €135,849,000, expenditure €173,729,000 (2014).

Supervisory Board: Harm Bruins Slot (Chair.); Prof. Jaap Verweij (Vice-Chair.); Prof. Tanja Bender (Sec.); Dr Paul H. J. M. Dirken (Treas.).

Principal Staff: Gen. Man. Dr Michel T. Rudolphie.

Address: Delflandlaan 17, 1062 EA Amsterdam; POB 75508, 1070 AM Amsterdam.

Telephone: (20) 5700500; **Fax:** (20) 6750302; **Internet:** www.kwfkankerbestrijding.nl; www.kwf.nl; **e-mail:** international@dutch-cancersociety.org.

Bernard van Leer Foundation

Established in 1949 by industrialist and philanthropist Bernard van Leer as a charitable foundation with broad humanitarian goals. After van Leer's death in 1958, his son Oscar van Leer reorganized the Foundation. From 1964 the Foundation focused on young children, primary education and youth, and since 1980 has concentrated exclusively on disadvantaged young children. It funded its first international project in Jamaica in 1966.

Activities: Seeks to improve opportunities for children up to the age of eight years who are growing up in socially and economically difficult circumstances. Grantmaking works primarily through supporting programmes implemented by local partners in selected countries. Partners include public, private and community-based organizations. The Foundation aims to build local capacity through partnerships, promote innovation and flexibility, and help to ensure that the work funded is culturally and contextually appropriate. Through its publications and advocacy, the Foundation aims to inform and influence policy and practice.

Geographical Area of Activity: International.

Restrictions: Unsolicited applications are not considered. Grants are the result of extensive consultations with organizations known by the Foundation.

Publications: *Early Childhood Matters* (journal, twice a year); *Early Childhood in Focus*; *Working Papers in Early Childhood Development* (series); *Practice and Reflections* (series); Annual Report; and other publications.

Finance: Annual income €18,571,700, expenditure €15,873,800 (2014).

Board of Trustees: Robert Swaak (Chair.).

Principal Staff: Exec. Dir Michael Feigelson.

Address: Lange Houtstraat 2, 2511 CW The Hague; POB 82334, 2508 EH The Hague.

Telephone: (70) 3312210; **Fax:** (70) 3502373; **Internet:** www.bernardvanleer.org; **e-mail:** info@bvleerf.nl.

Mama Cash

Founded in 1983 by Marjan Sax, Dorelies Kraakman, Tania Leon, Patti Slegers and Lida van den Broek to work for social transformation and the advancement of women's rights worldwide.

Activities: Core areas of activity are strategic grantmaking and resource mobilization; makes grants and provides accompaniment support to women's and girls' rights groups internationally. The organization promotes the human rights of women and girls by funding women-led organizations working in the thematic areas of body (safety from violence, sexual and reproductive rights, challenging harmful traditional practices); money (economic justice; workers' rights; property and inheritance rights); and voice (representation and participation, decision-making and leadership, and being seen and heard). It also provides support to local and regional women's funds around the world, which in turn raise money locally, regionally and internationally to support women's rights initiatives in their own communities; mobilizes resources from institutional and individual donors to increase the scale, influence and collective power of women's and girls' rights groups; and also works actively to engage more donors in the social justice philanthropy movement.

Geographical Area of Activity: Europe (including the Commonwealth of Independent States), Latin America and the Caribbean, Asia, Africa and the Middle East.

Restrictions: Does not fund: organizations whose mission and primary focus are not the promotion of women or girls' human rights; organizations that are led by men or based in the USA and Canada; organizations whose primary focus is development work, humanitarian assistance, poverty alleviation, or basic charity (e.g. income-generating activities and credit programmes, formal education, literacy programmes and traditional skills training, providing social services or regular medical care); organizations founded by, or structurally or economically dependent on, political parties government agencies or religious institutions; businesses; individuals; academic research; scholarships; or stand-alone travel grants.

Publications: Annual Report; *she has news* (newsletter); *she has e-news* (electronic newsletter).

Finance: Annual revenue, €4,340,866, expenditure €7,509,896 (31 Dec. 2014).

Board of Directors: Geetanjali Misra, Marieke van Doornick (Co-Chair.); Jacqueline Castelijns (Treas.).

Principal Staff: Exec. Dir Nicky McIntyre.

Address: POB 15686, 1001 ND Amsterdam; Eerste Helmersstraat 17, 1054 CX Amsterdam.

Telephone: (20) 5158700; **Fax:** (20) 5158799; **Internet:** www.mamacash.nl; **e-mail:** info@mamacash.nl.

MDF Training & Consultancy

Founded in 1984 in Ede, the Netherlands.

Activities: Provides training and consultancy to enhance the competencies of staff members; help organizations to enhance management capacities improve performance; maximize the impact of professional partnerships and organizations' networks; and focus on sustainable results in projects and programmes. The organization has regional offices in Belgium, Bolivia, the Democratic Republic of the Congo, Ghana, Indonesia, Sri Lanka, Tanzania and Viet Nam. There is also a special office to serve the Dutch development sector.

Geographical Area of Activity: Worldwide.

Publications: Monthly digital NewsLetter; annual programme and brochure; *Break the Ice Energise!; Tango Toolkit for Organizations.*

Principal Staff: Dir Herman Snelder; Man. Dir Mike Zuijderduijn.

Address: Bosrand 28, 6718 ZN Ede; Postbus 430, 6710 BK Ede.

Telephone: (318) 650060; **Fax:** (318) 614503; **Internet:** www.mdf.nl; **e-mail:** mdf@mdf.nl.

Milieukontakt International

Founded in 1988 as Milieukontakt Oost-Europa, by a group of foundations, including Friends of the Earth International (q.v.) and Stichting Natuur en Milieu, to strengthen the environmental movement in Europe and Asia.

Activities: Offers training and advice to NGOs in Europe and Asia, particularly at a local level, and fosters partnerships between Eastern and Western environmental groups. The organization encourages projects in the areas of the environment, sustainable agriculture, citizen participation, new technologies and NGO development. Maintains offices in Albania, the former Yugoslav republic of Macedonia and Moldova.

Geographical Area of Activity: Worldwide.

Publications: Annual Report; newsletter; fact sheets.

Finance: Annual income €227,201, expenditure €249,692 (2013).

Governing Board: A.T (Bram) de Borst (Chair.); André Schroer (Treas.); Willem Hendriks (Sec.).

Address: POB 20614, 1001 NP Amsterdam; Zekeringstraat 43 Amsterdam.

Telephone: (20) 5318930; **Fax:** (20) 5318940; **Internet:** milieukontakt.net; **e-mail:** info@milieukontakt.nl.

Nederlandsche Maatschappij voor Nijverheid en Handel—NMNH (Netherlands Society for Industry and Trade)

Founded in 1777 by the Hollandsche Maatschappij der Wetenschappen (Netherlands Society of Sciences) for the furtherance of common welfare by promoting industry, commerce, transport and communications, mining, agriculture and fisheries in the Netherlands and its overseas possessions.

Activities: Operates nationally and internationally in the fields of social welfare and studies, economic affairs and the conservation of natural resources, through self-conducted programmes, conferences, publications and lectures. The Society comprises 32 regional departments which, although responsible to the head office in The Hague, operate on an autonomous basis in their own area.

Geographical Area of Activity: Mainly the Netherlands and its overseas dependencies.

Publications: Annual Report; *Maatschappijbelangen* (monthly magazine).

Board: Dr Luuc Mannaerts (Chair.); Wouter Admiraal (Sec.); Jan Floris Holsteijn (Treas.).

Address: Jan van Nassaustraat 75, 2596 BP The Hague.

Telephone: (70) 3141940; **Fax:** (70) 3247515; **Internet:** www.de-maatschappij.nl; **e-mail:** info@de-maatschappij.nl.

Oranje Fonds

Founded in 1948 to support social welfare at home and, in exceptional cases, abroad. Formerly known as the Juliana Welzijn Fonds (Juliana Welfare Fund). Present name adopted in 2002.

Activities: Works in the field of social welfare. The Fund supports almost 7,000 social cohesion and integration projects, such as small-scale community initiatives, mentoring projects for young people, and language programmes. Its priorities are: to enable development and innovation within its field of activity; to initiate or develop executive activity; and to address the shortage of available activities and organizations.

Geographical Area of Activity: Netherlands and the Caribbean.

Restrictions: No grants are made to individuals, health, arts, education, environment or for development aid.

Publications: Annual Report; brochure; *Oranje fund reported*; *Appeltjes of oranje* (newsletter); newsletter.

Finance: Annual income €42,472,700, total expenditure €33,316,329 (31 Dec. 2014).

Board of Directors: Dr J. G. Wijn (Chair.); B. L. J. M. Beerkens (Treas.).

Principal Staff: Dir R. C. van der Giessen; Deputy Dir Dr Jonne Boesjes.

Address: Postbus 90, 3500 AB Utrecht; Maliebaan 18, 3581 CP Utrecht.

Telephone: (30) 6564524; **Fax:** (30) 6562204; **Internet:** www.oranjefonds.nl; **e-mail:** info@oranjefonds.nl.

Oxfam NOVIB—Nederlandse Organisatie voor Internationale Ontwikkelingssamenwerking (Oxfam NOVIB—Netherlands Organization for International Development Co-operation)

Founded in 1956 as NOVIB to promote sustainable development by supporting the efforts of poor people in developing countries; became part of the Oxfam confederation of 14 development agencies (qq.v.) in 1994.

Activities: Works to ensure that poor people have access to basic rights, through: support for local development projects initiated by private organizations in developing countries; advocacy through lobbying national governments, the European Union, and international organizations, including the World Bank, World Trade Organization and the UN. The organization co-operates with the sister organizations of Oxfam International and with around 3,000 local organizations across the world and in the Netherlands.

Geographical Area of Activity: Africa, Asia, Central and South America, Eastern Europe and the countries of the former USSR.

Publications: *Onze Wereld* (monthly magazine); *Novib Network;* Annual Report; series of novels from developing countries; newsletter.

Finance: Annual revenue €206,855,000, expenditure €201,246,000 (2013/14).

Board of Trustees: Hanzo van Beusekom (Chair.).

Principal Staff: Exec. Dir Farah Karimi.

Address: Postbus 30919, 2500 GX The Hague; Mauritskade 9, 2514 HD The Hague.

Telephone: (70) 3421777; **Fax:** (70) 3614461; **Internet:** www.oxfamnovib.nl; **e-mail:** info@oxfamnovib.nl.

Prins Claus Fonds Voor Cultuur en Ontwikkeling
(Prince Claus Fund for Culture and Development)

Established in 1996 to mark the 70th birthday of HRH Prince Claus of the Netherlands to expand insight into cultures and promoting interaction between culture and development.

Activities: Stimulates and supports activities in the field of culture and development by granting awards, funding and producing publications, and financing and promoting networks and innovative cultural activities. The Fund supports the organization of conferences or meetings, primarily in Africa, Asia and Central and South America, as well as funding innovative cultural activities and initiatives of people and organizations that involve creative processes leading to productions in the fields of theatre, music, art, architecture, design and audiovisual media. The Cultural Emergency Response Programme provides aid for cultural heritage damaged by man or nature. The Fund presents the annual Prince Claus Awards for outstanding achievements in culture and development.

Geographical Area of Activity: Africa, Central and South America, Asia and the Caribbean.

Publications: *The Prince Claus Fund Library*; *The Prince Claus Fund Journal*; *The Prince Claus Awards Book*; Annual Report.

Finance: Annual revenue €5,201,442, expenditure €5,132,129 (31 Dec. 2014).

Board of Trustees: Prince Constantijn (Hon. Chair.); Henk Pröpper (Chair.); Herman Froger (Vice-Chair.); Pascal Visée (Treas.).

Principal Staff: Dir Gitta Luiten.

Address: Herengracht 603, 1017 CE Amsterdam.

Telephone: (20) 3449160; **Fax:** (20) 3449166; **Internet:** www .princeclausfund.org; **e-mail:** info@princeclausfund.nl.

Rabobank Foundation

Established in 1973 by the Dutch Rabobank Group to help improve the position of socio-economic underprivileged people in society.

Activities: Operates nationally in the Netherlands and internationally in 25 countries in Africa, Central and South America, and South-East Asia, offering financial support and advice in two fields: microfinance (and micro insurance); and developing sustainable supply chains in coffee, cocoa, fruit, cotton, nuts and sugar. The Foundation works in partnership with local, national and international NGOs.

Geographical Area of Activity: Africa, Central and South America, and South-East Asia.

Finance: Rabobank Nederland and its branches donate a percentage of their profit annually to the Foundation. Annual income €14,706,525, expenditure €8,835,305 (31 Dec. 2013).

Board of Directors: Jorrit Jorritsma (Chair.).

Principal Staff: Dir Pierre Van Hedel.

Address: Postbus 17100, 3500 HG Utrecht; Croeselaan 18, 3521 CB Utrecht.

Telephone: (30) 2160000; **Fax:** (30) 2161937; **Internet:** www .rabobank.com/rabobankfoundation; **e-mail:** rabobankfoundation@rn.rabobank.nl.

Rutgers WPF

Founded in 1987, as the World Population Foundation. Present name adopted following merger with the Rutgers Nisso Group in 2010.

Activities: Aims to encourage sexual and reproductive health and rights throughout the world. The organization operates in less-developed countries of South and South-East Asia, and East and Southern Africa, through supporting local NGOs and governmental organizations in setting up and managing sexual and reproductive health projects. It provides information and training services and has developed an interactive CD-ROM to educate young people from the age of 10 years old. It also disseminates information and campaigns at national and international levels, and provides support to the

youth organizations CHOICE and YouAct. Maintains three field offices in Asia.

Geographical Area of Activity: Europe (especially the Netherlands), South and South-East Asia, and East and Southern Africa.

Publications: Annual Report.

Finance: Annual income €25,160,298, expenditure €25,019,274 (2013).

Supervisory Board: Andrée van Es (Chair.).

Principal Staff: Man. Dir Dianda Veldman.

Address: POB 9022, 3506 GA Utrecht; Oudenoord 176–178, 3513 EV, Utrecht.

Telephone: (30) 2313431; **Fax:** (30) 2319387; **Internet:** www .rutgerswpf.org; **e-mail:** office@rutgerswpf.nl.

ScriptumLibre Foundation

Established in 2003; the international branch of Stichting Vrijschrift.org in the Netherlands, established to raise awareness of freedom of information issues and promoting the sharing of software information.

Activities: Encourages and protects the freedom of digital creations. The Foundation raises awareness about the socio-economic implications of free knowledge and culture, and legislative infringement of privacy.

Geographical Area of Activity: Worldwide.

Board of Directors: Wiebe Van Der Worp (Chair.); Jeroen Dekkers (Treas.); Jeroen Hellingman (Sec.).

Address: Trekwei 7, 8711 GR Workum.

Telephone: (515) 543434; **Internet:** scriptumlibre.org; **e-mail:** office@scriptumlibre.org.

SIW Internationale Vrijwilligersprojecten (SIW International Volunteer Projects)

Established in 1953; a youth exchange organization aiming to promote international contact, personal growth and voluntary service.

Activities: Operates worldwide, in the fields of the arts and humanities, conservation, the environment and social welfare, through voluntary work. About 250 young Dutch volunteers work abroad annually, with projects operating in more than 50 countries. A number of projects operate in the Netherlands for around 200 overseas participants.

Geographical Area of Activity: Worldwide.

Restrictions: No direct applications from outside the Netherlands are accepted.

Finance: Financed through subsidies and an application fee.

Board: Tine Abbinga (Sec.); Maarten Bruna (Treas.).

Address: Willemstraat 7, 3511 RJ Utrecht.

Telephone: (30) 2317721; **Fax:** (30) 2343465; **Internet:** www .siw.nl; **e-mail:** info@siw.nl.

SOTA—Research Centre for Turkestan and Azerbaijan

Established in 1991 by Mehmet Tutuncu as a centre of research and study into the Turkic peoples of the former USSR, as the Foundation for the Research of Turkestan, Azerbaijan, Crimea, Caucasus and Siberia. Renamed in 2009.

Activities: Carries out research and analysis relating to Turkey and the Central Asian countries of the former USSR. The Centre promotes human rights and peace through democratic governance; and aims to inform public opinion in Western Europe and the USA. It organizes conferences and symposia; and maintains an archive and library containing more than 4,000 books and periodicals, and more than 10,000 pamphlets and newspaper articles.

Geographical Area of Activity: Turkey and the republics of Central Asia.

Publications: *BITIG* (quarterly journal); *Reform Movements and Revolution in Turkistan* (1900–1924); *Sefika Gaspirali and Turkic Women's Movement in Russia* (1893–1920); *Caucasus:*

War and Peace; *Turkey and Ataturk's Legacy*; *Geopolitical Importance of Central Asia*; *Pax Ottomana*; and others.

Principal Staff: Chair. Mehmet Tütüncü.

Address: Postbus 9642, 2003 LP Haarlem.

Telephone: (23) 5292883; **Fax:** (23) 5292883; **Internet:** www.turkistan.org/sotainfo.html; **e-mail:** sota@online.nl.

Stichting Agromisa (Agromisa Foundation)

Founded in 1934 to improve the lives of people in developing countries through providing information on small-scale sustainable agriculture.

Activities: Gives advice in the fields of nutrition, food processing, biogas, plant and animal husbandry, water and soil management, agricultural engineering, etc.; provides an Internet database on natural resource management; and maintains a library of books pertaining to small-scale agriculture. The Foundation also aims to raise awareness in the Netherlands of development problems.

Geographical Area of Activity: Africa, Asia, and Central and South America.

Restrictions: Not a grantmaking organization.

Publications: *Agrodok Series*; *AgroSpecials Series*; *Agro-Source: Educational Materials for agriculture & animal husbandry in warm climate zones*; Annual Report.

Finance: Total assets €48,495 (31 Dec. 2012).

Board: Ton van Schie (Chair.); Peter Holen (Sec.); Erni van Wingerden (Treas.).

Principal Staff: Team Co-ordinator and Publisher Eva Kok; Office Man. Lineke van Dongen.

Address: Postbus 41, 6700 AA Wageningen; Gebouw met de Klok (Clock House), WUR Bldg 351, Generaal Foulkesweg 37, 6703 BL Wageningen.

Telephone: (31) 7412217; **Fax:** (31) 7419178; **Internet:** www.agromisa.org; **e-mail:** agromisa@wur.nl.

Stichting DOEN (DOEN Foundation)

Established in 1991 by the Dutch Postcode Lottery to pursue the same objectives as the lottery (i.e. people and nature) and to complement the lottery's work.

Activities: Promotes sustainable, cultural and socially-minded pioneers. The Foundation defines pioneers as people who: take risks; have a creative or innovative approach; can transform pioneering concepts into concrete projects; can serve as an inspiring example to others; run sustainable and social business operations; put social and/or ecological objectives first and foremost, and/or create resourceful connections between sustainable, social and cultural interests. Since 2010, the Foundation has been active in three principal areas: climate change, the new economy, and culture and cohesion.

Geographical Area of Activity: International.

Restrictions: Grants made only to organizations.

Publications: Annual Report.

Finance: Receives funding from Dutch Postcode Lottery, FriendsLottery and the BankGiro Lottery. Annual income €25,905,152, expenditure €29,955,778 (2013).

Supervisory Board: Gert-Jan van der Vossen (Chair.).

Principal Staff: CEO Nina Tellegen; CFO Jasper Snoek.

Address: Postbus 75621, 1070 AP Amsterdam; Van Eeghenstraat 70, 1071 GK Amsterdam.

Telephone: (20) 5737333; **Fax:** (20) 5737370; **Internet:** www.doen.nl; **e-mail:** doen@doen.nl.

Stichting Fonds 1818 (1818 Fund Foundation)

Founded in 1990 as the VSB Fonds Den Haag by the VSB Bank to provide financial support to social, cultural and educational projects. Present name adopted in 2001.

Activities: Supports projects in The Hague, Netherlands, and surrounding areas in the fields of the arts and culture, economic affairs, conservation and the environment, medicine and health, sport and recreation, animal welfare and social welfare.

Geographical Area of Activity: Principally The Hague, Delft, Leiden and the Zoetermeer area of the Netherlands.

Restrictions: No grants to individuals and donates money only to projects that focus on the region in which the fund is established.

Publications: Annual Report; newsletter; information brochure; *Fonds 1818* (quarterly magazine); manuals.

Finance: Annual income €13,534,900, annual expenditure €14,334,900 (2012).

Board: Jan Schinkelshoek (Chair.).

Principal Staff: Dir Boudewijn de Blij; Gen.-Sec. Renée van Groeningen-Gentenaar; Exec. Sec. Rita Kas.

Address: POB 895, 2501 CW The Hague; Riviervismarkt 4, 2513 AM The Hague.

Telephone: (70) 3641141; **Fax:** (70) 3641891; **Internet:** www.fonds1818.nl; **e-mail:** info@fonds1818.nl.

Stichting voor Fundamenteel Onderzoek der Materie—FOM (Foundation for Fundamental Research on Matter)

Founded in 1946 by Dr H. Bruining, Prof. Dr H. J. Clay, Prof. Dr H. A. Kramers, Prof. Dr J. M. W. Milatz, Dr H. J. Reinink and Prof. G. van der Leeuw, for the advancement of fundamental scientific research on matter in the Netherlands for the general interest, higher education and industry.

Activities: Operates internationally in the field of physics through research, publications and lectures. The Foundation assists in the co-ordination of existing research projects and carries out its own work through research working groups (of which there are currently 214, spanning 11 Dutch universities). Research interests include: subatomic physics, atomic physics, optical physics, molecular physics, condensed matter physics, nanophysics, physical biology, thermonuclear research and plasma physics, applied and phenomenological physics. In addition, research is carried out in four institutes, which are financed completely or partly by FOM: the FOM Institute for Atomic and Molecular Physics; the FOM Institute for Plasma Physics; the Nuclear Accelerator Institute KVI; and the FOM Institute for Subatomic Physics.

Geographical Area of Activity: Europe.

Restrictions: Grants only to researchers with a working address in the Netherlands.

Publications: *FOM-jaarboek* (annual).

Finance: Funded by the Government, European Union, and industry and university contracts. Annual income €114,653,000, annual expenditure €102,306,000 (2014).

Executive Board: Prof. Dr N. J. Lopes Cardozo (Chair.); Prof. Dr N. H. Dekker (Vice-Chair.).

Principal Staff: Dir Dr Wim van Saarloos; Sec. Petra M. W. van Luling.

Address: POB 3021, 3502 GA Utrecht; Van Vollenhoven Ave 659, 3527 JP Utrecht.

Telephone: (30) 6001211; **Fax:** (30) 6014406; **Internet:** www.fom.nl; **e-mail:** info@fom.nl.

Stichting Max Havelaar (Max Havelaar Foundation)

Established in 1988 for fair and direct trade with small producers from developing countries.

Activities: Operates in developing countries in the areas of conservation and the environment, and international affairs. The Foundation promotes fair trade, co-operating with small-scale producers in developing countries, Dutch importers and consumers, and maintains a register of producers and checks on importers to insure fair trade principles are adhered to.

Geographical Area of Activity: Africa, Asia, and Central and South America; Netherlands.

Publications: *Handel onder Voorwaarden*; *Sinds maart* (yearly).

Finance: Annual income €3,770,097, annual expenditure €3,893,724 (2013).

Principal Staff: Man. Dir Peter d'Angremond.

Address: Lucasbolwerk 7, 3512 EG Utrecht.

Telephone: (30) 2337070; **Fax:** (30) 2332992; **Internet:** www.maxhavelaar.nl; **e-mail:** info@maxhavelaar.nl.

Stichting Liliane Fonds (Liliane Foundation)

Founded in 1980 by Liliane Brekelmans to provide aid for disabled children and young people (up to the age of 25 years) in developing countries.

Activities: Operates in Africa, Asia and Central and South America. Provides grants to individuals in the field of medical and social rehabilitation. Maintains office in Brussels, Belgium.

Geographical Area of Activity: Africa, Asia, and Central and South America.

Publications: Annual Report; newsletter (quarterly); *International* (newsletter); Newsflash; *Meedoen* (practical guidebook); brochures.

Finance: Funded by donations. Annual income €20,835,891, expenditure €19,954,076 (2013).

Board of Trustees: J. H. (Jack) van Ham (Chair.).

Principal Staff: Dir Kees van den Broek.

Address: Havensingel 26, 5211 TX 's-Hertogenbosch.

Telephone: (73) 5189420; **Fax:** (73) 5189421; **Internet:** www.lilianefonds.nl; **e-mail:** voorlichting@lilianefonds.nl.

Stichting Praemium Erasmianum (Praemium Erasmianum Foundation)

Founded in 1958 by HRH Prince Bernhard of the Netherlands to award one or more monetary prizes, if possible annually, to individuals or institutions that have made a particularly important contribution to Europe in the cultural, social or socio-scientific sphere.

Activities: Operates internationally in the fields of education, social welfare and studies, the arts and humanities, law and other professions, through the awarding of the Erasmus Prize, worth €150,000, to a person or institution for 'an exceptional contribution to culture, society or social science'. Previous prize winners include Wikipedia (2015), Frie Leysen (2014), Jurgen Habermas (2013), Daniel C. Dennett (2012) and Joan Busquets (2011).

Geographical Area of Activity: International.

Restrictions: No applications for grants are considered.

Publications: Annual Report; series of publications in connection with the laureates or theme of the prize.

Finance: Annual income €790,117, expenditure €597,269 (2013).

Governing Board: HRH the Prince of Orange (Patron); Dr Martin Sanders (Chair.); Margot Dijkgraaf (Vice-Chair.); Tom de Swaan (Treas.).

Principal Staff: Dir Dr Max Sparreboom; Exec. Sec. Lucia Aalbers.

Address: Jan van Goyenkade 5, 1075 HN Amsterdam.

Telephone: (20) 6752753; **Fax:** (20) 6752231; **Internet:** www.erasmusprijs.org; **e-mail:** spe@erasmusprijs.org.

Stichting Prins Bernhard Cultuurfonds (Prince Bernhard Cultural Foundation)

Established in London in 1940 to raise money to buy war material for the British and Dutch Governments. After the Second World War it was decided to continue the fund to rebuild cultural life in the Netherlands.

Activities: Works in the Netherlands, the Netherlands Antilles and Aruba, emphasising self-generated activity, private initiative and non-professional work. The Foundation currently supports initiatives in the fields of the visual arts; dance; theatre; literature; music; conservation of historic buildings and monuments; research in the humanities; cultural education; and nature conservation. Promotes Dutch culture abroad by providing financial support.

Geographical Area of Activity: Netherlands, Netherlands Antilles and Aruba.

Publications: Annual Report; newsletter.

Finance: Receives a share of the revenue of national lotteries, income from its own collections, and from assets and gifts. Total assets €205,973,545; annual income €49,926,426, expenditure €32,189,112 (2014).

Board of Trustees: Dr Alexander H. G. Rinnooy Kan (Chair.); Igno H. J. M. van Waesberghe (Vice-Chair.).

Principal Staff: Dir Dr Adriana Esmeijer.

Address: POB 19750, 1000 GT Amsterdam; Herengracht 476, 1017 CB Amsterdam.

Telephone: (20) 5206130; **Fax:** (20) 6238499; **Internet:** www.cultuurfonds.nl; **e-mail:** info@cultuurfonds.nl.

Stichting Triodos Foundation (Triodos Foundation)

Established in 1971 to mobilize gifts and loans for promising new social initiatives and enterprises. After the establishment of Triodos Bank in 1980, the Foundation limited its role to granting gifts to institutions.

Activities: Active in three main fields: nature and environment, people and society, and international co-operation. The Foundation prioritizes organic farming, renewable energy and solidarity with developing countries. It aims to stimulate national and international projects that initiate innovation. Branches of Triodos Bank in Belgium, Spain and the United Kingdom each have a similar foundation.

Geographical Area of Activity: Worldwide.

Finance: Annual income €3,521,578, expenditure €1,168,096 (2013).

Board of Directors: Pierre Aeby (Chair.); Gera van Wijk (Sec.); Kees Middendorp (Treas.).

Principal Staff: Man. Dir Ted van den Bergh.

Address: POB 55, 3700 AB Zeist.

Telephone: (30) 6936535; **Internet:** www.triodosfoundation.nl; **e-mail:** triodos.foundation@triodos.nl.

Stichting Vluchteling (Refugee Foundation)

Founded in 1976 by various churches and other groups in the Netherlands to provide assistance for refugees outside the Netherlands; restructured in 1982.

Activities: Provides assistance to refugees through grants to various organizations active overseas, providing both emergency aid and long-term self-reliance projects. The Foundation has no fieldworkers of its own, but attempts to co-ordinate assistance and to inform the public of the plight of refugees.

Geographical Area of Activity: International.

Restrictions: No assistance provided to refugees in the Netherlands.

Publications: *Jaarverslag* (annual report).

Finance: Annual income €10,949,000, annual expenditure €10,977,000 (2013).

Board: Femke Halsema (Chair.); Frank Bluiminck (Vice-Chair.); Guido Visser (Treas.).

Principal Staff: Dir Tineke Ceelen.

Address: Stadhouderslaan 28, 2517 HZ The Hague.

Telephone: (70) 3468946; **Fax:** (70) 3615740; **Internet:** www.vluchteling.nl; **e-mail:** info@vluchteling.nl.

Technologiestichting—STW (Technology Foundation)

Founded in 1981 by Prof. W. A. Koumans and Dr C. le Pair to promote research in technology. Formerly known as Stichting voor de Technische Wetenschappen.

Activities: Operates nationally in the field of applied science and engineering, through research, travel grants, lectures and publications. The Foundation subsidizes research projects at universities and technological institutes in the Netherlands; projects may be drawn from all technological fields, and are selected on the basis of both high scientific quality and applicability in industry.

Geographical Area of Activity: Netherlands.

Publications: Annual Report; project reports and others.

Finance: Annual revenue €89,693,000, expenditure €88,990,000 (2014).

Board: Prof. Dr Ton van der Steen (Chair.); Prof. Dr M. P. C. Weijnen (Vice-Chair.).

Principal Staff: Dir Dr Eppo E. W. Bruins; Deputy Dir Dr Chris Mombers.

Address: Postbus 3021, 3502 GA Utrecht; Van Vollenhovenlan 661, 3527 JP Utrecht.

Telephone: (30) 2116001; **Fax:** (30) 6014408; **Internet:** www .stw.nl; **e-mail:** info@stw.nl.

Tilapia International Foundation

Founded in 1952 by J. D. F. Heine to encourage the breeding of the tilapia fish to relieve malnutrition in developing countries.

Activities: Organizes training programmes designed to educate people in the breeding of tilapia; provides financial assistance for the establishment of fish farms and disseminates information.

Geographical Area of Activity: International.

Publications: Brochures.

Finance: Annual budget approx. €318,000.

Board: Mathieu J. H. P. Pinkers (Sec.-Gen. and Treas.).

Address: Postbus 2375, 3500 GJ Utrecht; Kanalstraat 20, 3531 BM Utrecht.

Telephone: (30) 2948700; **Fax:** (30) 2936810; **Internet:** www .tilapiastichting.nl; **e-mail:** infof@tilapiastichting.nl.

Universal Education Foundation—UEF

Established in 2004; an advocacy foundation that works towards the goal of learning for well-being, with a focus on children and young people.

Activities: Partners with organizations from different sectors and disciplines that share the common agenda of well-being for all. The Foundation focuses on cultivating capacities and environments that nurture personal potential; respect the uniqueness and diversity of each individual; emphasize the nature and quality of relationships; and support participation and engagement in the community and society. Through alliances, such as the Learning for Well-being Consortium in Europe, the Foundation seeks to develop a common agenda and mutually reinforcing activities to influence policies and funding; collect and promote inspiring practices; offer learning opportunities and support; and develop measurement, monitoring and evaluation approaches to create an inclusive society that invites the contribution of each child and young person and in which they live meaningful, happy and healthy lives. Core programmes are Elham Palestine, Voice of Children surveys and CATS (Children as Actors for Transforming Society).

Geographical Area of Activity: International.

Publications: *Elham Palestine 2009; Developing instruments to capture young people's perceptions of how school as a learning environment affects their well-being (2008); Lessons from the Voice of Children initiative: A sense of belonging as part of children's well-being (2008)*.

Board: Raymond Georis (Chair.); Corinne Evens (Treas.), Daniel Kropf (Founding Chair., Exec. Vice-Chair. and Sec.).

Principal Staff: Sec.-Gen. Dr Marwan Awartani.

Address: c/o Chamber of Commerce, Amsterdam, POB 34206704, Iepenlaan 47, 2061 GJ Bloemendaal.

Telephone: (0) 22230400; **Internet:** www .learningforwellbeing.org; **e-mail:** dkropf@dkropf.com.

XminusY Solidarity Fund

Established in 1968 to promote self-determination and social change worldwide.

Activities: Provides financial support to small local groups in Africa, Asia, Central and South America, and Eastern Europe that would otherwise not be able to exist. Funded groups operate in the areas of human rights and social and political justice. The Fund also works in Western Europe as an advocate for these goals and for international solidarity.

Geographical Area of Activity: Worldwide.

Restrictions: Does not usually finance conferences, research projects, educational trips, travel expenses or general office expenses. No grants for children's projects, health programmes or projects that are income-generating. Maximum grant awarded approx. US $3,000.

Publications: Annual Report; brochures; reports; CD-ROM on direct action; newsletter.

Board: Rosalie Smit (Chair.); Piet Schuijt (Treas.).

Principal Staff: Office Man. Cees Sies.

Address: De Wittenstr. 43–45, 1052 AL Amsterdam.

Telephone: (20) 6279661; **Fax:** (20) 6228229; **Internet:** www .xminy.nl; **e-mail:** info@xminy.nl.

Zero-Kap Foundation

Established in 1989 by private individuals who set up a fund to advance interest-free loans to groups and organizations of the least-privileged in developing countries to develop income-generating activities and home ownership. Merged with Stichting FEMI in 2011.

Activities: Operates in the fields of income generation (mainly in the area of primary production and the processing and trading of the resulting produce) and the construction of facilities to encourage income-generating activities and private housing. Loans are between €10,000 and €50,000 to be paid back over a period of from five years (income generation) up to nine years (private homes).

Geographical Area of Activity: Asia, Africa, and Central and South America.

Restrictions: No grants to individuals, and only to groups with a legal status, such as co-operatives and village communities.

Publications: Annual Report; newsletter.

Finance: Funded by private individuals or organizations which supply capital funding through donations. Total assets €1,165,473; annual income €101,303, annual expenditure €18,294 (2010).

Board: Ton Cools (Chair.); Erika van Scheijndel-Eelderink (Treas.); Dr Dik Stroband (Sec.).

Address: p/a FEMI Foundation, Torenlaan 15, 3742 CR Baarn.

Telephone: (35) 5488422; **Fax:** (35) 5488412; **Internet:** www .zero-kap.nl; www.femi.org; **e-mail:** info@zero-kap.nl.

ZOA

Founded in 1973 as Stichting Zuidoost Azië (South-East Asia Foundation) to provide assistance to people in need, as a sign of Christian compassion, through emergency relief, rehabilitation and reintegration programmes.

Activities: Aims to provide relief, hope and recovery. The organization supports people who suffer as a result of armed conflict or natural disasters and helps them to rebuild their livelihoods. Currently operates in 14 countries worldwide. Helped approx. 2m. people through its programmes in 2012.

Geographical Area of Activity: Africa, Asia, Central America.

Publications: Annual Report; *ZOA Magazine* (7 a year).

Finance: Receives funding from more than 50,000 private donors, governments, the European Union and the UN. Annual income €44,067,167, expenditure €41,315,830 (2014).

Supervisory Board: Dr H. Paul (Chair.).

Principal Staff: CEO Johan Mooij.

Address: Postbus 4130, 7320 AC Apeldoorn.

Telephone: (55) 3663339; **Fax:** (55) 3668799; **Internet:** www .zoa.nl; www.zoa-international.com; **e-mail:** info@zoa.nl.

New Zealand

FOUNDATION CENTRES AND CO-ORDINATING BODIES

Community Foundations of New Zealand

Established in 2012.

Activities: Comprises 11 mem. community foundations.

Geographical Area of Activity: New Zealand.

Finance: Annual income NZ $18,225, expenditure $17,285 (31 March 2014).

Principal Staff: Contact Nicky Wilkins.

Address: c/o Acorn Foundation, 78 First Ave, Tauranga; POB 13604, Tauranga 3141.

Telephone: (7) 579-9839; **Internet:** www .nzcommunityfoundations.org.nz; **e-mail:** nicky@ acornfoundation.org.nz.

Philanthropy New Zealand

Established in 1990 by patron Sir Roy McKenzie.

Activities: Operates projects in the areas of taxation, research and education, through working with other organizations in the voluntary and not-for-profit sector, networking with government departments, including lobbying for tax concessions for New Zealand foundations, supporting research, organizing seminars and conferences and issuing publications. The organization has 98 members.

Geographical Area of Activity: Asia-Pacific region.

Publications: Newsletter; *Philanthropy News.*

Finance: Annual income NZ $416,492, expenditure $552,284 (30 June 2014).

Board: Kate Frykberg (Chair.).

Principal Staff: Chief Exec. Liz Gibbs.

Address: POB 1521, Wellington; Level 4, Civic Assurance House, 114 Lambton Quay, Wellington.

Telephone: (4) 499-4090; **Fax:** (4) 472-5367; **Internet:** www .philanthropy.org.nz; **e-mail:** info@philanthropy.org.nz.

FOUNDATIONS, TRUSTS AND NON-PROFIT ORGANIZATIONS

Antarctic Heritage Trust (NZ)

Established to conserve expedition bases in the Antarctic.

Activities: Works to conserve expedition bases in the Antarctic.

Geographical Area of Activity: Antarctic regions.

Finance: Annual income NZ $4,795,125, expenditure $3,698,173 (30 June 2013).

Trustees: Paul East (Chair.); Anthony Wright (Deputy Chair.); Murray Harrington (Treas.).

Principal Staff: Exec. Dir Nigel Watson.

Address: Private Bag 4745, Christchurch 8140, New Zealand; Admin Bldg, Int Antarctic Centre, 38 Orchard Rd, Christchurch 8053.

Telephone: (3) 358-0212; **Fax:** (3) 358-0244; **Internet:** www .nzaht.org; **e-mail:** info@nzaht.org.

Cancer Society of New Zealand, Inc

Founded in 1929 by the British Empire Cancer Campaign Society, for the alleviation, prevention and cure of cancer.

Activities: Supports cancer research through grants to institutions and individuals in New Zealand, and through travelling fellowships enabling New Zealand graduates to travel abroad for study; it holds conferences with international participation, and disseminates the results of research. The Society also provides information and support services (including Living Well Programme and online forum, CancerChatNZ) to people affected by cancer.

Geographical Area of Activity: New Zealand.

Publications: Annual Report; Research Report; *Present State and Future Needs of Cancer Research in New Zealand;* press releases; information sheets.

Finance: Annual income NZ $5,979,000, expenditure $5,518,000 (31 March 2014).

National Board: Peter Hutchison (Acting Pres.).

Principal Staff: Chief Exec. Claire Austin.

Address: POB 12700, Wellington 6144; Red Cross House, Level 2, 69 Molesworth St, Wellington 6011.

Telephone: (4) 494-7270; **Fax:** (4) 494-7271; **Internet:** www .cancernz.org.nz; **e-mail:** admin@cancer.org.nz.

Family Planning

Established in 1936 to help women choose the size of their families and the spacing of their children.

Activities: Works to promote a positive view of sexuality and to enable people to make informed choices about their sexual and reproductive health and well-being. Clinical services include contraception, sexually-transmitted infection checks and treatment, advice around menopause, cervical screening, vasectomy, pregnancy testing and advice, etc. Health promotion services include parenting programmes, producing educational resources and workshops on adolescent sexuality. The organization also has an advocacy function to ensure sexual and reproductive health are well understood and supported in the community, makes submissions on proposed government legislation and works closely with appropriate government departments.

Geographical Area of Activity: New Zealand, South-East Asia and the Pacific region.

Publications: Annual Report; *Forum* (annual) newsletter (3 a year).

Finance: Annual income NZ $15,476,566, expenditure $15,542,945 (30 June 2014).

Council: Dr Tammy Steeves (Pres.); Marie Bismark (Deputy Pres.).

Principal Staff: Chief Exec. Jackie Edmond.

Address: POB 11515, Wellington; Level 6, Southmark House, 203–209 Willis St, Wellington 6142.

Telephone: (4) 384-4349; **Fax:** (4) 382-8356; **Internet:** www .familyplanning.org.nz; **e-mail:** national@familyplanning .org.nz.

Norman Kirk Memorial Trust

Founded in 1976 to promote the welfare and progress of the people of New Zealand and the South Pacific.

Activities: Within New Zealand, accepts direct applications from mature individuals who are either disadvantaged or disabled, and who are committed to taking advantage of education or training opportunities; or from mature applicants who are seeking a qualification or training that will enable them to assume a fuller role in the community, as well as supporting organizations helping people achieve these aims. The

Trust also funds a number of scholarships through other trusts focusing on education. Programme funding in the South Pacific region is made following the advice of other NGOs operating in the field; direct applications for these funds are not accepted.

Geographical Area of Activity: New Zealand and Oceania.

Restrictions: Does not consider direct applications from individuals or organizations based outside New Zealand. Grants to the South Pacific are allocated in co-operation with a partner agency working in the area.

Publications: Annual Report.

Finance: Funding from individual donations and from governments of New Zealand, Australia and several South Pacific nations. Annual income NZ $120,914, expenditure $51,337 (30 March 2014).

Trustees: Dr Peter Swain (Chair.).

Address: POB 805, Wellington 6140; 46 Waring Taylor St, Wellington 6011.

Fax: (4) 495-9444; **Internet:** www.communitymatters.govt .nz; **e-mail:** trusts@dia.govt.nz.

J. R. McKenzie Trust

Founded in 1940 by Sir John Robert McKenzie to assist national organizations and local community groups in New Zealand.

Activities: Supports those organizations working with people with special needs, especially children and young people, people 'at risk' or at significant social disadvantage. The Trust focuses on social, health and developmental needs supporting project-related costs, training of paid and unpaid staff, equipment, publications, administration, salaries, volunteer expenses and organizational development. It also supports new and innovative approaches to social problems and organizations seeking to make their services more effective and empowering.

Geographical Area of Activity: New Zealand.

Restrictions: No grants are made to individuals, sports groups, schools and early childhood centres, out-of-school care programmes, rest homes and hospitals, environmental groups or religious and campaigning groups.

Publications: Annual Report.

Finance: Annual income NZ $5,279,666, expenditure $3,838,250 (31 March 2014).

Board: Patrick Cummings (Chair.).

Principal Staff: Exec. Dir Iain Hines; Trust Admin. Alison Glen.

Address: POB 10-006, Wellington 6143; Level 4, 114–118 Lambton Quay, Wellington.

Telephone: (4) 472-8876; **Fax:** (4) 472-5367; **Internet:** www .jrmckenzie.org.nz; **e-mail:** info@jrmckenzie.org.nz.

National Heart Foundation of New Zealand

Established in 1968 to reduce premature deaths and suffering from diseases of the heart and circulation.

Activities: Operates in the area of medicine and health, through research, providing grants for research projects, training fellowships for cardiology trainees to study overseas, senior fellowships and a Chair in Cardiovascular Studies; health promotion, through programmes to promote good health for all and reduce underlying causes of the disease; and medical care to prevent people at high risk from developing heart and blood vessel disease, and to improve the care and rehabilitation of people with heart disease. The Foundation has around 20 brs.

Geographical Area of Activity: New Zealand.

Publications: Annual Report; newsletter.

Finance: Annual revenue NZ $21,952,000, expenditure $13,237,000 (30 June 2012).

Board of Directors: Michael Tomlinson (Chair.); Michael Benjamin (Deputy Chair.).

Principal Staff: Chief Exec. Tony Duncan; Medical Dir Norman Sharpe.

Address: POB 17160, Greenlane, 9 Kalmia St, Ellerslie, Auckland 1546.

Telephone: (9) 571-9191; **Fax:** (9) 571-9190; **Internet:** www .heartfoundation.org.nz; **e-mail:** info@heartfoundation.org .nz.

New Zealand Winston Churchill Memorial Trust

Founded in 1965 by Act of the New Zealand Parliament to give fellowships to New Zealand residents, for the advancement of any vocation carried out in New Zealand, or to the benefit in general of New Zealand.

Activities: Operates nationally in the fields of education, social welfare, economic affairs, science and medicine, the arts and humanities, and conservation of natural resources, and internationally in the field of international relations, through the award of up to 25 international fellowships each year. New Zealand residents may undertake an activity anywhere. Fellowships amount to as much as 80% of costs for short-term travel and activity followed by publication of a report within six months. Assistance is not renewable or extendable and is only available for travel outside New Zealand. The Trust is administered by the Department of Internal Affairs.

Geographical Area of Activity: New Zealand.

Restrictions: Fellowships are not granted for the gaining of academic or professional qualifications and funding is not normally granted for attending academic or professional conferences. Applications must be for travel between 1 January and 31 December in the year immediately after the year of application. Maximum individual grant disbursed NZ $10,000.

Publications: Annual Report and financial statement; Fellows' reports; bibliography reports.

Finance: Annual income NZ $207,067, expenditure $112,953 (31 March 2013).

Board of Trustees: Rachael Selby (Chair.); A. Graeme Hall (Deputy Chair.).

Address: POB 805, Wellington 6140; 46 Waring Taylor St, Wellington 6011.

Telephone: (4) 495-9431; **Fax:** (4) 495-9444; **Internet:** http:// www.communitymatters.govt.nz/Funding-and -grants—Trust-and-fellowship-grants—New-Zealand-W; **e-mail:** wcmt@dia.govt.nz.

NZIIA—New Zealand Institute of International Affairs

Founded in 1934 to promote an understanding of international questions and problems particularly in relation to New Zealand, the Commonwealth, and the countries of South-East Asia and the Pacific.

Activities: Operates internationally in the fields of economic affairs, law and other professions, international relations and aid to less-developed countries, through self-conducted programmes, research, conferences, publications and lectures. The Institute has eight branches throughout New Zealand.

Geographical Area of Activity: International.

Publications: *New Zealand International Review* (6 a year); pamphlet series; occasional papers and books.

Finance: Annual income NZ $191,391, expenditure $190,594 (31 Dec. 2013).

Standing Committee: Sir Douglas Kidd (Pres.); Prof. Roberto Rabel (Vice-Pres.); Prof. Athol Mann (Treas.).

Principal Staff: Exec. Dir Peter Kennedy; Exec. Officer Synonne Rajanayagam.

Address: c/o Victoria University of Wellington, POB 600, Wellington 6140; Rm 507, Level 5, Railway West Wing, Victoria University of Wellington, Pipitea Campus, Wellington.

Telephone: (4) 463-5356; **Fax:** (4) 463-5437; **Internet:** www .vuw.ac.nz/nziia; **e-mail:** nziia@vuw.ac.nz.

Oxfam New Zealand

Established in 1991 as part of the Oxfam confederation of organizations (qq.v.).

Activities: Works in partnership with local communities in the Pacific and South-East Asia, supporting long-term development and campaigning for economic and political change to combat poverty. Maintains offices in Wellington and in Papua New Guinea.

Geographical Area of Activity: Pacific and South-East Asia.

Publications: Reports.

Finance: Annual income NZ $10,790,009, expenditure $10,161,714 (31 March 2014).

Board of Trustees: Keith Johnston (Chair.); Joanna Collinge (Deputy Chair.); Felicity Hopkins (Treas.).

Principal Staff: Exec. Dir Rachael Le Mesurier.

Address: POB 68357, Newton, Auckland 1145; Level 1, 14 West St, Eden Terrace, Auckland 1010.

Telephone: (9) 355-6500; **Fax:** (9) 355-6505; **Internet:** www.oxfam.org.nz; **e-mail:** oxfam@oxfam.org.nz.

Pacific Development and Conservation Trust

Established in 1989 by the Government of New Zealand with funds from the French Government in recognition of the events surrounding the destruction of the Greenpeace ship the *Rainbow Warrior,* which French secret service agents blew up and sank in Auckland Harbour in 1985.

Activities: Operates in New Zealand and the South Pacific through self-conducted programmes, research and grants; grants are available for groups to use for charitable purposes to promote the enhancement and conservation of the environment, natural and historic resources and cultural heritage, and the peaceful, economic, physical and social development of the South Pacific and of its peoples, providing such development is consistent with sound conservation and resource management policies. Administered by Department of Internal Affairs.

Geographical Area of Activity: New Zealand and the South Pacific.

Restrictions: Projects must be charitable and promote the objectives of the Trust. The purchase of land and buildings will be funded only in exceptional circumstances. Applicants must be New Zealand or South Pacific citizens. Total average annual grant disbursements NZ $250,000.

Publications: Annual Report and financial statements.

Finance: Annual income NZ $367,806, expenditure $277,176 (30 June 2014).

Advisory Trustees: Peter Kiely (Chair.).

Address: POB 805, Wellington 6140; 46 Waring Taylor St, Wellington 6011.

Internet: www.communitymatters.govt.nz/Funding-and-grants—Trust-and-fellowship-grants—Pacific-development-; **e-mail:** trusts@dia.govt.nz.

Pacific Leprosy Foundation

Founded in 1939 to help people with leprosy; formerly known as the Makogai NZ Lepers' Trust Board.

Activities: Operates in the areas of medicine, health and social welfare, working to eliminate leprosy as a threat to public health, through research and attention to sanitation and health issues, and providing medical and social assistance to those affected by leprosy and their families.

Geographical Area of Activity: Australasia and the Pacific.

Publications: Newsletter; Annual Report.

Finance: Annual income NZ $1,669,946, expenditure $976,051 (30 June 2014).

Board: Richard C. Gray (Chair.); Andrew Tomlin (Treas.).

Principal Staff: Gen. Man. Jill Tomlinson; Relations Man. Lala Gittoes.

Address: Freepost Authority Number 204, Private Bag 4730, Christchurch Mail Centre, Christchurch 8140; 4 Anderson St, Addington, Christchurch 8140.

Telephone: (3) 343-3685; **Fax:** (3) 343-5525; **Internet:** www.leprosy.org.nz; **e-mail:** admin@leprosy.org.nz.

Peace and Disarmament Education Trust—PADET

Established in 1988 by the Government of New Zealand with funds from the French Government in recognition of the events surrounding the destruction of the Greenpeace ship the *Rainbow Warrior,* which was blown up and sunk in Auckland Harbour by French secret service agents in 1985.

Activities: Operates in New Zealand in the fields of education, international affairs, law and human rights, social studies and disarmament and arms control, through self-conducted programmes, research, grants to individuals and institutions, scholarships, conferences and training courses. The Trust aims to promote international peace, arms control and disarmament. It also offers scholarships for higher educational study in two categories: up to NZ $14,000 for a year's work towards a Master's thesis, and up to $21,000 (plus up to $5,000 for tuition fees) each year for up to three years' work towards a PhD doctoral thesis. Grants administered by the Department of Internal Affairs.

Geographical Area of Activity: New Zealand.

Restrictions: Will not fund the purchase of land, buildings, furniture or fittings, general running costs or day-to-day administration expenses; scholarship research topic must be relevant to current New Zealand disarmament and arms control policy.

Publications: Annual Report; theses.

Finance: Annual income NZ $193,329, expenditure $85,081 (31 March 2013).

Advisory Trustees: Wayne Mapp (Deputy Chair.).

Principal Staff: Co-ordinator Dalpat Nana.

Address: Trust and Fellowships Office, Department of Internal Affairs, POB 805, Wellington 6140; 46 Waring Taylor St, Wellington 6011.

Fax: (4) 495-9444; **Internet:** www.communitymatters.govt.nz/Funding-and-grants—Trust-and-fellowship-grants—Peace-and-Disarmamen; **e-mail:** community.matters@dia.govt.nz.

Royal Forest and Bird Protection Society of New Zealand

Established in 1923.

Activities: Operates nationally in the field of nature conservation, protecting natural areas, and plants and animals native to New Zealand. The Society promotes sustainability in farming and land management; works as an advocate for conservation by lobbying the Government on environmental issues; and supports the protection of Antarctica. It has more than 50 branches and runs the Kiwi Conservation Club for young people.

Geographical Area of Activity: New Zealand and Antarctica.

Publications: Annual Report; *Forest and Bird Magazine* (quarterly); *Best Fish Guide* (biennial consumer booklet); Kiwi Conservation Club magazine (5 a year); newsletters and e-newsletters; fact sheets.

Finance: Annual income NZ $6,239,735, expenditure $6,247,532 (28 Feb. 2014).

Executive: Andrew Cutler (Pres.); Mark Hanger (Deputy Pres.); Graham Bellamy (Treas.).

Principal Staff: Chief Exec. Hone McGregor.

Address: Level 1, 90 Ghuznee St, POB 631, Wellington 6140.

Telephone: (4) 385-7374; **Fax:** (4) 385-7373; **Internet:** www.forestandbird.org.nz; **e-mail:** office@forestandbird.org.nz.

Sutherland Self Help Trust

Founded in 1941 with funds donated by Arthur F. H. Sutherland; the Trust's purpose is to help people in need through gifts to relevant charities and organizations in New Zealand.

Activities: Provides capital and training/equipment grants to institutions in New Zealand operating in the fields of education, science and technology, medicine and health, and social welfare. The Trust focuses on the care and advancement of physically disabled and disadvantaged children, community youth work, care of the sick and elderly people, and the alleviation of social problems, including alcohol and drug abuse and sexual abuse.

Geographical Area of Activity: New Zealand.

Restrictions: No grants to individuals, nor for administration costs, vehicles or overseas travel nor for environmental, artistic, cultural or sporting purposes.

Finance: Annual income NZ $1,976,604, expenditure $1,268,639 (31 Dec. 2013).

Board of Trustees: John B. Sutherland (Chair.); David H. Gibbons (Sec.).

Address: POB 193, Wellington 6140; 7 Kenwyn Terrace, Newtown, Wellington 6021.

Telephone: (4) 385-1563; **Fax:** (4) 384-9515; **Internet:** ssht.co .nz; **e-mail:** ssht@ssht.co.nz.

Tindall Foundation

Established in 1994 by Stephen and Margaret Tindall with the aim of helping New Zealanders reach their full potential.

Activities: Active in five funding programme areas: family and social services; enterprise and employment; care of the environment and preservation of biodiversity; strengthening the community sector; and promoting philanthropy. A sizeable proportion of the Foundation's resources is allocated directly by appointed Fund Managers.

Geographical Area of Activity: New Zealand.

Publications: Annual Report.

Finance: Total assets NZ $17,471,641, annual expenditure $10,729,302 (31 March 2014).

Principal Staff: Man. John McCarthy.

Address: POB 33181, Takapuna, Auckland 0740; 1 Blomfield Spa, Takapuna, Auckland 0622.

Telephone: (9) 488-0170; **Internet:** www.tindall.org.nz; **e-mail:** admin.ttf@tindall.org.nz.

The Todd Foundation

Established in 1972 by the Todd family's corporate interests, for charitable purposes within New Zealand.

Activities: Provides funding to New Zealand organizations that contribute to 'inclusive communities where all families, children and young people can thrive and contribute'. The General Fund is the founding programme. It currently supports children, young people, their families and their communities. The Special Focus Fund is an invitation only fund, which is designed to provide support for selected social, economic, environmental and cultural issues. Awards and scholarships include a doctoral scholarship in energy research, and awards for excellence for research projects that are likely to directly benefit New Zealand and its people, carried out in approved universities and polytechnics.

Geographical Area of Activity: New Zealand.

Restrictions: Does not fund: anything not clearly linked to the Foundation's vision and main goals; capital items (buildings, vehicles, equipment); overseas organizations and overseas travel; fund-raising by third parties; individuals (except for tertiary research scholarships); sports organizations; individual schools and early childhood centres, toy libraries or out-of-school care programmes; projects already complete; the promotion of religious beliefs; organizations that focus on specific conditions and disabilities (the Foundation prefers initiatives that work more holistically to support 'a good life in an inclusive community').

Publications: Annual Report.

Finance: Annual income NZ $4,743,225, expenditure $5,227,943 (31 Dec. 2013).

Administration Board: Sir John Todd (Chair.).

Principal Staff: Exec. Dir Christina Howard.

Address: POB 3142, Wellington 6140; Level 15, Todd Bldg, 95 Customhouse Quay, Wellington 6011.

Telephone: (4) 931-6189; **Fax:** (4) 473-2836; **Internet:** www .toddfoundation.org.nz; **e-mail:** info@toddfoundation.org .nz.

Trade Aid NZ Inc—TANZ

Established in 1973 to encourage sustainable development through fair trade.

Activities: Operates in 30 developing countries in the area of aid to less-developed countries and economic affairs, by promoting self-reliance through fair trade. The organization imports products made by people from poor communities, offering a fair price for goods so as to provide a sustainable income. Also campaigns for a solution to the problem of 'third world debt'.

Geographical Area of Activity: Africa, Asia and Australasia, and Central and South America.

Publications: Annual Report; *Vital Magazine* (approx. 4 a year); *Pick of the Crop* (coffee-focused newsletter).

Finance: Annual income NZ $36,000, expenditure $36,000 (30 June 2014).

Board of Trustees: Lyn Jackson (Chair.).

Principal Staff: Gen. Man. Geoff White.

Address: POB 35049, Christchurch 8640; 174 Gayhurst Rd, Dallington, Christchurch 8061.

Telephone: (3) 385-3535; **Fax:** (3) 385-3536; **Internet:** www .tradeaid.org.nz; **e-mail:** customerservice@tradeaid.org.nz.

Volunteer Service Abroad—VSA

Established in 1962; a non-profit development agency that recruits skilled New Zealanders to work overseas.

Activities: Provides volunteers for local partner organizations in developing regions to assist local communities. Volunteers share knowledge and experience in a range of areas, including health, education and training, community development, economic development, enterprise, conservation and agriculture.

Geographical Area of Activity: Africa, Asia and Pacific.

Publications: *VISTA* (magazine, 2 a year); *Talk Talk* (bimonthly e-newsletter); media releases; Annual Review.

Finance: Annual income NZ $136,367, expenditure $164,578 (31 March 2014).

Council: Gordon Noble-Campbell (Chair.).

Principal Staff: CEO Gill Greer.

Address: POB 12246, Thorndon, Wellington 6144; Level 3, 32 Waring Taylor St, Wellington 6144.

Telephone: (4) 472-5759; **Fax:** (4) 472-5052; **Internet:** www .vsa.org.nz; **e-mail:** vsa@vsa.org.nz.

Nicaragua

FOUNDATIONS, TRUSTS AND NON-PROFIT ORGANIZATIONS

Fundación FAMA

Founded in 1991 (as Fundación para el Apoyo a la Microempresa) as a non-profit foundation to help small enterprises; affiliated to ACCION Network and the Network Micro Finance Network.

Activities: Supports small businesses (particularly those run by women) through micro-credit and training. Credit sources include the Foundation's own resources, commercial credit and funds from international organizations. Maintains 25 branches throughout Nicaragua.

Geographical Area of Activity: Nicaragua.

Finance: Assets US $26,590,729 (Dec. 2010); total funds disbursed $9,779,000 (2010).

Board of Directors: Dr Juan Álvaro Munguía Álvarez (Chair.); Eduardo Gurdián Ubago (Vice-Chair.).

Principal Staff: Gen. Man. Víctor Tellería Gabuardi.

Address: Apdo 3695, 3.5 cuadras al oeste de Montoya, sobre Carretera Sur, Managua.

Telephone: 268-4826; **Fax:** 266-5292; **Internet:** fundacionfama.org.ni; **e-mail:** info@fundacionfama.org.ni.

Nigeria

FOUNDATIONS, TRUSTS AND NON-PROFIT ORGANIZATIONS

Mike Adenuga Foundation

Established in 2009 by Mike Adenuga, founder and CEO of Globacom, a telecommunications company.

Activities: Partners with NGOs, public sector and community-based organizations with expertise in the fields of entrepreneurship and youth enterprise development, education, health, and rural development, including renewable energy and safe water projects. Through the Mike Adenuga Fellowship Programme, provides undergraduate and post-graduate scholarships, and research fellowships for study in Nigeria and abroad.

Geographical Area of Activity: Nigeria.

Restrictions: Does not fund political, religious or fundraising activities; sports; individual health or general grants.

Principal Staff: Chair. Dr Mike Adenuga, Jr.

Address: Mike Adenuga Towers, 1 Mike Adenuga Close, off Adeola Odeku St, Victoria Island, Lagos.

Internet: www.mikeadenugafoundation.org; **e-mail:** info@mikeadenugafoundation.org.

African Refugees Foundation—AREF

Established in 1993 by Chief Segun Olusola to assist refugees in Africa.

Activities: Helps refugees and displaced people in Africa, as well as organizing workshops on peace initiatives and conflict mediation, and seminars on conflict prevention and management; and working to develop policy for governments. The Foundation offers voluntary medical corps services. Sister organizations exist in the United Kingdom and the USA. The Foundation has UN accreditation.

Geographical Area of Activity: Africa.

Publications: Multimedia documentaries and periodic publications.

Principal Staff: Hon. Pres. Chief Opral M. Benson; Chair., Programmes Albert Alain Peters; Exec. Dir Olujimi Olusola, III.

Address: Lagos State Old Secretariat Rd, off Oba Akinjobi St, G. R. A. Ikeja, POB 5051, Lagos.

Telephone: (0) 8033067811; **Fax:** (1) 5850962; **Internet:** africanrefugeesfoundation.org; **e-mail:** jolusola@yahoo.com; aref24@hotmail.com; segun.olusola@yahoo.com.

Sir Ahmadu Bello Memorial Foundation

Established in 2009 to promote the legacies of the late Sir Ahmadu Bello, especially with regard to leadership, good governance and accountability.

Activities: Operates in the areas of human rights, conflict resolution, alleviation of poverty, health, education and conservation through research, financial aid, conferences, advocacy and workshops. The Foundation awards scholarships worth 100,000 naira for tertiary-level studies in science or technology.

Geographical Area of Activity: Nigeria.

Finance: Funded mainly by the Northern Governors' Forum, donations and independently generated through investments.

Board of Trustees: Alhaji Kashim Shettima (Chair.).

Principal Staff: Man. Dir and CEO Dr Shettima A. Ali.

Address: 13A Belel Close, off Ohinoyi St, Unguwan Rimi, Kaduna.

Telephone: (813) 5000001–4; **e-mail:** sabmfscholarship@gmail.com.

Dangote Foundation

Established in 1994 by Alhaji Aliko Dangote, Pres. of Dangote Group, an industrial conglomerate.

Activities: Operates internationally in the areas of education, health, and youth entrepreneurship, through the provision of small grants. It also makes grants to assist those affected by natural disasters. Alhaji Aliko Dangote endowed it with a gift of US $1,200m. in early 2014.

Geographical Area of Activity: International.

Address: Dangote Group, Union Marble House, 1 Alfred Rewane Rd, Ikoyi, Lagos.

Internet: dangote.com/touchinglives.aspx.

Tony Elumelu Foundation

Established in 2010 by Tony Elumelu, Chair. of Heirs Holdings, an investment company.

Activities: Promotes entrepreneurship in Africa. The Foundation invests in small and medium-sized enterprises, providing start-up funding and development opportunities. Initiatives include: the Entrepreneurship Programme; the Nigeria Empowerment Fund (f. 2014), which aims to bring economic sustainability to communities that have been affected by natural disasters or conflict; and the Africapitalism Institute (f. 2014), which conducts research on the importance of economic prosperity and the private sector to social and economic development in Africa. The Foundation awards the Tony & Awele Elumelu Prize (f. 2012 as the Elumelu Legacy Prize), which recognize academic excellence in students graduating from a selection of African tertiary institutions; prizes are worth US $1,400 for undergraduates and $2,800 for graduates.

Geographical Area of Activity: Africa.

Principal Staff: CEO Prof. Reid E. Whitlock; Dir of the Africapitalism Institute David A. Rice.

Address: Heirs Pl., 1 MacGregor Rd, Ikoyi, Lagos.

Telephone: (1) 27746415; **Internet:** www.tonyelumelufoundation.org; **e-mail:** info@tonyelumelufoundation.org.

Fate Foundation

Founded in 2000 by Fola Adeola to tackle the high rate of unemployment and poverty in Nigeria.

Activities: Aims to promote wealth creation in Nigeria through providing Nigerian young people with the skills, tools, networks and financing needed to create successful businesses that will in turn offer employment to other people. The Foundation makes annual awards to successful entrepreneurs.

Geographical Area of Activity: Nigeria.

Publications: *Impact Report* (annually); newsletter.

Board: Fola Adeola (Chair.).

Principal Staff: Exec. Dir Elizabeth Olofin.

Address: Water House, 1st Floor, Lagos State Water Corpn, Ijora Causeway, PMB 54495, Ikoyi, Lagos 101010.

Telephone: 07098123371 (mobile); **Internet:** www.fatefoundation.com; **e-mail:** info@fatefoundation.com.

Institute of Human Rights and Humanitarian Law

Established in 1988; a community-based human rights and education research network.

Activities: Operates in the field of human rights and humanitarian law, through education and training, advocacy, lobbying, dissemination of information, creating rural advice offices, research, and workshops, seminars and symposia. The Institute maintains the Human Rights Documentation Centre.

Geographical Area of Activity: Nigeria and Western Africa.

Publications: *Human Rights Defender* (quarterly journal) and other publications.

International Advisory Board: Prof. Akin Oyebode (Chair.).

Principal Staff: Exec. Dir Anyakwee S. Nsirimovu; Access to Justice Programmes Officer Courage Nsirimovu.

Address: National Secretariat: Humanity House, 1 Human Rights Close, off Ogworlu Rd, New Layout, off Int. Airport Rd, Rukpokwu Town, Obio/Akpor LGA, POB 2292, Port Harcourt.

Telephone: (0) 893029530; **Fax:** (84) 231716; **Internet:** ihrhl-ng.org; www.kabissa.org/directory/ihrhl; **e-mail:** ihrhl@ihrhl.org.

International Institute of Tropical Agriculture—IITA

Founded in 1967 by the Ford and Rockefeller Foundations (qq.v.) to contribute to the improvement of tropical farming techniques.

Activities: Conducts research, at its own stations and in collaboration with institutions in other countries. The Resource and Crop Management Programme aims to develop methods of land use and cropping systems that will enable efficient, economical and sustained production of food crops for the humid and sub-humid tropics, with particular emphasis on the problems of small farmers; co-operating programmes have been established in Cameroon and Ghana. Crop improvement programmes aim to bring about genetic improvements and control pests: the Root and Tuber Improvement Programme covers cassava and yams, and includes co-operation with similar programmes in Cameroon and the Democratic Republic of the Congo; the Cereals Improvement Programme (maize and rice) involves co-operation with the West Africa Rice Development Association (Côte d'Ivoire), the International Rice Research Institute (the Philippines), the International Maize and Wheat Improvement Centre in Mexico (q.v.) and African regional organizations; and the Grain Legume Improvement Programme (cowpeas and soybeans) is linked with projects in Brazil, Tanzania and Burkina Faso. The Institute's Genetic Resources Unit collects and stores germ-plasm for genetic research in collaboration with donors and recipients all over the world, and the Virology Unit studies virus diseases affecting crops. The Training Programme involves about 550 participants a year from African and other countries. Conferences and seminars are organized and the Institute also maintains a library and documentation centre.

Geographical Area of Activity: International.

Publications: Annual Report (in French and English); *IITA Research* (2 a year, in French and English); brochures, conference proceedings, technical papers, training manuals; newsletter (monthly).

Finance: Annual expenditure US $85,092,000 (2013).

Board of Trustees: Dr Bruce Coulman (Chair.).

Principal Staff: Dir-Gen. Dr Nteranya E. Sanginga.

Address: Oyo Rd, PMB 5320, Ibadan 200001, Oyo State.

Telephone: (2) 7517472; **Fax:** (2) 2412221; **Internet:** www.iita.org; **e-mail:** iita@cgiar.org.

A. G. Leventis Foundation Nigeria

Established in 1988; a subsidiary foundation of the A. G. Leventis Foundation (q.v.) in Greece.

Activities: Active in the fields of education, the environment, health care and culture, although principal support has been given to training young farmers in modern agricultural methods through the establishment of six schools in Nigeria and three schools in Ghana. The Foundation has also established an Environmental Resource Centre, in collaboration with the Nigerian Conservation Foundation, as well as developing an agro-forestry conservation programme, and donating equipment to technical colleges for vocational training of young Nigerians.

Geographical Area of Activity: Ghana and Nigeria.

Publications: *The Millennium Farmer* (newsletter, quarterly); *Small-scale Farming in West Africa*; *Agroforestry Guide – An Introductory Field Manual on Agroforestry Practices in Nigeria and Ghana*.

Principal Staff: Exec. Dir Dr Abimbola Ishola Adewumi.

Address: 4th Floor, Iddo House, Ebute-Metta, POB 159, Lagos.

Telephone: 08023003980 (mobile); **Fax:** (1) 4730968; **Internet:** www.leventisfoundation.org; **e-mail:** foundation@leventis-overseas.com.

Nigerian Conservation Foundation—NCF

Established in 1980 by Chief S. L. Edu, and registered as a Charitable Trust in 1982.

Activities: Pursues the conservation of nature and its resources with the aim of improving the quality of human life by: preserving the full range of Nigeria's biodiversity, which includes species, ecosystems and genetic diversity; promoting the sustainable use of natural resources for the benefit of the present and future generations; and advocating actions that minimize pollution and wasteful utilization of renewable and non-renewable resources. The Foundation runs participatory community-based projects, conducts research, organizes workshops, seminars, conferences and various other training courses. It is an affiliate of the WWF—World Wide Fund for Nature (WWF) and a partner of Birdlife International.

Geographical Area of Activity: Nigeria, West Africa.

Publications: Monthly newsletter.

Finance: Funded by donations, membership subscriptions and investment income.

Board of Trustees: Izoma Philip C. Asiodu (Pres.).

Principal Staff: Chair. of the Nat. Exec. Council Chief Ede Dafinone; Dir-Gen. Adeniyi Karunwi.

Address: Km 19, Lekki-Epe Expressway, POB 74638, Victoria Island, Lagos.

Telephone: (0) 7063369257; **Fax:** (1) 2642497; **Internet:** www.ncfnigeria.org; **e-mail:** info@ncfnigeria.org; media@ncfnigeria.org.

Nigerian Institute of International Affairs—NIIA

Established in 1961 to provide direction for Nigeria in international affairs.

Activities: Provides advice and guidance for foreign policy development. Organizes conferences, workshops and lectures.

Geographical Area of Activity: Nigeria.

Publications: *Nigerian Journal of International Affairs*; *Nigerian Forum*; *Nigerian Bulletin on Foreign Affairs*; *niianews* (newsletter).

Governing Council: Maj.-Gen. Ike O. S. Nwachukwu (Chair.).

Principal Staff: Dir-Gen. Prof. Bola A. Akinterinwa.

Address: 13–15 Kofo Abayomi St, Victoria Island, POB 1727, Lagos.

Telephone: (1) 9500983; **Fax:** (1) 2611360; **Internet:** www.niianet.org; **e-mail:** dgeneral@niianet.org; director-general1@hotmail.com.

Orji Uzor Kalu Foundation

Established by Orji Uzor Kalu, fmr governor of Abia State and Chair. of SLOK Holding and the *Daily Sun* and *New Telegraph* newspapers.

Activities: Main areas of interest are: health, building and supporting primary health-care centres; and education, supporting schools, teacher training, adult literacy programmes and vocational/technical training, building learning centres for people with disabilities, and providing university scholarships to disadvantaged students.

Geographical Area of Activity: Nigeria.

Board of Trustees: Dr Orji Uzor Kalu, Sweet Asouzu.

Address: 10 Randle Rd, Apapa, Lagos.

Internet: www.orjiuzorkalufoundation.org; **e-mail:** info@orjiuzorkalufoundation.org.

TY Danjuma Foundation

Established in 2008 by Theophilus Yakubu Danjuma, founder and Chair. of South Atlantic Petroleum (SAPETRO), to promote equal opportunities for all Nigerians.

Activities: Operates in three principal areas: community health; education; and income generation through working in partnership with Nigerian NGOs.

Geographical Area of Activity: Nigeria.

Trustees: Theophilus Yakubu Danjuma (Chair.).

Principal Staff: Exec. Dir. Dr Florence Etta-AkinAina.

Address: Plot 2015 Oda Cresc., off Dar Es Salaam St, off Aminu Kano Cresc., Wuse II, Abuja, Nigeria.

Internet: www.tydanjumafoundation.org; **e-mail:** contact@tydanjumafoundation.org.

Norway

FOUNDATIONS, TRUSTS AND NON-PROFIT ORGANIZATIONS

Environmental Foundation Bellona

Established in 1986 to raise awareness of environmental issues.

Activities: Operates in the field of the environment, especially in the areas of nuclear energy, fossil fuels and renewable energy. Maintains offices in the Russian Federation (Murmansk and St Petersburg), USA and Belgium.

Geographical Area of Activity: Worldwide.

Publications: Numerous reports and papers.

Principal Staff: Pres. Frederic Hauge; Man. Dir Nils Bøhmer.

Address: Postboks 2141, Grünerløkka, 0505 Oslo; Maridalsveien 17B, Oslo.

Telephone: 23-23-46-00; **Fax:** 22-38-38-62; **Internet:** www.bellona.org; **e-mail:** info@bellona.no.

Janson Johan Helmich og Marcia Jansons Legat (Janson Johan Helmich and Marcia Jansons Endowment)

Founded in 1949.

Activities: Operates in the field of education. The organization awards scholarships to Norwegian postgraduate students for advanced study abroad in any field, including doctoral or postgraduate study, and professional development. Some 66 grants of up to 100,000 krone are available.

Geographical Area of Activity: Worldwide.

Board: Gudmund Knudsen (Chair.).

Principal Staff: Admin. Reidun Haugen.

Address: Svensrud, Meieriveien 13, 3530 Røyse.

Telephone: 32-13-54-65; **Fax:** 32-13-56-26; **Internet:** www.jansonslegat.no; **e-mail:** post@jansonslegat.no.

Institusjonen Fritt Ord (Freedom of Expression Foundation)

Established in 1974 to promote freedom of speech in Norway and internationally.

Activities: Operates in the field of the arts and culture; supports the Norwegian Institute of Journalism and offers the annual Freedom of Expression Prize. Internationally, the Foundation offers the Gerd Bucerius Free Press of Eastern Europe Award (with the ZEIT-Stiftung, q.v.) and the Press Prize for Russia.

Geographical Area of Activity: Norway and international.

Publications: Annual Report.

Finance: Total assets 486.8m. krone (31 Dec. 2013).

Board of Trustees: Fr Georg Rieber-Mohn (Chair.); Prof. Grete Brochmann (Vice-Chair.).

Principal Staff: Dir Knut Olav Åmås; Project Dir Bente Roalsvig.

Address: Uranienborgveien 2, 0258 Oslo.

Telephone: 23-01-46-46; **Fax:** 23-01-46-47; **Internet:** www.fritt-ord.no; **e-mail:** post@fritt-ord.no.

Anders Jahres Humanitære Stiftelse (Anders Jahre's Foundation for Humanitarian Purposes)

Established in 1966 by Anders Jahre; the Foundation is managed by UNIFOR at the University of Oslo.

Activities: Operates in the field of the arts and humanities to promote Norwegian culture. The Foundation awards the annual Anders Jahre Prize for Culture.

Geographical Area of Activity: Norway.

Board: Svein Aaser (Chair.); Ellen Gjerpe Hansen (Vice-Chair.).

Principal Staff: Dir Anne-Merethe Lie Solberg.

Address: Postboks 440, Sentrum, 3201 Sandefjord.

Telephone: 33-46-02-90; **Fax:** 33-46-48-60; **Internet:** www.ajhs.no; **e-mail:** post@ajhs.no.

Chr. Michelsen Institute—CMI

Established in 1930.

Activities: An independent centre for research on international development and policy. The Institute conducts applied and theoretical research in 10 thematic research groups: aid, culture and politics of faith, gender politics, global health and development, governance and corruption, natural resources, peace and conflict, poverty dynamics, public finance management, and rights and legal institutions.

Geographical Area of Activity: Sub-Saharan Africa, Southern and Central Asia, the Middle East and Latin America.

Publications: Annual Report; CMI Report; CMI Working Paper; CMI Brief; books; reports.

Finance: Annual revenue 77,318,699 krone, expenditure 75,529,407 krone (2014).

Board of Directors: Prof. Lars G. Svåsand (Chair.).

Principal Staff: Dir Dr Ottar Mæstad; Deputy Dir Dr Arne Strand.

Address: Postboks 6033, Bedriftssenteret, 5892 Bergen; Jekteviksbakken 31, Bergen.

Telephone: 47-93-80-00; **Fax:** 47-93-80-01; **Internet:** www.cmi.no; **e-mail:** cmi@cmi.no.

Minor Foundation for Major Challenges

Established in 2000 by Peter Opsvik and members of his family.

Activities: Provides support to climate communication projects that aim to limit human-created climate change, through influencing public opinion and changing attitudes to these problems. The Foundation prioritizes projects that are innovative, experimental and untested; look likely to have the greatest impact; and would be difficult to achieve without the Foundation's assistance.

Geographical Area of Activity: International.

Restrictions: Does not support adaptation projects, mitigation technology, treeplanting or museum exhibitions.

Finance: Total annual grant expenditure approx. 1.5m. krone.

Board: Christian Bjornas (Chair.); Tore Braend (Exec. Dir and Sec.).

Address: c/o Grette DA, Postboks 1397, Vika, 0114 Oslo.

Internet: www.minor-foundation.no; **e-mail:** tore.braend@minor-foundation.no.

Fridtjof Nansen Institute—FNI

Founded in 1958 to conduct applied social science research on international issues in the fields of resource management, the environment and energy.

Activities: An independent foundation engaged in research on international environmental, energy and resource-management politics. Within this framework the Institute's research is mainly grouped around six focal points: Global Governance and Sustainable Development; Marine Affairs and Law of the Sea; Biodiversity and Biosafety; Polar and Russian Politics; European Energy and Environmental Politics; and Chinese Energy and Environmental Politics. Activities include academic studies, contract research, investigations and evaluations.

Geographical Area of Activity: International.

Restrictions: No grants to other organizations.

Publications: Books; peer-reviewed articles and chapters; FNI reports; *The FNI Newsletter* (2 a year); Annual Report.

Finance: Turnover 34m. krone (2012).

Board: Prof. Øyvind Østerud (Chair.); **Council:** Nils Holme (Chair.).

Principal Staff: Dir Geir Hønneland; Deputy Dir Lars H. Gulbrandsen.

Address: POB 326, 1326 Lysaker; Fridtjof Nansens vei 17, 1366 Lysaker.

Telephone: 67-11-19-00; **Fax:** 67-11-19-10; **Internet:** www.fni .no; **e-mail:** post@fni.no.

Norsk Utenrikspolitisk Institutt—NUPI (Norwegian Institute of International Affairs)

Founded in 1959 by the Stortinget (Parliament) to increase insight into questions concerning international relations by disseminating information, and to encourage the study of international problems of co-operation and the causes of international conflicts.

Activities: Operates nationally in the field of information and research, and nationally and internationally in the fields of foreign affairs and international relations, through self-conducted programmes, research, conferences, courses, publications and lectures.

Geographical Area of Activity: Norway and the Russian Federation.

Publications: Conference proceedings; *Internasjonal politikk* (quarterly journal); *Forum for Development Studies* (journal, 2 a year); *NUPI-notat* (20–30 a year); *NUPI-rapport* (10–15 a year); *Nordisk Østforum* (quarterly); *Caspian Energy Politics*; and other articles, papers and books.

Finance: Annual income 89,105,638 krone, expenditure 95,004,771 krone (2014).

Board of Directors: Kate Hansen Bundt (Chair.).

Principal Staff: Dir Ulf Sverdrup; Research Dir Ole Jacob Sending.

Address: POB 8159, 0033 Oslo; C. J. Hambros pl. 2D, Oslo.

Telephone: 22-99-40-00; **Fax:** 22-36-21-82; **Internet:** www .nupi.no; **e-mail:** info@nupi.no.

Henie Onstad Kunstsenter (Henie Onstad Art Centre)

Founded in 1968 by Sonja Henie and Niels Onstad to support and present international modern art in Norway.

Activities: Arranges exhibitions of modern and contemporary art. The Centre houses a collection of modern and contemporary paintings. It is cross-disciplinary and engages international artists for commissioned works, exhibitions, concerts and performances.

Geographical Area of Activity: Norway.

Publications: Annual Report; catalogues; CDs and videos.

Principal Staff: Dir Tone Hansen; Head of Admin. Siv Merethe Skorpen Brekke.

Address: Sonja Henies vei 31, 1311 Høvikodden.

Telephone: 67-80-48-80; **Fax:** 67-54-32-70; **Internet:** www .hok.no; **e-mail:** post@hok.no.

Peace Research Institute Oslo—PRIO

Founded in 1959; an independent research institution known for its effective synergy of basic and policy-relevant research.

Activities: Conducts research on the conditions for peaceful relations between states, groups and people. Researchers work to identify new trends in global conflict, as well as to formulate and document new understandings of and responses to armed conflict. The Institute seeks to understand how people are affected by, and cope with, armed conflict, and studies the normative foundations of peace and violence. Research at the Institute is multidisciplinary and concentrates on the driving forces as well as the consequences of violent conflict, and on ways that peace can be built, maintained and spread. Projects are organized within thematic research groups; in addition, researchers are organized into three administrative departments and the PRIO Cyprus Centre. From 2002 until 2012, PRIO hosted the Centre for the Study of Civil War (CSCW), a long-term, interdisciplinary initiative that was awarded Centre of Excellence status and core funding by the Research Council of Norway.

Geographical Area of Activity: Norway.

Publications: *Journal of Peace Research*; *Security Dialogue*; reports; papers; policy briefs.

Finance: Total assets 114,043,039 NOK; annual revenue 90,040,000 krone, expenditure 89,311,000 krone (31 Dec. 2013).

Board of Directors: Bernt Aardal (Chair.); Ragnhild Sohlberg (Deputy Chair.).

Principal Staff: Dir Kristian Berg Harpviken; Deputy Dir Inger Skjelsbæk; Admin Dir Lene Kristin Borg.

Address: Hausmanns Gate 7, 0186 Oslo; POB 9229, Grønland, 0134 Oslo.

Telephone: 22-54-77-12; **Fax:** 22-54-77-01; **Internet:** www .prio.org; **e-mail:** info@prio.no.

The Rafto Foundation

Established in 1986 to commemorate the life of Prof. Thorolf Rafto.

Activities: Main activity is the annual award of the Rafto Prize, to recognize the achievements of individuals and organizations fighting for human rights, freedom and democracy around the world. Previous winners include Agora (2014), the Bahrain Center for Human Rights (2013), Nnimmo Bassey (2012), Sexual Minorities Uganda (2011) and José Raúl Vera López (2010).

Geographical Area of Activity: International.

Restrictions: A candidate should be active in the struggle for the ideals and principles underlying the Human Rights Charter; a candidate's struggle for human rights should represent a non-violent perspective; a candidate may be a person or an organization; and two or more candidates may share the prize.

Publications: Newsletter; DVDs; books.

Board of Directors: Gunnar M. Sørbø (Chair.); Eva Tamber (Vice-Chair.).

Principal Staff: Exec. Dir (a.i.) Solveig Moldrheim.

Address: Rafto House, Menneskerettighetenes plass 1, 5007 Bergen.

Telephone: 55-21-09-30; **Fax:** 55-21-09-59; **Internet:** www .rafto.no; **e-mail:** rafto@rafto.no.

Regnskogfondet (Rainforest Foundation Norway)

Established in 1989 as part of the Rainforest Foundation network (qq.v.) to combat rainforest destruction and to support indigenous peoples of the world's rainforests in their effort to protect their forests; aims to strengthen national and international public awareness and action.

Activities: Operates in the field of conservation in rainforest areas of South America, Africa and South-East Asia to combat rainforest destruction.

Geographical Area of Activity: Rainforest areas of South America, Africa and South-East Asia, including Bolivia, Brazil, Democratic Republic of the Congo, Ecuador, Indonesia, Malaysia, Papua New Guinea, Paraguay, Peru and Venezuela.

Publications: Annual Report; *News Magazine* (quarterly newsletter).

Finance: Total income 127,564,302 krone, expenditure 126,837,953 krone (2012).

Principal Staff: CEO Dag Hareide.

Address: Mariboes gate 8, 0183 Oslo.

Telephone: 23-10-95-00; **Fax:** 23-10-95-01; **Internet:** www .regnskog.no; www.rainforest.no; **e-mail:** rainforest@ rainforest.no.

Sparebankstiftelsen DNB (Savings Bank Foundation DNB)

Established in 2002 to contribute to charitable causes in Norway.

Activities: Makes grants to not-for-profit organizations in Norway in fields including the arts and culture, environment and heritage.

Geographical Area of Activity: Norway.

Finance: Total assets 10,862.1m. krone, annual expenditure 34,603,667 krone (2013).

Board: Randi Eek Thorsen (Chair.); Elsbeth Tronstad Sande (Deputy Chair.).

Principal Staff: CEO André Støylen; Head of Communications Marit Fagnastøl.

Address: Postboks 555 Sentrum, Øvre Slottsgt. 3, 0105 Oslo.

Telephone: 90-24-41-00; **Internet:** www.sparebankstiftelsen .no; **e-mail:** post@sparebankstiftelsen.no.

Pakistan

FOUNDATION CENTRE AND CO-ORDINATING BODY

Pakistan Centre for Philanthropy—PCP

Established in 2001 as a membership organization serving grantmakers in Pakistan.

Activities: Provides a range of support services to foundations, philanthropists and corporate donors in Pakistan, as well as promoting the development of philanthropy. Work includes the Enabling Environment Initiative, aiming to establish dialogue between government and civil society organizations; Creating Linkages, which boosts corporate support for the education sector; and the NPO Certification System, which sets sector-wide standards of good internal governance, transparent financial management and effective programme delivery. The Centre also carries out research into the nature and scope of diaspora and corporate philanthropy.

Geographical Area of Activity: Pakistan.

Publications: Annual Report; reports and studies on philanthropy in Pakistan.

Finance: Total assets Rs 107,209,629, annual income Rs 50,427,307 (31 Dec. 2012).

Board of Directors: Dr Shamsh Kassim-Lakha (Chair.).

Principal Staff: Exec. Dir Shazia Maqsood Amjad.

Address: 1A St 14, F-8/3, Islamabad.

Telephone: (51) 2855903–4; **Fax:** (51) 2287073; **Internet:** www.pcp.org.pk; **e-mail:** mail@pcp.org.pk.

FOUNDATIONS, TRUSTS AND NON-PROFIT ORGANIZATIONS

Aman Foundation

Established in 2008.

Activities: Operates in the fields of health, nutrition and education, principally in Karachi. The Foundation awards grants to local and international organizations that focus on health care, education, sustainable livelihoods and capacity building. It operates an emergency medical and ambulance service, and a medical advice and diagnosis telephone service.

Geographical Area of Activity: Pakistan.

Finance: Annual income Rs 47,602,590, expenditure Rs 1,433.1m. (30 June 2013).

Trustees: Arif Naqvi (Chair.).

Principal Staff: CEO Malik Ahmad Jalal.

Address: Plot 333, Korangi Township, nr Pakistan Refinery Ltd, Karachi.

Telephone: (21) 111111823; **Internet:** theamanfoundation.org; **e-mail:** info@amanfoundation.org.

Foundation Open Society Institute—Pakistan

Established in 2003 as part of the Open Society Foundations (q.v.) network of foundations.

Activities: Promotes the development of an open, democratic and rights-based society. Operates in the areas of education, media, government transparency and accountability, justice and human rights, and economic policy.

Geographical Area of Activity: Pakistan.

Principal Staff: Country Dir Absar Alam.

Address: N Wing, L3, Serena Office Complex, Plot 17, Islamabad G-5/1 Ramna 5.

Telephone: (51) 2600192; **Internet:** www.opensocietyfoundations.org/about/offices-foundations/foundation-open-society-institute-pakistan.

Hamdard Foundation Pakistan

Founded in 1969 to administer and control the charitable and philanthropic works arising from the financial support of Hamdard Laboratories (Waqf) Pakistan; to advance learning and education, health and medical care, and emergency relief; to develop an indigenous or Eastern system of medicine and medical science; and to support general welfare and charitable purposes.

Activities: Supports the Pakistan Association of Eastern Medicine, Hamdard al-Majeed College of Eastern Medicine; established the Madinat al-Hikmah (City of Education, Science and Culture) in Karachi, comprising a library (Bait-al-Hikmah), institutes for education, medicine, science, Islamic studies and comparative religion, etc.; also provides medicine and health-care services in its clinics and through free mobile dispensaries. Initiated the Shura Hamdard (Hamdard Thinkers' Forum) a medico-scientific, educational and cultural service for the exchange of views on matters of national interest by leading intellectuals and business people, and the Naunehal Assembly for children and youth. Grants are made to individuals and institutions for research and education, particularly in the fields of medicine and pharmacy, and for general charitable purposes. Awards fellowships and scholarships, and sponsors publication of books.

Geographical Area of Activity: Pakistan.

Publications: Report of operations and financial statement; *Hamdard-i-Sehat* (monthly); *Hamdard Naunehal* (monthly); *Khaber Nama Hamdard* (monthly); *Hamdard Islamicus* (quarterly); *Hamdard Medicus* (quarterly); and other publications in Urdu and English.

Board of Trustees: Sadia Rashid (Pres.); Dr Navaid ul-Zafar (Vice-Pres.).

Address: Al-Majeed, Hamdard Centre, Nazimabad No. 3, Karachi 74600.

Telephone: (21) 6616001; **Fax:** (21) 6620945; **Internet:** www.hamdardfoundation.org; **e-mail:** hfp@hamdardfoundation.org.

Pakistan Institute of International Affairs—PIIA

Founded in 1947 with the aim of promoting interest and research in international affairs in Pakistan.

Activities: Operates internationally through research, publications, seminars, lectures and conferences. The Institute has a specialized library with more than 35,000 books and monographs. It assists the Institute's members and research staff, and helps Pakistani and foreign scholars in the field of international affairs and Pakistani foreign policy.

Geographical Area of Activity: South Asia.

Publications: *Pakistan Horizon* (quarterly journal); books; monographs.

Finance: Independent organization, funded by publication sales, rental income and membership fees.

Council: Dr Masuma Hasan (Chair.); Syed Mohammad Fazal (Hon. Treas.); Syed Abdul Minam Jafri (Hon. Sec.).

Address: Aiwan-e-Sadar Rd, POB 1447, Karachi 74200.

Telephone: (21) 35682891; **Fax:** (21) 35686069; **Internet:** www.piia.org.pk; **e-mail:** info@piia.org.pk.

Quaid-i-Azam Academy

Founded in 1976 by the Federal Government of Pakistan to undertake research on Quaid-i-Azam Mohammad Ali Jinnah (Founder of the Nation) and on the history of Pakistan.

Activities: Conducts and supports research on political, economic, social, religious and cultural aspects of the history of Pakistan; grants scholarships and professorships; sponsors and participates in lectures, conferences and seminars. The Academy awards seven prizes every three years to Pakistani or foreign scholars for work of academic merit on Quaid-i-Azam or on any aspects of modern Indo-Muslim history. It maintains a library and collection of research materials and archives, and publishes the results of research.

Geographical Area of Activity: International.

Publications: Studies, translations and bibliographies.

Principal Staff: Sec. Asaf Ghafoor; Dir Dr Shehla Kazmi (acting).

Address: 297 M. A. Jinnah Rd, Karachi 74800.

Telephone: (21) 99215234; **Fax:** (21) 99215236; **Internet:** www .quaidiazamacademy.com; **e-mail:** quaidazam1976@yahoo .com.

Zuleikhabai Valy Mohammad Gany (Z. V. M. G.) Rangoonwala Trust

Founded in 1967 by M. A. Rangoonwala to improve the life of indigent and deserving persons without any discrimination of caste, creed and colour, through the advancement of education and vocational training, the advancement of health and the prevention and relief of sickness, and through the care and comfort of the needy.

Activities: Operates nationally in the fields of education, social welfare, science and medicine, and the arts and humanities, and internationally in the fields of education, science and medicine, religion and the conservation of natural resources. Operates through self-conducted programmes, grants to institutions both at home and abroad, grants to individuals, fellowships, scholarships, conferences, courses, publications and lectures. Establishes, aids and maintains community centres, educational institutions, hospitals, dispensaries, maternity homes, nursing homes, clinics, sanatoria and medical research centres.

Geographical Area of Activity: International.

Publications: Report of operations and financial statement; Annual Report.

Finance: Funded by the Rangoonwala family.

Board of Trustees: Asif M. A. Rangoonwala (Man. Trustee); Mohammad Afzal Nagaria (Hon. Sec.).

Principal Staff: Exec. Chair. Mohammed Saleem Yousuf; Dir Saeed A. B. Mirza; Deputy Dir Arshad Jamil Bhatti.

Address: Plot Nos 4 and 5, K. D. A. Scheme No. 7, Block-4, Dhoraji Colony, Karachi 74800.

Telephone: (21) 34935168; **Fax:** (21) 34930534; **Internet:** www .rcc.com.pk; **e-mail:** zvmgrcc@yahoo.com.

Palestinian Territories

FOUNDATIONS, TRUSTS AND NON-PROFIT ORGANIZATIONS

Dalia Association

Established in 2007 as a community foundation, to help the development of civil society organizations in the Palestinian Territories.

Activities: Offers support and funding to NGOs in the Palestinian Territories for work within the community, providing advocacy and connecting resources and expertise. Programmes include Women Supporting Women, which provides women with training, advice and small grants to give them decision-making powers over community development resources; and The Village Decides, involving whole communities in decision-making processes over the distribution of community resources. The Association has an office in Brussels, Belgium, where it is also registered as a charity.

Geographical Area of Activity: Palestinian Territories.

Publications: Annual Report; newsletter.

Finance: Annual revenue US $311,384, expenditure $132,860 (31 Dec. 2013).

Board of Directors: Maha Mikhail (Chair.); Rula Muzaffer (Treas.).

Principal Staff: Exec. Dir Reem Qawasmi.

Address: POB 2394, 00972 Ramallah.

Telephone: (2) 298-9121; **Internet:** www.dalia.ps; **e-mail:** info@dalia.ps.

Panama

FOUNDATION CENTRES AND CO-ORDINATING BODIES

Consejo de Educación Popular de América Latina y el Caribe—CEAAL (Council for Popular Education in Latin America and the Caribbean)

Established in 1982, as the Consejo de Educación de Adultos de América Latina, an association of 195 civil organizations (located across 21 countries), to improve adult literacy and advance social development throughout Central and South America and the Caribbean. Present name adopted in 2012.

Activities: Operates in the field of education, consolidating the training and abilities of teaching staff in Central and South America and the Caribbean, promoting socio-cultural advancements in society, peace, human rights and democracy through education and raising adult literacy levels. The Council holds a General Assembly meeting every four years.

Geographical Area of Activity: Central and South America and the Caribbean.

Publications: *La Piragua; La Carta* (weekly); reports; books.

Executive Committee: Oscar Jara Holliday (Chair.); Edgardo Álvarez Puga (Treas.).

Principal Staff: Sec.-Gen. Nélida Céspedes Rossel.

Address: Apdo 0831-00817, Paitilla, Panama City; Oficina de la Secretaría General, Via Cincuentanario No. 84B, Coco del Mar, Corregimento de San Francisco, Panama City.

Telephone: 270-1085; **Fax:** 270-1084; **Internet:** www.ceaal .org; **e-mail:** info@ceaal.org.

Fundación AVINA (AVINA Foundation)

Founded in 1994 by Stephen Schmidheiny to build partnerships with the corporate sector and the leaders of civil society to promote sustainable development in Central and South America and parts of Europe.

Activities: Funds activities that promote relations between civil society and private sector leaders, principally change-orientated projects in the fields of formal and non-formal education and training, citizen participation and grassroots social involvement, eco-efficiency and effective management of natural resources, economic and community development, and corporate social responsibility.

Geographical Area of Activity: Argentina, Bolivia, Brazil, Chile, Colombia, Costa Rica, Ecuador, Guatemala, Nicaragua, Paraguay, Peru, Portugal, Uruguay, Venezuela, Spain and the USA.

Publications: Annual Report; books; *VIVA Publications*; *Informe de Odecu detectó altos niveles de caloría en leches saborizadas*; *Los Secretos del Eclipse*; *Informe de ODECU sobre los CFT de Chile*; *Revista Surcos; Conexion AVINA*.

Finance: Annual income US $27,833,540, expenditure $22,049,929 (31 Dec. 2014).

Board of Directors: Sean McKaughan (Chair.); Pamela Ríos (Sec.).

Principal Staff: Exec. Dir Gabriel Barracatt.

Address: Apdo 0832-0390 WTC, Panama City; Local 131B, Calle Evelio Lara, Ciudad del Saber, Clayton, Panama City.

Telephone: 317-0657; **Fax:** 317-0239; **Internet:** www.avina .net; **e-mail:** comunicaciones@avina.net.

FOUNDATIONS, TRUSTS AND NON-PROFIT ORGANIZATIONS

Fundación Dobbo Yala (Dobbo Yala Foundation)

Founded in 1990 to promote sustainable development for indigenous development and environmental conservation.

Activities: Provides administrative, technical and management support for environmental projects. Programmes include environmental education, training and extension of sustainable agriculture, socio-economic and environmental education, management of native forests projects, and training and support for indigenous micro-enterprises.

Geographical Area of Activity: Central America.

Publications: *Territorios Indigenas, Biodiversidad y Turismo; El valor del ambiente en los kunas desde una perspectiva de género; Minería en territorio indígena: Proyecto Cerro Colorado* (case study); *Diagnóstico Socio-Ambiental de la Actividad Minera en Panamá; Conflicto Socio-Ambiental en Panamá: Caso de Arimae y Emberá Puru; Aspecto legal sobre la protección de los Recursos Naturales; We Napa Nega Ibi Nuedi, Anmar Nue Sabgumala (Esta Tierra es Nuestra, Cuidémosla)*; and other publications.

Board of Directors: Pres. Aurelio Chiari.

Principal Staff: Exec. Dir Eligio Alvarado.

Address: Apdo 83-0308, Zona 3, Panama City; Calle Herbruger con Avda Ramón Arias,Casa 13B, Nuevo Reparto el Carmen, Urb. Linares.

Telephone: 261-6347; **Fax:** 261-7229.

Fundación Ricardo Martinelli por la Educación Caminando y Cumpliendo (Ricardo Martinelli Foundation for Education)

Established in 1991 as Fundación Super 99 to promote education as a fundamental tool for the betterment of society; present name adopted in 2004.

Activities: Offers scholarships to Panamanian students at all levels of education.

Geographical Area of Activity: Panama.

Address: Plaza Super 99, Costa del Este, Calle Principal, 2°, Local 1A, Panama City.

Telephone: 305-5005; **Internet:** www.ricardomartinelli.org; **e-mail:** info@ricardomartinelli.org.

Paraguay

FOUNDATIONS, TRUSTS AND NON-PROFIT ORGANIZATIONS

Fundación Moisés Bertoni—FMB (Moisés Bertoni Foundation)

Established in 1988 to protect animals and plants in Paraguay.

Activities: Promotes the conservation of nature and biodiversity; management of protected areas; sustainable use of resources; and education and training in environmental management. The Foundation also runs eco-tourism projects in managed private game reserves.

Geographical Area of Activity: Paraguay.

Publications: Annual Report; *Plantas Comunes del Mbaracayo*; *Helechos del Mbaracayo*; *Maniteros de la Reserva de Mbaracayo*; *Plantas Medicinales de la Comunidad Guarani*; *Membresías;* agreements of technical co-operation with numerous national and international organizations.

Finance: Annual revenue 13,084,232,053 guaranis, expenditure 9,217,041,118 guaranis (31 Dec. 2011).

Principal Staff: Exec. Dir Yan Speranza; Gen. Man. Daniel Jacquet.

Address: Prócer Carlos Argüello 208, POB 714, Asunción.

Telephone: (21) 60-8740; **Fax:** (21) 60-8741; **Internet:** www.mbertoni.org.py; **e-mail:** mbertoni@mbertoni.org.py.

Peru

FOUNDATION CENTRES AND CO-ORDINATING BODIES

Asociación Latinoamericana de Instituciones Financieras para el Desarrollo—ALIDE (Latin American Association of Development Financing Institutions)

Founded in 1968 to promote the participation of financial institutions in the social and economic progress of countries in Central and South America and the Caribbean.

Activities: Made up of public and private development financing institutions; it encourages members to co-operate and contribute to the development and integration of Central and South American economies. The Association disseminates information; reports on investment projects; supports the collaboration of members on projects; organizes training projects and seminars; works to strengthen banking institutions in Central and South America; and maintains an information network, documentation centre and database. It also acts as an executive institution for projects and programmes being funded by international co-operation organizations and agencies. The Association has more than 80 members within Central and South America and the Caribbean, but also in Canada, the People's Republic of China, Germany, Portugal, Spain, Sweden and the Russian Federation.

Geographical Area of Activity: Central and South America and the Caribbean.

Restrictions: Works only with member organizations and institutions.

Publications: Annual Report; *ALIDE Bulletin* (6 a year, in English and Spanish); *Anales Asamblea General* (annually); Alide Noticias (monthly); *Directorio de Instituciones de Desarrollo* (biennially); *Revista ALIDE* (bimonthly); *Boletín ALIDE-NOTICIAS* (monthly); *E-Banca* (monthly); *ALIDE E-News* (online bulletin, every four months); numerous technical papers and publications.

Finance: Annual income US $1,025,066, expenditure $1,025,066 (31 Dec. 2012).

Board of Directors: María Soledad Barrera Altamirano (Chair.); Enrique de la Madrid Cordero (Vice-Chair.).

Principal Staff: Sec.-Gen. Rommel Acevedo Fernández de Paredes.

Address: POB 3988, Lima 100; Avda Paseo de la República 3211, San Isidro, Lima 27.

Telephone: (1) 4422400; **Fax:** (1) 4428105; **Internet:** www.alide.org.pe; **e-mail:** sg@alide.org.pe.

CLADEM—Comité de América Latina y el Caribe para la Defensa de los Derechos de la Mujer (Latin American Committee for the Defence of Women's Rights)

Established in 1987; a network of individual women and women's organizations, to defend the rights of women in Central and South America and the Caribbean.

Activities: Operates in the field of women's rights, through education and information, proposals for legislative change and campaigning, solidarity activities, and through prizes awarded in recognition of women's achievements. The Committee has offices in 17 countries of Central and South America and the Caribbean, and a regional office in Peru.

Geographical Area of Activity: Central and South America and the Caribbean.

Publications: Books; reports; pamphlets; videos; CD-ROMs.

Principal Staff: Exec. Sec. Mery Elizabeth Cabero Calatayud; Regional Co-ordinator Elba Nuñez Ibáñez.

Address: Apdo 11-0470, Lima; Jr Estados Unidos 1295, Dpto. 702, Lima 11.

Telephone: (1) 4639237; **Fax:** (1) 4635898; **Internet:** www.cladem.org; **e-mail:** oficina@cladem.org.

FOUNDATIONS, TRUSTS AND NON-PROFIT ORGANIZATIONS

CEDRO—Centro de Información y Educación para la Prevención del Abuso de Drogas (Information and Education Centre for the Prevention of Drug Abuse)

Founded in 1986 to raise awareness of drug abuse in Peru, and to help people afflicted by drug addiction.

Activities: Disseminates information about the impact of drug use, production and commercialization, and works to overcome problems in society that are drug-related. The Centre funds community development projects in Peru, including working with 'street children' to overcome drug abuse through education and rehousing, where possible. It also provides vocational training and support, and funds research.

Geographical Area of Activity: Mainly Peru.

Publications: *Psychoactive Journal*.

Principal Staff: Exec. Dir Alejandro Vassilaqui; Deputy Dir Carmen Masías.

Address: Avda Roca y Boloña 271, San Antonio–Miraflores, Lima 18.

Telephone: (1) 4475130; **Fax:** (1) 4460751; **Internet:** www.cedro.org.pe; **e-mail:** postmast@cedro.org.pe.

ProNaturaleza—Fundación Peruana para la Conservación de la Naturaleza (Pro Nature—Peruvian Foundation for Nature Conservation)

Founded in 1984; a not-for-profit private organization dedicated to the conservation and protection of the environment in Peru.

Activities: Supports the conservation of soils, water resources, flora, fauna and other renewable natural resources in Peru, and promotes the development of a conservation culture. The Foundation works in conjunction with the Tropical Rainforest Coalition.

Geographical Area of Activity: Peru.

Publications: *Biodiversifica-t* (newsletter, 10–11 a year); *Diagnóstico Rural Participativo en las cuencas altas de los ríos Tambopata e Inambari*; *Estudio Etnobotánico en las cuencas altas de los ríos Tambopata e Inambari*; *Áreas de Conservación Privada en el Perú*; *Dos décadas de conservación en el Perú;* various documents and papers.

Finance: Annual income approx. US $4.5m. (2012).

Board of Directors: Manuel Ríos Rodríguez (Chair.); Enrique Agois Banchero (Vice-Chair.); Dr Fernando de Trazegnies Granda (Hon. Chair.).

Principal Staff: Exec. Dir Michael de la Cadena.

Address: Calle Doña Juana 137, Urb. Los Rosales, Santiago de Surco, Lima.

Telephone: (1) 2712662; **Fax:** (1) 4480947; **Internet:** www.pronaturaleza.org; **e-mail:** pronaturaleza@pronaturaleza.org.

PROTERRA

Established in 1983; a non-profit organization and centre of investigation and promotion of environmental and development issues, which aims to improve the quality of life through achieving sustainable development.

Activities: Operates nationally and internationally, throughout Central and South America, in the fields of environmental policies and law, and sustainable development, through research, projects, training, publications, information dissemination, conferences, workshops, seminars and lobbying. The organization co-operates with environmental workers and other national and international organizations; supports projects in Peru and Central and South America, especially in the Andes and Amazonia regions; and participated in the drafting of the Peruvian Environment and Natural Resources Code. It maintains a library of books, magazines, documents, photographs, videos, etc. on the environment, and a database of environmental legislation.

Geographical Area of Activity: Central and South America.

Publications: Annual Report; books on environmental law and the environment.

Principal Staff: Dir José Tedoro Maco García.

Address: c/o Instituto de Investigaciones de la Amazonía Peruana, Avda José Abelardo Quiñones km 2.5, Apdo 784, Iquitos, Loreto.

Telephone: (65) 265515; **Fax:** (65) 265516; **Internet:** www.iiap .org.pe/programas/proterra.htm; **e-mail:** proterra@iiap.org .pe.

Philippines

FOUNDATION CENTRES AND CO-ORDINATING BODIES

AF—Association of Foundations

Founded in 1972 to foster broader public understanding of the nature of foundations as institutions in nation-building; to promote co-ordination and co-operation among member foundations; to represent members; and to serve as a clearing house for information, establishing and maintaining a central file of foundation materials and a directory of Philippine foundations.

Activities: Operates nationally through the dissemination of information, organization of conferences and workshops, liaison among members and between members and government agencies, maintenance of an information centre, and through various publications. The Association hosts four major databanks, providing information on all indigenous and international grantmakers operating in the Philippines as well as on 941 social development organizations. It comprises the Philippine Foundation Center, a resource and information centre on NGOs, foundations and the civil society sector in general. Has approximately 135 member foundations and is one of six founding members of the Philippines Council for NGO Certification.

Geographical Area of Activity: Philippines.

Publications: Annual Report and financial statement; *AF Brochure*; *Foundation Bulletin*; *Directory of Philippine Foundations*; *Donor Trends: A Resource Book of Development Assistance in the Philippines*; *Philippines NGOs: A Resource Book of Social Development NGOs*.

Finance: Annual revenue 5,562,519 pesos, expenditure 5,036,353 pesos (2013).

Board of Trustees: Judy A. Roxas (Chair.); Fely C. Rixhon (Pres.); Danny Z. Urquico, Rose J. Depra, Joemil S. Montebon (Vice-Pres); Alex T. Escaño (Treas.); Cecile L. Alcantara (Sec.).

Principal Staff: Exec. Dir Oman Q. Jiao.

Address: Rm 1102, 11th Floor, Aurora Tower, Aurora Blvd, Cubao, 1109 Quezon City.

Telephone: (2) 9137231; **Fax:** (2) 9119792; **Internet:** www.afonline.org; **e-mail:** afonline@info.com.ph.

Asian NGO Coalition for Agrarian Reform and Rural Development—ANGOC

Founded in 1979 in Bangkok, Thailand.

Activities: Has two main programme areas: land and resource rights of the rural poor; and promoting smallholder agriculture for sustainable food systems and livelihoods. Member organizations operate in Bangladesh, Cambodia, the People's Republic of China, India, Indonesia, Laos, Nepal, Pakistan, the Philippines, Sri Lanka and Viet Nam.

Geographical Area of Activity: South-East, East and South Asia.

Publications: Annual Report; newsletter; *Land Governance in Asia: Understanding the debates on land tenure rights and land reforms in the Asian context*; *Securing the Right to Land: An Overview on Access to Land in Asia (2nd Edition)*; *Lokniti on Land Grabbing: Changing the terrain of land tenure*; *Chronicle of a land redeemed: The struggle for agrarian reform in Barobo, Valencia*.

Board of Directors: Rohini Reddy (Chair.); Chet Charya (Vice-Chair.).

Principal Staff: Exec. Dir Nathaniel Don E. Marquez.

Address: POB 3107, QCCPO 1103, Quezon City; 73-K Dr Lazcano St, Barangay Laging Handa, 1103 Quezon City.

Telephone: (2) 3510581; **Fax:** (2) 3510011; **Internet:** www.angoc.org; **e-mail:** angoc@angoc.org.

Asian Partnership for the Development of Human Resources in Rural Asia—AsiaDHRRA

Founded in 1975, as the Center for the Development of Human Resources in Rural Asia—CenDHRRA, to promote the establishment of rural development projects for rural communities in Asia. Present name adopted in 1994.

Activities: Activities focus on leadership and organizational development, regional advocacy and constituency building, resource development and information management; programmes include the Post-Yolanda (Haiyan) Fund for Local Initiatives and Farmers Fighting Poverty. It comprises 11 social development organizations from Cambodia, Indonesia, Japan, Laos, Malaysia, Myanmar, the Philippines, Taiwan, Thailand, the Republic of Korea and Viet Nam.

Geographical Area of Activity: Asia.

Publications: Annual Report; Farmers' Exchange Monographs; e-books; manuals.

Finance: Annual revenue US $1,063,751, expenditure $892,560 (2014).

Executive Committee: Dwi Astuti (Chair.); Kya Mu (Vice-Chair., Mekong Region); Saravanan Sinnapan (Vice-Chair., South-East Asia); Dr Sung Lee (Vice-Chair., North Asia).

Principal Staff: Sec.-Gen. Marlene D. Ramirez.

Address: Room 201, Partnership Center, 59 Salvador St, Loyola Heights, 1108 Quezon City.

Telephone: (2) 4364706; **Fax:** (2) 4266739; **Internet:** asiadhrra.org; **e-mail:** asiadhrra@asiadhrra.org.

League of Corporate Foundations

Established in 1991 within the Association of Foundations (q.v.); formally registered in 1996.

Activities: Promotes corporate social responsibility in the private sector. Comprises 70 grantmaking orgs.

Geographical Area of Activity: The Philippines.

Board of Trustees: Natalie Christine V. Jorge (Chair.); Rina Lopez-Bautista (Vice-Chair.); Monette Iturralde-Hamlin (Sec.); Carmen Linda M. Atayde (Treas.).

Principal Staff: Exec. Dir Helen O. Orande.

Address: Unit 305, Midland Mansions Condominium, 839 Arnaiz Ave, Legazpi Village, Makati City 1226.

Telephone: (2) 8929189; **Fax:** (2) 8925753; **Internet:** www.lcf.org.ph; **e-mail:** communications@lcf.org.ph.

National Council of Social Development Foundations

Established in 1949; formerly known as the Council of Welfare Agencies of the Philippines, Inc.

Activities: A network of social welfare and development agencies. Carries out capacity building, advocacy and social mobilization activities; lobbies to change national policies on behalf of children, their families and the wider community. Mem. of the Caucus of Development NGO Networks and Philippine Council for NGO Certification (q.v.).

Geographical Area of Activity: The Philippines.

Principal Staff: Pres. Sandra Camesa; Officer-in-Charge Marian Opeña.

Address: Unit 12, 12th Floor, Kassel Condominium, 2625 Taft Ave, Malate, Manila.

Telephone: 3542903; **Fax:** 3538466; **e-mail:** ncsdphils@yahoo.com.

Philippine Business for Social Progress

Established in 1970 by 50 Filipino businesspeople.

Activities: Promotes private sector support for poverty alleviation and programmes developing self-reliance. Its four main areas of interest are: health, with focus on tuberculosis, maternal and child health, and lifestyle diseases; education, building classrooms and providing scholarships; the environment, with a focus on watershed management, disaster risk reduction and climate change adaptation; and livelihood and enterprise development, providing vocational training, linking poverty groups with industry, and facilitating corporate social responsibility. Runs the Center for Corporate Citizenship, providing training, advocacy and consultancy services; and the Center for Social Development Management, supporting all aspects of public-private partnerships. Mem. of the Philippine Council for NGO Certification (q.v.).

Geographical Area of Activity: The Philippines.

Board of Trustees: Manuel V. Pangilinan (Chair.); Paul G. Domingues (Vice-Chair.); Ramon R. del Rosario, Jr (Treas.).

Principal Staff: Exec. Dir Rafael C. Lopa.

Telephone: (2) 527-7741; **Internet:** www.pbsp.org.ph; **e-mail:** pbsp@pbsp.org.ph.

Philippine Council for NGO Certification

Established in 1999 by the Association of Foundations (q.v.), Bishops-Businessmen's Conference for Human Development, Caucus of Development NGO Networks, League of Corporate Foundations (q.v.), National Council of Social Development Foundations (q.v.) and Philippine Business for Social Progress (q.v.).

Activities: Promotes NGO transparency and accountability through its certification mechanism; private-sector participation in social development; and greater collaboration between the Government and third-sector orgs.

Geographical Area of Activity: The Philippines.

Board of Trustees: Augusto P. I. Carpio, III (Chair.); Teresa Ang See (Vice-Chair.); Carmen Linda M. Atayde (Treas.); Fr Antonio Cecilio T. Pascual (Sec.).

Address: SCC Bldg, 6th Floor, CFA-MA Compound, 4427 Interior Old Sta. Mesa, 1016 Manila.

Telephone: (2) 782-1568; **Fax:** (2) 715-2783; **Internet:** www.pcnc.com.ph; **e-mail:** pcnc@pldtdsl.net.

FOUNDATIONS, TRUSTS AND NON-PROFIT ORGANIZATIONS

Ayala Foundation, Inc—AFI

Founded in 1961 by Col Joseph McMicking and his wife Mercedes Zobel to fund projects related to the arts, technology, social sciences and education. Formerly known as the Filipinas Foundation; now the socio-cultural development section of the Ayala Group of companies, one of the largest conglomerates in the Philippines.

Activities: Promotes and advances social development. Programmes focus on education, youth leadership, sustainable livelihoods, art and culture; special projects encompass strengthening the capacity of civil society organizations and disaster relief. The Foundation runs the Ayala Museum and also owns the Filipinas Heritage Library, the Center for Social Development and the Center of Excellence in Public Elementary Education.

Geographical Area of Activity: The Philippines.

Publications: Annual Report.

Finance: Annual revenue 921,699,877 pesos, expenditure 271,949,838 pesos (31 Dec. 2013).

Board of Trustees: Jaime Augusto Zobel de Ayala II, Fernando Zobel de Ayala (Co-Chair.); Ma. Cecilia Cruzabra (Treas.); Solomon Hermosura (Sec.); Nimfa Ambrosia Paras (Asst Sec.).

Principal Staff: Pres. Ruel Maranan.

Address: 111 Paseo Bldg, 8th Floor, Paseo de Roxas cnr Legaspi St, Legaspi Village 1229, Makati City.

Telephone: (2) 7521101; **Fax:** (2) 8134488; **Internet:** www.ayalafoundation.org; **e-mail:** info@ayalafoundation.org.

ChildHope Philippines

Established in 1989 as a branch office of ChildHope International (f. 1986) during the First Regional Conference on Street Children in Asia. In 1995, Childhope in the Philippines became an independent Philippine NGO.

Activities: Provides advocacy, capacity building and technical assistance, networking, databanking, and programme development and implementation. The organization's main programmes are the Baranggay Council for the Protection of Children and the Street Education Program. It also provides vocational/service skills training, psychosocial intervention, and health and medical services among the street children of Metro Manila.

Geographical Area of Activity: Metro Manila, the Philippines.

Publications: Annual Report; newsletter; narrative reports; directories; research series; guidebooks; workshop proceedings; manuals.

Board of Directors: Samuel Guevara (Chair.); Dr Jaime Galvez Tan (Vice-Chair.); Ginger Roxas-Arzt (Sec.); C. O. Sherwin (Treas.); Lester Joseph Castolo (Asst Treas.).

Principal Staff: Pres. and Exec. Dir Teresita Silva.

Address: 1210 Peñafrancia St, Paco 1007, Manila.

Telephone: (2) 5634647; **Fax:** (2) 5632242; **Internet:** www.childhope.org.ph; **e-mail:** chap@childhope.org.ph; childhope@hope.org.ph.

Communication Foundation for Asia

Established in 1973, but its origins go back to 1960, with the launch of the Philippine Catholic Digest, and the eventual establishment of the Social Communication Cente (SCC) in 1968. CFA and SCC were founded by Dutch missionary Fr Cornelio Lagerwey, in collaboration with journalist Genaro V. Ong and other lay Filipino communicators.

Activities: A multi-media centre with around 84 staff, producing video documentries and TV programmes, and publishing educational comics and magazines that reach an estimated readership of more than 1m. nationwide. The Foundation holds training workshops on communication skills and media education; and organizes media events such as film festivals, peace communication camps, environmental forums and travelling exhibits.

Geographical Area of Activity: Asia.

Publications: *Kidsmarts* (for pre-school, 5 isses a year); *Jesus Gospel Komiks Edition for Young Readers* (for early elementary readers, 5 issues a year); *Gospel Komiks* (for intermediate readers, 5 issues a year, in English and Filipino); *Gospel K Magazine for High School* (5 issues a year); Gospel Now (for high-school and early college readers, 5 issues a year).

Board of Trustees: Fr Gene Pejo, MSC (Chair.); Fr Filoteo C. Pelingon, MSC (Pres.); Fr Leonardo Cabrera (Vice-Chair. and Treas.); Francisco Gonzalez, V (Sec.).

Principal Staff: Exec. Dir Noel T. de Leon.

Address: 4427 Old Santa Mesa St, Santa Mesa, 1016 Manila.

Telephone: (2) 7132981; **Fax:** (2) 7132974; **Internet:** www.cfamedia.org; **e-mail:** info@cfamedia.org.

Cultural Center of the Philippines—CCP

Founded in 1966, the Center is mandated by Philippine law to preserve, promote and enhance the Filipino people's cultural heritage, and to encourage the evolution of the national culture of the Philippines.

Activities: Operates as a national centre for the performing arts; encourages, conserves and disseminates Filipino creativity and artistic experience, through providing artistic programmes, services and facilities. Maintains a library and organizes international exchanges.

Geographical Area of Activity: The Philippines.

Publications: Annual Report; catalogues on dance, theatre and music, and various monographs.

Finance: Annual income 426.3m. pesos, expenditure 436.5m. pesos (31 Dec. 2014).

Board of Trustees: Emily A. Abrera (Chair.).

Principal Staff: Pres. Dr Raul M. Sunico; Vice-Pres. Chris B. Millado.

Address: CCP Complex, Roxas Blvd, Pasay City 1300, Manila.

Telephone: (2) 8321125; **Fax:** (2) 8323683; **Internet:** culturalcenter.gov.ph; **e-mail:** ccp.publicrelations@gmail .com.

Haribon Foundation for the Conservation of Natural Resources, Inc

Established in 1972 by Alicia Busser, Dr Robert Kennedy and Pedro Gonzales to promote sustainable development for the Philippines, through community-based, socially equitable and scientifically-sound management of natural resources.

Activities: Operates nationally in the field of conservation and the environment, through self-conducted programmes, research, scholarships, conferences, training courses and community-based projects. Key programmes include the Marine Ecosystems Programme, the Institutional Partnership Development Programme and the Terrestrial Ecosystems Programme. The Foundation maintains links with local and international organizations.

Geographical Area of Activity: Asia-Pacific.

Publications: Annual Report; books on biodiversity; policy papers; research and educational materials; digital media; *Haring Ibon* magazine.

Finance: Annual revenue 39,724,835 pesos, expenditure 34,893,323 pesos (31 Dec. 2012).

Board of Directors: John Philip J. Lesaca (Chair.); Dante Francis M. Ang, II (Vice-Chair.); Teodulo Antonio G. San Juan, Jr (Sec.); Archimedes R. King (Treas.).

Principal Staff: COO Ma. Belinda E. de la Paz.

Address: 2F Santos and Sons Bldg, 973 Aurora Blvd, Cubao, Quezon City.

Telephone: (2) 4344642; **Fax:** (2) 4344696; **Internet:** www .haribon.org.ph; **e-mail:** act@haribon.org.ph.

IBON Foundation

Established in 1978 to provide advocacy, research, education and information.

Activities: Operates in the Philippines and abroad providing research, education, publications, information and advocacy. The Foundation is also involved in the education sector, providing non-formal education to people's organizations; conducting in-depth research and information services to various sectors; media education; and international networking. The international arm has an office in Belgium.

Geographical Area of Activity: Mainly the Philippines.

Publications: *Birdtalk: Economic and Political Briefing*; surveys.

Board of Directors: Prof. Judy Taguiwalo (Chair.); Bishop Solito Toquero (Vice-Chair.); Prof. Roland Simbulan (Sec.); Reynaldo Oliveros (Treas.).

Address: IBON Center, 114 Timog Ave., Quezon City 1103.

Telephone: (2) 9277060; **Fax:** (2) 9292496; **Internet:** www .ibon.org; **e-mail:** admin@ibon.org.

Integrated Rural Development Foundation

Established to promote sustainable development in the Philippines, especially with regard to the rural poor.

Activities: Operates nationally in the area of sustainable development through local community-based projects in natural resource management and food security. There are four main programmes: Sustainable Farming; Sustainable Community-based Resource Management; Rural Livelihood and Development; and Policy Research, Advocacy and Campaigns.

Geographical Area of Activity: The Philippines.

Principal Staff: Exec. Dir Arze Glipo-Carasco.

Address: POB 741, Araneta Center Post Office, Cubao, Quezon City; 87 Malakas St, Pinyahan, Quezon City 1100.

Telephone: (2) 4265518; **Fax:** (2) 9250987; **Internet:** irdf.org .ph; **e-mail:** info@irdf.org.ph.

International Institute of Rural Reconstruction— IIRR

Established in 1960 to bring about integrated community-based development and to generate models for reducing poverty based on participatory approaches to development.

Activities: Promotes people-centered development through capacity building for poor people and their communities, development organizations and agencies. The Institute shares its experiences and knowledge through training programmes and publications. Main themes of operation are: Education for Pastoralists and other Marginalized Communities; Food Security and Wealth Creation; Disaster Risk Reduction and Climate Change Adaptation; and Applied Learning. It maintains its Africa Regional Center in Kenya, a liaison office in New York, USA, and country offices in Cambodia, Ethiopia, Kenya, South Sudan, Uganda and Zimbabwe.

Geographical Area of Activity: Africa and Asia.

Publications: Annual Report; newsletters; publications relating to sustainable development.

Finance: Annual income US $54,094,886, expenditure $48,439,558 (31 Dec. 2013).

Board of Trustees: James F. Kelly (Chair.).

Principal Staff: Pres. Isaac B. Bekalo.

Address: Y. C. James Yen Center, Km 39 Aguinaldo Highway, Silang, Cavite 4118.

Telephone: (46) 4143216; **Fax:** (46) 4143216; **Internet:** www .iirr.org; **e-mail:** headquarters@iirr.org.

Ramon Magsaysay Award Foundation

Founded in 1957 by Belen H. Abreu, Paz Marquez Benitez, Jaime N. Ferrer, Jesus Magsaysay, Francisco Ortigas, Jr, Pedro Tuason and Leopoldo Uichanco, in memory of former President of the Philippines Ramon Magsaysay.

Activities: Confers the Ramon Magsaysay Award: six annual awards of US $50,000 each are offered in the fields of government service; public service; community leadership; journalism, literature and creative communication arts; international understanding; and since 2001, emergency leadership. The Foundation also runs the Programme for Asian Projects to enable awardees to develop their projects and runs an essay-writing competition. It maintains an Asian Library, housing an extensive collection of reference materials on contemporary Asia, as well as the Magsaysay Papers; organizes international seminars on issues affecting the Asian region; and offers presentations on the peoples and cultures of the region to secondary-school pupils. In 2011, the Foundation established the Ramon Magsaysay Transformative Leadership Institute as a hub to foster dialogue and the exchange of ideas between awardees and global leaders, organizing conferences, lectures and online fora.

Geographical Area of Activity: Asia.

Restrictions: Grants are made only to people or institutions that work in Asia.

Publications: Newsletter; *AwardeeLinks* (e-newsletter).

Finance: Funded by the Rockefeller Brothers Fund (q.v.) from 1958 to 1968, the Foundation is now supported by the income from the Ramon Magsaysay Center, which it owns. The Rockefeller Brothers Fund grants approx. US $150,000 annually to support the awards.

Board of Trustees: Juan B. Santos (Chair.); Fr Jose Ramon T. Villarin, S. J. (Vice-Chair.); Robina Y. Gokongwei-Pe (Treas.).

Principal Staff: Pres. and CEO Carmencita T. Abella.

Address: POB 3350, Manila; Ground Floor, Ramon Magsaysay Center, 1680 Roxas Blvd, 1004 Malate, Manila.

Telephone: (2) 5213166; **Fax:** (2) 4040926; **Internet:** www .rmaf.org.ph; **e-mail:** rmcenter@rmaf.org.ph; rmaf@rmaf .org.ph.

Philippine-American Educational Foundation— PAEF

Founded in 1948, as the US Educational Foundation in the Philippines, by the Governments of the USA and the Philippines to promote further mutual understanding by a wider exchange of knowledge and professional talents through educational contacts. Present name adopted in 1969.

Activities: Operates nationally and internationally in sponsoring research, educational conferences, lectures, seminars and scholarship and fellowship programmes, notably educational exchanges between students from the USA and the Philippines, the Philippine Fulbright Programme for study in the USA, the Hubert H. Humphrey North-South Fellowship Program for professional candidates, and the East-West Center student degree awards providing financial assistance to students from the Philippines studying at the University of Hawaii. The Foundation also provides information and counselling services, and maintains an information resource library on US universities.

Geographical Area of Activity: USA and the Philippines.

Finance: Income is derived from the Governments of the USA and the Philippines, from private agencies and individuals.

Board of Directors: Philip S. Goldberg (Hon. Chair.).

Principal Staff: Exec. Dir Dr Esmeralda S. Cunanan.

Address: 10th Floor Ayala Life–FGU Center-Makati, 6811 Ayala Ave, 1226 Makati City.

Telephone: (2) 8120919; **Fax:** (2) 8120822; **Internet:** www .fulbright.org.ph; **e-mail:** fulbright@fulbright.org.ph.

Tebtebba Foundation

Established in 1996.

Activities: Aims to resolve conflicts and promote sustainable development in indigenous communities. The Foundation works internationally in the field of law and human rights, as an advocate to attain peace and social justice in indigenous territories around the world, and to promote indigenous rights. It provides training for indigenous leaders and acts as a consultant to indigenous organizations; and also disseminates information about issues affecting indigenous people, carrying out research and holding conferences.

Geographical Area of Activity: Worldwide.

Publications: *Tebtebba* (magazine); *UN Declaration on the Rights of Indigenous Peoples and the Programme of the 2nd Decade of the World's Indigenous People*; *Capacity Building and Advocacy Report*; *Extracting Promises*; *Celebrating Diversity, Heightening Solidarity*; *Beyond the Silencing of the Guns*; *Engaging the UN Special Representative on Indigenous People: Opportunities and Challenges*; *The Kimberley Declaration and the Indigenous Peoples' Plan of Implementation on Sustainable Development; Indigenous Perspectives* (magazine).

Principal Staff: Exec. Dir Victoria Tauli-Corpuz.

Address: 1 Roman Ayson Rd, Baguio City 2600.

Telephone: (74) 4447703; **Fax:** (74) 4439459; **Internet:** www .tebtebba.org; **e-mail:** tebtebba@tebtebba.org.

Villar Foundation, Inc.

Established in 1995 by Manuel B. Villar, Jr and others to initiate, undertake, support or otherwise foster educational, cultural, scientific, charitable and civic activities aimed at benefiting the Filipino people, in particular the poor and needy.

Activities: Operates financial assistance or incentive programmes for young people, aimed at skills development and livelihood assistance; socio-civic, cultural, educational, religious, scientific and technological projects for the social or economic amelioration of poor and needy Filipino people; social welfare and relief services for the poor; and tree-planting and other conservation programmes, including historical preservation. In 2011, the Foundation established the Villar Social Institute for Poverty Alleviation and Governance (SIPAG) and in 2013 launched the Villar SIPAG Awards on Poverty Reduction, 20 prizes each worth 250,000 pesos, which recognize the achievements of community enterprises.

Geographical Area of Activity: The Philippines.

Publications: Annual Report; books.

Board of Trustees: Manuel B. Villar, Jr (Chair.); Mark A. Villar (Sec. and Treas.).

Principal Staff: Man. Dir Cynthia A. Villar.

Address: C. Masibay St, BF Resort Village, Talon, 1740 Las Piñas City.

Telephone: (632) 8728540; **Fax:** (632) 8725488; **Internet:** www .villarfoundation.org; **e-mail:** villarfoundationinc@gmail .com.

Poland

FOUNDATION CENTRES AND CO-ORDINATING BODIES

Akademia Rozwoju Filantropii w Polsce (Academy for the Development of Philanthropy in Poland)

Established in 1998.

Activities: Promotes philanthropy in Poland and supports the third sector, through a local grants programme; a grant programme for organizations promoting Polish-Jewish dialogue; a local youth fund; senior citizen programmes; scholarships for young gifted people; and participation in international philanthropy networks. The Academy also organizes the Benefactor of the Year competition, recognizing corporate philanthropists in Poland.

Geographical Area of Activity: Poland.

Publications: Annual Report; *The White Book of Philanthropy—Coalition for Better Law*; other publications.

Finance: Annual income 6,961,459 new złotys, expenditure 5,669,262 new złotys (31 Dec. 2013).

Board: Paweł Łukasiak (Chair.).

Principal Staff: Secretariat Co-ordinator Emilia Dmochowska.

Address: 00-590 Warsaw, ul. Marszalkowska 6/6.

Telephone: (22) 6220122; **Fax:** (22) 6220211; **Internet:** www.filantropia.org.pl; **e-mail:** arfp@filantropia.org.pl.

Federacja Funduszy Lokalnych w Polsce (Federation of Community Foundations in Poland)

Established in 2008.

Activities: Supports the development of community foundations. Provides training, advice, consultancy and other services. Nine mem. orgs.

Geographical Area of Activity: Poland.

Board of Directors: Irena Gadaj (Pres.); Krzystof Margol (Vice-Pres.); Maria Talarczyk (Sec.).

Principal Staff: Office Man. Maciej Mulawa.

Address: 23-400 Biłgoraj, ul. T. Kościuszki 65.

Telephone: (84) 6864877; **Internet:** www.ffl.org.pl; **e-mail:** ffl@ffl.org.pl.

Fundacja Rozwoju Demokracji Loaklnej (Foundation in Support of Local Democracy)

Founded in 1989 by Prof. Jerzy Regulski, Andrzej Celićski, Aleksander Paszyński, Walerian Paćko and Jerzy Stępień to promote civic self-government at local level.

Activities: Operates in the fields of education, and law and human rights, through self-conducted programmes, grants to institutions, conferences, training courses, publications, Internet information systems and offering technical assistance. The Foundation's main activities are training and education programmes for local government officers, councillors, NGOs, community leaders and local businesspeople; and consulting services in the technical areas of local government. Also involved in sharing the Polish experience in building democracy with other countries of Central, Eastern and Southern Europe and Kazakhstan. Maintains national network of 16 regional centres and branches and three Colleges of Public Administration.

Geographical Area of Activity: Central, Eastern and Southern Europe, Kazakhstan and Poland.

Publications: Publications on local government, management, legal and economic issues.

Finance: Annual revenue 53,617,303 new złotys, expenditure 55,768,984 new złotys (31 Dec. 2013).

Supervisory Board: Adam Kowalewski (Chair.); Jan Król (Vice-Chair.).

Principal Staff: CEO Irena Peszko; Vice-Pres. Witold Monkiewicz.

Address: 01-552 Warsaw, plac Inwalidów 10.

Telephone: (22) 3228440; **Fax:** (22) 3228441; **Internet:** www.frdl.org.pl; **e-mail:** zarzad@frdl.org.pl.

Grupa Zagranica (Zagranica Group)

Founded in 2001; a coalition of Polish NGOs operating outside Poland, originating from a conference held by the Stefan Batory Foundation (q.v.) in co-operation with the Ministry of Foreign Affairs.

Activities: Supports the exchange of information, experiences and common standards between Polish NGOs working abroad; fosters co-operation between the NGOs and other sectors; lobbies the Government on Polish foreign and development aid policy in countries where the NGOs are engaged; facilitates contacts between NGOs and potential partners; establishes contacts and co-operation with similar groups of NGOs in other countries and with European Union (EU) institutions, to exert influence on EU development aid policy and take part in its implementation; and disseminates information concerning the activities of Polish NGOs working abroad and campaigning for public support for their activities. Five working groups are currently active: Global Education, Polish Aid-Watch, Belarus, Eastern Partnership and Caucasus+. The General Meeting of the Members of the Group comprises 61 organizations.

Geographical Area of Activity: Poland.

Publications: *Guiding Principles of Polish Non-governmental Organisations Working Abroad.*

Principal Staff: Exec. Sec. Janek Bazyl.

Address: 00-666 Warsaw, ul. Noakowskiego 10/6A.

Telephone: (22) 2990105; **Fax:** (22) 2072560; **Internet:** www.zagranica.org.pl; **e-mail:** grupa@zagranica.org.pl.

Ogólnopolskie Forum Inicjatyw Pozarządowych— OFIP (National Forum of Polish Non-governmental Organisations)

Established in 1996 to promote civil society.

Activities: Supports the development of civil society and nonprofit organizations in Poland, and co-operation with governmental and private sector organizations through meetings and the exchange of information. Meetings take place every three years, organized since 2014 by the Ogólnopolska Federacja Organizacji (National Federation of NGOs).

Geographical Area of Activity: Poland.

Publications: Newsletter; bulletins and papers.

Principal Staff: Man. Dir Weronika Czyżewska.

Address: 00-031 Warsaw, ul. Strzelecka 3/12.

Telephone: (22) 2532856; **Fax:** (22) 8289129; **Internet:** ofip.eu; **e-mail:** ofip@ofip.eu.

OPUS—Centre for Promotion and Development of Civil Initiatives

Created in 1999 to support the development of civil society in Poland.

Activities: Supports civil society development in Poland through providing advice and consultancy services to NGOs, co-operating internationally in networks and with other organizations and channelling European Union programme funds to local Polish NGOs.

Geographical Area of Activity: Poland.

Publications: Annual Report.

Finance: Annual revenue 3,599,182 new złotys, expenditure 3,500,905 new złotys (2014).

Board of Directors: Łukasz Waszak (Chair.); Jolanta Woźnicka (Sec.); Wioletta Gawrońska (Treas.).

Address: 91-415 Łódź, pl. Wolności 2.

Telephone: (42) 2313101; **Fax:** (42) 2313102; **Internet:** www .opus.org.pl; **e-mail:** opus@opus.org.pl.

Polsko-Amerykańska Fundacja Wolności (Polish-American Freedom Foundation)

Established by the Polish-American Enterprise Fund in the USA in 1999; opened a Representative Office in Warsaw in 2000, and began operating activities in that year.

Activities: Aims to support the development of civil society, democracy and market economy in Poland, including efforts to equalize opportunities for personal and social development, as well as to support the transformation processes in other countries of Central and Eastern Europe. The Foundation runs programmes the following areas: Initiatives in Education; Development of Local Communities; Citizen in a Democratic State of Law; and Sharing the Polish Experiences in Transformation. In Poland, the Foundation currently focuses on initiatives that help level the playing field in education, as well as release and reinforce citizens' potential, particularly in villages and small cities.

Geographical Area of Activity: Poland.

Restrictions: No grants for commercial projects and grants only for Polish NGOs.

Publications: Annual Report; *10 years of the Polish-American Freedom Foundation*; general information brochures.

Finance: Financed through revenues generated by its endowment, the source of which is the Polish-American Enterprise Fund. Annual income US $3,720,725, expenditure $2,442,793 (31 Dec. 2013).

Board of Directors: Andrew Nagorski (Chair.).

Principal Staff: Pres. and CEO Jerzy Koźmiński.

Address: 02-954 Warsaw, ul. Królowej Marysienki 48.

Telephone: (22) 5502800; **Fax:** (22) 5502801; **Internet:** www .pafw.pl; **e-mail:** paff@pafw.pl.

Sieć Wspierania Organizacji Pozarządowych— SPLOT (Network of Information and Support for Non-governmental Organizations)

Established in 1994; comprises 14 independent NGOs aiming to promote the development of civil society in Poland.

Activities: Aims to support the development of civil society in Poland through providing funding and advisory services to associations, foundations, support groups and other civil initiatives, training and information.

Geographical Area of Activity: Poland.

Publications: Various manuals and studies.

Board: Arkadiusz Jachimowicz (Pres.); Monika Chrzczonowicz (Vice-Pres.).

Principal Staff: Dir Krzysztof Sawicki.

Address: 02-009 Warsaw, al. Niepodległości 245.

Telephone: (22) 8275211; **Internet:** www.siecsplot.pl; **e-mail:** biuro@siecsplot.pl.

Stowarzyszenie Klon/Jawor (Klon/Jawor Association)

Established in 1990 as part of the Regardless of the Weather Foundation to provide access to information so as to promote the development of civil society; became independent in 2000.

Activities: Promotes the development of civil society through maintaining a database of Polish NGOs (JAWOR); conducting research, especially on the third sector in the European Union and local government and NGOs; supporting NGOs; issuing

publications; promoting European networking; an Internet programme; and generally assisting NGOs in their operations.

Geographical Area of Activity: Poland.

Publications: *JAWOR; KLON; Citizen Information Center; Warsaw Information Guide for Senior; The Third Sector in the European Union; Know Your Rights* (series); *Know More* (series); and other publications on NGOs in Poland.

Finance: Annual income 3,349,703 new złotys, expenditure 3,299,583 new złotys (31 Dec. 2013).

Principal Staff: Chair. Urszula Krasnodębska-Maciuła; Sec. Alina Gałązka; Treas. Renata Niecikowska.

Address: 00-031 Warszawa, ul. Szpitalna 5/5.

Telephone: (22) 8289128; **Fax:** (22) 8289129; **Internet:** www .klon.org.pl; **e-mail:** klon@klon.org.pl.

FOUNDATIONS, TRUSTS AND NON-PROFIT ORGANIZATIONS

Fundacja Agory (Agora Foundation)

Established in 2004 to manage all charitable and social initiatives of the Agora and Agora Holding companies.

Activities: Provides support to educational and cultural initiatives. The Foundation provides fiancial support to disadvantaged individuals and families, and for health-care development and initiatives to save people's lives. It promotes entrepreneurship, professionalism and active living. It also sponsors *Zeszyty Literackie* (a literary periodical) and awards scholarships and a literary prize.

Geographical Area of Activity: Poland.

Publications: Annual Report.

Finance: Annual income 5,293,873 new złotys, expenditure 4,561,777 new złotys (31 Dec. 2012).

Board of Directors: Wojciech Kaminski (Chair.); Joanna Kosmal, Grzegorz Piechota (Vice-Chair.).

Address: 00-732 Warsaw, ul. Czerska 8/10.

Telephone: (22) 5555263; **Fax:** (22) 5558263; **Internet:** fundacjaagory.pl; **e-mail:** fundacja@agora.pl.

Fundacja Auschwitz-Birkenau (Auschwitz-Birkenau Foundation)

Established in 2009 by Prof. Władysław Bartoszewski to finance the upkeep and conservation work on the Auschwitz-Birkenau Memorial.

Activities: Established to raise €120m., the interest on which would be used to protect the remains of the Auschwitz concentration camp and their maintenance as a memorial and museum. The Foundation has been given funding by a number of governments, including those in Austria, Belgium, Germany, Israel, the Netherlands, New Zealand, Poland and the USA.

Geographical Area of Activity: Poland.

Publications: Annual Report.

Finance: Total assets 222,420,358 new złotys, net annual income 92,826,802 new złotys (31 Dec. 2013).

Principal Staff: Pres. Piotr M. A. Cywiński; Vice-Pres Rafał Pióro, Łukasz Rozdeiczer; Dir-Gen. Jacek Kastelaniec.

Address: 00-105 Warsaw, ul. Twarda 6.

Telephone: (22) 608 300 627; **Fax:** (22) 620 48 99; **Internet:** www.fundacja.auschwitz.org; **e-mail:** fundacja@fab.org.pl.

Fundacja im. Stefana Batorego (Stefan Batory Foundation)

Founded in 1988 by George Soros to support the development of Polish society in the areas of science, culture, education, information and civil society to strengthen democracy and a free market, and to encourage co-operation between the countries of Central and Eastern Europe; part of the Open Society Foundations (q.v.) network.

Activities: Supports the development of a democratic and open society in Poland and other Central and Eastern European countries. Through its grantmaking and operating programmes, the Foundation aims to enhance the role and involvement of civil society, promote civil liberties and the rule of law, and develop international co-operation and solidarity.

Geographical Area of Activity: Central and Eastern Europe, Poland.

Restrictions: Grants to organizations based in Poland. In some programmes also to organizations based in Ukraine, Belarus and in Kaliningrad District.

Publications: Annual Report; *Stefan Batory Foundation E-newsletter;* film on the Stefan Batory Foundation; numerous thematic publications.

Finance: Total annual expenditure 17,738,721 new złotys (31 Dec. 2013).

Board of Directors: Aleksander Smolar (Pres.).

Principal Staff: Exec. Dir. Ewa Kulik-Bielińska.

Address: 00-215 Warsaw, ul. Sapiezynska 10A.

Telephone: (22) 5360200; **Fax:** (22) 5360220; **Internet:** www .batory.org.pl; **e-mail:** batory@batory.org.pl.

Fundacja Biblioteka Ekologiczna (Ecological Library Foundation)

Founded in 1988 by Jacek Purat.

Activities: Operates in the fields of conservation and the environment and economic affairs, through research, conferences, publications and a library. The Foundation distributes books; conducts research; organizes conferences; presents films; has established an ecological library; and organizes projects for the protection of endangered species in Poland.

Geographical Area of Activity: Poland.

Publications: Annual Report.

Finance: Total assets 327,176 new złotys (31 Dec. 2013).

Board of Directors: Ryszard Gołdyn (Chair.); Stanisław Podsiadłowski (Vice-Chair.); Halina Szyper (Treas.).

Address: 61-715 Poznań, ul. Kościuszki 79.

Telephone: (61) 8521325; **Fax:** (61) 8528276; **Internet:** www.be .eko.org.pl; **e-mail:** fbercee@gmail.com.

Fundacja Centrum Prasowe (Central and Eastern European Media Centre Foundation)

Established in 1990 by the Polish Journalists' Association to support the development of an independent media in former communist countries.

Activities: Promotes the exchange of ideas and experiences between journalists; monitors and documents changes within the media and the social communication systems; lobbies governments with regard to media legislation and policies; organizes training courses for journalists and publishers; maintains a database; and conducts seminars and conferences. The Foundation also presents awards and prizes.

Geographical Area of Activity: Belarus, Poland, the Russian Federation and Ukraine.

Board of Trustees: Elżbieta Skotnicka-Illasiewicz (Chair.).

Principal Staff: CEO Stefan Bratkowski; Dir Joanna Olszewska.

Address: 00-363 Warsaw, ul. Nowy Świat 58 III p.

Telephone: (22) 8264557; **Fax:** (22) 8263002; **Internet:** www .fcp.edu.pl; **e-mail:** centrumprasowe@op.pl.

Fundacja Dobroczynności Atlas (Atlas Charity Foundation)

Established in 1996 by the Atlas Group for the alleviation of poverty.

Activities: Operates in the area of social welfare in Poland and Central and Eastern Europe, particularly children's welfare and Polish communities in Belarus, Kazakhstan, Lithuania, the Russian Federation and Ukraine.

Geographical Area of Activity: Eastern Europe and Poland.

Finance: Annual income 3,235,387 new złotys, expenditure 3,134,862 new złotys (31 Dec. 2013).

Principal Staff: Chair. Jolanta Rojek.

Address: 80-252 Gdańsk, ul. Jaśkowa Dolina 17.

Telephone: (58) 3421122; **Fax:** (58) 3430619; **Internet:** www .atlas.com.pl/pl/strona/fundacja_dobroczynnosci/63; **e-mail:** fundacja@atlas.com.pl.

Fundacja Gospodarcza (Economic Foundation)

Established in 1990 by the National Commission (NSZZ) of Solidarność (Solidarity) to confront the problems of unemployment and education.

Activities: Organizes programmes in the fields of trade union education and economic affairs. Projects include establishing an international system of exchange for economic information, promoting small businesses, programmes to reduce unemployment, and social activities programmes. The Foundation holds conferences; organizes consultancy programmes, providing information for people intending to start in business; and runs an occupational information centre for secondary-school students.

Geographical Area of Activity: Poland.

Publications: *Economics*; *Career Skills*; *Labour Code*; publications of interest to the unemployed and people in business.

Board of Trustees: Ewa Zydorek (Chair.); Bogdan Olszewski (Vice-Chair.).

Principal Staff: Chair. and CEO Irena Muszkiewicz-Herok; Dir Malgorzata Makiewicz.

Address: 81-538 Gdynia, ul. Olimpijska 2.

Telephone: (58) 6226017; **Fax:** (58) 6225985; **Internet:** www .fungo.com.pl; **e-mail:** sekretariat@fungo.com.pl.

Fundacja Bankowa im. Leopolda Kronenberga (Leopold Kronenberg Foundation)

Established in 1996 to mark the 125th anniversary of Bank Handlowy Warszawie SA to support general charitable work in Poland.

Activities: Operates in the areas of education, science, the arts and humanities, health care and social welfare, by supporting organizations and projects engaged in work in these areas. Also presents prizes for entrepreneurship.

Geographical Area of Activity: Poland.

Restrictions: Grants only to non-profit organizations in Poland.

Advisory Council: Prof. Daria Nałęcz (Pres.); Paweł Zegarłowicz (Vice-Pres.).

Principal Staff: Pres. of the Board Krzysztof Kaczmar; Dir Norbert Konarzewski.

Address: 00-067 Warsaw, ul. R. Traugutta 7–9.

Telephone: (22) 8268324; **Fax:** (22) 6925094; **Internet:** www .kronenberg.org.pl; **e-mail:** poczta@kronenberg.org.pl.

Fundacja Partnerstwo dla Środowiska (Polish Environmental Partnership Foundation)

Established in 1992 as a Programme Office of the German Marshall Fund of the USA; present name adopted in 1997 when it was registered as a foundation in Poland; operates as part of the Environmental Partnership Consortium (q.v.), which supports grassroots environmental action in Central Europe. Sister foundations operate within the framework of the Consortium in the Czech Republic, Slovakia and Hungary.

Activities: Supports non-profit organizations and communities that implement environmental projects, where these contribute to the development of democracy in Poland. The Foundation helps NGOs and local communities to solve environmental problems by supporting partnership action with the Government, businesses, universities and individuals. It provides direct financial support and technical assistance for community development; and maintains an Environmental

Information Centre, disseminating information through weekly and monthly bulletins, providing a helpline for members and access to information resources.

Geographical Area of Activity: Poland.

Restrictions: Grants made only to NGOs registered in, and operating in, Poland.

Publications: Annual Report; newsletter; *International Trails & Greenways Directory*; *A Decade of Nurturing the Grassroots*; *Ten Years of Community Revitalization in Central Europe.*

Finance: Annual expenditure 5,974,481 new złotys (2010).

Management Board: Rafał Serafin (Chair.); Joanna Węgrzycka (Vice-Chair.).

Address: 31-157 Kraków, pl. Matejki 5/6.

Telephone: (12) 4302443; **Fax:** (12) 4302465; **Internet:** www .fpds.pl; **e-mail:** biuro@fpds.pl.

Fundacja Pogranicze (Borderland Foundation)

Established in 1990 to carry out cultural activities in Central and Eastern Europe.

Activities: Operates in the countries of Central and Eastern Europe in the fields of the arts and humanities, education, and law and human rights, through self-conducted programmes, conferences, training courses and publications. Maintains a library and an arts and cultural centre.

Geographical Area of Activity: Central and Eastern Europe.

Publications: Annual Report; *Krasnogruda* (quarterly, in Polish and English); also history books, literary criticism, poetry; newsletters.

Finance: Annual revenue 1,735,829 new złotys, expenditure 1,475,267 new złotys (31 Dec. 2012).

Board of Directors: Krzysztof Czyżewski (Pres.).

Address: 16-500 Sejny, Krasnogruda 14; 16-500 Sejny, ul. Piłsudskiego 37.

Telephone: (87) 5650369; **Fax:** (87) 5162765; **Internet:** www .pogranicze.sejny.pl; **e-mail:** fundacja@pogranicze.sejny.pl.

Fundacja Pomocy Wzajemnej Barka (Barka Foundation)

Founded in 1989 by Tomasz Sadowski, Maria Garwolińska and Barbara Sadowska to promote improved living and working conditions.

Activities: Operates in Poland, France, Germany, the United Kingdom and the Netherlands in the field of social welfare, through self-conducted programmes, scholarships, prizes, conferences, training courses and publications. The Foundation runs four programmes in the fields of the community, social education, employment opportunity and housing. It assists the homeless through self-help projects throughout Poland and established the Poland-wide Confederation for Social Employment, which provides support to the long-term unemployed and homeless people.

Geographical Area of Activity: France, Germany, the Netherlands, the United Kingdom, Poland.

Publications: *Citizens' Initiatives of Greater Poland*; *Barka Bulletin*; conference proceedings.

Finance: The Government of Poland provides 5% of the Foundation's funds.

Trustees: Tomasz Sadowski (Pres.); Barbara Sadowska (Vice-Pres.).

Address: 61-003 Poznań, ul. św. Wincentego 6/9.

Telephone: (61) 6682300; **Fax:** (61) 8729050; **Internet:** www .barka.org.pl; **e-mail:** barka@barka.org.pl.

Fundacja Pro Bono II (Pro Bono Foundation)

Established in 1993 by a group of people connected with the pastoral services for the universities affiliated with the Rectory of St Ann's Academic Church in Warsaw.

Activities: Supports NGOs in Poland active in the areas of charity, cultural and educational work, as well as funding Catholic organizations, the conservation of works of art and the promotion of the Catholic press. Funded projects include orphanages, symposia and scholarships, medical costs and community centres. The Foundation has also established an art gallery to promote the work of young artists.

Geographical Area of Activity: Poland.

Principal Staff: Pres. Bogdan Bartołd.

Address: 00-322 Warsaw, ul. Krakowskie Przedmiescie 68, Kościół Akademicki św. Anny.

Telephone: (22) 8269977; **Fax:** (22) 8269977; **Internet:** www .probono.art.pl; **e-mail:** fundacja@probono.org.pl.

Fundacja Pro Bono PL

Established in 2001 by the J&S Group to support initiatives that help active and ambitious people and that hold a promise of success, as well as ideas and proposals designed to support the development of culture and combat all forms of social pathology, including intolerance and discrimination. Formerly known as J&S Pro Bono Poloniae Foundation.

Activities: Donates to NGOs running programmes in the areas of children and young people and culture, as well as funding educational scholarships for gifted young people.

Geographical Area of Activity: Poland.

Publications: Annual Reports.

Finance: Annual revenue 262,700 new złotys, expenditure 339,837 new złotys (31 Dec. 2013).

Principal Staff: Chair. Ryszard Romanowski; Vice-Chair. Izabela Smołokowska.

Address: 02-690 Warsaw, ul. Bokserska 64, pokój 124.

Telephone: (22) 8535407; **Fax:** (22) 8535408; **Internet:** www .probonopl.org; **e-mail:** fundacja@probonopl.org.

Fundacja Solidarności Polsko-Czesko-Słowackiej (Polish-Czech-Slovak Solidarity Foundation)

Established in 1990 by J. Broda, Z. Janas, M. Jasiński and M. Piotrowski 'Ducina' for the support of Polish-Czech-Slovak solidarity activities.

Activities: Operates in Central and Eastern Europe in the areas of aid to less-developed countries, the arts and humanities, education, independent media, international affairs, through self-conducted programmes, grants to institutions, conferences, training courses and publications.

Geographical Area of Activity: Central and Eastern Europe.

Publications: Newsletter.

Board: Jarosław Szostakowski (Chair.).

Address: 00-031 Warsaw, ul. Szpitalna 5/5.

Telephone: (22) 8289128; **Fax:** (22) 8289129; **Internet:** www .spczs.engo.pl; **e-mail:** spczs@szpitalna.ngo.pl; fundacja@ spczs.engo.pl.

Fundacja Współpracy Polsko-Niemieckiej/Stiftung für Deutsch-Polnische Zusammenarbeit (Foundation for German-Polish Co-operation)

Established in 1991 by the Governments of Poland and Germany to sponsor non-commercial projects of German-Polish interest.

Activities: Operates in Poland in the fields of the arts and humanities, conservation and the environment, education, international affairs, medicine and health, science and technology, and social welfare and social studies, through research, grants to institutions, scholarships and fellowships, conferences, training courses and publications. The Foundation has an office in Berlin. In 2010, it disbursed a total of 15,437,115 new złotys to 657 projects.

Geographical Area of Activity: Germany and Poland.

Publications: Annual Report; Polish foundation traditions; reports; analysis.

Finance: Annual revenue 318,906 new złotys, 13,384,089 new złotys (31 Dec. 2013).

Board of Trustees: Marek Krząkała, Markus Meckel (Co-Chair.).

Principal Staff: Dirs Krzysztof Miszczak, Cornelius Ochmann.

Address: 00-108 Warszawa, ul. Zielna 37.

Telephone: (22) 3386200; **Fax:** (22) 3386200; **Internet:** www.fwpn.org.pl; **e-mail:** sekretariat@fwpn.org.pl.

Fundacja Wspomagania Wsi (Rural Development Foundation)

Established in 1999 as a result of the merger of the Water Supply Foundation and the Agricultural Foundation.

Activities: Promotes the comprehensive, sustainable development of rural Poland. The Foundation supports economic, social, cultural, educational and pro-environmental initiatives of rural and small town inhabitants, providing loans and credit to businesses, local governments, public benefit agencies and individuals. It also awards grants for infrastructural development, including funding the construction of village clubs, and offers training and runs programmes for local young people. Programme themes are: micro-loans; development of information communication technology use in rural areas of Poland; training for local NGO leaders; support of children and young people in education; and local cultural heritage preservation. The Foundation also operates an exchange or partnership programme with organizations in other countries of Europe.

Geographical Area of Activity: Poland.

Publications: Annual Report; information brochures; manuals; e-books.

Finance: Annual revenue 22,736,371 new złotys, expenditure 22,736,371 new złotys (2013).

Council: Prof. Aleksander Szeptycki (Chair.).

Principal Staff: Pres. Piotr Szczepanski.

Address: 01-022 Warsaw, ul. Bellottiego 1.

Telephone: (22) 6362570; **Fax:** (22) 6366270; **Internet:** www.fundacjawspomaganiawsi.pl; **e-mail:** fww@fww.org.pl.

Institute for Private Enterprise and Democracy—IPED

Established in 1993 by the Polish Chamber of Commerce to carry out research into the Polish private sector and economic policy, and to support the development of the private sector.

Activities: Operates in Poland in the areas of economic affairs and social welfare, through research, conferences and the publication of policy and economic reports. Major projects include: a report on the state of the private sector in Poland; a study on the reform of the Polish tax system; business ethics and social responsibility; Polish women in private business; regional development and the promotion of entrepreneurship; legislative monitoring; and monitoring barriers to the development of small and medium-sized enterprises and their financing in Poland. The Institute supports the network of Chambers of Commerce in Poland.

Geographical Area of Activity: Poland.

Publications: Newsletter; *Influence of Justice on SME Development in Poland*; *Capital Investment Funding in Poland*; *Cooperation of NGOs with Local Self-Government*; *Economic Reform Today*; *Development of Entrepreneurship in Rural Areas*; *Sources of Inflation in Poland*; *Informal Labour Market*; *Dilemmas and Chances of Rural Development*; numerous other reports.

Board: Dr Mieczysław Bąk (Chair. and CEO); Prof. Tomasz Mroczkowski (Vice-Pres.).

Address: 00-074 Warsaw, ul. Trębacka 4, Rm 319.

Telephone: (22) 6309801; **Fax:** (22) 8262596; **Internet:** www.iped.pl; **e-mail:** iped@kig.pl.

Microfinance Centre—MFC

Established in 1997; a grassroots network of 105 member institutions that play an active role in shaping the microfinance sector, to advance economic development, improve employment, and alleviate poverty through microfinance in Europe and Central Asia.

Activities: Provides microfinance services, support and development to a wide range of financial institutions. Promotes microfinance among policy-makers, regulators, the formal banking sector and investors. Maintains office in Kyrgyzstan.

Geographical Area of Activity: Europe and Central Asia.

Publications: Annual Report; *MFC Newsletter*; *Policy Monitor*.

Finance: Annual revenue 6,208,512 new złotys, expenditure 5,273,727 new złotys (31 Dec. 2013).

Board of Directors: Cristian Jurma (Chair.).

Principal Staff: Exec. Dir Grzegorz Galusek; Deputy Dir Katarzyna Pawlak.

Address: 00-666 Warsaw, ul. Noakowskiego 10/38.

Telephone: (22) 6223465; **Fax:** (22) 6223485; **Internet:** www.mfc.org.pl; **e-mail:** microfinance@mfc.org.pl.

POLSAT Foundation

Established in 1996 by the television company POLSAT.

Activities: Operates in the areas of education and medicine and health, in particular for the benefit of children and young people.

Geographical Area of Activity: Poland.

Publications: Newsletter.

Finance: Annual revenue 12,307,632 new złotys, expenditure 9,347,448 (31 Dec. 2012).

Principal Staff: Exec. Pres. Krystyna Aldridge-Holc.

Address: 04-175 Warsaw, ul. Ostrobramska 77.

Telephone: (22) 5145555; **Fax:** (22) 5144730; **Internet:** www.fundacjapolsat.pl; **e-mail:** fundacja@polsat.com.pl.

Polska Fundacja Upowszechniania Nauki—PFUN (Polish Foundation for Science Advancement—PFSA)

Established in 1990 by the Polish Academy of Sciences, the Society for the Advancement of Sciences and Arts, the Society of the Polish Free University, the Scientific Publications Distribution Centre and the Polish Scientific Film Association to work for the dissemination of Polish science in Poland and abroad, and for the diffusion of foreign science in Poland.

Activities: Operates nationally and internationally in the fields of education and science and technology, through conducting research and promoting public understanding of science; publishing books and producing films and audio-visual materials for teaching and study; organizing courses, seminars and competitions; supporting the activities of Polish institutions and scientific associations in Poland and abroad in the advancement of science; and granting aid to foreign orgs seeking to promote knowledge in Poland of the scientific achievements of their respective countries. Major programmes include: Internet at Schools, a programme initiated by the President of Poland; the Postgraduate Science Communication and Media Studies programme undertaken jointly with the Institute for Literary Research of the Polish Academy of Sciences; and establishing the Open Television University in Poland.

Geographical Area of Activity: International.

Publications: Brochures and books; annual reports.

Principal Staff: Dir Wojciech Wiśniewski.

Address: 00-901 Warsaw, Pałac Kultury i Nauki, skr. poczt. 27, pok. 2104, 2105, 2107.

Telephone: (22) 6209174; **Fax:** (22) 6209174; **Internet:** pfun.pan.pl; **e-mail:** pfun@pan.pl.

Portugal

FOUNDATION CENTRE AND CO-ORDINATING BODY

Centro Português de Fundações—CPF (Portuguese Foundation Centre)

Established in 1993 by the Fundação Oriente (q.v.) in association with the Fundação Eng. António de Almeida and the Fundação Calouste Gulbenkian (qq.v.).

Activities: A membership organization of more than 100 foundations and trusts, which operates to promote the interests of foundations in Portugal through co-operation and support. Organizes meetings and conferences.

Geographical Area of Activity: Portugal.

Publications: Annual Report; *Portuguese Foundation Centre Directory.*

Board of Directors: Artur Santos Silva (Chair.).

Principal Staff: Gen. Sec. Mário Curveira Santos.

Address: Rua Rodrigo da Fonseca 178, 6º Esq., 1070-239 Lisbon.

Telephone: (21) 3538280; **Fax:** (21) 3538285; **Internet:** www.cpf.org.pt; **e-mail:** cpf@cpf.org.pt.

FOUNDATIONS, TRUSTS AND NON-PROFIT ORGANIZATIONS

Fundação Eng. António de Almeida (Eng. António de Almeida Foundation)

Founded in 1969 at the bequest of Eng. António de Almeida to promote art, culture and education for all people.

Activities: Sponsors art exhibitions and musical recitals; makes grants to cultural institutions in Portugal and to Portuguese graduates for research work; awards the Eng. António de Almeida Prize annually to students from six universities, who have excelled in dedication to their studies; holds international conferences; and issues cultural publications. The Foundation also maintains a museum of art to exhibit items collected by the founder, which include furniture, textiles, porcelain, paintings, timepieces and an important numismatic collection.

Publications: Annual Report; periodical magazines in the spheres of literature, philosophy, ethnography and museums, art, culture and science.

Board of Directors: Dr Fernando Aguiar-Branco (Chair.).

Principal Staff: Exec. Dir. Eugénia Aguiar-Branco.

Address: Rua Tenente Valadim 231–325, 4100-479 Porto.

Telephone: (22) 6067418; **Fax:** (22) 6004314; **Internet:** fcaa.pai.pt; **e-mail:** fundacao@feaa.pt.

Fundação Assistência Médica International—AMI (International Medical Assistance Foundation)

Established in 1984 by Dr Fernando de la Vieter Nobre to provide humanitarian aid worldwide.

Activities: Operates internationally in the fields of humanitarian aid to less-developed countries, education, medicine and health, and social welfare, through self-conducted programmes, grants to institutions, conferences, training courses and publications. AMI's activities are organized in four pillars: Medical Assistance; Social Action; Environmental Care; and Raising Awareness. Awards the AMI Journalism Against Indifference prize.

Geographical Area of Activity: Portugal and international.

Publications: *AMI Notícias* (quarterly).

Finance: Total assets €35,555,057, net annual income €166,872 (31 Dec. 2014).

Board of Directors: Prof. Dr Fernando José de La Vieter Ribeiro Nobre (Chair.); Maria Leonor de La Vieter Ribeiro Nobre (Vice-Chair.).

Principal Staff: Sec.-Gen. Maria Luísa Nemésio.

Address: Rua José do Patrocínio, 49, 1959-003 Lisbon.

Telephone: (21) 8362100; **Fax:** (21) 8362199; **Internet:** www.ami.org.pt; **e-mail:** fundacao.ami@ami.org.pt.

Fundação da Casa de Mateus (Mateus House Foundation)

Established in 1970 by Francisco de Sousa Botelho de Albuquerque, Count of Mangualde, Vila Real and Melo to maintain the Casa de Mateus, study and publish its archives, and promote scientific, cultural and pedagogical activities.

Activities: Operates in the fields of the arts and humanities, including music, history and literature; and science. Part of the House is maintained as a museum. The Foundation awards the Prémio D. Dinis and the Prémio Morgado de Mateus in the field of literature. Courses in theatre, sculpture, drawing and painting are also held at the Foundation, as are exhibitions and seminars. The Foundation chairs the International Institute Casa de Mateus, established in 1986 by Portuguese public universities, academies and scientific institutes, which organizes meetings of national and foreign scientists. It also set up an artists' residence for artists from any country.

Geographical Area of Activity: Portugal.

Publications: Annual Report.

Finance: Total assets €558,552, net annual income €432 (31 Dec. 2014).

Principal Staff: CEO Ana de Sousa Botelho de Albuquerque Paganini.

Address: 5000-291 Vila Real.

Telephone: (25) 9323121; **Fax:** (25) 9326553; **Internet:** www.casademateus.com; **e-mail:** casademateus@casademateus.pt.

Fundação Centro Cultural de Belém (Belém Cultural Centre Foundation)

Established in 1991 by the Government of Portugal and Portuguese companies to promote culture and the arts, especially Portuguese culture; formerly known as CCB—Belém Cultural Centre.

Activities: Manages the Belém Cultural Centre. The Foundation runs a conference centre, a performing arts centre and an exhibition centre, and facilitates exchanges with similar Portuguese and foreign institutions.

Geographical Area of Activity: Portugal.

Board of Directors: António Lamas (Chair.).

Address: Praça do Império, 1449-003 Lisbon.

Telephone: (21) 3612400; **Fax:** (21) 3612500; **Internet:** www.ccb.pt; **e-mail:** ccb@ccb.pt.

Fundação Champalimaud (Champalimaud Foundation)

Established in 2004 in accordance with the will of the late Portuguese industrialist and entrepreneur António de Sommer Champalimaud.

Activities: Primarily supports work in the areas of cancer and neuroscience. One of the Foundation's primary concerns is that research should benefit patients receiving clinical treatment. It also supports translational cancer research, linking the 'bench to the bedside', and bringing the most up-to-date scientific advances to those most in need. A particular focus of this work is the prevention, diagnosis and treatment of metastatic diseases. The Champalimaud Cancer Clinic, housed in the Champalimaud Centre for the Unknown, Lisbon, began receiving patients in 2011. The Foundation is also committed to driving forward advances in the area of neuroscience research. In addition to its in-house activities, the Foundation supports an outreach programme to aid the fight against global blindness. The €1m. Antonio Champalimaud Vision Award was launched in 2006 to support blindness prevention interventions in the developing world and vision research.

Geographical Area of Activity: Worldwide.

Finance: Total assets €956,927,720 (31 Dec. 2012).

Board of Directors: Leonor Beleza (Chair.).

Principal Staff: Dir of Champalimaud Centre for the Unknown Dr Zvi Fuks.

Address: Champalimaud Centre for the Unknown, Av. Brasilia s/n, 1400-038 Lisbon.

Telephone: (21) 480200; **Fax:** (21) 480299; **Internet:** www .fchampalimaud.org; **e-mail:** info@fundacaochampalimaud .pt.

Fundação Cidade de Lisboa (City of Lisbon Foundation)

Founded in 1989 by Nuno Krus Abecasis.

Activities: Operates nationally and in Angola, Cabo Verde, Mozambique, and São Tomé and Príncipe, in the fields of aid to less-developed countries and education, through self-conducted programmes, grants to individuals and institutions, scholarships and prizes, and conferences.

Geographical Area of Activity: Portugal, Angola, Cabo Verde, Mozambique, and São Tomé and Príncipe.

Publications: Annual Report; books.

Board of Trustees: Eugénio Anacoreta Correia (Chair.); **Board of Dirs:** Álvaro João Duarte Pinto Correia (Chair.).

Address: Campo Grande 380, 1700-097 Lisbon.

Telephone: (21) 7568241; **Fax:** (21) 7568248; **Internet:** www .fundacaocidadedelisboa.pt; **e-mail:** fclisboa@ fundacaocidadedelisboa.pt.

Fundação Dom Manuel II (Dom Manuel II Foundation)

Established in 1966 by Dona Augusta Viktoria, Duchess of Bragança, widow of King Dom Manuel II of Portugal, to help Portuguese emigrants.

Activities: Operates in the areas of aid to less-developed countries, conservation and the environment, education and social welfare, through self-conducted programmes, awarding prizes, and organizing conferences and training courses. The Foundation provides help in the areas of housing, integration of Portuguese emigrants into local communities, and education. It has established a subsidiary in Timor-Leste, the Timorese Cultural Foundation, which operates a printing factory.

Geographical Area of Activity: Europe, Portuguese-speaking Africa, Timor-Leste and Brazil.

Publications: *Futuro Real* (Bulletin).

Finance: Funded by donations and income from rented property.

Trustees: The Duke of Bragança (Pres.).

Principal Staff: Man. Nelson Figueiredo; Sec. Rosa Pratas; Contact Francisco de Mendia.

Address: Rua dos Duques de Bragança 10, 1200-162 Lisbon.

Telephone: (21) 3423705; **Fax:** (21) 3420225; **Internet:** www .fdommanuel.org; www.casarealportuguesa.org/ dynamicdata/funda.asp; **e-mail:** fdommanuel@portugalmail .pt.

Fundação EDP (EDP Foundation)

Established in 2004 to foster knowledge of science and technology in the areas of energy and the environment, preservation of historical heritage, and to promote culture and the arts.

Activities: Operates in the areas of culture and the arts, preservation of historical heritage and the environment; runs an Electricity Museum, Study Centre (Energy and Environment) and Documentation Centre. Aims to convert the campus at the Tejo Power Station into a scientific and cultural unit.

Geographical Area of Activity: Portugal (except the Azores and Madeira islands).

Publications: Annual Report.

Finance: Total assets €45,574,420, net annual income €1,585,368 (31 Dec. 2014).

Board of Trustees: Vasco Maria Guimarães José de Mello (Chair.); **Board of Directors:** António de Almeida (Chair.).

Principal Staff: Exec. Dir Miguel Coutinho.

Address: Av. de Brasília, Central Tejo, 1300-598 Lisbon.

Telephone: (210) 028130; **Fax:** (210) 028104; **Internet:** www .fundacaoedp.pt; **e-mail:** fundacaoedp@edp.pt.

Fundação Ricardo do Espírito Santo Silva (Ricardo do Espírito Santo Silva Foundation)

Founded in 1953 by Ricardo do Espírito Santo Silva to preserve the tradition of decorative arts and crafts threatened by modern industrial development.

Activities: Maintains 18 workshops devoted to producing reproductions and to restoration in 21 traditional crafts, including cabinetmaking, marquetry, decorative and enamel paintings, Arraiolos carpets, bookbinding, book decoration, chiselling, handmade gold leaf, etc. The Foundation runs workshops and restoration projects in Brazil, and collaborates with other organizations to form cultural associations and run exhibitions. It also runs the Portuguese Museum-School for Decorative Arts, the High School of Decorative Arts and the Arts and Crafts Institute.

Geographical Area of Activity: Portugal.

Publications: Newsletter; catalogues.

Board of Trustees: Dr José Manuel Pinheiro Espírito Santo Silva (Chair.).

Principal Staff: Exec. Dir Dr Maria da Conceição Alves Amaral.

Address: Rua de S. Tomé 90, 1100-564 Lisbon.

Telephone: (21) 8814600; **Fax:** (21) 8814637; **Internet:** www .fress.pt; **e-mail:** geral@fress.pt.

Fundação Calouste Gulbenkian (Calouste Gulbenkian Foundation)

Founded in 1956 by Calouste Sarkis Gulbenkian as a perpetual foundation to operate in the general fields of charity, art, education and science, in Portugal and abroad.

Activities: Provides grants on public health and social exclusion issues, focusing on a spectrum of activities, which includes health care, hospital services and equipment, preventive and palliative medicine, childcare and welfare of the elderly, and migrants, among other strategic priorities periodically reassessed. In the arts, the Foundation maintains a museum, containing the founder's private collection, and a Modern Art Centre, which comprises and exhibits the Foundation's collection of contemporary art works. The Foundation also supports the creation, dissemination and research on plastic arts architecture and design; history of art; archaeology and heritage; and cinema and theatre. The Foundation's Music Department manages two artistic groups, an orchestra and a choir, and annually promotes a music season. In education, the Foundation promotes educational development in Portugal, in particular through projects and activities in the area of lifetime training; the use of new technologies in education; the acquisition of new skills and know-how to increase the educational/training system effectiveness; the development of basic training areas; and all activities contributing to the full development of children, young people and adults, in emotional, cognitive, social and cultural terms. The Foundation also houses an art library with more than 220,000 documents, including books, audiovisual and multimedia records. In science, the Foundation provides grants for the stimulation of creativity and scientific research; supports the promotion of links between science and culture; supports the strengthening of interaction between science and society. The Instituto Gulbenkian de Ciência (IGC) undertakes scientific research and postgraduate training in biomedicine, helping to train new national scientific community leadership. It operates as a host institution, providing an intellectual environment in addition to premises and services to young Portuguese and overseas researchers for setting up autonomous research groups and developing their projects over specific time periods.

Geographical Area of Activity: International.

Publications: Annual Report; *Newsletter* (monthly); *Colóquio-Letras* (periodical).

Finance: Total assets €3,199,318 (31 Dec. 2014).

Board of Directors: Artur Santos Silva (Chair.).

Principal Staff: Sec.-Gen. Rui Esgaio.

Address: Av. de Berna 45a, 1067-001 Lisbon.

Telephone: (21) 7823000; **Fax:** (21) 7823021; **Internet:** www.gulbenkian.pt; **e-mail:** info@gulbenkian.pt.

Fundação Luso-Americana para o Desenvolvimento (Luso-American Development Foundation)

Founded in 1985 to assist Portugal in its development, mainly by building strong ties with the USA.

Activities: Operates in the fields of business, technology and science, education and culture. Provides funding for scholarships, internships, exchanges, conferences, publications, medical, scientific and technological research, business and trade development. The Foundation aims to implement projects in the following areas: research programmes and co-operation with US universities and other institutions; modernization of national and regional administration; environmental protection; cultural programmes; and co-operation with Portuguese-speaking African countries. Also maintains a documentation centre, housing around 6,000 items.

Geographical Area of Activity: Portugal, the USA and Portuguese-speaking countries in Africa.

Publications: Annual Report; brochures; newsletter; monographs; *Parallel Magazine* (in Portugese and English).

Finance: An initial fund of €85m. was provided by the Government of Portugal. Total assets €147,219,000, net annual income €1,343,000 (31 Dec. 2013).

Board of Directors: Vasco Rato (Chair.).

Principal Staff: Sec.-Gen. José Sá Carneiro.

Address: Rua do Sacramento à Lapa 21, 1249-090 Lisbon.

Telephone: (21) 3935800; **Fax:** (21) 3963358; **Internet:** www.flad.pt; **e-mail:** fladport@flad.pt.

Fundação Oriente (Orient Foundation)

Established in 1988 to encourage the maintenance and strengthening of historical and cultural ties between Portugal and Asia, particularly Macau, so as to bring the Macanese communities around the world into closer contact.

Activities: Supports cultural, educational, artistic and philanthropic activities. The Foundation awards funding to the following activities: exhibitions, cinema/video, theatre, music, dance, publications, conferences, festivals, health, philanthropic and social activities, and heritage recovery. It also provides support for Macau communities; conducts research; awards scholarships and prizes; and co-operates with other organizations. It established the Documentation Centre, which works to strengthen historical, cultural, scientific and artistic links between Portugal and countries and territories in the Far East. The Foundation operates primarily in Portugal but also in Macau, the People's Republic of China, India,

Timor-Leste, Japan, Thailand, Malaysia, and territories of the Far East that have cultural and historic links with Portugal and where Macanese communities exist. It was a founding member of the European Foundation Centre and the Portuguese Foundation Centre (qq.v.), which was established in 1993; and opened the Museu do Oriente in 2008.

Geographical Area of Activity: Europe, South-East Asia and the Far East.

Publications: Annual Report; publications relating to historical and cultural relations between Portugal and Asia; *Oriente Magazine.*

Finance: Total assets €304,666,040, net annual income €1,074,740 (loss) (31 Dec. 2013).

Board of Trustees: Mário José Brandão Ferreira (Chair.); **Board of Directors:** Carlos Augusto Pulido Valente Monjardino.

Address: Rua do Salitre 66–68, 1269-065 Lisbon.

Telephone: (21) 3585200; **Fax:** (21) 3527042; **Internet:** www.foriente.pt; **e-mail:** info@foriente.pt.

Fundação Eça de Queiroz (Eça de Queiroz Foundation)

Established in 1990 by the estate of Maria de Graça Salema de Castro, widow of the grandson of the novelist José Maria de Eça de Queiroz, and the J. P. Vinhos company.

Activities: Operates as a cultural organization that promotes the works of the novelist Eça de Queiroz nationally and internationally, maintains the Casa de Tormes museum and promotes the culture of the Tormes region. In addition, the Foundation promotes Portuguese culture, education, tourism and agriculture; summer courses for Portuguese and foreign university students and teachers; conferences about Eça de Queiroz in Portugal and abroad; and chamber concerts and educational activities.

Geographical Area of Activity: Portugal, Europe, USA and Brazil.

Publications: Annual Report; newsletter; *Queirosiana* (literary magazine, 2 a year).

Finance: Total assets €2,582,245 (31 Dec. 2014).

Board of Directors: Maria da Graça Salema de Castro (Chair.).

Principal Staff: Exec. Dir Dr Anabela Cardoso.

Address: Caminho de Jacinto, 3110 Quinta de Tormes, Santa Cruz do Douro, 4640-424 Baiao.

Telephone: (25) 4882120; **Fax:** (25) 4885205; **Internet:** www.feq.pt; **e-mail:** info@feq.pt.

Fundação de Serralves (Serralves Foundation)

Established in 1989 as a partnership between the Government of Portugal and a group of companies and other institutions (now numbering around 170) to promote contemporary art and to raise public awareness of environmental issues.

Activities: Operates nationally and internationally in the areas of the contemporary art and humanities, and conservation and the environment, through self-conducted programmes, conferences, environmental education programmes and publications. The Foundation organizes environmental conferences, seminars on the management of urban green areas and open-air classes and nature clubs; and promotes the arts through sponsorship of art exhibitions, conferences, dance, music and video production. Established a Museum of Contemporary Art in Porto in 1999.

Geographical Area of Activity: International.

Publications: Information brochures, exhibition catalogues; e-newsletter.

Finance: Total assets €67,572,745, net annual income €63,425 (31 Dec. 2014).

Board of Directors: Luís Braga da Cruz (Chair.); Rui Manuel Campos Guimarães, Adalberto Neiva de Oliveira (Vice-Chair.).

Principal Staff: Man. Dir Odete Patrício; Sec. Maria João Aguiar.

Address: Rua D. João de Castro 210, 4150-417 Porto.

Telephone: (22) 6156500; **Fax:** (22) 6156533; **Internet:** www
.serralves.pt; **e-mail:** serralves@serralves.pt.

Fundação Mário Soares (Mário Soares Foundation)

Founded in 1991 by Dr Mário Soares, the former President of
Portugal.

Activities: Promotes and sponsors cultural, scientific and
educational projects in the fields of political science, international relations and human rights. The Foundation awards the
Mário Soares Foundation Prize annually, holds conferences
and seminars in the areas of political science and contemporary history, and maintains an archive. It also funds the João
Soares Museum-House.

Geographical Area of Activity: Portugal.

Finance: Initial fund US $100m.

Board of Directors: Mário Alberto Nobre Lopes Soares
(Chair.); Maria Isabel Barroso Lopes Soares (Vice-Chair.).

Principal Staff: Sec.-Gen. Dr Carlos Barroso.

Address: Rua de S. Bento 176, 1200-821 Lisbon.

Telephone: (21) 3964179; **Fax:** (21) 3964156; **Internet:** www
.fmsoares.pt; **e-mail:** fms@fmsoares.pt.

Fundação Arpad Szenes–Vieira da Silva (Arpad
Szenes–Vieira da Silva Foundation)

Established in 1994 by the Portuguese Government, Lisbon
Municipal Council, the Luso-American Development
Foundation, the Fundação Cidade de Lisboa and the Calouste
Gulbenkian Foundation (qq.v.) to promote and study the work
of Arpad Szenes and Maria Helena Vieira da Silva.

Activities: Operates in the fields of the arts and humanities,
nationally through training courses, and nationally and internationally through research and conferences. The Foundation
comprises a museum of the artists' works and works of other
contemporary artists, and a study and documentation centre;
it organizes exhibitions and conferences on modern art and
cultural development, issues publications in the field of art criticism and 20th-century art history, and promotes exchanges
with similar national and international institutions.

Geographical Area of Activity: Mainly Portugal and South
America.

Publications: Annual Report; catalogues of temporary exhibitions.

Finance: Financed by the Ministry of Culture and other sponsors. Total assets €7,912,308, net annual income €6,312 (loss)
(31 Dec. 2014).

Board of Directors: António Gomes de Pinho (Chair.) João
Corrêa Nunes (Vice-Chair.).

Principal Staff: Dir and Curator Marina Bairrão Ruivo.

Address: Praça das Amoreiras 56/58, 1250-020 Lisbon.

Telephone: (21) 3880044; **Fax:** (21) 3880039; **Internet:** www
.fasvs.pt; **e-mail:** fasvs@fasvs.pt.

Puerto Rico

FOUNDATIONS, TRUSTS AND NON-PROFIT ORGANIZATIONS

Fundación Comunitaria de Puerto Rico—FCPR
(Puerto Rico Community Foundation)
Established in 1984.

Activities: Aims to promote community development, funding and philanthropy, so as to improve the socio-economic development of Puerto Rico. Operates nationally, through community development programmes in areas including the arts, business-community relations and young people. More than one-quarter of its annual expenditure is directed towards youth programmes, including a programme to provide alternative education to adolescents who have dropped out of formal education and a university-based programme of youth volunteer service. Supports other non-profit organizations in Puerto Rico, promoting charitable work to solve social problems on the island. Also operates a regional Institute for the Development of Philanthropy (IDEFI), which provides training and technical assistance to philanthropic initiatives in other Caribbean countries.

Geographical Area of Activity: Latin America, the Caribbean, Puerto Rico.

Publications: Annual Report; *Entrelazando*.

Finance: Annual revenue US $3,823,127, expenditure $3,601,080 (31 Dec. 2013).

Board of Directors: Dr Manuel Angel 'Coco' Morales (Pres.); Anitza Cox (Vice-Pres.); Aida Torres-Cruz (Sec.); Antonio Escudero Viera (Treas.).

Principal Staff: Chief Exec. Dir Dr Nelson I. Colón Tarrats; Admin. Dir Juan J. Reyes Rivera; Finance Dir Noelia Marín Oquendo.

Address: POB 70362, San Juan, PR 00936-8362; 1719 Avenue Ponce de León, San Juan 00909-1905.

Telephone: 721-1037; **Fax:** 982-1673; **Internet:** www.fcpr.org; **e-mail:** fcpr@fcpr.org.

Qatar

FOUNDATIONS, TRUSTS AND NON-PROFIT ORGANIZATIONS

Qatar Foundation

Established in 1995 by HH Sheikh Hamad bin Khalifa al-Thani, Emir of Qatar, to help convert the country's oil wealth into durable human capital.

Activities: Operates in the fields of education, scientific research and community development. The Foundation aims to change Qatar into an advanced knowledge-based society, as a major research base, with some commercialization, helping to diversify the economy. It established Education City in Doha, which hosts branches of eight international universities; and funds a number of science and technology research institutes and 'heritage centres', including the Qatar Philharmonic Orchestra, Qur'anic Botanic Garden, Mathaf: Arab Museum of Modern Art and the Qatar National Library. The Foundation has also set up a publishing venture in partnership with Bloomsbury Publishing.

Geographical Area of Activity: Qatar.

Publications: *Qatar Foundation Telegraph*; *Think*; *The Foundation* (magazine); radio channel QF Radio (93.7FM).

Board of Directors: HH Sheikha Mozah bint Nasser al-Missned (Chair.); HH Sheikha Hind bint Hamad al-Thani (Vice-Chair.).

Principal Staff: Pres. Saad Ebrahim al-Muhannadi.

Address: POB 5825, Doha; Education City, Al Huqoul St, Ar-Rayyan, Doha.

Telephone: 4540000; **Fax:** 4806117; **Internet:** www.qf.org.qa; **e-mail:** info@qf.org.qa.

Romania

FOUNDATION CENTRES AND CO-ORDINATING BODIES

CENTRAS—Assistance Centre for NGOs

Established in 1995 to promote freedom of thought and creativity, education and free exchange of opinion, and information based on democratic and humanitarian principles, through the development of Romania's non-profit sector.

Activities: Operates in the fields of NGO development, conservation and the environment, economic affairs, education, law and human rights, and social welfare, nationally through projects, research, conferences, training courses and publications, and internationally through projects and training courses.

Geographical Area of Activity: Romania.

Publications: *Attitudini* (magazine); *White Papers of the Romanian NGOs FORUM.*

Board of Trustees: Dorin Tudoran (Chair.).

Principal Staff: Exec. Dir Viorel Micescu.

Address: 011454 Bucharest, blvd Maresal Averescu 17, Pavilion F, et. 3, Sector 1.

Telephone: (21) 2230010; **Fax:** (21) 2230012; **Internet:** www.centras.ro; **e-mail:** office@centras.ro.

CIVITAS Foundation for Civil Society

Founded in 1992 to stimulate local and regional development.

Activities: Works through developing and implementing local and regional development programmes; supporting local initiatives that seek to develop relations between local governments and the local population; providing specialist consultancy services in various fields for local governments; running training courses for local public officials; and supporting the establishment and functioning of NGOs. The Foundation has offices in Cluj-Napoca and Odorheiu Secuiesc.

Geographical Area of Activity: Romania.

Publications: Annual Report; *Civil Forum* (twice a year, magazine); books.

Finance: Annual revenue 1,448,557 new lei, expenditure 1,370,620 new lei (2011).

Board of Trustees: Gábor Kolumbán (Chair.).

Principal Staff: Regional Dirs Márton Balogh, Árpád Orbán.

Address: 400124 Cluj-Napoca, blvd 21 Decembrie 1989 108/22.

Telephone: (264) 590554; **Fax:** (264) 590555; **Internet:** www.civitas.ro; **e-mail:** office@civitas.ro.

Forumul Donatorilor din România (Romanian Donors' Forum)

Established in 1999 to offer grantmaking instruments and services—the communication, co-ordination and advocacy means necessary for the development of foundations' capacity to act to support NGOs and the community.

Activities: Activities include: facilitating the exchange of information between grantmakers about their individual programmes and strategies; providing services to member foundations and promoting their interests; creating a framework for co-ordination and co-operation between grantmakers; promoting best practices in grantmaking; providing information about the NGO and donor community to existing and potential grantmakers; disseminating information about foreign grantmakers and their changing priorities; raising awareness of possible new sources of funding available to the NGO sector; raising public awareness about grantmakers and the general concept of philanthropy; creating a common platform for the protection and promotion of organized philanthropy; gathering and disseminating information about the problems and priorities of organized philanthropy; and promoting and assisting the development of corporate philanthropy in Romania.

Geographical Area of Activity: Romania.

Publications: Annual Report; *Review of Donor Support for Non-Profit Sector in Romania; Nine Steps towards a Successful Annual Report: A Guide to Writing an Annual Report; The 2001 Review of the Romanian NGO Sector; Tendencies in the Dynamic of the Romanian NGO Sector.*

Board of Directors: Tincuta Baltag (Chair.); Adriana Stoica (Vice-Chair.).

Principal Staff: Exec. Dir Magdalena Ciobanu Stoian.

Address: 010101 Bucharest, str. Stirbei Voda 29, et. 3, Apt 5, Sector 1.

Telephone: (21) 3118811; **Fax:** (21) 3118811; **Internet:** www.forumuldonatorilor.ro; **e-mail:** contact@donorsforum.ro.

Fundatia pentru Dezvoltarea Societatii Civile—FDSC (Civil Society Development Foundation)

Established in 1994 to offer information, financing, training and advocacy to develop the capacity of civil society organizations and communities and to improve people's lives.

Activities: Supports the development of civil society through consultancy and lobbying (adopting and amending those regulating acts regarding the way in which NGOs run their activity); information (NGO database, *Voluntar* publication); training and consultancy (Foundation trainers provide courses covering 30 topics); research (surveys on civil society, needs assessment, NGO sustainability, etc.); and technical assistance in European Union Phare programmes and structural funds.

Geographical Area of Activity: Romania.

Publications: *Voluntar* (weekly magazine for volunteers); studies, including *Civicus Index on Civil Society, Social Watch World Report.*

Finance: Receives funding from a number of governmental and non-governmental sources, including the European Union, Central and East European Trust, World Learning Romania, Netherlands Governement, USAID, Concorde and Eurostep. Annual income €1,899,370, expenditure €1,754,246 (2012).

Board of Directors: Cătălin R. Crețu (Chair.); Lorita Constantinescu, Mircea Kivu (Vice-Chair.).

Principal Staff: Exec. Dir Ionu Sibian.

Address: Bucharest, Blvd Nerva Traian 21, Sector 2.

Telephone: (21) 3100177; **Fax:** (21) 3100180; **Internet:** www.fdsc.ro; **e-mail:** office@fdsc.ro.

FOUNDATIONS, TRUSTS AND NON-PROFIT ORGANIZATIONS

Black Sea University Foundation—BSUF (Fundatia Universitara a Marii Negre)

Established in 1992 by 21 members of the Romanian scientific and cultural community to develop better professional skills and increase knowledge through regional and international co-operation.

Activities: Operates internationally in the field of education, through training courses and workshops run by the Black Sea University, on topics in areas such as Peace Diplomacy, Ecology and Sea Resources, Economy and Management, Advanced and Applied Science, and Culture, Contemporary Problems and Future Studies. Courses are attended by scholars, professionals, government experts, etc. from around the world. The Foundation, in co-operation with national and international institutions, has established a number of permanent institutions, including a Conflict Prevention Studies Centre, a Laboratory for Information Technologies in Education an Applied Economy Centre and a Black Sea Universities Network. It also collaborates with universities in other countries, and with international organizations. In 2007, the Foundation became the Head of Network of the Anna Lindh Foundation.

Geographical Area of Activity: Romania.

Publications: *Letter from the Black Sea University* (quarterly newsletter); *Millennium III* (quarterly, in English); papers and brochures.

Finance: European/international projects, donations.

Board: Prof. Mircea Malita (Founding Chair.); Liviu-Aurelian Bota (Chair.); Prof. Silviu Negu (Vice-Chair.).

Principal Staff: Pres. Dan Dungaciu; Exec. Dir Cosmin-Drago Dugan.

Address: 761172 Bucharest 5, calea 13 Septembrie 13, Casa Academiei Romane.

Telephone: (31) 4052542; **Fax:** (21) 2339125; **Internet:** www .bsuf.ro; **e-mail:** office@bsuf.ro.

Institutul Cultural Român (Romanian Cultural Institute)

Established in 2003 following the restructuring of the Romanian Cultural Foundation and of the Romanian Cultural Foundation Publishing House.

Activities: Operates in the fields of the arts and humanities, education and science, through self-conducted programmes, grants, research, scholarships and fellowships, prizes, training courses and publications. The Institute organizes several programmes, including grants to overseas students wishing to study in Romania; supports Romanian cultural institutes abroad; promotes relations with those interested in Romanian culture and civilization, and with Romanians living abroad; organizes international symposia, conferences and exhibitions; edits and distributes books, information bulletins, magazines, audio and video materials; encourages cultural exchange; and co-operates with similar institutions in other countries. The Institute also runs its own publishing venture.

Geographical Area of Activity: Romania.

Publications: Annual Report; *Curierul Românesc* (monthly); *Lettre Internationale* (quarterly); *Dilema* (weekly newspaper); *Transylvanian Review* (quarterly); *Contrafort* (monthly); *Destin Românesc* (quarterly); *Glasul Bucovinei* (quarterly); newsletter.

Finance: Partly self-financing; also receives government subsidies. Annual revenue 27,083,306 new lei, expenditure 27,083,306 new lei (31 Dec. 2014).

Board of Directors: Radu Boroianu (Chair.); Liviu Sebastian Jicman, Nagy Zoltan (Vice-Chair.).

Principal Staff: Sec.-Gen. Petrior Dumitrescu; Dep. Sec.-Gen. Valentin Iovan.

Address: 011824 Bucharest, Aleea Alexandru 38, Sector 1.

Telephone: (31) 7100625; **Fax:** (31) 7100607; **Internet:** www .icr.ro; **e-mail:** icr@icr.ro.

Dinu Patriciu Foundation (Fundatia Dinu Patriciu)

Established in 2007 to promote education in Romania.

Activities: Supports Romanian education by implementing two of the largest private scholarship programmes in the country.

Geographical Area of Activity: Romania.

Publications: Annual Report; *Stiinta & Tehnica* (monthly science and technology magazine).

Finance: Annual revenue 28,460,934 new lei, expenditure 27,932,913 new lei (2010).

Board: Dinu Patriciu (Chair.).

Principal Staff: Gen. Man. Tincuta Apateanu.

Address: 020276 Bucharest, Cladirea Lakeview, blvd Barbu Vacarescu 301–311, et. 14, Sector 2.

Telephone: (31) 4254120; **Fax:** (31) 4254127; **Internet:** www .fundatiadinupatriciu.ro; **e-mail:** office@ fundatiadinupatriciu.ro.

Soros Foundation Romania

Established in 1990 as the Soros Foundation for an Open Society Association, an independent foundation; renamed as Open Society Foundation in 1997; part of the Open Society Foundations (q.v.) foundations network. In 2000, the Foundation restructured its most important programmes as 13 independent organizations, which now function as centres of expertise and public policy development.

Activities: Focuses on institutional reform and democratization through advocacy, both directly and supporting other NGOs in their public initiatives. Current projects include the Migration and Development programme; the Arhipera Housing programme; the Transparency and Good Governance programme; and the Decade of Roma Inclusion (2005–2015). The Foundation also runs two European structural projects: Rures—on social economy in Romanian rural areas—and EU Inclusive—to share best practices on Roma work integration issues between Romania, Bulgaria, Spain and Italy.

Geographical Area of Activity: Romania.

Restrictions: Grants only to Romanian organizations or individuals.

Publications: Annual Report; *The Beneficial Regularisation of Immigration in Romania*; *Commentaries on the Romanian Constitution*; *Local Authorities face to face with the European Funds*; *Moldova: At the Crossroads; A Comparative Analysis of the Mining Fiscal Regime in Romania*; *Attitudes Towards Work in Romania*; *Political Culture in Romania*; *Immigrants in Romania: Perspectives and Risks*; *Enhancing the Contribution of Mining to Sustainable Development*; *Integrated Strategies for Natural Resource Exploitation*; *Roma: Life Stories*; *Effects of Migration: Children left at home: Risks and solutions*.

Finance: Annual budget US $3,404,000 (2013).

Council of Directors: Mircea Vasilescu (Pres.).

Principal Staff: Exec. Dir Gabriel Petrescu; Fin. Dir Ileana Muetescu.

Address: 010613 Bucharest, Sector 1, Str. Caderea Bastiliei 33.

Telephone: (21) 2121101; **Fax:** (21) 2121032; **Internet:** www .fundatia.ro; www.soros.ro; **e-mail:** info@soros.ro.

Russian Federation

FOUNDATION CENTRES AND CO-ORDINATING BODIES

CAF Russia—Charities Aid Foundation Russia

Established in 1993 by CAF—Charities Aid Foundation (q.v.).

Activities: Distributes grants provided by Russian and international donors, as well as providing support to companies and private philanthropists in the areas of planning of charitable and social projects that take into account the demands and interests of the donors, and the demands of the non-profit organizations in the regions where the projects are being carried out, and legal and financial advice in management of the projects. Also aims to develop new forms of philanthropy, including developing corporate giving, providing support to community foundations, and promoting payroll giving. Also carries out research work aimed at the study and development of different aspects of charitable activity in the Russian Federation, and promotes the development of civil society in the Russian Federation campaigning for improvement to Russian legislation regarding philanthropy and non-profit organizations and consultancy and training support for civil initiatives.

Geographical Area of Activity: Russian Federation.

Publications: Annual Report; *Money and Charity* (magazine, 6 a year); *World Giving Index*; industry reports; analysis; best practice guidelines.

Finance: Annual income £10,787,000, expenditure £10,787,000 (2013).

Principal Staff: Dir Maria Chertok.

Address: 101000 Moscow, ul. Myasnitskaya 24/7, Bldg 1, Entrance 10, Floor 4, Office 102.

Telephone: (495) 792-59-29; **Fax:** (495) 792-59-86; **Internet:** www.cafrussia.ru; **e-mail:** cafrussia@cafrussia.ru.

Community Foundation Partnership

Established in 2003.

Activities: Lobbies on behalf of community foundations. Aims to strengthen civil society and improve people's quality of life; and to guarantee the effective and transparent use of funds. Comprises 16 foundations.

Geographical Area of Activity: Russian Federation.

Principal Staff: Chair. Boris Tsyrulnikov; Vice-Chair. Ilia Chukalin.

Address: c/o Togliatti Community Foundation, Samara Oblast, ul. Ubileinaya, D. 31-E, Office 401.

Telephone: (8412) 260-120; **Internet:** www.p-cf.org; **e-mail:** bac@fondtol.org.

International Bank of Ideas

Founded in 1988 to register and develop ideas and projects relevant to Russian society.

Activities: Provides ideas for projects in all areas: cultural, political, commercial, scientific and ecological. The Bank develops ideas that are registered in a database and have received scientific and public support; established the Moscow Business Library, a joint project with the 22nd Century Foundation in the USA; and provides business literature, reference books, a database, fax and e-mail services to enable organizations to make contacts abroad. The Enterprise Development Programme is carried out in conjunction with the Center for Citizen Initiatives, providing training for participants from small businesses; and the Center of International Foundations project aims to set up an information centre on charity organizations worldwide, in co-operation with the Soros foundations and the Open Society Institute—Moscow, now the Open Society Institute—Russia (q.v.).

Geographical Area of Activity: Worldwide.

Principal Staff: Chair. Sergei S. Agapitov.

Address: 129301 Moscow, ul. Boris Galushkina 19, Bldg 1.

Telephone: (495) 283-09-19; **Fax:** (495) 283-09-19; **Internet:** www.bankideas.ru; **e-mail:** acn@aha.ru.

NGO Development Centre

Established in 1994; formerly the Russian-German Exchange Society.

Activities: Works as an information centre for the non-profit sector in the Russian Federation. Supports the development of a strong civil society in the Russian Federation through providing advice on forming an NGO, education, sector information exchange and organizational development, including advice on management, fund-raising, relations with the public and media, accountancy, taxation and legal matters. Also sponsors international, national and regional conferences on issues concerning non-profit sector development in the Russian Federation.

Geographical Area of Activity: Russian Federation.

Publications: Annual Report; *Pchela* (magazine); bulletins, brochures and booklets.

Finance: Annual income 25,989,913 roubles, expenditure 22,169,606 roubles (31 Dec. 2012).

Board: Anna Orlova (Chair.); Anna Kletsina (Sec.).

Principal Staff: Exec. Dir Anna Skvortsova.

Address: 191040 St Petersburg, pr. Ligovsky 87, Office 300.

Telephone: (812) 718-37-94; **Fax:** (812) 118-37-94; **Internet:** www.crno.ru; **e-mail:** crno@crno.ru.

Russian Donors Forum

Founded in 1996 as a membership organization of around 25 Russian and non-Russian grantmaking organizations.

Activities: Aims to enhance the effectiveness of organized grantmaking to support the development of a democratic civil society in the Russian Federation. The Forum organizes the exchange of information between grantmakers and facilitating networks; provides information on the grantmaking operating environment; provides services to support the development of member organizations; carries out research; organizes the Top Corporate Philanthropist Award.

Geographical Area of Activity: Russian Federation.

Publications: Annual Report.

Board: Oksana Oracheva (Chair.).

Principal Staff: Exec. Sec. Natalya Kaminarskaya.

Address: 127055 Moscow, ul. Sushevskaya 9, Bldg 4, Office 311.

Telephone: (499) 978-59-93; **Fax:** (499) 973-34-78; **Internet:** www.donorsforum.ru; **e-mail:** dfinfo@donorsforum.ru.

Union of Charitable Organizations of Russia

Established in 2000 as a membership organization to strengthen and develop philanthropy in the Russian Federation by establishing an efficient general system of charitable activity in Russia.

Activities: Aims to unite efforts of its members for the most efficient realization of charitable activity; supports members with legal, informational, financial and other kinds of support and protects interests of its members in relation to federal, regional and local authorities. The Union promotes members' interaction with public associations, commercial and non-profit organizations in the Russian Federation, with the countries of the Commonwealth of Independent States and also with Russian communities. It maintains a register of Russian Federation charitable organizations; and also campaigns on fiscal issues and laws on charities' regulation.

Geographical Area of Activity: Russian Federation and the Commonwealth of Independent States.

Board of Directors: Pyotr Anatolyevich Ishchenko (Pres.); Yevgeny Vladislavovich Vodopianov (Sr Vice-Pres.).

Principal Staff: Dir-Gen. Vladimir Erikovich Riabtsev; Dep. Dir-Gen. Renat Salavatovich Shayakhmetov.

Address: 127299 Moscow, ul. Kosmonavta Volkova 10.

Telephone: (495) 225-13-16; **Fax:** (495) 490-96-78; **Internet:** www.sbornet.ru; **e-mail:** sbor@sbornet.ru.

FOUNDATIONS, TRUSTS AND NON-PROFIT ORGANIZATIONS

Glasnost Defence Foundation—GDF

Established in 1991 to provide legal support to the media in Russia, and to monitor censorship.

Activities: Operates in the areas of the arts and humanities, and law and human rights, through providing legal and advocacy services to the media; and conducts day-to-day monitoring of abuses of media rights in the Russian Federation. The Foundation carries out research and analysis; runs projects; and organizes seminars for journalists, lawyers and human rights activists. Maintains a monitoring network in the Russian Federation.

Geographical Area of Activity: Russian Federation.

Publications: *Digest* (online, weekly) in Russuan and in English.

Finance: Receives funding from the MacArthur Foundation, Norwegian Helsinki Committee.

Principal Staff: Pres. Alexey Simonov; CEO Nataliya Y. Maksimova.

Address: 119021 Moscow, blvd Zubovsky 4, Rm 438, POB 536.

Telephone: (495) 637-44-20; **Fax:** (495) 637-49-47; **Internet:** www.gdf.ru; **e-mail:** fond@gdf.ru.

Gorbachev Foundation (The International Foundation for Socio-economic and Political Studies)

Founded in 1991 by M. S. Gorbachev, G. I. Revenko and A. N. Yakovlev to conduct socio-economic and political studies.

Activities: Operates in the fields of education, international affairs, medicine and health, welfare and social studies, through self-conducted programmes, research, conferences, training courses and publications. Research programmes include: the Twenty-First Century—a Century of Challenges and Responses (the principal international research project), Building a New Russia's Statehood, Russia, Greater Europe, the Asian Flank of the Commonwealth of Independent States (CIS), and Russia and Europe in a New World Order. The Foundation also undertakes humanitarian work, providing funds for medicines and equipment to treat children with blood diseases. It assists foreign businesses in finding partners in the countries of the former USSR. Maintains offices and has partner organizations in the Russian Federation, Canada, Germany, Switzerland and the USA. The Foundation's Public Affairs Center maintains an archive of more than 30,000 items and library, which contains around 6,000 publications.

Geographical Area of Activity: Worldwide.

Publications: Numerous books and information bulletins.

Executive Board: Mikhail Gorbachev (Pres.); Irina Virganskaya (Vice-Pres.).

Principal Staff: Exec. Dir Olga M. Zdravomyslova.

Address: 125167 Moscow, pr. Leningradsky 39, Bldg 14.

Telephone: (495) 945-38-20; **Fax:** (495) 945-78-99; **Internet:** www.gorby.ru; **e-mail:** gf@gorby.ru.

New Eurasia Foundation

Established in 2004 by the USA-based Eurasia Foundation, Brussels-based European Madariaga Foundation and Russia's Dynasty Foundation.

Activities: Implements territorial development projects; supports the modernization of regional education systems at all levels; supports the development of local self-governance and housing reform; supports the development of small and medium-sized businesses; creates programmes for young people; encourages the effective use of migrant workers; and improves the efficiency of the mass media.

Geographical Area of Activity: Russian Federation.

Restrictions: Does not accept grant applications, nor does it issue grants on the basis of the 'open door' principle. All grant programmes are only administered on the basis of competition and as part of the Foundation's current projects and programmes.

Publications: Annual Report; newsletter and numerous reports.

Finance: Annual income 133,695,000 roubles, expenditure 139,978,000 roubles (31 Dec. 2010).

Principal Staff: Pres. Andrei V. Kortunov.

Address: 105120 Moscow, per. Third Syromyatnichesky 3/9, Bldg 6.

Telephone: (495) 970-15-67; **Fax:** (495) 970-15-68; **Internet:** www.neweurasia.ru; **e-mail:** reception@neweurasia.ru.

Non-Governmental Ecological Vernadsky Foundation

Established in 1995 by the OAO Gazprom Company, OAO UKOIL Oil Company, RAO EES Russii, Russian Federation Savings Bank, the Ministry of Public Health of the Russian Federation and the Russian Academy of Medical Sciences.

Activities: Supports environmentally-orientated educational projects and represents the interests of people in Russia who are concerned about the environment, as well as socially responsible businesses. In 2000, the Foundation launched the idea of the Blue Corridor Project, to establish transport corridors for heavy-duty transport vehicles in central and eastern Europe using compressed natural gas. Each year, the Foundation supports events held in Russia and abroad, including conferences, fora and round tables on issues of sustainable development, with participation by scientists, representatives of government agencies and leaders of industry. A scholarship programme introduces talented young people to the scientific heritage of Academician V. I. Vernadsky, and encourages their interest in issues of environmental protection and balanced economic development. The Foundation has established 14 regional competition committees at leading universities in Russia, Ukraine, Belarus and Bulgaria. It also awards the V. I. Vernadsky Medal for Contributions to Sustainable Development, given for outstanding service in the area of sustainable economic, social and environmental development. The Foundation supports professional environmental experts, and efforts to bring them together to enhance the effectiveness of environmental protection in Russia. It also sponsors international exhibitions and promotes partnerships established with major foreign and domestic organizations.

Geographical Area of Activity: Russian Federation, Europe.

Restrictions: No grants to individuals.

Publications: *Noosphere* (journal); *The Ecological Encyclopedia*; *On the Way to Sustainable Development*; *Ecological Aspects of the Sustainable Development of Thermal Power Engineering in Russia*; Annual Report; scientific, educational, environmental and sustainable development literature.

Board of Trustees: Vitaly Markelov (Chair.).

Principal Staff: Chair. of the Exec. Cttee Oleg Aksyutin; Pres. and Dir-Gen. Vladimir A. Grachev.

Address: 119607 Moscow, ul. Udaltsov 44.

Telephone: (495) 953-75-62; **Internet:** www.vernadsky.ru; **e-mail:** info@vernadsky.ru.

The Vladimir Potanin Foundation

Established in 1999 by Vladimir Potanin, CEO of Norislk Nickel and founder of Interros Company, to promote higher education, arts and cultural projects, and the development of philanthropy in the Russian Federation.

Activities: Fosters the development of knowledge and professionalism, encourages volunteer activity and individual creativity, strengthens institutions, and promotes the development of philanthropy. The Foundation supports a number of programmes providing scholarships, promoting teacher training and awarding grants to socio-cultural projects. Federal scholarships are awarded to the best students from the leading state educational institutions in the Russian Federation who have strong organizational skills and can think creatively. The Foundation promotes the development of young university faculty members who successfully combine pedagogical and scientific activities and provides grants to the most innovative museum projects. In addition to grantmaking in core areas, the Foundation works to promote a common vision for strategic philanthropy, strengthen philanthropic collaboration and develop philanthropic infrastructure in Russia.

Geographical Area of Activity: Russian Federation.

Finance: Annual income 331,222,000 roubles, expenditure 292,109,000 roubles (2013).

Board of Trustees: Vladimir Potanin (Chair.).

Principal Staff: Pres. Larisa G. Zelkova; Exec. Dir Oksana I. Oracheva.

Address: 119180 Moscow, ul. Bolshaya Yakimanka 9.

Telephone: (495) 725-65-05; **Fax:** (495) 726-57-54; **Internet:** www.fondpotanin.ru; **e-mail:** info@fondpotanin.ru.

Russian Cultural Foundation

Founded in 1986, as the Cultural Foundation of the USSR, by prominent Soviet artists and scientists and by more than 50 public and government organizations, including unions of creative workers, major museums, research and education institutions, and ministries. Since 1996, the Foundation has operated as an NGO.

Activities: Engages in activities to preserve, assimilate and augment the cultural heritage of the past, and to promote the continuity of culture in the present and the future. The Foundation is particularly concerned with history, architecture, literature, music and education. It co-operates with the Government, companies, NGOs and the public to finance its numerous cultural programmes. Main programmes are: the church and culture; culture and society; culture and the state; culture and creativity; the nation and culture; culture, education and science; cultural ambassadorships; the return of Russian culture from abroad; cultural policies; and culture and publishing activities. The Foundation supports cultural activities through making grants in all these areas. It also offers a variety of scholarships, including the D. S. Likhachev Award, made to students at institutions of higher musical education in Russia. Runs the Pari-Parizh lottery, and the Prestizh-Tur agency for the development of cultural tourism. It has 52 regional offices within and outside the Russian Federation.

Geographical Area of Activity: Russian Federation.

Publications: *Our Heritage* (6 a year); *The Russian Archive* (20 vols completed by 2011).

Finance: Financed by voluntary donations from citizens, by the founding organizations and from the proceeds of its publishing and exhibition activities.

Board of Directors: Nikita S. Mikhalkov (Chair.).

Address: 119019 Moscow, blvd Gogolevskii 6/7.

Telephone: (495) 739-20-65; **Fax:** (495) 690-05-73; **Internet:** www.culture.ru; **e-mail:** info@culture.ru.

Victoria Children Foundation

Established in 2004 to ensure the well-being, equal opportunities and sustainable future of disadvantaged children in Russia and the former USSR.

Activities: Programmes include: prevention of abandonment of children; support and family placement services for abandoned children; life skills development for children in care; and advancing volunteerism and a supportive social environment for disadvantaged children.

Geographical Area of Activity: Russian Federation.

Publications: Annual Report.

Finance: Total expenditure 217,300,000 roubles (2012).

Board: Tatiana Letunova (Chair.); Galina V. Rakhmanov (Dep. Chair.).

Address: 119002 Moscow, ul. Arbat 36/2 Stroenie 6.

Telephone: (495) 705-92-66; **Fax:** (495) 960-29-11; **Internet:** www.victoriacf.ru; vk.com/cfvictoria; **e-mail:** info@victoriacf.ru.

Dmitry Zimin Dynasty Foundation

Established in 2002 by Dr Dmitry Zimin, President Emeritus of Vimpelkom, Inc., to support young and talented people in Russia and Russian research in the area of fundamental science.

Activities: Works in the fields of education, science and youth through science and education support programmes, and community and cultural programmes. Educational projects include support for tertiary-level science students, for the teaching of physics and mathematics, and for scientific research.

Geographical Area of Activity: Russian Federation.

Publications: Annual Report.

Finance: Annual budget US $10,268,147 (2010).

Board of Directors: Sergey Guriev (Chair.).

Principal Staff: Exec. Dir Anna Piotrovskaya; Dep. Exec. Dir Konstantin Petrov; Financial Dir Natalia Shustova.

Address: 127006 Moscow, ul. First Tverskaya-Yamskaya 2, Bldg 1, Office 400.

Telephone: (495) 969-28-83; **Fax:** (495) 969-28-84; **Internet:** www.dynastyfdn.ru; **e-mail:** apiotrovskaya@dynastyfdn.ru.

Saint Lucia

FOUNDATIONS, TRUSTS AND NON-PROFIT ORGANIZATIONS

National Community Foundation

Established in 2002 by the National Insurance Corpn.

Activities: Promotes local philanthropy. The Foundation receives and distibutes philanthropic funds; supports poor or disadvantaged people, and children's education. Main programmes include: Youth at Risk; Older Persons, providing food; Scholarship Program for secondary school pupils; Health Care, for seriously ill people; Homeless, providing grants to vicims of man-made and natural disasters; Persons with Disabilities, funding Special Education Centres; and Chess Program, promoting the game of chess in primary and secondary schools and the wider community.

Geographical Area of Activity: St Lucia.

Principal Staff: Exec. Dir Madonna Monrose.

Address: Godfrey James Bldg, 1st Floor, 19–23 High St, Castries.

Telephone: 453-6661; **Fax:** 456-0997; **Internet:** www.ncfstlucia.lc; **e-mail:** stluciancf@gmail.com.

San Marino

FOUNDATIONS, TRUSTS AND NON-PROFIT ORGANIZATIONS

Fondazione San Marino Cassa di Risparmio della Repubblica di San Marino

Established in 2001.

Activities: Operates in San Marino in the areas of the arts and culture, scientific research and education, and social affairs.

Geographical Area of Activity: San Marino.

Finance: Total assets €74,992,795 (31 Dec. 2013).

Board of Directors: Giovanni Nicolini (Chair.); Alessandro Scarano (Vice-Chair.).

Principal Staff: Gen. Sec. Dr Valentina Garavini.

Address: Palazzo SUMS, via G. B. Belluzzi 1, 47890 San Marino.

Telephone: (549) 872571; **Fax:** (549) 872575; **Internet:** www .fondazionesanmarino.sm; **e-mail:** marinorossi@ fondazionesanmarino.sm.

Saudi Arabia

FOUNDATIONS, TRUSTS AND NON-PROFIT ORGANIZATIONS

Gulf Research Center

Established in 2000 by Abdulaziz Sager in Dubai, United Arab Emirates; an independent research institute.

Activities: Carries out research on Gulf Co-operation Council countries and the wider Gulf region. The Center promotes co-operation, disseminates information and issues publications. The Gulf Research Centre Foundation (q.v.) operates in Switzerland.

Geographical Area of Activity: Gulf region.

Publications: Annual Report; research papers; *Araa magazine* (monthly).

Board: Dr Abdulaziz Sager (Chair.).

Principal Staff: Man. Salih Kourdi.

Address: 19 Rayat Al-Itihad St, POB 2134, Jeddah 21451.

Telephone: (12) 651-1999; **Fax:** (12) 653-0953; **Internet:** www .grc.net; **e-mail:** info@grc.net.

International Islamic Relief Organization of Saudi Arabia—IIROSA

Established in 1978 to alleviate suffering worldwide.

Activities: Aids victims of natural disasters and war, and other displaced people, on an international scale. The Organization runs programmes to provide education, medical aid and social support; and sponsors projects and small businesses whose work contributes to its objectives. It has more than 100 offices in Saudi Arabia and worldwide.

Geographical Area of Activity: Worldwide.

Publications: Annual Report (in Arabic, English and French); *Bulletin* (quarterly); newsletter (monthly); *Igatha* (magazine in Arabic); *Yanabie al-Khair* (newsletter in Arabic).

Principal Staff: Acting Sec.-Gen. Essan Saleh Taleb.

Address: POB 14843, Jeddah 21434; Hail St, al-Ruwais District, opp. the Presidency of Meteorology and Environment, Jeddah.

Telephone: (2) 651-2333; **Fax:** (2) 651-8491; **Internet:** www .iirosa.org; www.egatha.org/eportal; **e-mail:** relief@iirosa .org.

King Faisal Foundation—KFF

Founded in 1976 to use the estate of the late King Faisal bin Abdulaziz al-Saud for charitable purposes.

Activities: Operates nationally and internationally in the fields of science and medicine, and the arts and humanities, chiefly by awarding the King Faisal International Prizes (for Arabic Literature, Islamic Studies, Service to Islam, Science and Medicine), with prizes totalling approx. US $1m., and academic scholarships. The Foundation finances the King Faisal Centre for Research and Islamic Studies, the King Faisal School, the Effat University and the Alfaisal University (a private university established in partnership with a US technology institute).

Geographical Area of Activity: Worldwide.

Restrictions: Nominations for the King Faisal International Prize are not acceptable from political institutes.

Publications: *Al-Faisal*.

Finance: Total assets approx. 1,441m. Saudi riyals.

Board of Trustees: HRH Prince Muhammad al-Faisal (Chair.).

Principal Staff: Man. Dir HRH Prince Khalid al-Faisal; Deputy Man. Dir HH Prince Bandar bin Saud bin Khalid al-Saud.

Address: POB 352, Riyadh 11411.

Telephone: (1) 465-2255; **Fax:** (1) 465-6524; **Internet:** www .kff.com; **e-mail:** info@kff.com.

Sultan bin Abdulaziz al-Saud Foundation

Established in 1995 by HRH Prince Sultan bin Abdulaziz al-Saud, as a private non-profit organization, to provide humanitarian, social and cultural services, and to empower Saudi Arabia to participate in the spread of knowledge through modern means of communication.

Activities: Operates in the fields of social welfare and education through four principal programmes: the City for Humanitarian Services, the Science and Technology Centre, the Programme for Medical and Educational Telecommunications (Medunet) and the Special Education Programme.

Geographical Area of Activity: Saudi Arabia.

Board of Trustees: HRH Prince Khalid bin Sultan bin Abdulaziz (Chair.); HRH Prince Fahd bin Sultan bin Abdul-Aziz (Deputy Chair.).

Principal Staff: Sec.-Gen. HRH Prince Faisal bin Sultan bin Abdul-Aziz; Deputy Sec.-Gen. HRH Prince Saud bin Sultan bin Abdul-Aziz.

Address: POB 64400, Riyadh 11536.

Telephone: (1) 482-7663; **Fax:** (1) 482-2617; **Internet:** www .sultanfoundation.org; **e-mail:** question@sultanfoundation .org.

Senegal

FOUNDATION CENTRE AND CO-ORDINATING BODY

FAVDO—Forum for African Voluntary Development Organizations (Forum des Organisations Volontaires Africaines de Développement—FOVAD)

Established in 1986, an international association of c.450 African development organizations, to provide mutual support and co-operation and aid the general development of people in Africa.

Activities: Operates in the field of aid to less-developed countries, through establishing links and networks between NGOs, governments and governmental organizations in Africa and internationally.

Geographical Area of Activity: Africa.

Principal Staff: Pres. and CEO Abdou el Mazide Ndiaye.

Address: Immeuble Ndiaga Diop Colobane BP 12093, Dakar.

Telephone: 776-38-25-13; **Fax:** 338-25-88-81; **e-mail:** mazide@orange.sn.

FOUNDATIONS, TRUSTS AND NON-PROFIT ORGANIZATIONS

Association Nationale pour l'Alphabétisation et la Formation des Adultes—An@fa (Pan African Association for Literacy and Adult Education—PAALEA)

Established in 1984 as the African Association for Literacy and Adult Education by the merger of the African Adult Education Association and the Afrolit Society, which were both founded in 1968.

Activities: Promotes literacy and adult education, and aims to increase understanding of the concept of life-long learning within Africa. Conducts studies on educational problems and literacy, holds conferences and disseminates information. Educators form networks to develop programmes concerned with such issues as literacy, women in adult education and development, environmental education, training of trainers, artists for development, participatory research, and university, adult and continuing education. The Association provides professional training to educators. It maintains a reference library and pool of expert educators to act as consultants.

Geographical Area of Activity: Africa.

Finance: Funded through membership fees and grants and donations from sister organizations.

Principal Staff: Nat. Exec. Ousman Faty Ndongo.

Address: BP 10358, Dakar; Villa 17 bis, Patte d'Oie Builders Nord Extension, Dakar.

Telephone: 33-855-9450; **Fax:** 33-824-9460; **Internet:** www.anafa.org; **e-mail:** direction@anafa.org; anafa@sentoo.sn.

Enda Tiers Monde—Environnement et Développement du Tiers-Monde (Enda Third World—Environment and Development Action in the Third World)

Established in 1972 as an international associative organization active in combating poverty, and in the field of environmental development.

Activities: Operates in the fields of aid to less-developed countries and environmental development, through assisting local community organizations operating in areas such as cultural protection, urban economy, youth and energy. There are decentralized branches of the organization in Africa, South America and Asia, and representative offices in Europe.

Geographical Area of Activity: Africa, South America, Asia, the Caribbean and Europe.

Publications: Reports; *Trade Liberalisation and Sustainable Management of Fishery's Sector in West Africa: Case study of Gambia; Reconciling Countries through Culture; Contes seereer; Plantes médicinales du Sahel; Une Afrique s'invente.*

Board of Directors: Fatou Sow Sarr (Chair.).

Principal Staff: Exec. Sec. Masse Lô.

Address: Complexe SICAP Point E, Bâtiment B, 1er étage, ave Cheikh Anta Diop, BP 3370, Dakar.

Telephone: 33-869-9948; **Fax:** 33-860-5133; **Internet:** www.enda.sn; endatiersmonde.org; **e-mail:** se@endatiersmonde.org.

Fondation Rurale pour l'Afrique de l'Ouest (West African Rural Foundation)

Established in 1993 to promote rural development.

Activities: Operates internationally, supporting community organizations working in the fields of rural development, the environment and human rights. The Foundation promotes research and collaboration between researchers in the area of agricultural and rural development research; and provides training materials and technical and management advice. It also fosters links between organizations involved in rural development; and lobbies on behalf of rural organizations and individuals.

Geographical Area of Activity: West Africa.

Publications: *WARF Newsletter.*

Finance: Annual budget approx. US $1.5m.

Council of Governors: Dr Dominique Hounkonnou (Chair.); Saran Kourouma Thiam (Sec.-Gen.).

Principal Staff: Exec. Dir Ndèye Coumba Fall.

Address: Sacré Coeur 3, VDN Villa 10075, CP 13 Dakar-Fann.

Telephone: 33-865-0060; **Fax:** 33-860-6689; **Internet:** www.frao.info; www.frao.org; **e-mail:** secretary@frao.org.

Fondation Léopold Sédar Senghor (Léopold Sédar Senghor Foundation)

Founded in 1974 by Léopold Sédar Senghor, former President of Senegal, to preserve national heritage and support training and research, especially in the areas of culture and international co-operation.

Activities: Operates nationally and internationally in the fields of the arts and humanities, education, law and human rights, and science and technology, through self-conducted programmes, research, grants, literary prizes, conferences, training courses and publications. Maintains a library comprising approximately 2,500 volumes. Has membership organizations in Brazil, Côte d'Ivoire, France, Switzerland and the USA.

Geographical Area of Activity: Worldwide.

Publications: *Éthiopiques* (2 a year); *Lettres Majeures* (bulletin).

Principal Staff: Chair. Basile Senghor; Exec. Dir Alphonse Raphaël Ndiaye.

Address: rue Alpha Hachamiyou Tall et René Ndiaye, BP 2035, 2035 Dakar.

Telephone: 33-821-5355; **Fax:** 33-821-5355; **e-mail:** senghorf@syfed.refer.sn.

OSIWA—Open Society Initiative for West Africa

Established in 2000; part of the Open Society Foundations Network (q.v.).

Activities: Provides funding to organizations working in the areas of human rights (including women's political and economic empowerment), democracy and governance, media and technology (including information and communications technologies), legal reform and transitional justice, and HIV/AIDS. The organization supports national projects and those involving more than one country in West Africa. Maintains offices in Nigeria, Liberia and Sierra Leone. In 2005, it established the West Africa Civil Society Institute (WACSI) in Ghana to reinforce the capacities of civil society in the subregion. WACSI, which became operational in 2007, serves as a resource centre for training, research, experience-sharing and dialogue for civil society organizations in West Africa.

Geographical Area of Activity: West Africa.

Publications: Annual Report; *Osiwa News* (newsletter); reports; guides and handbooks; discussion papers.

Finance: Annual income US $20,303,015, expenditure $20,344,035 (2012).

Board of Directors: Akwasi Aidoo (Chair.).

Principal Staff: Exec. Dir Abdul Tejan Cole.

Address: BP 008, Dakar-Fann; Stèle Mermoz, rue El Hadj Ibrahima Niasse, MZ 83 X MZ 100, Dakar.

Telephone: 33-869-1024; **Fax:** 33-824-0942; **Internet:** www .osiwa.org; **e-mail:** osiwa-dakar@osiwa.org.

PAN Africa—Pesticide Action Network Africa

Founded in 1996, part of the PAN International network.

Activities: Works as one of the regional arms of PAN International (founded in Malaysia in 1982). The organization promotes the protection of the environment and pesticide-free sustainable agriculture, raises awareness of the problems and dangers related to pesticide use in agriculture, and raises awareness about the issues surrounding the indiscriminate use of pesticides. It disseminates information on the use of pesticides and their alternatives through the publication of journals, leaflets and audio-visual material, and a Regional Documentation Centre. It also organizes workshops and training sessions, and has set up a database on pesticides, sustainable agriculture and agro-ecology. The organization works to strengthen legislation in Africa regarding the use of toxic pesticides.

Geographical Area of Activity: Africa.

Publications: Annual Report; *Pesticides and Alternatives* (newsletter in French and English, 3 a year); brochures; Journal; *PAN Africa* bulletin.

Principal Staff: Regional Co-ordinator Dr Abou Thiam.

Address: POB 15938, Dakar-Fann; Siège Villa No. 15 Castors, rue 1 x J, Dakar.

Telephone: 33-825-4914; **Fax:** 33-825-1443; **Internet:** www .pan-afrique.org; **e-mail:** panafrica@pan-afrique.org.

Serbia

FOUNDATION CENTRES AND CO-ORDINATING BODIES

Centre for Development of Non-Profit Sector

Established in 1996 to aid in building and renewing the non-profit sector in Serbia and Montenegro and to promote the development of autonomous civil initiatives and civil society.

Activities: Initiatives include an information and documentation programme, including the development of a database of non-profit organizations in Serbia; publishing bulletins, brochures and books; operating a training and education programme to advance the development of NGOs; the provision of aid to NGOs in the form of counselling and information; helping NGOs find suitable volunteers; and a research programme. Operates a regional network that aims to develop NGOs in Serbia.

Geographical Area of Activity: Serbia.

Publications: *Third Sector in Serbia: Status and Prospects* (2001); *Civil Society Driving Development: An Assembly of Non-Governmental Organizations from Central Europe, Former Soviet Union and Turkey* (2002).

Finance: Funded by donations.

Board of Directors: Danilo Milić (Pres.).

Principal Staff: Dir Aleksandar Bratković.

Address: 11000 Belgrade, Gospodar Jevremova 47A, Stan. 2.

Telephone: (11) 2626113; **Fax:** (11) 3240128; **Internet:** www.crnps.org.rs; **e-mail:** info@crnps.org.rs.

Gradjanske inicijative—GI (Civic Initiatives)

Established in 1996 by a team of NGO activists who had contributed to non-nationalist democratic opposition and anti-war movements since 1990.

Activities: Works towards strengthening civil society in Serbia through promotion of democracy, education and supporting active citizenship. The organization provides development, training and relevant information to NGOs to enable them to develop the third sector in Serbia with enhanced sustainability. Activities carried out include providing education, professional advice, technical assistance and information pertinent to the areas of interest of NGOs.

Geographical Area of Activity: Serbia.

Publications: *NGO sector in Serbia*; *Civil Society and Democracy*; *Human Rights Monitoring*; *Little Dictionary of Parliamentary Terms*; *Market Democracy*; *Financing of the Political Parties in Europe*; *Membership in the Council of Europe*; *The Dictionary of Democracy*; *Trade Unions in Europe;* and other materials.

Finance: Total assets 16,521,000 Serbian dinars (31 Dec. 2012).

Principal Staff: Exec. Dir Maja Stojanović.

Address: Kneza Miloša 4, 11000 Belgrade.

Telephone: (11) 3284188; **Internet:** www.gradjanske.org; **e-mail:** civin@gradjanske.org.

FOUNDATIONS, TRUSTS AND NON-PROFIT ORGANIZATIONS

European Centre for Peace and Development—ECPD

Established in 1985 following an agreement between the UN University for Peace and the Government of Yugoslavia to contribute to peace and development in Europe and to international co-operation in the transfer of knowledge.

Activities: Works towards finding solutions for acute and chronic problems of development and the quality of life in specific regions of Europe, particularly South-Eastern Europe, with an emphasis on countries in transition. The Centre runs a series of inter-connected programmes: development of human resources; development of natural resources; economic development; scientific and technological development; social development; integrated development; development of international relations and co-operation; and management. It organizes and conducts postgraduate studies; research projects; international scientific meetings, conferences, symposia and seminars; provides consulting services; and publishes materials and papers relevant to its studies. The Centre has been involved in science and research in numerous areas, including sustainable development, environmental protection, banking, finance and international trade, the promotion of small and medium-sized enterprises, and the integration of modern and traditional medicine to preserve human resources for development. It runs projects in co-operation with universities and institutions in host countries, and with international organizations.

Geographical Area of Activity: Europe, with a current emphasis on South-Eastern Europe, and in the USA and Canada.

Publications: *Inter-ethnic Reconciliation, Religious Tolerance and Human Security in the Balkans; Organomatika i Sinergetika—Osnove društvenog Inženjerstva; Ekspertizna Medicina, Ekspertizna analiza; National Reconciliation, Religious Tolerance and Human Security in the Balkans.*

Finance: Funded through donations from national and international organizations, tuition and registration fees.

Executive Board: Prof. Jonathan Bradley (Pres.).

Principal Staff: Exec. Dir Dr Negoslav P. Ostojić.

Address: 11000 Belgrade, Terazije 41.

Telephone: (11) 3246041; **Fax:** (11) 3240673; **Internet:** www.ecpd.org.rs; **e-mail:** office@ecpd.org.rs.

Fondacija za otvoreno društvo, Srbija (Fund for an Open Society—Serbia)

Founded in 1991; an independent foundation, part of the Open Society Foundations network (q.v.), which aims to foster political and cultural pluralism and reform economic structures to encourage free enterprise and a market economy.

Activities: Operates in the fields of information and the independent media, education, economic reform, civil society, the arts and culture, science, law and criminal justice, public health, Roma and ethnic minorities, local government and public administration, and women's and youth programmes.

Geographical Area of Activity: Serbia.

Publications: *Open News.*

Principal Staff: Exec. Dir Jadranka Jelinčić.

Address: 11000 Belgrade, Kneginje Ljubice 14.

Telephone: (11) 3025800; **Fax:** (11) 3283602; **Internet:** www.fosserbia.org; **e-mail:** office@fosserbia.org.

Karić Foundation

Established in 1979, as the BK Foundation, by the Karić family with the goal of helping others, and the promotion of Serbian national culture and tradition.

Activities: Operates in Serbia and Montenegro, Europe and the USA in the areas of the arts and humanities, education, international affairs, law and human rights, medicine and health, and social welfare, through awarding prizes (the Karić Brothers Awards), humanitarian projects, publishing, international co-operation and family development. The Foundation has branches in Austria, Canada, Cyprus, the United Kingdom and the USA.

Geographical Area of Activity: USA, Europe, Montenegro and Serbia.

Publications: *Bulletin* (newsletter).

Board of Management: Milanka Karić (Founder); Danica Karić (Chair.).

Address: 11000 Belgrade, Terazije 28, 2 Sprat.

Telephone: (11) 3629193; **Fax:** (11) 3629194; **Internet:** www.karicfoundation.com; **e-mail:** kf@karicfoundation.com.

Singapore

FOUNDATION CENTRE AND CO-ORDINATING BODY

CAF South-East Asia

Established in 2008 as the Centre for Asian Philanthropy; renamed as CAF South-East Asia in 2011. Part of the CAF Global Alliance network of organizations.

Activities: Assists in the development of philanthropic programmes in collaboration with local NGOs.

Geographical Area of Activity: South-East Asia.

Address: 30 Raffles Place, Level 17 Chevron House, Singapore 048622.

Telephone: 31513112; **Internet:** cafsea.org; **e-mail:** enquiry@cafsea.org.

FOUNDATIONS, TRUSTS AND NON-PROFIT ORGANIZATIONS

Community Foundation of Singapore

Established in 2008.

Activities: Promotes local philanthropy, connecting donors to charitable organizations and non-profit orgs at community level; manages funds and makes grants.

Geographical Area of Activity: Singapore.

Finance: Total income 12,884,821 Singapore dollars, expenditure 8,343,010 Singapore dollars (31 March 2014).

Board of Directors: Laurence Lien (Chair.).

Principal Staff: CEO Catherine Loh.

Address: 6 Eu Tong Sen St, #04-88 The Central, Singapore 059817.

Telephone: 6550-9529; **Fax:** 6221-0625; **Internet:** www.cf .org.sg; **e-mail:** contactus@cf.org.sg.

Singapore International Foundation—SIF

Established in 1991 to promote greater understanding between Singaporeans and world communities by sharing ideas, skills and experiences.

Activities: Seeks to connect Singaporeans at home and abroad in a range of areas, including business development, the arts, culture and academia. The Foundation runs various programmes that focus on international vounteerism and networking.

Geographical Area of Activity: Singapore, South-East Asia, South Asia, Europe, the People's Republic of China, Japan.

Publications: Annual Report; *Singapore Magazine* (quarterly); research papers; *Singapore Insights from the Inside*; *DiverseCity*; *Utopias*; *Disappearing Moon*; *Inspirations for a Better World*.

Board of Governors: Ong Keng Yong (Chair.); Anita Fam (Deputy Chair.).

Principal Staff: Exec. Dir Jean Tan.

Address: International Involvement Hub, 60A Orchard Road, #04-01 Tower 1, Singapore 238890.

Telephone: 68378700; **Fax:** 68378710; **Internet:** www.sif.org .sg; **e-mail:** contactus@sif.org.sg.

Slovakia

FOUNDATION CENTRES AND CO-ORDINATING BODIES

Asociácia komunitných nadácií Slovenska—AKNS (Association of Slovakian Community Foundations)

Established in 2003 by eight Slovakian community foundations to promote the activities of its members and the concept of community philanthropy in Slovakia.

Activities: Promotes the community foundation movement in Slovakia, representing its members, informing the public about the activities of community foundations in Slovakia. The Association lobbies the Government for legislation favourable to the development of philanthropy in Slovakia. It co-operates with similar organizations internationally.

Geographical Area of Activity: Slovakia.

Principal Staff: Pres. Jozef Jarina; Co-ordinator Katarína Minárová.

Address: 811 03 Bratislava, Partizánska 2.

Telephone: (2) 5441-9998; **Fax:** (2) 5441-9998; **Internet:** www.asociaciakns.sk; **e-mail:** nkn@nkn.sk.

Nadácia Ekopolis (Ekopolis Foundation)

Established in 1991 to promote sustainable development, civil society development and public participation.

Activities: Operates in Central Europe making grants in the areas of civil society development, rural development, environmental protection, community foundation development and women's rights. 'Sister' foundations operate in the Czech Republic, Hungary, Poland and Romania. In 2013, the Foundation awarded grants amounting to €1,846,000.

Geographical Area of Activity: Central Europe.

Publications: Annual Report.

Finance: Annual income €3,929,335, expenditure €2,256,766 (2013).

Principal Staff: Dir Peter Medved; Finance Man. Lívia Haringová.

Address: 974 01 Banska Bystrica, Komenskeho 21.

Telephone: (48) 414-5478; **Fax:** (48) 414-5259; **Internet:** www.ekopolis.sk; **e-mail:** ekopolis@ekopolis.sk.

Nadácia Pontis (Pontis Foundation)

Established in 1997 as the successor to the Foundation for a Civil Society.

Activities: Encourages and supports the development and long-term financial sustainability of non-profit organizations in Slovakia and a number of other countries worldwide through the provision of grants and consultancy. The Foundation supports development of corporate philanthropy and social responsibility, provides consultancy for creating philanthropic strategies, undertakes research projects and organizes educational events. It awards the Via Bona Slovakia Award for philanthropic activity, and administers the Business Leaders Forum, an association of 21 businesses that promotes corporate social responsibility in Slovakia. In 2009, it launched a new programme of individual giving called Dobrá Krajina (Great Country).

Geographical Area of Activity: Mainly Slovakia, but also Belarus, Western Balkans, Moldova, Kenya, Egypt, Georgia and Cuba.

Restrictions: Grants are open only to registered NGOs in Slovakia. Restricted support available for individuals, travel grants and internships abroad.

Publications: Annual Report; reports; information brochures; e-newsletter.

Finance: Annual income €1,954,605, expenditure €1,969,916 (31 Dec. 2013).

Board of Directors: Luboš Vančo (Chair.).

Principal Staff: Dir Lenka Surotchak; Financial Dir Gabika Zúbriková.

Address: 821 08 Bratislava, Zelinárska 2.

Telephone: (2) 5710-8111; **Fax:** (2) 5710-8125; **Internet:** www.nadaciapontis.sk; www.pontisfoundation.sk; **e-mail:** pontis@pontisfoundation.sk.

NGDO—Non-Governmental Development Organizations Platform (Platforma Mimovládnych Rozvojovych Organizáchií—MVRO)

Established in 2002; an umbrella organization of non-profit organizations (23 full members and eight observers) focused on foreign development and humanitarian assistance.

Activities: Aims to contribute to public awareness in the field of solidarity, mutual assistance and to contribute to resolving the problem of global poverty and humanitarian crises, through supporting its member NGOs. The Platform represents its members' common interests in the field of international development co-operation and humanitarian aid, provides information to member organizations on developments within the field of international development co-operation and humanitarian aid and on co-operation possibilities, co-ordinates the common activities and projects of the its members; co-operates with national government and local governments; develops relations with foreign organizations; and issues publications.

Geographical Area of Activity: Slovakia.

Publications: Annual report.

Board: Ivana Raslavská (Chair.); Ján Mihálik (Vice-Chair.).

Address: 821 08 Bratislava, Mileticova 7.

Telephone: (2) 2044-5255; **Fax:** (2) 2044-5255; **Internet:** www.mvro.sk; **e-mail:** info@mvro.sk.

SAIA—Slovak Academic Information Agency

Established in 1990 to assist in the development of the education system and civil society in general.

Activities: Provides services for NGOs in Slovakia, including training and advisory services, a library on the third sector and an NGO database with approximately 3,000 entries. Also issues publications; organizes conferences and seminars; runs volunteer projects and grants the Heart on Palm volunteer awards; and collaborates regionally and internationally with other similar organizations on programmes. The Agency's educational services include providing information, scholarship competitions, seminars and workshops for those wishing to study abroad. Maintains five branch offices throughout Slovakia.

Geographical Area of Activity: Slovakia.

Publications: *SAIA Bulletin* (monthly information journal); *NonProfit* (monthly magazine); Annual Report; *International Students' Guide to the Slovak Republic*.

Finance: Annual income €2,0665,132, expenditure €1,395,769 (2013).

Board of Directors: Milan Žalman (Chair.); Stanislav Čekovský (Vice-Chair.).

Principal Staff: Exec. Dir Katarína Koštálová; Deputy Dirs Michal Fedák, Dr Karla Zimanová.

Address: 812 20 Bratislava 1, Nám. slobody 23.

Telephone: (2) 5930-4700; **Fax:** (2) 5930-4701; **Internet:** www .saia.sk; **e-mail:** saia@saia.sk.

Slovak Donors' Forum—SDF

Established in 1996 as an association of Slovak and foreign grantmaking organizations to promote effective grantmaking and support not-for-profit organizations in Slovakia.

Activities: Carries out research, promotes the work and effectiveness of its member foundations and implements outreach initiatives focused on development of corporate and individual philanthropy in Slovakia.

Geographical Area of Activity: Slovakia.

Publications: Annual report; newsletter; expert manuals.

Principal Staff: Pres. and Exec. Dir Sonya Lexmanová.

Address: 811 03 Bratislava, Baštová 5.

Telephone: (2) 5441-7917; **Fax:** (2) 5441-7917; **Internet:** www .donorsforum.sk; **e-mail:** donorsforum@donorsforum.sk.

Slovenská Humanitná Rada (Slovak Humanitarian Council)

Established in 1990 as the Czechoslovak Council for Humanitarian Co-operation—an independent non-governmental voluntary association of 169 organizations aiming to relieve human suffering, which, after the division of Czechoslovakia into the Czech Republic and Slovakia, became the Czech Council for Humanitarian Co-operation (now the Council of Humanitarian Associations, q.v.) and the Slovak Humanitarian Council.

Activities: Promotes the interests of the voluntary sector and provides humanitarian aid in collaboration with the state. The Council supports the projects of its member organizations; offers advice on management and fund distribution; organizes training courses; disseminates information; provides consultancy services; and issues publications.

Geographical Area of Activity: Slovakia.

Restrictions: Provides financial support, aid in kind and technical assistance only for projects in the social field.

Publications: *Humanita* (newsletter, monthly); Annual Report; electronic/online information; information brochures.

Governing Board: Ivan Sykora (Pres.); Jaroslav Hinšt (Vice-Pres.).

Principal Staff: Dir Eva Lysicanová.

Address: 821 08 Bratislava, Budyšínska 1.

Telephone: (2) 5020-0517; **Fax:** (2) 5020-0522; **Internet:** www .shr.sk; **e-mail:** shr@changenet.sk.

FOUNDATIONS, TRUSTS AND NON-PROFIT ORGANIZATIONS

Children of Slovakia Foundation (Nadácia pre deti Slovenska)

Established in 1995 by the International Youth Foundation (q.v.) as an independent NGO to support the positive development of children and young people in Slovakia.

Activities: Operates in the fields of education and social welfare, specifically in the area of children and young people, through self-conducted programmes, grants to institutions and training courses.

Geographical Area of Activity: Slovakia.

Restrictions: Projects are limited to Slovakia.

Publications: *Novo vynárajúce sa potreby detí na slovensku— prieskumná štúdia (newly emerging needs of children in Slovakia—exploratory study).*

Finance: Annual income €912,348, expenditure €941,681 (2013).

Board: Matej Ribanský (Chair.).

Principal Staff: Exec. Dir Dana Rusinová.

Address: 811 08 Bratislava, Heydukova 3.

Telephone: (2) 5263-6471; **Fax:** (2) 5263-6462; **Internet:** www .nds.sk; **e-mail:** nds@nds.sk.

International Visegrad Fund—IVF

Established in 2000 by the countries of the Visegrad Group: Czech Republic, Hungary, Poland and Slovakia.

Activities: Aims to promote regional co-operation among the Visegrad countries, as well other regions in Central and Eastern Europe, the Western Balkans and Southern Caucasus by supporting common cultural, scientific and research projects, educational projects, youth exchanges and cross-border co-operation. The Fund also awards individual postdoctoral scholarships, short-term research fellowships, and individual and group artist residencies.

Geographical Area of Activity: Czech Republic, Hungary, Poland and Slovakia, the Eastern Partnership countries (Armenia, Azerbaijan, Belarus, Georgia, Moldova, Ukraine), the Western Balkans (Albania, Bosnia and Herzegovina, Kosovo, former Yugoslav republic of Macedonia, Montenegro and Serbia); other countries.

Publications: *Two Decades of Visegrad Cooperation–The Visegrad Group; Visegrád 1335; The Visegrad Group–A Central European Constellation.*

Finance: Annual income €7,801,656, expenditure €7,801,656 (2013).

Principal Staff: Exec. Dir Karla Wursterová; Deputy Exec. Dir György Varga.

Address: 811 02 Bratislava, Kralovske udolie 8.

Telephone: (2) 5920-3811; **Fax:** (2) 5920-3805; **Internet:** www .visegradfund.org; **e-mail:** visegradfund@visegradfund.org.

Nadácia Aevis (Aevis Foundation)

Founded in 1991 to support environmental protection, primarily focusing on protection and regeneration of natural forests within a philosophy of deep ecology. Formerly known as Nadácia Zelená Nádej (Green Perspective Foundation); present name adopted in 2013.

Activities: Supports the activities of individuals, public initiatives and NGOs working in the above fields and education, through advisory, publishing, cultural, social and specific activities. The Foundation's main programmes include an annual award to the best forest protection activity open to applicants from the Czech Republic, Hungary, Poland and Slovakia; donations of books to rural libraries; financial help to students whose career goals meet the aims of the Foundation; and a small grant initiative for forest protection activities. It also runs the Wilderness Restoration nature tourism programme.

Geographical Area of Activity: Czech Republic, Hungary, Poland and Slovakia.

Publications: Several books.

Finance: Total assets €35,208,710 (31 Dec. 2012).

Board of Directors: Erik Balá (Chair.).

Principal Staff: Exec. Dir Rastislav Mičaník.

Address: Kpt. Nálepku 102, 069 01 Snina.

Telephone: (9) 07072863; **Internet:** www.aevis.org; **e-mail:** info@aevis.org.

Open Society Foundation—Bratislava (Nadácia Otvorenej Spoločnosti)

Founded in 1992; an independent foundation, part of the Open Society Foundations (q.v.) network, which aims to support, develop, protect and strengthen democratic and liberal values of open society through the implementation of programmes and projects.

Activities: Programme priorities include public administration, law and judiciary, Roma people, social integration, educational reform, education, co-operation between European countries, library support, Internet, publishing, public health, media, criminal justice, women, civil society and European integration. The Foundation also operates as a partner within the NGO sector, at governmental and donor level, and with individuals in Slovakia, as well as with international partners. In 2010, the Foundation awarded 142 grants worth more than €840,000 in total.

Geographical Area of Activity: Slovakia.

Publications: Annual Report; *Manual for Foundations*; *Free Access to Information Law*; *Prevention of HIV Epidemics in CEE and NIS*; *A Reader for Non-Profit Organizations*; and other publications.

Finance: Annual income €3,135,166, expenditure €1,273,815 (31 Dec. 2012).

Board of Directors: Zuzana Kušová (Chair.).

Principal Staff: Financial Dir Jana Dravecká.

Address: 811 03 Bratislava, Baštová 5.

Telephone: (2) 5441-6913; **Fax:** (2) 5441-8867; **Internet:** www.osf.sk; **e-mail:** osf@osf.sk.

Milan Simecka Foundation (Nadácia Milana Šimečku)

Founded in 1991 in memory of the Slovak philosopher, author, and democratic activist Milan Simecka.

Activities: Aims to initiate and promote activities leading to the development of democracy, culture, humanity and civil society. Supports those educational, publishing, training, and counselling activities that help to disseminate and strengthen democratic values in society and to apply ethical approaches in politics. The Foundation also funds activities focusing on mutual understanding and co-operation between states, nationalities, and ethnic groups, with special emphasis on the development of Czech and Slovak relations. It has initiated major projects in the field of human rights and civic education, community development, independent media support, and oral history research, and has established a Holocaust Documentation Centre.

Geographical Area of Activity: Czech Republic and Slovakia.

Publications: Annual Report; books; training manuals and handbooks.

Board: Eva Salnerová (Pres.).

Principal Staff: Exec. Dir Martina Mazenská; Programme Dir Laco Oravec.

Address: 811 03 Bratislava, Panenská 4.

Telephone: (2) 5443-3552; **Fax:** (2) 5443-3552; **Internet:** www.nadaciamilanasimecku.sk; **e-mail:** nms@nadaciams.sk.

SOSNA Foundation

Founded in 1992 to help the environment in Košice and its surroundings.

Activities: Encourages people to adopt alternative methods of solving environmental problems, primarily at local and regional levels. The Foundation runs programmes in the areas of environmental education, the sustainable development of the Košice region of Slovakia, and organic agriculture. It campaigns to solve environmental problems, funding pilot projects on principles of sustainable living; and organizes educational programmes, workshops, lectures and exhibitions, and producing publications. In 2010, it opened the Eco Centre in the village of Družstevná pri Hornáde.

Geographical Area of Activity: Slovakia.

Publications: Educational publications, teaching aids, training manuals.

Finance: Annual income €58,054, expenditure €64,004 (2012).

Principal Staff: Rep. Štefan Szabó.

Address: 044 31 Drustevná pri Hornáde, ul. Okruzná.

Telephone: (5) 5625-1903; **Fax:** (9) 0495-1139; **Internet:** www.sosna.sk; **e-mail:** omar.sosna@gmail.com.

Slovenia

FOUNDATION CENTRE AND CO-ORDINATING BODY

Zavod Center za Informiranje, Sodelovanje in Razvoj Nevladnih Organizacije—CNVOS (Centre for the Information Service, Co-operation and Development of NGOs)

Established in 2001 by 27 NGOs to promote the development of civil society in Slovenia.

Activities: Offers services to NGOs and develops NGOs' ability to take on activities carried out by public sector bodies. The Centre provides networking opportunities for Slovenian NGOs with European institutions and NGOs from other European countries. It also provides legal assistance to NGOs. Comprises more than 200 member organizations.

Geographical Area of Activity: Slovenia.

Publications: *NGO-ZINE = SEKTOR* (newsletter); *How to Write a Good Project*; *Ethical Code*; *Relations with Media: Handbook for NGOs; Actor in the Decision-making Process?*; *How to Use Smart EU Funding*; *NGO Networks in Slovenia*; *Strategic Planning for NGOs: Communication Tools*.

Finance: Annual income €395,806, expenditure €394,874 (2013).

Council: Majda Struc (Chair.); Tatjana Hvala (Vice-Chair.).

Principal Staff: Dir Goran Forbici; Deputy Dir Tina Divjak.

Address: 1000 Ljubljana, Povsetova 37.

Telephone: (1) 542 14 22; **Fax:** (1) 542 14 24; **Internet:** www.cnvos.si; **e-mail:** info@cnvos.si.

FOUNDATIONS, TRUSTS AND NON-PROFIT ORGANIZATIONS

Slovenska znanstvena fundacija (Slovenian Science Foundation)

Set up in 1994 by the Slovenian Government and prominent Slovenian organizations in the fields of education, research, economy, finance and the media to work towards the promotion of science in Slovenia.

Activities: Operates in the areas of science and technology and education, through offering professional training to develop existing as well as future research; conducting basic and applied research; extending scientific co-operation, such as synergizing with national science foundations including the European Science Foundation (q.v.); and organizing programmes to deepen public understanding of technology and science, including the Slovene Park of Science and Technology and the Slovene Science Festival. The Foundation also extends support to scientific training by providing scholarships and fellowships; makes research grants; issues publications; conducts conferences; and promotes joint research projects and interchange of scientific knowledge.

Geographical Area of Activity: Slovenia.

Publications: *Glasnik ustanove Slovenske znanstvene fundacije* (Slovenian Science Foundation Courier).

Principal Staff: Dir Dr Edvard Kobal.

Address: 1000 Ljubljana, Štefanova 15.

Telephone: (1) 426 35 90; **Fax:** (1) 426 35 91; **Internet:** www.szf.si; **e-mail:** info@szf.si.

South Africa

FOUNDATION CENTRES AND CO-ORDINATING BODIES

Association for Progressive Communications—APC

Established in 1990 by a group of seven computer networks from around the world to promote and facilitate information and communication technology use by groups and individuals working in the areas of human rights, environmental protection and peace, and use of the Internet to further the development of civil society.

Activities: Operates in various areas: the promotion of non-commercial Internet space for NGOs; network development, aiding existing communication service providers to expand; women, promoting gender-aware web design and use; improving networking capabilities in Africa; information dissemination; and special projects, including the APC Betinho Prize of US $7,500 awarded to groups or NGOs in any country that have used information and communication technology significantly and successfully in development work. The Association has 22 members in 20 countries.

Geographical Area of Activity: International.

Restrictions: Not a grantmaking organization.

Publications: *APCNews* (monthly newsletter); books; issue papers; research; toolkits.

Finance: Annual income US $2,072,071, expenditure $2,119,199 (31 Dec. 2012).

Board of Directors: Julián Casabuenas (Chair.); Valentina Pellizzer (Vice-Chair.); Liz Probert (Sec.); Osama Manzar (Treas.).

Principal Staff: Exec. Dir Anriette Esterhuysen.

Address: POB 29755, Melville 2109.

Telephone: (11) 7261692; **Fax:** (11) 7261692; **Internet:** www.apc.org; **e-mail:** info@apc.org.

CAF Southern Africa

Established in 2000; part of the CAF Global Alliance network of organizations.

Activities: Promotes and facilitates effective grantmaking.

Geographical Area of Activity: South Africa.

Board of Directors: Jo-Ann Pohl (Chair.).

Principal Staff: CEO Colleen du Toit.

Address: Postnet Suite #37, Private Bag X9, Melville 2109, Johannesburg; Studio 16, Arts on Main, Maboneng Precinct, 264 Fox St, City and Suburban, Johannesburg 2094.

Telephone: (11) 3340404; **Fax:** (11) 3340580; **Internet:** www.cafsouthernafrica.org; **e-mail:** info@cafsouthernafrica.org.

CIVICUS—World Alliance for Citizen Participation

Established in 1993; an international alliance dedicated to strengthening citizen action and civil society worldwide, in particular in areas where participatory democracy, freedom of association of citizens and their funds for public benefit are threatened.

Activities: Operates worldwide in the areas of the arts and humanities, conservation and the environment, international affairs and social welfare, through self-conducted programmes, research, conferences and publications. Through its programmes and actions the Alliance seeks an increased understanding and promotion of the nature and contributions of civil society; a political, legal and fiscal environment that enables freedom and autonomy of association; innovative forms of funding and partnership to enhance the resource base of civil society organizations; the strengthening of the institutional, leadership, networking and advocacy capacities of the sector; and increased partnerships among business, government and civil society institutions. It holds a World Assembly biennially, and sponsors regional meetings. Its current main focus is the CIVICUS Index on Civil Society project mapping the development of civil society worldwide.

Geographical Area of Activity: Worldwide.

Publications: *e-Civicus* (weekly bulletin); *Civil Society at the Millennium* (1999); *Promoting Corporate Citizenship: Opportunities for Business and Civil Society Engagement* (1999); *Sustaining Civil Society: Strategies for Resource Mobilization* (1997); *Legal Principles for Citizen Participation: Toward a Legal Framework for Civil Society Organizations* (1997); *Building Civil Society Worldwide: Strategies for Successful Communications* (1997); *The New Civic Atlas: Profiles of Civil Society in 60 Countries* (1997); *Cutting the Diamonds: Civil Society Index 2008–2011*; *CIVICUS World* (6 a year); and others.

Finance: Total assets US $992,627; annual income $3,034,868, expenditure $3,064,071 (31 Dec. 2012).

Board of Directors: Nyaradzayi Gumbonzvanda (Chair.); Feliciano J. Reyna (Vice-Chair.); Dr Uygar Özesmi (Treas.); Elisa Peter (Sec.).

Principal Staff: Sec.-Gen. Dr Dhananjayan (Danny) Sriskandarajah.

Address: POB 933, Southdale, Johannesburg 2135; 24 Gwigwi Mrwebi St, Newtown 2001, Johannesburg.

Telephone: (11) 8335959; **Fax:** (11) 8337997; **Internet:** www.civicus.org; **e-mail:** info@civicus.org.

Global Fund for Community Foundations—GFCF

Established in 2006, with funding from the World Bank, the Ford Foundation, Mott Foundation and other US and European funders (qq.v.) to support the development of community foundations worldwide (with particular focus on the global South and the emerging economies of Central and Eastern Europe).

Activities: Provides grants and technical support to community foundations and other local philanthropy institutions and support organizations in low- and middle-income countries. The Fund has an office in the United Kingdom.

Geographical Area of Activity: Low- and middle-income countries and occasionally in disadvantaged communities in the global North.

Restrictions: Does not make grants to NGOs for direct implementation of projects.

Board of Trustees: Gerry Salole (Chair.); Stephen Pittam (Treas.).

Principal Staff: Exec. Dir Jenny Hodgson.

Address: PostNet Suite 135, Private Bag X2600, Houghton, Johannesburg 2041; 4th Floor, 158 Jan Smuts Ave, Rosebank, Johannesburg 2196.

Telephone: (11) 4474396; **Internet:** www.globalfundcommunityfoundations.org; **e-mail:** info@globalfundcf.org.

Open Society Initiative for Southern Africa—OSISA

Founded in 1997; an African institution committed to deepening democracy and human rights in southern Africa; an independent foundation part of the Open Society network.

Activities: Promotes and sustains the ideals, values, institutions and practice of open society, with the aim of establishing a vibrant southern African society in which people, free from material and other deprivation, understand their rights and responsibilities and participate democratically in all spheres of life. The organization operates in 10 countries in southern Africa funding civil society projects and advocacy activities in the areas of education, human rights, democracy, HIV/AIDS, women's rights, media, economic justice, law, language rights and information and communication technology. It provides support to a wide range of civil society organizations across southern Africa.

Geographical Area of Activity: Southern Africa (Angola, Botswana, Democratic Republic of the Congo, Lesotho, Malawi, Mozambique, Namibia, Swaziland, Zambia and Zimbabwe).

Publications: *Openspace* (3 a year); *Buwa* (2 a year).

Finance: Annual income US $37,032,794, expenditure $36,845,855 (31 Dec. 2012).

Board of Trustees: Neville Gabriel (Chair.).

Principal Staff: Exec. Dir Siphosami Malunga; Deputy Dir Tiseke Kasambala.

Address: 1 Hood Ave/148 Jan Smuts Ave, Rosebank, Johannesburg 2196.

Telephone: (11) 5875000; **Fax:** (11) 5875099; **Internet:** www .osisa.org; **e-mail:** info@osisa.org.

Southern Africa Community Foundation Association—SACOFA

Established in 2005.

Activities: Supports the development of community foundations and other grantmaking organizations; provides advice, information, capacity building and technical services; mediates in political conflicts; carries out research into community needs. Member organizations include Greater Rustenburg Community Foundation, UThungulu Community Foundation and West Coast Community Foundation.

Geographical Area of Activity: South Africa.

Finance: Total assets US $3m.

Principal Staff: CEO Chris Mkhize.

Address: c/o Greater Rustenburg Community Foundation, POB 21553, Protea Park 305, North West; SACOFA Secretariat, 158 Leyd St, Rustenburg 299, North West.

Telephone: (14) 5921525; **Fax:** (35) 7973134; **Internet:** (14) 5921506; **e-mail:** christine@grcf.co.za.

FOUNDATIONS, TRUSTS AND NON-PROFIT ORGANIZATIONS

ActionAid

Founded in 1972 by Cecil Jackson Cole; in 2003, moved its head office from the United Kingdom to South Africa.

Activities: Works directly with poor communities and through local partner organizations in more than 40 countries of Africa, Asia, Central and South America and the Caribbean to improve access to food, water, education, health care, shelter and a livelihood. Programmes are designed to address the underlying causes of poverty by helping poor people to recognize, promote and secure their basic rights. The organization runs three major international campaigns: food; education; and HIV/AIDS. There are regional offices in Brazil, Thailand and Kenya, and offices in Washington, DC, and Brussels. Along with sister organizations in France, Greece, Ireland, Italy and Spain, they form the ActionAid Alliance.

Geographical Area of Activity: Worldwide.

Restrictions: Grants only to approved partner organizations.

Publications: *Global Progress Report*; *Common Cause* (supporters' magazine, 2 a year); Annual Report; numerous books.

Finance: Total income €225,179,000, expenditure €213,434,000 (31 Dec. 2013).

International Board: Irene Ovonji-Odida (Chair.); Michael D. Lynch-Bell (Treas.).

Principal Staff: International Chief Exec. Adriano Campolina; Deputy Chief Exec. Chris Kinyanjui.

Address: PostNet Suite No. 248, Private Bag X31, Saxonwold 2132, Johannesburg; 4th Floor, West Wing, 158 Jan Smuts Ave Bldg (entrance on Walters Ave), Rosebank, Johannesburg.

Telephone: (11) 7314500; **Fax:** (11) 8808082; **Internet:** www .actionaid.org; **e-mail:** mail.jhb@actionaid.org.

AISA—Africa Institute of South Africa

Founded in 1960 by the South African Academy of Arts and Science and the University of South Africa, the Institute is the principal nationally-based centre for the study of African affairs, whose role is to inform South African society about trends and events in Africa.

Activities: Collects, interprets and disseminates information and analyses on African, and especially Southern African, affairs. Information is disseminated through periodicals and other publications, commentary to the media, and through seminars, workshops and conferences. The Institute conducts research, and maintains a specialized reference library of around 60,000 vols and about 480 journals and a monitoring service. It collaborates with other institutions and with researchers and academics in the field of African studies worldwide, and has co-operation agreements with centres of African studies abroad (including joint research projects). The Institute focuses primarily on the political, socio-economic, international and developmental issues facing Africa. While the geographical scope of its interest covers the entire continent, its main concern is with Sub-Saharan Africa, and Southern Africa in particular.

Geographical Area of Activity: Africa.

Publications: Annual Report; *AISA Newsletter*; *AISA Brochure*; *Political Reforms in the Arab World*; *South Africa's Foreign Direct Investment in Africa*; *Somalia Peace Process*; *Elite Conflict in Botswana*; *Exploring Islamic Fundamentalist Ideologies in Africa*; *The New Partnership for Africa's Development*; *Defence, Militarism, Peace Building and Human Security in Africa*; *The Nature of the Conflict in Sudan*; *The Mazruiana Collection Revisited*; *The Social Sciences in South Africa Since 1994*; *Africa at a Glance 2006/2007*; *AISA Focus* (monthly newsletter).

Finance: Annual income 35,887,861 rand, expenditure 30,525,457 rand (2013).

Council: Dr Bekumuzi Hlatshwayo (Chair.).

Principal Staff: Exec. Dir Dr Thandi Sidzumo-Mazibuko.

Address: Bag X41, Pretoria 0001; HSRC Bldg, 134 Pretorious St, Pretoria 0002.

Telephone: (12) 3049700; **Fax:** (12) 3213164; **Internet:** www.ai .org.za; **e-mail:** bsuhlane@ai.org.za.

Eskom Development Foundation

Established in 1998.

Activities: Aims to contribute to the well-being of disadvantaged South Africans through the development and implementation of integrated and efficient social investment programmes. The Foundation focuses on poverty alleviation, income generation, job creation and social well-being. It is active in underdeveloped areas, particularly rural regions and new urban settlements, in all the provinces of South Africa. It supports social projects by offering donations and providing grants to enable economic development.

Geographical Area of Activity: South Africa.

Finance: Annual funds disbursed 87.9m. rand (31 March 2012).

Principal Staff: CEO Haylene Liberty.

Address: POB 1091, Johannesburg 2001; Eskom Megawatt Park, 2 Maxwell Dr., Sunninghill, Sandton, Johannesburg 2000.

Telephone: (11) 8008111; **Fax:** (11) 8002246; **Internet:** www .eskom.co.za/csi; **e-mail:** csi@eskom.co.za.

EWT—Endangered Wildlife Trust

Founded in 1973 as a non-profit NGO that aims to conserve the diversity of species in Southern Africa. It is a fully-accredited NGO member of the IUCN—World Conservation Union (q.v.).

Activities: Promotes the conservation of biological diversity in Southern Africa; conducts research; organizes practical conservation campaigns; aims to raise public awareness of conservation and environmental issues; and issues publications.

Geographical Area of Activity: Southern Africa.

Publications: *Vision* (annually); *EWT* (magazine); *Environment—people and conservation in Africa* (quarterly magazine); *Vulture News* (twice a year); *The Grus Grapevine; Indwa; Gabar.*

Board of Trustees: Dirk Ackermann (Chair.); Uwe Putlitz (Vice-Chair.); Paul Smith (Treas.).

Principal Staff: CEO Yolan Friedmann; COO Mandy Poole.

Address: Private Bag X11, Modderfontein, 1609, Gauteng; Bldg K2, Pinelands Office Park, Ardeer Rd, Modderfontein, 1645, Gauteng.

Telephone: (11) 3723600; **Fax:** (11) 6084682; **Internet:** www .ewt.org.za; **e-mail:** ewt@ewt.org.za.

FirstRand Foundation

Established in 1998 to support social causes and initiatives conducive to development, including educational as well as HIV/AIDS-combative initiatives. The Foundation receives an annual contribution of 1% from the after-tax profits of the FirstRand group companies (First National Bank—FNB, Momentum, FirstRand, Wesbank and Rand Merchant Bank—RMB).

Activities: Funding is categorized into four sections with each section focusing on specific areas. The Discovery Fund focuses on primary health care; the FNB Fund is concerned with safe community initiatives, education, hospice programmes, development of skill base and job creation; the Momentum Fund assists support programmes for those with AIDS, disabled people and early childhood issues; and the RMB Fund is aimed at conservation and the environment, community care projects, and art, music and culture.

Geographical Area of Activity: South Africa.

Publications: Annual Report.

Board of Trustees: Sizwe Nxasana (Chair.).

Address: POB 61713, Marshalltown 2107.

Telephone: (11) 3777360; **Fax:** (11) 8343682; **Internet:** www .firstrandfoundation.org.za; **e-mail:** firstrandfoundation@tsi .org.za.

Gift of the Givers Foundation

Established in 1992 by Dr Imtiaz Sooliman.

Activities: Aims to build bridges between peoples of different cultures and religions engendering goodwill, harmonious co-existence, tolerance and mutual respect; the largest disaster response NGO of African origin on the African continent. The Foundation is active nationally and internationally. It provides education, health care and humanitarian programmes; and supports a range of different projects, including bursaries for international study, HIV/AIDS workshops and anti-drug campaigns in South Africa. It has also funded projects in Afghanistan, Bosnia and Herzegovina, Chechnya, Haiti, India, Iran, Malawi, Mozambique, the Palestinian Territories, Rwanda, Somalia, Sudan and Turkey. In 2002, the Foundation launched the Millions for Africa Campaign. Other campaigns include South Africans Helping South Africans, which promotes corporate social responsibility in South Africa. It has branches in Johannesburg, Cape Town and Durban and an additional country office in Malawi.

Geographical Area of Activity: Worldwide.

Principal Staff: Chair. and Dir Dr Imtiaz Sooliman.

Address: 290 Prince Alfred St, Pietermaritzburg.

Telephone: (33) 3450175; **Fax:** (33) 3427489; **Internet:** www .giftofthegivers.org; **e-mail:** info@giftofthegivers.org; southafrica@giftofthegivers.org.

Global Water Foundation

Founded in 2005 by Johan Kriek and Minnie Hildebrand to provide technical assistance, facilitate the sharing of information and support technical innovation to provide humanitarian aid to the developing world.

Activities: Operates in the areas of aid and development to help provide sources of safe drinking water and sanitation. The Foundation has offices in Florida and North Carolina, USA.

Geographical Area of Activity: Africa.

Restrictions: Grants strictly limited to water and sanitation-related programmes and projects.

Principal Staff: Exec. Dirs Minnie Hildebrand, Johan Kriek.

Address: Chedza House, 95 Jan Smuts Ave, Saxonwold 2196, Johannesburg.

Telephone: (11) 4772441; **Internet:** www .globalwaterfoundation.org.

Lifeline Energy

Established in 1999 in the United Kingdom, as the Freeplay Foundation, to promote alternative energy sources in the developing world to assist the poor to access information sources. Present name adopted in 2010.

Activities: Created and distributes wind-up and solar-powered radios and media players, and renewable lighting. Has offices in the United Kingdom and the USA.

Geographical Area of Activity: Less-developed countries.

Publications: Newsletter.

Finance: Established Lifeline Technologies Trading Ltd in 2010; company profits revert to the charity in the form of dividend payments.

Board: Arthur Johnson (Chair.).

Principal Staff: CEO Kristine Pearson.

Address: 76 Arnold St, Observatory, Cape Town 7925.

Telephone: (21) 4476397; **Fax:** (86) 2197967; **Internet:** www .lifelineenergy.org; **e-mail:** fundraising@lifelineenergy.org.

Nelson Mandela Children's Fund

Established in 1994 by Nelson Mandela, who contributed one-third of his salary to the Fund for five years. The Fund works towards the empowerment and well-being of children and youth.

Activities: Supports children to combat poor economic and social circumstances, abuse and exploitation; supports the disadvantaged by providing education, counselling and care; focuses on initiatives pertaining to child welfare, leadership, disability, and education and development; works in partnership with similar organizations to implement projects empowering and bettering the lives of children and youth; advocates children and youth rights through awareness programmes and utilizing influence of public policies; and supports HIV/AIDS-affected children and families coping with debilitating illnesses. The Fund has offices in several countries including, the USA and the United Kingdom. It also operates in association with Nelson Mandela Children's Fund—in Canada, an independently-registered welfare organization.

Geographical Area of Activity: South Africa.

Publications: Annual Report; newsletter.

Finance: Annual income 94,960,000 rand, expenditure 42,579,000 rand (31 March 2014).

Board of Trustees: Judge Yvonne Mokgoro (Chair.).

Principal Staff: CEO Sibongile Mkhabela.

Address: 21 Eastwold Way, Saxonwold, POB 797, Highlands North, Johannesburg 2037.

Telephone: (11) 2745600; **Fax:** (11) 4863914; **Internet:** www .nelsonmandelachildrensfund.com; **e-mail:** tshidik@nmcf.co .za.

Nelson Mandela Foundation

Established following Nelson Mandela's retirement on 19 August 1999 to lead the development of a living legacy that captured the vision and values of his life and work: the spirit of reconciliation, *ubuntu* and social justice.

Activities: Core business is memory and dialogue work, with the key institutional vehicle being the Nelson Mandela Centre of Memory and Dialogue. In 2009, together with its sister charities the Foundation initiated Mandela Day, which takes place on 18 July every year, as a way of galvanizing members of the public towards community service. The UN has since declared it Nelson Mandela Internatonal Day.

Geographical Area of Activity: South Africa.

Publications: Financial reports; news; educational publications on the life and times of Nelson Mandela; publications on ongoing memory and dialogue work.

Finance: Annual income 26,265,151 rand, expenditure 31,676,006 rand (28 Feb. 2013).

Board of Trustees: Prof. Njabulo Ndebele (Chair.).

Principal Staff: CEO Sello Hatang.

Address: Private Bag X70000, Houghton 2041; 107 Central St, Houghton 2198.

Telephone: (11) 5475600; **Fax:** (11) 7281111; **Internet:** www .nelsonmandela.org; **e-mail:** nmf@nelsonmandela.org.

The Mandela Rhodes Foundation

Established by Nelson Mandela in 2002, in partnership with the Rhodes Trust (q.v.), to build exceptional leadership capacity in Africa.

Activities: Operating in the field of education, specifically postgraduate study in Africa, the Foundation awards scholarships on academic and leadership merit for Masters and Honours degrees at accredited South African tertiary education institutions. The Mandela Rhodes scholarship is open to applicants of any gender, race, culture, religion, class and field of academic study, aged 19–30 years and a citizen of an African country. Leadership development is promoted and supported by four supplementary residential courses annually and a mentor system.

Geographical Area of Activity: Africa.

Publications: Annual Yearbook.

Finance: Fund-raising toward a full endowment structure. Also Black Economic Empowerment partnership with Oxford University Press. Total assets 431,369,429 rand (31 Dec. 2013).

Board of Trustees: Prof. Njabulo Ndebele (Chair.).

Principal Staff: Exec. Dir Shaun Johnson.

Address: The Mandela Rhodes Bldg, 150 St George's Mall, Cape Town 8001, POB 15897, Vlaeberg 8018.

Telephone: (21) 4243346; **Fax:** (21) 4249617; **Internet:** www .mandelarhodes.org; **e-mail:** info@mandelarhodes.org.za.

Motsepe Foundation

Established in 1999 by Patrice Motsepe, founder and Exec. Chair. of African Rainbow Minerals (f. 1994), a mining company, and his wife Dr Precious Moloi Motsepe.

Activities: Promotes social and economic welfare at the community level through education and better health. Its main fields of interest are economic empowerment, women's empowerment, education and leadership, and sports. Provides scholarships for tertiary education and business grants to young entrepreneurs. Works with community- and faith-based organizations.

Geographical Area of Activity: South Africa.

Restrictions: Grants are awarded in the following areas: the arts and music; education; sport; traditional councils; women- or youth-owned businesses and co-operatives; workers'

organizations; public benefit organizations, religious organizations and NGOs.

Finance: In 2013, Patrice Motsepe signed Bill Gates' and Warren Bufett's Giving Pledge to give one-half of the income from his assets to philanthropic causes.

Address: 29 Impala Rd, Chislehurston, Johannesburg.

Telephone: (11) 7791520; **Fax:** (86) 5333127; **Internet:** www .motsepefoundation.org; **e-mail:** info@motsepefoundation .org.

NRF—National Research Foundation

Established in 1999 by the South African Government, replacing the former Foundation for Research Development, to support and promote research through funding, human resource development and the provision of the necessary research facilities to facilitate the creation of knowledge, innovation and development in all fields of science and technology, including indigenous knowledge, and thereby to contribute to the improvement of the quality of life of all the people of South Africa.

Activities: Offers research grants, scholarships and bursaries to researchers and students at the country's higher education institutions. All support programmes give high priority to the development of black and female researchers and building research capacity at previously disadvantaged institutions. The Foundation focuses on the development of skills and research related to South Africa's indigenous knowledge systems. Research and research skills are promoted across many disciplines; including natural sciences and engineering, agricultural and environmental sciences, health sciences, and social sciences and the humanities. Seven national research facilities also offer opportunities for research, advanced training and international collaboration. The Foundation also promotes collaboration between disciplines and institutions through international agreements and exchange programmes. Several research-related databases are maintained.

Geographical Area of Activity: South Africa.

Restrictions: Training of human resources through grants essential.

Publications: Annual Report; newsletter; research publications of national facilities; manuals and guidelines.

Finance: Total assets 2,480,337,000 rand; annual income 3,225,562,000 rand, expenditure 2,805,027,000 (2013/14).

Board of Directors: Prof. Loyiso Nongxa (Chair.); Magda Marx (Sec.).

Principal Staff: Deputy CEO Dr Gansen Pillay.

Address: Meiring Naudé Rd, Brummeria, POB 2600, Pretoria 0001.

Telephone: (12) 4814000; **Fax:** (12) 3491179; **Internet:** www .nrf.ac.za; **e-mail:** info@nrf.ac.za.

Open Society Foundation for South Africa—OSF-SA

Founded in 1993 by George Soros to support the promotion and protection of human rights and open, democratic society; an independent foundation, part of the Open Society Foundations network.

Activities: Operates in the fields of civil society, law and criminal justice, public health, youth and women, democracy building, economic reform, and information and the media.

Geographical Area of Activity: South Africa.

Publications: Annual Report; *Economic Justice and Development Programme*; *Criminal Justice Initiative*; *Human Rights and Governance Programme*; *Media Programme*; *Sentencing in South Africa—Conference Report* (2006); *The Effect of Sentencing on the Size of the South African Prison Population* (2006); *The Impact of Minimum Sentencing in South Africa* (2006).

Board of Directors: Isaac Oupa Shongwe (Chair.).

Principal Staff: Exec. Dir Fatima Hassan.

Address: POB 143, Howard Pl., Pinelands 7430; 2nd Floor, B2, Park Lane, c/o Park Rd and Alexandra Rd, Pinelands, Cape Town 7405.

Telephone: (21) 5111679; **Fax:** (21) 5115058; **Internet:** www.osf .org.za; **e-mail:** admin@osfsa.org.za.

Pitseng Trust

Established in 1998 by a group of women from historically disadvantaged communities; aims to facilitate, through funding, the work of autonomous women's organizations and groups striving to transform the subordinate condition of women in the socio-economic, political and cultural life of South Africa society.

Activities: Provides funding to women's community organizations, NGOs and grassroots organizations working in South Africa's most disadvantaged areas. The Trust also gives seed funding to new women's groups that adopt innovative and change-orientated strategies to attain human rights for women.

Geographical Area of Activity: South Africa.

Board of Trustees: Syriana Maesela (Chair.); Pani Tyalimpi (Treas.).

Principal Staff: Exec. Dir Dr Oshadi Maphefo Jane Mangena; Contact Fikile Dhlamini.

Address: Majestic Towers, 38 Empire Rd, 6th Floor, Room 605, Parktown Ext. 1, Johannesburg 2193.

Telephone: (11) 4847371; **Fax:** (86) 6698312.

SAASTA—South African Agency for Science and Technology Advancement

Established in 1955 to increase knowledge and understanding of the sciences; known as the Foundation for Education, Science and Technology—FEST until 2002.

Activities: A business unit of South Africa's National Research Foundation. The Agency promotes understanding of and engagement with science, engineering and technology among all South Africans; encourages young people into careers in science, technology and innovation; interacts with the public on issues of science, engineering and technology; and communicates advances in science and technology to the public.

Geographical Area of Activity: South Africa.

Publications: Newsletters; leaflets; posters; brochures.

Principal Staff: Man. Dir Dr Jabu Nukeri.

Address: POB 1758, Pretoria 0001; Didacta Bldg, 211 Skinner St, Pretoria.

Telephone: (12) 3929300; **Fax:** (12) 3207803; **Internet:** www .saasta.ac.za; **e-mail:** info@saasta.ac.za.

Shuttleworth Foundation

Set up in 2010 by Mark Shuttleworth to serve the cause of social development through grant of funds to social development projects and educational institutions.

Activities: Provides funding for leaders who are at the forefront of social change. The Foundation invests in initiatives and individuals who challenge the status quo and positively contribute to change. Fellowship grants are awarded to social innovators who are helping to change the world for the better. The Foundation is an experiment in open philanthropy and uses alternative funding methodologies, new technologies and collaborative ways of working to ensure that every initiative receives the best exposure and resources to succeed.

Geographical Area of Activity: Worldwide.

Publications: Annual Report.

Finance: Total assets 15,606,965 rand (Feb. 2010).

Trustees: Mark Shuttleworth (Founder).

Principal Staff: Chief Exec. Helen Turvey.

Address: POB 4615, Durbanville, Cape Town 7551.

Telephone: (21) 9701204; **Fax:** (21) 86 609 9205; **Internet:** www.shuttleworthfoundation.org; **e-mail:** info@ shuttleworthfoundation.org.

South African Institute of International Affairs

Founded in 1934 as an independent NGO to perform a public educational role by promoting an understanding of international questions, especially South Africa's foreign relations.

Activities: Key research areas are: South African foreign policy and African driver countries; governance and the African Peer Review Mechanism; governance of Africa's resources; economic diplomacy; relations of existing and emerging powers to Africa; and current global challenges. The Institute's activities include programmes of empirical research in-country, fellowships and awards, study and discussion groups, lectures, public addresses, conferences, symposia and publications. It maintains a library and information service, and runs a youth development programme. It has branches in East London, Pietermaritzburg and the Western Cape.

Geographical Area of Activity: Majority of research work conducted across Africa.

Publications: Annual Report; *South African Journal of International Affairs* (2 a year); occasional papers; special studies; reports; videos; podcasts; newsletters.

Finance: Annual revenue 27,173,276 rand, expenditure 27,728,677 rand (30 June 2011).

Council: Fred Phaswana (Chair.); Moeletsi Mbeki (Deputy Chair.); John Buchanan (Hon. Treas.).

Principal Staff: Chief Exec. Elizabeth Sidiropoulos.

Address: POB 31596, Braamfontein 2017; Jan Smuts House, East Campus, University of the Witwatersrand, Johannesburg.

Telephone: (11) 3392021; **Fax:** (11) 3392154; **Internet:** www .saiia.org.za; **e-mail:** info@saiia.org.za.

South African Institute of Race Relations

Founded in 1929 to encourage peace, goodwill and practical co-operation between the various races in South Africa, and to promote a free and open society based on liberal democratic values.

Activities: Conducts research on macro-economic, socio-economic, labour, constitutional and political trends, as well as on race relations in South Africa. The Institute also oversees a large bursary programme for students at universities and technikons, and provides a consultancy service.

Geographical Area of Activity: South Africa.

Publications: Annual Report; *South Africa Survey* (annually); *Fast Facts* (monthly); *Spotlight Series* (occasional); news releases, *South Africa Mirror* (briefing).

Finance: Annual income 11,483,659 rand, annual expenditure 12,691,777 rand (31 Dec. 2014).

Council: Prof. Jonathan Jansen; (Pres.); Prof. Hermann Giliomee (Vice-Pres.); **Board of Directors:** Theo Coggin.

Principal Staff: Chief Exec. Frans Cronje.

Address: POB 291722, Melville 2109; 2 Clamart Rd, Richmond, Johannesburg 2092.

Telephone: (11) 4827221; **Fax:** (11) 4827690; **Internet:** www .sairr.org.za; **e-mail:** prisca@sairr.org.za.

The Helen Suzman Foundation

Established in 1995 to promote liberal constitutional democracy and human rights in South Africa and other Southern African countries.

Activities: Promotes the values that underpin the liberal constitutional democracy and respect for human rights. The Foundation's research focuses on education, health, economic policy and wealth creation, institutional governance and South Africa's regional impact.

Geographical Area of Activity: Southern Africa.

Restrictions: Not a grantmaking organization.

Publications: *Focus* (quarterly); various monographs based on round tables and conferences.

Principal Staff: Dir Francis Antonie; Man. Rob Hewitt.

Address: Postnet Suite 130, Private Bag X2600, Houghton 2041; 2 Sherborne Rd, Parktown 2193.

Telephone: (11) 4822872; **Fax:** (11) 4828468; **Internet:** www .hsf.org.za; **e-mail:** roshan@hsf.org.za.

Transnet Foundation

Established in 1994 by Transnet, South Africa's government-owned transport and logistics organization, to promote initiatives conducive to organizational and national sustainability and development.

Activities: The goals of the Foundation are concomitant with the Government's integrated sustainable rural development (ISRDP) programme, which focuses on job creation; socio-economic development; transport heritage preservation; economic empowerment of black people; human capital development; and expanded public works programmes. The Foundation also supports projects in the areas of health, arts and culture, education, sports and under-used assets.

Geographical Area of Activity: South Africa.

Restrictions: No grants are made to individuals, or small groups in their personal capacity, political parties or groups with partisan political affiliations, professional fund-raising institutions, religious organizations for sectarian activities, institutions or bodies that are racially exclusive, profit-making concerns, trade unions, research projects, or for travel.

Board: Nunu R. Njeke (Chair.).

Principal Staff: Foundation Head Cynthia Mgijima.

Address: POB 72501, Parkview, Johannesburg 2122; 24th Floor, Carlton Centre, 150 Commissioner St, Johannesburg 2001.

Telephone: (11) 3082488; **Fax:** (11) 3082573; **Internet:** www .transnetfoundation.co.za; **e-mail:** eleanor.mthethwa@ transnet.net.

Desmond and Leah Tutu Legacy Foundation

Established as an umbrella organization for all the initiatives that bear the names of Desmond Tutu and Leah Tutu.

Activities: Aims to promote peace through conflict resolution and to foster reconciliation; to cultivate accountable leadership; to promote mutual respect and tolerance nationally and internationally; and to enhance the health and well-being of people and the planet.

Geographical Area of Activity: International.

Principal Staff: Exec. Dir Rev. Mpho A. Tutu.

Address: POB 1092, Milnerton, 7435 Cape Town; Suite 62 Frazzitta Business Park, Koeberg Rd and Freedom Way, Milnerton 7441.

Telephone: (21) 5527524; **Fax:** (21) 5527529; **Internet:** www .tutu.org.za; **e-mail:** info@tutu.org.za.

WHEAT Trust—Women's Hope Education and Training Trust

Established in 1988 on Women's Day with the aim of identifying and assisting women whose initiatives within their communities have a clear potential to transform, and promoting a culture of giving towards women's development initiatives.

Activities: Operates through sourcing donations to an endowment fund to pay for the training and education of individual women leaders or group members of viable community groups led by women, as well as supporting projects for women operating at grassroots level. Target areas for support are projects in the fields of health and social services, education, promotion of small, medium and micro enterprises, human rights and housing, and domestic violence.

Geographical Area of Activity: South Africa.

Publications: Newsletter.

Finance: Total assets 3,090,498 rand (Feb. 2011); annual income 1,861,721 rand, expenditure 2,015,390 rand (29 Feb. 2012).

Board of Trustees: Mpho Mashengete (Chair.).

Principal Staff: Exec. Dir Soraya Matthews.

Address: POB 18046, Wynberg, 7824 Western Cape; 4 Devonshire Ct, 20 Devonshire Rd, Wynberg, 7800 Western Cape.

Telephone: (21) 7626214; **Fax:** (21) 7972876; **Internet:** www .wheattrust.co.za; **e-mail:** communications@wheattrust.co .za.

WWF South Africa

A national organization of the WWF (q.v.), and until 1995 known as the Southern African Nature Foundation, which aims to assist in the protection and conservation of nature; raise awareness among the general public of nature conservation; and distribute and raise funds for urgent nature conservation projects in Southern Africa.

Activities: Works in South Africa to promote the conservation of natural resources to preserve species, and genetic and ecosystem diversity, through encouraging sustainable use of resources; lowering pollution; and supporting projects on freshwater, grasslands, flora and marine conservation. The Fund has assisted in the creation or development of 23 protected areas and 11 national parks; and has managed or funded more than 1,000 conservation projects, which include plant conservation projects and projects devised to save more than 70 species of endangered animals.

Geographical Area of Activity: South Africa.

Restrictions: Funding is restricted to South African conservation activities that fall within WWF South Africa's strategic focus.

Publications: Annual Report; *Panda Bulletin* (3 a year); *Living Planet Report (*2006); *State of Marine Protected Area Management in South Africa*; *Stock Assessment of Reef Fish Species along the Coast of the Cape Peninsula National Park*; *Status of Swordfish report in South Africa*; *Business Plan for the proposed Kogelberg Marine Park*; *Education in Africa Booklet; Coal & Water Futures in South Africa.*

Finance: Funded by membership fees, donations and sponsorship. Annual income 95,199,000 rand, disbursements 90,460,000 rand (30 June 2014).

Board: Valli Moosa (Chair.).

Principal Staff: CEO Dr Morné du Plessis.

Address: POB 23273, Claremont 7735; 1st Floor, Bridge House, Boundary Terraces, Mariendahl Lane, Newlands, Cape Town.

Telephone: (27) 216576600; **Internet:** www.wwf.org.za; **e-mail:** info@wwf.org.za.

Spain

FOUNDATION CENTRES AND CO-ORDINATING BODIES

Asociación Española de Fundaciones (Spanish Association of Foundations)

Established in 2003 following the merger of the Confederación Española de Fundaciones and the Centro de Fundaciones, to form a collective association of 1,050 member foundations.

Activities: Provides a forum for foundations and represents their common interests and needs to society, the media and the Government; co-ordinates initiatives and resolves problems. The Association promotes co-operation between foundations nationally and internationally, sharing experience and allowing co-ordinated work. It advises foundations on a range of legal, fiscal, economic, financial and telecommunication issues; operates training courses, conferences and seminars; and maintains a database of foundations and other funding sources. It represents the foundation sector in Spanish society, aiming to portray Spanish non-profit entities in a transparent and accurate manner.

Geographical Area of Activity: Spain.

Publications: *Cuadernos de la Asociación Española de Fundaciones* (quarterly); *Tribuna de las Fundaciones* (monthly bulletin); monographs; electronic bulletin; Annual Report.

Finance: Total assets €290,693 (2012).

Board of Directors: SAR Don Carlos de Borbón (Hon. Pres.); Javier Nadal Ariño (Pres.); Amadeo Petitbò Juan, Patricia Moreira Sánchez, Carlos Álvarez Jiménez, (Vice-Pres); Adolfo Menéndez Menéndez (Sec.); Íñigo Sáenz de Miera Cárdenas (Treas.).

Principal Staff: Dir-Gen. Silverio Agea Rodríguez.

Address: Calle Rafael Calvo, 18 – 4º B, 28010 Madrid.

Telephone: 91-310-63-09; **Fax:** 91-578-36-23; **Internet:** www.fundaciones.org; **e-mail:** info@fundaciones.org.

Foro Ubuntu (World Forum of Civil Society Networks—UBUNTU)

Constituted in 2001 within the UNESCO Chair in Technology, Sustainable Development, Imbalances and Global Change at the Technical University of Catalonia.

Activities: Promotes peace and human development in line with the principles established in the Universal Declaration of Human Rights. The Forum convenes annually or biennially.

Geographical Area of Activity: Worldwide.

Restrictions: No grants available.

Publications: Newsletter (quarterly); International Conference reports; Secretariat Position Document (2006); and other reports.

Finance: Funded by the Catalan Government, Barcelona City Council, Technical University of Catalonia and the Foundation for a Culture of Peace. Annual budget €200,000.

Board: Federico Mayor Zaragoza (Chair.).

Principal Staff: Dir Manuel Manonelles: Policy and Exec. Officer Janira Tor.

Address: Secretariado del Foro UBUNTU, Calle Jordi Girona 29, Nexus II (UPC), 08034 Barcelona.

Telephone: 93-413-77-80; **Fax:** 93-413-77-77; **Internet:** ubuntu.org; **e-mail:** info@ubuntu.upc.edu.

Fundación Lealtad (Loyalty Foundation)

Established in 2001 by a group of civic-minded businesspeople in Spain to promote trust among private donors and companies in NGOs active in the areas of social services, international development, humanitarian aid and environmental protection. Promotes donations and volunteer participation by individuals and the businesses in such NGOs.

Activities: Monitors the compliance of NGOs with nine standards of transparency and best practices; provides self-assessment and improvement workshops for NGOs that are not yet being monitored. The Foundation works with companies and corporate foundations with an interest in financing or working with NGOs in the framework of their social commitment strategy, and has developed several tools that help companies carry out their strategy. Also offers private donors specific knowledge and insight into charitable entities that have been monitored. The Foundation supports two projects in Mexico and Chile involving the adaptation of Spanish NGO analysis methodology in those countries. A member of the International Committee on Fundraising Organizations (ICFO).

Geographical Area of Activity: Chile, Mexico and Spain.

Publications: Annual Report; e-newsletter; *Solidarity Transparency*; *Transparency and Best Practices Guide to Spanish NGOs* (online); guides and other publications.

Finance: Total assets €363,534 (31 Dec. 2013).

Board of Trustees: Salvador García-Atance Lafuente (Chair.); Ignacio Garralda Ruiz de Velasco (Vice-Chair.); Cecilia Plañiol Lacalle (Treas.).

Principal Staff: Exec. Dir and Sec. Patricia de Roda García.

Address: Calle Velazquez 100, 1º dcha., 28006 Madrid.

Telephone: 91-789-01-23; **Fax:** 91-789-01-13; **Internet:** www.fundacionlealtad.org; **e-mail:** fundacion@fundacionlealtad.org.

FOUNDATIONS, TRUSTS AND NON-PROFIT ORGANIZATIONS

Anesvad

Founded in 1968 by José Luis Gamarra Aranoa to undertake health care and social development projects in less-developed countries.

Activities: Aims to balance the inequities between South and North and to promote sustainable development in less favoured countries and sectors. The organization works in the area of development co-operation, primarily in the health-care field, in particular those activities aimed at eliminating leprosy, Buruli's ulcer and other diseases that affect the most vulnerable groups of poor societies. Also considers social and educational projects related to children facing sexual exploitation or in emergency situations. It has an office in Madrid.

Geographical Area of Activity: Africa, Central and South America, Asia and Europe.

Publications: Magazines; leaflets; brochures; annual report.

Finance: Annual income €12,430,000, expenditure €18,508,000 (2012).

Board of Directors: Garbiñe Biurrun (Chair.).

Principal Staff: Gen. Man. Bernardo García Izquierdo.

Address: General Concha, 28 – 1º, Entrada calle Egaña, 48010 Bilbao.

Telephone: 94-44-18-008; **Fax:** 94-441-07-39; **Internet:** www.anesvad.org; **e-mail:** anesvad@anesvad.org.

Educo

Established in 2013 by the merger of Fundación Intervida (f. 1995) and Educación Sin Fronteras (f. 1988).

Activities: Priority areas are children and children's rights, in particular the right to a good quality education.

Geographical Area of Activity: Central and South America, West Africa, South Asia and South-East Asia.

Publications: Newsletter.

Finance: Total assets €118,999,000 (2012).

Board of Trustees: Julio Molinario Valls (Chair.); José M. Faura Messa (Vice-Chair.); Marcos Mas Rauchwerk (Sec.).

Principal Staff: Dir Josep M. Faura.

Address: Calle Pujades 77–79, 4°, 08005 Barcelona.

Telephone: 90-219-19-19; **Fax:** 93-309-68-68; **Internet:** www .educo.org; www.intervida.org; **e-mail:** educo@educo.org.

FRIDE—Fundación para las Relaciones Internacionales y el Diálogo Exterior (FRIDE—A European Think Tank for Global Action)

Established in 1999.

Activities: Conducts research and analysis, with a focus on: development co-operation; security and conflict; Europe and the international system; and democracy and human rights policies.

Geographical Area of Activity: Worldwide.

Publications: *Foreign Policy en Español* (online journal); *Challenges for European Foreign Policy in 2012; What kind of geo-economic Europe?*; numerous reports on international affairs; policy brief series; working papers series.

Board of Trustees: Diego Hidalgo (Founder and Hon. Pres.); Pedro Solbes (Pres.); José Manuel Romero (Vice-Pres.); Belén Galindo (Sec.).

Principal Staff: Dir Giovanni Grevi; Dep. Dir Magdalena Segre.

Address: Calle Felipe IV 9, 1° derecha, 28014 Madrid.

Telephone: 91-244-47-40; **Fax:** 91-244-47-41; **Internet:** www .fride.org; **e-mail:** fride@fride.org.

FUHEM Ecosocial

Established in 1984 by FUHEM (q.v.), a private NGO involved in conducting research in the fields of peace, ecology and education, and publishing the results of research. Formerly known as the Centro de Investigación para la Paz, CIP. Present name adopted in 2007.

Activities: Conducts research; publishes research findings; organizes conferences and seminars, and training courses for educating school teachers on peace; co-operates with international peace centres; maintains a documentation centre comprising 5,000 publications, and a press and communications office. The organization participates in national as well as international forums and networks. In 1988, it was awarded the Messengers of Peace award by the UN.

Geographical Area of Activity: Spain.

Publications: Annual Report; *Boletín ECOS; Guerra y Paz en el comienzo del siglo XXI; De Nueva York a Kabul; Políticas mundiales, tendencias peligrosas; Anuario sobre paz, militarización y conflictos; Papeles para la Paz; Colección de Economía Crítica* (series); *Ecología Política; CIP Reports on Peace and Ecology*; numerous books on peace studies and ecology.

Finance: Total assets €22,169,081 (31 Dec. 2011).

Principal Staff: Dir Santiago Álvarez Cantalapiedra; Sec. Carmen de Juan García.

Address: Calle Duque de Sesto 40, 28009 Madrid.

Telephone: 91-431-02-80; **Fax:** 91-577-33-13; **Internet:** www .fuhem.es/ecosocial; **e-mail:** fuhem@fuhem.es.

Fundació Agrupació Mútua (Agrupació Foundation)

Established in 1993 to promote social welfare.

Activities: Offers support to the elderly, children, young people and disabled people; promotes healthy living and personal autonomy; social and humanist programmes.

Geographical Area of Activity: Spain.

Finance: Total funds disbursed €65,000 (2013).

Board of Trustees: Josep Lluís Vilaseca Guasch (Chair.); Josep Verde Aldea (Treas.); Montserrat Serrallonga Sivilla (Sec.).

Principal Staff: Dir Imma Playà Pujols.

Address: Gran Via de les Corts Catalans 619, 08010 Barcelona.

Telephone: 93-482-67-01; **Fax:** 93-482-67-00; **Internet:** www .fundacioagrupacio.es; **e-mail:** fundacio@agrupacio.es.

Fundació Bancària 'La Caixa' ('La Caixa' Foundation)

Established in 1991 following the merger of Fundació Caixa de Barcelona and Fundació Caixa de Pensions.

Activities: Aims to address social needs unaddressed by other organizations in the areas of social aid, education, health care, science and culture, through self-devised programmes as well as through programmes carried out in collaboration with other organizations in Spain as well as in other countries where La Caixa savings bank operates. The Foundation manages funds allotted for social welfare by Caja de Ahorros y Pensiones de Barcelona. It runs two proprietary science museums, an art gallery exhibiting a collection of contemporary art, and a school of nursing.

Geographical Area of Activity: Spain and international, in countries where La Caixa operates.

Publications: *Estrella* (6 a year); Annual Report; brochures.

Finance: Funded by the Caixa d'Estalvis i Pensions de Barcelona. Welfare projects expenditure €361,015,000 (2012).

Board of Trustees: Isidre Fainé Casas (Chair.); Alejandro García-Bragado Dalmau (Vice-Chair and Asst Sec.); Óscar Calderón de Oya (Sec.).

Principal Staff: Exec. Dir Jaume Giró Ribas; Deputy Exec. Dirs Elisa Durán Montolio.

Address: Avda Diagonal 621–629, 08028 Barcelona.

Telephone: 93-404-60-00; **Fax:** 93-339-57-03; **Internet:** www .fundacio.lacaixa.es; obrasocial.lacaixa.es; **e-mail:** info .fundacio@lacaixa.es.

Fundació Jaume Bofill (Jaume Bofill Foundation)

Founded in 1969 by Teresa Roca Formosa and Josep Maria Vilaseca Marcet to encourage initiatives in the social sciences that seek to achieve a deeper understanding of society and to contribute in some tangible way towards its betterment. Merged with the Fundació Serveis de Cultura Popular in 2000.

Activities: Promotes initiatives that work towards a better understanding of society and improving it by eliminating all forms of inequality and discrimination and extending culture and education to those who are socially deprived. The Foundation awards scholarships and individual research grants in sociology, political science, demography, city planning, etc.; makes grants to research teams and centres to further the development of research in these areas; and supports meetings and discussions between social science researchers and co-operates with similar organizations, including those of international scope. Its activities come from the fields selected as a priority for successive four-year periods.

Geographical Area of Activity: Catalonia.

Publications: Newsletter (quarterly, in Catalan); books containing research projects of major contemporary relevance (also in Catalan).

Board of Trustees: Teresa Roca i Formosa (Founder-Pres.); Isabel Vilaseca i Roca (Pres.); Ignasi Carreras i Fisas, Joan Majó i Cruzate (Vice-Pres); Joan Manuel del Pozo i Álvarez (Sec.).

Principal Staff: Dir Ismael Palacín i Giner; Deputy Dir Josep Maria Bayer; Man. Eva Queralt Huguet.

Address: Provença 324, 08037 Barcelona.

Telephone: 93-458-87-00; **Fax:** 93-458-87-08; **Internet:** www
.fbofill.cat; **e-mail:** fbofill@fbofill.cat.

Fundació CIDOB (CIDOB Foundation)

Established in 1973 as a not-for-profit organization; became a
private foundation in 1979.

Activities: Operates in the areas of development studies, education and international affairs, through self-conducted programmes, research, conferences, training courses and
publications. Fields of interest are international politics, strategic studies, development and co-operation, intercultural
relations, migrations and population and development, with a
geographical focus on the Arab world, Asia, Sub-Saharan
Africa, Central and South America, Central and Eastern Europe, countries of the former USSR, and the Mediterranean
region. The Foundation also maintains a documentation centre.

Geographical Area of Activity: Spain, Latin America, the
Mediterranean and Arab world, Europe and Asia.

Publications: *Anuario Internacional*; *Afers Internationals;
CIDOB News* (monthly newsletter); Annual Report; monographs; yearbooks; books and special reports.

Board of Trustees: Dr Carles A. Gasòliba (Chair.); Javier
Solana Madariaga (Hon. Chair.).

Principal Staff: Dir Jordi Bacaria; Exec. Co-ordinator Anna
Estrada Bertran.

Address: Calle Elisabets 12 (Casa de la Misericòrdia), 08001
Barcelona.

Telephone: 93-302-64-95; **Fax:** 93-302-21-18; **Internet:** www
.cidob.org; **e-mail:** cidob@cidob.org.

Fundación Acción contra el Hambre

Established in 2013 by the merger of Acción contra el Hambre
with Fundación Luis Vives, which was founded in 1987 by the
merger of 11 private foundations.

Activities: Helps people experiencing social problems and
furthers social services through support to not-for-profit organizations. The Foundation offers consulting services and technical support to foundations involved in social services,
especially pertaining to programme design, management and
evaluation; works in collaboration with similar foundations to
support projects promoting social welfare; encourages the
development of new trusts and foundations; provides grants
to organizations to enable participation in international forums and for promoting international liaison; promotes
exchange of research at international level in social welfare
projects; supports and improves the employability of vulnerable young people. It comprises the Luis Vives Centre for
Social Studies.

Geographical Area of Activity: Spain.

Publications: Annual Report; brochures.

Finance: Total assets €72,323,499 (31 Dec. 2012).

Board of Trustees: José Luis Leal (Chair.); Emilio Aragón
(Vice-Chair.); Francisco Javier Ruiz Paredes (Sec.).

Principal Staff: Dir Olivier Longué.

Address: Duque de Sevilla 3, 28002 Madrid.

Telephone: 91-391-53-00; **Fax:** 91-391-53-01; **Internet:** www
.accioncontraelhambre.org; www.fundacionluisvives.org;
e-mail: ach@achesp.org.

Fundación AFIM—Ayuda, Formación e Integración del Discapacitado (Foundation for Assistance, Training and Integration of Disadvantaged People)

Established in 1992 as Fundación AFIM—Ayuda, Formación e
Integración del Minusválido to support the integration of people disadvantaged in society, whether through mental disability or their economic circumstances.

Activities: Promotes the reintegration in society of economically disadvantaged people or people with mental disabilities
through self-conducted and funded programmes in the fields
of training, rehabilitation and cultural visits.

Geographical Area of Activity: Spain.

Publications: Newsletter (quarterly); magazine.

Principal Staff: Dir Patricia Lacasa.

Address: Ctra de La Coruña km 18,200, Edif. D, 1º, 28231 Las
Rozas, Madrid.

Telephone: 91-710-58-58; **Fax:** 91-637-66-49; **Internet:** www
.fundacionafim.org.

Fundación de los Agentes Comerciales de España (Foundation of Spanish Commercial Agents)

Established in 1989 for cultural and social purposes.

Activities: Operates in the areas of economic affairs, education, international affairs and social welfare, nationally and
internationally through self-conducted programmes and conferences, and nationally through grants to individuals and
institutions, prizes and publications.

Geographical Area of Activity: Worldwide.

Publications: *La Gaceta del Agente Comercial* (journal, 6 a
year).

Board of Trustees: Francisco Manuel Maestre Barrajón
(Pres.); Lorenzo Galerón González (Vice-Pres.); Joaquín Pago
Torrén (Treas.); Alvaro Adrián de Castro Suárez (Sec.).

Address: Calle Goya 55, 5º piso, 28001 Madrid.

Telephone: 90-236-69-56; **Fax:** 91-577-00-84; **Internet:** www
.cgac.es; **e-mail:** fundacion.ac@cgac.es.

Fundación Albéniz (Albéniz Foundation)

Established in 1986 by Federico Sopeña, Paloma O'Shea, Elena
G. Botín, J. L. Martínez Marauri, Pedro Robles and Luis
Revenga to support the arts and humanities and education.

Activities: Operates in the areas of the arts and humanities
and education, through self-conducted programmes, research,
scholarships and fellowships, publications and training
courses. The Foundation's principal activities are the Con-
curso Internacional de Piano de Santander Paloma O'Shea,
supporting a music school, maintaining an archive and documentation centre and funding a music academy in Santander.

Geographical Area of Activity: Spain.

Publications: *Rubinstein y España; Albénez*; *Imágenes de la
Música Iberoamericana*; *Imágenes de Isaac Albéniz*.

Board of Trustees: HH Infanta Doña Margarita Duquesa de
Soria (Hon. Pres.); Paloma O'Shea (Pres.); José Luis de Zam-
bade (Sec.).

Address: Calle Requena 1, 28013 Madrid.

Telephone: 91-523-04-19; **Fax:** 91-532-96-61; **Internet:** www
.fundacionalbeniz.com; **e-mail:** fundacion@albeniz.com.

Fundación Alzheimer España—FAE (Alzheimer Spain Foundation)

Founded in 1991 to inform, assess, support and train families
and carers of those suffering from Alzheimer's Disease,
increase the possibilities of early diagnosis and disseminate
information about the disease.

Activities: Operates in the fields of medicine and health and
social welfare and social studies, through training courses,
consultancy, publications and international conferences. The
Foundation is a founding member of Alzheimer Europe. It
works in partnership with the Ministry of Health and a steering committee to develop an adecuate policy for neurodegen-
erative illnesses. Provides training for informal and
professional carers. Works to increase non-pharmacologial
therapies as a daily alternative for patients.

Geographical Area of Activity: Spain.

Publications: *Vivir con la enfermedad de Alzheimer*; *Vivencias
Familiares*; *Como cuidarse de sí mismo-Cuidador principal*;
*Cómo elegir la residencia adecuada al momento de institucionа-
lizar al paciente con EA*; *Proceedings of the European Conference on Alzheimer's Disease and Public Health*; Bulletin
(quarterly). Specificic Radio on-line 'Radio Alzheimer FAE'
designed by and for carers.

Finance: Total annual income c.€1m.

Governing Board: Micheline Antoine Selmes (Pres.); Adolfo Toledano Gasca (Vice-Pres.); Jacques Selmes Van den Bril (Sec.).

Address: Calle Pedro Muguruza 1, 6c, 28036 Madrid.

Telephone: 91-343-11-65; **Fax:** 91-343-11-75; **Internet:** www .alzfae.org; **e-mail:** fae@alzfae.org.

Fundación Carlos de Amberes (Carlos de Amberes Foundation)

Established in 1594 by Carlos de Amberes, a Flemish merchant living in Madrid, to support pilgrims from the then Spanish Low Countries. In 1988 the Foundation adapted its aims from acts of charity to cultural activities, aiming to build a united Europe.

Activities: Operates in the field of the arts and humanities, acting as a cultural link between Spain, Belgium, Luxembourg, France and the Netherlands, through organizing exhibitions, courses, seminars, conferences and music concerts, held at the Foundation's headquarters. Maintains a library specializing in European Union issues and organizes seminars on the construction of a new Europe.

Geographical Area of Activity: Spain.

Publications: *In the name of peace. The war of the Spanish Succession and the Treaties of Madrid, Utrecht, Rastatt and Baden (1713-1715); The Order of the Golden Fleece and its Sovereigns; James Ensor; African migrations; South to South Cooperation; Man Ray Lights and dreams; Monograph Felipe I the Beautiful one; 1506: European chronicles; Verse music; Madrid, mayo 1955 Cas Oorthuys; Anton van Dyck y el arte del grabado; Signos febriles y frágiles: Obra sobre papel de Henri Michaux; Paul Delvaux: Dibujos de una vida; Ceci n' est pas une pomme: Arte contemporáneo en Bélgica, etc.*

Trustees: HH King Juan Carlos (Pres.).

Principal Staff: Pres. Miguel Ángel Aguilar; Sec. Daniel de Busturia.

Address: Calle Claudio Coello 99, 28006 Madrid.

Telephone: 91-435-22-01; **Fax:** 91-578-10-92; **Internet:** www .fcamberes.org; **e-mail:** fca@fcamberes.org.

Fundación Ramón Areces (Ramón Areces Foundation)

Founded in 1976 by Ramón Areces Rodríguez to support scientific and technical research.

Activities: Co-operates with other organizations interested in the promotion and preservation of Spanish culture and scientific research. The Foundation awards research grants for scientific and technical projects, and scholarships to universities and research centres abroad. Its cultural programme includes lectures, symposia, conferences and inter-university courses.

Geographical Area of Activity: Spain.

Publications: Annual Report.

Finance: Annual expenditure approx. US $11m.

Board of Directors: Florencio Lasaga Munárriz (Chair.); Carlos Martínez Echavarría (Sec.).

Principal Staff: Dir Raimundo Pérez-Hernández y Torra.

Address: Calle Vitruvio 5, 28006 Madrid.

Telephone: 91-515-89-80; **Fax:** 91-564-52-43; **Internet:** www .fundacionareces.es; **e-mail:** info@fundacionareces.es.

Fundación Banco Bilbao Vizcaya Argentaria—Fundación BBVA (BBVA Foundation)

Founded in 1988 to create conditions that support discussion on the problems and challenges faced by society. Merged with the Fundación Argentaria in 2000.

Activities: Operates internationally and devotes a special interest to promoting scientific research in the areas of social science, biomedicine and the environment. The Foundation promotes knowledge as the most effective means to address the challenges facing contemporary society (environmental protection, sustainable development, health care, demographic change, globalization, social integration and innovation at the service of expanding opportunities for all members of society). It also seeks to promote analysis, reflection and debate in the areas of economic and international affairs, social science, and science and technology through programmes, conferences, publications and courses in collaboration with other groups and organizations. A series of major awards was launched in 2005, focusing on biodiversity conservation. Prizes are given in Spain and Central and South America to recognize achievement in excellence in scientific research, innovative action in nature conservation, and dissemination of knowledge in the area of environmental preservation.

Geographical Area of Activity: Spain, Europe, the USA, and Central and South America.

Restrictions: Research grants are open to Spanish organizations, but with an emphasis on international co-operation.

Publications: Annual Report; working papers; books; newsletter.

Board of Trustees: Francisco González Rodríguez (Pres.); Domingo Armengol Calvo (Sec.).

Principal Staff: Dir Rafael Pardo Avellaneda.

Address: Plaza de San Nicolás 4, 48005 Bilbao.

Telephone: 94-487-52-52; **Fax:** 94-424-46-21; **Internet:** www .fbbva.es; **e-mail:** informacion@fbbva.es.

Fundación José Miguel de Barandiarán (José Miguel de Barandiaran Foundation)

Established in 1988 by the Sociedad de Estudios Vascos–Eusko Ikaskuntza in conjunction with José Miguel de Barandiaran Ayerbe to promote science and culture.

Activities: Operates through organizing and funding programmes and awarding research grants in the fields of prehistory, archaeology, anthropology and ethnology. Also organizes courses, seminars, conferences and other related activities, and disseminates their results.

Geographical Area of Activity: Spain.

Publications: *Colección Sara; Colección Barandiaran; Yearbook of Eusko Folklore;* catalogues.

Board of Trustees: Josemari Velez de Mendizabal Azkarraga (Pres.); Susana Irigaray Soto (Sec.).

Address: Secretariat: Pedro Asua 2, 2º piso, of. 60, 01008 Vitoria-Gasteiz.

Telephone: 94-514-30-66; **Fax:** 94-514-13-64; **Internet:** www .barandiaranfundazioa.com; **e-mail:** gasteiz@ barandiaranfundazioa.com.

Fundación Barceló (Barceló Foundation)

Established in 1989 by the Barceló Oliver family.

Activities: Focuses on Central America but also provides some grants in Africa and South America. The Foundation operates in the areas of health, research, education, culture and art, aiming to contribute to the upliftment of people and society through its projects and resources. It offers microloans; provides medical equipment and assistance for medical training; extends financial support to housing projects and initiatives conducive to agricultural development; hosts art exhibitions; and extends support to educational projects aimed at developing countries.

Geographical Area of Activity: Central America and South America, Africa, and Mallorca, Spain.

Finance: Total assets €23,845,940 (31 Dec. 2012).

Board of Trustess: Antonia Barceló Tous (Chair.); Gabriel Barceló Oliver (Vice-Chair.); María Antonia Barceló Vadell (Sec.); María Luisa Barceló Vadell (Treas.).

Principal Staff: Dir-Gen. Rafael Torra Torreguitart.

Address: Casa del Marqués de Reguer-Rullán, Calle San Jaime 4, 07012 Palma de Mallorca.

Telephone: 97-172-24-67; **Fax:** 97-172-03-80; **Internet:** www .barcelo.com/barcelofoundation/es_es/home_fundacion.aspx; **e-mail:** fundacion@barcelo.com.

Fundación Barenboim-Said (Barenboim-Said Foundation)

Established in 2004 by the Andalusian regional government to develop a broad project promoting intercultural conciliation through music.

Activities: Promotes peace and reconciliation through music; promotes music education; and operates and promotes music education projects in Andalusia, Israel, Palestinian areas and Arab countries. Initiatives include the West-Eastern Divan Orchestra of musicians from Israel, the Middle East and Spain; the Academy of Orchestral Studies; a music education project in the Palestinian Territories; and an early childhood music education project that operates in Andalusian primary schools. The Foundation has representative offices in Berlin and Ramallah.

Geographical Area of Activity: Israel, the Palestinian Territories, Spain and the Middle East.

Publications: Annual Report; newsletter; *Parallels and Paradoxes*; *Humanism and Democratic Criticism*; *Musical Elaborations*; *Representations of the Intellectual*; *Music and Literature against the grain;* DVDs.

Board of Trustees: Mariam C. Said (Hon. Pres.); Reynaldo Fernández Manzano (Sec.).

Principal Staff: Pres. Daniel Barenboim Schuster; Man. Dir Muriel Páez Rasmussen.

Address: Patio de Banderas 14, 41004 Sevilla.

Telephone: 95-503-73-85; **Fax:** 95-503-73-84; **Internet:** www .barenboim-said.org; **e-mail:** info.fbs@juntadeandalucia.es.

Fundación Pedro Barrié de la Maza (Pedro Barrié de la Maza Foundation)

Founded in 1966 by Pedro Barrié de la Maza, Conde de Fenosa, to promote research in the sciences and in the field of arts and letters; to support deserving Spanish students; to promote the industrialization and prosperity of Spain in general and the Galicia region in particular; and to support charitable, educational and social institutions, prioritizing those in Galicia.

Activities: Operates mainly in Galicia in the fields of education, social welfare and studies, science, medicine and the arts and humanities, through self-conducted programmes, research, grants to individuals and institutions, conferences, courses and publications. The Foundation awards scholarships, prizes and research grants, and has financed the construction and equipment of technical schools and cultural and social institutions. In 1994, it established the Galician Institute of Economic Studies.

Geographical Area of Activity: Galicia, Spain.

Publications: Annual Report; books on humanities and economics; dictionaries.

Finance: Total assets €384,601,794 (31 Dec. 2013).

Board of Trustees: José María Arias Mosquera (Pres.); Pilar Romero Vázquez-Gulías (Vice-Pres.); Vicente Arias Mosquera (Sec.).

Principal Staff: Gen. Dir Javier López Martínez.

Address: Cantón Grande 9, 15003 A Coruña.

Telephone: 98-122-15-25; **Fax:** 98-122-44-48; **Internet:** www .fundacionbarrie.org; **e-mail:** info@fundacionbarrie.org.

Fundación José María Blanc (José María Blanc Foundation)

Established in 1982 by José María Blanc.

Activities: Operates in the field of conservation and the environment, through the study, conservation and promotion of wild fauna and game and their natural habitat. In 1988, the Foundation created the Cañada Real environmental centre in Peralejo, dedicated to the preservation of wildlife and the promotion of environmental education.

Geographical Area of Activity: Spain.

Principal Staff: Founding Pres. José María Blanc Díaz.

Address: Ctra. MV-533, km 16, 28211 Peralejo, Madrid.

Telephone: 91-890-87-48; **Fax:** 91-890-69-80; **Internet:** www .opennature.com; **e-mail:** contacto@opennature.com.

Fundación Marcelino Botín (Botín Foundation)

Established in 1964 by Marcelino Botin Sanz de Sautuola to promote social development in Cantabria, in the north of Spain.

Activities: Aims to stimulate the economic, social and cultural development of society. The Foundation is active in the fields of art and culture, education, science and rural development, supporting creative, progress-making talent and exploring new ways of generating wealth. It focuses primarily on Spain, and particularly on the region of Cantabria, but also on Latin America.

Geographical Area of Activity: Europe and Latin America.

Publications: Library includes a section on Cantabria in historical documents; art, the environment and sustainable development; music and education.

Finance: Annual expenditure €53,174,168 (2013).

Board of Trustees: Emilio Botín (Chair.).

Principal Staff: Exec. Dir and Sec.-Gen. Iñigo Saenz de Miera Cárdenas.

Address: Calle Pedrueca 1, 39003 Santander.

Telephone: 94-222-60-72; **Internet:** www.fundacionbotin .org; **e-mail:** info@fundacionbotin.org.

Fundación de las Cajas de Ahorros—FUNCAS (Foundation of Savings Banks)

Founded in 1968 by the Confederación Española de Cajas de Ahorros to study all scientific matters related to savings and savings banks; its research has been extended to include economics and financial systems, fiscal and taxation law, contemporary history and statistics, with special emphasis on their relation to the field of savings, and to similar European institutions.

Activities: Maintains close links with economic ministries and financial centres. The Foundation has an extensive library, a publishing fund that has produced more than 300 titles and a small grants fund for sustainable development projects in Spain. Awards annual Enrique Fuentes Quintana Prize (€4,000) for doctoral thesis.

Geographical Area of Activity: Spain.

Publications: Annual Report; *Papeles de Economía Española*; *Perspectivas del Sistema Financiero*; *Cuadernos de Información Económica*; *Panorama Social*; *Documentos de Trabajo*; *Economía de las Comunidades Autónomas; Estudios de la Fundación; El futuro del sector bancario;* and other publications.

Board of Trustees: Isidro Fainé Casas (Pres.); José Maria Méndez Álvarez-Cedrón (Vice-Pres.); Fernando Conlledo Lantero (Sec.).

Principal Staff: Dir-Gen. Carlos Ocaña Pérez de Tudela.

Address: Edificio Foro, Calle Caballero de Gracia 28, 28013 Madrid.

Telephone: 91-596-57-18; **Fax:** 91-596-57-96; **Internet:** www .funcas.es; **e-mail:** funcas@funcas.es.

Fundación Eduardo Capa (Eduardo Capa Foundation)

Established in 1998 by Eduardo Capa Sacristán and Julia Sanz Vaca to house the Eduardo Capa sculpture collection.

Activities: Operates in the areas of the arts and humanities, and education, through self-conducted programmes, conferences, training courses and publications; also holds a summer university of sculpture and organizes temporary sculpture exhibitions.

Geographical Area of Activity: Spain.

Publications: Newsletter; catalogues of temporary exhibitions; newsletter.

Finance: Financed by local government.

Principal Staff: Dir Fernando Capa Sanz.

Address: Carretera de Campo Real, 44ᴀ, 28500 Arganda del Rey, Madrid.

Telephone: 91-871-04-63; **Fax:** 91-870-20-16; **Internet:** capaesculturas.com/fundacion-capa; **e-mail:** fundicion@capaesculturas.com.

Fundación Carolina

Established in 2001.

Activities: Promotes cultural, educational and scientific co-operation between Spain and countries of the Organization of Ibero-American States. Since its inception the Foundation has disbursed grants worth a total of €136,717,738.

Geographical Area of Activity: Spain and Central and South America.

Finance: Annual income €18,346,096, expenditure €18,287,877 (31 Dec. 2010).

Board of Trustees: Mariano Rajoy Brey (Exec. Chair.).

Principal Staff: Dir Jesús Andreu Ardura; Sec.-Gen. and Man. Gustavo Rovira Salinas.

Address: Calle Gen. Rodrigo, 6, 4a°, Edif. Germania, 28003 Madrid.

Internet: www.fundacioncarolina.es; www.redcarolina.net; **e-mail:** informacion@fundacioncarolina.es.

Fundación Científica de la Asociación Española Contra el Cáncer—AECC (Scientific Foundation of the Spanish Cancer Association)

Established in 1971 to channel and manage the funds that the Spanish Cancer Association devotes to cancer research to promote and advance oncological research; and to link research and society through the spreading of scientific advances about cancer and involving society in research.

Activities: Offers funding for cancer research under the following programmes: stable research groups; child cancer research project; advanced cancer training programme; assistance for researchers.

Geographical Area of Activity: Mainly Spain.

Publications: *Estadística* (annually); information and monographs; *Cuidados Estéticos*; *Cómo ayudar tras el fallecimiento de un ser querido*; *InfoCáncer*; *Cómo hacer frente a la pérdida de un ser querido*.

Finance: Annual income €5,703,413, expenditure €5,522,758 (2012).

Executive Council: Isabel Oriol Díaz de Bustamante (Chair.); Reyes Artiñano Rodríguez de Torres (Vice-Chair.); Pilar López Sánchez (Treas.); José Palacios Pérez (Sec.-Gen.).

Principal Staff: Dir-Gen. Isabel Orbe Martínez Avial.

Address: Amador de los Ríos 5, 28010 Madrid.

Telephone: 91-310-82-54; **Fax:** 91-319-62-30; **Internet:** www.aecc.es/investigacion; **e-mail:** fundacion.cientifica@aecc.es; antonia.bordallo@aecc.es.

Fundación CODESPA—Futuro en Marcha (Co-operation for the Promotion and Development of Welfare Activities)

Established in 1985 to promote the economic and social development of the countries of Central and South America, Asia and Africa.

Activities: Operates nationally and internationally in the fields of aid to less-developed countries, economic affairs, education and social welfare. The Foundation awards grants to institutions; organizes conferences and training courses; and issues publications. Maintains offices in Guatemala, Nicaragua, Dominican Republic, Colombia, Peru, Morocco, the Philippines, Viet Nam and the USA.

Geographical Area of Activity: Asia, Central and South America, Africa and Spain.

Finance: Total assets €11,145,480 (31 Dec. 2013).

Board of Trustees: Manuel Herrando Prat de la Riba (Pres.); Pablo de la Esperanza Rodríguez (Sec.).

Principal Staff: Dir-Gen. José Ignacio González-Aller; Deputy Dir-Gen. Elena Martínez García.

Address: Rafael Bergamín 12, Bajo, 28043 Madrid.

Telephone: 91-744-42-40; **Fax:** 91-744-42-41; **Internet:** www.codespa.org; **e-mail:** codespa@codespa.org.

Fundación EAES

Established in 2002 by the Confederación de Entidades para la Economía Social de Andalucía and the Federación Andaluza de Empresas Cooperativas de Trabajo Asociado to support education, research, corporate development, innovation and international co-operation.

Activities: Runs a lifelong education centre and discussion groups.

Geographical Area of Activity: Spain.

Board of Trustees: Antonio Romero Moreno (Pres.); Manuel Mariscal Sigüenza (Vice-Pres.); Francisco Moreno Navajas (Sec.).

Address: Plaza de La Merced s/n, CP 41640, Osuna, Sevilla.

Telephone: 95-481-21-15; **Fax:** 95-582-05-63; **Internet:** www.escueladeeconomiasocial.es; **e-mail:** info@escueladeeconomiasocial.es.

Fundación Empresa y Sociedad (Business and Society Foundation)

Established in 1995 to encourage Spanish and foreign companies working in Spain to improve their corporate community involvement through social innovation.

Activities: Operates in the areas of research, debate and advice, promoting discussion on corporate community involvement in Spain. The Foundation carries out research on issues relevant to business, and acts as a source of information on community commitment, practice and experience. It links companies, NGOs and government agencies; advises companies on corporate community involvement and establishing community involvement initiatives; and manages projects. It also maintains a database on community programmes and the voluntary sector.

Geographical Area of Activity: Spain.

Publications: Annual Report; best practices guidelines.

Finance: Total assets €299,317 (31 Dec. 2013).

Board of Trustees: María Aparicio Rodrigo (Pres.).

Principal Staff: Dir Estela Fernández.

Address: Orense 29, 6°, 28020 Madrid.

Telephone: 91-435-89-97; **Fax:** 91-435-39-74; **Internet:** www.empresaysociedad.org/la-fundacion; **e-mail:** info@empresaysociedad.org.

Fundación Empresa-Universidad de Zaragoza—FEUZ (University of Zaragoza Business Foundation)

Founded in 1982 by the Universidad y Cámara de Comercio e Industria de Zaragoza to promote business research and training.

Activities: Operates nationally and internationally, in the fields of aid to less-developed countries; arts and humanities; conservation and the environment; economic affairs; education; international affairs; law and human rights; medicine and health; science and technology; and social welfare and social studies. The Foundation carries out research and awards grants, scholarships, fellowships and prizes. It also organizes conferences and training courses.

Geographical Area of Activity: International, with an emphasis on Central and South America and Europe.

Publications: Newsletter.

Trustees: Manuel López Pérez (Pres.); Manuel Teruel Izquierdo (Vice-Pres.); José Miguel Sánchez Muñoz (Sec.).

Principal Staff: Dir-Gen. José Javier Sánchez Asín.

Address: Paseo Fernando el Católico 2, 50005 Zaragoza.

Telephone: 97-635-15-08; **Fax:** 97-655-85-49; **Internet:** www.feuz.es; **e-mail:** feuz@feuz.es.

Fundación Entorno-BCSD España

Established in 1995, as Fundación Teneo para la Mejora del Medio Ambiente y la Conservación de la Naturaleza, with the support of 16 companies to advise businesses on environmental matters. Formerly known as the Fundación Entorno, Empresa y Desarrollo Sostenible. Present name adopted in 2006 after joining the World Business Council for Sustanaible Development.

Activities: Operates in Spain and in Central and South American countries in three main programme areas: information and training; research and education; and nature conservation. The Foundation organizes training programmes, workshops, conferences and seminars; supports research into environmental issues; and awards scholarships for environmental research carried out abroad. It maintains an online corporate database.

Geographical Area of Activity: Central and South America, Spain.

Publications: *Environmental Magazine*; conference reports and technical publications.

Finance: Total income €2,395,874. total expenditure €2,395,874 (2010).

Trustees: Javier Salas Collantes (Pres.); Miguel Cuenca Valdivia (Vice-Pres.); Félix Benítez de Lugo Guillén (Sec.).

Principal Staff: Man. Dir Cristina García-Orcoyen Tormo; Technical Dir Raquel Aranguren Diez.

Address: Calle Zurbarán 18, 1° derecha, 28010 Madrid.

Telephone: 91-575-63-94; **Fax:** 91-575-77-13.

Fundación Dr Antonio Esteve (Dr Antonio Esteve Foundation)

Established in 1983 primarily to promote advancement in pharmacotherapy through scientific communication and discussion.

Activities: Organizes multidisciplinary meetings on an international level where discussions are carried by groups of researchers about their findings, which are broadcast through the Esteve Foundation Symposia collection. The Foundation provides grants in support of pharmaceutical, biological and medical sciences; bestows a number of research awards on a biennial basis; and organizes conferences for Spanish researchers to discuss their findings, which are disseminated through Dr Antonio Esteve Monographs.

Geographical Area of Activity: Spain.

Publications: Monographs; booklets; articles; Foundation symposia; *Pharmacotherapy Revisited* (series); and other publications.

Board of Trustees: Josep Esteve Soler (Pres.); Joan Esteve Soler, Montserrat Esteve Soler (Vice-Pres); Josep Mª Ràfols Ferrer (Sec.).

Principal Staff: Dir Fèlix Bosch.

Address: Llobet i Vall-Llosera 2, 08032 Barcelona.

Telephone: 93-433-53-20; **Fax:** 93-450-48-99; **Internet:** www.esteve.org; **e-mail:** fundacion@esteve.org.

Fundación Gala–Salvador Dalí (Salvador Dalí Foundation)

Created in 1983 according to the wishes of artist Salvador Dalí.

Activities: Promotes the work of Dalí through the study and dissemination of his works, publishing books and articles and organizing conferences. The Foundation provides research grants and organizes international events such as the International Salvador Dalí Symposium, and temporary exhibitions. It holds and conserves the collections that the painter bequeathed to the Spanish Government on his death, including manuscripts, letters, photographs, books and films, which are made available to students and researchers. The Foundation also administers four museums dedicated to the artist's work.

Geographical Area of Activity: Spain.

Publications: Annual Report; *Catalogue Raisonné of paintings*; *Dalí Theatre-Museum, Figueres*; *Dalí: Joyas/Jewels*; *Dalí versus Schaal*; *Dallibres*; *Dalí Gaudí: The Revolution of the Feeling of Originality*; *Cadaqués, Scenario of Antoni Pitxot*; *Dalí: Elective Affinities*; *The Secret Life of Salvador Dalí*; *Dalí: Mass Culture*.

Finance: Total assets approx. €200m. (2012).

Board of Trustees: Rámon Boixadós Malé (Chair.); Antoni Pitxot Soler (Second Vice-Chair.); Lluís Peñuelas Reixach (Sec.-Gen.).

Principal Staff: Man. Dir Joan Manuel Sevillano.

Address: Torre Galatea, Pujada del Castell 28, 17600 Figueres.

Telephone: 97-267-75-05; **Fax:** 97-250-16-66; **Internet:** www.salvador-dali.org/fundacio-dali.

Fundación Hogar del Empleado—FUHEM (Workers' Centre Foundation)

Founded in 1965 (existed as an association since 1949) to promote solidarity, peace and justice.

Activities: Operates through editing magazines and other publications; creating educational and professional centres; organizing courses and conferences for professionals; and other activities directed at fostering employment and social participation, promoting tolerance, respect for human rights, peace, issues of co-operation for development, and humanitarian assistance initiatives. The Foundation owns seven schools, and in 1984 established the Centro de Investigación para la Paz—renamed FUHEM Ecosocial (q.v.) in 2007—which carries out research in the fields of international relations, environmental issues and economics, and the Centro de Innovación Educativa, which conducts educational programmes aimed at young people at risk of exclusion.

Geographical Area of Activity: Spain.

Publications: *Papeles de cuestiones internacionales*; *Ecología política*; *La situación del mundo (World Watch Institute Report)*; *Anuario CIP*; *Observatorio de conflictors*; *Guias didacticas de educación para el desarrollo*; *Colección de Economía Critica (2 a year)*; *Centro de Investigación para la Paz*; *Repensar, reorientar el CIP*.

Finance: Total assets €18,927,324 (31 Dec. 2013).

Board of Trustees: Ángel Martínez González-Tablas (Pres.); Javier Gutiérrez Hurtado (Vice-Pres.); Maria Luisa Rodríguez García-Robés (Sec.).

Principal Staff: Dir Yayo Herrero López; Gen. Man. José García del Pozo.

Address: Calle Duque de Sesto 40, 28009 Madrid.

Telephone: 91-431-02-80; **Fax:** 91-578-33-13; **Internet:** www.fuhem.es; **e-mail:** fuhem@fuhem.es.

Fundación IE (Business Institute Foundation)

Established in 1997 as the Fundación Instituto de Empresa to promote the training and involvement of young people in the business sector, and their continual training in relevant corporate areas.

Activities: Operates in the field of education. The Foundation awards aid and scholarships to Spanish and foreign students who wish to undertake studies at IE Business School, IE University or in other training centres; and to professors and researchers to undertake training or research work. It also finances research interns, seminars and conferences. Maintains a library and issues publications.

Geographical Area of Activity: Primarily Spain, but also North and South America, South-East Asia, the Middle East, North Africa and Europe.

Publications: *IDEAS* (quarterly magazine).

Finance: Annual revenue €3,792,334, annual expenditure €3,257,333 (2012).

Board of Governors: Diego del Alcázar Silvela (Pres.); Rafael Puyol Antolín (Vice-Pres.); Macarena Rosado (Sec.).

Principal Staff: Dir Margarita Alonso.

Address: María de Molina 6, 1°, 28006 Madrid.

Telephone: 91-787-01-00; **Fax:** 91-564-76-91; **Internet:** www
.ie.edu/es/ie-foundation; **e-mail:** fundacion.ie@ie.edu.

Fundación Innovación de la Economía Social—INNOVES

Established in 2006, with the backing of CEPES Andalucía
and FAECTA, to foster innovation and competition in the
Andalusian social economy.

Activities: Main objectives are to articulate, implement and
promote innovation and co-operation among, and the internationalization of, Andalusian social economy businesses.

Geographical Area of Activity: Spain.

Board of Trustees: Antonio Romero Moreno
(Chair.); Antonio Rivero López (Vice-Chair.); Mª del Mar García Torres (Sec.).

Principal Staff: Man. José Carlos Rodrigo.

Address: Parque Tecnológico de Andalucía, Calle Ivan Pavlov
8, Bloque 3, Bajo E, 29590 Campanillas.

Telephone: 95-227-22-53; **Fax:** 95-202-83-92; **Internet:** www
.innoves.es; **e-mail:** info@innoves.es.

Fundación para la Investigación Agraria de la Provincia de Almería—FIAPA (Foundation for Agricultural Research in the Province of Almería)

Established in 1988 to operate in the field of teaching, financing and promotion of research and development.

Activities: Operates in Almería (Andalusia region), North
Africa and South America in the field of science and technology, and specifically agricultural research. The Foundation
carries out research; awards grants, scholarships and fellowships; organizes conferences and training courses; and issues
publications. It also acts as an information and co-ordination
centre for the development of the agricultural economy.

Geographical Area of Activity: Almería, Spain; North
Africa and South America.

Publications: Numerous agricultural publications; books;
and research reports.

Principal Staff: Man. Dir Isabel M. Cuadrado Gómez.

Address: Carretera de la playa s/n, La Cañada de San Urbano,
04120 Almería.

Telephone: 95-029-19-81; **Fax:** 95-029-00-92; **e-mail:** info@
fiapa.es.

Fundación Yannick y Ben Jakober (Yannick and Ben Jakober Foundation)

Established in 1993 by Yannick Vu, Ben Jakober and Georges
Coulon Karlweis.

Activities: Conserves and restores Spanish heritage
and promotes the arts in general and painting and sculpture
in particular. The Foundation operates through self-conducted
programmes, conferences, publications and art exhibitions,
which are open to the public. It is active mostly in Spain, but
parts of the collection of portraits travel each year to museums
in other countries.

Geographical Area of Activity: Mainly Mallorca.

Restrictions: No grants available.

Publications: *Piccoli Principi Nella Grande Pittura Europea*;
Domenico Gnoli; *Ben Jakober, Yannick Vu*; *I Love Mallorca*; *Sa
Bassa Blanca*.

Board of Trustees: Marie-Claire Yannick Jakober (Pres.);
Firoz Ladak (First Vice-Pres.); Anthonie Stal (Second Vice-
Pres.); Benedict P. Jakober (Sec.).

Principal Staff: Man. Eva Mulet.

Address: Finca Sa Bassa Blanca, Apdo 10, camino del Coll
Baix, Es Mal Pas, 07400 Alcudia, Mallorca.

Telephone: 97-154-69-15; **Fax:** 97-189-71-63; **Internet:** www
.fundacionjakober.com; **e-mail:** secretario@
fundacionjakober.org.

Fundación Jiménez Díaz (Jiménez Díaz Foundation)

Founded in 1963 by Dr Carlos Jiménez Díaz for the education
of students, postgraduates, nurses and laboratory technicians
in medical and paramedical fields and techniques; for clinical
and basic investigation in existing departments of biochemistry, physiology, pathology and immunology, as well as in the
laboratories of other services; for the study of all kinds of
patients, both hospitalized and in out-patient departments.

Activities: Operates nationally in the fields of education,
science and medicine through funding research and awarding
prizes.

Geographical Area of Activity: Spain.

Publications: Annual Report.

Principal Staff: Man. Juan Antonio Álvaro de la Parra;
Assistant Man. Jesús María Rodríguez Alejandre.

Address: Avda Reyes Católicos 2, 28040 Madrid.

Telephone: 91-550-48-00; **Fax:** 91-544-26-36; **Internet:** www
.fjd.es; **e-mail:** fjd@fjd.es.

Fundación Laboral Sonsoles Ballvé Lantero (Sonsoles Ballvé Lantero Labour Foundation)

Established in 1974 by José Luis Ballvé and Eulalia Lantero for
the protection of mentally and physically disabled children,
and for the protection of pensioners and workers of food producer Campofrío Alimentación; and to support their children's
education in the arts, humanities, science, technology and
social welfare by offering scholarships, courses and seminars.

Activities: Operates nationally and internationally in the
fields of social welfare, training, education, the arts and humanities and recreational activities. Maintains library of more
than 6,000 volumes.

Geographical Area of Activity: Europe.

Publications: *ECOS* (monthly); Annual Report.

Principal Staff: Pres. Miguel Ángel Ortega Bernal.

Address: Calle Fundación Sonsoles Ballvé 2, 1º, 09007 Burgos.

Telephone: 94-728-31-03; **Fax:** 94-728-31-36; **e-mail:**
fundacion.sonsolesballve@campofriofg.com.

Fundación Loewe (Loewe Foundation)

Established in 1988 to promote culture.

Activities: Promotes culture and education of young people,
through awarding an international poetry prize, organizing a
piano competition, and promoting dance and design in Spain.

Geographical Area of Activity: Spain.

Board of Trustees: Lisa Montague (Chair.); Sheila Loewe
(Vice-Pres. and Dir).

Principal Staff: Gen. Co-ordinator Carla Fernández-Shaw.

Address: Carrera de San Jerónimo 15, 28014 Madrid.

Telephone: 91-204-13-00; **Internet:** www
.blogfundacionloewe.es; **e-mail:** fundacion@loewe.es.

Fundación MAPFRE (MAPFRE Foundation)

Founded in 1975 by the MAPFRE insurance company to promote safety at work, on the road and in the home. In 2006, the
Foundation expanded into areas previously covered by separate foundations.

Activities: Operates in Europe and Central and South America. The Foundation's main activities cover fields such as civil
society, insurance, culture, the prevention of environmental
pollution, health and security. It provides scholarships,
awards research grants and promotes the dissemination of
technical and scientific knowledge through publications.

Geographical Area of Activity: Central and South America, Portugal and Spain.

Publications: Annual Report; *MAPFRE Seguridad*; *Libros
de la Fundación*; *Proyectos de Investigación*; *LaFundación*
(quarterly review); books; brochures; newsletter.

Finance: Total assets €2,767.7m. (31 Dec. 2014).

Board of Trustees: Antonio Huertas Mejías (Chair.); Antonio Núñez Tovar, Francisco Vallejo Vallejo (Vice-Pres); Ángel Luis Dávila Bermejo (Sec.); Claudio Ramos Rodríguez (Asst Sec.).

Principal Staff: Dir Teófilo Domínguez Anaya.

Address: Paseo de Recoletos, 28004 Madrid.

Telephone: 91-602-52-21; **Fax:** 91-581-17-95; **Internet:** www.fundacionmapfre.com; **e-mail:** informacion.fundacion@mapfre.com.

Fundación Juan March (Juan March Foundation)

Founded in 1955 by Juan March Ordinas to stimulate studies of direct relevance and utility to Spanish scientific and cultural life; and to assist social institutions.

Activities: Organizes science courses and workshops, awards prizes, and makes grants for fellowships and group research programmes in the fields of scientific and technical research. The Centre for International Meetings on Biology, established in 1991 within the Juan March Institute for Study and Research, promotes collaboration between Spanish and foreign scientists working in the field of biology. A Centre for Advanced Study in the Social Sciences opened in 1987, within the Juan March Institute, to promote and conduct research, and offer postgraduate courses. Cultural activities include the organization of art exhibitions, music concerts, lectures, film projections, etc. The Programme for Cultural Advancement in Spanish Provinces operates with central, regional and local governments. Grants are made to institutions devoted to social welfare. The Foundation awards scholarships to artists and researchers in the visual arts undertaking work nationally and abroad. Maintains a library, research and documentation centre, including a specialized collection in Spanish contemporary theatre and music. Its Madrid headquarters serves as a cultural centre and the Foundation also directs the Museum of Spanish Abstract Art in Cuenca and Juan March Fundation Musuem in Palma de Mallorca.

Geographical Area of Activity: International.

Publications: *Anales* (annual report); *Revista de la Fundación Juan March* (monthly); *Calendario de actos* (monthly); *Center for Advanced Study in the Social Sciences*; brochures; catalogues and other publications.

Finance: Annual expenditure €13,924,660 (2013).

Board of Trustees: Juan March Delgado (Pres.); Carlos March Delgado (Vice-Pres.).

Principal Staff: Dir Javier Gomá Lanzón.

Address: Castelló 77, 28006 Madrid.

Telephone: 91-435-42-40; **Fax:** 91-576-34-20; **Internet:** www.march.es; **e-mail:** info@march.es.

Fundación Ana Mata Manzanedo (Ana Mata Manzanedo Foundation)

Established in 1977 by Ana Mata Manzanedo to provide assistance to those in need.

Activities: Operates mostly in Spain, particularly in the Burgos area, in the areas of education, social welfare and conservation of historic heritage, through grants to institutions and individuals, and through providing scholarships and fellowships.

Geographical Area of Activity: Mainly Spain.

Trustees: Moises Arroyo Alcalde (Pres.); Fernando Dancausa Treviño (Vice-Pres.).

Principal Staff: Sec. Gustavo Adolfo Burgos Peña.

Address: Of. 603, Calle Vitoria 4, 6º, 09004 Burgos.

Telephone: 94-727-67-16; **Fax:** 94-727-67-16.

Fundación Montemadrid (Montemadrid Foundation)

Established in 1991 by the Caja Madrid savings bank to operate in the fields of the arts and humanities; formerly known as the Fundación Caja Madrid.

Activities: Main programmes are Social Action, Education, Culture and Environment. The Foundation runs five nursery schools, five schools, three facilities for the elderly, four libraries, a sports centre, an employment centre and 35 social institution management centres. It awards 140 scholarships to graduates and post-graduates and supports emerging artists. It also organizes the Clásica x Contemporáneos music festival in Madrid, and runs a heritage conservation programme.

Geographical Area of Activity: Spain.

Publications: Annual Report.

Board of Trustees: Carmen Cafranga (Chair.).

Principal Staff: Dir-Gen. José Guirao.

Address: Casa de las Alhajas, Plaza de San Martín 1/Calle San Martín 5, 28013 Madrid.

Telephone: 90-224-68-10; **Fax:** 91-379-20-20; **Internet:** www.fundacionmontemadrid.es; **e-mail:** programasociales@montemadrid.es; proyectoseducativos@montemadrid.es; medioambiente@montemadrid.es.

Fundación Mujeres (Foundation for Women)

Established in 1994 to support women's participation in political and social affairs, to promote women in business and education and to promote co-operation between women in Spain and those in developing countries.

Activities: Operates nationally and internationally in the areas of international co-operation with less-developed countries, international affairs, social welfare and social studies, with an emphasis on promoting equal opportunities between men and women and preventing violence against women. The Foundation operates through self-conducted programmes, research, conferences, training courses and publications.

Geographical Area of Activity: International.

Publications: *Fundación Mujeres Bulletin* (2 a year); *El Libro del Buen Hablar: Una Apuesta por un Lenguaje no Sexista*; and others (see website).

Finance: Annual income €2,515,586, expenditure €3,041,630 (2012).

Board of Trustees: Carlota Bustelo García del Real (Hon. Chair.); Florentina Alarcón Hita (Chair.); María Luisa Soleto Ávila (Vice-Chair.).

Principal Staff: Sec.-Gen. Cristina García Comas.

Address: Calle Francisco de Rojas 2, 1º izquierda, 28010 Madrid.

Telephone: 91-591-24-20; **Fax:** 91-447-24-61; **Internet:** www.fundacionmujeres.es; **e-mail:** mujeres@fundacionmujeres.es.

Fundación Nantik Lum (Nantik Lum Foundation)

Established in 2003 by a group of Spanish businesspeople who wished to develop solutions for the world's poorest people through the promotion and research of micro-enterprise development and microfinance solutions.

Activities: Operates its own projects, and assists the development of activities of other organizations in Spain, Europe and the developing world that seek to achieve similar goals. The Foundation supports projects in areas of micro-enterprise, microfinance, research and training. It also funds projects that create self-employment, employment and income-generating opportunities for society's most underprivileged groups— particularly women, young people, farmers and immigrants— by supporting the development of microfinance systems that generate economic resources. The Foundation also operates a forum on microfinance, Foro Nantik Lum de Microfinanzas, which encourages open debate and the ongoing study of microfinance as a tool to fight poverty and the social exclusion of disadvantaged groups. The forum is an initiative in association with Universidad Pontificia Comillas (Madrid), the Spanish Red Cross and Fundación ONCE (q.v.).

Geographical Area of Activity: Spain and developing countries, including the Dominican Republic, Haiti and Mexico.

Publications: Research reports on microfinance (in Spanish and English); monographs; books; European micro-credit sector overviews.

Finance: Total assets €123,265 (31 Dec. 2013).

Board of Trustees: Juan Riva de Aldama (Chair.).

Principal Staff: Man. Dir Carmen Pérez.

Address: Calle Manuel Silvela 1, 1º, 28010 Madrid.

Telephone: 91-593-34-14; **Fax:** 91-411-46-59; **Internet:** www
.nantiklum.org; **e-mail:** nantiklum@nantiklum.org.

Fundación ONCE (ONCE—Spanish National Organization for the Blind—Foundation)

Founded in 1988 by ONCE, the Spanish National Organization for the Blind.

Activities: Assists people with disabilities and their integration in society. The Foundation operates primarily in Spain, co-operating with government agencies to help the disabled. It makes grants and low-interest loans for employment creation, education, rehabilitation and training; and to assist in social integration and the breaking down of barriers to communication. It also promotes sport for its role in the personal and social development of people with disabilities.

Geographical Area of Activity: Mainly Spain.

Publications: Annual Report; *Manual de Accesibilidad Global para la Formacion;* information brochures; books concerning disability and social issues.

Finance: Receives 3% of revenue from the lottery tickets sold by ONCE, equivalent to 20% of ONCE's operating revenue. Total project grants disbursed €536,860,123 (31 Dec. 2012).

Board of Trustees: HH Margarita de Borbón y Borbón (Hon. Chair.); Miguel Carballeda Piñeiro (Chair.); Alberto Durán López (Exec. Vice-Chair.).

Principal Staff: Dir-Gen. Luis Crespo Asenjo.

Address: Calle Sebastián Herrera 15, 28012 Madrid.

Telephone: 91-506-88-88; **Fax:** 91-539-34-87; **Internet:** www
.fundaciononce.es; **e-mail:** dae@fundaciononce.es.

Fundación Amancio Ortega (Amancio Ortega Foundation)

Founded in 2001 by Amancio Ortega Gaona.

Activities: Main fields of interest are education and social welfare. The Foundation designs, manages and evaluates its own initiatives, supporting pilot projects orientated towards the modernization of civil society, through public and private co-operation. Awards 200 grants annually to Spanish high-school students who wish to study in Canada and the USA.

Geographical Area of Activity: Galicia, Spain.

Restrictions: No grants available.

Publications: Press releases.

Board of Trustees: Amancio Ortega Gaona (Chair.); Flora Pérez Marcote (Vice-Pres.); Antonio Abril Abadin (Sec.).

Principal Staff: Dir Oscar Ortega Chávez.

Address: Avda Diputación s/n Arteixo, 15142 La Coruña.

Telephone: (981) 18-55-96; **Fax:** (981) 18-55-95; **Internet:**
www.faortega.org; www.becas.faortega.org; **e-mail:**
contacto@faortega.org.

Fundación José Ortega y Gasset–Gregorio Marañón (José Ortega y Gasset–Gregorio Marañón Foundation)

Established in 1978 by Soledad Ortega Spottorno as a private, non-profit-making academic research institute to further the cultural legacy of the philosopher and essayist José Ortega y Gasset; it comprises the Fundación Gregorio Marañón (f. 1988), dedicated to conserving the works of historian Gregorio Marañón.

Activities: Operates in the fields of the humanities and social sciences, through research and study activities, including postgraduate and doctoral research projects, seminars, lectures, exhibitions, and cultural and scientific meetings that cover unlimited topics. Emphasis is placed on subjects covering Iberia, Europe and Central and South America. The Foundation runs an International Programme of Spanish Language, Latin American and European Studies at its centre in Toledo, providing study opportunities for undergraduate and graduate students, as well as the annual Young Hispanic Leaders Programme, providing young US citizens of Hispanic origin with the opportunity to familiarize themselves with Spain's political, economic, social and cultural environment. It has headquarters in Madrid and Toledo in Spain. It has also established centres in Argentina, Colombia, Mexico and Peru; organizes events in other countries, including Chile and the Dominican Republic; and has established relations with several international universities. The Foundation also maintains the private library and archives of José Ortega y Gasset.

Geographical Area of Activity: Spain.

Publications: Annual Report; *Revista de Occidente* (monthly); papers and series.

Board of Trustees: José Varela Ortega (Pres.); Gregorio Marañón y Bertrán de Lis (Vice-Pres.); Jesús Sánchez Lambás (Second Vice-Pres.); Fernando Vallespín Oña (Sec.-Gen.).

Principal Staff: Dir-Gen. Lucía Sala Silveira.

Address: Calle Fortuny 53, 28010 Madrid.

Telephone: 91-700-41-00; **Fax:** 91-700-35-30; **Internet:** www
.ortegaygasset.edu; **e-mail:** comunicacion@fog.es.

Fundación Paideia Galiza (Paideia Galiza Foundation)

Founded in 1986 by Rosalía Mera Goyenechea to implement training, investigation and intervention initiatives in the field of social sciences; to implement programmes and dynamic tasks that are responsive to social issues; and to search for excellence in services and professional practices, from an inter-disciplinary, transversal and integrated point of view to promote social and scientific development.

Activities: Develops integrated training for a variety of professional sectors (in-service training); promotes projects and initiatives aimed at integration, both socially and in the workplace, for society's most vulnerable groups; and undertakes initiatives aimed at local, economic, cultural and environmental development of areas with little access to resources. The Foundation works in the following areas: social exclusion, disability, the social economy and development of rural and semi-urban zones, ethics and values, ongoing training and research, and inter-institutional co-operation. It has an office in Padrón.

Geographical Area of Activity: Spain.

Publications: *Código de Derecho Internacional Público en Materia de Discapacidad*; *Jurisprudencia de la Personas con Discapacidad (constitucional, civil, penal y laboral)*; *El Mayor Interés en la Esfera Personal del Incapaz*; *Normativa Jurídica Básica de las Personas con Discapacidad*; *Derecho y Retraso Mental*; *Hacia un Estatuto Jurídico de la Persona con Retraso Mental*; *Discursos Profesionales de las Ciencias de la Salud*; *Educación y Trabajo Social sobre la Discapacidad Psíquica*; *Antear un Modelo Integral*.

Board of Trustees: Sandra Ortega Mera (Chair.); Guillemo Vergara Muñoz (Vice-Chair.); María Cotón Fernández (Sec.).

Address: Plaza de María Pita 17, 15001 A Coruña.

Telephone: 98-122-39-27; **Fax:** 98-122-46-59; **Internet:** www
.paideia.es; **e-mail:** paideia@paideia.es.

Fundación Paz y Solidaridad Serafín Aliaga—FPyS (Serafín Aliaga Foundation for Peace and Solidarity)

Founded in 1989 to promote peace and solidarity worldwide; to support democratic freedom, especially in the area of labour and trade union rights; to promote the strengthening of labour and social organizations, and support social and economic development; and to promote international co-operation.

Activities: Provides resources to contribute to the social, cultural, economic and scientific and technical development of developing countries. The Foundation organizes training, educational activities, conferences and symposia on subjects related to peace and solidarity worldwide. It also publishes and distributes leaflets, essays and other publications relating to international co-operation, peace and solidarity.

Geographical Area of Activity: Central and South America, Western Africa, the Mediterranean region, the Middle East.

Publications: Annual Report; education and development publications.

Finance: Total assets €3,158,938 (Dec. 2011).

Board of Trustees: Monserrat Mir Roca (Chair.); Maria Engracia Cardeñosa Peñas (Treas.); Félix A. Ovejero Torres (Sec.).

Address: Calle Longares 6, 28022 Madrid.

Telephone: 91-444-09-50; **Fax:** 91-446-19-77; **Internet:** www.pazysolidaridad.ccoo.es; **e-mail:** pazysolidaridad@1mayo.ccoo.es.

Fundación Rafael del Pino (Rafael del Pino Foundation)
Established in 1999 by Rafael del Pino y Moreno.

Activities: Aims to contribute towards improving the knowledge of future Spanish, promote private initiative and foster free market and free enterprise principles. Operates in the fields of training, providing scholarships to Spanish students, funding research programmes and management training for NGOs, and organizing seminars, lectures and meetings, including the Free Enterprise Forum; Spanish cultural heritage, including lectures and conferences, and grants to projects aiming to protect and develop Spain's cultural heritage; and a series of awards and prizes, recognizing Spanish literature, dissertations in the fields of economy, law, business, politics, international relations, mass media and education, and initiatives aiming to eliminate inefficient regulations or foster competition within the goods and services markets.

Geographical Area of Activity: Spain.

Publications: Extensive publications on economics, business, law, history and other subjects.

Finance: Annual income €6,268,740, expenditure €10,192,330 (31 Dec. 2013).

Board of Trustees: Rafael del Pino y Moreno (Founder); María del Pino y Calvo-Sotelo (Chair.); José Ignacio Ysasi-Ysasmendi y Pemán (Sec.); Mª Teresa López de Silanes de Miguel (Deputy Sec.).

Principal Staff: Dir Vicente José Montes Gan.

Address: Rafael Calvo 39, 28010 Madrid.

Telephone: 91-396-86-00; **Fax:** 91-396-86-19; **Internet:** www.frdelpino.es; **e-mail:** info@frdelpino.es.

Fundación Princesa de Asturias (Princess of Asturias Foundation)
Founded in 1980 as the Príncipe de Asturias Foundation. The present name was adopted in 2014 following the proclamation of HM King Felipe VI as King of Spain.

Activities: Promotes scientific, cultural and humanist values. The Foundation presents the annual Princess of Asturias Awards in Communication and Humanities, Social Sciences, Arts, Literature, Technical and Scientific Research, International Co-operation, Concord, and Sports. The Awards recognize scientific, technical, cultural, social and humanist achievements by individuals or organizations at an international level. In 1983, the Foundation created a music department, which has three choirs and an international music school.

Geographical Area of Activity: International.

Finance: Annual income €5,588,700, expenditure €5,284,677 (2013).

Board of Trustees: HRH Leonor de Borbón, Princess of Asturias (Hon. Pres); Javier Fernández Fernández (Hon. Vice-Pres.); Matías Rodríguez Inciarte (Pres.).

Principal Staff: Gen. Sec. Adolfo Menéndez Menéndez; Dir Teresa Sanjurjo González.

Address: General Yagüe 2, 33004 Oviedo.

Telephone: 98-525-87-55; **Fax:** 98-524-21-04; **Internet:** www.fpa.es; **e-mail:** info@fpa.es.

Fundación Promi (Promi Foundation)
Founded in 1998.

Activities: Works to improve the quality of life of mentally disabled people throughout Europe, through projects, conferences and training programmes, concentrating on integration in work and society, and the rehabilitation of people with mental disabilities. The Foundation assists NGOs and other organizations with similar aims and lends its support to businesses employing people with mental disabilities. It has two research and information centres.

Geographical Area of Activity: Europe.

Publications: Annual Report; *Deficiencia, Enfermedad Mental y Senilidad: Mecanismos Legales de Protección*; and numerous other publications relating to disability.

Board of Trustees: Juan Antonio Pérez Benítez (Pres.); Juan de Dios Serrano González (Vice-Pres.); José María Castilla Martínez (Sec.).

Address: Ctra Madrid-Cádiz, km 396 (P. T. Rabanales), 14014 Córdoba.

Telephone: 95-732-53-80; **Internet:** www.promi.es; **e-mail:** infopromi@promi.es.

Fundación Fernando Rielo (Fernando Rielo Foundation)
Founded in 1982 by Fernando Rielo, a poet and philosopher, to promote understanding between different cultures and traditions.

Activities: Operates internationally, organizing conferences, seminars and concerts, and poetry, music, education and philosophy courses. The Foundation awards prizes, scholarships and grants to foster cultural activity, and in particular literature, including the annual Fernando Rielo World Mystical Poetry Prize. It maintains close ties with foundations and universities abroad, including establishing the Fernando Rielo Chair in Spanish Literature and Thought at the University of the Philippines; and operates exchange programmes with foreign universities for Spanish university teachers. The Foundation has 53 delegations worldwide.

Geographical Area of Activity: Worldwide.

Publications: *Equivalencias/Equivalences* (3 a year, in English and Spanish); several poetry collections and books on philosophy and education; *Dios y arbol*; *Lianto azul*; *Paisaje desnudo*; *Noche clara*; *Pasion y muerte*; *Transfiguration*; *Via lueis*.

Principal Staff: Dir Ascensión Escamilla Valera.

Address: Jorge Juan 82, 1° 6, 28009 Madrid.

Telephone: 91-575-40-91; **Fax:** 91-578-07-72; **Internet:** www.rielo.com; **e-mail:** fundacion@rielo.com.

Fundación María Francisca de Roviralta (María Francisca de Roviralta Foundation)
Established in 1959 by José María Roviralta and Manuel Roviralta for general charitable purposes.

Activities: Operates in Spain and internationally in the fields of aid to less-developed countries, education, medicine and health, science and technology, and social welfare, through making grants to institutions. The Foundation has four main programmes: social development; medicine and health; education and science; and other activities. In 2009, it was awarded the Medal of Honour by Asociación Española de Fundaciones.

Geographical Area of Activity: Spain and international.

Publications: Annual Report.

Finance: Total assets €33,587,993 (31 Dec. 2014).

Board of Trustees: Gerardo Salvador (Chair.); Augusto Testor (Vice-Chair. and Sec.).

Principal Staff: Dir Javier Serra.

Address: Correspondence: Calle Tuset 20-24, 08006 Barcelona; Avda Bruselas 15, 4°, 2810 Alcobendas, Madrid.

Telephone: 91-556-02-28; **Fax:** 91-556-37-36; **Internet:** www.roviralta.org; **e-mail:** fundacion@roviralta.org.

Fundación Santa María (Santa María Foundation)

Founded in 1977 by a religious order to provide the disadvantaged in society with access to education and culture, and to promote the development of pedagogic sciences and specialist training for teaching staff.

Activities: Operates programmes in four main areas. The Special Programmes aim to integrate marginalized groups at a social and cultural level; provide training for volunteers working in prisons; promote women; organize occupational workshops; and provide financial support for the construction of libraries, houses, etc. The Literature Programme organizes competitions for teenagers and children to stimulate artistic and literary creativity. The Social Research Programmes provide a platform for discussing the problems facing society from a Christian perspective. The Pedagogical Programmes organize training courses for teachers; provide research grants to centres whose interests are similar to those of the Foundation; and operate the Foundation's prize programme.

Geographical Area of Activity: Europe and South America.

Restrictions: Grants only to people who work or study in Spain.

Publications: Annual Report; brochures; grants list; monographs.

Finance: Funded by annual contributions from Ediciones SM. Annual project expenditure €2,477,037 (2011).

Board of Trustees: Miguel Ángel Cortés Soriano (Chair.); Rogelio Núñez Partido (Vice-Chair.); Miguel Agustí Martínez-Arcos (Sec.).

Principal Staff: Dir Leoncio Fernández Bernardo.

Address: Calle Joaquín Turina 39, 28044 Madrid.

Telephone: 91-535-96-00; **Fax:** 91-535-96-01; **Internet:** www.fundacion-sm.com; **e-mail:** fsm@fundacion-sm.com.

Fundación Santillana (Santillana Foundation)

Founded in 1979 to promote co-operation in education, the media and culture.

Activities: Supports experimental educational projects; conducts conferences and studies on educational policies; organizes cultural exhibitions; publishes educational materials; and conducts projects on the mass media. The Foundation operates nationally and in Central and South America, with a sister Fundación Santillana active in Colombia. It also co-operates with organizations in other European countries.

Geographical Area of Activity: Central and South America, Spain.

Publications: Catalogues; conference and symposia proceedings and results; *Documento Básico*; *Ponencias y Conclusiones*; *Seminario de Primavera*; *La Educación en España*; *La Educación que Queremos*; *Novedades de la Ocde*; *I Foro Latinoamericano de Educación*.

Board of Trustees: Ignacio Polanco Moreno (Pres.); Emiliano Martínez Rodríguez (Vice-Pres.); Bernardo García Granda (Sec.).

Principal Staff: Dir Basilio Baltasar.

Address: Calle Méndez Núñez 17, 28014 Madrid.

Telephone: 91-701-4800; **Internet:** www.fundacionsantillana.com; **e-mail:** secretaria@fundacionsantillana.com.

Fundación Juanelo Turriano (Juanelo Turriano Foundation)

Established in 1987 by José Antonio García-Diego.

Activities: Dedicated to studies of history of science, technology and engineering. For this purpose, the Foundation publishes books, awards study grants and organizes exhibitions and courses. It also maintains a library.

Geographical Area of Activity: Spain.

Publications: Books.

Finance: Annual budget €700,000.

Board of Trustees: Francisco Vigueras González (Hon. Chair.); Victoriano Muñoz Cava (Chair.); Pedro Navascués Palacio (Sec.).

Principal Staff: Dir-Gen. Bernardo Revuelta Pol.

Address: Calle Zurbano 41, 1º, 28010 Madrid.

Telephone: 91-531-30-05; **Fax:** 91-531-30-03; **Internet:** www.juaneloturriano.com; **e-mail:** fundacion@juaneloturriano.com.

Fundación Universidad-Empresa—UE (University-Industry Foundation)

Founded in 1973 by the universities of Madrid and the Chamber of Commerce and Industry to promote co-operation between the universities and industries of Madrid.

Activities: Aims to address the challenges and opportunities generated in the framework of university-business relations, with a special focus on: education; employment and career development; entrepreneurship; research and innovation.

Geographical Area of Activity: All regions, with a special focus on Europe.

Publications: *Guía de Empresas que Ofrecen Empleo* (annual job opportunities guide); books and reports in the field of university-business co-operation.

Board of Directors: Arsenio Huergo Fernández (Chair.).

Principal Staff: Exec. Dir Fernando Martínez Gómez.

Address: Calle Pedro Salinas 11, Edificio Anexo, 2º, 28043 Madrid.

Telephone: 91-548-98-60; **Fax:** 91-547-06-52; **Internet:** www.fue.es; **e-mail:** info@fue.es.

Fundación Víctimas del Terrorismo (Foundation for the Victims of Terrorism)

Established to promote democracy and human rights, and to support victims of terrorism.

Activities: Co-operates with a number of organizations to support victims of terrorism.

Geographical Area of Activity: Spain.

Publications: Annual Report; newsletter.

Board of Trustees: Adolfo Suárez González (Hon. Chair.); Mari Mar Blanco Garrido (Chair.); Ángeles Pedraza Portero, Tomás Caballero Martínez (Vice-Chair.); Montserrat Torija Noguerales (Sec.).

Address: Apdo 46.453, 28080 Madrid.

Internet: www.fundacionvt.org; **e-mail:** fundacionvt@fundacionvt.org.

Institut Europeu de la Mediterrània—IEMed (European Mediterranean Institute)

Founded in 1989; a consortium comprising the Catalan Government, the Spanish Ministry of Foreign Affairs and Co-operation, and Barcelona City Council.

Activities: Fosters actions and projects that contribute to mutual understanding, exchange and co-operation between the different Mediterranean countries, societies and cultures as well as to promote the progressive construction of a space of peace and stability, shared prosperity and dialogue between cultures and civilizations in the Mediterranean. As a think tank specializing in Mediterranean relations based on a multidisciplinary and networking approach, the Institute encourages analysis, understanding and co-operation through the organization of seminars, research projects, debates, conferences and publications, in addition to a broad cultural programme.

Geographical Area of Activity: The Mediterranean region.

Publications: Newsletter; *Mediterranean Yearbook*; *Afkar/Ideas*; *Quaderns de la Mediterrània*; *Mediterranean Monographies*; *Euromed Survey*; *afkar/ideas* (quarterly journal); *PapersIEMed*; *PapersIEMed/EuroMeSCo*; *Focus*; Joint Policy Studies; catalogues.

Board of Governors: Artur Mas (Chair.); José Manuel García-Margallo, Xavier Trias, Joana Ortega (Vice-Chair.).

Principal Staff: Exec. Pres. Senén Florensa; Man Dir Josep Ferré.

Address: Calle Girona 20, 5°, 08010 Barcelona.

Telephone: 93-244-98-50; **Fax:** 93-247-01-65; **Internet:** www .iemed.org; **e-mail:** info@iemed.org.

Instituto Europeo de Salud y Bienestar Social (European Institute of Health and Social Welfare)

Established in 1996 to encourage health, social health and environmental protection through multiple co-operation.

Activities: Focuses its activities on environmental protection, health and safety at work, health management and social protocol. The Institute organizes congresses, conferences and seminars and supports research in the area of environment and social issues.

Geographical Area of Activity: Europe.

Publications: Books include: *Obligaciones del empresario en prevención*; *Calidad en la asistencia sanitaria*; *La satisfacción de los Pacientes*.

Principal Staff: Pres. Dr Manuel de la Peña Castiñeira; Dir-Gen. Sonia Fernández-Durán.

Address: Calle Joaquín Costa 16, El Viso, 28002 Madrid.

Telephone: 91-411-80-90; **Fax:** 91-411-80-80; **Internet:** www .institutoeuropeo.es; **e-mail:** infcursos@institutoeuropeo .es; secretaria@institutoeuropeo.es.

Intermón Oxfam

Part of the Oxfam confederation of organizations (qq.v.).

Activities: Operates in 44 countries worldwide, in the areas of development, humanitarian assistance, fair trade and campaigning.

Geographical Area of Activity: International.

Publications: Monthly newsletter.

Finance: Annual income €75,922,028, expenditure €73,442,668 (31 March 2014).

Board of Trustees: Xavier Torra Balcells (Chair.); Ignasi Carreras Fisas (Vice-Chair.); Oriol Tuñí Vancells (Sec.); Ramon Casals Creus (Treas.).

Principal Staff: Dir-Gen. José María Vera Villacián.

Address: Gran Via de les Corts Catalanes 641, 08010 Barcelona.

Telephone: 90-233-03-31; **Fax:** 93-482-07-07; **Internet:** www .oxfamintermon.org; **e-mail:** info@oxfamintermon.org.

Open Society Initiative for Europe—OSIFE

Established in 2012; part of the Open Society Foundations (q.v.) network.

Activities: Promotes democratic participation; empowers civil society; and represents geographically peripheral and marginalized people, including minorities, migrants, refugees and stateless people.

Geographical Area of Activity: EU.

Publications: Reports and other publications.

Principal Staff: Dir Jordi Vaquer; Deputy Dir Susan Treadwell; Man. Belen Martin.

Address: Calle Elisabets 24, Barcelona, 08001.

Telephone: (93) 1593838; **Internet:** www .opensocietyfoundations.org/about/offices-foundations/open -society-initiative-europe.

Paz y Cooperación (Peace and Co-operation)

Founded in 1982 by Joaquin Antuña to promote disarmament, sustainable development in developing countries and human rights worldwide.

Activities: Organizes and manages co-operative projects in 27 countries around the world, which operate in the fields of human rights, co-operative development, children and young people, women and development, micro-credit, education, health, agriculture and the environment, and integral development with local communities and authorities. The organization also funds the International Peace and Co-operation School Award, an annual event that promotes education for peace and global solidarity.

Geographical Area of Activity: Worldwide, with an emphasis on Africa, Central and South America, Asia and the Middle East.

Publications: *Education and Solidarity*; *Another Mankind: Third Millennium* (weekly television debate show on issues including the peace culture, non-violence and solidarity); *Breaking Through* (20-year foundation review); *Verso Verso il Duemila* (in Italian); *The Strategy of Hope*.

Board of Governors: Joaquín Antuña (Pres. and Founder).

Address: Calle Meléndez Valdés 68, 4° izq., 28015 Madrid.

Telephone: 91-549-61-56; **Fax:** 91-543-52-82; **Internet:** www .peaceandcooperation.org; **e-mail:** pazycooperacion@ hotmail.com.

Sri Lanka

FOUNDATIONS, TRUSTS AND NON-PROFIT ORGANIZATIONS

International Water Management Institute—IWMI

Established in 1985 to improve water resources management and irrigated agriculture in developing countries, through research. Formerly known as the International Irrigation Management Institute.

Activities: A non-profit research organization working towards the sustainable management of land and water resources for food, livelihoods and the environment. The Institute has four research themes, which cover the following: water availability and access to water; productive use of water; water quality health and environment; and water and society. It aims to improve water productivity in agriculture and ensure future food security. The Institute also studies the implications of climate change and its impacts on water and land resources. It works with partners from the North and South, including national and international research institutes, government departments, universities and development organizations, and the private sector.

Geographical Area of Activity: Africa and Asia.

Publications: Annual Report; research report series; working papers; policy and issue briefs, brochures and newsletters.

Finance: Total assets US $38,340,000 (31 Dec. 2013).

Board of Governors: Dr Donald Blackmore (Chair.).

Principal Staff: Dir-Gen. Jeremy Bird.

Address: POB 2075, Colombo; 127 Sunil Mawatha, Pelawatte, Battaramulla.

Telephone: (11) 2880000; **Fax:** (11) 2786854; **Internet:** www .iwmi.org; **e-mail:** iwmi@cgiar.org.

Regional Centre for Strategic Studies—RCSS

Established in 1993 as an NGO to carry out collaborative research on international issues relating to Southern Asia, and to network and interact with similar organizations.

Activities: Operates in the field of international affairs, through carrying out research into issues relating to Southern Asia, including regional security, conflict and co-operation. The Centre facilitates communication exchange between organizations and individuals; organizes seminars and workshops; promotes research; and disseminates information through its publications. It also presents the Kodikara Awards to scholars from Bangladesh, Bhutan, India, Maldives, Nepal, Pakistan and Sri Lanka; the Mahbub ul Haq Research Awards for Non-Traditional Security Issues in South Asia, sponsoring collaborative research projects in the fields of governance in plural societies and security, environment and security, globalization and security, and conflict resolution; and the Mahbub ul Haq Award for collaborative research on non-traditional security issues that are relevant to contemporary South Asia, within the themes of Governance in Plural Societies and Security, Environment and Security, Globalization and Security, and Conflict Resolution.

Geographical Area of Activity: Southern Asia.

Publications: *RCSS Newsletter*; research papers; practice notes; books; reports.

Finance: Funded through grants from donor organizations.

Principal Staff: Exec. Dir (a.i.) Minna Thaheer.

Address: 20/73, Fairfield Gardens, Colombo 08.

Telephone: (11) 2690913; **Fax:** (11) 2690769; **Internet:** www .rcss.org; **e-mail:** rcss@rcss.org.

A. M. M. Sahabdeen Trust Foundation

Founded in 1991 by Dr A. M. M. Sahabdeen to advance knowledge, social development and to promote inter-cultural and international understanding through awards to outstanding scientists, scholars and community leaders.

Activities: Operates in the fields of education and social development by awarding educational scholarships, particularly to students in need. The Foundation makes grants to organizations in a variety of educational and social welfare fields including hostels, libraries, educational institutions, rehabilitation and refugee centres. In 1991, the Foundation established the Sri Lankan International Awards to honour scholars and scientists in the Asian region, and others who have made outstanding contributions to human progress in the fields of International Understanding, Science, Literature and Human Development. In 1998, it established the Mohamed Sahabdeen Institute for Advanced Studies and Research at Pahamune in the Kurunegala District. The Foundation established Pahamune House in 2005 to assist in the rehabilitation of destitute children affected by tsunamis in December 2004.

Geographical Area of Activity: Asia.

Publications: *The Sufi Doctrine in Tamil Literature*; *Iraivanum Pirapanjamum*; *God and the Universe*; *The Circle of Lives*.

Finance: Net assets 14.9m. rupees; annual expenditure 1.1m. rupees.

Board of Trustees: Dr A. M. M. Sahabdeen (Chair.).

Principal Staff: Dirs Rizvan Sahabdeen, S. R. Sahabdeen.

Address: 4th Floor, 86 Galle Rd, Colombo 03.

Telephone: (11) 2399601; **Fax:** (11) 2399603; **Internet:** www .ammstrustfoundation.org; **e-mail:** ammstrust@gmail.com.

Sweden

FOUNDATIONS, TRUSTS AND NON-PROFIT ORGANIZATIONS

Air Pollution and Climate Secretariat—AirClim

Established in 1982 as a collaborative venture between four Swedish environmental organizations, as the Swedish NGO Secretariat on Acid Rain. Present name adopted in 2008.

Activities: Raises awareness about, and campaigns to reduce, air pollution, including greenhouse gases. The Secretariat operates primarily in the European Union and Central and Eastern Europe, disseminating information, lobbying, supporting environmental organizations in other countries, and issuing publications.

Geographical Area of Activity: Worldwide (primarily in the European Union and Central and Eastern Europe).

Publications: *Acid News* (newsletter); fact sheets; briefings; leaflets; reports (in the Air Pollution & Climate series).

Principal Staff: Dir Christer Ågren.

Address: Första Långgatan 18, 413 28 Gothenburg.

Telephone: (31) 711 45 15; **Fax:** (31) 711 46 20; **Internet:** www.airclim.org; **e-mail:** info@airclim.org.

Folke Bernadottes Minnesfond (Folke Bernadotte Memorial Foundation)

Founded in 1948 by the Swedish Relief Committee for Europe, in memory of Count Folke Bernadotte, to promote understanding between nations, particularly through enabling young persons to become acquainted with the culture, ideals and social conditions of other countries, and to bring aid to those in need.

Activities: Offers scholarships to people living in Sweden, and under the age of 35 years, who want to travel outside Scandinavia to experience other cultural conditions. Some kind of exchange must be included, and the social aspect is important. Scholarships are also given to those taking part in camps and volunteering. The Foundation co-ordinates the activities of organizations abroad that commemorate Count Folke Bernadotte.

Geographical Area of Activity: Worldwide.

Restrictions: No scholarships for study.

Principal Staff: Dir Bernt Rehn; Sec. Helga Ponzio.

Address: POB 4309, 102 67 Stockholm.

Telephone: (8) 662 25 05; **Internet:** www.folkebernadottesminnesfond.se; **e-mail:** info@folkebernadottesminnesfond.se.

Cancerfonden (Swedish Cancer Society)

Founded in 1951 to support, organize and co-ordinate cancer research that is primarily concerned with basic medical and scientific research tasks; to promote the development of new research and treatment methods in cancer cases and to lend support to other measures in the interest of cancer patients; and to support educational activities concerned with the aims and means of cancer research and with the prevention, symptoms and treatment of cancer diseases.

Activities: Awards grants to individuals of any nationality to carry out cancer research, or research in a related science, including biochemistry, cell biology, pathology, virology, immunology, etc. The Society also disseminates information on cancer for public education purposes.

Geographical Area of Activity: Sweden.

Restrictions: No grants to individuals. Awards for Swedish researchers are tenable in countries outside Sweden; foreign recipients must carry out their research in Sweden.

Publications: Annual Report; *Rädda Livet* (quarterly); reports; newsletter; brochure.

Board of Directors: Wanja Lundy-Wedin (Pres.); Birgitta Lindholm (Vice-Pres.).

Principal Staff: Sec.-Gen. Stefan Bergh.

Address: David Bagares gata 5, 101 55 Stockholm.

Telephone: (8) 677 10 00; **Fax:** (8) 677 10 01; **Internet:** www.cancerfonden.se; **e-mail:** info@cancerfonden.se.

Crafoordska stiftelsen (The Crafoord Foundation)

Set up in 1980 by Holger Crafoord to support basic scientific research at both national and international level.

Activities: Focuses on geosciences, mathematics and astronomy, biosciences (particularly ecology), and medicine (rheumatoid arthritis); awards grants to individuals and organizations in Sweden pursuing scientific research; awards Nobel prizes in Chemistry and Physics totalling 9m. kronor each; and may also support education of, and assistance to, disadvantaged children and youngsters.

Geographical Area of Activity: Worldwide.

Publications: Annual Report.

Finance: Annual revenue 117,030,000 kronor, expenditure 6,398,000 kronor (2014).

Board of Trustees: Ebba Fischer (Chair.).

Principal Staff: Chief Exec. Lennart Nilsson.

Address: POB 137, 221 00 Lund; Malmövägen 8, 222 25 Lund.

Telephone: (46) 38 58 80; **Fax:** (46) 38 58 85; **Internet:** www.crafoord.se; **e-mail:** crafoord@crafoord.se.

Diakonia

Established in 1966 by five Swedish churches; a non-profit development organization, to promote dignity and equality for all people by actively supporting local civil society organizations.

Activities: Comprises two principal organizations: the Swedish Alliance Mission and the Uniting Church in Sweden. The organization operates in South and South-East Asia, Central and South America, Africa and the Middle East in the thematic areas of democratization and human rights, gender equality, social and economic justice, and peace and reconciliation, through making grants to organizations.

Geographical Area of Activity: Africa, Central and South America, South and South-East Asia and the Middle East.

Restrictions: Grants are not made to individuals, nor are they given to organizations in Europe, in the USA or in the countries of the former USSR.

Publications: Annual Report.

Finance: The Swedish Government provides 80% of the budget (through the Swedish International Development Co-operation Agency). EuropeAid, other governments, UN agencies and private donors provide the rest. Annual revenue 473,423 kronor, expenditure 470,108 kronor (2013).

Board: Oskar Permvall (Chair.); Ann-Sofie Lasell (Vice-Chair.).

Principal Staff: Sec.-Gen. Bo Forsberg; Deputy Sec.-Gen. and Admin. Man. Krister Adolfsson.

Address: Gustavslundsvägen 18, Alviks torg, Bromma; POB 14038, 167 14 Bromma.

Telephone: (8) 453 69 00; **Fax:** (8) 453 69 29; **Internet:** www .diakonia.se; **e-mail:** diakonia@diakonia.se.

Eden Foundation

Established in 1985 to show how underexploited plant species can be used to reverse desertification and bring welfare to the poorest people. The Foundation works on the premise that natural plants can feed the world's population in a way that is constructive for the environment, and pioneers this practice in drylands.

Activities: Operates in the field of conservation and the environment, and aid to less-developed countries. Runs a research project in Niger on how to combat desertification. The Foundation researches how to establish drought-tolerant perennial plants through rainfall only. It disseminates research results to local farmers and gives them seeds to establish plants on their own. Once established, these plants improve food security by stabilizing the environment and providing a supplemental, reliable food source. Projects are long term. The Foundation teaches villagers basic principles in preventive health, covering issues such as malaria, diarrhoea and HIV/AIDS.

Geographical Area of Activity: Niger.

Principal Staff: Founder and Exec. Dir Arne Victor Garvi.

Address: Skreavägen 45B, 311 72 Falkenberg.

Telephone: (346) 53 157; **Fax:** (346) 53 171; **Internet:** www .edenfoundation.com; www.eden-foundation.org; **e-mail:** project@edenfoundation.org.

Ekhagastiftelsen (Ekhaga Foundation)

Founded in 1944 by Gösta Videgård, an engineer, to support research into improvement and further development of ecological agriculture (ecologically well-suited agricultural systems where chemical compounds for fertilization and other uses are replaced with ecological and biological measures of promoting production) and research relating to the improvement and further development of such methods of healing that are natural and suited to promote the inherent human ability of self-healing.

Activities: Operates nationally and internationally in the fields of science and medicine, through grants to Scandinavian institutions and individuals, and the provision of fellowships and scholarships.

Geographical Area of Activity: Worldwide.

Restrictions: Applicants from outside Europe must be in co-operation with a European institution. No sponsorship of basic education at university level.

Finance: Total funds disbursed since 1999: 73m. kronor.

Board: Helena Dandenell (Chair.).

Address: POB 34012, 100 26 Stockholm.

Telephone: (70) 240 81 81; **Internet:** www.ekhagastiftelsen .se; **e-mail:** info@ekhagastiftelsen.se.

Föreningen Svenska Atheninstitutets Vänner (Association of the Friends of the Swedish Institute at Athens)

Founded in 1976 by Anders Sundberg and 13 others with the aim of supporting the Swedish Institute at Athens (q.v.) and promoting cultural contacts between Sweden and Greece.

Activities: Provides grants to institutions and individuals, and awards prizes and scholarships within Scandinavia. The Association also organizes conferences and training courses.

Geographical Area of Activity: Scandinavia.

Publications: *Hellenika* (quarterly).

Board of Directors: Krister Kumlin (Chair.); Bengt Ahlberg (Treas.).

Principal Staff: Sec. Ebba Fredin.

Address: POB 14 124, 104 41 Stockholm.

Telephone: (8) 667 64 55; **Fax:** (8) 25 95 91; **Internet:** www .athenvannerna.se; **e-mail:** info@athenvannerna.se.

Globetree Association

Founded in 1982 by Kajsa B. Dahlström and Ben van Bronckhorst to support the education of children, with particular emphasis on the environment with an international perspective.

Activities: Operates nationally and internationally in the fields of aid to less-developed countries, the arts and humanities, conservation and the environment, education, medicine and health. The Association runs self-conducted programmes, organizes training courses, conferences and research programmes, offers grants to individuals, and awards scholarships and fellowships.

Geographical Area of Activity: International.

Restrictions: No grants made.

Publications: *Meeting in the Globetree*; books and teaching aids.

Principal Staff: Chair. Kajsa B. Dahlström; Vice-Chair. Peroy Kirchner; Treas. Sam Samuelsson.

Address: POB 2048, 103 11 Stockholm; Bersgatan 3, Stockholm.

Telephone: (8) 652 35 27; **Fax:** (8) 420 212 30; **Internet:** www .globetree.org; **e-mail:** info@globetree.org.

Hjärt-Lungfonden (The Swedish Heart-Lung Foundation)

Established in 1904 as the Svenska Nationalföreningen mot Tuberkulos (the Swedish National Anti-tuberculosis Association); a charitable fund-raising organization.

Activities: Collects and distributes money for heart, lung and vascular research. Provides information about heart-lung disease.

Geographical Area of Activity: Mainly Sweden.

Publications: Report of operations and financial statement; annual review of heart disease in Sweden; information brochures on heart and lung diseases.

Finance: Depends on donations from private individuals and companies.

Board: Mari Andersson (Chair.); Anders Westerberg (Vice-Chair.); Lars Lundquist (Treas.).

Principal Staff: Sec.-Gen. Kristina Sparreljung.

Address: POB 5413, Biblioteksgatan 29, 114 84 Stockholm.

Telephone: (8) 566 242 00; **Fax:** (8) 566 242 29; **Internet:** www .hjart-lungfonden.se; **e-mail:** info@hjart-lungfonden.se.

H & M Conscious Foundation

Established in 2007 to make long-lasting impact in the areas of education, clean water and women's empowerment.

Activities: Offers funding to organizations working in the areas of education, access to clean water, and women's empowerment. In addition, country-specific programmes operate in areas where H & M is present.

Finance: Since 2013, the Persson family has given 700m. kronor to the Foundation.

Board of Directors: Stefan Persson (Chair.).

Principal Staff: Man. Helena Thybell.

Address: H & M Hennes & Mauritz AB, Mäster Samuelsgatan 46 A, 106 38 Stockholm.

Telephone: (8) 796 55 00; **Fax:** (8) 796 57 03; **Internet:** www .hm.com/consciousfoundation.

Institut Mittag-Leffler (Mittag-Leffler Foundation of the Royal Swedish Academy of Sciences)

Founded in 1916 by Gösta Mittag-Leffler and Signe Lindfors Mittag-Leffler to promote pure mathematics in Sweden and Scandinavia with international co-operation.

Activities: Conducts research in pure mathematics; awards grants and scholarships open to researchers who have recently obtained a doctorate, and to advanced graduate students researching within the topic of the year.

Geographical Area of Activity: International.

Restrictions: Grants restricted to the annual theme.

Publications: *Acta Mathematica*; *Arkiv för Matematik* (journals); books; research papers.

Finance: Funded by the research councils of Denmark, Norway and Sweden, the Ministry of Education of Finland, the Icelandic Mathematical Society and foundations. Annual income 20,562,683 kronor, expenditure 18,065,000 kronor (31 Dec. 2014).

Board: Anders Björner (Chair.).

Principal Staff: Dir Prof. Ari Laptev; Deputy Dir Prof. Tobias Ekholm.

Address: Auravägen 17, 182 60 Djursholm.

Telephone: (8) 622 05 60; **Fax:** (8) 622 05 89; **Internet:** www .mittag-leffler.se; **e-mail:** info@mittag-leffler.se.

International Foundation for Science—IFS

Founded in 1972 by the national academies or research councils of 12 countries to encourage scientific work in developing countries.

Activities: Provides young scientists and technologists of outstanding merit from developing countries with financial and other support in their work. The sharing of scientific information between researchers and advisers is encouraged by regional meetings and visits to project sites. The Foundation has 135 member organizations (scientific academies, research councils and national and international organizations) in 86 countries (mainly in the developing world).

Geographical Area of Activity: International.

Restrictions: Researchers must carry out the work in their own country, and research is restricted to biological and agricultural sciences, and the chemistry of natural resources.

Publications: Report of operations and financial statement; electronic newsletter; Annual Reports; *IFS Impact Studies (MESIA)*; *External Evaluations of IFS*; *IFS Strategic Plans*; *IFS Work Plans*.

Finance: Core contributions to the budget come from France, Germany, the Netherlands, Norway, Sweden, Switzerland and the USA; restricted contributions are made by several other organizations. Annual budget approx.5m. kronor (2015).

Board of Trustees: Prof. Olanrewaju Babatunde Smith (Chair.); Professor Torbjörn Fagerström (Vice-Chair.).

Principal Staff: Dir Dr Graham Haylor.

Address: Karlavägen 108, 5th Floor, 115 26 Stockholm.

Telephone: (8) 545 818 00; **Fax:** (8) 545 818 01; **Internet:** www .ifs.se; **e-mail:** info@ifs.se.

KK-stiftelsen (Knowledge Foundation)

Set up in 1994 to improve the potential of business sectors and higher education to enable healthy co-operation in pursuing common goals.

Activities: Increases communication between academic and business sectors by developing research in Sweden's universities and colleges. The Foundation invests resources in postgraduate programmes to promote competence in business; supports advancement in Swedish schools; and works towards improving health care with new technologies. Since its inception, the Foundation has disbursed funds amounting to more than 7.5m. kronor.

Geographical Area of Activity: Sweden.

Publications: Annual Report.

Finance: Annual income 629,982,000 kronor, expenditure 50,670,000 kronor (2013).

Board of Directors: Kerstin Eliasson (Chair.).

Principal Staff: CEO Madelene Sandström.

Address: POB 3222, 103 64 Stockholm; Mäster Samuelsgatan 60, 9 tr, Stockholm.

Telephone: (8) 566 481 00; **Fax:** (8) 24 75 09; **Internet:** www .kks.se; **e-mail:** info@kks.se.

Konung Gustaf V's 90-Årsfond (King Gustaf V 90th Birthday Foundation)

Founded in 1949 by the Swedish people, in honour of King Gustaf's 90th birthday, to support voluntary youth activities.

Activities: Awards grants to Swedish youth organizations for their international exchange programmes with focus on leadership training. The Foundation particularly emphasizes leadership training programmes in Europe. It awards the annual Ernst Killander Scholarship, recognized as the foremost award to a voluntary Swedish youth leader.

Geographical Area of Activity: Mainly Europe.

Restrictions: No grants to individuals.

Finance: Total disbursements: more than 4m. kronor (2013).

Board of Trustees: Gunnar Björk (Chair.); Bengt Sevelius (Sec.-Gen. and Vice-Chair.) Inger Persson (Treas.).

Address: Kungliga Slottet, 111 30 Stockholm.

Telephone: (8) 108 433; **Fax:** (8) 108 433; **Internet:** www.gv90 .a.se; **e-mail:** suzanne.fredborg@gv90.se.

Kulturfonder for Sverige och Finland (Swedish and Finnish Cultural Foundation)

Established in 1960.

Activities: Grants are provided for a broad range of activities that aim to increase contact and understanding between the people of Sweden and Finland, especially in the fields of culture, the environment and industry. The Foundation also works to promote the Finnish language in Sweden.

Geographical Area of Activity: Sweden and Finland.

Restrictions: No grants made to municipalities, counties or state agencies.

Finance: Assets 150m. kronor in Sweden and €33.9m. in Finland (2012).

Board of Directors: Jan-Erik Enestam (Chair.); Chris Heister (Vice-Chair.).

Principal Staff: Dir Gunvor Kronman (Finland); Dir Mats Wallenius (Sweden).

Address: Föreningen Norden, POB 22087, 102 44 Stockholm; Hanasaarenranta 5, 02100 Esbo, Finland.

Telephone: (8) 506 113 00; **Fax:** (8) 506 113 20; **Internet:** www .kulturfonden.net; www.nordiskafonder.se; **e-mail:** anni@ kulturfonden.net.

Kvinna till Kvinna Foundation

Founded in 1993 in response to the war in the Balkans and the atrocities committed against women.

Activities: Supports a range of projects targeting women living in conflict or post-conflict areas. The projects cover areas such as women's participation in peace processes and crisis mangagement; sexual and reproductive health and rights; psychological health care; training for empowerment and employment; addressing domestic violence and trafficking; legal advice; and other issues that arise in conflict and post-conflict situations. The Foundation also seeks to build networks among women's groups across conflict borders and raise awareness on developing issues. maintains regional offices in the Balkans, South Caucasus and the Middle East.

Geographical Area of Activity: Albania, Bosnia and Herzegovina, Kosovo, the former Yugoslav republic of Macedonia, Montenegro, Serbia, Georgia, Armenia, Azerbaijan, Israel, the Palestinian Territories, Iraq, Lebanon, Jordan, Egypt, the Democratic Republic of the Congo, Liberia.

Restrictions: No unsolicited proposals accepted.

Publications: Annual Report; newsletter; thematic reports.

Finance: Funding from the Swedish International Development Agency and other trusts and foundations. Public fundraising activities. Annual revenue 133,961,000 kronor, expenditure 132,709,000 kronor (31 Dec. 2014).

Board of Directors: Birgit Hansson (Chair.); Viola Furubjelke (Vice-Chair.).

Principal Staff: Sec.-Gen. Lena Ag.

Address: Slakthusplan 3, 121 62 Johanneshov.

Telephone: (8) 588 891 00; **Fax:** (8) 588 891 01; **Internet:** www .kvinnatillkvinna.se; **e-mail:** info@kvinnatillkvinna.se.

Nobelstiftelsen (Nobel Foundation)

Founded in 1900 in accordance with the will of Alfred Nobel to award annual prizes to those who, during the preceding year, are judged to have conferred the greatest benefit on mankind in each of the following fields: physics, chemistry, physiology or medicine, literature and peace.

Activities: Operates internationally in the fields of science and medicine, literature and peace promotion, through the prizes to individuals, a peace prize to institutions or individuals, conferences and publications. Prizewinners are chosen by the Royal Academy of Sciences, Stockholm (Physics, Chemistry), the Nobel Assembly at the Karolinska Institutet, Stockholm (Physiology or Medicine), the Swedish Academy, Stockholm (Literature) and the Norwegian Nobel Committee (Peace). In 1968, the Central Bank of Sweden instituted an Alfred Nobel Memorial Prize in Economic Sciences of the same value as the Nobel Prize—the prizewinner of this award is chosen by the Royal Swedish Academy of Sciences.

Geographical Area of Activity: International.

Publications: Annual Report and financial statement; *Les Prix Nobel; Nobel Lectures;* books and journals.

Finance: Total assets 2,740,596,000 kronor (31 Dec. 2014).

Board of Directors: Carl-Henrik Heldin (Chair.); Göran K. Hansson (Deputy Chair.).

Principal Staff: Exec. Dir Lars Heikensten.

Address: POB 5232, 102 45 Stockholm; Sturegatan 14, Stockholm.

Telephone: (8) 663 09 20; **Fax:** (8) 660 38 47; **Internet:** www .nobelprize.org/nobel_organizations/nobelfoundation; **e-mail:** info@nobel.se.

Nordiska Afrikainstitutets Stipendier (Nordic Africa Institute Scholarships)

Founded in 1962 to provide funds for researchers associated with universities and other research institutions in the Nordic countries (Denmark, Finland, Iceland, Norway and Sweden) to conduct fieldwork in Africa.

Activities: Provides grants for those preparing and conducting research projects concerned with development issues in Africa. The Institute emphasizes the social sciences and closely related fields. The main programmes are: the Travel Scholarship Programme; Study Scholarship Programme; Scholarship for PhD Candidates; African Guest Researchers' Scholarship Programme; Nordic Guest Researchers' Scholarship Programme; and Claude Ake Visiting Chair at Uppsala University, a collaboration between the Department of Peace and Conflict Research, Uppsala University and the Institute.

Geographical Area of Activity: The Nordic countries (Denmark, Finland, Iceland, Norway and Sweden) and Africa.

Restrictions: Grants only to researchers associated with institutions in the Nordic countries.

Publications: Published more than 600 academic titles on African politics, economics, social issues and modern history.

Principal Staff: Dir Iina Soiri.

Address: POB 1703, 751 47 Uppsala; Villavägen 6, 752 36 Uppsala.

Telephone: (18) 56 22 00; **Fax:** (18) 56 22 90; **Internet:** www .nai.uu.se/scholarships; **e-mail:** nai@nai.uu.se.

NORDITA—Nordisk Institut for Teoretisk Fysik (Nordic Institute for Theoretical Physics)

Founded in 1957 by the Governments of Denmark, Finland, Iceland, Norway and Sweden to undertake research, provide training to young physicists from the Nordic countries, and promote co-operation between institutes in member countries. The Institute is run jointly by the Royal Institute of Technology (KTH) and Stockholm University and is located on the premises of AlbaNova University Center in Stockholm.

Activities: Carries out research and strengthens Nordic collaboration within the basic areas of theoretical physics. The main research areas are: Astrophysics and Astrobiology; Condensed Matter and Statistical and Biological Physics; and Subatomic Physics.

Geographical Area of Activity: Scandinavia.

Publications: *Nordita News* (online newsletter, approx. four a year); research reports.

Finance: Funded by the Nordic Council of Ministers together with the Swedish Research Council, KTH and Stockholm University. Annual budget approx. 19.8m. kronor.

Board: Prof. Kalle-Antti Suominen (Chair.).

Principal Staff: Dir Prof. Katherine Freese; Dep. Dir Prof. Axel Brandenburg.

Address: Roslagstullsbacken 23, 106 91 Stockholm.

Telephone: (5) 537 84 44; **Fax:** (5) 537 84 04; **Internet:** www .nordita.org; **e-mail:** info@nordita.org.

Olof Palmes Minnesfond (Olof Palme Memorial Fund)

Established in 1986 by Olof Palme's family and by the Social Democratic Party to honour his memory.

Activities: Awards the annual Olof Palme prize, worth US $75,000, for an outstanding achievement, as well as awarding scholarships in the fields of peace and disarmament, anti-racism and hostility to foreigners and supporting projects ranging from advanced research to simple individual projects, including trade union and cultural exchanges between young people in different countries, and studies and research, principally for young people in Sweden. The Fund supports initiatives by schools and youth organizations, both at a national and a local level. Also works to promote international understanding in other ways, by actively seeking out and supporting suitable projects in Sweden and elsewhere.

Geographical Area of Activity: Sweden and international.

Finance: Capital 70m. kronor.

Board: Pierre Schori (Chair.); Joakim Palme (Vice-Chair.); Björn Wall (Treas.).

Address: POB 836, 101 36 Stockholm.

Telephone: (8) 677 57 90; **Fax:** (8) 677 57 71; **Internet:** www .palmefonden.se; **e-mail:** palmefonden@palmecenter.se.

Reumatikerförbundet (Swedish Rheumatism Association)

Founded in 1945 by the Swedish Confederation of Trade Unions, the Co-operative Union and Wholesale Society, the Federation of Swedish Farmers' Associations, the Federation of Swedish Trade Unions, and different associations of workers in social welfare to combat rheumatic diseases in Sweden.

Activities: Operates nationally running a hospital for rheumatic patients; enables information to be exchanged among members and others interested; makes grants for research in rheumatology, and participates in international conferences.

Geographical Area of Activity: Sweden.

Publications: *Reumatikertidningen* (periodical); Annual Report and financial statement.

Finance: Total operating income 51,442,000 kronor, expenditure 57,519,000 kronor (31 Dec. 2014).

Board: Anne Carlsson (Chair.); Beryl Svanberg, Bo Jonsson (Vice-Chair.).

Principal Staff: Gen. Sec. Leif Salmonsson.

Address: Alströmergatan 39, POB 12851, 112 98 Stockholm.

Telephone: (8) 505 805 00; **Fax:** (8) 505 805 50; **Internet:** www.reumatikerforbundet.org; **e-mail:** info@ reumatikerforbundet.org.

Right Livelihood Award Foundation

Established in 1980 by Jakob von Uexkull.

Activities: Presents the Right Livelihood Awards annually to honour and support those 'offering practical and exemplary answers to the most urgent challenges facing us today'. The Foundation also supports and reports about its Laureates.

Geographical Area of Activity: International.

Restrictions: Anyone can propose almost anyone else (individuals or organizations), though not themselves, close relatives nor their own organization.

Publications: Brochures; bibliographies of Laureates (mainly online); DVDs and CDs.

Finance: Funded by private donations.

Board of Trustees: Jakob von Uexkull, Monika Griefahn (Co-Chair.).

Principal Staff: Exec. Dir Ole von Uexkull.

Address: Stockholmsvägen 23, 122 62 Enskede.

Telephone: (8) 70 20 340; **Fax:** (8) 70 20 338; **Internet:** www .rightlivelihood.org; **e-mail:** info@rightlivelihood.org.

SNF—Swedish Nutrition Foundation

Founded in 1961 by 14 food and related industries and associations to further scientific nutrition research of interest to the food industry and other allied producers, and the practical utilization of advances in nutritional science.

Activities: Operates nationally in the field of education, and nationally and internationally in the fields of science and medicine and international relations. The Foundation awards scholarships and supports research in basic and applied nutrition through grants to Swedish students. Travel grants enable researchers to participate in congresses and conferences and to visit laboratories abroad. International symposia are organized, and extracts of the proceedings are published. Information and advice is provided to sponsors enabling them to profit from the results of nutrition research. The Foundation has around 40 member organizations.

Geographical Area of Activity: Sweden.

Publications: Report of operations and financial statement; *Symposia of the Swedish Nutrition Foundation* (series); *Food & Nutrition Research* (open access journal); *Nordisk Nutrition* (quarterly).

Finance: Annual income 3,660,900 kronor, expenditure 4,152,409 kronor (2011).

Board of Directors: Annika Åhnberg (Chair.).

Principal Staff: CEO Dr Susanne Bryngelsson.

Address: Ideon Science Park, 17, 223 70 Lund; Beta hus 5, Scheelevägen 17, Lund.

Telephone: (46) 286 22 82; **Fax:** (46) 286 22 81; **Internet:** www .snf.ideon.se; **e-mail:** info@snf.ideon.se.

Erik Philip-Sörensens Stiftelse (Erik Philip-Sörensen Foundation)

Founded in 1976 to promote research into genetic science and the humanities.

Activities: In the field of genetic science, research grants are made to individuals or groups regardless of the institute where they choose to operate. Both basic and specialized research are supported. Grants in the field of the humanities are awarded on the recommendation of Lund University. In 2014, the Foundation disbursed research grants amounting to 3.4m. kronor.

Geographical Area of Activity: Sweden.

Restrictions: Does not give grants for research work outside Sweden; accepts applications only from Swedish universities.

Principal Staff: Dir Sven Philip-Sorensen.

Address: SEB Kapitalförvaltning, Institutioner & Stiftelser, 205 20 Malmö.

Internet: www.epss.se.

Stiftelsen Blanceflor Boncompagni-Ludovisi, född Bildt (Blanceflor Boncompagni-Ludovisi, née Bildt Foundation)

Founded in 1955 to promote scientific and education research for Swedish and Italian citizens under the age of 35 years.

Activities: Grants are provided to individuals under the age of 35 years for study in scientific fields (for example, chemistry, physics, medicine, dentistry and engineering) where study abroad is seen to be of specific value. Grants are awarded for higher education (at university or the equivalent) to those not eligible for state or community grants. The preferred host countries are Canada, Germany, Italy, Japan, Sweden, Switzerland, the United Kingdom and the USA.

Geographical Area of Activity: International.

Restrictions: No grants to groups or associations, nor for undergraduate study. Grants are made for study in certain disciplines only.

Finance: Total annual grants 3m.–4m. kronor.

Address: c/o CERTA Advokatbyrå, Grev Turegatan 13,B, 114 46 Stockholm.

Telephone: (8) 678 01 65; **Fax:** (8) 679 84 98; **Internet:** www .blanceflor.se; **e-mail:** info@blanceflor.se.

Stiftelsen Dag Hammarskjölds Minnesfond (Dag Hammarskjöld Foundation)

Established in 1962 in memory of the second Secretary-General of the UN.

Activities: Provides a forum for free and frank debate, stimulating Another Development for the future. The Foundation promotes the values of Dag Hammarskjöld, the second UN Secretary-General, within the current global development discourse and activities focus on UN-related issues.

Geographical Area of Activity: International.

Restrictions: An operating and not a grantmaking foundation; its work programmes are carried out under its own auspices.

Publications: Two series: *Development Dialogue* (2 a year) and *Critical Currents*; seminar papers; reports.

Board of Trustees: Prof. Göran Bexell (Chair.).

Principal Staff: Exec. Dir. Henrik Hammargren.

Address: Övre Slottsgatan 2, 753 10 Uppsala.

Telephone: (18) 410 10 00; **Fax:** (18) 12 20 72; **Internet:** www .daghammarskjold.se; www.dhf.uu.se; **e-mail:** secretariat@ dhf.uu.se.

Stiftelsen för Miljöstrategisk Forskning—Mistra (Swedish Foundation for Strategic Environmental Research)

Founded in 1994 to encourage research, especially in the field of the environment.

Activities: Supports environmental research programmes in the area of sustainable development, and promotes co-operation between universities, industry and international centres of research.

Geographical Area of Activity: International.

Publications: Annual Report; brochures; conference and reports.

Finance: Annual income 23,864,078 kronor, expenditure 21,642,676 kronor (31 Dec. 2014).

Board: Lena Treschow Torell (Chair.); Bengt Söderström (Vice-Chair.).

Principal Staff: CEO Åke Iverfeldt.

Address: Gamla Brogatan 36–38, 111 20 Stockholm.

Telephone: (8) 791 10 20; **Fax:** (8) 791 10 29; **Internet:** www .mistra.org; **e-mail:** mail@mistra.org.

Stiftelsen Riksbankens Jubileumsfond

Established in 1964 by the Swedish Parliament and the Bank of Sweden to commemorate the tercentenary of the bank, and to support scientific research.

Activities: Supports research in the humanities and social sciences through grants and scholarships. Programmes include the Nils-Eric Svensson Fund, which promotes educational exchanges between young researchers in Sweden and the rest of Europe, and several grants that support research projects and programmes in the humanities and social sciences. Internationally, the Foundation funds the Swedish–German Research Awards for Scientific Co-operation programme in conjunction with the Alexander-von-Humboldt-Stiftung, and is one of a number of foundations funding the Collegium Budapest for Advanced Study. The Foundation is also involved in several projects with VolkswagenStiftung, Compagnia di San Paolo, Bosch Stiftung, European Cultural Foundation and the European Foundation Centre.

Geographical Area of Activity: Sweden and worldwide.

Restrictions: No grants to undergraduate students, nor to doctoral students.

Publications: Annual Report and financial statement; conference reports; Yearbook.

Finance: Annual income 477,258,000 kronor, expenditure 533,509,000 kronor (2014).

Board of Directors: Prof. Maarit Jänterä-Jareborg (Chair.).

Principal Staff: Chief Exec. Dr Göran Blomqvist.

Address: Kungsträdgårdsgatan 18, POB 5675, 114 86 Stockholm.

Telephone: (8) 506 264 00; **Fax:** (8) 506 264 31; **Internet:** www.rj.se; **e-mail:** rj@rj.se.

Stockholm Environment Institute

Founded in 1989 by the Swedish Parliament.

Activities: A research organization that works on environmental and development issues from local to global policy levels. The Institute combines scientific research with policy analysis, working collaboratively to inform and influence decision-makers and civil society; link science with development; promote social and environmental sustainability; and build capacity, strengthen institutions, and equip partners for the long term. Research addresses overarching issues such as climate change, energy systems, food security, water and urbanization, as well as specific problems such as air pollution at the local level. In addition, the Institute has developed modelling tools that help practitioners around the globe to make decisions about water and energy use. Maintains offices in Stockholm, Tallinn (Estonia), Bangkok (Thailand), Nairobi (Kenya), Boston, Davis and Seattle (USA), and Oxford and York (United Kingdom).

Geographical Area of Activity: International.

Publications: Newsletters; fact sheets; *Renewable Energy for Development*; *Urban Air Pollution in Asian Cities: Status Challenge and Management*; *Sun, Sea, Sand and Tsunamis: Examining Disaster Vulnerability in the Tourism Community of Khao Lak, Thailand*; *Greening the Greys: Climate Change and the Over 50s*; *Sustainable Energy for All: from Basic Access to a Shared Development Agenda*; *Climate Policy in India: What Shapes International, National and State Policy?*; *The Baltic-Climate toolkit: Bringing data and resources to key actors in the public and private sectors*.

Finance: Total assets 66,987,578 kronor, annual income 107,885,149 kronor (31 Dec. 2013).

Board: Kerstin Niblaeus (Chair.); Andreas Carlgren (Vice-Chair.).

Principal Staff: Exec. Dir Johan L. Kuylenstierna; Deputy Dir Måns Nilsson.

Address: Headquarters: Linnégatan 87D, 115 23 Stockholm.

Telephone: (8) 30 80 44; **Internet:** www.sei-international.org; **e-mail:** info@sei-international.org.

Stockholm International Peace Research Institute—SIPRI

Established in 1966 as an independent international institute dedicated to research into conflict, armaments, arms control and disarmament.

Activities: Provides data, analysis and recommendations, based on open sources, to policy-makers, researchers, the media and members of the public. The Institute operates internationally in the fields of regional and global security, armed conflict and conflict management, military spending and armaments and arms control, disarmament and non-proliferation. Programmes include China and Global Security, and Global Health and Security. The Institute maintains a number of databases on international arms transfers, military expenditure, multilateral peace operations, and international arms embargoes. Other activities include seminars and conferences, as well as advice and consultancy.

Geographical Area of Activity: International.

Publications: Annual Review; *SIPRI Yearbook*; monographs and research reports; policy papers; peace and security policy briefs; fact sheets; special reports and handbooks.

Finance: The Swedish Government provides a substantial part of the Institute's funding through an annual grant. The Institute also seeks financial support from other organizations. Annual income 53,885,755 kronor (2014).

Governing Board: Sven-Olof Petersson (Chair.).

Principal Staff: Dir (a.i.) Ian Anthony; Deputy Dir Jakob Hallgren.

Address: Signalistgatan 9, 169 70 Solna.

Telephone: (8) 655 97 00; **Fax:** (8) 655 97 33; **Internet:** www.sipri.org; **e-mail:** sipri@sipri.org.

Sverige-Amerika Stiftelsen (Sweden-America Foundation)

Founded in 1919 by representatives and leaders of society, private business and culture to develop understanding between Sweden and the USA and Canada by promoting the exchange of scientific, cultural and practical experiences between the countries.

Activities: Provides scholarships to Swedish citizens for advanced study and research in the USA or Canada.

Geographical Area of Activity: Sweden, the USA and Canada.

Publications: Annual Report.

Board of Directors: Mariana Burenstam Linder (Chair.); Magnus Sjöqvist (First Vice-Chair.); Harald Mix (Second Vice-Chair.).

Principal Staff: Exec. Dir Anna Rosvall Stuart.

Address: Grev Turegatan 14, POB 5280, 102 46 Stockholm.

Telephone: (8) 611 46 11; **Fax:** (8) 611 40 04; **Internet:** www.sweamfo.se; **e-mail:** info@sweamfo.se.

Sweden-Japan Foundation—SJF

Founded in 1971 with the purpose of increasing understanding between the people of Sweden and Japan.

Activities: Operates in the fields of research and development, industry, science, commerce and culture. The Foundation organizes courses, seminars and study trips, and the publication of relevant documentation. It also encourages cultural exchange and co-operation between the two countries. Each year, the Fouondation awards around 50 scholarships to Swedish students who wish to study or work in Japan.

Geographical Area of Activity: Sweden and Japan.

Publications: *Japan-Nytt* (monthly newsletter); papers.

Board of Directors: Bo Dankis (Chair.).

Address: Grev Turegatan 14, 114 46 Stockholm.

Telephone: (8) 611 68 73; **Fax:** (8) 611 73 44; **Internet:** www.swejap.a.se; **e-mail:** info@swejap.a.se.

Transnationella Stiftelsen för Freds- och Framtidsforskning—TFF (Transnational Foundation for Peace and Future Research)

Founded in 1986 by Christina Spännar and Jan Øberg to promote conflict mitigation, peace research and education; to improve conflict understanding; and to promote alternative security and global development based on non-violent politics and economics.

Activities: Runs the following programmes: EU peace and conflict; Ukraine and the New Cold War; Iran and Iranian nuclear issues; world images and peace thinking; European orders of peace and co-operation; reconciliation and forgiveness; Mahatma Gandhi's relevance in the contemporary world; conflict mitigation—theory and practice in the former Yugoslavia, Iraq, Burundi and Greenland; and the role of the UN in the emerging world order.

Geographical Area of Activity: International.

Restrictions: Not a grantmaking organization.

Publications: Books, research reports, occasional papers and annual reports and three free mail services: *TFF Press-Info* (analyses and debate articles).

Board of Directors: Jan Øberg (Chair.).

Principal Staff: Dir Jan Øberg.

Address: Vegagatan 25, 224 57 Lund.

Telephone: 738 525200; **Internet:** www.transnational.org; **e-mail:** tff@transnational.org.

Knut och Alice Wallenbergs Stiftelse (Knut and Alice Wallenberg Foundation)

Founded in 1917 by Knut Agathon Wallenberg and Alice O. Wallenberg to promote research and education of value to Sweden.

Activities: Operates primarily nationally in the fields of education, medicine, the natural sciences and the arts and humanities, through grants to institutions, particularly for high-value equipment and laboratories.

Geographical Area of Activity: Sweden.

Restrictions: Grants are not made to private individuals without connection to a research institution, with the exception of scholarship programmes established by or supported by the Foundation. Only Swedish applications are considered.

Finance: Total annual grants 1,300m. kronor.

Board of Directors: Peter Wallenberg (Chair.); Marcus Wallenberg (Vice-Chair.).

Principal Staff: Exec. Dir Göran Sandberg.

Address: Knut och Alice Wallenberg Stiftelse, POB 16066, 103 22 Stockholm.

Telephone: (8) 545 017 80; **Fax:** (8) 545 017 85; **Internet:** www.wallenberg.com/kaw; **e-mail:** kaw@kaw.se.

Dr Marcus Wallenbergs Stiftelse för Utbildning i Internationellt Industriellt Företagande (Dr Marcus Wallenberg Foundation for Further Education in International Industry)

Founded in 1982 with the aim of providing financial assistance for education in industry and business.

Activities: Awards grants to Swedish citizens for study abroad. Grants are also made to educational institutions.

Geographical Area of Activity: Sweden.

Restrictions: Grants are available to Swedish citizens with a university degree and two years' experience in business or public administration; only accepts electronic applications made online.

Finance: Annual grants approved 1,000m. kronor (2013).

Board of Directors: Peter Wallenberg (Chair.).

Address: POB 16066, 103 22 Stockholm.

Telephone: (8) 54 50 17 77; **Fax:** (8) 54 50 17 85; **Internet:** www.wallenberg.com/tmw; **e-mail:** tmw@fam.se.

Wenner-Gren Foundations

Established in 1955 to promote international co-operation in scientific research in Sweden, and organize symposia and conferences in the sciences. The organization comprises the Wenner-Gren Centre Foundation for Scientific Research and the Axel-Wenner-Gren Foundation for International Exchange of Scientists.

Activities: Provides guest apartments for foreign researchers in Stockholm; awards fellowships to Swedish researchers wanting to go abroad, and to guest scientists who wish to visit Sweden; supports the invitation of foreign guest lecturers; organizes international symposia; and facilitates the exchange of knowledge between researchers in different countries.

Geographical Area of Activity: International.

Restrictions: All applications for fellowships must come through Swedish institutions.

Publications: *Eye Movements in Reading*; *Active Hearing*; *Challenges and Perspectives in Neuroscience*; *Life and Death in the Nervous System*; *Molecular mechanisms of Neuronal Communication*; *Goals and Purposes of Higher Education in the 21st Century*; *Politics and Culture in the Age of Christina*; *Genetics and Psychiatric Disorders*; *Basic Sensory Mechanisms in Cognition and Language*; *Connective Tissue Biology: Integration and Reductionism*; *The Chemistry, Biology and Medical Applications of Hyaluronan and its Derivatives*; *The Impact of Electronic Publishing on the Academic Community*.

Board of Directors: Dan Brändström (Chair.); Kerstin Eliasson (Vice-Chair.).

Principal Staff: CEO Britt-Marie Sjöberg; Man. Dir Susan Ludvigsson.

Address: Sveavägen 166, 23rd Floor, 113 46 Stockholm.

Telephone: (8) 736 98 00; **Fax:** (8) 31 86 32; **Internet:** www.swgc.org; **e-mail:** maria.helgostam@swgc.org.

Switzerland

FOUNDATION CENTRES AND CO-ORDINATING BODIES

Alliance Sud—Swiss Alliance of Development Organisations

Established in 1971 to pursue development projects common to the six member organizations; SWISSAID (q.v.), the Catholic Lenten Fund, Bread for All, Swiss Interchurch Aid, Helvetas (q.v.) and Caritas (q.v.). Formerly known as the Swiss Coalition of Development Organisations.

Activities: Focuses on development policy, acting as an advocate within Switzerland for disadvantaged social classes in the Global South. The Alliance works through a combination of lobbying, public relations works and grassroots mobilization in activities designed to be politically effective. It maintains information and documentation centres in Berne and Lausanne.

Geographical Area of Activity: Worldwide.

Restrictions: No grants available.

Publications: Annual Report; *Social Watch Report*; *The Reality of Aid Report*; newsletters.

Finance: Funded by member organizations; annual budget approx. US $3.2m.

Principal Staff: Dir Peter Niggli.

Address: Monbijoustr. 31, POB 6735, 3001 Berne.

Telephone: 313909330; **Fax:** 313909331; **Internet:** www.alliancesud.ch; **e-mail:** mail@alliancesud.ch.

Fondation Philias (Philias Foundation)

Established in 1997 by Bettina Ferdman Guerrier to promote Corporate Social Responsibility (CSR) in Switzerland and help companies to put CSR into practice.

Activities: Provides information to its members, organizes workshops, and provides consultancy services on corporate community involvement and CSR strategy. Through its corporate network, the Foundation acts as a catalyst and unifying force on various CSR projects and issues. It is a member of CSR Europe (q.v.) network.

Geographical Area of Activity: Switzerland.

Publications: Annual Report; *Philgood* (quarterly newsletter).

Finance: Annual revenue 892,447 Swiss francs, expenditure 856,838 Swiss francs (31 Dec. 2013).

Board of Trustees: Philippe Nordmann (Chair.); Claude Bébéar (Hon. Chair.); Charles Firmenich (Vice-Chair. and Treas.).

Principal Staff: Founder and CEO Bettina Ferdman Guerrier.

Address: Clos de la Fonderie 17, 1227 Carouge.

Telephone: 223084650; **Fax:** 223084656; **Internet:** www.philias.org; **e-mail:** info@philias.org.

International Council of Voluntary Agencies—ICVA

Founded in 1962.

Activities: Functions as an advocacy network adding value to the work of the NGOs that form its membership. The Council facilitates partnerships between NGOs and international agencies, and the accurate, timely and effective exchange of information, concerns and issues among member NGOs, international humanitarian agencies and governments working towards common objectives. These objectives include the alleviation of human suffering in disaster areas, protection and promotion of human rights. The Council facilitates access and NGO input to the Standing and Executive Committees of the UN High Commissioner for Refugees (UNHCR). As one of the three NGO networks on the UN Inter-Agency Standing Committee, the Council facilitates dialogue between NGOs and the main international body for humanitarian co-ordination and is also involved in the Sphere Project. It has more than 75 members.

Geographical Area of Activity: International.

Restrictions: Not a grantmaking agency.

Publications: Annual Report; *Monthly Bulletin* (newsletter, e-mail or online).

Finance: Annual income 3,131,334 Swiss francs, expenditure 3,101,967 Swiss francs (31 Dec. 2014).

Board of Directors: Dr Ahmad Faizal Mohd Perdaus (Chair.).

Principal Staff: Exec. Dir Nan Buzard.

Address: ave Giuseppe-Motta 26–28, 1202 Geneva.

Telephone: 229509600; **Fax:** 229509609; **Internet:** www.icvanetwork.org; **e-mail:** secretariat@icvanetwork.org.

proFonds

Established in 1990 to support the development and activities of foundations and associations in Switzerland.

Activities: Promotes the rights and activities of foundations and associations in Switzerland, through networking at national and international level, lobbying government on legal and fiscal issues relating to the non-profit sector, and promoting and facilitating the exchange of information between non-profit organizations. Also issues publications and carries out research.

Geographical Area of Activity: Switzerland.

Publications: *Stiftungsland Schweiz* (annual); *proFonds-Info* (quarterly newsletter); publications on management, law and tax issues related to the non-profit sector.

Finance: Annual income 420,082 Swiss francs, expenditure 416,379 Swiss francs (2014).

Board of Directors: François Geinoz (Chair.); Dr Harold Grüninger (Vice-Chair.).

Principal Staff: Dir Dr Christoph Degen.

Address: Dufourstr. 49, 4052 Basel.

Telephone: 612721080; **Fax:** 612721081; **Internet:** www.profonds.org; **e-mail:** info@profonds.org.

RedR International

Established in 1993.

Activities: Supports and accredits RedR member organizations. Currently composed of six federated member organizations: RedR Australia, RedR India, RedR Lanka, RedR Malaysia, RedR New Zealand and RedRUK.

Geographical Area of Activity: International.

Principal Staff: International Co-ordinator and Sec. Robert L. P. Hodgson.

Address: RedR International Secretariat, Ch. du Molard 6, 1278 La Rippe.

Internet: www.redr.org/international.html.

SwissFoundations—Verband der Schweizer Förderstiftungen/Association des Fondations Donatrices Suisses (Association of Grantmaking Foundations in Switzerland)

Established in 2001; an initiative of 11 large Swiss grantmaking foundations.

Activities: Represents member organizations in Switzerland (96 in 2012). The Association is a platform for inter-foundation interaction where experiences of foundations can be exchanged. It shares technical expertise and experience, promotes transparency and encourages involvement of new foundations.

Geographical Area of Activity: Switzerland.

Publications: Annual Report; *Swiss Foundation Code 2009* (in German).

Finance: Annual income 733,872 Swiss francs, expenditure 723,731 Swiss francs (2014).

Board of Directors: Dr Antonia Jann (Chair.); Peter Brey (Vice-Chair.).

Principal Staff: Exec. Dir Beate Eckhardt; Deputy Exec. Dir Claudia Genier.

Address: Kirchgasse 42,8001 Zürich.

Telephone: 444400010; **Fax:** 444400011; **Internet:** www.swissfoundations.ch; **e-mail:** info@swissfoundations.ch.

FOUNDATIONS, TRUSTS AND NON-PROFIT ORGANIZATIONS

Abegg-Stiftung (Abegg Foundation)

Founded in 1961 by Werner Abegg for the collection and restoration of ancient woven fabrics dating up to the 18th century; the collection and display of works of minor arts, sculptures and paintings from the Near East, Byzantium, the European Middle Ages, and the Renaissance and Baroque periods; the education of textile restorers; and research in the fields of textiles and minor arts.

Activities: Supports textile restoration projects and students of textile restoration, through creating and running a degree course in textile art at the University of Applied Science, Berne. The Foundation maintains a library and a museum. Promotes scientific exchange in textile art by founding a research institute, organizing conferences and issuing publications.

Geographical Area of Activity: Switzerland.

Publications: Collection catalogues and other specialist publications; *Riggisberger Berichte*; *Schriften*.

Board: Dominik Keller (Chair.); Hermann Fillitz (Vice-Chair.).

Principal Staff: Dir Dr Regula Schorta.

Address: Werner Abegg-Str. 67, 3132 Riggisberg.

Telephone: 318081201; **Fax:** 318081200; **Internet:** www.abegg-stiftung.ch; **e-mail:** info@abegg-stiftung.ch.

Aga Khan Agency for Microfinance

Established in 2004; a private, not-for-profit, non-denominational international development agency.

Activities: Aims to alleviate poverty, diminish the vulnerability of poor populations and reduce economic and social exclusion. The Agency aims to accomplish the following: help people become self-reliant and eventually gain the skills needed to graduate into the mainstream financial sector; achieve long-term sustainability covering costs and contributing to expansion; reach out as broadly as possible, in terms of geographical coverage and range of services offered; and maximize the impact on intended beneficiaries by ensuring that resources flow primarily to the poor and the excluded.

Geographical Area of Activity: Asia, Africa and the Middle East.

Publications: Annual Report; brochures.

Finance: Loans disbursed US $226.6m. (2010).

Board of Directors: HH the Aga Khan (Chair.).

Principal Staff: Gen. Man. Mwaghazi Mwachofi.

Address: Aga Khan Development Network, POB 2049, ave de la Paix 1–3, 1202 Geneva 2.

Telephone: 229097200; **Fax:** 229097292; **Internet:** www.akdn.org/akam.asp; **e-mail:** akam@akdn.org.

Aga Khan Development Network—AKDN

Launched by HH Prince Karim Aga Khan as a body of development agencies working together to execute welfare activities mainly in the poorest Asian and African regions.

Activities: Focuses on promoting education, health and welfare, economic development, culture and NGO development, mainly in Asia and Africa. The Network comprises the Aga Khan Foundation (q.v.), Aga Khan Education Services, Aga Khan Academies, Focus Humanitarian Assistance, Aga Khan Health Services, Aga Khan Trust for Culture (qq.v.), Aga Khan University and University of Central Asia, Aga Khan Fund for Economic Development, Aga Khan Planning and Building Services, and the Aga Khan Agency for Microfinance (q.v.).

Geographical Area of Activity: Worldwide, but primarily Africa and Asia.

Restrictions: No grants to individuals or for research; grants made in specific countries or regions only; no grants for construction.

Publications: Brochures; calendars; bulletins.

Finance: Funded by individual agencies. Annual budget US $625m.

Board of Directors: HH the Aga Khan (Chair.); Jane Piacentini-Moore (Sec.).

Address: POB 2049, ave de la Paix 1–3, 1202 Geneva 2.

Telephone: 229097200; **Fax:** 229097292; **Internet:** www.akdn.org; **e-mail:** afk@akdn.org.

Aga Khan Foundation—AKF

Founded in 1967 by HH Prince Karim Aga Khan to promote new and effective solutions to certain well-defined problems that impede social development in developing countries. The Bellerive Foundation merged with the Foundation in 2006 to become the Prince Sadruddin Aga Khan Fund for the Environment within the AKF. An agency of the Aga Khan Development Network (q.v.).

Activities: Operates nationally and internationally in the fields of health, education, rural development, the strengthening of civil society and related concerns, including community participation, gender and the environment, through grants to institutions, fellowships and scholarships, and publications. The Foundation prefers to fund innovative solutions to generic problems. With few exceptions, the Foundation provides funding for programmes in countries where it has branch offices and local professional staff to monitor implementation. Travel and study awards are made only to sponsored staff directly involved in programme implementation. The Foundation has offices in Afghanistan, Bangladesh, Canada, Egypt, India, Kenya, Kyrgyzstan, Madagascar, Mali, Mozambique, Pakistan, Portugal, the Russian Federation, Syria, Tajikistan, Tanzania, Uganda, United Kingdom and the USA.

Geographical Area of Activity: International.

Restrictions: No grants to individuals or for research; grants made in specific countries or regions only; no grants for construction.

Publications: Annual Report; numerous reports and evaluations.

Board of Directors: HH the Aga Khan (Chair.); André Ardoin (Sec.).

Principal Staff: Dir Christopher Beck.

Address: Aga Khan Development Network, POB 2049, ave de la Paix 1–3, 1202 Geneva 2.

Telephone: 229097200; **Fax:** 229097291; **Internet:** www.akdn.org/akf; **e-mail:** akf@akdn.ch.

Aga Khan Fund for Economic Development

Established in 1984.

Activities: An international development agency promoting entrepreneurship and economically sound enterprise in the developing world, with a network of more than 90 project companies in areas including banking, electricity, agricultural processing, tourism, airlines and telecommunications. The Fund also runs social programmes in microfinance, education and health. It is active in 17 countries.

Geographical Area of Activity: Afghanistan, Bangladesh, Burkina Faso, Burundi, the Democratic Republic of the Congo, India, Ivory Coast, Kenya, Kyrgyzstan, Mali, Mozambique, Pakistan, Senegal, Syria, Tajikistan, Tanzania and Uganda.

Finance: Revenue US $3,500m. (2013).

Board of Directors: HH the Aga Khan (Chair.).

Principal Staff: Exec. Dir Prince Rahim Aga Khan; Dirs Mahmud Janmohamed, Lutaf Kassam.

Address: Aga Khan Development Network, POB 2049, ave de la Paix 1–3, 1202 Geneva 2.

Telephone: 229097200; **Fax:** 229097200; **Internet:** www .akdn.org/akfed; **e-mail:** afk@akdn.org; akfed@akdn.org.

Aga Khan Trust for Culture—AKTC

Established in 1988 to promote a deeper understanding of the role of the built environment in society, and the development of Muslim societies.

Activities: Main activities focus on architecture and its importance in cultural and social development; the Trust supports enterprises that it expects to become self-sustaining in time. The Trust supports the Aga Khan Program for Islamic Architecture at Harvard University and Massachusetts Institute of Technology (MIT), USA, and the Historic Cities Support Program. It runs a Music Initiative in Central Asia, offers the Aga Khan Award for Architecture and maintains a documentation centre.

Geographical Area of Activity: International, in countries where Muslims have a significant presence, with an emphasis on Asia and Africa.

Publications: Publishes international and regional seminar proceedings.

Finance: Funds are provided by private donations and international development organizations.

Trustees: HH Prince Karim Aga Khan (Chair.).

Principal Staff: Man. Dir Luis Monreal; Dir Nicholas Bulloch.

Address: Aga Khan Development Network, POB 2049, ave de la Paix 1–3, 1202 Geneva 2.

Telephone: 229097200; **Fax:** 229097292; **Internet:** www .akdn.org/aktc; www.archnet.org; **e-mail:** aktc@akdn.ch.

Aide et Action International

Established initially in 1981 as a national NGO in France by Pierre-Bernard Le Bas to improve standards of education in less-developed countries. Aide et Action International was established in Switzerland in 2007.

Activities: Operates in less-developed countries in the fields of education, development, training and solidarity, through defending children's right to education, particularly the most disadvantaged children; contributing to children's basic education in developing countries where there are low levels of schooling (with the help of partner organizations, parents, teachers, local education authorities, NGOs, etc.); promoting self-development within communities; teacher training; and creating solidarity between the northern and southern hemispheres through sponsorship. The organization ran 98 projects in 24 countries in 2013.

Geographical Area of Activity: International.

Publications: Annual Report; *Aide et Action* (quarterly); e-newsletter on various issues; reports; books.

Finance: Annual revenue €22.3m., expenditure €21.6m. (2012).

Board of Directors: Jacques Le Marechal (Chair.); Daniel Després (Sec.); Aïcha Bah Diallo (Treas.).

Principal Staff: Dir-Gen. Gunilla Björner; Sec.-Gen. Sabine Boyé-Gonçalves.

Address: Route des Morillons 15, 1218 Le Grand Saconnex.

Telephone: 225442980; **Internet:** www.aide-et-action.org; **e-mail:** contact.int@aide-et-action.org.

Kofi Annan Foundation

Established in 2010 to promote peace and conflict resolution.

Activities: Aims to promote better global governance and strengthen the capacities of people and countries to achieve a fairer, more secure world. The Foundation has developed programmes and partnerships in three main focus areas: Sustainable Development; Human Rights and the Rule of Law; and Peace and Security.

Geographical Area of Activity: International.

Restrictions: Not a grantmaking organization.

Publications: Newsletter (quarterly).

Finance: Funded by public and private donors.

Board of Directors: Kofi Annan (Chair.).

Principal Staff: Exec. Dir Alan Doss.

Address: CP 157, 1211 Geneva 20.

Telephone: 229197520; **Fax:** 229197529; **Internet:** www .kofiannanfoundation.org; **e-mail:** info@ kofiannanfoundation.org.

Associazione Donatella Flick

Established in 1990 by Donatella Flick.

Activities: Promotes the arts, including sponsoring concerts of contemporary music, exhibitions, opera, etc., and supports the European Union-wide Donatella Flick Conducting Competition, begun in 1991. The Association has also funded research into genetic disease.

Geographical Area of Activity: Europe.

Board of Directors: Donatella Flick (Chair.).

Address: c/o ribo Treuhand AG, Chalet Litzi, 3780 Gstaad.

Sophie und Karl Binding-Stiftung (Sophie and Karl Binding Foundation)

Established in 1963 to extend support to projects concerned with the environmental, social and cultural development of Switzerland.

Activities: Provides financial and technical support to projects aimed at achieving social welfare, as well as environmental, educational, art and cultural development. The Foundation extends holiday accommodation for the challenged and their families; awards the Prix Binding pour la Forêt annually; grants educational scholarships; and supports inter-ethnic cultural exchanges in Switzerland.

Geographical Area of Activity: Switzerland.

Restrictions: Grants for organizations based in Switzerland only.

Publications: Annual reports; *Medienmitteilung 'Binding Sélection d'Artistes' – ein neues Förderprogramm für Schweizer Künstler* (2004); *Die Konferenz Schweizer Kunstmuseen (KSK)* (2004); *Kurzportrait der Stiftung*; *Portrait der Stiftung*; *Fakten zur Stiftung*; *Stiftungsflyer*.

Finance: Annual expenditure 3,332,533 Swiss francs (2013).

Foundation Council: Dr Ueli Vischer (Pres.); Dr Carl Binding (Vice-Pres.).

Principal Staff: Man. Dir Dr Benno Schubiger.

Address: Rennweg 50, 4020 Basel.

Telephone: 613171239; **Fax:** 613131200; **Internet:** www .binding-stiftung.ch; **e-mail:** contact@binding-stiftung.ch.

Ludwig-Borchardt-Stiftung (Ludwig Borchardt Foundation)

Founded in 1931 by Ludwig Borchardt and Emily Borchardt-Cohen to promote architectural research in Ancient Egypt; to maintain the Swiss Institute for Architectural and Archaeological Research of Ancient Egypt in Cairo; and to assist similar institutes as well as researchers. Originally known as the Borchardt-Cohen'sche Stiftung.

Activities: Supports the Institute's excavations and research in Egypt, which are partly undertaken in collaboration with other archaeological institutes in Egypt.

Geographical Area of Activity: Egypt.

Publications: *Beiträge zur Aegyptischen Bauforschung und Altertumskunde* (Contributions on Ancient Egyptian Architecture and Archaeology); reports and articles.

Finance: Funded through privately-held assets of the Foundation.

Board: Hans Rudi Alder (Chair.).

Principal Staff: Dir Dr Cornelius von Pilgrim.

Address: c/o Kanzlei Peyer-Alder-Keiser-Lämmli, Pestalozzistr. 2, Postfach 395, 8200 Schaffhausen.

Telephone: 526300620; **Fax:** 526256240; **Internet:** swissinst.ch/html/stiftung.html; **e-mail:** cvpilgrim@swissinst.ch.

CARE International—CI

Founded in 1945 in Washington, DC, as Co-operative for American Remittances to Europe; registered under present name in 1981.

Activities: Provides disaster relief and aims to improve social and economic conditions in developing countries. The organization promotes the use of indigenous resources, and provides disaster relief and rehabilitation support. Development activities include: agriculture and environment; small business development; health, including immunization, water and sanitation, family planning services and AIDS education; and food security. Its network comprises 13 national member organizations and one affiliate.

Geographical Area of Activity: Africa, Central and South America, Asia, Eastern Europe, Middle East.

Restrictions: Does not normally award grants; funds its own programmes.

Publications: Annual Report; member publications.

Finance: The organization is financed through: donations from individuals and the private sector; grants from CARE member governments and multilateral agencies; host government support; and donations-in-kind. Annual income €576,789,000, expenditure €626,703,000 (30 June 2013).

International Board: Ralph Martens (Chair.).

Principal Staff: Sec.-Gen. Dr Wolfgang Jamann.

Address: chemin de Balexert 7–9, 1219 Chatelaine Geneva.

Telephone: 227951020; **Fax:** 227951029; **Internet:** www.care-international.org; **e-mail:** cisecretariat@careinternational.org.

Centre Écologique Albert Schweitzer—CEAS (Albert Schweitzer Ecological Centre)

Founded in 1980 to promote ecological solutions to agricultural problems.

Activities: Encourages ecologically sound practices in agriculture through the application of appropriate technology. Projects include: promoting solar energy; the reduction of desertification; and the production and distribution of water pumps, solar heaters and dryers, in collaboration with African organizations. The Centre organizes training, compiles documentation and maintains a library. It has an office in Burkina Faso.

Geographical Area of Activity: Burkina Faso, Senegal and Madagascar.

Publications: *L'Avenir est entre vos mains* (periodic, in French and German); *Tropical Fruits Processing Manual* (in English and French).

Finance: Annual revenue 1,829,872 Swiss francs, expenditure 1,820,089 Swiss francs (31 Dec. 2013).

Board: Armand Gillabert (Chair.); Philippe Dind (Vice-Chair.).

Principal Staff: Dir Daniel Schneider.

Address: rue de la Côte 2, 2000 Neuchâtel.

Telephone: 327250836; **Fax:** 327251507; **Internet:** www.ceas.ch; **e-mail:** info@ceas.ch.

Centre Européen de la Culture—CEC (European Centre of Culture)

Founded in 1950 by Denis de Rougemont and Salvador de Madariaga to contribute to the unification of Europe by encouraging cultural pursuits.

Activities: Conducts training programmes for young people through its Euroateliers programme. Previously, the Centre housed a number of other cultural events, workshops and festivals, but in 2001 these activities were curtailed. Members of the Centre are national and international cultural institutions established by the Centre, and other individuals and organizations.

Geographical Area of Activity: Europe.

Publications: *Newsletter* (periodical, in English, French and German); *Temps Européens*; various books.

Finance: Annual budget approx. 800,000 Swiss francs.

Board: Prof. Dusan Sidjanski (Hon. Chair.); Prof. Charles Mélà (Chair.); François Saint-Ouen (Sec.-Gen.).

Address: Institut d'Études Globales, rue de l'Ecole-de-Médecine 20, 1211 Geneva 4.

Telephone: 227106603; **Fax:** 227880449; **Internet:** www.ceculture.org; **e-mail:** contact@ceculture.org.

the cogito foundation

Established in 2001 to encourage a dialogue between science and technology on the one hand and humanities and the social sciences on the other hand. It also strives to make scientific thinking better known and understood by the public.

Activities: Aims to bridge the gap between science and technology, and the humanities and social sciences, through funding of research projects, scholarships for postdoctorate researchers, fellowships, conferences, seminars and publications that are in line with the mission statement of the foundation. Every two years, the cogito prize is awarded to a distinguished scientist whose work fulfills the foundation's goals.

Geographical Area of Activity: Switzerland and international.

Publications: Annual reports; press releases, articles.

Finance: Annual budget 650,000 Swiss francs.

Council: Dr Christof Aegerter (Pres.); Dr Irene Aegerter (Vice-Pres.).

Address: Säumerstr. 26, 8832 Wollerau.

Telephone: 447877676; **Fax:** 447877677; **Internet:** www.cogitofoundation.ch; **e-mail:** info@cogitofoundation.ch.

Defence for Children International—DCI

Founded in 1979 to provide practical help to children internationally, and to promote and protect the rights of the child.

Activities: Initiates worldwide action in response to abuses of children's human rights, and generally seeks to improve children's rights internationally. The organization promotes issues involving children that are inadequately documented and takes up specific cases regarding violations of human rights. It publishes information about children's rights, and monitors the implementation of laws that should protect children. It has 47 sections and associate members worldwide.

Geographical Area of Activity: International.

Publications: *DCI Monitor* (quarterly magazine); newsletter; reports; *The World of the Defenseless*; *The Monitor, The Child Labour Problem*; *Regional Analysis on Child Labor in Western* *and Eastern Europe; Can there be a life during and after detention?; STOP for political abuse of children during the electoral campaign; Children's rights and juvenile justice; The World of Working Children.*

Executive Council: Benoît Van Keirsbilck (Pres.); Aloys van Rest (Treas.).

Principal Staff: Exec. Dir Ileana Bello.

Address: rue de Varembé 1, CP 88, 1211 Geneva 20.

Telephone: 227340558; **Fax:** 227401145; **Internet:** www .defenceforchildren.org; **e-mail:** info@defenceforchildren .org.

European Foundation for the Sustainable Development of the Regions—FEDRE

Established in 1996 as a network for the promotion of exchanges and economic, environmental and social partnerships to promote the regions of Europe.

Activities: Works in the fields of conservation and the environment through operating three main programmes: local and regional democracy in the Balkans; energy and sustainable development; and cities and nature ('Salève in another way'), which promotes public transport around Mt Salève. The Foundation organizes annual Economic Forums of the Regions of Europe.

Geographical Area of Activity: Eastern, Central and Western Europe.

Publications: Articles and magazines.

Board of Directors: Claude Haegi (Chair.); Yves Berthelot, Daniel Goeudevert (Vice-Chair.).

Principal Staff: Sec.-Gen. François Saint-Ouen.

Address: rue François-Dussaud 17, 1227 Acacias-Geneva.

Telephone: 228071717; **Fax:** 228071718; **Internet:** www.fedre .org; **e-mail:** info@fedre.org.

The Evian Group@IMD

Founded in 1995 by the late Katsuo Seiki, founding Executive Director of the Tokyo-based Global Industrial and Social Progress Research Institute (GISPRI) and Jean-Pierre Lehmann, Professor of International Political Economy at IMD (International Institute for Management Development).

Activities: Aims to build confidence and create knowledge among its members, stakeholders and constituents; to establish vision and direction by formulating agendas for action; to enhance global leadership and business statesmanship; to influence policy-makers; and to promote its ideas. The Group convenes an annual plenary meeting in Europe and round-table meetings in the Arab Region, Greater China and South Asia, in addition to ad hoc meetings, fora and symposia.

Geographical Area of Activity: The Middle East, Europe, South Asia, the People's Republic of China.

Publications: Policy briefs; position papers, reports and communiqués; Web-based newsletter.

Finance: Relies on a pool of corporate and institutional members, as well as ad hoc sponsorships.

Faculty Advisory Board: Prof. Maury Peiperl (Chair.).

Principal Staff: Dir Prof. Carlos A. Primo Braga.

Address: chemin de Bellerive 23, POB 915, 1001 Lausanne.

Telephone: 216180551; **Fax:** 216180619; **Internet:** www.imd .org/eviangroup; **e-mail:** emily.banks@imd.org.

Focus on Hope—Nana Mouskouri Foundation

Established in 1994.

Activities: Set up to support cultural and arts projects, particularly in the areas of cinema and music, to provide advice and financial help to young artists, and to award cultural prizes including the Nana Mouskouri Foundation Prix 'Focus Hope'. Also sponsors exhibitions and cultural events, including a travelling exhibition on the Parthenon Marbles.

Geographical Area of Activity: International.

Principal Staff: Founder and Pres. Nana Mouskouri; Sec. Juliette Guggenbuhl.

Address: c/o Étude Oberson Avocats, rue de Candolle 20, 1205 Geneva.

Telephone: 228071888; **Fax:** 223201670.

Fondation pour le Développement de la Psychothérapie Médicale, spécialement de la Psychothérapie de Groupe (Foundation for the Development of Medical Psychotherapy, especially Group Psychotherapy)

Founded in 1982 with the aim of promoting the development of medical psychotherapy.

Activities: Finances and organizes activities aiming to help people who are mentally ill. The Foundation is particularly interested in supporting projects involving group therapy. It awards prizes, and holds conferences and seminars.

Board: Dr Édouard de Perrot (Chair.); Cosette Guex (Treas.); Daniel Peter (Sec.).

Address: chemin des Noisetiers 2, 1271 Givrins.

Telephone: 223691295; **Fax:** 223691295; **e-mail:** edep@ bluewin.ch.

Fondation Hindemith (Hindemith Foundation)

Founded in 1968 in execution of the will of Johanna-Gertrud Hindemith, widow of the composer Paul Hindemith, to maintain his musical and literary heritage; to encourage interest and research in the field of music, in particular contemporary music; and to disseminate the results of this research.

Activities: Operates mainly in Western Europe in the field of music, through self-conducted programmes, research, publications, courses, lectures and concerts. The Foundation maintains a course centre, the Hindemith Music Center Blonay, near Vevey, Switzerland; and a centre of archives, documentation and publication, the Hindemith-Institut Frankfurt, Germany.

Geographical Area of Activity: International.

Restrictions: No grants to outside organizations currently available.

Publications: *Hindemith General Original Edition; Les Annales Hindemith; Hindemith-Forum.*

Foundation Council: Prof. Dr Andreas Eckhardt (Chair.); François Margot (Vice-Chair.).

Principal Staff: Dir Hindemith Music Center Blonay Marcel Lachat; Dir Hindemith-Institut Frankfurt Dr Susanne Schaal-Gotthardt; Sec. and Admin. Sylvia Rumo.

Address: champ Belluet 41, 1807 Blonay.

Telephone: 219430528; **Fax:** 219430529; **Internet:** www .hindemith.org; **e-mail:** administration@hindemith.org.

Fondation Hirondelle: Media for Peace and Human Dignity

Established in 1995 to establish and support information media in war zones, zones in crisis and post-conflict zones; Hirondelle USA was established in 2008.

Activities: Supports the development of the media, including radio stations, in countries affected by war, or in post-conflict situations. Works in partnership with the UN and local journalists.

Geographical Area of Activity: International.

Restrictions: Does not make grants.

Finance: Projects are primarily financed by governments and institutional donors. Annual income 10,345,639 Swiss francs (2013).

Principal Staff: CEO Jean-Marie Etter.

Address: ave du Temple 19c, 1012 Lausanne.

Telephone: 216542020; **Internet:** www.hirondelle.org; **e-mail:** info@hirondelle.org.

Fondation Internationale Florence Nightingale (Florence Nightingale International Foundation)

Founded in 1934 in memory of Florence Nightingale.

Activities: Aims to support the advancement of nursing education, research and services for the public good. Leading foundation of the International Council of Nurses (ICN), supporting and complementing the work and objectives of ICN. The Girl Child Education Fund, a signature initiative of the Foundation, supports the primary and secondary schooling of girls under the age of 18 years in developing countries whose nurse parent or parents have died. The Foundation recognizes the contributions of nurses who make a difference. The International Achievement Award is given biennially to a mid-career practising nurse who is currently influencing nursing internationally in two of nursing's four domains: direct care, education, research and management. The Award accords worldwide recognition of the recipient's achievements and contribution to nursing internationally.

Geographical Area of Activity: International.

Publications: Project publications.

Board of Directors: Judith Sharmian (Pres.); Rosemary Bryant (Immediate Past Pres.).

Address: International Council of Nurses, pl. Jean-Marteau 3, 1201 Geneva.

Telephone: 229080100; **Fax:** 229080101; **Internet:** www.fnif.org; **e-mail:** williamson@icn.ch.

Fondation ISREC (ISREC Foundation)

Established in 1964 by G. Candardjis, J.-L. de Coulon, H. Isliker, P. Mercier, A. de Muralt, A. Sauter, P. Schumacher, R. Stadler and F. Zumstein to carry out experimental research on cancer Formerly known as the Fondation Institut Suisse de Recherche Expérimentale sur le Cancer (Swiss Institute for Experimental Cancer Research/Schweizerisches Institut für Experimentelle Krebsforschung).

Activities: Operates through research and teaching. The Foundation selects and supports cancer research projects that help the transfer of knowledge and collaboration between fundamental research and clinical research; and supports projects encouraging scientific and academic development in cancer research, in particular supporting PhD students in biology or medicine taking part in doctoral programmes.

Geographical Area of Activity: Switzerland.

Publications: Annual Report.

Finance: Capital 36,650,327 Swiss francs (2013).

Board of Trustees: Yves J. Paternot (Chair.).

Principal Staff: Chair. of Scientific Bd Prof. Franco Cavalli; Dir Francis-Luc Perret; Sec.-Gen. Aylin Niederberger.

Address: rue du Bugnon 27, 1005 Lausanne.

Telephone: 216530716; **Fax:** 216526933; **Internet:** www.isrec.ch; **e-mail:** aylin.niederberger@isrec.ch.

Fondation Louis-Jeantet de Médecine (Louis-Jeantet Medical Foundation)

Established in 1982 to promote basic and clinical medical research, with additional support given for teaching and research at the Faculty of Medicine at the University of Geneva.

Activities: Within Switzerland, the Foundation awards the annual Prix Louis-Jeantet de Médecine at the Faculty of Medicine, University of Geneva; and within Europe, the Foundation awards prizes in recognition of medical research work.

Geographical Area of Activity: Switzerland and Europe.

Publications: Brochures, books, audio and video publications.

Finance: Annual research budget 4m. Swiss francs (2015).

Board of Trustees: Prof. Jean-Louis Carpentier (Chair.); Prof. Jürg A. Schifferli (Vice-Chair.).

Principal Staff: Admin. Inge-Marie Campana.

Address: chemin Rieu 17, CP 270, 1211 Geneva 17.

Telephone: 227043636; **Fax:** 227043637; **Internet:** www.jeantet.ch; **e-mail:** info@jeantet.ch.

Fondation Latsis Internationale (International Latsis Foundation)

Established in 1975 by the Greek family Latsis in Geneva.

Activities: Operates in the field of science and technology. Annually awards four University Latsis Prizes (25,000 Swiss francs each) and the National Latsis Prize (100,000 Swiss francs). The Fondation Européenne de la Science (q.v.) awards the annual European Latsis Prize (100,000 Swiss francs), funded by the Foundation, which is made in recognition of an individual under the age of 40 years or an organization's contribution to research in a particular scientific field.

Geographical Area of Activity: Europe.

Board: Prof. Denis Duboule (Chair.); Verena Lenz (Sec.).

Principal Staff: Dir David Byrom.

Address: rue Le Corbusier 40, 1208 Geneva.

Internet: www.fondationlatsis.org; **e-mail:** info@fondationlatsis.org.

Fondation Charles Léopold Mayer pour le Progrès de l'Homme—FPH (Charles Léopold Mayer Foundation for the Progress of Humankind)

Founded in 1982 by Charles Léopold Mayer (1881–1971) to fund projects that would contribute to the progress of humanity.

Activities: Focuses on three main areas: new forms of governance; common ethical principles; and transition towards more sustainable modes of living and societies. Set up a grants programme for young people with French newspaper *Le Monde*. Approximately two-thirds of the annual budget is allocated to grants and the remaining one-third spent on Foundation-initiated programmes. Maintains office in Paris, France.

Geographical Area of Activity: International.

Restrictions: Does not accept unsolicited individual applications for scholarships, fellowships or travel grants.

Publications: Newsletters; books and brochures.

Finance: Annual budget 10m. Swiss francs.

Board of Trustees: Pierre Calame (Hon. Chair.); Christian Mouchet (Chair.); Bruno Descroix (Vice-Pres.).

Principal Staff: Dir Matthieu Calame.

Address: ave Charles Dickens 6, 1006 Lausanne.

Telephone: 213425010; **Fax:** 213425011; **Internet:** www.fph.ch; **e-mail:** contact.lausanne@fph.ch.

Fondation Jean Monnet pour l'Europe (Jean Monnet Foundation for Europe)

Founded in 1978 by Jean Monnet, who gave the organization his archives.

Activities: Aims to contribute to building a united Europe in accordance with Jean Monnet's thoughts, methods and actions. The Foundation maintains archives of several protagonists of European unification, conducts research and holds international conferences on topics related to European political and economic unity; publishes the results of research. It also awards the Jean Monnet Medal.

Geographical Area of Activity: Europe.

Publications: Cahiers rouges (series); books on European topics.

Finance: Funded through public and private sources. Annual budget 1.2m. Swiss francs.

Executive Council: Pat Cox (Chair.); Patrick Piffaretti (Vice-Chair.).

Principal Staff: Dir Dr Gilles Grin; Deputy Dir Dr Hervé Bribosia.

Address: Ferme de Dorigny, 1015 Lausanne.

Telephone: 216922090; **Fax:** 216922095; **Internet:** www.jean-monnet.ch; **e-mail:** secr@fjme.unil.ch.

Fondation Nestlé pour l'Etude des Problèmes de l'Alimentation dans le Monde (Nestlé Foundation for the Study of the Problems of Nutrition in the World)

Founded in 1966 by Nestlé Alimentana SA, Vevey, to improve nutrition, particularly in those areas of the world suffering from malnutrition, by encouraging directly connected basic and applied research.

Activities: Operates internationally by developing and sponsoring nutrition-related research projects, awarding research grants to individuals and institutions, and awarding scholarships for postgraduate studies in nutrition to candidates from selected nutrition units. The Fundation also organizes scientific conferences, and publishes and disseminates scientific literature.

Geographical Area of Activity: Low and lower-middle-income countries.

Publications: Annual Report; scientific publications.

Council: Prof. Susanne Suter (Pres.).

Principal Staff: Dir Prof. Paolo M. Suter.

Address: pl. de la Gare 4, POB 581, 1001 Lausanne.

Telephone: 213203351; **Fax:** 213203392; **Internet:** www.nestlefoundation.org; **e-mail:** nf@nestlefoundation.org.

Fondation Simón I. Patiño (Simón I. Patiño Foundation)

Established in 1958 in memory of the Bolivian industrialist, Simón I. Patiño, by his heirs.

Activities: Operates internationally in the fields of education, culture, research, health, nutrition, hygiene, agriculture and ecology, through self-conducted programmes and publications, at a number of operational centres. The Albina R. de Patiño Paediatric Centre, in Cochabamba, provides medical care, and carries out training and research; it also runs a nutritional centre for malnourished children. The Simón I. Patiño Pedagogical and Cultural Centre, also in Cochabamba, offers literacy programmes through a network of village-based libraries, a central library and cultural events. In Pairumani, the Foundation conducts agricultural research at its Phyto-ecogenetic Research Centre, and at its Seed Centre, and applied programmes at the Pairumani Model Farm. In Santa Cruz and Concepción, the Foundation develops applied agro-biological programmes aimed at sustainable agricultural and environmental development, at the Centre for Applied Ecology. A cultural centre is managed in La Paz, which also hosts the Documentation Centre for Latin American Arts and Literature. Internationally, in particular in Switzerland, the Foundation provides university scholarships for high-potential Bolivian students, who will return to help in Bolivian development. It is also active in the field of arts and culture, through organizing visual arts exhibitions and musical events and offering scholarships for young artists. The Foundation's publishing house publishes books on philosophy and Latin American culture, poetry and literature.

Geographical Area of Activity: Central and South America (with an emphasis on Bolivia), Europe.

Restrictions: Principally establishes and maintains its own programmes.

Publications: Annual Report; *Bolivia Ecológica* (monthly); *Revista Boliviana de Ecología y Conservación Ambiental* (quarterly); other publications.

Governing Board: Olivier Mach (Chair. and Sec.); Nicolas du Chastel (Vice-Chair.).

Principal Staff: Exec. Dir Grégoire de Sartiges.

Address: rue Giovanni-Gambini 8, 1206 Geneva.

Telephone: 223470211; **Fax:** 227891829; **Internet:** www.fundacionpatino.org; **e-mail:** fondpatino@bluewin.ch.

Fondation Pro Victimis Genève (Pro Victimis Foundation)

Established in 1988.

Activities: Operates internationally to bring about lasting changes in the lives of the most disadvantaged and vulnerable communities in developing countries. The Foundation funds projects or programmes implemented by NGOs, community-based organizations or social entrepreneurs. It gives priority to population groups and issues that receive little or no attention.

Geographical Area of Activity: International.

Restrictions: Grants not awarded for: emergency relief activities in the immediate wake of a disaster (natural or man-made); projects related to disaster situations with a large media coverage; activities entirely and permanently dependent on international funding; projects with religious or political objectives; general fund-raising drives or events; individual cases; scholarships/fellowships. Applications are discouraged from organizations with no history of prior donor funding, unless the project is carried out in partnership with a more experienced organization or from organizations with an annual budget of more than €10m.

Board of Trustees: René Merkt (Hon. Chair.); Jean Bonna (Chair.).

Principal Staff: Exec. Dir Nicolas Borsinger.

Address: rue St Ours 5, 1205 Geneva.

Fax: 227814261; **Internet:** www.provictimis.org; **e-mail:** contact@provictimis.org.

Fondation Denis de Rougemont pour l'Europe

Founded in 1987; named after Denis de Rougemont, the founder of the Centre Européen de la Culture (European Cultural Centre, q.v.).

Activities: Focuses on federalism, the European regions and sustainable development. The Foundation awards the Denis de Rougemont Prize in Geneva.

Geographical Area of Activity: Europe.

Publications: *Denis de Rougemont et l'Europe des Régions*; *Denis de Rougemont: Introduction à sa vie et son œuvre*; *Denis de Rougemont: de la Personne à l'Europe* (2000).

Finance: Annual budget approx. 30,000 Swiss francs.

Board of Directors: Claude Haegi (Chair.).

Principal Staff: Sec.-Gen. François Saint-Ouen.

Address: c/o Claude Haegi, rue de l'Arquebuse 12, 1204 Geneva.

Telephone: 223200493; **Fax:** 228002201; **Internet:** www.fondationderougemont.org; **e-mail:** contact@fondationderougemont.org.

Fondation Charles Veillon

Established in 1972 to promote dialogues in which opinion, experience and philosophy can be linked together.

Activities: Operates in the fields of international relations and culture, through promoting dialogue covering European culture, philosophy, federalism and interdisciplinary studies. The Foundation offers the prestigious Prix Européen de l'Essai Charles Veillon for an essay dealing with contemporary society. The award, worth 30,000 Swiss francs, is given every year, in collaboration with Lausanne University, to a European writer.

Geographical Area of Activity: Europe.

Board of Directors: Pascal Veillon (Chair.).

Principal Staff: Sec. Sarah Gumy.

Address: 1012 Lausanne.

Telephone: 788700092; **Internet:** www.fondation-veillon.ch; **e-mail:** info@fondation-veillon.ch.

Fondation Franz Weber—FFW (Franz Weber Foundation)

Founded in 1975 by Franz Weber.

Activities: Operates in the field of conservation and the environment. Promotes the protection of nature and wildlife and defence of animal rights. The Foundation runs a series of national and international campaigns fighting the destruction of natural habitats, campaigning for the rights of indigenous species and to obtain legal status for animals.

Geographical Area of Activity: International.

Publications: *Journal Franz Weber.*

Finance: Funded by contributions, donations and legacies. Annual expenditure approx. 2m. Swiss francs.

Board: Vera-Franziska Weber (Chair.); Judith Weber-Stähli (Sec.); Christian Landolt (Treas.).

Address: Case Postale, 1820 Montreux.

Telephone: 219642424; **Fax:** 219645736; **Internet:** www.ffw .ch; **e-mail:** ffw@ffw.ch.

Fondation Hans Wilsdorf—Montres Rolex (Hans Wilsdorf Foundation)

Established in 1945 and the sole owner of the share capital of Montres Rolex SA.

Activities: Funds projects and organizations in the fields of social welfare, arts and culture, and scientific and medical research.

Geographical Area of Activity: Mainly Switzerland.

Finance: Total assets approx. €9,000m.

Board: Costin van Berchem (Chair.).

Principal Staff: Sec.-Gen. Marc Maugué.

Address: pl. d'Armes 20, POB 1432, 1227 Carouge.

Telephone: 227373000; **Fax:** 227002956; **e-mail:** fhw@ swissonline.ch.

Fonds für Entwicklung und Partnerschaft in Africa—FEPA (Fund for Development and Partnership in Africa)

Founded in 1963 by Hans and Hedwig Meyer-Schneeberger to support self-help projects in Africa.

Activities: Operates in Zimbabwe, Tanzania, South Africa and Mozambique, providing grants to self-help projects, especially youth and women. The Fund provides financing for local development NGOs to promote empowerment of marginalized groups through skills-training, workshops in life skills and advocacy.

Geographical Area of Activity: South Africa, Tanzania, Zimbabwe and Mozambique.

Restrictions: No grants to individuals.

Publications: *FEPA—Mitteilungsblatt* (twice a year).

Finance: Total assets 188,167 Swiss francs (31 Dec. 2012).

Principal Staff: Man. Dir Marcel Dreier.

Address: Drahtzugstr. 28, POB 195, 4005 Basel.

Telephone: 616818084; **Fax:** 616834312; **Internet:** www .fepafrika.ch; **e-mail:** info@fepafrika.ch.

Foundation for Environmental Conservation

Founded in 1975 by the International Union for Conservation of Nature and Natural Resources—IUCN (now the World Conservation Union, q.v.), the World Wildlife Fund—WWF (now the WWF—World Wide Fund for Nature, q.v.) and the late Prof. Dr Nicholas Polunin to undertake, in co-operation with appropriate individuals, organizations and other groups, all possible activities to maintain the biosphere and further environmental conservation.

Activities: Owns, manages and undertakes publications on the environment, and organizes conferences (notably the International Conferences on Environmental Future), lectures and specialist workshops.

Geographical Area of Activity: International.

Publications: *Environmental Conservation* (quarterly journal); occasional books, notably those arising from the ICEF conferences.

Board: Prof. Nick V. C. Polunin (Chair.).

Address: 1148 Moiry, 1110 Morges.

Fax: 2186666616; **Internet:** www.ncl.ac.uk/icef; **e-mail:** envcons@ncl.ac.uk.

Anne Frank-Fonds (Anne Frank Fund)

Founded in 1963 by Otto H. Frank, father of Anne Frank, to promote charitable, social and cultural activities and tolerance in the spirit of Anne Frank, and protect the literary heritage and rights of the author.

Activities: Operates in the fields of the arts and humanities and social welfare, support of 'righteous gentiles' through the Anne Frank Medical Fund for the Righteous (f. 1987); sponsoring the Anne Frank-Shoah Library, which specializes in the Nazi Holocaust period; providing finance for exchange visits and meetings of young Israelis, Germans and Arabs; providing support to Israeli and Palestinian peace organizations; supporting educational projects; and other related organizations and projects. The Fund also makes grants to the Anne Frank Museum in Amsterdam and financed a professorship in ethics at the University of Basel.

Geographical Area of Activity: International.

Publications: Annual Report.

Finance: Total grants 300,000 Swiss francs (2010).

Board of Trustees: Buddy Elias (Pres.); John D. Goldsmith (Vice-Pres.).

Principal Staff: Exec. Sec. Barbara Eldridge-Bächlin.

Address: Steinengraben 18, 4051 Basel.

Telephone: 612741174; **Fax:** 612741175; **Internet:** www .annefrank.ch; **e-mail:** info@annefrank.ch.

Gebert Rüf Stiftung

Established by Heinrich Gebert in 1997.

Activities: Supports scientific research projects at institutions of higher education in Switzerland related to innovation and transfer of science. Since its inception, the Foundation has disbursed approx 167m. Swiss francs.

Geographical Area of Activity: Mainly Switzerland.

Publications: Annual Report.

Finance: Total assets approx. 220m. Swiss francs.

Board of Trustees: Prof. Dr Rudolf Marty (Chair.); Prof. Dr Peter Forstmoser (Deputy Chair.).

Principal Staff: Dir Dr Philipp Egger; Deputy Dir Dr Pascale Vonmont.

Address: Bäumleingasse 22/4, 4051 Basel.

Telephone: 612708822; **Fax:** 612708823; **Internet:** www .grstiftung.ch; **e-mail:** info@grstiftung.ch.

Fritz-Gerber-Stiftung für Begabte Junge Menschen (Fritz Gerber Foundation for Gifted Young People)

Established in 1999 by Fritz Gerber to assist talented young people.

Activities: Offers grants to young gifted people between the ages of 10 and 25 years, in need of financial assistance to develop a specific talent. The Foundation makes grants in areas outside formal education, including sport, and the arts and culture.

Geographical Area of Activity: Switzerland.

Publications: Activity report.

Finance: A donation of €12.4m. from Fritz Gerber to establish the foundation. Has supported more than 1,650 young people and disbursed funds totalling 20.4m. Swiss francs (March 2015).

Trustees: Dr Fritz Gerber (Hon. Chair.); Urs Lauffer (Chair.); Renate Gerber (Vice-Chair.).

Address: Kirchgasse 38, Postfach 373, 8024 Zürich.

Telephone: 442605383; **Fax:** 442546035; **Internet:** www.fritz -gerber-stiftung.ch; **e-mail:** lauffer@bluewin.ch.

Global Harmony Foundation—GHF

Established in 1989 by B. Affolter, R. Boschi, N. Dajani, C. Pfluger, and the late Sir Peter Ustinov to promote sustainable development for underprivileged people, charitable work and conservation of the environment.

Activities: Operates in the fields of aid to less-developed countries, conservation of the environment and functional education, through self-conducted programmes, conferences, training courses and publications. The Foundation's programmes aim to foster greater self-efficiency, self-reliance and self-esteem using traditional practices and with regard for local cultural frameworks. Areas of interest include pre-schooling, nutritional and health care; improvement of nutrition, health and hygiene; education of women; and facilitation of the development of schools, institutions and communities.

Geographical Area of Activity: Programmes operate in Brazil, Costa Rica, Dominican Republic, India and Mexico.

Publications: Training booklets and documents; annual calendar.

Finance: Annual budget approx. 500,000 Swiss francs.

Trustees: Naseeb Dajani (Chair.); Igor Ustinov (Hon. Chair.).

Address: World Trade Centre, ave Gratta-Paille 2, 1018 Lausanne.

Telephone: 216411088; **Fax:** 216411089; **Internet:** www.global-harmony.org; **e-mail:** admin@global-harmony.org.

Gulf Research Center Foundation

Established in Geneva in 2007 by Abdulaziz Sager to gather and disseminate knowledge on the Gulf region.

Activities: Carries out research on political, economic, social and security issues; organizes workshops and conferences; issues publications; and maintains a library. Associated with the Gulf Research Center in Dubai, United Arab Emirates (q.v.).

Finance: Current assets 764,987 riyals.

Council: Dr Abdulaziz Sager (Founder and Chair.); Mustafa Alani (Treas.).

Principal Staff: Dir Prof. Dr Christian Koch.

Address: ave Blanc 49, 1202 Geneva.

Telephone: 227162730; **Fax:** 227162739; **Internet:** www.grc.ae/index.php?sec_code=foundationcouncil; **e-mail:** info@grc.net.

Helvetas Swiss Intercooperation

Established in 2011 following merger of Helvetas, which was founded in 1955, and Intercooperation, founded in 1982; a network of independent affiliates.

Activities: Co-ordinates development projects, offers advisory services to governmental and NGOs, and raises awareness concerning the problems faced by people in developing countries. The organization's main programmes are Water and Infrastructure; Rural Economy; Environment and Climate Change; Skills Development and Education; and Governance and Peace. It is active in some 30 countries, in Africa, Asia, Latin America and Eastern Europe.

Geographical Area of Activity: Africa, Asia, Latin America and Eastern Europe.

Restrictions: No grants to individuals.

Publications: Annual Report and financial statement; position papers and archives.

Finance: Annual revenue 133,332,902 Swiss francs, expenditure 134,913,584 Swiss francs (2014).

Board of Directors: Elmar Ledergerber (Chair.); Therese Frösch (Vice-Chair.).

Principal Staff: Exec. Dir Melchior Lengsfeld.

Address: Weinbergstr. 22A, 8021 Zürich.

Telephone: 443686500; **Fax:** 443686580; **Internet:** www.helvetas.ch; **e-mail:** info@helvetas.org.

Hilfswerk der Evangelischen Kirchen Schweiz—HEKS (Swiss Church Aid)

Set up in 1946 by the Federation of Swiss Protestant Churches (FSPC) to contribute to the reconciliation and reconstruction of Europe in co-operation with the Protestant churches of the respective partner countries.

Activities: Provides humanitarian and emergency aid and fights the causes of hunger, injustice and social deprivation in more than 200 projects in Switzerland and other countries. Internationally, focuses on the development of rural communities, the promotion of peace and conflict resolution, humanitarian aid and collaboration with church groups; and in Switzerland on the social integration of disadvantaged people and advocacy for the socially disadvantaged. Maintains five regional offices in Switzerland and co-ordination offices in 21 key countries.

Geographical Area of Activity: Africa, Central and South America, Asia, Europe.

Publications: Annual Report (in French, German and English); *HEKS-Magazin handeln and agir* (quarterly).

Finance: Annual income approx. 69.2m. Swiss francs (2013).

Board of Trustees: Dr Claude Ruey (Chair.); Doris Amsler-Thalmann (Vice-Chair.).

Principal Staff: Dir Ueli Locher.

Address: Seminarstr. 28, Postfach, 8042 Zürich.

Telephone: 443608800; **Fax:** 443608801; **Internet:** www.heks.ch; **e-mail:** info@heks.ch.

Helmut-Horten-Stiftung (Helmut Horten Foundation)

Founded by Helmut Horten in 1971 to support health care research and related initiatives.

Activities: Provides support to the health care system in Switzerland, through financial contributions to medical research facilities, hospitals, and other health care institutions, as well as to individuals who are in need of medical care. Preference is given to funding large-scale research projects, particularly where the Foundation is the sole funder. Significant initiatives funded by the Foundation include the Horten Center for Applied Research and Science and the Institute for Research in Biomedicine in Bellinzona, Switzerland. Scholarships are also occasionally awarded.

Geographical Area of Activity: Mainly Switzerland.

Board of Directors: Arthur Decurtins (Chair.).

Principal Staff: Gen. Man. Bernard Keller.

Address: World Trade Center, 6982 Agno/Lugano.

Telephone: 916102280; **Fax:** 916001212; **Internet:** www.helmut-horten-stiftung.org; **e-mail:** info@helmut-horten-stiftung.org.

Institut Universitaire de Hautes Etudes Internationales et du Développement (Graduate Institute of International Studies and Development Studies)

Founded in 1927 by Prof. W. Rappard and Prof. P. Mantoux to carry out teaching and research devoted to the scientific study of contemporary international relations, and to contribute to the advancement of international fellowship through the impartial observation and objective analysis of ideas and events. Merged with the Institut Universitaire du Développement in 2008.

Activities: Operates internationally, as a teaching and research institution, in the fields of history of international relations, international economics, international law, and political science. The Institute's curriculum enables students of any nationality to qualify for the Diploma and Doctor's degrees in international relations, both conferred by the University of Geneva, and a Certificate in international relations, conferred by the Institute. Scholarships are available only to students of the Institute. It maintains a library that owns the printed documents of the League of Nations and serves as a depository of the publications of the UN.

Geographical Area of Activity: International.

Publications: Brochure; books; working papers.

Foundation Board: Rolf Soiron (Chair.); Beth Krasna (Vice-Chair.).

Principal Staff: Dir Prof. Philippe Burrin; Deputy Dir Elisabeth Prügl.

Address: rue de Lausanne 132, CP 136, 1211 Geneva 21.

Telephone: 229085700; **Fax:** 229085710; **Internet:** graduateinstitute.ch; **e-mail:** info@graduateinstitute.ch.

International Baccalaureate Organization—IBO

Founded in 1968 to promote international secondary education and administer an international examination giving access to higher education in all countries, and to undertake educational research in relation to this objective, as well as for other educational purposes.

Activities: Offers the Primary Years Programme for children between the ages of three and 11 years; the Middle Years Programme for those aged between 11 and 16 years; and the Diploma Programme for students aged between 16 and 19 years. Operates through four regional offices, serving North America; Central and South America; Africa, Europe and the Middle East; and the Asia-Pacific region.

Geographical Area of Activity: International.

Publications: *IB World*; *Statistical Bulletin;* Annual Review; curriculum support materials.

Finance: Annual income US $167.7m., expenditure $158.4m. (31 Dec. 2013).

Board of Governors: Dr George Rupp (Chair.); Sally Holloway (Vice-Chair.).

Principal Staff: Dir-Gen. Dr Siva Kumari.

Address: route des Morillons 15, Grand-Saconnex, 1218 Geneva.

Telephone: 223092540; **Fax:** 227910277; **Internet:** www.ibo .org; **e-mail:** ibhq@ibo.org.

International Balzan Foundation—Fund

Founded in 1956 by Angela Lina Balzan to honour the memory of her father, Eugenio Balzan, a famous Italian journalist, who died in 1953.

Activities: Acts through two foundations jointly, the International Balzan Foundation—Fund under Swiss law, which manages the estate of Eugenio Balzan, and the International Balzan Foundation—Prize under Italian law. The Foundation awards four prizes each worth 750,000 Swiss francs: two in social sciences, literature and the arts; and two in physical, mathematical and natural sciences and medicine. Since 1979, on six occasions the Foundation has also awarded a prize for Humanity, Peace and Fraternity among Peoples, which is worth 1m. Swiss francs.

Geographical Area of Activity: Worldwide.

Publications: Newsletter; *Premi Balzan* (published each February with information on the winners and the Foundation, in English, French, German and Italian); *Balzan's One Hundred Prize Winners*.

Board: Achille Casanova (Chair.).

Principal Staff: Sec.-Gen. Dr Suzanne Werder.

Address: Claridenstrasse 35, Postfach 2448, 8022 Zürich.

Telephone: 442014822; **Fax:** 442014829; **Internet:** www .balzan.org; **e-mail:** balzan@balzan.ch.

International Council on Alcohol and Addictions—ICAA

Founded in 1907 to reduce and prevent the harmful effects of the use of alcohol and other drugs.

Activities: Conducts training programmes for health professionals on drug and alcohol problems, with particular reference to basic health care, socio-cultural and other relevant factors, and studies methods of prevention, treatment and rehabilitation. The Council organizes an Annual International Congress on Alcohol, Drugs, Tobacco and Gambling, and other international conferences, symposia and study groups. It works with the World Health Organization and other international, regional and national bodies: there are member organizations and individual members in 90 countries. The Council also maintains a library of approximately 6,000 volumes on drug dependence, approximately 12,000 pamphlets, reprints, etc., and 120 periodicals. It has regional offices in Argentina, Azerbaijan and Egypt.

Geographical Area of Activity: International.

Publications: *ICAA News* (quarterly); *Book of Abstracts* (annually); *Report of Plenary Sessions* (annually).

Board of Directors: Dr Arthur Guerra de Andrade (Chair.).

Address: c/o Addiction-Info Suisse, ave Louis-Ruchonnet 14, POB 870, 1001 Lausanne.

Telephone: 213209865; **Fax:** 213209817; **Internet:** www.icaa .ch; **e-mail:** secretariat@icaa.ch; icaamailbox@aol.com.

Institut International des Droits de l'Enfant (International Institute for the Rights of the Child)

Founded in 1995 by Dr Bernard Comby and Jean Zermatten and the merger of the International Association of Youth and Family Judges and Magistrates to promote children's rights at an international level.

Activities: Operates in the field of law and human rights, specifically for children. The Institute holds international seminars, provides training nationally and internationally, publishes a number of books on the subject of children's rights in the law, and maintains an interactive website.

Geographical Area of Activity: International.

Publications: Newsletter; books; working reports; documentary films.

Finance: Funded by the Swiss Confederation and by individual companies.

Board of Directors: Christophe Darbellay (Chair.); Michel Lachat (Vice-Chair.); Philip Jaffé (Sec./Treas.).

Principal Staff: Deputy Dir Paola Riva Gapany.

Address: CP 4176, 1950 Sion 4.

Telephone: 272057303; **Fax:** 272057302; **Internet:** www .childsrights.org; **e-mail:** info@childsrights.org.

International Red Cross and Red Crescent Movement—ICRC

Comprises the National Red Cross and Red Crescent Societies, the International Committee of the Red Cross (ICRC), founded in 1863 to help wounded soldiers on the battlefield, and the International Federation of Red Cross and Red Crescent Societies (the Federation), founded in 1919 (as the League of Red Cross and Red Crescent Societies) to promote humanitarian activities in peacetime.

Activities: An impartial, neutral and independent organization whose exclusively humanitarian mission is to protect the lives and dignity of victims of war and internal violence, and to provide them with assistance. The Movement directs and co-ordinates international relief activities in situations of conflict. It also endeavours to prevent suffering by promoting and strengthening humanitarian law and universal humanitarian principles. Comprises 176 National Red Cross and Red Crescent Societies; acts as a permanent body for liaison, co-ordination and study, advising members on the development of their services to the community. It also organizes international emergency relief operations for the victims of natural disasters, and co-ordinates relief preparedness programmes.

Geographical Area of Activity: International.

Publications: ICRC: *International Review of the Red Cross* (quarterly); *Red Cross Red Crescent* (quarterly, magazine produced jointly with the Federation, in English, French and Spanish); *Forum* (annually); Annual Report; Federation: Annual Review; *Handbook of the International Red Cross and Red Crescent Movement* (with the ICRC); *Weekly News*; *World Disasters Report* (annually); newsletters, guides and manuals.

Finance: Annual budget 1,600m. Swiss francs (2015).

International Committee: Peter Maurer (Pres.); Christine Beerli (Vice-Pres.).

Principal Staff: Dir-Gen. Yves Daccord.

Address: ave de la Paix 19, 1202 Geneva.

Telephone: 227346001; **Fax:** 227332057; **Internet:** www.icrc .org; **e-mail:** press.gva@icrc.org.

International Service for Human Rights—ISHR

Established in 1984.

Activities: Supports and facilitates the work of human rights defenders with the UN human rights system and regional human rights systems. The Service operates worldwide, at national, regional and international levels, with the aim of safeguarding human rights by publishing news updates and analytical reports on developments in key human rights systems; providing training for human rights defenders on international and regional human rights mechanisms; and providing information, support and advisory services. It builds human rights defenders' capacity effectively to engage with human rights systems and advocates for the improvement of these systems. It has a branch office in New York.

Geographical Area of Activity: International.

Restrictions: Not a grantmaking organization; does not campaign on individual cases.

Publications: Annual Report; *Human Rights Monitor Quarterly* (quarterly); *Simple Guide to the UN Treaty Bodies; Road map for civil society: State reporting procedure of the African Commission on Human and Peoples Rights*; manuals; handbooks; reports briefing papers.

Finance: Annual revenue 1,760,667 Swiss francs, expenditure 1,711,496 Swiss francs (31 Dec. 2014).

Board of Directors: Rosemary McCreery (Chair.); Chris Sidoti (Vice-Chair.); Pierre Avanzo (Treas.).

Principal Staff: Exec. Dir Phil Lynch.

Address: rue de Varembé 1, CP 16, 1211 Geneva 20.

Telephone: 229197100; **Fax:** 229197125; **Internet:** www.ishr.ch; **e-mail:** information@ishr.ch.

International Union Against Cancer—UICC

Founded in 1933 as a world federation of non-governmental agencies and organizations that combat cancer.

Activities: Promotes collaboration between cancer organizations, among cancer investigators, physicians and allied health professionals and experts. The Union focuses on four priority areas: building and enhancing cancer control capacity; tobacco control; population-based cancer prevention and control; and transfer of cancer knowledge and dissemination. It conducts research and information programmes covering: tumour biology; epidemiology and prevention; treatment and rehabilitation; detection and diagnosis; professional education; campaigns and public education; patient support; international collaborative activities; tobacco and cancer. It also organizes international conferences, study groups and courses, and administers the following fellowships: UICC International Cancer Technology Transfer Fellowships; Yamagiwa-Yoshida Memorial International Cancer Study Grants; American Cancer Society UICC International Fellowships for Beginning Investigators; AstraZeneca and Novartis UICC Translational Cancer Research Fellowship; UICC Trish Greene International Oncology Nursing Fellowships; UICC Asia-Pacific Cancer Society Training Grants; and UICC Latin America COPES Education and Training Fellowships. The Union manages GLOBALink, a computer communications system.

Geographical Area of Activity: International.

Publications: Annual Report; *UICC International Directory of Cancer Institutes and Organizations* (electronic); *International Journal of Cancer and Predictive Oncology* (30 a year); *UICC News* (quarterly); Annual Report; *International Calendar of Meetings on Cancer* (2 a year); manuals.

Finance: Income from membership dues, national subscriptions, grants and donations. Annual income US $11,776,044, expenditure $8,892,380 (2013).

Board of Directors: Dr Tezer Kutluk (Pres.); Prof. Sanchia Aranda (Pres.-elect); Mary Gospodarowicz (Immediate Past Pres.).

Principal Staff: CEO Cary Adams; Deputy CEO and Advocacy Officer Dr Julie Torode; Deputy CEO and COO Maria Barbara Leon.

Address: route de Frontenex 62, 1207 Geneva.

Telephone: 228091811; **Fax:** 228091810; **Internet:** www.uicc.org; **e-mail:** info@uicc.org.

Internationale Stiftung Hochalpine Forschungsstationen Jungfraujoch und Gornergrat (International Foundation of the High-Altitude Research Stations Jungfraujoch and Gornergrat)

Founded in 1930 by representatives of scientific institutions in Belgium, Germany, Austria, France, the United Kingdom and Switzerland to promote high-altitude research. Italy is also a member of the Foundation.

Activities: Supports the research station and Sphinx laboratory on the Jungfraujoch, and the two astronomical observatories Gornergrat South and Gornergrat North. Research is undertaken in the fields of physiology, physics, environment, astronomy and astrophysics.

Geographical Area of Activity: International.

Publications: Annual Report; white papers.

Board: Prof. Dr Hans Balsiger (Hon. Pres.); Prof. Dr Erwin O. Flückiger (Pres.); Karl Martin Wyss (Treas.).

Principal Staff: Dir Prof. Dr Markus Leuenberger.

Address: Sidlerstr. 5, 3012 Berne.

Telephone: 316314052; **Fax:** 316314405; **Internet:** www.ifjungo.ch; **e-mail:** markus.leuenberger@climate.unibe.ch.

IUCN/UICN (International Union for Conservation of Nature)

Founded in 1948.

Activities: Works in the areas of biodiversity, climate change, livelihoods, energy and green markets. It supports scientific research; manages field projects all over the world; and brings governments, NGOs, businesses, the UN, international conventions and community organizations together to develop policy, legislation and best practice. It is the world's largest professional global environmental network, a democratic union with more than 1,000 government and NGO member organizations, and almost 11,000 volunteer scientists in more than 160 countries. In addition, the Union works closely with a wide range of leading companies in a variety of sectors, academic organizations, social and indigenous groups and UN organizations.

Geographical Area of Activity: International.

Publications: *World Conservation/Planète conservation/Conservacíon mundial* (three times a year); *The Red List of Threatened Species*; *Best Practice Guidelines on Protected Areas series*; *Environmental Policy and Law Papers; Species Conservation and Action Plans*; reports and other specialist publications.

Finance: Income from membership, framework agreements and project agreements. Annual income approx. 113,599,000 Swiss francs, expenditure 105,197,000 Swiss francs (31 Dec. 2012).

Council: Xinsheng Zhang (Pres.); Jenny Gruenberger, Malik Amin Aslam Khan, John Robinson, Marina von Weissenberg (Vice-Pres); Patrick de Heney (Treas.).

Principal Staff: Dir-Gen. Inger Andersen; Deputy Dir-Gen. Poul Engberg-Pedersen.

Address: rue Mauverney 28, 1196 Gland.

Telephone: 229990000; **Fax:** 229990002; **Internet:** www.iucn.org; **e-mail:** mail@iucn.org.

Jacobs Foundation

Established in 1988 by Klaus J. Jacobs to foster child and youth development.

Activities: Supports research and intervention projects in the field of child and youth development. The Foundation focuses on the value chain paradigm: innovative research, practical testing of the findings in pilot interventions and market introduction, which ensures the systematic application of tested models on a larger scale. It funds projects that stand a strong chance of delivering a positive outcome and demonstrate potential for implementation elsewhere, pursuing the majority of projects in close collaboration with established partners.

Geographical Area of Activity: International.

Restrictions: No support is given for endowments, regular operating budgets, religious organizations, construction projects, or for financial aid/tuition assistance or scholarships.

Publications: Annual Report; brochure.

Finance: Total assets 1,601,8m. Swiss francs, net annual income 34,032,000 Swiss francs (2013).

Board of Directors: Lavinia Jacobs (Chair.); Dr Joh. Christian Jacobs (Hon. Chair.).

Principal Staff: Man. Dir Sandro Giuliani.

Address: Seefeldquai 17, POB, 8034 Zürich.

Telephone: 443886123; **Fax:** 443886137; **Internet:** www.jacobsfoundation.org; **e-mail:** jf@jacobsfoundation.org.

C. G. Jung-Institut Zürich

Founded in 1948 by Prof. C. G. Jung, C. A. Meier, K. Binswanger, L. Frey-Rohn and J. Jacobi; a training institute for education and research in the field of analytical psychology.

Activities: Operates internationally in the fields of analytical psychology, education, science and medicine, through research, courses and contacts with others interested in psychology and the publication of scientific works. The Institute also maintains a library containing some 15,000 volumes.

Geographical Area of Activity: Training and classes are in German and English with the English Programme being entirely international. Iran, India, Ireland, South Africa, Brazil, the United Kingdom, the USA, as well as all of the Asian countries are currently represented.

Restrictions: Applicants are required to apply to study.

Publications: A number of lectures, most of Marie-Louise von Franz's work and transcripts of classes are held at the Jung Institute. Major authors are: Jung, von Franz, Neumann, Edinger, Harding, C.A. Meier, Kast, Leonard, Woodman, Estes, Frey-Rhon, Ulanov, Wilmer, van der Post and Guggenbühl-Craig; newsletter.

Finance: Financed through tuition and endowments. The Institute is a non-profit educational foundation.

Board of Trustees: Prof. Dr Verena Kast (Pres.); Philip L. Kime (Vice-Pres.).

Principal Staff: Head of Admin. Eveline Ryser.

Address: Hornweg 28, 8700 Küsnacht.

Telephone: 449141040; **Fax:** 449141050; **Internet:** www.junginstitut.ch; **e-mail:** cg@junginstitut.ch.

Landis & Gyr Stiftung (Landis & Gyr Foundation)

Established in 1971, as the Zuger Kulturstiftung Landis & Gyr, by the firm Landis & Gyr Ltd to promote and develop activities in culture, science and social concerns.

Activities: Operates in the field of the arts and humanities, through project support, as well as through a studio programme in fine arts, literature and culture criticism, linked exclusively to accommodation in Berlin, London or Zug. The Foundation also lends support to specific scientific institutions such as Collegium Budapest, New Europe College, Bucharest, and the Centre for Advanced Study, Sofia, to strengthen scientific exchange with Eastern Europe. Awards the Landis & Gyr Stiftung Prize every two years to an individual or group for outstanding services of social benefit.

Geographical Area of Activity: Switzerland, Europe.

Restrictions: No project support outside Switzerland; studio programme through official application only; no applications accepted from outside Switzerland.

Finance: Annual expenditure approx. 3m. Swiss francs.

Trustees: Bruno Bonati (Pres.); Dr Thomas Sprecher (Vice-Pres.).

Principal Staff: Man. Dir Regula Koch.

Address: Dammstr. 16, Postfach 4858, 6304 Zug.

Telephone: 417242312; **Fax:** 417245383; **Internet:** www.lg-stiftung.ch; **e-mail:** regula.koch@lg-stiftung.ch.

Limmat Stiftung (Limmat Foundation)

Founded in 1972 by Dr Arthur Wiederkehr to promote initiatives for the common good in Switzerland and abroad, especially by offering the necessary organizational infrastructure.

Activities: Operates nationally and internationally in the fields of education, health, advancement of the poor (especially women) and vocational training. Programmes are instruction orientated and encourage self-help.

Geographical Area of Activity: International.

Publications: Annual Report; articles.

Finance: Average annual project income 7,400m. Swiss francs; expenditure 7,800m. Swiss francs (2010–14).

Board: Elisabeth András (Pres.), Franz Stirnimann (Sec.).

Principal Staff: Exec. Dir François Geinoz; Project Dir Juan J. Alarcon; Financial Dir André Meier.

Address: Rosenbühlstr. 32, 8044 Zürich.

Telephone: 442662030; **Fax:** 442662031; **Internet:** www.limmat.org; **e-mail:** limmat@limmat.org.

The Lutheran World Federation (Lutherischer Weltbund/Fédération Luthérienne Mondiale//Federación Luterana Mundial)

Founded in 1947 to serve Lutheran churches as an instrument for humanitarian assistance, mission and development, ecumenism, communication and theological study.

Activities: Operates internationally in the fields of humanitarian assistance, communication, mission and development, human rights, ecumenical and interfaith relations. The Federation offers annual scholarships (mainly at graduate level) in theology and other disciplines, and vocational courses for members of Lutheran churches throughout the world. It also organizes study programmes and seminars to advance its theological, ecumenical and development work in the different world contexts. Maintains a Peace Fund, supporting the human rights ministries of member churches with training, financial and other assistance. The Federation has an international news service in English and German, and publishes studies and specialized publications on development, human rights and theological issue. In 2014, the Federation comprised 144 member churches in 79 countries.

Geographical Area of Activity: International.

Publications: *Lutheran World Information* (electronic); *Lutherische Welt-Information* (news bulletin); *LWF Annual Report*; *LWF Documentation/LWB Dokumentation*; *LWF Studies/LWB-Studien*; *LWF Women*; *LWF Youth*; departmental and office reports and working papers.

Finance: Annual income €105.6m., expenditure €101.5m. (2013).

Principal Staff: Pres. Bishop Dr Munib A. Younan; Gen. Sec. Rev. Martin Junge.

Address: 150 route de Ferney, POB 2100, 1211 Geneva 2.

Telephone: 227916111; **Fax:** 227916630; **Internet:** www.lutheranworld.org; **e-mail:** info@lutheranworld.org.

MAVA Fondation pour la Nature

Established in 1994 by Dr Luc Hoffmann.

Activities: Promotes the conservation of nature through the protection of rare or threatened species and their habitats; the preservation of biodiversity and landscapes; and the sustainable management of natural resources.

Geographical Area of Activity: Mediterranean Basin, Switzerland and the Alpine Arc, and West African coastal zone.

Publications: Annual Report.

Finance: Annual project expenditure 60m. Swiss francs (2013).

Board of Directors: André Hoffmann (Chair.); Luc Hoffman (Chair. Emeritus); Hubert du Plessix (Treas.).

Principal Staff: Dir-Gen. Lynda Mansson.

Address: rue Mauverney 28, 1196 Gland.

Telephone: 215441600; **Fax:** 215441616; **Internet:** www.mava-foundation.org; **e-mail:** info@fondationmava.org.

Médecins Sans Frontières International—MSF International (Doctors Without Borders International)

Founded in 1971 in Paris to provide medical care to populations in times of crisis in any part of the world.

Activities: Works in the fields of medicine and health, aid to less-developed countries, and law and human rights, through self-conducted programmes, conferences, training courses and publications. The organization relies on volunteer health professionals, and provides medical aid to those in need worldwide, in countries at war or coping with disaster. It runs missions in refugee camps and long-term operations in countries where health structures have broken down; promotes human rights; helps to secure long-term rehabilitation of health structures; organizes the training of staff; and operates two centres for surveillance and applied research in epidemiology and public health. The international network comprises 24 independent operational sections and delegate offices in Europe, North America and Asia; there are missions in more than 70 countries and territories worldwide. It was awarded the Nobel Peace Prize in 1999.

Geographical Area of Activity: International.

Publications: Annual Report; *MSF International Newsletter*; *Développement durable: espace de démocratie et d'intégration citoyenne*; *Populations in Danger* (annually); bulletins; Annual Report; activity reports.

Finance: More than 90% of funding comes from private sources. Annual income €1,008.5m., expenditure €952.5m. (2013).

Principal Staff: International Pres. Dr Joanne Liu; Sec.-Gen. Jérôme Oberreit.

Address: rue de Lausanne 78, CP 116, 1211 Geneva 21.

Telephone: 228498400; **Fax:** 228498404; **Internet:** www.msf.org; **e-mail:** webmaster@msf.org.

Christoph-Merian-Stiftung (Christoph Merian Foundation)

Established in 1886.

Activities: Aims to assist those in need and promote a healthy environment, quality of life and culture in Basle, Switzerland. The basis for Foundation activities is provided by the assets bequeathed to it by Christoph Merian (1800–58) and Margaretha Merian-Burckhardt (1806–1886). Only the income from those assets may be used for the Foundation and its diverse activities; the capital itself must be left intact.

Geographical Area of Activity: Basel, Switzerland.

Restrictions: No grants to individuals and no grants to organizations outside Basel.

Publications: Annual Report.

Finance: Annual revenue 64,730,228 Swiss francs, expenditure 56,502,365 Swiss francs (2014).

Foundation Commission: Dr Lukas Faesch (Chair.); Prof. Dr Leonhard Burckhardt (Gov.).

Principal Staff: Dir Dr Beat von Warburg.

Address: St Alban-Vorstadt 5, Postfach, 4052 Basel.

Telephone: 612263333; **Fax:** 612263344; **Internet:** www.merianstiftung.ch; **e-mail:** info@merianstiftung.ch.

Novartis Foundation

Began in 1973 as a department within the Novartis company for relations with developing countries; name changed in 1979 to the Ciba-Geigy Foundation for Co-operation with Developing Countries and subsequently to the Novartis Foundation for Sustainable Development. Present name adopted in 2015.

Activities: Does not make grants, but supports the implementation of health initiatives financially and technically. The Foundation operates in three overlapping areas: developing and supporting health-care projects that focus on people in low-income settings and improve access to health care, strengthening human resources and empowering vulnerable groups; serving as a think tank on international health and corporate responsibility; and fostering dialogue between the private sector, government and civil society regarding global development and corporate responsibility.

Geographical Area of Activity: Sub-Saharan Africa, Indian subcontinent.

Restrictions: No unsolicited applications normally accepted. Not a grantmaking organization.

Publications: Annual Report; symposium reports; *Project Management Handbook*; *Leisinger: On Corporate Responsibility for Human Rights*.

Finance: Annual budget 10,610,000 Swiss francs (2013).

Board of Trustees: Andrin Oswald (Chair.).

Principal Staff: Head of Foundation Dr Ann Aerts.

Address: Novartis Campus, WSJ-210.10.26, 4002 Basel.

Telephone: 616962300; **Fax:** 616962333; **Internet:** www.novartisfoundation.org; **e-mail:** info@novartisfoundation.org.

Oak Foundation

Formally established in 1998; a group of charitable and philanthropic organizations.

Activities: Programmes include climate change, marine conservation, human rights, child abuse, women's issues, homelessness and learning differences. The Foundation runs special programmes in Denmark and Zimbabwe. Has offices in Belize, Bulgaria, Denmark, Ethiopia, the United Kingdom, the USA and Zimbabwe.

Geographical Area of Activity: International.

Restrictions: No grants are made to religious organizations, for general funding, or for supporting political candidates; no grants under US $25,000.

Board of Trustees: Kristian Parker (Chair.); Natalie Shipton, Caroline Turner (Vice-Chair.).

Principal Staff: Pres. Kathleen Cravero-Kristoffersson; Sec. Gary Goodman.

Address: ave Louis Casaï 58, CP 115, 1216 Cointrin, Geneva.

Internet: www.oakfnd.org; **e-mail:** info@oakfnd.ch.

Pro Helvetia (Swiss Arts Council)

Founded in 1939 to promote the arts and cultural exchange.

Activities: Promotes creative cultural activities and cultural works relating to Switzerland nationally and internationally. The Council maintains a network of liaison offices and partner institutes worldwide.

Geographical Area of Activity: International.

Publications: *Passages* (Swiss cultural magazine, 3 a year); information sheets; Swiss cultural policy glossary; information series on Swiss culture; newsletters.

Finance: Receives a global budget from parliament every four years. Global budget 35.9m. Swiss francs (2015); total assets 23,133,000 Swiss francs (31 Dec. 2014).

Board of Trustees: Charles Beer (Pres.).

Principal Staff: Dir Andrew Holland; Deputy Dir Madeleine Betschart.

Address: Schweizer Kulturstiftung, Hirschengraben 22, 8024 Zürich.

Telephone: 442677171; **Fax:** 442677106; **Internet:** www.prohelvetia.ch; **e-mail:** info@prohelvetia.ch.

Pro Juventute

Established in 1912 by Dr Carl Horber for the promotion of children and youth in personal development.

Activities: Focuses on protecting children and adolescents and improving their quality of life in the family and in society in general. The organization works in the fields of education, human rights, health care and social welfare. It funds projects, makes grants to individuals, organizes conferences, and develops its own programmes.

Geographical Area of Activity: Switzerland.

Publications: Annual Report; *Futura* (quarterly magazine); brochures and fact sheets.

Finance: Funded by donations and the sale of stamps, cards and other products, co-operation with businesses. Annual income 17,944,000 Swiss francs, expenditure 18,910,000 Swiss francs (31 Dec. 2014).

Board of Trustees: Josef Felder (Pres.); Reto Medici (Vice-Pres.).

Principal Staff: Dir Robert Schmuki.

Address: Thurgauerstr. 39, CP 8050 Zurich.

Telephone: 442567777; **Fax:** 442567778; **Internet:** www .projuventute.ch; **e-mail:** info@projuventute.ch.

Ramsay Foundation

Established in 1998 by Freda Ramsay to support educational and cultural activities.

Activities: Aims to advance education, through support for pedagogy, training and post-training initiatives, as well as through funding for art and cultural activities, in Switzerland and overseas. Outside of Switzerland, the Foundation has awarded grants to projects in Africa, Brazil, Bulgaria, Croatia, Germany, India, Israel, the Russian Federation, the United Kingdom and Ukraine. In 2013, its annual disbursements amounted to more than 100,000 Swiss francs.

Geographical Area of Activity: Switzerland and international, incl. Africa, Brazil, Bulgaria, Croatia, Germany, India, Israel, the Russian Federation, the United Kingdom and Ukraine.

Restrictions: No grants made to individuals, target groups comprising people over the age of 20 years, commercial projects and events, film or musical recording productions or large-scale projects.

Board of Trustees: Don Vollen (Chair.).

Address: Postfach, 4001 Basel.

Telephone: 612263321; **Internet:** www.ramsayfoundation.ch; **e-mail:** info@ramsayfoundation.ch.

Marc Rich Foundation for Education, Culture and Welfare

Founded in 1988 by Marc and Denise Rich to promote Jewish cultural, artistic, educational, social and scientific awareness within a broad humanitarian framework.

Activities: Offers support in the areas of education, culture and social welfare worldwide. Since its inception, the Foundation has disbursed more than US $150m.

Geographical Area of Activity: International.

Board: Kathrin Genovese (Chair.); Georg Stucky (Vice-Chair.).

Principal Staff: Man. Dir Avner Azulay.

Address: c/o Dr Margrit Meyer Hirschengraben 7 6003 Luzern.

Telephone: 417090700; **Fax:** 417090799.

Rroma Foundation

Established in 1993 to support the Roma in Central and Eastern Europe; the Foundation was part of the Soros network of foundations, but is now a fully independent foundation.

Activities: Supports programmes in the fields of culture, education, community development, and human rights, including the training of Roma as teachers, journalists and human rights advisers. The Foundation provides support for schools and summer schools; grants for publishing projects, offering scholarships and supporting bilingual journals and newspapers; and grants for arts projects. It offers legal advice and assistance; and promotes interaction between majority populations and the Roma minority. The Foundation established a Roma Social Bureau in Bulgaria, which offers advice on civil rights issues, and was planning to establish a similar bureau in Ukraine. It also supports Roma refugees in Switzerland.

Geographical Area of Activity: Mainly Central and Eastern Europe.

Publications: Background reports.

Board of Trustees: Judith C. Kruck (Chair.).

Principal Staff: Exec. Dir Dr Stéphane Laederich.

Address: Gladbachstr. 67, 8044 Zürich.

Telephone: 13836326; **Fax:** 13836302; **Internet:** foundation .rroma.org; **e-mail:** admin@rroma.org.

Sandoz Fondation de Famille (Sandoz Family Foundation)

Established in 1964 by Marcel Edouard Sandoz, the son of the founder of Sandoz SA of Basle (now Novartis SA), to hold the Sandoz family's company shareholding.

Activities: Seeks to encourage entrepreneurial commitment through its commercial shareholdings, as well as encouraging creativity and private initiative. In 1982, the Foundation established the Fondation Edouard et Maurice Sandoz (FEMS), which awards the annual FEMS Prize to support artistic development, as well as supporting a range of cultural events and organizations. In 1999, it launched a programme funding science professorships at Swiss universities.

Geographical Area of Activity: Mainly Switzerland.

Board of Directors: Dr Pierre Landolt (Pres.); Olivier Verrey (Sec.).

Principal Staff: Media Contact Jörg Denzler.

Address: Sandoz Family Office SA, ave Général-Guisan 85, 1009 Pully; Bahnhofstrasse 15, 8750 Glarus.

Telephone: 217211336; **Internet:** www.sandozfondation.ch; **e-mail:** j.denzler@sandozfamilyoffice.ch.

Max Schmidheiny-Stiftung (Max Schmidheiny Foundation)

Established in 1978 at the University of St Gallen by Max Schmidheiny to promote individual, social and economic freedom.

Activities: Promotes valuable endeavours towards the preservation and further development of a free market economy and society, especially initiatives safeguarding individual freedom, the responsibility of the individual for his/her own welfare and the guaranteed maintenance of social security. The Foundation focuses on entrepreneurship and risk, and on the analysis of business in the socio-economic context, including the promotion of exchanges and collaboration between the younger generation of entrepreneurs, business people and politicians. It funds the Max Schmidheiny Foundation Professorship at the University of St Gallen.

Geographical Area of Activity: Switzerland and international.

Board of Trustees: Dr Thomas Schmidheiny (Chair.); **Board of Directors:** Thomas Bieger.

Address: Dufourstr. 83, CP 1045, 9001 St Gallen.

Telephone: 712272070; **Fax:** 712272075; **Internet:** www.ms -foundation.org; **e-mail:** msf@ms-foundation.org.

Schwab Foundation for Social Entrepreneurship

Established in 1998.

Activities: Provides platforms at regional and global levels to promote leading models of sustainable social innovation. The Foundation identifies a select community of social entrepreneurs and engages it in shaping global, regional and industry agendas that improve the state of the world, in collaboration with other World Economic Forum stakeholders.

Geographical Area of Activity: Switzerland.

Publications: Manuals; reports.

Board: Hilde Scwab (Chair. and Co-Founder); Klaus Schwab (Co-Founder).

Principal Staff: Man. Dir David Aikman.

Address: route de la Capite 91–93, 1223 Cologny/Geneva.

Telephone: 228691212; **Fax:** 227862744; **Internet:** www
.schwabfound.org; **e-mail:** info@schwabfound.org.

Schweizerisch-Liechtensteinische Stiftung für Arch-äologische Forschungen im Ausland—SLSA (Swiss-Liechtenstein Foundation for Archaeological Research Abroad—SLFA)

Established in 1986 with the participation of HSH Prince Hans-Adam II of Liechtenstein to assist developing countries to preserve their national heritage and contribute to international solidarity in the field of archaeological research.

Activities: Carries out research in the areas of archaeological, ethnographical and cultural research in developing countries, including Bhutan, the People's Republic of China, Ecuador, Indonesia, Jordan, Mali, Mongolia, Peru and Syria, in collaboration with local research organizations and universities.

Geographical Area of Activity: Croatia, Jordan, Mali, Peru, Syria, Switzerland.

Restrictions: Supports only its own research.

Publications: Annual Report; research publications; *Terra Archaeologica* (monograph series); *Ergebnisse der Schweizerisch-Liechtensteinischen Ausgrabungen* (2000); *Sauvegarde et Conservation du Patrimoine Archéologique* (2000); *Ergebnisse der Schweizerisch-Liechtensteinischen Ausgrabungen* (2006); *Cinq mille ans d'histoire au pied des volcans en Equateur* (2008); and other publications.

Finance: Funding from Prince Hans-Adam II of Liechtenstein, private sponsors and the Swiss State. Total assets 2,258,865 Swiss francs (31 Dec. 2013).

Board of Trustees: Dr Hans Heinrich Coninx (Chair.); Dr Egmond Frommelt, Danielle Ritter (Vice-Chair.).

Principal Staff: Sec.-Gen. Dr Eberhard Fischer.

Address: Generalsekretariat SLSA, Museum Rietberg Zürich, Gablerstr. 15, 8002 Zürich.

Telephone: 442017669; **Fax:** 442010548; **Internet:** www.slsa
.ch; **e-mail:** postfach@slsa.ch.

Schweizerische Akademie der Medizinischen Wissenschaften (Swiss Academy of Medical Sciences)

Founded in 1943 to promote medical research in Switzerland and research carried out by the Swiss in other countries; to promote medico-scientific co-operation in Switzerland; to issue ethical guidelines for the medical profession; and to award prizes for medical scholars.

Activities: Supports advanced medical research. The Academy awards a limited number of grants and scholarships for research and several prizes, including the Bing Prize and the Ott Prize. It organizes scientific meetings and symposia, and produces medico-scientific publications.

Geographical Area of Activity: Switzerland.

Restrictions: Support restricted to Switzerland.

Publications: Annual Report (in French and German); *Ethical Guidelines for Physicians*; *SAMW Bulletin* (quarterly, in German and French); various information brochures.

Finance: Total assets 1,574,987 Swiss francs (31 Dec. 2014).

Executive Board: Prof. Peter Meier-Abt (Pres.); Prof. Martin Schwab, Prof. Martin G. Täuber (Vice-Pres); Prof. Urs Brügger (Treas.).

Principal Staff: Sec.-Gen. Dr Hermann Amstad; Deputy Sec.-Gen. Michelle Salathé.

Address: Haus der Akademien, Laupenstrasse 7, Postfach 3001 Bern.

Telephone: 313069270; **Internet:** www.samw.ch; **e-mail:** mail@samw.ch.

Schweizerische Herzstiftung (Swiss Heart Foundation)

Founded in 1967 to promote research and prevention in the field of cardiovascular disease and stroke; and to support researchers and encourage co-ordinated research.

Activities: Committed to reducing the number of people suffering from cardiovascular diseases or remaining disabled by them, and to helping those affected to cope. The Foundation's main activities are promoting scientific research; informing patients and the general public about cardiovascular diseases; diagnosis; treatment; life-saving (HELP programme); heart groups; and prevention.

Geographical Area of Activity: Switzerland.

Publications: Annual Report; information brochures; magazine for donors.

Finance: Annual income 8,102,332 Swiss francs, expenditure 7,485,256 Swiss francs (31 Dec. 2013).

Board of Trustees: Prof. Dr Ludwig von Segesser (Chair.); Prof. Dr Rubio Mordasini (Vice-Chair.).

Principal Staff: Chief Exec. Therese Junker; Deputy Chief Exec. Martin Zimmerman.

Address: Schwarztorstr. 18, POB 368, 3000 Berne 14.

Telephone: 313888080; **Fax:** 313888088; **Internet:** www
.swissheart.ch; www.helpbyswissheart.ch; www
.swissheartgroups.ch; **e-mail:** info@swissheart.ch.

Schweizerische Stiftung für Alpine Forschungen (Swiss Foundation for Alpine Research)

Founded in 1939 to organize, finance and equip expeditions to mountains outside Europe and to the Arctic and Antarctic regions, and for Alpine research.

Activities: Operates internationally in the fields of science, mountaineering and alpine safety (high-altitude medicine, glaciology, geology, avalanches, ecological deterioration of high-altitude regions, etc.) through self-conducted programmes and research, and disseminating publications and topographical maps.

Geographical Area of Activity: International.

Publications: Annual Report; newsletter; maps; books; DVDs; brochure.

Foundation Council: Étienne Gross (Chair.).

Principal Staff: Man. Dir Thomas Weber-Wegst.

Address: Stadelhoferstr. 42, 8001 Zürich.

Telephone: 442531200; **Fax:** 442531201; **Internet:** www
.alpinfo.ch; **e-mail:** mail@alpinfo.ch.

Schweizerischer Nationalfonds zur Förderung der Wissenschaftlichen Forschung/Fonds National Suisse de la Recherche Scientifique—SNF (Swiss National Science Foundation—SNSF)

Founded in 1952 by the Schweizerische Naturforschende Gesellschaft, the Akademie der Medizinischen Wissenschaften, the Schweizerische Geisteswissenschaftliche Gesellschaft, the Schweizerischer Juristenverein and the Schweizerische Gesellschaft für Statistik und Volkswirtschaft to grant financial support to basic research in all scientific disciplines, at Swiss universities and other scientific institutions.

Activities: Operates nationally and internationally in the fields of education, science and medicine, the arts and humanities, law and other professions. The Foundation awards grants to individuals and institutions, as well as fellowships and scholarships; it conducts research; organizes conferences, courses and lectures; and disseminates publications. It is responsible for several national research programmes and implements the National Centres of Competence in Research (NCCR). It also maintains a database of funded projects, containing approximately 3,500 entries.

Geographical Area of Activity: Mainly Switzerland.

Restrictions: To be eligible for a research grant, candidates must be resident in Switzerland (regardless of citizenship); candidates for fellowships must be resident in Switzerland or have Swiss or Liechtenstein nationality.

Publications: Annual Report; *SNSF Profile including Facts and Figures*; *Horizonte/Horizons* (quarterly); *SNF/FNSinfo*; *Multi-annual programme*; *NCCR Portrait: Cutting-edge research made in Switzerland*; *Guide: The NCCR at a glance*; *NRP Portrait: Research for you*; *Prospectus on the different Funding Instruments of the SNSF.*

Finance: Annual income 1,086.3m. Swiss francs, expenditure 1,086.3m. Swiss francs (2014).

Board: Gabriele Gendotti (Pres. of the Foundation Council); Martin Vetterli (Pres. of the Research Council); Daniel Höchli (Man. Dir).

Address: Wildhainweg 3, POB 8232, 3001 Berne.

Telephone: 313082222; **Fax:** 313013009; **Internet:** www.snf.ch; **e-mail:** com@snf.ch.

Secours Dentaire International (International Dental Rescue)

Founded in 1981 to support co-operation and development in medical dentistry in less-developed countries.

Activities: Operates in Africa and the Caribbean in the field of dentistry. The organization teaches and trains staff for dental clinics; and provides technical skills and trains school teachers. It has clinics in Benin, Burkina Faso, Cameroon, the Congo, Gabon, Haiti, Madagascar, Tanzania and Zimbabwe.

Geographical Area of Activity: Sub-Saharan Africa and Haiti; Switzerland.

Restrictions: No grants to individuals.

Publications: *SDI News 1*; *SDI News 2*; *Prophylactic Lessons in SDI clinics*; *Outreach Work in Zimbabwe*; statistics; posters; leaflets.

Finance: Funded by donations.

Board of Directors: Dr Michael Willi (Chair.); Quentin Voellinger (Vice-Chair.).

Address: c/o Q. Voellinger, Le Bourg 11, 1610 Oron-la-Ville.

Telephone: 219462532; **Internet:** www.secoursdentaire.ch; **e-mail:** info@secoursdentaire.ch.

Stiftung zur Förderung der Ernährungsforschung in der Schweiz—SFEFS (Swiss Nutrition Foundation)

Founded in 1969 by Nestlé SA, Hoffmann-La Roche & Cie, AG, and Wander AG to further scientific research in the field of nutrition.

Activities: Operates mainly nationally in the field of human nutrition, focusing on its physiological, medical and social aspects. The Foundation supports research projects; awards grants to individuals and institutions, and fellowships and scholarships; and sponsors publications. Grants are provided to Swiss nationals for postgraduate studies and research abroad or research projects in Switzerland.

Geographical Area of Activity: Switzerland.

Publications: Annual Report.

Principal Staff: Pres. Prof. Dr Caspar Wenk; Sec. Monique Dupuis.

Address: c/o Institute of Animal Sciences, Nutrition Biology, ETH Zentrum LFW B 57, 8092 Zurich.

Telephone: 446323269; **Fax:** 446321128; **Internet:** www.sfefs.ethz.ch; **e-mail:** cwenk@ethz.ch; monique.dupuis@inw.agrl.ethz.ch.

Stiftung Kinderdorf Pestalozzi (Pestalozzi Children's Foundation)

Founded in 1946 by Walter Robert Corti to provide help for children in need and distress, and to be a place of meeting and co-operation, a centre of mutual understanding beyond all national, religious and linguistic barriers.

Activities: Operates in the fields of access to education, intercultural coexistence, and addressing the needs of disadvantaged children and young people. All the Foundation's programmes and projects are partner-based: it does not operate and implement projects directly, but co-operates with local structures (government and NGO). Co-operation projects are currently running in Ethiopia, El Salvador, Guatemala, Honduras, Laos, the former Yugoslav republic of Macedonia, Moldova, Myanmar, Serbia, Thailand and Tanzania. The Foundation also operates a village in Trogen, Switzerland as a facility for exchange projects, bringing together approx. 2,500 children and young people each year from around the world for inter-cultural activities.

Geographical Area of Activity: East Africa, Central America, South-East Asia, South-Eastern Europe and Switzerland.

Restrictions: Project proposals that are outside the Foundation's range of activities and supported countries will not be considered.

Publications: Annual Report (available in English, French and German); other publications; newsletter.

Finance: Main financial support comes from donations, sponsorships and legacies. Annual income 16,665,895 Swiss francs, expenditure 16,113,956 Swiss francs (2014).

Trustees: Rosmarie Quadranti (Pres.).

Principal Staff: Exec. Dir Dr Urs Karl Egger.

Address: Kinderdorfstr. 20, 9043 Trogen.

Telephone: 713437373; **Fax:** 713437300; **Internet:** www.pestalozzi.ch; **e-mail:** info@pestalozzi.ch.

Stiftung Klimarappen (Climate Cent Foundation)

Founded in 2005; a voluntary initiative of four major Swiss business associations.

Activities: Aims to contribute to Switzerland's fulfilment of its climate policy targets as set by the Swiss CO2 Law and the Kyoto Protocol. Between 2013 and 2022, the Foundation intends to concentrate its activities abroad.

Geographical Area of Activity: Switzerland and international.

Publications: Annual Report; newsletter.

Finance: Total assets 126,922,004 Swiss francs (31 Dec. 2012).

Foundation Council: Dr David Syz (Chair.); Dr Rolf Harti (Vice-Chair.).

Principal Staff: Man. Dir Dr Marco Berg.

Address: Freiestr. 167, 8032 Zürich.

Telephone: 443879900; **Fax:** 443879909; **Internet:** www.klimarappen.ch; **e-mail:** info@stiftungklimarappen.ch.

Stiftung Szondi-Institut (Szondi Institute Foundation)

Founded in 1969 by Dr Leopold Szondi to promote in-depth research in psychology.

Activities: Conducts research on the influence of heredity and environment on neuroses, psychoses and criminality, and on psychological tests, in particular the Szondi test. The Institute trains future psychotherapists and collaborates with researchers from other countries.

Geographical Area of Activity: Switzerland.

Publications: Books by Leopold Szondi and by other authors.

Board of Trustees: Alois Altenweger (Chair. and Dir).

Principal Staff: Sec. Manuela Eccher.

Address: Krähbühlstr. 30, 8044 Zürich.

Telephone: 442524655; **Fax:** 442529188; **Internet:** www.szondi.ch; **e-mail:** info@szondi.ch.

Stiftung Vivamos Mejor (Vivamos Mejor Foundation)

Established in 1981 to aid social groups in Central and South America.

Activities: Co-finances and supervises development projects in the fields of: education (pre-school and school advancement, fostering of caring, responsible and non-violent behaviour); training (adult education, professional training and advancement, organizational development and gender); employment (nutritional safety, earnings promotion and sustainable handling of natural resources); and health (hygiene, health care, pregnancy, AIDS, combat of maternal and infant mortality, and balanced diet).

Geographical Area of Activity: Central and South America, Switzerland.

Publications: Annual report, newsletter (bi-annual), several brochures and flyers.

Finance: Annual income 2,276,099 Swiss francs (31 Dec. 2014).

Board of Trustees: Dr Andreas Gubler (Chair.); Jean-Pierre Remund (Treas.).

Principal Staff: Man. Markus Burri.

Address: Fabrikstr. 31, POB 873, 3000 Berne 9.

Telephone: 313313929; **Fax:** 313320309; **Internet:** www .vivamosmejor.ch; **e-mail:** info@vivamosmejor.ch.

SWISSAID Foundation

Established in 1948 to work towards a peaceful world, free from violence, war, poverty and hunger.

Activities: Operates in collaboration with local partner organizations in Africa (Chad, Guinea-Bissau, Niger and Tanzania), Asia (India and Myanmar) and Central and South America (Colombia, Ecuador and Nicaragua) to assist in sustainable development. Maintains offices in 10 countries.

Geographical Area of Activity: Chad, Colombia, Ecuador, Guinea-Bissau, India, Myanmar, Nicaragua, Niger, Tanzania.

Publications: *SWISSAID Spiegel/Le Monde* (quarterly, in German and French).

Finance: Receives donations and government contributions. Annual revenue 19,431,107 Swiss francs, expenditure 18,495,238 Swiss francs (2014).

Board of Trustees: Rudolf Rechsteiner (Chair.).

Principal Staff: Dir Caroline Morel.

Address: Lorystr. 6A, POB 3000, Bern 5.

Telephone: 313505353; **Fax:** 313512783; **Internet:** www .swissaid.ch; **e-mail:** info@swissaid.ch.

Swisscontact—Swiss Foundation for Technical Co-operation

Established in 1959 by notable figures from the worlds of commerce and science in Switzerland.

Activities: Promotes economic, social and ecological development by supporting people to integrate successfully into local commercial life and improve their living conditions as a result through their own efforts. The Foundation focuses on strengthening local and global value chains. It concentrates on four core areas: Vocational Education and Training—enabling access to the labour market and creating the conditions for gaining an occupation and earning an income; SME Promotion—promoting local entrepreneurship with the goal of strengthening competitiveness; Financial Services—creating access to local financial service providers who offer credit, savings, leasing and insurance products; and Resource Efficiency—promoting the efficient use of resources through production methods that are efficient in their use of energy and materials, and by taking measures to promote clear air and sustainable waste disposal.

Geographical Area of Activity: Asia, Central and South America, Africa and Eastern Europe.

Restrictions: No grants to individuals.

Publications: Annual Report (in English, Spanish, French and German).

Finance: Total assets 36,921,000 Swiss francs (2014).

Board of Trustees: Heinrich M. Lanz (Chair.).

Principal Staff: CEO Samuel Bon.

Address: Döltschiweg 39, 8055 Zürich.

Telephone: 444541717; **Fax:** 444541797; **Internet:** www .swisscontact.ch; **e-mail:** info@swisscontact.ch.

Syngenta Foundation for Sustainable Agriculture

Established in 2001 by Syngenta AG to assist in the development of smallholders and rural communities, improving livelihoods through innovation in sustainable agriculture.

Activities: Operates in agricultural development in less-developed, often semi-arid areas of Africa, Latin America and Asia to reduce poverty. The Foundation runs projects with local partners to increase smallholder productivity through access to technologies and markets. It also contributes to the agricultural development debate worldwide.

Geographical Area of Activity: Africa, Latin America, Asia.

Finance: Annual budget approx. €9m.

Board of Directors: Michel Demaré (Chair.).

Principal Staff: Exec. Dir Marco Ferroni.

Address: WRO-1002.11.52, Schwarzwaldallee 215, POB 4002, 4068 Basel.

Telephone: 613235634; **Fax:** 613237200; **Internet:** www .syngentafoundation.org; **e-mail:** syngenta.foundation@ syngenta.com.

Terre des Hommes Foundation

Founded in 1960 by Edmond Kaiser to support children in distress.

Activities: Provides short-term and long-term direct help to children in need without racial or religious prejudices. The Foundation conducts projects in more than 30 countries all over the world in the following priority intervention areas: health, social work and children's rights. It operates through self-conducted programmes and grants to institutions and individuals. All projects have an emphasis on the protection and support of children in need. Also provides emergency humanitarian aid.

Geographical Area of Activity: Over 30 countries in Eastern Europe, Africa, Latin America and Asia.

Publications: Annual Report; general brochure; country information sheets; various publications on thematic issues.

Finance: Annual income 67.5m. Swiss francs, expenditure 64.9m. Swiss francs (2013).

Council: Beat Mumenthaler (Pres); Félix Bollman, Thomas Harder (Vice-Pres).

Principal Staff: CEO Vito Angelillo; Dir Operations Philippe Buchs.

Address: ave de Montchoisi 15, 1006 Lausanne.

Telephone: 586110666; **Fax:** 586110677; **Internet:** www.tdh .ch; **e-mail:** info@tdh.ch.

Tibet-Institut Rikon (Tibetan Monastic Institute in Rikon, Switzerland)

Founded in 1967 by Henri Kuhn-Ziegler and Jacques Kuhn.

Activities: Aims to take care of the spiritual and religious needs of Tibetans living in exile in Switzerland; to enable Tibetan scholars and learned priests to teach compatriots the values of their ancient culture; and to enable Tibetan scholars and priests to learn Western sciences and languages to become informed about the Western way of living and thinking. The Institute operates internationally in the fields of education, social welfare and studies, science and the arts, and humanities, through research carried out in Switzerland and in co-operation with European and American institutions, and conferences, courses, publications and lectures. It undertakes research in the fields of history of religion, literature, cultural anthropology, linguistics and related disciplines. Courses are held on Tibetan religion, history, script and language, and basic instruction is given in the techniques of meditation. Formal opinions and reports on Tibetan affairs are prepared by the monks. Maintains a library of more than 12,000 titles, and film and photograph archives.

Geographical Area of Activity: International.

Publications: Annual Report and financial statement; *Opuscula Tibetana* (series of publications); *A Waterdrop from the Glorious Sea*; *Textbook of Colloquial Tibetan Language*; *Testimonies of Tibetan Tulkus*; *Political Officers, Sikkim, and Heads of British Mission, Lhasa*; *Tibetan songs from Dingri*; *The Historical Kingdom of Mili*; *Five Tibetan Legends from the Avadana*

Kalpalata; *Transformation into the Exalted State*; *Tibetan Ritual Music*; *Samatha*.

Governing Board: Dr Rudolf Högger (Pres.).

Principal Staff: Man. Dir and Curator Philip Hepp; Sec. Barbara Ziegler.

Address: Wildbergstr. 10, 8486 Rikon im Tösstal, Switzerland.

Telephone: 523831729; **Internet:** www.tibet-institut.ch; **e-mail:** info@tibet-institut.ch.

Volkart-Stiftung (Volkart Foundation)

Founded in 1951 on the 100th anniversary of the foundation of the Volkart Group.

Activities: Supports selected ideas, projects and organizations in the fields of sustainability, civil society, ecology, education, health, youth, and the arts and culture.

Geographical Area of Activity: Brazil, India, Portugal and Switzerland.

Restrictions: Does not accept applications for funding.

Publications: Annual Report.

Finance: Annual disbursements 625,596 Swiss francs (2012).

Foundation Council: Marc Reinhart (Chair.).

Principal Staff: Man. Dir Judith Forster.

Address: Volkart Haus, Postfach, 8401 Winterthur.

Telephone: 522686868; **Fax:** 522686889; **Internet:** www.volkartstiftung.ch; **e-mail:** stiftung@volkart.ch.

Welfare Association (Ta'awoun)

Founded in 1983.

Activities: Dedicated to the progress of Palestinians by preserving their heritage and identity, supporting their living culture and building civil society. The Association supports sustainable development initiatives through high-impact projects and solutions to complex problems. It is committed to sustainable Palestinian development and focuses on four main sectors: education, culture, community development, and emergency and humanitarian assistance. Other programmes include the revitalization of the Old City of Jerusalem and the Palestinian Remembrance Museum. Has offices in Geneva, Ramallah, Jerusalem, Gaza, Beirut, Amman and London.

Geographical Area of Activity: Palestinian Territories and Palestinian refugee camps in Lebanon.

Restrictions: No grants are made to individuals.

Publications: *Ta'awoun* (newsletter, in Arabic); Annual Report; other publications.

Finance: Annual disbursements US $38,490,000 (2013).

Board of Trustees: Faisa S. Alami (Chair.).

Principal Staff: Dir-Gen. Tafeeda Jarbawi.

Address: POB 3765, 1211 Geneva 3.

Internet: www.welfareassociation.org; **e-mail:** dg-office@jwelfare.org.

World Alliance of YMCAs—Young Men's Christian Associations

Founded in 1844 by George Williams and centred on the Christian faith.

Activities: Works for the physical, emotional and spiritual welfare of people of all faiths and of none. The Alliance runs programmes worldwide in the areas of youth, emergency aid, peacebuilding, education, food security, climate change, migration, leadership development, inter-faith dialogue, gender equality and globalization. It operates in 119 countries. The national associations of countries form the World Alliance, which holds consultative status with the UN.

Geographical Area of Activity: Africa, Americas, Asia, Europe, Middle East and the Pacific.

Restrictions: Does not make grants.

Publications: *YMCA World*; *World Week of Prayer*; *Living in Hope*; directory; reports.

Finance: Annual income 3,524,514 Swiss francs, expenditure 2,463,622 Swiss francs (31 Dec. 2013).

Executive Committee: Peter Posner (Pres.); Evelyne Gueye (Deputy Pres.); Leopoldo Moacir (Treas.).

Principal Staff: Sec.-Gen. Rev. Johan Vilhelm Eltvik.

Address: clos Belmont 12, 1208 Geneva.

Telephone: 228495100; **Fax:** 228495110; **Internet:** www.ymca.int; **e-mail:** office@ymca.int.

World Economic Forum

Founded in 1971 by Prof. Klaus M. Schwab to contribute to the growth of worldwide prosperity through economic co-operation and the promotion of enterprise. Supervised by the Swiss Federal Council, with consultative status with the UN.

Activities: Encourages the direct exchange of information between world leaders in business, politics and the academic sphere, to promote worldwide prosperity, particularly through engaging its corporate members in global citizenship. The Forum holds an annual meeting, the World Business Summit, in Davos, Switzerland, and arranges Industry Summits and conferences geared to the requirements of the specific needs of individual countries or regions. The Trustees '21' Project seeks to improve the state of the world in the transition from the 20th to the 21st century, through networking of global decision-makers, creating task forces comprising people from all sections of humanity.

Geographical Area of Activity: International.

Publications: *Global Competitiveness Report* (annually, in collaboration with the International Monetary Fund—IMF); *World Link* (magazine, 6 a year); Annual Meeting and Summit Reports; annual reports; institutional brochure; newsletters (institutional publications).

Principal Staff: Founder and Exec. Chair. Prof. Klaus M. Schwab.

Address: route de la Capite 91–93, 1223 Cologny/Geneva.

Telephone: 228691212; **Fax:** 227862744; **Internet:** www.weforum.org; **e-mail:** contact@weforum.org.

World Scout Foundation—Fondation du Scoutisme Mondial

Founded in 1969.

Activities: Finances scouting activities and provides support to the World Organization of the Scout Movement. The Foundation comprises 161 National Scout Organizations in 223 countries and territories. In 2014, the total amount of grants disbursed amounted to US $8.9m.

Geographical Area of Activity: Worldwide.

Publications: Annual Report; *One Promise, One Image*; *28 million young people are changing the world*; *The World Scouting Report*; copyrights; Baden-Powell's writings; catalogue.

Board: HM The King of Sweden (Hon. Chair.); Siegfried Weiser (Chair.)l; Wayne M. Perry (Chair.-elect); Mike Bosman (Past Chair.); Fredrik Gottlieb (Treas.); Dr Jens Ehrhardt (Sec.).

Principal Staff: Man. Tom Marsden.

Address: 1 rue de la Navigation, POB 2116, 1211 Geneva 1.

Telephone: 227051090; **Fax:** 227051099; **Internet:** www.scout.org; **e-mail:** info@worldscoutfoundation.org.

Worlddidac Foundation (Worlddidac-Stiftung)

Established in 1984 by Worlddidac—the World Association of Publishers, Manufacturers and Distributors of Educational Materials.

Activities: Presents the Worlddidac Award to the manufacturers of the best educational materials to promote creativity and innovation in the production of educational materials.

Geographical Area of Activity: International.

Publications: *Worlddidac Award Booklet;* newsletter.

Executive Council: Prof. Dr Wassilios E. Fthenakis (Pres.); Dr Chula Kumara Gangoda (Vice-Pres.) Reinhard Koslitz (Treas.).

Principal Staff: Dir-Gen. Beat Jost.

Address: Bollwerk 21, 3011 Berne.

Telephone: 313117682; **Fax:** 313121744; **Internet:** www.worlddidac.org; www.worlddidacaward.org; **e-mail:** info@worlddidac.org.

WWF International

Founded in 1961 by Sir Peter Scott and others to promote the conservation of natural resources and the diversity of species and ecosystems worldwide; originally known as the World Wildlife Fund.

Activities: Aims to stop the degradation of natural environments, conserve biodiversity, ensure the sustainable use of renewable resources, and promote the reduction of both pollution and wasteful consumption. The organization addresses the following priority issues: forests; freshwater and marine species; and climate change and toxics. It has identified and focuses its activities on 200 'ecoregions' the ('Global 200') believed to contain the world's remaining biological diversity, and actively supports and operates conservation programmes in more than 90 countries. The organization has 54 offices worldwide and five associate organizations.

Geographical Area of Activity: Worldwide.

Publications: *WWF News* (quarterly); *Living Planet Report* (periodically updated); *Wildlife of India* (CD-ROM); Annual Report.

Finance: Anual income €653,584,000, expenditure €614,105,000 (2013).

Board of Trustees: Yolanda Kakabadse Navarro (Pres.); André Hoffmann (Vice-Pres.); Markus Joytak Shaw (Treas.).

Principal Staff: Dir-Gen. Marco Lambertini.

Address: Secretariat, ave du Mont-Blanc 27, 1196 Gland.

Telephone: 223649111; **Fax:** 223648836; **Internet:** www.panda.org.

WWSF—Women's World Summit Foundation (Frauen Weltgipfel Stiftung/Fondation Sommet Mondial des Femmes)

Founded in 1991 by Elly Pradervand after the 2000 UN Childrens' Summit in support of the implementation of women and children's rights and the UN Development Goals.

Activities: Operates through two principal sections: the WWSF Women's Section and the WWSF Children-Youth Section. The Women's Section includes an annual prize for women's creativity in rural life; the International Day of Rural Women—15 October (since 2007 a UN Resolution Day); the Micro-credit Sheep Project in Mali; the Numbers Must Change campaign, which advocates greater gender equality; and the White-Ribbon Campaign Switzerland, which aims to create community dialogues for the elimination of violence against women. The WWSF Children-Youth section concentrates on prevention of abuse and violence against children and youth, and includes an international coalition of relevant actors around the world, an annual prize for innovative prevention activities, an International Clearinghouse, the Yellow-Ribbon campaign, a TV slot and signature cards. In 2010, the Foundation launched a YouthEngage website for the empowerment of young people to become involved in prevention of violence against children and young people.

Geographical Area of Activity: International.

Publications: Annual Report; *Empowering Women and Children* (newsletter, 2 a year); publicity materials.

Finance: Public support, memberships and government contributions.

Board of Directors: Bunny McBride (Pres.); Filomina Choma Steady (Vice-Pres.).

Principal Staff: Exec. Dir and Founder Elly Pradervand.

Address: POB 143, 1211 Geneva 20.

Telephone: 227386619; **Fax:** 227388248; **Internet:** www.woman.ch; white-ribbon.ch; youthengage.com; **e-mail:** info@woman.ch.

Taiwan

FOUNDATION CENTRES AND CO-ORDINATING BODIES

Himalaya Foundation

Established in 1990; a corporate foundation which aims to enable capable people of Chinese ancestry to develop their talents and participate broadly in the world community.

Activities: Operates in the fields of Chinese studies, economic affairs and civil society, through research, grants, exchanges, publications and involvement in international philanthropic associations. Also involved in the development of civil society and the third sector, setting up the Taiwan Philanthropy Information Center (q.v.) which informs on the non-profit sector in Taiwan and elsewhere by maintaining a database of foundations, as well as a library on philanthropy and the third sector. The Foundation has established the NPO Development Center for not-for-profit organization IT capacity building and the NPO book website providing publications relating to the third sector or published by not-for-profit organizations.

Geographical Area of Activity: Taiwan, Asia and the USA.

Restrictions: Prefers to fund projects which have tangible and far-reaching benefits for society.

Publications: *Directory of Foundations in Taiwan*; *Handbook on Good Practices for Laws Relating to Non-Governmental Organizations* (Chinese translation); series of books on the non-profit sector.

Board of Trustees: S. Gong (Chair.).

Principal Staff: Exec. Dir S. Gong; Asst Exec. Dir Andy Kao.

Address: 67 Fu Hsing North Rd, 9th Floor, Taipei 105.

Telephone: (2) 2544-8296; **Fax:** (2) 2718-5850; **Internet:** www.himalaya.org.tw; www.npo.org.tw; **e-mail:** hmfdtion@himalaya.org.tw.

Taiwan NPO Information Platform

Established in 1999 by the Himalaya Foundation (q.v.) as the Taiwan Philanthropy Information Center, a centre of information on the non-profit sector in Taiwan.

Activities: Provides information on the non-profit sector in Taiwan and elsewhere by maintaining a database of not-for-profit organizations operating in Taiwan and a library on philanthropy and the third sector.

Geographical Area of Activity: Taiwan.

Publications: *Newsletter* (weekly).

Address: c/o Himalaya Foundation, 167 Fu Hsing North Rd, 9th Floor, Taipei 105.

Telephone: (2) 2544-8296; **Fax:** (2) 2718-5850; **Internet:** www.npo.org.tw; **e-mail:** webmaster@npo.org.tw.

FOUNDATIONS, TRUSTS AND NON-PROFIT ORGANIZATIONS

Advantech Foundation

Founded in 1997 by Advantech Corpn.

Activities: Provides support to educational research in Taiwan and overseas, aiming to put the results into practice at individual, social and corporate level to improve people's standard of living. Active in the areas of entrepreneurship education as well as running a thesis programme and a technology innovation competition (TiC100).

Geographical Area of Activity: Taiwan and Malaysia.

Board of Directors: Ke Cheng Liu (Chair.).

Principal Staff: Contact Wendy Chen.

Address: 1 Alley 20, Lane 26, Rui-Kuan Rd, Nai-Hou, Taipei.

Telephone: (2) 2792-7818; **Fax:** (2) 2794-7327; **Internet:** www.tic100.org.tw; **e-mail:** tic100@advantech.com.tw.

AVRDC—The World Vegetable Center

Founded in 1971 as the Asian Vegetable Research and Development Center to encourage research and development of safe vegetable farming in the tropics and subtropics; and to help improve nutrition, health, employment and income of small-scale farmers in developing countries. As the organization's scope of work expanded over time, the name was changed to AVRDC—The World Vegetable Center.

Activities: Conducts research into vegetable development; maintains the world's largest public sector gene bank of vegetable germplasm, with more than 58,000 accessions; holds training workshops, seminars and conferences; operates regional vegetable research and development networks; maintains an information database and a library of about 45,000 books and periodicals.

Geographical Area of Activity: International, with an emphasis on developing countries. Headquarters are in Taiwan, with four regional centres, in Thailand, Tanzania, India and Dubai, and offices or staff in many other developing countries in Africa and Asia.

Publications: Annual Report; AVRDC newsletter; seminar proceedings; technical bulletins; production manuals; field guides.

Finance: Annual revenue US $19,343,655, expenditure $19,475,782 (31 Dec. 2014).

Board: Dr Yu-Tsai Huang (Chair.); Dr David Sammons (Vice-Chair.); Dolores Ledesma (Sec.).

Principal Staff: Dir-Gen. Dyno Keatinge; Deputy Dir-Gen. (Research) Dr Jacqueline d'Arros Hughes; Deputy Dir-Gen. (Administration and Services) Dr Yin-Fu Chang.

Address: POB 42, Shanhua, Tainan 74199; 60 Yin-Min Liao, Shanhua, Tainan 74151.

Telephone: (6) 583-7801; **Fax:** (6) 583-0009; **Internet:** www.avrdc.org; **e-mail:** info@worldveg.org.

Chang Yung-Fa Foundation

Established in 1985 by Chang Yung-Fa, founder and Chair. of Evergreen Group, a shipping and logistics co.

Activities: Provides maritime education and training to personnel, and scholarships to study in Taiwan and abroad; supports social welfare initiatives and public health programmes; and funds disaster relief. The Foundation has its own symphony orchestra (f. 2002), which performs c.100 times a year; runs the Evergreen Maritime Museum (f. 2008); and maintains an international conference centre.

Geographical Area of Activity: East Asia.

Publications: *Morals* (monthly magazine).

Finance: Total assets US $435m.; total expenditure since 1985 $130m.

Principal Staff: Exec. Dir Demie Chung.

Address: Zhongshan South Rd, Zhongzheng District, Taipei 11.

Telephone: (2) 2351-6699; **Fax:** (2) 2391-5175; **Internet:** www.cyff.org.tw; **e-mail:** cyff@cyff.org.tw.

Chia Hsin Foundation

Founded in 1963 by Dr Ming-Yu Chang and Ming-Chong Oung, Chairman of the Board of Directors and Managing Director, respectively, of the Chia Hsin Cement Corporation, for the promotion of culture in Taiwan.

Activities: Operates nationally in the fields of the arts and humanities, social studies, science and medicine, law and education, through research projects, courses, conferences, lectures, publications, fellowships and scholarships, and grants to individuals and institutions. Grants the Chia Hsin Technology Award, the Distinguished Contribution Award, the Chia Hsin Prize for Journalism and the Chia Hsin Athletics Award. Also facilitates and finances study abroad for a limited number of students, and provides universities with free copies of Master of Arts and doctoral theses.

Geographical Area of Activity: Taiwan.

Publications: Report of operations.

Board of Directors: An-Ping Chan (Chair.); Chang-Wen Chen (Vice-Chair.).

Address: 96 Chung Shan North Rd, Section 2, Taipei 10449.

Telephone: (2) 2523-1461; **Fax:** (2) 2511-4002; **Internet:** www .chcgroup.com.tw; **e-mail:** ch_found@chcgroup.com.tw.

Chiang Ching-Kuo Foundation for International Scholarly Exchange—CCKF

Founded in 1989 by the Government of Taiwan and the private sector to promote Chinese studies and scholarly exchange.

Activities: Operates internationally in the fields of the arts and humanities, economic affairs, education, international affairs, law and human rights, medicine and health, and social welfare and social studies, through research, grants to institutions and individuals, and awarding scholarships and fellowships. Programmes cover the American Region (including North, Central and South America), the Asian/Pacific Region, the European Region and the Republic of China. Maintains an office in the USA and has overseas centres at universities in the Czech Republic, Germany, Hong Kong and the USA.

Geographical Area of Activity: International.

Publications: Annual Report (in Chinese and English); newsletter (quarterly); *Building for the Future: the First Decade.*

Finance: Operational funds derive from interest generated by original endowment of US $86m. Annual revenue US $8,689,805, expenditure $6,887,096 (31 Dec. 2012).

Board of Directors: Kao-Wen Mao (Chair.).

Principal Staff: Pres. Yun-Han Chu; Vice-Pres Chun-I Chen, Gang Shyy.

Address: 65 Tun Hua South Rd, 13th Floor, Section 2, Taipei 106.

Telephone: (2) 2704-5333; **Fax:** (2) 2701-6762; **Internet:** www .cckf.org; **e-mail:** cckf@ms1.hinet.net.

Pacific Cultural Foundation

Founded in 1974 to promote international cultural exchange.

Activities: Operates through organizing and participating in international academic and cultural conferences; organizing international artists' or performing groups' visits to Taiwan; hosting exhibitions at the Foundation's Cultural Center in Taipei; and promoting international academic and cultural exchange initiatives.

Geographical Area of Activity: International.

Board of Trustees: Huan Lee (Chair.).

Principal Staff: Pres. Yu-Sheng Chang; Vice-Pres. Wu-Jian Guo.

Address: 2F-1, 180 Chang-An West Rd, Taipei 103, Taiwan.

Telephone: (2) 2555-3927; **Fax:** (2) 2555-3927; **Internet:** www .pcf.org.tw; **e-mail:** pcfarts@pcf.org.tw.

Syin-Lu Social Welfare Foundation

Founded in 1987 by Jing-Yi Zong.

Activities: Works through campaigning for the rights of physically and mentally disabled people to ensure their entitlement to social benefits; funds education, rehabilitation, housing, leisure and counselling services for physically and mentally disabled people; trains professionals to mobilize community services on behalf of people with disabilities; and publishes relevant information.

Geographical Area of Activity: Taiwan.

Finance: Annual expenditure NT $323,849,493, expenditure $304,737,605 (2012).

Principal Staff: CEO Jing-Yi Zong.

Address: 364 Jilin Rd, 4th Floor, Zhongshan District, Taipei 104.

Telephone: (2) 2592-9778; **Fax:** (2) 2592-8514; **Internet:** www .syinlu.org.tw; **e-mail:** isyinlu@gmail.com.

Tajikistan

FOUNDATIONS, TRUSTS AND NON-PROFIT ORGANIZATIONS

OSIAF—Open Society Institute Assistance Foundation—Tajikistan

Founded in 1996 to promote the development of open society in Tajikistan. An independent foundation, part of the Soros foundations network, which aims to foster political and cultural pluralism and reform economic structures to encourage free enterprise and a market economy.

Activities: Works in the fields of public health, educational and electoral reform, human rights and legal reform, regional co-operation, information and the media, and arts and culture.

Geographical Area of Activity: Tajikistan.

Publications: Annual Report; reports on education, capacity-building and e-readiness.

Board of Directors: Parviz Mullojanov (Chair.).

Principal Staff: Exec. Dir Dr Zuhra S. Halimova.

Address: 37/1 Bokhtar St, Vefa Business Centre, 4th Floor, 734002 Dushanbe.

Telephone: (372) 441-07-28; **Fax:** (372) 51-01-42; **Internet:** www.soros.tj; **e-mail:** osi@osi.tajik.net.

Tanzania

FOUNDATIONS, TRUSTS AND NON-PROFIT ORGANIZATIONS

Mo Dewji Foundation

Established in 2014 by Mohammed Dewji, CEO of MeTL Group.

Activities: Active in the fields of: education, building and equipping schools, training teachers, and supporting literacy initiatives; and health care, building hospitals, providing subsidized health care and cataract operations, raising awareness about contraception and HIV/AIDS, and donating mosquito nets. The Foundation also fosters local entrepreneurship. Other areas of interest include sports and access to water.

Geographical Area of Activity: Tanzania.

Address: PSPF Golden Jubilee Towers, 20th Floor, Ohio St, POB 20660, Dar es Salaam.

Telephone: (22) 2122830; **Internet:** www.modewjifoundation .org; **e-mail:** info@modewjifoundation.org.

Mwalimu Nyerere Foundation—MNF

Established in 1996 in memory of Mwalimu Julius Nyerere, the country's first President; it is an independent body not linked to any political party, and its aim is to promote 'peace, unity and people-centred development in Africa'.

Activities: Seeks to carry out its aims through encouraging and organizing dialogues within Africa, among and between governments, people, NGOs and local institutions; co-operating with other similar institutions within and outside Africa; collecting, analysing and disseminating information; and establishing a specialist library. Operates three programmes, the African Unity Programme, Institutional Capacity Building, and Justice for All. Also aims to promote the study of the principles adopted and practised by Nyerere, through collecting, analysing and cataloguing documents, letters, reports, etc., concerning him, and to make available to the public all such information. The Foundation took a leading role in facilitating Burundi peace talks in 1999. Maintains a Documentation Research Centre.

Geographical Area of Activity: Africa.

Publications: *The Work of the Mwalimu Nyerere Foundation* (Swahili version); *Africa Today and Tomorrow* (collection of speeches by Mwalimu Julius Nyerere); *South Bulletin.*

Board of Trustees: Dr Salim Ahmed Salim (Chair.).

Principal Staff: Exec. Dir Joseph W. Butiku.

Address: India/Makunyanga/Bridge Sts, POB 71000, Dar es Salaam.

Telephone: (22) 2118354; **Fax:** (22) 2119216; **Internet:** www .nyererefoundation.org; **e-mail:** info@nyererefoundation.org.

Tanzania Millennium Hand Foundation—TAMIHA

Established in 2007 to further the Millennium Goals in Tanzania.

Activities: Operates HIV/AIDS awareness and prevention campaigns, and provides health care; promotes environmental conservation; and runs community programmes in the areas of gender empowerment and poverty reduction, through the promotion of micro-enterprises. Runs an orphanage and a vocational school.

Geographical Area of Activity: Tanzania.

Principal Staff: Founder and Pres. Crispin K. Mugarula; Sr Man. Moody Orondi.

Address: POB 541, Usa River, Arusha; Alliance Bldg, Leganga-Usa River, 3rd Floor, Nos 6, 8 and 9.

Telephone: (732) 971394; **Fax:** (787) 474341; **Internet:** www .tanzaniavolunteer.info; **e-mail:** crispin@tanzaniavolunteer .info; ceo@tanzaniavolunteer.info.

Thailand

FOUNDATION CENTRE AND CO-ORDINATING BODY

CPCS—Center for Philanthropy and Civil Society

Established in 1997 under the National Institute of Development Administration, for the support of the third sector.

Activities: Aims to encourage the development of philanthropy and the third sector in Thailand, through carrying out research; maintaining databases; training and advisory services; lobbying; co-ordinating the activities and programmes of third-sector organizations; and educational programmes. Maintains an information centre.

Geographical Area of Activity: Thailand.

Executive Board: Prof. Dr Juree Vichit-Vadakan (Chair.).

Principal Staff: Dir Dr Kanokkan Anukansai.

Address: National Institute of Development Administration, 118 Seri Thai Rd, Klongchan Bangkapi, Bangkok 10240.

Telephone: (2) 727-3504/5; **Fax:** (2) 374-7399; **Internet:** www.cpcs.nida.ac.th; **e-mail:** juree@cpcsnida.com.

FOUNDATIONS, TRUSTS AND NON-PROFIT ORGANIZATIONS

AIT—Asian Institute of Technology

Founded in 1959 as the SEATO Graduate School of Engineering; present name adopted in 1967 when it became fully independent.

Activities: Aims to help meet the growing need for advanced engineering education and research in Asia in engineering, technology, planning and management. Provides advanced (postgraduate) education in engineering, science and allied fields, through academic programmes leading to higher degrees, through research by students, faculty and research staff directed towards the solution of technological problems relevant to Asia, and through special programmes, including conferences, seminars and short courses. The Institute provides scholarships and grants to assist well-qualified students from the region. The Institute comprises four schools—the School of Advanced Technologies, the School of Civil Engineering, the School of Environment, Resources and Development, and the School of Management—and an AIT extension. There are also a number of academic centres. Maintains databases and a library comprising more than 230,000 vols.

Geographical Area of Activity: Africa, Asia, Europe and the USA.

Publications: *Annual Report on Research and Activities*; *AIT Review* (3 a year); Annual Report.

Board of Trustees: Dr Supin Pinkayan (Chair.); Dr Sohail Khan, Gen. Dr Boonsrang Niampradit, Dr John Nelson (Vice-Chair.); Kulvimol Wasuntiwongse (Sec.).

Principal Staff: Interim Pres. Prof. Worsak Kanok-Nukulchai; Interim Vice-Pres Prof. Sivanappan Kumar, Prof. Kanchana Kanchanasut, Prof. Kazuo Yamamoto.

Address: 58 Moo 9, Km 42, Paholyothin Highway; POB 4, Klong Luang, Pathumthani 12120.

Telephone: (2) 524-5000; **Fax:** (2) 516-2126; **Internet:** www.ait.asia; www.ait.ac.th; **e-mail:** admissions@ait.ac.th.

ECPAT International

Established in 1991, originally as a three-year project to combat child prostitution. In 1996, it became a NGO and is now a network of organizations and individuals around the world working together for the elimination of child prostitution, child pornography and trafficking of children for sexual purposes.

Activities: Carries out local, national and international activities aimed at protecting children in every part of the world, including the whole range of issues revolving around the commercial sexual exploitation of children. Organizes conferences, operates an information and resource centre, carries out research, develops models of prevention and disseminates information. The ECPAT Network comprises 86 independent groups in more than 78 different countries across Asia, Central, South and North America, Eastern and Western Europe, the Middle East, North Africa and the Pacific. Holds a General Assembly every three years.

Geographical Area of Activity: International.

Publications: *Stay safe from online sexual exploitation: a guide for young people*; *Implementation of the Agenda for Action Against the Commercial Sexual Exploitation of Children* (annual); *ECPAT Newsletter* (quarterly); *Questions and Answers About the Commercial Sexual Exploitation of Children*; *Protecting Children Online: An ECPAT Guide*; *Regional Situational Analysis Reports*; Annual Report; research reports.

Finance: Annual revenue US $3,359,000, expenditure $2,487,000 (30 June 2014).

Board: Carol Bellamy (Chair.).

Principal Staff: Exec. Dir Dorothy Rozga.

Address: 328 Phaya Thai Rd, Rachathewi, Bangkok 10400.

Telephone: (2) 215-3388; **Fax:** (2) 215-8272; **Internet:** www.ecpat.net; **e-mail:** info@ecpat.net.

The Education for Development Foundation—EDF

Established in 1987. Works in the socio-educational field, with an emphasis on poverty reduction, education development and international peacebuilding. Provides educational opportunities to children in countries in the Greater Mekong region.

Activities: Activities include a scholarship programme, which enables students to continue their education beyond primary school; educational development projects, which aim to improve students' agricultural knowledge, vocational skills and health education, and improve school infrastructure and facilities; and helping schools to become community learning centres which promote innovation and self-reliance.

Geographical Area of Activity: Thailand, Laos, Cambodia, Viet Nam, Myanmar.

Restrictions: Scholarships available only for poor students.

Publications: Newsletter; videos; CD-ROMs and multimedia.

Finance: Total assets 94,304,974 baht; annual income 59,287,572 baht, expenditure 58,429,443 baht (31 March 2014).

Board of Directors: Col Somkid Sreesangkom (Chair.); Nartrudee Nakornvacha (Sec. and Treas.).

Principal Staff: Man. Dir Sunphet Nilrat.

Address: Kasetsart University Alumni Bldg, 3rd Floor, 50 Paholyothin Rd, Jatujak, Bangkok 10900.

Telephone: (2) 940-5265; **Fax:** (2) 940-5266; **Internet:** www.edfthai.org; **e-mail:** public@edfthai.org.

Empower Foundation

Founded in 1994.

Activities: Active in two main programme areas: women and prostitution, and AIDS prevention and problem solving.

Carries out educational activities in the fields of legal rights, social benefits and AIDS prevention; grants scholarships; and provides medical fees and emergency funds for prostitutes. Also provides leadership training.

Geographical Area of Activity: Thailand.

Restrictions: Applications from domestic organizations for projects seeking to combat prostitution are rarely approved.

Publications: *Life Leading.*

Finance: Annual revenue approx. 800,000 baht.

Principal Staff: Founder and Sec.-Gen. Chantawipa Apisuk.

Address: 57/60 Tivanond Rd, Nonthaburi 11000.

Telephone: (2) 526-8311; **Fax:** (2) 526-3294; **Internet:** www.empowerfoundation.org; **e-mail:** badgirls@empowerfoundation.org.

Foundation for Children

Founded in 1978 to support the welfare of children in Thailand.

Activities: Focuses on the welfare of children in Thailand. Activities are within three programme areas: Educational and Cultural Institute Programmes, including support for village schools and projects helping homeless children; Children's Welfare and Education Institute, meeting basic needs of children; and the Children's Institute, developing knowledge in the community. Promotes physical and mental development of children, co-ordinates educational activities, provides scholarships and works in partnership with other NGOs. Also provides humanitarian relief and supports environmental preservation activities. Runs its own publishing house.

Geographical Area of Activity: Thailand.

Restrictions: Projects must be practical, transparent and simple enough to be monitored and evaluated.

Executive Committee: Prof. Sem Pringpuangkaew (Hon. Pres.); Prof. Prawase Wasi (Pres.).

Address: 95/24 Moo 6, Soi Katoomlom 18, Buddha Monthon 4, Sampharn, Nakhon Pathom 73220.

Telephone: (2) 814-1481; **Fax:** (2) 814-0369; **Internet:** www.ffc.or.th; **e-mail:** children@ffc.or.th; donation@ffc.or.th.

Foundation for Women

Founded in 1984 to support women's development, help women and children victimized by violence, and to promote and support women's rights and equality.

Activities: Provides grants to projects promoting women's rights and equality, and to organizations helping marginalized women, particularly in the north and north-east of Thailand. Also provides training for women and young people in the areas of violence against young people, women and their rights; provides technical assistance and temporary accommodation to women who have experienced violence; and carries out research and data collection activities on various kinds of problems affecting women, including female trafficking, as well as disseminating this information to government and private organizations.

Geographical Area of Activity: Thailand.

Publications: *Voices of Thai Women* (newsletter).

Finance: Annual income approx. 3m. baht.

Principal Staff: Chair. Siriporn Skrobanek; Dir Usa Lerdsrisuntad.

Address: POB 47 Bangkoknoi, Bangkok 10700.

Telephone: (2) 433-5149; **Fax:** (2) 434-6774; **Internet:** www.womenthai.org; **e-mail:** info@womenthai.org.

Sem Pringpuangkeo Foundation

Established in 1995 to assist people who suffer from illness, in particular HIV/AIDS, and to ensure an adequate education for children orphaned as a result of these illnesses through a comprehensive fostering programme.

Activities: Operates in the areas of social welfare, conservation and the environment, and medicine and health. Works with hill tribes and other lowland peoples of northern Thailand to preserve natural environment; and encourages and supports education and religious work, including preserving local culture, customs and traditions. The Foundation's Foster Parents Programme provides education and training to children affected by HIV/AIDS in the six upper northern provinces of Thailand to prevent them from entering the cycle of drug abuse, homelessness, crime and child prostitution; operates a scholarship scheme; and educates children in agricultural skills and introduces children to traditional Thai cultural values. The Environmental Programme promotes family planning in the hill tribes; encourages the use of biological agriculture; and develops mutual co-operation on environmental preservation by establishing a house-temple-school network.

Geographical Area of Activity: Thailand.

Board of Directors: Kasem Snidvongs (Chair.); Isara Vongkusolkit (Vice-Chair.); Achara Soontornvatin (Sec. and Treas.).

Principal Staff: Man. Santi Leksakun; Asst Man. Ridthirong Santhabut.

Address: 46/3 Moo 10, Rob Wiang Subdistrict, Muang District, Chiang Rai 57000.

Telephone: (5) 202-0506; **Fax:** (5) 202-0506; **Internet:** www.sem-foundation.org; **e-mail:** admin@sem-foundation.org.

Seub Nakhasathien Foundation

Founded in 1990, in memory of conservationist Seub Nakhasathien, to promote the environment.

Activities: Operates in the field of conservation of forest and natural resources through providing youth training programmes, teacher-training programmes, exhibitions on environmental issues, and campaigning on environmental and conservation issues.

Geographical Area of Activity: Western Thailand.

Publications: *Seub Journal*; leaflets; and strategy reports.

Finance: Annual revenue approx. 3m. baht.

Principal Staff: Sec.-Gen. Sasin Chalermlab.

Address: Dept of Medical Science, 4th Bldg, 693 Bumrungmuang Rd, Pombrab District, Bangkok 10100.

Telephone: (2) 224-7838/9; **Internet:** www.seub.or.th; **e-mail:** snf@seub.or.th.

Siam Society

Founded in 1904 to investigate and encourage the arts and sciences in relation to Thailand and its neighbouring countries.

Activities: Operates internationally in the fields of education, economic affairs, the arts and humanities, religion, international relations and the conservation of natural resources, through self-conducted programmes, research, grants to institutions and individuals, fellowships, scholarships, conferences, courses, publications and lectures. Maintains a library.

Geographical Area of Activity: South-East Asia.

Publications: *Journal of the Siam Society* (2 a year); *Natural History Bulletin of the Siam Society* (2 a year); books; monographs; report of operations and financial statement; *The Customs of Cambodia*; *The Royal Chronicles of Ayutthaya*; *Footprints of The Buddhas of This Era in Thailand*; *Witnesses to a Revolution: Siam 1688*; *The Society of Siam: Selected Articles for The Siam Society's Centenary*; *Art and Art-Industry in Siam*; *Thai Culture in Transition*.

Council: Bilaibhan Sampatisiri (Pres.); Dr Weerachai Nankorn, Suraya Supanwanich (Vice-Chair. and Hon. Treas); Jumbhot Chuasai (Hon. Sec.).

Principal Staff: Gen. Man. Kanitha Kasina-Ubol.

Address: 131 Asoke Montri Rd (Sukhumvit 21), Bangkok 10110.

Telephone: (2) 661-6470; **Fax:** (2) 258-3491; **Internet:** www.siam-society.org; **e-mail:** info@siam-society.org.

Thairath Foundation

Originally founded in 1979 by Kampon Watcharaphon, former director of the daily newspaper *Thai Rath*; approved as a public charity organization in 1999.

Activities: Oversees and supports 101 Thai-Rath Witthaya Schools, provides humanitarian relief and awards the Kampon Wacharapon prize for an outstanding journalistic thesis. Also carries out research, including research into the development of arithmetic studies for primary school children, as well as providing training to teachers.

Geographical Area of Activity: Thailand.

Finance: Total endowment approx. 25m. baht.

Board of Directors: Khun Ying Praneetsilp Vacharaphol (Chair.); Wimol Yimlamai (Vice-Chair.); Yinglak Vacharaphol (Vice-Chair. and Treas.); Somboon Woraphong (Sec.).

Principal Staff: Dir Manich Sooksomchitra.

Address: Thai Rath Foundation Bldg 12 (Bldg AD), 1st Floor, 4th Floor, Chom Phon, Chatuchak, Bangkok 10900.

Telephone: (2) 272-1030; **Fax:** (2) 272-1754; **Internet:** www .thairath-found.or.th; **e-mail:** sirikanya@thairath-found.or .th.

TISCO Foundation

Founded in 1982 by the TISCO Financial Group.

Activities: Provides support for social and economic development activities, through the award of scholarships, medical funding for patients in need, and grants for employment activities and business start-ups by poor people. Also provides humanitarian relief.

Geographical Area of Activity: Thailand.

Finance: Net income approx. 120m. baht.

Board of Directors: Sivaporn Dardarananda (Chair.); Pliu Mangkornkanok (Vice-Chair.); Vannee Uboldejpracharak (Sec.); Duangrat Kittivittayakul (Treas.).

Principal Staff: Advisor Pattira Wattanawarangkul; Man. Apapan Kulapongse; Asst Man. Yongyuth Lewrojskul.

Address: 5th Floor, TISCO Tower, 48/11 North Sathorn Rd, Bangkok 10500.

Telephone: (2) 633-7501; **Fax:** (2) 638-0554; **Internet:** www .tiscofoundation.org; **e-mail:** tiscofoundation@ tiscofoundation.org.

TTF—Toyota Thailand Foundation

Established in 1992 by the Toyota Company in Thailand.

Activities: Active in the fields of education, social welfare and community development in Thailand, through funding NGOs and training schemes. Projects include an initiative to encourage children to eat more green vegetables, provision of scholarships in engineering at the Institute of Traffic and Transport Engineering at Chulalongkorn University, support for orphans whose parents have died from AIDS and a programme to empower young women.

Geographical Area of Activity: Thailand.

Finance: Total capital 400m. baht.

Principal Staff: Chair. Dr Sanor Unakul; Vice-Chair. Kyoichi Tanada; Treas. Kohei Nakao.

Address: 186/1 Moo 1, Old Railway Rd, Samrong Tai, Phrapadaeng, Samut Prakarn.

Telephone: (2) 386-1393; **Fax:** (2) 386-1885; **Internet:** www .toyota.co.th/ttf/en/about.php; **e-mail:** tff@toyota.co.th.

Timor-Leste

FOUNDATIONS, TRUSTS AND NON-PROFIT ORGANIZATIONS

Haburas Foundation (Fundasaun Haburas)

Founded in 1998 by Demetrio do Amaral de Carvalho to promote and protect the environment in Timor-Leste; a member of Friends of the Earth International (q.v.).

Activities: Initiates and funds projects designed to help Timor-Leste develop sustainably and equitably. The Foundation promotes reforestation and the establishment of the country's first national park; educates people about environmental issues; and mediates in environmental disputes.

Geographical Area of Activity: Timor-Leste.

Publications: *Verde* (monthly bulletin); brochures.

Principal Staff: Exec. Dir Virgilio da Silva Guterres.

Address: POB 390, rua Celestino da Silva, Farol, Dili.

Telephone: 331-0103; **Internet:** haburas.org; **e-mail:** haburaslorosae@yahoo.com; haburass@hotmail.com.

Turkey

FOUNDATION CENTRES AND CO-ORDINATING BODIES

Sivil Toplum Geliştirme Merkezi—STGM (Civil Society Development Centre)

Formed in 2004 to enable civil and participatory democracy in Turkey.

Activities: Maintains a library and a database of NGOs. Runs a support centre for NGOs to meet and exchange information and experiences, and holds events and conferences for Turkish NGOs. Regional offices in the provinces of Adana, Denizli, Diyarbakır and Eskişehir.

Geographical Area of Activity: Turkey.

Publications: *Siviliz* (bulletin, 2 a month, in Turkish and English); *Gender Guide for Non-governmental Organizations*; *Voluntary Participation and Volunteer Management Guide for NGOs*; *Advocacy Guide for NGOs*; *Communication and Campaigning Guide for NGOs*; *Social Entrepreneurship Guide for Social Change*; *Legal Handbook for Non-governmental Organizations*; *Guide for Civil Networks in the World, in Europe and in Turkey*; *Story of Civil Society in Turkey: An Oasis Amidst Constraints*; *Feeling of Always Starting as Loser-Discriminatory Practices in Turkey: Victims and Specialists Tell About it*; *Issues and Resolutions of Rights Based NGOs in Turkey* (in Turkish and English); *Project Stories from Civil Society*; *Civil Life in Turkey*; *Handbook of Civil Society Activist*; *Project Cycle Management: Logical Framework Approach, Informatics Guide for NGOs, Governance Guide for NGOs*.

Finance: Funded by the European Union.

Administrative Board: Levent Korkut (Chair.).

Principal Staff: Gen. Co-ordinator Tezcan Eralp Abay.

Address: Tunus Cad. 85/8, 06680 Kavaklıdere, Ankara.

Telephone: (312) 4424262; **Fax:** (312) 4425755; **Internet:** www.stgm.org.tr; **e-mail:** bilgi@stgm.org.tr.

Third Sector Foundation of Turkey—TÜSEV

Established in 1993 by civil society organizations to strengthen the non-profit sector in Turkey.

Activities: A network of some 107 associations and foundations that share a vision of strengthening the legal, fiscal and operational infrastructure of the third (non-profit) sector in Turkey. Programmes include civil society law reform, social investment, international relations and networking research.

Geographical Area of Activity: Turkey.

Publications: *TUSEV e-newsletter* (quarterly); *Turkish Foundations during the Republican Period*; *Directory of Member Foundations and Associations of the Third Sector Foundation of Turkey*; *Philanthropy in Turkey: Citizens, Foundations and the Pursuit of Social Justice*; *The Landscape of Philanthropy and Civil Society in Turkey: Key Findings, Reflections and Recommendations*; periodicals; monographs; information brochures.

Executive Board: Prof. Dr Üstün Ergüder (Chair.); İnal Avcı, Timur Erk (Vice-Chair.).

Principal Staff: Sec.-Gen. Tevfik Başak Ersen; Deputy Sec.-Gen. Liana Varon.

Address: Bankalar Cad. No. 2, Minerva Han Kat 5, 34420 Karaköy, İstanbul.

Telephone: (212) 2438307; **Fax:** (212) 2438305; **Internet:** www.tusev.org.tr; **e-mail:** info@tusev.org.tr.

FOUNDATIONS, TRUSTS AND NON-PROFIT ORGANIZATIONS

Açık Toplum Enstitüsü (Open Society Institute—Turkey)

Established in 2001 as a member of the Soros foundations network, with the purpose of acting as a liaison office enhancing partnerships with Turkish donors and facilitating collaboration between Turkish civil society and the Open Society Foundations network (q.v.).

Activities: Provides direct support and acts as a liaison organization in the fields of social, economic and European Union membership research, human rights, educational reform and co-operation among NGOs. In its first year of operation, support included a scholarship programme for graduate-level study of human rights law offered by the Human Rights Center at Bilgi University and, in collaboration with the Open Society Foundation—Sofia; the organization also co-sponsored competitions for joint projects between Bulgarian and Turkish NGOs.

Geographical Area of Activity: Turkey.

Publications: E-newsletter.

Finance: Total budget 36,295,926 Turkish lira; grants awarded 11,617,688 Turkish lira (2009–13).

Principal Staff: Exec. Dir Gökçe Tüylüoğlu.

Address: Cevdet Pasa Cad., Mercan Apt No. 85, D11, 34342 Bebek, İstanbul.

Telephone: (212) 2879986; **Fax:** (212) 2879967; **Internet:** www.aciktoplumvakfi.org.tr; **e-mail:** info@aciktoplumvakfi.org.tr.

Beyaz Nokta Gelişim Vakfi (White Point Development Foundation)

Established in 1994 by Ishak Alaton, M. Tinaz Titiz, Faruk Ekinci, Yuksel Domaniç, Mümin Erkunt and Ibrahim Kocabas to promote problem-solving in society.

Activities: Operates throughout Turkey in the field of education, through self-conducted programmes, research, prizes, conferences, training courses and publications. Projects include non-formal education for children unable to remain in the education system, a civic education project, a campaign to encourage responsible driving and donations of science equipment to develop children's interest in science education.

Geographical Area of Activity: Turkey.

Restrictions: Grants to foundation members only.

Publications: *Beyaz Bülten* (newsletter).

Finance: Total assets 141,674 Turkish lira (31 Dec. 2013).

Board of Directors: H. Kamil Tanriverdi (Chair.); Faruk Ekinci (Vice-Chair.).

Principal Staff: Gen. Co-ordinator Güler Yüksel.

Address: Sedat Simavi Sok., Çankaya Sitesi No. 29/Z-1, 06550 Çankaya, Ankara.

Telephone: (312) 4420760; **Fax:** (312) 4420776; **Internet:** www.beyaznokta.org.tr; **e-mail:** bnv@beyaznokta.org.tr.

Çevre Koruma ve Ambalaj Atiklari Değerlendirme Vakfi—CEVKO (Environmental Protection and Packaging Waste Recovery and Recycling Trust)

Established in 1991 by a number of national and multinational companies to promote and organize economically efficient and environmentally friendly packaging, waste recovery and recycling based on the principle of co-responsibility.

Activities: Operates in the field of conservation and the environment, through research and training courses, public awareness raising activities, and organizing national and international conferences. Co-ordinates implementation of the European Green Dot packaging recycling initiative in Turkey.

Publications: Bulletin; Annual Report.

Finance: Total assets approx. US $400,000.

Management Board: Okyar Yayalar (Chair.); Mehmet H. Erbak (Vice-Chair.).

Principal Staff: Gen. Sec. Mete İmer.

Address: Cenap Şahabettin Sok. 94, 81020 Koşuyolu, Kadiköy, Istanbul.

Telephone: (216) 4287890; **Fax:** (216) 4287895; **Internet:** www .cevko.org.tr; **e-mail:** cevko@cevko.org.tr.

Anne Çocuk Eğitim Vakfi—AÇEV (Mother Child Education Foundation)

Founded in 1993 with a mission to empower people through family-based education.

Activities: Main focus is on early childhood education and family literacy programmes, which aim to provide equal opportunity in education to all by targeting pre-school children and their families in disadvantaged communities. The main education programmes include the Mother and Child Education Programme, the Father Support Programme and the Functional Literacy and Women's Empowerment Programme. The Foundation conducts research, and develops and implements programmes in two main areas of expertise: early childhood and adult education. Implements programmes using a variety of models and mediums, including training courses, seminars and awareness-raising programmes through the television and media. Programmes are free and aim to reach the most vulnerable families and disadvantaged communities in Turkey. Programmes try to provide a 'fair start' to schooling for all children by empowering families to support the development of their children in pre-school years. The Foundation collaborates with governmental agencies, local and international NGOs and organizations, universities and private businesses to fund its programme activities.

Geographical Area of Activity: Turkey.

Publications: *An Evaluation of the Mother Support Programme in South-Eastern Turkey* (2008); *Girls' Access to Primary Education Best Practices from Turkey* (2008); *Girls' Access to Primary Education Best Practices from the World* (2008); *Providing Access to Basic Literacy Education with Educational TV* (2008); *Early Childhood Education in Turkey: Access, Equality and Quality* (2009); *Mothers from Five Countries Reporting: Mother-Child Education Program* (2009); and others.

Finance: Annual income 9,060,019 Turkish lira, expenditure 9,027,485 Turkish lira (2013).

Board of Trustees: Ayşen Özyeğin (Pres.).

Principal Staff: Vice-Pres. Dr Çiğdem Kağıtçıbaşı; Vice-Pres. and CEO Ayla Göksel; Gen. Man. Nalan Yalçın.

Address: Büyükdere Cad., Stad Han. 85, Kat 2, 34387 Mecidiyeköy, İstanbul.

Telephone: (212) 2134220; **Fax:** (212) 2133660; **Internet:** www .acev.org; **e-mail:** acev@acev.org.

Aydın Doğan Vakfi (Aydın Doğan Foundation)

Established in 1996 by businessman and newspaper publisher Aydın Doğan to contribute to the development of Turkey in the areas of education and culture.

Activities: Operates nationally in the fields of education and culture. The Foundation has built a number of schools and dormitories, and libraries, sports and cultural centres. Makes a number of awards, including the Aydın Doğan International Cartoon Prize, Young Communicators' awards, and various awards in the areas of architecture, social services, literature and music. Maintains an art gallery.

Geographical Area of Activity: Turkey.

Finance: Annual expenditure €1,962,000 (2010).

Board of Directors: Aydın Doğan (Hon. Chair.); Hanzade V. Boyner (Pres.); Vuslat Doğan Sabanci (Deputy Chair.).

Principal Staff: Exec. Dir Candan Fetvaci.

Address: Burhaniye Mahallesi Kisikli Cad. 65, 34676 Üsküdar, İstanbul.

Telephone: (216) 5569176; **Fax:** (216) 5569147; **Internet:** www .aydindoganvakfi.org.tr; **e-mail:** advakfi@advakfi.org.

Hisar Education Foundation—HEV

Established in 1970 by a number of individuals to contribute to the implementation of advanced education systems in Turkey and to provide institutions of all levels with funds for grants, scholarships and equipment.

Activities: Operates nationally in the field of education, through self-conducted programmes, scholarships and fellowships, conferences, training courses and publications. As well as making educational grants to various schools, the Foundation runs its own primary school.

Geographical Area of Activity: Turkey.

Publications: *Educating Young Children.*

Board of Directors: Feyyaz Berker (Hon. Pres.); Jak Baruh (Pres.); İzi Kohen (Vice-Pres.); Mehmet Taki (Sec.); Birsen Uzun (Treas.).

Principal Staff: Gen. Dir David Cardenas.

Address: Göktürk Merkez Mahallesi İstanbul Cad. No. 3, 34077 Eyüp, İstanbul.

Telephone: (212) 3640000; **Fax:** (212) 3220307; **Internet:** www.hisarschool.k12.tr; **e-mail:** kurumsalgelistirme@ hisarschool.k12.tr.

İktisadi Kalkınma Vakfı (Economic Development Foundation)

Founded in 1965 by the Istanbul Chamber of Commerce and the Istanbul Chamber of Industry to monitor and evaluate Turkey-European Union (EU) relations, to inform the public and to represent Turkish business in dealings with the EU.

Activities: Conducts research on Turkey-EU relations; formulates and expresses opinions and proposals on behalf of the Turkish private sector on EU and Turkey-EU relations; carries out projects which aim to address general and technical issues related to Turkey-EU integration, and help inform and involve businesses, NGOs, media and the public. Organizes conferences, seminars and panels on EU and Turkey-EU relations. Ensures a regular flow of information, including activities undertaken by Turkey in the harmonization process, to the European Commission and Parliament, as well as to European NGOs and the media, and carries out lobbying activities promoting Turkey. Maintains a library which is the depository library of EU publications in Turkey and permanent representation in Brussels, the first representation of the Turkish private sector in the EU.

Geographical Area of Activity: Turkey, EU member states.

Publications: Research studies on EU policies, their effects on Turkey, and the level of harmonization with these policies; studies on all aspects of Turkey-EU relations; *IKV Monthly* (newsletter); *IKV Brief Notes*; annual almanac; various reports.

Finance: Fully financed by the private sector; does not receive any financial support from the Government.

Board of Directors: Ömer Cihad Vardan (Pres.); Zeynep Bodur Okyay, Prof. Dr Halûk Kabaalioğlu (Vice-Chair.).

Principal Staff: Sec.-Gen. Assoc. Prof. Çiğdem Nas; Dep. Sec.-Gen. and Research Dir Melih Özsöz.

Address: Esentepe Mah. Harmann Sok., TOBB Plaza No. 10, K 7–8 Şişli, İstanbul.

Telephone: (212) 2709300; **Fax:** (212) 2703022; **Internet:** www .ikv.org.tr; **e-mail:** ikv@ikv.org.tr.

İnsan Hak ve Hürriyetleri İnsani Yardım Vakfı (IHH Humanitarian Relief Foundation)

Established in 1995 by Bulent Yildirim and Mehmet Kose to support people affected by conflict or disaster.

Activities: Operates in the areas of aid to less-developed countries, education, law and human rights, medicine and health, and social welfare, by making grants to individuals, offering scholarships, carrying out emergency relief, and defending human rights.

Geographical Area of Activity: South-Eastern Europe, Central and South Asia, the Middle East, Africa, the Far East, and Central and South America.

Publications: Annual Report; booklets; periodicals: *Düşünce Gündem* and *İnsani Yardım*.

Finance: Annual income 150,738,405 Turkish lira, expenditure 119,126,575 Turkish lira (31 Dec. 2011).

Board of Trustees: Fehmi Bülent Yıldırım (Pres.); Huseyin Oruç (Dep. Pres.).

Address: Büyük Karaman Cad. Taylasan Sok., No. 3 Pk, 34230 Fatih, İstanbul.

Telephone: (212) 6312121; **Fax:** (212) 6217051; **Internet:** www .ihh.org.tr; **e-mail:** info@ihh.org.tr.

İnsan Kaynağını Geliştirme Vakfı—IKGV (Human Resource Development Foundation)

Founded in 1988 by a group of academics and business people to contribute to the solution of health, education and employment problems that have a negative impact on the economic, social and cultural development of society.

Activities: Works to empower people (women and children in particular), through advocacy, training and service provision in the areas of population and sustainable development.

Geographical Area of Activity: Turkey.

Publications: Books, bulletins, leaflets, newsletters and training manuals on reproductive health and sex education (in Turkish; some manuals are available in Azeri and Russian) and human trafficking.

Board of Directors: Turgut Tokuş (Chair.); Prof. Dr Ayşen Bulut (Dep. Chair.); Hasip Buldanlıoğlu (Treas.).

Principal Staff: Exec. Dir Dr Muhtar Çokar.

Address: Yeniçarşı Cad. 34, 34425 Beyoğlu, İstanbul.

Telephone: (212) 2931605; **Fax:** (212) 2931009; **Internet:** www .ikgv.org; **e-mail:** ikgv@ikgv.org.

International Blue Crescent Relief and Development Foundation—IBC (Uluslararası Mavi Hilal İnsani Yardım ve Kalkınma Vakfı)

Established in 1999 to provide humanitarian relief in Turkey and worldwide to alleviate human suffering caused by war, hunger, natural disasters, environmental problems and disease.

Activities: Operates humanitarian relief programmes in the fields of disaster relief and rehabilitation; post-emerency housing and reconstruction; rural social and economic development; supporting civil society and community development through technical and financial capacity-building; formal and informal education and training; and renovating, building and managing public health facilities.

Geographical Area of Activity: Central and South-Eastern Europe, Central Asia, the Middle East and Africa.

Publications: Books, reports, brochures, posters.

Board of Directors: Recep Üker (Pres.); Muzaffer Baca (Vice-Pres.).

Address: Bagdat Cad. Fistikli Sok. Dilek Apt. No. 3/5, Suadiye, İstanbul.

Telephone: (216) 3841486; **Fax:** (216) 3615745; **Internet:** www .ibc.org.tr; **e-mail:** ibc@ibc.org.tr.

Kadın Emeğini Değerlendirme Vakfı—KEDV (Foundation for the Support of Women's Work)

Established in 1986 to support low-income women's groups to improve the quality of their lives, their communities and their leadership.

Activities: Runs programmes in the areas of early childcare and education services for the poor, capacity building, economic empowerment and natural disasters. Has a craft shop.

Geographical Area of Activity: Turkey.

Publications: Books and manuals.

Board of Directors: Berrin Bal (Pres.).

Address: Istiklal Cad. Bekar Sok. No. 17, Beyoğlu, İstanbul.

Telephone: (212) 2922672; **Fax:** (212) 2491508; **Internet:** www .kedv.org.tr; **e-mail:** kedv@kedv.org.tr.

Open Society Foundation—Turkey

Established in 2008; part of the Open Society Foundations network (q.v.).

Activities: Operates in Turkey in the areas of financial and technical assistance in the areas of political reform and the European Union, media, gender, public health and minority rights. Supports research on issues including women's participation in the public sphere, the development of a local governance participation model, urban sustainability processes, and the use of information technology in democratization. Also promotes social inclusion and equality, including people with mental health problems, people living with HIV/AIDS, and women facing gender-based violence; the Foundation also promotes increasing access to education and political mobilization among Roma people.

Geographical Area of Activity: Turkey.

Restrictions: Only provides institutional support for scholarships on a project basis.

Finance: Annual budget 88,500 Turkish lira.

Board of Directors: İshak Alaton (Chair.).

Principal Staff: Gen. Sec. Gökce Tüylüoglu.

Address: Cevdet Pasa Cad., Mercan Apt, No. 85, D.11, 34342 Bebek, İstanbul.

Telephone: (212) 2879986; **Fax:** (212) 2879967; **Internet:** www .aciktoplumvakfi.org.tr; **e-mail:** info@aciktoplumvakfi.org .tr.

Sabancı Vakfı—Hacı Ömer Sabancı Foundation (Sabancı Foundation)

Established in 1974 by the Sabanci family to further Turkey's social and economic development.

Activities: Promotes social development and social awareness among current and future generations by supporting initiatives that affect and bring change to people's lives by creating authentic, innovative and lasting values. In addition to supporting institutions, arts and culture, and providing scholarships and awards, the Foundation supports civil society organizations in promoting equality and active participation for young people, women and people with disabilities.

Geographical Area of Activity: Turkey.

Restrictions: Only organizations in Turkey are eligible for funding.

Finance: Total assets €364,272,747 (31 Dec. 2014).

Board of Trustees: Guler Sabanci (Chair.), Husnu Pacacioğlu (Vice-Chair.).

Principal Staff: Gen. Man. Zerrin Koyunsağan.

Address: Sabancı Centre 4, 34330 Levent, İstanbul.

Telephone: (212) 3858800; **Fax:** (212) 3858811; **Internet:** www .sabancivakfi.org; **e-mail:** info@sabancivakfi.org.

Tarih Vakfı (History Foundation of Turkey)

Established in 1991, as the Economic and Social History Foundation of Turkey, by 264 members of the scientific and cultural community to create an archival and library collection of sources relating to the economic and cultural heritage of Turkey, and to promote historical study.

Activities: Operates in the area of history and the preservation of historical heritage, and the development of NGOs, nationally and internationally, through self-conducted programmes, research, conferences and publications. Co-operates with similar national and international organizations. Maintains an information and documentation centre, a liaison office in Ankara and an online database of Turkish NGOs.

Geographical Area of Activity: Turkey.

Publications: Books; magazines; journals; newsletters; encyclopedia; Latin script; *Istanbul* (periodical, 2 a year); *Toplumsal Tarih* (social, periodical, monthly); *Tarih Vakfi'ndan Haberler* (monthly bulletin); *Istanbul'u Gezerken (Strolling through Istanbul)*; illustrated scholarly books.

Board of Directors: Bülent Bilmez (Chair.); Evangelos Kechriotis (Vice-Chair.); Işık Tamdoğan (Gen. Sec.); Erol Köroğlu (Treas.).

Principal Staff: Gen. Man. Münevver Eminoğlu.

Address: Sarıdemir Mah. Ragıp Gümüşpala Cad. Değirmen Sok. No. 10 Eminönü, Fatih, İstanbul.

Telephone: (212) 5220202; **Fax:** (212) 5135400; **Internet:** www .tarihvakfi.org.tr; **e-mail:** tarihvakfi@tarihvakfi.org.tr.

Türkiye Aile Sağlığı ve Planlaması Vakfı—TAPV (Turkish Family Health and Planning Foundation)

Established in 1985 by Vehbi Koç to increase the quality and accessibility of reproductive health care information and services for women in Turkey.

Activities: Operates nationally in the fields of women's and children's health care, reproductive health and family planning, and the enhancement of women's status in society. Publishes information, holds conferences and engages in projects to carry out its mission.

Geographical Area of Activity: Turkey.

Publications: *Görünüm* (quarterly newsletter); books, reports, brochures.

Finance: Total assets 6,309,971 Turkish lira (31 Dec. 2012).

Board of Directors: Caroline Koç (Chair.); Prof. Dr Baran Tuncer (Pres. and Vice-Chair.).

Address: Güzel Konutlar Sitesi, A Blok D3–4, Ulus Mahallesi, 34760 Etiler, İstanbul.

Telephone: (212) 2577941; **Fax:** (212) 2577943; **Internet:** www .tapv.org.tr; **e-mail:** info@tapv.org.tr.

Türkiye Çevre Vakfı (Environment Foundation of Turkey)

Founded in 1978 by Dr Cevdet Aykan, Serbülent Bingöl, Muslih Fer, Ertugrul Soysal, Prof. Dr Necmi Sönmez, Engin Ural and Altan Zeki Ünver to establish a documentation centre on the environmental problems of Turkey and of other countries; to prepare and release articles and programmes for the mass media; to sponsor, carry out and publish research on environmental issues; to co-operate with institutions in other countries dealing with environmental problems; and to play an advocacy role in promoting the quality of the environment.

Activities: Operates in the field of conservation and the environment, through research, organizing national and international conferences and seminars, publications, environmental advice, promoting public awareness of environmental issues, and co-operation with the media and with international organizations. Maintains a library. Grants scholarships to Turkish university students studying in Turkey.

Geographical Area of Activity: Turkey, Central Asia and the Black Sea region.

Restrictions: Grants made only to specific NGOs working in Central Asia and the Black Sea region.

Publications: Newsletter (quarterly, in Turkish); books on the environment, agriculture, renewable energy.

Trustees: Prof. Koray Haktanır (Chair.).

Address: Tunalı Hilmi Cad. 50/20, 06660 Ankara.

Telephone: (312) 4255508; **Fax:** (312) 4185118; **Internet:** www .cevre.org.tr; **e-mail:** cevre@cevre.org.tr.

Türkiye Erozyonla Mücadele Ağaçlandırma ve Doğal Varlıkları Koruma Vakfı—TEMA (Turkish Foundation for Combating Soil Erosion, for Reforestation and the Protection of Natural Habitats)

Established in 1992 to draw attention to soil erosion, land degradation and their associated effects.

Activities: Supports projects such as education programmes, local conservation and development, rural development and land rehabilitation; as well as lobbying for sustainable policies and collaborating with similar NGOs and government agencies.

Geographical Area of Activity: Turkey.

Publications: Annual Report.

Finance: Financed by membership subscriptions. Total assets 21,237,151 Turkish lira (31 Dec. 2014).

Board of Trustees: A. Doğan Arikan (Chair.).

Address: Çayır Çimen Sok. Emlak Kredi Blokları A-2, Blok Kat:2 Daire:8, 34330 Levent, İstanbul.

Telephone: (212) 2837816; **Fax:** (212) 2811132; **Internet:** www .tema.org.tr; **e-mail:** tema@tema.org.tr.

Türkiye İnsan Hakları Vakfi (Human Rights Foundation of Turkey)

Established in 1990 to provide treatment and rehabilitation services for torture survivors and to document human rights violations in Turkey.

Activities: Operates in Turkey in the field of human rights, through supporting measures against torture; protecting the rights of refugees and asylum seekers; running treatment and rehabilitation centres; and maintaining a documentation centre.

Geographical Area of Activity: Turkey.

Publications: Reports.

Executive Board: Şebnem Korur Fincanci (Pres.).

Principal Staff: Sec.-Gen. Dr Metin Bakkalci.

Address: Mithatpaşa Cad. 49/11, 6. Kat 06420 Kızılay, Ankara.

Telephone: (312) 3106636; **Fax:** (312) 3106463; **Internet:** www .tihv.org.tr; **e-mail:** tihv@tihv.org.tr.

Türkiye Kalkinma Vakfi (Development Foundation of Turkey)

Founded in 1969 to alleviate poverty and improve the quality of life among resource-poor rural families, through small-scale agricultural investment projects and agricultural vocational training.

Activities: Develops and manages a wide range of agricultural development programmes in five regions of rural Turkey. Two of the Foundation's programmes, bee-keeping development and broiler production, have become national programmes. Others include dairy farming, introduction of fodder crops, work with fruit and vegetables, sericulture improvement, development of small-scale irrigation schemes, introduction of better-yielding varieties of wheat, combating internal and external parasites in sheep, and assistance to rural communities in cheese production. The Foundation manages centres for training young women in rug-weaving, and assists with the marketing of the rugs. Many of the projects involve supervision of credits provided by the Agricultural Bank to participating farmers. The Foundation maintains regional offices and has 32 centres for developing the social and economic status of women in the Eastern Anatolia region.

Geographical Area of Activity: Eastern and South-Eastern Turkey.

Publications: *Mellifera* (annually); books and reports on specific areas of activity.

Finance: Funds are derived from the Turkish Government, institutions and individuals in Turkey, Europe and the USA, bilateral technical assistance programmes with Germany and Switzerland, and loans from national and international agencies.

Board of Directors: Rıfat Dağ (Chair.); İbrahim Tuğrul (Vice-Chair.); Rahmi Demir (Treas.).

Principal Staff: Gen. Man. İsmail Mihrace Erdoğan.

Address: Fatih Mahallesi Vakif Cad. 43ʙ Kazan, 06980 Ankara.

Telephone: (312) 8141119; **Fax:** (312) 8141590; **Internet:** www .tkv-dft.org.tr; **e-mail:** info@tkvbal.com.tr.

Umut Vakfi (Umut Foundation)

Established in 1993 to promote conflict resolution and peace.

Activities: Promotes peaceful conflict resolution and individual disarmament; helps young people develop strong leadership skills; promotes the rule of law; and co-operates with similar NGOs.

Geographical Area of Activity: Turkey, South-Eastern Europe and the Middle East.

Publications: *Who's Who in Europe in the Science and Art of Peace and Reconciliation*; *Terror and Struggle Against Organised Crime*; *Individual Disarmament*; *Criminology*; *Criminal Law Reform*; *To Be A Citizen: Teachers' Hand Manual*; *To Be A Citizen: Student Book*; *Individual Disarmament: Give life a chance!* (cartoons).

Principal Staff: Pres. Nazire Dedeman Çağatay.

Address: Yıldız Posta Cad. 52, 34340 Esentepe, İstanbul.

Telephone: (212) 2160670; **Fax:** (212) 2160678; **Internet:** www .umut.org.tr; **e-mail:** vakif@umut.org.tr.

Vehbi Koç Vakfı (Vehbi Koç Foundation)

Founded in 1969 by Vehbi Koç, and supported by Koç Holding SA, for the allocation of financial support in education, medicine, culture and related areas.

Activities: Operates nationally in the fields of education, social welfare, science, arts and culture, and medicine and health, through research, conferences, courses, seminars, lectures, awards, scholarships and travel grants. Provides grants for social welfare, buildings and medical equipment for hospitals in Turkey. Supports public museums, including the Sadberk Hanım Müzesi, which exhibits collections in the fields of ethnography, archaeology and artistic cultural traditions; the Rahim H. Koç Museum, the first Turkish museum to be devoted to the history of technology and industry; and the Suna-Inan Kiraç Research Institute on Mediterranean Civilisations, which researches archaeology and indigenous cultures. Also funds the building of schools, established the Koç University, as well as funding the Vehbi Koç Professorship of Turkish Studies at Harvard University's Faculty of Arts and Sciences. In 1990 the Tofaş Fiat Fund was created in conjunction with the Turkey Fiat Group to provide scholarships to students in Italy and Turkey to support conservation work and to sponsor bilingual (Italian and Turkish) art publications.

Geographical Area of Activity: Mainly Turkey and Western Europe.

Publications: Annual Report.

Finance: Annual expenditure 188,508,000 Turkish lira (2013); budget 179,808,000 Turkish lira (2014).

Board of Directors: Semahat Arsel (Chair.); Rahmi M. Koç (Vice-Chair.).

Principal Staff: Gen. Man. Erdal Yıldırım.

Address: Nakkaştepe, Azizbey Sok. 1, Kuzguncuk, 81207 İstanbul.

Telephone: (216) 5310000; **Fax:** (216) 4925872; **Internet:** www .vkv.org.tr; **e-mail:** info@vkv.org.tr.

Uganda

FOUNDATIONS, TRUSTS AND NON-PROFIT ORGANIZATIONS

Kulika Charitable Trust (Uganda)

Founded in 1981 by Patricia Brenninkmeyer in the United Kingdom for general charitable purposes. In 2005, the operational management of Kulika was transferred to the Uganda office.

Activities: Operates in the fields of education, sustainable agriculture and development in Uganda. Currently concentrating on providing scholarships, running a training and awareness programme in sustainable agriculture, supporting poverty alleviation and development projects, and funding environment and conservation projects.

Geographical Area of Activity: East Africa, mainly Uganda.

Publications: Newsletter.

Principal Staff: Chief Exec. Christine Ssempebwa.

Address: Plot 472, Nsambya Rd, POB 11330, Kampala.

Telephone: (41) 4266261; **Fax:** (41) 4510005; **Internet:** www.kulika.org; **e-mail:** kulikauganda@kulika.org.

Mara Foundation

Established in 2009 by Ashish J. Thakkar, CEO of conglomerate Mara Group.

Activities: Fosters local entrepreneurship, mentoring and funding business people, and providing business training facilities. Runs the Mara Mentor online social network and Mara One-to-One mentoring programme. Plans to establish the Mara Ad-Venture Fund to invest in new businesses in Kenya, Nigeria, South Africa, Tanzania and Uganda.

Geographical Area of Activity: Kenya, Nigeria, South Africa, Tanzania, Uganda.

Address: Ham Towers, 3rd Floor, Makerere Hill Rd, Kampala.

Telephone: (756) 707224; **Internet:** www.mara-foundation.org; **e-mail:** info@mara-foundation.org.

Ruparelia Foundation

Established in 2012 by Dr Sudhir Ruparelia, founder of Crane Bank Ltd (f. 1995) and Goldstar Insurance Co Ltd (f. 1996), and Jyotsna Ruthpareli.

Activities: Active in the fields of education, funding school infrastructure and students' fees; environmental preservation, and wildlife and forest conservation; health, funding medical research, primary and maternal and child health care, and subsidizing medical bills; social welfare, through poverty alleviation and sustainable livelihoods initiatives; religion, supporting multi-faith activities; and sports, sponsoring local and national teams and sportspeople.

Geographical Area of Activity: Uganda.

Board of Trustees: Dr Sudhir Ruparelia (Chair.).

Principal Staff: Dir Rajiv Ruparelia.

Address: c/o Ruparelia Group, Crane Chambers, 1st Floor, Plot 38, Kampala Rd, Kampala; POB 3673, Kampala.

Internet: rupareliafoundation.com; **e-mail:** fundraising@rupareliafoundation.com.

Ukraine

FOUNDATION CENTRES AND CO-ORDINATING BODIES

Centre for Philanthropy

Established in 1998 to support non-profit organizations in Ukraine.

Activities: Aims to develop Ukrainian philanthropy and to provide a supporting environment, through carrying out research, issuing publications, providing a library and information service to both philanthropists and NGOs, providing technical support, and organizing international fund-raising workshops and conferences.

Geographical Area of Activity: Ukraine.

Publications: Handbooks and training materials.

Principal Staff: Dir Svitlana Kuts.

Address: c/o Institute of Professional Fund-raising, 04211 Kyiv, POB 83.

Telephone: (44) 231-26-77; **Fax:** (44) 212-31-50.

Ednannia: Initiative Centre to Support Social Action—ISAR Ednannia

Launched in 1997 as a not-for-profit NGO aiming to strengthen civil society through social initiatives, and improve Ukrainian quality of life.

Activities: Provides grants, consultations, training, information, networking, research and numerous other services to NGOs and other interested parties. The Centre maintains an online NGO database, a library and a database of NGO experts in Ukraine; runs an NGO support network of 15 Centres for NGO Expertise and nine regional NGO Support Centres.

Geographical Area of Activity: Ukraine.

Publications: *Bulletin for NGOs* (monthly); *NGO Success Stories*; Annual Report.

Advisory Board: Iryna Belashova (Hon. Chair.).

Principal Staff: Exec. Dir Vladimir Sheyhus.

Address: 03150 Kyiv, POB 447, str. Predlsavinskaya 26.

Telephone: (44) 201-01-60; **Fax:** (44) 201-01-60; **Internet:** isar.net.ua; **e-mail:** ednannia@isar.net.ua.

GURT Resource Centre for NGO Development

National information and support centre established in 1995 to provide a range of services to strengthen civil society organizations of all types and sizes.

Activities: Operates through three main programmes: the Societal Information Programme, which includes the collection, processing and dissemination of information about different events, projects, programmes and other activities of Ukrainian NGOs; the Civil Society Organizations Sustainability Programme, which aims to provide training and consultancy support to civil society organizations, NGOs, charitable foundations, political parties, local governments, etc., and also assist in establishing contacts with organizations abroad; and the Social Partnership Programme, which aims to research information on and implement different schemes of social partnership, establishing co-operative relations between NGOs and local government and businesses.

Geographical Area of Activity: Ukraine.

Publications: *GURT Bulletin* (weekly e-mail newsletter); publications on volunteering, NGO governance, public relations and fund-raising; Annual Report.

Finance: Total income US $333,000, total expenditure $316,000 (2011).

Board: Oleksiy Meleschuk (Chair.).

Principal Staff: Exec. Dir Bohdan Maslych.

Address: 01025 Kyiv, POB 126, str. Popudrenka 52, Rm 609.

Telephone: (44) 296-10-52; **Fax:** (44) 296-10-52; **Internet:** www.gurt.org.ua; **e-mail:** info@gurt.org.ua.

Ukrainian Philanthropists Forum

Established in 2004.

Activities: Provides information, skills and professional knowledge, and communications services. Programmes include Na Vchis'!, comprising monthly training seminars, workshops and peer-learning events; the Hard Talks on Philanthropy discussion platform; and the Starting Point for Philanthropy seminar series. The Forum's Information Resource Centre promotes research into philanthropy. Composed of 21 mem. orgs.

Geographical Area of Activity: Ukraine.

Publications: *Chronicles of Philanthropy* (weekly e-digest); *Philanthroscop* (monthly newsletter).

Principal Staff: Dir Anna Gulevskaya-Chernish.

Address: 04070 Kyiv, St Elias 18-1.

Telephone: (44) 425-92-94; **Fax:** (44) 425-92-95; **Internet:** www.ufb.org.ua; **e-mail:** info@ufb.org.ua.

FOUNDATIONS, TRUSTS AND NON-PROFIT ORGANIZATIONS

International Charitable Fund 'Ukraine 3000'

Established in 2001 to assist in the development of Ukrainian society.

Activities: Operates in three principal areas: Yesterday (heritage, archaeology, ethnography); Today (health, social welfare); and Tomorrow (development of Ukraine).

Geographical Area of Activity: Ukraine.

Board of Directors: Maryna Antonova (Chair.); Oleksandr Maksymchuk (Vice-Chair.).

Principal Staff: Head of Supervisory Board Kateryna Yushchenko.

Address: 04070 Kyiv, POB 159, str. Spaska 37.

Telephone: (44) 390-05-44; **Fax:** (44) 390-05-49; **Internet:** www.ukraine3000.org.ua; **e-mail:** info@ukraine3000.org.ua.

International Renaissance Foundation—IRF

Established in 1990; part of the Open Society Foundations (q.v.) network, founded by George Soros.

Activities: Aims to provide financial and efficient assistance to the development of an open, democratic society in Ukraine by supporting key civil initiatives. The Foundation is supported by international donors as well as by Ukrainian and foreign organizations. Throughout the period of its activity, the Foundation has offered grants to various Ukrainian NGOs, scientific research and educational institutions, and publishing houses totalling more than US $95m. The Foundation has allocated approximately $6m. to projects promoting European integration, strengthening civil society, the advocacy system and securing the principle of the rule of law in Ukraine, implementation of the judicial and penitentiary reforms, fostering freedom of speech and information, promoting the civil activism of ethnic minorities and tolerance, educational and public health reforms, the translation of important academic works, and the development of Ukrainian publishing. The Foundation traditionally supports public initiatives during elections such as national exit polls, monitoring and supporting independent coverage of election campaigns in the mass media.

Geographical Area of Activity: Primarily Ukraine.

Publications: Annual Report; IRF Newsletter; brochures and leaflets.

Finance: Annual income US $10,420,034, expenditure $10,498,193 (31 Dec. 2012).

Supervisory Board: Roman Shporlyuk (Chair.); **Executive Board:** Oleksandr Sushko (Chair.).

Principal Staff: Exec. Dir Yevhen Bystrytsky; Deputy Exec. Dir Inna Pidluska.

Address: 04053 Kyiv, str. Artema 46.

Telephone: (44) 461-97-09; **Fax:** (44) 486-76-29; **Internet:** www.irf.kiev.ua; **e-mail:** irf@irf.kiev.ua.

Victor Pinchuk Foundation

Established in 2006 to organize Victor Pinchuk's philanthropic projects.

Activities: Aims to develop a new generation of leaders within Ukraine through strategic modernization projects.

Geographical Area of Activity: Ukraine.

Publications: Annual Report.

Finance: Annual income US $16,889,064, expenditure $17,239,105 (31 Dec. 2012).

Board: Thomas Weihe (Chair.).

Principal Staff: Exec. Dir Victoria Chernyavska.

Address: 01601 Kyiv, str. Mechnikova 2.

Telephone: (44) 490-48-35; **Fax:** (44) 490-48-78; **Internet:** www.pinchukfund.org; **e-mail:** info@pinchukfund.org.

Ukrainian Women's Fund

Founded in 2000 to provide financial and consultational support and information to public organizations, particularly women's organizations, from Ukraine, Moldova and Belarus.

Activities: Facilitates the consolidation of the women's movement in Ukraine, Moldova and Belarus; promotes issues of gender and diversity; and works to attract more resources to support women's initiatives by developing a culture of philanthropy in Ukraine. The Fund has made grants to projects for expanding economic opportunities for women, developing businesses run by women and reducing unemployment among women, increasing women's political participation and gender equality. Promotes information exchange between women's organizations, which can facilitate the establishment and development of networks of NGOs that work on women's and gender issues; aims to increase the activity of young women in the community life of Ukraine, preparing future female leaders, and promoting the formation of a women's movement among the younger generation.

Geographical Area of Activity: Belarus, Moldova and Ukraine.

Publications: *Directory of non-governmental organizations of Ukraine working on women's and gender issues*; *Basic strategies and methodologies of gender mainstreaming*; *Training manual for civil servants* (in Ukrainian).

Finance: Annual income US $409,060 (2013).

Board of Directors: Natalia Karbowska (Chair.).

Principal Staff: Dir Olesya Bondar.

Address: 04050 Kyiv, vul. Artema 79, Office 38.

Telephone: (44) 568-53-89; **Fax:** (44) 484-62-05; **Internet:** www.uwf.kiev.ua; **e-mail:** uwf@uwf.kiev.ua.

United Arab Emirates

FOUNDATIONS, TRUSTS AND NON-PROFIT ORGANIZATIONS

Emirates Foundation

Established in 2005, and funded by the United Arab Emirates Government and the private sector in UAE, to improve the quality of life in the country.

Activities: Focuses on helping young people, associated institutions and community organizations through three core programmes—Leadership and Empowerment, Social Inclusion and Community Engagement—delivered through social enterprise.

Geographical Area of Activity: UAE.

Publications: Newsletter.

Board of Directors: HH Sheikh Abdullah bin Zayed Al Nahyan (Chair.); HE Sheikh Sultan bin Tahnoon Al Nahyan (Man. Dir).

Principal Staff: CEO Clare Woodcraft-Scott.

Address: POB 111445, Mezzanine Floor, Al Mamoura Bldg, 4th and 15th Sts, Abu Dhabi.

Telephone: (2) 404-2994; **Fax:** (2) 404-2901; **Internet:** www.emiratesfoundation.ae; **e-mail:** information@emiratesfoundation.ae.

Muhammad bin Rashid Al Maktoum Foundation

Established in 2007 by HH Sheikh Muhammed bin Rashid Al Maktoum, Vice-President and Prime Minister of the United Arab Emirates and Ruler of Dubai.

Activities: Operates in the areas of the arts and culture, business and education. Runs the Dubai International Poetry Festival and the Dubai International Children's Book Fair. Other intiatives include the Arab German Dialogue, the Translate and Write Program, and Business Incubators scholarships for Arab students who wish to study at universities abroad.

Geographical Area of Activity: UAE.

Publications: *Arab Knowledge Reports*; books.

Finance: Initial endowment of AED 37,000m. (US $10,000m.).

Principal Staff: Chair. HH Sheikh Muhammad bin Rashid Al Maktoum; Man. Dir HE Jamal bin Huwaireb.

Address: POB 214444, Bldg 7, Dubai Outsource Zone, Dubai.

Telephone: (14) 423-3444; **Fax:** (14) 368-7777; **Internet:** www.mbrfoundation.ae; **e-mail:** info@mbrf.ae.

United Kingdom

FOUNDATION CENTRES AND CO-ORDINATING BODIES

Association of Charitable Foundations

Formed in 1989.

Activities: Open to any charitable organization based in the United Kingdom whose principal function is grantmaking, supported by income from property or another assured source (except for grants from government or other grantmaking trusts). Associate membership is open to other grantmakers. The Association aims to support charitable grantmaking trusts by: seeking a constructive influence on the law and public policy affecting grantmaking charities, and providing relevant information to the membership; enabling trusts and foundations to learn from each other's experience, to discuss matters of common concern, to confer with funders from other sectors, and to achieve good practice in grantmaking; encouraging philanthropy and promoting the development of new grantmaking foundations; and seeking to improve understanding of trusts and foundations, among grant-seekers and the general public. Activities include lobbying for public policy and legislation affecting grantmaking charities; running a varied meeting programme; liaising with government departments concerned with grantmaking and with other organizations of the voluntary sector; assisting individuals and corporations planning to set up new foundations; and research. Member foundations convene interest groups on areas such as the arts, education, the environment, penal affairs, children and young people, housing, and international funding. The Association also maintains contacts with a variety of relevant bodies in the USA, Europe, Australia and elsewhere, and with WINGS and the European Foundation Centre (qq.v.). The Association has more than 300 members.

Geographical Area of Activity: United Kingdom.

Restrictions: Does not make grants, nor does it give individual advice to grant-seeking organizations or individuals.

Publications: *Trust & Foundation News* (quarterly).

Finance: Annual income £853,908, expenditure £893,766 (31 Dec. 2013).

Trustee Board: Amanda Jordan (Chair.); Sara Llewellin (Vice-Chair.); Lucy Palfreyman (Treas.).

Principal Staff: Chief Exec. David Emerson; Deputy Chief Exec. Carol Mack.

Address: Acorn House, 314–320 Gray's Inn Rd, London WC1X 8DP.

Telephone: (20) 7255-4499; **Fax:** (20) 7255-4496; **Internet:** www.acf.org.uk; **e-mail:** acf@acf.org.uk.

Association of Medical Research Charities—AMRC

Formally established in 1987 to further medical research in the United Kingdom generally and in particular to advance the effectiveness of United Kingdom medical research charities.

Activities: Aims to support the medical and health research charities sector's effectiveness and advance medical research by developing best practice, providing information and guidance, improving public dialogue about research and science, and influencing government. The Association has more than 120 member charities, which contribute more than £1,000m. annually to research aimed at tackling diseases such as heart disease, cancer and diabetes, as well as rarer conditions, including cystic fibrosis and motor neurone disease.

Geographical Area of Activity: United Kingdom.

Restrictions: United Kingdom only. Does not fund medical research itself, or assist grant applicants with finding grants from member charities.

Finance: Annual income £721,109, expenditure £653,506 (31 March 2014).

Executive Council: Lord Willis of Knaresborough (Chair.); John Moore (Vice-Chair.); Martin Richardson (Hon. Treas.).

Principal Staff: Chief Exec. Sharmila Nebhrajani.

Address: Charles Darwin House, 12 Roger St, London WC1N 2JU.

Telephone: (20) 7685-2620; **Fax:** (20) 7685-2621; **Internet:** www.amrc.org.uk; **e-mail:** info@amrc.org.uk.

CAF—Charities Aid Foundation

Established in 1924 in its original form, as part of the National Council of Social Service; launched as an independent foundation in 1974, under a Declaration of Trust between the NCSS (now the National Council for Voluntary Organisations, q.v.) and the Trustees of the Foundation.

Activities: Aims to increase the resources available to the voluntary sector. The Foundation operates the CAF Charity Account scheme for private and corporate donors, manages Give As You Earn, a payroll deduction scheme, and provides financial and administrative services to charities. It also publishes research findings and statistics concerning the voluntary sector and organizes annual conferences on matters of current concern to charities and voluntary organizations. All CAF surpluses are distributed in grants, throughout the voluntary sector. Maintains a number of overseas offices.

Geographical Area of Activity: North and South America, Southern Africa, Australia, Europe, India and United Kingdom.

Restrictions: No grants to individuals.

Publications: *Charity Trends*; publications on the non-profit sector.

Finance: Annual income £418,213,000, expenditure £406,991,000 (30 April 2014).

Trustees: Dominic Casserley (Chair.); Sue Ashtiany (Vice-Chair.).

Principal Staff: Chief Exec. Dr John Low.

Address: 25 Kings Hill Ave, Kings Hill, West Malling ME19 4TA.

Telephone: (3000) 123000; **Fax:** (3000) 123001; **Internet:** www.cafonline.org; **e-mail:** enquiries@cafonline.org.

Charities Advisory Trust

Established in 1979 as the Charity Trading Advisory Group to render unbiased information on all aspects of charity trading.

Activities: Aims to redress injustice and inequality through practical approaches. The Trust conducts research on all aspects of charity trading to provide authentic information on the sector and provides information on proposals made by governments, as well as by NGOs, on third sector reform and income generation. It makes charitable donations in areas including peace and reconciliation projects, and in medical research including diabetic prevention and control, prevention of blindness and early detection of cancer; and also focuses on urban tree-planting and tackling homelessness. The Trust funded The Green Hotel venture in Mysore, in southern India, the proceeds of which are channelled to environmental and charitable projects in India; the Hotel also hosts training courses for graduates interested in careers in international development.

Geographical Area of Activity: Mainly United Kingdom and India.

Restrictions: No grants to individuals, large fund-raising organizations or to missionary charities. Grants considered for any charitable purpose; unsolicited applications are rarely responded to.

Publications: *The Charity Shops Handbook*; *Charities, Trading and the Law*; *Trading by Charities: A Statistical Analysis*; and other publications.

Finance: Annual income £2,065,516, expenditure £1,420,994 (30 June 2014).

Trustees: Dame Hilary Blume (Sec.).

Address: Radius Works, Back Lane, London NW3 1HL.

Telephone: (20) 7794-9835; **Fax:** (20) 7431-3739; **Internet:** www.charitiesadvisorytrust.org.uk; **e-mail:** people@charitiesadvisorytrust.org.uk.

DEC—Disasters Emergency Committee

Established in 1963 to provide support for relief sector charities in the United Kingdom dealing with the effects of major overseas disasters.

Activities: Operates through providing an accredited national forum for fund-raising and a focal point for public response, facilitating co-operation, co-ordination and communication, and ensuring that funds are used effectively and properly. The Committee has a Rapid Response Network of partners which provides free facilities as and when required, comprising television and radio, the banking sector, the Royal Mail, regional and national telephone companies, and a range of organizations in the corporate sector. The aid agencies that meet the Committee's membership criteria are Actionaid, the British Red Cross Society, CAFOD—Catholic Agency for Overseas Development, CARE International, Christian Aid, Concern Worldwide, Help the Aged, Islamic Relief, MERLIN—Medical Emergency Relief International, Oxfam, Save the Children, Tearfund and World Vision.

Geographical Area of Activity: United Kingdom.

Publications: *DEC Policy Handbook;* Annual Review.

Finance: Annual income £70,028,000, expenditure £29,125,000 (31 March 2014).

Board of Trustees: Clive Jones (Chair.); Jeremy Bennett (Deputy Chair.); Clare Thompson (Hon. Treas.).

Principal Staff: Chief Exec. Saleh Saeed.

Address: 43 Chalton St, Ground Floor, London NW1 1DU.

Telephone: (20) 7387-0200; **Internet:** www.dec.org.uk; **e-mail:** info@dec.org.uk.

Directory of Social Change

Founded in 1975.

Activities: Strives to be independent source of information and advocate of international recognition to voluntary and community sectors worldwide. The charity promotes the voluntary sector by running conferences; conducting practical training courses, briefings and seminars on current issues influencing the sector; researching and publishing handbooks and reference guides, online information, CD-ROMs and journals; organizing Charityfair; encouraging voluntary groups to communicate and share information; and campaigning to nurture the interests of the voluntary sector. It also issues publications and conducts training courses on management, fundraising, organizational and personal development, finance, law and communication.

Geographical Area of Activity: United Kingdom.

Publications: Annual Report; *A Guide to Grants for Individuals in need* (2007); *The Educational Grants Directory* (2007); books and information catalogue.

Finance: Annual income £2,500,724, expenditure £2,353,078 (31 Dec. 2013).

Principal Staff: Chief Exec. Debra Allcock Tyler.

Address: 24 Stephenson Way, London NW1 2DP.

Telephone: (20) 7391-4800; **Fax:** (20) 7391-4808; **Internet:** www.dsc.org.uk; **e-mail:** enquiries@dsc.org.uk.

International NGO Training and Research Centre—INTRAC

Established in 1991.

Activities: Carries out specialist training, and provides consultancy and research services to organizations executing international development and relief programmes. The Centre provides specially designed training, consultancy and research services to organizations involved in international development and relief. It aims to improve civil society performance by strengthening management and organizational effectiveness, and exploring policy issues. It promotes enhanced organizational and managerial capacity for NGOs and civil society organizations; researches global NGO trends and conducts analyses; and extends support for the advancement of the NGO sector.

Geographical Area of Activity: Central Asia, South America, countries of the former USSR, Africa, Cyprus, and Central and Eastern Europe.

Restrictions: Does not make grants.

Publications: *ONTRAC* (newsletter, 3 a year); Annual Report; notes and papers for practitioners on issues affecting NGOs in development; occasional papers; resource materials; policy briefing papers.

Finance: Annual income £2,041,347, expenditure £2,039,149 (31 March 2014).

Board of Trustees: Paul Thornton (Chair.); Tom Travers (Hon. Treas.).

Principal Staff: Exec. Dir Michael Hammer.

Address: Oxbridge Ct, Osney Mead, Oxford OX2 0ES.

Telephone: (1865) 201851; **Fax:** (1865) 201852; **Internet:** www.intrac.org; **e-mail:** info@intrac.org.

National Council for Voluntary Organisations—NCVO

Established in 1919 as the National Council of Social Services by a £1,000 legacy from Edward Vivian Birchall, who was killed during the Battle of the Somme in France in 1916.

Activities: A lobbying organization that represents the views of its members, and the wider voluntary sector, to government, the European Union and other bodies. The Council also researches and analyses the voluntary sector; and campaigns on generic issues affecting the voluntary sector, such as the role of voluntary organizations in public service delivery and the future of local government. It has several specialist teams that provide information, advice and support to others working in or with the voluntary sector; runs networking and training events; manages and facilitates a wide range of forums and networks for staff and volunteers working in specific areas such as policy, planning, ICT, membership, publishing and public service delivery; provides direct support to organizations through the NCVO Consultancy service' and runs a helpdesk providing information and support for NCVO members.

Geographical Area of Activity: United Kingdom.

Publications: Reports, toolkits, briefing papers and books.

Finance: Annual income £9,588,000, expenditure £8,868,000 (31 March 2014).

Trustee Board: Baroness Grey-Thompson (Pres.); Martyn Lewis (Chair.); Jules Mason (Vice-Chair.); Bruce Gordon (Hon. Treas.).

Principal Staff: Chief Exec. Sir Stuart Etherington.

Address: National Council for Voluntary Organisations Society Building, 8 All Saints St, London N1 9RL.

Telephone: (20) 7713-6161; **Fax:** (20) 7713-6300; **Internet:** www.ncvo.org.uk; **e-mail:** ncvo@ncvo.org.uk.

UK Community Foundations—UKCF

Established in 1991 as the Community Foundation Network (CFN). Present name adopted in 2013.

Activities: Co-ordinating organization supporting the 48 community foundations operating in the United Kingdom.

Geographical Area of Activity: United Kingdom.

Finance: Annual income £11,427,000, expenditure £10,537,000 (31 March 2013).

Trustees: David Sheepshanks (Chair.); Hamish Buchan (Treas.).

Principal Staff: Chief Exec. Fabian French.

Address: 12 Angel Gate, 320–326 City Rd, London EC1V 2PT.

Telephone: (20) 7713-9326; **Internet:** ukcommunityfoundations.org; **e-mail:** network@ ukcommunityfoundations.org.

FOUNDATIONS, TRUSTS AND NON-PROFIT ORGANIZATIONS

Action for Children

Founded in 1869 and formerly known as NCH (National Children's Home). Present name adopted in 2008.

Activities: Helps children and young people suffering as a result of poverty, disability, abuse, neglect and social exclusion. The organization operates across the United Kingdom, through campaigning for policy changes to benefit children and young people. It works in the following areas: ending child poverty and social exclusion; providing safeguards for children and young people at risk of abuse; promoting education and health; preventing youth crime and homelessness; improving the quality of life for children in care; foster care; family centres and residential homes; mediation services; and ensuring safe use of the Internet for children. Runs short-break projects, residential centres and community centres. Has offices in Wales, Scotland and Northern Ireland.

Geographical Area of Activity: United Kingdom.

Publications: *Adoption*; *Care leavers*; *Child migration*; *Children's rights*; *Children in care*; *Commissioning services*; *Education*; *Family support*; facts and statistics; complaints.

Finance: Annual income £179,670,000, expenditure £168,484,000 (31 March 2014).

Council of Trustees: John O'Brien (Chair.); Catherine Dugmore (Vice-Chair.).

Principal Staff: Chief Exec. Sir Tony Hawkhead.

Address: 3 The Boulevard, Ascot Rd, Watford WD18 8AG.

Telephone: (1923) 361500; **Internet:** www.actionforchildren.org.uk; **e-mail:** ask.us@actionforchildren.org.uk.

The Sylvia Adams Charitable Trust

Established in 1995 to make grants to charities working to alleviate poverty and disease, in particular among children, and to support charities working with the homeless, projects in developing countries and health education.

Activities: Provides start-up and time-limited funding for a wide variety of purposes and causes.

Geographical Area of Activity: Hertfordshire, United Kingdom; Africa, South Asia and South America.

Restrictions: Closed to new applications for grants.

Finance: Annual income £209,273, expenditure £1,500,131 (31 March 2014).

Trustees: Jerry Golland (Chair.).

Principal Staff: Dir Jane Young.

Address: Sylvia Adams House, 24 The Common, Hatfield AL10 0NB.

Telephone: (1707) 259259; **Fax:** (1707) 259268; **Internet:** www.sylvia-adams.org.uk; **e-mail:** info@sylvia-adams.org.uk.

Afghanaid

Established in 1983 to provide humanitarian relief to Afghans in hardship and distress, and to assist with the rehabilitation and development of Afghanistan.

Activities: Operates in Afghanistan through major infrastructure work such as building and maintaining roads and bridges; macro-irrigation structures; and sustainable community development projects, including agriculture, microfinance, income generation, animal health, health and basic literacy education and skills training for women.

Geographical Area of Activity: Afghanistan.

Restrictions: Currently funding only its own projects.

Publications: Annual Report; regular newsletters.

Finance: Annual income £5,049,749, expenditure £6,503,958 (31 Dec. 2014).

Trustees: Chris Kinder (Chair.); Elizabeth Winter (Vice-Chair.); Mary Mountain (Treas.).

Principal Staff: Man. Dir Charles R. Davy.

Address: Development House, 56–64 Leonard St, London EC2A 4LT.

Telephone: (20) 7065-0825; **Internet:** www.afghanaid.org.uk; **e-mail:** info@afghanaid.org.uk.

Africa Educational Trust

Founded in 1958 by Rev. Michael Scott to support education in and outside Africa, for persons who, in the opinion of the trustees, are wholly or partly of African descent, and to advise on educational immigration and welfare provisions for African students.

Activities: Operates in Africa in the field of education, especially non-formal education and skills training; primary and secondary education; and development of local NGOs. The Trust implements activities directly and does not provide grants. It provides training to African community organizations in the United Kingdom and maintains a regional office in Kenya.

Geographical Area of Activity: Africa, United Kingdom and Ireland.

Publications: Annual Report; *The Situation of AET Sponsored Namibians After their Return Home*.

Finance: Annual income £4,316,501, expenditure £4,605,672 (31 Aug 2013).

Trustees: Sally Healy (Chair.); Prof. Francis Katamba (Vice-Chair.); Prof. Richard Hodder-Williams (Treas.).

Principal Staff: Exec. Dir Sara Cottingham; Finance and Admin. Dir Ed Helmer.

Address: 18 Hand Ct, London WC1V 6JF.

Telephone: (20) 7831-3283; **Fax:** (20) 7242-3265; **Internet:** www.africaeducationaltrust.org; **e-mail:** info@ africaeducationaltrust.org.

Africa Foundation (UK)

Founded in 1992 to facilitate the empowerment and development of individuals, living in, or adjacent to, protected areas in Africa, by forging unique partnerships between conservation initiatives and local communities. Formerly known as the Rural Investment Trust, an independent arm of CC Africa, a South Africa-based safari company.

Activities: Supports projects in the fields of education, health care and small business development. In the field of education, support includes building classrooms, pre-schools, laboratories and media centres, and the provision of educational bursaries to community leaders; health care activities include building medical clinics, AIDS prevention programmes, hosting educational workshops and providing family planning; and in the area of small business development, funding is given to promising entrepreneurs, supporting community centres and small businesses, and encouraging eco-tourism and community development initiatives. The Foundation provides conservation lessons for local children to further knowledge of the environment and the value of conservation. Projects are currently run in Kenya, Tanzania, Zanzibar, Zimbabwe, Namibia, South Africa and Botswana. Also maintains an office in the USA.

Geographical Area of Activity: Botswana, Kenya, Namibia, South Africa, Tanzania, Zanzibar, Zimbabwe.

Finance: Annual income £226,532, expenditure £256,266 (30 June 2014).

Board of Trustees: Robin James (Chair.); C. L. Creasey (Sec.).

Address: c/o Sutton Place (UK) Ltd, 26 Curzon St, London W1J 7TQ.

Telephone: (20) 3137-9942; **Internet:** www.africafoundation.org; **e-mail:** info@africafoundation.org.

Aga Khan Foundation (UK)—AKF

Established in 1967 by HH the Aga Khan to promote social development in developing countries of Asia and Africa by funding health, education and rural development programmes, without regard to race, religion or background. An affiliate of the Aga Khan Foundation in Switzerland (q.v.).

Activities: Channels funds to support organizations and programmes principally in less-developed countries in Asia and Africa, and also in Canada, Portugal, Tajikistan, Switzerland, the United Kingdom and the USA. The Foundation is involved in conservation and the environment, education, medicine and health, and social welfare, through grants to institutions, promoting community self-help projects, scholarships and fellowships, conferences and publications. It operates programmes to aid child development and education, especially by improving the quality of formal education and early childhood education; family health and nutrition through community-orientated health development; and rural development through income-generation and the management of renewable resources. Promotes skills development, training and technical exchanges internationally.

Geographical Area of Activity: International.

Restrictions: Does not solicit applications for funding, nor will it respond positively to any such requests.

Publications: Project briefings; information sheets on Foundation activities; and evaluation reports on Foundation-supported projects; Annual Report.

Finance: Annual income £15,688,000, expenditure £14,066,000 (31 Dec. 2013).

National Committee: Naguib Kheraj (Chair.), Yasmin Jetha (Vice-Chair.); Habib Motani (Sec.).

Principal Staff: Chief Exec. Aly Nazerali.

Address: 210 Euston Rd, London NW1 2DA.

Telephone: (20) 7383-9090; **Fax:** (20) 7589-0641; **Internet:** www.akf.org.uk; www.akdn.org/akf.

Al Fayed Charitable Foundation

Established in 1987 for general charitable purposes.

Activities: Operates nationally in the fields of medicine, health and social welfare. The Foundation awards grants to children's hospitals and hospices.

Geographical Area of Activity: United Kingdom.

Publications: Press releases.

Finance: Annual income £1,668,342, expenditure £1,673,879 (31 Dec. 2013).

Trustees: Mohamed Al Fayed; Camilla Fayed; H. Fayed.

Principal Staff: Contact Kate Lovell.

Address: c/o Charity Man., Hyde Park Residence, 55 Park Lane, London W1K 1NA.

Telephone: (20) 7225-6673; **Fax:** (20) 7225-6872; **Internet:** www.the-acf.com; **e-mail:** acf@alfayed.com.

The Al-Khoei Benevolent Foundation

Established in 1989.

Activities: Aims to advance the Islamic religion. The Foundation operates schools, a nursery, a mosque and a library. It organizes religious and social meetings, and interfaith activities; and also provides advice on good practice and capacity building to mosques and Islamic teaching institutions in the United Kingdom. Has offices in Canada, France, Pakistan, Thailand and the USA.

Geographical Area of Activity: Worldwide.

Publications: *Dialogue* (in English); *Al-Ghadeer* (in Arabic).

Finance: Annual income £1,715,760, expenditure £2,264,177 (31 Aug. 2013).

Principal Staff: Finance Dir M. Mousavi; Public Relations Dir Y. A. Al-Khoei; Sec.-Gen. Seyed Saheb Khoei.

Address: Stone Hall, Chevening Rd, London NW6 6TN.

Telephone: (20) 7372-4049; **Fax:** (20) 7372-0694; **Internet:** www.khoei.net; **e-mail:** sajad@alkhoei.org.

Alchemy Foundation

Founded in 1985 by Richard and Annabel Stilgoe as the Starlight Foundation to support mental and physical health care of the elderly and children, and to assist in famine relief.

Activities: Operates worldwide in the fields of aid and development, arts and humanities, education, medicine and health, and social welfare. The Foundation promotes self-conducted programmes and aims in particular to aid people (especially children) suffering from mental or physical illness or disability, and people suffering from the effects of famine.

Geographical Area of Activity: International.

Restrictions: Grants only to other registered charities.

Finance: Annual income £303,571, expenditure £292,135 (5 April 2014).

Trustees: Sir Richard H. Z. S. Stilgoe (Chair.).

Address: Trevereux Manor, Limpsfield Chart, Oxted RH8 0TL.

Telephone: (1883) 730600.

All Saints Educational Trust

Founded in 1979 to promote the training of teachers and research and development in education.

Activities: Aims to promote education, principally in schools—both maintained and independent—through: making awards to those undertaking professional teacher training and to teachers who wish to gain further qualifications; providing resources to encourage innovative classroom activity, the establishment of libraries and other pedagogical initiatives; and promoting research, particularly in home economics and religious education.

Geographical Area of Activity: Europe and all other countries.

Restrictions: Courses must lead to degrees awarded by institutions in the United Kingdom. Applications from citizens from outside the United Kingdom or European Union must be for one year, full-time Master's programmes only.

Publications: Annual Report.

Finance: Annual income £524,732, expenditure £607,723 (30 June 2013).

Trustees: Rev. Dr Keith G. Riglin (Chair.); D. J. Trillo (Vice-Chair.).

Principal Staff: Clerk K. D. Mitchell.

Address: Knightrider House, 2 Knightrider Court, London EC4V 5AR.

Telephone: (20) 7248-8380; **Internet:** www.aset.org.uk; **e-mail:** aset@aset.org.uk.

Amnesty International

Founded in 1961 by Peter Benenson and others to secure throughout the world the provisions of the UN Universal Declaration of Human Rights (1948) and other internationally recognized human rights instruments.

Activities: Operates internationally in the field of human rights. The organization works against the imprisonment, detention or other physical restrictions imposed on any person by reason of their political, religious or conscientiously held beliefs; or by reason of their ethnic origin, gender, colour, language, national or social origin, economic status, birth or other status, provided that he or she has not used or advocated violence ('prisoners of conscience'). It also works against the detention of any political prisoner without fair trial or any trial procedures that do not conform to internationally recognized norms; the death penalty, and the torture or other cruel, inhuman or degrading treatment or punishment of prisoners, whether or not they have used or advocated violence; and the extrajudicial execution of persons whether or not detained, and 'disappearances', whether or not the persons affected have used or advocated violence. Also seeks to co-operate with other not-for-profit organizations, the UN and regional inter-governmental organizations, and to ensure control of international military, security and police relations to prevent human rights abuses. Organizes human rights education and awareness-raising programmes. Has more than 50 national sections and in excess of 2.8m. members and subscribers in more than 150 countries and territories worldwide.

Geographical Area of Activity: International.

Publications: *Amnesty International Report* (annually); *The Wire* (2 a month); annual reports; thematic and regional reports on human rights issues.

Finance: Annual income £59,001,000, expenditure £53,437,000 (31 March 2013).

Principal Staff: Sec.-Gen. Salil Shetty.

Address: International Secretariat, 1 Easton St, London WC1X 0DW.

Telephone: (20) 7413-5500; **Fax:** (20) 7956-1157; **Internet:** www.amnesty.org; **e-mail:** contactus@amnesty.org.

Ancient India and Iran Trust

Established in 1978 by Prof. Sir Harold Bailey, Prof. Joan van Lohuizen, Dr Jan van Lohuizen, Dr Raymond Allchin and Dr Bridget Allchin.

Activities: Promotes public and academic interest in the early cultures and languages of the Indo-Iranian world. The Trust maintains a library of more than 30,000 volumes open to the public; runs courses and lectures; and organizes regular symposia and seminars on related subjects.

Geographical Area of Activity: Central and South Asia.

Restrictions: Small research grants only to researchers in the regions covered, when funds permit.

Publications: *The Crossroads of Asia: Transformation in Image and Symbol*; *Living Traditions: Studies in the Ethnoarchaeology of South Asia*; *Gandharan Art in Context: East-West Exchanges at the Crossroads of Asia*; paper and online newsletter, INDIRAN.

Finance: Annual revenue £192,842, expenditure £110,461 (31 March 2014).

Trustees: Prof. Nicholas Sims-Williams (Hon. Chair.); Prof. Almut Hintze (Hon. Treas.); Dr Christine van Ruymbeke (Sec.); Ursula Sims-Williams (Hon. Librarian).

Principal Staff: Admin. Brendan Griggs; Custodian James Cormick.

Address: 23 Brooklands Ave, Cambridge CB2 8BG.

Telephone: (1223) 356841; **Fax:** (1223) 361125; **Internet:** www.indiran.org; indiairantrust.wordpress.com; **e-mail:** info@indiran.org.

Andrews Charitable Trust—ACT

Founded by C. Jackson-Cole in 1965 to alleviate suffering and to advance Christianity. Formerly known as the Phyllis Trust and later as World in Need. The ACT is the majority shareholder of Andrews & Partners estate agency business, which was also set up by Jackson-Cole and which now has 100% charitable ownership. The minority shares are held by the ACT's sister trusts, Christian Initiative Trust and Christian Book Promotion Trust.

Activities: Supports initiatives that are innovative, replicable and sustainable. The Trust looks for ideas that will make a difference to the world and are a significant addition to existing approaches to address an identified need. Works with founders of new organizations or those that wish to make a step change

in the delivery of services. Provides pro-bono support in business planning, governance and other organizational development skills, in addition to grant funding.

Geographical Area of Activity: United Kingdom and international.

Restrictions: Supports the above activities only. Does not accept unsolicited applications.

Finance: Annual income £599,945 expenditure £247,692 (31 Dec. 2013).

Board: Andrew Radford (Chair.); Paul Heal (Chair.-elect); Nick Wright (Treas.).

Principal Staff: Dir Siân Edwards.

Address: The Clockhouse, Bath Hill, Keynsham, Bristol BS31 1HL.

Telephone: (117) 9461834; **Internet:** www.andrewscharitabletrust.org.uk; **e-mail:** info@andrewscharitabletrust.org.uk.

Antarctic Heritage Trust

Established in 1993 to preserve Antarctic buildings and heritage.

Activities: Promotes study of Antarctic regions through providing information and supporting institutions with a connection to Antarctic heritage.

Geographical Area of Activity: Antarctic regions.

Finance: Annual income £239,551, expenditure £399,305 (30 April 2014).

Trustees: Donald Lamont (Chair.); Ian Rushby (Treas.).

Principal Staff: Chief Exec. Camilla Nichol.

Address: High Cross, Madingley Rd, Cambridge CB3 0ET.

Telephone: (1223) 355049; **Internet:** www.ukaht.org; **e-mail:** info@ukaht.org.

Anti-Slavery International

Founded in 1839 (known as the Anti-Slavery Society for the Protection of Human Rights until 1990).

Activities: Aims to eradicate slavery and forced labour in all their forms through: research and the publication of information about all forms of slavery throughout the world; generating greater awareness of such abuses; campaigning nationally and internationally; and working with local partners to help the victims of human rights injustices. The organization has consultative status with the UN Economic and Social Council (ECOSOC), and has members worldwide. Launched the annual Anti-Slavery Award in 1991.

Geographical Area of Activity: International.

Restrictions: Does not make grants.

Publications: *Anti-Slavery Reporter* (twice-yearly newsletter); various other publications on issues including bonded, forced and child labour; Annual Report and Accounts.

Finance: Annual income £2,561,851, expenditure £1,907,647 (31 March 2014).

Board of Trustees: Tanya English (Chair.); Malcolm John (Vice-Chair.); Richard Ratcliffe (Treas.).

Principal Staff: Dir Dr Aidan McQuade.

Address: Thomas Clarkson House, The Stableyard, Broomgrove Rd, London SW9 9TL.

Telephone: (20) 7501-8920; **Fax:** (20) 7738-4110; **Internet:** www.antislavery.org; **e-mail:** info@antislavery.org.

ARK—Absolute Return for Kids

Established in 2002 as an international charity to transform the lives of children.

Activities: Programmes include: HIV/AIDS (Southern Africa)—helping prevent children from being orphaned or dying from AIDS; Education—developing leadership in inner-city schools in the United Kingdom, improving the educational opportunities of deprived children in India, and opening a network of state-funded secondary schools in rural Uganda over the next five years; and Children in Care

(Romania)—reforming child-care systems, and assisting in the closure of institutions and the placement of children with families or small group homes. Operates a network of 27 primary and secondary schools in the United Kingdom.

Geographical Area of Activity: Sub-Saharan Africa, United Kingdom, India, Eastern Europe.

Publications: Annual Report.

Finance: Annual income £9,503,000, expenditure £13,979,000 (31 Aug. 2014).

Board of Trustees: Ian Wace (Chair.).

Principal Staff: Chief Exec. Lucy Heller; CFO Micky Sandall.

Address: 65 Kingsway, London WC2B 6TD.

Telephone: (20) 3116-0700; **Fax:** (20) 7831-9469; **Internet:** www.arkonline.org; www.arkschools.org; **e-mail:** info@arkonline.org.

Art Fund—National Art Collections Fund

Founded in 1903 to foster the visual arts and to help public museums, galleries and historic houses to acquire works of art.

Activities: Operates in the United Kingdom in the arts, through grants or bequests to regional and national institutions for the acquisition of works of art of national and historical importance. Campaigns on behalf of museums and galleries, particularly on issues such as free admission to national collections and funding for acquisitions, as well as promoting art to a wider audience.

Geographical Area of Activity: United Kingdom.

Publications: Annual Report and Accounts; *Review* (annually); *Art Quarterly*.

Finance: Annual income £10,558,000, expenditure £10,746,000 (31 Dec. 2013).

Board of Trustees: Lord Smith of Finsbury (Chair.); Jeremy Palmer (Treas.); Linda Ashworth (Sec.).

Principal Staff: Dir Dr Stephen Deuchar.

Address: Millais House, 7 Cromwell Pl., London SW7 2JN.

Telephone: (20) 7225-4800; **Fax:** (20) 7225-4848; **Internet:** www.artfund.org; **e-mail:** info@artfund.org.

Arthritis Research UK

Founded in 1936 as the Empire Rheumatism Council to promote medical research into the cause, treatment and cure of arthritis and musculoskeletal conditions. Previously known as Arthritis Research Campaign.

Activities: A leading authority on arthritis in the United Kingdom. Conducts scientific and medical research into all types of arthritis and musculoskeletal conditions. Committed to funding high-quality research into the cause, treatment and cure of arthritis.

Geographical Area of Activity: United Kingdom.

Publications: Range of publications and resources aimed at general practitioners, hospital doctors, allied health professionals and medical students; over 90 patient information booklets on arthritis and musculoskeletal conditions; quarterly research magazine.

Finance: Annual income £37,016,000, expenditure £33,611,000 (31 July 2014).

Board of Trustees: Charles Maisey (Chair.).

Principal Staff: Chief Exec. Liam O'Toole.

Address: Copeman House, St Mary's Gate, Chesterfield, Derbyshire, S41 7TD.

Telephone: (300) 790-0400; **Fax:** (300) 790-0401; **Internet:** www.arthritisresearchuk.org; **e-mail:** enquiries@arthritisresearchuk.org.

Arts Council England

Established in 1946; the national development agency for the arts in England.

Activities: Operates in England in the area of the arts. The Council distributes both national lottery and government funds to artists and arts organizations (see also Lottery Arts Fund for England, Scotland, Wales and Northern Ireland). Funding programmes seek to support the highest artistic achievements and to make these available to as many people as possible; to encourage new work and new audiences; to bring challenging art to all sectors of the community; and to celebrate the diversity of cultures contributing to artistic life in England. Current programmes include the Creative Partnerships initiative, which will develop long-term partnerships between schools, cultural and creative organizations and artists; Decibel, a project funding culturally diverse projects; and Artsmark, a national arts award for schools.

Geographical Area of Activity: England.

Publications: *Audience Development, and Resource Development*; Annual Review; publications on different arts activities; information sheets; newsletters.

Finance: Annual income £694,686,000, expenditure £638,712,000 (31 March 2014).

National Council: Sir Peter Bazalgette (Chair.).

Principal Staff: Chief Exec. Alan Davey; Deputy Chief Exec. Althea Efunshile.

Address: 14 Great Peter St, London SW1P 3NQ.

Telephone: (845) 300-6200; **Fax:** (161) 934-4426; **Internet:** www.artscouncil.org.uk; **e-mail:** chiefexecutive@artscouncil.org.uk.

Ashden Charitable Trust

Established in 1989 for general charitable purposes. One of the Sainsbury Family Charitable Trusts, all of which share a common administration.

Activities: Operates the following projects: conservation and the environment overseas; environmental projects in the United Kingdom; sustainable regeneration; People at Risk; community arts; a Social Investment Fund; and a Low Carbon Fund. Offers small grants to organizations. Co-funds the Ashden Awards for sustainable energy, in association with other Sainsbury Family Charitable Trusts.

Geographical Area of Activity: United Kingdom, Africa, Asia and developing countries.

Restrictions: No grants are made to individuals.

Publications: Annual Report; *The Ashden Directory*; reports.

Finance: Annual income £1,605,129, expenditure £1,564,635 (5 April 2014).

Principal Staff: Dir Alan P. Bookbinder; Finance Dir Paul Spokes.

Address: c/o Sainsbury Family Charitable Trusts, The Peak, 5 Wilton Rd, London SW1V 1AP.

Telephone: (20) 7410-0330; **Internet:** www.ashdentrust.org.uk; **e-mail:** ashdentrust@sfct.org.uk.

Asthma UK

Established in 1989 by the merger of the Asthma Research Council (f. 1927) and the Friends of Asthma Research Council (f. 1972). Present name adopted in 2004.

Activities: Funds scientific research; operates the Asthma UK Adviceline; runs activity holidays for children; and produces publications for health professionals and people with asthma. Maintains offices in London, Edinburgh, Cardiff and Belfast.

Geographical Area of Activity: United Kingdom.

Publications: Annual Report; information booklets; posters; fact sheets; and other publications.

Finance: Annual income £7,626,000, expenditure £10,078,000 (30 Sept. 2013).

Trustees: Dr Rob Wilson (Chair.).

Principal Staff: Chief Exec. Kay Boycott.

Address: 18 Mansell St, London E1 8AA.

Telephone: (20) 7786-4900; **Fax:** (20) 7256-6075; **Internet:** www.asthma.org.uk; **e-mail:** mediaoffice@asthma.org.uk.

The Andrew Balint Charitable Trust

Founded in 1961 to provide funds for general charitable purposes.

Activities: Awards grants to recognized charities, nationally and internationally, aiming to assist them with achieving their respective objectives. Linked to The George Balint Charitable Trust, The Paul Charitable Trust and The Trust for Former Employees of Balint Companies, all of which are jointly administered.

Geographical Area of Activity: International.

Restrictions: No grants are made to individuals.

Finance: Annual income £21,149, expenditure £47,794 (5 April 2014).

Trustees: Agnes Balint; Dr Gabriel G. Balint-Kurti; Roy David Balint-Kurti; Daniel M. Balint-Kurti; Peter J. Balint-Kurti.

Principal Staff: Contact David P. Kramer.

Address: c/o Carter, Backer, Winter, Enterprise House, 21 Buckle St, London E1 8NN.

Telephone: (20) 7309-3800.

Baring Foundation

Established in 1969 to give money to charities and voluntary organizations pursuing charitable purposes.

Activities: Runs three core grant programmes: the Joint International Development Programme, in collaboration with the John Ellerman Foundation, which aims to improve the effectiveness of non-governmental organizations and community-based organizations in Sub-Saharan Africa, and to address problems arising from long-term forced migration; the Arts Programme, which provides development funding for arts organizations in the United Kingdom already producing and presenting arts made by older people; and the Strengthening the Voluntary Sector Programme, which works on the theme of independence in the voluntary sector. The Foundation is working on three special initiatives: African Diaspora-African Development, Climate Change, and the Third Sector and Interculturality.

Geographical Area of Activity: United Kingdom and Sub-Saharan Africa.

Restrictions: No grants to individuals. Applicant organizations must be charities or voluntary sector not-for-profit organizations registered in the United Kingdom.

Publications: *Report on Activities* (annual); *Housing Associations in England and the Future of the Voluntary Sector; An Unexamined Truth.*

Finance: Annual income £2,516,063, expenditure £3,049,986 (31 Dec. 2013).

Trustees: Janet Morrison (Chair.).

Principal Staff: Dir David Cutler; Deputy Dir David Sampson.

Address: 60 London Wall, London EC2M 5TQ.

Telephone: (20) 7767-1348; **Fax:** (20) 7767-7121; **Internet:** www.baringfoundation.org.uk; **e-mail:** baring.foundation@uk.ing.com.

Barnardo's

Established in 1867 to help children, young people and their families in the United Kingdom.

Activities: Provides guidance, support and care to young people and their families, including counselling for abused children; support for families with disabled children; family centres; fostering and adoption schemes; help for homeless young people; schools and shared houses for those leaving care; support for children and families with HIV/AIDS; and research and lobbying activities. The organization has regional offices throughout the United Kingdom and international offices in Australia, Ireland and New Zealand.

Geographical Area of Activity: United Kingdom.

Publications: *What Works?* (series); *Counting the Cost of Child Poverty*; *Joined-Up Youth Research, Policy and Practice: A New Agenda for Change?*; and other publications.

Finance: Annual income £285,774,000, expenditure £278,422,000 (31 March 2014).

Trustees: Tony Cohen (Chair.); Judy Clements (Deputy Chair.); Neil Braithwaite (Hon. Treas.).

Principal Staff: Chief Exec. Javed Khan.

Address: Tanners Lane, Barkingside, Ilford IG6 1QG.

Telephone: (20) 8550-8822; **Fax:** (20) 8551-6870; **Internet:** www.barnardos.org.uk; **e-mail:** info@barnardos.org.uk.

The Batchworth Trust

Founded in 1965 for general charitable purposes worldwide.

Activities: Operates in the fields of the environment, education, medicine and health, and social welfare. The Trust makes donations to institutions worldwide that are recognized as exclusively charitable.

Geographical Area of Activity: International, with an emphasis on England and Wales, Africa and Asia.

Restrictions: Unsolicited applications are not considered.

Finance: Annual income £398,907, expenditure £472,085 (5 April 2013).

Trustees: J. A. N. Campbell (Chair.).

Principal Staff: Admin. Exec. Martin Neve.

Address: c/o Reeves & Co LLP, Griffin House, 135 High St, Crawley RH10 1DQ.

Telephone: (1293) 776411; **Fax:** (1293) 820161.

BBC Children in Need Appeal

Established in 1980.

Activities: Aims to give every child in the United Kingdom a childhood that is safe, happy and secure, and allows them the chance to reach their potential. The organization provides grants to projects in the United Kingdom that focus on disadvantaged children and young people. It supports organizations that empower children and extend their life choices.

Geographical Area of Activity: United Kingdom.

Restrictions: Please see our website for full guidance on applying and eligibility criteria.

Publications: Annual Report; newsletters.

Finance: Annual income £55,564,000, expenditure £46,464,000 (30 June 2014).

Board: Sir Terry Wogan (Life Pres.); Stevie Spring (Chair.); Daniel Cohen (Vice-Chair.); Beverly Tew (Treas.).

Principal Staff: Chief Exec. David Ramsden.

Address: POB 1000, London W12 7WJ.

Telephone: 0345 609 0015; **Internet:** www.bbc.co.uk/pudsey; **e-mail:** pudsey@bbc.co.uk.

BBC Media Action

Founded in 1992 by the BBC (British Broadcasting Corporation) as the BBC Marshall Plan of the Mind Trust. Name changed to BBC World Service Trust in 1999. Present name adopted in 2012.

Activities: Uses media to enable people in the developing world to have access to life-changing information that can help them survive, shape their lives and thrive. The organization operates in the following principal areas: Education, through radio broadcasts and tutorials; Emergency Response, through broadcasting information; the Environment in partnership with local NGOs to offer information; Governance and Human Rights; Health; and Livelihoods. Works in partnership with local NGOs and broadcasters.

Geographical Area of Activity: Africa, Asia, Eastern Europe and the Middle East.

Publications: Newsletter; Annual Report; fact sheets and workbooks to accompany programmes broadcast.

Finance: Annual income £40,381,000, expenditure £40,094,000 (31 March 2014).

Trustees: Francesca Unsworth (Chair.); Alison Evans (Vice-Chair.); Lindsey North (Sec.).

Principal Staff: Exec. Dir Caroline Nursey.

Address: MC3A BBC Media Centre, 201 Wood Lane, London, W12 7TQ.

Telephone: (20) 8008-0001; **Fax:** (20) 7379-1622; **Internet:** www.bbcmediaaction.org; **e-mail:** media.action@bbc.co.uk.

Beaverbrook Foundation

Founded in 1954 by Lord Beaverbrook for general charitable purposes.

Activities: Provides funds to charities.

Geographical Area of Activity: United Kingdom and Canada (New Brunswick and Nova Scotia).

Restrictions: Does not make grants to individuals.

Finance: Annual income £39,309, expenditure £429,149 (30 Sept. 2014).

Trustees: Lord Beaverbrook (Chair.); Lady Aitken (Deputy Chair.).

Principal Staff: Sec. and Chief Exec. Jane S. Ford.

Address: 11–12 Dover St, London W1S 4LJ.

Telephone: (20) 7042-9435; **Internet:** www.beaverbrookfoundation.org; **e-mail:** jane@beaverbrookfoundation.org.

Beit Trust

Founded in 1906 by Alfred Beit for charitable purposes of an educational or public nature that will best promote the welfare of the inhabitants of Zimbabwe, Zambia and Malawi.

Activities: Works in Zimbabwe, Zambia and Malawi in the fields of education and health and welfare, usually in the form of building grants. The Truat operates a secondary school bursary scheme and also a Postgraduate Scholarships scheme for students from Zimbabwe, Zambia and Malawi at universities in the United Kingdom, Ireland and South Africa. The Beit Memorial Fellowships for Medical Research transferred all its undertakings to the Wellcome Trust on 1 October 2009.

Geographical Area of Activity: Malawi, Zambia and Zimbabwe.

Restrictions: Grants are not made to undergraduates.

Publications: Annual Report.

Finance: Annual income £2,451,103, expenditure £2,515,736 (31 Dec. 2013).

Trustees: Sir Alan Munro (Chair.).

Principal Staff: Sec. Maj.-Gen. Angus I. Ramsay; Rep. Tim M. Johnson.

Address: Beit House, Grove Rd, Woking, Surrey GU21 5JB.

Telephone: (1483) 772575; **Fax:** (1483) 725833; **Internet:** www.beittrust.org.uk; **e-mail:** enquiries@beittrust.org.uk.

Benesco Charity Limited

Founded in 1970 to advance medical research and education.

Activities: Provides funds to registered charities to support medical research, education and welfare, in particular the Charles Wolfson Charitable Trust.

Geographical Area of Activity: Worldwide.

Restrictions: No grants to individuals; grants made to United Kingdom-based charities only.

Publications: Annual Report.

Finance: Annual income £8,547,082 expenditure £7,387,743 (5 April 2014).

Board of Trustees: Michael M. Franks (Sec.).

Principal Staff: Correspondent Joanne Cowan.

Address: 8–10 Hallam St, London W1W 6NS.

Big Lottery Fund

Founded in 1994, as the National Lottery Charities Board, to help meet the needs of the most disadvantaged in society and improve the quality of life of the community. Name changed in April 2001 to the Community Fund. Merged with the New Opportunities Fund in 2004 to become the Big Lottery Fund.

Activities: Operates nationally and internationally through capital grants and revenue funding. The principal grants programmes are: main grants (funding projects that help people or communities overcome problems that stop them from playing a full part in economic, social and community activities); grants of up to £60,000 for projects; international grants (for NGOs based in the United Kingdom to work in collaboration with NGOs abroad in the area of development education and addressing the causes of poverty and inequality); research grants (for social and medical research, in particular in the areas of young and old people, minority ethnic groups and people with learning disabilities); small grants; and Awards for All (for small groups involved in areas such as sports, heritage and the arts, and community and voluntary activities).

Geographical Area of Activity: International.

Restrictions: Only funds United Kingdom-based charities and voluntary groups.

Publications: Magazine *Big Times;* regional newsletters; corporate reports.

Finance: Annual income £756,640,000, expenditure £970,506,000 (31 March 2014).

Board: Peter Ainsworth (Chair.); Anna Southall (Vice-Chair.); Nat Sloane (England Chair.); Frank Hewitt (Northern Ireland Chair.); Maureen McGinn (Scotland Chair.); Sir Adrian Webb (Wales Chair.).

Principal Staff: Chief Exec. Dawn Austwick.

Address: 1 Plough Pl., London EC4A 1DE.

Telephone: (20) 7211-1800; **Fax:** (20) 7211-1750; **Internet:** www.biglotteryfund.org.uk; **e-mail:** general.enquiries@biglotteryfund.org.uk.

Biotechnology and Biological Sciences Research Council—BBSRC

Established in 1994; one of the organizations formed by the splitting up of the Science and Engineering Research Council (SERC).

Activities: The United Kingdom funding agency for research in the life sciences. Sponsored by the Government, the Council annually invests in a wide range of research on the agriculture, food, chemical, health care and pharmaceutical sectors. It funds internationally competitive research; provides training in the biosciences; fosters opportunities for knowledge transfer and innovation; and promotes interaction with the public and other stakeholders on issues of scientific interest in universities, centres and institutes. Institutes of the BBSRC include the Babraham Institute, the Institute for Animal Health, the Institute of Food Research, the John Innes Centre and Rothamsted Research.

Geographical Area of Activity: United Kingdom.

Publications: Annual Report and accounts; policy and planning documents; corporate brochures; business, knowledge transfer and innovation documents; *BBSRC Business* (quarterly magazine).

Finance: Financed by the British Government; budget £484m. (2013–14).

Council: Prof. Sir Tom Blundell (Chair.).

Principal Staff: Chief Exec. Prof. Jackie Hunter; Deputy Chief Exec. Steve Visscher.

Address: Polaris House, North Star Ave, Swindon SN2 1UH.

Telephone: (1793) 413200; **Fax:** (1793) 413201; **Internet:** www.bbsrc.ac.uk; **e-mail:** external.relations@bbsrc.ac.uk.

BirdLife International

Founded in 1922 as the International Council for Bird Preservation; renamed BirdLife International in 1993.

Activities: A worldwide partnership of organizations working for the diversity of all life through the conservation of birds and their habitats. The organization operates internationally in the field of conservation, through programmes (e.g. bird surveys and studies; conservation programmes for particular species or areas and for the sustainable use of natural resources; public education campaigns; and the provision of expert advice to governments on bird conservation issues); support for local societies and their projects; international conferences; conservation expeditions; compiling and disseminating information, including a computer database, international data books and other publications. It supports more than 100 member organizations through regional offices in Belgium, Ecuador, Fiji, Japan, Singapore, Jordan and Kenya. Maintains a reference library of 5,000 volumes.

Geographical Area of Activity: International.

Publications: *Bird Red Data Book*; *Bird Conservation International* (quarterly); BirdLife Conservation Series; Annual Report; newsletter; technical publications; study reports; surveys; conference proceedings; *World Birdwatch* (quarterly magazine); *Rare Birds Yearbook*; partner journals.

Finance: Annual income £16,412,142, expenditure £14,118,759 (31 Dec. 2013).

Global Council: Khaled Anis Irani (Chair.); Nick Prentice (Treas.).

Principal Staff: Chief Exec. Patricia Zurita.

Address: Wellbrook Ct, Girton Rd, Cambridge CB3 0NA.

Telephone: (1223) 277318; **Fax:** (1223) 277200; **Internet:** www .birdlife.org; **e-mail:** birdlife@birdlife.org.

Tony Blair Faith Foundation

Established by Tony Blair in 2008 to promote the belief that understanding and respecting different faiths is central to securing sustained and informed peace in the world.

Activities: Aims to inform present and future leaders; to educate the next generation on religion and respect for others; and to show how faith can be a transformative force for progress. The Foundation operates a schools programme (Face to Faith); university programme (Faith and Globalisation); and health and social action programme (Faiths Act), which shows how faith's role in communities can bring about positive social change.

Geographical Area of Activity: International.

Finance: Annual income £1,618,000, expenditure £2,836,000 (30 Dec. 2013).

Trustees: Robert Clinton (Chair.).

Principal Staff: Chief Exec. Charlotte Keenan.

Address: POB 60519, London W2 7JU.

Telephone: (203) 3701959; **Internet:** www .tonyblairfaithfoundation.org; **e-mail:** info@ tonyblairfaithfoundation.org.

The Body Shop Foundation

Established in 1990 to provide a means of gathering together funds raised by directors, employees, national and international franchisees and friends of The Body Shop to allocate these to social, human and environmental welfare.

Activities: Operates nationally and internationally in the fields of human rights, and animal and environmental protection.

Geographical Area of Activity: International.

Restrictions: Does not accept unsolicited applications for funding.

Finance: Annual income £1,523,675 expenditure £1,524,945 (28 Feb. 2014).

Principal Staff: CEO Lisa Jackson.

Address: Watersmead, Littlehampton, West Sussex BN17 6LS.

Telephone: (1903) 844039; **Fax:** (1903) 844202; **Internet:** www .thebodyshopfoundation.org; **e-mail:** bodyshopfoundation@ thebodyshop.com.

Book Aid International—BAI

Founded in 1954 by Hermione, Countess of Ranfurly as the Ranfurly Library. Present name adopted in 1994.

Activities: Works in partnership with organizations in developing countries to support local initiatives in literacy, education and publishing. The organization provides more than 600,000 selected books and journals each year to support learning and skills development in 12 countries in Sub-Saharan Africa, the Palestinian Territories and Sri Lanka. It responds to requests from organizations that urgently need up-to-date information resources. Partners include library networks, schools, universities, vocational colleges and hospitals. Launched the Books Change Lives campaign in 2008.

Geographical Area of Activity: America, Sub-Saharan Africa, South-East Asia and the Caribbean.

Publications: *Book Mark* (newsletter); Annual Review; Report and Accounts.

Finance: Annual income £8,258,566, expenditure £8,392,253 (31 Dec. 2013).

Board of Trustees: Lord Paul Boateng (Chair.); Fergus Cass (Hon. Treas.).

Principal Staff: Dir Alison Hubert.

Address: 39–41 Coldharbour Lane, Camberwell, London SE5 9NR.

Telephone: (20) 7733-3577; **Fax:** (20) 7978-8006; **Internet:** www.bookaid.org; **e-mail:** info@bookaid.org.

Born Free Foundation Limited

Founded in 1984 by actors Bill Travers and Virginia McKenna to co-ordinate and develop effective campaigns to prevent animal suffering, protect endangered species and their habitats, and keep wildlife in the wild.

Activities: Programmes include Zoo Check, to monitor conditions of wildlife in zoos, safari parks and circuses, with the aim of preventing the abuse of captive animals; ELEFRIENDS Elephant Protection Group, aiming to combat poachers and end trade in ivory; Big Cat Campaign, to rescue big cats in captivity and protect those in the wild; Wolf Campaign, to save Ethiopian wolves from extinction and provide information on the species; Dolphin Campaign, to bring about an end to the practice of holding dolphins and whales captive in marine parks, and to protect orca in the wild; Primate Campaign, to protect orphaned and abused baby chimpanzees at a sanctuary in Uganda, and to protect primates in the wild; and Bear Campaign, to return orphaned bears to the wild and campaign against the exploitation of bears. Maintains offices in Kenya and the USA.

Geographical Area of Activity: Worldwide.

Publications: Newsletters; Annual Report.

Finance: Annual income £3,761,783, expenditure £3,297,777 (31 March 2014).

Trustees: Virginia McKenna (Founder); Michael Reyner (Chair.); Brian Bergin (Sec. and Treas.).

Principal Staff: Pres. Will Travers; CEO Adam Roberts.

Address: 3 Grove House, Foundry Lane, Horsham, West Sussex RH13 5PL.

Telephone: (1403) 240170; **Internet:** www.bornfree.org.uk; **e-mail:** info@bornfree.org.uk.

Britain-Nepal Medical Trust

Founded in 1968 by Dr J. Cunningham to assist the people of Nepal to improve their health.

Activities: Operates in Nepal in the fields of health and community development through self-conducted programmes, research, training and capacity building. The Trust works in collaboration with Nepal's Ministry of Health and Population, international and local NGOs, local committees and communities.

Geographical Area of Activity: Nepal and Europe.

Restrictions: Funds currently restricted to the Trust's own work.

Publications: Annual Report.

Finance: Annual revenue £615,313, expenditure £889,335 (31 Dec. 2013).

Trustees: Dr Gillian M. C. Holdsworth, Prof. Surya P. Subedi (Co-Chair.).

Principal Staff: Sec. and Admin. Adele G. Peck.

Address: Export House, 130 Vale Rd, Tonbridge, Kent TN9 1SP.

Telephone: (1732) 360284; **Fax:** (1732) 363876; **Internet:** www .britainnepalmedicaltrust.org.uk; www.bnmt.org.np; **e-mail:** info@britainnepalmedicaltrust.org.uk.

British Academy

Established in 1902 to promote the study of the humanities and social sciences.

Activities: The United Kingdom national academy for the humanities and social sciences. The Academy operates nationally and internationally in the fields of academic research in the humanities and social sciences. It provides grants to British scholars for a wide range of personal research projects, for conference attendance and for international collaboration. Supports research posts (post-doctoral and senior level) and a series of scholarly projects; and also funds a number of British institutes abroad and in the United Kingdom. Publishes monographs or serial publications relating to various aspects of the social sciences. Organizes and publishes papers from lectures, conferences and symposia. Maintains links with international partners (academies and research councils) and supports international scholarly collaboration. Member of international organizations, including the European Science Foundation (q.v.), ALLEA and the Union Académique Internationale.

Geographical Area of Activity: International.

Restrictions: In most cases, only offers awards for post-doctoral research in the humanities and social sciences undertaken by scholars normally resident in the United Kingdom.

Publications: Monographs and other scholarly publications; annual proceedings; biannual review; editions; catalogues; conference proceedings, lectures and biographies.

Finance: Annual income £31,665,115, expenditure £31,605,735 (31 March 2014).

Council: Lord Stern of Brentford (Pres.); Prof. Michael Fulford (Treas.).

Principal Staff: Chief Exec. and Sec. Dr Robin Jackson.

Address: 10–11 Carlton House Terrace, London SW1Y 5AH.

Telephone: (20) 7969-5200; **Fax:** (20) 7969-5300; **Internet:** www.britac.ac.uk; **e-mail:** thefellowship@britac.ac.uk.

The British Council

Established in 1934 to promote educational and cultural relations between the United Kingdom and other countries worldwide. Incorporated by Royal Charter in 1940.

Activities: Operates internationally through cultural, educational, English language and information programmes. Maintains 227 offices and teaching centres in 110 countries.

Geographical Area of Activity: International.

Publications: Numerous publications in the fields of English language, education and the arts; Annual Report.

Finance: Annual income £864,289,000, expenditure £880,410,000 (31 March 2014).

Board of Trustees: Sir Vernon Ellis (Chair.); Baroness Prashar of Runnymede (Deputy Chair.); Alison Coutts (Sec.).

Principal Staff: Chief Exec. Ciarán Devane.

Address: 10 Spring Gardens, London SW1A 2BN.

Telephone: (20) 7389-4385; **Fax:** (20) 7389-6347; **Internet:** www.britishcouncil.org; **e-mail:** general.enquiries@ britishcouncil.org.

British Gas Energy Trust

Established in 2004.

Activities: Makes grants to individuals and families facing fuel poverty to help with the clearance of energy and other debts.

Geographical Area of Activity: England, Scotland and Wales.

Finance: Annual income £18,175,810, expenditure £10,048,144 (31 Dec. 2013).

Board of Trustees: Imelda Redmond (Chair.).

Address: 3rd Floor, Midgate House, Midgate, Peterborough PE1 1TN; POB 42, Peterborough PE3 8XH.

Telephone: (1733) 421060; **Fax:** (1733) 421020; **Internet:** www .britishgasenergytrust.org.uk; **e-mail:** bget@charisgrants .com.

British Heart Foundation

Founded in 1961; the leading British medical research charity working in the field of cardiovascular disease.

Activities: Funds medical research into the causes, prevention, diagnosis and treatment of heart disease. The Foundation provides support and information to sufferers and their families, through British Heart Foundation nurses, rehabilitation programmes and support groups. It educates the public and health professionals about heart disease prevention and treatment; promotes training in emergency life-support skills for the public and health professionals; and provides equipment to hospitals and other health providers.

Geographical Area of Activity: United Kingdom.

Publications: Leaflets and videos for members of the public, patients and their families, schools, hospitals and doctors' surgeries.

Finance: Annual income £275.1m., expenditure £312.8m. (31 March 2014).

Board of Trustees: Phil Yea (Chair.).

Principal Staff: CEO Simon Gillespie.

Address: Greater London House, 180 Hampstead Rd, London NW1 7AW.

Telephone: (20) 7554-0000; (300) 330-3311; **Fax:** (20) 7554-0100; **Internet:** www.bhf.org.uk; **e-mail:** supporterservices@bhf.org.uk.

British Institute at Ankara

Founded in 1948.

Activities: Supports, promotes and publishes British research focused on Turkey and the Black Sea littoral in all academic disciplines within the arts, humanities and social sciences, while maintaining a centre of excellence in Ankara focused on the archaeology and related subjects of Turkey. A small staff at the Institute's premises in Ankara conducts research, assists scholars and maintains the centre of excellence, which houses a library of more than 60,000 volumes, research collections of botanical, faunal, epigraphic and pottery material, together with collections of maps, photographs and fieldwork archives, and a laboratory and computer services. In 2013, the following initiatives were supported: habitat and settlement in prehistoric, historical and environmental perspective; migration, minorities and regional identities; climate and its historical and current impact; religion and politics in historical perspective; and cultural heritage, society and economy in Turkey.

Geographical Area of Activity: United Kingdom, Turkey and the Black Sea region.

Publications: *Anatolian Studies* (annually); *Heritage Turkey* (previously *Anatolian Archaeology*) (annually); monograph series.

Finance: Annual income £701,405, expenditure £743,592 (31 March 2014).

Council of Management: Sir David Logan (Chair.); Prof. Stephen Mitchell (Hon. Sec.); Anthony Sheppard (Hon. Treas.).

Principal Staff: Dir Dr Lutgarde Vandeput; Man. Claire McCafferty.

Address: 10 Carlton House Terrace, London SW1Y 5AH; Tahran Caddesi 24, Kavaklıdere, 06700 Ankara, Turkey.

Telephone: (20) 7969-5204; **Fax:** (20) 7969-5401; **Internet:** www.biaa.ac.uk; **e-mail:** biaa@britac.ac.uk.

British Institute of International and Comparative Law

Founded in 1958 to provide an international centre for the study of the practical application to current problems of public international law, private international law, European Community (now European Union) law and comparative law.

Activities: Carries out independent research; organizes lectures, seminars and conferences; and publishes books and periodicals in its fields of interest.

Geographical Area of Activity: International.

Publications: *International and Comparative Law Quarterly* and monographs.

Finance: Annual income £1,668,901, expenditure £1,775,410 (31 Dec. 2013).

Trustees: Sir Franklin Berman (Chair.).

Principal Staff: Pres. Dame Rosalyn Higgins; Dir Prof. Robert McCorquodale.

Address: Charles Clore House, 17 Russell Sq., London WC1B 5JP.

Telephone: (20) 7862-5151; **Fax:** (20) 7862-5152; **Internet:** www.biicl.org; **e-mail:** info@biicl.org.

British Red Cross

Founded in 1870 by Royal Charter.

Activities: Provides emergency services and skilled care for those in need and crisis in their local community and overseas. The organization operates through local branches and centres to provide a full range of services in the community, which include: medical loans; home from hospital; therapeutic care; emergency response; fire and emergency support services; event first aid; ambulance support; international tracing and messaging; refugee services; youth and schools services; and first aid training. It raises funds to provide aid in the form of money, materials or personnel to disaster-stricken areas of the United Kingdom or abroad. Part of the International Red Cross and Red Crescent movement (q.v.).

Geographical Area of Activity: International.

Restrictions: No grants are made to individuals.

Publications: Annual Report and Review.

Finance: Annual income £228.4m., expenditure £231.7m. (31 Dec. 2013).

Board of Trustees: David Bernstein (Chair.).

Principal Staff: Pres. HRH The Prince of Wales; Chief Exec. Mike Adamson.

Address: 44 Moorfields, London EC2Y 9AL.

Telephone: (20) 7138-7900; **Fax:** (20) 7562-2000; **Internet:** www.redcross.org.uk; **e-mail:** information@redcross.org.uk.

CABI

Established in 1913 as the Commonwealth Agricultural Bureaux (CAB), it became an international non-profit organization with a new constitution in 1986, called the Centre for Agricultural Bioscience International. Present name adopted in 2006.

Activities: Disseminates scientific knowledge to promote sustainable development and human welfare. The organization operates in four principal areas: scientific research, international development, knowledge management and publishing. Operates in more than 70 countries worldwide, with centres in Brazil, the People's Republic of China, Ghana, India, Kenya, Malaysia, Pakistan, Switzerland, Trinidad and Tobago, the USA and the United Kingdom.

Geographical Area of Activity: International.

Publications: Abstracts; Annual Review.

Finance: Annual income £25,182,000, expenditure £24,544,000 (31 Dec. 2012).

Executive Board: John Ripley (Chair.).

Principal Staff: CEO Dr Trevor Nicholls; CFO Ian Barry.

Address: Nosworthy Way, Wallingford, Oxfordshire OX10 8DE.

Telephone: (1491) 832111; **Fax:** (1491) 829292; **Internet:** www.cabi.org; **e-mail:** enquiries@cabi.org.

William Adlington Cadbury Charitable Trust

Founded in 1923 by William C. Cadbury to provide funds for general charitable purposes, with preference given to the West Midlands.

Activities: Main funding areas are: the West Midlands, the rest of the United Kingdom, as well as cross-community projects between Northern Ireland and the Republic of Ireland, and national charities working overseas (Africa). The Trust operates in the fields of the Society of Friends and other religious organizations, social welfare, health and medicine, conservation of the environment, sustainable development, and education, through grants to registered charities.

Geographical Area of Activity: United Kingdom and Africa.

Restrictions: Grants only to charities registered in the United Kingdom; no funding for individuals. International grants currently to organizations known to the Trust.

Publications: Annual Report; grant policy and guidelines.

Finance: Annual income £929,305, expenditure £927,293 (31 March 2014).

Trustees: Sarah Stafford (Chair.).

Principal Staff: Trust Admin. Carolyn Bettis.

Address: Rokesley, Univ. of Birmingham, Bristol Rd, Selly Oak, Birmingham B29 6QF.

Telephone: (121) 4721464; **Internet:** www.wa-cadbury.org.uk; **e-mail:** info@wa-cadbury.org.uk.

Edward Cadbury Charitable Trust, Inc

Founded in 1945 for general charitable purposes.

Activities: Principally supports the voluntary sector in the Midlands region. The Trust focuses grants on education, interfaith and multifaith relations, the oppressed and disadvantaged, the arts and the environment.

Geographical Area of Activity: United Kingdom (Midlands).

Restrictions: Grants are made to registered charities only: grants are not made to students or to individuals.

Finance: Annual income £943,662, expenditure £795,828 (5 April 2014).

Trustees: N. R. Cadbury (Chair.).

Principal Staff: Trust Man. Sue Anderson.

Address: Rokesley, University of Birmingham, Selly Oak, Bristol Rd, Birmingham B29 6QF.

Telephone: (121) 4721838; **Fax:** (121) 4721838; **Internet:** www.edwardcadburytrust.org.uk; **e-mail:** ecadburytrust@btconnect.com.

CAFOD—Catholic Agency for Overseas Development

Established in 1962 as the official organization of the Roman Catholic Bishops' Conference of England and Wales.

Activities: Shares its resources with sister churches and other partners throughout the world to combat poverty, hunger, ignorance, disease and suffering. The Agency operates in partnership with local NGOs in more than 40 developing countries in Africa, Central and South America and the Caribbean, and Asia. Its main work is in the funding of development projects in food production; preventive health; vocational training; community development; non-formal education; and block grants made to Church development agencies. Specialized fields include emergency aid and projects concerned with AIDS. The Agency conducts campaigns in the United

Kingdom to raise awareness of the causes of poverty and injustice worldwide; and also co-funds with the United Kingdom's Department for International Development and the European Union. Maintains offices in Bolivia, the Democratic Republic of the Congo, Ethiopia, Kenya, Mozambique, Nicaragua, Nigeria, Sierra Leone and Sudan, with staff in a number of other countries worldwide.

Geographical Area of Activity: International.

Restrictions: Projects involving heavy construction costs are not undertaken, nor are funds provided for primary or secondary education.

Publications: Trustees' Report and Financial Statements; *Side by Side*; *CAFOD Bulletin*.

Finance: Annual income £51,287,000, expenditure £51,459,000 (31 March 2014).

Trustees: Rt Rev. John Arnold (Chair.); Charles Reeve-Tucker (Hon. Treas.).

Principal Staff: Dir Chris Bain.

Address: Romero House, 55 Westminster Bridge Rd, London SE1 7JB.

Telephone: (20) 7733-7900; **Fax:** (20) 7274-9630; **Internet:** www.cafod.org.uk; **e-mail:** cafod@cafod.org.uk.

Cambridge Commonwealth, European and International Trust

Formed in 2013 by a merger of the Cambridge Commonwealth Trust (f. 1982) and the Cambridge Overseas Trust (f. 1989), which were established to give financial support to international students studying at the University of Cambridge.

Activities: Awards grants and scholarships to students of outstanding merit to pursue study or research courses. The Trust awarded 527 scholarships for 2014/15.

Geographical Area of Activity: International.

Restrictions: Awards some scholarships based on academic merit only; however, in some cases, the Trust also takes financial need into account.

Trustees: Dr Rowan Williams (Chair.); Sarah Squire (Deputy Chair.).

Principal Staff: Dir Helen Pennant.

Address: 53–54 Sidney St, Cambridge CB2 3HX.

Telephone: (1223) 338498; **Fax:** (1223) 760618; **Internet:** www.cambridgetrust.org; **e-mail:** cambridge.trust@admin.cam.ac.uk.

Cancer Research UK

Formed in 2002 by the merger of the Cancer Research Campaign and the Imperial Cancer Research Fund to investigate all matters connected with or bearing on the causes, prevention, treatment and cure of cancer.

Activities: Supports and undertakes a comprehensive programme of research in institutes, hospitals, universities and medical schools throughout Britain and Northern Ireland. The organization works in anti-cancer drug development and to ensure cancer sufferers receive new treatments as quickly as possible; carries out research into the psychological impact of cancer and improving communication between doctor and patient; provides a wide range of authoritative cancer information publications and guidelines for general practitioners; and promotes cancer prevention through education and research. It also trains cancer scientists and doctors.

Geographical Area of Activity: United Kingdom.

Publications: Annual Report; scientific report; brochures; leaflets; fact sheets; accounts.

Finance: Annual income £665,410,600, expenditure £540,260,360 (31 March 2014).

Council of Trustees: Michael Pragnell (Chair.).

Principal Staff: Chief Exec. and Exec. Chair. Harpal Kumar.

Address: Angel Bldg, 407 St John St, London EC1V 4AD.

Telephone: (20) 7242-0200; **Fax:** (20) 7121-6700; **Internet:** www.cancerresearchuk.org; **e-mail:** secretariat@cancer.org.uk.

Carnegie Trust for the Universities of Scotland

Founded in 1901 to promote the development of Scottish universities.

Activities: Provides grants to Scottish undergraduates to help with university fees and to staff and graduates of Scottish universities to fund study and research. Also makes a number of larger grants to projects of interest to Scottish universities as a whole.

Geographical Area of Activity: Scotland.

Publications: Books.

Finance: Annual income £2,718,718, expenditure £2,630,863 (30 Sept. 2013).

Trustees: Prof. Sir David Edward (Chair.).

Principal Staff: Sec. and Treas. Prof. Andy Walker.

Address: Andrew Carnegie House, Pittencrieff St, Dunfermline, Fife KY12 8AW.

Telephone: (1383) 724990; **Fax:** (1383) 749799; **Internet:** www.carnegie-trust.org; **e-mail:** admin@carnegie-trust.org.

Carnegie UK Trust

Founded in 1913 by Andrew Carnegie and one of a network of 22 Carnegie foundations worldwide, the Trust works to improve the well-being of people living in the United Kingdom and Ireland.

Activities: Aims to change minds through influencing policy, and change lives through innovative practice and partnership work. The Trust works under three broad themes: people and place, knowledge and culture, enterprise and society.

Geographical Area of Activity: Mainly United Kingdom and Ireland; also works with international partners on issues of a more global nature that affect the United Kingdom and Ireland.

Restrictions: No unsolicited requests accepted. Mainly operates through partnership working. Currently one grant scheme for public debates called the Carnegie Challenge.

Publications: Annual Review; policy and practice reports, consultation responses, project leaflets.

Finance: Annual income £1,553,611, expenditure £1,753,849 (31 Dec. 2013).

Trustees: William Thomson (Pres.); Angus Hogg (Chair.); Jane Steele (Vice-Chair.).

Principal Staff: Chief Exec. Martyn Evans.

Address: Andrew Carnegie House, Pittencrieff St, Dunfermline, Fife KY12 8AW.

Telephone: (1383) 721445; **Fax:** (1383) 749799; **Internet:** www.carnegieuktrust.org.uk; **e-mail:** info@carnegieuk.org.

Sir Ernest Cassel Educational Trust

Founded in 1919 by Sir Ernest Cassel to promote adult education by voluntary bodies, and the higher education of women.

Activities: Awards Mountbatten Memorial Grants to Commonwealth students experiencing hardship in their final year of higher education; and the Mountbatten Memorial Award at Christ's College, Cambridge. Overseas research grants are administered by the British Academy. The Trust awards grants to organizations providing opportunities for young people to serve overseas and for adult education in the United Kingdom.

Geographical Area of Activity: United Kingdom.

Finance: Annual income £65,254, expenditure £63,021 (31 May 2014).

Trustees: Prof. Francis Robinson (Chair.); Lady Amanda Ellingworth (Deputy Chair.).

Principal Staff: Sec. Kathryn Hodges.

Address: 5 Grimston Park Mews, Grimston Park, Tadcaster LS24 9DB.

Telephone: (1937) 834730; **Internet:** www.casseltrust.co.uk; **e-mail:** casseltrust@btinternet.com.

Charity Islamic Trust Elrahma

Established in 1993 to assist the needy in the Muslim community in the United Kingdom and internationally.

Activities: Operates in the fields of social welfare, education and religion nationally and internationally, through grants for the building of schools, mosques and institutions for orphans, and for the relief of poverty.

Geographical Area of Activity: International.

Finance: Annual income £1,169,723, expenditure £1,301,659 (31 Dec. 2013).

Trustees: Abubaker Megerisi (Chair.); Patrick D. Daniels (Sec.).

Principal Staff: Contact A. A. Naib.

Address: 3 The Avenue, London NW6 7YG.

Telephone: (20) 8459-3331; **Fax:** (20) 8451-7993; **Internet:** www.elrahma.org.uk; **e-mail:** projects@elrahma.org.uk.

Leonard Cheshire Disability International

Founded in the United Kingdom in 1948 by Group Capt. Leonard Cheshire, the organization has undertaken international work since 1955.

Activities: Works with disabled people throughout the world by providing the environment necessary for each individual's physical, mental and spiritual well-being. The organization provides support and guidance to more than 250 locally-run programmes for disabled people and their families, in 57 countries outside the United Kingdom; programmes include rehabilitation centres, skills training centres, community-based support services and residential homes. It also advises local communities on obtaining grants for new developments.

Geographical Area of Activity: International.

Restrictions: Grants only to Leonard Cheshire Services.

Publications: Annual Report; *Disability and Inclusive Development*; *Compass* (quarterly).

Finance: Annual income £154,559,000, expenditure £153,541,000 (31 March 2014).

Trustees: Ilyas Khan (Chair.); Tom Bartlam, Susan Douglas-Scott (Vice-Chair.); Alan Cruickshank (Sec.).

Principal Staff: Chief Exec. Clare Pelham.

Address: 66 South Lambeth Rd, London SW8 1RL.

Telephone: (20) 3242-0200; **Fax:** (20) 3242-0250; **Internet:** www.lcint.org; **e-mail:** international@lcdisability.org.

Child Migrants Trust

Established in 1987 by Margaret Humphreys as an advisory and support organization for former child migrants who were sent abroad from the United Kingdom between the end of the Second World War and 1970.

Activities: Operates as a counselling and advisory organization in the United Kingdom, Australia, Canada, New Zealand, USA and Zimbabwe for former child migrants and their families. Maintains offices in Perth and Melbourne (Australia).

Geographical Area of Activity: Australia, Canada, New Zealand, United Kingdom, USA and Zimbabwe.

Publications: *Empty Cradles*; *Lost Children of the Empire*.

Finance: Annual income £683,973, expenditure £1,011,422 (31 March 2014).

Principal Staff: Dir Margaret Humphreys; Asst Dirs Ian Thwaites, Mervyn Humphreys.

Address: 28A Musters Rd, West Bridgford, Nottingham NG2 7PL.

Telephone: (115) 9822811; **Fax:** (115) 9817168; **Internet:** www.childmigrantstrust.com; **e-mail:** enquiries@childmigrantstrust.com.

ChildHope (UK)

Established in 1989; supports children and young people who face injustice, violence and abuse.

Activities: Works closely with local organizations to understand and tackle the root causes of poverty and injustice, ensuring that the children and young people themselves have a say in how their lives should change for the better. The organization operates in the fields of human rights and social welfare through financial support and providing training for projects helping children, in particular 'street-connected children' in developing countries. Operates in partnership with local NGOs in three main areas: participation and inclusion; protection from all forms of violence; and access to quality education.

Geographical Area of Activity: Asia, Africa and South America.

Publications: Annual Report; *Child protection toolkit; Children and young people's participation (CYPP) training and workshop guide*; newsletters.

Finance: Annual income £2,016,259; expenditure £1,995,376 (31 Dec. 2014).

Trustees: Paul Marvell (Chair.); Philippa Hurst (Treas.).

Principal Staff: Exec. Dir and Sec. Jill Healey.

Address: Development House, 56–64 Leonard St, London EC2A 4LT.

Telephone: (20) 7065-0950; **Fax:** (20) 7065-0951; **Internet:** www.childhope.org.uk; **e-mail:** info@childhope.org.uk.

The Children's Investment Fund Foundation

Established in 2004 by Chris and Jamie Cooper-Hohn to improve children's lives in less-developed countries.

Activities: Operates in less-developed countries in partnership with organizations and governments to help alleviate poverty and hunger, improve education, and lessen the effects of climate change. Has offices in Nairobi, Kenya, and New Delhi, India.

Geographical Area of Activity: Africa, East and South-East Asia.

Finance: Annual revenue £99,871,418, expenditure £98,119,243 (31 Aug. 2014).

Trustees: Mark Malloch-Brown (Acting Chair.).

Principal Staff: CEO Michael Anderson; COO Hunada Nouss.

Address: 7 Clifford St, London W1S 2FT.

Telephone: (20) 3740-6100; **Internet:** ciff.org; **e-mail:** info@ciff.org.

Childwick Trust

Founded in 1985.

Activities: Operates in the following main areas: to assist elderly people in need; charities connected with thoroughbred horse breeding or racing; Jewish charities in the United Kingdom; charities involved in education and assistance for people who have worked in the mining industry in South Africa; and charities benefiting disabled people in the United Kingdom. The Trust also operates in South Africa in the field of pre-school education and training.

Geographical Area of Activity: United Kingdom and South Africa.

Restrictions: No grants to individuals, and grants are made to United Kingdom-based organizations only.

Finance: Annual income £79,978,556, expenditure £3,441,162 (31 March 2014).

Trustees: Anthony R. G. Cane (Chair.).

Principal Staff: Trust Admin. Karen Groom.

Address: 9 The Green, Childwick Bury, St Albans, Hertfordshire AL3 6JJ.

Telephone: (1727) 844666; **Internet:** www.childwicktrust.org; **e-mail:** karen@childwicktrust.org.

Christian Aid

Founded in 1945 as Christian Reconstruction in Europe to assist refugees; became a department of the British Council of Churches and was subsequently renamed the Department of Interchurch Aid and Refugee Service. Present name adopted in 1964.

Activities: Finances practical programmes of aid, development and relief for the neediest people across the world, including disaster victims and refugees; and improves understanding of poverty by carrying out educational work in the United Kingdom. The organization works mainly in developing countries, through regional and local organizations involved in relief, resettlement, development (in spheres of health, urban welfare, agriculture and water resources) and education programmes. Some funds are granted to race relations, community and development education projects in the United Kingdom.

Geographical Area of Activity: International.

Publications: Annual Report; audited accounts; quarterly list of grants; *Christian Aid News*; catalogue of current publications and resources list.

Finance: Annual income £103,604,000, expenditure £100,403,000 (31 March 2014).

Trustees: Dr Rowan Williams (Chair.); Charlotte Seymour Smith (Vice-Chair.).

Principal Staff: Chief Exec. Loretta Minghella.

Address: 35 Lower Marsh, Waterloo, London SE1 7RL.

Telephone: (20) 7620-4444; **Fax:** (20) 7620-0719; **Internet:** www.christianaid.org.uk; **e-mail:** info@christian-aid.org.

Winston Churchill Memorial Trust

Founded in 1965 to provide travelling fellowships.

Activities: Awards about 100 fellowships annually to British citizens, resident in the United Kingdom, of any age, for a stay overseas of four to eight weeks. Also funds up to 10 undergraduate bursaries at Churchill College Cambridge each year, and an Archive By-Fellowship at the Churchill Archives Centre.

Publications: Newsletter (1 a year); explanatory leaflet and brochure; project reports.

Finance: Annual income £2,013,360, expenditure £1,675,288 (30 Sept. 2014).

Board of Trustees: Robert Fellowes (Chair.).

Principal Staff: Dir-Gen. Maj.-Gen. Jamie Balfour; Sec. Alexandra Sibun.

Address: South Door, 29 Great Smith St, London SW1P 3BL.

Telephone: (20) 7799-1660; **Fax:** (20) 7799-1667; **Internet:** www.wcmt.org.uk; **e-mail:** office@wcmt.org.uk.

Citizenship Foundation

Founded in 1989 to improve understanding of citizenship, political, social and legal systems, and participation in community and voluntary projects. The Foundation had as its predecessor the Law in Education Project, established in 1984 to develop teaching materials that introduce students to the notions of responsibilities and rights, and the role of law in democratic society.

Activities: Operates a wide range of educational programmes in the field of law and human rights, including public debates, competitions and training initiatives.

Geographical Area of Activity: International.

Publications: *Passport to Life*; Annual Report; educational resources and publications; newsletter; books; pamphlets; papers.

Finance: Annual income £1,206,323, expenditure £1,272,371 (31 March 2014).

Board of Trustees: Martin Bostock (Chair.); Susan Simmonds (Treas.).

Principal Staff: Chief Exec. Andy Thornton.

Address: 63 Gee St, London EC1V 3RS.

Telephone: (20) 7566-4141; **Fax:** (20) 7566-4131; **Internet:** www.citizenshipfoundation.org.uk; **e-mail:** info@ citizenshipfoundation.org.uk.

The City Bridge Trust

Traces its origins to 1097, when a special tax was raised to help repair the wooden London Bridge. Name changed from Bridge House Trust in 2006.

Activities: Maintains five bridges that cross the river Thames into the City of London: Blackfriars Bridge, the Millennium Bridge, Southwark Bridge, London Bridge and Tower Bridge. Through a Charitable Scheme set up in 1995, the Trust uses its surplus money for the benefit of Greater London. It makes grants and funds strategic work for the benefit of London and the wider charity sector in the form of research, learning events and feasibility studies.

Geographical Area of Activity: London, United Kingdom.

Restrictions: Grants are made in London only. No grants made to individuals, statutory bodies, political parties, for medical or academic research, to churches or religious bodies for religious purposes or maintenance of religious buildings, or to educational establishments.

Publications: Annual Review; Annual Report and Financial Statements; *Working with Londoners—Programme Guidelines*; *The Knowledge—Learning from London*.

Finance: Annual income £40.9m., expenditure £39.3m. (31 March 2014).

Trust Committee: William H. Dove (Chair.); Jeremy Paul Mayhew (Deputy Chair.); Chris Bilsland, Dr Peter Kane (Treas).

Principal Staff: Chief Exec. John Barradell; Chief Grants Officer David Farnsworth.

Address: City of London, POB 270, Guildhall, London EC2P 2EJ.

Telephone: (20) 7332-3710; **Fax:** (20) 7332-3127; **Internet:** www.citybridgetrust.org.uk; **e-mail:** citybridgetrust@ cityoflondon.gov.uk.

CLIC Sargent

Formed in 2005 after a merger between CLIC (Cancer and Leukaemia in Childhood, founded in 1976 by Bob Woodward following the death of his son) and Sargent Cancer Care for Children (founded in 1968 by Sylvia Darley in memory of conductor Sir Malcolm Sargent).

Activities: Provides clinical, practical, financial and emotional support to children and young people, and their families, who are affected by cancer.

Geographical Area of Activity: United Kingdom.

Restrictions: Applications must be made through a hospital social worker.

Publications: Annual report; storybooks; guides; booklets; leaflets.

Finance: Annual income £25,485,000, expenditure £24,531,000 (31 March 2014).

Board of Trustees: Peter Hollins (Chair.); Graham Clarke (Treas.).

Principal Staff: Chief Exec. Lorraine Clifton.

Address: Horatio House, 77–85 Fulham Palace Rd, London W6 8JA.

Telephone: (20) 8752-2878; **Fax:** (20) 8752-2806; **Internet:** www.clicsargent.org.uk; **e-mail:** info@clicsargent.org.uk.

Clore Duffield Foundation—CDF

Founded in 1964, as the Clore Foundation, to provide financial assistance for general charitable purposes. Money is donated at the discretion of the trustees.

Activities: Funds registered charities, usually in the United Kingdom, with a particular focus on supporting children, young people and society's most vulnerable individuals, principally in the fields of museum and gallery education, art and design education, performing arts education, health, social welfare and disability. The Foundation operates a main grants programme, with grants ranging between £10,000 and £2.5m.; a small grants programme for museum and gallery education; an Artworks Programme making awards for high-quality art teaching and funding art research; and, since 2004, the Clore Cultural Leadership Programme, promoting the leadership and management of cultural organizations in the United Kingdom.

Geographical Area of Activity: Mainly United Kingdom.

Restrictions: No funding for individuals and only rarely for organizations working outside the United Kingdom.

Publications: Annual Report and Accounts; *Space for Learning: A Handbook for Education Spaces in Museums, Heritage Sites and Discovery Centres (2004)*; *The Clore Small Grants Programme for Museum*; *Gallery Eduction, 1999–2004*; *State of the Art*.

Finance: Annual income £659,977, expenditure £30,025,905 (31 Dec. 2013).

Trustees: Dame Vivien Duffield (Chair.).

Principal Staff: Exec. Dir Sally Bacon.

Address: Studio 3, Chelsea Manor Studios, Flood St, London SW3 5SR.

Telephone: (20) 7351-6061; **Fax:** (20) 7351-5308; **Internet:** www.cloreduffield.org.uk; **e-mail:** info@cloreduffield.org.uk.

Colt Foundation

Established in 1978.

Activities: Promotes research into social, medical and environmental problems created by commerce and industry, and supports the publication of the results of such research. The Foundation finances research projects, especially concerning occupational health, carried out at universities and research establishments in the United Kingdom. It also awards Fellowships to PhD students whose subjects are relevant to occupational and environmental medicine, and supports the MSc in Human and Applied Physiology at King's College London. Recent projects include: research on particle toxicology at Edinburgh Napier University; work on nanoparticles and nanotubes at the University of Edinburgh; the Centre for Occupational and Environmental Health, University of Manchester; work on the effects of metal particles on inflammatory response at the University of Aberdeen; and work on capacity to work in an ageing population at the NHLI at Imperial College.

Geographical Area of Activity: United Kingdom.

Restrictions: Grants are not made to individuals, to projects outside the United Kingdom, or to the general funds of charities.

Publications: Annual Report.

Finance: Annual income £450,767, expenditure £380,318 (31 Dec. 2014).

Trustees: Prof. Sir Anthony Newman Taylor (Chair.).

Principal Staff: Dir Jackie Douglas.

Address: New Lane, Havant, Hampshire PO9 2LY.

Telephone: (23) 9249-1400; **Fax:** (23) 9249-1363; **Internet:** www.coltfoundation.org.uk; **e-mail:** jackie.douglas@uk.coltgroup.com.

Comic Relief

Established in 1984, as Charity Projects, to provide aid for disadvantaged people in the United Kingdom and Africa.

Activities: Operates in the United Kingdom and internationally, principally in Africa (one-third of grants are made in the United Kingdom, and two-thirds in Africa, although a new International Grants programme has been established to make grants internationally). Grants programmes in the United Kingdom and in Africa focus on social welfare, giving grants to small organizations. International projects support children, incl. those affected by conflict and orphans. The organization runs the Red Nose Day fund-raising campaign biennially and in 2002 launched the Sport Relief fund-raiser.

Geographical Area of Activity: International (mainly Africa and the United Kingdom).

Publications: Annual Report and accounts; information leaflet.

Finance: Annual income £114,166,636, expenditure £126,434,005 (31 July 2013).

Trustees: Tim Davie (Chair.); Richard Curtis (Vice-Chair.); Mike Harris (Treas.).

Principal Staff: CEO Kevin Cahill.

Address: 1st Floor, 89 Albert Embankment, London SE1 7TP.

Telephone: (20) 7820-5555; **Fax:** (20) 7820-5500; **Internet:** www.comicrelief.com; **e-mail:** info@comicrelief.com.

Commonwealth Foundation

Founded in 1965 as an inter-governmental organization to support the work of the non-governmental sector within the Commonwealth, in particular the strengthening of civil society, sustainable development and poverty eradication; and to facilitate pan-Commonwealth and inter-country connections between people, their associations and communities at all levels.

Activities: The Foundation's work is guided by Commonwealth values and programme priorities. These relate to democracy and good governance, respect for human rights and gender equality, poverty reduction, and sustainable, people-centred development. The Foundation supports civil society activities that contribute to the achievement of the Millennium Development Goals. It funds inter-country networking (particularly between developing countries), training, capacity building and information exchange. In particular, it targets activities that strengthen civil society organizations in their work on poverty eradication, good governance and sustainable development; and it places emphasis and importance on using culture as a tool in development. Works in four programme areas: communities and livelihoods, culture, governance and democracy, and human development.

Geographical Area of Activity: Commonwealth countries.

Publications: Annual Report; *Educating Girls: A foundation for development*; *Putting Culture First: Commonwealth perspectives on culture and development*; *Breaking the Taboo: Perspectives of African civil society on innovative sources of finance for development*; *The Implications of High Food and Energy Prices for Economic Management*; *Multi-Stakeholder Partnerships for Gender Equality—Perspectives from Government*; *Climate Change and Its Implications: Which Way Now?*; *Engaging with Faith: Report of the Foundation project on improving understanding and co-operation between different faith communities*; *Transforming Commonwealth Societies to Achieve Political, Economic and Human Development: Civil Society Perspectives*.

Trustees: Sir Anand Satyanand (Chair.).

Principal Staff: Dir Vijay Krishnarayan; Deputy Dir Myn Garcia.

Address: Marlborough House, Pall Mall, London SW1Y 5HX.

Telephone: (20) 7930-3783; **Fax:** (20) 7839-8157; **Internet:** www.commonwealthfoundation.com; **e-mail:** foundation@commonwealth.int.

Community Foundation for Northern Ireland

Founded in 1979 to support voluntary and community projects in Northern Ireland; until 2003, known as the Northern Ireland Voluntary Trust.

Activities: Emphasizes community empowerment and social justice, supporting projects that deal with social problems in urban and rural areas: young people, women's groups, unemployed people, community care, the arts, education, welfare rights and inter-community activity. Also maintains an office in Derry.

Geographical Area of Activity: Northern Ireland.

Publications: Annual Report and accounts; *Infonotes* (publication series); *In Brief* (report series).

Finance: Annual income £7,664,835, expenditure £11,609,265 (31 March 2013).

UNITED KINGDOM

Trustees: Tony McCusker (Chair.); Les Allamby (Vice-Chair.).

Principal Staff: Chief. Exec. Andrew McCracken.

Address: Community House, Citylink Business Park, Albert St, Belfast BT12 4HQ.

Telephone: (28) 9024-5927; **Fax:** (28) 9032-9839; **Internet:** www.communityfoundationni.org; **e-mail:** info@ communityfoundationni.org.

Concern Universal

Founded in 1976 to provide aid to less-developed countries.

Activities: Promotes development and improved living conditions in less-developed countries, particularly among refugees, victims of war, people with AIDS and their children. The organization supports environmental conservation efforts, adult literacy and basic education training; provides emergency humanitarian relief; promotes children's rights; and develops food security and sustainable agriculture initiatives. Currently working in Bangladesh, Brazil, Colombia, Gambia, Ghana, Guinea, India, Kenya, Malawi, Mozambique, Nigeria, Senegal and the United Kingdom.

Geographical Area of Activity: Sub-Saharan Africa, Central and South America, Asia and Europe.

Restrictions: Does not make grants.

Finance: Annual income £23,182,149, expenditure £22,330,588 (31 March 2014).

Governing Council: Peter Ayres (Chair.).

Principal Staff: Exec. Dir Kathryn Llewellyn.

Address: 21 King St, Hereford HR4 9BX.

Telephone: (1432) 355111; **Fax:** (1432) 355086; **Internet:** www.concern-universal.org; **e-mail:** cu.uk@concern-universal.org.

Conservation Foundation

Founded in 1982 by Prof. David Bellamy and David Shreeve to provide a means for interested parties—governments, corporations, institutions, organizations and associations—to collaborate on environmental causes in which common ground can be found.

Activities: Works nationally and internationally in the fields of conservation and the environment; working with commercial and environmental organizations to create award schemes; research and information programmes; conferences; educational materials; multimedia presentations and publications. The Foundation supports ethno-medical research by young scientists in rainforests, and local conservation projects in the United Kingdom and Europe.

Geographical Area of Activity: International.

Publications: *Network 21* (environmental news service); *Parish Pump* (newsletter).

Finance: Annual income £185,301, expenditure £203,825 (28 Feb. 2014).

Council: William Moloney (Sec.).

Principal Staff: Pres. Prof. David Bellamy; Dir David Shreeve.

Address: 1 Kensington Gore, London SW7 2AR.

Telephone: (20) 7591-3111; **Fax:** (20) 7591-3110; **Internet:** www.conservationfoundation.co.uk; **e-mail:** info@ conservationfoundation.co.uk.

Marjorie Coote Animal Charities Trust

Founded in 1954 for the benefit of all or any of five named charities and of any other charitable organization that has as its main purpose the care and protection of horses, dogs or other animals or birds.

Activities: Concentrates on funding research into animal health problems and on the protection of species. A small proportion of the grants expenditure goes towards general animal welfare, including sanctuaries.

Geographical Area of Activity: Worldwide.

Restrictions: No grants are made to individuals; applications must be made in writing to the correspondent, to arrive during the month of September.

Finance: Annual income £136,805, expenditure £118,037 (5 April 2014).

Principal Staff: Contact Jill P. Holah.

Address: End Cottage, Terrington, York YO60 6PU.

e-mail: info@mcacharity.org.uk.

Marie Curie Cancer Care

Founded in 1948 by T. B. Robinson and four others to provide in-patient and community care for cancer patients. Previously known as the Marie Curie Memorial Foundation.

Activities: Cares for people affected by cancer and improves their quality of life, through its caring services, cancer research and education. The organization operates hospices throughout the United Kingdom and provides a network of nurses, giving practical nursing care at home to people with cancer, free of charge. It also has its own Marie Curie Research Institute at Oxted in Surrey, and runs education and training courses for health professionals involved in cancer care. Maintains an office in Scotland.

Geographical Area of Activity: United Kingdom.

Publications: Annual Report and accounts; other leaflets and brochures; e-newsletter; *Shine On* (magazine).

Finance: Annual income £154,805,000, expenditure £164,920,000 (31 March 2014).

Trustees: John Varley (Chair.); David Ereira (Vice-Chair.); Tim Breedon (Hon. Treas.); Penny Laurence-Parr (Gen. Counsel and Sec.).

Principal Staff: Chief Exec. Dr Jane Collins.

Address: 89 Albert Embankment, London SE1 7TP.

Telephone: (20) 7599-7777; **Fax:** (20) 7599-7788; **Internet:** www.mariecurie.org.uk; **e-mail:** supporter.services@ mariecurie.org.uk.

Cystic Fibrosis Trust

Founded in 1964 to finance medical and scientific research aimed at understanding, treating and curing cystic fibrosis and ensuring that people with cystic fibrosis receive the best possible care and support in all aspects of their lives.

Activities: Main aims are to fund research to find a cure for cystic fibrosis and to improve symptom control; ensure appropriate clinical care for those with cystic fibrosis; and to support those affected by cystic fibrosis by providing information, support and, where appropriate, financial assistance.

Geographical Area of Activity: Mainly United Kingdom.

Publications: Report of operations and financial statement; *CF Today* (5 a year); *CF Talk; Focus on Fundraising;* extensive booklet series; booklets; fact sheets; consensus documents.

Finance: Annual income £10,806,000, expenditure £10,123,000 (31 March 2014).

Trustees: George R. Jenkins (Chair.); Allan Gormly (Deputy Chair.); Rupert Pearce Gould (Hon. Treas.).

Principal Staff: Pres. Dr Jim Littlewood; Chief Exec. Ed Owen.

Address: 11 London Rd, Bromley, Kent BR1 1BY.

Telephone: (20) 8464-7211; **Fax:** (20) 8313-0472; **Internet:** www.cysticfibrosis.org.uk; **e-mail:** enquiries@cysticfibrosis.org.uk.

Roald Dahl's Marvellous Children's Charity

Founded in 1991 as the Roald Dahl Foundation. Present name adopted in 2010.

Activities: Improves the lives of children and young people in the United Kingdom who have significant unmet needs because of serious health problems. The Charity prioritizes those: in poverty; with rare conditions; without a diagnosis; culturally excluded from support networks; in care; and with very severe and complex conditions. It makes grants to families where a child or young person has significant unmet needs and is experiencing financial hardship; and also to small and new organizations, and for specialist professional support workers (e.g. nurses, therapists, social workers).

Geographical Area of Activity: United Kingdom.

Restrictions: Makes grants in the United Kingdom only to NHS hospitals and charitable organizations. Grant applications are not considered for general appeals from large, well-established charities, nor for education fees.

Finance: Annual income £868,730, expenditure £876,513 (31 March 2014).

Board of Trustees: Martin A. F. Goodwin (Chair).

Principal Staff: Chief Exec. Dr Richard Piper.

Address: 81A High St, Great Missenden, Buckinghamshire HP16 0AL.

Telephone: (1494) 890465; **Fax:** (1494) 890459; **Internet:** www .roalddahlcharity.org.

Daiwa Anglo-Japanese Foundation

Established in 1988 with a benefaction from Daiwa Securities Co Ltd to support closer links between the United Kingdom and Japan.

Activities: Aims to enhance the United Kingdom's and Japan's understanding of each other's people and culture; to enable British and Japanese students and academics to further their education through exchanges and co-operation; and to make grants available to individuals and organizations to promote links between the United Kingdom and Japan at all levels. The Foundation carries out its work principally through the awarding of Daiwa Scholarships, grant-giving and a year-round programme of events. For the Daiwa Scholarship programme, up to 10 talented British graduates are chosen each year to spend 19 months in Japan. The scholarship has three elements: language study, homestay and work placement. The Foundation headquarters in central London acts as a centre for academic and cultural activities relating to Japan. It provides a forum for discussion and exchange, meeting rooms for Japan- and United Kingdom-Japan-associated activities and a Centre for Visiting Academics.

Geographical Area of Activity: United Kingdom and Japan.

Restrictions: Grants are made for United Kingdom-Japanese exchange only.

Finance: Annual income £236,351, expenditure £1,307,687 (31 March 2014).

Trustees: Sir Peter Williams (Chair.); Shigeharu Suzuki (Vice-Chair.).

Principal Staff: Dir-Gen. Jason James.

Address: Daiwa Foundation Japan House, 13–14 Cornwall Terrace, London NW1 4QP.

Telephone: (20) 7486-4348; **Fax:** (20) 7486-2914; **Internet:** www.dajf.org.uk; **e-mail:** office@dajf.org.uk.

Miriam Dean Fund

Founded in 1964, as the Miriam Dean Refugee Trust Fund, to provide aid to victims of war or other disasters.

Activities: Awards grants to charitable organizations abroad, particularly in South India and Africa.

Geographical Area of Activity: South India, Kenya, South Africa.

Restrictions: No grants to individuals; grants only to specific NGOs.

Publications: Annual report; bi-annual newsletter.

Finance: Annual income £252,949, expenditure £218,209 (31 Dec. 2013).

Principal Staff: Contact Andy Moore.

Address: Hidden House, 3 Ladwell Close, Newbury, Berkshire RG14 6PJ.

Telephone: (1635) 34979; **Internet:** www.miriamdeanfund .org.uk; **e-mail:** trustees@miriamdeanfund.org.uk.

The Delius Trust

Founded in 1935 according to the will of Jelka Delius to promote the music of Frederick Delius by providing financial aid for performances and recordings and by publishing a collected edition of his works.

Activities: Operates nationally and internationally in the field of the arts and humanities, through providing grants to individuals and institutions towards the cost of performances and to finance recordings.

Publications: *The Collected Edition of the Works of Frederick Delius*; several other books on the life and works of Frederick Delius; collected works.

Finance: Annual income £83,334, expenditure £110,863 (31 Dec. 2013).

Trustees: Martin Williams; David Lloyd-Jones.

Principal Staff: Sec. Helen Faulkner.

Address: 7–11 Britannia St, London WC1X 9JS.

Telephone: (20) 7239-9143; **Internet:** www.delius.org.uk; **e-mail:** deliustrust@mbf.org.uk.

Diabetes UK

Founded in 1934, and previously known as the British Diabetic Association, to fund research into the prevention, treatment and cure of diabetes; and to provide information and support to people living with diabetes.

Activities: Funds and initiates research into the causes and treatment of diabetes (about 38% of expenditure); provides advice and information to people with diabetes, and to health-care professionals; campaigns against discrimination; and promotes improved services for people with diabetes.

Geographical Area of Activity: United Kingdom.

Publications: Annual Report and accounts; *Diabetes Update* (quarterly journal); *Balance* (magazine, 2 a month); publications and leaflets; newsletters.

Finance: Annual income £38,840,000, expenditure £33,531,000 (31 Dec. 2013).

Trustees: Sir Peter Dixon (Chair.); Julian Baust (Vice-Chair.); Noah Franklin (Treas.).

Principal Staff: Pres. Richard Lane; Chief Exec. Barbara Young.

Address: Macleod House, 10 Parkway, London NW1 7AA.

Telephone: (20) 7424-1000; **Fax:** (20) 7424-1001; **Internet:** www.diabetes.org.uk; **e-mail:** info@diabetes.org.uk.

Diageo Foundation

Established in 1998 by Diageo PLC, with a commitment to contribute 1% of Diageo's worldwide trading profit, less interest, to the community.

Activities: Acts as a primary funding and support organization for social investment programmes and charitable giving. The Foundation works internationally, principally where Diageo PLC businesses operate, through the following main programmes: Local Citizens; Alcohol Education; Our People (i.e. employee involvement); and Water of Life. Aspects of former programmes Global Brands and Skills for Life are incorporated into the current programmes. Works in collaboration with community charitable groups.

Geographical Area of Activity: International.

Restrictions: Does not fund individuals, medical charities, religious or political organizations, or animal welfare charities.

Finance: Annual income £803,917, expenditure £1,453,697 (30 June 2014).

Trustees: Geoffrey T. Bush (Chair.).

Principal Staff: Man. Lynne Smethurst; Sec. Victoria Cooper.

Address: 7 Lakeside Dr., Park Royal, London NW10 7HQ.

Telephone: (20) 8978-6000; **Internet:** www.diageo.com/en-sc/csr/community/Pages/diageo-foundation.aspx; **e-mail:** diageofoundation@diageo.com.

Ditchley Foundation

Founded in 1958 by Sir David Wills to promote, carry out or advance any charitable objects, and in particular any branches or aspects of education likely to be for the common benefit of British subjects and citizens of the USA.

Activities: Exclusively supports in-house activities; maintains Ditchley Park as a conference centre and supports the Ditchley conference programme. Facilities are available to other bodies on a fee-paying basis. The Foundation organizes invitation-only conferences on topics of international concern to the British and American peoples, with the participation of other nationalities, particularly from member states of the European Union. US and Canadian Ditchley Foundations exist with similar aims, and to assist in the work of the United Kingdom Ditchley Foundation.

Restrictions: No grants to individuals or groups unless at Ditchley.

Publications: Annual Report and financial statement; newsletters and conference reports.

Finance: Annual income £651,777, expenditure £1,540,750 (31 March 2014).

Council of Management: Lady Wills (Hon. Life Pres.); Lord Robertson (Chair.); Philip Stephens (Vice-Chair.).

Principal Staff: Dir Sir John Holmes; Deputy Dir Sarah Puntan-Galea.

Address: Ditchley Park, Enstone, Chipping Norton OX7 4ER.

Telephone: (1608) 677346; **Fax:** (1608) 677399; **Internet:** www.ditchley.co.uk; **e-mail:** info@ditchley.co.uk.

Dulverton Trust

Founded in 1949 by the first Lord Dulverton for general charitable purposes at the discretion of the trustees.

Activities: Operates nationally in the fields of youth and education, conservation, general welfare, religion, preservation, peace and security. The Trust also funds charities working in Kenya and Uganda with which it has long-standing relations, usually in the fields of education and conservation.

Geographical Area of Activity: United Kingdom, Kenya, Uganda.

Restrictions: No grants in area of medicine and health, nor to organizations based in Greater London or Northern Ireland, nor to museums, arts organizations, expeditions, schools, colleges or universities. Grants made only to registered charities and never to individuals.

Publications: Annual Report.

Finance: Annual income £3,539,384, expenditure £4,059,287 (31 March 2014).

Trustees: Christopher Wills (Chair.); Sir John Kemp-Welch (Vice-Chair.).

Principal Staff: Dir Andrew Stafford.

Address: 5 St James's Pl., London SW1A 1NP.

Telephone: (20) 7629-9121; **Fax:** (20) 7495-6201; **Internet:** www.dulverton.org; **e-mail:** trust@dulverton.org.

John Ellerman Foundation

Formed in 1992 by the merger of the New Moorgate Trust Fund and the Moorgate Trust Fund, for general charitable purposes.

Activities: Works in the mainland United Kingdom and, to a limited extent, in UK overseas territory. Foundation grants are made, based on merit and worthiness, in three categories: arts, environment and welfare.

Geographical Area of Activity: United Kingdom.

Restrictions: Grants are not made to individuals, nor for education; only supports organizations with an office in the United Kingdom.

Publications: Annual Report.

Finance: Annual income £3,496,000, expenditure £4,516,000 (31 March 2015).

Trustees: Lady Sarah Riddell (Chair.).

Principal Staff: Dir Nicola Pollock.

Address: Aria House, 23 Craven St, London WC2N 5NS.

Telephone: (20) 7930-8566; **Fax:** (20) 7839-3654; **Internet:** www.ellerman.org.uk; **e-mail:** enquiries@ellerman.org.uk.

Embrace the Middle East

Founded in 1854 as the Turkish Missions Aid Society; also formerly known as the Bible Lands Society. Its original aim was to support existing Christian missions in the lands of the Bible. Present name adopted in 2012.

Activities: Supports overseas partners who provide health, education and community development programmes for the most disadvantaged people in the lands of the Bible, regardless of their faith or nationality. The organization aims to increase the working capacity and resources of local Christian partners so that they are able to respond strategically and effectively to the needs in the region.

Geographical Area of Activity: Egypt, Lebanon, Israel and Palestinian Territories.

Restrictions: No grants are made to individuals.

Publications: *The Star in the East* (3 a year); *Life Lines*; *The Child Sponsor*; *The Care Sharer*; Annual Review.

Finance: Annual income £3,475,517, expenditure £4,373,341 (31 Dec. 2013).

Council of Trustees: Rev. Brian Jolly (Chair.); Anthony Ball (Vice-Chair.); Vicky Smith (Treas.).

Principal Staff: CEO Jeremy Moodey.

Address: 24 London Rd West, Amersham, Buckinghamshire HP7 0EZ.

Telephone: (1494) 897950; **Fax:** (1494) 897951; **Internet:** www.embraceme.org; **e-mail:** info@embraceme.org.

EMI Music Sound Foundation

Established in 1997 as an independent charity dedicated to the improvement of music education. Formerly known as the Music Sound Foundation.

Activities: Operates in the United Kingdom in the areas of primary, secondary and tertiary education in the field of music, through making grants to schools, to music students to pay for instruments, and to music teachers for training. Sponsors specialist performing arts colleges.

Geographical Area of Activity: United Kingdom and Ireland.

Restrictions: Does not currently fund community projects or music therapy.

Publications: Annual Review.

Finance: Annual income £374,027, expenditure £594,970 (31 July 2013).

Trustees: David Hughes (Chair.).

Principal Staff: Chief Exec. Janie Orr; Man. Louisa Taylor.

Address: Beaumont House, Avonmore Rd, Kensington Village, London W14 8TS.

Telephone: (20) 7795-7000; **Fax:** (20) 7795-7296; **Internet:** www.emimusicsoundfoundation.com; **e-mail:** enquiries@emimusicsoundfoundation.com.

Emunah (Faith)

Founded in 1933 to promote the welfare of underprivileged and vulnerable children in Israel, provide funds for education and therapy, and help dysfunctional families.

Activities: Operates in Israel in the above areas, providing funding for special needs centres, residential homes, schools, after-school activities, community centres, sports centres and day-care centres. British Emunah funds 35 of 225 Emunah projects in Israel and is part of World Emunah, which has more than 180,000 members in 30 countries.

Geographical Area of Activity: Israel.

Publications: Newsletter (quarterly); legacy information leaflet plus other information showing various ways to support the charity.

Finance: Annual revenue £942,821, expenditure £1,286,814 (31 Dec. 2013).

Trustees: Rochelle Selby (Chair.).

Principal Staff: Hon. Pres. Lady Elaine Sacks; Chair. Hilary Pearlman; Dir Deborah Nathan.

Address: Shield House, Harmony Way, off Victoria Rd, Hendon, London NW4 2BZ.

Telephone: (20) 8203-6066; **Fax:** (20) 8203-6668; **Internet:** www.emunah.org.uk; **e-mail:** info@emunah.org.uk.

Engineering and Physical Sciences Research Council—EPSRC

The Science Research Council (SRC) was formed in 1965 to address issues highlighted by the Trend Committee concerning the organization of civil science in the United Kingdom. In 1981, the SRC became the Science and Engineering Research Council (SERC) to reflect the increased emphasis on engineering research, and was responsible for all publicly-funded scientific engineering and research activities, including astronomy, biotechnology and biological sciences, space research and particle physics in the United Kingdom. In 1994, the SERC was split into discipline-specific areas, resulting in the formation of the Engineering and Physical Sciences Research Council (EPSRC).

Activities: Promotes and supports high-quality, basic, strategic and applied research and related postgraduate training in engineering and the physical sciences; advances knowledge and technology (including the promotion and support of the exploitation of research outcomes); and provides trained scientists and engineers. The Council aims to meet the needs of users and beneficiaries (including the chemical, communications, construction, electrical, electronic, energy, engineering, information technology, pharmaceutical, process and other industries), thereby contributing to the economic competitiveness of the United Kingdom and the quality of life. The Council may also: generate public awareness, communicate research outcomes, encourage public engagement and dialogue, disseminate knowledge and provide advice. Its vision is for the United Kingdom to be the most dynamic and stimulating environment in which to engage in research and innovations.

Geographical Area of Activity: United Kingdom.

Restrictions: Grants only to universities.

Finance: Annual income £907,249,000, expenditure £936,072,000 (31 March 2014).

Principal Staff: Chair. Paul Golby; Chief Exec. Prof. Philip Nelson.

Address: Polaris House, North Star Ave, Swindon SN2 1ET.

Telephone: (1793) 444000; **Internet:** www.epsrc.ac.uk; **e-mail:** pressoffice@epsrc.ac.uk.

English-Speaking Union

Founded in 1918 by Sir Evelyn Wrench to promote the mutual advancement of the education of the English-speaking peoples of the world.

Activities: Operates internationally through groups in more than 40 countries in the fields of education, the arts and humanities, science, environment, and international affairs, through self-conducted programmes and conferences. Provides scholarships and fellowships for British graduates and teachers to pursue research at US universities and institutions, for study trips to the USA, and awards for British graduates or holders of professional qualifications to work on projects in developing countries.

Geographical Area of Activity: International.

Publications: Annual Report; *Concord* (magazine, 2 a year); *ESU Newsletter* (6 a year).

Finance: Annual income £3,576,165, expenditure £3,134,779 (31 March 2014).

Trustees: Lord Paul Boateng (Chair.); Prof. James Raven, Coral Sebag-Montefiore (Deputy Chair.); Roderick Chamberlain (Hon. Treas.).

Principal Staff: Pres. HRH The Princess Royal; Dir-Gen. Jane Easton.

Address: Dartmouth House, 37 Charles St, London W1J 5ED.

Telephone: (20) 7529-1550; **Fax:** (20) 7495-6108; **Internet:** www.esu.org; **e-mail:** esu@esu.org.

Environmental Justice Foundation—EJF

Established in 2000 with the aim of empowering people most affected by environmental abuses to prevent such abuses.

Activities: Provides training to organizations in the southern hemisphere in finding solutions to environmental abuses; promotes environmental security; produces films; campaigns internationally on issues including illegal fishing, agricultural production, pesticide use and wildlife depletion. The Foundation works with partner organizations in Brazil, Indonesia, Mali, Mauritius, Sierra Leone, Uzbekistan and Viet Nam.

Geographical Area of Activity: International.

Finance: Annual income £693,362, expenditure £849,038 (31 Dec. 2013).

Principal Staff: Exec. Dir Steve Trent.

Address: 1 Amwell St, London EC1R 1UL.

Telephone: (20) 7239-3310; **Internet:** www.ejfoundation.org; **e-mail:** info@ejfoundation.org.

European Association for Cancer Research

Founded in 1968 to advance cancer research by facilitating communication between scientists.

Activities: Advances cancer research, from basic research to prevention, treatment and care. The Association operates internationally (mainly in Europe) in the fields of medicine and science, by organizing conferences, sponsoring researchers, awarding fellowships and issuing publications. There are more than 9,000 members from more than 80 countries both within and outside Europe.

Geographical Area of Activity: International (mainly Europe).

Publications: *EACR Yearbook* (annually); *European Journal of Cancer* (18 a year).

Board: Richard Marais (Pres.); Anton Berns (Pres.-Elect); Moshe Oren (Past Pres.); Clare Isacke (Sec.-Gen.); Christof von Kalle (Treas.).

Principal Staff: Exec. Dir Robert Kenney.

Address: School of Pharmacy, University of Nottingham, Nottingham NG7 2RD.

Telephone: (115) 9515114; **Fax:** (115) 9515115; **Internet:** www.eacr.org; **e-mail:** eacr@nottingham.ac.uk.

The Eveson Charitable Trust

Founded in 1994 according to the will of Violet Eveson for general charitable purposes.

Activities: Provides grants to organizations working in Herefordshire, Worcestershire and the West Midlands, including Birmingham and Coventry, in the fields of the physically or mentally disabled, hospitals and hospices, the elderly, blind and deaf people, children, the homeless and medical research.

Geographical Area of Activity: United Kingdom (Herefordshire, Worcestershire and the West Midlands).

Restrictions: Grants are made only in Herefordshire, Worcestershire and the West Midlands; no grants for individuals.

Finance: Annual income £1,260,413, expenditure £2,499,641 (31 March 2014).

Trustees: Richard Mainwaring (Chair.).

Principal Staff: Admin. Alex D. Gay.

Address: 45 Park Rd, Gloucester GL1 1LP.

Telephone: (1452) 501352; **Fax:** (1452) 302195; **e-mail:** admin@eveson.plus.com.

Esmée Fairbairn Foundation

Founded in 1961 as the Esmée Fairbairn Charitable Trust. Present name adopted in 2001.

Activities: Funds the charitable activities of organizations that have the ideas and ability to achieve change for the better. The Foundation supports work that might otherwise be considered difficult to fund. Primary interests are in the arts, children and young people, the environment, food and social change.

Geographical Area of Activity: United Kingdom.

Restrictions: Guidance notes can be viewed on the Foundation's website and there is an online application process.

Finance: Annual income £8,948,000, expenditure £39,370,000 (31 Dec. 2013).

Trustees: James Hughes-Hallett (Chair.).

Principal Staff: CEO Caroline Mason.

Address: Kings Pl., 90 York Way, London N1 9AG.

Telephone: (20) 7812-3700; **Internet:** www.esmeefairbairn .org.uk; **e-mail:** info@esmeefairbairn.org.uk.

Farm Africa

Established in 1985 to assist African farming and forest communities to reduce poverty through the development of agriculture and the effective use of natural resources.

Activities: Promotes effective agricultural development in East Africa. Maintains regional offices in Ethiopia, Kenya, South Sudan and Tanzania.

Geographical Area of Activity: East Africa.

Finance: Annual income £12,822,000, expenditure £12,510,000 (31 Dec. 2013).

Board: Richard Macdonald (Chair.); John Young (Sec.); John Shaw (Treas.).

Principal Staff: Pres. Sir Martin Wood; Chief Exec. Nigel Harris.

Address: 9th Floor, Bastion House, 140 London Wall, London EC2Y 5DN.

Telephone: (20) 7430-0440; **Fax:** (20) 7430-0460; **Internet:** www.farmafrica.org.uk; **e-mail:** farmafrica@farmafrica.org .uk.

The Federal Trust for Education and Research

Founded in 1945 under the auspices of William Beveridge to explore, through research and education, the suitability of federal solutions to problems of governance at national, continental and global level.

Activities: Involved in carrying out and promoting research, nationally and internationally, in the fields of international citizenship, constitutional developments, good governance at European and global level, European Union (EU) enlargement and various aspects of EU policy, through self-conducted programmes, conferences and publications. The Trust currently conducts research into the issue of devolution in the United Kingdom, democracy and stakeholder participation in the United Kingdom, the United Kingdom's relationship with the countries of the EU, EU policy, the role of international organizations such as the International Monetary Fund, the UN, and the World Trade Organization in developing global governance.

Geographical Area of Activity: United Kingdom, Europe.

Publications: *Europe, Parliament and the Media*; *European Futures*; *The Euro Debate*; *Treaty of Nice Explained*; newsletter; books; reports; policy reports; papers; European policy briefs; catalogue.

Finance: Annual income £53,217, expenditure £66,933 (31 Dec. 2013).

Advisory Council: Peter Sutherland (Pres.); Sir Stephen Wall (Chair.); John Cooke (Treas.).

Principal Staff: Dir and Sec. Brendan Donnelly.

Address: 31 Jewry St, London EC3N 2EY.

Telephone: (20) 7320-3045; **Internet:** www.fedtrust.co.uk; **e-mail:** info@fedtrust.co.uk.

Feed the Minds

Founded in 1964 by Lord Coggan to support the development of Christian literature programmes in less-developed countries.

Activities: Runs practical education programmes with partners in some of the world's poorest communities to bring about sustainable change.

Geographical Area of Activity: Developing countries.

Finance: Annual income £987,946, expenditure £879,945 (30 April 2014).

Board of Trustees: Christine Elliott (Chair.); Rev. Jonathan Kerry (Treas.); Rev. Canon Mark Oxbrow (Pres.).

Principal Staff: Chief Exec. Josephine Carlsson.

Address: The Foundry, 17 Oval Way, London SE11 5RR.

Telephone: (20) 3725-5800; **Internet:** www.feedtheminds .org; **e-mail:** info@feedtheminds.org.

Finnish Institute in London Trust

Founded in 1990 to identify emerging issues in contemporary society and to facilitate social change.

Activities: Works with artists, researchers, experts and policy-makers in Finland, the United Kingdom and Ireland to promote strong networks in the fields of culture and social studies. The Institute encourages new, unexpected collaborations and supports artistic interventions and social innovation. There are two main programme strands: Culture and Society. Within the field of culture, the Institute works to facilitate cultural export, artist exchange and innovative collaborations across the arts and across borders. Within social studies, it invites broad participation to focus on challenges and opportunities in contemporary society to turn research results into evidence for policy-makers.

Geographical Area of Activity: United Kingdom, Republic of Ireland and Finland.

Publications: E-newsletter.

Finance: Financed by the Finnish Ministry of Education and Culture, with projects funded from various sources.

Executive Board: Juhana Aunesluoma (Chair.); Marianna Kajantie (Vice-Chair.).

Principal Staff: Dir Pauliina Ståhlberg.

Address: Unit 1, 3 York Way, London N1C 4AE.

Telephone: (20) 3764-5090; **Internet:** www.finnish-institute .org.uk; **e-mail:** info@finnish-institute.org.uk.

FORWARD—Foundation for Women's Health, Research and Development

Founded in 1983 by Efua Dorkenoo to promote improved reproductive health among African women and their children, and education to counter traditional practices that are prejudicial to the health of women and children.

Activities: Campaigns for the elimination of female genital mutilation through: sponsoring local health and education programmes; supporting community self-help groups; facilitating the development of co-ordinated policies on the issue within local authorities in the United Kingdom; disseminating information to professionals and students working on the issue; and providing training for professionals, including health workers, to provide better services to affected women.

Geographical Area of Activity: United Kingdom and Africa.

Restrictions: Does not make grants.

Publications: *Voices of Tarime Girls: Views on Child Marriage, Health and Rights*; *Child Protection and Female Genital Mutilation*; *Holistic Care for Women: A Practical Guide for Midwives*; *Female Genital Mutilation: Proposals for Change*; *Out of Sight, Out of Mind*; *Another Form of Physical Abuse: Prevention of Female Genital Mutilation in the United Kingdom* (video); online newsletter and other publications; newsletters (annually); Annual Report.

Finance: Annual income £1,347,225, expenditure £1,187,249 (31 March 2014).

Board of Trustees: Dr Soheil Elneill (Chair.); Lisa Smith (Treas.).

Principal Staff: Exec. Dir Naana Otoo-Oyortey.

Address: Suite 2.1, Chandelier Bldg, 8 Scrubs Lane, London NW10 6RB.

Telephone: (20) 8960-4000; **Fax:** (20) 8960-4014; **Internet:** www.forwarduk.org.uk; **e-mail:** forward@forwarduk.org.uk.

Foundation for International Environmental Law and Development—FIELD

Founded in 1989 by James Cameron and Philippe Sands to contribute to the progressive development of international law for the protection of the environment and the attainment of sustainable development.

Activities: Brings together public international lawyers committed to the promotion of environmental protection and sustainable development through law; promotes the development of the law through research; disseminates the law through teaching, training and publishing; and applies the law through advocacy, advice and assistance. The Foundation runs three core programmes: Biodiversity and Marine Resources; Climate Change and Energy; and Trade, Investment and Sustainable Development.

Geographical Area of Activity: International.

Restrictions: Does not make grants.

Publications: *FIELD in Brief* (newsletter); Annual Report; and other publications.

Finance: Annual income £70,681, expenditure £100,142 (31 March 2014).

Trustees: Kate Gilmore (Chair.).

Principal Staff: Exec. Dir Joy Hyvarinen.

Address: Cityside House, 3rd Floor, 40 Adler St, London E1 1EE.

Telephone: (20) 7096-0277; **Internet:** www.field.org.uk; **e-mail:** field@field.org.uk.

The Anne Frank Trust UK

Founded in 1991 to advance public education in the United Kingdom in the principles of racial and religious tolerance and democracy.

Activities: Organizes travelling exhibitions and educational workshops.

Geographical Area of Activity: Europe, United Kingdom.

Restrictions: Does not make grants.

Finance: Annual income £1,206,281, expenditure £1,182,069 (31 Dec. 2013).

Board of Trustees: Daniel Mendoza (Chair.); Zac Mockton (Treas.).

Principal Staff: Co-Founder and Exec. Dir Gillian Walnes; COO Robert Posner.

Address: Star House, 104–108 Grafton Rd, London NW5 4BA.

Telephone: (20) 7284-5858; **Fax:** (20) 7428-2601; **Internet:** www.annefrank.org.uk; **e-mail:** info@annefrank.org.uk.

The Gaia Foundation

Founded in 1985 to show how human development and well-being are linked to the health and understanding of the living planet; began its work in the Amazon region.

Activities: Collaborates with projects in Europe, Central and South America, Africa and Asia to protect biodiversity and promote sustainable living. The Foundation co-ordinates information and seeks to create links between communities, individuals and organizations in the North and communities in the South, and to encourage financial collaboration in projects in developing countries.

Geographical Area of Activity: Central and South America, Africa, Asia and Europe.

Restrictions: Does not make grants to individuals.

Publications: *Opening Pandora's Box*; *Short Circuit*; *Under-Mining Agriculture; Cool Tobacco, Sweet Coca*; *Biopiracy–The Plunder of Nature and Knowledge*; *Indigenous Peoples of Colombia and the Law*; *The Forest Within*; *The Movement for Collective Intellectual Rights*; *Raiding the Future: Patent Truths or Patent Lies*; briefings; papers.

Finance: Annual income £1,462,434, expenditure £1,408,511 (31 Dec. 2013).

Trustees: Roger Northcott (Sec.).

Principal Staff: Dir Liz Hosken.

Address: 6 Heathgate Pl., Agincourt Rd, Hampstead, London NW3 2NU.

Telephone: (20) 7428-0055; **Fax:** (20) 7428-0056; **Internet:** www.gaiafoundation.org; **e-mail:** info@gaianet.org.

Garden Organic/Henry Doubleday Research Association—HDRA

Founded in 1958 by Lawrence Hills to research and promote organic gardening, farming and food; officially known as the Henry Doubleday Research Association; working name Garden Organic since 2005.

Activities: Operates in the fields of conservation and the environment and education, through self-conducting programmes nationally and internationally, research, conferences and training courses. The Association runs organic gardens, an education and conference centre, and a consultancy department on organic waste disposal. It collaborates with other organic research centres and groups in the United Kingdom and overseas. Also maintains a Heritage Seed Library and trades through Organic Enterprises Ltd; maintains the Vegetable Kingdom visitor centre.

Geographical Area of Activity: International.

Publications: *The Organic Way* (quarterly); step-by-step guides; organic gardening books; composting manuals.

Finance: Annual income £2,900,377, expenditure £2,905,701 (31 Dec. 2013).

Board: Roger Key (Chair.); John Milligan, Mattin Stott (Vice-Chair.); John Brown (Hon. Treas.); Julie Court (Sec.).

Principal Staff: Pres. Prof. Tim Lang; Chief Exec. James Campbell.

Address: Ryton Organic Gardens, Ryton on Dunsmore, Coventry CV8 3LG.

Telephone: (24) 7630-3517; **Fax:** (24) 7663-9229; **Internet:** www.gardenorganic.org.uk; **e-mail:** enquiry@gardenorganic .org.uk.

The Gatsby Charitable Foundation

Founded in 1967 to provide funds for general charitable purposes. One of the Sainsbury Family Charitable Trusts, all of which share a common administration.

Activities: Gives grants for work in the areas of: aid to less-developed countries (Africa); economic and social research; mental health; plant science; technical education; cognitive neuroscience; disadvantaged children and young people; local economic renewal; and the arts. The Foundation also funds the Sainsbury Centre for Mental Health. Local trusts, directed by local trustees, have been established in Cameroon, Kenya, Tanzania and Uganda to fund development projects.

Geographical Area of Activity: Africa and the United Kingdom.

Restrictions: Unsolicited applications are not normally considered for funding. Grants are not normally made to individuals.

Publications: *Gatsby Papers*; *Technology Transfer: Report on Six Pilot Projects*; Annual Report; newsletters.

Finance: Annual income £64,065,000, expenditure £50,560,000 (5 April 2014).

Principal Staff: Head of the Sainsbury Family Charitable Trusts Alan Bookbinder; Dir Peter Hesketh; Deputy Dir P. Hesketh; Finance Dir Paul Spokes.

Address: The Peak, 5 Wilton Rd, London SW1V 1AP.

Telephone: (20) 7410-0330; **Fax:** (20) 7410-0332; **Internet:** www.gatsby.org.uk; **e-mail:** contact@gatsby.org.uk.

J. Paul Getty Jnr Charitable Trust

Founded in 1985 to support general charitable purposes in areas of deprivation in the United Kingdom.

Activities: Involved in projects assisting the homeless, offenders and ex-offenders, the mentally ill, drug and alcohol addicts, community groups, self-help groups, and projects working with young people and ethnic minorities. The Trust may also give some support to conservation projects.

Geographical Area of Activity: United Kingdom.

Restrictions: Does not accept unsolicited applications. Financial assistance is provided only to registered charities, not individuals. Charities already widely supported are unlikely to be considered. Preference is given to projects outside the South-East of the United Kingdom; no funds are offered outside the United Kingdom; closed online applications for grants in early 2013 with the intention of winding up the Trust by the end of 2015.

Publications: Annual Reports.

Finance: Annual income £185,233, expenditure £11,865,181 (31 Dec. 2013).

Trustees: Christopher Gibbs (Chair.).

Principal Staff: Dir Elizabeth Rantzen.

Address: 1 Park Sq. West, London NW1 4LJ.

Telephone: (20) 7486-1859; **Internet:** www.jpgettytrust.org.uk.

The Glass-House Trust

Established in 1993 (as the Alex Sainsbury Charitable Trust) to work in the areas of parenting, family welfare and child development. One of the Sainsbury Family Charitable Trusts, all of which share a common administration.

Activities: Operates in the above areas through making grants to United Kingdom organizations working nationally and internationally. The Trust also supports projects in the areas of childcare and family support, education and research/policy development. Co-funder of the Ashden Awards for Sustainable Energy.

Geographical Area of Activity: International.

Finance: Annual income £321,513, expenditure £1,377,882 (5 April 2014).

Principal Staff: Exec. Mathew Williams; Dir Alan Bookbinder; Finance Dir Paul Spokes.

Address: The Sainsbury Family Charitable Trusts, The Peak, 5 Wilton Rd, London SW1V 1AP.

Telephone: (20) 7410-0330; **Fax:** (20) 7410-0332; **Internet:** www.sfct.org.uk/glass_house.html; **e-mail:** info@sfct.org.uk.

Goodenough College

Established in 1930 to provide a collegial environment for international graduates studying in London, and to promote tolerance and understanding by providing a forum in which they could interact.

Activities: An independent residential community of international postgraduate students, the College organizes workshops, seminars, conferences and public events, cultural, artistic, community volunteering and sporting activities.

Geographical Area of Activity: International.

Restrictions: Open to graduate students by application.

Publications: Newsletter (2 a year); brochures; Yearbook.

Finance: Annual income £8,483,308, expenditure £10,595,128 (31 March 2014).

Board: Jonathan Hirst (Chair.).

Principal Staff: Pres. Advisory Council René Weis; Dir Andrew Ritchie.

Address: Mecklenburgh Sq., London WC1N 2AB.

Telephone: (20) 7837-8888; **Fax:** (20) 7833-5829; **Internet:** www.goodenough.ac.uk; **e-mail:** appointments@goodenough.ac.uk.

Great Britain Sasakawa Foundation

Founded in 1985 to enhance mutual appreciation and understanding in the United Kingdom and Japan of each other's institutions, culture and achievements.

Activities: Operates principally in the United Kingdom and Japan, especially favouring projects involving reciprocal action between the two countries. Special awards include the Butterfield Awards for collaboration in medicine and health; and the Programme for Japanese Studies, which seeks to promote the study of Japanese contemporary issues in British universities.

Geographical Area of Activity: Japan and United Kingdom.

Restrictions: Makes grants to institutions and organizations of the United Kingdom or Japan.

Publications: Annual Report.

Finance: Annual income £1,198,242, expenditure £1,341,614 (31 Dec. 2014).

Trustees: Prof. Peter Mathias (Hon. Pres.); Earl of St Andrews (Chair.); Jeremy Brown (Vice-Chair.); Michael French (Treas.).

Principal Staff: Chief Exec. and Sec. Stephen McEnally.

Address: Dilke House, 1 Malet St, London WC1E 7JN.

Telephone: (20) 7436-9042; **Internet:** www.gbsf.org.uk; **e-mail:** gbsf@gbsf.org.uk.

HALO Trust

Established in 1989.

Activities: Specializes in the removal of the debris of war, particularly mine clearance. The Trust operates in countries of Africa, South-East and Central Asia, and the Caucasus and Balkans, through training local teams of managers, mine clearers, mechanics, medical staff, technicians and drivers. It also uses teams of Mine Awareness trainers.

Geographical Area of Activity: Africa, South-East and Central Asia, and the Caucasus and Balkans.

Restrictions: No grants are disbursed.

Publications: Annual Report.

Finance: Annual income £24,157,000, expenditure £25,526,000 (31 March 2014).

Trustees: Amanda Pullinger (Chair.); Anthony J. Wigan (Sec.).

Principal Staff: Chief Exec. Guy Willoughby.

Address: Carronfoot, Thornhill, Dumfries DG3 5BF.

Telephone: (1848) 331100; **Fax:** (1848) 331122; **Internet:** www.halotrust.org; **e-mail:** mail@halotrust.org.

Paul Hamlyn Foundation—PHF

Founded in 1987 (incorporating an earlier Paul Hamlyn Foundation, f. 1972) to contribute to developments in the areas of the arts, education, social justice and overseas projects in India.

Activities: Helps people fulfil their potential and improve their quality of life, particularly children and young people, and disadvantaged people. The Foundation currently operates three United Kingdom programmes: Arts, Education and Learning, and Social Justice, each of which runs an open grants scheme alongside special initiatives that focus on particular issues. It also operates a grants programme for NGOs in India.

Geographical Area of Activity: United Kingdom and India.

Restrictions: Grants do not support: individuals or proposals for the benefit of one individual; funding for work that has already started; general circulars/appeals; proposals about property or those that are mainly about equipment or other capital items; overseas travel, expeditions, adventure and residential courses; promotion of religion; animal welfare; medical/health/residential or day care; proposals from organizations outside the United Kingdom, except under the India programme; or proposals that benefit people living outside the United Kingdom, except under the India programme.

Publications: *PHF Yearbook; PHF Strategic Plan 2006–12; PHF Awards Made.*

Finance: Annual income £17,936,011, expenditure £26,588,980 (31 March 2013).

Trustees: Jane Hamlyn (Chair.).

Principal Staff: Dir Moira Sinclair.

Address: 18 Queen Anne's Gate, London SW1H 9AA.

Telephone: (20) 7227-3500; **Fax:** (20) 7222-0601; **Internet:** www.phf.org.uk; **e-mail:** information@phf.org.uk.

Headley Trust

Founded in 1973 for general charitable purposes. One of the Sainsbury Family Charitable Trusts, all of which share a common administration.

Activities: Operates nationally and internationally in a variety of fields, including arts and heritage, aid to less-developed countries, education, health and social welfare. Co-funder of the Ashden Awards for Sustainable Energy.

Geographical Area of Activity: International.

Restrictions: Unsolicited applications are not normally accepted. Grants are not normally made to individuals.

Publications: Annual report.

Finance: Annual income £2,235,000, expenditure £5,911,000 (5 April 2014).

Principal Staff: Dir Alan P. Bookbinder; Finance Dir Paul Spokes.

Address: c/o The Sainsbury Family Charitable Trusts, The Peak, 5 Wilton Rd, London SW1V 1AP.

Telephone: (20) 7410-0330; **Fax:** (20) 7410-0332; **Internet:** www.sfct.org.uk/headley.html; **e-mail:** info@sfct.org.uk.

Health Foundation

Founded in 1983 as the PPP Medical Trust; became fully independent in 1998 with an endowment of approx. £560m. following the sale of the PPP Healthcare group to Guardian Royal Exchange.

Activities: Works to improve the quality of health care across the United Kingdom. The Foundation supports people working in health care practice and policy to make lasting improvements to health services. It carries out research and in-depth policy analysis; runs improvement programmes to put ideas into practice in the National Health Service; supports and develops leaders; and shares evidence to encourage wider change.

Geographical Area of Activity: United Kingdom.

Restrictions: No grants for capital building.

Publications: Briefings; research reports; corporate publications; Annual Report.

Finance: Annual income £14,405,000, expenditure £32,068,000 (31 Dec. 2013).

Board of Governors: Sir Alan Langlands (Chair.).

Principal Staff: Chief Exec. Dr Jennifer Dixon.

Address: 90 Long Acre, London WC2E 9RA.

Telephone: (20) 7257-8000; **Fax:** (20) 7257-8001; **Internet:** www.health.org.uk; **e-mail:** info@health.org.uk.

HelpAge International

Founded in 1983 by Help the Aged (Canada), HelpAge (India), HelpAge (Kenya), Help the Aged (United Kingdom) and Pro Vida Colombia.

Activities: A global network of non-profit-making organizations with a mission to improve the lives of disadvantaged older people. HelpAge International provides expertise and grants to organizations serving the needs of older people in 80 developing countries, assisting them to help the most disadvantaged to lead independent lives. It promotes a positive image of old people worldwide, assisting them to achieve their full potential; provides advocacy, training and research, disaster relief, refugee resettlement and rehabilitation; and develops and supports programmes designed to meet the financial, material, medical and social needs of older people worldwide. Maintains regional offices in Central and South America, the Caribbean, East and Central Europe, Africa and Asia, in Belgium, Bolivia, Kenya, South Africa, St Lucia and Thailand. Also runs country development programmes in Cambodia, Ethiopia, Mozambique, Rwanda, Sudan and Tanzania.

Geographical Area of Activity: International.

Restrictions: Grants only to older people and those working with them. Mainly funds its own projects.

Publications: Newsletter; briefings; research papers on rights abuses, access to services, health and social protection; *The Madrid International Plan of Action on Ageing*; Annual Report.

Finance: Annual income £26,658,000, expenditure £26,417,000 (31 March 2014).

Governing Board: Cynthia Cox Roman (Chair.).

Principal Staff: CEO Toby Porter.

Address: POB 70156, London WC1A 9GB; 3rd Floor, Tavis House, 1–6 Tavistock Sq., London WC1H 9NA.

Telephone: (20) 7278-7778; **Fax:** (20) 7387-6992; **Internet:** www.helpage.org; **e-mail:** info@helpage.org.

Heritage Lottery Fund—HLF

Under the National Lottery etc. Act 1993, the Trustees of the National Heritage Memorial Fund became responsible for the distribution of that proportion of the National Lottery proceeds allocated to heritage in the United Kingdom.

Activities: Makes grants for a wide range of heritage projects, including countryside, parks and gardens; objects and sites that are linked to the United Kingdom's industrial, transport and maritime history; records such as local history archives, photographic collections or oral history; historic buildings; and museum and gallery collections.

Geographical Area of Activity: United Kingdom.

Publications: *Strategic Framework 2013–2018*; Annual Report; application guidance and forms; good practice guidance documents.

Finance: Annual income £333,764,000, expenditure £411,911,000 (31 March 2014).

Trustees: Sir Peter Luff (Chair.).

Principal Staff: Chief Exec. Carole Souter.

Address: 7 Holbein Pl., London SW1W 8NR.

Telephone: (20) 7591-6000; **Fax:** (20) 7591-6001; **Internet:** www.hlf.org.uk; **e-mail:** enquire@hlf.org.uk.

Terrence Higgins Trust—THT

Founded in 1982.

Activities: Operates in England, Wales and Scotland with people infected by HIV, people affected by HIV and those concerned about their sexual health. The Trust aims to reduce the spread of HIV and to promote good sexual health; to provide services and support for those affected to improve their quality of life; and to campaign for greater public understanding of HIV and AIDS and sexual health in general. It runs a national helpline, a Web-based service and a network of local centres.

Geographical Area of Activity: United Kingdom.

Publications: Publications about living with HIV; publications that have a sexual health promotion function (i.e. about preventing HIV), and reports produced by the policy team, supporting campaigns; DVD aimed at people living with HIV, *Positively Living*.

Finance: Annual income £19,646,000, expenditure £19,388,000 (31 March 2014).

Trustees: Robert Glick (Chair.).

Principal Staff: Chief Exec. Dr Rosemary Gillespie.

Address: 314–320 Gray's Inn Rd, London WC1X 8DP.

Telephone: (20) 7812-1600; **Fax:** (20) 7812-1601; **Internet:** www.tht.org.uk; **e-mail:** info@tht.org.uk.

Hilden Charitable Fund

Founded in 1963 by Tony Rampton for general charitable purposes.

Activities: Principally involved in supporting projects in the United Kingdom in the areas of homelessness, asylum seekers and refugees, penal affairs and community-based initiatives for disadvantaged young people; and in developing countries in the areas of community development, education and health.

Geographical Area of Activity: United Kingdom and developing countries.

Restrictions: No grants are made to individuals.

Publications: Annual Report.

Finance: Annual income £435,261, expenditure £626,685 (5 April 2014).

Trustees: Prof. M. B. H. Rampton (Chair.).

Principal Staff: Sec. Rodney J. R. Hedley.

Address: 34 North End Rd, London W14 0SH.

Telephone: (20) 7603-1525; **Fax:** (20) 7603-1525; **Internet:** www.hildencharitablefund.org.uk; **e-mail:** hildencharity@hotmail.com.

Jane Hodge Foundation

Founded in 1962 to provide funds for the advancement of medical research and medical and surgical science, education and religion.

Activities: Provides grants to registered charities throughout the world, with particular emphasis on those supporting research into cancer, diseases affecting children, polio and tuberculosis.

Geographical Area of Activity: Worldwide.

Restrictions: Grants only to exempt or registered charities.

Publications: *Annual Memorial Lecture.*

Finance: Annual income £1,097,783, expenditure £880,011 (31 Oct. 2013).

Principal Staff: Contact Derreck L. Jones.

Address: 31 Windsor Pl., Cardiff CF1 3UR.

Telephone: (29) 2076-6521; **Fax:** (29) 2075-7009; **e-mail:** info@janehodgefoundation.co.uk.

A. S. Hornby Educational Trust

Founded in 1961 for the advancement of the English language, and its teaching and learning as a foreign language.

Activities: Provides scholarships (approx. 10 a year) and grants for foreign teachers to study teaching English as a foreign language in the United Kingdom. Awards include the English Speaking Union Summer School Bursary and British Council Summer School Scholarships. Works in collaboration with the British Council (q.v.).

Geographical Area of Activity: International.

Restrictions: Grants are made through the British Council; there are no direct grants.

Finance: Annual income £325,765, expenditure £458,561 (31 March 2014).

Trustees: Dr Roger Bowers (Chair.); Dr Richard Smith (Deputy Chair.); Tricia Alfreds (Sec.).

Address: c/o Kingston Smith LLP, Orbital House, 20 Eastern Rd, Romford RM1 3PJ.

Telephone: (1708) 759759; **Internet:** www.hornby-trust.org.uk; **e-mail:** admin@hornby-trust.org.uk.

The Hunter Foundation

Established in 1998 by Sir Tom Hunter to promote equality of opportunity for children worldwide.

Activities: Operates through proactive venture philanthropy.

Geographical Area of Activity: United Kingdom (especially Scotland), Rwanda.

Finance: Annual income £1,257,340, expenditure £962,181 (31 March 2014).

Trustees: Sir Tom Hunter (Chair.).

Principal Staff: CEO Ewan Hunter.

Address: Marathon House, Olympic Business Park, Drybridge Rd, Dundonald KA2 9AE.

Internet: www.thehunterfoundation.co.uk; **e-mail:** info@thehunterfoundation.co.uk.

Mo Ibrahim Foundation (Fondation Mo Ibrahim)

Established in 2006 to stimulate debate on governance in Africa, and to support leadership that will improve the economic and social prospects of the people of Africa.

Activities: Awards the Ibrahim Prize for Achievement in African Leadership; the Ibrahim Index of African Governance; the Ibrahim Scholarship Programme; and the Ibrahim Fellowship Programme.

Geographical Area of Activity: Africa.

Publications: Ibrahim Index of African Governance.

Board: Mo Ibrahim (Chair.).

Address: 3rd Floor North, 35 Portman Sq., London W1H 6LR.

Telephone: (20) 7535-5063; **Internet:** www.moibrahimfoundation.org; **e-mail:** info@moibrahimfoundation.org.

Inclusion International—II

Established in 2004.

Activities: A federation of family-based organizations campaigning on behalf of the human rights of people with intellectual disabilities worldwide. The organization hosts regional forums for families and self-advocates to learn from each other about initiatives in different countries that promote and implement aspects of the organization's Convention. The organization draws on the knowledge and expertise of its volunteers and member organizations to support country-level initiatives. It works in partnership with the International Disability Alliance, and with UN agencies and development agencies to identify opportunities to include and promote the rights of people with intellectual disabilities in their work, and campaigns to promote their right to live within the community. Represents more than 200 member federations in 115 countries.

Geographical Area of Activity: International.

Publications: *Inclusion Around the World* (newsletter); *Global Report on Poverty and Disability—Hear Our Voices*; *Global Report on Education—Better Education for All, when we are included too*; *Priorities for People with Intellectual Disabilities in implementing the UNCRPD*; *The implication of the CRPD*.

Finance: Annual income £586,327, expenditure £545,689 (31 Dec. 2013).

Council: Klaus Lachwitz (Pres.); Fadia Farah (Vice-Pres.); Ralph Jones (Sec.-Gen.); Diane Richler (Past Pres.); Tim Gadd (Treas.).

Principal Staff: Exec. Dir Connie Laurin-Bowie; Admin. Coordinator Raquel Gonzalez.

Address: KD.2.03, University of East London, Docklands Campus, 4–6 University Way, London E16 2RD.

Telephone: (20) 8223-7709; **Fax:** (20) 8223-6081; **Internet:** www.inclusion-international.org; **e-mail:** info@inclusion-international.org.

John Innes Foundation—JIF

Formed in 1910 following a bequest from John Innes, a landowner in the City of London.

Activities: In 1910 the trustees of the Foundation founded the John Innes Horticultural Institution at Merton, London, John Innes's home. In 1945, finding those premises too restrictive, the Institution purchased an estate at Bayfordbury, Hertfordshire, and then, in 1967 moved to its present site in Colney,

Norfolk. The Foundation provides grants to students for the advancement of education in agriculture, horticulture and bio-technology. It also provides land and buildings for research at the John Innes Centre in Norwich and supports a library there, containing material on the history of genetics and rare botanical books. The Foundation supports Emeritus Fellows and PhD studentships at JIC and it also makes a contribution to a variety of on-site amenities, including sport and environment.

Geographical Area of Activity: United Kingdom.

Finance: Annual income £904,505, expenditure £1,281,098 (31 March 2014).

Trustees: John F. Oldfield (Sec.).

Principal Staff: Clerk to the Trustees J. P. Webster.

Address: Oriel House, 5 Nethergate St, Bungay NR35 1HE.

Telephone: (1986) 894111; **Internet:** www .johninnesfoundation.org.uk; **e-mail:** mail@jpwebster.co.uk.

Institute for European Environmental Policy—IEEP

Established in 1990 as an office of the European Cultural Foundation (q.v.); became independent in 1990.

Activities: Carries out research and promotes strategies and alternatives for dealing with environmental problems in Europe, and proposes solutions to national governments, the European Parliament and other institutions. The Institute's research covers a number of areas, including agriculture, environmental governance, fisheries, marine conservation, nature conservation and biodiversity, climate change, rural development and transport. Also operates from Belgium and Finland.

Geographical Area of Activity: Europe.

Publications: *The Environment in Europe* (in English, French and German); *Manual of Environmental Policy: the EU and Britain* (updated twice yearly); Annual Reports.

Finance: Annual income £2,146,097, expenditure £2,130,167 (31 Dec. 2013).

Board of Trustees: Sir John Harman (Chair.).

Principal Staff: Exec. Dir David Baldock.

Address: 11 Belgrave Rd, IEEP Offices, Floor 3, London SW1V 1RB.

Telephone: (20) 7799-2244; **Fax:** (20) 7799-2600; **Internet:** www.ieep.eu; **e-mail:** jlindblad@ieep.eu.

International Alert—Alert

Founded in 1986 by Martin Ennals, Archbishop Desmond Tutu and other human rights advocates.

Activities: Promotes resolution of differences without resorting to violent conflict. The organization has three main aims: to work with people who live in areas affected or threatened by armed conflict to make a positive difference for peace; to work at government, European Union and UN levels to improve both the substance and implementation of international policies that affect prospects for peace; and to strengthen the peacebuilding sector through increasing its effectiveness and profile so that more people recognize the necessity of peace-building, what can be done to address violent conflict and the realities involved. It runs a body of programmes on conflict in the Great Lakes region of Africa, West Africa, Eurasia, South Asia and on peacebuilding issues, including aid effectiveness, climate change, gender, security and economy/business.

Geographical Area of Activity: More than 20 countries and territories around the world, including West Africa (Guinea, São Tomé and Príncipe, Liberia and Sierra Leone), the Great Lakes region (Burundi, Rwanda, Uganda and the Democratic Republic of the Congo), Caucasus (Georgia, Armenia, Azerbaijan, Abkhazia and Nagorny Karabakh), Central Asia, the Philippines, Nepal and Sri Lanka.

Restrictions: Not a grantmaking organization.

Publications: Annual Report; Annual Review; resource packs, research reports and other publications.

Finance: Annual income £12,962,000, expenditure £13,502,000 (31 Dec. 2013).

Board of Trustees: Pierre Schori (Chair.); Gregor Stewart (Hon. Treas.).

Principal Staff: Sec.-Gen. Dan Smith.

Address: 346 Clapham Rd, London SW9 9AP.

Telephone: (20) 7627-6800; **Fax:** (20) 7627-6900; **Internet:** www.international-alert.org; **e-mail:** info@international -alert.org.

International Institute for Environment and Development—IIED

Founded in 1971 by economist and policy adviser Barbara Ward.

Activities: Promotes sustainable world development through research, policy studies, networking and information dissemination. Provides leadership in researching and promoting sustainable development at a local, national and global level, with the aim of shaping a future that ends global poverty and sustains fair and sound management of the world's resources. Partnerships are key to the Institute. By forging alliances with individuals and organizations ranging from urban slum-dwellers to global institutions, it ensures that national and international policy reflects the agendas of marginalized people. Played key roles in the Stockholm Conference of 1972, the Brundtland Commission of 1987, the 1992 Earth Summit and the 2002 World Summit on Sustainable Development.

Geographical Area of Activity: Primarily Africa, Asia, and Central and South America.

Publications: IIED produces a range of books, journals, briefing papers, DVDs and CD-ROMs. Publications include: *Environment and Urbanization (Human Settlements)*; *Participation, Learning and Action (Natural Resources)*; *Haramata (Climate Change)*; *Gatekeeper (Natural Resources)*; *Tiempo (Climate Change Group)*; *The Earthscan Reader in Rural-Urban Linkages*; *Reducing Poverty and Sustaining the Environment*; *Evidence for Hope*; *Words Into Action*; *Pelican Man—A Video Documentary*; *Sustainable Development Opinion Papers*.

Finance: Total revenue £19,400,435, expenditure £19,384,840 (31 March 2014).

Trustees: Rebeca Grynspan (Chair.); Ian Rushby (Vice-Chair.); Frank Kirwan (Treas.).

Principal Staff: Dir Camilla Toulmin; COO Chris Wilde.

Address: 80–86 Grays Inn Rd, London WC1X 8NH.

Telephone: (20) 3463-7399; **Fax:** (20) 3514-9055; **Internet:** www.iied.org.

The International Institute for Strategic Studies—IISS

Founded in 1958.

Activities: Promotes, on a non-party basis, the study and discussion of, and exchange of information on, military strategy, weapons control, regional security and conflict resolution. The Institute operates in the field of international affairs by providing an independent centre for research, debate and the dissemination of information. Various foundations fund its research, which a team of Research Fellows and Research Associates carries out, mainly in three interrelated areas: the changing nature of international security; national and regional security; and arms control and demilitarization. The Institute, which is a membership organization, holds several conferences a year, including a major annual conference for members, and an annual memorial lecture (given by a leading international figure) in memory of the first Director, Alastair Buchan, and discussion meetings and seminars. Maintains a library and information centre.

Geographical Area of Activity: United Kingdom, USA, Asia, Middle East.

Publications: *The Military Balance* (annually); *Strategic Survey* (annually); *Survival* (bi-monthly); *Adelphi Papers* (monographs, 8–10 a year); *Strategic Comments* (10 a year); *Strategic Dossier*; newsletters.

Finance: Annual income £16,020,000, expenditure £15,916,000 (30 Sept. 2013).

Board of Trustees: Fleur de Villiers (Chair.).

Principal Staff: Dir-Gen. and Chief Exec. Dr John Chipman.

Address: Arundel House, 13–15 Arundel St, Temple Pl., London WC2R 3DX.

Telephone: (20) 7379-7676; **Fax:** (20) 7836-3108; **Internet:** www.iiss.org; **e-mail:** iiss@iiss.org.

International Maritime Rescue Foundation—IMRF

Founded in 1924 as the International Lifeboat Federation, to co-ordinate the activities of national non-government and government lifeboat organizations; formally incorporated in 2003.

Activities: Provides technical assistance to countries exploring how to start a marine search and rescue service to meet the International Maritime Organization's World Maritime Search and Rescue Regional Plan, through operating training programmes, search and rescue services, medical care, communications and finance. The Foundation finances research into lifeboat design; promotes exchange of information; and maintains a reference library.

Geographical Area of Activity: International.

Publications: *Conference Report* (every 4 years); IMRF Lifeline Newsletter (6 a year).

Finance: Annual income £258,063, expenditure £353,316 (31 Dec. 2013).

Trustees: Michael Vlasto (Chair.).

Principal Staff: CEO Bruce Reid.

Address: 50 Allardice St, Stonehaven AB39 2RA.

Telephone: (1569) 767405; **Internet:** www.international-maritime-rescue.org; **e-mail:** info@imrf.org.uk.

International Planned Parenthood Federation—IPPF

Founded in 1952; a federation of autonomous family planning associations.

Activities: Works in sexual and reproductive health, choice and rights. The Federation promotes and defends the rights of women and men, including young people, to decide freely the number and spacing of their children, and the right to the highest possible level of sexual and reproductive health. It initiates and supports the promotion of sexual and reproductive health worldwide, including family planning; and highlights these and related issues, including human rights, HIV/AIDS, gender, young people, refugees, violence against women, and poverty, to the media, governmental organizations, NGOs and the general public. It also works to mobilize financial resources to fund programmes and materials, and provides training on issues relating to adolescents, HIV/AIDS, abortion, access to contraception and global advocacy. The Federation's International Medical Panel, which comprises leading medical experts, provides guidelines and statements on current medical and scientific thinking and the best practices. The Federation offers contraceptive services and equipment, ranging from clinical and office equipment to vehicles, for member associations and other public health bodies. A Youth Working Group ensures programmes are accessible to young people and to promote young people's rights. Links member organizations in 172 countries.

Geographical Area of Activity: Europe, Asia (South and South-East), Oceania, Africa, the Middle East, the USA, and Central and South America.

Restrictions: Only funds member family planning associations.

Publications: *Newsletter for Donors* (quarterly); *Family Planning Handbook for Health Professionals*; *IPPF Directory of Hormonal Contraceptives* (online publication); *IPPF Medical Bulletin* (6 a year, in English, French and Spanish); *News, News, News* (online publication); *Mezzo* (in English, French and Spanish); *Press* (2 a year, in English, French and Spanish); *Voice* (in English, French and Spanish); books, fact sheets, audiovisual materials and cassettes.

Finance: Annual income £82,536,753, expenditure £80,514,651 (31 Dec. 2013).

Governing Council: Dr Naomi Seboni (Pres./Chair.); Sujatha Natarajan (Hon. Treas.); Jacqueline Sharp (Immediate Past Pres.).

Principal Staff: Dir-Gen. Tewodros Melesse.

Address: 4 Newhams Row, London SE1 3UZ.

Telephone: (20) 7939-8200; **Fax:** (20) 7939-8300; **Internet:** www.ippf.org; **e-mail:** info@ippf.org.

International Refugee Trust—IRT

Established in 1989 to support refugees overseas.

Activities: Funds small-scale projects. The Trust emphasizes health, medicine, training, education and well-being of refugees; promotes projects operated by local people aimed at attaining self-sufficiency. It supports two orphanages in Uganda, which help Sudanese refugee children; carries out development programmes in Sudan, including a health clinic for the aged, children and mothers; operates a medical care programme in Jordan to provide medical aid to refugee mothers and infants from Palestinian Territories and Iraq; and assists Myanma refugees residing on the Thai–Myanmar border by providing medical and food aid.

Geographical Area of Activity: Africa, Asia and the Middle East.

Restrictions: No grants to individuals; grants made only overseas.

Publications: Appeals; newsletter; Annual Report.

Finance: Annual income £760,953, expenditure £797,756 (31 March 2014).

Trustees: Simon Whitfield (Chair.).

Principal Staff: CEO Adrian Hatch.

Address: POB 31452, Chiswick, London W4 4JG; 11 Heathfield Terrace, London W4 4JE.

Telephone: (20) 8994-9120; **Fax:** (20) 8742-0315; **Internet:** www.irt.org.uk; **e-mail:** info@irt.org.uk.

International Tree Foundation—ITF

Founded in 1924 by Dr Richard St Barbe Baker. Formerly known as Men of the Trees.

Activities: Aims to sustain and enhance the environment through the planting and protection of trees. The Foundation plants trees worldwide to increase land fertility and is particularly active in desert areas and tropical rain forests. It supports sustainable projects in developing countries.

Geographical Area of Activity: International.

Publications: Annual Journals; e-bulletins.

Finance: Annual income £143,267, expenditure £163,263 (30 Sept. 2013).

Trustees: Timothy Hornsby (Chair.); Roger Leakey (Vice-Chair.); Maria Grecna (Treas.).

Principal Staff: Dir Andy Egan.

Address: Crawley Business Centre, Stephenson Way, Three Bridges, Crawley, West Sussex RH10 1N.

Telephone: (1342) 717300; **Fax:** (1342) 718282; **Internet:** www.internationaltreefoundation.org; **e-mail:** info@internationaltreefoundation.org.

Iran Heritage Foundation—IHF

Established in 1995 to promote and preserve the history, languages and cultures of Iran and the Persian world.

Activities: Organizes activities of cultural or scholarly merit worldwide. The Foundation organizes conferences, symposiums, seminars and workshops; publishes conference proceedings and monographs; and funds research and travel grants. Its Institutional Partnerships Programme (IPP) supports fellowships, teaching positions, curatorial positions and centres dedicated to the Iranian studies at academic and cultural institutions based in the United Kingdom and abroad. The Foundation collaborates with institutional partners to help sustain posts in Iranian studies and culture that would otherwise be unsustainable.

Geographical Area of Activity: Mainly in the United Kingdom.

Publications: *Forough Farrokhzad, Poet of Modern Iran: Iconic Woman and Feminine Pioneer of New Persian Poetry* (eds Dr P. Brookshaw and Dr N. Rahimieh); *Iran's Constitutional Revolution: Popular Politics, Cultural Transformations amd Transnational Connections* (eds Prof. H. Chehabi and Prof. V. Martin).

Finance: Annual income £721,334, expenditure £690,769 (31 Dec. 2013).

Board of Trustees: Sedigheh Rastegar (Pres.); Vahid Alaghband (Chair.); Dr Kimya Kamshad (Sec.).

Principal Staff: CEO Dr John Curtis.

Address: 63 New Cavendish St, London W1G 7LP.

Telephone: (20) 7493-4766; **Fax:** (844) 871-2210; **Internet:** www.iranheritage.org; **e-mail:** info@iranheritage.org.

Islamic Relief Worldwide

Established in 1984 by Dr Hany El Banna; an international relief and development charity.

Activities: Operates in the areas of social welfare, disaster management and sustainable development. Partner organizations operate in Australia, Belgium, Canada, France, Germany, Malaysia, Mauritius, the Netherlands, Sweden, Switzerland, the USA and the Middle East.

Geographical Area of Activity: International.

Finance: Annual income £82,814,292, expenditure £87,284,642 (31 Dec. 2013).

Board of Trustees: Ibrahim El-Zayat (Chair.); Mohammed El-Alfy (Vice-Chair.); Adnan Saif (Sec.); Tahir Salie (Treas.).

Principal Staff: CEO Dr Mohamed Ashmawey.

Address: 19 Rea St South, Digbeth, Birmingham B5 6LB.

Telephone: (121) 6055555; **Fax:** (121) 6225003; **Internet:** www.islamic-relief.com.

IVS—International Voluntary Service

Founded in 1931 by Pierre Cérésole and Jean Inebnit as the British branch of Service Civil International (q.v.) to provide opportunities for men and women, young and old, irrespective of their race, nationality, creed or politics to join together in giving useful voluntary service to the community in a spirit of friendship and international understanding.

Activities: Provides volunteer help to local and global communities in more than 45 countries, and works to promote greater inter-cultural understanding by bringing people from different cultures and backgrounds to live and work together. Supported projects are within the areas of environment and conservation, children, people with disabilities, culture and peace, and solidarity.

Geographical Area of Activity: International.

Restrictions: Does not make grants.

Publications: Annual Report; *International Volunteer Projects Directory*; quarterly newsletter.

Finance: Annual income £89,485, expenditure £164,608 (31 Dec. 2013).

Governing Board: Hilary Campbell (Chair.); Ben Moon (Deputy Chair.); Geraldine Lowery (Sec.); Mahrouf Shafi (Treas.).

Principal Staff: Development Dir Helen Wass O'Donnell.

Address: Thorn House, 5 Rose St, Edinburgh EH2 2PR.

Telephone: (131) 2432745; **Fax:** (131) 2432747; **Internet:** www.ivsgb.org; **e-mail:** info@ivsgb.org.

Japan Foundation Endowment Committee—JFEC

Founded in 1974 by the University Grants Committee (UGC) to administer an endowment made by the Japanese Government through the Japan Foundation (q.v.) for the promotion of Japanese studies within universities in the United Kingdom.

Activities: Provides small grants to support academic research in Japanese studies by staff and doctoral research students in higher education institutions in the United Kingdom, covering research on any aspect of Japan within the humanities and social sciences (including comparative studies where Japan is a major element). Applications are considered for funding for fieldwork in Japan, other forms of research support, and the partial support of doctoral students.

Geographical Area of Activity: United Kingdom.

Restrictions: Applications must be made by staff of United Kingdom higher education institutions; applications may not be made directly by students. Funding is not available for coursework or Master's dissertations.

Publications: Annual Report.

Finance: Grants disbursed approx. £50,000 per year.

Trustees: Prof. Ian Neary (Chair.).

Principal Staff: Exec. Sec. Lynn Baird.

Address: c/o JFEC, Lynn Baird, University of Essex, Colchester CO4 3SQ.

Telephone: (1206) 872543; (0) 7580 178960; **Fax:** (1206) 873965; **Internet:** www.bajs.org.uk/funding/jfec; www.jfec.org.uk; **e-mail:** admin@jfec.org.uk.

JCA Charitable Foundation

Founded in 1891 as the Jewish Colonization Association by Baron Maurice de Hirsch to assist Jews in need, particularly in those countries where they were oppressed.

Activities: Provides funds to organizations involved in assisting Jewish refugees; finances agricultural institutions and research in Israel, and international school networks for Jewish students; and encourages the formation of Jewish groups within institutions throughout the world.

Geographical Area of Activity: Worldwide.

Restrictions: Does not make grants to individuals; nor does it usually accept applications from bodies not currently linked to the Foundation.

Publications: Annual Report; *Centenary Brochure*.

Finance: Annual income £407,000, expenditure £1,109,000 (31 Dec. 2013).

Council of Administration: Sir Stephen Waley Cohen (Pres.); Baron Alain Philippson (Vice-Pres.); Yehiel Admoni (Hon. Pres.).

Principal Staff: Sec. Timothy R. Martin.

Address: 11 Garnick St, London WC2E 9A.

Telephone: (20) 7828-0600; **Fax:** (20) 7828-6882; **e-mail:** thejcafoundation@aol.com.

Jephcott Charitable Trust—JCT

Founded in 1965 by Sir Harry Jephcott for general charitable purposes.

Activities: Main areas of interest are projects in developing countries to improve quality of life, especially in the fields of population control, education, health and the environment. The Trust gives grants mainly to charities involved in smaller projects.

Geographical Area of Activity: Worldwide.

Restrictions: Does not make grants to large national organizations, to those concerned with education or alleviating poverty in the United Kingdom, to individuals, or for animal welfare, or heritage.

Publications: Annual Report.

Finance: Annual income £127,757, total expenditure £118,604 (30 June 2014).

Trustees: Lady Jephcott (Chair.); District Judge A. North (Deputy Chair.).

Principal Staff: Sec. Dr Felicity Gibling.

Address: The Threshing Barn, Ford, Kingsbridge, Devon TQ7 2LN.

Internet: www.jephcottcharitabletrust.org.uk.

Jerusalem Trust

Founded in 1982 for the advancement of Christian religion; the advancement of Christian education and learning; and for the benefit of charitable purposes or charitable institutions determined by the trustees. One of the Sainsbury Family Charitable Trusts, all of which share a common administration.

Activities: Operates internationally in the areas of Christian evangelism and relief work; Christian media; Christian education; and Christian art. Within the United Kingdom it operates in the areas of Christian evangelism and social responsibility work with children and young people, and prisoners and ex-prisoners.

Geographical Area of Activity: Worldwide.

Restrictions: Unsolicited applications are unlikely to be successful. No grants are made to individuals.

Finance: Annual income £3,590,000, expenditure £4,511,000 (5 April 2014).

Principal Staff: Dir Alan P. Bookbinder; Finance Dir Paul Spokes.

Address: c/o The Sainsbury Family Charitable Trusts, The Peak, 5 Wilton Rd, London SW1V 1AP.

Telephone: (20) 7410-0330; **Fax:** (20) 7410-0332; **Internet:** www.sfct.org.uk/the-jerusalem-trust/; **e-mail:** jerusalemtrust@sfct.org.uk.

JNF Charitable Trust—JNFCT

Founded in 1901 as a fund to help establish a Jewish state.

Activities: Raises funds in the United Kingdom to support a range of environmental and humanitarian projects in Israel.

Geographical Area of Activity: Israel and the Middle East.

Restrictions: No grants are made to individuals.

Publications: Annual Report; books.

Finance: Annual income £13,855,000, expenditure £13,485,000 (31 Dec. 2013).

Executive Board: Samuel Hayek (Chair.); Dr Michael Sinclair (Vice-Chair.); David Berens (Sec.).

Principal Staff: Contact Jonathan Levy.

Address: JNF House, Spring Villa Park, Spring Villa Rd, Edgware HA8 7ED.

Telephone: (20) 8732-6100; **Fax:** (20) 8732-6111; **Internet:** www.jnf.co.uk; **e-mail:** info@jnf.co.uk.

Elton John AIDS Foundation—EJAF

Founded in 1993 by Sir Elton John as an international non-profit organization funding direct patient care services that help to alleviate the physical, emotional and financial hardship of those living with HIV/AIDS, as well as AIDS prevention programmes. A sister organization with offices in Los Angeles, USA, was established in 1992 to fund programmes in North America.

Activities: Funds programmes that help to alleviate the physical, emotional and financial hardship of those living with, affected by or at risk of HIV/AIDS. The Foundation was formed primarily to look after the needs of people with HIV/AIDS living in the United Kingdom. It has extended the scope of its work and now provides funds in 15 countries across four continents. The Foundation has raised more than £113m., which has been used to support more than 1,300 projects reaching millions of people infected, affected or at risk of HIV/AIDS, including: providing information about HIV/AIDS to more than 150m. people around the globe, including 5m. children; giving 185,000 people with AIDS in South Africa proper palliative care; providing 10,000 adults with antiretroviral treatment in Sub-Saharan Africa; supporting more than 57,000 people in need to access income generation programmes, vocational training, grants or loans; and enabling more than 200,000 people living with HIV/AIDS to be supported through positive people's groups and networks.

Geographical Area of Activity: International.

Restrictions: Grants are restricted to selected countries in Africa, Asia and Europe.

Finance: Annual income £7,136,999, expenditure £7,790,105 (31 Dec. 2013).

Trustees: David Furnish (Chair.); George Kangis (Sec.).

Principal Staff: Exec. Dir Anne Aslett.

Address: 1 Blythe Rd, London W14 0HG.

Telephone: (20) 7603-9996; **Fax:** (20) 7348-4848; **Internet:** ejaf.org; **e-mail:** grants@ejaf.com.

Karuna Trust

Established in 1980 as Aid for India for the relief of poverty through educational, medical and skills projects, particularly in India.

Activities: Operates in India in the fields of aid to less-developed countries, education, and medicine and health, through self-conducted programmes and grants; also issues publications.

Geographical Area of Activity: India.

Publications: Annual Report.

Finance: Annual income £1,855,505, total expenditure £1,598,173 (31 March 2014).

Trustees: Ulla Brown (Chair.).

Principal Staff: CEO Ciaran Maguire.

Address: 72 Holloway Rd, London N7 8JG.

Telephone: (20) 7700-3434; **Fax:** (20) 7700-3535; **Internet:** www.karuna.org; **e-mail:** info@karuna.org.

Kennedy Memorial Trust

Founded in 1966 from the proceeds of a National Memorial Appeal launched by the Lord Mayor of London following the assassination of US President John F. Kennedy in 1963 to enable graduates from the United Kingdom to spend one year studying at one of the faculties of Harvard University or the Massachusetts Institute of Technology.

Activities: Administers the Kennedy Memorial Fund. The Trust works in the field of education, through granting about 10 scholarships annually tenable by British citizens ordinarily resident in the United Kingdom, and wholly or mainly educated there. Scholarships are tenable in all areas of the arts, sciences, social sciences and political studies.

Geographical Area of Activity: United Kingdom.

Restrictions: Fellowships to British citizens only.

Finance: Kennedy Memorial Fund: annual income £314,394, expenditure £647,337 (30 April 2014).

Trustees: Prof. Tony Badger (Chair.).

Principal Staff: Sec. Annie Thomas.

Address: 3 Birdcage Walk, Westminster, London SW1H 9JJ.

Telephone: (20) 7222-1151; **Fax:** (20) 7222-7189; **Internet:** www.kennedytrust.org.uk; **e-mail:** annie@kennedytrust.org.uk.

The King's Fund

Founded in 1897 (as King Edward's Hospital Fund for London) by King Edward VII, then Prince of Wales, originally for the support, benefit and extension of the hospitals of London, now interpreted broadly to include all the health services in Greater London.

Activities: Supports the health of Londoners through policy analysis, service development and education. The Fund operates in seven main areas: health and social care; health-care policy; primary care; public health; leadership development; rehabilitation; and health systems. Activities include giving grants to innovative health projects in London, running leadership courses for National Health Service (NHS) managers, and producing frequent publications on key policy issues. Also provides conference and library facilities, and distributes King's Fund Millennium Awards.

Geographical Area of Activity: London, United Kingdom.

Publications: Annual Report; *Funding Health Care: 2008 and beyond*; *An Anatomy of GP Referral Decisions: A qualitative study of GPs' views on their role in supporting patient choice*;

How to Regulate Health Care in England? An international perspective; *NHS Reform: Getting back on track*; *Future Trends and Challenges for Cancer Services in England: A review of literature and policy*; *Grow Your Own: Creating the conditions for sustainable workforce development*; *Clearing the Air: Debating smoke-free policies in psychiatric units*; *Designing the 'new NHS: Ideas to make a supplier market in health care work*; *Assessing the New NHS Consultant Contract: A something for something deal?*.

Finance: Annual income £13,491,000, total expenditure £15,834,000 (31 Dec. 2013).

Board of Trustees: Sir Christopher Kelly (Chair.); Strone Macpherson (Treas.).

Principal Staff: Chief Exec. Chris Ham.

Address: 11–13 Cavendish Sq., London W1G 0AN.

Telephone: (20) 7307-2400; **Fax:** (20) 7307-2801; **Internet:** www.kingsfund.org.uk; **e-mail:** enquiry@kingsfund.org.uk.

Ernest Kleinwort Charitable Trust

Founded in 1963 for general charitable purposes.

Activities: Principally operates internationally in the fields of wildlife, environmental conservation and family planning; and nationally in the fields of the disabled, medical research, elderly and youth welfare.

Geographical Area of Activity: International.

Restrictions: Preference is given to charities operating in Sussex.

Finance: Annual income £1,761,550, expenditure £1,717,373 (11 March 2014).

Trustees: Lord Thomas Orlando, 3rd Viscount Chandos (Chair.).

Principal Staff: Trust Officer Scott Rice.

Address: 14 St George St, London W1S 1FE.

Telephone: (20) 3207-7008; **Internet:** www.ekct.org.uk.

Frank Knox Memorial Fellowships

Founded in 1945 by Annie Reid Knox as the Frank Knox Memorial to enable students from Australia, Canada, New Zealand and the United Kingdom to undertake graduate study at Harvard University.

Activities: Operates in the field of education, through fellowships.

Geographical Area of Activity: United Kingdom.

Restrictions: Awards fellowships only to citizens of Australia, Canada, New Zealand and the United Kingdom. Preference given to degree applicants.

Principal Staff: Sec. (United Kingdom applicants) Annie Thomas.

Address: 3 Birdcage Walk, Westminster, London SW1H 9JJ.

Telephone: (20) 7222-1151; **Fax:** (20) 7222-7189; **Internet:** www.frankknox.harvard.edu & www.frankknoxfellowships.org.uk; **e-mail:** annie@frankknoxfellowships.org.uk.

Heinz, Anna and Carol Kroch Foundation

Founded in 1962 by Falk Heinz Kroch and Anna Kroch to further medical research, and relieve individuals suffering severe poverty and financial hardship who have ongoing medical problems.

Activities: Assists people who are experiencing severe poverty, financial hardship, domestic violence and homelessness.

Geographical Area of Activity: United Kingdom and Ireland.

Restrictions: Grants are not made for projects, nor for medical research. No grants for holidays or education projects. Applications must come through the social services or another recognized agency.

Finance: Annual income £190,257, expenditure £195,244 (5 April 2014).

Principal Staff: Admin. Beena Astle.

Address: POB 462, Teddington TW11 1BS.

Telephone: (20) 8979-0609; **Fax:** (20) 8979-7479; **e-mail:** hakf50@hotmail.com.

Maurice and Hilda Laing Charitable Trust

Established in 1996 as the Hilda Laing Charitable Trust.

Activities: Supports organizations promoting Christianity throughout the world, through funding religious education as well as funding projects working to combat poverty and support people with physical and mental disabilities. Most overseas grants are channelled through United Kingdom-registered charities. Grants are co-ordinated with the Beatrice Laing Trust and the Kirby Laing Foundation (q.v.).

Geographical Area of Activity: International.

Restrictions: No grants to individuals.

Finance: Annual income £1,516,562, expenditure £3,851,018 (31 Dec. 2013).

Trustees: Peter J. Harper (Chair.).

Principal Staff: Dir Elizabeth A. Harley.

Address: 33 Bunns Lane, Mill Hill, London NW7 2DX.

Telephone: (20) 8238-8890; **Fax:** (20) 8238-8897; **Internet:** www.laingfamilytrusts.org.uk/maurice_hilda_laing.html.

Kirby Laing Foundation

Founded in 1972 for general charitable purposes and promotion of the evengelical Christian faith.

Activities: Operates nationally and internationally, making donations to registered charities. Most donations overseas are channelled through United Kingdom-registered charities. The Foundation co-ordinates its grants with the Beatrice Laing Trust and the Maurice and Hilda Laing Charitable Trust (qq.v.).

Geographical Area of Activity: United Kingdom.

Restrictions: No grants to individuals.

Finance: Annual income £1,856,408, expenditure £2,523,578 (31 Dec. 2013).

Principal Staff: Dir Elizabeth A. Harley.

Address: 33 Bunns Lane, Mill Hill, London NW7 2DX.

Telephone: (20) 8238-8890; **Fax:** (20) 8238-8897.

Beatrice Laing Trust

Founded in 1952 for the relief of poverty, and for the advancement of the evangelical Christian faith internationally.

Activities: Grants are made to charities working in deprived sections of the community in the United Kingdom, to missionary societies and, less frequently, to individuals working in the field of missions, in the United Kingdom and abroad. Most donations overseas are channelled through United Kingdom-registered charities. The Trust co-ordinates donations with the Kirby Laing Foundation and the Maurice and Hilda Laing Charitable Trust (qq.v.).

Geographical Area of Activity: Europe, United Kingdom.

Restrictions: No grants to individuals.

Finance: Annual income £2,553,397, expenditure £1,919,902 (5 April 2014).

Principal Staff: Dir Elizabeth Anne Harley.

Address: 33 Bunns Lane, Mill Hill, London NW7 2DX.

Telephone: (20) 8238-8890; **Fax:** (20) 8238-8897; **Internet:** www.laingfamilytrusts.org.uk/beatrice_laing_trust.html.

Allen Lane Foundation

Founded in 1966 by Sir Allen Lane to support general charitable purposes.

Activities: Funds a variety of projects in the United Kingdom. Current priorities include: refugees and asylum seekers; migrant workers; elderly people; those experiencing mental health problems; those experiencing violence or abuse; offenders and former offenders; gay, lesbian, bisexual or transgender people; and gypsies and travellers. Priority is given to projects that will make a long-term difference to the problems addressed.

Geographical Area of Activity: United Kingdom.

Restrictions: No grants are made to individuals or to organizations outside of the United Kingdom. There are a number of other restrictions, and applicants should request the full guidelines before applying.

Finance: Annual income £642,969, expenditure £963,910 (31 March 2014).

Trustees: Philip Walsh (Chair.).

Principal Staff: Exec. Sec. Tim Cutts.

Address: 90 The Mount, York YO24 1AR.

Telephone: (1904) 613223; **Fax:** (1904) 613133; **Internet:** www.allenlane.org.uk; **e-mail:** info@allenlane.org.uk.

Laureus Sport for Good Foundation

Established in 2000 to use sport to change the lives of disadvantaged children and young people.

Activities: Funds and promotes the use of sport as a tool for social change. Supports more than 140 sporting projects worldwide that bring about social change. Key project areas are: social exclusion; gun and gang violence; discrimination; community integration and cohesion; peace and reconciliation; and education and health.

Geographical Area of Activity: Worldwide.

Restrictions: Applicants must be community-based organizations or legally registered NGOs. The Foundation does not fund certain types of organizations or activities, including: statutory bodies or profit-making organizations; organizations working purely with élite sport or promoting specific sporting talent; individual athletes or professional sports teams; individuals for their sole benefit; major infrastructural projects or large capital grants; or disaster or emergency humanitarian relief projects.

Publications: Regular publications; magazine.

Finance: Annual income £2,477,308, expenditure £4,545,626 (31 Dec. 2013).

Trustees: Edwin Moses, Tanni Grey-Thompson, Boris Becker (Vice-Chair.).

Principal Staff: Sec. Nicholas Garside.

Address: 460 Fulham Rd, London SW6 1BZ.

Telephone: (20) 7514-2762; **Fax:** (20) 7514-2837; **Internet:** www.laureus.com; **e-mail:** foundation@laureus.com.

Law Society Charity

Established in 1974 to offer support in the field of law and justice nationally and internationally.

Activities: Operates in the United Kingdom and abroad in the field of law, offering grants to organizations furthering law and justice, including support for legal education, the welfare of members of the profession and the promotion of human rights.

Geographical Area of Activity: England and Wales.

Restrictions: Grants are usually made only to United Kingdom organizations.

Publications: Annual Report.

Finance: Annual income £29,331, expenditure £135,613 (5 April 2014).

Trustees: Nigel Dodds (Chair.).

Principal Staff: Sec. Andrew Dobson.

Address: 113 Chancery Lane, London WC2A 1PL.

Telephone: (20) 7316-5631; **Internet:** www.lawsociety.org.uk/law-society-charity; **e-mail:** lawsocietycharity@lawsociety.org.uk.

Leprosy Mission International

Established in 1874 by Wellesley Bailey as an international Christian charity that provided ministry to people affected by leprosy worldwide.

Activities: Works in co-operation with national governments and with other organizations to improve the quality of life of people affected by leprosy, by dealing with the detection, treatment, care, rehabilitation and reintegration of people affected by leprosy. This includes raising awareness of leprosy in all areas, removing stigma attached to the disease and reducing discrimination. The organization runs centres to provide suitable treatment and carries out surgery; engages in research into leprosy and its treatment; provides socio-economic assistance to patients in developing countries; and supports community-based rehabilitation and self-help initiatives.

Geographical Area of Activity: Leprosy-related projects in Africa, and South and South-East Asia. National support offices in Europe, South Africa, America, Canada, Australia and New Zealand.

Publications: *Ask Prayer Guide.*

Finance: Annual income £14,072,849, expenditure £13,938,006 (31 Dec. 2013).

Board of Trustees: Kenneth W. Martin (Chair.); Nalini Abraham (Vice-Chair.); Gordon Brown (Hon. Treas.).

Principal Staff: Gen. Dir and Sec. Geoffrey L. Warne.

Address: 80 Windmill Rd, Brentford TW8 0QH.

Telephone: (20) 8326-6767; **Fax:** (20) 8326-6777; **Internet:** www.leprosymission.org; **e-mail:** friends@tlmint.org.

Leukaemia and Lymphoma Research

Founded in 1960 as Leukaemia Research. Present name adopted in 2010.

Activities: Dedicated exclusively to researching blood cancers and disorders including leukaemia, Hodgkin's and other lymphomas, and myeloma. The foundation's doctors work in more than 50 research centres across the United Kingdom, seeking to improve diagnosis of blood disorders and treatments for patients, and to understand why and how cells become cancerous.

Geographical Area of Activity: United Kingdom.

Restrictions: Grants for research only.

Publications: Annual review; information for health professionals; patient information booklets; newsletters.

Finance: Annual income £21,656,000, expenditure £26,565,000 (31 March 2014).

Board of Trustees: Pelham Allen (Chair.); Jeremy Bird (Vice-Chair.); Peter Burrell (Hon. Treas.).

Principal Staff: Pres. Sir Ian Botham; Chief Exec. Cathy Gilman.

Address: 39–40 Eagle St, London WC1R 4TH.

Telephone: (20) 7405-0101; **Fax:** (20) 7405-3139; **Internet:** www.beatbloodcancers.org; leukaemialymphomaresearch.org.uk; **e-mail:** info@beatbloodcancers.org.

Leverhulme Trust

Founded in 1925 under the provisions of the will of the first Viscount Leverhulme to provide scholarships for research and education.

Activities: Grants are made to institutions and charitable organizations in the United Kingdom and abroad for specific research projects, for educational innovations and for Trust-approved schemes of academic interchange between the United Kingdom and other countries. A number of smaller individual awards of research fellowships and grants, emeritus fellowships and studentships for study abroad are made under annually publicized schemes. The Trust also provides grants to support artists' residencies. Grants to institutions are made by the Trust Board, meeting three times a year; awards to individuals are made annually on the recommendation of the Trust's Research Awards Advisory Committee.

Geographical Area of Activity: Mainly United Kingdom.

Restrictions: Does not give support in the areas of medicine or social policy. Grants for endowments, buildings, equipment or general funds are excluded.

Publications: Brochure; Guide for Applicants; Newsletter (3 a year); Annual Report; recently awarded and previously awarded grants; RAAC awards; major research fellowships; Philip Leverhulme Prize recipients.

Finance: Annual income £78,794,000, expenditure £84,864,000 (31 Dec. 2014).

Trust Board: Niall W. A. FitzGerald (Chair.).

Principal Staff: Dir Prof. Gordon Marshall.

Address: 1 Pemberton Row, London EC4A 3BG.

Telephone: (20) 7042-9888; **Fax:** (20) 7042-9889; **Internet:** www.leverhulme.ac.uk; **e-mail:** enquiries@leverhulme.ac.uk.

Joseph Levy Foundation

Founded in 1965 for general charitable purposes. Formerly known as the Joseph Levy Charitable Foundation.

Activities: Operates mainly in the areas of medicine, health, and children and young people.

Geographical Area of Activity: United Kingdom.

Restrictions: No grants are made to individuals.

Finance: Annual income £808,316, expenditure £339,419 (5 April 2014).

Principal Staff: Dir Sue Nyfield.

Address: 1 Bell St, London NW1 5BY.

Telephone: (20) 7616-1200; **Fax:** (20) 7616-1206; **Internet:** www.jlf.org.uk; **e-mail:** info@jlcf.org.uk.

Linbury Trust

Founded in 1973 for general charitable purposes. One of the Sainsbury Family Charitable Trusts, all of which share a common administration.

Activities: Operates in the fields of the arts, education including arts education, museums and heritage, the environment, social welfare, and medicine and health.

Geographical Area of Activity: International.

Restrictions: No grants are made directly to individuals.

Publications: Annual report; charity information.

Finance: Annual income £8,784,000, expenditure £8,724,000 (5 April 2014).

Principal Staff: Dirs Philip Lawford, Alan Bookbinder; Finance Dir Paul Spokes.

Address: c/o The Sainsbury Family Charitable Trusts, The Peak, 5 Wilton Rd, London SW1V 1AP.

Telephone: (20) 7410-0330; **Fax:** (20) 7410-0332; **Internet:** www.linburytrust.org.uk; **e-mail:** info@sfct.org.uk.

Lloyd Foundation

Founded in 1972 to enable children of British citizens whose families are living by necessity overseas to obtain a British education.

Activities: Awards grants to enable the children of British citizens whose families are living by necessity abroad to attend the nearest English-language school; when there is no alternative, the Foundation assists with boarding fees for children to study in the United Kingdom.

Geographical Area of Activity: Worldwide.

Publications: Annual Report.

Finance: Annual income £157,423, expenditure £128,629 (31 Aug. 2014).

Board of Trustees: Joan H. Caesar (Chair.), Hilary A. Dibble (Vice-Chair.).

Principal Staff: Sec. Margaret E. Keyte.

Address: 1 Churchill Cl., Breaston DE72 3UD.

Telephone: (1332) 873772; **e-mail:** keytelloyd@btinternet.com.

Lloyds Bank Foundation for England and Wales

Established in 1986 to alleviate community and social need. Formerly known as the Lloyds TSB Foundation for England and Wales.

Activities: Operates in England and Wales in the area of social welfare. The Foundation makes grants to registered charities that work in England and Wales in the area of social welfare, and supports organizations helping people, especially those who are disadvantaged, play a fuller role in their communities. Grants are available for local, regional and national projects through the Community Programme. Lloyds TSB Foundations also operate in Northern Ireland, Scotland and the Channel Islands.

Geographical Area of Activity: England and Wales.

Restrictions: See guidelines online.

Publications: Annual Review; guidelines; grants list.

Finance: Annual income £26,758,000, expenditure £24,071,000 (31 Dec. 2013).

Trustees: Prof. Sir Ian Diamond (Chair.).

Principal Staff: CEO Paul Streets; COO Andrew Clapham.

Address: Pentagon House, 52–54 Southwark St, London SE1 1UN.

Telephone: (870) 411-1223; **Fax:** (870) 411-1224; **Internet:** www.lloydsbankfoundation.org.uk; **e-mail:** enquiries@lloydsbankfoundation.org.uk.

Lullaby Trust

Founded in 1971 as the Foundation for the Study of Infant Deaths by Mrs J. Hunter-Gray to raise funds for research into sudden infant death syndrome (SIDS—cot death), to support bereaved families and to act as an information centre. Present name adopted in 2013.

Activities: Operates in England, Wales and Northern Ireland in the fields of medicine and health, and social welfare and studies, through self-conducted programmes, research, grants to institutions and individuals, conferences, training courses and publications. The Trust supports research programmes in various areas concerning the sudden and unexplained death of infants, including epidemiology, immunology, pathology, statistics and infection. Research grants relevant to SIDS are offered to researchers in the United Kingdom and elsewhere. The Trust also provides support to families whose babies have died suddenly and unexpectedly, and disseminates information about cot death and baby care among professionals and the public.

Geographical Area of Activity: England, Wales and Northern Ireland.

Publications: E-newsletters and numerous leaflets.

Finance: Annual income £1,461,396, expenditure £1,283,646 (30 June 2014).

Board of Trustees: Terry Hebden (Chair.).

Principal Staff: CEO Francine Bates.

Address: 11 Belgrave Rd, London SW1V 1RB.

Telephone: (20) 7802-3200; **Fax:** (20) 7802-3229; **Internet:** www.lullabytrust.org.uk; **e-mail:** office@lullabytrust.org.uk.

The Mackintosh Foundation

Founded in 1988 by Sir Cameron Mackintosh for general charitable purposes.

Activities: Operates in the fields of the arts and humanities (in particular the performing arts), education, and medicine and health. Provides funding through grants to institutions and individuals.

Geographical Area of Activity: United Kingdom and overseas.

Restrictions: No grants for individual, politics or religion.

Publications: Information sheet.

Finance: Annual income £56,157, expenditure £687,319 (31 March 2014).

Trustees: Cameron Mackintosh (Chair.).

Principal Staff: Appeals Dir Nicholas Mackintosh; Company Sec. Richard T. Knibb; Admin. Amanda Parker.

Address: 1 Bedford Sq., London WC1B 3RB.

Telephone: (20) 7637-8866; **Fax:** (20) 7436-2683; **Internet:** www.cameronmackintosh.com.

Macmillan Cancer Support

Founded in 1911 by Douglas Macmillan for the purpose of engaging in any activities that may lessen the suffering of cancer patients, including the protection and preservation of the health of their families and carers.

Activities: Operates training courses for doctors and nurses in the care of patients, particularly pain control; funds specialist Macmillan nurses and doctors; provides care in the home and, through special units, within hospitals; provides cash grants to patients in need, grants and scholarships for relevant study, and academic appointments; provides a telephone helpline; and funds certain charities in the United Kingdom that offer support and information to cancer sufferers.

Geographical Area of Activity: East Anglia, London, Northern Ireland, Northern England, South-East England, Scotland, Wales.

Restrictions: Activities are restricted to the United Kingdom and Ireland (where funds are provided for patient support only).

Publications: *Macmillan News* (quarterly); Annual Review; booklets; cancer publications; *Talking to children when an adult has cancer* (2004); *Macmillan spokespeople* (newsletter); *Resources and contacts for journalists* (newsletter); *Cancer Services and Campaigns* (newsletter); *Cancer Voice News* (newsletter).

Finance: Annual income £189,709,000, expenditure £181,074,000 (31 Dec. 2013).

Trustees: Julia Palca (Chair.); Victoria Benson (Sec.); Simon Heale (Treas.).

Principal Staff: Pres. The Countess of Halifax; Deputy Pres. Jamie Dundas; Chief Exec. Lynda Thomas.

Address: 89 Albert Embankment, London SE1 7UQ.

Telephone: (20) 7840-7840; **Fax:** (20) 7840-7841; **Internet:** www.macmillan.org.uk; **e-mail:** webmanager@macmillan.org.uk.

MAG—Mines Advisory Group

Founded in 1989 after Soviet troops left Afghanistan, to deal with the legacy of landmines and other unexploded ordnance.

Activities: An international humanitarian organization that has operated in more than 40 countries. The organization works in countries left with landmines and unexploded ordnance. It collects and analyses information on incidents; educates local communities about safe practices; provides training and employment to local people; clears unexploded ordnance and landmines; and aims to restore a healthy land.

Geographical Area of Activity: Worldwide, in particular Angola, Burundi, Cambodia, Chad, Colombia, the Democratic Republic of the Congo, the Republic of the Congo, Iraq, Laos, Lebanon, Pakistan, Rwanda, Somalia, Sri Lanka, Sudan and Viet Nam.

Publications: Country reports; Annual Report; grant list; news articles.

Finance: Annual income £33,907,726, expenditure £32,720,649 (30 June 2014).

Trustees: Lord Williams of Baglan (Chair.); Colin Rowe (Vice-Chair.); Paul Nielsen (Treas.).

Principal Staff: Chief Exec. Nick Roseveare.

Address: 68 Sackville St, Manchester M1 3NJ.

Telephone: (161) 2364311; **Fax:** (161) 2366244; **Internet:** www.maginternational.org; **e-mail:** info@maginternational.org.

Mayfair Charities Ltd

Founded in 1968 for the benefit of charitable organizations promoting orthodox Judaism.

Activities: Grants are made to charities nationally and internationally for educational and religious purposes in Israel, the United Kingdom and the USA.

Geographical Area of Activity: United Kingdom, Israel and the USA.

Finance: Annual income £4,389,000, expenditure £6,330,000 (31 March 2014).

Trustees: Benzion S. E. Freshwater (Chair.).

Principal Staff: Sec. Mark R. M. Jenner.

Address: Freshwater Group of Companies, Freshwater House, 158–162 Shaftesbury Ave, London WC2H 8HR.

Telephone: (20) 7836-1555; **Fax:** (20) 7379-6365.

Medical Foundation for the Care of Victims of Torture

Established in 1985 by Helen Bamber to provide medical and psychological care to victims of torture and their families, alongside practical support, welfare advice and forensic examination of injuries sustained under torture that can be used as documentary evidence in support of an individual's claim for refugee protection.

Activities: Aims to protect survivors and prevent torture through policy, advocacy and communications work. The Foundation operates in the United Kingdom, aiming to provide survivors of torture with medical treatment, practical assistance and psychotherapeutic support; document evidence of torture; provide training for health professionals working with torture survivors; educate the public and decision-makers about torture and its consequences; and ensure that the United Kingdom offers support to asylum seekers and refugees. Maintains centres in London, Manchester (North West), Glasgow (Scotland), Newcastle (North East) and Birmingham (West Midlands).

Geographical Area of Activity: United Kingdom.

Restrictions: Services are for the victims of torture and organized violence, including individuals and their families.

Publications: Annual Review; *Supporter* (e-newsletter); country reports; thematic reports.

Finance: Annual income £7,759,137, expenditure £7,693,391 (31 Dec. 2013).

Board of Trustees: Dr Frank Margison (Chair.); Gillian Fawcett (Treas.).

Principal Staff: CEO Susan Monroe.

Address: 111 Isledon Rd, Islington, London N7 7JW.

Telephone: (20) 7697-7777; **Fax:** (20) 7697-7799; **Internet:** www.freedomfromtorture.org; www.torturecare.org.uk; **e-mail:** info@freedomfromtorture.org.

MENCAP

Founded in 1946 to campaign for equal rights for people with learning difficulties.

Activities: Campaigns locally, nationally and in Europe to highlight learning disability issues; provides residential, education and employment services, leisure opportunities, and support and advice for those with learning disabilities and their families and carers. The organization's leisure division, Gateway, supports approx. 400 clubs and projects throughout the United Kingdom, which provide sport, music, dance and drama facilities. Runs a helpline to deal with issues relating to benefits, employment, housing and other issues. Has around 50,000 members.

Geographical Area of Activity: Mainly England, Northern Ireland and Wales.

Publications: *Viewpoint* (newspaper); campaign reports.

Finance: Annual income £201,195,000, expenditure £192,512,000 (31 March 2013).

Trustees: Derek Lewis (Chair.).

Principal Staff: Pres. Lord Rix; Chief Exec. Jan Tregelles.

Address: 123 Golden Lane, London EC1Y 0RT.

Telephone: (20) 7454-0454; **Fax:** (20) 7608-3254; **Internet:** www.mencap.org.uk; **e-mail:** info@mencap.org.uk.

Mental Health Foundation

Founded in 1949 to support research into learning disabilities and mental health problems. Incorporates the Foundation for People with Learning Disabilities.

Activities: Takes an integrated approach to mental health and mental illness. The Foundation bases its activity on the understanding that social or biological factors are crucial in understanding mental health. Work topics include: nutrition; exercise; alcohol; family situations; parenting; schools; acute services; early intervention; and cultural diversity. It aims to help the general public to understand and manage their own mental health. Carries out its own research, and generates new findings that inform its policy, service development and campaign work.

Geographical Area of Activity: United Kingdom.

Publications: *Fundamental facts: all the latest facts and figures on mental illness; Bright futures: promoting children and young people's mental health; Building expectations: opportunities and services for people with a learning disability*; information booklets; research and policy briefings.

Finance: Annual income £4,218,429, expenditure £4,268,821 (31 March 2014).

Trustees: Keith Leslie (Chair.); Prof. Dinesh Bhugra (Pres.).

Principal Staff: Chief Exec. Jenny Edwards.

Address: Colechurch House, 1 London Bridge Walk, London SE1 2SX.

Telephone: (20) 7803-1100; **Fax:** (20) 7803-1111; **Internet:** www.mentalhealth.org.uk; **e-mail:** mhf@mhf.org.uk.

Mentor Foundation

Established in 1994; works in the field of drug misuse prevention at a global level, with a focus on identifying and disseminating best practice in drug prevention methods. The founding members were HM Queen of Sweden, HRH Grand Duke Henri of Luxembourg, HM Queen Noor of Jordan, HRH Prince Talal Bin Abdul Aziz as-Saud, Bertil Hult, Stefan Persson, Nino Cerruti, Corinne Schuler-Voith, Princess Anni-Frid Reuss and Ivan Pictet.

Activities: Operates through the Mentor Prevention Academy, the Mentor Prevention Awards and field-based projects, aiming to help practitioners, policy-makers and those who care and have responsibility for children and young people to be more focused and effective in their drug prevention work, as well as to ensure young people are fully informed about the dangers of drugs and that they are better equipped to make responsible decisions. The Foundation supports drug prevention practitioners by identifying and sharing advice and information that will help them develop promising and effective practices in drug misuse prevention at a global level. It also initiates and runs its own projects and supports other field-based work aimed at preventing drug use. Most of the project work is undertaken with support from the Foundation's network of national centres, based in the Arab world, Belgium (in development), Colombia, Germany, Lithuania, Sweden, the United Kingdom and the USA.

Geographical Area of Activity: International.

Finance: Annual income £628,672, expenditure £621,23 (31 March 2014).

Board of Trustees: Sim Scavazza (Chair.).

Principal Staff: Chief Exec. Michael O'Toole.

Address: CAN-Mezzanine, 49–51 East Rd, London N1 6AH.

Telephone: (20) 7553-9920; **Internet:** www.mentoruk.org.uk; **e-mail:** admin@mentoruk.org.

Mercers' Charitable Foundation

Founded in 1983 by the Worshipful Company of Mercers (City of London) to make grants for charitable purposes according to English law.

Activities: Operates nationally in the fields of the arts, conservation, education, the advancement of religion, medicine and social welfare. The Foundation makes grants to education, heritage, arts, medical and social welfare projects. The co-administered Mercers' Educational Trust Fund provides grants to individuals for educational purposes, while welfare projects are funded by the Whittington Charity and the Earl of Northampton's Charity.

Geographical Area of Activity: United Kingdom.

Restrictions: No grants are made to individuals.

Finance: Annual income £7,813,000, expenditure £3,379,000 (31 March 2014).

Principal Staff: Clerk Menna McGregor; Head of Finance Trevor Sykes.

Address: Mercers' Hall, Ironmonger Lane, London EC2V 8HE.

Telephone: (20) 7726-4991; **Fax:** (20) 7600-1158; **Internet:** www.mercers.co.uk; **e-mail:** info@mercers.co.uk.

Mercury Phoenix Trust

Established in 1992 in memory of Freddie Mercury, principal singer of the pop group Queen, by the remaining members of the group and the group's manager to assist people with AIDS and HIV worldwide.

Activities: Operates worldwide in the areas of medicine and health, and social welfare, through making grants to relieve the poverty and distress of people with HIV and AIDS, and to increase awareness of AIDS. The Trust has funded projects in collaboration with the World Health Organization, and projects in various African countries, India and Nepal.

Geographical Area of Activity: International.

Finance: Annual income £761,035, expenditure £670,110 (31 March 2014).

Principal Staff: Admin. Peter Chant.

Address: The River Wing, Latimer Park, Latimer, Chesham HP5 1TU; POB 704, Chesham HP 1XF.

Telephone: (1494) 766799; **Internet:** www .mercuryphoenixtrust.com; **e-mail:** funding@ mercuryphoenixtrust.com.

MERLIN—Medical Emergency Relief International

Established in 1993 by Merlin Board Ltd to provide health care in areas in crisis around the world. Became part of Save the Children (q.v.) in 2013.

Activities: Operates mostly in Africa, South-East Asia and the countries of the former USSR in the areas of aid to less-developed countries, and medicine and health, through international programmes and projects, including projects in emergency medical relief, health education and infrastructure, and strategic development. Projects are currently active in Afghanistan, the Democratic Republic of the Congo, Ethiopia, Georgia, Iran, Iraq, Kenya, Liberia, Palestinian Territories, the Russian Federation, Sierra Leone and Tajikistan. MERLIN assists the World Health Organization (WHO) in implementing the Roll Back Malaria campaign, and promotes cost-effective treatment for tuberculosis, improved access to primary health care, and training for health professionals. A member of the Disasters Emergency Committee—DEC (q.v.).

Geographical Area of Activity: Africa, Middle East, South-East Asia and the countries of the former USSR.

Restrictions: Does not make grants.

Publications: Annual Report; *Response Newsletter*.

Finance: Annual income £62,303,583, expenditure £62,608,183 (31 Dec. 2013).

Principal Staff: Chief Exec. David Alexander; Sec. Chris Lane.

Address: 12th Floor, 207 Old St, London EC1V 9NR.

Telephone: (20) 7014-1600; **Fax:** (20) 7014-1601; **Internet:** www.merlin.org.uk; **e-mail:** hq@merlin.org.uk.

Minority Rights Group International

Established in 1981 to support the rights of ethnic, religious and linguistic minority groups worldwide.

Activities: Carries out research and publishes reports on minorities worldwide; lobbies the UN, international organizations and governments on behalf of the rights of minority groups; networks with similar organizations internationally; and educates on the rights of minority groups. Main programmes operate in Europe and Central Asia, Asia and the Pacific, and Africa and the Middle East. There are also specific programmes for Roma people and inter-regional programmes. Maintains a co-ordination office in Budapest, Hungary.

Geographical Area of Activity: International.

Publications: *Outsider* (newsletter); *World Directory of Minorities*; Annual Report; reports; training manuals; workshop reports.

Finance: Annual income £2,340,408, expenditure £2,400,776 (31 Dec. 2013).

Council: Gay J. McDougall (Chair.); Arjan Buteijn (Treas.).

Principal Staff: Exec. Dir and Sec. Mark Lattimer.

Address: 54 Commercial St, London E1 6LT.

Telephone: (20) 7422-4200; **Fax:** (20) 7422-4201; **Internet:** www.minorityrights.org; **e-mail:** minority.rights@mrgmail.org.

The Mission to Seafarers

The Mission was founded in 1856, under the name The Mission to Seamen Afloat, at Home and Abroad. It was renamed The Missions to Seamen in 1858. Present name adopted in 2000.

Activities: Works in more than 260 ports in 71 countries caring for seafarers of all ranks, nationalities and beliefs. Through its global network of chaplains, staff and volunteers the Mission offers practical, emotional and spiritual support to seafarers through ship visits, drop-in centres and a range of welfare and emergency support services.

Geographical Area of Activity: International.

Finance: Annual income £5,087,000, expenditure £5,636,000 (31 Dec. 2013).

Board of Trustees: Robert B. Woods (Chair.).

Principal Staff: Pres. HRH The Princess Royal; Sec.-Gen. Rev. Andrew Wright; Exec. Dir Martin Sandford.

Address: St Michael Paternoster Royal, College Hill, London EC4R 2RL.

Telephone: (20) 7248-5202; **Fax:** (20) 7248-4761; **Internet:** www.missiontoseafarers.org; **e-mail:** pressoffice@missiontoseafarers.org.

Monument Trust

Founded in 1965 for general charitable purposes. One of the Sainsbury Family Charitable Trusts, all of which share a common administration.

Activities: Operates nationally in the fields of the arts, the environment, health and community care, AIDS and social development.

Geographical Area of Activity: United Kingdom.

Restrictions: Unsolicited applications are unlikely to be successful. No grants are made directly to individuals.

Publications: Annual Report.

Finance: Annual income £4,440,372, expenditure £36,145,136 (5 April 2014).

Principal Staff: Dir Alan P. Bookbinder; Finance Dir Paul Spokes.

Address: c/o The Sainsbury Family Charitable Trusts, The Peak, 5 Wilton Rd, London SW1V 1AP.

Telephone: (20) 7410-0330; **Fax:** (20) 7410-0332; **Internet:** www.sfct.org.uk/monument.html; **e-mail:** sfct@sfct.org.uk.

The Henry Moore Foundation

Founded in 1977 by Henry Moore for the education of the public in the appreciation of the fine arts and the works of Henry Moore in particular.

Activities: Operates nationally and internationally through self-conducted programmes, and nationally through research, grants to institutions, scholarships, bursaries and fellowships, and publications.

Geographical Area of Activity: International.

Restrictions: No grants are made to individuals.

Publications: Bibliographies; catalogues; *Celebrating Moore*; books; *Henry Moore: Complete Sculpture*; essays on sculptors; The British Sculptors and Sculpture Series; *Henry Moore: War and Utility*; exhibition catalogues; Annual Report and financial statement.

Finance: Annual income £6,349,092, expenditure £5,828,556 (31 March 2014).

Trustees: Nigel Carrington (Chair.); David Wilson (Vice-Chair.).

Principal Staff: Dir Richard Calvocoressi.

Address: Dane Tree House, Perry Green, Much Hadham SG10 6EE.

Telephone: (1279) 843333; **Fax:** (1279) 843647; **Internet:** www.henry-moore.org; **e-mail:** info@henry-moore.org.

John Moores Foundation

Founded in 1964 to provide funding for general charitable purposes.

Activities: Awards grants to voluntary organizations in Northern Ireland and on Merseyside working in the following areas: local community groups, women's groups; ethnic minorities; advice on welfare rights; second chance learning; and community work. On Merseyside, the Foundation also awards grants to voluntary organizations providing grassroots social health initiatives, family support, services for carers, homeless people, refugees and young people.

Geographical Area of Activity: Northern Ireland and Merseyside, United Kingdom.

Restrictions: No grants to individuals; grants to organizations only awarded on Merseyside and in Northern Ireland.

Finance: Annual income £818,672, expenditure £1,015,483 (5 April 2014).

Principal Staff: Grants Dir Phil Godfrey.

Address: 7th Floor, Gostins Bldg, 32–36 Hanover St, Liverpool L1 4LN.

Telephone: (151) 707-6077; **Fax:** (151) 707-6066; **Internet:** www.jmf.org.uk; **e-mail:** info@johnmooresfoundation.com.

Multiple Sclerosis Society of Great Britain and Northern Ireland

Founded in 1953 by Sir Richard Cave to promote research into the cause and cure of multiple sclerosis (MS), and to provide a welfare and support service for people with MS and their friends, families and carers.

Activities: Conducts and supports research within the United Kingdom. The Society also holds international conferences, disseminates information and runs a national helpline for people affected by MS.

Geographical Area of Activity: United Kingdom.

Restrictions: Unable to fund research grant applications where the principal investigator is based outside the United Kingdom. However, collaborative applications (with United Kingdom-based research groups) are encouraged and, where there is genuine participation of research groups outside the United Kingdom, welcomed.

Publications: *MS Matters* (member magazine, 6 a year); Annual Report; information booklets.

Finance: Annual income £24,093,000, expenditure £28,016,000 (31 Dec. 2013).

Board of Trustees: Hilary Sears (Chair.); John Litchfield (Vice-Chair.); Paul Cooper (Treas.).

Principal Staff: Chief Exec. Michelle Mitchell.

Address: MS National Centre, 372 Edgware Rd, London NW2 6ND.

Telephone: (20) 8438-0700; **Fax:** (20) 8438-0701; **Internet:** www.mssociety.org.uk; **e-mail:** info@mssociety.org.uk.

Gilbert Murray Trust

Founded in 1956 to promote the study of ancient Greek literature and thought, and the propagation of Hellenic culture; and to promote, with the help of travelling fellowships, scholarships, grants or other means, the study of the purpose and work of the United Nations.

Activities: Operates internationally in the fields of international relations and Hellenic culture, through grants to institutions and organizations, and to individuals. The Trust has two committees: the Classical Committee, which awards annual grants for travel to Greece and for activities such as summer schools; and the International Committee, which offers awards of up to £500 to students aged under 25 years, who are or have been students at a university or similar institution in the United Kingdom to travel abroad to study international affairs.

Geographical Area of Activity: International.

Publications: Annual Report.

Finance: Annual income £16,023, expenditure £10,467 (5 April 2014).

Trustees: Prof. Edith Hall (Chair.); Prof. Mike Edwards (Hon. Sec.); Peter Wilson (Hon. Treas.).

Address: The Hon. Secretary of the Gilbert Murray Trust, Prof. Mike Edwards, Dept of Humanities, University of Roehampton, Digby Stuart College, Roehampton Lane, London SW15 5PH.

Telephone: (20) 8392-5143; **Internet:** www .gilbertmurraytrust.org.uk; **e-mail:** mike.edwards@ roehampton.ac.uk.

Muscular Dystrophy UK

Founded in 1959 as the Muscular Dystrophy Group of Great Britain and Northern Ireland to fund medical research into muscular dystrophy and allied diseases, and to offer support to those affected and to their families. Present name adopted in 1999 to reflect its active role in lobbying and campaigning. Formerly known as the Muscular Dystrophy Campaign.

Activities: Finances research by means of grants to individuals and United Kingdom institutions, and organizes conferences. The organization is a member of the Founding Board of the European Neuromuscular Centre, and collaborates with and promotes the exchange of information between similar associations in other countries. Provides a range of information to people living with muscular dystrophy and related muscle diseases.

Geographical Area of Activity: United Kingdom.

Publications: *Target MD* (quarterly magazine); fact sheets and other publications.

Finance: Annual income £6,660,000, expenditure £4,937,000 (31 March 2014).

Trustees: Bill Ronald (Chair.).

Principal Staff: Pres. Sue Barker; Chief Exec. Robert Meadowcroft.

Address: 61A Great Suffolk St, London SE1 0BU.

Telephone: (20) 7803-4800; **Fax:** (20) 7401-3495; **Internet:** www.muscular-dystrophy.org; **e-mail:** info@ musculardystrophyuk.org.

Muslim Aid

Established in 1985 to alleviate poverty.

Activities: Distributes grants through partner organizations in the fields of emergency relief, health care, education, water conservation, skills training, orphan care and shelter.

Geographical Area of Activity: Africa, Asia, Europe, South America, Middle East.

Restrictions: Aid distributed through partner and local community organizations only.

Publications: Annual Review.

Finance: Annual income £26,683,444, expenditure £26,567,699 (31 Dec. 2013).

Board of Trustees: Dr Manazir Ahsan (Chair.); Dr Suhaib Hasan (Vice-Chair.); Dr Muhammad Bari (Sec.); Saleem Asghar Kidwai (Treas.).

Principal Staff: CEO Hamid Azad.

Address: POB 3, London E1 1WP; LMC Business Wing, 1st Floor, 38–44 Whitechapel Rd, Tower Hamlets, London E1 1JX.

Telephone: (20) 7377-4200; **Fax:** (20) 7377-4201; **Internet:** www.muslimaid.org; **e-mail:** mail@muslimaid.org.

National Foundation for Educational Research–NFER

Founded in 1946 as an independent education and children's services research body.

Activities: Gathers, analyses and disseminates research-based information to improve children's services, education and training. The Foundation undertakes research on behalf of government, local authorities, professional associations and external clients in all areas of children's services and education, from pre-school and primary to further and higher education. It provides evaluation services on the impact of various education and training programmes at local and national levels; and develops and researches tests of all types, including those for the National Curriculum. Maintains a full range of support services, including library, national and international information services, in-house publishing unit, computing and statistics, and survey administration. Also works internationally in co-operation with overseas partner organizations.

Geographical Area of Activity: International.

Publications: Research findings; *NFER News* (newsletter, 2 a year); practical research for education; *nferdirect* (monthly updates); CERUK Plus database; international education current awareness bulletin.

Finance: Annual income £11,309,000, expenditure £11,213,000 (31 March 2014).

Trustees: Richard Bunker (Chair.); Jon Harris (Vice-Chair.); Neal Hollister (Hon. Treas.).

Principal Staff: CEO Carole Willis.

Address: The Mere, Upton Park, Slough SL1 2DQ.

Telephone: (1753) 574123; **Fax:** (1753) 691632; **Internet:** www .nfer.ac.uk; **e-mail:** enquiries@nfer.ac.uk.

The National Trust for Places of Historic Interest or Natural Beauty

Founded in 1895 to support the preservation of historic buildings or sites of natural beauty in England, Wales and Northern Ireland.

Activities: Maintains historically or architecturally important buildings, as well as parks, gardens, coast and countryside to which it may provide public access; also conducts educational programmes. The Trust has more than 3.9m. members.

Geographical Area of Activity: England, Wales and Northern Ireland.

Restrictions: Does not normally make grants.

Publications: Annual Reports; magazine (3 a year); *National Trust Handbook for Members and Visitors* (annually); *Information for Visitors with Disabilities* (annually); more than 70 further publications promoting the work of the Trust.

Finance: Annual income £460,298,000, expenditure £467,937,000 (28 Feb. 2014).

Board of Trustees: Tim Parker (Chair.); Orna NiChonna (Deputy Chair.).

Principal Staff: Pres. HRH Prince Charles; Dir-Gen. Dame Helen Ghosh.

Address: Kemble Dr., Swindon SW2 2NA.

Telephone: (1793) 817400; **Fax:** (1793) 817401; **Internet:** www.nationaltrust.org.uk; **e-mail:** enquiries@nationaltrust.org.uk.

Airey Neave Trust

Founded in 1979, in memory of Airey Neave, by Sir John Tilney, and the late Baroness Airey of Abingdon and Lord McAlpine of Moffat, for the furtherance of research into personal freedom under the law, and for financial help for the educational needs of refugees.

Activities: Funds research projects into all aspects of individual freedom under the law, of which approximately half are related to terrorism. Gives direct help to refugees by contributing towards their postgraduate fees so that they can qualify or requalify in their trades or professions.

Geographical Area of Activity: United Kingdom.

Restrictions: Grants to individuals are made to refugees and to Fellows attached to law faculties only.

Publications: *Children Enslaved*; *The Victims of Terrorism*; *The International Covenant on Civil and Political Rights and the UK*; *Study of the Operation and Impact of the Council of Europe Committee for the Prevention of Torture*; *Political Violence and Commercial Victims*; *The Position of Refugees in British and European Law and Practice*; *Terrorist Use of Weapons of Mass Destruction*; *Walking Away from Terrorism*.

Finance: Annual income £26,145, expenditure £60,638 (31 March 2014).

Trustees: John Giffard (Chair.); Hugh Tilney (Vice-Chair.); Howard Dawson (Hon. Treas.).

Principal Staff: Pres. Baron Bew of Donegore.

Address: POB 111, Leominster HR6 6BP.

Internet: www.aireyneavetrust.org.uk; **e-mail:** aireyneavetrust@gmail.com.

NESTA—National Endowment for Science, Technology and the Arts

Established in 1998 as a national endowment under the National Lottery Act 1998.

Activities: Aims to be the strongest single catalyst for innovation in the United Kingdom, seeking to increase the country's capacity to fulfil its vast innovative potential. Through a blend of early-stage investment, practical programmes and policy and research, the Endowment aims to show how innovation can help solve some of the major economic and social challenges facing the United Kingdom.

Geographical Area of Activity: United Kingdom.

Restrictions: Restricted to the United Kingdom only.

Publications: Annual Report; research papers; policy briefings.

Finance: Annual income £15,974,000, expenditure £28,528,000 (31 March 2014).

Board of Trustees: Sir John Chisholm (Chair.).

Principal Staff: CEO Geoff Mulgan; Gen. Counsel and Sec. Clare Goodman.

Address: 1 Plough Pl., London EC4A 1DE.

Telephone: (20) 7438-2500; **Fax:** (20) 7438-2501; **Internet:** www.nesta.org.uk; **e-mail:** information@nesta.org.uk.

Network for Social Change

Founded in 1986 as Network Foundation, for general charitable purposes.

Activities: Seeks out projects to fund rather than responding to applications from charities or individuals; unsolicited applications are not accepted; operates nationally and internationally.

Geographical Area of Activity: United Kingdom and international.

Finance: Annual income £1,255,355, expenditure £1,322,181 (31 Aug. 2014).

Principal Staff: Admin. Tish McCrory.

Address: BM Box 2063, London WC1N 3XX; Vantage Point, Woodwater Park, Pynes Hill, Exeter EX2 5FD.

Telephone: (1647) 61106; **Internet:** thenetworkforsocialchange.org.uk; **e-mail:** thenetwork@gn.apc.org.

New Economics Foundation—NEF

Established in 1984 as a think tank aiming to develop practical and enterprising solutions to the social, environmental and economic challenges facing the local, regional, national and global economies.

Activities: Carries out research and policy work, which principally focus on well-being, the environment, finance and banking, local economic renewal, impact measurement, public service reform, macroeconomics and training in economics. The Foundation is involved in the development of alternative currency schemes, as well as community time banks, and introducing benchmark surveys on ethical consumption and corporate performance.

Geographical Area of Activity: United Kingdom.

Publications: *Ghost Town Britain*; *Real World Economic Outlook*; *Profiting from Poverty*; *Radical Economics*; *Are You Happy? New economics past, present and future*; *Hooked on Oil: Breaking the habit with a windfall tax*; *A Long Row to Hoe: Family farming and rural poverty in developing countries*; *Aspects of Co-production: The implications for work, health and volunteering*; *Migration and the Remittance Euphoria: Development or dependency?*; *Odious Lending: Debt relief as if morals mattered*.

Finance: Annual income £3,556,076 expenditure £3,351,832 (30 June 2014).

Board of Trustees: Tess Gill (Chair.); Martin Gillie (Treas.).

Principal Staff: Exec. Dir Stewart Wallis.

Address: 10 Salamanca Pl., London SE1 7HB.

Telephone: (20) 7820-6300; **Fax:** (20) 7820-6301; **Internet:** www.neweconomics.org; **e-mail:** info@neweconomics.org.

Northern Rock Foundation

Established in 1997 by the former Northern Rock Building Society to support disadvantaged people in the North-East of England and Cumbria.

Activities: Operates in the North-East of England and Cumbria to combat disadvantage and to improve quality of life, through making grants under five programmes: Changing Lives (personalized support for disadvantaged young people, substance misusers, and people facing prejudice and discrimination); Enabling Independence and Choice (services for older people, learning-disabled people, people with mental health problems, and carers); Safety and Justice for Victims of Abuse (tackling domestic abuse, sexual violence and exploitation, child abuse and hate crimes); Managing Money (helps people who are in debt or have other financial problems); and Having a Home (helps vulnerable people who are homeless or in danger of becoming homeless). Although Northern Rock was taken into temporary public ownership in 2008, it was announced by the Treasury that the company would provide the Foundation with a minimum of £15m. a year during 2008–10, and that the Board of the bank would consider the Foundation's longer-term future.

Geographical Area of Activity: North-East of England and Cumbria.

Restrictions: Only supports projects in the North-East of England (Northumberland, Tyne and Wear, County Durham and the Tees Valley) and Cumbria, and organizations whose purposes are recognized as charitable in law.

Publications: *Rock Reports* (newsletter); *Think* (research series); *Insight* (learning from grants made); Annual Report; media guide.

Finance: Annual income £493,000, expenditure £9,652,000 (31 Dec. 2013).

Trustees: Alastair Balls (Chair.).

Principal Staff: Chief Exec. Penny Wilkinson.

Address: The Old Chapel, Woodbine Rd, Gosforth, Newcastle upon Tyne NE3 1DD.

Telephone: (191) 284-8412; **Fax:** (191) 284-8413; **Internet:** www.nr-foundation.org.uk; **e-mail:** generaloffice@nr -foundation.org.uk.

NSPCC—National Society for the Prevention of Cruelty to Children

The London Society of Prevention of Cruelty to Children was founded in 1884 by the Reverend Benjamin Waugh. Changed its name to the National Society of Prevention of Cruelty to Children in 1889.

Activities: Runs a national Helpline, which offers advice and support to anyone concerned about the welfare of a child, and ChildLine, a free helpline for children and young people in the United Kingdom. The Society also provides local services throughout the United Kingdom to help children and families recover from their experiences.

Geographical Area of Activity: United Kingdom.

Publications: Annual Report; Annual Review; parenting and information leaflets; and numerous other specialist publications.

Finance: Annual income £125,877,000, expenditure £124,528,000 (31 March 2014).

Board of Trustees: Mark Wood (Chair.); Locksley Ryan, Ann Morrison, Sir David Normington (Vice-Chairmen); Jonathan Bloomer (Hon. Treas.).

Principal Staff: CEO Peter Wanless.

Address: Weston House, 42 Curtain Rd, London EC2A 3NH.

Telephone: (20) 7825-2500; **Fax:** (20) 7825-2525; **Internet:** www.nspcc.org.uk; **e-mail:** info@nspcc.org.uk.

Nuffield Foundation

Founded in 1943 by Lord Nuffield for the advancement of social well-being, particularly through scientific research. The Commonwealth Relations Trust (f. 1937) is now formally part of the Foundation.

Activities: Grants are awarded through institutions in the United Kingdom. Major grants are for experimental or development projects in education or social welfare; small grants and fellowships in science and social science are also offered under research grant schemes, which are open to members of universities and other research institutions in the United Kingdom. The Foundation also sponsors the Africa Programme (formerly run by the Commonwealth Relations Trust).

Geographical Area of Activity: United Kingdom and countries of Eastern and Southern Africa.

Restrictions: No grants to individuals for financial assistance.

Publications: Annual Report; various publications produced by the Foundation, the Council on Bioethics and the Curriculum Programme.

Finance: Annual revenue £17,232,000, expenditure £30,875,000 (31 Dec. 2013).

Trustees: Prof. David Rhind (Chair.).

Principal Staff: Dir Sharon Witherspoon.

Address: 28 Bedford Sq., London WC1B 3JS.

Telephone: (20) 7631-0566; **Fax:** (20) 7323-4877; **Internet:** www.nuffieldfoundation.org; **e-mail:** info@ nuffieldfoundation.org.

The Officers' Association

Founded in 1919 by Admiral of the Fleet Earl Beatty, Field Marshal Earl Haig and Air Marshal Sir Hugh Trenchard for the relief of financial distress among male or female former officers of HM Naval, Military or Air Forces, their widows and dependants.

Activities: Operates in the United Kingdom and abroad in the field of social welfare, through grants to individuals. The Assocation provides advice on finding accommodation in homes for the elderly; and its Employment Department helps officers leaving the Services and former officers to find employment in 'civilian life'.

Geographical Area of Activity: International.

Publications: Report of operations and financial statement.

Finance: Annual income £3,038,000, expenditure £3,581,000 (30 Sept. 2014).

Exec. Committee: Dominic Fisher (Chair. and Hon. Treas.).

Principal Staff: CEO Lee Holloway.

Address: Mountbarrow House, First Floor, 6–20 Elizabeth St, London SW1W 9RB.

Telephone: (20) 7808-4160; **Internet:** www .officersassociation.org.uk; **e-mail:** info@officersassociation .org.uk.

OneWorld International Foundation

Founded in 1999 to promote sustainable use of resources and the protection of human rights and democratic structures, through operating as an online media gateway without regard to geographic or linguistic barriers.

Activities: Operates a network of 11 OneWorld Centres (in Austria, Canada, Costa Rica, Finland, India, Italy, the Netherlands, Spain, the United Kingdom, the USA and Zambia) dedicated to the promotion of human rights and sustainable development. OneWorld International Ltd, a not-for-profit company, carries out the day-to-day support and co-ordination of the network; the company also undertakes production contracts for like-minded organizations.

Geographical Area of Activity: Austria, Central and South America, Finland, India, Italy, the Netherlands, Spain, the USA and Zambia.

Publications: Annual Report; archive.

Finance: Annual income £200,434, expenditure £199,210 (31 March 2014).

Trustees: Rosemary O'Mahony (Chair.).

Principal Staff: Exec. Mike Yates.

Address: CAN Mezzanine, 32–36 Loman St, London SE1 0EH.

Telephone: (20) 7922-7844; **Fax:** (20) 7922-7706; **Internet:** www.oneworldgroup.org; **e-mail:** hello@oneworld.org.

Open Society Foundation—London

An independent charity; part of the Soros foundations network.

Activities: Manages Soros initiative programmes, including Central Eurasia Project, Early Childhood Programme, Open Society Initiative for Eastern Africa, and scholarship, education and information programmes in collaboration with other Soros foundations and organizations in the United Kingdom.

Geographical Area of Activity: International.

Finance: Annual income £14,347,074, expenditure £14,633,295 (31 Dec. 2013).

Trustees: Martin Graf Saurma-Jeltsch (Sec.).

Principal Staff: Dir Darius Cuplinskas.

Address: 7th Floor, Millbank Tower, 21–24 Millbank, London SW1P 4QP.

Telephone: (20) 7031-0200; **Fax:** (20) 7031-0201; **Internet:** www.soros.org/about/locations/london.

Opportunity International UK

Founded in 1992 as Opportunity Trust to empower people and communities in developing countries, and to overcome poverty and secure sustainable improvement in the quality of life in these countries.

Activities: Operates in the fields of aid to less-developed countries, economic affairs and education, through self-conducted programmes, research, grants to institutions and publications. The organization works through 40 partner organizations in 27 countries, providing small business loans to those without access to the formal banking sector.

Geographical Area of Activity: Africa, Asia, Eastern Europe, and Central and South America.

Restrictions: Grants only to Opportunity International implementing partner organizations.

Publications: Annual Report; *Impact* (newsletter).

Finance: Annual income £5,003,935, expenditure £2,835,988 (31 Dec 2013).

Board of Trustees: Terry Watson (Chair.); Adrian Hill (Treas.).

Principal Staff: CEO Edward Fox.

Address: Angel Ct, 81 St Clements St, Oxford OX4 1AW.

Telephone: (1865) 725304; **Fax:** (1865) 295161; **Internet:** www.opportunity.org.uk; **e-mail:** impact@opportunity.org.uk.

Our Spaces—Foundation for the Good Governance of International Spaces (International Spaces—Foundation for the Good Governance of International Spaces)

Founded in 2009 to focus on the nearly 70% of the Earth's surface that lies outside national boundaries and thus outside national laws and governance, called international spaces.

Activities: Aims to stimulate discussion between disciplines and nationalities to further environmental protection or improvement. The Foundation educates and raises awareness; and promotes research (the results of which will be publicly available) on the governance of international spaces. In 2010, it initiated Antarctica Day on 1 December to celebrate the signing of the Antarctic Treaty on 1 December 1959.

Geographical Area of Activity: Worldwide, with particular emphasis on polar regions.

Finance: Annual revenue £721, expenditure £1,171 (31 Dec. 2013).

Board: Prof. Paul A. Berkman (Chair.).

Principal Staff: Man. Dir Dr Julie A. Hambrook Berkman.

Address: 20 Chishill Rd, Heydon, Herts SG8 8PW.

Internet: www.internationalspaces.org; **e-mail:** director@internationalspaces.org.

Overseas Development Institute—ODI

Founded in 1960 as an independent non-governmental centre for development research and a forum for discussion of the problems facing developing countries.

Activities: Operates nationally and internationally in the fields of economic affairs, development policy and social studies, through research, publications and the ODI Fellowship Scheme. The Institute's main research and policy programmes are: Agricultural Development; Centre for Aid and Public Expenditure; Climate & Environment; Growth, Poverty & Inequality; Humanitarian Policy; International Economic Development; Politics & Governance; Private Sector & Markets; Research and Policy in Development; Social Development; Social Protection; and Water & Sanitation. It manages international networks of practitioners, policy-makers and researchers, including the Humanitarian Practice Network and Evidence-based Policy in Development Network. It also hosts the Secretariat of the Active Learning Network for Accountability and Performance in Humanitarian Action. The Institute undertakes policy-related research and evaluations, provides advisory services and stages public events.

Geographical Area of Activity: International.

Publications: *Reports; Briefing Papers; Development Policy Review* (quarterly)*; Disasters* (quarterly)*; Natural Resources Perspectives; Annual Report; Working Papers; Network Publications*; *Humanitarian Publications*; practical toolkits; journals.

Finance: Annual income £28,541,000, expenditure £26,692,000 (31 March 2014).

Board: James Cameron (Chair.); Moira Malcolm (Sec.).

Principal Staff: Exec. Dir Kevin Watkins.

Address: 203 Blackfriars Rd, London, SE1 8NJ.

Telephone: (20) 7922-0300; **Fax:** (20) 7922-0399; **Internet:** www.odi.org.uk; **e-mail:** odi@odi.org.uk.

Oxfam GB

Founded in 1942, as the Oxford Committee for Famine Relief, to relieve poverty, distress and suffering in any part of the world. Part of the Oxfam confederation of 17 organizations (qq.v.).

Activities: Supports poor people, regardless of race or religion, in their struggle against hunger, disease, exploitation and poverty worldwide, particularly by tackling the impacts of climate change. The organization provides relief in emergencies, especially through the fast provision of clean drinking water and sanitation facilities; works with local partners on sustainable development programmes that empower people to work their way out of poverty; and campaigns and runs educational programmes to raise public awareness and tackle the underlying practices that create and sustain poverty.

Geographical Area of Activity: International.

Publications: Annual Report and accounts; *Inside Oxfam* (quarterly); general and technical publications; business papers; educational and audio-visual materials.

Finance: Annual income £389.1m., expenditure £365.1m. (31 March 2013).

Trustees: Karen Brown (Chair.); James Darcy (Vice-Chair.); David Pitt-Watson (Hon. Treas.).

Principal Staff: Dir Mark Goldring.

Address: Oxfam House, John Smith Dr., Cowley, Oxford OX4 2JY.

Telephone: 0300 200 1292; (1865) 473727; **Internet:** www.oxfam.org.uk; **e-mail:** enquiries@oxfam.org.uk.

Oxfam International

Established in 1942 as The Oxford Committee of Famine Relief to provide relief for women and children in occupied Greece. Now an international confederation of 17 organizations, its international secretariat was established in 1995.

Activities: Works to find practical, innovative ways for people to lift themselves out of poverty and thrive. The organization provides assistance during and after crises, and campaigns against injustice on behalf of the poor. Has campaigning offices in Geneva, Brussels, New York and Washington, D.C., and a liaison with the African Union office in Addis Ababa.

Geographical Area of Activity: International.

Restrictions: Affiliate organizations make grants.

Publications: Annual Report; *Strategic Plan 2013–2019: The power of people against poverty*; policy papers and reports.

Finance: Annual income €947.1m., expenditure €915.0m. (31 March 2014).

Inetrnational Secretariat: Juan Alberto Fuentes (Chair.); Chi Kin Lo (Deputy Chair.); Joris Voorhoeve (Interim Treas.).

Principal Staff: Exec. Dir Winnie Byanyima.

Address: Suite 20, 266 Banbury Rd, Oxford, OX2 7DL; 2nd Floor, 228–240 Banbury Rd, Oxford OX2 7BY.

Telephone: (1865) 339100; **Fax:** (1865) 339101; **Internet:** www.oxfam.org; **e-mail:** information@oxfaminternational.org.

Peace Brigades International—PBI

Founded in 1981 to promote non-violence and protect human rights.

Activities: Works at local, regional and international levels to protect human rights defenders and communities whose lives and work are threatened by political violence. An international political support network reinforces physical accompaniment by trained international volunteers to deter attacks against human rights defenders. The organization has programmes in Guatemala, Mexico, Colombia, Indonesia and Nepal and country groups in Argentina, Australia, Belgium, Canada, France, Germany, Italy, Luxembourg, the

Netherlands, Norway, Portugal, Spain, Sweden, Switzerland and the USA.

Geographical Area of Activity: Worldwide.

Restrictions: No funding is given to groups or individuals.

Publications: Annual Review; *Special report: breaking cycles of repression, ending impunity;* project publications.

Finance: Annual income £401,779, expenditure £339,452 (31 Dec. 2013).

International Council: Dana Brown (Pres.); John Carlarne (Vice-Pres.); Michael Bluett (Sec.); Ellen Kaas (Treas.).

Principal Staff: International Co-ordinator Laura Clarke.

Address: PBI International Office, Development House, 56–64 Leonard St, London EC2A 4LT.

Telephone: (20) 7065-0775; **Fax:** (20) 7065-0779; **Internet:** www.peacebrigades.org; **e-mail:** admin@peacebrigades.org .uk.

Penal Reform International—PRI

Founded in 1989.

Activities: Develops and promotes international standards for the administration of justice; reduces the unnecessary use of imprisonment; and promotes the use of alternative sanctions that encourage reintegration while taking into account the interests of victims. The organization has programmes in Africa, the Middle East and the former USSR, and offices in Georgia, Jordan, Kazakhstan, the Russian Federation, Rwanda and the United Kingdom. It has consultative status at the UN Economic and Social Council (ECOSOC) and the Council of Europe, and observer status with the African Commission on Human and Peoples' Rights.

Geographical Area of Activity: Worldwide.

Finance: Annual income £4,619,670, expenditure £4,261,736 (31 Dec. 2013).

Executive Board: David Daubney (Chair.); Prof. Dirk van Zyl Smit (Deputy Chair.); Juliet Lyon (Sec.-Gen.); Olawale Fapohunda (Deputy Sec.-Gen.); Prof. Anton Van Kalmthout (Treas.).

Principal Staff: Exec. Dir Alison Hannah.

Address: 60–62 Commercial St, London E1 6LT.

Telephone: (20) 7247-6515; **Fax:** (20) 7377-8711; **Internet:** www.penalreform.org; **e-mail:** info@penalreform.org.

Pesticide Action Network UK—PAN UK

Founded in 1987, as part of PAN International, to promote healthy food, sustainable agriculture and a safe environment without using hazardous pesticides.

Activities: Supports projects with partner organizations in developing countries; researches related issues; engages with retailers and producers on supply chain issues; and undertakes policy advocacy. The Network provides information through publishing briefings, books and journals.

Geographical Area of Activity: International.

Restrictions: Not a grantmaking organization.

Publications: *Pesticides News*; *Current Research Monitor*; Annual Report.

Finance: Annual income £455,813, expenditure £437,532 (31 Dec. 2013).

Board of Directors: Jeanette Longfield (Chair.); Natasha Clayton (Treas.).

Principal Staff: Dir Keith Tyrell.

Address: The Brighthelm Centre, North Rd, Brighton BN1 1YD.

Telephone: (1273) 964230; **Internet:** www.pan-uk.org; **e-mail:** admin@pan-uk.org.

PHG Foundation

Established in 2007; an independent not-for-profit public health organization.

Activities: Works in the field of science and biomedical innovation to improve health, especially genome-based science and technologies. The Foundation carries out research in the areas of biomedical science.

Geographical Area of Activity: England and Wales.

Finance: Annual income £1,088,658, expenditure £1,061,237 (31 March 2014).

Board of Trustees: Dr Ron Zimmern (Chair.).

Principal Staff: Dir Dr Hilary Burton.

Address: 2 Worts Causeway, Cambridge CB1 8RN.

Telephone: (1223) 761-900; **Fax:** (1223) 740-892; **Internet:** www.phgfoundation.org.

Pilgrim Trust

Founded in 1930 by Edward Stephen Harkness for such charitable purposes within Great Britain and Northern Ireland as the trustees may from time to time determine.

Activities: Operates nationally in the fields of: Art and Learning, through funding scholarships, academic research, cataloguing and conservation within museums, galleries, libraries and archives; Preservation, in particular architectural or historical features on historic buildings or the conservation of individual monuments or structures that are of importance to the surrounding environment; Records, encompassing the cataloguing and conservation of records associated with archaeology, marine archaeology, historic buildings and designed landscapes; and Places of Worship, through annual block grants for the repair of the fabric of historic churches of any denomination to the Historic Churches Preservation Trust for churches in England and Wales and to the Scottish Churches Architectural Heritage Trust.

Geographical Area of Activity: United Kingdom.

Restrictions: No grants to individuals or organizations outside the United Kingdom.

Publications: Annual Report and financial statement; guidelines.

Finance: Annual income £1,886,604, expenditure £2,605,586 (31 Dec. 2013).

Trustees: Sir Mark Jones (Chair.).

Principal Staff: Dir Georgina Nayler.

Address: 55A Catherine Pl., London SW1E 6DY.

Telephone: (20) 7834-6510; **Internet:** www.thepilgrimtrust .org.uk; **e-mail:** info@thepilgrimtrust.org.uk.

PLAN International—PI

Established in 1937 by John Langdon-Davies and Eric Muggeridge.

Activities: Creates child-focused development programmes to aid communities worldwide. The organization operates internationally in less-developed countries, through child sponsorship to assist in community development. It has programmes in five priority areas: health, education, habitat, livelihood and building relationships. Health programmes include: safe motherhood and child survival, early childhood care and development, reproductive health and HIV/AIDS; education programmes include: access to quality education, out of school education, and adult literacy and vocational skills; habitat programmes include: land and housing tenure, sanitation, and managing natural resources; livelihood programmes include: improved agricultural production, credit and financial services, and vocational training; and building relationships programmes aim to ensure that children and their communities play a leading part in all development projects, and promote the relationships between sponsors and their sponsored children. Sister organizations operate in 15 other countries.

Geographical Area of Activity: Worldwide.

Publications: Annual Report; *Count me in!*; *Tradition and Rights: Female genital cutting in West Africa*; *Plan's Global AIDS Framework*; *1-year on from the tsunami: the children's* *stories*; *Water and environmental sanitation*; *Improving schools*; *Gender Equality Report*; *Violence against teenagers*.

Finance: Annual income £63,170,000, expenditure £63,479,000 (31 Dec. 2014).

International Board of Directors: Joshua Liswood (Chair.); Gunvor Kronman (Vice-Chair.); Werner Bauch (Treas.).

Principal Staff: CEO Nigel Chapman.

Address: Dukes Court, Block A, Duke St, Woking, Surrey GU21 5BH.

Telephone: (1483) 755155; **Fax:** (1483) 756505; **Internet:** www.plan-international.org; **e-mail:** info@plan-international.org.

Plunkett Foundation

Founded in 1919 by Sir Horace Curzon Plunkett to promote and disseminate information regarding the principles of co-operative business systems.

Activities: Undertakes training courses, consultancy projects and research studies on co-operative development and management in the United Kingdom and in developing countries. The Foundation helps rural communities to establish and run enterprises that provide essential services. It conducts study programmes for organizations and individuals; and maintains a library of more than 20,000 books, pamphlets, reports and periodicals on co-operation worldwide, with plans to make the collection available online. The Foundation's international work is supported by partners and agencies including the British Overseas Development Agency and British Government's Know-How Fund, the European Commission, World Bank and UN.

Geographical Area of Activity: International, mainly the United Kingdom.

Publications: Annual Report; *The Journal of Co-operative Studies*; *Directory and Statistics of Agricultural Co-operatives and Farmer Controlled Businesses in the UK*; *Rural Connections* (quarterly newsletter); *Plunkett Weekly News* (newsletter); *Village e-news* (newsletter); *Organisational Structures for Rural Social Enterprises*; *The Real Choice: How local foods can survive the supermarket onslaught*; *Enterprising Approaches to Rural Community Transport*; *Supporting Rural Enterprise in England*; *Rural Lifelines: Older People and Rural Social Enterprises*; *The Co-operative Opportunity*; *Farming Together for Profit*.

Finance: Annual income £1,014,512, expenditure £1,254,681 (31 Dec. 2013).

Board of Trustees: Margaret Clark (Chair.); Tom Scanlon, Dr Wil Gibson (Co-Vice-Chair.); David Dickman (Treas.).

Principal Staff: Chief Exec. Peter Couchman.

Address: The Quadrangle, Woodstock, Oxfordshire OX20 1LH.

Telephone: (1993) 810730; **Internet:** www.plunkett.co.uk; **e-mail:** info@plunkett.co.uk.

Polden-Puckham Charitable Foundation—PPCF

Founded in 1991 for general charitable purposes.

Activities: Funds projects in peace and sustainable security. The Foundation supports the development of ways of resolving violent conflicts peacefully, and of addressing their underlying causes. It also supports environmental sustainability work that addresses pressures and conditions that are leading towards global environmental breakdown, particularly national initiatives in the United Kingdom that promote sustainable living. The Foundation is linked with the Society of Friends (Quakers).

Geographical Area of Activity: United Kingdom.

Restrictions: Does not fund: organizations that work outside the United Kingdom (unless they are of international focus); grants to individuals; travel bursaries (including overseas placements and expeditions); study; academic research; capital projects (e.g. building projects or purchase of nature reserves); community or local practical projects (except

innovative projects for widespread application); environmental/ecological conservation; international agencies and overseas appeals; human rights work (except where it relates to peace and environmental sustainability).

Publications: Annual Report; *Review of Grant Giving 2000–2010*.

Finance: Annual income £536,396, expenditure £495,494 (5 April 2014).

Principal Staff: Exec. Sec. Bryn Higgs.

Address: BM PPCF, London WC1N 3XX.

Telephone: (20) 7193-7364; **Internet:** www.polden-puckham.org.uk; **e-mail:** ppcf@polden-puckham.org.uk.

Policy Studies Institute—PSI

Founded in 1978 (formerly known as Political and Economic Planning—PEP, founded in 1931) as an independent research organization, undertaking studies of social, economic and cultural policy. Merged with the University of Westminster in 2009.

Activities: Operates nationally and internationally, carrying out research in the fields of the arts and humanities, education, training, economic affairs, and social and political studies, examining selected problems. Research areas include arts and culture, communications, criminal justice, disability, education and training, employment, ethnic minorities, evaluation, family life, health, household budgets, income and wealth, industrial relations, information, the legal system, local and regional studies, new technology, policing, social care, social security, women and young people. The Institute publishes the results of its research.

Geographical Area of Activity: United Kingdom.

Publications: Annual Report; *Policy Studies* (quarterly journal); *Cultural Trends* (quarterly journal); *Changing priorities*; *Transformed opportunities*; *Why people work after state pension age*; *Green taxes and charges: Reducing their impact on low-income households*; *Job Satisfaction and Employer Behaviour*; *Climate change and fuel poverty*; *The Benefits of Public Arts*; *Amateur Arts in the UK*; *Research Discussion Series* (reports).

Principal Staff: Admin. Tim Edwards.

Address: 35 Marylebone Rd, London NW1 5LS.

Telephone: (20) 7911-7500; **Fax:** (20) 7911-7501; **Internet:** www.psi.org.uk; **e-mail:** admin@policystudiesinstitute.org.uk.

The Porter Foundation

Founded in 1970 by Sir Leslie Porter and Dame Shirley Porter to support projects in the fields of education, culture, conservation and the environment, and health and welfare.

Activities: Operates in the United Kingdom and Israel in the fields of the arts, conservation and the environment, education and medicine, through grants to institutions.

Geographical Area of Activity: Israel and United Kingdom.

Finance: Annual income £162,223, expenditure £73,926 (5 April 2014).

Trustees: Dame Shirley Porter (Chair.).

Address: 16 Gt Queen St, Covent Garden, London WC2B 5AH.

Telephone: (20) 7544-8863; **Internet:** www.dameshirleyporter.net.

Practical Action

Established in 1966 as the Intermediate Technology Development Group—ITDG by the economist Dr E. F. Schumacher and others to promote development.

Activities: An international development agency working with poor communities to help them choose and use technology to improve their lives.

Geographical Area of Activity: International.

Publications: Annual Reports (international and by region); *Waterlines* (journal); *Enterprise Development & Microfinance* (journal); *Food Chain* (journal); books on development, including analytical texts, handbooks, manuals and reference works; briefing papers.

Finance: Annual income £30,252,000, expenditure £27,824,000 (31 March 2014).

Board of Trustees: Helena Molyneux (Chair.); Dr Roger Clarke (Vice-Chair.); Nigel Saxby-Soffe (Treas.).

Principal Staff: Chief Exec. Simon Trace (until Oct. 2015).

Address: The Schumacher Centre, Bourton on Dunsmore, Rugby CV23 9QZ.

Telephone: (1926) 634400; **Fax:** (1926) 634401; **Internet:** www.practicalaction.org.uk; **e-mail:** enquiries@practicalaction.org.uk.

The Prince's Trust

Founded in 1976 by HRH The Prince of Wales to enable young people, in particular the most disadvantaged, to develop themselves and serve the community.

Activities: Operates in the United Kingdom to encourage young people aged 13–30 years into employment, education, training or volunteering via Trust programmes. Particular emphasis is placed on projects to aid the community, education, training and employment programmes, and helping young offenders and the homeless. The Trust is an operational charity rather than a grantmaking trust.

Geographical Area of Activity: United Kingdom.

Finance: Annual income £60,583,000, expenditure £63,517,000 (31 March 2013).

Council: Sir Charles Dunstone (Chair.).

Principal Staff: Pres. HRH Prince Charles; Chief Exec. Martina Milburn.

Address: Prince's Trust House, 9 Eldon St, London EC2M 7LS.

Telephone: (20) 7543-1234; **Fax:** (20) 7543-1200; **Internet:** www.princes-trust.org.uk; **e-mail:** info@princes-trust.org.uk.

Progressio

Established in 1940 as The Sword of the Spirit; changed its name to the Catholic Institute for International Relations in 1965; present name adopted in 2006. The organization now operates as an international development agency.

Activities: Operates programmes in Central America and the Caribbean, South America, Africa and the Middle East, and Asia. The organization provides skilled development workers to work with grassroots organizations in developing countries and improve the lives of poor people.

Geographical Area of Activity: South and Central America, Africa.

Finance: Annual income £5,727,671, expenditure £6,015,546 (31 March 2014).

Board: Martin McEnery (Chair.); Michael Doris (Treas.).

Principal Staff: Chief Exec. Mark Lister.

Address: Unit 3, Canonbury Yard, 190A New North Rd, London N1 7BJ.

Telephone: (20) 7354-0883; **Fax:** (20) 7359-0017; **Internet:** www.progressio.org.uk; **e-mail:** enquiries@progressio.org.uk.

Project Trust

Founded in 1967 to promote a broader education for young people through volunteer work-experience schemes abroad, and for general charitable purposes.

Activities: Sends European school leavers overseas to take part in voluntary work, usually in developing countries.

Geographical Area of Activity: Africa, South and Latin America, Asia.

Restrictions: Not a grantmaking organization.

Publications: *Project Post* (quarterly newsletter).

Finance: Annual income £1,884,956, expenditure £1,929,165 (30 Sept. 2013).

Board of Directors: Ivor Dunbar (Chair.).

Principal Staff: Dir Ingrid Emerson.

Address: The Hebridean Centre, Isle of Coll, Argyll PA78 6TE.

Telephone: (1879) 230444; **Fax:** (1879) 230357; **Internet:** www.projecttrust.org.uk; **e-mail:** info@projecttrust.org.uk.

PRS for Music Foundation

Established in 1999.

Activities: Aims to stimulate and support the creation and performance of new music throughout the United Kingdom. Since 2000, has funded more than 4,600 new music initiatives, at a cost of more than £19.5m., through open grant schemes, which are available to musicians and organizations four times a year, and partnership programmes, which respond to specific needs and gaps in funding.

Geographical Area of Activity: United Kingdom.

Finance: Annual income £2,249,912, expenditure £2,531,204 (31 Dec. 2014).

Board of Trustees: Royce Bell (Chair.).

Principal Staff: Exec. Dir Vanessa Reed.

Address: 2 Pancras Sq., London N1C 4AG.

Telephone: (20) 7306-4044; **Fax:** (20) 7306-4814; **Internet:** www.prsformusicfoundation.com; **e-mail:** info@prsformusicfoundation.com.

A. M. Qattan Foundation

Founded in 1993 by Abdul Mohsen and Leila Al-Qattan to advance education, cultural development and awareness; preserve the cultural values and heritage and enrich the social fabric of Palestinian communities worldwide.

Activities: Operates in the United Kingdom and the Middle East in the fields of culture and education, with offices in London, Ramallah and Gaza City. Projects include the Qattan Centre for Educational Research and Development; the Qattan Centre for the Child, Gaza City; the Culture and Arts Programme, including Palestinian Audio-Visual Project (recently renamed the Production Support Project); the Gaza Music School; and The Mosaic Rooms, an exhibition and events space in London.

Geographical Area of Activity: Palestinian Territories, Lebanon, Jordan, Syria, the United Kingdom.

Publications: *Flowers of Palestine*; *Young Artist of the Year Award* (catalogue); research reports; and numerous other publications; educational quarterly *Rua Tarbawiyyah (Educational Outlooks)*.

Finance: Annual income £4,000,907, expenditure £3,922,212 (31 March 2014).

Trustees: Abdel Mohsin Al-Qattan (Pres.); Omar Al-Qattan (Chair.).

Principal Staff: Dir-Gen. Ziad Khalaf.

Address: Tower House, 226 Cromwell Rd, London SW5 0SW.

Telephone: (20) 7370-9990; **Fax:** (20) 7370-1606; **Internet:** www.qattanfoundation.org; **e-mail:** info@uk.qattanfoundation.org.

Quilliam Foundation

Established in 2008 by Muslim scholars as a think tank to counter extremism and terrorism.

Activities: Works in the fields of civil society, community cohesion and Muslim integration, through research projects, media campaigns and other events, publications and training.

Geographical Area of Activity: United Kingdom.

Finance: Annual income £690,641, expenditure £631,780 (31 March 2013).

Advisory Board: Maajid Nawaz (Co-Founder and Chair.).

Principal Staff: Pres. Noman Benotman; Man. Dir Haras Rafiq.

Address: POB 60380, London WC1A 9AZ; 35–50 Rathbone Pl., London WC1A 9AZ.

Telephone: (20) 7182-7280; **Fax:** (20) 7637-4944; **Internet:** www.quilliamfoundation.org; **e-mail:** information@ quilliamfoundation.org.

The Rainforest Foundation

Founded in 1989 by Gordon Sumner (Sting) and Trudie Styler.

Activities: Aims to support indigenous people and traditional populations of the world's rainforests in their efforts to protect their environment and fulfil their rights by assisting them in: securing and controlling the natural resources necessary for their long-term well-being and managing these resources in ways that do not harm their environment, violate their culture or compromise their future; and developing the means to protect their individual and collective rights and to obtain, shape and control basic services from the state. Currently funding projects and campaigns in Cameroon, Guyana, Madagascar, Peru, Thailand, the United Kingdom and Venezuela. Works in conjunction with affiliate foundations in Austria, Japan, Norway and the USA, and partner organizations in Brazil.

Geographical Area of Activity: International.

Publications: Annual Report; *The Myth and Reality of the Forest Stewardship Council*; *Life After Logging* (report); *Out of Commission*; *Forest in Focus* (newsletter, 2 a year); *Conflict Timber—Africa Case Studies*; *Congo Basin Forests and the Law*; *Divided Forests—Towards Fairer Zoning*; *Forest Law Rights and Poverty*; *Strengthening the Rights of Pygmy Peoples*.

Finance: Annual income £2,255,298, expenditure £2,144,165 (31 Dec. 2013).

Board of Trustees: John Paul Davidson (Chair.); Dr John Hemming (Sec.); Mark Campanale (Treas.).

Principal Staff: Exec. Dir Simon Counsell.

Address: 223A Kentish Town Rd, London NW5 2JT.

Telephone: (20) 7485-0193; **Fax:** (20) 7485-0315; **Internet:** www.rainforestfoundationuk.org; **e-mail:** info@ rainforestuk.com.

The Rank Foundation

Founded in 1953 by Lord and Lady Rank to promote the Christian religion, education and general charitable purposes in the United Kingdom and overseas.

Activities: Provides funds to organizations working in the promotion of Christianity (funds in this area are committed to an associated charity, the Foundation for Christian Communication Ltd). The Foundation also makes grants in the areas of education, including educational programmes for young offenders; youth; and other charitable projects, including the elderly and the disabled.

Geographical Area of Activity: United Kingdom.

Restrictions: No grants are made to individuals; only one unsolicited application in four is successful.

Publications: Annual Report.

Finance: Annual income £820,000, expenditure £12,693,000 (31 Dec. 2013).

Trustees: R.F.H. Cowen (Life Pres.); Joey R. Newton (Chair.); M.E.T. Davies (Deputy Chair.).

Principal Staff: CEO David J. Sanderson.

Address: 12 Warwick Sq., London SW1V 2AA.

Telephone: (20) 7834-7731; **Internet:** www.rankfoundation .com; **e-mail:** natalie.kay@rankfoundation.co.uk.

Sigrid Rausing Trust

Established in 1995 by Dr Sigrid Rausing.

Activities: Operates nine main programmes: Advocacy, Research and Litigation; Detention, Torture and the Death Penalty; Human Rights Defenders; Free Expression; Transitional Justice; Women's Rights; LGBTI Rights; Xenophobia and Intolerance; Transparency and Accountability.

Geographical Area of Activity: International.

Restrictions: No grants to individuals; does not generally accept unsolicited applications.

Finance: Annual income £23,680,665, expenditure £19,949,364 (31 Dec. 2013).

Board of Trustees: Sigrid Rausing (Chair.); Andrew Puddephatt (Deputy Chair.).

Principal Staff: Dir of Programmes Julie Broom; Admin. Dir Elizabeth Wedmore.

Address: 12 Penzance Pl., London W11 4PA.

Telephone: (20) 7313-7720; **Fax:** (20) 7313-7721; **Internet:** www.sigrid-rausing-trust.org; **e-mail:** info@srtrust.org.

Rayne Foundation

Founded in 1962 by Lord Rayne for general charitable purposes.

Activities: Operates nationally in the fields of the arts, education, health and medicine, and social welfare and development, through grants to charitable and voluntary organizations.

Geographical Area of Activity: United Kingdom.

Restrictions: No grants are made for work outside the United Kingdom or to individuals.

Publications: Annual Report.

Finance: Annual income £1,411,421, expenditure £4,430,394 (30 Nov. 2013).

Trustees: Robert A. Rayne (Chair.).

Principal Staff: Dir Amelia Fitzalan Howard.

Address: 100 George St, London W1U 8NU.

Telephone: (20) 7487-9650; **Fax:** (20) 7935-3737; **Internet:** www.raynefoundation.org.uk; **e-mail:** info@ raynefoundation.org.uk.

Reall—Real Equity for All

Founded in 1989, as Homeless International, for the relief of poverty following the 1987 UN International Year of Shelter for the Homeless. Present name adopted in 2015.

Activities: Operates internationally supporting community-led housing and infrastructure-related development, through grants to organizations, working in collaboration with local partners on long-term development. The organization also provides advisory and financial services, carries out research, and gives specialist technical assistance.

Geographical Area of Activity: Africa and Asia.

Publications: Annual Report; CLIFF Annual Report.

Finance: Annual income £11,656,544, expenditure £4,696,928 (31 March 2014).

Council of Management: David Orr (Chair.); Suzanne Forster (Hon. Treas.).

Principal Staff: Chief Exec. Larry English.

Address: Queens House, 16 Queens Rd, Coventry CV1 3EG.

Telephone: (24) 7663-2802; **Fax:** (24) 7663-2911; **Internet:** reall.xyz; **e-mail:** info@reall.net.

RedR UK

Founded in 1980 as an international disaster relief charity, following engineer Peter Guthrie's experiences working in a refugee camp during the Vietnamese Boat People crises. Oxfam (q.v.) provided RedR with a start-up fund.

Activities: Trains aid workers and provides skilled professionals to humanitarian programmes worldwide. The organization has permanent humanitarian training programmes in Pakistan, Sudan, South Sudan, Kenya and the United Kingdom. It also delivers tailor-made humanitarian training to aid agencies worldwide. Has 1,700 members, experienced humanitarians with wide-ranging skills, who work in more than 80 countries each year and respond to disasters, wherever they occur.

Geographical Area of Activity: International.

Publications: RedAlert magazine (2 a year), Annual Report; handbooks, reports, aid-related materials and guides.

Finance: Annual income £5,485,677, expenditure £5,261,925 (31 March 2014).

Board of Trustees: Ian Smout (Chair.); Jenny Mills (Vice-Chair.); P. J. Greeves (Treas.).

Principal Staff: Chief Exec. Martin McCann.

Address: 250A Kennington Lane, London SE11 5RD.

Telephone: (20) 7840-6000; **Fax:** (20) 7582-8669; **Internet:** www.redr.org.uk; **e-mail:** info@redr.org.uk.

Rhodes Trust

Founded in 1902 by Cecil John Rhodes, for educational and general purposes.

Activities: Operates internationally in the field of education, by awarding 82 Rhodes Scholarships annually for overseas graduates (mainly from the Commonwealth, the USA and Germany) to study at the University of Oxford.

Geographical Area of Activity: International.

Restrictions: Applicants must be between the ages of 19 and 25 years (those applying from Kenya must be under the age of 27). Scholarships cover tuition fees, a maintenance allowance and travel costs.

Finance: Annual income £11,886,206, expenditure £11,035,331 (30 June 2013).

Board of Trustees: Dr John Hood (Chair.).

Principal Staff: Warden and Sec. Charles Conn.

Address: Rhodes House, South Parks Rd, Oxford OX1 3RG.

Telephone: (1865) 270902; **Fax:** (1865) 270914; **Internet:** www.rhodeshouse.ox.ac.uk; **e-mail:** admin@rhodeshouse.ox.ac.uk.

Joseph Rowntree Charitable Trust

Founded in 1904 by Joseph Rowntree, who placed particular emphasis on justice, equal opportunity and the unique value of each individual.

Activities: As a Quaker trust, seeks to transform the world by supporting people who address the root causes of conflict and injustice. The Trust makes grants, mainly in the United Kingdom and Ireland, supporting work on the peaceful resolution of international and other conflicts; racial justice; democratic process; human rights; corporate responsibility; and work connected with the Religious Society of Friends (Quakers).

Geographical Area of Activity: United Kingdom and Ireland.

Restrictions: Does not award grants to/for: larger, older national charities that have an established constituency of supporters and substantial levels of reserves; work in mainstream education; medical research; academic research, except as an integral part of policy and campaigning work that is central to the Trust's areas of interest; building, buying or repairing buildings; business development or job creation schemes; providing care, support or training services, such as for elderly people, children and young people, people with learning difficulties, people with physical disabilities, people using mental health services, refugees or asylum seekers; housing and homelessness; the arts, except where a project is specifically concerned with issues of interest to the Trust; travel or adventure projects; educational bursaries; the personal support of individuals in need; general appeals; work that the Trust believes should be funded from statutory sources, or which has been in the recent past; work that has already been done; work that tries to make a problem easier to live with, rather than getting to the root of it; local work in the United Kingdom (except racial justice work in West Yorkshire); work in the United Kingdom that aims to raise public awareness or change policy concerning injustices in other nations; work outside the United Kingdom (except for groups working elsewhere within the European Union—EU—on EU policy).

Publications: Annual reports.

Finance: Annual income £4,917,000, expenditure £8,635,000 (31 Dec. 2013).

Trustees: Margaret Bryan (Chair.); Peter Coltman (Vice-Chair.).

Principal Staff: Trust Sec. Nick Perks; Asst Trust Sec. Maureen Grant.

Address: The Garden House, Water End, York YO30 6WQ.

Telephone: (1904) 627810; **Fax:** (1904) 651990; **Internet:** www.jrct.org.uk; **e-mail:** enquiries@jrct.org.uk.

Joseph Rowntree Foundation

Founded in 1904 by Joseph Rowntree. Also comprises, and shares trustees and directors with the Joseph Rowntree Housing Trust, a registered housing association and provider of care services which manages around 2,500 homes.

Activities: Aims to find out the underlying causes of poverty and inequality in the United Kingdom, and identify solutions through research and learning from experience; show solutions by developing and running services, innovating and supporting others to innovate; influence positive and lasting change, publishing and promoting evidence to policy-makers, and bringing people together to share ideas.

Geographical Area of Activity: United Kingdom.

Restrictions: No grants to individuals.

Publications: Research findings.

Finance: Annual income £8,747,000, expenditure £10,032,000 (31 Dec. 2013).

Board of Trustees: Tony Stoller (Chair.).

Principal Staff: Chief Exec. Julia Unwin.

Address: The Homestead, 40 Water End, York YO30 6WP.

Telephone: (1904) 629241; **Fax:** (1904) 620072; **Internet:** www.jrf.org.uk.

Joseph Rowntree Reform Trust Ltd (including the JRSST Charitable Trust)

Founded in 1904 by Joseph Rowntree to promote political reform, constitutional change and social justice.

Activities: Operates in the field of politics, campaigning activities, and pressure groups; through self-conducted programmes and through grants to organizations and individuals. Note: Although the Joseph Rowntree Reform Trust is not charitable in law, its subsidiary, the JRSST Charitable Trust, makes charitable grants for purposes closely related to those of the Joseph Rowntree Reform Trust.

Geographical Area of Activity: Mainly United Kingdom.

Restrictions: Does not provide funding for research; nor does it fund work that can be funded from charitable sources.

Publications: *State of the Nation* (2014); *Privacy & Personal Data Poll* (2014); *Speaking Truth to Power*; *Ipsos MORI report on Intergenerational Justice* (2014); *The Bradford Earthquake—Full report* (2013).

Finance: Grants disbursed approx. £1m. JRSST Charitable Trust annual income £112,372, expenditure £140,812 (31 Dec. 2013).

Directors: Tina Day (Chair.); Andrew Neal (Vice-Chair.).

Principal Staff: Trust Sec. Tina Walker.

Address: The Garden House, Water End, York YO30 6WQ.

Telephone: (1904) 625744; **Fax:** (1904) 651502; **Internet:** www.jrrt.org.uk; **e-mail:** info@jrrt.org.uk.

Royal Aeronautical Society—RAES

Founded in 1866 for the general advancement of aeronautical art, science and engineering. Incorporates the Royal Aeronautical Society Foundation (f. 2006).

Activities: Promotes the highest professional standards in all aerospace disciplines. The Society provides specialist information and acts as a central forum for the exchange of ideas. It also plays a leading role in influencing opinion on aerospace matters.

Geographical Area of Activity: International.

Publications: *The Aeronautical Journal*; AEROSPACE (both monthly).

Finance: Annual income £4,314,294, expenditure £3,991,750 (31 Dec. 2013).

Council: Bill Tyack (Pres.); Martin Broadhurst (Pres.-elect); Jenny Body (Chair.).

Principal Staff: Chief Exec. Simon Luxmoore.

Address: 4 Hamilton Pl., London W1J 7BQ.

Telephone: (20) 7670-4300; **Fax:** (20) 7670-4309; **Internet:** www.aerosociety.com; **e-mail:** raes@aerosociety.com.

Royal Air Force Benevolent Fund

Founded in 1919 by Lord Trenchard for the relief of distress experienced by anyone who has entered productive service in the Royal Air Force, or any of its associated Forces, as well as their immediate dependants. The Fund also maintains the RAF Memorial on the Victoria Embankment, London.

Activities: Operates internationally, providing financial, practical and emotional support to all members of the RAF family, from childhood through to old age. The Fund owns homes in Sussex, offering short-term respite care, as well as jointly owning homes in Northumberland, Avon and Lancashire. It also manages the Royal Air Force Benevolent Fund Housing Trust.

Geographical Area of Activity: United Kingdom and international.

Restrictions: Only serving or former member of the RAF or their partners may be eligible.

Publications: Report of operations and financial statement; newsletters.

Finance: Annual income £19,253,000, expenditure £21,871,000 (31 Dec. 2013).

Board of Trustees: Lawrie Haynes (Chair.); The Viscount Trenchard of Wolfeton (Deputy Chair.); Tony Lea (Hon. Treas.).

Principal Staff: Controller Air Marshal Christopher Nickols.

Address: 67 Portland Pl., London W1B 1AR.

Telephone: (20) 7580-8343; **Fax:** (20) 7636-7005; **Internet:** www.rafbf.org; **e-mail:** info@rafbf.org.uk.

Royal Anthropological Institute of Great Britain and Ireland—RAI

Founded in 1871 by the merger of the Ethnological Society and the Anthropological Society.

Activities: Operates nationally and internationally in anthropology, through publications; conferences and lectures; the provision of library facilities for research; the promotion of anthropological film; and grants and scholarships to individual researchers from trust funds. The Institute also manages a photographic archive, and raises funds. It awards several international prizes, such as the Curl Essay Prize, the Wellcome Medal for Medical Anthropology, the Lucy Mair Medal for Applied Anthropology, and the J. B. Donne Essay Prize in the Anthropology of Art.

Geographical Area of Activity: International.

Restrictions: Grants and scholarships are open only to those replying to published advertisements.

Publications: Report of operations and financial statement; *The Journal of the Royal Anthropological Institute* (quarterly journal, incorporating *Man*); *Anthropology Today* (6 a year); *Anthropological Index Online* (internet service); *Discovering Anthropology;* occasional papers.

Finance: Annual income £964,932, expenditure £813,875 (31 Dec. 2013).

Council: Dr André Singer (Pres.); Prof. Raymond Apthorpe, Dr Lissant Bolton, Dr Simon Underdown (Vice-Pres); Eric Hirsch (Hon. Sec.); Dr Michael Scott (Hon. Librarian); Julie Scott (Hon. Treas.).

Principal Staff: Dir Dr David Shankland; Asst Dir Christine M. R. Patel.

Address: 50 Fitzroy St, London W1T 5BT.

Telephone: (20) 7387-0455; **Fax:** (20) 7388-8817; **Internet:** www.therai.org.uk; **e-mail:** admin@therai.org.uk.

Royal Asiatic Society of Great Britain and Ireland

Founded in 1823 by Henry Thomas Colebrooke to promote the study of Asia.

Activities: Main activities are publishing journals and books, managing a library and collection, organizing lectures, seminars and exhibitions, and operating a fellowship programme. The Society has around 700 members, one-half of whom are based outside the United Kingdom.

Geographical Area of Activity: Asia.

Publications: *Journal of the Royal Asiatic Society Third Series* (quarterly); books; monographs.

Finance: Annual income £429,651, expenditure £407,013 (31 Dec. 2013).

Council of Management: Prof. Peter Robb (Pres.); Lionel Knight (Treas.).

Principal Staff: Dir and Sec. Dr Alison Ohta.

Address: 14 Stephenson Way, London NW1 2HD.

Telephone: (20) 7388-4539; **Fax:** (20) 7391-9429; **Internet:** www.royalasiaticsociety.org; **e-mail:** info@royalasiaticsociety.org.

Royal British Legion

Founded in 1921 by Field Marshal Earl Haig to promote the welfare of ex-service people and their dependants.

Activities: Provides assistance to those serving, or who have served in the armed forces and to their dependants. The Legion assists disabled and needy ex-servicemen and women, and their dependants, by running residential homes; providing sheltered employment and special housing; proving entitlement to pensions and assisting individual cases of hardship; advising on small businesses and providing resettlement training; it also arranges visits to war graves abroad. There are more than 3,000 branches in the United Kingdom and more than 50 overseas.

Geographical Area of Activity: International.

Publications: Annual Report and accounts; *Legion* (magazine); leaflets; fact sheets; newsletters.

Finance: Annual income £124,558,000, expenditure £122,483,000 (30 Sept. 2013).

Board of Trustees: John Crisford (Chair.); Terry Whittles (Vice-Chair.).

Principal Staff: Dir-Gen. Chris Simpkins; Deputy Dir-Gen. John Graham.

Address: 199 Borough High St, London SE1 1AA.

Telephone: (20) 3207-2100; **Internet:** www.britishlegion.org.uk; **e-mail:** info@britishlegion.org.uk.

Royal Commission for the Exhibition of 1851

Founded in 1850 to organize the Great Exhibition; a supplementary charter was granted in 1851 to use surplus funds of the Exhibition to extend industrial education and the influence of science and art on productive industry.

Activities: Operates in the fields of the physical and biological sciences, pure and applied, and engineering and industrial design, principally through postgraduate research awards and fellowships. Some other special awards are made.

Publications: Annual Report; *Record of Award Holders in Science, Engineering and the Arts, 1891–2000; The Crystal Palace and the Great Exhibition, Art, Science and Productive Industry—A History of the Royal Commission for the Exhibition of 1851.*

Finance: Annual income £2,714,294, expenditure £2,682,322 (31 Dec. 2014).

Commission: HRH The Princess Royal (Pres.); Bernard Taylor (Chair.).

Principal Staff: Sec. and Chief Exec. Nigel Williams.

Address: 453 Sherfield Bldg, Imperial College, London SW7 2AZ.

Telephone: (20) 7594-8790; **Fax:** (20) 7594-8794; **Internet:** www.royalcommission1851.org.uk; **e-mail:** royalcom1851@imperial.ac.uk.

The Royal Commonwealth Society—RCS

Founded in 1868; present name adopted in 1956.

Activities: A network of individuals and organizations committed to improving the lives and prospects of Commonwealth citizens across the world. The Society promotes the value and the values of the Commonwealth through youth empowerment, education and advocacy. It campaigns for human rights, democracy and sustainable development across the 53 member states, which are intrinsically linked through their common history and shared values.

Geographical Area of Activity: International.

Restrictions: Not a grantmaking organization.

Publications: Annual Report; newsletters; thematic reports.

Finance: Annual income £729,873, expenditure £937,178 (31 Dec. 2013).

Board: Claire Whitaker (Chair.); Michael Bostelmann (Treas.).

Principal Staff: Dir Michael Lake; COO Carolyn Jack.

Address: Award House, 7–11 St Matthew St, London SW1P 2JT.

Telephone: (20) 3727-4300; **Internet:** www.thercs.org; **e-mail:** info@thercs.org.

Royal Geographical Society (with The Institute of British Geographers)

Founded in 1830 by Sir John Barrow and others for the 'advancement of geographical science'.

Activities: Learned society and professional body for geography that supports and promotes geographical research, expeditions and fieldwork, education, public engagement and geography input to policy. The Society aims to foster an understanding and informed enjoyment of our world. Maintains the world's largest private geographical collection.

Geographical Area of Activity: International.

Publications: *The Geographical Journal; Geographical Magazine; Area; Transactions; WIRES Climate Change* (online).

Finance: Annual income £4,318,997, expenditure £4,660,803 (31 Dec. 2013).

Council: Prof. Dame Judith Rees (Pres.); Michael Palin (Immediate Past Pres.).

Principal Staff: Hon. Pres. HRH The Duke of Kent; Dir and Sec. Dr Rita Gardner.

Address: 1 Kensington Gore, London SW7 2AR.

Telephone: (20) 7591-3000; **Fax:** (20) 7591-3001; **Internet:** www.rgs.org; **e-mail:** info@rgs.org.

Royal Institute of International Affairs—RIIA—Chatham House

Founded in 1920 to encourage and facilitate the scientific study of international questions. The Institute is precluded by its charter from expressing opinions of its own.

Activities: Operates as an independent centre for the study of international political and economic affairs, through self-conducted programmes of research, discussion, exposition and publication, designed to serve an informed public in general and the Institute's 3,000 members in particular. The Institute maintains a library and information service, and runs an active programme of meetings for its members. Its research programme includes work on Europe, the countries of the former USSR, South Asia, Japan and East Asia, Africa, the Middle East, international economic relations, international security questions, and international energy and environmental issues. All research is directed towards publication; meetings, seminars and conferences related to research are organized at home and abroad.

Geographical Area of Activity: International.

Restrictions: The Institute is exclusively an operating body, and does not give grants.

Publications: *The World Today* (monthly); *International Affairs* (six a year); books; *Chatham House Reports*; briefing papers; programme papers; Annual Report.

Finance: Annual income £12,766,000, expenditure £11,685,000 (31 March 2014).

Board of Trustees: Stuart Popham (Chair.); Sir Roderic Lyne (Deputy Chair.); Ed Smith (Hon. Treas.).

Principal Staff: Pres Lord Ashdown, Sir John Major, Baroness Scotland; Dir Dr Robin Niblett.

Address: Chatham House, 10 St James's Sq., London SW1Y 4LE.

Telephone: (20) 7957-5700; **Fax:** (20) 7957-5710; **Internet:** www.chathamhouse.org.uk; **e-mail:** contact@chathamhouse.org.uk.

Royal National Institute of Blind People—RNIB

Founded in 1868.

Activities: Provides advice, information and services to enable blind and partially sighted people to take charge of their own lives; and challenges the underlying causes of blindness by helping to prevent, cure or alleviate it. The Institute provides access to Braille, large print, 'talking' books and computer training. Seeks innovative and imaginative solutions to everyday challenges, as well as campaigning to change society's attitudes, actions and assumptions, so that people with sight problems can enjoy the same rights, freedoms and responsibilities as fully sighted people. It also funds pioneering research into the prevention and treatment of eye disease and promotes eye health by running public health awareness campaigns.

Geographical Area of Activity: United Kingdom.

Publications: *RNIB Hotel Guide 2006; Patient Focus; The Accessible Office; The See it Right pack; Vision Magazine; The See Change pack*; Annual Report.

Finance: Annual income £118,647,000, expenditure £120,604,000 (31 March 2014).

Board of Trustees: Kevin Carey (Chair.); Ellie Southwood (Vice-Chair.); Alan Tinger (Hon. Treas.).

Principal Staff: Chief Exec. Lesley-Anne Alexander.

Address: 105 Judd St, London WC1H 9NE.

Telephone: (20) 7388-1266; **Fax:** (20) 7388-2034; **Internet:** www.rnib.org.uk; **e-mail:** helpline@rnib.org.uk.

Royal Over-Seas League—ROSL

Established by Sir Evelyn Wrench in 1910. Holds a Royal Charter, and is pledged to work for the service of others, the good of the Commonwealth, and humanity in general.

Activities: Supports classical music and the arts, and contributes to worldwide humanitarian relief. The League provides scholarships and opportunities to young professional artists and musicians from across the Commonwealth. Organizes concerts, exhibitions, readings and book events. Conducts education and humanitarian projects, such as providing school bursaries and resources in Namibia and Kenya, and travelling eye clinics in Sri Lanka.

Geographical Area of Activity: International.

Publications: *Overseas* (quarterly journal).

Principal Staff: Dir-Gen. Maj.-Gen. Roddy Porter.

Address: Over-Seas House, Park Pl., St James's St, London SW1A 1LR.

Telephone: (20) 7408-0214; **Fax:** (20) 7499-6738; **Internet:** www.rosl.org.uk; **e-mail:** info@rosl.org.uk.

Royal Society

Founded in 1660 to promote natural knowledge. Granted a Royal Charter by King Charles II in 1662.

Activities: Operates nationally and internationally in the fields of education, natural and applied science (including mathematics, engineering and medicine), international scientific relations and the conservation of natural resources. The Society carries out self-conducted programmes and research; awards grants to institutions and individuals; awards fellowships and scholarships; organizes conferences and lectures; and issues publications. It provides an independent source of advice on scientific matters, notably to the British Government.

Geographical Area of Activity: International.

Publications: *Proceedings of the Royal Society A: Mathematical, Physical & Engineering Sciences; Proceedings of the Royal Society B: Biological Sciences; Philosophical Transactions of the Royal Society A: Mathematical, Physical & Engineering Sciences; Philosophical Transactions of the Royal Society B: Biological Sciences; Biology Letters; Journal of the Royal Society Interface; Interface Focus; Notes & Records of the Royal Society; Biographical Memoirs of Fellows of the Royal Society; Year Book of the Royal Society.*

Finance: Annual income £70,626,000, expenditure £77,891,000 (31 March 2013).

Council: Sir Paul Nurse (Pres.); Sir Venkatraman (Venki) Ramakrishnan (Pres.-elect); Prof. Anthony Cheetham (Treas.).

Principal Staff: Exec. Dir Dr Julie Maxton.

Address: 6–9 Carlton House Terrace, London SW1Y 5AG.

Telephone: (20) 7451-2500; **Fax:** (20) 7930-2170; **Internet:** royalsociety.org; **e-mail:** grants@royalsociety.org.

Royal Society for the Encouragement of Arts, Manufactures and Commerce—RSA

Founded in 1754 by William Shipley for the encouragement of the arts, manufactures and commerce.

Activities: Operates nationally and internationally in the arts, manufactures, commerce, design, education and the environment. The Society works to remove barriers to social progress. It drives ideas, innovation and social change through its ambitious programme of projects, events and lectures, and with the support of a 27,000-strong fellowship.

Geographical Area of Activity: International.

Restrictions: Not a grantmaking organization.

Publications: *RSA Journal* (every quarter); other reports and publications.

Finance: Annual income £9,730,000, expenditure £9,608,000 (31 March 2014).

Trustee Board: Vikki Heywood (Chair.); Suzy Walton (Deputy Chair.); Sarah Ebanja, Hanif Virji (Treas).

Principal Staff: Chief Exec. Matthew Taylor; COO Carol Jackson.

Address: 8 John Adam St, London WC2N 6EZ.

Telephone: (20) 7930-5115; **Fax:** (20) 7839-5805; **Internet:** www.thersa.org; **e-mail:** general@rsa.org.uk.

The Royal Society of Medicine—RSM

Founded in 1805 to promote the interests of medical science, using its neutrality to encourage co-operation in medicine and provide education through a wide variety of means, including meetings, debates, conferences, publications and a library.

Activities: Operates nationally and internationally in medicine and science, through meetings, conferences, publications, e-learning, prizes for doctors and students across 58 specialties and providing members (those involved in medicine, science and health care-related professions) with access to the library, online journals and databases, and use of club facilities in central London.

Geographical Area of Activity: United Kingdom.

Publications: *Journal of the RSM*; JRSM Short Reports, *Tropical Doctor; AIDS and Hepatitis Digest; International Journal of STD and AIDS; Journal of Medical Biography; Journal of Telemedicine and Telecare; Annals of Clinical Biochemistry; Clinical Risk; Handbook of Practice Management; Journal of Health Services Research and Policy; Journal of Integrated Care Pathways; Journal of Laryngology and Otology.*

Finance: Annual income £16,630,000, expenditure £16,526,000 (30 Sept. 2014).

Council: Babulal Sethia (Pres.); Martin Bailey (Hon. Sec.); Dr Gillian Leng (Hon. Librarian); Rachel Hargest (Hon. Treas.); Adrian Beckingsale (Chair. of Academic Board).

Principal Staff: CEO Ian Balmer.

Address: 1 Wimpole St, London W1G 0AE.

Telephone: (20) 7290-2900; **Fax:** (20) 7290-2989; **Internet:** www.rsm.ac.uk; **e-mail:** membership@rsm.ac.uk.

Royal Society for the Prevention of Cruelty to Animals—RSPCA

Founded in 1824 as the Society for the Prevention of Cruelty to Animals. Present name adopted in 1840.

Activities: Prevents cruelty and promotes kindness to, and alleviates the suffering of, all animals. The Society encourages responsible pet care, supports animal welfare projects and operates a 24-hour cruelty and advice line. It campaigns to improve the welfare of pets and wild animal; improve the lives and reduce the suffering of farm animals; and reduce the suffering of animals used in research. The Society educates in schools and through its network of educational professionals; and also carries out scientific and technical research on all aspects of farm, wild, laboratory and companion animal welfare.

Geographical Area of Activity: England and Wales, with some international activity.

Publications: *Science Review; Animal Life; Animal Action; The Welfare State: Measuring Animal Welfare in the UK;* Annual Review; Trustees' Report and Accounts.

Finance: Annual income £121,245,000, expenditure £117,377,000 (31 Dec. 2013).

Governing Council: Michael Tomlinson (Chair.); Paul Draycott (Vice-Chair.) Karen Harley (Treas.); Paul Baxter (Deputy Treas.).

Address: Wilberforce Way, Southwater, Horsham, West Sussex RH13 9RS.

Telephone: (300) 123-0100 (switchboard); (300) 1234-555 (enquiries); **Fax:** (303) 123-0100; **Internet:** www.rspca.org.uk; **e-mail:** executive@rspca.org.uk.

Royal Society for the Protection of Birds—RSPB

Founded in 1889 as the Society for the Protection of Birds; became the Royal Society for the Protection of Birds in 1904 to campaign against the killing of wild birds for their plumage for use in the millinery trade.

Activities: Promotes the conservation of birds and wildlife throughout the United Kingdom and worldwide. The Society works to protect and recreate habitats for endangered birds and wildlife. It acquires land and manages many nature reserves; campaigns for better protection and management of wildlife sites not in conservation ownership; works in partnership with conservation organizations, including BirdLife International (q.v.), in Europe, Africa and Asia; and aims to develop awareness of conservation issues through education, and to influence education in agriculture, planning and other key professions. Programmes include birds and biodiversity, biodiversity and sustainability, and collaboration with local communities on issues of national importance. Also seeks to influence national and international government policy.

Geographical Area of Activity: United Kingdom, Europe, Africa, Asia and Middle East.

Publications: Annual Review and Annual Report; *Birds* (members' magazine).

Finance: Annual income £127,045,000, expenditure £126,779,000 (31 March 2014).

Council: Prof. Steve Ormerod (Chair.).

Principal Staff: Pres. Miranda Krestovnikoff; Chief Exec. Mike Clarke.

Address: The Lodge, Potton Rd, Sandy SG19 2DL.

Telephone: (1767) 680551; **Internet:** www.rspb.org.uk; **e-mail:** membership@rspb.org.uk.

The Rufford Foundation

Established in 2013 by the merger of the Rufford Small Grants Foundation, which was founded in 2007, and the Rufford Foundation, founded in 1982 by John Hedley Laing.

Activities: Supports nature conservation projects, predominantly in developing countries. The main area of giving is through the Foundation's small grants programme, which targets individuals and small organizations in developing countries.

Geographical Area of Activity: Mainly the developing world.

Restrictions: Only funds nature/biodiversity conservation projects. Rarely funds projects in developed countries.

Finance: Annual income £3,656,366, expenditure £4,373,972 (5 April 2014).

Board of Trustees: John H. Laing (Chair.).

Principal Staff: Dir Terry Kenny.

Address: 248 Tottenham Court Rd, 6th Floor, London W1T 7QZ.

Telephone: (20) 7436-8604; **Internet:** www.rufford.org; **e-mail:** admin@rufford.org.

Bertrand Russell Peace Foundation—BRPF

Founded in 1963 by Bertrand Russell to campaign for international disarmament, peace and social justice.

Activities: Organizes campaigns for peace and disarmament and for political prisoners, and the European Peace and Human Rights Conference.

Geographical Area of Activity: Europe.

Publications: *The Spokesman* (quarterly); leaflets, letters, books and pamphlets.

Principal Staff: Dir and Sec. Ken Fleet; Publisher Tony Simpson.

Address: Russell House, Bulwell Lane, Nottingham NG6 0BT.

Telephone: (115) 970-8318; **Fax:** (115) 942-0433; **Internet:** www.spokesmanbooks.com; www.russfound.org; **e-mail:** elfeuro@compuserve.com.

Saïd Foundation

Founded in 1982 to alleviate poverty and suffering among children and young people in the Middle East.

Activities: Operates in the fields of education and disability through grants to institutions working with disadvantaged children and young people. Grants are usually made to experienced NGOs in Jordan, Lebanon, the Palestinian Territories and Syria. Awards scholarships to students from the Middle East for postgraduate study in the United Kingdom. The Foundation supports the Saïd Business School (at the University of Oxford) Strategic Development Fund. It encourages the development of Syria, particularly in the areas of disability, health, education and culture; and supports the Saïd Foundation for Development, which was established in 2010 in Syria.

Geographical Area of Activity: Middle East (in particular Syria, as well as Jordan, Lebanon and the Palestinian Territories) and the United Kingdom.

Publications: E-newsletter; annual printed newsletter; brochure.

Finance: Annual income £3,432,192, expenditure £5,908,110 (31 Aug. 2013).

Trustees: Wafic R. Saïd (Chair.).

Principal Staff: CEO Neville McBain.

Address: 24 Queen Anne's Gate, London SW1H 9AA.

Telephone: (20) 7593-5420; **Fax:** (20) 7593-5429; **Internet:** www.saidfoundation.org; **e-mail:** admin@saidfoundation.org.

St John Ambulance

Founded in the United Kingdom in 1877 to provide care for the sick and organize classes in first aid. A foundation of the Order of St John, which traces its roots back to the 11th-century Crusades, and subsidiary of the Priory of England and the Islands of the Most Venerable Order of the Hospital of St John of Jerusalem.

Activities: Provides first aid and care training to almost 500,000 people every year in the United Kingdom. Care programmes include: primary health care for the homeless; training courses for those working with the homeless; conferences to promote healthy lifestyles, aimed at young people; care courses; care handbook; young carers' support groups; and young carers' resource pack. The association runs first aid courses for young people through co-operation with schools; develops new courses and course materials to meet the needs of communities and customers; and provides first aid cover at sporting and entertainment events, at national and local levels. It is supported by more than 47,000 volunteer workers, more than one-half of whom are under the age of 18 years. Also provides dental and ophthalmic care; relief and disaster planning; primary health care; youth programmes; and, in some cases, provides the statutory ambulance service. Has members in 42 countries. Maintains a reference library.

Geographical Area of Activity: Worldwide.

Publications: Annual Review.

Finance: Annual income £91.4m., expenditure £97.1m. (31 Dec. 2013).

Board of Trustees: Rodney Green (Chair.).

Principal Staff: Chief Exec. Sue A. Killen.

Address: 27 St John's Lane, London EC1M 4BU.

Telephone: (8700) 104950; **Fax:** (8700) 104065; **Internet:** www.sja.org.uk; **e-mail:** info@sja.org.uk.

The Salvation Army

Founded in 1865 by William Booth for the advancement of the Christian religion as promulgated in the religious doctrines that are professed, believed and taught by the Army and, pursuant thereto, the advancement of education, the relief of poverty and other charitable objects beneficial to society or the community of mankind as a whole. A quasi-military command structure was introduced in 1878.

Activities: Promotes the advancement of the Christian religion. The organization also carries out specific projects around the world, including emergency housing, feeding and clothing; medical and educational work; agricultural training and social welfare programmes. Operates in 119 countries.

Geographical Area of Activity: International.

Finance: Annual income £196,265,000, expenditure £166,957,000 (31 March 2014).

Trustees: Cmmr Clive Adams (Chair); Col David Hinton (Deputy Chair.); Lt-Col Alan Read (Man. Dir).

Principal Staff: High Council Gen. André Cox.

Address: 101 Queen Victoria St, London EC4P 4EP.

Telephone: (20) 7332-0101; **Fax:** (20) 7236-4681; **Internet:** www.salvationarmy.org; **e-mail:** info@salvationarmy.org.

Save the Children

Established in 1919 by Eglantyne Jebb and her sister Dorothy Buxton, as the international arm of Save the Children (q.v.), to promote a world view that respects and values each child; listens to and learns from children; and where all children have hope and opportunity. Formerly known as International Save the Children Alliance.

Activities: Operates internationally through 27 member organizations in more than 110 countries, promoting children's rights, assisting children involved in war or natural disasters, and delivering immediate and lasting improvements to children's lives worldwide. The organization works through both domestic and international programmes. Promotes the International Convention on the Rights of the Child. Maintains a regional office in Brussels, Belgium.

Geographical Area of Activity: International.

Publications: *Children's Rights: A Second Chance*; *UN study on violence against children*; *Forgotten Casualties of War*; *Child Protection Policy*; Annual Reports and other publications.

Finance: Annual income £559,141,304 expenditure £555,684,783 (31 Dec. 2013).

Board: Charles R. Perrin (Chair.).

Principal Staff: CEO Jasmine Whitbread.

Address: St Vincent House, 30 Orange St, London WC2H 7HH.

Telephone: (20) 8748-2554; **Fax:** (20) 8237-8000; **Internet:** www.savethechildren.net; **e-mail:** info@savethechildren.org.

Save the Children (UK)

Established in 1919 to assist disadvantaged and vulnerable children worldwide.

Activities: Commited to the rights of children, as enshrined in the UN Convention on the Rights of the Child. The organization runs programmes nationally and internationally to help children in the areas of social protection; welfare and inclusion; education; health; food security and nutrition; HIV/AIDS and children; and work. It provides emergency relief as well as long-term development and prevention work. Collaborates in its work with local, national and international organizations and governments. Supports projects in around 70 countries.

Geographical Area of Activity: International.

Restrictions: No grants to individuals; works in partnership with other NGOs, governments and local, national and international organizations.

Publications: Annual Report; financial accounts; subject-specific publications: *What makes me happy*; *The Right Not to Lose Hope*; *Safe Learning*; *Paying with their lives*.

Finance: Annual income £342,594,000, expenditure £308,912,000 (31 Dec. 2013).

Board of Trustees: Sir Alan Parker (Chair.); Mark Esiri, Fiona MacBain (Vice-Chair.); Richard Winter (Hon. Treas.).

Principal Staff: Chief Exec. Justin Forsyth; COO Jennifer Geary.

Address: 1 St John's Lane, London EC1M 4AR.

Telephone: (20) 7012-6400; **Fax:** (20) 7012-6963; **Internet:** www.savethechildren.org.uk; **e-mail:** supporter.care@savethechildren.org.uk.

Science and Technology Facilities Council—STFC

Established in 2007 following the merger of the Council for the Central Laboratory of the Research Councils and the Particle Physics and Astronomy Research Council, and the transfer of responsibility for nuclear physics from the Engineering and Physical Sciences Research Council.

Activities: Funds researchers in universities directly through grants, particularly in astronomy, particle physics, space science and nuclear physics. The Council provides access to facilities that include ISIS, the Central Laser Facility, and High-End Computing Terascale Resource (HECToR). It is also a major stakeholder in the Diamond Light Source, which started operations in 2007. The Council provides a broad range of scientific and technical expertise in space and ground-based astronomy, microelectronics, wafer-scale manufacturing, particle and nuclear physics, alternative energy production, radio communications and radar. It provides access to facilities overseas, including through the European Organization for Nuclear Research (CERN); the European Space Agency; the European Southern Observatory; the European Synchrotron Radiation Facility; the Institut Laue-Langevin and telescope facilities in Chile, Hawaii and La Palma; and the MERLIN/VLBI National Facility, which includes the Lovell Telescope at Jodrell Bank Observatory.

Geographical Area of Activity: United Kingdom; funding for telescopes in Australia, Chile and the Canary Islands (Spain); international research partnerships.

Finance: Funded by the United Kingdom Government. Annual budget £489m. (2013–14).

Council: Prof. Sir Michael Sterling (Chair.).

Principal Staff: CEO Prof. John Womersley.

Address: Polaris House, North Star Ave, Swindon SN2 1SZ.

Telephone: (1793) 442000; **Fax:** (1793) 442125; **Internet:** www.stfc.ac.uk; **e-mail:** enquiries@stfc.ac.uk.

Scope

Established in 1952 for the public benefit and for general charitable purposes according to the laws of England and Wales and in particular, but not exclusively, for the promotion of equality, diversity, independence and health of disabled people, especially those with cerebral palsy.

Activities: Works with disabled people and their families to give them the same opportunities as everyone else. The charity offers practical support, from information services to education and everyday care; and seeks to influence decision-makers.

Geographical Area of Activity: England and Wales.

Finance: Annual income £102,635,000, expenditure £103,295,000 (31 March 2014).

Board of Trustees: Alice Maynard (Chair.); Vicky McDermott (Vice-Chair.); John Gilbert (Hon. Treas.).

Principal Staff: Chief Exec. Richard Hawkes.

Address: 6 Market Rd, London N7 9PW.

Telephone: (20) 7619-7100; **Fax:** (1908) 321051; **Internet:** www.scope.org.uk; **e-mail:** response@scope.org.uk.

Scottish Catholic International Aid Fund—SCIAF

Founded in 1965 as the overseas relief development agency of the Scottish Catholic Church.

Activities: Provides support to poor communities in developing countries, raises awareness of the underlying causes of poverty, and campaigns for a fairer world.

Geographical Area of Activity: Developing countries.

Publications: Annual Report; mission statement; newsletter; *Review* magazine.

Finance: Annual income £7,725,053, expenditure £7,220,031 (31 Dec. 2013).

Board of Directors: Bishop Peter A. Moran (Pres.).

Principal Staff: Dir Alistair Dutton.

Address: 19 Park Circus, Glasgow G3 6BE.

Telephone: (141) 3545555; **Fax:** (141) 3545533; **Internet:** www.sciaf.org.uk; **e-mail:** sciaf@sciaf.org.uk.

Scouloudi Foundation

Founded in 1962 by Irene Scouloudi, a historian and philanthropist, for general charitable purposes; formerly known as the Twenty-Seven Foundation.

Activities: Operates in the United Kingdom. The Foundation distributes funds in the following areas: annual donations to the Institute of Historical Research of the University of London for research, publications and historical awards fellowships; regular donations to a selected list of national charities; and donations for special needs as they arise.

Geographical Area of Activity: United Kingdom.

Finance: Annual income £239,438, expenditure £261,674 (7 Feb. 2014).

Trustees: Sarah E. Baxter (Chair.).

Address: c/o Haysmacintyre, 26 Red Lion Sq., London WC1R 4AG.

Telephone: (20) 7969-5500; **Fax:** (20) 7969-5600.

Seafarers UK

Founded in 1917 by HM King George V to raise funds to support Marine Benevolent and Welfare Institutions throughout the United Kingdom and the Commonwealth. Granted a

Royal Charter in 1920. Formerly known as the King George's Fund for Sailors.

Activities: Works to unite the maritime charity sector to address the specific needs of all seafarers and their families.

Geographical Area of Activity: United Kingdom and Commonwealth.

Restrictions: No grants to individuals.

Publications: *Flagship* (supporter magazine, 3 a year); *Nautical Welfare Guide* (every 2–3 years); Annual Report and accounts.

Finance: Annual income £2,862,000, expenditure £4,541,000 (31 Dec. 2013).

General Council: HRH The Earl of Wessex (Pres.); Vice-Adm. Peter J. Wilkinson (Chair.); Peter Mamelok (Deputy Chair.).

Principal Staff: Dir-Gen. Commodore Barry W. Bryant; Exec. Man. Robina Whitehorn.

Address: 8 Hatherley St, London SW1P 2YY.

Telephone: (20) 7932-0000; **Fax:** (20) 7932-0095; **Internet:** www.seafarers-uk.org; **e-mail:** seafarers@seafarers-uk.org.

Shackleton Foundation

Established in 2007 to support individuals of all ages, nationalities and backgrounds who exemplify the spirit of Sir Ernest Shackleton: inspirational leaders aiming to assist the disadvantaged.

Activities: Commemorates the life of Sir Ernest Shackleton. Also offers Leadership Awards.

Finance: Annual income £56,720, expenditure £53,753 (31 March 2014).

Board of Trustees: Bill Shipton (Chair.).

Address: 52 Mount St, London W1K 2SF.

Internet: www.shackletonfoundation.org; **e-mail:** info@shackletonfoundation.org.

Shell Foundation

Established in 2000 by the Royal Dutch/Shell Group to support initiatives worldwide in the area of sustainable development.

Activities: Operates worldwide in the field of conservation and the environment, mainly through its Sustainable Energy Programme, but also through two further programmes, the Sustainable Communities and the Promoting Youth Enterprise Programmes. The Foundation offers grants for projects carried out by non-profit-making groups or organizations.

Geographical Area of Activity: Worldwide.

Publications: Financial Report; newsletter.

Finance: Annual income £16,288,679, expenditure £25,516,753 (31 Dec. 2013).

Trustees: Malcolm Brinded (Chair.).

Principal Staff: Dir Sam Parker; Deputy Dir Pradeep Pursnani.

Address: Shell Centre, London SE1 7NA.

Telephone: (20) 7934-2727; **Fax:** (20) 7934-7348; **Internet:** www.shellfoundation.org; **e-mail:** info@shellfoundation.org.

Shelter—National Campaign for Homeless People

Founded to improve the quality of life of homeless people and those with inadequate housing.

Activities: Supports homeless people through the following programmes: Shelterline, a free national telephone helpline, which provides advice and information; Housing Aid Centres at 59 locations, which provide information, advice and advocacy; Homeless to Home Projects, which aim to resettle homeless families; the Street Homelessness Project, which works with local authorities and voluntary organizations to help reduce the number of people sleeping in the street; the National Homelessness Advice Service; and the Homework Project, which aims to prevent homelessness through educating children and providing educational materials to schools. In addition to these programme areas, the organization runs Shelter Training; works with politicians at all levels on housing and welfare issues; and is closely involved with initiatives dealing with social exclusion.

Geographical Area of Activity: United Kingdom.

Publications: *Roof* (newsletter, 6 a year); policy reports, briefings and fact sheets; Annual Report; and other publications on housing-related subjects.

Finance: Annual income £57,540,000, expenditure £59,845,000 (31 March 2014).

Board of Trustees: Sir Derek Myers (Chair.); Jon Kenworthy (Vice-Chair.); Daniel Oppenheimer (Sec.).

Principal Staff: Chief Exec. Campbell Robb.

Address: 88 Old St, London EC1V 9HU.

Telephone: (20) 7505-2162; (808) 800-4444 (helpline); **Fax:** (20) 7505-2030; **Internet:** www.shelter.org.uk; **e-mail:** info@shelter.org.uk.

Archie Sherman Charitable Trust

Founded in 1967 for general charitable purposes.

Activities: Operates nationally and internationally in the fields of health and education.

Geographical Area of Activity: International.

Finance: Annual income £1,426,830, expenditure £1,413,397 (5 April 2014).

Trustees: Michael J. Gee; A. H. S. Morgenthau; E. A. Charles; R. Freedman.

Principal Staff: Sec. Archana Vishnu.

Address: Flat 27, Berkeley House, 15 Hay Hill, London W1J 8NS.

Telephone: (20) 7493-1904; **e-mail:** trust@sherman.co.uk.

Sight Savers International

Founded in 1950 to prevent and cure blindness and promote the welfare, education and employment of blind people in developing countries.

Activities: Operates in 32 developing countries in the field of blindness prevention and cure. The organization works in co-operation with the World Health Organization and major international NGOs. It designs and delivers projects with the help of local and regional organizations and national agencies to bring services to the maximum number of people.

Geographical Area of Activity: Africa, Southern Asia, the Caribbean and Europe.

Publications: Annual Report; newsletter (monthly).

Finance: Annual income £199,688,000, expenditure £200,406,000 (31 Dec. 2013).

Trustees: Lord Crisp (Chair.); Martin Dinham (Vice-Chair.); Mike Chilton (Hon. Treas.).

Principal Staff: Chief Exec. Dr Caroline Harper.

Address: Grosvenor Hall, Bolnore Rd, Haywards Heath RH16 4BX.

Telephone: (1444) 446600; **Fax:** (1444) 446688; **Internet:** www.sightsavers.org; **e-mail:** info@sightsavers.org.

Sino-British Fellowship Trust—SBFT

Founded in 1948 to provide educational scholarships dedicated to the advancement of human welfare.

Activities: Provides scholarships for postgraduate students from, and for British postgraduate students proceeding to, the People's Republic of China. The majority of grants are made to allied organizations; a small amount is available for individual grants in special circumstances, incl. grants made from the Katherine Whitaker Bequest for postgraduate scholars of Chinese medicine, Chinese arts and humanities, and Tibetan Buddhism.

Geographical Area of Activity: People's Republic of China and Europe.

Restrictions: Candidates must be over 27 years of age.

Publications: Annual Report.

Finance: Annual income £439,671, expenditure £507,032 (31 Dec. 2013).

Council: Anne Elizabeth Ely (Chair.); P.J. Ely (Deputy Chair.).

Address: c/o Flat 23, Bede House, Manor Fields, London SW15 3LT.

Telephone: (20) 8788-6252.

The Henry Smith Charity

Established in 1628 for the relief of the poor kindred of Henry Smith, the relief and maintenance of 'Godly preachers', and limited charitable purposes.

Activities: Operates in the United Kingdom (with local programmes in certain United Kingdom counties), in the areas of medicine and health, and social welfare. The Charity makes grants for projects in the fields of hospitals; hospices; young people; the elderly; disabled people; counselling and family advice; homelessness; drugs and alcohol; community service; general welfare; and medical research.

Geographical Area of Activity: United Kingdom.

Restrictions: Does not make grants to individuals, except for the relief of the poor kindred of Henry Smith and clergy of the Church of England; grants are made to charitable organizations only, and no grants are made for purposes outside the Charity's objectives. Grants are usually made to small charities, not to other grantmaking organizations.

Publications: Annual Report.

Finance: Annual income £10,621,000, expenditure £40,621,000 (31 Dec. 2013).

Trustees: Jamie D. Hambro (Chair.).

Principal Staff: Dir Nick A. B. Acland.

Address: 6th Floor, 65–68 Leadenhall St, London EC3A 2AD.

Telephone: (20) 7264-4970; **Fax:** (20) 7488-9097; **Internet:** www.henrysmithcharity.org.uk.

Sobell Foundation

Founded in 1977 by the late Sir Michael Sobell for general charitable purposes.

Activities: Operates in the fields of medicine and health, and social welfare, through supporting projects that benefit children, the elderly, the poor, the ill and the disabled. The Foundation supports Jewish charities and non-Jewish charities in England, Wales, Israel and the Commonwealth of Independent States.

Geographical Area of Activity: England, Wales, Israel, Commonwealth of Independent States.

Restrictions: No grants to individuals; applicants must be United Kingdom-registered charities.

Finance: Annual income £2,100,201, expenditure £5,219,165 (5 April 2014).

Trustees: Roger K. Lewis; Susan G. Lacroix; Andrea G. Scouller.

Principal Staff: Admin. Penny Newton.

Address: POB 2137, Shepton Mallet, Somerset BA4 6YA.

Telephone: (1749) 813135; **Fax:** (1749) 813136; **Internet:** www.sobellfoundation.org.uk; **e-mail:** enquiries@sobellfoundation.org.uk.

Soroptimist International

An NGO established in 1921 to strive for human rights and advance the status of women.

Activities: Has more than 90,000 female members in 124 countries worldwide. Operates internationally in the areas of aid to less-developed countries, humanities, conservation, environment, education, international affairs, human rights, health, and through projects, grants and seminars. The organization consists of four federations: the Americas, Europe, Great Britain and Ireland, and the South-West Pacific.

Geographical Area of Activity: Worldwide.

Publications: *The International Soroptimist* and *Federation* magazines.

Principal Staff: Int. Pres. Yvonne Simpson; Int. Treas. Patricia Carruthers.

Address: 87 Glisson Rd, Cambridge CB1 2HG.

Telephone: (1223) 311833; **Fax:** (1223) 467951; **Internet:** www.soroptimistinternational.org; **e-mail:** hq@soroptimistinternational.org.

Spinal Research

Established in 1980 by Stewart Yesner to fund research nationally and internationally with the aim of ending permanent paralysis caused by spinal cord injury.

Activities: Operates nationally and internationally in the field of medical research into spinal cord injury, through funding laboratories in its research network.

Geographical Area of Activity: Worldwide.

Publications: Newsletters; Annual Review; research updates; *Annual Research Review.*

Finance: Annual income £2,072,271, expenditure £2,201,845 (31 March 2014).

Board of Trustees: John W. A. Hick (Chair.); Philippa Herbert (Deputy Chair.).

Principal Staff: Exec. and Scientific Dir Mark Bacon.

Address: Bramley Business Centre, Station Rd, Bramley, Guildford, Surrey GU5 0AZ.

Telephone: (1483) 898786; **Fax:** (1483) 898763; **Internet:** www.spinal-research.org; **e-mail:** info@spinal-research.org.

Staples Trust

Established in 1992, as one of the Sainsbury Family Charitable Trusts, all of which have a joint administration. Formerly known as the Jessica Sainsbury Charitable Trust.

Activities: Active in the fields of gender issues, human rights and civil liberties. The Trust operates in the United Kingdom, Brazil and Guatemala. It also runs the Frankopan Fund (f. 1999), which awards educational grants to students from Croatia.

Geographical Area of Activity: International.

Restrictions: No grants are made to individuals.

Publications: Annual Report.

Finance: Annual income £505,146, expenditure £667,401 (5 April 2014).

Principal Staff: Dir Alan P. Bookbinder; Finance Dir Paul Spokes.

Address: c/o The Sainsbury Family Charitable Trusts, The Peak, 5 Wilton Rd, London SW1V 1AP.

Telephone: (20) 7410-0330; **Fax:** (20) 7410-0332; **Internet:** www.sfct.org.uk/staples.html; **e-mail:** info@sfct.org.uk.

Stewards Company Limited

Founded in 1898 for general charitable purposes.

Activities: Provides grants to religious charitable organizations throughout the world, particularly those involved in missionary work.

Geographical Area of Activity: International.

Finance: Annual income £1,826,325, expenditure £6,475,305 (30 June 2014).

Board of Trustees: Alexander L. Mcilhinney (Chair.); Glyn J. Davies (Vice-Chair.).

Principal Staff: Dir of Operations Andrew B. Griffiths.

Address: 124 Wells Rd, Bath BA2 3AH.

Telephone: (1225) 427236; **e-mail:** stewardsco@stewards.co.uk.

Sir Halley Stewart Trust

Established in 1924 by Sir Halley Stewart to promote and support pioneering research in the medical, social, educational and religious fields, and help prevent human suffering, on a Christian basis.

Activities: Promotes and assists innovative research and groundbreaking developments, and aims to make these self-sustaining. The Trust emphasizes the prevention rather than alleviation of suffering.

Geographical Area of Activity: United Kingdom, Burkina Faso, northern Ghana.

Restrictions: No gap-year projects supported. Only grants to United Kingdom-registered charities; not individuals.

Finance: Annual income £1,063,000, expenditure £917,000 (31 March 2014).

Senior Trustees: Lord Stewartby (Pres.); Prof. Phillip Whitfield (Chair.); Joanna Womack (Hon. Treas.).

Principal Staff: Sec. Vicky Chant.

Address: 22 Earith Rd, Willingham, Cambridge CB24 5LS.

Telephone: (1954) 260707; **Fax:** (1954) 260707; **Internet:** www.sirhalleystewart.org.uk; **e-mail:** email@sirhalleystewart.org.uk.

Marie Stopes International—MSI

Founded in 1921 by Marie Stopes as the Mothers' Clinic.

Activities: Supports the right to have children by choice, not by chance, through the provision of information and services. The MSI lobbies governments and international organizations to influence policy and allocation of resources in the areas of family-planning services and reproductive health care. It provides information, and family-planning and health-care services, in 37 countries worldwide, working in collaboration with local organizations. Each programme is managed and run by a local team, and meets the specific needs of the country with the focus on building the capacity of indigenous organizations.

Geographical Area of Activity: Worldwide.

Publications: Annual Report; *First People* (newsletter); *Handbook on European Community Support*; *Abortion*; *Female sterilisation*; *Fees*; *Health screening*; *Sex education*; *Vasectomy*.

Finance: Annual income £211,928,000, expenditure £203,310,000 (31 Dec. 2013).

Board of Trustees: Timothy M. Rutter (Chair.).

Principal Staff: CEO Simon Cooke; Deputy CEO Michael Holscher.

Address: 1 Conway St, Fitzroy Sq., London W1T 6LP.

Telephone: (20) 7636-6200; **Fax:** (20) 7034-2370; **Internet:** www.mariestopes.org.uk; **e-mail:** info@mariestopes.org.uk.

The Stroke Association

Established in 1899 as the National Association for the Prevention of Tuberculosis, becoming the Stroke Association in 1992.

Activities: Provides practical support to people who have had strokes, and their families; and increases awareness of strokes in society. The Association operates in England and Wales; provides community services; maintains a central information service and a network of regional information centres; offers support to families, and to those suffering from dysphasia; provides welfare grants; and makes grants for stroke research.

Geographical Area of Activity: England and Wales.

Publications: *Stroke News* (quarterly); leaflets and booklets; Annual review and accounts.

Finance: Annual income £33,546,000, expenditure £31,930,000 (31 March 2014).

Board of Trustees: Sir David Varney (Chair.); Richard Polson (Sec.).

Principal Staff: Chief Exec. Jon Barrick.

Address: Stroke Association House, 240 City Rd, London EC1V 2PR.

Telephone: (20) 7566-0300; **Fax:** (20) 7490-2686; **Internet:** www.stroke.org.uk; **e-mail:** info@stroke.org.uk.

The Bernard Sunley Charitable Foundation

Founded in 1960 to provide funds for general charitable purposes.

Activities: Seeks to raise the quality of life, particularly for those who are young, disadvantaged, deprived, disabled or elderly. The Foundation provides financial assistance to charitable projects in the United Kingdom in areas including education for those with special needs, activities for young people to realise their potential, the arts and humanities, wildlife and the environment, hospices and medical research, encouraging community cohesion and youth training, and provision for the elderly.

Geographical Area of Activity: United Kingdom.

Restrictions: No grants made to individuals.

Publications: Annual Report.

Finance: Annual income £3,802,000, expenditure £3,414,000 (31 March 2014).

Trustees: Anabel Knight (Chair.).

Principal Staff: Chief Exec. John A. Rimington.

Address: 20 Berkeley Sq., London W1J 6LH.

Telephone: (20) 7408-2198; **Internet:** www.bernardsunley.org; **e-mail:** office@bernardsunley.org.

Survival International

Founded in 1969; a worldwide organization supporting the rights of tribal peoples to decide their own future, and to protect their lives, lands and human rights.

Activities: Runs campaigns to attract international support for indigenous peoples under threat; provides information and educational materials; and supports health and educational projects that benefit indigenous peoples. Has members in more than 90 countries.

Geographical Area of Activity: Worldwide.

Publications: News releases; background materials.

Finance: Annual income £1,120,111, expenditure £987,480 (31 Dec. 2013).

Board of Trustees: Robin Hanbury-Tenison (Pres.); Michael Davis (Treas.).

Principal Staff: Dir-Gen. Stephen Corry.

Address: 6 Charterhouse Bldgs, London EC1M 7ET.

Telephone: (20) 7687-8700; **Fax:** (20) 7687-8701; **Internet:** www.survivalinternational.org; **e-mail:** info@survivalinternational.org.

John Swire 1989 Charitable Trust

Founded in 1989.

Activities: Awards grants for general charitable purposes.

Geographical Area of Activity: International.

Restrictions: Individual applications are not accepted.

Finance: Annual revenue £1,163,100, expenditure £1,623,125 (31 Dec. 2013).

Principal Staff: Settlor Sir John Swire.

Address: Swire House, 59 Buckingham Gate, London SW1E 6AJ.

Telephone: (20) 7834-7717; **Fax:** (20) 7630-5534.

Tearfund

Founded in 1968 by the Evangelical Alliance to serve churches in the United Kingdom and Ireland.

Activities: A relief and development agency, working for the relief of poverty, suffering and distress; involved in disaster response, disaster risk reduction and advocacy. The organization supports local churches to help transform lives materially and spiritually. Its 10-year vision is to see 50m. people released from material and spiritual poverty through a worldwide network of 100,000 local churches.

Geographical Area of Activity: Worldwide.

Publications: *Tear Times*; Annual Report; policy reports and research papers on issues including climate change, disaster risk reduction, food security, governance and corruption, HIV, sustainable economics, and water and sanitation.

Finance: Annual income £59,372,000, expenditure £62,324,000 (31 March 2014).

Board of Directors: Clive Mather (Chair.); John Shaw (Treas.).

Principal Staff: Chief Exec. Matthew Frost.

Address: 100 Church Rd, Teddington, TW11 8QE.

Telephone: (20) 8977-9144; **Fax:** (20) 8943-3594; **Internet:** www.tearfund.org; **e-mail:** enquiries@tearfund.org.

Thomson Foundation

Founded in 1962 by Roy Thomson (later Lord Thomson of Fleet) to provide training facilities for journalism and television in developing countries.

Activities: Practical training is given in the United Kingdom for media management and senior journalists, and specialized training in television production and engineering by arrangement; training teams are provided to help overseas media and media institutions to raise professional standards. More recently, the emphasis has been on providing experienced trainers to supply in-country training. The Foundation works in collaboration with UNESCO and other organizations to provide training advisory services to developing countries.

Geographical Area of Activity: International.

Restrictions: Grants only for Thomson courses.

Publications: Training manuals for journalism; television engineering videotapes; news archive.

Finance: Annual income £1,353,000, expenditure £1,567,000 (31 Dec. 2013).

Board of Trustees: Lord (Tom) Chandos of Aldershot (Chair.).

Principal Staff: CEO Nigel Baker.

Address: 46 Chancery Lane, London WC2A 1JE.

Telephone: (20) 3440-2440; **Internet:** www .thomsonfoundation.org; **e-mail:** enquiries@ thomsonfoundation.org.

Thomson Reuters Foundation

Founded in 1982 by Reuters, the international news and information organization, to aid the media in developing countries, and to narrow the gap in information technology between developed and developing countries.

Activities: Organizes training courses for practising journalists from developing countries and Eastern Europe in subjects including international, environmental, HIV/AIDS and business news-writing, photographic and television journalism. Reuters Foundation Fellowships are offered to journalists for study at the University of Oxford. The Foundation operates AlertNet, an Internet service aimed at providing news, field reports and forums to the international disaster relief community, and the AIDfund programme, which funds aid organizations dealing with large-scale natural disasters.

Geographical Area of Activity: International.

Restrictions: Does not make grants. Local causes are supported by the giving of Reuters' time, skills and talents through volunteering engagement.

Finance: Annual income £8,371,000, expenditure £8,873,000 (31 Dec. 2013).

Board of Trustees: David W. Binet (Chair.); Susan Jenner (Sec.).

Principal Staff: CEO Monique Villa.

Address: 30 South Colonnade, Canary Wharf, London E14 5EP.

Telephone: (20) 7542-7015; **Internet:** www.trust.org; **e-mail:** foundation@reuters.com.

The Sir Jules Thorn Charitable Trust

Founded in 1964 by Sir Jules Thorn to improve the quality of life for the sick and disadvantaged.

Activities: Funds medical research in universities and National Health Service organizations, and humanitarian work undertaken by registered charities. In 2001, the Trust launched the annual Sir Jules Thorn Award for Biomedical Research, which provides a grant of up to £1.25m. over five years for a programme of translational research. Its humanitarian grants include an annual Special Project award or awards up to a maximum of approximately £500,000 linked to a theme, selected by the Trustees, and numerous small donations to a wide range of charities.

Geographical Area of Activity: United Kingdom.

Restrictions: Grants are not made to individuals, nor to applicants from countries other than the United Kingdom.

Finance: Annual income £2,438,336, expenditure £13,594,052 (31 Dec. 2013).

Trustees: Elizabeth Charal (Chair.).

Principal Staff: Dir David H. Richings; Sr Exec. Andrew Elliot.

Address: 24 Manchester Sq., London W1U 3TH.

Telephone: (20) 7487-5851; **Fax:** (20) 7224-3976; **Internet:** www.julesthorntrust.org.uk; **e-mail:** info@julesthorntrust .org.uk.

Trans-Antarctic Association—TAA

Founded in 1962 by the Committee of Management of the Trans-Antarctic Expedition to further research in subjects relating to the Antarctic.

Activities: Makes annual awards to individuals for research and exploration in the Antarctic regions, publication of results, cost of travel to Antarctica, or attendance at international meetings concerned with Antarctic science.

Geographical Area of Activity: Antarctica.

Restrictions: Awards are made to citizens of the United Kingdom, Australia, New Zealand and South Africa only.

Finance: Annual income £12,372, expenditure £16,386 (31 Dec. 2013).

Trustees: Dr Peter D. Clarkson (Chair.).

Principal Staff: Company and Grants Sec. Dr James Smith.

Address: c/o British Antarctic Survey, High Cross, Madingley Rd, Cambridge, CB3 0ET.

Telephone: (1223) 221429; **Fax:** (1223) 362616; **Internet:** www .transantarctic.org.uk; **e-mail:** taagrants@bas.ac.uk.

Trust for London

Founded in 1891 as the City Parochial Foundation (CPF) for general charitable purposes in the Metropolitan Police District of London and the City of London. Present name adopted in 2010 following merger with Trust for London.

Activities: Operates within all London boroughs and the City of London; main priority areas are tackling poverty and inequality. Grants are made to organizations working in these areas.

Geographical Area of Activity: London Boroughs and City of London.

Restrictions: No grants are made to individuals, nor for medical research or equipment, trips abroad, one-off events, major capital appeals, the direct replacement of public funds, publications or endowment appeals.

Publications: *LSE analysis of UK Social Policy; LivingWage; Poverty and Austerity*; Annual Report; grant guidelines; grants review.

Finance: Annual income £9,090,334, expenditure £14,940,457 (31 Dec. 2013).

Board of Trustees: Jeff Hayes (Chair.); Loraine Martins (Vice-Chair.).

Principal Staff: Chief Exec. Bharat Mehta; Dir of Finance and Admin. Carol Harrison.

Address: 6 Middle St, London EC1A 7PH.

Telephone: (20) 7606-6145; **Fax:** (20) 7600-1866; **Internet:** www.trustforlondon.org.uk; **e-mail:** info@trustforlondon .org.uk.

Trusthouse Charitable Foundation

Established in 1997 following the takeover of the Forte company by Granada (and superseding the non-charitable but grant-distributing Council of Forte, established in 1904 to promote temperance), for general charitable purposes.

Activities: The Council of Forte makes grants mainly to medical projects and for the support of former members of the armed forces. Applications should specify the specific project and normally be for a small amount of funding. Awards around 300 grants annually.

Geographical Area of Activity: United Kingdom.

Restrictions: Does not normally support the following: small local charities; applications from individuals; foreign charities (although applications are considered from United Kingdom-based organizations that operate overseas). No grants to other grantmaking bodies; medical research projects; animal welfare; revenue funding for more than one year; social research; training professionals within the United Kingdom.

Publications: Annual Report.

Finance: Annual income £1,895,000, expenditure £2,838,000 (30 June 2014).

Board of Trustees: Olga Polizzi (Chair.).

Principal Staff: Dir Nick Acland.

Address: 65 Leadenhall St, 6th Floor, London EC3A 2AD.

Telephone: (20) 7264-4990; **Fax:** (20) 7488-9097; **Internet:** trusthousecharitablefoundation.org.uk.

Tudor Trust

Founded in 1955 for general charitable purposes.

Activities: An independent grantmaking trust that supports organizations working across the United Kingdom. The Trust aims to fund a wide range of organizations that are working to achieve lasting change in their communities. It is most interested in supporting smaller, under-resourced organizations that provide direct services to marginalized people, and that involve the people they work with in their planning.

Geographical Area of Activity: United Kingdom.

Restrictions: Applications for funding from outside the United Kingdom are not accepted. No grants are made to individuals, and demand for funding greatly exceeds the available finance.

Publications: *Funding Guidelines*; Annual Report.

Finance: Annual income £6,898,000, expenditure £21,617,000 (31 March 2014).

Board of Trustees: Nell Buckler (Chair.); James Long (Vice-Chair.).

Principal Staff: Dir Christopher Graves.

Address: 7 Ladbroke Grove, London W11 3BD.

Telephone: (20) 7727-8522; **Fax:** (20) 7221-8522; **Internet:** www.tudortrust.org.uk.

Turquoise Mountain Foundation

Established in 2006 to promote the regeneration and preservation of old Kabul, Afghanistan.

Activities: Works to preserve historic buildings and culture in Kabul. Maintains an office in Kabul. A separate US foundation operates in the USA.

Geographical Area of Activity: Afghanistan.

Finance: Annual income £2,444,362, expenditure £2,268,980 (31 Dec. 2013).

Trustees: Richard Keith (Chair.).

Principal Staff: Pres HRH Prince of Wales, HE Hamid Karzai.

Address: c/o Turcan Connell, Princes Exchange, 1 Earl Grey St, Edinburgh EH3 9EE.

Telephone: (1764) 650888; **Internet:** www.turquoisemountain.org; **e-mail:** contact@turquoisemountain.org.

Tutu Foundation UK

Established in 2007 to assist in peacebuilding in communities in the United Kingdom.

Activities: Works in the United Kingdom to build peace and reconciliation in communities in, or at risk of, conflict.

Geographical Area of Activity: United Kingdom.

Finance: Annual income £83,298, expenditure £104,187 (31 March 2014).

Board of Trustees: Clive Conway (Chair.); Dr Isaac John (Vice-Chair.); Edith Slee (Treas.); Peter King (Sec.).

Principal Staff: Interim CEO Prof. Surinder Sharma.

Address: c/o The Young Foundation, 18 Victoria Park Sq., Bethnal Green, London E2 9PF.

Telephone: (20) 8980-9737; **Internet:** www.tutufoundationuk.org; **e-mail:** info@tutufoundationuk.org.

tve—Television for the Environment

Founded in 1984 by Central Independent Television (now part of ITV), WWF and the UN Environment Programme to inspire change towards a greener, fairer world, through the production and distribution of films.

Activities: Editorially independent, functions as a producer and distributor, encouraging film-makers to make new programmes and promoting the distribution of finished films. Since 1985, the Trust has produced and co-produced more than 3,000 films that focus on the environment, development, human rights and health. It distributes programmes either free or on a subsidized basis to television stations in developing countries, and sells films to channels in high-income countries; its films are also used in schools and universities and are available online. The Trust works with a network of more than 45 long-standing partners in Asia, Africa, Latin America, the Caribbean and the Middle East, and with other film-makers and distributors around the world.

Geographical Area of Activity: Worldwide.

Publications: *Why Women Count; tvebiomovies; YouTube Relay; Future Food; Reframing Rio—Life Apps; Voices; Zero Ten Twenty; Looting the Pacific; Earth Reporters; Early Life.*

Finance: Annual income £865,905, expenditure £884,457 (31 Dec. 2013).

Trustees: Richard Creasey (Chair.).

Principal Staff: Exec. Dir Cheryl Campbell.

Address: 292 Vauxhall Bridge Rd, London SW1V 1AE.

Telephone: (20) 7147-7420; **Internet:** www.tve.org; **e-mail:** tve@tve.org.uk.

Twenty-Ninth May 1961 Charity

Founded anonymously on 29 May 1961 for general charitable purposes.

Activities: Operates nationally in the fields of education, social welfare, science and medicine, and the arts and humanities, through grants to institutions.

Geographical Area of Activity: United Kingdom.

Restrictions: Grants are not made to individuals.

Publications: List of grants awarded.

Finance: Annual income £3,416,822, expenditure £6,141,248 (5 April 2014).

Principal Staff: Contact Vanni Emanuele Treves.

Address: Ryder Ct, 14 Ryder St, London SW1Y 6QB.

Telephone: (20) 7024-9034; **e-mail:** enquiries@29may1961charity.org.uk.

UJIA—United Jewish Israel Appeal

Founded in 1968 to ensure a positive future for young people in the United Kingdom and Israel.

Activities: Operates numerous school and after-school programmes for pupils and teachers; runs Jewish youth movements and the UJIA Israel Experience; supports the Union of Jewish Students and young people in the United Kingdom; and educational initiatives for young people in Israel.

Geographical Area of Activity: United Kingdom and the Galil, northern Israel.

Finance: Annual income £10,180,000, expenditure £10,661,000 (30 Sept. 2013).

Trustees: Bill Benjamin (Chair.).

Principal Staff: Chief Exec. Michael Wegier.

Address: 37 Kentish Town Rd, London NW1 8NX.

Telephone: (20) 7424-6400; **Fax:** (20) 7424-6401; **Internet:** www.ujia.org; **e-mail:** central@ujia.org.

UNA Trust—United Nations Association Trust

Established in 1968; a registered charity, independent of the UN and not funded by it.

Activities: Strives to make reality of the UN's aim to promote peace, justice and development for all. The Trust operates nationally and internationally in the fields of education and international relations, through self-conducted programmes.

Geographical Area of Activity: International.

Restrictions: Funds are used almost exclusively to assist the educational work of the UN Association (UNA) and the work of UNA International Service (UNAIS).

Publications: *New World* (magazine).

Finance: Annual income £318,500, expenditure £407,700 (30 June 2013).

Board of Directors: Rodney Fielding (Chair.); Sally Kakar (Hon. Treas.); Anthony Donnelly (Sec.).

Principal Staff: Exec. Dir Natalie Samarasinghe.

Address: 3 Whitehall Ct, London SW1A 2EL.

Telephone: (20) 7766-3454; **Fax:** (20) 7000-1381; **Internet:** www.una.org.uk; **e-mail:** membership@una.org.uk.

United Society for Christian Literature—USCL

Founded in 1799 (incorporated 1899) to disseminate the Christian message through the use of the printed word, and thus to serve Churches at home and abroad. Present name adopted in 1935.

Activities: Operates internationally in the fields of religion and education, by making grants to institutions for the production and dissemination of Christian literature in developing countries, principally through Feed the Minds (q.v., founded in 1964 to raise funds for literature and communication programmes in developing countries).

Geographical Area of Activity: International.

Restrictions: No grants are made to individuals.

Publications: Report of operations and financial statement.

Finance: Annual income £162,571, expenditure £178,616 (30 April 2014).

Committee: John Clark (Chair.); Dr Frances Shaw, Rev Joanna Yates (Hon. Secs); Edward Duffield (Hon. Treas.).

Principal Staff: Dir and Sec. Josephine Carlsson.

Address: Park Pl., 12 Lawn Lane, London SW8 1UD.

Telephone: (20) 7582-3535; **Fax:** (20) 7735-7617; **Internet:** www.uscl.org.uk; **e-mail:** info@feedtheminds.org.

Us.

Founded in 1701 by Dr Thomas Bray, DD, as the Society for the Propagation of the Gospel in Foreign Parts, it merged with the Universities' Mission to Central Africa (f. 1857) in 1965 to become the United Society for the Propagation of the Gospel. Present name adopted in 2012.

Activities: Partners with Anglican churches worldwide. The organization works alongside local communities to improve health, put children in school, tackle discrimination, nurture leaders, and give a voice to women.

Geographical Area of Activity: International.

Publications: *Transmission* magazine (3 times a year); educational, promotional and prayer material, DVDs and online films.

Finance: Annual income £3,752,000, expenditure £4,283,000 (31 Dec. 2013).

Trustees: Rev Canon Christopher Chivers (Chair.); Rev Richard Bartlett (Vice-Chair.).

Principal Staff: Chief Exec. and Gen. Sec. Janette O'Neill.

Address: Harling House, 47–51 Great Suffolk St, London SE1 0BS.

Telephone: (20) 7921-2200; **Fax:** (20) 7378-5650; **Internet:** www.weareus.org.uk; **e-mail:** info@weareus.org.uk.

Van Neste Foundation

Founded in 1959 for general charitable purposes.

Activities: Operates nationally and internationally, especially in developing countries and Eastern Europe, in the areas of assisting the disabled and the elderly, and the promotion of religion, the community and the family.

Geographical Area of Activity: International.

Finance: Annual income £295,724, expenditure £330,775 (5 April 2014).

Principal Staff: Sec. Fergus J. F. Lyons.

Address: 15 Alexandra Rd, Clifton, Bristol BS8 2DD.

Telephone: (117) 973-5167.

Victoria League for Commonwealth Friendship

Founded in 1901 to promote friendship and understanding among the peoples of the Commonwealth.

Activities: Runs a hostel in London, providing student accommodation, and organizes trips and events for United Kingdom and Commonwealth members and guests in the United Kingdom. The League operates autonomously in Australia, New Zealand, Scotland, South Africa and Zimbabwe. There are affiliated organizations in Canada and the USA.

Geographical Area of Activity: International.

Publications: Report of operations and financial statement; newsletter.

Finance: Total income £314,205, expenditure £309,920 (31 Dec. 2013).

Board of Trustees: Lyn D. Hopkins (Chair.); Caroline Roughton (Treas.).

Principal Staff: Gen. Man. Doreen Henry.

Address: Victoria League House, 55 Leinster Sq., London W2 4PW.

Telephone: (20) 7243-2633; **Fax:** (20) 7229-2994; **Internet:** www.victorialeague.co.uk; **e-mail:** membership@victorialeague.co.uk.

Vodafone Foundation

Established in 2001 to offer disaster relief, and to fund cultural and sports projects for disadvantaged young people and communities.

Activities: Works in countries where the Vodafone companies operate, in a number of areas, including health, social welfare, the arts and culture, and conservation and the environment. Grants are made through 28 local Vodafone foundations and social investment programmes, which distribute two-thirds of the Foundation's funding. One-third of grants are awarded for disaster relief and preparedness, and for sport and music projects for disadvantaged young people. In 2008, the Foundation announced that it would co-operate with the UN World Food Programme and the UN Foundation (q.v.) to establish an information technology training programme to help agencies respond to disasters and emergencies worldwide.

Geographical Area of Activity: International.

Finance: Annual income £22,026,277, expenditure £22,507,711 (31 March 2014).

Trustees: Nick Land (Chair.).

Principal Staff: Dir Andrew Dunnett.

Address: Vodafone House, The Connection, Newbury RG14 2FN.

Telephone: (1635) 33251; **Internet:** www.vodafone.com/start/foundation.html; **e-mail:** groupfoundation@vodafone.com.

VSO—Voluntary Service Overseas

Founded in 1958.

Activities: Operates in around 44 of the world's disadvantaged countries in Europe, Africa, Asia, the Pacific, Latin America and the Carribean, working with local organizations to tackle poverty. Volunteers share their skills in education, health, business, management, technical and natural resources placements to achieve specific goals in education,

HIV and AIDS, disability, health and social well-being, secure livelihoods, and participation and governance. The organization adopts three approaches in its work: empowerment, partnership and commitment to training through a range of approaches, including international volunteering, networking and alliance-building, awareness-raising and advocacy.

Geographical Area of Activity: Africa, Eastern Europe, South and South-East Asia, Latin America and the Pacific.

Restrictions: Does not make grants.

Publications: Annual Report; education and development publications for development practitioners; advocacy papers; working papers.

Finance: Annual income £68,713,000, expenditure £68,227,000 (31 March 2014).

International Board: Mari Simonen (Chair.); Sam Younger (Vice-Chair.); John Bason (Hon. Treas.).

Principal Staff: Chief Exec. Dr Philip Goodwin.

Address: 100 London Rd, Kingston upon Thames, Surrey KT2 6QJ.

Telephone: (20) 8780-7500; **Internet:** www.vso.org.uk; **e-mail:** enquiry@vso.org.uk.

Charles Wallace India Trust

Founded in 1982 to provide funds to enable citizens of India to undertake study or research, or to gain professional experience in the United Kingdom.

Activities: Provides grants in the areas of the performing and visual arts, Indian artistic and cultural heritage, and the humanities.

Geographical Area of Activity: India and the United Kingdom.

Restrictions: Grants made only to Indian citizens normally resident and domiciled in that country.

Finance: Annual income £293,617, expenditure £237,381 (5 April 2014).

Trustees: Richard Alford (Sec.).

Address: British Council, 10 Spring Gardens, London SW1A 2BN.

Telephone: (20) 7389-4385; **Internet:** www.britishcouncil.org/india-scholarships-cwit; **e-mail:** cwit@in.britishcouncil.org.

War on Want

Founded in 1951 by Harold Wilson and Victor Gollancz to campaign against world poverty.

Activities: Operates nationally and internationally in the fields of aid to less-developed countries and development studies, through grants to institutions, and organizing training courses and conferences. Current campaign programmes include: supermarkets and sweatshops; corporations and conflict; trade justice; fighting occupation in Palestinian Territories, Iraq and Western Sahara; tax avoidance; financial crisis.

Geographical Area of Activity: International.

Restrictions: No unsolicited applications accepted.

Publications: *Upfront* (magazine); reports; Annual Report.

Finance: Total income £1,816,009, expenditure £1,666,876 (31 March 2014).

Council: Steve Preston (Chair.); David Hillman, Gaynelle Samuel (Vice-Chair.); Sue Branford (Treas.); Ben Birnberg (Sec.).

Principal Staff: Exec. Dir John Hilary.

Address: 44–48 Shepherdess Walk, London N1 7JP.

Telephone: (20) 7324-5040; **Fax:** (20) 7324-5041; **Internet:** www.waronwant.org; **e-mail:** support@waronwant.org.

WaterAid

Founded in 1981 at the start of the UN International Drinking Water Decade (1981–1990) to help ensure access to safe water and sanitation for the world's poorest people.

Activities: Enables the world's poorest people to gain access to safe water and sanitation as a first step in overcoming poverty. The organization works with local partners who understand local issues, and provides them with the skills and support to help communities set up and manage practical and sustainable projects that meet their real needs. Also works locally and internationally to change policy and practice, and ensure that water, hygiene and sanitation's vital role in reducing poverty is recognized.

Geographical Area of Activity: Africa and southern Asia.

Restrictions: Grants only to specific (partner) organizations.

Publications: *Oasis* (journal, 2 a year); Annual Report; other resources, such as country information sheets and issue sheets.

Finance: Annual income £73,695,000, expenditure £71,923,000 (31 March 2014).

Board of Trustees: Tim Clark (Chair.); Peter Newman (Hon. Treas.).

Principal Staff: Chief Exec. and Sec. Barbara Frost.

Address: 47–49 Durham St, London SE11 5JD.

Telephone: (20) 7793-4500; **Fax:** (20) 7793-4545; **Internet:** www.wateraid.org; **e-mail:** wateraid@wateraid.org.

Wates Foundation

Founded in 1966 for the improvement of quality of life, and to alleviate stress, particularly in the urban community.

Activities: Grants are allocated in five broad programme areas: Community Support and Development; Aid to Ethnic and Immigrant Communities; Foundations of Society; Arts, Heritage and the Environment; and Areas of Special Focus. There is also an emphasis on the physical, mental and spiritual welfare of young and disadvantaged people aged between 8 and 25 years, and racial equality is addressed throughout. Grants are concentrated on projects in the Greater London area, particularly South London and South-East England. Preference is given to projects that seek to comply with recognized quality assurance and accreditation schemes.

Geographical Area of Activity: Greater London.

Publications: Annual Report.

Finance: Annual income £392,005, expenditure £1,018,344 (31 March 2014).

Trustees: William Wates (Chair.).

Principal Staff: Dir Brian Wheelwright.

Address: Wates House, Station Approach, Leatherhead, Surrey KT22 7SW.

Telephone: (1372) 861251; **Fax:** (1372) 861252; **Internet:** www.watesfoundation.org.uk; **e-mail:** director@watesfoundation.org.uk.

Webb Memorial Trust

Founded in 1947 in memory of Beatrice Webb.

Activities: Finances projects furthering the cause of economic and social justice, in Eastern Europe and the United Kingdom, and funds fellowships at Ruskin College, Oxford.

Geographical Area of Activity: Eastern Europe and the United Kingdom.

Finance: Annual income £32,603, expenditure £257,056 (31 July 2014).

Board of Trustees: Richard Rawes (Chair.); Michael Parker (Hon. Sec.).

Address: Crane House, Unit 19, Apex Business Village, Annitsford, Newcastle NE23 7BF.

Internet: www.webbmemorialtrust.org.uk; **e-mail:** webb@cranehouse.eu.

Wellbeing of Women

Established in 1964 to support research concerned with better health of women and babies. Formerly known as WellBeing and prior to that as Birthright.

Activities: Raises money to improve women's health through research, training and education. The organization funds medical research to develop treatments, supports specialist training to improve doctors' effectiveness, and provides education for women so that they can stay well.

Geographical Area of Activity: United Kingdom and the Republic of Ireland.

Publications: Health information.

Finance: Annual income £2,125,273, expenditure £2,807,631 (31 Dec. 2013).

Trustees: Sir Marcus Setchell (Hon. Pres.); Sir Victor Blank (Chair.); Eve Pollard (Vice-Chair.).

Principal Staff: Chief Exec. Fiona Leishman.

Address: 1st Floor, Fairgate House, 78 New Oxford St, London WC1A 1HB.

Telephone: (20) 7697-7000; **Internet:** www .wellbeingofwomen.org.uk; **e-mail:** hello@ wellbeingofwomen.org.uk.

Wellcome Trust

Founded in 1936 by the will of the late Sir Henry Wellcome to support clinical and basic scientific research into human and veterinary medicine.

Activities: Supports research in all branches of clinical medicine (except cancer research) and basic biomedical sciences, through the provision of clinical and non-clinical research fellowships and postgraduate studentships, and programme, travel, project, refurbishment and equipment grants. Special interests include support of research into tropical medicine, population issues and the history of medicine. Special initiative funding includes the Joint Infrastructure Fund, University Challenge Fund, functional genomics, pathogen genome sequencing, United Kingdom Population Biomedical Collections and the Cardiovascular Initiative; the Trust is currently providing a significant contribution to the Human Genome Project. In 2009, the Beit Memorial Fellowships for Medical Research transferred all their undertakings to the Wellcome Trust.

Geographical Area of Activity: International.

Publications: *Wellcome News* (quarterly magazine); Annual Report and accounts; grants information booklet.

Finance: Annual income £337,962,640, expenditure £869,843,888 (30 Sept. 2014).

Board of Governors: Sir William Castell (Chair.).

Principal Staff: Dir Jeremy Farrar.

Address: Gibbs Bldg, 215 Euston Rd, London NW1 2BE.

Telephone: (20) 7611-8888; **Fax:** (20) 7611-8545; **Internet:** www.wellcome.ac.uk; **e-mail:** contact@wellcome.ac.uk.

Westminster Foundation for Democracy—WFD

Founded in 1992 to strengthen pluralist democratic development overseas.

Activities: An independent public body sponsored by the Foreign and Commonwealth Office (FCO), specializing in parliamentary strengthening and political party development. The Foundation is uniquely placed to draw directly on the expertise and involvement of all the Westminster political parties and works both on a party-to-party and cross-party basis to develop the capacity of local political parties and politicians to operate effectively in pluralistic and vibrant democracies. Its parliamentary work aims to strengthen good governance through developing sustainable capacity among parliamentarians, parliamentary staff and parliamentary structures to ensure transparency and accountability. The three main political parties in the United Kingdom are represented on the Governing Board, which also includes a representative of the smaller parties and independent members. Has worked on programmes in more than 40 countries.

Geographical Area of Activity: Has historically worked in three key regions: Eastern Europe, Sub-Saharan Africa and the Middle East and North Africa. However, there is considerable potential and demand to expand further into Africa and Asia, in particular in Commonwealth countries.

Publications: Annual Report; Annual Review; Newsletter; *Democracy in the Doldrums?*; *WFD's Strategic Framework 2015–2020*; *Supporting Democracy and Good Governance*; *Human Rights Handbook*; *Handbook on Ethics and Conduct*; *Building Better Democracies*.

Finance: Receives core funding from the United Kingdom FCO, as well as funding for specific programmes from the United Kingdom Department for International Development, the European Union and the British Council. Annual income £2,817,483, expenditure £3,499,742 (31 March 2014).

Board of Governors: Henry Bellingham (Chair.); Ann McKechin (Vice-Chair.).

Principal Staff: CEO Anthony Smith.

Address: Artillery House, 11–19 Artillery Row, London SW1P 1RT.

Telephone: (20) 7799-1311; **Fax:** (20) 7799-1312; **Internet:** www.wfd.org; **e-mail:** wfd@wfd.org.

Garfield Weston Foundation

Founded in 1958 for general charitable purposes.

Activities: Makes grants for the support of activities in the areas of religion, conservation and the environment, education, the arts, medicine and health, and welfare, community and youth. The Foundation's current focus is on welfare, youth and community, and economically disadvantaged regions.

Geographical Area of Activity: Mainly United Kingdom, with limited funding available overseas.

Restrictions: Grants are made to registered charities only (with the exception of applications from churches). No grants are made for animal welfare projects.

Publications: Annual Report.

Finance: Annual income £51,790,000, expenditure £54,531,000 (5 April 2014).

Trustees: Guy H. Weston (Chair.).

Principal Staff: Dir Philippa Charles.

Address: Weston Centre, 10 Grosvenor St, London W1K 4QY.

Telephone: (20) 7399-6565; **Fax:** (20) 7399-6580; **Internet:** www.garfieldweston.org.

Whitley Fund for Nature

Established in 1994 by Edward Whitley to offer awards in the area of conservation.

Activities: Offers awards and grants in the area of conservation to nature conservationists worldwide. Whitley Awards are worth £30,000 each; the Gold Award of an additional £30,000 is offered annually to one recipient.

Geographical Area of Activity: International.

Finance: Annual income £1,480,171, expenditure £1,567,875 (30 June 2014).

Trustees: Edward Whitley (Chair.).

Principal Staff: Dir Georgina Domberger.

Address: 6 Walmer Courtyard, 225 Walmer Rd, London W11 4EY.

Telephone: (20) 7221-9752; **Internet:** www.whitleyaward.org; **e-mail:** info@whitleyaward.org.

Harold Hyam Wingate Foundation

Founded in 1960 by Harold Hyam Wingate, the principal objective being the general advancement of Jewish and other charitable purposes.

Activities: Supports Jewish organizations, the performing arts, music, and problems associated with social exclusion.

Geographical Area of Activity: United Kingdom, Israel, developing countries.

Publications: Annual Accounts.

Finance: Annual income £260,418, expenditure £780,460 (5 April 2014).

Principal Staff: Admin. Karen C. Marshall.

Address: Golden Cross House, 8 Duncannon St, London WC2N 4JF.

Internet: www.wingatefoundation.org.uk.

The Wolfson Family Charitable Trust

Founded in 1958, and formerly known as the Edith and Isaac Wolfson Charitable Trust, for the advancement of health, education, the arts and humanities. The Trust shares objectives and joint administration with the Wolfson Foundation.

Activities: Operates through grants to institutions, in the United Kingdom and Israel in the above areas.

Geographical Area of Activity: United Kingdom and Israel.

Restrictions: No grants to individuals.

Publications: Annual Report and accounts.

Finance: Annual income £832,000, expenditure £1,582,000 (5 April 2014).

Trustees: Laura Wolfson Townsley (Chair.).

Principal Staff: Chief Exec. Paul Ramsbottom.

Address: 8 Queen Anne St, London W1G 9LD.

Telephone: (20) 7323-5730; **Fax:** (20) 7323-3241; **Internet:** www.wolfson.org.uk/about-us/wolfson-family-charitable-trust.

The Wolfson Foundation

Founded in 1955 for the support of science and medicine, health, education and the arts.

Activities: Supports excellence in science and medicine, health, education and the arts, usually through the provision of infrastructure.

Geographical Area of Activity: United Kingdom, the Commonwealth and Israel.

Restrictions: No grants to individuals.

Publications: Annual Report and accounts.

Finance: Annual income £19,765,000, expenditure £32,823,000 (5 April 2014).

Trustees: Dame Janet Wolfson de Botton (Chair.).

Principal Staff: Chief Exec. Paul Ramsbottom.

Address: 8 Queen Anne St, London W1G 9LD.

Telephone: (20) 7323-5730; **Fax:** (20) 7323-3241; **Internet:** www.wolfson.org.uk.

The Wood Foundation

Established in 2007 by Sir Ian Wood, former Chair. of the Wood Group oil company, as the Wood Family Trust. Present name adopted in 2014.

Activities: Main programmes are Making Markets Work for the Poor in Sub-Saharan Africa, Developing Young People in Scotland, and the Youth and Philanthropy Initiative Scotland.

Geographical Area of Activity: Sub-Saharan Africa and Scotland.

Restrictions: The Trust does not accept unsolicited applications.

Finance: Annual income £5,066,000, expenditure £3,635,000 (31 March 2014).

Trustees: Sir Ian Wood (Chair.).

Principal Staff: Dir Africa David Knopp; UK Man. Alison MacLachlan.

Address: Blenheim House, Fountainhall Rd, Aberdeen AB15 4DT.

Telephone: (1224) 373516; **Fax:** (1224) 851211; **Internet:** www.thewoodfoundation.org.uk; **e-mail:** info@thewoodfoundation.org.uk.

World Land Trust—WLT

Established in 1989 to purchase and protect critically threatened tropical forests and other endangered habitats.

Activities: Concerned with conservation initiatives, including land purchase and protection of threatened areas in partnership with overseas project partner organizations. The Trust raises funds and public awareness to support its conservation aims and objectives. Its Carbon Balanced programme delivers carbon offsets through restoration ecology and avoided deforestation. Also runs outreach and training local to its office in East Anglia, United Kingdom.

Geographical Area of Activity: Central and South America, India, South-East Asia and Kenya.

Restrictions: No grants to individuals. All funds go directly to WLT projects.

Publications: *WLT News* (3 a year); monthly e-mail bulletins.

Finance: Annual income £3,477,900, expenditure £2,193,713 (31 Dec. 2013).

Board of Trustees: Dr Gerard Bertrand (Hon. Pres.); Dr Simon Lyster (Chair.).

Principal Staff: Chief Exec. John A. Burton.

Address: Blyth House, Bridge St, Halesworth IP19 8AB.

Telephone: (1986) 874422; **Fax:** (1986) 874425; **Internet:** www.worldlandtrust.org; www.carbonbalanced.org; www.wildlifefocus.org; www.focusonforests.org; **e-mail:** info@worldlandtrust.org.

World Animal Protection

Founded in 1981 by the merger of the World Federation for the Protection of Animals (f. 1950) and International Society for the Protection of Animals (f. 1959). Present name adopted in 2014; fmrly know as the World Society for the Protection of Animals—WSPA.

Activities: Promotes effective means for the protection of animals, for the prevention of cruelty to and the relief from suffering and exploitation of animals. The organization operates internationally, in the fields of protection of animals and conservation of their environment; and in related areas of education, international relations and international law, through self-conducted programmes, education campaigns, research, conferences and courses, publications and lectures. Current projects include campaigns in the areas of whaling, disaster management, bullfighting, working horses, bears, stray animals and factory farming. Has more than 900 member animal welfare societies in more than 150 countries.

Geographical Area of Activity: International.

Publications: *Animals International*; Annual Report.

Finance: Annual income £27,892,000, expenditure £28,981,000 (31 Dec. 2013).

Trustees: Mark Watts (Pres.); Hanja Maij-Weggen (Deputy Pres.).

Principal Staff: CEO Mike Baker.

Address: 5th Floor, 222 Grays Inn Rd, London WC1X 8HB.

Telephone: (20) 7239-0500; **Fax:** (20) 7239-0653; **Internet:** www.wspa.org.uk; **e-mail:** wspa@wspa.org.uk.

Worldwide Cancer Research

Founded in 1979 as a branch of a US charity; now an independent United Kingdom-registered charity. Formerly known as the Association for International Cancer Research.

Activities: Aims to save lives by investing in basic and translational research to improve the prevention, diagnosis and treatment of cancer. Has funded projects in 24 countries around the world.

Geographical Area of Activity: International.

Publications: Newsletters; leaflets; Annual Report.

Finance: Annual income £16,985,080, expenditure £17,494,865 (30 Sept. 2013).

Board of Directors: J. C. Murray (Chair.).

Principal Staff: Chief Exec. Norman Barrett.

Address: Madras House, St Andrews, Fife KY16 9EH.

Telephone: (1334) 477910; **Fax:** (1334) 478667; **Internet:** www.worldwidecancerresearch.org; www.aicr.org.uk; **e-mail:** enquiries@worldwidecancerresearch.org.

YMCA—Young Men's Christian Association

Founded in 1844 by George Williams. Aims to be an inclusive Christian Movement, transforming communities so that all young people truly belong, contribute and thrive.

Activities: Works to empower young people with the right skills and education; support families; provide suitable accommodation for young people; and promote physical activity as a key part of the preventative health agenda. In England there are 135 YMCAs working in more than 250 communities, offering more than 7,000 bed spaces every night. The YMCA is an international movement with more than 45m. members and volunteers working in more than 125 countries worldwide.

Geographical Area of Activity: International.

Publications: Annual review and summary accounts.

Finance: Each of the 135 YMCAs is an independent charity. In the year ending 31 March 2013 the YMCA England (The National Council of YMCAs) had a total income of £24,132,000 and total expenditure of £24,087,000.

Trustees: Peter Jeffrey (Chair.); Nick Mourant (Hon. Treas.).

Principal Staff: Pres. Most Rev. John Sentamu; Chief Exec. Denise Hatton.

Address: YMCA England, 29–35 Farringdon Rd, London EC1M 3JF.

Telephone: (20) 7070-2160; **Internet:** www.ymca.org.uk; **e-mail:** enquiries@ymca.org.uk.

Zochonis Charitable Trust

Founded in 1977 to provide funds for general charitable purposes.

Activities: Operates nationally and internationally in the fields of education, social welfare, and the arts and humanities, with a focus on children's education and welfare.

Geographical Area of Activity: England and Wales.

Restrictions: Awards grants to registered charities only.

Finance: Annual income £26,377,248, expenditure £3,904,777 (5 April 2014).

Principal Staff: Contact Marie E. Gallagher.

Address: Manchester Business Park, 3500 Aviator Way, Manchester M22 5TG.

Telephone: (161) 435-1005.

Zurich Community Trust

Founded in 1973, and formerly known as the Allied Dunbar Charitable Trust, for general charitable purposes and to help the most disadvantaged in the community move from dependence to independence locally, nationally and in developing countries.

Activities: Operates nationally and in developing countries in the fields of law and human rights, and medicine and health. Current programmes include: the India Programme, which combines funding and management development opportunities; the Breaking the Cycle Programme, which is providing £1.2m. to break the generational cycle of drug abuse; the Mental Health and Families Programme, which involves £1.1m. in funding over five years; and the Older People programme, which is making grants of £2.2m. over five years to tackle the issues facing older people. Incorporates Zurich Cares, a staff volunteering and payroll-giving programme, and the Openwork Foundation, supported by more than 3,000 members of the financial advisers and employees of Openwork, and currently involved in the Cares 4 Kids theme, which supports children and young people aged 0–18 years who are disadvantaged in some way—socially, mentally or physically.

Geographical Area of Activity: International.

Restrictions: No grants to individuals, for research, animal welfare, emergency or disaster appeals, nor to political, religious or mainstream educational institutions (unless directly benefiting people with disabilities).

Finance: Annual income £3,697,000, expenditure £3,848,000 (31 Dec. 2013).

Trustees: Tim Culling (Chair.).

Principal Staff: Head of Team Pam Webb.

Address: POB 1288, Swindon SN1 1FL.

Telephone: (1793) 502450; **Internet:** www.zurich.co.uk/zurichcommunitytrust; **e-mail:** zct@zct.org.uk.

United States of America

FOUNDATION CENTRES AND CO-ORDINATING BODIES

Africa Grantmakers' Affinity Group—AGAG

Originally established in the 1980s as the South Africa Grantmakers Affinity Group (SAGAG); adopted current name in 2000 following expansion of remit.

Activities: Operates as a membership network of grantmakers currently funding in Africa or interested in funding in Africa, promoting greater foundation interest and more effective grantmaking in Africa.

Geographical Area of Activity: Africa, USA, Europe.

Restrictions: No grants awarded.

Publications: Newsletter; research findings.

Steering Committee: Sarah Hobson, Vuyiswa Sidzumo (Co-Chair.).

Principal Staff: Exec. Dir Niamani Mutima; Communications and Programme Man. Talaya Grimes.

Address: 1776 I St NW, Suite 900, Washington, DC 20006.

Telephone: (202) 756-4835; **Fax:** (202) 403-3207; **Internet:** www.africagrantmakers.org; **e-mail:** contactus@agag.org.

CAF America

Established in 1993; part of the CAF Global Alliance network of organizations.

Activities: Helps donors with their grantmaking.

Geographical Area of Activity: International.

Finance: Annual revenue US $78,259,788, expenditure $69,669,501 (30 April 2013).

Board of Directors: Rob Buchanan (Pres.); Chris Clouse (Treas.); Char Mollison (Sec.).

Principal Staff: CEO Ted Hart; CFO David Venne.

Address: King St Station, 1800 Diagonal Rd, Suite 150, Alexandria, VA 22314.

Telephone: (703) 837-9512; **Fax:** (703) 549-8934; **Internet:** www.cafamerica.org; **e-mail:** info@cafamerica.org.

Community Foundations of Florida

Merged with the Florida Philanthropic Network in 2009.

Activities: Promotes local philanthropy, and connects donors with community foundations. Comprises 28 community foundations.

Geographical Area of Activity: Florida.

Finance: Total assets US $1,840m.; annual giving $161m.

Principal Staff: Chair. Roxie Jerde.

Address: Florida Philanthropic Network, 1211 N. Westshore Blvd, Suite 314, Tampa, FL 33607.

Telephone: (813) 983-7399; **Fax:** (813) 527-9502; **Internet:** www.fpnetwork.org; **e-mail:** admin@fpnetwork.org.

Council on Foundations, Inc

Founded in 1949 and incorporated in 1957 as a publicly supported charitable organization.

Activities: Members (more than 2,100 grantmakers) include private, community- and company-sponsored foundations and corporate contributors; regional associations of grantmakers are also affiliated with the Council and work closely with it in providing information and services. The Council provides a variety of technical and advisory services to guide its members on matters ranging from legal and tax issues to investment management, programme development and grantmaking principles and practices. It maintains regular liaison with other parts of the philanthropic sector, including the Foundation Center (q.v.), through direct communication and participation in conferences and 'umbrella' organizations; conducts an annual conference and other meetings throughout the year to assist its members in their grantmaking activities; and sponsors research and educational programmes. Awards offered include the Wilmer Shields and Distinguished Grantmaker Awards.

Geographical Area of Activity: USA.

Publications: Annual Report; *Council Columns*; *Foundation News and Commentary Magazine*; *Principles and Practices for Effective Grantmaking*; and numerous other publications.

Finance: Annual revenue US $14,267,716, expenditure $16,710,304 (31 Dec. 2013).

Board of Directors: Dr Sherry P. Magill (Chair.); Akhtar Badshah (Vice-Chair.); Sherry Elise Ristau (Sec.); Eugene W. Cochrane, Jr (Treas.).

Principal Staff: Pres. and CEO Vikki Spruill.

Address: 2121 Crystal Dr., Suite 700, Arlington, VA 22202.

Telephone: (800) 673-9036; **Internet:** www.cof.org; **e-mail:** membership@cof.org.

Council of Michigan Foundations

Established in 1972.

Activities: Promotes philanthropy in Michigan and supports charitable orgs. Members include community, corporate, family, independent and public foundations. In 2013, the Council comprised more than 330 members.

Geographical Area of Activity: Michigan.

Restrictions: Does not make grants.

Finance: Total revenue US $8,949,159, expenditure $6,181,635 (31 March 2014).

Board of Trustees: Ellen E. Crane (Chair.); Marsha J. Smith (Sec.); Neal R. Hegarty (Treas.).

Principal Staff: Pres. and CEO Robert S. Collier.

Address: One South Harbor Dr., Suite 3, Grand Haven, MI 49417.

Telephone: (616) 842-7080; **Fax:** (616) 842-1760; **Internet:** www.michiganfoundations.org; **e-mail:** info@michiganfoundations.org.

Edge Funders Alliance

Formed in 2012 by a merger of the Funders Network on Transforming the Global Economy and Grantmakers without Borders to address social, economic and ecological issues worldwide.

Activities: Operates in three main areas: organizing and networking; philanthropic learning and advocacy; and information services. Organizes the annual Just Giving conference.

Geographical Area of Activity: Worldwide.

Restrictions: Not a funding organization.

Publications: *Funding the Movement: Occupy and Beyond*; *Funders Network Alliance in Support of Grassroots Organizing and Movement Building*; *A Perfect Storm: Lessons from the Defeat of Proposition 23*; case studies, online directories, working group reports and briefings.

Finance: Annual revenue US $288,338, expenditure $274,708 (31 Dec. 2013).

Board of Directors: Shalini Nataraj, Eileen Jamison Tyrer (Co-Chair.).

Principal Staff: Dir Mark Randazzo.

Address: POB 559, 60 29th St, San Francisco, CA 94110.

Telephone: (617) 894-1423; **Internet:** www.edgefunders.org; **e-mail:** contactus@edgefunders.org.

Foundation Center

Opened in 1956 as the Foundation Library Center, with founding president F. Emerson Andrews of the Russell Sage Foundation and author of *Foundation Watcher*. To achieve its goal of providing broad, open access to information on foundations, the Center began in 1959 to establish depositories of information in other libraries—now known as the Funding Information Network—nationwide. In 1960, it published the first *Foundation Directory*, which is still published annually. Present name adopted in 1968.

Activities: Operates five library/learning centres in New York City, Washington, DC, Atlanta, Cleveland and San Francisco. These offer free access to information resources and educational programmes. Access is also available internationally through more than 450 funding information centres. The Center maintains unique databases of information on the entire universe of foundations, corporate donors and grantmaking public charities in the USA and their grants; conducts research and publishes reports on the growth of the foundation field and on trends in foundation support of the non-profit sector, including the annual *Foundations Today Series*; and educates thousands of people each year through a full curriculum of training courses in the classroom and online.

Geographical Area of Activity: USA.

Restrictions: Does not direct applications for funds to particular foundations, nor does it arrange introductions to foundation officials or assist persons seeking positions in foundations.

Publications: *Foundation Directory Online*; *Map of Cross-Border Giving*.

Finance: Annual revenue US $30,244,244, expenditure $25,008,492 (31 Dec. 2013).

Board of Trustees: P. Russell Hardin (Chair.).

Principal Staff: Pres. Bradford K. Smith.

Address: 79 Fifth Ave/16th St, New York, NY 10003.

Telephone: (212) 620-4230; **Fax:** (212) 807-3677; **Internet:** foundationcenter.org; grantspace.org; **e-mail:** communications@foundationcenter.org.

Give2Asia

Established in 2011 following the acquisition of the Asia Pacific Philanthropy Consortium (f. 1994) by Give2Asia (f. 2001).

Activities: Assists foundations and corporate donors in the Asia-Pacific region, through technical support, training, research, information services, networking, exchanges and conferences. Works in 25 countries.

Geographical Area of Activity: Asia-Pacific region.

Publications: Reports.

Finance: Annual revenue US $32,016,909, expenditure $31,929,046 (30 Sept. 2013).

Board of Directors: Tan-lin Hsu (Chair.); Bill S. Kim (Hon. Chair.); William P. Fuller, Teresa Orr (Vice-Chair.); Eugene Hong (Treas.); Joe Lumarda (Sec.).

Principal Staff: Pres. and CEO Birger Stamperdahl; Vice-Pres. Pamela Calvert.

Address: 340 Pine St, Suite 501, San Francisco, CA 94104.

Telephone: (415) 9676300; **Fax:** (415) 9676290; **Internet:** www.give2asia.org; **e-mail:** info@give2asia.org.

Independent Sector

Founded in 1980; a national coalition of foundations, non-profit organizations and corporations that aims to strengthen philanthropy and citizen action in the USA.

Activities: Acts as a forum for member organizations, as a source of information and as a mediator between the grant-making and grantseeking communities. The organization also works to encourage volunteer work and community action in society. It supports and engages in non-profit initiatives in areas such as public policy, research and communications.

Geographical Area of Activity: USA.

Publications: *Principles for Good Governance and Ethical Practice: A Guide for Charities and Foundations (2007)*; *Giving and Volunteering Signature Series*; *Giving and Volunteering in the United States*; *The New Nonprofit Almanac and Desk Reference*; *Outcome Measurement in Nonprofit Organizations: Current Practices and Recommendations*; *What You Should Know About Nonprofits*; *Facts and Finding Series* (series of research reports); Annual Report; numerous reports, papers and other publications.

Finance: Annual US $9,049,878, expenditure $9,635,030 (31 Dec. 2013).

Board of Directors: Neil Nicoll (Chair.); Steven J. McCormick (Vice-Chair.); Lorie A. Slutsky (Treas.); Kelvin H. Taketa (Sec.).

Principal Staff: Pres. and CEO Diana Aviv.

Address: 1602 L St NW, Suite 900, Washington, DC 20036.

Telephone: (202) 467-6100; **Fax:** (202) 467-6101; **Internet:** www.independentsector.org; **e-mail:** info@independentsector.org.

InterAction American Council for Voluntary International Action

Formed in 1984 by the merger of the American Council of Voluntary Agencies for Foreign Service and Private Agencies Collaborating Together, InterAction is a coalition of more than 190 US private and voluntary organizations dedicated to international humanitarian issues. Its main purpose is to enhance the effectiveness and professional capacities of its members while fostering partnership, collaboration and leadership within the voluntary organization community.

Activities: Member organizations' activities include disaster relief, refugee protection, assistance and resettlement, sustainable development, public policy and educating the American public on global development issues.

Geographical Area of Activity: USA.

Publications: *Gender Mainstreaming*; *Global Works*; *Foreign Assistance in Focus: Monday Developments* (2 a month); *InterAction Member Profiles* (biennially); newsletters and media guides.

Finance: Annual revenue US $9,717,409, expenditure $9,637,110 (31 Dec. 2013).

Board of Directors: Neal-Keny Guyer (Chair.); Carolyn Miles (Vice-Chair.); Tressie San Martin (Treas.).

Principal Staff: Pres. and CEO Sam Worthington; Exec. Vice-Pres. Lindsay Coates.

Address: 1400 16th St NW, Suite 210, Washington, DC 20036.

Telephone: (202) 667-8227; **Fax:** (202) 667-8236; **Internet:** www.interaction.org; **e-mail:** ia@interaction.org.

International Society for Third-Sector Research—ISTR

Founded in 1992, as an international association promoting research and education in the fields of civil society, philanthropy and the non-profit sector.

Activities: Committed to building a global community of scholars and interested others dedicated to the creation, discussion and advancement of knowledge relating to the third sector and its impact on human and global well-being and development internationally. The Society's mission is to promote the development of high-quality research and education internationally on third sector-related issues, theories and policies; and to enhance the dissemination and application of knowledge about the third sector as widely as possible throughout the world. It strives to broaden the participation of researchers in all parts of the world and in all disciplines, with special emphasis given to expanding the number of third sector researchers in developing nations and Central and Eastern Europe. Has members in 85 countries. Holds conferences biennially to promote the exchange of ideas and research findings in the voluntary sector, and promotes discussion and co-operation between researchers and scholars. The Society has established a number of regional research networks and has one formal Affinity Group (Gender).

Geographical Area of Activity: International.

Publications: *Inside ISTR* (quarterly newsletter); *ISTR Report*; *Voluntas* (journal); membership directory (online); Annual Report; Working Papers.

Finance: Supported by membership dues, conference fees and grants.

Board of Directors: Annette Zimmer (Pres.); Steven Rathgeb Smith (Pres.-elect); Bhekinkosi Moyo (Sec.); Hagai Katz (Treas.).

Principal Staff: Exec. Dir Margery B. Daniels.

Address: 624 N Broadway Hampton House, Suite 356, Baltimore, MD 21205.

Telephone: (410) 516-4678; **Fax:** (410) 516-4870; **Internet:** www.istr.org; **e-mail:** istr@jhu.edu.

League of California Community Foundations

Established in 1994.

Activities: Promotes the development of community foundations. Comprises 29 member foundations.

Geographical Area of Activity: California.

Finance: Total assets US $7,600m.; grants disbursed $654m. (2011).

Board: John Kobara (Chair.); Dan Baldwin (Vice-Chair.); Jeff Pickering (Treas.); Ron Gallo (Sec.).

Principal Staff: Contact Patricia Jones.

Address: POBB 1303, Jamestown, CA 95327.

Telephone: (209) 984-3955; **Internet:** lccf.org; **e-mail:** info@lccf.org.

FOUNDATIONS, TRUSTS AND NON-PROFIT ORGANIZATIONS

ACCION International

Founded in 1961; an independent agency that aims to help local organizations reach small businesses in urban and rural areas of North, Central and South America, South and East Asia and Sub-Saharan Africa.

Activities: Advises on issues affecting small businesses; assists in employment and financial projects, small business development and micro-credit loan programmes; and provides management assistance for development agencies. The organization maintains a small reference library and publishes a monthly e-mail newsletter. In 2001, it launched the Citi-ACCION Outstanding Microentrepreneur Prize with Citigroup and the Citigroup Foundation (q.v.). Also operates offices in Washington, DC, and Colombia and India.

Geographical Area of Activity: North, Central and South America, Sub-Saharan Africa, South and East Asia.

Restrictions: Neither lends to nor funds individuals directly.

Publications: *InSight* (bulletin); *ACCION International Publications* (annual); Annual Report; and other leaflets, manuals, discussion papers and publications on microfinance.

Finance: Annual revenue US $31,362,274, expenditure $46,665,061 (31 Dec. 2013).

Board of Directors: Diana Taylor (Chair.); Titus Brenninkmeijer, Henry Miller (Vice-Chair.); Tara Kenney (Treas.); Paul Tregidgo (Sec.).

Principal Staff: Pres. and CEO Michael Schlein; COO Esteban A. Altschul.

Address: 56 Roland St, Suite 300, Boston, MA 02129.

Telephone: (617) 625-7080; **Fax:** (617) 625-7020; **Internet:** www.accion.org; **e-mail:** info@accion.org.

ACDI/VOCA

Established in 1963 as the International Cooperative Development Association by major US farm co-operatives. Present name adopted following the merger in 1997 with Volunteers in Overseas Co-operative Assistance—VOCA to promote economic opportunities for co-operatives, enterprises, and communities through the innovative application of sound business practice.

Activities: Aims to provide farmers with the necessary resources to succeed in the world economy. The organization blends business and technical acumen with humanitarian concern, implementing large-scale projects that address the most pressing and intractable development challenges. It does not rely on short-term interventions or supply-driven technology transfer directed at single problems in isolation, but treats problems holistically to provide lasting results. Has worked in 146 countries.

Geographical Area of Activity: International.

Publications: *Global Connections* (monthly subscription e-mail newsletter); Annual Report.

Finance: Annual revenue US $169,008,107, expenditure $174,000,000 (31 Dec. 2013).

Board of Directors: Mortimer H. Neufville (Chair.); Deborah Atwood (Vice-Chair.).

Principal Staff: Pres. and CEO Bill Polidoro.

Address: 50 F St NW, Suite 1075, Washington, DC 20001.

Telephone: (202) 469-2000; **Fax:** (202) 469-6257; **Internet:** www.acdivoca.org; **e-mail:** webmaster@acdivoca.org.

Acumen Fund

Founded in 2001 with seed money from the Rockefeller Foundation (q.v.), the Cisco Systems Foundation and a group of individual investors.

Activities: Invests patient capital in innovative businesses that have high potential to solve social and economic problems. The Fund provides financial and technical support to these investments; develops talent and leaders through its Fellows programme; and leads development in the social impact investing sector. It invests in five sectors: water, health, housing, energy and agriculture. Has offices in New York (USA), New Delhi (India), Karachi (Pakistan) and Nairobi (Kenya).

Geographical Area of Activity: Africa, India, Pakistan.

Publications: Newsletter (quarterly).

Finance: Annual revenue US $10,644,819, expenditure $11,581,021 (31 Dec. 2013).

Board of Directors: Robert H. Niehaus (Chair.).

Principal Staff: CEO Jacqueline Novogratz.

Address: 76 Ninth Ave, Suite 315, New York, NY 10011.

Telephone: (212) 566-8821; **Fax:** (212) 566-8817; **Internet:** www.acumenfund.org; **e-mail:** info@acumenfund.org.

Adventist Development and Relief Agency International—ADRA

Formed in 1956 by the Seventh-day Adventist Church as an independent humanitarian agency to provide disaster relief and individual and community development.

Activities: Works in disaster areas and parts of the developing world, providing aid and support. The Agency's development programmes help to improve education, health care, food supplies and economic and social well-being for people in more than 120 countries and territories, helping to achieve sustainable change and long-term humanitarian solutions.

Geographical Area of Activity: International.

Publications: *ADRA Works* (quarterly newsletter); Annual Report.

Finance: Annual revenue US $58,877,101, expenditure $54,121,244 (31 Dec. 2013).

Board of Directors: Geoffrey Mbwana (Chair.); Ella Simmons (Vice-Chair.); Robert Lemon (Treas.).

Principal Staff: Pres. Dr Jonathan Duffy.

Address: 12501 Old Columbia Pike, Silver Spring, MD 20904.

Telephone: (301) 680-6380; **Fax:** (301) 680-6370; **Internet:** www.adra.org; **e-mail:** response@adra.org.

Africa-America Institute—AAI

Founded in 1953 to help further development in Africa, improve African-American understanding and inform Americans about Africa.

Activities: Engages in educational training, development assistance and informational activities in two areas: African Higher Education and Training, and Educational Outreach and Policy. The Institute sponsors African-American Conferences, media workshops and regional conferences and seminars. Maintains a presence in more than 50 countries in Africa, including offices in Mozambique and South Africa.

Geographical Area of Activity: Southern Africa and the USA.

Publications: *AAIONLINE* (quarterly newsletter); *African Perspectives*; *Africa Report* magazine; Biennial Report; also policy forum, symposium and conference reports; art exhibit catalogues, bulletins and educational materials.

Finance: Annual revenue US $1,826,409, expenditure $1,909,374 (30 Sept. 2013).

Board: Kofi Appenteng (Chair.); Joseph Moodhe (Sec.).

Principal Staff: Pres. and CEO Amini Kajunju.

Address: 420 Lexington Ave, Suite 1706, New York, NY 10170-0002.

Telephone: (212) 949-5666; **Fax:** (212) 682-6174; **Internet:** www.aaionline.org; **e-mail:** aainy@aaionline.org.

African Development Institute

Established in 1995 as a public policy research institute to promote the human and material development of Africa through education, research and policy analysis.

Activities: Promotes alternative development strategies by three methods: problem-orientated research; empowering education; and advocacy of self-reliant and endogenous development policies. Has special consultative status with the Economic and Social Council of the UN.

Geographical Area of Activity: Africa and the USA.

Publications: *SANKOFA: African Visions* (quarterly newsletter).

Board of Directors: Kwame Akonor (Chair.).

Principal Staff: Exec. Dir Enock Mensah.

Address: POB 1644, New York, NY 10185.

Telephone: (201) 838-7900; **Fax:** (908) 850-3016; **Internet:** www.africainstitute.net; **e-mail:** office@africainstitute.net.

African Wildlife Foundation—AWF

Founded in 1961 as the African Wildlife Leadership Foundation, Inc; present name adopted in 1982.

Activities: Promotes wildlife management and conservation in Africa.

Geographical Area of Activity: Botswana, the Democratic Republic of the Congo, Kenya, Mozambique, Namibia, Rwanda, South Africa, Tanzania, Uganda, Zambia and Zimbabwe.

Publications: Annual Report; *African Wildlife News* (quarterly newsletter); *African Heartland News* (newsletter); fact sheets, wall calendar; reports and periodic publishings in peer-reviewed journals.

Finance: Annual revenue US $19,711,708, expenditure $22,803,798 (30 June 2013).

Board of Trustees: David Thomson (Chair.); Benjamin W. Mkapa (Vice-Chair.); Dr Myma Belo-Osagie (Sec.); Maureen Groen (Treas.).

Principal Staff: Chief Exec. Dr Patrick J. Bergin.

Address: 1400 16th St NW, Suite 120, Washington, DC 20036.

Telephone: (202) 939-3333; **Fax:** (202) 939-3332; **Internet:** www.awf.org; **e-mail:** africanwildlife@awf.org.

Africare

Founded in 1971, originally in response to severe droughts in West Africa.

Activities: Helps families and communities in every major region of Sub-Saharan Africa and also works in a number of countries in North Africa. The organization supervises development and self-help programmes in aid, medicine and health, conservation and environment, and social welfare and studies. Has operated in 36 countries.

Geographical Area of Activity: Africa.

Publications: *Africare* (online newsletter); Annual Report.

Finance: Annual revenue US $60,221,407, expenditure $61,631,906 (30 June 2013).

Board of Directors: Stephen D. Cashin (Chair.); Dr Joseph C. Kennedy (Sec.); Peter Francis (Treas.).

Principal Staff: Pres. Darius Mans.

Address: Africare House, 440 R St NW, Washington, DC 20001-1935.

Telephone: (202) 462-3614; **Fax:** (202) 387-1034; **Internet:** www.africare.org; **e-mail:** info@africare.org.

Daniele Agostino Derossi Foundation

Founded in 1991 by Flavia Robinson to promote the well-being of Mayan women and children.

Activities: Aims to promote the well-being of Mayan women and children through grants to support projects active in the fields of education, health and women's co-operatives.

Geographical Area of Activity: Primarily Guatemala.

Restrictions: No grants to individuals.

Finance: Annual revenue US $42,388, expenditure $151,334 (30 June 2013).

Board of Directors: Daniele C. Derossi (Pres.); David J. Pollack (Vice-Pres. and Treas.); Flavia Derossi Robinson (Sec. and Pres. Emeritus).

Address: 40 Wachusett Dr., Lexington, MA 02421-6936.

Internet: www.dafound.org; **e-mail:** dafound@dafound.org.

The Ahmanson Foundation

Founded in 1952 by Howard F. Ahmanson, Dorothy G. Sullivan and others for general charitable services.

Activities: Operates mainly in Los Angeles, CA, in the fields of education, arts and culture, medicine and health, and science and welfare. Foundation support includes programme support, capital, research, endowment and scholarships.

Geographical Area of Activity: USA (primarily Los Angeles).

Restrictions: No grants are made to individuals. Grants are made only to organizations that are tax-exempt.

Publications: Annual Report.

Finance: Annual revenue US $82,051,000, expenditure $58,019,000 (31 Oct. 2014).

Principal Staff: Pres. William H. Ahmanson; Man. Dir and Sec. Karen Ahmanson Hoffman; CFO and Treas. Kristen K. O'Connor.

Address: 9215 Wilshire Blvd, Beverly Hills, CA 09210.

Telephone: (310) 278-0770; **Internet:** www.theahmansonfoundation.org; **e-mail:** info@theahmansonfoundation.org.

Alavi Foundation

Founded in 1973, and formerly known as the Mostazafan Foundation of New York, with religious, philanthropic and educational aims.

Activities: Operates its own programmes emphasizing research into the Islamic religion; publishes and distributes educational and religious material. The Foundation contributes to educational centres and Sunday schools for the teaching of Middle Eastern languages and of the Islamic religion and culture. Contributes to disaster relief funds; provides student loans.

Geographical Area of Activity: USA.

Publications: *Fundamentals of Islamic Teachings*; *A Glance at the Life of Prophet Mohammed.*

Finance: Annual revenue US $1,610,510, expenditure $4,426,052 (31 March 2013).

Board of Trustees: Dr Houshang Ahmadi (Pres.); Misriya Chatoo (Sec.).

Address: 650 Fifth Ave, Suite 2406, New York, NY 10019.

Telephone: (212) 944-8333; **Fax:** (212) 921-0325; **Internet:** www.alavifoundation.org; **e-mail:** info@alavifoundation.org.

Alcoa Foundation

Founded in 1952 by the Aluminum Company of America (Alcoa) to improve the quality of life for people in communities where Alcoa plants or offices are located, and for the public at large.

Activities: Operates nationally and internationally (in countries where Alcoa operates), principally in the fields of global education and workplace skills, conservation and sustainability, business and community partnerships, and safe and healthy children and families. The Foundation makes grants to educational institutions for equipment, improvement of facilities, and the provision of fellowships and scholarships. It also makes grants for cultural events and to health and welfare organizations, hospitals and medical centres, civic and community organizations, and youth organizations.

Geographical Area of Activity: International.

Restrictions: No grants are made to individuals, other than through the Sons and Daughters Scholarship programme for the children of Alcoa employees, and only certified charitable organizations are considered.

Publications: Annual Report.

Finance: Annual revenue US $18,413,783, expenditure $28,141,313 (2013).

Principal Staff: Pres. Esra Ozer; Exec. Vice-Pres Roy Harvey, William F. Oplinger.

Address: Alcoa Corporate Center, 201 Isabella St, Pittsburgh, PA 15212-5858.

Telephone: (412) 553-4545; **Fax:** (412) 553-4498; **Internet:** www.alcoa.com/global/en/community/foundation.asp; **e-mail:** alcoa.foundation@alcoa.com.

The George I. Alden Trust

Founded in 1912 by George I. Alden for the promotion of education in schools, colleges or other educational institutes, with a preference for industrial, vocational or professional education; for the promotion of work carried out by the Young Men's Christian Association in Massachusetts; and for the benefit of the Worcester Trade Schools and the Worcester Polytechnic Institute.

Activities: Involved in the fields of higher and vocational education in the USA, through funding, research, conferences, scholarships and endowment funds.

Geographical Area of Activity: USA.

Publications: Annual Report; information brochure; Financial Report.

Finance: Annual revenue US $19,445,588, expenditure $10,445,440 (2013).

Board of Trustees: Warner S. Fletcher (Chair.); Gail T. Randall (Vice-Chair.); Douglas Q. Meystre (Clerk); James E. Collins (Treas.).

Address: 370 Main St, 11th Floor, Worcester, MA 01608.

Telephone: (508) 459-8005; **Fax:** (508) 459-8305; **Internet:** www.aldentrust.org; **e-mail:** trustees@aldentrust.org.

The Paul G. Allen Family Foundation

Established in 1990 by Paul G. Allen and Jo Lynn Allen.

Activities: Operates in the areas of community development and social change; arts and culture; science and technology; education and youth engagement; and emergency relief.

Geographical Area of Activity: Primarily north-west USA.

Publications: Research and reports.

Finance: Annual revenue US $245,516,014, expenditure $20,511,753 (2013).

Board of Directors: Paul G. Allen (Chair.); David R. Stewart (Sec.); Allen D. Israel (Asst Sec.).

Principal Staff: Pres. Jo Lynn Allen; Co-Mans Dune Ives, Bert Kolde.

Address: 505 Fifth Ave South, Suite 900, Seattle, WA 98104.

Telephone: (206) 342-2030; **Fax:** (206) 342-3030; **Internet:** www.pgafoundations.com; **e-mail:** info@ pgafamilyfoundation.org.

Isabel Allende Foundation

Established in 1996 to promote social and economic justice for women.

Activities: Operates in the San Francisco Bay area of the USA and in Chile to promote the empowerment of women and girls.

Restrictions: Grants are typically of US $1,000–$5,000.

Finance: Annual revenue US $637,094, expenditure $947,522 (30 Nov. 2013).

Board of Trustees: Isabel Allende (Pres.); William C. Gordon (Sec.).

Principal Staff: Exec. Dir Lori Barra.

Address: 116 Caledonia St, Sausalito, CA 94965.

Telephone: (415) 289-0992; **Fax:** (415) 298-1154; **Internet:** www.isabelallendefoundation.org; **e-mail:** lori@ isabelallendefoundation.org.

Alliance for International Educational and Cultural Exchange

Formed in 1992 by a group of US international exchange organizations to create and promote public policies that facilitate international cultural exchanges between the USA and other countries around the world to improve cultural understanding between people of different nations.

Activities: Supports the interests of 76 international exchange organizations in the USA, through advocacy, information services and networking. The Alliance also organizes a programme of government relations activities, and provides a place where the issues and concerns of leaders of international exchange groups can be discussed and addressed. It endeavours to inform the public about the importance of the role of international exchange globally, nationally and in terms of individuals.

Geographical Area of Activity: USA.

Publications: *The Policy Monitor* (quarterly journal); *News News News* (bulletin); *Action Alerts*; *International Exchange Locator: a Resource Directory for Educational and Cultural Exchange* (2005 edition).

Finance: Annual revenue US $791,478, expenditure $783,803 (31 Dec. 2013).

Board of Directors: Lynn Shotwell (Chair.); Laura Rose (Vice-Chair.); Ellen Hoggard (Treas.).

Principal Staff: Exec. Dir Michael McCarry; Deputy Dir Marc Overmann.

Address: 1828 L St NW, Suite 1150, Washington, DC 20036.

Telephone: (202) 293-6141; **Fax:** (202) 293-6144; **Internet:** www.alliance-exchange.org; **e-mail:** information@alliance -exchange.org.

Jenifer Altman Foundation—JAF

Founded in 1991.

Activities: Makes grants within the fields of environmental health and mind-body health, primarily supporting work on the impact of endocrine disrupting chemicals and other foetal contaminants on human health and on biodiversity. The Foundation also administers the Mitchell Kapor Foundation (q.v.). Grants range from US \$1,000 to \$10,000.

Geographical Area of Activity: Central and South America, USA, Europe, Asia.

Restrictions: No grants to individuals.

Publications: Annual report; grants list; programme policy statement; application guidelines.

Finance: Annual revenue US \$470,000, expenditure \$740,000 (30 June 2014).

Board of Directors: Michael Lerner (Pres.); Catherine Porter (Sec.).

Principal Staff: Exec. Dir Marni Rosen.

Address: Thoreau Center for Sustainability, Presidio Bldg 1016, First Floor, POB 29209, San Francisco, CA 04129.

Telephone: (415) 561-2182; **Fax:** (415) 561-6480; **Internet:** www.jaf.org; **e-mail:** info@jaf.org.

American Association of University Women Educational Foundation—AAUW

Founded in 1959 by the American Association of University Women to encourage, among the members of the AAUW and the community, the continuation of education beyond college; to enable women scholars to carry on advanced research, study and creative work; to engage in and promote studies and research in education; to provide for the diffusion of knowledge obtained thereby, and to foster intellectual and educational growth; to encourage standards of excellence in public school education and in higher education; and to co-operate with other organizations with similar purposes and activities.

Activities: Operates nationally and internationally in the field of education. Provides one-year, non-renewable fellowships to American women for dissertation writing and post-doctoral research, as well as short-term publications fellowships. Career Development Grants support women who hold a Bachelor's degree and who are preparing to advance or change their careers, or re-enter the workforce. Selected Professions Fellowships are awarded to women who are US citizens or permanent residents and who intend to pursue a full-time course of study (during the fellowship year) in designated degree programmes, where traditionally women's participation has been low. One-year non-renewable International Fellowships are awarded to women who are not US citizens or permanent residents of the USA for study in the USA at the Master's, PhD or postdoctoral levels. Six fellowships are awarded annually to women who are members of organizations affiliated with the International Federation of University Women—IFUW—for one year of graduate study anywhere in the world. The Foundation also makes several prestigious national awards recognizing excellence in achievement and the AAUW Legal Advocacy Fund supports women fighting sex discrimination cases in higher education.

Geographical Area of Activity: International.

Restrictions: Grants only to women.

Publications: Report of operations and financial statement; *Action Alert* (newsletter).

Finance: Annual revenue US \$25,893, expenditure \$26,835 (31 Dec. 2013).

Board of Directors: Patricia Fae Ho (Pres.); Sandra Camillo (Sec.).

Principal Staff: Exec. Dir Linda D. Hallman.

Address: 1111 16th St NW, Washington, DC 20036.

Telephone: (202) 785-7700; **Fax:** (202) 872-1425; **Internet:** www.aauw.org; **e-mail:** connect@aauw.org.

American Council of Learned Societies—ACLS

Founded in 1919 (incorporated in 1924) for the advancement of humanistic studies in all fields of learning and the maintenance and strengthening of relations among the national societies devoted to such studies.

Activities: Comprises 72 US scholarly organizations concerned with the humanities and related social sciences. The Council offers fellowships to US citizens or permanent residents to carry out post-doctoral research in the humanities. Internationally, it supports various research and planning activities to encourage research on specific countries or regions of the world, as well as comparative and transnational research projects.

Geographical Area of Activity: International.

Restrictions: No funding for fellowships or scholarships for undergraduate study and no grants for creative work.

Publications: Annual Report; occasional paper series; newsletter; ACLS Humanities E-Book Project; white papers and other publications.

Finance: Annual revenue US \$17,472,283, expenditure \$22,760,388 (30 June 2012).

Board of Directors: James J. O'Donnell (Chair.); Nicola Courtright (Vice-Chair.); Jonathan D. Culler (Sec.); Nancy J. Vickers (Treas.).

Principal Staff: Pres. Pauline Yu; Vice-Pres. Steven C. Wheatley.

Address: 633 Third Ave, 8th Floor, New York, NY 10017-6795.

Telephone: (212) 697-1505; **Fax:** (212) 949-8058; **Internet:** www.acls.org.

American Councils for International Education—ACTR/ACCELS

Established in 1974 as an international not-for-profit organization working to advance education, research and mutual understanding across the USA and the nations of Eastern Europe, Eurasia and South-Eastern Europe.

Activities: Operates in the field of education, funding academic exchanges, professional training, institution building, research, materials development, technical assistance and consultation. The organization's mission is to foster democratic development and civil societies by advancing education and research, cultivating leadership and empowering individuals and institutions through learning. It designs, implements and supports innovative programmes in education, community outreach and scholarly research. Currently, ACTR (American Council of Teachers of Russian) is the professional association that focuses on educational, research and training programmes for citizens of the USA, while ACCELS (American Council for Collaboration in Education and Language Study) deals with exchanges, training and technical assistance programmes in Eastern Europe, the Russian Federation and Central Asia. ACCELS also runs more than 40 educational programmes in the countries of the former USSR.

Geographical Area of Activity: USA, Afghanistan, countries of the former USSR, South-Eastern Europe and South Asia.

Restrictions: Not a grantmaker in its own right; administers government funding.

Publications: Annual Report; specialist videos, papers, journals and books in fields of interest; *Predictors of Foreign Language Gain during Study Abroad*; *Journal of Eurasian Research*.

Finance: Annual revenue US \$81,393,449, expenditure \$80,900,734 (30 June 2013).

Board of Trustees: Robert M. Rhea (Chair.); Edith Falk (Vice-Chair.).

Principal Staff: Pres. Dr Dan E. Davidson; Exec. Vice-Pres. David Patton, Lisa Choate.

Address: 1828 L St NW, Suite 1200, Washington, DC 20036.

Telephone: (202) 833-7522; **Fax:** (202) 833-7523; **Internet:** www.americancouncils.org; **e-mail:** info@americancouncils.org.

American Express Foundation

Founded in 1850 in New York by the American Express Co and its subsidiaries for charitable purposes in the areas of community service, education and employment, cultural programmes, historic preservation and economic independence.

Activities: Supports projects worldwide within the themes of community service, cultural heritage and economic independence. Projects include those involved with the arts and humanities, education, historic conservation, community welfare, minorities, AIDS, drug abuse, child development and welfare, and the disabled. The Foundation aims to create partnerships between public and private organizations, especially in the fields of education, employment and training programmes; and programmes to promote understanding of the world's cultural diversity and heritage. It promotes the tourism industry through its Academies of Travel and Tourism in the USA and its international Travel and Tourism Programme. The Economic Independence Fund supports community development and financial literacy programmes, and the Performing Arts Fund helps performing arts organizations across the USA to attract broader audiences.

Geographical Area of Activity: International.

Restrictions: Grants made only to non-profit organizations.

Publications: *Philanthropy at American Express Report.*

Finance: Annual revenue US $10,115,389, expenditure $8,750,591 (2013).

Board of Directors: Thomas Schick (Chair.); Mary Ellen Craig (Sec.); Richard A. Brown (Asst Sec.); David L. Yowan (Asst Treas.).

Principal Staff: Pres. Tim McClimon.

Address: 200 Vesey St, 48th Floor, New York, NY 10285.

Telephone: (212) 640-5661; **Fax:** (212) 693-1033; **Internet:** www.americanexpress.com/csr.

American Foundation for the Blind, Inc—AFB

Founded in 1921 to support visually impaired people and to educate the general public about blindness.

Activities: Provides educational, vocational, advisory and social services, and publications (including 'talking books') related to blindness. The Foundation awards a number of scholarships for undergraduate and graduate visually impaired and blind students, including: the Delta Gamma Foundation Florence Margaret Harvey Memorial Scholarship and the Rudolph Dillman Memorial Scholarship for students in the field of rehabilitation or education of blind or visually impaired people; the Gladys C. Anderson Memorial Scholarship and the R. L. Gillette Scholarship for female students studying religious music, classical music or literature; the Karen D. Carsel Memorial Scholarship and the Ferdinand Torres AFB Scholarship for full-time students in economic need; and the Paul W. Ruckes Scholarship for students pursuing a degree in engineering or in computer, physical or life sciences. It also distributes Helen Keller Achievement Awards promoting achievement of individuals who act as role models or improve the quality of life of individuals with visual impairment. Maintains offices in Washington, DC, Atlanta, GA, Dallas, TX (the AFB Center on Vision Loss), Huntington, WV (AFB TECH, working with manufacturers to increase accessibility to technology for blind people) and San Francisco, CA.

Geographical Area of Activity: USA.

Publications: *Access World: Technology for Consumers with Visual Impairment* (6 a year); *AFB Directory of Services for Blind and Visually Impaired Persons in the US and Canada*; *Journal of Visual Impairment and Blindness* (10 a year); Annual Report.

Finance: Annual revenue US $7,859,816, expenditure $3,092,888 (30 June 2014).

Board of Trustees: Larry Kimbler (Chair.); James H. McLaughlin (Vice-Chair.); Peter D. Tonks (Treas.); Elaine J. Pommells (Sec.).

Principal Staff: Pres. and CEO Carl R. Augusto.

Address: 2 Penn Plaza, Suite 1102, New York, NY 10121.

Telephone: (212) 502-7600; **Fax:** (212) 502-7777; **Internet:** www.afb.org; **e-mail:** info@afb.org.

American Foundation for Pharmaceutical Education—AFPE

Founded in 1942 to provide support for graduate study of pharmaceutical science.

Activities: Funds research and offers grants, fellowships and scholarships in the field of pharmaceutical sciences, particularly pharmaceutics, pharmacology, manufacturing pharmacy, pharmaco-economics and medicinal chemistry. Awards include Student Gateway Research Scholarships, First Year Graduate School Scholarships, Pre-Doctoral Graduate Scholarships in the Pharmaceutical Sciences, Clinical Pharmacy Post-Pharmaceutical Doctoral Fellowships in the Biomedical Research Sciences, and Pharmacy Faculty Investigator Grants.

Geographical Area of Activity: USA.

Restrictions: Grants are usually open only to those studying in the USA.

Finance: Annual revenue US $863,398, expenditure $1,121,431 (31 Dec. 2013).

Board of Directors: Dr Ernest Mario (Chair.); Dr J. Lyle Bootman (Vice-Chair.); Dr George J. Vuturo (Treas.); Ellen J. Woods (Pres. and Sec.).

Address: 6076 Franconia Rd, Suite C, Alexandria, VA 22310-1758.

Telephone: (703) 875-3095; **Fax:** (703) 875-3098; **Internet:** www.afpenet.org; **e-mail:** info@afpenet.org.

American Friends Service Committee—AFSC

Founded in 1917; a Quaker organization that aims to overcome poverty, injustice and strife in the world through practical aid and non-violent means, based on the belief in the good of every person, regardless of race or religion.

Activities: Operates in 14 countries in Africa, Asia, Latin America and the Caribbean, the Middle East and the USA, in the areas of peacebuilding, conflict resolution, demilitarization, community development, economic and social justice, and supporting transformational youth leadership. The Committee aims to address the root causes of poverty, injustice and conflict, working for relief both through immediate aid and long-term development projects.

Geographical Area of Activity: Africa, Asia, Latin America and the Caribbean, the Middle East and the USA.

Publications: *Quaker Action* (periodical, 3 a year); *Wage Peace* (e-mail newsletter); and other regional and issue area newsletters and e-newsletters.

Finance: Annual revenue US $32,325,160, expenditure $33,853,122 (30 Sept. 2014).

Board of Directors: Phil Lord (Presiding Clerk); Lisa L. Gasstrom, Dan Seeger (Asst Secs); David S. Henkel (Recording Clerk); Susan Cozzens (Treas.).

Principal Staff: Gen. Sec. Shan Cretin.

Address: 1501 Cherry St, Philadelphia, PA 19102.

Telephone: (215) 241-7000; **Fax:** (215) 241-7275; **Internet:** www.afsc.org; **e-mail:** afscinfo@afsc.org.

American Heart Association, Inc

Founded in 1948 with the aim of preventing premature strokes and cardiovascular disease.

Activities: The Association awards fellowships for US undergraduate research, and grants-in-aid to support research in the fields of cardiovascular disease and strokes. International Research Fellowships enable researchers who are US citizens or permanent residents to study in foreign institutions, or foreign citizens to study at US institutions. The Association also bestows awards aimed at encouraging clinically trained physicians to pursue careers in cardiovascular and stroke research, as well as supporting stroke survivors and their families; maintains eight affiliate offices in USA and Puerto Rico.

Geographical Area of Activity: International.

Restrictions: No grants to individuals working at private companies, nor to organizations receiving funding from a different source.

Publications: *Stroke Connection* (magazine, 2 a month); *Traditional Cookbooks*; *Health Information Publications*; *Heart and Stroke Facts*; *Magazine Cookbooks*.

Finance: Annual revenue US $632,636,617, expenditure $591,341,173 (30 June 2014).

Board of Directors: Bernard P. Dennis (Chair.); Alvin S. Royse (Chair.-elect); Ron W. Haddock (Immediate Past Chair.); David A. Bush (Sec.-Treas.).

Principal Staff: Pres. Mariell Jessup; Pres.-elect Elliot Antman; CEO Nancy Brown.

Address: National Center, 7272 Greenville Ave, Dallas, TX 75231-4596.

Telephone: (214) 360-6106; **Fax:** (214) 360-6124; **Internet:** www.heart.org; **e-mail:** aha.nsc.general@heart.org.

American Historical Association—AHA

Founded in 1884 for the promotion of historical studies, the collection and preservation of historical manuscripts, and the dissemination of historical research.

Activities: Operates mainly nationally in the field of education and historical studies, by supporting research, awarding prizes, research grants and fellowships for work on various aspects of history, and issuing publications.

Geographical Area of Activity: USA.

Restrictions: Research grants made only to AHA members.

Publications: *American Historical Review*; *Perspectives on History* (newsletter); *Directory of History Departments and Organizations in the United States and Canada*; Annual Report; essays, studies, doctoral dissertations, details of grants and fellowships for historians.

Finance: Annual revenue US $3,776,172, expenditure $3,827,489 (30 June 2013).

Council: Vicki L. Ruiz (Pres.); Patrick Manning (Pres.-elect); Jan E. Goldstein (Past Pres.).

Principal Staff: Exec. Dir James Grossman.

Address: 400 A St SE, Washington, DC 20003-3889.

Telephone: (202) 544-2422; **Fax:** (202) 544-8307; **Internet:** www.historians.org; **e-mail:** info@historians.org.

American Hungarian Foundation

Founded in 1955 to further the understanding and appreciation of the Hungarian cultural and historical heritage in the USA.

Activities: Provides educational scholarships and grants, and conducts lectures, exhibitions and special events to further understanding of Hungarian heritage and culture; maintains a library containing more than 60,000 volumes, an exhibition space and a museum; has established several academic institutions as well as programmes promoting Hungarian studies, such as the Institute for Hungarian Studies at Rutgers, the State University of New Jersey.

Geographical Area of Activity: Hungary and the USA.

Finance: Annual revenue US $201,627, expenditure $370,359 (30 June 2013).

Board of Directors: Dr Zsolt Harsanyi (Chair.); August J. Molnar (Co-Chair.); Thomas G. Gaspar, Michael Kaufman, Laszlo Papp (Vice-Chair.); James F. Horvath (Sec.); John M. Kerekes (Asst Sec.); Scott B. Lukacs (Treas.).

Principal Staff: Man. Dir Melissa Pepin.

Address: 300 Somerset St, POB 1084, New Brunswick, NJ 08903.

Telephone: (732) 846-5777; **Fax:** (732) 249-7033; **Internet:** www.ahfoundation.org; **e-mail:** info@ahfoundation.org.

American Institute of Pakistan Studies

Founded in 1973 by Dr Hafeez Malik, the Institute aims to promote scholarly exchange between the USA and Pakistan, and to support research on issues relevant to Pakistan.

Activities: Offers pre-doctoral and post-doctoral research fellowships to scholars who are US citizens and are engaged in research on Pakistan, in all fields of the humanities and social sciences. Also administers lectureships and organizes academic conferences. Maintains an office in Islamabad, Pakistan.

Geographical Area of Activity: USA.

Restrictions: Grants made only to US citizens.

Publications: *The Annual of Urdu Studies; Modern Asian Studies; Pakistan Studies News* (newsletter).

Finance: Annual revenue US $754,157, expenditure $772,792 (30 Sept. 2013).

Principal Staff: Pres. Dr Kamran Asdar Ali; Vice-Pres. Farina Mir; Sec. Cabeiri deBergh Robinson; Treas. Farhat Haq.

Address: 203 Ingraham Hall, 1155 Observatory Dr., Madison, WI 53706.

Telephone: (608) 261-1194; **Fax:** (608) 265-3062; **Internet:** www.pakistanstudies-aips.org; **e-mail:** aips@pakistanstudies-aips.org.

American Jewish Joint Distribution Committee—JDC

Founded in 1914 to distribute funds raised by the Orthodox Central Committee for the Relief of Jews, the American Jewish Relief Committee and the People's Relief Committee; the organization aims to provide aid to Jews in need in a non-partisan and non-political way, in every continent outside North America.

Activities: Represents the American Jewish community overseas and works by funding programmes of relief, rescue and reconstruction in a number of countries. The Committee works to ensure that all elderly survivors of the Holocaust are able to live out their lives in dignity; revives and strengthens Jewish communities; and endeavours to help social service concerns in Israel.

Geographical Area of Activity: International.

Publications: *American Jewry and The Holocaust*; *Archives of the Holocaust*; *A Continuing Task*; *I Seek My Brethren*; *My Brother's Keeper*; *Out of the Ashes*; *Renewal*; *The Saving Remnant*; *To Save a World*; *To the Rescue.*

Finance: Annual revenue US $352,594,099, expenditure $22,587,281 (31 Dec. 2013).

Board: Dr Irving A. Smokler (Chair.); Stanley A. Rabin (Treas.); Nancy Grand (Sec.).

Principal Staff: Pres. Penny Blumenstein; Exec. Vice-Pres. and CEO Alan H. Gill.

Address: POB 530, 132 East 43rd St, New York, NY 10017.

Telephone: (212) 687-6200; **Internet:** www.jdc.org; **e-mail:** info@jdc.org.

American Jewish World Service—AJWS

Founded in 1985 as an international development organization motivated by Judaism's imperative to pursue justice.

Activities: Works to alleviating poverty, hunger and disease among the people of the developing world regardless of race, religion or nationality. Through grants to grassroots organizations, volunteer service, advocacy and education, the AJWS fosters civil society, sustainable development and human rights for all people, while promoting the values and responsibilities of global citizenship within the Jewish community. It works with women, young people, ethnic, religious and sexual minorities, indigenous people, refugees and internally displaced people, and people living with HIV/AIDS. Volunteer service programmes are designed to increase the impact of its grants and to create a cadre of global social justice leaders. The organization also advocates US engagement to find peaceful and just resolutions to conflicts, and to provide support to rebuild societies devastated by crisis. Current advocacy work focuses on the genocide in Darfur (Sudan), HIV/AIDS, debt relief, women's rights, and universal access to education.

Geographical Area of Activity: International.

Publications: *AJWS Reports* (magazine); Annual Report.

Finance: Annual revenue US $15,954,955, expenditure $9,662,985 (30 April 2014).

Board of Trustees: Kathleen Levin (Chair.); Jolie Schwab, James Dubey (Vice-Chair.); Monte Dube (Sec.); James Koshland (Treas.).

Principal Staff: Pres. Ruth W. Messinger; Exec. Vice-Pres. Robert Bank.

Address: 45 West 36th St, New York, NY 10018-7904.

Telephone: (212) 792-2900; **Fax:** (212) 792-2930; **Internet:** www.ajws.org; **e-mail:** ajws@ajws.org.

American Near East Refugee Aid—ANERA

Established in 1968.

Activities: Works towards improving the lives of the people of the Middle East by reducing poverty and suffering. The organization aims to address long-term issues relating to Palestinian and Lebanese people, as well as providing emergency aid in time of war. It operates in various fields in the Middle East, providing humanitarian aid and relief and partial funding to community, micro-credit and environmental services; working with local organizations to improve community services and health care; providing education for all; increasing employment; providing sustainable agricultural solutions; developing infrastructure; and advancing information technology resources. Maintains additional offices in Gaza, Hebron, Nablus, Ramallah, Jerusalem, Amman and Beirut.

Geographical Area of Activity: Palestinian Territories, Israel, Jordan, Lebanon.

Publications: Annual Report; newsletter (quarterly).

Finance: Annual revenue US $52,050,493, expenditure $59,591,797 (31 May 2014).

Board of Directors: Prof. Joseph P. Saba (Chair.); Jean Black (Vice-Chair.); Teresa Barger (Treas.); Murad Siam (Sec.).

Principal Staff: Pres. and CEO William D. Corcoran; CFO Donna Diane.

Address: 1111 14th St NW, Suite 400, Washington, DC 20005.

Telephone: (202) 266-9700; **Fax:** (202) 266-9701; **Internet:** www.anera.org; **e-mail:** anera@anera.org.

American Philosophical Society—APS

Founded in 1743 by Benjamin Franklin.

Activities: Promotes scholarly research in the sciences and humanities through grants and fellowships. The Society makes about 185 awards each year that are open to US citizens, and to foreign nationals for research in the USA. The grant and fellowship programmes include: Franklin Research Grants; Daland Fellowships in Clinical Investigation; Lewis and Clark Fund for Exploration and Field Research; Lewis and Clark Fund for Exploration and Field Research in Astrobiology; Phillips Fund Grants for Native American Research; Sabbatical Fellowships in the Humanities and Social Sciences; and Library Resident Research Fellowships. Holds two annual conferences or symposia and has a library of 350,000 volumes and around 11m. manuscripts, specializing in the history of science.

Geographical Area of Activity: Worldwide.

Restrictions: Institutions are not eligible to apply. Grants available to residents of the USA or to US citizens abroad. Foreign nationals whose research is to be carried out in the USA may also apply.

Publications: *Proceedings* (quarterly); *Transactions* (2 a month); *Mendel Newsletter* (annually); memoirs; yearbook; *News* (2 a year).

Finance: Annual revenue US $17,265,388, expenditure $8,987,920 (31 Dec. 2013).

Council: Clyde F. Barker (Pres.); John W. O'Malley, Barbara J. Grosz, Linda Greenhouse (Vice-Pres); Richard E. Quandt (Treas.); Carl F. Miller (Sec.).

Principal Staff: Exec. Officer Keith S. Thomson.

Address: 104 South Fifth St, Philadelphia, PA 19106-3387.

Telephone: (215) 440-3400; **Fax:** (215) 440-3450; **Internet:** www.amphilsoc.org; **e-mail:** LMusumeci@amphilsoc.org.

American Refugee Committee—ARC

Established in 1978 by Neal Ball; a non-profit, non-sectarian organization.

Activities: Aims to improve the quality of life of refugees, asylum seekers and displaced persons, and to enable them to rebuild their lives with dignity and purpose. The Committee sends medical teams and other specialists to refugee camps in a number of countries to provide adequate health care and humanitarian assistance. It runs programmes to improve water and sanitation in refugee camps; teaches shelter repair and construction; gives resettlement advice and assistance; offers micro-credit and vocational training; provides psychosocial services; looks after primary health care concerns; and works towards enabling refugees to return home. Works in collaboration with other international organizations, such as the UN High Commissioner for Refugees (UNHCR). Maintains field offices in Haiti, Liberia, Rwanda, South Sudan, Uganda, Pakistan, Somalia, Thailand and Darfur (Sudan).

Geographical Area of Activity: Worldwide.

Publications: Annual Report.

Finance: Annual revenue US $38,018,523, expenditure $35,586,045 (31 Dec. 2014).

Board of Directors: Ben Boyum (Chair.); Neal Ball (Hon. Chair.); Sheila Leatherman (Vice-Chair.); Holly Robbins (Sec.); Perry Witkin (Treas.).

Principal Staff: Pres. and CEO Daniel Wordsworth; CFO Mark White.

Address: 615 1st Ave NE, Suite 500, Minneapolis, MN 55413-2681.

Telephone: (612) 872-7060; **Fax:** (612) 607-6499; **Internet:** www.arcrelief.org; **e-mail:** info@archq.org.

American Scandinavian Foundation—ASF

Founded in 1910 (incorporated in the State of New York in 1911) to promote international understanding through educational and cultural exchange between the USA and Denmark, Finland, Iceland, Norway and Sweden.

Activities: Awards fellowships and grants; sponsors cultural programmes, sponsors internship/training, issues publications; operates Scandinavia House: the Nordic Center in America, which presents exhibitions, films, concerts, lectures, and has a gallery, auditorium and library. The Foundation makes several awards, including an annual Translation Prize.

Geographical Area of Activity: USA and Scandinavia.

Publications: *Scandinavian Review* (3 a year); *Scan* (quarterly newsletter); Bi-Annual Report.

Finance: Annual revenue US $3,802,118, expenditure $3,954,541 (30 June 2014).

Board: Bente Svensen Frantz (Chair.); Steven B. Peri (Deputy Chair.); Edward E. Elson (Vice-Chair. for Denmark); Dr Aili Flint (Vice-Chair. for Finland); Dr Kristjan T. Ragnarsson (Vice-Chair. for Iceland); Giacomo Landi (Vice-Chair. for Norway); Monika Heimbold (Vice-Chair. for Sweden); Linda Nordberg (Vice-Chair. for the USA); Bård E. Bunaes (Treas.); Lynn Carter (Exec. Vice-Pres. and Sec.).

Principal Staff: Pres. Edward P. Gallagher.

Address: Scandinavia House, 58 Park Ave, between 37th and 38th Sts, New York, NY 10016-3007.

Telephone: (212) 779-3587; **Fax:** (212) 686-1157; **Internet:** www.amscan.org; **e-mail:** info@amscan.org.

American Schools of Oriental Research—ASOR

Founded in 1900 by the Society of Biblical Literature, the Archaeological Institute of America and the American Oriental Society to support research into the peoples and cultures of the Near East.

Activities: Operates internationally in the fields of education and the humanities by conducting and supporting research into Middle Eastern culture, especially through archaeological, anthropological and historical projects. ASOR runs research institutes in the Near East (the W. F. Albright Institute of Archaeological Research, Jerusalem, the American Center of Oriental Research, Amman and the Cyprus American Archaeological Research Institute, Nicosia); awards research fellowships, publishes the results of research, and holds an Annual Meeting.

Geographical Area of Activity: USA and the Middle East.

Publications: *Bulletin of the American Schools of Oriental Research*; *ASOR Newsletter*; *Near Eastern Archaeology*; *Journal of Cuneiform Studies; Archaeological Report Series.*

Finance: Annual revenue US $1,199,091, expenditure $152,276 (30 June 2014).

Board of Trustees: B. W. Ruffner (Chair.); Lynn Swartz Dodd (Sec.); Richard Coffman (Treas.).

Principal Staff: Pres. Susan Ackerman; Vice-Pres. Sharon Herbert; Past. Pres. Tim Harrison; Exec. Dir Dr Andrew G. Vaughn.

Address: Boston University, 656 Beacon St, 5th Floor, Boston, MA 02215-2010.

Telephone: (617) 353-6570; **Fax:** (617) 353-6575; **Internet:** www.asor.org; **e-mail:** asor@bu.edu.

AmeriCares Foundation, Inc

Officially founded in 1982, having been initiated in 1975 by Robert C. Macauley and Alma Jane (Leila) Macauley.

Activities: Provides immediate response to emergency medical needs and supports long-term humanitarian assistance programmes for people around the world irrespective of race, creed or political persuasion. The Foundation provides aid to people affected by famine, civil conflict and natural disasters internationally with emergency relief supplies, including medicines and medical supplies. It also operates nationally, responding to disaster and crisis as well as supporting three community programmes that mobilize volunteers to deliver health-care services to the uninsured.

Geographical Area of Activity: International.

Publications: Annual Report; financial statements.

Finance: Annual revenue US $521,176,478, expenditure $64,795,170 (30 June 2014).

Board of Directors: C. Dean Maglaris (Chair.); Alma Jane Macauley (Vice-Chair.); Jerry Leamon (Vice-Chair.).

Principal Staff: Pres. and CEO Michael J. Nyenhuis.

Address: 88 Hamilton Ave, Stamford, CT 06902.

Telephone: (203) 658-9500; **Fax:** (203) 327-5200; **Internet:** www.americares.org; **e-mail:** info@americares.org.

America's Children

Established in 1984 by Dr William and Judy Schwank as a national network of volunteers who provide free medical care to children worldwide, and especially in Guatemala; known as Children of The Americas—COTA until 2012.

Activities: Operates in the fields of medicine and health, and social welfare. Medical teams travel to Guatemala regularly to provide medical treatment. Children are also referred to the organization's medical team in Kentucky from throughout the world. Has established an orphanage and a surgical centre in Guatemala. Also provides educational services and scholarships in Mexico and Central America.

Geographical Area of Activity: International.

Publications: *One Child* (quarterly newsletter); Annual Report.

Finance: Annual revenue US $920,342, expenditure $924,558 (31 Dec. 2013).

Board of Directors: Dave Brisbin (Pres.); Eugene Spann (Treas.); Marian Brisbin (Sec.).

Address: 67 Gingham St, Trabuco Canyon, CA 92679.

Telephone: (949) 709-0673; **Fax:** (949) 709-0674; **Internet:** www.americaschildren.org; **e-mail:** 4kids@americaschildren.org.

Amerind Foundation, Inc

Founded in 1937 by William Shirley Fulton to promote anthropological studies of the native peoples of America, the preservation and conservation of their material culture and the development of related educational programmes.

Activities: Organizes anthropological field research, collections study, seminars and visiting scholar programmes, and co-operates with organizations and individuals engaged in similar work. The Foundation maintains an anthropological research facility; archaeological, ethnographic and fine arts museum complex; archaeological site files, photographic collections and a library.

Geographical Area of Activity: USA, Mexico.

Restrictions: Grants are made only for advanced seminars.

Publications: *Amerind New World Studies Series*; *Amerind Studies in Archaeology*; and other publications.

Finance: Annual revenue US $1,012,265, expenditure $1,126,794 (31 Dec. 2013).

Board of Directors: Dr George Gumerman (Chair.); Marilyn Fulton (Sec.); James Quirk (Treas.).

Principal Staff: Pres. John H. Davis; Vice-Pres. Dr Dan Shilling; Exec. Dir Dr Christine Szuter.

Address: 2100 North Amerind Rd, POB 400, Dragoon, AZ 85609.

Telephone: (520) 586-3666; **Fax:** (520) 586-4679; **Internet:** www.amerind.org; **e-mail:** amerind@amerind.org.

amfAR—The Foundation for AIDS Research

Founded in 1985 by the merger of the AIDS Medical Foundation and the National AIDS Research Foundation to prevent HIV infection and the death and disease associated with HIV/AIDS and to protect the human rights of all people threatened by HIV/AIDS.

Activities: Raises funds to provide grants and awards to support AIDS research, AIDS prevention and treatment education, and the advocacy of sound AIDS-related public policy. Awards grants to non-profit institutions for basic biomedical and clinical research in fields related to HIV/AIDS and for postdoctoral investigators to study at other institutions; office in Washington, DC.

Geographical Area of Activity: International.

Restrictions: Grants only to non-profit organizations.

Publications: *amfAR e-News* (e-mail newsletter); *amfAR News* (biannual newsletter); *Treat Asia Report* (quarterly); Annual Report; and other publications.

Finance: Annual revenue US $29,914,632, expenditure $29,258,665 (30 Sept. 2013).

Board of Trustees: Kenneth Cole (Chair.); Patricia J. Matson, John C. Simons (Vice-Chair.); Wallace Sheft (Treas.); Mervyn F. Silverman (Sec.).

Principal Staff: CEO Kevin R. Frost.

Address: 120 Wall St, 13th Floor, New York, NY 10005-3908.

Telephone: (212) 806-1600; **Fax:** (212) 806-1601; **Internet:** www.amfar.org; **e-mail:** information@amfar.org.

AMIDEAST—America-Mideast Educational and Training Services, Inc

Founded in 1951 by Dorothy Thompson to strengthen mutual understanding and co-operation between Americans and peoples of the Middle East and North Africa.

Activities: Administers publicly and privately sponsored programmes in the Middle East and North Africa in the areas of professional training and development, English language training, institutional development, educational advising and testing, and international educational exchange. The organization also administers 'study abroad' programmes for US citizens, and develops and distributes educational resources on the Middle East and North Africa to US schools and libraries.

Geographical Area of Activity: North Africa, the Middle East and USA.

Restrictions: Not a grantmaking organization.

Publications: *The Advising Quarterly*; Annual Report.

Finance: Annual revenue US $75,035,971, expenditure $75,045,416 (30 Sept. 2013).

Board of Directors: Dr Mary W. Gray (Chair.); Nicholas A. Veliotes (Vice-Chair.); Robert H. Pelletreau (Treas.).

Principal Staff: Pres. and CEO Theodore H. Kattouf; Vice-Pres. and CFO Linda DeNicola.

Address: 1730 M St, NW, Suite 1100, Washington, DC 20036-4505.

Telephone: (202) 776-9600; **Fax:** (202) 776-7000; **Internet:** www.amideast.org; **e-mail:** inquiries@amideast.org.

Ananda Marga Universal Relief Team—AMURT

Founded in 1965 in India.

Activities: Improves the quality of life of the poor and underprivileged, and offers long-term solutions to break the poverty cycle. AMURT aims to provide opportunities for everyone regardless of race, religion, sex or social status. It also provides emergency supplies for victims of natural and manmade disasters. Works in approx. 80 countries in the fields of education, health, micro-enterprise and community development. A sister organization, AMURTEL (f. 1975), concentrates on problems affecting women and children.

Geographical Area of Activity: International.

Finance: Annual revenue US $913,323, expenditure $940,157 (31 Dec. 2013).

Board: Steven Landau (Pres.); David Grau (Vice-Pres.); Peter Dodge (Treas.); Diane Alcantara (Sec.).

Principal Staff: Exec. Dir Peter Sage.

Address: 2502 Lindley Terrace, Rockville, MD 20850.

Telephone: (301) 738-7122; **Fax:** (301) 738-7123; **Internet:** www.amurt.net; **e-mail:** info@amurt.net.

The Annenberg Foundation

Founded in 1989 by Walter H. Annenberg, who died in 2002, for general charitable purposes.

Activities: Operates mainly in the fields of education, especially early childhood and pre-collegiate education and cultural programmes, primarily in the USA. The Foundation also supports other arts and cultural initiatives, health programmes, and civic and community projects.

Geographical Area of Activity: Primarily USA.

Restrictions: Unsolicited requests from organizations outside the USA are not accepted; no grants are made to individuals; no grants for scholarships or book publications.

Publications: Application Guidelines.

Finance: Annual revenue US $24,657,507, expenditure $124,531,748 (1 July 2013).

Board of Directors: Wallis Annenberg (Chair.).

Principal Staff: Pres. and CEO Wallis Annenberg; Vice-Pres Gregory Annenberg Weingarten, Charles Annenberg Weingarten, Lauren Bon; Exec. Dir Leonard J. Aube.

Address: 2000 Ave of the Stars, Suite 1000 S, Los Angeles, CA 90067.

Telephone: (310) 209-4560; **Fax:** (310) 209-1631; **Internet:** www.annenbergfoundation.org; **e-mail:** info@annenbergfoundation.org.

Anti-Defamation League of B'nai B'rith—ADL

Founded in 1913 to counter the defamation of Jewish people; aims to identify and combat anti-Semitic and bigoted sentiments, and promote democratic ideals and civil rights for all.

Activities: Operates internationally through carrying out research on and monitoring anti-Semitic and racist groups all over the world, and disseminating information. Also serves as a resource for governments, media and the public, runs courses educating people about the Holocaust and related issues, and works towards safeguarding religious liberty in the world. Carries out an annual audit of anti-Semitic incidents in the USA. Also supports peace talks in the Middle East. Maintains offices throughout the USA, and in Israel and Russia.

Geographical Area of Activity: International.

Publications: Annual Report, ADL on the Frontline, HeADLines.

Finance: Annual revenue US $61,366,360, expenditure $58,137,559 (31 Dec. 2013).

National Commission: Barry Curtiss-Lusher (Nat. Chair.).

Principal Staff: Nat. Dir Abraham Foxman; Deputy Nat. Dir Kenneth Jacobson.

Address: 605 Third Ave, New York, NY 10158.

Telephone: (212) 885-7700; **Fax:** (212) 867-9406; **Internet:** www.adl.org.

Arca Foundation

Founded in 1952 by Nancy S. Reynolds to promote the well-being of humanity throughout the world.

Activities: Seeks to influence public policy, especially economic and political issues in the USA. The Foundation supports projects in Central and South America and the Caribbean that promote a foreign policy based on respect for human rights, national sovereignty and international law. It currently focuses on US policy towards Cuba; reform of political party funding; education; fighting deterioration in conditions for working people; capital punishment; and the need for strong coalitions to create equality for all individuals in society.

Geographical Area of Activity: USA, and Central and South America and the Caribbean.

Restrictions: Does not extend grants to direct social services or research fellowships. No grants made to individuals, groups outside the USA, scholarship funds or scholarly research, government programmes, nor to capital projects/endowments.

Publications: Annual Report.

Finance: Annual revenue US $27,083,555, expenditure $25,987,500 (30 June 2014).

Board of Directors: Nancy R. Bagley (Pres.); Nicole Bagley (Vice-Pres.); Mary E. King (Sec.).

Principal Staff: Exec. Dir Anna Lefer Kuhn.

Address: 1308 19th St, NW, Washington, DC 20036.

Telephone: (202) 822-9193; **Fax:** (202) 785-1446; **Internet:** www.arcafoundation.org; **e-mail:** proposals@arcafoundation.org.

Arcus Foundation

Established in 2000 by Jon Stryker.

Activities: Promotes the idea that respect for diversity among peoples and in nature is essential to a positive future for the planet and all of its inhabitants. Has offices in New York City and Cambridge, United Kingdom.

Geographical Area of Activity: International.

Restrictions: Does not fund individuals or support requests to pay off debts. In addition, the foundation does not support political activities or attempts to influence specific legislation.

Publications: Annual Report; *Politics of Species, State of the Apes Volume 1: Extractive Industries and Ape Conservation*; *Bordered Lives*; *Lyudmila and Natasha*.

Finance: Annual revenue US \$19,328,996, expenditure \$39,776,167 (2013).

Board of Directors: Jon Stryker (Pres.).

Principal Staff: Exec. Dir Kevin Jennings.

Address: 44 W 28th Street, 17th Floor, New York, NY.

Telephone: (212) 488-3000; **Fax:** (212) 488-3010; **Internet:** www.arcusfoundation.org; **e-mail:** contact@ arcusfoundation.org.

Arthritis Foundation

Founded in 1948 to improve lives through leadership in the prevention, control and cure of arthritis and related diseases.

Activities: Operates nationally in the fields of education, science and medicine, through self-conducted programmes, research, grants to institutions and individuals, fellowships, scholarships, conferences, courses, publications and lectures. The Foundation works in five key areas: increasing funding to arthritis-related research; building awareness; empowering health actions, through involving everyone in healthy behaviour; influencing national health policy; and exploring all possible research angles. It awards the Russell L. Cecil Arthritis Medical Journalism Awards, the Arthritis Investigator Award and the Segal Clinical Scientist Grants for Osteoarthritis Biomarkers. Maintains 46 local offices around the USA.

Geographical Area of Activity: USA.

Publications: *Arthritis Today* (6 a year); Annual Report; consumer health magazine.

Finance: Annual revenue US \$10,651,940, expenditure \$9,665,698 (31 Dec. 2013).

Board of Directors: Michael V. Ortman (Chair.); Rowland W. (Bing) Chang (Vice-Chair.); Catherine T. (Cathy) Dunlay (Sec.); Laurie Stewart (Treas.); Daniel T. McGowan (Immediate Past Chair.).

Principal Staff: Pres. and CEO Ann M. Palmer.

Address: 1330 W. Peachtree St, Suite 100, Atlanta, GA 30309; POB 7669, Atlanta, GA 30357-0669.

Telephone: (800) 283-7800; **Internet:** www.arthritis.org.

Asia Foundation

Established in 1954; a private non-profit NGO.

Activities: Dedicated to advancing the mutual interests of the USA and the Asia-Pacific region. The Foundation works in four main areas: governance, law and civil society; economic reform and development; women's political participation; and international relations. Collaborates with partner organizations from the public and private sectors to support institutional development, exchanges and dialogue, technical assistance, research and policy engagement. It also makes grants to organizations based in Asia. Maintains a network of 17 offices throughout Asia, as well as an office in Washington, DC. In 2001, the Foundation launched the Give2Asia fund-raising initiative and since 1954 has been running its Books for Asia initiative, distributing books, software programmes, and other educational materials to educational institutions in 40 countries in Asia.

Geographical Area of Activity: USA and the Asia-Pacific region.

Restrictions: No grants to individuals.

Publications: Annual Report; *Asian Perspectives Series*; numerous reports and publications.

Finance: Annual revenue US \$137,309,886, expenditure \$138,906,281 (30 Sept. 2013).

Board of Trustees: David M. Lampton (Chair.); Kenneth I. Juster, Sunder Ramaswamy, Mary Brown Bullock (Vice-Chair.); Teresita C. Schaffer (Sec.); Thomas P. Rohlen (Treas.).

Principal Staff: Pres. and CEO David D. Arnold; Exec. Vice-Pres. and COO Suzanne E. Siskel.

Address: 465 California St, 9th Floor, San Francisco, CA 94104; POB 193223, San Francisco, CA 94119-3223.

Telephone: (415) 982-4640; **Fax:** (415) 392-8863; **Internet:** www.asiafoundation.org; **e-mail:** sf.general@asiafoundation .org.

Asia Society

Founded in 1956 by John D. Rockefeller, II to promote greater knowledge of Asia in the USA.

Activities: Works to strengthen relations and promote understanding among the people, leaders and institutions of the USA and Asia. The Society seeks to increase knowledge and enhance dialogue; encourage creative expression; and generate new ideas across the fields of arts and culture, policy and business, and education. It fulfills its educational mandate through a wide range of cross-disciplinary programmes, incl. Asian-American issues, the effects of globalization and pressing concerns in Asia. In 2014, it established the Asia Society Policy Institute, with a focus on regional security, prosperity and environmental sustainability.

Geographical Area of Activity: USA, South-East Asia and Australasia.

Finance: Annual revenue US \$137,309,886, expenditure \$138,906,281 (30 Sept. 2013).

Board of Trustees: Ronnie C. Chan, Henrietta H. Fore (Co-Chair.).

Principal Staff: Pres. Josette Sheeran; Exec. Vice-Pres. Tom Nagorski.

Address: 725 Park Ave/70th St, New York, NY 10021.

Telephone: (212) 288-6400; **Fax:** (212) 517-8315; **Internet:** www.asiasociety.org; **e-mail:** info@asiasociety.org.

Asian Cultural Council—ACC

Founded in 1963 by John D. Rockefeller, III, to support cultural exchange in the visual and performing arts between the USA and Asia. Originally known as the JDR 3rd Program, it has been formally affiliated to the Rockefeller Brothers Fund (q.v.) since 1991.

Activities: The emphasis of the grant programme is on providing individual fellowship awards to artists, scholars, students and specialists in the visual and performing arts for research, travel, study and creative work involving cultural exchange between Asia and the USA. The Council also makes a limited number of grants to arts organizations and educational institutions for specific projects of Asian-American cultural exchange. It currently prioritizes individuals in East and South-East Asia seeking grant assistance for research, travel, study, training or creative activity in the USA. Has additional offices in Taiwan, Hong Kong and Japan.

Geographical Area of Activity: Mainly Asia, from Pakistan eastwards to Japan.

Restrictions: No grants to individuals for lecture programmes, personal exhibitions, individual performance tours, undergraduate studies, nor for activities by individuals within their home countries. No grants to organizations for publications, film and video productions, capital campaigns or general programme or administrative costs.

Publications: Annual Report; information brochure.

Finance: Received initial support for administrative expenses from the JDR 3rd Fund, but has to raise funds for grant programmes from other foundations, government agencies, corporations and individuals. Annual revenue US \$3,234,832, expenditure \$4,960,505 (31 Dec. 2013).

Board of Trustees: Wendy O'Neill (Chair.); Valerie Rockefeller Wayne, Hans Michael Jebsen (Vice-Chair.); Richard S. Lanier (Pres.); Stephen B. Heintz (Vice-Pres.); Pauline R. Yu (Sec.); Jonathan Fanton (Treas.).

Principal Staff: Exec. Dir Miho Walsh.

Address: 6 West 48th St, 12th Floor, New York, NY 10036-1802.

Telephone: (212) 843-0403; **Fax:** (212) 843-0343; **Internet:** www.asianculturalcouncil.org; **e-mail:** acc@accny.org.

Asian Youth Center

Established in 1989.

Activities: Advocates and extends support for international laws that address local and regional issues of poverty and privation. The Center promotes regional federation of development, peace and youth organizations, and runs programmes to create awareness and new opportunities to uplift the deprived sections of society. It focuses on youth empowerment by providing a platform for information exchange for organizations all over Asia; raises awareness of issues of poverty in Asia; works towards making social justice accessible to all; promotes volunteerism and involvement of youngsters in welfare activities; and finances educational schemes.

Geographical Area of Activity: South-East Asia.

Publications: Annual Report; *Asian Youth News* (newsletter).

Finance: Annual revenue US $4,005,204, expenditure $3,680,451 (30 June 2014).

Board of Directors: Jim Smith (Pres.); Ken Tcheng (Past Pres.); Helen Romero Shaw (First Vice-Pres.); David Lawton (Sec.); K. T. Leung (Treas.).

Principal Staff: Exec. Dir Michelle L. Freridge.

Address: 100 West Clary Ave, San Gabriel, CA 91776.

Telephone: (626) 309-0622; **Fax:** (626) 309-0717; **Internet:** www.asianyouthcenter.org; **e-mail:** admin@asianyouthcenter.org.

Aspen Institute

Founded in 1950 as a global forum for world leaders and policy-makers to discuss issues affecting the human condition.

Activities: Runs a series of Seminar Programs and Policy Programs to encourage corporate leaders to act responsibly and provide a forum for debates on domestic and international issues, ranging from the growth of micro-enterprises to the control of nuclear weapons. The Institute operates internationally through a network of partner organizations in Europe and Asia.

Geographical Area of Activity: International.

Restrictions: Not a grantmaking organization.

Publications: *The Aspen Idea*.

Finance: Annual revenue US $93,242,479, expenditure $82,126,112 (31 Dec. 2013).

Board of Trustees: Robert K. Steel (Chair.); James Schine Crown (Vice-Chair.).

Principal Staff: Pres. and CEO Walter Isaacson.

Address: One Dupont Circle NW, Suite 700, Washington, DC 20036-1133.

Telephone: (202) 736-5800; **Fax:** (202) 467-0790; **Internet:** www.aspeninstitute.org; **e-mail:** info@aspeninstitute.org.

Atkinson Foundation

Founded in 1939 by George H. Atkinson and Mildred M. Atkinson for general charitable purposes.

Activities: Priority areas of interest are: tax-exempt, not-for-profit organizations, mainly in San Mateo County, CA, working in the areas of the disadvantaged, the homeless, child welfare, family planning, the disabled, education, welfare and AIDS; and international development, technical assistance, population and health education projects in Mexico and Central America.

Geographical Area of Activity: USA, Central and South America.

Restrictions: Does not give directly to individuals or finance research; grants are made only to US charitable, tax-exempt organizations.

Publications: Annual Report.

Finance: Annual revenue US $1,280,250, expenditure $794,230 (31 Dec. 2013).

Board of Directors: Linda Lanier (Pres.); Jean Atkinson (Sec.); James Avedisian (Treas.); William Crandall, Jr (Asst Treas.).

Principal Staff: Vice-Pres. and Admin. Elizabeth H. Curtis.

Address: 1720 South Amphlett Blvd, Suite 100, San Mateo, CA 94402-2710.

Telephone: (650) 357-1101; **Fax:** (650) 357-1101; **Internet:** atkinsonfdn.org; **e-mail:** atkinfdn@aol.com.

Atlantic Philanthropies

Established in 1982 by Charles F. Feeney to bring about lasting changes that will improve the lives of disadvantaged and vulnerable people. Consists of the Atlantic Foundation and the Atlantic Trust, both domiciled in Bermuda, several smaller foundations based in Bermuda, the United Kingdom, Ireland and the USA, and regional service companies that select and evaluate potential grant recipients, oversee grants once awarded, and manage the endowment.

Activities: Grants are made to projects in Bermuda, the United Kingdom (Northern Ireland), Ireland, South Africa, the USA and Viet Nam in the fields of ageing, disadvantaged children and young people, health of populations in developing countries, and reconciliation and human rights. The organization focuses on tackling the root causes of big and neglected problems that are amenable to solution, and where grants can make lasting contributions and achieve enduring change. In 2002, the Board of Directors decided to reduce the endowment gradually over an expected 12–15 years.

Geographical Area of Activity: Bermuda, Northern Ireland and United Kingdom, Ireland, South Africa, USA, Viet Nam.

Restrictions: Proposals are considered by invitation only.

Publications: Annual Report; *Atlantic Reports*.

Finance: Annual revenue US $160,940, expenditure $583,726 (31 Dec. 2012).

Board of Directors: Peter Smitham (Chair.); Thomas N. Mitchell, Sara Lawrence-Lightfoot (Deputy Chair.); Sarah Cooke (Sec.).

Principal Staff: Pres. and CEO Christopher G. Oechsli.

Address: 75 Varick St, New York, NY 10013-1917.

Telephone: (212) 916-7300; **Fax:** (212) 922-0360; **Internet:** www.atlanticphilanthropies.org; **e-mail:** usa@atlanticphilanthropies.org.

Atlantis Blue Project Foundation, Inc.

Established in 2005 as Kerzner Marine Foundation by the Kerzner International group of companies to assist in the protection of marine habitats.

Activities: Operates in the field of conservation of tropical marine ecosystems, through scientific research, education and community projects. The Foundation especially favours projects in the areas of development and management of marine protected areas, and conservation of coral reefs and cetaceans, as well as research.

Geographical Area of Activity: Marine environments in the Caribbean, the Indian Ocean and the Pacific.

Restrictions: Does not fund litigation, political activities, fund-raising, scholarships, endowment and university overhead costs.

Finance: Annual revenue US $250,203, expenditure $386,586 (2012).

Board of Directors: George Markantonis (Pres.); Mark Gsellman (Vice-Pres. and Sec); Carlos Hernandez (Treas.).

Principal Staff: Exec. Dir Debra Erickson.

Address: 1000 S Pine Island Rd, Suite 800, Plantation, FL 33324-3907.

Telephone: (954) 809-2000; **Fax:** (954) 809-2303; **Internet:** blueprojectatlantis.org.

Atlas Economic Research Foundation

Founded in 1981 by the late Sir Antony Fisher to develop and strengthen a global network of market-orientated think tanks.

Activities: Aims to discover intellectual entrepreneurs, support the development and dissemination of their work to current and potential opinion leaders, and to support the development of think tanks. The Foundation makes grants to think tanks and similar institutions; funds international travel for young people wishing to develop the ideas of the free market; and through its Health and Welfare Program provides start-up grants to encourage and facilitate think-tank work on health and welfare issues, especially work concerning more 'vulnerable' sectors of society. It also funds workshops and teaching initiatives; makes prizes for publications; and operates the Templeton Freedom Awards and Program, which recognizes new institutes with exceptional future promise, as well as outstanding work by leading think tanks in the areas of free-market solutions to poverty, ethics and values, social entrepreneurship, and outreach to students.

Geographical Area of Activity: International.

Publications: *Highlights* (newsletter); *Atlas Investor Reports* (newsletter); *AZAD Newsletter*; Annual Report.

Finance: Annual revenue US $11,596,955, expenditure $8,627,157 (31 Dec. 2013).

Board of Directors: Dan Grossman (Chair.).

Principal Staff: Pres. Dr Alejandro (Alex) A. Chafuen; CEO Brad Lips.

Address: 1201 L St NW, Washington, DC 20005.

Telephone: (202) 449-8449; **Fax:** (202) 280-1259; **Internet:** atlasnetwork.org; **e-mail:** info@atlasnetwork.org.

AT&T Foundation

Founded in 1984 by AT&T Corporation as a philanthropic organization dedicated to the support of education, arts and culture, and civic and community services nationally and internationally.

Activities: Operates in the fields of education, arts and culture, and civic and community service, and provides 33% of its budget to a local grants initiative, operated by local offices supporting communities in their area. Within the field of education, the Foundation supports projects focusing on the use of technology to enhance teaching and learning, and promoting family involvement in education, providing professional development opportunities for educators and promoting life-long learning and community collaboration. Civic and community service programme grants are given to health services for those in need; diversity in the workplace; environmental projects; national US organizations conducting public policy research; and projects enhancing the effectiveness of the voluntary sector. The arts and culture programme assists the production and creation of new artistic work; brings the work of women artists and artists of diverse cultures to a wider public; and mobilizes new technologies to promote artistic innovation and increase access to the arts. Local grants are given within areas where the company operates or has a significant presence.

Geographical Area of Activity: International.

Restrictions: Prefers to work with charitable organizations that have clearly stated objectives, long-range planning, active participation of the governing board and strategies that incorporate diversified sources of support. Also considers grants to organizations that qualify as government bodies.

Publications: Biennial Report; newsletters.

Finance: Annual revenue US $5,334,376, expenditure $4,828,713 (2013).

Board of Trustees: James W. Cicconi (Chair.); Jonathan P. Klug (Treas.); Thomas R. Giltner (Sec.); Daniel O'Grady (Asst Treas.).

Principal Staff: Pres. Beth Shiroshi.

Address: 32 Ave of the Americas, 6th Floor, New York, NY 10013.

Telephone: (212) 387-6555; **Fax:** (212) 387-4882; **Internet:** about.att.com/csr; **e-mail:** sustainability@attnews.us.

The Francis Bacon Foundation, Inc

Founded in 1937 by Walter Conrad Arensberg and Louise Stevens Arensberg to conduct and promote research in history, philosophy, science and literature, with special reference to the life and works of Francis Bacon, and his influence on his own and succeeding times; to make grants to colleges and universities; and to create and operate a library for those purposes.

Activities: Operates in the fields of education and the arts and humanities, nationally through self-conducted programmes, grants to institutions, particularly in southern California, conferences and courses, and nationally and internationally through publications and lectures. Awards Visiting Professorships and Lectureships in the Humanities to smaller colleges and universities to enable them to attract outstanding scholars, as well as the biennial Francis Bacon Award in the history of science, the history of technology, or historically engaged philosophy of science, in conjunction with the California Institute of Technology, worth US $20,000. Maintains the Huntington Library with a collection of almost 13,000 vols in San Marino, CA.

Geographical Area of Activity: USA.

Publications: Annual Report.

Finance: Annual revenue US $466,565, expenditure $133,672 (31 Dec. 2013).

Trustees: Karl I. Swaidan (Sec.).

Principal Staff: Pres. Henry J. Gibbons.

Address: 301 E. Colorado Blvd, Pasadena, CA 9101.

Telephone: (626) 795-5894; **Internet:** www.sirfrancisbacon.org.

Bank of America Charitable Foundation

Founded in 1998 by Bank of America Corporation to fund private, non-profit, tax-exempt organizations providing services to communities nationally and internationally in areas where the company operates.

Activities: Provides grants, investments and loans within three main areas: preserving local communities, equipping people to be economically self-sufficient, and helping those most in need. The Foundation makes education grants to a variety of learning, educator development and literacy projects. A Volunteer Grants Program supports non-profit organizations where company associates volunteer their time. The Joe Martin Scholarship Program offers financial assistance to students who are dependants of company employees.

Geographical Area of Activity: USA and areas where the Bank of America operates.

Publications: Newsletter (quarterly); Annual Report.

Finance: Annual revenue US $274,950,638, expenditure $198,332,854 (2011).

Trustees: Anne M. Finucane (Chair.); Colleen O. Johnson (Sec.); Pamela Grotsky (Asst Sec.); Suzette Finger (Treas.).

Principal Staff: Pres. Kerry H. Sullivan.

Address: 100 North Tryon St NC1-007-18-01, Charlotte, NC 28288.

Telephone: (980) 388-5138; **Internet:** www.bankofamerica.com/foundation.

Baptist World Aid—BWAid

Established in 1905 to work in the field of international relief and development; a division of the Baptist World Alliance.

Activities: Operates, without regard to race or religion, in famine, disaster and refugee relief work. BWAid funds long-term development programmes in the areas of training in self-sufficiency, agriculture, health and education in developing countries. It also offers fellowship assistance to Baptists across the world.

Geographical Area of Activity: International.

Restrictions: Works through member bodies of the Baptist World Alliance.

Publications: Newsletter; *Baptist World Centenary Congress: Official Report*; *Baptists Together in Christ 1905–2005*; numerous studies and research papers.

Finance: Annual revenue US $2,761,104, expenditure $3,313,554 (31 Dec. 2013).

Principal Staff: Pres. John Upton; Gen. Sec. Neville G. Callam; First Vice-Pres. Daniel Carro; Treas. Carolyn Fossen.

Address: 405 North Washington St, Falls Church, VA 22046.

Telephone: (703) 790-8980; **Fax:** (703) 893-5160; **Internet:** www.bwanet.org; **e-mail:** bwa@bwanet.org.

Benton Foundation

Founded in 1981, following the principles of William Benton relating to the use of communications to benefit society and help solve social problems.

Activities: Works in three areas: defines and advocates public policies that recognize new media's capacity for working in the public interest; helps NGOs use the media and communications technologies to best provide information for the public; and works to create Internet-based 'knowledge networks' that are accessible sources of information for non-profit action groups, journalists and educators. The Foundation established the Richard M. Neustadt Center for Communications in the Public Interest.

Geographical Area of Activity: USA.

Restrictions: No unsolicited or general grant applications accepted.

Publications: *Technology Literacy Benchmarks for Nonprofit Organizations*; *Benton Foundation 20 Year Report*; *Youth Activism and Global Engagement*; *Networking for Better Care: Health Care in the Information Age*; *Native Networking: Telecommunications and Information Technology in Indian Country*; *Losing Ground Bit by Bit: Low-Income Communities in the Information Age*; *Effective Language for Discussing Early Childhood Education and Policy*; *Universal Service: A Historical Perspective and Policies for the 21st Century*.

Finance: Annual revenue US $388,921, expenditure $786,968 (2012).

Board of Directors: Charles Benton (Chair.); Michael Smith (Treas.); Robert A. Cohen (Sec.).

Principal Staff: Exec. Dir Adrianne Benton Furniss.

Address: 1250 Connecticut Ave NW, Suite 200, Washington, DC 20036.

Telephone: (202) 638-5770; **Fax:** (240) 235-5024; **Internet:** www.benton.org; **e-mail:** info@benton.org.

Better World Campaign—BWC

Established in 1997 as the Better World Fund along with its sister organization, the UN Foundation (q.v.), following a gift of US $1,000m. to the UN by R. E. (Ted) Turner.

Activities: Conducts and finances projects aimed at educating the public about the work and role of the UN in addressing global issues, and building public support for the organization, in particular highlighting the UN's work to strengthen international security through global co-operation. In conjunction with the UN Foundation, it sponsors the daily *UN Wire* news summary on UN and global affairs. Promotes US engagement with the UN and educates the American public about the benfits.

Geographical Area of Activity: International.

Finance: Annual revenue US $6,098,949, expenditure $12,278,465 (31 Dec. 2013).

Board of Directors: Re Turner (Chair.); Gro Harlem Brundtland, Timothy E. Wirth (Vice-Chair.).

Principal Staff: Pres. and CEO Kathryn Calvin Walters; Vice-Pres. and Exec. Dir Peter Yeo.

Address: 1750 Pennsylvania Ave, NW, Suite 300, Washington, DC 20006.

Telephone: (202) 462-4900; **Fax:** (202) 462-2686; **Internet:** www.betterworldcampaign.org; **e-mail:** info_bwc@betterworldcampaign.org.

Blue Moon Fund, Inc

Founded in 2002 by Diane Edgerton Miller and Patricia Jones Edgerton, following the restructuring of the W. Alton Jones Foundation (f. 1944 to promote environmental conservation and world peace).

Activities: Provides grants to organizations concerned with the protection and conservation of environmental resources. Funded initiatives include sustainable economic development projects in Brazil; the promotion of green energy schemes in the People's Republic of China and the establishment of a carbon trading facility to finance small renewable energy and energy efficiency projects in developing countries, initially in India, China and the Americas. The Fund also sponsors an urban initiative and fellowship programme aimed at promoting cutting-edge approaches providing solutions to the questions of human consumption, the natural world, and economic advancement, placing fellows employed in the private or governmental sectors in non-profit organizations.

Geographical Area of Activity: Asia, North America, Central America and South America.

Restrictions: No grants are made to individuals, for building construction, endowment funds, basic research, scholarships, fellowships, international exchanges or conferences.

Finance: Annual revenue US $6,896,566, expenditure $16,060,173 (2013).

Board of Trustees: Ethan A. Miller (Sec.).

Principal Staff: Pres. and CEO Diane Edgerton Miller.

Address: 222 W South St, Charlottesville, VA 22902.

Telephone: (434) 295-5160; **Fax:** (434) 295-6894; **Internet:** www.bluemoonfund.org; **e-mail:** info@bluemoonfund.org.

Born This Way Foundation

Established in 2011 by the singer Lady Gaga and her mother, Cynthia Germanotta, to foster a society that embraces difference and individuality.

Activities: Carries out its own campaigning and advocacy projects.

Geographical Area of Activity: USA.

Finance: Annual revenue US $1,838,756, expenditure $4,048,687 (31 Dec. 2013).

Board of Directors: Cynthia Germanotta (Pres.); Joseph A. Germanotta (Treas.).

Address: 10736 Jefferson Blvd, No. 525, Culver City, CA 90230.

Internet: bornthiswayfoundation.org; **e-mail:** info@bornthiswayfoundation.org.

Lynde and Harry Bradley Foundation, Inc

Founded in 1942 as the Allen-Bradley Foundation, Inc to support local and national initiatives. Converted to a private foundation and present name adopted in 1985.

Activities: Operates locally in the fields of the arts, education, social welfare and public policy, and promotes citizenship and civil society. The Foundation gives support to US organizations involved in research into national and international public policy, and grants are made to institutes of higher education on a national level, especially in the field of the arts and humanities.

Geographical Area of Activity: USA.

Publications: Annual Report; *Donor Intent Program*; *Intellectual Infrastructure*; *Improve Education*; *Revitalize Civil Society*; *Legacy of Milwaukee*; *Fifteen Years of Giving* (report).

Finance: Annual revenue US $19,942,000, expenditure $50,010,000 (31 Dec. 2014).

Board of Directors: Dennis J. Kuester (Chair.); David V. Uihlein, Jr (Vice-Chair.).

Principal Staff: Pres. and CEO Michael W. Grebe.

Address: The Lion House, 1241 North Franklin Pl., Milwaukee, WI 53202-2901.

Telephone: (414) 291-9915; **Fax:** (414) 291-9991; **Internet:** www.bradleyfdn.org.

Bridge to Asia—BTA

Founded in 1987 by Jeffrey Smith to aid the modernization of education in the People's Republic of China and other Asian countries.

Activities: Helps libraries at universities and research institutes upgrade their collections, through donations of books, journals and other materials in China, Viet Nam and other countries.

Geographical Area of Activity: China, South-East Asia and USA.

Finance: Annual revenue US \$522,651, expenditure \$513,303 (31 Dec. 2012).

Board of Directors: Geraldine Kunstadter (Chair.).

Principal Staff: Pres. Jeff Smith; Vice-Pres. Newton Liu.

Address: 1505 Juanita Way, Berkeley, CA 94702-1103.

Telephone: (510) 665-3998; **Internet:** www.bridge.org; **e-mail:** asianet@bridge.org.

BrightFocus Foundation

Established in 1973 as American Health Assistance Foundation. Present name adopted in 2013.

Activities: Supports scientific investigation of Alzheimer's disease, glaucoma and macular degeneration, and has a strong public outreach mission to inform people about these age-related, degenerative diseases. The Foundation grants awards to peer-reviewed and selected researchers around the world through three programmes: Alzheimer's Disease Research, National Glaucoma Research and Macular Degeneration Research. It also provides vital information to the public, especially those affected by these three age-related, degenerative diseases.

Geographical Area of Activity: International.

Publications: Publications include booklets on all three diseases, shorter brochures, and newsletters with research updates.

Finance: Annual revenue US \$26,723,642, expenditure \$25,127,380 (31 March 2013).

Board of Directors: Grace Frisone (Chair.); Michael H. Barnett (Vice-Chair.); Nicholas W. Raymond (Treas.); Scott Rodgville (Sec.).

Principal Staff: Pres. and CEO Stacy Pagos Haller.

Address: 22512 Gateway Center Dr., Clarksburg, MD 20871.

Telephone: (301) 948-3244; **Fax:** (301) 258-9454; **Internet:** www.brightfocus.org; www.ahaf.org; **e-mail:** info@brightfocus.org.

Bristol-Myers Squibb Foundation

Established in 1982 to fund and support projects that enhance and extend human lives around the world.

Activities: Supports a broad range of initiatives that deal with important health and social matters around the world, including women's health education and biomedical research. Support includes research grants and donations of medical supplies and pharmaceutical products. One of the Foundation's largest projects is the US \$115m. Secure the Future programme to reduce the impact of the HIV/AIDS epidemic in Southern and Western African countries, funding research, training, education and community outreach work. In 2010, the Foundation launched an initiative to help people with diabetes.

Geographical Area of Activity: International.

Restrictions: Does not award grants to individuals; political, social, fraternal or veterans' organizations; religious or sectarian organizations unless engaged in action significantly beneficial to the community; organizations in receipt of funds from United Way; endowments; advertising; conferences, videos or special events.

Publications: Annual Report.

Finance: Annual revenue US \$2,828,834, expenditure \$34,554,247 (31 Dec. 2013).

Board of Directors: Lamberto Andreotti (Chair.); Mary Van-Hatten (Sec.); Jeffrey Galik (Treas.).

Principal Staff: Pres. John L. Damonti.

Address: 345 Park Ave, 43rd Floor, New York, NY 10154-0037.

Telephone: (212) 546-4000; **Fax:** (609) 252-6031; **Internet:** www.bms.com/foundation/pages/home.aspx.

British Schools and Universities Foundation, Inc—BSUF

Founded in 1961 to promote closer relations between the USA and the British Commonwealth, through educational assistance.

Activities: A charitable foundation that makes grants to educational institutions in the United Kingdom and the British Commonwealth, and supports reciprocal Anglo-American education.

Geographical Area of Activity: United Kingdom, the Commonwealth and the USA.

Publications: Annual Report.

Finance: Annual revenue US \$3,905,658, expenditure \$3,802,620 (31 Dec. 2013).

Board of Directors: David Lipson (Chair.); Patrick M. Russell (Treas.); Allerton G. Smith, John G. Stiller, Daniel O'Day, Jr, David W. Webber (Vice-Pres); Rosalind C. Benedict (Sec.); Jay H. McDowell (Gen. Counsel).

Principal Staff: Pres. Roger H. Martin; Exec. Dir James E. Marlow.

Address: 575 Madison Ave, Suite 1006, New York, NY 10022-2511.

Telephone: (212) 662-5576; **Internet:** www.bsuf.org; **e-mail:** info@bsuf.org.

The Broad Foundations

Established in 1999 by Eli and Edythe Broad, the Foundations include the Broad Education Foundation and Broad Art Foundation.

Activities: The Foundations operate in the fields of public education in the USA, scientific and medical research, contemporary arts worldwide, and civic projects in Los Angeles.

Geographical Area of Activity: USA and international.

Finance: Total assets US \$2,766m. (2014).

Trustees: Eli Broad, Edythe L. Broad.

Principal Staff: Pres. Bruce Reid; Man. Dir of Policy Gregory McGinty (Broad Education Foundation); Man. Dir of Programs Rebecca Wolf DiBiase (Broad Education Foundation); Dir/Chief Curator Joanne Heyler (Broad Art Foundation).

Address: 10900 Wilshire Blvd, 12th Floor, Los Angeles, CA 90024.

Telephone: (310) 954-5000; **Fax:** (310) 954-5051; **Internet:** www.broadfoundation.org; **e-mail:** info@broadfoundation.org.

Brookings Institution

Founded in 1927 by Robert S. Brookings and others to conduct and foster research, education, training and publication on public policy issues in the broad fields of economics, government administration, foreign policy and the social sciences.

Activities: Activities organized in three main programmes: the Economic Studies programme, for policy-orientated research and analysis on labour economics, social and urban economics, public finance, economic growth and stability, international economics, and industrial organization and regulation; the Governmental Studies programme, which focuses on social policy, political institutions and regulation and economic policy; and the Foreign Policy Studies programme, looking at issues of international economic policy, national security policy and energy and regional studies. The Institution organizes educational conferences for leaders in business and government professions on issues of public policy; research fellowships are granted in support of policy-orientated pre-doctoral research in national security policy, government and economics.

Geographical Area of Activity: USA.

Publications: *Brookings Papers on Economic Activity* (2 a year); *Brookings Review* (quarterly); Annual Report; periodic journals, policy briefs, analysis and commentary.

Finance: Annual revenue US $106,526,578, expenditure $99,568,578 (30 June 2014).

Board of Trustees: John L. Thornton, David M. Rubenstein (Co-Chair.); Glenn Hutchins, Suzanne Nora Johnson (Vice-Chair.).

Principal Staff: Pres. Strobe Talbott; Exec. Vice-Pres. Martin S. Indyk.

Address: 1775 Massachusetts Ave NW, Washington, DC 20036-2188.

Telephone: (202) 797-6000; **Fax:** (202) 797-6004; **Internet:** www.brookings.edu; **e-mail:** communications@brookings.edu.

Brother's Brother Foundation

Founded in 1958 by Dr Robert Hingson to distribute donated educational, medical, agricultural and humanitarian aid to those in need internationally.

Activities: Requests and distributes donated aid shipments of medical, educational and humanitarian resources to those in need, whether because of war, or natural or man-made disasters, and without regard to race, religion or political affiliation.

Geographical Area of Activity: International.

Publications: Newsletters; Annual Report.

Finance: Annual revenue US $295,883,198, expenditure $285,042,211 (31 Dec. 2013).

Board of Trustees: Thomas Wentling, Jr (Chair.); Charles Stout (Vice-Chair.); Louann Tronsberg-Deihle (Treas.); John P. Tymitz (Sec.).

Principal Staff: Pres. Luke L. Hingson.

Address: 1200 Galveston Ave, Pittsburgh, PA 15233-1604.

Telephone: (412) 321-3160; **Fax:** (412) 321-3325; **Internet:** www.brothersbrother.org; **e-mail:** mail@brothersbrother.org.

The Brush Foundation

Founded in 1929 by Charles F. Brush.

Activities: Aims to ensure that family planning worldwide becomes acceptable, available, accessible, affordable, effective and safe. The Foundation funds national and international innovative family-planning projects that: protect and enhance people's ability to manage their reproductive health; carry out public policy analysis and/or public education in areas related to reproductive behaviour and its social implications; and advance the knowledge and purposeful behaviour of young people regarding sexuality within both a social and health context. Annual project grants generally range from US $5,000 to $25,000.

Geographical Area of Activity: International.

Restrictions: No unsolicited proposals accepted; no funding normally for videos, conferences, pre- or post-natal care, or youth theatre groups.

Finance: Annual revenue US $344,058, expenditure $384,376 (2013).

Board of Managers: Abigail English (Pres.); Stacey Easterling (Pres.-elect); Ellen Rome (Treas.); Rev. Henry C. Doll (Sec.).

Principal Staff: Programme Officer Kate Ingersoll.

Address: 25350 Rockside Rd, 3rd Floor, Bedford Heights, OH 44146-3704.

Telephone: (216) 334-2209; **Fax:** (216) 334-2211; **Internet:** fdnweb.org/brush; **e-mail:** brushfoundation@hotmail.com.

Pearl S. Buck International

Established in 1964 by Nobel and Pulitzer prize-winning author and humanitarian Pearl S. Buck; an international development and humanitarian organization dedicated to helping children and promoting intercultural understanding.

Activities: Works to improve the quality of life and available opportunities for children who suffer discrimination related to the circumstances of their birth, by promoting tolerance and human rights, mitigating the effects of injustices suffered by children, and supporting many related programmes around the world, with a particular emphasis on projects working in South-East Asia.

Geographical Area of Activity: Worldwide, with an emphasis on the People's Republic of China, the Philippines, the Republic of Korea, Taiwan, Thailand and Viet Nam.

Restrictions: Grants to affiliated and partner organizations.

Publications: Annual Report; *Connections* (biennial newsletter).

Finance: Annual revenue US $1,685,971, expenditure $2,372,538 (30 June 2014).

Board of Directors: David R. Breidinger (Chair.); David Ballai (Vice-Chair.); Helen Ljungdahl Round (Sec.); Frederick Schea (Treas.).

Principal Staff: Pres and CEO Janet L. Mintzer.

Address: 520 Dublin Rd, Perkasie, PA 18944.

Telephone: (215) 249-0100; **Fax:** (215) 249-9657; **Internet:** www.psbi.org; **e-mail:** info@pearlsbuck.org.

The Howard G. Buffett Foundation

Established in 1999 to improve the lives of impoverished and marginalized peoples.

Activities: Operates in Central and South America, Africa and the USA in the areas of food and water security, conflict resolution and post-conflict development, and conservation of the environment.

Geographical Area of Activity: Central and South America, the Great Lakes region of Africa, southern Africa and the USA.

Restrictions: No unsolicited requests for funding are accepted.

Finance: Annual revenue US $171,086,763, expenditure $113,651,674 (31 Dec. 2013).

Trustees: Howard G. Buffett (Chair., CEO and Pres.).

Principal Staff: Pres. Ann M. Kelly.

Address: 145 N. Merchant St, Decatur, IL 62523-1442.

Telephone: (217) 423-9286; **Internet:** www.thehowardgbuffettfoundation.org.

Burroughs Wellcome Fund—BWF

Founded in 1955 by the Burroughs Wellcome Co, USA, as a private non-profit foundation to advance medical science by supporting research and other scientific and educational activities.

Activities: Has two primary goals: to help outstanding scientists early in their career; and to advance fields in the basic medical sciences that are undervalued or in need of particular encouragement. The Fund makes grants primarily to institutions within the USA and Canada for research in the basic biomedical sciences through a series of competitive award programmes in: infectious diseases; interfaces in science; translational research; population and laboratory-based sciences; reproductive sciences; biomedical sciences and science education. Most grants are made on a competitive basis, but they are also made to non-profit organizations conducting activities to improve the general environment for science.

Geographical Area of Activity: USA and Canada.

Restrictions: No grants are made to individuals.

Publications: Annual Report; *FOCUS* (e-newsletter); programme brochures; special reports.

Finance: Annual revenue US $53,316,304, expenditure $45,902,360 (31 Aug. 2013).

Board of Directors: Dr Dianne F. Wirth (Chair.).

Principal Staff: Pres. Dr John E. Burris.

Address: POB 13901, 21 T. W. Alexander Dr., Research Triangle Park, NC 27709-3901.

Telephone: (919) 991-5100; **Fax:** (919) 991-5160; **Internet:** www.bwfund.org; **e-mail:** info@bwfund.org.

The Bydale Foundation

Founded in 1965 by James P. Warburg to support various charitable purposes.

Activities: Provides support for programmes in the areas of the environment, social justice, women's rights, human rights and poetry.

Geographical Area of Activity: USA.

Restrictions: No grants made to individuals. Unsolicited proposals for organizations outside the Foundation's areas of interest are unlikely to receive funding.

Finance: Annual revenue US $699,019, expenditure $557,239 (2013).

Board: Joan M. Warburg (Pres. and Sec.); Frank J. Kick (Treas.).

Principal Staff: Agent Christine O'Donnell.

Address: 1 Bryant Park, NY1-100-28-05, New York, NY 10036-6715.

Telephone: (646) 855-1011; **Fax:** (646) 855-5463; **Internet:** foundationcenter.org/grantmaker/bydale; **e-mail:** bydale@ustrust.com.

California Community Foundation

Established in 1915 as a public charitable organization.

Activities: Administers more than 1,700 charitable funds. The Foundation provides financial, technical and managerial support to non-profit organizations. It has five core programmes: Arts, Education, Health Care, Transition Aged Youth, and Housing and Economic Development; and also provides scholarships to students in need.

Geographical Area of Activity: Mainly Los Angeles County.

Finance: Annual revenue US $232,617,162, expenditure $179,800,155 (30 June 2013).

Board of Directors: Dr Cynthia A. Telles (Chair.); Tom Unterman (Chair.-elect).

Principal Staff: Pres and CEO Antonia Hernández; Exec. Vice-Pres. and COO John E. Kobara.

Address: 221 S. Figueroa St, Ste 400, Los Angeles, CA 90012.

Telephone: (213) 413-4130; **Fax:** (213) 383-2046; **Internet:** www.calfund.org; **e-mail:** info@calfund.org.

Carnegie Corporation of New York

Founded in 1911 by Andrew Carnegie to promote the advancement and diffusion of knowledge and understanding among the peoples of the USA, Russia and of certain countries that are, or have been, members of the British Commonwealth.

Activities: Current areas of interest are education; international peace and security; international development; and strengthening US democracy. Also operates the Carnegie Corporation Scholars Program, supporting research by outstanding young scholars, as well as a Special Opportunities Fund for projects falling outside the main areas of interest. Support is directed towards the development of children and youth, childhood health and development, educational achievement, science education and the reform of education; the development of human resources in less-developed countries; and co-operative security and the avoidance of conflict between nations. Grant programmes support: science-based analyses of the ways in which the risk of nuclear war can be diminished; projects linking educational reform to social and economic changes; research into the prevention of problems for children and young teenagers such as school failure, school-age

pregnancy, childhood injury and substance abuse; and efforts to improve maternal and infant health in English-speaking countries of Africa and to strengthen indigenous scientific capacity to solve development problems. Most grants are made to organizations in the USA, but support is also given overseas with a current focus on Commonwealth Africa. Projects involving both Russian and American participants are also funded. Supports conferences and seminars, exchange programmes and publications.

Geographical Area of Activity: USA and countries that are, or have been, members of the British Commonwealth, with a current emphasis on Commonwealth Africa, and the Russian Federation.

Restrictions: No grants to individual schools.

Publications: Annual Report; *New Directions for Carnegie Corporation of New York*; *Carnegie Quarterly*; newsletters (quarterly); magazines (quarterly).

Finance: Annual revenue US $257,346,063, expenditure $156,112,963 (30 Sept. 2013).

Board of Trustees: Thomas H. Kean (Chair.); Kurt L. Schmoke (Vice-Chair.).

Principal Staff: Pres. Vartan Gregorian.

Address: 437 Madison Ave, New York, NY 10022.

Telephone: (212) 371-3200; **Fax:** (212) 754-4073; **Internet:** www.carnegie.org.

Carnegie Endowment for International Peace

Founded in 1910 by Andrew Carnegie; a private non-profit organization dedicated to advancing co-operation between nations and promoting active international engagement by the USA.

Activities: Conducts research, publishes information, holds meetings, and occasionally creates new institutions and international networks. The Endowment's activities include the China Program, the Democracy and Rule of Law Program, the Energy and Climate Program, the Middle East Program, the Nonproliferation Program, the Russia and Eurasia Program, the Carnegie South Asia Program, and the Trade, Equity and Development Program. Its interests are international and concentrate on relations between governments, businesses, international organizations and civil society, focusing on the economic, political and technological forces driving global change. Through the Carnegie Moscow Center, founded in 1992, the Endowment helps to develop a tradition of public policy analysis in the states of the former USSR, and to improve relations between the Russian Federation and the USA.

Geographical Area of Activity: USA, the People's Republic of China, Middle East, South Asia and the Russian Federation.

Restrictions: Not a grantmaking organization.

Publications: *Foreign Policy* (6 a year); monographs, books, newsletters, working papers, reports and other publications on international relations and foreign policy.

Finance: Annual revenue US $26,767,015, expenditure $32,939,297 (30 June 2014).

Board of Trustees: Harvey V. Fineberg (Chair.); Shirley M. Tilghman (Vice-Chair.); Paul Balaran (Exec. Vice-Pres. and Sec.).

Principal Staff: Pres. William J. Burns.

Address: 1779 Massachusetts Ave NW, Washington, DC 20036-2103.

Telephone: (202) 483-7600; **Fax:** (202) 483-1840; **Internet:** www.carnegieendowment.org; **e-mail:** info@carnegieendowment.org.

Carnegie Hero Fund Commission

Founded in 1904 by Andrew Carnegie to recognize, with the award of medals and sums of money, heroism voluntarily performed by civilians in the USA and Canada, in saving, or attempting to save, the lives of others at extraordinary risk to the life of the rescuer.

Activities: Operates in the USA and Canada in the field of social welfare, through grants to individuals, including scholarship assistance and continuing aid to those disabled in their attempts to save others, and grants to the dependants of those who died in such attempts. National Carnegie Hero Fund Foundations were established in 1908 in the United Kingdom, 1909 in France and 1911 in Belgium, Denmark, Italy, the Netherlands, Norway, Sweden and Switzerland. These foundations also award medals and diplomas to individuals in those countries who have risked or lost their lives, as well as cash grants.

Geographical Area of Activity: USA and Canada.

Restrictions: Act of heroism must have occurred in the USA or Canada and the Commission must be notified within two years.

Publications: Annual Report; newsletter; leaflets.

Finance: Annual revenue US $2,368,730, expenditure $1,870,991 (2013).

Commission: Mark Laskow (Chair.); Walter F. Rutkowski (Pres. and Sec.); Jeffrey A. Dooley (Asst Sec.); Priscilla J. McCrady (Vice-Pres.); Dan D. Sandman (Treas.).

Address: Koppers Bldg, 436 Seventh Ave, Suite 1101, Pittsburgh, PA 15219-1841.

Telephone: (412) 281-1302; **Fax:** (412) 281-5751; **Internet:** www.carnegiehero.org; **e-mail:** carnegiehero@carnegiehero.org.

The John W. Carson Foundation

Established in 1981 by entertainer Johnny Carson to support children, education and health services. On his death in 2005, he left US $156m. to the Foundation.

Activities: Supports non-profit organizations.

Geographical Area of Activity: Principally Los Angeles and Nebraska.

Finance: Annual revenue US $10,459,228, expenditure $11,991,455 (30 June 2013).

Principal Staff: CEO and Pres. Allan L. Alexander; COO, CFO and Sec. Lawrence L. Witzer.

Address: 16000 Ventura Blvd, Suite 900, c/o Allan L. Alexander, Encino, CA 91436.

Telephone: (310) 288-9966.

The Carter Center

Established in 1982 to work in partnership with Emory University, with a fundamental commitment to human rights and the alleviation of human suffering.

Activities: Seeks to prevent and resolve conflicts, enhance freedom and democracy, and improve health worldwide. The Center operates peace programmes in the areas of democracy, human rights, conflict resolution, the Americas and the People's Republic of China; and health programmes to fight six preventable diseases—Guinea worm, river blindness, trachoma, schistosomiasis, lymphatic filariasis and malaria—by using health education and simple, low-cost methods.

Geographical Area of Activity: Less-developed countries worldwide.

Finance: Annual revenue US $109,098,852, expenditure $78,898,319 (31 Aug. 2013).

Board of Trustees: Jimmy Carter (Founder); Rosalynn Carter (Founder); Kent C. 'Oz' Nelson (Chair.); Kathryn E. Cade (Vice-Chair.).

Principal Staff: CEO Mary Ann Peters.

Address: One Copenhill, 453 Freedom Parkway, Atlanta, GA 30307.

Telephone: (404) 420-5100; **Internet:** www.cartercenter.org; **e-mail:** carterweb@emory.edu.

Caterpillar Foundation

Established in 1952 to make sustainable communities possible through advancing knowledge, protecting the environment and conserving resources, and promoting access to basic human needs.

Activities: Operates internationally in the areas of education, health and social welfare, and civic, cultural and environmental causes.

Geographical Area of Activity: International.

Finance: Annual revenue US $60,400,244, expenditure $57,564,907 (2013).

Principal Staff: Pres., Chair. and CEO; Doug R. Oberhelman; Exec. Vice-Pres. James B. Buda.

Address: 100 NE Adams St, Peoria, IL 61629-1480.

Telephone: (309) 675-5941; **Internet:** www.caterpillar.com/sustainability/caterpillar-foundation.

Center for Citizen Initiatives—CCI

Founded in 1983.

Activities: Works to support democracy in post-communist Russia and encourage economic reform; and to provide aid to disadvantaged people in the Russian Federation. The Center funds volunteer programmes in the Russian Federation, including a Productivity Enhancement Program (PEP), providing US-based management training for Russian entrepreneurs; the Advanced Business Management Program for Russian Executives and their Team of Top Managers (ABMP); the Entrepreneur-to-Entrepreneur Business Training (EEBT); and the Russian Youth Program (RYP). Operates six partner offices in the Russian Federation.

Geographical Area of Activity: Russian Federation.

Publications: *PEP Brochure 2000*; *PEP Profiles 2000;* newsletter (quarterly).

Finance: Annual revenue US $11,481, expenditure $99,268 (31 Dec. 2013).

Board of Directors: Arlie Schardt (Chair.); Don Chapman (Treas.); Nancy Glaser (Sec.).

Principal Staff: Pres. Sharon Tennison; Program Officer Masha Maslova.

Address: Presidio of San Francisco, POB 29249, San Francisco, CA 94129-0249.

Telephone: (415) 561-7777; **Fax:** (415) 561-7778; **Internet:** www.ccisf.org; **e-mail:** info@ccisf.org.

Center for Communications, Health and the Environment—CECHE

Founded in 1990; a private non-profit institution.

Activities: Aims to help underserved communities in the USA, Central and Eastern Europe, India and developing countries worldwide. The Center operates in underserved communities worldwide supporting programmes that improve lifestyles, reduce health risks and counteract the harmful effects of pollution. Main programme areas, with an emphasis on the use of mass media, focus on nutrition, tobacco control, public health, democracy and health, private voluntary action and environmental health.

Geographical Area of Activity: Developing countries, underserved communities in Europe, and the USA.

Restrictions: Grants only to non-profit organizations for joint projects.

Publications: *In Focus* (online periodical); fact sheets; project reports; Annual Report.

Finance: Annual revenue US $483,125, expenditure $71,219 (31 Dec. 2013).

Board of Directors: Dr Sushma Palmer (Chair.); Mark Palmer (Vice-Chair.).

Principal Staff: Dir Dr Leonard Silverstein.

Address: 4437 Reservoir Rd, NW, Washington, DC 20007.

Telephone: (202) 965-5990; **Fax:** (202) 965-5996; **Internet:** www.ceche.org; **e-mail:** ceche@comcast.net.

The Center for International Humanitarian Cooperation—CIHC

Founded in 1992 by a group of physicians and diplomats to promote healing and peace in countries affected by conflict, ethnic violence or natural disaster.

Activities: Aims to professionalize training in the humanitarian field. Foundation programmes cover a variety of topics, incl. disaster management, mental health issues and negotiation, to prepare members of international relief organizations and humanitarian workers to be effective in their work in conflict and post-conflict areas.

Geographical Area of Activity: International.

Publications: *Technology for Humanitarian Action; Human Security for All; Emergency Relief Operations*; *Traditions, Values and Humanitarian Actions*; *Basics of International Humanitarian Missions*; *Preventive Diplomacy*; *Clearing the Fields*; *A Framework for Survival*; *The Pulse of Humanitarian Assistance*; *Even in Chaos: Education in Times of Emergency*; *The Open Door*; newsletters.

Board of Directors: Kevin M. Cahill (Pres.).

Principal Staff: Humanitarian Programs Dir Larry Hollingworth; Deputy Humanitarian Programs Dir Gonzalo Sánchez-Terán.

Address: 850 Fifth Ave, New York, NY 10065.

Telephone: (212) 636-6294; **Fax:** (212) 636-7060; **Internet:** www.cihc.org; **e-mail:** mail@cihc.org.

Center for Victims of Torture—CVT

Founded in 1985.

Activities: Provides direct care for victims of politically motivated torture and their families in St Paul, MN, the Democratic Republic of the Congo, Kenya and Jordan. The Center evaluates and monitors the progress of survivors in its care programmes; runs training programmes for health care, education and social work professionals in the USA and abroad; and works towards the elimination of torture through public policy initiatives and education campaigns, in collaboration with other human rights and civic organizations.

Geographical Area of Activity: International.

Publications: Annual Report; *Storycloth* (newsletter); training materials for social workers, physicians, health workers and educators.

Finance: Annual revenue US $10,777,726, expenditure $10,290,624 (31 Dec. 2013).

Board of Directors: C. Scott Cooper (Chair.); Samuel Heins (Vice-Chair.); Babette Apland (Past Chair.); Richard Senese (Treas.).

Principal Staff: Exec. Dir Curt Goering; Deputy Dir Ruth Barrett Rendler.

Address: 649 Dayton Ave, St Paul, MN 55104.

Telephone: (612) 436-4800; **Fax:** (612) 436-2600; **Internet:** www.cvt.org; **e-mail:** cvt@cvt.org.

Centre for Development and Population Activities—CEDPA

Founded in 1975; a non-profit international organization.

Activities: Aims to help and empower women at all levels of society and to involve them in development work. The Centre operates internationally in collaboration with partner NGOs and networks, in the areas of gender equality and developing the role of women in society, through linking reproductive health care with women's empowerment; improving facilities and capabilities of development centres and networks; increasing women's involvement in policy-making; and promoting youth involvement in development agendas. Maintains country offices in India and Nigeria.

Geographical Area of Activity: International.

Publications: Project reports; fact sheets; newsletter (quarterly); booklets; Annual Report.

Finance: Annual revenue US $5,674,841, expenditure $7,057,853 (2012).

Board of Directors: Ann Van Dusen (Chair.); Barie Carmichael (Sec.).

Principal Staff: Pres. and CEO Carol A. Peasley; Vice-Pres. Doris Mason Martin.

Address: 1120 20th St NW, Suite 720, Washington, DC 20036.

Telephone: (202) 667-1142; **Fax:** (202) 332-4496; **Internet:** www.cedpa.org; **e-mail:** info@cedpa.org.

The Century Foundation

Founded in 1919 by Edward A. Filene for research on major economic, political and social institutions and issues. Formerly known as the Twentieth Century Fund, Inc.

Activities: Conducts research nationally and internationally in the fields of communications, international affairs and economic development, and on major political, economic and social institutions. The Foundation's main programme areas are Economics and Inequality, Retirement Security, Education, Health Care, Homeland Security, Election Reform, Media and Politics and International Affairs. Research results are published in book form. Awards the Leonard Silk Journalism Fellowship to an established journalist producing a book on what the Foundation considers an important contemporary issue. Maintains office in Washington, DC.

Geographical Area of Activity: International, USA.

Restrictions: Not a grantmaking foundation.

Publications: Annual Report; newsletter; studies and paperback series.

Finance: Annual revenue US $7,067,972, expenditure $4,370,531 (30 June 2014).

Trustees: Bradley Abelow (Chair.); Alan Brinkley (Vice-Chair.); Lewis B. Kaden (Treas.); Alicia H. Munnell (Sec. and Clerk).

Principal Staff: Pres. Mark Zuckerman.

Address: 1 Whitehall St, 15th Floor, New York, NY 10004.

Telephone: (212) 535-4441; **Fax:** (212) 879-9197; **Internet:** www.tcf.org; **e-mail:** info@tcf.org.

CGIAR Fund

Founded in 1971 by the International Bank for Reconstruction and Development (World Bank) and other UN agencies to improve the quantity and quality of food in developing countries and eradicate poverty.

Activities: Comprises a network of 15 autonomous international agricultural research centres and organizations in Central and South America, Asia, Africa, the Middle East, Europe and the USA. Research programmes focus on increasing productivity, protecting the environment, saving biodiversity, improving policies and strengthening national research. The Group also makes the biennial King Baudouin Award to recognize and stimulate agricultural research, Third World development and the agricultural production of ordinary farmers.

Geographical Area of Activity: International.

Publications: *CGIAR News*; Annual Report; study papers; research documents; and other publications.

Finance: Financing since inception: inflows US $1,812m., disbursements $1,718.2m. (30 Sept. 2014).

Fund Council: Rachel Kyte (Chair.).

Principal Staff: Exec. Sec. Jonathan Wadsworth.

Address: The World Bank, MSN P6–601, 1818 H Street, NW, Washington, DC 20433.

Telephone: (202) 473-8951; **Fax:** (202) 473-8110; **Internet:** www.cgiar.org/who-we-are/cgiar-fund; **e-mail:** cgiarfund@cgiar.org.

Chatlos Foundation, Inc

Founded in 1953 by William F. Chatlos.

Activities: Operates nationally and internationally, providing funding in the fields of bible colleges and seminaries (amounting to 33% of funding), religious causes (30% of funding), medicine and health, liberal arts colleges (principally private colleges) and social welfare.

Geographical Area of Activity: Worldwide.

Restrictions: Only non-profit organizations that are tax exempt for US federal income tax purposes may apply. No grants directly to international organizations, to individual churches, secondary schools, arts or medical research organizations. No grants to individuals, endowment funds, medical research, conferences, bricks and mortar, or multi-year grants; no loans.

Publications: Information brochure; application guidelines.

Finance: Annual revenue US $2,794,869, expenditure $3,935,533 (2013).

Principal Staff: Pres., CEO and Chief Investment Officer William J. Chatlos; Sr Vice-Pres. Michele Roach.

Address: POB 915048, Longwood, FL 32791-5048.

Telephone: (407) 862-5077; **Internet:** www.chatlos.org; **e-mail:** info@chatlos.org.

Global Communities

Founded in 1952; formerly known as CHF International.

Activities: Helps people in in low- and moderate-income communities around the world improve their economic circumstances, environment and infrastructure. The organization provides technical expertise and leadership in international development, including development finance, housing and entrepreneurship. It works in partnership with other organizations to develop systems, policies and practices that increase access to affordable housing, community services and finance. Has worked in around 100 countries.

Geographical Area of Activity: International.

Restrictions: No grants to individuals; grants are given only to project-specific local organizations. Global Communities does not accept unsolicited proposals or requests for support.

Publications: *Building a Better World* (annual international programme report); fact sheets; bulletins; booklets, including *International Development Matters*.

Finance: Annual revenue US $158,951,725, expenditure $146,665,815 (30 Sept. 2013).

Board of Trustees: Robert A. Mosbacher, Jr (Chair.); Lauri Fitz-Pegado (Vice-Chair.); Richard F. Celeste (Treas.); Caroline Blakely (Sec.).

Principal Staff: Pres. and CEO David A. Weiss; Exec. Vice-Pres. and COO Chris Sale.

Address: 8601 Georgia Ave, Suite 800, Silver Spring, MD 20910.

Telephone: (301) 587-4700; **Fax:** (301) 587-7315; **Internet:** www.globalcommunities.org; **e-mail:** mailbox@globalcommunities.org.

The Chicago Community Trust

Founded in 1915 for such charitable purposes as would best make for the mental, moral, intellectual and physical improvement, assistance and relief of the inhabitants of Cook County, IL.

Activities: Operates mainly in Greater Chicago in the fields of education, health, basic human needs, the arts and humanities, and community development, through grants for both general operating support and specific programmes.

Geographical Area of Activity: USA.

Restrictions: No grants are made to individuals.

Publications: Annual Report; *Trust News* (3 a year); grant guidelines; financial statement.

Finance: Annual revenue US $299,248,702, expenditure $174,173,335 (30 Sept. 2013).

Executive Committee: Frank M. Clark (Chair.).

Principal Staff: Pres. and CEO Terry Mazany.

Address: 111 East Wacker Dr., Suite 1400, Chicago, IL 60601.

Telephone: (312) 616-8000; **Fax:** (312) 616-7955; **Internet:** www.cct.org; **e-mail:** info@cct.org.

Child Health Foundation—CHF

Founded in 1985 to promote better health of children and their mothers in developing countries and medically underserved populations.

Activities: Operates mainly in the area of diarrhoeal diseases, malnutrition and poverty. The Foundation develops low-cost technologies; conducts health, educational and training programmes; promotes research capabilities in institutions in developing countries; and carries out charitable activities. It maintains a speakers' bureau and through its Innovative Small Grant Program awards grants of up to US $5,000 to research or service projects aiming to improve the health of children.

Geographical Area of Activity: International.

Publications: Annual Report; newsletter.

Finance: Annual revenue US $188,535, expenditure $225,710 (31 Dec. 2013).

Board of Directors: Dr Maureen Black (Chair.); Dr Pamela Johnson (Vice-Chair.); William B. Greenough, III (Sec.); Nathaniel F. Pierce (Treas.).

Principal Staff: Dir R. Bradley Sack; Dir of Admin. Jonathan Sack.

Address: 10630 Little Patuxent Parkway, Century Plaza, Suite 126, Columbia, MD 21044.

Telephone: (410) 992-5512; **Fax:** (410) 992-5641; **Internet:** www.childhealthfoundation.org; **e-mail:** contact@childhealthfoundation.org.

ChildFund International

Founded in 1938 by a Presbyterian minister. Prior names include Christian Children's Fund and China's Children Fund.

Activities: An international child development and protection organization that works in 31 countries, including the USA. The Fund promotes positive outcomes for children in every stage of their lives from infancy to young adulthood. It works with families and communities to promote the development and protection of children, and works with supporters dedicated to the well-being and rights of children. Areas of focus include basic education, health and sanitation, early childhood development, emergencies, micro-enterprise and nutrition.

Geographical Area of Activity: Africa, America, Asia, the Caribbean, Belarus.

Restrictions: No grants to individuals.

Publications: Annual Report, newsletter, booklets, studies.

Finance: Annual revenue US $238,552,752, expenditure $239,297,115 (30 June 2013).

Board of Directors: Marilyn Grist (Chair.); John L. Lewis, IV (Vice-Chair.); Nancy Hill (Sec.).

Principal Staff: Pres. and CEO Anne Lynam Goddard; Exec. Vice-Pres. Isam G. Ghanim.

Address: 2821 Emerywood Parkway, POB 26484, Richmond, VA 23294.

Telephone: (804) 756-2700; **Fax:** (804) 756-2719; **Internet:** www.childfund.org; **e-mail:** questions@childfund.org.

Children International—CI

Established in 1936; a non-profit humanitarian organization.

Activities: Aims to help children around the world to overcome the effects of poverty to become healthy, well-educated, self-sustaining and integrated members of society. The organization runs child sponsorship projects in Central and South America, Asia, Africa and the USA for the benefit of children, providing the opportunity for people to support children in the developing world. Sponsor contributions are used to help children, particularly in the fields of health and education, as well as to buy basic provisions such as food and clothing.

Geographical Area of Activity: Central and South America, Asia, Africa and the USA.

Restrictions: Does not provide individual educational benefits to children who are not yet enrolled in school.

Publications: *Children International* (newsletter); Annual Report.

Finance: Annual revenue US $180,378,425, expenditure $180,270,784 (30 Sept. 2013).

Board of Directors: Gordon Bailey (Chair.); David Cacioppo (Treas.).

Principal Staff: CEO Susana Eshleman; Exec. Vice-Pres. and COO David Houchen.

Address: 2000 East Red Bridge Rd, POB 219055, Kansas City, MO 64121.

Telephone: (816) 942-2000; **Fax:** (816) 942-3714; **Internet:** www.children.org; **e-mail:** children@children.org.

Children's Wish Foundation International—CWFI

Founded in 1985 by Linda Dozoretz.

Activities: Aims to distract critically ill children from the anxieties of treatment and empower them to face the difficulties ahead. Programmes include once-in-a-lifetime wish fulfillment; and hospital enrichment, sending educational and entertainment gift packages to paediatric hospitals, and running in-patient events help counter feelings of isolation and build a natural support group for children and their families. Has worked in 53 countries.

Geographical Area of Activity: International.

Restrictions: No minimum age; however, if the child's health allows, the Foundation tries to wait to fulfill the wish until the child is old enough to enjoy fully and remember the experience.

Publications: Newsletter.

Finance: Annual revenue US $8,762,838, expenditure $9,182,802 (30 June 2013).

Principal Staff: Exec. Dir Linda Dozoretz.

Address: 8615 Roswell Rd, Atlanta, GA 30350.

Telephone: (770) 393-9474; **Fax:** (770) 393-0683; **Internet:** www.childrenswish.org; **e-mail:** info@childrenswish.org.

Jane Coffin Childs Memorial Fund for Medical Research

Founded in 1937 by Alice S. Coffin and Starling W. Childs to further research into the causes, origins and treatment of cancer.

Activities: Operates nationally and internationally in the field of cancer research, through post-doctoral fellowships; US citizens may hold fellowships in any country, foreigners must study in the USA.

Geographical Area of Activity: Worldwide.

Publications: Newsletter.

Finance: Annual revenue US $5,610,481, expenditure $4,801,697 (30 June 2014).

Board of Directors: Dr James E. Childs (Chair.); Dr Bronwen A. Childs (Treas.).

Principal Staff: Admin. Dir Kim E. Roberts.

Address: 333 Cedar St, SHM L300, New Haven, CT 06510.

Telephone: (203) 785-4612; **Fax:** (203) 785-3301; **Internet:** www.jccfund.org; **e-mail:** jccfund@yale.edu.

China Medical Board

Founded in 1928 by the Rockefeller Foundation (q.v.) to provide financial support to the Peking Union Medical College and similar institutions in the Far East.

Activities: Helps health profession institutions to enhance educational and research activities in medicine, nursing and public health. The Board makes grants to designated national medical, nursing and public health educational institutions in Hong Kong, Indonesia, the Republic of Korea, Malaysia, the Philippines, Singapore, China (Taiwan), Laos, Myanmar, Thailand and the People's Republic of China (including Tibet).

Geographical Area of Activity: East and South-East Asia.

Restrictions: Does not accept unsolicited grant applications. No support for governments, professional societies, or research institutes not directly under medical school control.

No grants to individuals (except for scholarships and fellowships), nor for capital funds, operating budgets for medical care, special projects, or the basic equipping of medical schools, nursing schools, or schools of public health that are the responsibility of various governments or universities; no loans.

Publications: include Annual Report; *The China Medical Board: 50 Years of Programs, Partnerships and Progress 1950–2000;* numerous research papers and speeches.

Finance: Annual revenue US $13,016,215, expenditure $12,623,441 (1 July 2013).

Board of Trustees: Mary Brown Bullock (Chair.); Thomas S. Inui (Sec. and Treas.); Sarah Wood (Asst Sec.); Sally Paquet (Asst Treas.).

Principal Staff: Pres. Lincoln C. Chen.

Address: 2 Arrow St, Cambridge, MA 02138.

Telephone: (617) 979-8000; **Internet:** www.chinamedicalboard.org; **e-mail:** info@chinamedicalboard.org.

Winston Churchill Foundation of the United States

Founded in 1959, having been authorized by Sir Winston Churchill; a charitable organization granting scholarships to US students.

Activities: Awards scholarships to students of outstanding calibre to pursue graduate studies in mathematics, engineering, or the sciences. The Foundation offers at least 14 scholarships annually to postgraduates in engineering, biological and natural sciences and mathematics at the University of Cambridge.

Geographical Area of Activity: USA.

Restrictions: Eligible candidates are aged between 19 and 26 years with US citizenship, holding a Bachelor's degree from a US university or college and enrolled at one of the more than 100 US institutions taking part in the programme.

Finance: Annual revenue US $1,334,951, expenditure $1,142,123 (31 Dec. 2013).

Board of Trustees: Hon. John L. Loeb, Jr (Chair.); David D. Burrows (Treas.); James A. FitzPatrick, Jr (Sec.).

Principal Staff: Pres. Patrick A. Gerschel; Exec. Dir Peter C. Patrikis.

Address: 600 Madison Ave, 16th Floor, New York, NY 10022-1737.

Telephone: (212) 752-3200; **Fax:** (212) 246-8330; **Internet:** www.winstonchurchillfoundation.org; **e-mail:** info@winstonchurchillfoundation.org.

Citi Foundation

Established in 1995 to improve the quality of life of children, families and communities worldwide, through supporting organizations contributing to education, economic and community development, and quality of life. Formerly known as Citigroup Foundation.

Activities: Operates worldwide in the areas of education and community development, with a small amount of funding for arts education, and health and welfare. In the area of education, the Foundation operates through funding projects in early childhood, technology for the classroom, higher education for minority groups and women, and financial literacy. In community development, it supports organizations funding affordable housing, small business loans in the USA, micro-credit in less-developed countries and welfare-to-work initiatives. In 2004, the Foundation committed US $200m. for the following 10 years to support financial education initiatives.

Geographical Area of Activity: International.

Restrictions: Grants are not made to individuals, to political causes, religious organizations, nor for fund-raising events; prospective grantees are usually approached by the Foundation; unsolicited applications are less likely to succeed.

Publications: Annual Report.

Finance: Annual revenue US $78,042,098, expenditure $79,704,566 (2013).

Board of Directors: Lewis B. Kaden (Chair.); Graham Mac-Millan (Vand Sec.); Shelly Dropkin (Asst Sec.); Karen Valencia Wright (Treas.).

Principal Staff: Pres. Brandee McHale.

Address: 1 Court Sq, 43rd Floor, Long Island City, NY 11120.

Telephone: (212) 793-8451; **Fax:** (212) 793-5944; **Internet:** www.citifoundation.com/citi/foundation; **e-mail:** citizenship@citi.com.

Civitas International

Inaugurated in 1995; an international consortium comprising individuals, governmental and non-governmental organizations, and international organizations, promoting civic education and supporting education for citizenship in new and established democracies worldwide.

Activities: Operates a worldwide network to promote civic education, through computer networking and international exchange of educators. The organization maintains the Civnet website for civic education practitioners, administrators, NGOs, etc., containing resources and other information on civic education and society.

Geographical Area of Activity: Worldwide.

Publications: *Civnet Journal* (6 a year); Activity Report.

Board: Charles N. Quigley (Chair.).

Principal Staff: Dir Jack N. Hoar; Asst Dir Alissa Irion.

Address: c/o Center for Civic Education, 5145 Douglas Fir Rd, Calabasas, CA 91302-1467.

Telephone: (818) 591-9321; **Fax:** (818) 591-9330; **Internet:** www.civnet.org; new.civiced.org/civitas-program/civitas -programs; **e-mail:** info@civnet.org.

Liz Claiborne and Art Ortenberg Foundation

Founded in 1984 to foster natural resource and wildlife conservation and protection.

Activities: Main programmes are: the mitigation of conflict between the land and the resource needs of local communities and the preservation of biological diversity; the implementation of scientific, technical and practical conservation of biological diversity in rural landscapes outside parks and reserves; and the implementation of relevant, field-based, scientific, technical and practical training programmes for local people. The Foundation runs programmes in the Rocky Mountain region of the USA and in developing countries in Africa, Central and South America and Asia, as well as the Russian Far East.

Geographical Area of Activity: Africa, Central and South America, USA (Rocky Mountains), Asia, and Russian Far East.

Restrictions: No grants are provided for general support for underwriting of overheads.

Finance: Annual revenue US $6,506,241, expenditure $6,806,558 (31 Dec. 2012).

Principal Staff: Programme Dir Jim Murtaugh.

Address: 650 Fifth Ave, 15th Floor, New York, NY 10019.

Telephone: (212) 333-2536; **Fax:** (212) 956-3531; **Internet:** www.lcaof.org; **e-mail:** lcaof@lcaof.org.

Clean Water Fund—CWF

Established in 1978.

Activities: Aims to help people campaign for clean, safe water, clean air and protection from pollution everywhere. The Fund is involved in training, research and education to ensure safe drinking water and clean seas. It promotes safe solid waste management, control of workplace and community toxic hazards, and the conservation of natural resources; protects public health and environmental safety; and builds on and complements the work of Clean Water Action, a 700,000-member national organization that has helped develop, pass, strengthen and defend the USA's major water and toxics laws such as the Clean Water Act, Safe Drinking Water Act, Superfund and others.

Geographical Area of Activity: USA only.

Restrictions: No large grants available.

Publications: Reports; fact sheets.

Finance: Annual revenue US $4,089,663, expenditure $4,086,153 (31 Dec. 2013).

Principal Staff: Pres. and CEO Robert Wendelgass; Sec. Dianne Akabli; Asst Sec. Kathy Aterno.

Address: 1010 Vermont Ave NW, Suite 400, Washington, DC 20005.

Telephone: (202) 895-0432; **Fax:** (202) 895-0438; **Internet:** www.cleanwaterfund.org; **e-mail:** cwf@cleanwater.org.

Cleveland Foundation

Founded in 1914 by Frederick Harris Goff as the world's first community foundation.

Activities: Helps individuals contribute to philanthropies in the Cleveland area, and provides leadership in dealing with community problems. The Foundation operates principally for the benefit of citizens of the Greater Cleveland community with broad purposes in the fields of economic transformation, public school improvement, youth development, neighbourhoods and arts advancement, through scholarships; and grants, which are made primarily to tax-exempt private agencies, and in some cases to governmental agencies. It also administers the annual Anisfield-Wolf Book Awards, presented to authors of books that address the issue of racism or expand appreciation of human diversity.

Geographical Area of Activity: USA.

Restrictions: No grants for religious purposes, and not normally for endowments, membership drives, fund-raising projects, travel, publications and videos.

Publications: *Donor Connections* (quarterly newsletter); *Giving Voice* (quarterly newsletter); annual report; application guidelines; financial statement; informational brochures; information for donors, attorneys and financial planners; grant list.

Finance: Annual revenue US $90,734,443, expenditure $98,827,499 (31 Dec. 2013).

Board of Directors: James A. Ratner (Chair.); Paul J. Dolan (Vice-Chair.).

Principal Staff: Pres. and CEO Ronald B. Richard; Exec. Vice-Pres. Robert E. Eckardt.

Address: 1422 Euclid Ave, Suite 1300, Cleveland, OH 44115.

Telephone: (216) 861-3810; **Fax:** (216) 861-1729; **Internet:** www.clevelandfoundation.org; **e-mail:** contactus@clevefdn .org.

William J. Clinton Foundation

Founded in 2002.

Activities: Operates internationally in the areas of medicine and health (especially in the areas of HIV/AIDS), sustainable development, economic development, and ethnic, racial and religious reconciliation, through carrying out programmes in the USA and worldwide. Maintains offices in New York City, NY, Boston, MA, and Little Rock, AR.

Restrictions: Does not usually make grants to outside organizations.

Finance: Annual revenue US $54,712,950, expenditure $58,751,898 (31 Dec. 2013).

Board of Directors: Bruce R. Lindsey (Chair.); Chelsea Clinton (Vice-Chair.).

Principal Staff: CEO (a.i.) Maura Pally; Exec.Dir Stephanie S. Streett.

Address: 1271 Ave of the Americas, 42nd Floor, New York, NY 10020.

Telephone: (212) 348-8882; **Internet:** www .clintonfoundation.org.

The Coca-Cola Foundation, Inc

Founded in 1984 by the Coca-Cola Co to improve the quality of life in the community and support education.

Activities: Gives primarily to initiatives concerned with: HIV/AIDS, water stewardship, education, community recycling, and healthy and active lifestyles; also provides emergency relief.

Geographical Area of Activity: International.

Restrictions: No grants are made to individuals.

Publications: Annual Report.

Finance: Annual revenue US \$19,337,361, expenditure \$99,352,162 (2013).

Board of Directors: Lisa M. Borders (Chair.); Gary P. Fayard (Treas.); William Hawkins (Asst Treas.); Alexander B. Cummings (Sec.).

Principal Staff: Exec. Dir Helen Smith Price.

Address: 1 Coca-Cola Plaza, Atlanta, GA 30313-2420.

Telephone: (404) 676-2568; **Fax:** (404) 676-8804; **Internet:** www.thecoca-colacompany.com/citizenship/foundation_coke .html; **e-mail:** cocacolacommunityrequest@na.ko.com.

Cogitare Foundation

Founded in 1998 by Peter Cooper and Elaine Scialo as the Leonard and Charlotte S. Cooper Foundation. Present name adopted in 2000.

Activities: Funds programmes to alleviate problems faced by the poor, including house building, education and health care. Has an office in Zambia.

Geographical Area of Activity: Africa.

Restrictions: Does not provide assistance to religious organizations.

Finance: Annual revenue US \$226,928, expenditure \$370,846 (31 March 2014).

Principal Staff: Pres. Elaine Scialo; Vice-Pres. Peter D. Cooper.

Address: 9 Waccabuc River Lane, South Salem, NY 10590.

Telephone: (212) 362-2136; **Internet:** www .cogitarefoundation.org; **e-mail:** info@cogitarefoundation .org.

The Commonwealth Fund

Founded in 1918 by Anna M. Harkness and others to enhance the common good.

Activities: Major programme areas include: improving health insurance coverage and access to medical care; improving the quality of health care services; promoting ways for elderly Americans to participate more fully in community life; developing the capacities of children and young people; and improving the health of minorities. The Fund also supports related projects in these areas. It promotes innovative health care policy and practice in the USA and abroad. Operates internationally in the field of education, through the Harkness Fellowships Program, which provides health policy fellowships to potential leaders from Australia, New Zealand and the United Kingdom for study and research in the USA. Also makes grants to enhance the quality of life in New York City.

Geographical Area of Activity: International.

Publications: Annual Report; grants list; newsletters.

Finance: Annual revenue US \$92,047,038, expenditure \$30,777,222 (30 June 2014).

Board of Directors: Benjamin K. Chu (Chair.); Cristine Russell (Vice-Chair.).

Principal Staff: Pres. David Blumenthall; Exec. Vice-Pres. and COO John E. Craig.

Address: 1 E 75th St, New York, NY 10021.

Telephone: (212) 606-3800; **Fax:** (212) 606-3500; **Internet:** www.commonwealthfund.org; **e-mail:** info@cmwf.org.

Compton Foundation, Inc

Founded in 1973 by members of the Compton family, as the successor to the Compton Trust (f. 1946), to address community, national and international concerns in the areas of peace and world order, population and the environment.

Activities: Operates nationally and internationally in the fields of peace and world order; family planning; the environment; equal educational opportunity; community welfare and social justice; and culture and the arts.

Geographical Area of Activity: Sub-Saharan Africa, Central America, USA, Mexico.

Restrictions: Does not make grants to individuals.

Publications: Report (biennially); information brochure.

Finance: Annual revenue US \$10,094,883, expenditure \$5,270,823 (2013).

Board of Directors: Vanessa Compton (Pres.); Rebecca DiDomenico (Vice-Pres.); W. Danforth Compton (Sec.); Emilie Cortes (Treas.).

Principal Staff: Exec. Dir Ellen Friedman; Programme Dir Jennifer L. Sokolove.

Address: 101 Montgomery St, Suite 850, San Francisco, CA 94104.

Telephone: (415) 391-1001; **Fax:** (650) 508-1191; **Internet:** www.comptonfoundation.org; **e-mail:** info@ comptonfoundation.org.

Conservation International Foundation

Founded in 1987 for conservation and environmental purposes.

Activities: Collaborates with governments and other organizations to promote sustained biological diversity and ecosystems and prevent species extinction, along with basic economic and social requirements. The Foundation runs programmes in North, Central and South America, Africa, Asia and the Pacific; carries out research; promotes educational projects and eco-tourism; researches and markets rain forest products; and assists in the formulation of policy. It makes grants to individuals and local not-for-profit organizations in all countries or regions that are hot spots or wilderness areas. Active in more than 30 countries.

Geographical Area of Activity: International.

Publications: Annual Report; newsletters; *A Climate for Life; A Perfect Storm in the Amazon Wilderness; Lemurs of Madagascar; Consuming Nature.*

Finance: Annual revenue US \$96,823,379, expenditure \$143,663,423 (30 June 2013).

Board of Directors: Peter A. Seligmann (Chair.); Harrison Ford, André Esteves (Vice-Chair.); Dr Russell Mittermeier (Exec. Vice-Chair.).

Principal Staff: CEO Peter A. Seligmann; COO Jennifer Morris; Pres. Gary Edson.

Address: 2011 Crystal Dr., Suite 500, Arlington, VA 22202.

Telephone: (703) 341-2400; **Internet:** www.conservation.org; **e-mail:** inquiry@conservation.org.

Consuelo Foundation

Founded in 1988 as the Consuelo Zobel Alger Foundation. Affiliated since 1993 with the International Youth Foundation (q.v.), which shares a common mission to improve the conditions and prospects of youth by fostering their positive development. Formerly known as the Children and Youth Foundation of the Philippines. Present name adopted in 2004.

Activities: Oversees children's and youth programmes in the Philippines, specifically those below 25 years of age who are victims of abuse and neglect, street children, children of indigenous people, out-of-school youth, child labourers, and those exposed to violence and armed conflict. The Foundation also supports programmes on women, families and communities so they may attain dignity, self-esteem and self-sufficiency, working with more than 100 community-based partner organizations. It also manages a Resource Center and conducts the annual Consuelo Awards to recognize outstanding NGOs in the Philippines that have made a significant difference to the lives of disadvantaged Philippine children, women and families. In Hawaii, promotes community development and self-help projects.

Geographical Area of Activity: Hawaii and the Philippines.

Restrictions: Contracts, financial and technical support are given only to partner organizations, which must maintain excellent levels of organizational and service delivery standards.

Publications: *Building Bridges: The Development of a Leadership Training Program for Indigenous Youth; Looking After Filipino Children: A Compendium of Philippine Laws and Policies on Youth and Children; A Profile Report of Child and Women Abuse in the Province of Albay 1994–1999; On Their Own Behalf: Case Studies of Child and Youth Participation in the Philippines.*

Finance: Annual revenue US $7,777,208, expenditure $7,238,764 (2013).

Board of Directors: Constance H. Lau (Chair.); Patti J. Lyons (Sec.).

Principal Staff: Pres. and CEO Dr Jon Matsuoka; CFO Jonathan San Vuong; Man. Dir Carmela Andal-Castro.

Address: 110 N Hotel St, Honolulu, HI 96817.

Telephone: (808) 532-3939; **Fax:** (808) 532-3930; **Internet:** www.consuelo.org; **e-mail:** info@consuelo.org.

Council on International Educational Exchange—CIEE

Founded in 1947 by organizations active in the fields of international education and student travel to improve understanding and co-operation between countries, and help re-establish student exchanges after the Second World War.

Activities: Represents educational institutions in developing educational exchange policy; provides consultation services and evaluation of exchange programmes; and acts as a clearing-house for information. The Council organizes conferences and seminars, and administers Study Abroad Programs in some 35 countries. Includes the Ping Foundation (f. 2004).

Geographical Area of Activity: International.

Publications: *Journal of Studies in International Education* (bi-annual); *Council–ISP News* (monthly newsletter); *Update* (monthly); *Work, Study, Travel Abroad: The Whole World Handbook; Volunteer! The Comprehensive Guide to Voluntary Service in the US and Abroad; Going Places; The High School Student's Guide to Study, Travel and Adventure Abroad; Basic Facts on Study Abroad; Where to Stay USA and Smart Vacations: The Traveler's Guide to Learning Adventures Abroad.*

Finance: Annual revenue US $264,160, expenditure $274,191 (31 Aug. 2013).

Board of Directors: Robert E. Fallon (Chair.); Thomas Mooney (Vice-Chair. and Sec.).

Principal Staff: Pres. and CEO James P. Pellow.

Address: 300 Fore St, Portland, ME 04101.

Telephone: (207) 553-4000; **Fax:** (207) 553-4299; **Internet:** www.ciee.org; **e-mail:** contact@ciee.org.

Council for International Exchange of Scholars—CIES

Founded in 1947 to assist the US Government in administering the Fulbright Scholar Program.

Activities: Aims to increase mutual understanding between the people of the USA and those of other nations; to strengthen the ties that unite the USA with other nations; and promote international co-operation for educational and cultural advancement. The Council awards about 800 Fulbright Scholar Awards for research and lecturing abroad annually, open to US citizens holding a doctorate or comparable professional qualification, along with university or college teaching experience, for research or teaching in any discipline, in more than 140 countries worldwide. The Awards are also open to nationals of those same 140 countries to conduct research or lecture within the USA.

Geographical Area of Activity: International.

Publications: *Fulbright Online Awards Catalog; Fulbright Scholar Program: Grants for Faculty and Professionals;* Annual Report.

Finance: Funded by the US Dept of State, Bureau of Educational and Cultural Affairs.

Principal Staff: Exec. Dir María de los Ángeles Crummett.

Address: 1400 K St NW, Suite 700, Washington, DC 20005.

Telephone: (202) 686-4000; **Fax:** (202) 686-4029; **Internet:** www.cies.org; **e-mail:** scholars@iie.org.

Counterpart International, Inc.

Founded in 1965; a diverse, non-profit, international development organization.

Activities: Helps people in need in the areas of civil society, food security, private enterprise, environmental resource management, humanitarian relief and health care. The organization builds the capacity of local partner NGOs, lenders, businesses, governments and other institutions to solve their own self-defined economic, ecological, political and social problems in ways that are sustainable, practical and independent.

Geographical Area of Activity: International.

Publications: Annual Report; newsletters.

Finance: Annual revenue US $78,381,754, expenditure $78,472,532 (30 Sept. 2013).

Board of Directors: Deborah Nolan (Chair.).

Principal Staff: Pres. and CEO Joan C. Parker.

Address: 2345 Crystal Dr., Suite 301, Arlington, VA 22202.

Telephone: (703) 236-1200; **Fax:** (703) 412-5035; **Internet:** www.counterpart.org; **e-mail:** communications@counterpart.org.

Covenant Foundation

Established in 1990 by the Crown Family Foundation in partnership with the Jewish Education Service of North America.

Activities: Aims to build on strengths within the field of Jewish education in North America, and thus perpetuate the identity and cultural heritage of Jewish people. The Foundation supports innovative programmes in Jewish schools and institutions, and funds creative Jewish educators for the development and implementation of significant and cost-effective approaches to Jewish education. The maximum grant available over five years is US $250,000. Also distributes information about effective programmes through publications and conferences.

Geographical Area of Activity: USA and Canada.

Restrictions: No funding for endowments, building funds or tuition fees.

Publications: *A Covenant of Dreams: Realizing the Promise of Jewish Education; The Covenant Foundation: The First Ten Years 1990–2000.*

Finance: Annual revenue US $9,847,199, expenditure $10,726,493 (31 Dec. 2013).

Board of Directors: Eli N. Evans (Chair.).

Principal Staff: Exec. Dir Harlene Winnick Appelman; Associate Dir Joni Blinderman.

Address: 1270 Ave of the Americas, Suite 304, New York, NY 10020-1702.

Telephone: (212) 245-3500; **Fax:** (212) 245-0619; **Internet:** www.covenantfn.org; **e-mail:** info@covenantfn.org.

CRDF Global

Established in 1995 by the National Science Foundation (q.v.) to promote international scientific and technical collaboration. Formerly known as the US Civilian Research & Development Foundation.

Activities: Promotes peace and prosperity through international science collaboration. The Foundation offers grants, technical resources and training to promote scientific and technical collaboration. Maintains offices in the Russian Federation, Ukraine, Kazakhstan and Jordan.

Geographical Area of Activity: International.

Publications: Newsletter and fact sheets.

Finance: Annual revenue US $22,288,495, expenditure $28,789,832 (31 Dec. 2013).

Board of Directors: Paul Longsworth (Chair.); Dr Rodney Nichols (Vice-Chair.); Dr Anne C. Petersen (Sec.); Catherine Mannick (Treas.).

Principal Staff: Pres. and Chief Exec. Cathleen A. Campbell; Sr Vice-Pres. John Hurley.

Address: 1776 Wilson Blvd, Suite 300, Arlington, VA 22209.

Telephone: (703) 526-9720; **Fax:** (703) 526-9721; **Internet:** www.crdfglobal.org; **e-mail:** information@crdfglobal.org.

Creating Hope International—CHI

Founded in 1982.

Activities: Aims to help victims of war, political unrest and natural disasters through grassroots programmes so that they can rebuild their lives for a better future. The organization provides technical and financial assistance to raise the level of education, health and economy throughout parts of the world where people, particularly women and children, are underprivileged, poor, oppressed or generally in need. It fosters worldwide interest in these causes to increase funding for those who lack basic health care, educational and training opportunities. Currently concentrates on assisting women and children in Afghanistan, through the Afghan Institute of Learning, and Tibetan refugees in India.

Geographical Area of Activity: International, including Afghanistan, Pakistan and Tibet.

Finance: Annual revenue US $2,309,654, expenditure $837,489 (31 Dec. 2013).

Principal Staff: Pres. and Exec. Dir Carolyn 'Toc' Dunlap; Vice-Pres. and Sec. Prof. Sakena Yacoobi.

Address: POB 1058, Dearborn, MI 48121.

Telephone: (313) 278-5806; **Internet:** www.creatinghope.org; **e-mail:** chi@creatinghope.org.

Crown Family Philanthropies

Founded in 1947 as the Arie and Ida Crown Memorial by members of the Crown family for general charitable purposes. Present name adopted in 2009.

Activities: Operates primarily in the metropolitan Chicago area, with emphasis on Jewish welfare funds in the fields of social welfare, education, the arts and humanities, health care, community development, inner cities, youth, the elderly and the disabled.

Geographical Area of Activity: USA (Chicago area) and Israel.

Restrictions: No grants are made to individuals; no unsolicited applications accepted.

Finance: Annual revenue US $109,909,345, expenditure $32,611,691 (30 June 2013).

Board of Directors: Barbara Goodman Manilow (Pres.); Sara Crown Star (Vice-Pres. and Sec.); Caren Yanis (Vice-Pres. and Asst Sec.); James S. Crown (Vice-Pres. and Treas.).

Principal Staff: Exec. Dir Caren Yanis.

Address: 222 North LaSalle St, Suite 2000, Chicago, IL 60601-1109.

Telephone: (312) 750-6671; **Fax:** (312) 984-1499; **Internet:** www.crownmemorial.org; **e-mail:** aicm@crown-chicago.com.

Cystic Fibrosis Foundation

Established in 1955 to fund research into finding the means to cure and control cystic fibrosis, and to assist those with the disease.

Activities: Funds research into cystic fibrosis, care centres for those with cystic fibrosis, and adult care programmes. Has more than 75 chapters and branch offices in the USA.

Geographical Area of Activity: USA.

Finance: Annual revenue US $297,690,483, expenditure $75,047,721 (31 Dec. 2013).

Board: Catherine C. McLoud (Chair.).

Principal Staff: Pres. and Chief Exec. Dr Robert J. Beall; Exec. Vice-Pres. and COO C. Richard Mattingly.

Address: 6931 Arlington Rd, 2nd Floor, Bethesda, MD 20814.

Telephone: (301) 951-4422; **Fax:** (301) 951-6378; **Internet:** www.cff.org; **e-mail:** info@cff.org.

The Baron de Hirsch Fund

Founded in 1891 by Baron Maurice de Hirsch and Baroness Clara de Hirsch to assist in the economic assimilation of Jewish immigrants in the USA and Israel, and in providing them with vocational training in trade and agriculture.

Activities: Makes grants, primarily in the New York area and Israel, for the above purposes, and assists agencies helping to obtain education and employment for immigrants. The Fund awards fellowships to Israeli agriculturalists.

Geographical Area of Activity: USA and Israel.

Finance: Annual revenue US $153,595, expenditure $49,009 (30 June 2012).

Board of Trustees: Lois Conway (Pres.); Stanley Baumblatt (Sec. and Treas.).

Principal Staff: Man. Dir Lauren Katzowitz Shenfield.

Address: 130 East 59th St, 12th Floor, New York, NY 10022-1302.

Telephone: (212) 836-1358; **Fax:** (212) 453-6512.

Charles Delmar Foundation

Founded in 1957 by Charles Delmar for general charitable purposes to be undertaken mainly in the Washington area and in Puerto Rico and Central and South America.

Activities: Operates nationally and internationally in the fields of education and social welfare, with emphasis on inter-American studies, higher education, literacy, the arts, hospitals, and youth and child welfare agencies.

Geographical Area of Activity: Central and South America, USA, India.

Restrictions: No grants are made to individuals.

Finance: Annual revenue US $1,377,021, expenditure $356,211 (2013).

Trustees: Mareen Delmar Hughes (Pres.); Christopher Braddock (Asst Treas.).

Address: c/o Mareen Hughes, POB 1501, Pennington, NJ 08534-0671.

Arthur S. DeMoss Foundation

Founded in 1955 as the National Liberty Foundation of Valley Forge Inc to support Christian agency and church programmes in the USA and abroad, mainly in developing countries.

Activities: Offers financial support to set up and run Christian evangelical programmes, incl. Literature for Little Ones, in the USA and developing countries. The Foundation operates a fund-matching programme.

Geographical Area of Activity: International.

Finance: Annual revenue US $36,593,783, expenditure $30,141,073 (2013).

Board of Directors: Nancy S. DeMoss (Chair. and Treas.); Robert G. DeMoss (Pres.); Charlotte A. DeMoss (Sec. and Asst Treas.); Elisabeth DeMoss (Asst Sec.).

Principal Staff: Exec. Asst Derrick Max.

Address: Phillips Point-W. Twr, 777 South Flagler Dr., Suite 1600W, West Palm Beach, FL 33401-6158.

Telephone: (561) 804-9000.

Deutsche Bank Americas Foundation

Established in 1999.

Activities: Provides loans, investment and grants for sustainable community development, the arts and access to education.

Geographical Area of Activity: Canada, Central and South America, USA.

Publications: Annual Report; guidelines; *Community Focus* (newsletter).

Finance: Annual revenue US $12,190,273, expenditure $12,054,238 (2012).

Trustees: Jacques Brand (Chair.); Alessandra Digiusto (Treas./Sec.); Sam Marks (Asst Treas.).

Principal Staff: Pres. Gary S. Hattem.

Address: 60 Wall St, NYC60–2112, New York, NY 10005.

Telephone: (212) 250-0539; **Fax:** (212) 797-2255; **Internet:** www.db.com/usa/content/en/responsibility.html; www.db.com/cr/en/strategy/cr-worldwide.htm.

Development Gateway—DG

Established in 2001 in partnership with the International Bank for Reconstruction and Development (World Bank); an international non-profit organization with dual expertise in information solutions and international development.

Activities: Designs and provides information management solutions to manage aid more effectively and transparently, facilitate the interactive exchange of information and good practice, and improve tendering. The organization creates cost-effective Web-based information systems to enhance decision-making at the local, national and international level. It enhances local capacity and leverages a strong user network to create sustainable solutions. Programmes include: the Aid Management Platform (AMP), Web-based software that enables recipient governments to manage foreign aid flows; AidData, an online portal for information on development finance; Zunia, an online platform for knowledge-exchange between development actors; dgMarket, an online tender information service; and Country Gateways, locally owned public-private partnerships that facilitate access to and use of ICT. Also provides consulting services, and partners with development actors to generate custom technology solutions tailored to unique needs and problems.

Geographical Area of Activity: International.

Publications: Newsletter (quarterly); Annual Report.

Finance: Annual revenue US $6,459,818, expenditure $6,531,175 (30 June 2013).

Board of Directors: Mary O'Kane (Chair.).

Principal Staff: CEO Jean-Louis Sarbib.

Address: 1889 F St, NW, 2nd Floor, Washington, DC 20006.

Telephone: (202) 572-9200; **Fax:** (202) 572-9290; **Internet:** www.developmentgateway.org; **e-mail:** info@developmentgateway.org.

Cleveland H. Dodge Foundation, Inc

Founded in 1917 by Cleveland H. Dodge to promote the well-being of mankind throughout the world.

Activities: Makes grants to selected international organizations active in the Middle East, to selected national agencies in the USA, and to organizations based in New York City. Grants in the USA are mainly for education, youth programmes, child welfare and cultural programmes.

Geographical Area of Activity: USA and the Middle East.

Restrictions: No grants are made to individuals.

Publications: Annual Report; programme policy statement.

Finance: Annual revenue US $794,732, expenditure $2,115,589 (2013).

Board of Directors: William D. Rueckert (Pres.); Katherine O. Kerr (Vice-Pres.); Louis E. Black (Sec.).

Principal Staff: Exec. Dir and Treas. Phyllis Criscuoli.

Address: 420 Lexington Ave, Suite 2331, New York, NY 10170.

Telephone: (212) 972-2800; **Fax:** (212) 972-1049; **Internet:** www.chdodgefoundation.org; **e-mail:** info@chdodgefoundation.org.

The William H. Donner Foundation, Inc

Founded in 1961 with funds originally donated by William Donner.

Activities: Operates nationally, through funding programmes to support the growth of undergraduate and graduate studies programmes in Canadian affairs at US universities; and to support experimental grants in fields such as international affairs, education and public affairs.

Geographical Area of Activity: USA and Canada.

Restrictions: Does not accept or acknowledge unsolicited proposals for grants.

Publications: Annual Report.

Finance: Annual revenue US $24,351,388, expenditure $7,718,970 (31 Oct. 2013).

Board: Rebecca D. Winsor (Pres.); William M. Spencer, III (Vice-Pres. and Asst Treas.); Curtis Winsor, Jr (Treas.).

Address: 520 White Plains Rd, Suite 500, Tarrytown, NY 10591.

Telephone: (914) 524-0404; **Fax:** (914) 524-0407; **Internet:** www.donner.org; **e-mail:** dfeeney@donner.org.

The Camille and Henry Dreyfus Foundation, Inc

Founded in 1946 by Camille E. Dreyfus to advance the sciences of chemistry, biochemistry, chemical engineering and related sciences as a means of improving human relations and circumstances throughout the world.

Activities: Helps academic institutions to foster research and train students for graduate study for doctoral degrees in chemistry; other qualifying organizations, such as research institutes with similar goals, are also eligible for grant consideration. The Foundation sponsors the Post-doctoral Program in Environmental Chemistry, the Dreyfus Teacher-Scholar Awards Program, the Dreyfus Prize in the Chemical Sciences and the Special Grant Program in the Chemical Sciences. It also sponsors the ACS Awards administered by the American Chemical Society: the ACS Award for Encouraging Women into Careers in the Chemical Sciences and the ACS Award for Encouraging Disadvantaged Students into Careers in the Chemical Sciences.

Geographical Area of Activity: USA.

Restrictions: Grants are not made to individuals.

Publications: Annual Report; programme brochures.

Finance: Total assets US $1,436,961; annual expenditure $5,521,625 (2013).

Board of Directors: Henry C. Walter (Pres.); Dorothy Dinsmoor (Vice-Pres. and Sec.); H. Scott Walter (Treas.).

Principal Staff: Exec. Dir Mark J. Cardillo; Assoc. Dir Gerard L. Brandenstein; Operations Man. Adam J. Lore.

Address: 555 Madison Ave, 20th Floor, New York, NY 10022-3301.

Telephone: (212) 753-1760; **Fax:** (212) 593-2256; **Internet:** www.dreyfus.org; **e-mail:** admin@dreyfus.org.

Dreyfus Health Foundation—DHF

Founded in 1965 as the Dreyfus Medical Foundation; a division of The Rogosin Institute, an independent, non-profit institution for scientific and medical research, treatment and education, which is affiliated with New York-Presbyterian Hospital (NYPH) and Weill Cornell Medical College. Renamed in 1988.

Activities: Aims for better health worldwide by optimizing available resources. The Foundation supports innovative scientific and health projects through its own programme, which include: Problem Solving for Better Health (PSBH), which aims to improve health at the local level and promote an international exchange of ideas; and Problem Solving for Better Health—Nursing, raising the role of the nurse in global health provision.

Geographical Area of Activity: Africa, North, Central and South America, Asia, the Caribbean, Central and Eastern Europe, and the Middle East.

Publications: Articles; special publications such as *Problem Solving for Better* Health: A Global Perspective (2010).

Finance: Annual expenditure US $1,237,988 (31 Dec. 2013).

Board of Directors: Richard Hall (Chair.).

Principal Staff: Dir Dr Barry H. Smith.

Address: 205 East 64th St, Suite 404, New York, NY 10065.

Telephone: (212) 750-5075; **Fax:** (212) 371-2776; **Internet:** www.dhfglobal.org; **e-mail:** info@dhfglobal.org.

Drug Policy Alliance—DPA

Established in 2000 by a merger between the Lindesmith Center, a drug policy think tank set up in 1994 by Ethan Nadelmann, and Drug Policy Foundation, a grantmaking and membership organization launched in 1987.

Activities: Promotes drug policy reforms in political discourse as well as the mainstream public. The Alliance provides research fellowships and grants; analyses government drug policies and their ramifications; maintains an information centre and a library; promotes reforms in drug policies; and conducts conference and seminars on topics of interest. It is associated with the Open Society Institute's programme—International Harm Reduction Development, which is aimed at reducing individual and social damage consequent to the use of drugs in the former USSR and Eastern Europe by offering grants to projects working on alleviation of drug impact.

Geographical Area of Activity: USA, Eastern Europe and the countries of the former USSR.

Publications: Journal articles; reports; testimonies; fact sheets; working papers; bibiliographies; research briefs and monographs.

Finance: Annual revenue US $6,813,891, expenditure $12,175,728 (31 May 2014).

Board of Directors: Ira Glasser (Pres.); Richard B. Wolf (Treas.); Rev. Edwin Sanders (Sec.).

Principal Staff: Exec. Dir Dr Ethan Nadelmann.

Address: 131 W 33rd St, 15th Floor, New York, NY 10001.

Telephone: (212) 613-8020; **Fax:** (212) 613-8021; **Internet:** www.drugpolicy.org; **e-mail:** nyc@drugpolicy.org.

Duke Endowment

Founded in 1924 by James B. Duke to provide in some measure for the physical, mental and spiritual needs of mankind.

Activities: Operates four grant programmes in North and South Carolina: supporting education, health care, child care and rural church initiatives.

Geographical Area of Activity: USA (North and South Carolina).

Restrictions: No awards are made outside the states of North and South Carolina or outside the four established grant programmes.

Publications: *Issues* (newsletter); Annual Report; reports on foundation programmes; *Guidelines for Environmentally Friendly Structures*; *The Indenture of Trust; A New Effort*.

Finance: Annual revenue US $262,400,431, expenditure $151,278,838 (2013).

Board of Trustees: Minor M. Shaw (Chair.); Mary D.T. Jones, Dennis M. Campbell (Vice-Chair.); Terri W. Honeycutt (Corporate Sec.).

Principal Staff: Pres. Eugene W. Cochrane, Jr; Vice-Pres. and Gen. Counsel Arthur E. Morehead, IV.

Address: 800 East Morehead St, Charlotte, NC 28202.

Telephone: (704) 376-0291; **Fax:** (704) 376-9336; **Internet:** www.dukeendowment.org; **e-mail:** infotde@tde.org.

Dumbarton Oaks

Founded in 1940 by Mr and Mrs Robert Woods Bliss to promote research and study in the areas of Byzantine, pre-Columbian, and garden and landscape studies.

Activities: The Dumbarton Oaks Research Library and Collection houses important research and study collections in the above three fields; it is administered by the Trustees for Harvard University. The institute offers residential summer fellowships, as well as one-year junior and postdoctoral fellowships. It also makes grants to assist scholarly projects in the three fields with which it is concerned, and organizes conferences and symposia.

Geographical Area of Activity: USA and Canada.

Restrictions: Grants are limited to applicants holding a doctorate or the equivalent for research purposes or to fund a suitable project. Grants are not normally made for the purchase of computers or the salary of the principal investigator.

Publications: *Lighting in Early Byzantium; Three Byzantine Military Treatises; Byzantine Magic; Dumbarton Oaks Papers 61; Gardens and Imagination: Cultural History and Agency; Gardens, City Life and Culture: A World Tour; Palace of the Ancient New World; Script and Glyph: Pre-Hispanic History, Colonial Bookmaking, and the Historia Tolteca-Chichimeca.*

Finance: Annual expenditure US $20,932,650 (30 June 2013).

Trustees: Drew Gilpin Faust (Pres.); James F. Rothenberg (Treas.).

Principal Staff: Exec. Dir Yota Batsaki; Dir Jan M. Ziolkowski.

Address: 1703 32nd St NW, Washington, DC 20007.

Telephone: (202) 339-6401; **Fax:** (202) 339-6419; **Internet:** www.doaks.org; **e-mail:** museum@doaks.org.

Earhart Foundation

Founded in 1929 by Harry Boyd Earhart to support education and research.

Activities: Awards fellowships and grants for graduate study and research in the fields of history, economics, political science and international affairs. The Foundation makes grants to individuals and institutions.

Geographical Area of Activity: Worldwide.

Restrictions: Not for general operating support, endowment or building programmes.

Publications: Annual Report.

Finance: Annual revenue US $2,417,788, expenditure $7,985,144 (31 Dec. 2013).

Board of Trustees: Dennis L. Bark (Chair.); John. H. Moore (Vice-Chair.); Montgomery B. Brown (Sec.); Elayne J. Ellis (Asst Sec.); Kathleen B. Richeson (Treas.); Cheryl D. Gorski (Asst Treas.).

Principal Staff: Pres. Ingrid Ann Gregg.

Address: 2200 Green Rd, Suite H, Ann Arbor, MI 48105-1569.

Telephone: (734) 761-8592; **Fax:** (734) 761-2722.

Earth Island Institute—EII

Established in 1982 by David Brower to develop conservation and environment projects.

Activities: Operates in the field of conservation, preservation and restoration of the environment, by promoting citizen action and incubating a diverse group of global projects. The Institute provides mentoring, training and support for more than 40 projects in more than 25 countries, including Indonesia (Borneo), the Russian Federation, Taiwan and the USA. Supported projects include Baikal Watch; Bay Area Wilderness Training; the Fiji Organic Project; the International Marine Mammal Project; Global Services Corps; Reef Protection International; SAVE International; and the Tibetan Plateau Project. Makes annual Brower Youth Awards for environmental leadership.

Geographical Area of Activity: International.

Publications: *Earth Island Journal*; Annual Report; *Island-Wire* (e-bulletin, 6 a year); *Borneo Wire*; *ECO; Global Service Corps*; *INLAKECH!*; *Kids for the Bay*; *Late Friday* (newsletter); electronic publications.

Finance: Annual revenue US $11,557,597, expenditure $12,144,021 (31 Dec. 2013).

Board of Directors: Michael Mitrani (Pres.); Martha Davis, Kenneth Brower (Vice-Pres); Jennifer Snyder (Sec.); Alex Giedt (Treas.).

Principal Staff: Exec. Dirs John A. Knox, Dave Phillips.

Address: 2150 Allston Way, Suite 460, Berkeley, CA 94704-1375.

Telephone: (510) 859-9100; **Fax:** (510) 859-9091; **Internet:** www.earthisland.org.

Earthrights International—ERI

Founded in 1995 by Ka Hsaw Wa and Katie Bedford along the Thai–Myanmar border, with a focus on using innovative legal strategies and mechanisms to bring justice to indigenous Myanmar communities abused by the military regime and its corporate partners in the name of development.

Activities: Represents and partners with individuals and communities around the world who are victims, survivors, or at risk of human rights and environmental abuses that occur during natural resource extraction projects such as oil and gas development, water diversion projects, logging and mining. ERI uses legal actions, media campaigns, public education and organizing strategies to hold corporate and government human rights and environmental offenders to account. It has pioneered corporate accountability litigation in US courts, winning landmark judgments and successful settlements, most notably in its actions against Unocal and Shell; and also advocates the introduction of strong domestic and international legal mechanisms for corporate accountability. Has two EarthRights Schools and a Regional Legal Training Program and Mekong Legal Advocacy Institute.

Geographical Area of Activity: South-East Asia, South America and the USA.

Publications: *Gaining Ground: Earth Rights Abuses in Burma Exposed*; *Litigation Manual* (2nd edn); *Oil Impacts in the Territory of the Native Communities of Peru*; *Flooding the Future: Hydropower and Cultural Survival in the Salween River Basin*; *If We Dont Have Time to Take Care of Our Fields Our Rice Will Die*; *Shock and Law: George W. Bush's Attack on Law and Universal Human Rights*.

Finance: Annual revenue US $1,966,113, expenditure $2,426,386 (31 Jan. 2013).

Board of Directors: Kate Tillery, Laura Levine (Co-Chair.); Stanley L. Korfman (Treas.).

Principal Staff: Exec. Dir Ka Hsaw Wa; Dir Katie Redford; Man. Dir Marie Soveroski.

Address: 1612 K Street, NW, Suite 401, Washington, DC 20006.

Telephone: (202) 466-5188; **Fax:** (202) 466-5189; **Internet:** www.earthrights.org; **e-mail:** infousa@earthrights.org.

EarthTrust, Inc

Established in 1976 by DJ White.

Activities: Dedicated to the preservation of wildlife and the natural environment. The organization co-ordinates international campaigns against whaling and damage to dolphin stocks through the use of drift nets and ocean acidification; programmes include the Flipper Fund, Save the Whale International, Impossible Missions, FutureSeas, Endangered Wildlife and the Bottleneck Foundation. It is also involved in research and environmental education. Founding member of the Flipper Foundation (f. 1993).

Geographical Area of Activity: Worldwide.

Publications: Annual Report; newsletter.

Finance: Annual revenue US $174,330, expenditure $121,031 (31 Dec. 2013).

Board of Directors: Sue White (Sec. and Treas.).

Principal Staff: Pres. DJ (Don) White.

Address: Windward Environmental Center, 1118 Maunawili Rd, Kailua, HI 96734.

Telephone: (415) 662-3264; **Fax:** (206) 202-3893; **Internet:** www.earthtrust.org; **e-mail:** info@earthtrust.us.

East-West Center—EWC

Founded in 1960 by the US Congress with a mandate 'to promote better relations and understanding between the USA and the nations of Asia and Pacific through co-operative study, training and research'; a public, non-profit national and international research and education institution.

Activities: Receives most of its financial support from the US Congress, but there are also contributions from Asian and Pacific governments, as well as from private agencies and corporations. The Center's staff regularly co-operate in study, research and training with research fellows, graduates and professionals in business and government in the areas of economic change; international co-operation; national economic development strategies; energy policy; politics and security; environmental issues; behaviour and health; and Pacific islands development. Its facilities include administrative and research offices, three residential halls and an international conference centre equipped for simultaneous translation. Maintains an office in Washington, DC.

Geographical Area of Activity: South-East, East and Southern Asia, the Pacific and USA.

Restrictions: Grants only for degree and non-degree scholarships, workshop participants and visiting fellowships.

Publications: Annual Report; *International Production Networks in Asia: Rivalry or Riches?*; *Regional Dynamics and Future US Policy*; *Population Aging Raises Questions for Policymakers*; *AsiaPacific Issues*; *Asia-Pacific Population and Policy*; *East-West Center Observer* (quarterly newsletter); conference proceedings.

Finance: Annual revenue US $1,026,850, expenditure $616,345 (30 Sept. 2013).

Board of Governors: R. Brian Tsujimura (Chair.); Margaret Carpenter, Richard Turbin (Vice-Chair.); Ricky Kubota (Treas.); Clinton Nonaka (Asst Treas.); Carleen G. Gumapac (Sec.).

Principal Staff: Pres. Dr Charles E. Morrison.

Address: 1601 East-West Rd, Honolulu, HI 96848.

Telephone: (808) 944-7111; **Fax:** (808) 944-7376; **Internet:** www.eastwestcenter.org; **e-mail:** fellowships@eastwestcenter.org.

Easter Island Foundation

Established in 1989 to promote the conservation and protection of the cultural heritage of Easter Island (Rapa Nui).

Activities: Created and helps to support the William Mulloy Library on Easter Island. The Foundation provides scholarships to academically promising students of Rapanui ancestry (under 30 years of age) for further education. It publishes books and a biannual journal, and sponsors conferences on Easter Island and the Pacific. Assists with educational, archaeological and environmental research projects on Easter Island.

Geographical Area of Activity: Easter Island and Polynesia.

Publications: *Rapa Nui Journal*; series of books about Easter Island and other Polynesian islands.

Finance: Annual revenue US $29,062, expenditure $65,877 (31 Dec. 2013).

Board of Directors: David Rose (Pres.); Kay Sanger (First Vice-Pres.); Michael Chamberlain (Treas.); Elaine Dvorak (Sec.).

Address: POB 6774, Los Osos, CA 93412.

Telephone: (805) 528-8558; **Fax:** (805) 534-9301; **Internet:** www.islandheritage.org; **e-mail:** books@islandheritage.org.

eBay Foundation

Founded in 1998 to contribute to the economic and social well-being of local communities.

Activities: Makes grants to non-profit organizations and NGOs that strengthen the local communities where eBay employees live and work. Strategic grants have a focus in fostering economic opportunity.

Geographical Area of Activity: USA and international.

Restrictions: No grants for fund-raising events; advertising; government agencies; sponsorships; individuals; organizations with a limited constituency (such as fraternities or veterans' groups); organizations that limit their services to members of one religious group; political organizations.

Finance: Annual revenue US $3,300,003, expenditure $3,947,391 (31 Dec. 2013).

Board of Directors: Beth Axelrod (Chair.); Amyn Thawer (Sec.); Lydia Ventura (Treas.).

Principal Staff: Pres. Amy Millington.

Address: 2065 Hamilton Ave, San Jose, CA 95125.

Telephone: (650) 450-5400; **Internet:** blog.ebay.com/category/ebay-foundation-2/.

EcoHealth Alliance

Established in 1971 by British naturalist Gerald M. Durrell as Wildlife Trust, a sister organization to the Jersey Wildlife Preservation Trust (now the Durrell Wildlife Conservation Trust). Formerly known as Wildlife Preservation Trust International. Present name adopted in 2010.

Activities: Aims to protect endangered species, promote biodiversity conservation and training for local scientists, and promote the development of conservation organizations. The Alliance makes grants to around 65 environmental projects in more than 20 countries in North, Central and South America and the Caribbean, Africa and Asia. It supports research in the field of captive breeding of endangered species, the reintroduction of captive-bred animals to the wild, conservation, and associated environmental education programmes; and trains local conservation professionals. Jointly administers the Gerald Durrell Memorial Funds in conjunction with the Durrell Wildlife Conservation Trust and the Wildlife Preservation Trust Canada, supporting endangered species conservation projects by International Conservation Center graduates. Also makes small grants through the Species Survival Fund. Edge of the Sea Aquatic Conservation Program based in St Petersburg, Florida.

Geographical Area of Activity: North, Central and South America, the Caribbean, Africa and Asia.

Publications: *EcoHealth Journal*; *Wildlife Trust Magazine*; *Conservation Medicine-Ecological Health in Practice*; *Wildlife Trust* (e-newsletter); *Edge of the Sea* (brochure).

Finance: Annual revenue US $8,712,682, expenditure $8,362,573 (30 June 2013).

Board of Directors: Ellen Shedlarz (Chair.); Olivia Engert (Vice-Chair.); Marc O'Donnell (Treas.); Ann B. Moore (Sec.).

Principal Staff: Pres. Dr Peter Daszak; Exec. Vice-Pres. Dr William Karesh.

Address: 460 W 34th St, 17th Floor, New York NY 10001-2320.

Telephone: (212) 380-4460; **Fax:** (212) 380-4465; **Internet:** www.ecohealthalliance.org; **e-mail:** homeoffice@ecohealthalliance.org.

ECOLOGIA—Ecologists Linked for Organizing Grassroots Initiatives and Action

Founded in 1989.

Activities: Provides training, technical advice and assistance in environmental conservation to grassroots groups in Eastern Europe and the countries of the fomer USSR. ECOLOGIA promotes the development of democratic and informed decision-making skills on environmental matters. It established the Virtual Foundation (q.v.), which supports grassroots community-based initiatives and funds organizations in countries where ECOLOGIA acts as a full partner. The organization has extended its activities to the People's Republic of China where it operates a number of programmes to promote sustainable development among local communities. Maintains offices in Moscow and Chengdu.

Geographical Area of Activity: Eastern Europe, countries of the former USSR and the People's Republic of China.

Restrictions: No grants to independent organizations or individuals except via the Virtual Foundation.

Finance: Annual revenue US $114,472, expenditure $95,454 (30 June 2014).

Board of Directors: Randy Kritkausky (Pres. and Exec. Dir); Carolyn Schmidt (Sec.); Ed Shoener (Treas.).

Address: POB 268, Middlebury, VT 05753.

Telephone: (802) 623-8075; **Fax:** (802) 623-8075; **Internet:** www.ecologia.org; **e-mail:** ecologia@ecologia.org.

Albert Einstein Institution

Founded in 1983 to promote the strategic use and study of non-violence as a means of achieving effective results in international conflicts and struggles.

Activities: Promotes the use of non-violent solutions to conflicts throughout the world. The Institution also advances the study of non-violence as a means of defending democratic freedoms and institutions, examining the past use of non-violent action and dedicating itself to finding how peace, freedom and justice can be achieved without the need for violence and war. It communicates the results of its research to the general public through the media, conferences and its own publications as well as running a policy and outreach programme advising groups involved in conflict about the potential effectiveness of non-violent action, through courses, workshops, consultations and dissemination of written materials.

Geographical Area of Activity: International.

Publications: Annual Report; *Nonviolent Action* (newsletter); monographs and handouts; papers, reports and publications on non-violent action.

Finance: Annual revenue US $428,638, expenditure $316,188 (30 June 2013).

Board of Directors: Cornelia Sargent (Chair.).

Principal Staff: Exec. Dir and Sec. Jamila Raqib.

Address: POB 455, East Boston, MA 02128.

Telephone: (617) 247-4882; **Fax:** (617) 247-4035; **Internet:** www.aeinstein.org; **e-mail:** einstein@igc.org.

endPoverty.org

Established in 1985 as Enterprise Development International, a faith-based organization dedicated to enabling the working poor in the developing world to lift themselves out of poverty.

Activities: Provides small loans to poor entrepreneurs with limited access to capital. The organization offers vocational training to individuals in impoverished communities expressing a desire to start and maintain their own businesses. Provides ongoing mentorship and community support networks to borrowers to help ensure their micro-business success and personal growth. Closely partnered with local microfinance and development institutions in 12 countries in Africa, Asia, South America and Eastern Europe.

Geographical Area of Activity: International.

Publications: Annual Report.

Finance: Annual revenue US $464,664, expenditure $501,055 (31 Dec. 2013).

Board of Directors: Larry Roadman (Chair. and Interim Exec. Dir); Richard Dean, Paul Vinogradov, Charles 'Chaz' Seale (Vice-Chair.); C. W. 'Kip' Gardner (Treas.); Colby M. May (Sec.).

Principal Staff: COO Tammy Wang.

Address: POB 3380, Oakton, VA 22124; 7910 Woodmont Ave, Suite 800, Bethesda, MD 20814.

Telephone: (240) 396-1146; **Fax:** (240) 235-3550; **Internet:** www.endpoverty.org; **e-mail:** for-more-info@endpoverty .org.

EngenderHealth

Established in 1943 as a non-profit organization that aims to improve reproductive health services around the world and make them safe, reliable and available to everyone. Formerly known as AVSC International, until 2001.

Activities: Works in more than 20 countries in the area of health, improving family planning and reproductive health care, working with governments, health institutions and clinic staff to develop services where none currently exist, and improving care in already existing facilities. The organization does this through technical assistance and training; running training seminars and providing on-site help for health-care workers on safe medical techniques; management and supervision; research on family planning issues and attitudes; and through publications that make technical reference material and information accessible to those working in the area of reproductive health. Also involved in women's general health care, including HIV/AIDS issues and maternity services.

Geographical Area of Activity: Worldwide.

Publications: *EngenderHealth Update* (quarterly newsletter); *EngenderHealth Connect* (monthly electronic newsletter); *Client-Education Materials*; *Counselling, Informed Choice, and Informed Consent*; *Medical and Surgical Guidelines*; *Service Management/Quality of Care*; *About EngenderHealth*; Annual Report.

Finance: Annual revenue US $63,026,244, expenditure $56,503,575 (30 June 2013).

Board of Directors: Robert D. Petty (Chair.); Francine Coeytaux (Chair., Exec. Cttee); Rosemary Ellis (Sec.); Margaret Neuse (Asst Sec.); Janice Hansen Zakin (Vice-Chair.).

Principal Staff: Pres. and CEO Pamela W. Barnes; COO Daniel Doucette.

Address: 440 Ninth Ave, New York, NY 10001.

Telephone: (212) 561-8000; **Fax:** (212) 561-8067; **Internet:** www.engenderhealth.org; **e-mail:** info@engenderhealth.org.

EnterpriseWorks/VITA—EWV

Established in 1998; a non-profit organization. Formerly known as Appropriate Technology International. Became a division of Relief International following merger in 2009.

Activities: Aims to provide economic opportunity for all as a long-term solution to poverty in the developing world. The organization operates in the field of economic development in more than 60 countries in Africa, Asia, and Central and South America, supporting small businesses to increase the earning power, income and quality of life of the world's 2,000m. small producers, with the aim of breaking the poverty cycle and enabling the underprivileged to provide their families with a better quality of life. It focuses on producers in the areas of small-scale irrigation, energy, oilseeds and staple foods, tree crops, dairy and other livestock, and natural products.

Geographical Area of Activity: Worldwide.

Publications: E-newsletter; various manuals and proceedings.

Finance: Annual revenue US $479,002, expenditure $453,137 (30 Sept. 2013).

Board of Directors: Paul Levengood (Chair.).

Address: 1100 H St, NW, Suite 1200, Washington, DC 20005.

Telephone: (202) 639-8660; **Fax:** (202) 639-8664; **Internet:** www.enterpriseworks.org; **e-mail:** info@enterpriseworks .org.

Epilepsy Foundation

Founded in 1968 by merger of the Epilepsy Foundation (f. 1954) and the Epilepsy Association of America (f. 1965) as the national, voluntary health organization for the prevention and cure of seizure disorders, the alleviation of their effects, and improvement of the quality of life for people who have these disorders.

Activities: Operates mainly nationally in the field of medicine and health. The Foundation conducts and supports research, awards fellowships for research and exchange of expertise (incl. the Fritz E. Dreyfuss International Travel Program); supports training programmes for sufferers from epilepsy; holds conferences; and disseminates information through its publications.

Geographical Area of Activity: Mainly USA.

Publications: Annual Report; *Between Us* (quarterly); *Epilepsy USA* (2 a month and online newsletter); *Kids News* (quarterly); brochures and specialist publications.

Finance: Annual revenue US $14,896,869, expenditure $15,121,223 (30 June 2013).

Board of Directors: Warren Lammert (Chair.); Roger Heldman (Treas.); May J. Liang (Sec.); Brien J. Smith (Immediate Past Chair.).

Principal Staff: Pres. and CEO Phil Gattone.

Address: 8301 Professional Pl., East Suite 200, Landover, MD 20785-2353.

Telephone: (301) 459-3700; **Fax:** (301) 577-2684; **Internet:** www.epilepsyfoundation.org; **e-mail:** contactus@efa.org.

Esperança, Inc

Founded in 1970 to support the work of Fr Luke Tupper. The organization aims to provide adequate health care for children around the world.

Activities: Operates in the field of medicine and health in developing countries, working to improve health care, particularly focusing on reducing child mortality. The organization currently runs projects in Bolivia, Nicaragua and the USA, incl. training doctors and nurses to improve the quality of health services, informing mothers on disease-prevention methods, and funding health education.

Geographical Area of Activity: USA, Africa, Central and South America.

Restrictions: No grants available.

Publications: Annual Report; newsletters.

Finance: Annual revenue US $6,257,988, expenditure $6,008,392 (30 Sept. 2013).

Board of Directors: Mark Williams (Chair.); Rosary Hernandez (Sec.); Jeremy Smith (Treas.) .

Principal Staff: Pres. and CEO James Hoyt.

Address: 1911 West Earll Dr., Phoenix, AZ 85015.

Telephone: (602) 252-7772; **Fax:** (602) 340-9197; **Internet:** www.esperanca.org; www.wetransformlives.org; **e-mail:** info@esperanca.org.

Etruscan Foundation

Founded in 1958 to support the work of students and scholars interested in classical archaeology, especially the history of ancient Etruscan civilization, and the preservation of the natural and cultural heritage of Tuscany, ancient land of the Etruscans.

Activities: Provides annual fellowships for conservation, fieldwork and research activities at Etruscan sites across Italy. The Cinelli Lecture Series provides annual lecture programmes on Etruscan and Italic archaeology through the Archaeological Institute of America. *Etruscan Studies: Journal of the Etruscan Foundation* is the leading scholarly publication on Etruscology and related disciplines in the English language.

Geographical Area of Activity: USA and Italy.

Publications: *Etruscan Studies: Journal of the Etruscan Foundation*.

Finance: Annual revenue US $87,619, expenditure $93,572 (31 Dec. 2012).

Board of Directors: Kenneth B. Katz (Pres.); P. Gregory Warden (Vice-Pres.); Wendy Walker (Sec.); Peter Cinelli (Treas.).

Principal Staff: Exec. Dir Richard F. String.

Address: POB 26, Fremont, MI 49412.

Telephone: (231) 519-0675; **Fax:** (231) 924-0777; **Internet:** www.etruscanfoundation.org; **e-mail:** office@etruscanfoundation.org.

Eurasia Foundation

Founded in 1992 with funds from the US Agency for International Development (USAID) to promote the advancement of democratic institutions and private enterprise in the countries of the former USSR.

Activities: Works to empower communities to take responsibility for their own civic and economic prosperity. The Foundation helps small businesses to succeed, local governments to become more responsive, and builds the leadership skills of young people. Since 1992, it has invested more than US $400m. in building civil societies through the Eurasia Foundation Network: locally registered organizations in the Russian Federation, Central Asia, the South Caucasus, Ukraine and Moldova. The Foundation applies best practices in advocacy, institutional development and online education to promote civil society across the Eurasia region, the Middle East and North Africa, and the People's Republic of China.

Geographical Area of Activity: The Russian Federation, Eastern Europe and Central Asia, the Middle East and North Africa, the People's Republic of China.

Restrictions: Does not fund political parties or movements and activities of a religious nature.

Publications: Annual Report; information brochure; application guidelines; newsletter.

Finance: Annual revenue US $5,365,252, expenditure $9,365,970 (30 Sept. 2013).

Board of Trustees: Jan Kalicki (Chair.); Daniel Witt (Vice-Chair.).

Principal Staff: Pres. W. Horton Beebe-Center.

Address: 1350 Connecticut Ave NW, Suite 1000, Washington, DC 20036.

Telephone: (202) 234-7370; **Fax:** (202) 234-7377; **Internet:** www.eurasia.org; **e-mail:** eurasia@eurasia.org.

Feed the Children

Founded in 1979; a Christian, non-profit charitable organization.

Activities: Supports children, families and people in need all over the world. The organization works in the USA and internationally in four main fields: food supply; sustainable development; medical care; and emergency relief. It distributes food, provides medical assistance and educational opportunities to children, and financially supports orphanages, schools and other charities and NGOs. Sends medical teams and supplies to developing regions, and promotes self-sustaining development for families, so as to provide a long-term solution to poverty and hunger.

Geographical Area of Activity: International.

Publications: Financial statements.

Finance: Annual revenue US $453,867,785, expenditure $411,604,686 (30 June 2013).

Board of Directors: Rick England (Chair.); Gregg Yeilding (Treas.).

Principal Staff: Pres. and CEO Kevin Hagan; COO Travis Arnold.

Address: 333 N. Meridian, Oklahoma City, OK 73107; POB 36, Oklahoma City, OK 73101-0036.

Telephone: (405) 942-0228; **Fax:** (405) 945-4177; **Internet:** www.feedthechildren.org; **e-mail:** ftc@feedthechildren.org.

Feed My Hungry People, Inc

Established in 1990 as an international organization. Formerly known as Feed My People International.

Activities: Stores and distributes food, commodities and disaster relief to thousands of the most impoverished people in Arizona and the South-West of the USA. Works through the Northern Arizona Food Bank (f. 1986), which merged with the Flagstaff Food Center in 2013.

Geographical Area of Activity: Mainly Arizona and the South-West USA.

Publications: Newsletter.

Finance: Annual revenue US $4,844,502, expenditure $4,851,516 (30 Sept. 2012).

Board of Dirs: Tim McCullough (Pres.); Stacey Button (Vice-Pres.); Derek Turner (Sec.); Mickey Abeshaus (Treas.).

Principal Staff: Exec. Dir Steve Saville.

Address: 3805 East Huntington Dr., Flagstaff, AZ 86004; POB P, Flagstaff, Arizona 86002.

Telephone: (928) 774-3188; **Fax:** (928) 774-7469; **Internet:** www.feedmypeople.org; www.nafoodbank.org; **e-mail:** info@hotfood.org.

FHI 360

Established in 2011 as a global development organization following the takeover of Academy for Educational Development (AED, f. 1961) by Family Health International (FHI, f. 1971).

Activities: Works in collaboration with local and national partner organizations. Operates in some 125 countries.

Geographical Area of Activity: International.

Publications: Annual Report.

Finance: Annual revenue US $664,065,312, expenditure $653,826,994 (30 Sept. 2013).

Board of Directors: Edward W. Whitehorne (Chair. and CEO); Paul R. De Lay (Vice-Chair.); Martin Mittag-Lenkheym (Treas.); Helga Ying (Sec.).

Principal Staff: CEO Patrick C. Fine.

Address: 2224 E NC Highway 54, Durham, NC 27713.

Telephone: (919) 544-7040; **Fax:** (919) 544-7261; **Internet:** www.fhi360.org.

FINCA International

Founded in 1984 to support the economic and human development of families trapped in severe poverty to enable them to create their own jobs, raise household incomes and improve their standard of living.

Activities: Supports economic self-sufficiency in less-developed countries, through the creation of sustainable development projects, including village banks to provide loans of US $50–$1,000 to individuals and to initiate savings programmes. Operates in North, Central and South America, and the Caribbean, Africa, the Middle East, certain countries of the former USSR, and Kosovo and Metohija.

Geographical Area of Activity: North, Central and South America, and the Caribbean, Africa, the Middle East, Kosovo and Metohija, and countries of the former USSR.

Publications: *Village Bank Notes* (quarterly newsletter).

Finance: Annual revenue US $72,202,657, expenditure $64,169,620 (31 Dec. 2013).

Board of Directors: Robert W. Hatch.

Principal Staff: Pres. and CEO Rupert W. Scofield; Vice-Pres. and COO Andrée Simon; Vice Pres. and CFO Dane Steven McGuire.

Address: 1101 14th St NW, 11th Floor, Washington, DC 20005.

Telephone: (202) 682-1510; **Fax:** (202) 682-1535; **Internet:** www.finca.org; **e-mail:** info@finca.org.

Firefly, Inc.

Established in 2000 by Jonathan and Julie Baker.

Activities: Works to help local governments in the Russian Federation develop programmes that will keep children in their birth families. The organization promotes the establishment of foster homes, small group homes, and domestic adoption when living with birth families is not an option. By offering technical assistance, best practices, and targeted capacity building to local leaders, it assists local champions who wish to create a Russia without orphanages.

Geographical Area of Activity: Russia.

Publications: *Firefly Newsletter.*

Finance: Annual revenue US $27,977, expenditure $68,827 (31 Dec. 2012).

Board of Directors: Nicole Levine (Pres.); Diana England (Sec.); J. Jonathan F. Baker (Treas.).

Principal Staff: Programme Dir Melinda Richards.

Address: 8317 Woodhaven Blvd, Bethesda, MD 20817.

Telephone: (917) 359-7207; **Fax:** (240) 396-2107; **Internet:** www.fireflykids.org; **e-mail:** mrichards@fireflykids.org.

Firelight Foundation

Founded in 1999 by Kerry Olson to identify, fund and strengthen promising community organizations that support the health, resilience and education of children in Africa.

Activities: Supports vulnerable children and families in Sub-Saharan Africa by funding community-based organizations that work directly and effectively to support the fundamental needs and rights of children orphaned or otherwise affected by poverty and HIV and AIDS. The Foundation prioritizes grass-roots projects developed in direct response to local community needs, particularly organizations that raise resources from within the local community. It provides initial one-year grants of US $1,000–$10,000, with subsequent grants of up to $15,000.

Geographical Area of Activity: Sub-Saharan Africa.

Restrictions: Priority countries for grantmaking are Lesotho, Malawi, Rwanda, Tanzania, Zambia and Zimbabwe. From Ethiopia, Kenya, South Africa and Uganda, Firelight accepts only renewal requests and solicited proposals.

Publications: Annual Report; *Protecting Our Children: How African Community Organizations Improve Child Protection Systems* (e-book).

Finance: Annual revenue US $9,136,713, expenditure $5,117,044 (30 June 2014).

Board of Directors: Catherine Milton (Chair.) Dick Staufenberger (Vice-Chair. and Treas.); David Katz (Sec.).

Principal Staff: Finance Man. Jane Stokes.

Address: 740 Front St, Suite 380, Santa Cruz, CA 95060.

Telephone: (831) 429-8750; **Fax:** (831) 429-2036; **Internet:** www.firelightfoundation.org; **e-mail:** info@firelightfoundation.org.

First Peoples Worldwide—FPW

Established in 1997 by the First Nations Development Institute to work as an advocate for indigenous rights worldwide.

Activities: Operates worldwide in the field of human rights for indigenous peoples. The organization works to help sustain the land and culture of indigenous peoples in a number of ways, incl. encouraging and enabling indigenous peoples to take an active role in issues concerning the environment, the economy and the legal system; providing technical and financial support for culturally-appropriate development programmes; advocating self-governance; building and maintaining a database containing information on indigenous land rights and self-governance; and operating a fellowship programme for community leaders. It has been engaged in direct work in Southern Africa and Australia, and is currently operating projects in South America. Since 2007, the Tides Center has provided financial and administrative support.

Geographical Area of Activity: Africa, South America, Australia.

Publications: *Indigenous Peoples Funding and Resource Guide.*

Finance: Annual revenue US $700,340, expenditure $919,396 (31 Dec. 2013).

Principal Staff: Founder and Pres. Rebecca Adamson.

Address: 857 Leeland Rd, Fredericksburg, VA 22405-6005.

Telephone: (540) 899-6545; **Fax:** (540) 899-6501; **Internet:** www.firstpeoples.org; **e-mail:** info@firstpeoples.org.

Flight Safety Foundation

Founded in 1947 by R. Crane, H. DeHaven and J. Morrison to promote and foster improvements in international conditions of air safety.

Activities: Publishes, and distributes to members, bulletins on aviation safety and accident prevention. The Foundation conducts specialized research and flight safety analyses for operators. It organizes annual business air safety seminars and annual awards. Its members include more than 1,200 organizations, individuals, companies, etc. from some 150 countries. Maintains a library of approximately 1,000 volumes and a regional office in Melbourne, Australia.

Geographical Area of Activity: Worldwide.

Publications: *Annual Index*; *Accident Prevention* (monthly); *Airport Operations* (6 a year); *Aviation Mechanics Bulletin* (6 a year); *Cabin Crew Safety* (6 a year); *Flight Safety Digest* (monthly); *Helicopter Safety* (6 a year); *Human Factors and Aviation Medicine* (6 a year); seminar and workshop proceedings, special reports, technical manuals and studies, membership directory; Annual Report.

Finance: Annual revenue US $2,838,676, expenditure $3,466,041 (31 Dec. 2013).

Board of Governors: Ken Hylander (Chair.); Kenneth P. Quinn (Gen. Counsel and Sec.); David Barger (Treas.).

Principal Staff: Pres. and CEO Jon Beatty.

Address: 801 N Fairfax St, Suite 400, Alexandria, VA 22314-1774.

Telephone: (703) 739-6700; **Fax:** (703) 739-6708; **Internet:** www.flightsafety.org; **e-mail:** mcgee@flightsafety.org.

Food for the Hungry—FH

Founded in 1971 as a Christian organization to relieve poverty worldwide.

Activities: Operates programmes in the fields of health care, community development, nutrition and emergency relief. The organization provides an information and education service; organizes seminars and workshops; provides training for farmers; promotes child sponsorship; and gives financial assistance to other development organizations.

Geographical Area of Activity: Asia, Africa and Latin America.

Publications: *Food for the Hungry Story* (newsletter); Annual Report.

Finance: Annual revenue US $82,094,970, expenditure $83,556,516 (30 Sept. 2013).

Board of Directors: Larry Jones, Laurent Mbanda (Co-Chair.).

Principal Staff: Pres. and CEO Gary Edmonds; Chief International Operations Officer Luis Noda.

Address: 1224 East Washington St, Phoenix, AZ 85034-1102.

Telephone: (480) 998-3100; **Internet:** www.fh.org; **e-mail:** webquestions@fh.org.

Food for the Poor, Inc

Established in 1982 by Robin Mahfood; an NGO that seeks to link the Church in developed countries with that in less-developed areas and help the poor.

Activities: Works internationally to support the poor in developing countries. The organization has links with 12,000 primarily religious and indigenous NGOs worldwide. It works with them to raise funding and develop projects to improve conditions in Central and South America and the Caribbean, especially in the areas of food supplies, education, health care and social welfare.

Geographical Area of Activity: Central and South America and the Caribbean.

Restrictions: Operates only in Central and South American and Caribbean countries.

Publications: Annual Report; newsletters.

Finance: Annual revenue US $938,210,756, expenditure $950,853,360 (31 Dec. 2013).

Board of Directors: P. Todd Kennedy (Chair.); Bill Benson (Vice-Chair.); David T. Price (Sec.); Most Rev. Burchell McPherson (Treas.).

Principal Staff: Pres. and CEO Robin G. Mahfood; Exec. Dir Angel Aloma.

Address: 6401 Lyons Rd, Coconut Creek, FL 33073.

Telephone: (954) 427-2222; **Fax:** (954) 570-7654; **Internet:** www.foodforthepoor.org; **e-mail:** info@foodforthepoor.com.

Ford Foundation

Founded in 1936 by Henry Ford and his son Edsel B. Ford.

Activities: Aims to strengthen democratic values, reduce poverty and injustice, promote international co-operation and advance human achievement. The Foundation makes grants to institutions primarily within three programme areas: Asset Building and Community Development, which incorporates Community and Resource Development and Economic Development; Peace and Social Justice, which comprises two units—Human Rights and Governance and Civil Society; and Knowledge, Creativity and Freedom, which also comprises two units—Education, Sexuality and Religion, and Media, Arts and Culture. The Foundation provides support for: conferences and seminars; general purposes; matching funds; publications; research; programme-related investments; seed money; special projects; technical assistance; endowment funds; fellowships; and individual grants. Has field offices in Brazil, Chile, the People's Republic of China, Egypt, India, Indonesia, Kenya, the Philippines, Mexico, Nigeria, the Russian Federation, South Africa and Viet Nam, and associations in Israel and Eastern Europe.

Geographical Area of Activity: Worldwide.

Restrictions: Support not given for personal needs, religious activities or building construction.

Publications: Annual Report; magazine (quarterly); *Current Interests* (biennially).

Finance: Annual revenue US $689,997,536, expenditure $685,564,893 (30 Sept. 2013).

Board of Trustees: Kofi Appenteng (Chair.).

Principal Staff: Pres. Darren Walker.

Address: 320 East 43rd St, New York, NY 10017.

Telephone: (212) 573-5000; **Fax:** (212) 351-3677; **Internet:** www.fordfoundation.org; **e-mail:** office-of-communications@fordfoundation.org.

Foreign Policy Association

Founded in 1918 to educate Americans about international events and issues and to encourage them to participate in the foreign policy process.

Activities: Seeks to educate Americans about US foreign policy and global affairs, principally through its Great Decisions programme, which consists of an annual impartial briefing of eight key foreign policy issues, discussed by groups, and at seminars and public forums aimed at both students and adults. The Association also publishes books, leaflets and produces other educational online resources.

Geographical Area of Activity: Worldwide, but mostly in the USA.

Restrictions: Not a grantmaking organization.

Publications: *Great Decisions* (annual programme guide); online newsletters; Annual Report; other publications.

Finance: Annual revenue US $4,345,699, expenditure $4,418,291 (30 June 2013).

Board of Directors: Jillian Sackler (Chair.).

Principal Staff: Pres. and CEO Noel V. Lateef.

Address: 470 Park Ave S, New York, NY 10016.

Telephone: (212) 481-8100; **Fax:** (212) 481-9275; **Internet:** www.fpa.org; **e-mail:** info@fpa.org.

Foundation for a Civil Society—FCS

Founded in 1990 to act as a co-ordinating body to promote civil society, democracy and the market economy. Formerly known as the Foundation for a Civil Society (Charter 77 Foundation-New York).

Activities: Has two main functions: to act as a catalyst, initiating and supporting projects; and to act as facilitator, connecting funding sources with institutions and individuals wishing to establish programmes and projects. The Foundation has an extensive network of high-level contacts in the USA and other parts of the world. Its major programmes include the New Slovakia initiative designed to ensure that the new governments in the Slovak Republic move smoothly toward European integration. The Foundation's offices in the Czech Republic and Slovakia became independent NGOs known as VIA Foundation (q.v.) and Nadácia Pre Občiansku Spoločnost.

Geographical Area of Activity: International, with an emphasis on Central and Eastern Europe, Northern Ireland and Central America.

Publications: Annual Report.

Finance: Annual revenue US $579,200, expenditure $454,173 (31 Dec. 2013).

Board of Directors: Carolyn Seely Wiener (Chair.).

Principal Staff: Pres. Wendy W. Luers.

Address: 25 East End Ave, 1B, New York, NY 10028.

Telephone: (212) 980-4584; **Fax:** (212) 980-4583; **Internet:** www.fcsny.org; **e-mail:** info@fcsny.org.

Foundation for Deep Ecology

Established in 1990.

Activities: Focuses on fundamental ecological issues in three areas: Biodiversity and Wilderness, incl. protection of forests, aquatic ecosystems and other habitats, wildlands philanthropy (i.e. buying land to save it), wilderness recovery (supporting the design and implementation of large-scale wilderness recovery networks), funding for activists campaigning for full protection of species and ecosystems, and funding efforts to eliminate resource extraction on public lands; Ecological Agriculture, incl. support for alternative models of agriculture that support biodiversity, local self-reliance and healthy agrarian communities, support for efforts to combat industrialization of agriculture, and support for efforts to link conservationists with farmers and activists to integrate habitat preservation and restoration with diverse farming practices; and Education, incl. campaigns to educate the public about and to resist the growth of the new macro-economic trends and the technological systems that drive these trends (e.g. international free-trade agreements), and providing aid to groups working towards viable local economic systems (for example community-building, local currencies and defining new technological and economic systems). From 2003, the Foundation increased its focus on wildlands philanthropy, with a resulting reduction in available grants in the remaining grant programmes.

Geographical Area of Activity: USA, South America and Canada (primarily Chile and Argentina). Grants to some groups in the Netherlands, Spain and the United Kingdom.

Restrictions: No new grant proposals accepted.

Publications: *Century of Failed Forest Policy*; *Fatal Harvest*; *The Tragedy of Industrial Agriculture*.

Finance: Annual revenue US $103,645, expenditure $1,921,519 (30 June 2014).

Board of Directors: Douglas R. Tompkins (Pres.); Quincey Tompkins Imhoff, Kristine McDivitt Tompkins (Vice-Pres); Debra B. Ryker (Sec. and Treas.).

Principal Staff: Editorial Projects Dir Tom Butler.

Address: 1606 Union St, San Francisco, CA 94123.

Telephone: (415) 229-9339; **Fax:** (415) 229-9340; **Internet:** www.deepecology.org; **e-mail:** info@deepecology.org.

FLAAR—Foundation for Latin American Anthropological Research

Founded in 1969 by Dr Nicholas M. Hellmuth to engage in academic research in the fields of archaeology, art history and tropical flora and fauna.

Activities: Operates in the fields of the arts and humanities, with respect to ancient cultures of Central America, especially in the areas of archaeology; ethno-zoology; ethno-botany; ethno-history of sports; conservation and the environment; and education. The Foundation focuses on evaluation of digital camera equipment and wide-format inkjet printers to assist museums, zoos, national parks, botanical gardens, and university research institutes with knowledge on digital imaging related to anthropology broadly defined. It organizes conferences and training courses, and field trips to Central America. Most research is carried out in Mexico, Guatemala, Honduras and Belize, but the Foundation also carries out studies of Mesoamerican art in museums worldwide. Maintains libraries in Austria and Guatemala, and a photographic archive. Established the Asociación FLAAR Mesoamérica (f. 2006) in Guatemala.

Geographical Area of Activity: Mainly Central America, Mexico.

Publications: Electronic reports on archaeology, pre-Columbian art, ancient architecture and sports in Pre-Hispanic America, and on digital imaging to record and exhibit these subjects.

Finance: Annual revenue US $236,192, expenditure $342,584 (31 Dec. 2013).

Board of Directors: Dr Nicholas M. Hellmuth (Pres. and Dir); Lawrence Katzenstein (Sec.).

Address: 12317 Inletridge Dr., Maryland Heights, MO 63043.

Telephone: (419) 823-9218; **Internet:** www.flaar.org; maya-archaeology.org; **e-mail:** frontdesk@flaar.org.

Foundation for Middle East Peace—FMEP

Founded in 1979 by Merle Thorpe, Jr to assist in an understanding of Israeli-Palestinian relations, including the identification of US interests, and to contribute to a just and peaceful resolution.

Activities: Carries out research into Middle East peace, and supports elements in the Arab and Jewish communities that are working towards peace between Israelis and Palestinians. Grants have supported educational, humanitarian, public affairs, civil rights and Palestinian-Israeli reconciliation activities, as well as small-scale economic projects that meet the needs of victims of the current conflict.

Geographical Area of Activity: Israel and Palestinian Territories.

Restrictions: No grants are made to individuals; grants are made only to organizations and projects that contribute to Israeli-Palestinian peace.

Publications: *The West Bank: Hostage of History*; *Prescription for Conflict: Israel's West Bank Settlement Policy*; *Error and Betrayal in Lebanon*; *Facing the PLO Question*; *A Policy for the Moment of Truth*; *No Trumpets, No Drums*; *Report on Israeli Settlement in the Occupied Territories* (6 a year); settlement reports.

Finance: Funded by endowment and annual income; total revenue US $887,567, expenditure $937,000 (30 Sept. 2012).

Board of Trustees: Nicholas A. Veliotes (Chair.).

Principal Staff: Pres. Matthew Duss.

Address: 1761 N St NW, Washington, DC 20036.

Telephone: (202) 835-3650; **Fax:** (202) 835-3651; **Internet:** www.fmep.org; **e-mail:** info@fmep.org.

Michael J. Fox Foundation for Parkinson's Research

Established in 2000 by actor Michael J. Fox and Deborah W. Brooks to find a cure for Parkinson's disease.

Activities: Funds research into Parkinson's disease.

Publications: *Accelerating the Cure* (newsletter, 3 a year); *Fox-Flash* (e-newsletter).

Finance: Annual revenue US $91,460,361, expenditure $83,700,634 (31 Dec. 2013).

Board of Directors: Woody Shackleton (Chair.); George E. Prescott (Vice-Chair.).

Principal Staff: CEO Dr Todd Sherer; Exec. Vice-Chair. Deborah W. Brooks.

Address: Grand Central Station, POB 4777, New York, NY 10163-4777.

Telephone: (212) 509-0995; **Fax:** (212) 509-2390; **Internet:** www.michaeljfox.org; **e-mail:** info@michaeljfox.org.

Francis Family Foundation

Founded in 1989 by the merger of the Parker B. Francis Foundation and the Parker B. Francis, III Foundation.

Activities: Funds medical fellowships in pulmonary medicine and anaesthesiology, and supports principal educational and cultural institutions within the Greater Kansas City metropolitan area. The Foundation awards fellowships to citizens of the USA or Canada (or to foreign nationals intending to take up permanent residence in the USA or Canada) for postdoctoral research related to pulmonary disease. It also supports child and youth development programmes in the areas of life-long learning and arts and culture in the Greater Kansas City metropolitan area.

Geographical Area of Activity: North America.

Publications: Annual Report.

Finance: Annual revenue US $4,986,404, expenditure $6,955,371 (2012).

Board of Directors: David V. Francis (Chair.); Ann Barhoum (Vice-Chair.); Charles Schellhorn (Treas.).

Principal Staff: Exec. Dir and Sec. Jim Koeneman.

Address: 800 West 47th St, Suite 717, Kansas City, MO 64112.

Telephone: (816) 531-0077; **Fax:** (816) 531-8810; **Internet:** www.francisfoundation.org; **e-mail:** info@francisfoundation.org.

Franciscans International

Established in 1984.

Activities: Works in collaboration with other NGOs, the UN and Franciscans around the world on global issues, especially relating to peacemaking and concern for the poor, incl. projects on religious intolerance, human rights, migration and development in Africa. The organization also runs an internship programme. It aims to represent the poor at the UN. Maintains offices in Geneva and Bangkok.

Geographical Area of Activity: Worldwide.

Publications: Annual Report; *Pax et Bonum* (newsletter); *West Papua Factsheet; World Poverty—Franciscan Reflections.*

Finance: Annual revenue 852,275 Swiss francs, expenditure 682,196 Swiss francs (2013).

Board of Directors: Doug Clorey (Pres.); Averil Swanton (Vice-Pres.); Jude Winkler (Sec.); Elias Mallon (Interim Treas.).

Principal Staff: Dir Markus Heinze.

Address: 246 E 46th St, Suite 1F, New York, NY 10017-2937.

Telephone: (212) 490-4624; **Fax:** (212) 490-4626; **Internet:** www.franciscansinternational.org; **e-mail:** newyork@fiop.org.

The Freedom Forum

Established by Allen H. Neuharth in 1991; a non-partisan, international foundation and successor to a foundation started in 1935 by newspaper publisher Frank E. Gannett.

Activities: Dedicated to free press, free speech and free spirit for all people. Focuses on four priority areas: the Newseum, First Amendment issues, newsroom diversity and world press freedom. The Newseum is an independent affiliate, funded by the Freedom Forum, an interactive museum of news, based in Arlington, VA. The Freedom Forum also funds the First

Amendment Center, another independent affiliate, with offices at Vanderbilt University in Nashville, TN, New York City and Arlington, which works to preserve and protect First Amendment freedoms through information and education. The Center serves as a forum for the study and exploration of free-expression issues, including freedom of speech, of the press and of religion, the right to assemble and to petition the government. It makes several annual awards in recognition of quality journalism and to promote freedom of speech. The Freedom Forum has operating offices in Buenos Aires, Hong Kong, Johannesburg, London and Cocoa Beach, FL, but operates principally in the USA.

Geographical Area of Activity: Mainly USA.

Restrictions: Does not accept unsolicited requests for funding.

Publications: Annual Report; information brochures; conference and seminar reports; video and audio tapes of programmes; *Media Ethics and Fairness*; *Media Studies Journal*; *World Press Freedom*; *Newsroom Diversity*.

Finance: Annual revenue US $21,191,788, expenditure $49,467,918 (31 Dec. 2013).

Principal Staff: CEO and Chair. Jan A. Neurath.

Address: 555 Pennsylvania Ave NW, Washington, DC 20001.

Telephone: (202) 292-6100; **Internet:** www.freedomforum .org; www.newseum.org/about/freedom-forum/; **e-mail:** news@freedomforum.org.

Freedom House, Inc

Founded in 1943 by Eleanor Roosevelt, Wendell Willkie and other Americans concerned with the mounting threats to peace and democracy to promote democratic values and oppose dictatorships of the far left and the far right. In 1997, incorporated the programmes of the National Forum Foundation.

Activities: Promotes the development of the world's young democracies, which are coping with the debilitating legacy of statism, dictatorship and political repression. The organization conducts US and overseas research, advocacy, education and training initiatives that promote human rights, democracy, free-market economics, the rule of law, independent media, and US engagement in international affairs. Its regional programmes cover a range of issues, incl. raising the sustainability of independent local media, reducing violence against women, torture treatment and prevention, and human-rights training. Also maintains offices in Almaty, Amman, Belgrade, Bishkek, Bucharest, Budapest, Dushanbe, Kiev, Lagos, Mexico City, Tashkent, Warsaw and New York.

Geographical Area of Activity: Worldwide.

Publications: *Freedom in the World* (annually); *Freedom of the Press*; special reports; *Nations in Transit* (annually); *Countries at the Crossroads* (annually); *Women's Rights Survey*; Annual Report.

Finance: Annual revenue US $106,480, expenditure $115,382 (30 June 2013).

Board of Trustees: Kenneth I. Juster (Chair.); Charles Davidson, D. Jeffrey Hirschberg (Vice-Chair.); David Nastro (Treas.); James H. Carter (Sec.).

Principal Staff: Pres. Mark P. Lagon; Exec. Vice-Pres. Daniel Calingaert.

Address: 1301 Connecticut Ave NW, 6th Floor, Washington, DC 20036.

Telephone: (202) 296-5101; **Fax:** (202) 293-2840; **Internet:** www.freedomhouse.org; **e-mail:** info@freedomhouse.org.

Freedom from Hunger

Founded in 1946.

Activities: Fights chronic hunger with sustainable self-help solutions. The organization works with partners to provide small cash loans and education to women's groups in poor rural villages of developing countries. It works with about 150 local partner organizations, including NGOs, rural banks and credit unions, in 24 developing countries.

Geographical Area of Activity: Africa, Asia and Latin America.

Publications: Annual Report; newsletters, white papers.

Finance: Annual revenue US $5,206,800, expenditure $6,321,920 (30 June 2013).

Board of Trustees: Marianne Udow-Phillips (Chair.); Richard C. Auger (Vice-Chair.); Catherine C. Roth (Sec.); William B. Robinson (Treas.).

Principal Staff: Pres. Steve Hollingworth.

Address: 1644 Da Vinci Ct, Davis, CA 95618.

Telephone: (530) 758-6200; **Fax:** (530) 758-6241; **Internet:** www.freedomfromhunger.org; **e-mail:** info@ freedomfromhunger.org.

Freeman Foundation

Established in 1994 by Houghton Freeman and other Freeman family members in memory of Mansfield Freeman.

Activities: Focuses on environmental protection, conservation of natural resources and promotion of international studies. The Foundation aims to deepen mutual appreciation and understanding of cultures, economies and histories, existing institutions and their purpose of establishment, between the USA and the East Asian countries; and supports projects that contribute to the development of an international free enterprise system. It runs an exchange programme, extends general support and provides funds.

Geographical Area of Activity: International.

Finance: Annual revenue US $25,871,506, expenditure $15,096,319 (31 Dec. 2013).

Principal Staff: Exec. Dir Graeme Freeman; Programme Dir Dr Jue-Fei Wang.

Address: c/o Rockefeller Trust Co, 10 Rockefeller Plaza, 3rd Floor, New York, NY 10020; 1601 East West Rd, Honolulu, HI 96848.

Telephone: (808) 944-7663; **Internet:** www.macalester.edu/ freemangrant/about_freeman.html.

French-American Foundation—FAF

Established in 1976 to enhance relations between France and the USA and to promote a mutual active dialogue.

Activities: Acts as a platform for leaders, policy-makers and professionals of France and the USA where problems of concern to both countries are put forward for discussion, opinions are shared on common issues, productive relationships are created between people of both nations, and attempts are made to bring about a change through mutual harmony. The Foundation devises various programmes that address cultural, business, social, political and educational issues through lectures, conferences, exchanges and study tours that are conducive to the adoption of innovative practices being implemented in both nations.

Geographical Area of Activity: USA and France.

Restrictions: No grants available.

Publications: Annual Report; project reports; newsletter.

Finance: Annual revenue US $1,366,947, expenditure $1,853,693 (31 Dec. 2012).

Board of Directors: Allan M. Chapin (Chair.); François Bujon de l'Estang, James G. Lowenstein (Vice-Chair.).

Principal Staff: Vice-Pres. and COO Dana Arifi.

Address: 28 West 44th St, Suite 1420, New York, NY 10036.

Telephone: (212) 829-8800; **Fax:** (212) 829-8810; **Internet:** www.frenchamerican.org; **e-mail:** info@frenchamerican.org.

Freshwater Society

Established in 2003.

Activities: A not-for-profit organization that promotes the protection and judicious use and management of fresh water resources. The Society focuses on the environment and conservation through educational programmes, research and demonstration projects to encourage protection of fresh water resources, and resource management. As part of fresh water resource protection, the Society restores and conserves such resources together with the surrounding watersheds. It also initiates programmes in surface water and groundwater stewardship activities, freshwater resource management, conducts conferences, carries out public education, and issues publications.

Geographical Area of Activity: Worldwide.

Publications: Annual Report; *Minnesota Weatherguide Environment Calendar*; *Guide to Lake Protection and Management*; *ANS Digest* (quarterly); *Facets of Freshwater* (newsletter).

Finance: Annual revenue US $980,626, expenditure $937,505 (30 June 2013).

Board of Directors: Stuart E. Grubb (Chair.); Rick Bateson (Vice-Chair.); Lisa Whalen (Sec.); Corrine D. Ricard (Treas.).

Principal Staff: Exec. Dir Steve Woods.

Address: 2500 Shadywood Rd, Excelsior, MN 55331.

Telephone: (952) 471-9773; **Fax:** (952) 471-7685; **Internet:** www.freshwater.org; **e-mail:** freshwater@freshwater.org.

Alfred Friendly Press Partners

Founded in 1983 by the late Alfred Friendly to promote a free press, and co-operation between the press and other institutions in the USA and abroad.

Activities: Provides work experience in the USA for foreign journalists through a fellowship programme. Applications are accepted from journalists from Eastern Europe and less-developed countries with an emerging free press. The Foundation awards the Alfred Friendly Press Fellowships for professional journalists to work for six months at US host news organizations.

Geographical Area of Activity: International.

Restrictions: Fellowship applicants must have an excellent command of English, at least three years' experience as a print journalist, a demonstrated commitment to journalism in his or her home country, and be currently employed as a journalist.

Publications: Newsletter.

Finance: Annual revenue US $199,731, expenditure $405,404 (2012).

Foundation Board: Jonathan Friendly (Chair.); Patrick J. Stueve (Treas.); Susan Talalay (Sec.).

Principal Staff: Pres. Randall D. Smith; Exec. Dir Kathleen Graham; Program Dir David Reed.

Address: 1100 Connecticut Ave NW, Suite 440, Washington, DC 20036.

Telephone: (202) 429-3740; **Fax:** (202) 429-3741; **Internet:** www.pressfellowships.org; **e-mail:** info@pressfellowships.org.

FXB International—Association François-Xavier Bagnoud

Established in 1989 in Switzerland to commemorate François-Xavier Bagnoud, a helicopter pilot who died at the age of 24 years, by his mother Countess Albina du Boisrouvray, members of her family and friends. Formerly known as the François-Xavier Bagnoud Foundation, it promotes social welfare and studies, education, and science and technology.

Activities: Carries out its activities on a national as well as an international level in the fields of science and technology, education, and health and welfare. Promotes efforts to alleviate poverty and HIV/AIDS; and supports orphans and vulnerable children, their families and communities. In 1992, the François-Xavier Bagnoud Center for Health and Human Rights was launched at Harvard University School of Public Health. The Association has financed a Chair in Aerospace Engineering at the University of Michigan College of Engineering, awards the François-Xavier Bagnoud Aerospace Prize (US $250,000), and also strives to defend children's rights, as well as health and human rights, and carries out some 100 projects supporting child HIV/AIDS victims and families subjected to social ostracism in 15 countries. FXB supports orphans and susceptible child victims of AIDS by voicing their concerns and extending direct assistance to communities and families who are involved in nurturing such victims. It carries out projects to support children exploited as prostitutes, soldiers or terrorists.

Geographical Area of Activity: International.

Restrictions: Grants are made only to pre-selected organizations, and no grants are made to individuals.

Publications: Annual Report; articles.

Finance: Annual revenue US $86,428, expenditure $484,045 (31 Dec. 2013).

Board: Khadija Rejto (Pres.); Jean-Louis Sarbib (Treas.).

Principal Staff: Pres. Albina du Boisrouvray; CEO (a.i.) Bilge Bassant.

Address: 115 W 30th Street, Suite 1103, New York, NY 10017.

Telephone: (212) 697-3566; **Fax:** (212) 697-2065; **Internet:** fxb.org/foundation; **e-mail:** info@fxb.org.

Bill & Melinda Gates Foundation

Established in 1994 by William (Bill) Gates and Melinda Gates to help improve the lives of people worldwide through health and learning; the Gates Learning Foundation (f. 1997 as the successor to the Microsoft/American Library Association) and the William H. Gates Foundation (f. 1994) were integrated into the Bill and Melinda Gates Foundation in 1999.

Activities: Works in the areas of medicine and health, education and community welfare, through three main projects: Global Health (especially projects in the areas of vaccine-preventable diseases, reproductive and child health, and conditions associated with poverty, including a US $100m. donation over 10 years to the Global Fund for AIDS and Health and the $1m. Gates Award for Global Health administered by the Global Health Council—q.v.), Global Development and the US Program. The Foundation established a scholarship programme in 2000, setting up the Gates Cambridge Trust, endowed with $210m., to enable gifted graduate students from any country outside the United Kingdom to study at the University of Cambridge. In 2002, the Foundation announced that more than $40m. was to be used to establish a network of small schools in the USA offering college courses; and in 2003 launched the Grand Challenges in Global Health initiative, in partnership with the National Institutes of Health (NIH), with a grant of $200m.

Geographical Area of Activity: International.

Restrictions: Currently not accepting grant applications for Global Libraries and Education initiatives.

Publications: Annual Report; newsletters.

Finance: Annual revenue US $4,927m., expenditure $4,235m. (31 Dec. 2013).

Board of Trustees: Bill Gates, Melinda Gates, William Gates, Sr (Co-Chair.); Keith Traverse (Sec.).

Principal Staff: CEO William H. Gates, III; CFO Richard Henriques.

Address: 500 Fifth Ave North Seattle, WA 98109; POB 23350, Seattle, WA 98102.

Telephone: (206) 709-3100; **Fax:** (206) 709-3180; **Internet:** www.gatesfoundation.org; **e-mail:** info@gatesfoundation.org.

GE Foundation

Founded in 1952 as the General Electric Foundation for the support of education in the USA. Present name adopted in 1994 following the merger of the General Electric Foundation and the General Electric Foundation, Inc.

Activities: Provides financial assistance in the fields of the environment, education and public policy. The Foundation focuses primarily on the field of education and provides financial assistance to institutions for general education; graduate research and teaching; minority group education; physical science, engineering, computer science, mathematics, industrial management and business administration education;

selected public schools; and arts and cultural centres. It also awards grants to other US organizations, incl. those concerned with international understanding and culture; and internationally to support higher education institutions and government-run schools and community organizations working to improve access to education for disadvantaged people, to raise educational achievement, to test innovative solutions and to implement best practices.

Geographical Area of Activity: International.

Restrictions: Unlikely to make grants to unsolicited projects.

Publications: Annual Report; archives.

Finance: Annual revenue US $133,429,041, expenditure $132,456,263 (2013).

Board of Directors: Susan Peters (Chair.); Michael J. Cosgrove (Treas.); Janine Rouson (Sec.).

Principal Staff: Pres. Deborah A. Elam.

Address: 3135 Easton Turnpike, Fairfield, CT 06431.

Telephone: (203) 373-3216; **Fax:** (203) 373-3029; **Internet:** www.gefoundation.com; **e-mail:** gefoundation@ge.com.

General Service Foundation

Founded in 1946 by Clifton R. Musser and Margaret Kulp Musser.

Activities: Makes grants to charitable organizations that operate in the fields of: international peace, particularly in Central America, Mexico and the Caribbean; reproductive health and rights in the USA and Mexico; and Western water, in the interior west of the USA.

Geographical Area of Activity: North and Central America and the Caribbean.

Restrictions: Grants are not made to individuals, for annual campaigns, capital expenditures or relief.

Finance: Annual revenue US $1,733,958, expenditure $3,764,874 (2013).

Board of Directors: Robin Snidow (Chair.); Zoe Estrin (Vice-Chair.); Marcie J. Musser (Sec.); Sara Samuels (Asst Sec.); Will Halby (Treas.).

Principal Staff: CFO and Asst Treas. William M. Repplinger.

Address: 557 North Mill St, Suite 201, Aspen, CO 81611.

Telephone: (970) 920-6834; **Fax:** (970) 920-4578; **Internet:** www.generalservice.org; **e-mail:** sara@generalservice.org.

German Marshall Fund of the United States—GMF

Created in 1972 by a gift from the German people as a permanent memorial to the Marshall Plan.

Activities: Promotes understanding and co-operation between the USA and Europe in the spirit of the post-war Marshall Plan. The Fund encourages the study of international and domestic policies, supports comparative research and debate on key issues, and assists policy and opinion leaders' understanding of these issues. It makes grants in the following areas: foreign policy; economics; the environment; civic participation and democratization; and immigration and integration. Projects must address issues important to European countries and the USA, and they must involve people or institutions on both sides of the Atlantic. The Fund has a particular interest in leadership development. It gives special attention to programmes that involve political, media and other professionals who have a strong interest in transatlantic relations and leadership potential. Projects normally include the transfer of experience and innovations, preferably involving practitioners and policy-makers. In 2003, the Fund launched the Balkan Trust for Democracy, in a funding partnership with the US Agency for International Development (USAID) and the Charles Stewart Mott Foundation (q.v.). Maintains offices in Ankara, Belgrade, Berlin, Bratislava, Brussels, Bucharest and Paris.

Geographical Area of Activity: USA and Europe.

Publications: Annual Report; special reports.

Finance: Annual revenue US $41,616,944, expenditure $37,633,741 (31 May 2013).

Board of Trustees: Dr Guido Goldman (Founder and Chair. Emeritus); J. Robinson West, Marc Leland (Co-Chair.).

Principal Staff: Pres. Karen Donfried; Exec. Vice-Pres. Barry Lowenkron.

Address: 1744 R St NW, Washington, DC 20009.

Telephone: (202) 683-2650; **Fax:** (202) 265-1662; **Internet:** www.gmfus.org; **e-mail:** info@gmfus.org.

J. Paul Getty Trust

Founded as a small museum in 1954 by J. Paul Getty (as the J. Paul Getty Museum). The Getty Center, a hilltop campus designed by Richard Meier, opened in 1997. The Getty Villa in Malibu, CA, the original location of the J. Paul Getty Museum, reopened in 2006 with a new mission as an educational centre and museum dedicated to the arts and cultures of ancient Greece, Rome and Etruria. In 1982 the Trustees sought to make a greater contribution to the visual arts through an expanded museum as well as a range of new programmes. The Getty Conservation Institute, the Getty Research Institute and the Grant Program were founded in the 1980s. The Grant Program became the Getty Foundation in 2005.

Activities: Operates through four programmes: the J. Paul Getty Museum (in two locations); the Getty Research Institute, which includes the Research Library; the Getty Conservation Institute, which advances conservation knowledge and practice worldwide; and the Getty Foundation, which provides grants to further the understanding and preservation of the visual arts throughout the world.

Geographical Area of Activity: International.

Publications: Annual Report; numerous museum and conservation publications through Getty Publications.

Finance: Annual revenue $469,390,127, expenditure $281,926,505 (30 June 2013).

Board of Trustees: Mark S. Siegel (Chair.); Neil L. Rudenstine (Vice-Chair.); Stephen W. Clark (Sec.); James M. Williams (Treas.).

Principal Staff: Pres. and CEO James Cuno; Dir Deborah Marrow; Deputy Dir Joan Weinstein.

Address: 1200 Getty Center Dr., Los Angeles, CA 90049-1679.

Telephone: (310) 440-7320; **Fax:** (310) 440-7703; **Internet:** www.getty.edu/foundation; **e-mail:** GettyFoundation@getty.edu.

Howard Gilman Foundation, Inc

Established in 1981 by the Gilman Paper and Investment Corporation to nurture and conserve a vibrant natural and cultural environment.

Activities: Operates in the fields of the arts and humanities, conservation and the environment, and medicine and health, through research, offering grants to institutions, and conferences.

Geographical Area of Activity: USA and the countries of the former USSR.

Restrictions: No grants are made to individuals.

Publications: Application guidelines.

Finance: Annual revenue US $4,085,304, expenditure $6,814,141 (31 Dec. 2012).

Board of Directors: Mary C. Farrell (Pres.); Daniel L. Kurz (Sec.); Marvin S. Rosen (Treas.).

Principal Staff: Exec. Dir Laura Aden Packer.

Address: 1 Rockefeller Plaza, Suite 1701, New York, NY 10020.

Telephone: (212) 408-0400; **Internet:** www.gilmanfoundation.org; **e-mail:** info@howardgilmanfoundation.org.

Giving USA Foundation

Founded in 1985 by the American Association of Fund-Raising Counsel as the AAFRC Trust for Philanthropy.

Activities: Aims to increase public awareness and understanding of philanthropy through conducting programmes; funds and commissions research into philanthropy; and promotes projects set up by other similar organizations. The Foundation develops and conducts college courses on philanthropy in conjunction with the American Association of Colleges; and sponsors the John Grenzebach awards for outstanding research in the field. Co-ordinates Giving USA, an annual analysis of all sources of philanthropic funding in the USA.

Geographical Area of Activity: USA.

Publications: *Giving USA* (annually); *Giving USA Update* (irregular); newsletters (quarterly).

Finance: Annual revenue US $129,858, expenditure $166,017 (31 July 2013).

Board of Directors: David H. King (Chair.); Jeffrey D. Byrne, Rachel Hutchisson (Vice-Chair.); Derek Alley (Sec.); Sarah J. Howard (Treas.); Thomas W. Mesaros (Past Chair.).

Principal Staff: Exec. Dir Erin Berggren.

Address: 225 West Wacker Dr., Suite 2650, Chicago, IL 60606.

Telephone: (312) 981-6794; **Fax:** (312) 265-2911; **Internet:** www.givinginstitute.org; **e-mail:** info@givinginstitute.org.

Elizabeth Glaser Pediatric AIDS Foundation

Founded in 1988 to support paediatric AIDS research.

Activities: Aims to eradicate paediatric AIDS. The Foundation provides care and treatment for people with HIV/AIDS and aims to accelerate the discovery of new treatments for other serious and life-threatening paediatric illnesses. It advocates for public policies that support children's health in the USA and worldwide, funds research and makes awards.

Geographical Area of Activity: Worldwide.

Publications: Annual Reports.

Finance: Annual revenue US $119,164,859, expenditure $121,432,406 (31 Dec. 2013).

Board of Directors: Paul Glaser (Hon. Chair.); Russ Hagey (Chair.); Annie Hill (Sec.).

Principal Staff: Pres. and CEO Charles Lyons; COO Brad Kiley.

Address: 1140 Connecticut Ave NW, Suite 200, Washington, DC 20036.

Telephone: (202) 296-9165; **Fax:** (202) 296-9185; **Internet:** www.pedaids.org; **e-mail:** info@pedaids.org.

Global Alliance for Women's Health—GAWH

Established in 1994 for the advancement of women's health worldwide.

Activities: Works in co-operation with national and international NGOs, women's groups and other organizations to advance women's health in all areas of the world. The Alliance promotes the implementation of improvements to health care services and research into women's health. It distributes women's health care information and organizes health conferences and symposia on a variety of health policy issues.

Geographical Area of Activity: International.

Publications: Annual Report; newsletter; reports; seminar proceedings.

Finance: Annual revenue US $24,000, expenditure $12,527 (31 Dec. 2012).

Executive Board: Dr Elaine M. Wolfson (Founding Pres.); Fantaye Mekbeb (Vice-Pres.); Kenneth L. Brown (Treas.).

Address: 777 United Nations Plaza, 7th Floor, New York, NY 10017.

Telephone: (212) 286-0424; **Fax:** (212) 286-9561; **Internet:** www.gawh.org; **e-mail:** wolfson@gawh.org.

Global Fund for Women—GFW

Founded in 1987 by Anne Firth Murray to promote the growth of women's groups and links between groups worldwide.

Activities: Operates in the fields of economic affairs, education, human rights, medicine and health, and social welfare and studies, by assisting grassroots women's organizations outside the USA. Maintains an office in New York.

Geographical Area of Activity: International.

Restrictions: Operates internationally, but does not support individuals or groups based in the USA.

Publications: *Raising Our Voices* (newsletter); *Women's Fundraising Handbook*; *Caught in the Storm: The Impact of Natural Disasters; What Girls Need to Grow: Lessons for Social Change Philanthropy; More Than Money: Strategies to Build Women's Economic Power;* Annual Report; information brochure.

Finance: Annual revenue US $16,779,184, expenditure $16,579,005 (30 June 2014).

Board of Directors: Leila Hessini (Chair.); Marissa Wesely (Treas.); Linda Gruber (Sec.).

Principal Staff: Pres. and CEO Dr Musimbi Kanyoro; CFO Elizabeth Schaffer.

Address: 222 Sutter St, Suite 500, San Francisco, CA 94108.

Telephone: (415) 248-4800; **Fax:** (415) 248-4801; **Internet:** www.globalfundforwomen.org; **e-mail:** info@globalfundforwomen.org.

Global Greengrants Fund

Established in 1993.

Activities: Aims to protect the global environment by strengthening grassroots movements in developing countries working on environmental sustainability and human rights issues. The Fund awards small grants, typically ranging from US $500 to $5,000, throughout the world to grassroots NGOs working for environmental and social justice causes.

Geographical Area of Activity: International, working in over 120 countries worldwide.

Restrictions: No unsolicited proposals accepted.

Publications: Annual Report; feature pieces on sustainability, energy, water, indigenous peoples and women; e-newsletter.

Finance: Annual revenue US $9,765,964, expenditure $8,740,910 (2014).

Board of Directors: Nnimmo Bassey (Chair.); Mele Lau Smith (Former Chair.); Maxine A. Burkett (Vice-Chair.); Jake Beinecke (Sec.); Larry Kressley (Treas.).

Principal Staff: Exec. Dir and CEO Terry Odendahl.

Address: 2840 Wilderness Pl., Suite A, Boulder, CO 80301.

Telephone: (303) 939-9866; **Fax:** (303) 939-9867; **Internet:** www.greengrants.org; **e-mail:** info@greengrants.org.

Global Health Council

Established in 1972, as the National Council for International Health; a membership organization of individuals, organizations and communities working in the field of health internationally. Present name adopted in 1999.

Activities: Operates in the field of health and works in collaboration with local partner organizations. The Council's main areas of activity are HIV/AIDS (the Global AIDS Program), reproductive and maternal health, infectious diseases, child health and nutrition, disaster and refugee health, and health systems. Holds an annual conference to promote human development. Administers the Gates Award for Global Health, funded by the Bill & Melinda Gates Foundation (q.v.); and the Jonathan Mann Award for Global Health and Human Rights in partnership with Doctors of the World and FXB International (q.v.); as well as making other awards that recognize excellence in global health issues.

Geographical Area of Activity: International.

Restrictions: Not a funding organization.

Publications: *Global Health Magazine.*

Finance: Annual revenue US $336,900, expenditure $431,308 (31 Dec. 2013).

Board of Directors: Dr Jonathan Quick (Chair.).

Principal Staff: Exec. Dir Dr Christine Sow.

Address: Main office: 1875 Connecticut Ave, NW, 10th Floor, Washington, DC 20009; Mailing: 1199 N. Fairfax St, Suite 300, Alexandria, VA 22314.

Telephone: (703) 717-5200; **Fax:** (703) 717-5215; **Internet:** www.globalhealth.org; **e-mail:** membership@globalhealth.org.

Global Impact

Established in 1956.

Activities: Builds partnerships and raises resources by providing integrated, partner-specific advisory and secretariat services; campaign design, marketing and implementation for workplace and signature fund-raising campaigns; fiscal agency, technology services and integrated giving platforms; revenue diversification strategies; employee engagement programmes; corporate social responsibility strategies; and custom philanthropic funds. The organization works with around 450 public- and private-sector workplace giving campaigns to generate funding for an alliance of more than 120 international charities; and supports programmes on clean water, disaster relief and resiliency, economic development, education, environmental sustainability, global health and child survival, human trafficking, hunger, and women and girls. It serves as the secretariat of the Global Health Council, the Hilton Humanitarian Prize Laureates Collaborative and the Central America Donors Forum; and also as administrator for one of the world's largest workplace giving campaigns, the Combined Federal Campaign-Overseas.

Geographical Area of Activity: International.

Publications: Annual Report; *The Corporate Signature Program: A Custom Approach*.

Finance: Annual revenue US $16,722,539, expenditure $16,534,781 (30 June 2014).

Board of Directors: Steve Polo (Chair.); Nancy A. Kelly (Vice-Chair.); James B. Kanuch (Sec. and Treas.).

Principal Staff: Pres. and CEO Scott Jackson.

Address: 1199 N Fairfax St, Suite 300, Alexandria, VA 22314.

Telephone: (703) 717-5200; **Fax:** (703) 717-5215; **Internet:** www.charity.org; **e-mail:** mail@charity.org.

Global Links

Established in 1989 to assist health-care institutions in developing countries regardless of nationality, or religious or political affiliation.

Activities: Collects donations of a wide variety of surplus medical supplies, including equipment, instruments, sutures, and other supplies and hospital furnishings from the USA and distributes them to health care facilities in underserved communities to improve the medical care. Donations are currently sent to institutions in Bolivia, Cuba, the Dominican Republic, Guatemala, Guyana, Haiti, Honduras, Jamaica and Nicaragua, although sutures are donated throughout the world and some donations are for organizations serving resource-poor communities in Western Pennsylvania.

Geographical Area of Activity: Mainly Central and South America and the Caribbean.

Publications: Annual Report; *Global Links News* (newsletter).

Finance: Annual revenue US $6,303,377, expenditure $4,172,111 (31 Dec. 2013).

Board of Directors: Jeffrey Ford (Chair.); Charles Vargo (Vice-Chair.); Steve Frank (Treas.); Rev. Eugene F. Lauer (Sec.).

Principal Staff: CEO Kathleen Hower; Dep. Dir Angela Garcia.

Address: 700 Trumbull Dr., Pittsburgh, PA 15205.

Telephone: (412) 361-3424; **Fax:** (412) 875-6150; **Internet:** www.globallinks.org; **e-mail:** info@globallinks.org.

The Goldman Sachs Foundation

Established in 1999 by the Goldman Sachs banking and securites firm to assist in the creation of partnerships in the public, private and non-profit sectors to promote innovation and excellence in education and youth development throughout the world. Formerly known as the Goldman Sachs Charitable Fund.

Activities: Operates nationally and internationally, supporting projects in the field of education through promoting partnerships between the public, private and non-profit sectors. The Foundation helps large projects that enhance academic outcomes and offer educational opportunities in the field of business and entrepreneurship. Major programme areas are Developing High Potential Youth, Promoting Entrepreneurship and Leadership, and Advancing Academic Achievement.

Geographical Area of Activity: International.

Publications: Annual Report; *Highlights of the Portfolio*; *Ideas into Action*.

Finance: Annual revenue US $40,661,682, expenditure $42,328,801 (2013).

Board of Directors: Dina H. Powell (Pres.); Emmett C. St John (Treas.); Beverly L O'Toole (Sec.); Benjamin J. Rader (Gen. Counsel).

Address: 200 West St, 29th Floor, New York, NY 10282.

Telephone: (212) 902-4223; **Internet:** www.goldmansachs.com/foundation.

Horace W. Goldsmith Foundation

Founded in 1955 by Horace W. Goldsmith.

Activities: Provides support for cultural activities, Jewish welfare funds and temple support, hospitals (particularly for the elderly) and education (especially higher education).

Geographical Area of Activity: USA and Israel.

Restrictions: No grants are made to individuals.

Finance: Annual revenue US $30,810,763, expenditure $25,114,152 (2012).

Principal Staff: CEO William A. Slaughter; Man. Dir (Operations) Thomas R. Slaughter; Man. Dir (Finance) Charles L. Slaughter; Sec. R. James Slaughter.

Address: 375 Park Ave, Suite 1602, New York, NY 10152-1600.

Telephone: (212) 319-8700.

Good360

Established in 1984, as Gifts in Kind International, to promote the donation of products from the private and commercial sectors to charitable causes around the world. Present name adopted in 2011.

Activities: A global network that co-ordinates and distributes donated products from the private sector, providing quality services and goods for poorer communities in different countries. These donations include computers for education, clothing for the homeless, products for disaster relief and construction materials for the rehabilitation of residential areas.

Geographical Area of Activity: International.

Publications: Annual Report; newsletter.

Finance: Annual revenue US $310,014,786, expenditure $322,701,484 (31 Dec. 2013).

Board of Directors: Carly Fiorina (Chair.); Mikel Durham (Vice-Chair.).

Principal Staff: Pres. and CEO Cindy Hallberlin.

Address: 1330 Braddock Pl., Suite 600, Alexandria, VA 22314.

Telephone: (703) 836-2121; **Fax:** (703) 798-3192; **Internet:** www.good360.org; **e-mail:** serviceteam@good360.org.

Goodwill Industries International, Inc

Established in 1902 by Rev. Edgar Helms to assist in training and finding jobs for people who would otherwise have difficulty in finding employment.

Activities: Aims to ensure that all people have the opportunity to achieve their fullest potential as individuals and to participate and contribute fully in all aspects of a productive life. The organization operates internationally, running employment and training programmes to increase the self-sufficiency of people with barriers to work, such as people with disabilities, and illiterate or homeless people. It seeks to create opportunities for vocational training and employment through its network of 165 autonomous, community-based agencies in the USA and Canada, and by creating alliances with other NGOs, foundations and companies. Affiliated with 14 organizations in countries around the world. Runs a chain of more than 1,900 Goodwill charity shops in the USA and Canada to raise funds. Goodwill Global, with an office in Washington, DC, seeks to foster the organization's entrepreneurial efforts outside the USA and Canada.

Geographical Area of Activity: International.

Publications: *Working!* (quarterly magazine); Annual Report.

Finance: Annual revenue US $46,058,697, expenditure $43,065,887 (31 Dec. 2013).

Board of Directors: Dr A. Gidget Hopf (Chair.); Larry Ishol (Vice-Chair.); Michelle Belknap (Treas.); Belinda Gumbs (Sec.).

Principal Staff: Pres. and CEO Jim Gibbons.

Address: 15810 Indianola Dr., Rockville, MD 20855.

Telephone: (301) 530-6500; **Fax:** (301) 530-1516; **Internet:** www.goodwill.org; **e-mail:** contactus@goodwill.org.

Google.org

Established in 2005.

Activities: Uses information and technology to build products and advocate for policies that address global challenges. Programmes include empowering women and girls; combatting human trafficking and child abuse; protecting wildlife; and advancing computer science education. Manages the Google Foundation.

Geographical Area of Activity: Worldwide.

Finance: Annual revenue US $30,393,596, expenditure $14,208,388 (2013).

Board of Directors: Matthew Stepka (Pres.).

Address: 1600 Amphitheatre Parkway, Mountain View, CA 94043-1351.

Telephone: (650) 253-0000; **Internet:** www.google.org; **e-mail:** press@google.com.

The Adolph and Esther Gottlieb Foundation, Inc

Founded in 1976 to assist artists in financial need.

Activities: Conducts two grant programmes to assist painters, sculptors and printmakers in a mature phase of their art who are in current financial need: the Emergency Assistance Programme available throughout the year; and the Individual Support Grant awarded on an annual basis.

Geographical Area of Activity: USA.

Restrictions: No grants to organizations, students, educational institutions, to those working in crafts, graphic artists or for projects.

Finance: Annual revenue US $824,622, expenditure $1,244,487 (30 June 2013).

Board of Directors: Sanford Hirsch (Exec. Dir, Sec. and Treas.).

Principal Staff: Pres. Robert Mangold; Vice-Pres Gordon Marsh, Charlotta Kotik.

Address: 380 West Broadway, New York, NY 10012-5115.

Telephone: (212) 226-0581; **Fax:** (212) 226-0584; **Internet:** www.gottliebfoundation.org; **e-mail:** sross@gottliebfoundation.org.

Florence Gould Foundation

Founded in 1957 by Florence J. Gould to promote good relations between France and the USA, and for general charitable purposes.

Activities: Offers fellowships for research to be carried out in France, and a translation prize.

Geographical Area of Activity: USA and France.

Finance: Annual revenue US $5,627,760, expenditure $8,382,762 (2013).

Board of Directors: John R. Young (Pres.); Walter C. Cliff (Vice-Pres., Sec. and Asst Treas.).

Address: c/o Cahill, Gordon & Reindel LLP, 80 Pine St, Suite 1548, New York, NY 10005-1702.

Telephone: (212) 701-3400.

Graham Foundation for Advanced Studies in the Fine Arts

Founded in 1956.

Activities: Produces public programmes to foster the development and exchange of diverse and challenging ideas about architecture and its role in the arts, culture and society. The Foundation supports investigations into architecture; architectural history, theory and criticism; design; engineering; landscape architecture; urban planning; urban studies; visual arts; and related fields of inquiry. Its interest also extends to work being done in the fine arts, humanities and sciences that expands the boundaries of thinking about architecture and space. Its grantmaking focuses on the public dissemination of ideas and supports individuals and organizations.

Geographical Area of Activity: USA, international.

Finance: Annual revenue US $1,115,295, expenditure $2,599,250 (31 Aug. 2012).

Board of Trustees: Ross Wimer (Pres.); Chandra Goldsmith Gray (Vice-Pres.); Rena Conti (Treas.); Sean Keller (Sec.).

Principal Staff: Dir Sarah Herda.

Address: Madlener House, 4 West Burton Pl., Chicago, IL 60610-1416.

Telephone: (312) 787-4071; **Internet:** www.grahamfoundation.org; **e-mail:** info@grahamfoundation.org.

Grameen Foundation—GF

Founded in 1997 by a group of friends who were inspired by the work of Grameen Bank in Bangladesh, with the aim of combating poverty in the USA and worldwide.

Activities: Grew from the Grameen Bank, offering small amounts of credit, and has now become a worldwide movement. The Foundation supports the Grameen Bank in its anti-poverty programmes, which include support for micro-credit institutions; projects in the areas of education and technical assistance; establishing joint ventures with the private sector; marketing products produced by small enterprises; and educating the public and government in the USA about poverty and its alleviation through micro-credit. Established the Grameen Technology Center in Bangladesh.

Geographical Area of Activity: Middle East and North Africa, Sub-Saharan Africa, Latin America and the Caribbean, USA, East Asia, South Asia.

Publications: Papers; *Village Computing: A State of the Field, Reflections on the Village Computing Consultation*; *Measuring the Impact of Microfinance*; *Thinking About Microfinance Through a Commercial Lens*; *Banker to the Poor: Microlending and the Battle Against World Poverty*; *More Pathways Out of Poverty*; Annual Report; books.

Finance: Annual revenue US $20,100,040, expenditure $22,390,842 (31 March 2014).

Board of Directors: Robert Eichfeld (Chair.); Peter Cowhey, Ricki Tigert Helfer (Vice-Chair.); Si White (Treas.).

Principal Staff: Pres. and CEO Alex Counts.

Address: 1101 15th St NW, 3rd Floor, Washington, DC 20005.

Telephone: (202) 628-3560; **Fax:** (202) 628-3880; **Internet:** www.grameenfoundation.org; **e-mail:** development@grameenfoundation.org.

William T. Grant Foundation

Founded in 1936 by William T. Grant to promote the research capacity of promising scholars who investigate the understanding and promotion of the well-being and healthy development of children and adolescents, and generally to help young people reach their full potential.

Activities: Aims to create a society that values young people and enables them to reach their full potential. The Foundation pursues this goal by investing in research and in people and projects that use evidence-based approaches. Supports research on how contexts such as families, programmes and policies affect young people; how these contexts can be improved; and how scientific evidence affects influential adults. Funded research outside the USA must clearly address an issue or question affecting a large number of young people aged 8 to 25 years in the USA or a particularly vulnerable sub-group of US young people.

Geographical Area of Activity: Mainly USA.

Restrictions: Funded to a limited number of communications activities.

Publications: Annual Report; brochures.

Finance: Annual revenue US $26,925,210, expenditure $17,481,122 (31 Dec. 2013).

Board of Trustees: Henry E. Gooss (Chair.).

Principal Staff: Pres. Adam Gamoran.

Address: 570 Lexington Ave, 18th Floor, New York, NY 10022-6837.

Telephone: (212) 752-0071; **Fax:** (212) 752-1398; **Internet:** www.wtgrantfoundation.org; **e-mail:** info@wtgrantfdn.org.

The Grass Foundation

Founded in 1955 by Albert and Ellen Grass to support research and education in neuroscience.

Activities: Operates in the fields of medicine and science through a fellowship programme offering summer fellowships for young researchers conducting independent research at the Marine Biological Laboratory, Woods Hole, MA. The Foundation also supports several courses in neuroscience, provides annual funding of lectureships, awards prizes and organizes annual lectures.

Geographical Area of Activity: USA.

Restrictions: Applicants from overseas are eligible for fellowships, but work must be carried out at a North American institution. No support for ongoing research, full-time students, symposia or conferences.

Publications: Application guidelines; programme policy statement; information brochure.

Finance: Annual revenue US $2,838,970, expenditure $1,207,949 (31 Dec. 2013).

Board of Trustees: Dr Felix Schweizer (Pres.); Dr Bernice Grafstein (Vice-Pres.).

Address: POB 241458, Los Angeles, CA 90024.

Telephone: (424) 832-4188; **Fax:** (310) 986-2252; **Internet:** www.grassfoundation.org; **e-mail:** info@grassfoundation.org.

Grassroots International—GRI

GRI was set up in 1983 as an autonomous, not-for-profit agency to attain positive social transformation.

Activities: Active in the fields of social welfare and human rights in partnership with organizations in Latin America, Asia, Africa, the Caribbean and the Middle East. GRI supports community development works by providing grants through partner NGOs to bring about a positive social change; carries out advocacy and educational activities on behalf of its partner organizations; and directs world attention to issues of power, social change and poverty through media.

Geographical Area of Activity: Africa (Horn), Asia, Middle East, Latin America and the Caribbean.

Restrictions: Grants are only made to specific organizations in specific regions.

Publications: *Insights* (newsletter); *GrassrootsONLINE*; fact sheets; reports and summaries; Annual Report.

Finance: Annual revenue US $2,552,644, expenditure $2,604,386 (31 Oct. 2013).

Board of Directors: Soya Jung (Chair.); David Holmstrom (Treas.); Anil Naidoo (Sec.).

Principal Staff: Exec. Dir Chung-Wha Hong.

Address: 179 Boylston St, 4th Floor, Boston, MA 02130.

Telephone: (617) 524-1400; **Fax:** (617) 524-5525; **Internet:** www.grassrootsonline.org; **e-mail:** info@grassrootsonline.org.

Greater Kansas City Community Foundation

Established in 1978.

Activities: Aims to improve the quality of life in Greater Kansas City. The Foundation administers more than 3,300 charitable funds. Regional affiliates include the Black Community Fund, Catholic Community Foundation, Eastland Community Foundation, Hispanic Development Fund, Community Foundation of Johnson County, Northland Community Foundation and Community Foundation of Wyandotte County. Maintains a database of more than 600 non-profit organizations.

Geographical Area of Activity: Greater Kansas City.

Finance: Annual revenue US $334,669,972, expenditure $159,909,166 (31 Dec. 2012).

Board of Directors: Robert D. Regnier (Chair.); Dr Jim Hinson (Vice-Chair.); William S. Berkley (Past Chair.); Deryl W. Wynn (Sec.); Jeannine Strandjord (Treas.).

Principal Staff: Pres. and CEO Debbie Wilkerson.

Address: 1055 Broadway, Ste 130, Kansas City, MO 64105.

Telephone: (816) 842-0944; **Fax:** (816) 842-8079; **Internet:** www.gkccf.org; www.growyourgiving.org; **e-mail:** info@growyourgiving.org.

William and Mary Greve Foundation, Inc

Founded in 1964 by Mary P. Greve.

Activities: Operates in the fields of education, international relations, especially between the USA and Eastern Europe, the environment and the performing arts, through grants to organizations.

Geographical Area of Activity: USA.

Restrictions: Does not generally accept unsolicited applications for grants. No grants are made to individuals, nor for scholarships or fellowships.

Finance: Annual revenue US $1,997,817, expenditure $2,666,524 (2012).

Board of Directors: John W. Kiser, III (Chair.); Jennifer Franklin (Sec.).

Principal Staff: Pres. Anthony C. M. Kiser.

Address: 665 Broadway, Suite 1001, New York, NY 10112.

Telephone: (212) 307-7850; **Internet:** wmgreve.org.

Solomon R. Guggenheim Foundation

Established in 1937 for the collection and preservation of, and research into, modern and contemporary art.

Activities: Funds the Solomon R. Guggenheim Museum, New York; the Peggy Guggenheim Collection, Venice, Italy; the Guggenheim Museum Bilbao, Spain; and the Guggenheim Abu Dhabi, United Arab Emirates. The Foundation also supports international partnerships and the development of new museums in other regions of the world, special exhibitions, conservation efforts, educational initiatives and research.

Geographical Area of Activity: International.

Finance: Annual revenue US $77,901,649, expenditure $75,582,888 (31 Dec. 2013).

Trustees: William L. Mack (Chair.); Jennifer Blei Stockman (Pres.); John Calicchio, Wendy L.-J. McNeil, Edward H. Meyer, Denise Saul (Vice-Pres); Robert C. Baker (Treas.); Edward F. Rover (Sec.); Sara G. Austrian (Asst Sec.).

Principal Staff: Dir Richard Armstrong; Sr Deputy Dir and COO Marc Steglitz.

Address: Solomon R. Guggenheim Museum, 1071 Fifth Ave (at 89th St), New York, NY 10128-0173.

Telephone: (212) 423-3500; **Internet:** www.guggenheim.org/guggenheim-foundation; **e-mail:** visitorinfo@guggenheim.org.

The Harry Frank Guggenheim Foundation

Founded in 1929 by Harry Frank Guggenheim to study and research'Man's Relation to Man', the Foundation supports specific and innovative projects that seek to promote understanding of human social problems related to violence, aggression and dominance.

Activities: Operates nationally and internationally in the field of science, through research and grants to individuals for research; also makes awards for support during the writing of doctoral theses. Grants are available for holders of a doctorate or professional equivalent, and for doctoral candidates for the writing of their dissertation. Support is given mainly for basic research in the social, behavioural and biological sciences.

Geographical Area of Activity: International.

Restrictions: No grants to institutions, nor for programmes.

Publications: *HFG Review of Research;* Annual Report; research reports.

Finance: Annual revenue US $5,042,905, expenditure $4,472,219 (2013).

Board of Trustees: Peter Lawson-Johnston (Chair.); Deirdre Hamill (Treas.).

Principal Staff: Pres. Josiah Bunting, III.

Address: 25 W 53rd St, 16th Floor, New York, NY 10019-5401.

Telephone: (646) 428-0971; **Fax:** (646) 428-0981; **Internet:** www.hfg.org; **e-mail:** info@hfg.org.

John Simon Guggenheim Memorial Foundation

Founded in 1925 by Senator and Mrs Simon Guggenheim to improve the quality of education and the practice of the arts and professions; to foster research; and to provide for the cause of better international understanding.

Activities: Operates nationally and internationally in all fields of science, the humanities and the creative arts, through fellowships and grants to individuals who have demonstrated exceptional capacity for productive scholarship or exceptional creative ability in the arts. Fellowships are open to all citizens and permanent residents of the USA, Canada, and Central and South America and the Caribbean.

Geographical Area of Activity: North, Central and South America and the Caribbean.

Restrictions: No grants to organizations or institutions, only to individuals. No grants for the performing arts.

Publications: Annual Report; brochures.

Finance: Annual revenue US $13,266,751, expenditure $11,187,724 (31 Dec. 2013).

Board of Trustees: William P. Kelly (Chair.).

Principal Staff: Pres. Edward Hirsch.

Address: 90 Park Ave, New York, NY 10016.

Telephone: (212) 687-4470; **Fax:** (212) 697-3248; **Internet:** www.gf.org; **e-mail:** fellowships@gf.org.

Habitat for Humanity International

Founded in 1976 by Millard and Linda Fuller to provide affordable homes for families in need by building and rehabilitating simple housing.

Activities: Operates in the USA and less-developed countries in the field of social welfare, in particular housing, by providing volunteers to work alongside those in need of shelter to build adequate basic houses. Homes are then sold to families at no profit or interest. The organization also promotes sustainable building, providing education and training to local affiliates, and conducts programmes in more than 90 countries. Regional headquarters for Europe and Central Asia are located in Bratislava, Slovakia.

Geographical Area of Activity: International.

Publications: *Habitat World Magazine*; Annual Report.

Finance: Annual revenue US $268,201,897, expenditure $256,437,490 (30 June 2014).

Board of Directors: Renee Glover (Chair.); Henry Cisneros, Alex Silva (Vice-Chair.); Bradford L. Hewitt (Sec.); Joe Price (Treas.).

Principal Staff: CEO Jonathan Reckford.

Address: 121 Habitat St, Americus, GA 31709.

Telephone: (229) 924-6935; **Fax:** (229) 924-6541; **Internet:** www.habitat.org; **e-mail:** publicinfo@habitat.org.

The John A. Hartford Foundation

Founded in 1929 for general charitable purposes.

Activities: Operates two programmes in the field of Ageing and Health: the Academic Geriatrics and Training Initiative and the Integrating and Improving Services Initiative. The Foundation provides grants to US organizations aiming to improve the efficacy and affordability of health care for the increasingly ageing population in the USA.

Geographical Area of Activity: USA.

Restrictions: No grants are made directly to individuals.

Publications: Annual Report; E-newsletter; articles include *Decades of Focus: Grant Making at the John A. Hartford Foundation*; *Strategies to Advance Geriatric Nursing: The John A. Hartford Foundation Initiatives*; *The John A. Hartford Geriatric Social Work Initiatives*; *Views from Funding Agencies: The John A. Hartford Foundation*; *Foundation Funding for Geriatric Training*.

Finance: Annual revenue US $44,712,351, expenditure $23,615,867 (31 Dec. 2013).

Board of Trustees: Norman H. Volk (Chair.); Barbara Paul Robinson (Vice-Chair. and Sec.).

Principal Staff: Pres. Corinne H. Rieder.

Address: 55 E 59th St, 16th Floor, New York, NY 10022-1713.

Telephone: (212) 832-7788; **Fax:** (212) 593-4913; **Internet:** www.jhartfound.org; **e-mail:** mail@jhartfound.com.

Hasbro Children's Fund, Inc

Established in 2006 by Hasbro, Inc to improve quality of life for disadvantaged children aged 12 years and under, their families and communities in the USA. The Fund includes giving formerly carried out by the Hasbro Children's Foundation (f. 1984) and the Hasbro Charitable Trust.

Activities: Supports programmes in the USA and worldwide that assist disadvantaged and seriously ill children, and work in the areas of children's education and social welfare.

Geographical Area of Activity: USA and international.

Restrictions: No grants are made to individuals, to religious or political organizations, or to schools.

Publications: Annual Report.

Finance: Annual revenue US $1,661,060, expenditure $3,344,944 (30 Dec. 2013).

Board of Directors: Barbara Finigan (Sec.); Deborah Thomas (Treas.).

Principal Staff: Pres. Karen Davis.

Address: 1027 Newport Ave, Pawtucket, RI 02862.

Telephone: (401) 727-5429; **Fax:** (401) 727-5089; **Internet:** www.hasbro.com/corporate/community-relations/about.cfm; **e-mail:** hcfinfo@hasbro.com.

Health Alliance International—HAI

Established in 1987 as the Mozambique Health Committee; name changed in 1993 to reflect the expanding reach of its activities.

Activities: Aims to improve the health and welfare of those in need around the world; and to educate North Americans about social, economic and political issues that affect those in Southern Africa. The Alliance operates in the field of health care internationally in collaboration with local organizations. It works to identify economic, social and political factors that cause poor health care for marginalized peoples, and to raise public awareness of these matters; provides direct technical and material assistance in support of basic health services; engages in research and training in public health care in the USA and abroad (incl. parts of Sub-Saharan Africa, Central and South America, the Caribbean, Asia and the Middle East); and supports graduate training in public health at the University of Washington. Also tries to ensure the equal distribution and efficient delivery of quality health care worldwide and seeks to support policies that promote health, equality, social justice and self-sufficiency. Has offices in Côte d'Ivoire, Mozambique and Timor-Leste.

Geographical Area of Activity: International.

Publications: *Sickness and Wealth—The Corporate Assault on Global Health*; books; editorials; lectures; papers; presentations; newsletters (quarterly); Annual Report.

Finance: Annual revenue US $8,496,099, expenditure $8,407,690 (31 Dec. 2013).

Board of Directors: Jo Anne Myers-Ciecko (Pres.); Paul Thottingal (Vice-Pres.); Julie West (Sec.); Terri Kitto (Treas.).

Principal Staff: Exec. Dir Dr James Pfeiffer; Deputy Dir Mara Child.

Address: 4534 11th Ave NE, Seattle, WA 98105.

Telephone: (206) 543-8382; **Fax:** (206) 685-4184; **Internet:** www.healthallianceinternational.org; **e-mail:** info@ healthallianceinternational.org.

Health Volunteers Overseas—HVO

Established in 1986 as a private non-profit organization to improve health care in developing countries through training and education.

Activities: Operates in the fields of health care and international development, working to improve the accessibility and quality of health care in developing countries in a number of ways. Volunteer professionals train local people in pathologies and medical problems they might encounter in their area, providing a self-sustaining, long-term medical presence in underdeveloped areas using local available supplies and equipment. Programmes specialize in child health, primary care, trauma and rehabilitation, essential surgical care, nursing education, oral health, blood disorders and cancer, infectious disease and wound management.

Geographical Area of Activity: Africa, Central and South America, Asia.

Restrictions: Not a grantmaking organization.

Publications: *The HVO Guide to Volunteering Overseas*; *The Volunteer Connection* (newsletter, biannual); The Net Connection (monthly e-newsletter); Annual Report.

Finance: Annual revenue US $2,749,182, expenditure $2,686,877 (2013).

Board of Directors: Richard Fisher (Chair.).

Principal Staff: Exec. Dir Nancy A. Kelly.

Address: 1900 L St NW, Suite 310, Washington, DC 20036.

Telephone: (202) 296-0928; **Fax:** (202) 296-8018; **Internet:** www.hvousa.org; **e-mail:** info@hvousa.org.

The Hearst Foundation, Inc

Founded in 1945 by William Randolph Hearst to support general charitable purposes in the USA. Shares administration with The William Randolph Hearst Foundation (q.v.).

Activities: Supports programmes in the USA and its overseas dependencies in the fields of higher and private secondary education, health care, social welfare, and culture, through the provision of funds. Maintains an office in San Francisco, CA.

Geographical Area of Activity: USA and its dependencies.

Restrictions: Grants are not made to individuals.

Finance: Annual revenue US $31,883,198, expenditure $16,846,482 (2013).

Board of Directors: Virginia H. Randt (Pres.); James M. Asher (Sec.); Catherine A. Bostron, Eve B. Burton (Asst Secs); Ralph Cuomo (Treas.); Carlton J. Charles, Mitchell Scherzer, Roger Paschke, Mary Fisher (Asst Treas).

Principal Staff: Exec. Dir Paul 'Dino' Dinovitz.

Address: 300 West 57th St, 26th Floor, New York, NY 10019-3741.

Telephone: (212) 649-3750; **Fax:** (212) 586-1917; **Internet:** www.hearstfdn.org; **e-mail:** hearst.ny@hearstfdn.org.

The William Randolph Hearst Foundation

Established in 1948 by William Randolph Hearst, as the California Charities Foundations, to carry out general charitable activities; shares a common administration with The Hearst Foundation, Inc (q.v.).

Activities: Extends financial support to organizations implementing projects in the areas of culture, social welfare, education and health care. The Foundation makes miscellaneous grants, and offers scholarships through its US Senate Youth Program and Journalism Awards Program.

Geographical Area of Activity: USA and its dependencies.

Restrictions: No grants are made to individuals, for loans and programme-related investments, multi-year grants, startup or seed funding, equipment of any kind, publishing projects, radio, film, television or other media-related projects, conferences, workshops or seminars, public policy research, special events, tickets, tables or advertising for fund-raising events.

Finance: Annual revenue US $69,492,065, expenditure $33,041,455 (2013).

Board of Directors: William R. Hearst, III (Pres.); James M. Asher (Sec.); Ralph Cuomo (Treas.).

Principal Staff: Exec. Dir Paul 'Dino' Dinowitz.

Address: 300 West 57th St, 26th Floor, New York, NY 10019.

Telephone: (212) 586-5404; **Fax:** (212) 586-1917; **Internet:** www.hearstfdn.org; **e-mail:** hearst.ny@hearstfdn.org.

Heart to Heart International

Founded in 1992 by Gary Morsch; an international development and relief organization that aims to alleviate human suffering.

Activities: Operates programmes worldwide in the fields of international development and relief. The organization's work includes educational and medical supplies projects in developing countries; an international food programme; disaster relief for the victims of natural and man-made disasters; and domestic projects to help the poor, neglected and abused in the USA. Works in around 100 countries worldwide.

Geographical Area of Activity: International.

Publications: *The Link* (quarterly newletter); special reports.

Finance: Annual revenue US $94,533,819, expenditure $137,616,981 (31 Dec. 2014).

Board of Directors: Gary Morsch (Chair.); Bob Lambrechts (Vice-Chair.).

Principal Staff: CEO Jim Mitchum.

Address: 13250 West 98th St, Lenexa, KS 66215.

Telephone: (913) 764-5200; **Fax:** (913) 764-0809; **Internet:** www.hearttoheart.org; **e-mail:** info@hearttoheart.org.

Hebrew Immigrant Aid Society—HIAS

Founded in 1881.

Activities: A global Jewish agency that protects and advocates for refugees on a non-sectarian basis. The Society helps refugees to integrate in countries of asylum by providing legal services, trauma counselling, and livelihood programmes, and resettles the most vulnerable refugees to the USA. It also reunites refugee families separated during migration; advocates for increased refugee protection and funding; and engages the Jewish community in its mission.

Geographical Area of Activity: International.

Publications: Annual Report; reports and policy papers.

Finance: Annual revenue US $36,802,659, expenditure $31,098,519 (31 Dec. 2013).

Board of Directors: Dale Schwartz (Chair.); René Lerer (Sec./Treas.); Dianne F. Lob, Neil M. Moss (Vice-Chair.).

Principal Staff: Pres. and CEO Mark Hetfield; Sr Vice-Pres. Sussan Khozouri.

Address: 333 Seventh Ave, 16th Floor, New York, NY 10001.

Telephone: (212) 967-4100; **Fax:** (212) 967-4483; **Internet:** www.hias.org; **e-mail:** info@hias.org.

Heifer International

Founded in 1944 by Dan West to provide long-term solutions to hunger and poverty.

Activities: Operates in the field of aid to less-developed countries and social welfare, by providing animals as a source of food and income to families in need (incl. heifers, goats, llamas, geese, sheep, buffalos, rabbits and pigs) and training. In this way, families receive a nutritious long-term food source and a potential income for better education, housing and health care, and learn sustainable agricultural techniques. Recipients pass on offspring of donated animals to others. Established the Heifer International Foundation in 1990 to provide an ongoing endowment for the Heifer International and to educate people about charitable giving and estate planning. Operates active projects in 23 US states and maintains 38 field offices around the world.

Geographical Area of Activity: Africa, America, Asia and Eastern Europe.

Publications: *The Exchange* (quarterly newsletter); Annual Report.

Finance: Annual revenue US $7,147,681, expenditure $2,734,626 (30 June 2013).

Board of Directors: Norman Doll, Arlene Withers (Chair.); George Petty, Susan Grant (Vice-Chair.).

Principal Staff: Pres. and CEO Pierre Ferrari.

Address: 1 World Ave, POB 727, Little Rock, AR 72202.

Telephone: (888) 422-1161; **Fax:** (501) 907-2606; **Internet:** www.heifer.org; **e-mail:** info@heifer.org.

The Heinz Endowments

Founded in 1941 as the Howard Heinz Endowment and incorporating the Vera Heinz Endowment (f. 1986).

Activities: Works through five programme areas seeking innovative ways of improving the quality of life in Pennsylvania, supporting organizations that are concerned with the arts and culture, education, the environment, innovation economy and children, youth and families.

Geographical Area of Activity: USA, Pennsylvania.

Restrictions: No grants to individuals; grants only to non-profit organizations with an emphasis on programmes either in south-western Pennsylvania or of clear benefit to the region.

Publications: Annual Report; programme policy statement.

Finance: Annual revenue US $120,540,889, expenditure $77,981,577 (2013).

Board of Directors: Teresa Heinz (Chair.); James M. Walton (Vice-Chair.).

Principal Staff: Pres. Grant Oliphant; Vice-Pres. Edward Kolano.

Address: 30 Dominion Tower, 625 Liberty Ave, Pittsburgh, PA 15222.

Telephone: (412) 281-5777; **Fax:** (412) 281-5788; **Internet:** www.heinz.org; **e-mail:** info@heinz.org.

Heiser Program for Research in Leprosy

Founded in 1972 by Dr Victor G. Heiser to support biomedical research into leprosy (research into tuberculosis was added in 1992). Part of the New York Community Trust, a public non-profit organization.

Activities: Operates internationally, through post-doctoral research fellowships awarded to biomedical students beginning post-doctoral training in research in leprosy. In 2014, the Program was offering two-year grants to research laboratories of US $70,000, up to a maximum of $35,000 per year. The Program has also funded a project to determine the DNA sequence of the entire genome of *Mycobacterium leprae*.

Geographical Area of Activity: International.

Restrictions: Grants for research fellowships only.

Publications: Annual Reports; grants newsletters; financial statements; guidelines for grant applicants; handbook; brochure; professional notes; newsletters.

Scientific Advisory Committee: Stewart T. Cole (Chair.).

Address: c/o The New York Community Trust, 909 Third Ave, 22nd Floor, New York, NY 10022.

Telephone: (212) 686-0010; **Fax:** (212) 532-8528; **Internet:** www.nycommunitytrust.org; **e-mail:** programinitiatives@nyct-cfi.org.

The Leona M. and Harry B. Helmsley Charitable Trust

Established in 1999 by Leona Helmsley.

Activities: Leona Helmsley died in 2007 and bequeathed her estate, estimated at more than US $4,000m., to the Trust, which was to continue the Helmsleys' philanthropic legacy.

Geographical Area of Activity: USA.

Finance: Annual revenue US $175,457,200, expenditure $326,139,149 (31 March 2013).

Principal Staff: CEO John R. Ettinger.

Address: 230 Park Ave, New York, NY 10169-0698.

Telephone: (212) 679-3600; **Internet:** helmsleytrust.org; **e-mail:** info@helmsleytrust.org.

HELP International

Founded in 1999 in reponse to the suffering caused by Hurricane Mitch in Honduras.

Activities: Aims to facilitate the elimination of poverty worldwide. The organization runs various projects, incl. earthquake relief, microfinance impact assessment, family gardening, adobe stoves, libraries, business training and teaching English as a second language.

Geographical Area of Activity: Belize, El Salvador, Peru, Fiji, India, Thailand, Uganda, Tanzania.

Finance: Annual revenue US $462,051, expenditure $506,681 (30 Sept. 2013).

Principal Staff: Exec. Dir Arturo Adan Fuentes.

Address: 455 North University Ave, Suite 212, Provo, UT 84601.

Telephone: (801) 374-0556; **Fax:** (801) 374-0457; **Internet:** www.help-international.org; **e-mail:** office@help-international.org.

The William and Flora Hewlett Foundation

Founded in 1966 by William R. Hewlett, Flora Lamson Hewlett and Walter B. Hewlett to promote the well-being of humanity by supporting selected activities of a charitable, religious, scientific, literary or educational nature as well as organizations or institutions engaged in such activities.

Activities: Operates primarily in the fields of education, environment, global development, performing arts, population and philanthropy, through the provision of grants to relevant institutions and regional grants. Activities are restricted to the USA. A proportion of the Foundation's funds are given to projects in the San Francisco Bay area, CA.

Geographical Area of Activity: USA.

Restrictions: Makes grants to non-profit charitable organizations. The Foundation normally does not make grants intended to support basic research, capital construction funds, endowment, general fund-raising drives, or fund-raising events; nor does it make grants intended to support candidates for political office, to influence legislation, or to support sectarian or religious purposes.

Publications: Annual Report; brochures and programme reports; newsletter.

Finance: Annual revenue US $289,396,942, expenditure $303,616,986 (31 Dec. 2013).

Board: Walter B. Hewlett (Chair.); Elizabeth Peters (Sec.); Susan Ketcham (Treas.).

Principal Staff: Pres. Larry D. Kramer; Vice-Pres. and Chief Investment Officer Ana Marshall.

Address: 2121 Sand Hill Rd, Menlo Park, CA 94025.

Telephone: (650) 234-4500; **Fax:** (650) 234-4501; **Internet:** www.hewlett.org; **e-mail:** ebrown@hewlett.org.

Conrad N. Hilton Foundation

Founded in 1944 by hotel entrepreneur Conrad N. Hilton. Funds non-profit organizations that improve the lives of disadvantaged and vulnerable people worldwide.

Activities: Conducts strategic initiatives in six priority areas: providing safe water; ending chronic homelessness; preventing substance abuse; helping children affected by HIV/AIDS; supporting transition-age youth in foster care; and extending the Catholic Sisters Initiative. Following selection by an independent international jury, the Foundation annually awards the US $1.5 million Conrad N. Hilton Humanitarian Prize to a non-profit organization that reduces human suffering.

Geographical Area of Activity: Worldwide.

Restrictions: Does not accept unsolicited proposals; no grants to individuals.

Publications: Annual Report.

Finance: Annual revenue US $275,790,594, expenditure $156,678,289 (2013).

Principal Staff: Chair., Pres. and CEO Steven M. Hilton.

Address: 30440 Agoura Rd, Agoura Hills, CA 91301.

Telephone: (818) 851-3700; **Internet:** www.hiltonfoundation.org; **e-mail:** communications@hiltonfoundation.org.

Hitachi Foundation

Founded in 1985 by Hitachi Ltd, Japan.

Activities: Has three major activities: a grant programme for business and communities; Yoshiyama Awards for exemplary services; and a community action partnership. The Foundation aims to support grassroots non-profit organizations throughout the USA, through its general grants programme; work with employees of the Hitachi companies in its Matching Funds Program; and makes 10 annual Yoshiyama Awards to senior school students in recognition of their community activities.

Geographical Area of Activity: USA.

Restrictions: Does not accept unsolicited proposals.

Finance: Annual revenue US $4,094,082, expenditure $3,100,365 (2013).

Board of Directors: Patrick Gross (Chair.); Takashi Kawamura (Hon. Chair.).

Principal Staff: Pres. and CEO Barbara Dyer.

Address: 1215 17th St, NW, Washington, DC 20036.

Telephone: (202) 457-0588; **Fax:** (202) 296-1098; **Internet:** www.hitachifoundation.org; **e-mail:** info@hitachifoundation.org.

Holt International

Established in 1956 as Holt International Children's Services—HICS.

Activities: Operates in the field of child welfare, specifically national and international adoption and family preservation. The organization supports adopting families; funds staff training in child welfare; and recommends policies related to children's rights and those of adoptive and birth parents to national governments and the UN. Runs programmes in 10 countries, maintaining a network of its own offices, agencies and affiliated organizations around the world.

Geographical Area of Activity: USA, Asia, Africa.

Publications: Annual Report; *Holt International Magazine*; *Gifts of Hope Catalog*; *E-News Updates* (quarterly).

Finance: Annual revenue US $20,470,668, expenditure $19,529,774 (31 Dec. 2013).

Board of Directors: Clay Henderson (Chair.); Chuck Mittman (Vice-Chair.); Ken Matsurra (Treas.).

Principal Staff: Pres. and CEO Phillip Littleton.

Address: POB 2880, 250 Country Club Rd, Eugene, OR 97401.

Telephone: (541) 687-2202; **Fax:** (541) 683-6175; **Internet:** www.holtinternational.org; **e-mail:** info@holtinternational.org.

J. Homer Butler Foundation, Inc

Founded in 1961 with donations from the late Mabel A. Tod to assist projects that care for sick people, especially leprosy patients and those with HIV/AIDS.

Activities: Funds projects helping seriously ill people, with a particular emphasis on the relief of people with leprosy and HIV/AIDS.

Geographical Area of Activity: Central and South America, Africa, Asia (the Philippines, India).

Restrictions: No grants to individuals, nor for education or construction.

Finance: Annual revenue US $191,280, expenditure $167,509 (31 Dec. 2013).

Board of Directors: James J. Yannarell (Pres.); James F. Keenan (Vice-Pres.); Nicholas T. Montalto (Sec.); Dorothy F. Montalto (Asst Sec.); John J. Emmanuel (Treas.).

Principal Staff: Grants Admin. Dorothy F. Montalto.

Address: 523 E 14th St, Apt 1ꜰ, New York, NY 10009.

Telephone: (718) 356-9293; **Fax:** (718) 442-5088.

Houston Endowment, Inc

Founded in 1937 by Mr and Mrs Jesse H. Jones for the support of any charitable, educational or religious undertaking.

Activities: Operates nationally, with greatest priority on local and state needs, in the fields of education and health, through grants to institutions, scholarships and the construction and equipping of educational establishments and hospitals. The Endowment also makes grants in the areas of arts and culture, community enhancement, and medical facilities and research.

Geographical Area of Activity: USA.

Restrictions: No grants to individuals; grants only to non-profit organizations.

Publications: Annual Report and financial statement.

Finance: Annual revenue US $105,208,393, expenditure $97,503,062 (2013).

Board of Directors: David L. Mendez (Chair.).

Principal Staff: Pres. Ann B. Stern.

Address: 600 Travis, Suite 6400, Houston, TX 77002-3000.

Telephone: (713) 238-8100; **Fax:** (713) 238-8101; **Internet:** www.houstonendowment.org; **e-mail:** info@houstonendowment.org.

The George A. and Eliza Gardner Howard Foundation

Founded in 1952 by Nicea Howard to aid the personal development of promising individuals at the crucial middle stage of their careers.

Activities: Awards a limited number of one-year fellowships for independent projects in a five-year rotation of categories: creative non-fiction, literary translation into English, literary studies, film studies; photography, anthropology, archaeology; painting, sculpture, history of art and architecture; playwriting, music, musicology, theatre studies, history; and creative writing in English, including fiction and poetry, philosophy.

Geographical Area of Activity: USA.

Restrictions: Fellowships are tenable anywhere in the world, but are restricted to candidates who, regardless of their country of citizenship, are professionally based in the USA. Fellowships are not given to support degree candidates.

Finance: Annual revenue US $870,624, expenditure $450,657 (31 Dec. 2013).

Board of Trustees: William W. Kenyon (Chair.).

Principal Staff: Admin. Dir Prof. William C. Crossgrove.

Address: Brown University, Box 1945, Providence, RI 02912; Howard Foundation, 2000 Chapel View Blvd, Suite 350, Cranston, RI 02920.

Telephone: (401) 863-2640; **Fax:** (401) 863-6280; **Internet:** www.brown.edu/initiatives/howard-foundation; **e-mail:** howard_foundation@brown.edu.

Howard Hughes Medical Institute—HHMI

Founded in 1953 by Howard R. Hughes to support the field of science, particularly medical research and education.

Activities: Operates a Medical Research Program conducting biomedical research in the USA in such fields as cell biology, genetics, immunology, neuroscience, structural biology and bioinformatics/computational biology. The Institute makes grants to promote education in the biological sciences in the USA and supports research abroad, particularly in Central and South America, Canada, Europe (incl. the United Kingdom), the Russian Federation and Australia. It also helps scientists in the Czech Republic, Hungary and Poland through grants to the European Molecular Biology Organization. Fellowships are awarded for research training for medical students. Also interested in minority issues, notably Asian/Pacific islanders, African Americans, Latinos and Native Americans.

Geographical Area of Activity: Worldwide.

Restrictions: Grants are made primarily within defined competitive programmes; rarely funds unsolicited proposals.

Publications: Annual Report; *HHMI Bulletin*; occasional reports; quarterly magazine; grant programme announcements.

Finance: Annual revenue US $1,353m., expenditure $1,054m. (31 Aug. 2013).

Board of Trustees: Kurt L. Schmoke (Chair.).

Principal Staff: Pres. Dr Robert Tjian; Exec. Vice-Pres. and COO Cheryl A. Moore.

Address: 4000 Jones Bridge Rd, Chevy Chase, MD 20815-6789.

Telephone: (301) 215-8500; **Fax:** (301) 215-8863; **Internet:** www.hhmi.org; **e-mail:** webmaster@hhmi.org.

Human Rights Watch—HRW

Established in 1978 as Helsinki Watch, with the aim of assisting in the protection of human rights worldwide; it does not accept direct or indirect funding from any government.

Activities: Operates in the field of human rights internationally in collaboration with other NGOs. The organization has five offices in the USA, and offices in London, Berlin, Toronto, Paris, Johannesburg, Moscow, Tokyo, Geneva and Brussels, which collect information on human rights, in areas such as executions, torture, restrictions on religious organizations, children's and women's rights, refugees, prisons, landmines and discrimination. It also carries out research; disseminates information; and lobbies national governments and international organizations.

Geographical Area of Activity: Worldwide.

Publications: *World Report 2012 Arms; Business and Human Rights; Children's Rights; Emergencies; Health and Human Rights; International Justice; Lesbian, Gay, Bisexual & Transgender Rights; Refugee Policy; Terrorism/Counterterrorism; Women's Rights*; and numerous other publications.

Finance: Annual revenue US $16,235,448, expenditure $69,173,905 (30 June 2013).

Board of Directors: Hassan Elmasry, Joel Motley (Co-Chair.); Wendy Keys, Susan Manilow, Jean-Louis Servan-Schrieber; Sid Sheinberg, John J. Studzinski (Vice-Chair.); Bruce Rabb (Sec.).

Principal Staff: Exec. Dir Kenneth Roth.

Address: 350 Fifth Ave, 34th Floor, New York, NY 10118-3299.

Telephone: (212) 290-4700; **Fax:** (212) 736-1300; **Internet:** www.hrw.org; **e-mail:** hrwpress@hrw.org.

The Humana Foundation, Inc

Founded in 1981 by Humana, Inc for general charitable purposes.

Activities: Operates mainly in Kentucky in the fields of the arts and culture, health and human services, education, community development and international projects; awards scholarships; operates institutes for medical research and training, and funds medical schools. The Foundation runs a widespread humanitarian aid project in Romania.

Geographical Area of Activity: USA, Poland and Romania.

Restrictions: Focuses on organizations supporting communities where Humana, Inc has a business presence.

Finance: Annual revenue US $2,944,545, expenditure $8,594,966 (2013).

Board of Directors: Michael B. McCallister (Chair.); Joan O. Lenahan (Sec.).

Principal Staff: Pres. and CEO Michael B. McCallister; Exec. Dir Virginia K. Judd.

Address: 500 W. Main St, Suite 208, Louisville, KY 40202; POB 740026, Louisville, KY 40201.

Telephone: (502) 580-4140; **Fax:** (502) 580-1256; **Internet:** www.humanafoundation.org; **e-mail:** humanafoundation@humana.com.

Humanity United

Established in 2005 to advocate for peace and the advancement of humanity worldwide; part of the Omidyar Group.

Activities: A grantmaking private foundation, social welfare organization and charity which operates through making grants, its own projects and advocacy. Campaigns to end slavery and human trafficking, and to advance peace and human freedom.

Geographical Area of Activity: International, especially Asia and Africa.

Finance: Annual income US $30,091,060, expenditure $26,956,400 (31 Dec. 2013).

Trustees: Pam Omidyar (Chair.); Susan McCue (Vice-Chair.).

Principal Staff: Pres. and CEO Randy Newcomb.

Address: 1 Letterman Dr., Bldg D, Suite D3100, San Francisco, CA 94129.

Telephone: (415) 426-6300; **Internet:** www.humanityunited.org; **e-mail:** info@humanityunited.org.

The Hunger Project

Established in 1982; dedicated to eliminating chronic hunger around the world by focusing on the human issues that cause it.

Activities: Operates in the fields of aid to less-developed countries and social welfare, through seeking to empower disadvantaged people in Africa, Asia and Central and South America to improve their own health, education, nutrition and income in collaboration with local grassroots organizations. The Project is also committed to gender equality and the reduction of infant mortality. Awards the annual Africa Prize for Leadership for the Sustainable End of Hunger. Maintains offices in Australia, Bangladesh, Belgium, Benin, Bolivia, Burkina Faso, Canada, Ethiopia, Germany, Ghana, India, Japan, Malawi, Mexico, Mozambique, the Netherlands, New Zealand, Peru, Senegal, Sweden, Switzerland, Uganda and the United Kingdom.

Geographical Area of Activity: Africa, South Asia, and Central and South America, Latin America.

Publications: Newsletter (monthly); Annual Report.

Finance: Annual revenue US $16,260,086, expenditure $14,637,711 (31 Dec. 2013).

Board of Directors: Steven J. Sherwood (Chair.); Lena Ariola (Treas.).

Principal Staff: Pres. and CEO Åsa Skogström Feldt; Exec. Vice-Pres. John Coonrod.

Address: 5 Union Sq. West, New York, NY 10003.

Telephone: (212) 251-9100; **Fax:** (212) 532-9785; **Internet:** www.thp.org; **e-mail:** info@thp.org.

IAPA Scholarship Fund

Founded in 1954 by the Inter American Press Association (IAPA) to support the exchange of journalists and journalism students between Western hemisphere countries.

Activities: Operates internationally (in the Western hemisphere) in the field of journalism, through exchange programmes and scholarships (at least 10 a year) awarded to residents of North, Central and South America and the Caribbean for study at university schools of journalism abroad. In 2013, the Fund awarded four scholarships, each worth US $20,000.

Geographical Area of Activity: North, Central and South America and the Caribbean.

Restrictions: Open to English- and Spanish-speaking journalists and journalism school graduates aged 21–35 years.

Board of Governors: Gerardo García Gamboa (Pres.); Ernesto Kraiselburd, Pamela Howard (Vice-Pres); Ildefonso Chávez Olveda (Treas.); María Catalina Saieh (Sec.).

Principal Staff: Co-ordinator Mauricio J. Montaldo.

Address: 1801 SW Third Ave, Miami, FL 33129.

Telephone: (305) 634-2465; **Fax:** (305) 635-2272; **Internet:** www.sipiapa.org/en/scholarships/descripcion-becas; **e-mail:** becas@sipiapa.org.

IBM International Foundation

Founded in 1985 for general charitable purposes in South Africa. In 1992, the Foundation's charter was amended to allow charitable giving worldwide.

Activities: Operates nationally and internationally, mainly in the field of education. Foundation projects also include: global initiatives in early learning and the arts and culture; and grants to organizations working in Africa, Asia and Europe. Launched the Smarter Cities Initiative in 2010 to assist in the technological development of 100 cities worldwide.

Geographical Area of Activity: Worldwide.

Restrictions: Does not consider requests from individuals, or for individual endeavours.

Publications: Information brochure.

Finance: Annual revenue US $37,522,336, expenditure $26,670,135 (2013).

Board of Directors: Virginia Rometty (Chair.); John Iwata (Vice-Chair.); Robert del Bene (Treas.); Gregory C. Hubertus (Asst Treas.); Michelle H. Browdy (Sec.).

Principal Staff: Pres. Stanley S. Litow.

Address: c/o IBM Corporation, New Orchard Rd, Armonk, NY 10504-1709.

Telephone: (914) 766-1900; **Fax:** (914) 499-7624; **Internet:** www.ibm.com/ibm/ibmgives.

IMA World Health—Interchurch Medical Assistance, Inc

Founded in 1960.

Activities: Provides essential health care services and supplies to people in need in developing countries, through direct provision to hospitals, clinics, programmes and other health care providers; and by strengthening health care systems through training, education, and oversight. Faith-based organizations are key partners.

Geographical Area of Activity: Worldwide.

Restrictions: Not a grantmaking organization; channels grant monies to identified local partners as appropriate.

Publications: Annual Report.

Finance: Annual revenue US $49,033,919, expenditure $49,463,716 (30 June 2013).

Board: Lisa Rothenberger (Chair.); Rev. Amy Gopp (Vice-Chair.); Sarah Newhall (Sec.); William C. Clarke, III (Treas.).

Principal Staff: Pres. and CEO Richard L. Santos.

Address: 500 Main St, Building Old Main, New Windsor, MD 21776; POB 429, New Windsor, MD 21776.

Telephone: (410) 635-8720; **Fax:** (410) 635-8726; **Internet:** www.imaworldhealth.org; **e-mail:** imainfo@imaworldhealth.org.

India Partners

Founded in 1984 to support self-help ministry projects in India through partner organizations that are committed to providing long-term solutions to poverty for every individual, regardless of race, religion, caste or sex.

Activities: Supports work in the fields of development assistance, leadership training, disaster relief, education and health work. The organization also works on short-term projects (incl. programmes related to agriculture, construction and water resource management among others) and runs a child sponsorship programme.

Geographical Area of Activity: India.

Publications: Annual Report; newsletter.

Finance: Annual revenue US $906,449, expenditure $932,993 (30 June 2014).

Board of Directors: Susan Cannon (Chair.); Mark De Lucia (Vice-Chair.).

Principal Staff: Pres. and CEO John Sparks.

Address: POB 5470, Eugene, OR 97405.

Telephone: (877) 874-6342; **Fax:** (541) 683-2773; **Internet:** www.indiapartners.org; **e-mail:** info@indiapartners.org.

INMED Partnerships for Children

Established in 1986 to rescue children from the immediate and irreversible harm of disease, hunger, abuse, neglect or violence.

Activities: Works through a broad range of health, social, education, violence prevention and community development programmes focused on: securing children's health, development and safety; developing skills, knowledge and opportunities for children and youth; and building family and community capacity to support and sustain positive change.

Geographical Area of Activity: USA, Brazil, Peru, Jamaica, Trinidad and Tobago, South Africa.

Publications: *Home Visitors Handbook*; *Women's Wellness Sourcebook*; *Curriculum Sourcebook*; Annual Report; newsletters.

Finance: Annual revenue US $5,690,559, expenditure $4,081,050 (31 Dec. 2013).

Board of Directors: Paul C. Bosland (Chair.); James R. Rutherford (Treas.); Wendy Balter (Sec.).

Principal Staff: Pres. and CEO Dr Linda Pfeiffer; Exec. Vice-Pres. Dr Thad M. Jackson.

Address: 21630 Ridgetop Circle, Suite 130, Sterling, VA 20166.

Telephone: (703) 729-4951; **Fax:** (703) 858-7253; **Internet:** www.inmed.org; **e-mail:** contact@inmed.org.

Institute of Current World Affairs—ICWA

Founded in 1925 by Charles R. Crane and Walter S. Rogers (and also known as the Crane-Rogers Foundation) to provide opportunity and full financial support to a few persons of high character and unusual promise to enable them to observe and study at first hand particular areas and problems of contemporary significance outside the USA.

Activities: Operates through the granting of a limited number of long-term fellowships to promote a thorough and balanced knowledge of particular areas or problems outside the USA and the effective communication of this knowledge. The Institute awards Fellowships for study in Eastern Europe, the Middle East and Sub-Saharan Africa, and for outside these areas.

Geographical Area of Activity: Worldwide, excluding USA.

Restrictions: Fellowship candidates must be fluent in the English language and under 36 years of age. Fellowships are not awarded to support work towards academic degrees, nor to underwrite specific studies or programmes of research as such, but for independent self-designed programmes of study.

Publications: Information brochure.

Finance: Annual revenue US $952,793, expenditure $884,830 (31 Dec. 2013).

Board of Trustees: Dirk Vandewalle (Chair.); Cynthia Caron (Vice-Chair.); Neri Zilber (Sec.); Virginia R. Foote (Treas.).

Address: 1779 Massachusetts Ave, NW, Suite 615, Washington, DC 20036.

Telephone: (202) 364-4068; **Fax:** (202) 364-0498; **Internet:** www.icwa.org; **e-mail:** icwa@icwa.org.

Institute of International Education—IIE

Founded in 1919, following the First World War, by Dr Stephen Duggan, Dr Nicholas Murray Butler and Elihu Root, and based on the belief that the sharing of knowledge and skills is the only road to lasting peace and international understanding.

Activities: An independent non-profit organization dedicated to increasing the capacity of people to think and work on a global basis. The Institute implements 250 international exchange programmes, benefiting more than 20,000 people from 175 countries. On behalf of the US Department of State, it has administered the Fulbright Program since the latter's inception in 1947. The Institute also serves corporations, foundations and government agencies worldwide, making available testing and advisory services, scholarships, information on opportunities for international study, emergency assistance to students and scholars, and the IIE Network membership programme, which links colleges and universities worldwide.

Geographical Area of Activity: International.

Publications: Annual Report; *Open Doors* (annually); *Funding for U.S. Study* (annually); *IIE Passport Study Abroad Directory* (annually); *IIENetwork Membership Directory* (annually); studies, handbooks, surveys and leaflets on international education.

Finance: Annual revenue US $438,617,954, expenditure $436,192,243 (30 Sept. 2013).

Board of Trustees: Thomas S. Johnson (Chair.); Henry Kaufman (Chair. Emer.); Thomas A. Russo (Chair., Exec. Cttee); Ruth Hinerfeld, Henry G. Jarecki (Vice-Chair.); Mark A. Angelson (Treas.).

Principal Staff: Pres. and CEO Dr Allan E. Goodman.

Address: 809 United Nations Plaza, New York, NY 10017.

Telephone: (212) 883-8200; **Fax:** (212) 984-5496; **Internet:** www.iie.org; **e-mail:** info@iie.org.

Institute for Sustainable Communities—ISC

Established in 1991 to address environmental, economic and social challenges worldwide. Merged with the Advocacy Institute in 2006.

Activities: Works to build capacity, infrastructure and strong comunity leadership. Operates within five core programmes: Climate & Environment; Community Building; Civil Society; Education for Sustainability; and Advocacy & Leadership. The Institute also runs the Advocacy and Leadership Center; Environmental Health and Safety Academy (in the People's Republic of China); Climate Leadership Academy and Urban Sustainability Leadership Academy programmes; and Advocacy Fellows Program; and provides support to USAID on specific topics. Has offices in China and Serbia.

Geographical Area of Activity: International.

Finance: Annual revenue US $16,086,739, expenditure $11,893,290 (30 Sept. 2013).

Board of Directors: Richard D. Paisner (Chair.); Jonathan Lash (Vice-Chair.); Elizabeth Knup (Sec.); John A. Dooley (Treas.).

Principal Staff: Pres. George Hamilton.

Address: 535 Stone Cutters Way, Montpelier, VT 05602.

Telephone: (802) 229-2900; **Fax:** (802) 229-2919; **Internet:** www.iscvt.org; **e-mail:** isc@iscvt.org.

Inter-American Foundation—IAF

Founded in 1969 by the US Congress (as an independent agency, so that its operations would not be affected by short-term US policy considerations) to support the self-help efforts of disadvantaged people in Central and South America and the Caribbean.

Activities: An independent agency of the US Government that provides grants to non-governmental and community-based organizations in Latin America and the Caribbean for innovative, sustainable and participatory self-help programmes. The Foundation primarily funds partnerships among grassroots and non-profit organizations, businesses and local governments, directed at improving the quality of life of poor people and strengthening participation, accountability and democratic practices. To contribute to a better understanding of the development process, the Foundation also shares its experiences and the lessons it has learned.

Geographical Area of Activity: Central and South America and the Caribbean.

Restrictions: Supports projects only in Central and South America and the Caribbean. Funding in the Caribbean is currently restricted to the Dominican Republic, Haiti and Jamaica. Does not accept grant applications from individuals, governments, political parties, groups based outside the region or that do not contribute their own resources to projects; or projects for welfare or purely religious or research purposes. Grant requests must be between US $25,000 and $400,000.

Publications: *Grassroots Development* (journal, 2 a year in English, Spanish and Portuguese); annual review; fact sheets.

Finance: Receives about 60% of its annual budget from the US Congress; also receives funding from the Social Progress Trust Fund of the Inter-American Development Bank. Total funding available US $36,415,538 (2014/15).

Board of Directors: Eddy Arriola (Chair.); Thomas J. Dodd (Vice-Chair.); Jack C. Vaughn, Jr (Sec.).

Principal Staff: Pres. Robert N. Kaplan.

Address: 1331 Pennsylvania Ave, NW, Suite 1200, North Washington, DC 20004.

Telephone: (202) 360-4530; **Internet:** www.iaf.gov; **e-mail:** inquiries@iaf.gov.

International Aid, Inc—IA

Established in 1980; a non-profit Christian relief and development agency.

Activities: Works globally to improve the health of the world's poorest people. Programmes include the HydrAidTM BioSand Water Filter, which provides households throughout the developing world with safe drinking water, as well as the distribution of new and refurbished medical equipment and supplies to hospitals and clinics in developing countries. The agency also partners with academia, corporations and NGOs to develop and implement training programmes for health professionals throughout the world. Has field staff in Central America, Africa and Asia.

Geographical Area of Activity: International.

Publications: Annual Report.

Finance: Annual revenue US $79,926,307, expenditure $79,785,197 (30 June 2014).

Board of Directors: Luke Nieuwenhuis (Chair.); Roger W. Spoelman; (Vice-Char.); James R. Batten (Treas.); Mike Houskamp (Sec.).

Principal Staff: Pres. and CEO Brian Anderson.

Address: 17011 Hickory St, Spring Lake, MI 49456-9712.

Telephone: (616) 846-7490; **Fax:** (616) 846-3842; **Internet:** www.internationalaid.org; **e-mail:** ia@internationalaid.org.

International Center for Not-for-Profit Law—ICNL

Established in 1992.

Activities: Promotes development of civil society and its participation in public decision-making. Programmes and research focus on promoting an enabling legal environment for civil society and public participation worldwide. The Center works in more than 90 countries, co-operating with national and international organizations in the area of third-sector law. It provides technical legal assistance, training and educational materials for legal professionals; organizes conferences; hosts senior research fellowships; and publishes research. Maintains an online library and resource centre with more than 2,300 materials. Has offices in Washington DC, Budapest, Almaty, Kiev, Sofia, Ashgabat, Kabul, Moscow, Baku, Bishkek and Dushanbe.

Geographical Area of Activity: Worldwide.

Publications: Annual Reports; *Defending Civil Society: A Report of the World Movement for Democracy*; *International Investment Treaty Protection of Not-for-Profit Organizations*; *Safeguarding Civil Society in Politically Complex Environments*; *Recent Laws and Legislative Proposals to Restrict Civil Society and Civil Society Organizations*; *Handbook on Freedom of Association under the European Convention of Human Rights and Fundamental Freedoms*; *The International Journal of Not-for-Profit Law*; *International Investment Treaty Protection of Not-for-Profit Organizations*; *NGO Laws in Select Arab States*; *Development of Noncommercial Law in Kazakhstan*; *Freedom of Association in Central Asia*; *Law and Civil Society in the South Pacific*.

Finance: Annual revenue US $15,923,396, expenditure $10,232,814 (31 Dec. 2013).

Board of Directors: Betsy Buchalter Adler (Chair.); Feliciano Reyna Ganteaume (Vice-Chair.); Adam Kolker (Sec. and Treas.).

Principal Staff: Pres. Douglas Rutzen.

Address: 1126 16th St NW, Suite 400, Washington, DC 20036.

Telephone: (202) 452-8600; **Fax:** (202) 452-8555; **Internet:** www.icnl.org; **e-mail:** infoicnl@icnl.org.

International Center for Research on Women—ICRW

Founded in 1976.

Activities: Works with governments and partner organizations worldwide to reduce poverty, promote development and improve the lives of women. Through research, direct action and advocacy, the Center supports work on issues that affect women everywhere, incl. HIV/AIDS; economic growth; poverty reduction; reproductive health and nutrition; policy and communications; population and social transition; and social struggle and transformation. Maintains a country office in New Delhi, India, and project offices in Secunderabad, India, and Kampala, Uganda.

Geographical Area of Activity: Worldwide.

Publications: Annual Report; research reports; newsletters.

Finance: Annual revenue US $8,595,711, expenditure $9,641,629 (30 Sept. 2013).

Board of Directors: Elizabeth Griffith (Chair.); Scott Jackson (Vice-Chair.); Patricia Daunas (Treas.); Kristin Fack (Sec.).

Principal Staff: Pres. Sarah Degnan Kambou.

Address: 1120 20th St NW, Suite 500 North, Washington, DC 20036.

Telephone: (202) 797-0007; **Fax:** (202) 797-0020; **Internet:** www.icrw.org; **e-mail:** info@icrw.org.

International Center for Transitional Justice—ICTJ

Established in 2002 to assist societies in transition to address legacies of massive human rights violations and protect human rights.

Activities: Offers advice, carries out research and advises victims' groups in the area of human rights. Maintains offices in Belgium, Colombia, Indonesia, Kenya, Lebanon, Nepal, Switzerland and Uganda.

Finance: Annual revenue US $9,310,270, expenditure $11,653,492 (31 March 2013).

Board of Directors: Kofi Appenteng (Chair.).

Principal Staff: Pres. David Tolbert; Vice-Pres. and Gen. Counsel Paul Seils.

Address: 5 Hanover Sq., 24th Floor, New York, NY 10004.

Telephone: (917) 637-3800; **Fax:** (917) 637-3900; **Internet:** ictj.org; **e-mail:** info@ictj.org.

International Child Art Foundation

Founded in 1997 by Ashfaq Ishaq as a charity to harness children's imagination for positive social change.

Activities: Operates the Arts Olympiad, World Children's Festival, Healing Arts Program and Peace Through Art Program.

Geographical Area of Activity: International.

Restrictions: Arts Olympiad restricted to children aged 8–12 years. No grants to individuals or non-profit organizations.

Publications: *ChildArt* (quarterly magazine); *Sketches* (newsletter).

Finance: Annual revenue US $115,687, expenditure $115,202 (31 Dec. 2013).

Executive Board: Dr Ashfaq Ishaq (Chair.); Katty Guerami (Sec.).

Address: 2540 Virginia Ave NW, Washington, DC 20037; POB 58133, Washington, DC 20037.

Telephone: (202) 530-1000; **Fax:** (202) 530-1080; **Internet:** www.icaf.org; **e-mail:** childart@icaf.org.

International College of Surgeons—ICS

Founded in 1935 by Dr Max Thorek.

Activities: A worldwide federation of organizations that aims to encourage worldwide surgical excellence through training, humanitarian work, education and fellowship. The College operates in the field of medicine and health, through the exchange of surgical knowledge and techniques, and assisting in surgical missions in developing countries around the world, incl. disaster relief work and providing surgical care alongside other humanitarian agencies. It offers scholarships for surgical training, funds surgical research and lectureships. Has 60 national sections, of which ICS–USA is the largest. Maintains the International Museum of Surgical Science, in Chicago, IL.

Geographical Area of Activity: Worldwide.

Publications: *International Surgery* (bimonthly journal).

Finance: Annual revenue US $835,979, expenditure $963,190 (31 Dec. 2013).

Principal Staff: Exec. Dir Max C. Downham.

Address: 1516 N Lakeshore Dr., Chicago, IL 60610.

Telephone: (312) 642-3555; **Fax:** (312) 787-1624; **Internet:** www.icsglobal.org; **e-mail:** info@icsglobal.org.

International Education Research Foundation, Inc—IERF

Founded in 1969 as a public-benefit, non-profit agency.

Activities: Evaluates international education credentials in terms of US equivalence for employment purposes, for colleges, universities, licensing agencies, professional organizations and the armed services. The Foundation also conducts workshops and research, maintains a library on international education, and operates a research grant programme. Has a library of more than 30,000 publications.

Geographical Area of Activity: Worldwide.

Finance: Annual revenue US $2,587,078, expenditure $2,460,818 (30 June 2014).

Board of Directors: Leo A. Van Cleve (Chair.); Satpal Nagpal (Treas.); Christopher T. Krug (Sec.).

Principal Staff: Exec. Dir Susan J. Bedil.

Address: POB 3665, Culver City, CA 90231-3665.

Telephone: (310) 258-9451; **Fax:** (310) 342-7086; **Internet:** www.ierf.org; **e-mail:** info@ierf.org.

International Executive Service Corps— IESC

Founded in 1964 by David Rockefeller; a private, not-for-profit organization.

Activities: Capitalizes on the skills of industry-expert volunteers, consultants and professional staff to promote economic growth around the world. The Corps promotes economic development worldwide by providing technical or managerial experts to assist in enterprise projects in the developing world, thus ultimately increasing employment and standards of living. Skills Bank registry of more than 8,500 volunteer and consultant experts, and alliances with more than 15 similar organizations worldwide.

Geographical Area of Activity: Worldwide.

Publications: IESC Update Newsletter; mid-year reports.

Finance: Annual revenue US $28,086,192, expenditure $28,116,102 (31 Dec. 2013).

Board of Directors: Don B. Taggart (Chair.); Wing Keith (Vice-Chair.).

Principal Staff: Pres. and CEO Thomas Miller.

Address: 1900 M St NW, Suite 500, Washington, DC 20036.

Telephone: (202) 589-2600; **Fax:** (202) 326-0289; **Internet:** www.iesc.org; **e-mail:** iesc@iesc.org.

International Eye Foundation—IEF

Founded in 1961 as the International Eye Bank by Dr John Harry King, Jr, to promote the prevention and cure of blindness in developing countries, through the provision of training; clinical, surgical and preventive services; equipment, supplies and medication; public education; and technical assistance in the development of health infrastructure. Present name adopted in 1969.

Activities: Operates internationally in the fields of medicine, public health and education, through co-operative programmes with health ministries and private indigenous organizations, as well as through fellowships for ophthalmic training and scientific conferences. The Foundation addresses the prevention and amelioration of conditions such as onchocerciasis (river blindness), xerophthalmia, glaucoma, cataracts and other major eye diseases, through projects in Africa, Asia, Central and South America, and Eastern Europe.

Geographical Area of Activity: Worldwide.

Publications: *Eye to Eye*; *Eye Care in Developing Nations*; *IEF Fact Sheets*; Annual Report.

Finance: Annual revenue US $5,673,697, expenditure $5,957,495 (30 June 2014).

Board of Directors: Kathryn D. Leckey (Chair.); Steve Dick Tennyson Matenje (Vice-Chair.); Frances R. Pierce (Treas.); Dr Ralph J. Helmsen (Sec.).

Principal Staff: Pres. and CEO Victoria M. Sheffield.

Address: 10801 Connecticut Ave, Kensington, MD 20895.

Telephone: (240) 290-0263; **Fax:** (240) 290-0269; **Internet:** www.iefusa.org; **e-mail:** ief@iefusa.org.

The International Foundation

Founded in 1948 to support projects in developing countries that promote sustainable development in agriculture, education, health, social development and the environment.

Activities: Makes grants only to US-headquartered non-profit agencies or institutions engaged in aid to developing countries in Asia, Central and South America, the Caribbean, the Middle East, the South Pacific and Sub-Saharan Africa.

The Foundation prioritizes agricultural research and production; medicine and health (incl. sanitation and nutrition); education and research; and social welfare and development.

Geographical Area of Activity: Sub-Saharan Africa, the Middle East, Central and South America, Asia and the South Pacific.

Restrictions: Makes grants only to 501C3 organizations headquartered in the USA.

Finance: Annual revenue US $1,936,500, expenditure $1,472,787 (31 Dec. 2013).

Board of Trustees: Frank H. Madden (Pres.); John D. Carrico (Sec. and Treas.); John D. Carrico, II (Asst Sec./Treas.).

Principal Staff: Grants Chair. Dr William M. McCormack.

Address: 1700 Route 23 North, Suite 300, Wayne, NJ 07470.

Telephone: (973) 406-3970; **Fax:** (973) 406-3969; **Internet:** www.intlfoundation.org; **e-mail:** info@intlfoundation.org.

International Foundation for Art Research—IFAR

Founded in 1969 by John Rewald, Harry Bober and the New York State Attorney General to research authentication questions and provide other impartial and scholarly information to the art world, including on art theft and looting, art law and ethics.

Activities: Operates in the field of the arts and humanities, nationally through self-conducted programmes, and internationally through research, publications, online resources and training courses. The Foundation has an Art Advisory Council and a Law Advisory Council. Provides an art authentication research service and provenance research services; hosts an annual public lecture series and conferences; maintains a free online Catalogues Raisonnés Database and an online Art Law & Cultural Property Database for annual subscribers.

Geographical Area of Activity: Worldwide.

Publications: *IFAR Journal* (quarterly), incorporating *Stolen Art Alert* (in co-operation with the Art Loss Register, the art community, insurance companies, the police, the Federal Bureau of Investigation—FBI, and Interpol).

Finance: Annual revenue US $873,192, expenditure $789,206 (31 Dec. 2013).

Board of Directors: Anthony Williams (Chair.).

Principal Staff: Exec. Dir Dr Sharon Flescher.

Address: 500 Fifth Ave, Suite 935, New York, NY 10110.

Telephone: (212) 391-6234; **Fax:** (212) 391-8794; **Internet:** www.ifar.org; **e-mail:** kferg@ifar.org.

International Foundation for Education and Self-Help—IFESH

Founded in 1983 by the Rev. Leon H. Sullivan to reduce poverty and unemployment in Sub-Saharan Africa, and improve links between Africa and the USA.

Activities: Operates in the fields of agriculture, business and economic development, democracy and governance, education and health to improve the quality of life in developing countries, with a particular focus on Sub-Saharan Africa. Foundation programmes include: reducing hunger and poverty; increasing literacy levels through better education; providing training to the unemployed and unskilled; helping to reduce the spread of HIV/AIDS; providing basic health care; and encouraging cultural, social and economic relations between Africans and African-Americans.

Geographical Area of Activity: Côte d'Ivoire, Djibouti, Ghana, Guinea, Ethiopia, Kenya, Liberia, Malawi, Nigeria, Senegal.

Restrictions: Operates its own programmes.

Publications: Annual newsletter; Annual Report.

Finance: Annual revenue US $4,824,699, expenditure $5,160,954 (30 Sept. 2012).

Board of Directors: Dr Eamon M. Kelly (Chair.); Esther B. Ferguson (Sec.).

Principal Staff: Pres. and CEO Dr Julie H. Sullivan.

Address: 5040 East Shea Blvd, Suite 260, Scottsdale, AZ 85254.

Telephone: (480) 443-1800; **Fax:** (480) 443-1824; **Internet:** www.ifesh.org; **e-mail:** information@ifesh.org.

International Foundation for Electoral Systems—IFES

Established in 1987 as a private non-profit organization to provide technical assistance in the promotion of democracy worldwide.

Activities: Operates worldwide in the fields of education, international affairs, law and human rights, politics and civil society, through self-conducted programmes, research, grants to institutions, scholarships and fellowships, conferences, training courses and publications. The Foundation also offers information about democratic development and elections. It has developed methodologies that promote the understanding of the political, social and economic background to international electoral events; organizes training courses for election officials and NGOs; and supports civil society, rule of law and the strengthening of international governance. Has worked in more than 100 countries.

Geographical Area of Activity: Worldwide.

Restrictions: Not a grantmaking institution; however, public funds are expended to carry out programmes internationally, and sub-grants are made to in-country partners.

Publications: Annual Report; *Elections Today* (quarterly); *Money and Politics in Nigeria*; *The Resolution of Election Disputes: Legal Principles That Control Election Challenges* (2nd edn); *International Directory of Election Offices*; *Afro-Ecuadorians Strive for Political Rights*; *The Right Time for Re-engagement*; *Buyer's Guide to Election Suppliers*.

Finance: Annual revenue US $79,322,838 expenditure $80,176,830 (30 Sept. 2013).

Board of Directors: Donald R. Sweitzer (Chair.); Judy A. Black (Vice-Chair.); Lesley Israel (Treas.); J. Kenneth Backwell (Sec.).

Principal Staff: Pres. and CEO Bill Sweeney; COO Jim Johnson.

Address: 1850 K St NW, 5th Floor, Washington, DC 20006.

Telephone: (202) 350-6700; **Fax:** (202) 350-6701; **Internet:** www.ifes.org; **e-mail:** info.communications@ifes.org.

International Foundation for Ethical Research

Founded in 1985 to support basic and applied research into valid alternatives to the use of live animals for research, testing and educational purposes.

Activities: Operates in the area of scientific research, through grants of up to US $15,000 per award and renewal postgraduate fellowships of up to $15,000. The Foundation awards grants to scientists who are developing credible alternatives to live animal research, and to postgraduate students seeking to incorporate animal welfare issues into their studies. It also disseminates information designed to increase awareness of alternatives through seminars, publications and workshops.

Geographical Area of Activity: International.

Publications: Newsletter; workshop proceedings.

Finance: Annual revenue US $98,161, expenditure $120,634 (2013).

Board of Directors: Peggy Cunniff (Pres.).

Principal Staff: Exec. Dir Peter O'Donovan.

Address: 53 West Jackson Blvd, Suite 1552, Chicago, IL 60604.

Telephone: (312) 427-6025; **Fax:** (312) 427-6524; **Internet:** www.ifer.org; **e-mail:** ifer@navs.org.

International Fund for Animal Welfare—IFAW

Founded in 1969 by Brian Davies to campaign for animal welfare.

Activities: Operates in the field of animal welfare, seeking to improve conditions for wild and domestic animals all over the world. The Fund aims to reduce commercial exploitation of animals, protect natural habitats, and help animals in distress through campaigning and research. It seeks to motivate the public to prevent cruelty to animals and promote animal welfare and conservation policies that advance the well-being of both animals and people. Works closely with a number of non-profit organizations, government leaders and volunteers to protect animals worldwide.

Geographical Area of Activity: Worldwide.

Publications: Annual Report; *Our Shared World* (quarterly magazine); animal fact sheets; programme publications.

Finance: Annual revenue US $19,180,462, expenditure $19,762,270 (30 June 2013).

Board of Directors: Kathleen Savesky (Chair.).

Principal Staff: Pres. and CEO Azzedine Downes; CFO Thom Maul.

Address: 290 Summer St, Yarmouth Port, MA 02675.

Telephone: (508) 744-2000; **Fax:** (508) 744-2009; **Internet:** www.ifaw.org; **e-mail:** info@ifaw.org.

International Orthodox Christian Charities, Inc—IOCC

Established in 1992; serves as the official humanitarian arm of the Assembly of Canonical Orthodox Bishops of the USA.

Activities: Provides humanitarian relief, sustainable development and self-help programmes to people in need. The organization provides assistance solely on the basis of need, and benefits families, refugees and displaced persons, the elderly, school children, orphans and people with disabilities.

Geographical Area of Activity: Africa, USA, Europe and the Middle East.

Restrictions: Does not support church mission programmes.

Publications: *News and Needs* (newsletter); Annual Report; Prayer Journal; Year in Review; IOCC in Brief.

Finance: Annual revenue US $53,911,175, expenditure $52,450,373 (2013).

Board of Directors: Mark Stavropoulos (Chair.); Maria Z. Mossaides (Vice-Chair); John Sobchak (Treas.); Thomas M. Suehs (Sec.).

Principal Staff: Exec. Dir and CEO Constantine M. Triantafilou.

Address: 110 West Rd, Suite 360, Baltimore, MD 21024.

Telephone: (410) 243-9820; **Fax:** (410) 243-9824; **Internet:** www.iocc.org; **e-mail:** relief@iocc.org.

International Relief & Development—IRD

Established in 1988 by Rev. Dr Arthur B. Keys, Jr.

Activities: Aims to improve the quality of life of people living in developing countries throughout the world. The IRD works in the fields of international aid and development, implementing programmes in less-developed countries with the support of other aid organizations, government agencies and private business sources. It works in more than 30 countries in Central and Eastern Europe and Central and South-East Asia in the areas of democracy and governance, economic growth, emergency response, food and agriculture, health and hygiene, and rebuilding infrastructure. Maintains field offices in Armenia, Azerbaijan, Georgia, Indonesia, Montenegro, Serbia and Ukraine.

Geographical Area of Activity: USA (Gulf Coast), Central and South-East Asia, and Central and Eastern Europe.

Restrictions: No grants are made.

Publications: Information bulletin; Annual Report and newsletters.

Finance: Annual revenue US $336,018,740, expenditure $330,512,078 (31 Dec. 2012).

Principal Staff: Pres. and CEO Roger Ervin.

Address: 1621 North Kent St, Fourth Floor, Arlington, VA 22209.

Telephone: (703) 248-0161; **Fax:** (703) 248-0194; **Internet:** www.ird.org; **e-mail:** communications@ird.org.

International Relief Teams

Established in 1988.

Activities: Alleviates human suffering by providing health services and humanitarian assistance to victims of disaster, neglect, and profound poverty worldwide. The organization focuses on two core activities: disaster relief, which includes deploying medical and reconstruction teams, providing relief supplies and financing the restoration of livelihoods and infrastructure; and building healthy communities, by providing medical training to save babies' lives, surgeries for the poor, eye glasses to improve sight, medicines for rural hospitals and clinics, and nutrition and education support for abused, abandoned and homeless children.

Geographical Area of Activity: International.

Publications: *TEAMNews* (newsletter); Annual Report.

Finance: Total revenue US $29,760,208, expenditure $29,750,816 (30 June 2014).

Board of Directors: Richard Yousko (Chair.).

Principal Staff: Exec. Dir Barry La Forgia.

Address: 4560 Alvarado Canyon Rd, Suite 2G, San Diego, CA 92120-4309.

Telephone: (619) 284-7979; **Fax:** (619) 284-7938; **Internet:** www.irteams.org; **e-mail:** info@irteams.org.

International Rescue Committee, Inc—IRC

Founded in 1933 as a voluntary organization at the suggestion of Albert Einstein to help Germans suffering under the Nazi regime in Germany.

Activities: Works internationally to help those fleeing victimization, oppression and conflict. The Committee resettles and rehouses refugees; and provides emergency shelter and supplies for homeless and displaced people, and health services and health care training in areas suffering the effects of violent conflict. Also awards the annual IRC Freedom Award.

Geographical Area of Activity: Worldwide.

Publications: Annual Report.

Finance: Annual revenue US $563,536,000, expenditure $549,208,000 (30 Sept. 2014).

Board of Directors: Sarah O'Hagan, Tom Schick (Co-Chair.); Liv Ullmann (Vice-Chair.); Glenda Burkhart (Sec.); Gordon Smith (Treas.).

Principal Staff: Pres. and CEO David Miliband.

Address: 122 East 42nd St, New York, NY 10168.

Telephone: (212) 551-3000; **Fax:** (212) 551-3179; **Internet:** www.rescue.org; **e-mail:** donorservices@rescue.org.

International Rivers

Founded in 1985 to protect river systems and the communities that depend on them, and to fight for worldwide environmental integrity, social justice and human rights.

Activities: Works with environmental and human rights organizations around the world to campaign for community-based river development, and with people who are directly affected by dams and other large-scale water intervention projects. The organization fosters greater understanding and respect for rivers, and participates in research and project analyses. It makes recommendations for alternative solutions to international environmental problems caused by governments' environmental policies.

Geographical Area of Activity: Worldwide.

Publications: *World Rivers Review* (2 a month); *River Revival Bulletin*; Annual Report; special reports; fact sheets; working papers; information resources.

Finance: Annual revenue US $2,419,862, expenditure $1,934,132 (31 Dec. 2013).

Board of Directors: Deborah Moore (Chair.); Leonard Sklar (Vice-Chair.); Leslie Leslie (Sec.); Susan Kopman (Treas.).

Principal Staff: Exec. Dir Peter Bosshard (a.i.).

Address: 2150 Allston Way, Suite 300, Berkeley, CA 94704-1378.

Telephone: (510) 848-1155; **Fax:** (510) 848-1008; **Internet:** www.irn.org; **e-mail:** contact@internationalrivers.org.

International Snow Leopard Trust—ISLT

Established in 1981.

Activities: Operates in Central Asia, dedicated to the conservation of the snow leopard and its mountain ecosystem, through conservation, research, education and information exchange, symposia, running projects in collaboration with local organizations, and publications. The Trust carries out certain environmental education, captive breeding and research programmes outside Central Asia.

Geographical Area of Activity: Mainly Central Asia.

Publications: *Conservation Handbook*; symposia proceedings; scholarly articles; pamphlets; annual reports; annual conservation reports; newsletters (monthly).

Finance: Annual revenue US $1,456,544, expenditure $1,367,489 (31 Dec. 2013).

Board of Directors: Rhetick Sengupta (Pres.); Andrea Gates Sanford, Gayle Podrabsky (Vice-Pres); Steven Kearsley (Sec./Treas.).

Principal Staff: Exec. Dir Brad Rutherford.

Address: 4649 Sunnyside Ave North, Suite 325, Seattle, WA 98103.

Telephone: (206) 632-2421; **Fax:** (206) 632-3967; **Internet:** www.snowleopard.org; **e-mail:** info@snowleopard.org.

International Women's Health Coalition—IWHC

Founded in 1980 to improve reproductive and sexual education and health in the developing world.

Activities: Operates in the fields of medicine and health, and social welfare, in Bangladesh, Brazil, Cameroon, Chile, Nigeria and Peru to reduce preventable deaths and illnesses by providing better reproductive and sexual health information and services. The IWHC promotes women's rights; provides technical, practical and financial support to grassroots organizations that work in reproductive and sexual health care and women's rights; holds meetings and conferences; publishes books and information papers; raises awareness in the USA of the problems facing women in these areas; acts as an advocate for new and improved health and population policies to benefit the lives of women and their communities; and provides grants for organizations engaging in innovative health care schemes, training, public education and advocacy.

Geographical Area of Activity: Selected countries in Africa, Asia and Central and South America.

Publications: *Positively Informed: Lesson Plans and Guidance for Sexuality Educators and Advocates*; *Twenty Years One Goal: 20th Anniversary Report 2004*; *Reproductive Health and Human Rights*; *My Father Didn't Think This Way*; *Nigerian Boys Contemplate Gender Equality*; Annual Report; and other publications.

Finance: Annual revenue US $4,171,840, expenditure $5,548,408 (30 Sept. 2014).

Board of Directors: Marlene Hess (Chair.); Debora Diniz, Marnie S. Pillsbury, Susan Nitze (Vice-Chair.); John E. Craig, Jr (Treas.); Catherine A. Gellert (Sec.).

Principal Staff: Pres. Françoise Girard.

Address: 333 Seventh Ave, 6th Floor, New York, NY 10001.

Telephone: (212) 979-8500; **Fax:** (212) 979-9009; **Internet:** www.iwhc.org; **e-mail:** info@iwhc.org.

International Women's Rights Action Watch—IWRAW

Established in 1985 at the World Conference on Women in Nairobi, Kenya. Joined the University of Minnesota Human Rights Center in 2006.

Activities: A resource centre for activists, academics and organizations concerned with the advancement of women's human rights internationally. The organization supports NGOs throughout the globe in their work to improve women's status, advocating for positive change in government policy and law. It monitors the implementation of the Convention on the Elimination of All Forms of Discrimination Against Women—CEDAW—and the implementation of women's human rights under other human rights treaties.

Geographical Area of Activity: International.

Publications: Guides and tools for using international human rights principles and procedures to advance women's human rights; special projects.

Principal Staff: Dir Prof. Marsha Freeman.

Address: University of Minnesota Human Rights Center, 229 19th Ave South, Minneapolis, MN 55455.

Telephone: (612) 625-4985; **Fax:** (612) 625-2011; **Internet:** www.iwraw.net; **e-mail:** mfreeman@umn.edu.

International Youth Foundation—IYF

Founded in 1990. Builds and maintains a worldwide community of businesses, governments and civil society organizations committed to empowering young people to be healthy, productive and engaged citizens.

Activities: Runs programmes that help young people obtain a quality education, gain employability skills, make healthy choices and improve their communities. The Foundation collaborates with businesses, governments and civil society organizations in more than 70 countries that share a common desire to improve the life conditions and prospects of young people, by building effective, sustainable and scalable programmes that positively impact the lives of young people worldwide.

Geographical Area of Activity: International.

Restrictions: Grants directed towards partner foundations only. The Foundation does not accept unsolicited proposals.

Publications: Annual Report; *Youth* (magazine); case studies, assessments and other reports.

Finance: Annual revenue US $24,507,699, expenditure $34,551,614 (31 Dec. 2013).

Board of Directors: Douglas L. Becker (Chair.).

Principal Staff: Pres. and CEO William S. Reese; CFO Samantha Barbee.

Address: 32 South St, Baltimore, MD 21202.

Telephone: (410) 951-1500; **Fax:** (410) 347-1188; **Internet:** www.iyfnet.org; **e-mail:** youth@iyfnet.org.

IREX—International Research & Exchanges Board

Established in 1968; a non-profit organization committed to international education in its broadest sense.

Activities: Operates in the field of education. Administers programmes in academic research, professional training, institution-building, technical assistance and policy-making, which operate collaboratively between the USA and 125 countries.

Geographical Area of Activity: USA, Middle East and North Africa, Asia, Central and Eastern Europe and Central Asia.

Publications: *Frontline* (newsletter); Annual Report; policy papers; online newsletter; conference reports.

Finance: Annual revenue US $75,911,178, expenditure $76,030,770 (30 June 2014).

Board of Directors: Edward M. Fouhy (Chair.).

Principal Staff: Pres. and CEO Kristin Lord.

Address: 1275 K St NW, Suite 600, Washington, DC 20005.

Telephone: (202) 628-8188; **Fax:** (202) 628-8189; **Internet:** www.irex.org; **e-mail:** irex@irex.org.

The James Irvine Foundation

Founded in 1937 by James Irvine for charitable purposes.

Activities: Operates within California in the fields of arts, education, civic participation, culture and youth services not receiving government support, through grants to institutions. Maintains an office in Los Angeles.

Geographical Area of Activity: California, USA.

Restrictions: No grants are made to individuals, private secondary schools, for sectarian religious activities, normal operating expenses, nor for general support.

Publications: Annual Report; information brochure; publications relating to areas of interest; *Irvine Quarterly* online newsletter.

Finance: Total assets US $148,321,958; annual expenditure $97,676,430 (31 Dec. 2013).

Board of Directors: Gregory M. Avis (Chair.); Steven A. Schroeder (Vice-Chair.).

Principal Staff: Pres. and CEO Don Howard.

Address: 1 Bush St, Suite 800, San Francisco, CA 94104.

Telephone: (415) 777-2244; **Fax:** (415) 777-0869; **Internet:** www.irvine.org; **e-mail:** communications@irvine.org.

Ittleson Foundation

Founded in 1932 by Henry Ittleson for the promotion of the well-being of humanity throughout the world, including, as means to that end, research, publication, the establishment and maintenance of charitable, religious and educational activities, agencies and institutions; and the aid of any such activities, agencies and institutions already established.

Activities: Operates nationally in the fields of the environment, health, welfare and education for health and welfare, with special emphasis on mental health and psychiatric research, through research grants to institutions, conferences, courses, publications and lectures. The Foundation currently focuses on AIDS, the environment and mental health.

Geographical Area of Activity: USA.

Restrictions: No fellowships or scholarships, travel grants or grants-in-aid to individuals; with a limited budget, the Foundation is unable to fund individuals, direct service programmes, continuing support or capital campaigns. Only making grants under its environmental programme in 2015.

Publications: Annual Report.

Finance: Annual revenue US $677,491, expenditure $1,152,706 (2013).

Board of Directors: H. Anthony Ittleson (Chair.); Anthony C. Wood (Sec.); Henry P. Davison, II (Treas.).

Principal Staff: Pres. H. Anthony Ittleson; Vice-Pres. Pamela Syrmis; Exec. Dir Anthony C. Wood.

Address: 15 East 67th St, New York, NY 10021.

Telephone: (212) 794-2008; **Fax:** (212) 794-0351; **Internet:** www.ittlesonfoundation.org.

Izumi Foundation

Established in 1998 to support and enhance the goals of Shinnyo-en USA, which are to address the root causes of human suffering, increase compassion and caring among all human beings, and promote a society that respects all living things.

Activities: Focuses on the alleviation of human suffering through improved health care, in particular for the poorest and most vulnerable members of society. The Foundation primarily operates through supporting efforts to reduce infectious diseases in less-developed and low-income countries in Sub-Saharan Africa and Central and South America, in particular projects that recognize the inter-relationship between disease and poverty; address the underlying causes of diseases and persistent health care problems; use innovative solutions to promote and help ensure sustainable outcomes; and increase collaboration and partnerships among local health care providers.

Geographical Area of Activity: Considers support for projects in Sub-Saharan Africa and Central and South America.

Restrictions: No unsolicited proposals accepted. No funding for medical research or other research-related activities;

endowments, capital costs or fund-raising activities; ongoing general operating expenses or existing deficits; lobbying of any kind; individuals; religious activities; or indirect costs. Maximum grant available US $100,000.

Finance: Annual revenue US $3,287,572, expenditure $1,644,698 (31 Dec. 2013).

Board of Directors: Shinrei Ito (Pres.); Ko Yamamoto (Treas.); Yuko Yoshida (Clerk).

Principal Staff: Programme Director Gretchen Stoddard.

Address: 1 Financial Center, 28th Floor, Boston, MA 02111.

Telephone: (617) 292-2333; **Fax:** (617) 292-2315; **Internet:** www.izumi.org; **e-mail:** info@izumi.org.

Lyndon Baines Johnson Foundation

Founded in 1969; responsible for managing gifts that benefit two institutions at the University of Texas at Austin—the Lyndon B. Johnson Library and Museum and the Lyndon B. Johnson School of Public Affairs.

Activities: Makes grants for living and travel expenses incurred by researchers of any nationality while conducting research on the life and career of Lyndon B. Johnson at the Johnson Library. The Foundation also awards fellowship for work to be done in National Archives facilities, including Presidential Libraries.

Geographical Area of Activity: USA.

Finance: Annual revenue US $15,534,267, expenditure $11,198,258 (31 Aug. 2013).

Board: Larry E. Temple (Chair.); Elizabeth Christian (Pres.); Ben Barnes, Lyndon L. Olson (Vice-Chair.).

Principal Staff: Exec. Dir Amy Barbee.

Address: LBJ Library and Museum, 2313 Red River St, Austin, TX 78705.

Telephone: (512) 232-2266; **Fax:** (512) 232-2285; **Internet:** www.lbjfoundation.org; **e-mail:** info@lbjfoundation.org.

Robert Wood Johnson Foundation—RWJF

Founded in 1936 for the improvement of health care in the USA.

Activities: Operates through grants to hospitals, medical, nursing and public schools, hospices, professional associations, research organizations, local and government agencies and community groups. The Foundation has three primary concerns: to ensure that Americans of all ages have access to basic health care at reasonable cost; to improve the organization and provision of services to people with chronic health conditions; and to promote health and reduce the personal, social and economic harm caused by substance abuse (tobacco, alcohol and illicit drugs).

Geographical Area of Activity: USA.

Publications: Annual Report; *Advance* (newsletter); books; occasional reports.

Finance: Annual revenue US $391,495,552, expenditure $543,066,787 (2013).

Board of Trustees: Roger S. Fine (Chair.).

Principal Staff: Pres. and CEO Risa Lavizzo-Mourey.

Address: POB 2316, Route 1 and College Rd East, Princeton, NJ 08543-2316.

Telephone: (609) 452-8701; **Fax:** (609) 452-1865; **Internet:** www.rwjf.org; **e-mail:** mail@rwjf.org.

The Johnson Foundation at Wingspread

Founded in 1958 by Herbert F. Johnson to promote international understanding, educational excellence, intellectual and cultural growth, and improvement of the human environment.

Activities: Aims to serve as a catalyst for innovative public and private solutions to healthy environments and healthy local communities. The Foundation plans and hosts conferences at Wingspread, its educational conference centre in Racine, WI.

Geographical Area of Activity: USA.

Restrictions: Supports conference-related activities by non-profit organizations.

Publications: *Wingspread Journal*; Annual Report; information brochure.

Finance: Annual revenue US $9,076,812, expenditure $5,803,738 (30 June 2014).

Board: Helen Johnson-Leipold (Chair.).

Principal Staff: Pres. Roger C. Dower.

Address: 33 E Four Mile Rd, Racine, WI 53402-2621.

Telephone: (262) 639-3211; **Fax:** (262) 681-3327; **Internet:** www.johnsonfdn.org; **e-mail:** info@johnsonfdn.org.

Joyce Foundation

Established in 1948 by Beatrice Joyce Kean, as an independent private foundation, to promote conservation, culture, economic development, education, campaign finance reform and the prevention of gun violence in the Great Lakes area.

Activities: Awards grants to not-for-profit organizations whose aims are to improve public policies in the areas of education, employment, environment, gun violence, campaign finance and culture. The Foundation also works to reduce poverty, to protect the natural environment of the Great Lakes and to prevent political corruption. In 2003, it initiated the Joyce Awards, an annual competition open to major and mid-size cultural organizations in mid-West cities. Operates in the mid-West states and in Canada.

Geographical Area of Activity: USA and Canada.

Publications: Annual Report; newsletters; *Welfare to Work: What Have We Learned*.

Finance: Annual revenue US $149,319,684, expenditure $44,604,619 (31 Dec. 2013).

Board of Directors: Roger R. Fross (Chair.); Charles U. Daly (Vice-Chair.).

Principal Staff: Pres. Ellen S. Alberding.

Address: 321 N. Clark St, Suite 1500, Chicago, IL 60654.

Telephone: (312) 782-2464; **Fax:** (312) 595-1350; **Internet:** www.joycefdn.org; **e-mail:** info@joycefdn.org.

Juvenile Diabetes Research Foundation International—JDRF

Founded in 1970 to support research into the causes, treatment, prevention and cure of type 1 diabetes and its complications.

Activities: Promotes research and education in the area of medicine and health, as well as outreach to those affected by diabetes and the general public. The Foundation offers grants and awards incl.: the Career Development Award in diabetes research for post-doctoral study in any country; the New Training for Established Scientist Award to provide assistance for visiting scholars carrying out research in any country, in a field different from, but related to, the diabetes-related area in which the applicant normally works; the Summer Student Program in diabetes research to assist colleges, universities, medical schools, etc., in supporting student research work; and fellowships and research awards tenable in any country for research into diabetes and its complications.

Geographical Area of Activity: International.

Publications: Annual Report; *Online Countdown*; *Emerging Technologies E-Newsletter; Life with Diabetes E-Newsletter*; fact sheets.

Finance: Annual revenue US $225,228,000, expenditure $214,896,840 (30 June 2014).

Board of Directors: Mary Tyler Moore (Int. Chair.); Robert Wood Johnson IV (Chair. of JDRF); John Brady (Chair. International Bd of Dirs); Stephen Newman (Vice-Chair. International Bd of Dirs) Max C. (Tom) Chapman III (Sec. and Chair. Nominating and Governance); Karen Case (Treas. and Chair. Finance).

Principal Staff: Pres. and CEO Derek K. Rapp.

Address: 26 Broadway, 14th Floor, New York, NY 10004.

Telephone: (800) 533-2873; **Fax:** (212) 785-9595; **Internet:** www.jdrf.org; **e-mail:** info@jdrf.org.

Max Kade Foundation, Inc

Founded in 1944 by Max Kade for general charitable purposes.

Activities: Operates nationally and internationally in the field of education, by sponsoring post-doctoral research exchange programmes between the USA and Europe in medicine and in the natural and physical sciences. The Foundation's particular focus is on developing relations between Germany and the USA.

Geographical Area of Activity: USA and Europe.

Restrictions: No grants or loans are made to individuals, only to publicly supported charitable organizations.

Finance: Annual revenue US $2,032,569, expenditure $6,294,481 (31 Dec. 2013).

Board of Directors: Lya Friedrich Pfeifer (Pres. and Treas.); Berteline Baier Dale (Sec.).

Address: 6 E. 87th St, 5th Floor, New York, NY 10128-0505.

Telephone: (646) 672-4354; **Internet:** www.maxkadefoundation.org.

The Henry J. Kaiser Family Foundation

Founded in 1948 by Henry J. Kaiser and his family members principally to support medical care programmes.

Activities: Operates in the areas of health policy, media and public education, and health and development in South Africa, through the provision of funds for research grants, special projects, fellowships, scholarships, professorships, seminars, conferences and technical assistance. Grants in the Community Grants Program are limited to California, other grants are made in the USA and Canada. The Foundation awards the annual Nelson Mandela Award for Health and Human Rights.

Geographical Area of Activity: North America and South Africa.

Restrictions: No grants are made to individuals and no unsolicited requests for funding accepted.

Publications: Annual Report; news releases; fact sheets.

Finance: Annual revenue US $33,881,978, expenditure $46,951,664 (31 Dec. 2013).

Board of Trustees: Richard T. Schlosberg, III (Chair.).

Principal Staff: Pres. and CEO Dr Drew E. Altman; Exec. Vice-Pres. Diane Rowland.

Address: 2400 Sand Hill Rd, Menlo Park, CA 94025.

Telephone: (650) 854-9400; **Fax:** (650) 854-4800; **Internet:** www.kff.org; **e-mail:** kffhelp@kff.org.

Kapor Center for Social Impact

Founded in 1997 as the Mitchell Kapor Foundation to protect the environment, improve quality of life for all people and help sustain healthy ecosystems. Present name adopted in 2013.

Activities: Seeks to use technology to bring about positive social change in under-represented communities, with a focus on closing academic, political, health and economic gaps. The Center operates in three core programme areas: Educational Access; Tech Tools for Social Impact; and Diversifying Tech.

Geographical Area of Activity: USA.

Publications: Biennial Report.

Finance: Annual revenue US $1,119,114, expenditure $3,627,730 (31 Dec. 2013).

Board of Directors: Mitch Kapor, Dr Freada Kapor Klein (Chair.); Mitchell D. Kapor (Pres.).

Principal Staff: Managing Partners Cedric Brown, Nicole Sanchez.

Address: 2201 Broadway, Suite 727, Oakland, CA 94612.

Telephone: (510) 255-4650; **Internet:** www.kaporcenter.org.

Howard Karagheusian Commemorative Corporation—HKCC

Founded in 1921 by Mihran Karagheusian and others to promote child welfare, public health services and international relief programmes in the Armenian refugee communities of Lebanon and Syria, and, on a smaller scale, in native Muslim Arab groups in the same communities.

Activities: Priority areas include: children's and community health care; distribution of medical equipment and medication; afterschool programmes for at-risk youths; vocational training and recreational programmes; social and housing assistance; and funding for social and medical institutions.

Geographical Area of Activity: Armenia, Lebanon and Syria.

Restrictions: No grants are made to individuals or organizations.

Publications: Annual Report.

Finance: Annual revenue US $2,156,733, expenditure $3,532,915 (2013).

Board of Directors: Michael Haratunian (Pres.); H. Irma Der Stepanian (Vice-Pres.); Harry A. Dorian (Treas.); Richard J. Varadian (Sec. and Asst Treas.).

Principal Staff: Man. Dir Irina Lazarian.

Address: 381 Park Ave S, Suite 1601, New York, NY 10016-8804.

Telephone: (212) 725-0973; **Fax:** (212) 447-0378; **Internet:** www.thkcc.org; **e-mail:** info@thkcc.org.

Ewing Marion Kauffman Foundation

Established in 2010 by Ewing Marion Kauffman to foster economically independent citizens engaged in their communities.

Activities: Operates in the areas of education and entrepreneurship through the provision of grants.

Geographical Area of Activity: USA, mainly Kansas City area.

Finance: Annual revenue US $215,950,094, expenditure $146,575,441 (31 Dec. 2013).

Board of Trustees: Janice Kreamer (Chair.).

Principal Staff: Pres. and CEO Farhan Latif.

Address: 4801 Rockhill Rd, Kansas City, MO 64110.

Telephone: (816) 932-1000; **Internet:** www.kauffman.org; **e-mail:** wbentrop@kauffman.org.

Helen Keller International—HKI

Founded in 1915.

Activities: Works to prevent blindness and reduce malnutrition. The organization runs programmes in 22 countries in Africa and the Asia-Pacific region, incl. USA, in two major areas of expertise: Eye Health, to prevent and treat cataracts, onchocerciasis—river blindness—trachoma and diabetic retinopathy by providing equipment and training; and Nutrition, providing Vitamin A supplements and leading food fortification initiatives, and promoting homestead food production, consumption of orange-fleshed sweet potatoes (OFSPs), and community management of malnutrition. It focuses on the major causes of blindness in the world that have been identified as priority eye diseases by the VISION 2020 global initiative to eliminate avoidable blindness.

Geographical Area of Activity: Africa, Asia, USA and Europe, encompassing 22 nations.

Restrictions: Does not distribute grants.

Publications: Bulletins and reports; Annual Report; research, resources and publications on: anaemia; food fortification; general health and nutrition; eye health; homestead food production; micronutrients; nutrition surveillance; and onchocerciasis.

Finance: Annual revenue US $59,388,476, expenditure $53,227,490 (30 June 2013).

Board of Trustees: Henry C. Barkhorn, III (Chair.); Desmond G. FitzGerald (Vice-Chair.); Mary F. Crawford (Sec.); Robert M. Thomas, Jr (Treas.).

Principal Staff: Pres. and CEO Kathy Spahn.

Address: 352 Park Ave South, 12th Floor, New York, NY 10010.

Telephone: (212) 532-0544; **Fax:** (212) 532-6014; **Internet:** www.hki.org; **e-mail:** info@hki.org.

W. K. Kellogg Foundation

Founded in 1930 by W. K. Kellogg, the breakfast cereal pioneer, to build the capacity of individuals, communities and institutions to solve their own problems.

Activities: Operates with the aim of improving human well-being in the USA, Central and South America, the Caribbean and Southern African countries (Botswana, Lesotho, Mozambique, South Africa, Swaziland and Zimbabwe). The Foundation's current aims are to support children, families and communities to help vulnerable children to achieve success as individuals and as members of society. It also supports the needs of young people through its other areas for assistance: health; youth and education; rural development; food systems; philanthropy and volunteerism. Kellogg International Fellowship programmes run worldwide.

Geographical Area of Activity: USA, Central and South America and the Caribbean, and Southern Africa.

Restrictions: Does not support research or endowment projects, nor does it award grants for operational phases of established programmes, capital facilities, equipment, conferences, films, television or radio programmes (unless these are an integral phase of a project the Foundation is already supporting), planning and studies, religious purposes, nor to individuals except for fellowships in specific areas of Foundation programming.

Publications: Annual Report; newsletter; brochures and reports.

Finance: Annual revenue US \$329,050,483, expenditure \$258,933,861 (31 Aug. 2013).

Board of Trustees: Bobby D. Moser (Chair.); Kathryn A. Kreckejnh (Sec.).

Principal Staff: Pres. and CEO La June Montgomery Tabron.

Address: 1 Michigan Ave E, Battle Creek, MI 49017-4012.

Telephone: (269) 968-1611; **Fax:** (269) 968-0413; **Internet:** www.wkkf.org; **e-mail:** int@wkkf.org.

Kennan Institute

Established in 1974 to increase American understanding and knowledge of the Russian Federation and the former USSR.

Activities: Hosts US-based scholars selected through a competition, so that they can conduct their individual research on the countries of the former USSR. The Institute also provides scholarships to researchers from these countries and runs a public lecture series during the academic year. It has a publication programme, and other activities include a junior scholar workshops series and a human rights fellowship in memory of former scholar Galina Starovoitova. Maintains offices in Moscow and Kiev.

Geographical Area of Activity: Russia and other countries of the former USSR (excluding the Baltic states).

Restrictions: Short-term grants only to individuals from the USA and former USSR.

Publications: *Kennan Cable*; monthly calendar/meeting reports; occasional paper series; commercially published books.

Finance: Receives funding from the US Dept of State, Carnegie Corporation of New York and Woodrow Wilson International Center for Scholars (qq.v.), federal appropriation and income from endowment.

Council: Christopher Kennan (Chair.).

Principal Staff: Dir Matthew Rojansky; Deputy Dir William E. Pomeranz.

Address: Woodrow Wilson Center, 1 Woodrow Wilson Plaza, 1300 Pennsylvania Ave NW, Washington, DC 20004-3027.

Telephone: (202) 691-4100; **Fax:** (202) 691-4247; **Internet:** www.wilsoncenter.org/index.cfm?fuseaction=topics .home&topic_id=1424; **e-mail:** kennan@wilsoncenter.org.

Joseph P. Kennedy Jr Foundation

Founded in 1946 for the prevention of mental disability by identifying its causes, and for the improvement of the means by which society deals with its mentally disabled citizens.

Activities: Makes grants for research, special projects, advisory services, conferences and seminars involving medicine and health, education and welfare of people with mental disability. The Foundation limits grants to proposals in the field of mental disability. It awards scholarships for a one-week bioethics course held at the Kennedy Institute of Ethics at Georgetown University, and Public Policy Leadership Fellowships for professionals and parents involved in the field of mental disability.

Restrictions: Does not fund specialized, local projects; does not provide funds to individuals.

Publications: *The New Housing Choice Voucher Program*; *Improved Care for Neglected Population Must Be 'Rule Rather Than Exception'*; *Putting Mental Retardation and Mental Illness on Health Care Professionals' Radar Screen*.

Finance: Annual revenue US \$1,572,124, expenditure \$555,082 (2013).

Board of Trustees: Jean Kennedy Smith (Vice-Chair.).

Principal Staff: Man. Steven M. Eidelman.

Address: 1133 19th St NW, 12th Floor, Washington, DC 20036-3604.

Telephone: (202) 393-1250; **Fax:** (202) 824-0351; **Internet:** www.jpkf.org; **e-mail:** eidelman@jpkf.org.

Kettering Foundation

Founded in 1927 by Charles F. Kettering. Deals with questions associated with governing, educating and science, all in relation to one another and in an international perspective, with attention to both formal and informal institutions to learn how democracy can work better.

Activities: Conducts projects that aim to find solutions to fundamental problems in the areas of governance, education and science. Carries out research in six inter-related areas: citizens and public choice; community politics and community leadership; the public and public schools; institutions, professionals and the public; public-government relations; and the international and the civil. As an operating, rather than a grantgiving, foundation, it pursues its projects in collaboration with organizations sharing its interests. It maintains a publications programme and holds training workshops in the USA and abroad.

Geographical Area of Activity: Mainly USA.

Restrictions: Not a grantmaking organization.

Publications: *Voices of Hope: The Story of the Jane Addams School for Democracy*; *Collective Decision Making Around the World*; *When Citizens Deliberate: Russian and American Citizens Consider Their Relationship*; *Reclaiming Public Education by Reclaiming Our Democracy*; *Citizens and Public Choice*; *Civil Investing*; *Community Politics and Leadership*; *International and the Civil*; *Journalism and Democracy*.

Finance: Annual revenue US \$20,605,926, expenditure \$21,553,478 (30 June 2013).

Board of Directors: Ed Dorn (Chair.).

Principal Staff: Pres. and CEO David Mathews; Vice-Pres. and Treas. Brian T. Cobb; Vice-Pres. and Program Dir John R. Dedrick; Vice-Pres., Sec. and Gen. Counsel Maxine S. Thomas.

Address: 200 Commons Rd, Dayton, OH 45459.

Telephone: (937) 434-7300; **Fax:** (937) 439-9804; **Internet:** www.kettering.org; **e-mail:** info@kettering.org.

Koch Foundation, Inc

Established in 1979 by Carl E. Koch and Paula Koch to promote Roman Catholicism.

Activities: Awards grants to Catholic organizations, nationally and internationally, that propagate the Catholic faith. Grants are made for different evangelization programmes, educational and spiritual formation of evangelists, resource-poor Catholic schools that are the principal means of evangelization in the community, a Catholic presence in the media, and capital expenditures. Priority is given to situations involving financially distressed, underdeveloped areas.

Geographical Area of Activity: International.

Restrictions: No grants are made to individuals; no loans or scholarships.

Publications: Annual Report.

Finance: Annual revenue US $15,222,426, expenditure $7,887,324 (31 March 2014).

Officers and Directors: William A. Bomberger (Pres.); Inge L. Vraney (Vice-Pres.); Dorothy Bomberger (Treas.); Lawrence Vraney, Michelle H. Bomberger (Asst Treas); Rachel A. Bomberger (Sec.).

Principal Staff: Exec. Dir Carolyn A. Young.

Address: 4421 NW 39th Ave, Bldg 1, Suite 1, Gainesville, FL 32606.

Telephone: (352) 373-7491; **Internet:** www.thekochfoundation.org; **e-mail:** staff@thekochfoundation.org.

Susan G. Komen for the Cure

Established in 1982 by Nancy Brinker.

Activities: Aims to eradicate breast cancer as a life-threatening disease. The organization funds breast cancer research, education, screening and treatment programmes, as well as operating a community-based grant programme, funding breast cancer health education and screening projects aimed at disadvantaged people. Funding is provided to non-profit organizations, educational institutions and government agencies. Also funds fellowships designed to improve the quality of care for breast cancer patients and operates an International Grant Fund. Operates a national telephone helpline.

Geographical Area of Activity: USA.

Publications: Annual Report.

Finance: Annual revenue US $123,039,886, expenditure $125,757,674 (31 March 2014).

Board of Directors: Linda Custard (Chair.).

Principal Staff: CEO Judy A. Salerno.

Address: 5005 LBJ Freeway, Suite 250, Dallas, TX 75244.

Telephone: (972) 855-1600; **Fax:** (972) 855-1605; **Internet:** www.komen.org; **e-mail:** grants@komen.org.

Koret Foundation

Founded in 1966 by Joseph Koret and Stephanie Koret for general charitable purposes.

Activities: Operates in California, mainly in the San Francisco Bay area, and Israel, in the fields of community development and Jewish life and culture. The Foundation's initiatives include the Koret Israel Economic Development Funds, the Koret Jewish Studies Publications Program, the Koret Jewish Book Awards, the Koret Israel Emergency Fund, the Koret Synagogue Initiative, Routes to Learning and the Koret Prize.

Geographical Area of Activity: USA and Israel.

Restrictions: No support is given to private foundations, nor to individuals.

Publications: *Catalyst* (newsletter); community reports; *Perspectives*.

Finance: Annual revenue US $38,592,603, expenditure $47,210,194 (2013).

Board of Directors: Susan Koret (Chair.); Michael J. Boskin, Dr Anita Friedman (Pres).

Principal Staff: CEO Jeffrey A. Farber.

Address: 33 New Montgomery St, Suite 1090, San Francisco, CA 94105.

Telephone: (415) 882-7740; **Fax:** (415) 882-7775; **Internet:** www.koretfoundation.org; **e-mail:** info@koretfoundation.org.

The Kosciuszko Foundation, Inc

Founded in 1925 to promote a better knowledge of their Polish heritage among Americans of Polish descent, and develop a sense of pride in the accomplishment of their ancestors, which is basic to an appreciation of their American heritage; to promote understanding between the USA and Poland; to encourage younger generations of Americans of Polish descent into higher education and contribute to the educational level in the USA; and to promote the growth of Polish studies in the USA.

Activities: Operates nationally and internationally in the fields of education, science and medicine, and the arts and humanities, through grants to institutions and individuals, fellowships, scholarships, conferences, courses, publications and lectures. The Foundation awards grants for Polish Americans to enter medical schools in Poland; and to enable writers, artists and students to complete scholarly, artistic or literary projects that would serve to implement the purposes of the Foundation. It also awards scholarships for Polish Americans to go on to higher education, and for Americans of non-Polish background to undertake Polish studies. The Chopin Piano Competition and the Marcella Sembrich Competition in Voice are held annually, as well as the Metchie J. E. Budka Award for outstanding scholarly work.

Geographical Area of Activity: Poland and USA.

Publications: Newsletters; Annual Report; and other publications.

Finance: Annual revenue US $3,479,999, expenditure $2,106,959 (30 June 2013).

Board of Trustees: William J. Nareski (Chair.); Wanda M. Senko, Cynthia Rosicki, Alex Storozynski (Vice-Chair.); Joseph E. Gore (Sec.).

Principal Staff: Pres. and Exec. Dir Prof. John S. Micgiel.

Address: 15 East 65th St, New York, NY 10065.

Telephone: (212) 734-2130; **Fax:** (212) 628-4552; **Internet:** www.thekf.org; **e-mail:** alex@thekf.org.

Kresge Foundation

Founded in 1924 by Sebastian S. Kresge for general charitable purposes.

Activities: Provides challenge grants only towards projects involving construction or renovation of facilities; purchase of major items of equipment or an integrated equipment at a cost of at least US $300,000 (which may include computer software expenses, if applicable); or the purchase of real estate. Those eligible to apply are well-established, financially sound, tax-exempt charitable organizations operating in the fields of higher education (awarding baccalaureate and/or graduate degrees), health and long-term care, human services, science and the environment, the arts and humanities, and public affairs. Full accreditation is required for higher education and hospital applicants. The Foundation also supports development at historically black colleges and universities and makes local grants in Detroit and South-Eastern Michigan. Office in Detroit opened in 2012.

Geographical Area of Activity: Canada, Mexico, South Africa, USA, United Kingdom.

Restrictions: Requests towards debt retirement or completed projects are not eligible.

Publications: Annual Report.

Finance: Annual revenue US $179,728,575, expenditure $170,639,271 (2013).

Board of Trustees: Elaine D. Rosen (Chair.).

Principal Staff: Pres. and CEO Rip Rapson; Vice-Pres. Ariel H. Simon.

Address: 3215 W. Big Beaver Rd, Troy, MI 48084.

Telephone: (248) 643-9630; **Fax:** (248) 643-0588; **Internet:** www.kresge.org; **e-mail:** info@kresge.org.

Samuel H. Kress Foundation

Founded in 1929 to promote education in the history of art and advanced training in fine arts conservation.

Activities: Provides grants for individuals and institutions to conduct research in European art from antiquity to 1850 and in the conservation of works of art; for the conservation and restoration of monuments in Western Europe; and for the development of scholarly resources in the areas of art history and conservation. The Foundation awards scholarships, fellowships for study and travel, and supports conferences and publications.

Geographical Area of Activity: USA, Europe.

Restrictions: No grants to artists or for the purchases of art. Grants only to organizations with US non-profit status.

Publications: Annual Report; articles.

Finance: Annual revenue US $6,224,914, expenditure $5,002,884 (30 June 2013).

Board of Trustees: Frederick W. Beinecke (Chair.); David Rumsey (Sec. and Treas.).

Principal Staff: Pres. Max Marmor; Dep. Dir L. W. Schermerhorn.

Address: 174 East 80th St, New York, NY 10075.

Telephone: (212) 861-4993; **Fax:** (212) 628-3146; **Internet:** www.kressfoundation.org; **e-mail:** info@kressfoundation .org.

KRS Education and Rural Development Foundation, Inc

Established in 1991 by the KRS Group to support projects relating to the environment, education and development, mainly in India.

Activities: Aims to improve education and health conditions for women and children in rural parts of India. The Foundation sponsors activities in the USA to advance global awareness and human understanding. It runs the Centre for Environment, Education and Development, which carries out research and development, as well as providing consultancy and information and running training courses and seminars.

Geographical Area of Activity: India and USA.

Finance: Annual revenue US $85,255, expenditure $85,255 (30 Nov. 2013).

Board of Directors: Sharada Rajanna (Pres.); Dr Bettalya Rajanna (Treas.).

Address: POB 820932, Vicksburg, MS 39182.

Telephone: (601) 638-5459; **Internet:** www.krsfoundation .org; **e-mail:** info@krsfoundation.org.

La Leche League International—LLLI

Established in 1956 to promote breastfeeding and to help breastfeeding mothers around the world.

Activities: Operates internationally in the area of health and social welfare. The League provides encouragement, education and information on topics and issues related to breastfeeding and parenting help, shared knowledge and support. It raises awareness of breastfeeding as an important element in the healthy development of the baby, the mother and the relationship between them.

Geographical Area of Activity: Worldwide.

Publications: Annual Report; *New Beginnings* (2 a month); *Leaven* (quarterly); *Abstracts* (quarterly); archives of breastfeeding information; books, fact sheets and other educational materials.

Finance: Annual revenue US $1,323,839, expenditure $1,652,915 (31 March 2014).

Board of Directors: Linda Anderson, Lydia de Raad (Co-Chair.); Anne Batterjee (First Vice-Chair.); Carolyn Driver-Burgess (Second Vice-Chair.); Catherine Marquis (Treas.); Diane Jeffer (Sec.); Villy Kaltsa (Member at Large).

Principal Staff: Exec. Dir Katie Keel.

Address: 35 E Wacker Dr., Suite 850, Chicago, IL 60601.

Telephone: (312) 646-6260; **Fax:** (312) 644-8557; **Internet:** www.llli.org; **e-mail:** info@llli.org.

Landesa—Rural Development Institute

Established in 1981 by Roy Prosterman as the Rural Development Institute to work with governments to give land rights to the world's poorest people.

Activities: Operates in the field of land rights through research, advocacy and programmes. The Institute maintains the Center for Women's Land Rights. Runs offices in the People's Republic of China and India.

Geographical Area of Activity: People's Republic of China, India and Sub-Saharan Africa.

Finance: Annual revenue US $10,999,903, expenditure $9,708,695 (30 June 2014).

Board of Directors: Christine Grumm (Chair.).

Principal Staff: Pres. and CEO Tim Hanstad.

Address: 1424 Fourth Ave, Suite 300, Seattle, WA 98101.

Telephone: (206) 528-5880; **Internet:** www.landesa.org; **e-mail:** info@landesa.org.

Lannan Foundation

Founded in 1960 by J. Patrick Lannan, Sr.

Activities: Supports the visual and literary arts and rural Native American communities. Through its visual arts programme, the Foundation makes awards, grants and fellowships with the aim of promoting, exhibiting, studying and discussing contemporary art. A literary programme fosters the writing of prose and poetry through grants and projects, and attempts to bring literature to a wider audience. The programme has awarded more than US $3.4m. to 75 writers of fiction, non-fiction and poetry since 1989 through its annual literary awards, which include a $200,000 Lifetime Achievement Award. The Foundation also awards the Lannan Prize for Cultural Freedom. The Indigenous Communities Program supports the efforts of Native Americans to continue their traditions by funding projects that revive and preserve languages and culture.

Geographical Area of Activity: USA.

Publications: Audio and bookworm archives; programme statements.

Finance: Annual revenue US $22,424,746, expenditure $29,570,667 (2013).

Board of Directors: Patrick Lannan (Pres.); Frank C. Lawler (Vice-Pres.).

Address: 313 Read St, Santa Fe, NM 87501-2628.

Telephone: (505) 986-8160; **Fax:** (505) 986-8195; **Internet:** www.lannan.org; **e-mail:** info@lannan.org.

Latter-day Saint Charities—LDSC

Established in 1996 to provide life-sustaining resources to people in emergencies, help strengthen families to help them become self-reliant, and offer opportunities for giving and service.

Activities: Provides emergency relief response, and builds self-reliance through health promotion and disease prevention initiatives. The organization also provides literacy, English language, and other training for teachers; and training in gardening and food production. It helps children to live within loving families, or in appropriate institutions when necessary. In 2014, the organization was present in 131 countries.

Geographical Area of Activity: Worldwide.

Restrictions: No grants to individuals.

Finance: Funded by public donations and by the Church of Jesus Christ of Latter-day Saints.

Principal Staff: Dir Sharon Eubank.

Address: 50 E. North Temple St, Floor 7, Salt Lake City, UT 84150-6890.

Telephone: (801) 240-1201; **Fax:** (801) 240-1964; **Internet:** ldscharities.org; **e-mail:** lds-charities@ldschurch.org.

Leakey Foundation

Founded in 1968 to increase scientific knowledge, education, and public understanding of human origins, evolution, behaviour and survival.

Activities: Supports postgraduate research (principally doctoral candidates and scientists with professional qualifications and demonstrated capability) in human origins and evolution, and human behaviour and survival, especially in the areas of: the ecology, archaeology and human paleontology of the Miocene, Pliocene and Pleistocene eras; great apes and primate behaviour; and the ecology of contemporary hunter-gatherer societies. Also awards the Franklin Mosher Baldwin Memorial Fellowships to students with citizenship in an African country who wish to obtain an advanced degree or carry out specialist training in an area of study related to human origins research.

Geographical Area of Activity: USA.

Publications: *AnthroQuest* (newsletter); news articles; press releases; podcast: DigDeeper.

Finance: Annual revenue US $1,749,857, expenditure $1,627,695 (31 Aug. 2013).

Board of Trustees: Gordon P. Getty (Chair.); Donald E. Dana (Pres.); J. Michael Gallagher (Vice-Pres.); Dr Diana McSherry (Vice-Pres., Grants Chair.); Camilla Smith (Vice-Pres., Public Outreach Chair.); G. Robert Muehlhauser (Governance Chair.); Julie M. LaNasa (Development Chair.); Dr Diana McSherry (Grants Chair.); Alice M. Corning (Sec.); William P. Richards, Jr (Treas., Investment Chair.); Cole Thomson (Finance Chair.).

Principal Staff: Man. Dir Sharal Camisa.

Address: 1003B O'Reilly Ave, San Francisco, CA 94129-1359.

Telephone: (415) 561-4646; **Fax:** (415) 561-4647; **Internet:** www.leakeyfoundation.org; **e-mail:** info@leakeyfoundation.org.

Levi Strauss Foundation

Founded in 1952 by Levi Strauss & Co.

Activities: Since 1982 has contributed approximately US $45m. to HIV/AIDS service organizations in more than 40 countries. In 2010, the Foundation dedicated roughly $2.1m. to this area. It has been committed to asset-building programmes since 1997, and in 2010 it devoted approximately $1.6m. of grant funds to advance its goals in asset building in the USA and abroad. The Foundation also supports programmes that reach approximately 300,000 apparel and textile workers annually in 15 countries where the company's products are made. Programmes range from asset building and financial literacy programmes to address the impact of the expiration of the Multi-Fiber Arrangement (MFA) in Latin America, to helping the significant female migrant labour force in the People's Republic of China. The Foundation aims to educate workers and factory management on labour rights and responsibilities; improve the health of workers (incl. hygiene, reproductive health and HIV/AIDS); provide asset-building opportunities for workers; and enhance oversight of labour laws through support for factory-level dispute resolution mechanisms, legal aid and arbitration channels.

Geographical Area of Activity: Worldwide.

Restrictions: Does not accept unsolicited proposals. Does not make grants to individuals, nor does it fund capital or endowment campaigns or building funds; recreational activities, sporting events or athletic associations; advertising; sectarian or religious activities; political campaigns or causes; or organizations that do not comply with the Foundation's non-discrimination policy.

Publications: Annual Report.

Finance: Annual revenue US $8,894,516, expenditure $9,913,803 (30 Nov. 2013).

Board of Directors: Robert D. Haas (Pres.); Jennifer Haas, Seth Jaffe (Vice-Pres); John Nystedt (Treas.).

Principal Staff: Exec. Dir and Sec. Daniel Jae-Won Lee.

Address: 1155 Battery St., Levi Plaza, San Francisco, CA 94111-1230.

Internet: levistrauss.com/about/foundations/levi-strauss-foundation.

Liberty Fund, Inc

Founded in 1960 by Pierre F. Goodrich.

Activities: Publishes print and electronic scholarly resources, incl. new editions of classic works in American constitutional history, European history, law, political philosophy and theory, economics, and education. The Fund also conducts around 165 conferences annually throughout the USA, Canada, Central and South America, and Europe.

Geographical Area of Activity: Worldwide.

Restrictions: Not a grantmaking organization.

Publications: *AMAGI* books (around 20 titles).

Finance: Annual revenue US $41,460,077, expenditure $22,204,112 (30 April 2014).

Board of Directors: T. Alan Russell (Chair.); Sandra J. Schaller (Sec.-Treas.).

Principal Staff: Pres. and CEO Chris L. Talley; Exec. Vice-Pres. and COO Emilio J. Pacheco.

Address: 8335 Allison Pointe Trail, Suite 300, Indianapolis, IN 46250.

Telephone: (317) 842-0880; **Fax:** (317) 579-6060; **Internet:** www.libertyfund.org; **e-mail:** info@libertyfund.org.

Life Sciences Research Foundation—LSRF

Founded in 1981 by Dr Donald D. Brown to administer an international programme of post-doctoral fellowships in all areas of life sciences.

Activities: Operates nationally and internationally in the fields of conservation and the environment, education, medicine and health, and science and technology. The Foundation provides grants to institutions and individuals, and funding for research. It accepts applications from US and foreign candidates conducting their research in US laboratories.

Geographical Area of Activity: USA.

Restrictions: Applications from non-US citizens must be for study in the USA.

Publications: Financial statements; information brochure.

Finance: Annual revenue US $4,055,939, expenditure $4,381,454 (31 May 2014).

Principal Staff: Pres. Donald D. Brown; Vice-Pres. Douglas E. Koshland; Treas. Christine Pratt.

Address: Admin. Office: 3520 San Martin Dr., Baltimore, ML 21218.

Telephone: (410) 467-2597; **Internet:** www.lsrf.org; **e-mail:** pratt@lsrf.org.

Lifebridge Foundation, Inc

Established in 1992 to promote holistic life, and to support individuals and organizations working to develop deeper understanding among people regarding the wholeness of humanity and the interdependence of all life.

Activities: Finances organizations working in: community service; science; the environment; youth and education; arts and culture; and world goodwill.

Geographical Area of Activity: Worldwide, but 95% of funded projects are in the USA.

Restrictions: Since 2005, the Foundation has been unable to accept any requests for funding because it is using funds to establish the Lifebridge Sanctuary.

Publications: *The Bridging Tree* (newsletter, 2 a year).

Finance: Annual revenue US $445,253, expenditure $372,078 (2013).

Board of Directors: Evelyn W. Hancock (Chair.); Stephen Nation (Sec.).

Principal Staff: Pres. and Treas. Barbara L. Valocore.

Address: POB 327, High Falls, NY 12440.

Telephone: (845) 658-3439; **Internet:** www.lifebridge.org; **e-mail:** info@lifebridge.org.

Lifewater International—LI

Founded in 1979 by William A. Ashe; a non-profit Christian organization.

Activities: Aims to help poor people living in rural areas around the world to obtain safe water, sanitation systems and hygiene education. Lifewater International works in less-developed countries through providing volunteers to train local organizations and people in the technical skills necessary to improve water supplies and sanitation, and donating equipment and financial support to assist communities to become self-sufficient and to provide a long-term solution to the problems caused by unclean water.

Geographical Area of Activity: East Africa, West Africa, Latin America and Caribbean, North America, Asia Pacific.

Publications: *Lifewater International Newsletter* (quarterly); *Water For The World Technical Notes*.

Finance: Annual revenue US $1,685,611, expenditure $1,435,229 (31 March 2014).

Board of Directors: Gene Ashe (Chair.); Tim Geisse (Vice-Chair.); Josh Brown (Treas.); Dr Jeff Bjorck (Sec.).

Principal Staff: Pres. and CEO Justin Narducci; Gen. Man. Shaun Russell.

Address: POB 3131, San Luis Obispo, CA 93403.

Telephone: (805) 541-6634; **Fax:** (805) 541-6649; **Internet:** www.lifewater.org; **e-mail:** info@lifewater.org.

Lilly Endowment, Inc

Founded in 1937 by the Lilly family for the promotion and support of religious, educational or charitable programmes.

Activities: Operates mainly in the fields of religion, education and community development (incl. social welfare and the arts and humanities). The Endowment gives special attention to programmes in Indianapolis and Indiana. It prioritizes projects that depend on private support, but a limited number of grants are made to governmental institutions and tax-supported programmes. International projects that the Endowment supports are limited to a small number of emergency relief efforts and public policy programmes, mostly in Canada and Mexico. Projects in health care, biological and physical science research, housing, transport, environment and population are usually not funded.

Geographical Area of Activity: Mainly Indiana, USA; some funding to Canada and Mexico.

Restrictions: Grants are not made to individuals.

Publications: Annual Report; occasional report; newsletter.

Finance: Annual revenue US $284,418,612, expenditure $295,277,886 (31 Dec. 2013).

Board of Directors: Thomas M. Lofton (Chair.); David D. Biber (Sec.); Diane M. Stenson (Vice-Pres. and Treas.).

Principal Staff: Pres. N. Clay Robbins.

Address: 2801 N Meridian St; Indianapolis, IN 46208; POB 88068, Indianapolis, IN 46208.

Telephone: (317) 924-5471; **Fax:** (317) 926-4431; **Internet:** www.lillyendowment.org.

Charles A. and Anne Morrow Lindbergh Foundation

Founded in 1977 by members of the Explorers Club, incl. Gen. James H. Doolittle and astronaut Neil Armstrong, to further Charles and Anne Morrow Lindbergh's vision of a balance between the advance of technology and the preservation of the environment.

Activities: Operates nationally and internationally in the fields of conservation and the environment; runs the Air Shepherd anti-poaching initiative in southern Africa. The Foundation funds grants and sponsors other educational and motivational efforts designed to honour the legacy of Charles and Anne Lindbergh and advance their vision of balance, incl. grants, awards and educational programmes. It funds around 8–10 Lindbergh Grants each year of amounts up to US $10,580 each.

Geographical Area of Activity: International.

Restrictions: Grants to individuals whose work demonstrates a balance between the innovative use or advancement of technology with the preservation of the environment.

Publications: Newsletter (3 a year); Annual Report; financial statements.

Finance: Annual revenue US $274,029, expenditure $348,393 (31 Dec. 2012).

Governing Board of Directors: John L. Petersen (Chair.); Gregg E. Maryniak (Vice-Chair.).

Principal Staff: Exec. Dir, Pres. and CEO Yolanka Wulff.

Address: 2150 Third Ave, N, Suite 310, Anoka, MN 55303-2200; POB 861, Berkeley Springs, WV 25411.

Telephone: (763) 576-1596; **Fax:** (763) 576-1664; **Internet:** www.lindberghfoundation.org; **e-mail:** info@lindberghfoundation.org.

Lucius N. Littauer Foundation, Inc

Founded in 1929 to enlarge the realms of human knowledge and to promote the general moral, mental and physical improvement of society.

Activities: Makes grants in the areas of education, social welfare, health care, the environment, arts and culture, Jewish communal life and Jewish studies. Most grants are made to organizations in the New York Metropolitan area and in Israel. The Foundation also supports organizations that work nationally, particularly in the fields of education and Jewish studies. Most Jewish studies work focuses on large-scale digitization and processing projects in Judaica libraries and archives.

Geographical Area of Activity: USA (mainly NY metropolitan area) and Israel.

Restrictions: No grants to individuals, or for religious activities or publishing of monographs and exhibition catalogues; grants only to non-profit organizations in the USA.

Publications: Guidelines.

Finance: Annual revenue US $1,812,033, expenditure $2,979,350 (2013).

Trustees: Noah B. Perlman (Sec.); Geula R. Solomon (Treas.).

Principal Staff: Pres. and CEO Robert D. Frost; Program Officer Alan Divack.

Address: 220 Fifth Avenue, 19th Floor, New York, NY 10001.

Telephone: (212) 697-2677; **e-mail:** info@littauerfoundation.org.

Livestrong Foundation

Established in 1997 to support people with cancer. Formerly known as the Lance Armstrong Foundation.

Activities: Helps people affected by cancer. The Foundation provides education, information, referral and support services; and makes grants for cancer survivorship research, community programmes, and survivorship centres at academic medical institutions.

Geographical Area of Activity: USA.

Publications: Newsletter.

Finance: Annual revenue US $38,077,668, expenditure $38,210,018 (31 Dec. 2013).

Board of Directors: Jeffery C. Garvey (Chair. and Founding Chair.); Michael Sherwin (Vice-Chair.); Dr Amelie G. Ramirez (Treas.); Blaine P. Rollins (Sec.).

Principal Staff: Pres and CEO Chandini Portteus.

Address: 2201 E. Sixth St, Austin, TX 78702.

Telephone: (877) 236-8820; **Internet:** www.livestrong.org; **e-mail:** livestrong@livestrong.org.

The Long Now Foundation—LNF

Established in 1996 to develop the 10,000 Year Old Clock and Library projects, which aim to become the basis of a long-term cultural institution.

Activities: Organizes seminars about long-term thinking, which aim to build a coherent and compelling body of ideas to help promote the Foundation's goal of making long-term thinking automatic and common. The 10,000 Year Old Clock project, conceived by Danny Hillis, aims to be a monument to long-term thinking. The Rosetta Project website is currently the largest collection of linguistic data on the Internet, containing collected material in more than 2,300 languages.

Geographical Area of Activity: USA.

Publications: Audio downloads.

Finance: Annual revenue US $2,632,883, expenditure $1,713,421 (31 Dec. 2013).

Board of Directors: Danny Hillis, Stewart Brand (Co-Chair.); Kevin Kelly (Sec.); David Rumsey (Treas.).

Principal Staff: Exec. Dir Alexander Rose.

Address: 2 Marina Blvd, Bldg A, San Francisco, CA 94123.

Telephone: (415) 561-6582; **Fax:** (415) 561-6297; **Internet:** www.longnow.org; **e-mail:** services@longnow.org.

Henry Luce Foundation, Inc

Founded in 1936 by Henry Robinson Luce to make grants for specific projects in the broad areas of Asian affairs, higher education and scholarship, theology, American arts and public affairs.

Activities: The Luce Scholars Program gives a select group of young Americans, who are not Asian specialists, a year's work/study experience in East and South-East Asia. Funding in the arts focuses on research, scholarship and exhibitions in American art; direct support for specific projects at major museums and service organizations; and dissertation support for topics in American art history through the American Council of Learned Societies (q.v.). The Clare Boothe Luce Program is designed to enhance the careers of women in science and engineering by offering scholarships, fellowships and professorships at invited institutions. Grants are also available in the fields of public policy, the environment and theology. The Henry R. Luce Professorship Program, which until 2004 provided six- to nine-year support for a limited number of integrative academic programmes in the humanities and social sciences at private colleges and universities, is currently on hold.

Geographical Area of Activity: USA.

Publications: American Art Press releases; financial reports.

Finance: Annual revenue US $29,178,984, expenditure $33,550,772 (31 Dec. 2013).

Board of Directors: Margaret Boles Fitzgerald (Chair.); Staci M. Salomon (Treas.).

Principal Staff: Pres. Michael Gilligan; Vice-Pres. Sean Buffington.

Address: 51 Madison Ave, 30th Floor, New York, NY 10010.

Telephone: (212) 489-7700; **Fax:** (212) 581-9541; **Internet:** www.hluce.org; **e-mail:** hlf1@hluce.org.

Ludwig Institute for Cancer Research—LICR

Established in 1971 by Daniel K. Ludwig, a US business tycoon; an international non-profit institute dedicated to understanding and controlling cancer.

Activities: Carries out research in collaboration with medical centres and hospitals. In Europe, the Institute has branches at the University of Oxford (United Kingdom), the Karolinska Institute and Uppsala University (Sweden), the Louvain Catholic University (Belgium), and the University of Lausanne and Swiss Institute for Vaccine Research (Switzerland). Five more branches outside Europe.

Geographical Area of Activity: Australasia, Europe, North and South America.

Publications: Annual and financial reports; news archive.

Finance: Annual revenue US $106,821,104, expenditure $108,070,010 (31 Dec. 2013).

Board of Directors: John L. Notter (Chair.).

Principal Staff: Pres. and CEO Edward A. McDermott, Jr.

Address: 666 Third Ave, 28th Floor, New York, NY 10017.

Telephone: (212) 450-1500; **Fax:** (212) 450-1565; **Internet:** www.licr.org.

Georges Lurcy Charitable and Educational Trust

Founded in 1985 to support educational purposes.

Activities: Provides grants to students of US and French universities and colleges for educational exchanges. The Trust also supports cultural organizations and secondary education.

Geographical Area of Activity: France and USA.

Finance: Annual revenue US $2,448,105, expenditure $1,488,264 (30 June 2014).

Principal Staff: Contact Seth E. Frank.

Address: 1633 Broadway, 32nd Floor, New York, NY 10019.

Telephone: (212) 660-3000; **Internet:** www.lurcy.org.

LWR—Lutheran World Relief

Established in 1945 to provide humanitarian aid around the world.

Activities: Works to improve the lives of smallholder farmers and people experiencing poverty in Africa, Asia and the Middle East, and Latin America, both in times of emergencies and for the long term. With the financial support of US Lutherans and other donors, the LWR strengthens communities through programmes in agriculture, climate and emergency support.

Geographical Area of Activity: Africa, Latin America, Asia and the Middle East.

Restrictions: No funding to US-based organizations.

Publications: Annual Report; *LWR eNews* (e-newsletter); *LWR Special Reports* (newsletter); *Faith in Action* (newsletter for LWR Quilters and Personal and School Kit Makers).

Finance: Annual revenue US $37,462,091, expenditure $45,226,311 (30 Sept 2013).

Board of Directors: Dr Gloria S. Edwards (Chair.); Jayesh Hines-Shah (Vice-Chair.); Jonathan D. Schultz (Sec.); JoAnn Theys (Treas.).

Principal Staff: Pres. and CEO Daniel V. Speckhard; Exec. Vice-Pres. Jeff Whisenant.

Address: 700 Light St, Baltimore, MD 21230; POB 17061 Baltimore, MD 21298-9832.

Telephone: (410) 230-2800; **Fax:** (410) 230-2882; **Internet:** lwr.org; programs.lwr.org; **e-mail:** lwr@lwr.org.

The John D. and Catherine T. MacArthur Foundation

Founded in 1978 by John D. and Catherine T. MacArthur to support creative people and effective institutions committed to building a just and peaceful world.

Activities: Fosters the development of knowledge, nurtures individual creativity, strengthens institutions, helps improve public policy, and provides information to the public, primarily through support for public interest media. The Foundation makes grants and loans through four programmes: the Program on Global Security and Sustainability focuses on international issues, such as human rights and international justice, peace and security, conservation and sustainable development, higher education in Nigeria and the Russian Federation, migration and human mobility, and population and reproductive health; the Program on Human and Community Development addresses issues in the USA, incl. community and economic development, housing, with a focus on the preservation of affordable rental housing, juvenile justice reform, education, with an emerging interest in digital media and learning, and policy research and analysis; the General Program supports public interest media, radio, documentary programming and work to explore the use of digital technologies to reach and engage the public; and the MacArthur Fellow

Program awards five-year, unrestricted fellowships to individuals across all ages and fields who show exceptional merit and promise of continued creative work.

Geographical Area of Activity: International.

Restrictions: The Foundation does not support political activities or attempts to influence action on specific legislation; nor provides scholarships or tuition assistance for undergraduate, graduate, or postgraduate studies.

Publications: Annual Report.

Finance: Annual revenue US $430,126,421, expenditure $286,012,311 (31 Dec. 2013).

Board of Directors: Marjorie M. Scardino (Chair.).

Principal Staff: Pres. Julia M. Stasch; Sec. Elizabeth Kane.

Address: 140 S. Dearborn St, Chicago, IL 60603-5285.

Telephone: (312) 726-8000; **Fax:** (312) 920-6258; **Internet:** www.macfound.org; **e-mail:** 4answers@macfound.org.

The Craig and Susan McCaw Foundation

Established in 1998 to carry out philanthropic activities in the areas of education, child development and environment.

Activities: Focuses on poverty reduction, economic development, and helping people gain access to technology worldwide. The Foundation also contributes a significant amount of its grants to organizations that implement an entrepreneurial and innovative approach to achieve their goals. It provides aid to under-developed countries for health and welfare; offers grants to organizations serving in Africa, incl. the Foundation for Community Development (qq.v.) and the Nelson Mandela Foundation; provides small-scale loans in support of technology development in Asia.

Geographical Area of Activity: Africa and South-East Asia.

Finance: Annual revenue US $9,717,6751, expenditure $3,769,775 (2012).

Board of Directors: Craig O. McCaw (Pres.); Susan R. McCaw, Amit Mehta (Vice-Pres); Teresa Mason (Sec.).

Address: POB 2908, Kirkland, WA 98083-2908.

Telephone: (425) 828-8000; **Internet:** mccawfoundation.org; **e-mail:** contact@mccawfoundation.org.

The Edna McConnell Clark Foundation

Established in 1969 by Edna McConnell Clark, daughter of the founder of Avon Products, David H. McConnell.

Activities: Seeks to transform the life prospects of economically disadvantaged young people in the USA. The Foundation works with other funders to make large, long-term investments to expand programmes that offer compelling evidence that they can help vulnerable young people, aged between nine and 24 years, to become successful adults by receiving an education, finding employment, and/or avoiding risky behaviours such as teen pregnancy and crime. Its investment approach incorporates four major components: flexible growth capital to strengthen a grantee's organizational and effectiveness capacity; assistance with business and evaluation planning; relationship management and strategic counsel and support provided by an experienced Foundation portfolio manager; and performance measurement that makes payout contingent on a grantee's progress towards quantifiable, mutually agreed goals.

Geographical Area of Activity: USA.

Restrictions: Grants are not made to individuals, nor for scholarships.

Publications: Annual Reports; evaluation reports; programme assessments and related materials.

Finance: Annual revenue (excl. unrealized gains) US $44,825,989, expenditure (incl. investment management expense) $54,920,476 (30 Sept. 2013).

Board of Trustees: H. Lawrence Clark (Chair.).

Principal Staff: Pres. Nancy Roob.

Address: 415 Madison Ave, 10th Floor, New York, NY 10017.

Telephone: (212) 551-9100; **Fax:** (212) 421-9325; **Internet:** www.emcf.org; **e-mail:** info@emcf.org.

Robert R. McCormick Foundation

Established as the Robert R. McCormick Charitable Trust in 1955 by Robert R. McCormick; became a foundation in 1990.

Activities: Aims to improve the social and economic development, encourage a free and responsible discussion of issues affecting the USA, enhance the effectiveness of US education and to stimulate responsible citizenship. The Foundation operates mainly in the Chicago metropolitan area supporting work in the fields of communities, citizenship, education and journalism. It runs a Journalism Program nationally and in Central and South America.

Geographical Area of Activity: USA, and Central and South America.

Restrictions: No grants are made to individuals.

Publications: Annual Report; information brochure.

Finance: Annual revenue US $135,028,877, expenditure $33,777,120 (31 Dec. 2013).

Board of Directors: Dennis J. FitzSimons (Chair.); Melinda Rosebraugh (Treas.).

Principal Staff: Pres. and CEO David D. Hiller.

Address: 205 N. Michigan Ave, Suite 4300, Chicago, IL 60601.

Telephone: (312) 445-5000; **Fax:** (312) 445-5001; **Internet:** www.rrmtf.org; **e-mail:** info@mccormickfoundation.org.

James S. McDonnell Foundation

Founded in 1950 by aerospace pioneer James S. McDonnell to 'improve the quality of life'.

Activities: Operates in the fields of biological and behavioural sciences. The Foundation runs the 21st Century Science Initiative, which supports individual and collaborative research in two areas: Studying Complex Systems; and Brain Cancer Research. Individual grants are awarded over a period of three to six years. International applications are invited.

Geographical Area of Activity: International.

Restrictions: Grants only to not-for-profit (501 (c)3) organizations or foreign equivalent.

Finance: Annual revenue US $28,176,681, expenditure $32,678,774 (2013).

Board of Directors: James S. McDonnell, III (Sec.); Jeffrey M. McDonell (Asst Sec.); John F. McDonnell (Treas.).

Principal Staff: Pres. Dr Susan M. Fitzpatrick.

Address: 1034 S Brentwood Blvd, Suite 1850, St Louis, MO 63117.

Telephone: (314) 721-1532; **Fax:** (314) 721-7421; **Internet:** www.jsmf.org; **e-mail:** info@jsmf.org.

McKnight Foundation

Founded in 1953 by William L. and Maude L. McKnight and Virginia M. and James M. Binger for general charitable purposes.

Activities: Gives funding in the fields of children and families; communities and regions; the arts; environment; research; and international funding. Scientific research is divided into two main areas: neuroscience, particularly diseases affecting the memory; and crop research, particularly in developing countries. The Foundation has interests in Tanzania, Uganda, Zimbabwe, Cambodia, Laos and Viet Nam, where the emphasis is on agricultural development, community development, health care, assistance for landmine victims, and micro-enterprise development.

Geographical Area of Activity: Mainly USA (Minnesota); some grants in Cambodia, Laos, Tanzania, Uganda, Viet Nam and Zimbabwe.

Restrictions: Grants are rarely made outside the state of Minnesota.

Publications: Annual Report; grants list; occasional report; information brochure.

Finance: Annual revenue US $198,507,550, expenditure $137,763,820 (2013).

Board of Directors: Meghan Binger Brown (Chair.); Rick Scott (Sec.); Bill Gregg (Asst Treas.).

Principal Staff: Pres. Kate Wolford.

Address: 710 South Second St, Suite 400, Minneapolis, MN 55401.

Telephone: (612) 333-4220; **Fax:** (612) 332-3833; **Internet:** www.mcknight.org; **e-mail:** grants@mcknight.org.

Maclellan Foundation, Inc

Incorporated in 1945 by Robert J. Maclellan and family; provides funding for Christian ministries worldwide. Part of the Maclellan Family Foundations group, which includes the Robert L. and Kathrina H. Maclellan Foundation (f. 1972), which supports evangelical Christian ministries in the Greater Chattanooga area, with an emphasis on youth, family, education and leadership; and the Christian Education Charitable Trust (f. 1974), which explores the use of technology in Christian education.

Activities: Invests in faith-based solutions throughout the world and encourages wise giving.

Geographical Area of Activity: Worldwide.

Restrictions: No grants are made to individuals. All ministries must have a 501 (c) 3 tax-exempt status or be in a fiscal sponsor relationship with a US tax-exempt group.

Finance: Annual revenue US $15,976,404, expenditure $31,834,860 (2013).

Board of Trustees: Hugh O. Maclellan, Jr (Exec. Chair. and Treas.); Robert H. Maclellan (Vice-Chair.); Christopher H. Maclellan (Sec.).

Principal Staff: Exec. Dir David G. Denmark.

Address: 820 Broad St, Suite 300, Chattanooga, TN 37402.

Telephone: (423) 755-1366; **Fax:** (423) 755-1640; **Internet:** www.maclellan.net; **e-mail:** support@maclellan.net.

Josiah Macy, Jr Foundation

Founded in 1930 by Kate Macy Ladd to advance medicine and health in the USA and abroad.

Activities: Operates nationally and internationally in the fields of science and medicine, through health programmes, grants to institutions, conferences and publications. The Foundation's major interest is in medical education. It is particularly concerned with African American, Latino and Native American health issues, and enhancing the representation of minorities in the health profession. Currently focused on improving health professional education, increasing teamwork between and among multiple health professions, educational strategies that increase access and use of health-care facilities by underserved communities, and increasing diversity among health-care professionals.

Geographical Area of Activity: Mainly USA.

Restrictions: No grants are given for building, endowment, annual fund appeals or individual travel.

Publications: Annual Report; *Continuing Education in the Health Professions: Improving Healthcare through Lifelong Learning*; *Women and Medicine*; *The Convergence of Neuroscience, Behavioral Science, Neurology, and Psychiatry*; *The Future of Pediatric Education in the 21st Century*; *Macy-Morehouse Conferences on Primary Care for the Underserved*; *Modern Psychiatry: Challenges in Educating Health Professionals to Meet New Needs*; *Education of Health Professionals in Complementary/Alternative Medicine*; *Enhancing Interactions Between Nursing and Medicine: Opportunities in Health Professional Education*; *Education for More Synergistic Practice of Medicine and Public Health*; *The Implications of Genetics for Health Professional Education*.

Finance: Annual revenue US $18,333,936, expenditure $8,764,878 (30 June 2014).

Board of Directors: William H. Wright, II (Chair.); Peter Goodwin (Treas.).

Principal Staff: Pres. George E. Thibault.

Address: 44 East 64th St, New York, NY 10065.

Telephone: (212) 486-2424; **Fax:** (212) 644-0765; **Internet:** macyfoundation.org; **e-mail:** info@macyfoundation.org.

MADRE

Founded in 1983 by a group of women to advance women's human rights by meeting urgent needs in communities and building lasting solutions to the crises women face.

Activities: Operates in the field of international human rights by working with grassroots women's organizations in communities around the world, focusing on health, combating violence against women, peacebuilding, economic and environmental justice and other basic human rights. The organization provides financial and technical support for these partner groups, while raising awareness of relevant issues within the USA. Programmes currently operate in Afghanistan, Colombia, Guatemala, Haiti, Iraq, Kenya, Mexico, Nicaragua, Palestinian Territories, Peru and Sudan.

Geographical Area of Activity: South America, Central America and the Caribbean, Asia, Africa and the Middle East.

Restrictions: Grants only to partner organizations.

Publications: Newsletter; position papers; articles.

Finance: Annual revenue US $2,156,553, expenditure $1,819,688 (31 Dec. 2013).

Board of Directors: Anne H. Hess, Blaine Bookey (Co-Chair.).

Principal Staff: Exec. Dir Yifat Susskind.

Address: 121 W 27th St, Suite 301, New York, NY 10001.

Telephone: (212) 627-0444; **Fax:** (212) 675-3704; **Internet:** www.madre.org; **e-mail:** madre@madre.org.

A. L. Mailman Family Foundation, Inc

Established in 1980 by Abraham Mailman to support communities and families in providing care and stability for young children.

Activities: Funds national projects in the USA to improve the quality of early child care and education, with a specific emphasis on advocacy projects. In 2000, the Foundation launched the Early Childhood Leadership Award, accompanied by a grant to support leadership development and mentorship activities.

Geographical Area of Activity: USA.

Restrictions: No grants for direct services, local programmes, individuals or scholarships, childcare centres and schools, capital campaigns and endowments, deficit reduction or general operating expenses.

Finance: Annual revenue US $293,622, expenditure $720,914 (2013).

Board of Directors: Dr Wendy S. Masi (Chair.); Michael Walden (Sec./Treas.).

Principal Staff: Pres. Richard D. Segal.

Address: 707 Westchester Ave, White Plains, NY 10604.

Telephone: (914) 683-8089; **Fax:** (914) 686-5519.

MAP International—Medical Assistance Programs

Established in 1954 by Dr J. Raymond Knighton; a Christian relief and development organization that aims to promote the health of people living in developing countries.

Activities: Operates in developing countries in Africa and Central and South America in the area of medicine and health, through works in partnership with other organizations to provide essential medicines to those in need, so as to prevent and eradicate diseases (particularly addressing the problem of HIV/AIDS) and to promote community health development in less-developed countries. The organization also provides emergency health care in areas suffering from the effects of natural and man-made disasters. It offers scholarships to medical students from North America to travel to developing countries to work at hospitals helping people in financial need. Maintains overseas offices in Bolivia, Ecuador, Indonesia, Côte d'Ivoire, Kenya and Uganda.

Geographical Area of Activity: Africa, Central and South America and South-East Asia.

Finance: Annual revenue US $348,887,499, expenditure $352,622,111 (30 Sept. 2014).

Board of Directors: Phillip J. Mazzilli (Chair.); Mary Jane Lindholm (Vice-Chair.); Dr Mark R. Bell (Treas.); Cheryl Vaught (Sec.).

Principal Staff: Pres. and CEO Steve Stirling.

Address: 4700 Glynco Parkway, Brunswick, GA 31525-6901.

Telephone: (912) 265-6010; **Fax:** (912) 265-6170; **Internet:** www.map.org; **e-mail:** map@map.org.

March of Dimes Foundation

Founded in 1938 by US President Franklin Roosevelt as the National Foundation for Infantile Paralysis to combat polio; later renamed March of Dimes Birth Defects Foundation. The foundation's current aim is to help prevent birth defects and infant mortality through education and research.

Activities: Promotes the continuing education of professionals in the field of perinatal care, and the expansion of education programmes for the general public. Makes grants to organizations for research in aspects of birth defects; and various research awards for research in the USA, including Clinical Research Grants, Pre-doctoral Graduate Research Training Fellowships, Social and Behavioral Sciences Research Grants, the Summer Science Research Program for Medical Students, the Basil O'Connor Starter Scholar Research Award Program, and the Research Support Program on Reproductive Hazards in the Workplace, Home, Community and Environment.

Geographical Area of Activity: Africa, Latin America, Asia, Central and Eastern Europe.

Publications: Annual Report; newsletter.

Finance: Annual revenue US $217.3m., expenditure $216.1m. (31 Dec. 2013).

Board of Trustees: LaVerne H. Council (Chair.); Gary Dixon, Jonathan Spector, H. Edward Hanway (Vice-Chair.); Monica Luechtefeld (Sec.); Deirdra Merriwether (Treas.).

Principal Staff: Pres. Dr Jennifer L. Howse; Exec. Vice-Pres. and COO Lisa Bellsey.

Address: 1275 Mamaroneck Ave, White Plains, NY 10605.

Telephone: (914) 997-4488; **Fax:** (914) 997-4650; **Internet:** www.marchofdimes.org.

Marisla Foundation

Founded in 1986 to provide funding to preserve individual rights to have a safe place to live to organizations that work to preserve the world's natural resources.

Activities: Operates in the field of environmental conservation and protection on the West Coast of the USA, Hawaii and the Pacific. The Foundation has a special interest in programmes promoting marine conservation. It is also concerned with women's centres and services in Los Angeles County and Orange County in Southern California.

Geographical Area of Activity: USA, Hawaii and the Pacific.

Finance: Annual revenue US $41,002,238, expenditure $43,816,500 (2013).

Board of Directors: Anne G. Earhart (Pres.); Oliver N. Crary (Treas.); Glenda S. Menges (Sec. and Admin.).

Principal Staff: Exec. Dir Herbert M. Bedolfe, III.

Address: 668 North Coast Highway, PMB 1400, Laguna Beach, CA 92651.

Telephone: (949) 494-0365; **Fax:** (949) 494-8392; **Internet:** online.foundationsource.com/public/home/marisla; **e-mail:** glenda@marisla.org.

Markle Foundation

Founded in 1927 by John and Mary R. Markle to promote the advancement and diffusion of knowledge and the general good of humanity.

Activities: Focuses on the potential of mass communications and information technology to enhance learning, and improving the mass media, incl. services growing out of new technologies for the processing and transfer of information. The Foundation operates throughout the USA in the fields of health and national security, through self-conducted programmes, research and grants to institutions. It has made substantial commitments to the following programme areas: developing policies for a networked society, promoting information technologies for better health, as well as operating an Opportunity Fund.

Geographical Area of Activity: USA.

Restrictions: No grants are made to individuals.

Publications: Financial documents; *Health; A Model for Remote Health Care in the Developing World: The Markle Foundation Telemedicine Clinic in Cambodia; Connecting for Health; Time Series Modeling for Syndromic Surveillance; It is about Health: Securing a National Health Information Infrastructure; The Quality Case for Information Technology in Healthcare; Creating a Trusted Information Network for Homeland Security.*

Finance: Annual revenue US $8,526,354, expenditure $12,597,600 (30 June 2013).

Board of Directors: Lewis B. Kaden (Chair.).

Principal Staff: CEO and Pres. Zoë Baird.

Address: 10 Rockefeller Plaza, 16th Floor, New York, NY 10020-1903.

Telephone: (212) 713-7600; **Fax:** (212) 765-9690; **Internet:** www.markle.org; **e-mail:** info@markle.org.

The Max Foundation

Established in 1997 by Pedro José Rivarola to improve the quality of life and the treatment of patients suffering from leukaemia, and other blood diseases and rare cancers, especially children of Hispanic and Latino origin.

Activities: Operates in Asia, the USA and in Central and South America in the field of medicine and health. The Foundation provides information about treatment options; offers advice and emotional and financial support to sufferers of blood-related diseases; and raises awareness of the importance of becoming a bone marrow donor. It is also working to establish the VidaMax-MaxLife Bone Marrow and Cord Blood Registry to increase patients' chances of survival and successful treatment; and operates the Max For Life community fundraising programme, encouraging individuals to donate small amounts of funds to support the improvement of the health care system in some of the regions of the world most in need. Maintains satellite MaxStations in Argentina, Bolivia, Chile, India, Malaysia, Mexico, Pakistan, Paraguay, Peru, the Philippines, the Russian Federation, Singapore, South Africa, Thailand, Turkey and Uruguay.

Geographical Area of Activity: Worldwide.

Publications: Newsletter.

Finance: Annual revenue US $2,800,980, expenditure $2,454,817 (31 Dec. 2013).

Board of Directors: Pat Garcia-Gonzalez (Pres. and CEO); Jenny Scott (Treas.); Robert Farmer (Sec.).

Address: 110 West Dayton St, Suite 205, Edmonds, WA 98020.

Telephone: (425) 778-8660; **Fax:** (425) 778-8760; **Internet:** www.themaxfoundation.org; **e-mail:** info@themaxfoundation.org.

MDA—Muscular Dystrophy Association

Founded in 1950 by a group of New York parents and relatives of young people affected by muscular dystrophy.

Activities: Aims to combat neuromuscular disease through worldwide support of basic and clinical research directed at developing affective treatments for neuromuscular disorders.

The Association also operates a national programme of medical services and clinical care, incl. diagnostic services and rehabilitative follow-up care through a nationwide network of hospital-affiliated clinics; provides selected medical equipment; and offers support groups and summer camp programmes. It attempts to broaden public awareness of neuromuscular disease through its publications, video presentations and press releases, and offers online information services.

Geographical Area of Activity: Conducts research worldwide; services available only in the USA.

Restrictions: Grants to individual scientific investigators affiliated with academic institutions or qualified research facility.

Publications: Annual Report; brochures; *ALS Newsletter*; *Quest; Quest Magazine*; *MDA/ALS Newsmagazine*; *Facts About* (booklets); publications about MDA programmes; publications about daily living with neuromuscular diseases.

Finance: Annual revenue US $150,325,720, expenditure $148,005,192 (31 Dec. 2013).

Board: R. Rodney Howell (Chair.); Timmi Masters (Sec.); Charles D. Schoor (Treas.).

Principal Staff: Pres. and CEO Stephen M. Derks.

Address: 3300 East Sunrise Dr., Tucson, AZ 85718-3208.

Telephone: (520) 529-2000; **Fax:** (520) 529-5300; **Internet:** www.mdausa.org; **e-mail:** mda@mdausa.org.

Richard King Mellon Foundation

Founded in 1947 by Richard King Mellon for general charitable purposes.

Activities: Operates programmes in the fields of conservation; regional economic development; children, youth and young adults; education and human services; and non-profit capacity building. The Foundation focuses mainly on quality of life in Pittsburgh and south-west Pennsylvania, but also promotes national conservation programmes.

Geographical Area of Activity: USA (particularly southwestern Pennsylvania).

Restrictions: Will not consider requests on behalf of individuals or from outside the USA. Funding is mainly restricted to Southwestern Pennsylvania.

Publications: Annual Report and financial statement; information brochure.

Finance: Annual revenue US $173,661,730, expenditure $115,995,253 (2013).

Trustees: Seward Prosser Mellon (Chair. and CEO); Douglas L. Sisson (Vice-Pres. and Treas.); Lawrence S. Busch (Asst Treas.); Lisa Kuzma (Sec.).

Principal Staff: Pres. W. Russell G. Byers, Jr; Dir Scott D. Izzo.

Address: BNY Mellon Center, 500 Grant St, Suite 4106, Pittsburgh, PA 15219; POB 945 Ligonier, PA 15658.

Telephone: (412) 392-2800; **Fax:** (412) 392-2837; **Internet:** foundationcenter.org/grantmaker/rkmellon.

The Andrew W. Mellon Foundation

Founded in 1969 by the merger of the Avalon Foundation (f. 1940 by Ailsa Mellon Bruce) and the Old Dominion Foundation (f. 1941 by Paul Mellon) to support higher education and cultural institutions.

Activities: Operates five programmes nationally: higher education and scholarship; scholarly communications and information technology; art history, museums and art conservation; performing arts; and conservation and the environment. Offers Distinguished Achievement in the Humanities awards annually to academics holding tenured positions at US universities.

Geographical Area of Activity: Mainly USA.

Restrictions: Makes few grants to non-US organizations, and no grants to individuals.

Publications: Annual Report; *Equity and Excellence*; *Reclaiming the Game*; *JSTOR: A History*; *Stand and Prosper*; *The Game of Life*; *Library Automation in Transitional Societies*; *Promise and Dilemma*; *Technology and Scholarly Communication*; *The Shape of the River*; *Universities and Their Leadership*; *Crafting a Class*; *What's Happened to the Humanities*; *The New-York Historical Society*; *Managing Change in the Nonprofit Sector*; *Inside the Boardroom*; *The Charitable Nonprofits*; *University Libraries and Scholarly Communication*; *In Pursuit of the PHD*; *Prospects for Faculty in Arts and Sciences*.

Finance: Annual revenue US $568,858,344, expenditure $293,893,892 (2013).

Trustees: Danielle S. Allen (Chair.).

Principal Staff: Pres. Earl Lewis; Deputy to the Pres. Makeba Morgan Hill.

Address: 140 East 62nd St, New York, NY 10065.

Telephone: (212) 838-8400; **Fax:** (212) 888-4172; **Internet:** www.mellon.org; **e-mail:** inquiries@mellon.org.

Memorial Foundation for Jewish Culture

Founded in 1965 by Dr Nahum Goldmann with reparation funds from the Government of West Germany.

Activities: Aims to encourage and assist Jewish scholarship and education; and to contribute to the preservation, enhancement and transmission of Jewish culture throughout the world. The Foundation awards scholarships to prepare future scholars, researchers and rabbinical leaders, and fellowships to aid scholars, writers and artists.

Geographical Area of Activity: Worldwide.

Finance: Annual revenue US $3,610,671, expenditure $2,289,707 (30 Sept. 2013).

Board of Trustees: Ismar Schorsch (Pres.); Salomon Rytz (Sec.); Fernando Lottenberg (Treas.).

Principal Staff: Exec. Dir Jennifer S. Friedman.

Address: 50 Broadway, 34th Floor, New York, NY 10004.

Telephone: (212) 425-6606; **Fax:** (212) 425-6602; **Internet:** www.mfjc.com; **e-mail:** office@mfjc.org.

The John Merck Fund

Founded in 1970 by the late Serena S. Merck for charitable purposes.

Activities: Operates nationally and internationally in the areas of developmental disabilities, the environment, reproductive health, providing job opportunities, and human rights, through awarding grants to medical teaching hospitals and small organizations; offers support for conferences, seminars and research, and fellowships. The Fund also awards the annual Serena Merck Memorial Award to an exceptional individual who has demonstrated long-term, selfless dedication and compassion in the care or service to children who are mentally disabled and have significant mental health problems.

Geographical Area of Activity: International, mainly USA.

Restrictions: Endowment or capital-fund projects; large organizations with well-established funding sources (except those that need help launching promising new projects for which funding is not readily available); general support (except in the case of small organizations whose entire mission coincides with one of the Fund's areas of interest); individuals (except if his or her project is sponsored by a domestic or foreign educational, scientific or charitable organization).

Publications: Grant reports.

Finance: Annual revenue US $7,579,266, expenditure $10,726,695, (2013).

Board of Trustees: Olivia H. Farr (Chair.); Anne Stetson (Treas.).

Principal Staff: Exec. Dir and Sec. Ruth G. Hennig; Dep. Dir and Asst Treas. Nancy Stockford.

Address: 2 Oliver St, 8th Floor, Boston, MA 02109.

Telephone: (617) 556-4120; **Fax:** (617) 556-4130; **Internet:** www.jmfund.org; **e-mail:** info@jmfund.org.

Mercy Corps

Founded in 1981 by Dan O'Neill and Ellsworth Culver to alleviate suffering around the world. Merged with NetAid (f. 1999 to help alleviate poverty worldwide) in 2007.

Activities: Operates as a network of organizations with offices in more than 40 countries working internationally in the fields of sustainable community development, civil society and emergency relief. Programmes are primarily targeted at providing long-term solutions for people suffering the effects of poverty, oppression and conflict, through health care, housing, education, economic and community development, material aid and micro-enterprise schemes. The organization provides emergency relief for those affected by natural and man-made disasters and also works to promote citizen participation, the accountability of governments and conflict management.

Geographical Area of Activity: Worldwide.

Publications: Annual Report.

Finance: Annual revenue US $275,451,652, expenditure $278,519,140 (30 June 2014).

Board of Directors: Allen S. Grossman (Chair.); Linda A. Mason (Hon. Chair.); Robert D. Newell (Treas.).

Principal Staff: CEO Neal L. Keny-Guyer.

Address: 45 SW Ankeny St, Portland, OR 97204; Dept W, POB 2669, Portland, OR 97208-2669.

Telephone: (503) 796-6800; **Internet:** www.mercycorps.org; **e-mail:** donorservices@mercycorps.org.

Mercy-USA for Aid and Development—M-USA

Incorporated in 1988; a non-profit international relief and development organization dedicated to alleviating human suffering and supporting people in their efforts to become more self-sufficient.

Activities: Operates in the areas of aid to less-developed countries, education, medicine and health, and social welfare, through a number of projects, incl. promoting economic and educational growth, disaster relief, reconstruction and rehabilitation, and international development projects.

Geographical Area of Activity: Africa, Central and South-Eastern Europe, Central and Southern Asia, and the USA.

Restrictions: No grants are made to individuals.

Publications: *Mercy News* (newsletter); Annual Report.

Finance: Annual revenue US $8,973,281, expenditure $9,200,168 (31 Dec. 2013).

Board of Directors: Iman Elkadi (Chair.); Dr Ali el-Menshawi (Vice-Chair.); Melvin Bilal (Treas.).

Principal Staff: Pres., CEO and Sec. Umar al-Qadi; CFO Anas Alhaidar.

Address: 44450 Pinetree Dr., Suite 201, Plymouth, MI 48170-3869.

Telephone: (734) 454-0011; **Fax:** (734) 454-0303; **Internet:** www.mercyusa.org; **e-mail:** info@mercyusa.org.

Mertz Gilmore Foundation

Founded in 1959 by Joyce Mertz-Gilmore for general charitable purposes.

Activities: Currently makes grants to non-profit organizations active in the following programme areas: Climate Change Solutions; Human Rights in the USA; New York City Communities; New York City Dance.

Geographical Area of Activity: USA.

Restrictions: No grants are made for individuals, sectarian religious concerns, conferences, film or media projects, endowments, publications or for single-country projects.

Publications: Report (biennially); information brochure; grants list; staff departure.

Finance: Annual revenue US $21,818,969, expenditure $8,245,627 (2013).

Board of Directors: Mikki Shepard (Chair.); Laura Butzel (Sec.); Rini Banerjee (Treas.).

Principal Staff: Pres. Jay Beckner.

Address: 218 East 18th St, New York, NY 10003-3694.

Telephone: (212) 475-1137; **Fax:** (212) 777-5226; **Internet:** www.mertzgilmore.org; **e-mail:** info@mertzgilmore.org.

The Michael Fund—International Foundation for Genetic Research

Founded in 1978 by Randy Engel and the late Dr Jerome Lejeune to promote cure and treatment research programmes for genetic disorders, including Down's Syndrome.

Activities: Operates in the area of medicine and health internationally, carrying out research and awarding grants to individuals for research and defending the rights of physically and mentally disabled people.

Geographical Area of Activity: Worldwide.

Publications: *The Friends of the Michael Fund* (newsletter); *Non-Directive Counselling*; *Obstetric Genetic Counselling for Lethal Anomalies*; *Little David*; *A March of Dimes Primer*; *The A–Z of Eugenic Killing*.

Finance: Annual revenue US $13,115, expenditure $52,263 (2013).

Board of Trustees: Randy Engel (Pres.); James R. Grab (Treas.).

Principal Staff: Exec. Dir Randy Engel; Dir of Medical Research Dr Paddy Jim Baggot.

Address: 4371 Northern Pike, Monroeville, PA 15146.

Telephone: (412) 374-0111; **Internet:** www.michaelfund.org; **e-mail:** randy@michaelfund.org.

Milbank Memorial Fund

Founded in 1905 by Elizabeth Milbank Anderson to improve the physical, mental and moral condition of humanity.

Activities: Works in three areas: improving health-care and related services for patients; protecting and improving the health of people in communities and workplaces; and improving the governance of public and private organizations to offer more effective care and health protection, as well as opportunities for health improvement. The Fund is an endowed foundation that engages in non-partisan analysis, study, research and communication on significant issues in health policy. Results are made available to decision-makers and in publications. Most of the Fund's work is collaborative, involving strategic relationships with decision-makers in the public and private sectors. It uses its resources to complement its partners' resources, not making grants in the traditional sense.

Geographical Area of Activity: USA.

Publications: *The Milbank Quarterly*; reports, briefs and books.

Finance: Annual revenue US $3,845,703, expenditure $4,096,193 (2013).

Principal Staff: Pres. Christopher F. Koller; Vice-Pres. and COO Kathleen S. Andersen.

Address: 645 Madison Ave, 15th Floor, New York, NY 10022-1095.

Telephone: (212) 355-8400; **Fax:** (212) 355-8599; **Internet:** www.milbank.org; **e-mail:** info@milbank.org.

MIUSA—Mobility International USA

Founded in 1981 by Susan Sygall and Barbara Williams to empower people with disabilities.

Activities: Operates internationally to provide people with disabilities with equal opportunities. MIUSA promotes their inclusion in development programmes through international exchange, information, technical assistance and training. It also manages the National Clearinghouse on Disability and Exchange.

Geographical Area of Activity: Worldwide.

Publications: Books, fact sheets and videos, including *A World Awaits You*, *A Practice of Yes*, *Survival Strategies for Going Abroad: A Guide for People with Disabilties*, *Building* *an Inclusive Development Community, Rights and Responsibilities, Building Bridges.*

Finance: Annual revenue US $2,299,383, expenditure $2,325,147 (31 Dec. 2013).

Board of Directors: Shelley Snow (Pres.); Molly Rogers (Vice-Pres.); Linda Phelps (Sec.); Patty Prather (Treas.).

Principal Staff: CEO Susan Sygall.

Address: 132 East Broadway, Suite 343, Eugene, OR 97401.

Telephone: (541) 343-1284; **Fax:** (541) 343-6812; **Internet:** www.miusa.org; **e-mail:** info@miusa.org.

The Ambrose Monell Foundation

Established in 1953 to contribute to religious, charitable, scientific, literary and educational purposes in New York, the USA in general, and worldwide. Shares an administration with the G. Unger Vetlesen Foundation (q.v.).

Activities: Operates in New York, the USA in general and internationally; makes grants to organizations operating in the above fields.

Geographical Area of Activity: International.

Restrictions: No grants are made to individuals.

Finance: Annual revenue US $7,135,091, expenditure $12,342,966 (2013).

Board of Directors: Ambrose K. Monell (Pres. and Treas.); Maurizio J. Morello (Exec. Vice-Pres. and Asst Treas.); Kristen G. Pemberton (Sec.).

Address: 1 Rockefeller Plaza, Suite 301, New York, NY 10020-2002.

Telephone: (212) 586-0700; **Fax:** (212) 245-1863; **Internet:** www.monellvetlesen.org; **e-mail:** info@monellvetlesen.org.

Moody Foundation

Founded in 1942 by William Lewis Moody, Jr, and Libbie Shearn Moody.

Activities: Operates in Texas primarily in the fields of conservation and renovation, with organizations involved in social services, education or the arts, through research, grants to institutions, fellowships, scholarships, publications, conferences and lectures. Established the Moody Gardens complex in Galveston Island, and the Transitional Learning Center, which offers facilities for the rehabilitation of people with brain injuries.

Geographical Area of Activity: USA (Texas).

Restrictions: No grants to individuals, except for scholarships to Galveston County students. Grants only to organizations in Texas.

Publications: Annual Report; application guidelines.

Finance: Annual revenue US $86,923,516, expenditure $62,643,810 (2013).

Board of Trustees: Robert L. Moody, Sr (Chair.).

Principal Staff: Exec. Dir Frances A. Moody-Dahlberg; CFO Garrik Addison.

Address: 2302 Post Office St, Suite 704, Galveston, TX 77550.

Telephone: (409) 797-1500; **Fax:** (409) 763-5564; **Internet:** www.moodyf.org.

Gordon and Betty Moore Foundation

Established in 2000.

Activities: Seeks to improve the quality of life for future generations. The Foundation operates in three specific areas of focus where a significant and measurable impact can be achieved: environmental conservation, science and the San Francisco Bay area, CA. Distinct initiatives have been created within these programme areas. Each initiative employs a portfolio of grants that are expected to help achieve targeted, large-scale outcomes in a specific time frame.

Geographical Area of Activity: USA.

Restrictions: Does not accept unsolicited proposals. Instead, funds Foundation-generated initiatives, commitments and special opportunities within the areas of focus, and makes local grants through the San Francisco Bay area programme.

Publications: Annual Report; financial documents; data-sharing policy and guidelines.

Finance: Annual revenue US $430,418,414, expenditure $330,074,433 (31 Dec. 2013).

Board of Trustees: Gordon Moore (Chair.).

Principal Staff: Pres. Dr Harvey V. Fineberg.

Address: 1661 Page Mill Rd, Palo Alto, CA 94304-1209.

Telephone: (650) 213-3000; **Fax:** (650) 213-3003; **Internet:** www.moore.org; **e-mail:** info@moore.org.

Morehead-Cain Foundation

Founded in 1945 by John Motley Morehead, III, a prominent philanthropist. Renamed in 2007 following a US $100m. grant from the Gordon and Mary Cain Foundation.

Activities: Awards merit scholarships for undergraduate study at the University of North Carolina at Chapel Hill (UNC-CH). In addition to covering the full cost of attending UNC-CH, the scholarship includes four summer enrichment programmes across the country and around the world. Morehead-Cain Scholars are selected from North Carolina high schools, British and Canadian secondary schools, and selected high schools across the USA. Selected international secondary schools are also permitted to nominate candidates. Modelled on the Rhodes Scholarship at Oxford University, United Kingdom, the Morehead-Cain is the oldest merit scholarship in the USA.

Restrictions: Awards scholarships for undergraduate study at the University of North Carolina at Chapel Hill.

Publications: Annual Report; electronic newsletters, online multimedia resources for scholars, prospective scholars and program alumni.

Finance: Annual revenue US $13,342,661, expenditure $11,214,270 (30 June 2013).

Board of Trustees: Lucy Hanes Chatham (Chair.); Timothy B. Burnett (Vice-Chair.); Steve Michalak (Treas.).

Principal Staff: Exec. Dir Charles 'Chuck' E. Lovelace, Jr; Assoc. Dir Megan Mazzocchi.

Address: Morehead Planetarium Bldg, East Wing, Ground Floor, 222 East Franklin St, Chapel Hill, NC 27514; POB 690, Chapel Hill, NC 27514-0690.

Telephone: (919) 962-1201; **Fax:** (919) 962-1615; **Internet:** www.moreheadcain.org; **e-mail:** moreheadcain@unc.edu.

The J. P. Morgan Chase Foundation

Established in 1956 as the Manufacturers Hanover Foundation, becoming the Chemical Bank Foundation in 1993. Merged with the J. P. Morgan Charitable Trust, following the merger of J. P. Morgan and Chase Manhattan Bank in 2000.

Activities: Operates in the fields of the arts and culture, community development and education (especially early childhood and youth). The Foundation makes grants mainly in the New York City area and parts of New York state where the Chemical Bank operates, but also internationally through US-based non-profit organizations.

Geographical Area of Activity: International.

Restrictions: Programmes outside the geographic markets served; individuals; fraternal organizations; athletic teams or social groups; public agencies; private schools; public schools (K-12), unless in partnership with a qualified not-for-profit organization; parent-teacher associations; scholarships or tuition assistance; fund-raising events (e.g. golf outings, school events); advertising, including advertisements in event, performance or athletic programmes; volunteer-operated organizations; funds to pay down operating deficits; programmes designed to promote religious or political doctrines; endowments or capital campaigns (exceptions are made by invitation only). In general, also higher education, organizations that discriminate on the basis of race, sex, sexual orientation, age or religion, and health- or medical-related organizations.

Publications: *Community Development Group News* (Annual Report).

Finance: Annual revenue US $48,909,121, expenditure $186,834,333 (31 Dec. 2013).

Board of Directors: Peter Scher (Chair.); Neila B. Radin (Sec.); John C. Marion (Treas.).

Principal Staff: CEO Bruce McNamer; Pres. Dalila Wilson-Scott.

Address: 1 Chase Manhattan Plaza, 5th Floor, New York, NY 10081.

Telephone: (212) 552-1112; **Internet:** www.jpmorganchase .com/corporate/Corporate-Responsibility/global -philanthropy.htm.

Morgan Stanley Foundation

Established in 1963.

Activities: Operates in the USA and internationally, through the Morgan Stanley Global Alliance for Children's Health. The Foundation provides scholarships to university students from minorities through the Richard B. Fisher Scholarship programme. Affiliated with the Morgan Stanley International Foundation (f. 1994), which operates in Europe, the Middle East and Africa.

Geographical Area of Activity: International.

Finance: Annual revenue US $7,744,995, expenditure $9,026,357 (31 Dec. 2013).

Principal Staff: Pres. Joan Steinberg.

Address: Morgan Stanley, 1633 Broadway, 25th Floor, New York, NY 10019.

Telephone: (212) 537-1555; **Internet:** www.morganstanley .com/globalcitizen/ms_guidelines.html; **e-mail:** whatadifference@morganstanley.com.

Charles Stewart Mott Foundation—CSMF

Founded in 1926 by Charles Stewart Mott for charitable purposes.

Activities: Operates nationally and (on a limited basis) internationally, in the fields of social welfare, education, the environment and civil society, through grants to institutions. The Foundation supports projects that lead to better community and family relations, more inter-agency co-operation, and the strengthening of the non-profit sector. It also supports community education programme development in Canada, the United Kingdom, South Africa, Eastern and Central Europe, the countries of the former USSR and other countries. Maintains additional offices in South Africa and the United Kingdom, and has staff representatives in Hungary and Ireland. The four main programme areas of the Foundation are: Civil Society; the Environment; the town of Flint, MI; and Pathways out of Poverty. Also supports Exploratory and Special Projects. Maintains an online grants database on grants made by the Foundation since 1993.

Geographical Area of Activity: North America, Central and Eastern Europe, Western Europe, South Africa.

Restrictions: Grants are not made to individuals, nor to religious organizations for religious purposes.

Publications: Annual Report; occasional reports.

Finance: Annual revenue US $154,404,515, expenditure $129,164,070 (2013).

Board of Trustees: William H. Piper (Vice-Chair.).

Principal Staff: Chair. and CEO William S. White; Pres. Ridgway H. White.

Address: Mott Foundation Bldg, 503 S Saginaw St, Suite 1200, Flint, MI 48502-1851.

Telephone: (810) 238-5651; **Fax:** (810) 766-1753; **Internet:** www.mott.org; **e-mail:** info@mott.org.

The Mountain Institute—TMI

Non-profit educational and scientific organization founded in 1972 that aims to help and protect mountain environments and cultures around the world.

Activities: Operates in the core regions of the Appalachians, Andes and Himalayas, all of which harbour severe poverty and serious environmental challenges. The Institute works in five major programmatic areas: sustainable livelihoods for marginalized communities; cultural empowerment; education and public outreach; sustaining natural resources and environmental security; and policy and governance.

Geographical Area of Activity: Asia, North and South America.

Finance: Annual revenue $2,850,554, expenditure $2,813,051 (2014).

Board: William W. Beddow (Chair.); Dr Augusta Molnar, Dr John 'Jed' Shilling (Vice-Chair.)

Principal Staff: Exec. Dir Andrew Taber.

Address: 3000 Connecticut Ave NW, Suite 101, Washington, DC 20008.

Telephone: (202) 234-4050; **Fax:** (202) 234-4054; **Internet:** www.mountain.org; **e-mail:** summit@mountain.org.

Ms Foundation for Women

Founded in 1972 to improve the lives of women and girls.

Activities: Operates in three project areas: Women's Economic Security; Women's Health and Safety; and Girls, Young Women and Leadership. The Foundation conducts advocacy and public education campaigns, provides technical assistance, and directs resources to organizations operating in these project areas. Also administers the Katrina Women's Response Fund and established Take Our Daughters To Work Day.

Geographical Area of Activity: USA.

Restrictions: No grants to direct service organizations, individuals, for scholarships, university-based research, state agencies, religious institutions, cultural or media projects, publications or conferences, nor to applications not submitted in response to a request for proposals.

Publications: Annual Report; newsletter.

Finance: Annual revenue US $9,430,338, expenditure $8,409,224 (30 June 2013).

Board of Directors: Heather Arnet (Chair.); Susan Dickler (Vice-Chair.); Eve Ellis, Kathleen Stephansen (Co-Treas); Verna L. Williams (Sec.).

Principal Staff: Pres. and CEO Teresa C. Younger; Vice-Pres Rosina Barba, Carolyn Cavicchio.

Address: 12 MetroTech Center, 26th Floor, New York, NY 11201.

Telephone: (212) 742-2300; **Fax:** (212) 742-1653; **Internet:** forwomen.org; **e-mail:** info@ms.foundation.org.

National Fish and Wildlife Foundation

Founded in 1984 by the US Congress for the conservation of natural resources through grantmaking to effective and innovative projects.

Activities: Runs projects concerned with habitat protection, environmental education, public policy development, natural resource management, ecosystem rehabilitation and leadership training for conservation workers. The Foundation operates nationally and internationally, although with a focus on the USA, through matching grant and special grant programmes for institutions and individuals.

Geographical Area of Activity: Mainly USA.

Restrictions: No awards for lobbying, political activism or litigation.

Publications: Annual Report.

Finance: Annual revenue US $183,101,882, expenditure $119,947,894 (30 Sept. 2013).

Board of Directors: John V. Faraci, Jr (Chair.); Patsy Ishiyama, Paul Tudor Jones, II, Carl R. Kuehner, III, Charles D. McCrary, Don J. McGrath (Vice-Chair.).

Principal Staff: Exec. Dir and CEO Jeff Trandahl.

Address: 1133 Fifteenth St NW, Suite 1100, Washington, DC 20005.

Telephone: (202) 857-0166; **Fax:** (202) 857-0162; **Internet:** www.nfwf.org; **e-mail:** info@nfwf.org.

National Humanities Center

Incorporated in 1978 by the American Academy of Arts and Sciences to support advanced post-doctoral scholarship in the humanities and to foster the influence of the humanities in the USA.

Activities: Awards up to 40 fellowships annually for post-doctoral scholars in the humanities, including history, philosophy, languages, literature, classics, religion, history of art, etc. Fellowships are open to students of any nationality for study in the USA.

Geographical Area of Activity: USA.

Restrictions: Grants only for study in the USA.

Publications: *News of the National Humanities Center* (newsletter); *Ideas* (2 a year); Annual Report; conference reports; occasional papers.

Finance: Annual revenue US $7,918,555, expenditure $5,345,184 (30 June 2014).

Trustees: Patricia R. Morton (Chair.); William C. Jordan (Vice-Chair.); John F. Adams (Sec.); Lawrence R. Ricciardi (Treas.).

Principal Staff: Pres. and Dir Geoffrey G. Harpham.

Address: 7 T.W. Alexander Dr., POB 12256, Research Triangle Park, NC 27709-2256.

Telephone: (919) 549-0661; **Fax:** (919) 990-8535; **Internet:** nationalhumanitiescenter.org; **e-mail:** nhc@nationalhumanitiescenter.org.

National Kidney Foundation, Inc

Established in 1950 to prevent kidney and urinary tract diseases, improve the health and well-being of individuals and families affected by these diseases, and increase the availability of all organs for transplantation.

Activities: As a US-based public health organization, the Foundation serves those at risk and those diagnosed with chronic kidney disease through education, programmes and support services. The Foundation develops accredited medical education programmes and clinical decision-making materials for health-care professionals. Also awards grants for nephrology research, including clinicial scientist grants and young investigator grants; a Research Award Committee reviews applications and selects awardees on an annual basis.

Geographical Area of Activity: USA.

Restrictions: Grants only for study in the USA.

Publications: Periodicals and specific publications; Annual Report.

Finance: Annual revenue US $37,346,000, expenditure $34,552,000 (30 June 2014).

Board of Directors: Gregory W. Scott (Chair.); Art Pasquarella (Chair.-elect); W. Edward Walter (Immediate Past Chair.); Jeffrey S. Berns (Pres.); Michael J. Choi (Pres.-elect); Beth Piraino (Immediate Past Pres.); William G. Dessoffy (Sec.).

Principal Staff: CEO Kevin Longino (acting).

Address: 30 East 33rd St, New York, NY 10016.

Telephone: (212) 889-2210; **Fax:** (212) 779-0068; **Internet:** www.kidney.org; **e-mail:** info@kidney.org.

National Organization for Women Foundation, Inc—NOW Foundation

Established in 1966 to advance women's rights and promote equality in the USA and around the world.

Activities: Operates in the field of women's rights through education, advocacy, conferences, publications, training and leadership development. The Foundation runs projects in areas incl. women's reproductive rights, women with disabilities, prevention of violence against women, sexual harassment, lesbian rights, global feminism and other related issues. Affiliated with the National Organization for Women—NOW.

Geographical Area of Activity: Worldwide.

Publications: Annual Report.

Finance: Annual revenue US $769,107, expenditure $814,595 (31 Dec. 2013).

Principal Staff: Pres. Tery O'Neill; Exec. Vice-Pres. Bonnie Grabenhofer.

Address: 1100 H St NW, Washington, DC 20005.

Telephone: (202) 628-8669; **Fax:** (202) 785-8576; **Internet:** www.nowfoundation.org; **e-mail:** now@now.org.

National Science Foundation

Established in 1950 as an independent US government agency to facilitate and fund research into all areas of science and engineering except for human health and medical research.

Activities: Supports research in the areas of biological sciences, computers, information science and engineering, education, envirional research, geosciences, mathematics, physical sciences, polar research, social, behavioural and economic sciences. Also supports co-operative research between US scientists and those in other countries.

Geographical Area of Activity: Mainly USA.

Publications: General information, including a toolkit; news releases; fact sheets; budget information; policies and procedures; programme announcements and information; reports; statistical reports on US science and engineering; award abstracts.

Finance: Funding of approx. US $7,172m. for the 2014 fiscal year.

National Science Board: Dr Dan E. Arvizu (Chair.); Dr Kelvin K. Droegemeier (Vice-Chair.).

Principal Staff: Dir France A. Córdova.

Address: 4201 Wilson Blvd, Arlington, VA 22230.

Telephone: (703) 292-5111; **Fax:** (703) 292-9041; **Internet:** www.nsf.gov; **e-mail:** info@nsf.gov.

National Wildlife Federation—NWF

Founded in 1936 to promote the study of wildlife, conservation and the environment, and to increase public awareness of such issues.

Activities: Provides fellowships, internships and awards. Environmental Conservation Fellowships are open to Canadian, Mexican and US citizens for advanced study in the USA or abroad. Internships are for work in the Resources Conservation Department in Washington, DC, and for research in the Institute for Wildlife Research. Environmental Publication Awards are offered to student publications in the field of environmental science. The Federation runs various environmental educational programmes, incl. the Environmental Education Division Internships. Maintains the Institute for Wildlife Research.

Geographical Area of Activity: North America and Mexico.

Publications: Annual Report; books, directories and reports; *Conservation Directory* (annually); *Conservation Exchange* (quarterly); *EYAS* (newsletter, 3 a year); *International Wildlife* (6 a year); *National Wildlife* (6 a year); *Ranger Rick* (monthly); *Your Big Backyard* (monthly); *Animal Baby Magazine* (10 a year).

Finance: Annual revenue US $85,431,000, expenditure $66,325,000 (31 Aug. 2013).

Board of Directors: Deborah Spalding (Chair.); Bruce Wallace (Chair.-elect).

Principal Staff: Pres. and CEO Collin O'Mara.

Address: 11100 Wildlife Center Dr., Reston, VA 20190-5362.

Telephone: (703) 438-6000; **Fax:** (703) 438-6045; **Internet:** www.nwf.org; **e-mail:** info@nwf.org.

The Nature Conservancy

Established in 1951 with the aim of saving the world's most beautiful areas for future generations.

Activities: Works in the field of international conservation with governments, corporations and landowners, as well as local people, to help save and preserve land including forests, aquatic areas, prairies and deserts and the communities that support such areas.

Geographical Area of Activity: North, Central and South America and the Caribbean, USA, Asia and the Pacific.

Publications: *Nature Conservancy* (newsletter); Annual Report; financial statements.

Finance: Annual revenue US $976,103, expenditure $757,871 (30 June 2014).

Board of Directors: Craig O. McCaw (Chair.); James E. Rogers (Vice-Chair.); Muneer A. Satter (Treas.); Frank E. Loy (Sec.).

Principal Staff: Pres. and CEO Mark R. Tercek; Chief Conservation Officer Brian McPeek.

Address: 4245 North Fairfax Dr., Suite 100, Arlington, VA 22203-1606.

Telephone: (703) 841-5300; **Internet:** www.nature.org; **e-mail:** member@tnc.org.

NCSJ—National Conference on Soviet Jewry

Created in 1971. Aims to safeguard the individual and communal political rights of Jews living in the former USSR, as well as working to secure their religious and political freedoms.

Activities: Advocates on behalf of Jews in the Russian Federation, Ukraine, the Baltic states and the republics of Central Asia, and represents the American Jewish community abroad. The Conference monitors compliance by the governments of the former USSR in the areas of free emigration and religious and cultural rights, and also monitors developments related to anti-Semitism in the former USSR. It runs Operation Lifeline, which provides materials, kosher food, and religious and cultural objects to Jews in the countries of the former USSR; and holds conferences, seminars and special events.

Geographical Area of Activity: USA, the republics of Central Asia, the Baltic states, Russia, Ukraine.

Restrictions: Not a grantmaking organization.

Publications: *Newswatch*; country reports; weekly bulletin; resources: *History of Soviet Jewry* (March 1999); *Listen to Moscow Synagogue Choir*; *Russian Federal Law on Religion* (1997); state department documents: *Global Anti-Semitism Report* (2005); *International Religious Freedom Report*; *US on Human Rights Abroad*; *Human Rights Report*.

Finance: Annual revenue US $923,993, expenditure $898,060 (31 Dec. 2013).

Executive Committee: Stephen M. Greenberg (Chair.); Max R. Schrayer (Treas.); Karen Moss (Sec.).

Principal Staff: Pres. Alexander Smukler; Exec. Dir Mark B. Levin.

Address: 2020 K St, NW, Suite 7800, Washington, DC 20006.

Telephone: (202) 898-2500; **Fax:** (202) 898-0822; **Internet:** www.ncsj.org; **e-mail:** ncsj@ncsj.org.

NDI—National Democratic Institute for International Affairs

Created as part of the 1984 statute that set up the National Endowment for Democracy. Affiliated to the US Democratic Party and set up as an independent organization to expand and strengthen democracy worldwide.

Activities: Provides practical assistance to civic and political leaders advancing democratic values, practices and institutions. The Institute has worked in more than 100 countries, building political and civic organizations, safeguarding elections, and promoting citizen participation, openness and accountability in government through the provision of expert volunteers, technical resources and training. Its programmes focus on citizen participation, civil-military relations, election and political processes, democratic governance, political party development and women's participation. Has more than 60 field offices.

Geographical Area of Activity: Worldwide.

Restrictions: Not a grantmaking organization.

Publications: include *NDI Reports: A review of political developments in new democracies* (newsletter); *Constituent Relations Manual: a Guide to Best Practices*; *Assessing Women's Political Party Programs: Best Practices and Recommendations 2008*; *New Mandate, New Opportunities: Evaluation of the Work of the Assembly of Kosovo*.

Finance: Annual revenue US $140,131,576, expenditure $140,180,419 (30 Sept. 2013).

Board of Directors: Madeleine K. Albright (Chair.); Thomas A. Daschle, Harriet C. Babbitt, Marc B. Nathanson (Vice-Chair.); Patrick J. Griffin (Sec.); Robert G. Liberatore (Treas.).

Principal Staff: Pres. Kenneth D. Wollack; Vice-Pres. Shari K. Bryan.

Address: 455 Massachusetts Ave, NW, 8th Floor, Washington, DC 20001-2621.

Telephone: (202) 728-5500; **Fax:** (888) 875-2887; **Internet:** www.ndi.org; **e-mail:** info@ndi.org.

NEF—Near East Foundation

Founded in 1915 to offer people of developing nations technical assistance in the implementation of programmes of rural and community improvement.

Activities: Works in the Middle East and Africa on projects to increase food production, with related activities in rural and community development, and primary health care. The Foundation sends qualified technicians overseas to assist with technical-skills transfer and human-resource development. It provides start-up funds for projects until support is available from local sources, and often works in co-operation with other donor agencies. The Foundation has offices in Egypt, Jordan, Mali, Morocco, Sudan and the Palestinian Territories.

Geographical Area of Activity: Africa and Middle East.

Restrictions: Operating rather than grantmaking foundation.

Publications: Annual Report; brochures.

Finance: Annual revenue US $6,131,798, expenditure $5,188,581 (30 June 2013).

Board of Directors: Shant Mardirossian (Chair.); Johnson Garrett (Vice-Chair.); Haig Mardikian (Sec.).

Principal Staff: Pres. Dr Charles Benjamin; Vice-Pres. and CFO John Ashby.

Address: 230 Euclid Ave, Syracuse, New York, NY 13210.

Telephone: (315) 428-8670; **Internet:** www.neareast.org; **e-mail:** info@neareast.org.

The New World Foundation

Founded in 1954 by Anita McCormick Blaine for the support of equal rights, public education, health care, community development and peaceful international relations.

Activities: Operates through four main programmes: the Global Environmental Health and Justice Fund; the Phoenix Fund for Workers and Communities; the New Majority Fund; and the Arts for Justice Program. The Foundation focuses on young people, the community, enfranchisement of voters and democracy.

Geographical Area of Activity: Worldwide.

Restrictions: No grants are made to individuals; no unsolicited proposals.

Publications: Biennial Report; articles; books; reports.

Finance: Annual revenue US $9,624,818, expenditure $10,208,695 (30 Sept. 2013).

Board of Directors: Kent Wong (Chair.); Lisa Abbott (Vice-Chair.); Bill Dempsey (Treas.); Peggy Saika (Sec.).

Principal Staff: Pres. Dr Colin Greer.

Address: 666 West End Ave, New York, NY 10025.

Telephone: (212) 497-3470; **Fax:** (212) 472-0508; **Internet:** www.newwf.org; **e-mail:** recept@newwf.org.

The New York Community Trust—NYCT

Established in 1924.

Activities: Administers more than 2,000 charitable funds. The Trust operates four programmes: Community Development and the Environment; Health and People with Special Needs; Education, Arts and Human Justice; and Children, Youth and Families. It focuses its grantmaking within New York City, and also has two divisions: the Westchester Community Foundation and the Long Island Community Foundation.

Geographical Area of Activity: New York City.

Publications: Annual Report; Biographical Sketches; brochures, guidelines and planning notes.

Finance: Annual revenue US $451,724,161, expenditure $156,377,606 (31 Dec. 2013).

Board of Directors: Charlynn Goins (Chair.); Jane L. Wilton (Gen. Counsel and Sec.); Alan Holzer (Treas.).

Principal Staff: Pres. Lorie A. Slutsky.

Address: 909 Third Ave, New York, NY 10022.

Telephone: (212) 686-0010; **Fax:** (212) 532-8528; **Internet:** www.nycommunitytrust.org; **e-mail:** aw@nyct-cfi.org.

Newberry Library

Founded in 1887 at the bequest of Walter Loomis Newberry to collect, preserve and make available to readers books, journals, newspapers, maps, manuscripts and other library materials in history and the humanities; and to foster the use of these materials by all available means, including fellowships, lectures, seminars, exhibitions and publications.

Activities: Offers fellowships for scholars proposing to work in residence, and sponsors conferences, courses, publications, lectures and four research centres. The Library comprises more than 1.5m. volumes, 5m. manuscripts and 500,000 historic maps, and has strong general collections embracing history and the humanities within Western Europe and the Americas from the late Middle Ages to the early 20th century, and a specialization in genealogy. Also operates research and education programmes.

Publications: Atlas of Historical County Boundaries.

Finance: Annual revenue US $11,517,247, expenditure $10,790,630 (30 June 2014).

Trustees: Victoria J. Herget (Chair.); David C. Hilliard (Vice-Chair.); David E. McNeel (Treas.); Mark Hausberg (Sec.).

Principal Staff: Pres. and Librarian David Spadafora.

Address: 60 West Walton St, Chicago, IL 60610.

Telephone: (312) 255-3666; **Fax:** (312) 255-3680; **Internet:** www.newberry.org; **e-mail:** research@newberry.org.

NFCR—National Foundation for Cancer Research

Founded in 1973 by Nobel Prize winner Albert Szent-Gyorgyi to provide seed-funding for basic scientific research toward the better understanding of and cures for cancer.

Activities: Funds nearly 50 laboratories around the world in a variety of scientific disciplines. The Foundation holds conferences and symposia; and awards the annual Albert Szent Györgyi Prize for Progress in Cancer Research—an award of US $25,000 to a researcher who has made an outstanding contribution in the field of cancer research. Has provided more than $275m. for basic cancer research science.

Geographical Area of Activity: USA, Europe and Asia.

Publications: *Research for a Cure* (newsletter); website, booklets and papers; newsletters and e-newsletter.

Finance: Annual revenue US $13,693,930, expenditure $13,790,230 (31 Dec. 2012).

Board of Directors: Joseph F. Franlin (Chair.); Mark Baran (Treas.).

Principal Staff: CEO Franklin C. Salisbury, Jr; Pres. and COO Dr Sujan Ba.

Address: 4600 East West Highway, Suite 525, Bethesda, MD 20814.

Telephone: (301) 654-1250; **Fax:** (301) 654-5824; **Internet:** www.nfcr.org; **e-mail:** info@nfcr.org.

Nonprofit Enterprise and Self-sustainability Team—NESsT

Founded in 1997 in Hungary by Lee Davis and Nicole Etchart to solve critical social problems in emerging market countries, by developing and supporting social enterprises that strengthen the financial sustainability of civil society organizations to maximize their social impact.

Activities: Works in three main areas: applied research; capacity building; and policy and outreach. Aims to increase awareness, critical analysis and understanding of non-profit enterprise, and to attract new leaders to the emerging field. Operates in a variety of areas, including offering internships to young and mid-career professionals, and encouraging the integration of the teaching of non-profit enterprise into the formal curricula of graduate-level non-profit management and business schools. Has launched initiatives promoting self-financing for non-profit enterprises in both South America and Central Europe, as well as the NESsT Venture Fund providing targeted finance and capacity building support to non-profit enterprises in Central Europe and Central and South America. Maintains offices in Chile, Hungary and the USA.

Geographical Area of Activity: Argentina, Brazil, Chile, Ecuador, Croatia, Czech Republic, Hungary, Peru, Romania, Slovakia.

Publications: *All in the Same Boat: An Introduction to Engaged Philanthropy*; *Commitment to Integrity: Guiding Principles for Nonprofits in the Marketplace*; *Enterprising Mentality: A Social Enterprise Guide for Mental Health and Intellectual Disabilities Organizations*; *Get Ready, Get Set: Starting Down the Road to Self-Financing*; *Hit the Ground Running: Getting a Head Start with Local Lessons for Sustainable Social Enterprise*; *Legal Guides*; *Risky Business: The Impacts of Merging Mission and Market*.

Finance: Annual revenue US $2,959,408, expenditure $3,161,698 (31 Dec. 2013).

Principal Staff: Co-CEOs Loïc Comolli, Nicole Etchart.

Address: 5917 Jordan Ave, El Cerrito, CA 94530.

Telephone: (503) 704-9195; **Fax:** (815) 846-1775; **Internet:** www.nesst.org; **e-mail:** nesst@nesst.org.

Novartis US Foundation

Established in 1997 by Novartis Corporation.

Activities: Aims to support social, health and education ventures initiated by communities and organizations. The Foundation supports innovative biomedical science programmes and effective education to encourage the advancement of the life sciences. It also works to ensure that every young person in the USA has a good start in life with sufficient care and support for a healthy development.

Geographical Area of Activity: USA.

Restrictions: Grants only to US programmes.

Finance: Annual revenue US $1,537,809, expenditure $1,417,493 (2012).

Board of Trustees: Robert Pelzer (Chair.); Barry Rosenfeld (Sec.); Kenneth Schuster (Treas.).

Principal Staff: Exec. Dir Edgar Butz.

Address: 230 Park Ave, 21 Floor, New York, NY 10169.

Telephone: (212) 766-9800; **Internet:** www.us.novartis.com/novartis-us-foundation/index.shtml.

NoVo Foundation

Established to assist in the creation of a peaceful society through focusing on improving the status and well-being of girls and women worldwide.

Activities: Makes grants to USA-based charities carrying out projects in the areas of promoting gender equality, ending violence against women and girls, and the empowerment of girls in less-developed countries. The Foundation also make grants to projects that advance social and emotional learning in the USA. In 2011, the Foundation announced that US $80m. was to be spent over the following 10 years to help end violence against women in the USA.

Geographical Area of Activity: International.

Restrictions: Does not currently accept unsolicited proposals or requests for funding.

Finance: Annual revenue US $150,280,680, expenditure $115,717,881 (31 Dec. 2013).

Board of Directors: Jennifer Buffett (Co-Chair. and Treas.); Peter Buffett (Co-Chair.); Aaron Stern (Sec.).

Principal Staff: Co-Pres Jennifer Buffet, Peter Buffet.

Address: 535 Fifth Ave. 33rd Floor, New York, NY 10017.

Internet: novofoundation.org.

The Ocean Foundation

Established in 2002 as the Coral Reef Foundation; a community foundation with a mission to support, strengthen and promote those organizations working to reverse the destruction of ocean environments around the world.

Activities: Operates in four main areas: conserving marine habitats and special places; protecting species of concern; building the capacity of the marine conservation community; and expanding ocean literary and public awareness. The Foundation does this through field of interest funds, special initiatives, fiscal sponsorship and donor funds.

Geographical Area of Activity: International.

Publications: Annual Report; newsletter.

Finance: Annual revenue US $5,264,763, expenditure $5,401,568 (30 June 2014).

Board of Directors: Mark J. Spalding (Chair. and Pres.); Angel Braestrup (Acting Sec.); Joshua Ginsberg (Acting Treas.).

Principal Staff: Vice-Pres. Karen Muir.

Address: 1990 M St NW, Suite 250, Washington, DC 20036.

Telephone: (202) 887-8992; **Internet:** www.oceanfdn.org; **e-mail:** info@oceanfdn.org.

Omidyar Network

Established in 2004 by Pam and Pierre Omidyar, the founder of eBay, based on the belief that every person has the potential to make a difference.

Activities: Funds for-profit and non-profit organizations to create opportunities for people, enabling them to improve their lives and make powerful contributions to their communities.

Geographical Area of Activity: Worldwide.

Finance: Annual revenue US $129,956,770, expenditure $68,117,774 (2013).

Board of Trustees: Pierre M. Omidyar (Chair.); William Fitzpatrick (Sec.).

Principal Staff: Man. Partner and Pres. Matthew Bannick.

Address: 1991 Broadway St, Suite 200, Redwood City, CA 94063.

Telephone: (650) 482-2500; **Fax:** (650) 482-2525; **Internet:** www.omidyar.com; **e-mail:** info@omidyar.com.

Open Society Foundations

Founded in 1993 by George Soros as the Open Society Institute. Present name adopted in 2011.

Activities: Promotes the development of open societies, encourages public debate on policy alternatives in controversial areas and manages regional programmes conducted throughout Central and Eastern Europe and the countries of the former USSR. The New York office acts as the administrative, financial and communications headquarters of the Foundations' network. The network provides administrative, financial and technical support; addresses specific issues on a regional or network-wide basis; and also operates a series of programmes that focus principally on the USA, which include criminal and civil justice reform, women's rights, and US policy in Colombia and Central Eurasia. In 2008, the organization established the Open Society Fellowships for work on open society challenges that is innovative and unconventional.

Geographical Area of Activity: Europe, the countries of the former USSR, Africa, Latin America and the Caribbean, the Middle East, Asia and the USA.

Restrictions: Fellowship projects should address at least two areas of interest to the organization, which include human rights, government transparency, access to information and justice, civil society and inclusion.

Publications: Annual Report; *Open Society News* (quarterly newsletter); leaflets, articles and other publications.

Finance: Annual revenue US $155,644,135, expenditure $190,444,407 (31 Dec. 2013).

Trustees: George Soros (Chair.).

Principal Staff: Pres. Prof. Christopher Stone.

Address: 224 West 57th St, New York, NY 10019.

Telephone: (212) 548-0600; **Fax:** (212) 548-4600; **Internet:** www.opensocietyfoundations.org; **e-mail:** osfellows@ opensocietyfoundations.org.

Open Society Policy Center

Established in 1997 to address civil liberties violations in the USA and expand the Open Society Institute's policy and advocacy work in the areas of criminal and civil justice reform. The Center is part of the Open Society Foundations (q.v.) network.

Activities: Works to influence US government policy on domestic and international issues in the fields of: civil rights and liberties; criminal justice reform; immigration; multilateralism; development assistance; health; human rights; and government transparency and accountability.

Geographical Area of Activity: USA.

Finance: Annual revenue US $5,200,000, expenditure $4,558,517 (2013).

Board of Directors: Prof. Christopher Stone (Chair.); Lynthia Gibson-Price (Treas.); Asia Johnson (Sec.).

Principal Staff: Exec. Dir Stephen Rickard; Deputy Dir Caroline Chambers.

Address: 1730 Pennsylvania Ave, NW, 7th Floor, Washington, DC 20006.

Telephone: (202) 721-5600; **Fax:** (202) 530-0128; **Internet:** opensocietypolicycenter.org.

Operation Rainbow, Inc

Founded in 1978 by Dr William B. Riley, Jr to provide free reconstructive surgery for underprivileged children in the USA and in developing countries around the world.

Activities: Operates in the field of medicine and health care, by raising money from individuals, foundations and corporations to fund reconstructive surgery (plastic and orthopaedic) to be performed by volunteer surgeons on children with medical problems primarily in Asia, Central and South America and the USA. The organization also provides teaching and training for local medical staff overseas, and runs a sponsorship programme, so that nurses and physicians from abroad are sponsored to come to the USA for additional training.

Geographical Area of Activity: Asia, Central and South America, and the USA.

Finance: Annual revenue US $602,296, expenditure $598,696 (30 June 2014).

Board of Directors: Dr Gus Gialamas (Chair.); Dr Taylor R. Smith (Sec. and Treas.).

Principal Staff: Pres. David M. Atkin; Exec. Dir Laura Escobosa.

Address: 4200 Park Blvd, PMB 157, Oakland, CA 94602.

Telephone: (510) 273-2485; **Internet:** www.operationrainbow .org; **e-mail:** laura@operationrainbow.org.

Operation USA

Established in 1979 as Operation California.

Activities: Aims to mitigate the effects of poverty and the results of natural and man-made disasters in the USA and abroad. The organization provides emergency medical, nutritional and shelter supplies to victims of poverty and disaster throughout Asia, Africa, Central and South America and the Caribbean, Eastern Europe and the Balkans. It also runs a domestic disaster response programme, micro-enterprise initiatives, a community clinic support programme in the USA, and initiated Operation Landmine in 1995 to engage in de-mining activities around the world.

Geographical Area of Activity: International; USA.

Publications: Annual Report.

Finance: Annual revenue US $12,656,001, expenditure $10,309,748 (30 June 2014).

Board of Directors: Michael Mahdesian (Chair.); Dave Brubaker (Vice-Chair.); Bob L. Johnson (Treas.); Tom Moore, Jr (Sec.).

Principal Staff: CEO and Pres. Richard M. Walden.

Address: 7421 Beverly Blvd, Los Angeles, CA 90036.

Telephone: (323) 413-2353; **Fax:** (323) 931-5400; **Internet:** www.opusa.org; **e-mail:** info@opusa.org.

Opportunity International USA

Established in 1973 to transform the lives of those living in chronic poverty, through job creation, small business development and community support.

Activities: A network of 45 autonomous affiliated implementing partners in developing countries worldwide and seven support partners in developed countries. The organization operates internationally in collaboration with indigenous partner organizations in the areas of aid to less-developed countries and social welfare, through promoting micro-enterprise schemes to combat poverty, and offering loans and basic business training. It founded the Women's Opportunity Network, and in 2003 launched the US $25m. Lending Hope to Africa Campaign. Other members of the network operate from Australia, Canada, Germany and the United Kingdom (q.v.).

Geographical Area of Activity: Africa, Asia, Central and South America, the Caribbean, Central and Eastern Europe.

Publications: *Impact* (newsletter, 2 a year); Annual Report.

Finance: Annual revenue US $132,668,569, expenditure $122,556,963 (31 Dec. 2013).

Board of Directors: Carly Fiorina (Chair.).

Principal Staff: CEO Vicki Escarra.

Address: 2122 York Rd, Suite 150, Oak Brook, IL 60523.

Telephone: (630) 242-4100; **Fax:** (630) 645-1458; **Internet:** www.opportunity.org.

Orbis International

Established in 1982 to reduce preventable blindness throughout the world through training, health education and improved access to eye care.

Activities: Originally, a mobile teaching eye hospital—a fully equipped aeroplane—to travel around the world training doctors and medical staff in developing countries, transferring knowledge and skills through lectures and training. Since then, the organization has expanded to include specialized training programmes and community health projects to further improve the standard of eye care in less-developed countries where a large percentage of blindness is because of preventable conditions. Currently operates projects in Africa (including Botswana, Burkina Faso, Cameroon, Ethiopia, Ghana, Kenya, Mali, Malawi, Nigeria, Tanzania and Uganda), Asia (Bangladesh, the People's Republic of China, India and Viet Nam), and Latin America and the Caribbean (Jamaica and Peru).

Geographical Area of Activity: Worldwide.

Publications: Annual Report; brochures; posters and advertisements; *Vision for the World* (brochure); *Aviation advertisement poster*; fact sheet; *Observer* (newsletter).

Finance: Annual revenue US $147,036,403, expenditure $146,247,183 (31 Dec. 2013).

Board of Directors: Kevin McAllister (Chair.); James R. Parker (Vice-Chair.); Diana Wheeler (Sec.); John Howitt (Interim Treas.).

Principal Staff: Pres. and CEO Jenny Hourihan.

Address: 520 Eighth Ave, 11th Floor, New York, NY 10018.

Telephone: (646) 674-5500; **Fax:** (646) 674-5599; **Internet:** www.orbis.org; **e-mail:** info@orbis.org.

Orentreich Foundation for the Advancement of Science, Inc—OFAS

Founded in 1961 and classified as an operating private foundation in 1972.

Activities: Carries out its own research and collaborates with other institutions on projects that aim to prevent or reverse disorders decreasing length or quality of life. The Foundation operates in the field of medicine and health, through conferences, seminars and research, which it carries out at its biomedical research centre in New York state. It also makes occasional grants to help fund joint or collaborative research in fields of substantial research interest.

Geographical Area of Activity: Mainly USA.

Restrictions: Recipients are typically at or above post-graduate level in science or medicine at accredited universities or research institutions in the USA.

Publications: Annual Directors' Report; *VitaLongevity News Letters*.

Finance: Annual revenue US $1,480,541, expenditure $3,346,913 (31 Dec. 2013).

Board of Directors: Norman Orentreich (Chair.).

Principal Staff: Pres. David Orentreich; Deputy Dir Dr Bernardita Calinao.

Address: 910 Fifth Ave, New York, NY 10021-4187.

Telephone: (212) 606-0850; **Internet:** www.orentreich.org; **e-mail:** library@orentreich.org.

Outreach International

Incorporated in 1979 as an international development organization that aims to alleviate suffering in the world.

Activities: Works to eliminate the poverty, hunger and disease suffered by people around the world by providing long-term solutions, through Participatory Human Development, a non-directive process designed to involve the poor in the decisions that affect them in order that they can learn to sustain themselves. The organization focuses on three main areas: Human and Community Development; Literacy and Child Survival; and Civil Society. Currently operates programmes in 13 countries around the world.

Geographical Area of Activity: North, Central and South America, Africa, Asia and the Caribbean.

Publications: *Outreach Developments* (quarterly newsletter); Annual Report.

Finance: Annual revenue US $2,800,261, expenditure $2,650,283 (30 Sept. 2013).

Board of Directors: Randall Pratt (Chair.); Constance L. Thatcher (Vice-Chair.); Richard Lindgren (Sec.); Karen Mercer (Treas.).

Principal Staff: Pres. and CEO Kevin Prine; Chief Development Officer Mary Eisenhower; COO Orval Fisher.

Address: 129 W Lexington, Independence, MO 64050.

Telephone: (816) 833-0883; **Fax:** (816) 833-0103; **Internet:** www.outreach-international.org; **e-mail:** info@outreach-international.org.

Oxfam America

Established in 1970, part of the Oxfam confederation of organizations (qq.v.).

Activities: Assists people affected by emergencies, conflicts and natural disasters worldwide; campaigns on issues including food security and aid.

Geographical Area of Activity: International.

Publications: Annual Report; OXFAMExchange (magazine, 3 a year); fact sheets, papers, etc.

Finance: Annual revenue US $67,958,480, expenditure $81,768,356 (31 March 2014).

Board of Directors: Joseph Loughrey (Chair.); Smita Singh (Vice-Chair.); Joe H. Hamilton (Treas. and Sec.).

Principal Staff: Pres. Raymond C. Offenheiser.

Address: 226 Causeway St., 5th Floor, Boston, MA 02114-2206.

Telephone: (617) 482-1211; **Internet:** www.oxfamamerica.org; **e-mail:** info@oxfamamerica.org.

David and Lucile Packard Foundation

Founded in 1964 by David and Lucile Packard to support projects in the areas of child development and health, family planning, education, the environment and conservation, marine sciences and global population studies.

Activities: Primarily concerned with supporting local projects; however, the Foundation also offers support in the fields of conservation and science, population studies, children, family and communities, and capacity building in Central and South America, particularly Mexico and Colombia. It also operates a Local Area Fund.

Geographical Area of Activity: North, Central and South America.

Restrictions: No grants are made to individuals.

Publications: Annual Report and financial statement; grants list; occasional reports; information brochures; programme policy statements; programme area publications; Foundation e-newsletter.

Finance: Annual revenue US $283,023,038, expenditure $353,894,166 (31 Dec. 2013).

Board of Trustees: Susan Packard Orr (Chair.); Julie E. Packard, Nancy Packard Burnett (Vice-Chair.); Mary Anne Rodgers (Sec. and Gen. Counsel).

Principal Staff: Pres. and CEO Carol S. Larson.

Address: 343 Second St, Los Altos, CA 94022.

Telephone: (650) 948-7658; **Fax:** (650) 948-2957; **Internet:** www.packard.org; **e-mail:** inquiries@packard.org.

Pact

Established in 1971 to assist indigenous organizations working for development.

Activities: Runs its own development programmes throughout Africa, Asia, and South America alongside partner organizations and local NGOs. Projects deal with areas incl. food security, education, health (HIV/AIDS), micro-credit and small enterprise, capacity building, women's empowerment, increasing the effectiveness of grassroots civil society organizations, and rural development. Maintains 24 field offices.

Geographical Area of Activity: Worldwide.

Restrictions: Not a grantmaking organization, although does provide financial resources to local partner organizations.

Publications: Annual Report; and a number of books related to the areas in which Pact works.

Finance: Annual revenue US $145,626,909, expenditure $146,020,920 (30 Sept. 2013).

Board of Directors: Nancy Murphy (Chair.).

Principal Staff: Pres. and CEO Mark Viso; CFO and Exec. Vice-Pres. Alik Hinckson.

Address: 1828 L St NW, Suite 300, Washington, DC 20036.

Telephone: (202) 466-5666; **Fax:** (202) 466-5669; **Internet:** www.pactworld.org; **e-mail:** info@pactworld.org.

PADF—Pan American Development Foundation

Founded in 1962 to promote social and economic development of the Americas.

Activities: Primarily focuses on bringing technical expertise and resources to Central and South America and the Caribbean, as well as providing disaster assistance. Main project areas are the strengthening of local civic institutions, sustainable agricultural production, increasing family incomes, and family health promotion. The Foundation operates in partnership with local organizations, with multinational corporations, private businesses and NGOs in the region, along with the US Government and inter-American NGOs. Maintains offices in Colombia and Haiti.

Geographical Area of Activity: Central and South America and the Caribbean.

Publications: Annual Report; *PADF Newsletter*; technical publications.

Finance: Annual revenue US $69,042,877, expenditure $68,367,425 (30 Sept. 2013).

Board of Trustees: José Miguel Insulza (Chair.); Albert R. Ramdin (Vice-Chair.); Gladys Coupet (Acting Pres. and Treas.); Carlos Mariño García (First Vice-Pres.); Edouard Baussan (Second Vice-Pres. and Treas.); Precious Murchison Gittens (Sec.).

Principal Staff: Exec. Dir John Sanbrailo; Dep. Exec. Dir and COO Dr Judith Hermanson.

Address: 1889 F St NW, Washington, DC 20006.

Telephone: (202) 458-3969; **Fax:** (202) 458-6316; **Internet:** www.padf.org; **e-mail:** info@padf.org.

PAHO Foundation (Fundación Panamericana de la Salud y Educación—PAHEF)

Founded in 1968 to promote and stimulate efforts to combat disease, lengthen life, improve health-care services, foster health research, and enhance the capabilities of health workers in the Americas; formerly known as PAHEF—Pan American Health and Education Foundation.

Activities: Works wiith the Pan American Health Organization, the Regional Office for the Americas of the World Health Organization (WHO), and shares the vision of health for all. The Foundation promotes healthy living (prevention of chronic disease, healthy ageing, prevention of childhood obesity) and enhances the training of medical professionals and health workers. It operates, mainly in Latin America and the Caribbean, in the field of public health, through self-conducted programmes, awarding prizes, and issuing publications. Programmes include: Expanded Textbook and Instructional Materials Program (PALTEX); Awards for Excellence in Inter-American Public Health Program; and PAHEF Grants Program.

Geographical Area of Activity: Latin America and the Caribbean.

Restrictions: Only accepts proposals that respond to its annual call for proposals.

Publications: Numerous publications and manuals; brochures; other promotional materials.

Finance: Annual revenue US $1,170,315, expenditure $1,483,106 (2012).

Board of Directors: Simone Acha (Chair.); Harold Hamana (Vice-Chair.); David Aiken (Treas.).

Principal Staff: Pres. and CEO Dr Jennie Ward-Robinson.

Address: 1889 F St, NW, Suite 312, Washington, DC 20006.

Telephone: (202) 974-3416; **Fax:** (202) 974-3636; **Internet:** www.pahofoundation.org; **e-mail:** info@pahofoundation.org.

PAI—Population Action International

Founded in 1965; a private, non-profit group.

Activities: An independent policy advocacy group working to strengthen political and financial support worldwide for population programmes grounded in individual rights. PAI is committed to advancing universal access to family planning and related health services, and to educational and economic opportunities, especially for girls and women. It seeks to make clear the linkages between population, reproductive health, the environment and development. It also fosters the development of US and international policy on population and reproductive health issues through an integrated programme of research, advocacy and communications; and serves as a bridge between the academic and policy-making communities. Disseminates strategic, action-orientated research publications; participates in and sponsors conferences, meetings and seminars; and works to educate and inform policy-makers and international colleagues in related fields.

Geographical Area of Activity: International.

Publications: *Countdown 2015: Sexual & Reproductive Health & Rights For All*; *What You Need to Know About the Global Gag Rule and US HIV/AIDS Assistance: An Unofficial Guide*; *The Security Demographic: Population and Civil Conflict After the Cold War*; *Access Denied: US Restrictions on International Family Planning*; *Condoms Count: Meeting the Need in the Era of HIV/AIDS*; *In This Generation: Sexual & Reproductive Health Policies for a Youthful World*; newsletter; other fact sheets, books and charts; Annual Report.

Finance: Annual revenue US $6,146,974, expenditure $7,164,246 (31 Dec. 2013).

Board of Directors: Harriet C. Babbitt (Chair.); Victoria P. Sant (Vice-Chair.); Moses Naim (Former Chair.); Dr Pouru Bhiwandi (Treas.); Susan Esserman (Sec.).

Principal Staff: Pres. and CEO Suzanne Ehlers; COO Carolyn Gibb Vogel.

Address: 1300 19th St NW, Suite 200, Washington, DC 20036.

Telephone: (202) 557-3400; **Fax:** (202) 728-4177; **Internet:** pai.org; www.populationaction.org; **e-mail:** info@pai.org.

Panasonic Foundation

Established in 1984 by Matushita Electrical Corporation of America (MECA), and formerly known as the Matsushita Foundation, a subsidiary company of the Japan-based Matsushita Electrical Industrial Co Ltd.

Activities: Operates in the field of education through partnerships with a small number of school districts, which are provided with direct technical assistance to bring about school reform.

Geographical Area of Activity: USA.

Restrictions: Does not award grants.

Publications: Newsletter; articles and books; *The Panasonic Foundation and School Reform: 20 Years of Corporate Commitment*; *The Panasonic Foundation 25 Years*; *Learning by Doing: Panasonic Partnerships and Systemic School Reform*.

Finance: Annual revenue US $375,000, expenditure $2,015,046 (2013).

Officers and Trustees: Dr Milton Chen (Chair.); Michael Riccio (Treas.); Gordon Kyvik (Asst Treas.): Sandra Karriem (Sec.).

Principal Staff: Exec. Dir Larry Leverett; Asst Exec. Dir Scott Thompson.

Address: 2 Riverfront Plaza, 11th Floor, Newark, NJ 07102.

Telephone: (201) 392-4132; **Fax:** (201) 392-4126; **Internet:** www.panasonicfoundation.net; **e-mail:** info@foundation.us.panasonic.com.

Parkinson's Disease Foundation, Inc—PDF

Founded in 1957 by William Black to raise funds to plan, undertake, support and promote investigation into the cause and cure of Parkinson's disease and related disorders, and to provide patients suffering from the disease with a better quality of life. Merged with the United Parkinson Foundation, Chicago in 1999.

Activities: Operates nationally and internationally in the fields of research, education and advocacy. The Foundation makes grants to institutions and individuals, awards scholarships and fellowships, holds conferences, runs advisory services and issues publications. Programmes include the International Research Grants Program; the H. Houston Merritt Fellowship Program; the Summer Fellowship Program; and a post-doctoral programme.

Geographical Area of Activity: Mainly USA, although international grants are available.

Publications: Annual Report; *PDF Newsletter*; *PDF Science Bulletin*; *Progress, Promise and Hope!*; *Exercises for the Parkinson Patient*; *The Parkinson Patient at Home*; leaflets and brochures.

Finance: Annual revenue US $9,777,656, expenditure $9,764,203 (30 June 2012).

Board of Directors: Howard D. Morgan (Chair.); Dr Constance Woodruff Atwell (Vice-Chair.); Stephen Ackerman (Treas.); Isobel Robins Konecky (Sec.); Stanley Fahn (Scientific Dir).

Principal Staff: Pres. Robin Anthony Elliot; Vice-Pres. Dr James Beck.

Address: 1359 Broadway, Suite 1509, New York, NY 10018.

Telephone: (212) 923-4700; **Fax:** (212) 923-4778; **Internet:** www.pdf.org; **e-mail:** info@pdf.org.

Partners in Health—PIH

Established in 1987 by Ophelia Dahl and Paul E. Farmer to provide primary health care in less-developed countries, counter the causes of disease and alleviate poverty that can exacerbate disease.

Activities: Operates some 50 health centres and hospitals in 11 countries in Africa, Central and South America and the Caribbean, and countries of the former USSR to help counter diseases such as tuberculosis and HIV.

Geographical Area of Activity: Guatemala, Haiti, Lesotho, Malawi, Mexico, Peru, the Russian Federation, Rwanda.

Finance: Annual revenue US $88,865,208, expenditure $88,925,980 (30 June 2014).

Board of Trustees: Ophelia Dahl (Chair.).

Principal Staff: CEO Gary Gottlieb; Chief Strategist Paul E. Farmer.

Address: 888 Commonwealth Ave, 3rd Floor, Boston, MA 02215.

Telephone: (617) 998-8922; **Fax:** (617) 998-8973; **Internet:** www.pih.org; **e-mail:** info@pih.org.

PATH—Program for Appropriate Technology in Health

PATH was founded in 1977 as PIACT, the Program for the Introduction and Adaptation of Contraceptive Technology. Present name adopted in 1981.

Activities: An international non-profit organization that creates sustainable, culturally relevant solutions, enabling communities to break long-standing cycles of poor health. By collaborating with diverse public and private sector partners, the Program provides appropriate health technologies and strategies that change the way people think and act, and improves global health and well-being. Currently works in more than 70 countries in the areas of health technologies, maternal and child health, reproductive health, vaccines and immunization, and emerging and epidemic diseases. Has offices in 34 cities in 23 countries.

Geographical Area of Activity: International.

Restrictions: Not a grantmaking organization.

Publications: More than 800 publications, including: *Directions in Global Health*; *Outlook* (on reproductive health issues); *PATH Today* (newsletter); Annual Report; other resources.

Finance: Annual revenue US $315,128,000, expenditure $314,015,000 (31 Dec. 2013).

Board of Directors: Dean Allen (Chair. and Treas.).

Principal Staff: Pres. and CEO Steve Davis.

Address: 2201 Westlake Ave, Suite 200, Seattle, WA 98121; POB 900922, Seattle, WA 98109.

Telephone: (206) 285-3500; **Fax:** (206) 285-6619; **Internet:** www.path.org; **e-mail:** info@path.org.

Pathfinder International

Incorporated in 1957 by Dr Clarence Gamble as the Pathfinder Fund to introduce better family planning information and facilities around the world.

Activities: Works to improve reproductive health services in the developing world. The organization aims to improve the lives of women and their families, particularly in the areas of improving access to services, advocacy work, AIDS and abortion services. It funds and participates in national family planning programmes in Africa, Central and South America, Asia and the Caribbean.

Geographical Area of Activity: Africa, Central and South America, Asia and the Caribbean.

Publications: Annual Report, *Reproductive Health Resources, Guides and Tools*; technical guidelines, training curricula, articles, working papers, reports; *Pathways* (newsletter).

Finance: Annual revenue US $99,900,027, expenditure $100,953,003 (30 June 2014).

Board: Richard Nekowitz, Jessica J. Druga (Chair.); Roslyn Watson (Vice-Chair.); Jane Havemeyer (Sec.).

Principal Staff: Pres. and CEO Purnima Mane; Sr Vice-Pres. Caroline Crosbie.

Address: 9 Galen St, Suite 217, Watertown, MA 02472.

Telephone: (617) 924-7200; **Fax:** (617) 924-3833; **Internet:** www.pathfinder.org; **e-mail:** information@pathfind.org.

Alicia Patterson Foundation—APF

Founded in 1965 by members of the Albright and Patterson families to support print journalists.

Activities: Awards one-year and six-month fellowships to print journalists with at least five years' experience who are US citizens. Fellowship recipients pursue independent projects of significant interest in the USA or overseas.

Geographical Area of Activity: USA.

Restrictions: Fellowships open only to US citizens, or non-US citizens who work on US print publications. No grants are made for academic study.

Publications: *APF Reporter* (quarterly); web magazine; Annual Report; information brochure.

Finance: Annual revenue US $286,332, expenditure $432,635 (2013).

Board of Directors: Alice Arlen (Chair.); Adam Albright (Treas.); Margaret Engel (Sec.); Michael Massing, Frances Fitzgerald (Co-Treas.).

Principal Staff: Pres Robert Lee Hotz; Vice-Pres. Patrick Hoge; Exec. Dir Margaret Engel.

Address: 1090 Vermont Ave NW, Suite 1000, Washington, DC 20005.

Telephone: (202) 393-5995; **Fax:** (301) 951-8512; **Internet:** www.aliciapatterson.org; **e-mail:** info@aliciapatterson.org.

PCI-Media Impact

Founded in 1985 as Population Communications International (PCI).

Activities: Aims to work creatively with the media and other organizations to influence population trends. The organization promotes sustainable development through the research, production and broadcast of locally run and culturally appropriate radio and television serial dramas. These productions inform and educate local communities in Africa, Asia, Central and South America, and the USA about population and development issues through popular entertainment, and work to enhance communications between NGOs. Issues covered include reproductive health and family planning, HIV prevention, gender equality, social welfare and the protection of the environment. Also acts as the Secretariat for the NGO Committee on Population and Development, which encourages co-operation between the UN and NGOs.

Geographical Area of Activity: International.

Restrictions: Does not make grants.

Publications: *Mónica en busca de amor*; *Jam Packed*; *Time to Act*; *The Cost of Cool*; *Telling Stories, Saving Lives;* Annual Report; research papers; *PCI Strengthens HIV/AIDS Initiative in Peru*; *PCI partner stays on the air despite violence in Oaxaca, Mexico*.

Finance: Annual revenue US $2,580,043, expenditure $2,543,348 (31 Dec. 2013).

Board of Directors: Sally Timpson, Dr Lynne Yeannakis (Co-Chair.); Rita Fredricks Salzman (Vice-Chair.); Alan Court (Treas.); Richard Stone (Sec.).

Principal Staff: Exec. Dir Sean Southey.

Address: 777 United Nations Plaza, 5th Floor, New York, NY 10017.

Telephone: (212) 687-3366; **Fax:** (212) 661-4188; **Internet:** mediaimpact.org; **e-mail:** info@mediaimpact.org.

PepsiCo Foundation, Inc

Founded in 1962 by PepsiCo, Inc, and Frito-Lay, Inc.

Activities: Provides financial support to non-profit organizations primarily where employees of PepsiCo are involved as volunteers. The Foundation prioritizes organizations concerned with Nutrition and Activity, Safe Water and Usage Efficiencies, and Education and Empowerment. It is also involved in disaster response.

Geographical Area of Activity: Worldwide.

Restrictions: Only considers grant applications made online. No grants are made to individuals.

Finance: Annual revenue US $15,218,356, expenditure $32,323,539 (31 Dec. 2013).

Board of Directors: Indra K. Nooyi (Chair.); Christine C. Griff (Sec.); Tessa Hilado (Treas.).

Principal Staff: Pres. Larry Thompson; Vice-Pres., Global Citizenship and Sustainability Sue Tsokris.

Address: c/o PepsiCo, Inc, 700 Anderson Hill Rd, Purchase, NY 10577.

Telephone: (914) 253-2000; **Internet:** www.pepsico.com/purpose/global-citizenship.

Pesticide Action Network North America—PANNA

Founded in 1982 as a regional centre of the PAN International network to campaign for safer forms of pest control in Canada, Mexico and the USA.

Activities: Promotes healthier and more effective methods of pest control to replace harmful pesticides, through research, policy development, media coverage, education and international advocacy campaigns. The Network provides activists, researchers and policy-makers with technical information, analysis, training, campaign support and policy guidance. It enlists the support of numerous health, consumer, agricultural and environmental groups throughout North America to eliminate harmful pesticide use.

Geographical Area of Activity: North and Central America.

Publications: *PAN Magazine*.

Finance: Annual revenue US $2,946,088, expenditure $2,646,652 (30 June 2014).

Board of Directors: Polly Hoppin (Pres.); Mary Brune (Vice-Pres.); Susan Baker (Treas.); Ana Pardo (Sec.).

Principal Staff: Exec. Dir Judy Hatcher.

Address: 49 Powell St, Suite 500, San Francisco, CA 94102.

Telephone: (415) 981-1771; **Fax:** (415) 981-1991; **Internet:** www.panna.org; **e-mail:** panna@panna.org.

Peter G. Peterson Foundation

Established in 2008 by Peter G. Peterson to support all forms of sustainability in the USA.

Activities: Operates in the USA to draw attention to future problems in the areas of social welfare, medicine and health, and conservation and the environment, including costs of welfare and health care, energy consumption, global warming, and nuclear and biological weapons.

Geographical Area of Activity: USA.

Restrictions: Proposals are currently by invitation only.

Finance: Annual revenue US $1,691,883, expenditure $22,578,080 (31 March 2013).

Board of Directors: Peter G. Peterson (Chair.); Michael A. Peterson (Vice-Chair.).

Principal Staff: Pres. and CEO Michael A. Peterson; Exec. Vice-Pres. Loretta Ucelli.

Address: 888-C Eighth Ave, Box 144, New York, NY 10019.

Internet: www.pgpf.org; **e-mail:** inquiries@pgpf.org.

The Pew Charitable Trusts

Including the Pew Memorial Trust (f. 1948), the J. N. Pew, Jr Charitable Trust (f. 1956), the J. Howard Pew Freedom Trust, the Mabel Pew Myrin Trust and the Mary Anderson Trust (all f. 1957), the Knollbrook Trust (f. 1965) and the Medical Trust (f. 1979).

Activities: Support non-profit activities in three main areas: informing the public, through the Pew Research Center, based in Washington, DC, which explores important issues and trends that affect public opinion; improving public policy nationally and globally by helping to find non-partisan solutions for the problems affecting communities; and stimulating civic life including by supporting organizations in Philadelphia concerned with encouraging the participation of local citizens in the city's arts and culture community.

Geographical Area of Activity: USA, with a special emphasis on the Philadelphia area.

Restrictions: No grants are made to individuals, for scholarships, nor for endowment funds; non-applied research; land acquisition; equipment purchases; capital projects; debt reduction.

Publications: *Program Resource Guide*; *Trust* (quarterly magazine); strategy papers; reports; and other publications.

Finance: Annual revenue US $321,776,712, expenditure $300,296,337 (30 June 2013).

Board of Directors: J. Howard Pew, II (Chair.).

Principal Staff: Pres. and CEO Rebecca W. Rimel.

Address: 1 Commerce Sq., 2005 Market St, Suite 1700, Philadelphia, PA 19103-7077.

Telephone: (215) 575-9050; **Fax:** (215) 575-4939; **Internet:** www.pewtrusts.org; **e-mail:** info@pewtrusts.org.

Pfizer Foundation

Founded in 1953 by Pfizer Inc, a pharmaceuticals company.

Activities: Operates in areas where the Pfizer company has offices. The Foundation promotes access to health care and education, encourages and develops innovation, and supports the community involvement of Pfizer workers. Internationally, programmes focus on the donation of medicines and providing support to train health care workers in diagnosis and treatment, and help patients understand how to live healthier lives to prevent the spread of preventable diseases. A worldwide programme with a budget of US $33m. to improve the diagnosis and treatment of cancer and to support tobacco control was announced in 2008. Also provides disaster relief in the form of funding and gifts-in-kind.

Geographical Area of Activity: Worldwide.

Restrictions: Unsolicited proposals are discouraged, but not refused.

Finance: Annual revenue US $5,456,227, expenditure $17,753,103 (2013).

Board: Ian C. Read (Chair. and CEO).

Address: 235 East 42nd St, New York, NY 10017-5703.

Telephone: (212) 733-4250; **Internet:** www.pfizer.com/responsibility.

The Carl and Lily Pforzheimer Foundation, Inc

Founded in 1942 by members of the Pforzheimer family for general charitable purposes.

Activities: Operates primarily in the field of American and English literature, in collaboration with libraries and educational institutions, through publications and through the Carl H. Pforzheimer Library. The Foundation supports certain selected institutions active in the fields of education, medicine, social welfare and the arts.

Geographical Area of Activity: USA.

Finance: Annual revenue US $874,069, expenditure $529,350 (31 Dec. 2013).

Board of Directors: Carl H. Pforzheimer, III (Pres. and Treas.); Nancy P. Aronson (Vice-Pres.); George L. K. Frelinghuysen (Asst Treas. and Asst Sec.); Jennifer Lui (Sec.).

Principal Staff: Comptroller Anthony L. Ferranti.

Address: 950 3rd Ave, 30th Floor, New York, NY 10022-2705.

Telephone: (212) 223-6500.

PH International

Founded in 1985 by Charles Hosford as Project Harmony to create a stronger global community. Present name adopted in 2009.

Activities: Co-ordinates cultural, educational and professional exchanges to enhance international understanding, strengthen communities and nurture personal friendships. The organization also carries out programmes in: youth leadership; civic participation; combating domestic violence; reparative justice; digital literacy; social media for social change; economic development and projects that use information technology for these purposes. Offices in the USA, Armenia, Georgia, the former Yugoslav republic of Macedonia, the Russian Federation and Ukraine, with additional projects in Turkey and Kazakhstan.

Geographical Area of Activity: Worldwide, with special focus on Eurasia, the Middle East and USA.

Restrictions: None.

Publications: E-newsletter; Annual Report; financial summary.

Finance: Annual revenue US $6,161,122, expenditure $6,493,646 (31 Dec. 2014).

Board of Directors: Philip R. Smith (Chair.); Jeanne Keller (Co-Chair.); Jim Reardon (Sec.).

Principal Staff: Exec. Dir Ann Martin.

Address: 5197 Main St, Unit 6, Waitsfield, VT 05673.

Telephone: (802) 496-4545; **Fax:** (802) 496-4548; **Internet:** www.ph-int.org; **e-mail:** ph-vt@ph-int.org.

Philippine Development Foundation—PhilDev

Established in 2000 as the Ayala Foundation USA to build links between Filipino communities in the USA and the Philippines. Linked to the Ayala Foundation in the Philippines (q.v.). Present name adopted in 2010.

Activities: Assists the development of philanthropic giving for the Philippines in partnership with individuals and organizations/networks of Filipinos in the USA. The Foundation aims to increase awareness of socio-economic issues affecting poverty, hunger, illiteracy, environmental degradation and homelessness. Raises funds to support projects in the Philippines, including assistance to poor communities; education, technological and business skills development to help economically disadvantaged young people and adults to find employment; and enhancing cultural, historical and environmental conservation awareness through communication, publication and governance. Maintains a database on donor opportunities in the Philippines.

Geographical Area of Activity: USA and the Philippines.

Restrictions: Grants are made in the Philippines to non-profit organizations engaged in social development.

Publications: Annual Report; newsletter; e-bulletin (monthly).

Finance: Annual revenue US $949,849, expenditure $1,630,784 (31 Dec. 2013).

Board of Trustees: Dado Banatao (Chair.); Jones Castro (Exec. Vice-Pres.); Josie Chernoff (Sec.); Danilo Lopez (Treas.).

Principal Staff: Pres. Catherine Buan Peterson.

Address: 3000 Sand Hill Rd Bldg 3, Suite 240 Menlo Park, CA 94025.

Telephone: (650) 288-3937; **Fax:** (650) 288-3916; **Internet:** www.phildev.org; **e-mail:** info@phildev.org.

Physicians for Human Rights—PHR

Founded in 1986.

Activities: Uses medical and scientific methods to research and expose human rights violations around the world. The organization works in four programme areas: mass atrocities, such as attacks on civilians, their dwellings and infrastructure, intentional starvation, forced labour and displacement, disappearance, detention and enslavement; sexual violence in conflict zones and rape used as a weapon of war; persecution of health professionals and other violations of medical neutrality, such as attacks on hospitals, clinics, medical transport and interference with the impartial care of the sick and wounded in conflict situations; and torture—detention, cruel inhuman degrading treatment, mutilation and unethical scientific experimentation. Has offices in Boston, MA and Washington, DC.

Geographical Area of Activity: Worldwide.

Publications: *Doctors in the Crosshairs: Four Years of Attacks on Health Care in Syria*; *Doing Harm: Health Professionals' Central Role in the CIA Torture Program*; *A Foreseeable Disaster in Burma*; *Impunity in Honduras: Torture and Ill-Treatment after the Coup d'État*; *Contempt for Freedom*; *Patterns of Anti-Muslim Violence in Burma: A Call for Accountability and Prevention*; *Massacre in Central Burma*; *Buried Alive: Solitary Confinement in the US Detention System*; *Securing Afghanistan's Past: Human Remains Identification Needs and Gap Analysis*; *Libyan Human Identification Needs Assessment and Gap Analysis*; *Ending Impunity: The Use of Forensic Medical Evaluations to Document Torture and Ill Treatment in Kyrgyzstan*; *Under the Gun: Ongoing Assaults on Bahrain's Health System*. Also publishes fact sheets, programme brochures, newsletters and an Annual Report.

Finance: Annual revenue US $7,619,206, expenditure $7,108,144 (30 June 2014).

Board of Directors: Deborah D. Ascheim (Chair.); Kerry J. Sulkowicz (Vice-Chair.); David Dantzker (Treas.); Joel Lamstein (Clerk).

Principal Staff: Exec. Dir Donna McKay.

Address: 256 W 38th Street, 9th Floor, New York, NY 10018.

Telephone: (646) 564-3720; **Fax:** (646) 564-3750; **Internet:** phr.org; physiciansforhumanrights.org; **e-mail:** info@phrusa.org.

Plenty International

Established in 1974 by The Farm community, a non-government alternative organization aiming to help share the world's resources and knowledge.

Activities: Facilitates the exchange of technology, skills, information and friendship between communities and cultures by sending volunteers to areas of need around the world who work on sustainable development projects relating to health care, education, food and nutrition (particularly soya nutrition), alternative energy, protection of the environment and disaster relief. The organization works on long-term projects in Central America, West Africa and the USA, especially with Native Americans.

Geographical Area of Activity: North and Central America, Mexico, the Caribbean and West Africa.

Publications: *The Plenty Bulletin* (quarterly newsletter).

Finance: Annual revenue US $224,820, expenditure $277,471 (31 Dec. 2013).

Board of Directors: Lisa Wartinger (Pres.); Carol Nelson (Sec. and Treas.).

Principal Staff: Exec. Dir Peter Schweitzer.

Address: POB 394, Summertown, TN 38483.

Telephone: (931) 964-4323; **Fax:** (931) 964-4864; **Internet:** www.plenty.org; **e-mail:** info@plenty.org.

Ploughshares Fund

Founded in 1981 to help prevent the spread of nuclear weapons, control the sale of conventional weapons, take steps toward preventing armed conflict, and build global and regional security.

Activities: Operates internationally in the fields of weapons control and conflict resolution, particularly in the USA, Europe, Asia, the Middle East, the Russian Federation, the Democratic People's Republic of Korea and Japan. The Fund makes grants for projects, research, conferences and to individuals.

Geographical Area of Activity: Worldwide.

Publications: Annual Report; newsletter.

Finance: Annual revenue US $7,830,020, expenditure $6,808,686 (30 June 2013).

Board of Directors: Mary Lloyd Estrin (Chair.); Doug Carlston (Treas.); Terry Gamble Boyer (Sec.).

Principal Staff: Pres. Joseph Cirincione; Exec. Dir and COO Philip W. Yun.

Address: 1808 Wedemeyer St, Suite 200, The Presidio of San Francisco, San Francisco, CA 94129.

Telephone: (415) 668-2244; **Fax:** (415) 668-2214; **Internet:** www.ploughshares.org; **e-mail:** ploughshares@ploughshares.org.

Pollock–Krasner Foundation, Inc

Founded in 1985 by Lee Krasner to support artists.

Activities: Awards grants to professional, working artists in the fields of sculpture, painting, works on paper and printmaking. Since 1985 the Foundation has awarded more than 3,850 grants totalling more than US $58m. to artists in 75 countries.

Geographical Area of Activity: Worldwide.

Restrictions: No grants are made for academic study, nor to commercial artists, photographers, performance artists, video artists, film-makers or artisans.

Publications: Grant Report.

Finance: Annual revenue US $3,911,762, expenditure $5,015,860 (30 June 2013).

Board of Directors: Charles C. Bergman (Chair. and CEO).

Principal Staff: Pres. Samuel Sachs, II; Exec. Vice-Pres. Kerrie Buitrago.

Address: 863 Park Ave, New York, NY 10021.

Telephone: (212) 517-5400; **Fax:** (212) 288-2836; **Internet:** www.pkf.org; **e-mail:** grants@pkf.org.

Wladyslaw Poniecki Foundation, Inc

Founded in 1990 by W. I. Poniecki; previously known as the Wladyslaw Poniecki Charitable Foundation.

Activities: Aims to enhance education through technology, and support activities in developing countries, especially emerging market economies. The Foundation's main programmes concentrate on Internet training for librarians. Other work includes the translation of workbooks relating to technology and software; publishing educational books in the areas of medicine, business, the environment and education; and stimulating grassroots, professional, non-profit associations. Work is principally centred on Central and Eastern Europe, but the Foundation is not restricted to this area and its expertise is also applicable to other parts of the developing world.

Geographical Area of Activity: Mainly Central and Eastern Europe.

Finance: Annual revenue US $6,263, expenditure $12,651 (31 Dec. 2013).

Board of Directors: Wandzia Rose (Pres.); Andrzej Witkowski (Treas.).

Principal Staff: Exec. Dir Czeslaw Jan Grycz.

Address: 3020 El Cerrito Plaza, Suite 311, El Cerrito, CA 94530-2728.

Telephone: (510) 621-3498; **Fax:** (510) 588-4670; **Internet:** www.poniecki.org; **e-mail:** info@poniecki.org.

Population Council

Founded in 1952 by John D. Rockefeller, III.

Activities: Seeks to improve the well-being and reproductive health of current and future generations around the world, and to help achieve a humane, equitable and sustainable balance between people and resources. The Council conducts research in three areas: HIV and AIDS; poverty, gender and youth; and reproductive health. It improves the research capacity of reproductive and population scientists in developing countries through grants, fellowships and support of research centres.

Geographical Area of Activity: Africa, Asia, Middle East, North and South America, and the Caribbean.

Restrictions: Grants only in the form of doctoral and post-doctoral fellowships in the biomedical, health and social sciences.

Publications: *Studies in Family Planning* (quarterly); *Population and Development Review* (quarterly); Annual Report; books; newsletters; regional monographs; *Poverty, Gender and Youth Working Papers.*

Finance: Annual revenue US $81,701,469, expenditure $87,349,595 (31 Dec. 2013).

Board of Trustees: Mark A. Walker (Chair.).

Principal Staff: Pres. Julia Bunting.

Address: 1 Dag Hammarskjöld Plaza, New York, NY 10017.

Telephone: (212) 339-0500; **Fax:** (212) 755-6052; **Internet:** www.popcouncil.org; **e-mail:** pubinfo@popcouncil.org.

Pro Mujer International (Pro Women International)

Established in 1990 by Lynne Patterson and Carmen Velasco.

Activities: A women's development, health and microfinance non-profit social enterprise that provides more than 270,000 clients in Latin America with a set of integrated services: small loans, savings and insurance; business and empowerment training; and high-quality, low-cost primary health care.

Geographical Area of Activity: USA, Argentina, Bolivia, Mexico, Nicaragua and Peru.

Publications: Newsletter; Annual Report and financial statement.

Finance: Annual revenue US $41,934,131, expenditure $33,604,876 (31 Dec. 2013).

Board of Directors: Gail Landis (Chair.); Joel Landis (Interim Vice-Chair.); Ana Demel (Sec.); Mary McCaffrey (Treas.).

Principal Staff: Pres. and CEO Rosario Pérez.

Address: 253 West 35th St, 11th Floor South, New York, NY 10001.

Telephone: (646) 626-7000; **Fax:** (212) 904-1038; **Internet:** www.promujer.org; **e-mail:** promujer@promujer.org.

Project Concern International—PCI

Established in 1961 by Dr James Turpin to help the world's vulnerable children, families and communities, provide access to health resources, prevent disease and promote development through dynamic partnerships that build local capacity in efficient and measurable ways.

Activities: Works in four key areas; Women and Children's Health, incl. child survival interventions (immunizations, breastfeeding, control of diarrhoeal disease and acute respiratory infections, integrated management of childhood illnesses and provision of Vitamin A) as well as family planning, reproductive health, prenatal care and men's health education; Food Security, improving access, availability and use of food resources, promoting home gardens, nutritional education programmes, community infrastructure development, school feeding programmes and food aid for households affected by HIV/AIDS; Disease Prevention and Mitigation, preventing the spread of communicable and vector-borne diseases, as well as the activities that mitigate their impact, home-based care for people with AIDS, community-based programmes that address the needs of orphans and vulnerable children, tuberculosis and leprosy screening and treatment; and Water and Sanitation, improving access to potable water and sanitation facilities, incl. the construction and training in community management of wells, gravity-fed arrangements and rainwater catchment systems, small-scale municipal sewerage systems and solid waste disposal systems.

Geographical Area of Activity: International, with an emphasis on Bolivia, Central America, Ghana, India, Indonesia, Romania, the USA and Zambia.

Restrictions: No grants to individuals.

Publications: *CONCERNews* (quarterly newsletter); Annual Report.

Finance: Annual revenue US $48,696,031, expenditure $47,003,273 (30 Sept. 2013).

Board of Directors: Gaddi Vasquez (Chair.); Nancy Plaxico (Man. Dir); Judith A. Ettinger (Immediate Past Man. Dir); Anne Otterson (Chair. Emerita).

Principal Staff: CEO and Pres. George Guimaraes; CFO Nikolos Oakley.

Address: 5151 Murphy Canyon Rd, Suite 320, San Diego, CA 92123.

Telephone: (858) 279-9690; **Fax:** (858) 694-0294; **Internet:** www.projectconcern.org; **e-mail:** postmaster@pciglobal.org.

Project HOPE

Project HOPE (Health Opportunity for People Everywhere) is the principal activity of the People-to-People Health Foundation, founded in 1958 by William B. Walsh.

Activities: Promotes the development of health system infrastructure, the training of local health workers in modern medical techniques in developing countries worldwide, and assists in the development of medical facilities. The foundation distributes medical textbooks and journals to institutions throughout the world. It also holds conferences. The foundation's Center for Health Affairs carries out research in health policy. Has established national organizations in Germany, Hong Kong, Japan, Switzerland, the United Kingdom and the USA.

Geographical Area of Activity: Africa, Asia, Central and Eastern Europe, the Russian Federation and Central Asia, the Americas and the Caribbean, and the Middle East.

Publications: Annual Report; newsletter; brochures.

Finance: Annual revenue US $290,389,000, expenditure $276,962,000 (30 June 2013).

Board of Directors: Richard T. Clark (Chair.); George B. Abercrombie (Vice-Chair.); William F. Brandt, Jr (Treas.); Dayton Ogden (Sec.).

Principal Staff: Pres. and CEO John P. Howe, III; Exec. Vice-Pres. Linda N. Heitzman.

Address: 255 Carter Hall Lane, Millwood, VA 22646.

Telephone: (540) 837-2100; **Fax:** (540) 837-1813; **Internet:** www.projecthope.org; **e-mail:** hope@projecthope.org.

ProLiteracy

Formed in 2002 by the merger of Laubach Literacy International and Literacy Volunteers of America.

Activities: Monitors public policy and legislation concerning adult learners and literacy providers. The organization's projects in the USA are concerned with: Performance Accountability; Volunteers in Adult Basic Education; National Referral Service; Increasing Intensity of Instruction; Literacy and Home Safety; and Reducing Student Waiting Lists. It runs a Literacy for Social Change project, training projects, initiatives and partner programmes in more than 50 developing countries, and also credentialling programmes. Administers the National Book Fund and the Charles Evans Book Fund. Holds an annual conference.

Geographical Area of Activity: Worldwide.

Publications: Books; educational materials; documentaries.

Finance: Annual revenue US $7,726,245, expenditure $8,956,048 (30 June 2013).

Board of Directors: John Ward (Chair.); Nikki Zollar (Sec.); Thomas Fiscoe (Treas.); Seetha Srinivasan (Sec.).

Principal Staff: Pres. and CEO Kevin Morgan; Assoc. Exec. Dir Peter Waite.

Address: 104 Marcellus St, Syracuse, NY 13204.

Telephone: (315) 422-9121; **Fax:** (315) 422-6369; **Internet:** www.proliteracy.org; **e-mail:** info@proliteracy.org.

Prudential Foundation

Founded in 1977 by the Prudential Insurance Co of America and the Prudential Property & Casualty Co for general charitable purposes.

Activities: Involved in the fields of education, economic development and civic infrastructure, mainly in areas of company operations.

Geographical Area of Activity: USA, Brazil, Mexico, Japan, the Republic of Korea, India, Taiwan and the People's Republic of China.

Restrictions: No grants are made to individuals; generally no funding for capital campaigns or endowments.

Publications: Annual Report.

Finance: Annual revenue US $15,440,227, expenditure $29,792,437 (31 Dec. 2013).

Board of Trustees: Sharon C. Taylor (Chair.); James McCarthy (Treas.); Shane Harris (Vice-Pres. and Sec.).

Principal Staff: Pres. Lata Reddy.

Address: 213 Washington St, Newark, NJ 07102.

Telephone: (973) 802-4791; **Internet:** www.prudential.com/view/page/public/12373; **e-mail:** community.resources@prudential.com.

Public Welfare Foundation, Inc

Established in 1947 by Charles Edward Marsh, a newspaper publisher, and his wife Claudia.

Activities: Operates in the USA in three programme areas: criminal justice, juvenile justice and workers' rights. The Foundation provides grants to organizations.

Geographical Area of Activity: USA.

Restrictions: No grants to individuals, nor for scholarships, graduate work, government projects, research or capital projects or foreign study.

Publications: Annual Report; guidelines.

Finance: Annual revenue US $42,195,670, expenditure $24,205,537 (30 Sept. 2013).

Board of Directors: Lydia M. Marshall (Chair.).

Principal Staff: Pres. Mary E. McClymont; Chief Financial and Admin. Officer Phillipa Taylor.

Address: 1200 U St NW, Washington, DC 20009-4443.

Telephone: (202) 965-1800; **Fax:** (202) 265-8851; **Internet:** www.publicwelfare.org; **e-mail:** info@publicwelfare.org.

Rainforest Action Network—RAN

Founded in 1985 by Randy Hayes to protect the Earth's rainforests and support the rights of their inhabitants through education, local community organization and non-violent direct action.

Activities: A non-profit organization working nationally and internationally with other environmental and human rights organizations to protect rainforests. The Network runs four primary campaigns: Freedom from Oil; Global Finance; Old Growth; and Rainforest Agribusiness. The Protect-an-Acre programme provides grant funding directly to organizations and communities in rainforest regions. The Network is also involved in negotiation, research, conferences and seminars, and education. It issues publications and maintains a speakers' bureau and library. In 2007, the Network launched Action Tank, a project designed to provide training for activists and develop effective techniques for grassroots action. There are some 25,000 active members and more than 175 Rainforest Action Groups worldwide.

Geographical Area of Activity: International.

Publications: *Cut Waste, Not Trees: a wood use reduction guide*; *Importing Destruction*; *Drilling to the Ends of the Earth*; *500 Year Plan*; *Action Alerts* (2 a month); Annual Report; fact sheets and information packs.

Finance: Annual revenue US $3,705,572, expenditure $3,775,400 (30 June 2013).

Board of Directors: André Carothers (Chair.); Jodie Evans, Anna Hawken McKay (Development Co-Chair.); Stephen Stevick (Governance Chair.); Allan Badiner (Program Chair.); Scott B. Price (Treas. and Finance Chair.); James D. Gollin (Pres.).

Principal Staff: Exec. Dir Lindsey Allen.

Address: 221 Pine St, 5th Floor, San Francisco, CA 94104.

Telephone: (415) 398-4404; **Fax:** (415) 398-2732; **Internet:** www.ran.org; **e-mail:** answers@ran.org.

Rainforest Foundation US

Established in 1989, as part of the Rainforest Foundation group of organizations (qq.v.), to conserve rainforests and their indigenous peoples.

Activities: Operates in Central and South America, working in partnership with indigenous groups and local organizations to help secure land rights, advocate for policies to protect resources and build community leadership.

Geographical Area of Activity: Brazil, Guyana, Panama and Peru.

Finance: Annual revenue US $1,075,087, expenditure $1,045,777 (31 Dec. 2012).

Board of Directors: John W. Copeland (Chair.); S. Todd Crider (Vice-Chair.).

Principal Staff: Exec. Dir Suzanne Pelletier.

Address: 180 Varick St, Suite 528, New York, NY 10014.

Telephone: (212) 431-9098; **Internet:** www.rainforestfoundation.org; **e-mail:** spelletier@rffny.org.

RARE

Established in 1985 to promote conservation to benefit inhabitants and nature.

Activities: Designs conservation programmes in more than 50 countries through the training of local partners in the implementation of 'Pride' campaigns (to inspire local pride in natural resources). Maintains offices in the People's Republic of China, Indonesia, Mexico, the Philippines and Micronesia.

Geographical Area of Activity: Worldwide.

Finance: Annual revenue US $12,369,587, expenditure $18,130,046 (30 Sept. 2013).

Board of Dirs: Edward Soule (Chair.); Scott M. Amero (Chair.); Vadim Nikitine (Sec.); Duncan M. McFarland (Treas.).

Principal Staff: Pres. and CEO Brett Jenks.

Address: 1310 North Courthouse Rd, Suite 110, Arlington, VA 22201.

Telephone: (703) 522-5070; **Internet:** www.rareconservation.org; **e-mail:** info@rareconservation.org.

Reef Ball Foundation

Established in 1993 by Todd Barber to support ocean reef systems through the use of artificial reefs and related technologies for betterment of marine ecosystems.

Activities: Operates internationally using artificial reefs to rehabilitate natural reef systems. To date, the Foundation has placed around 500,000 artificial reefs in more than 59 countries. The Foundation is also involved in conservation projects incl. coral propagation, mangrove plantings, and oyster reef conservation, development and erosion control, and collaborates with other organizations.

Geographical Area of Activity: International.

Publications: *Step by Step Guide to Reef Rehabilitation for Grassroots Organization.*

Finance: Annual revenue US $358,723, expenditure $334,139 (30 Sept. 2013).

Board of Directors: Todd Barber (Chair.); Larry Beggs (Vice-Pres.).

Principal Staff: Exec. Dir Kathy Kirbo.

Address: 890 Hill St, Athens, GA 30606.

Telephone: (706) 714-4399; **Fax:** (509) 357-2722; **Internet:** www.reefball.org; **e-mail:** reefball@reefball.com.

Christopher and Dana Reeve Foundation

Established in 1999 following the merger of the American Paralysis Association (f. 1982) and the Christopher Reeve Paralysis Foundation.

Activities: Operates in the field of medical research, especially in the area of spinal cord injury research. The Foundation offers two-year research awards of a maximum of US $75,000 per award: to encourage new research on regeneration and recovery, in particular on spinal cord injuries; to encourage established researchers to transfer their research efforts to spinal cord research; and to assist researchers with new ideas to seek awards from other sources of funding. It funds activities that hold the promise of identifying therapies for paralysis and other sequelae of spinal cord injury. Development of effective therapies for chronic injury is a priority for the organization, though funding is also provided for studies more relevant to the acute phase of injury. Basic research is supported if it has clear potential to accelerate progress at the applied end of the continuum and/or if it reflects a research change in direction. The Quality of Life Program includes health promotion programmes for people with paralysis-related disabilities, which aim to remove societal and environmental barriers that limit an individual's ability to participate in life's activities; grants are made to regional and local organizations. Maintains a Paralysis Resource Center and offices in Westlake Village, CA and Washington, DC.

Geographical Area of Activity: USA.

Restrictions: Does not make grants to individuals.

Publications: Annual Report; *The Spinal Cord: A Christopher and Dana Reeve Foundation Text and Atlas*; informational brochures, including the Reeve Report and Progress in Research.

Finance: Annual revenue US $12,395,586, expenditure $13,154,273 (31 Dec. 2013).

Board of Directors: John M. Hughes (Chair.); John E. McConnell, Matthew Reeve, Henry G. Stifel, III (Vice-Chair.); Jeffrey P. Cunard (Sec.); Joel M. Faden (Treas.).

Principal Staff: Pres. and CEO Peter T. Wilderotter.

Address: 636 Morris Turnpike, Suite 3A, Short Hills, NJ 07078.

Telephone: (973) 225-0292; **Fax:** (973) 912-9433; **Internet:** www.christopherreeve.org; **e-mail:** media@christopherreeve.org.

Refugees International—RI

Established in 1979 to act as an independent voice for humanitarian action on behalf of the least-known and most vulnerable victims of war, famine and disaster.

Activities: Operates in areas of war and crisis, providing direct aid to refugees and people who have been displaced from their homes, including emergency relief, repatriation and protection. The organization also provides on-site field assessments and reports to policy- and opinion-makers worldwide to mobilize help for the victims. Since 2000, it has worked towards reforms in six areas designed to help avoid or alleviate chronic, continuing refugee crises: improvement of the UN peacekeeping capability through the creation of an established rapid-reaction peace and security force; new protection for internally displaced people; increased attention to the needs of refugee women; an end to the recruitment and use of child soldiers; more attention to the transition between relief operations and economic development; and building local capacity and institutions.

Geographical Area of Activity: International.

Publications: Newsletter (monthly); Annual Report; bulletins; articles; videos.

Finance: Annual revenue US $2,985,176, expenditure $3,239,647 (31 Dec. 2013).

Board of Directors: Eileen Shields-West (Chair.); Elizabeth Galvin (Vice-Chair.); L. Craig Johnstone (Sec.); Jeffrey Tindell (Treas.).

Principal Staff: Pres. Michael Gabaudan.

Address: 2001 S St NW, Suite 700, Washington, DC 20009.

Telephone: (202) 828-0110; **Fax:** (202) 828-0819; **Internet:** www.refugeesinternational.org; **e-mail:** ri@refugeesinternational.org.

Rehabilitation International—RI

Founded in 1922 to assist and act as an advocate for disabled people around the world. Present name adopted in 1972.

Activities: A federation of more than 1,000 organizations in 96 countries, promoting and implementing the rights and inclusion of people with disabilities. The organization acts as an open forum for the exchange of information and experience on research and practice. It has regional offices in Africa, the Middle East, Asia, Europe, North America, South America and Central America.

Geographical Area of Activity: International.

Publications: *Rehabilitation Review* (annually); *One in Ten*; bulletins; reviews; catalogues.

Finance: Annual revenue US $497,135, expenditure $291,777 (31 Dec. 2013).

Principal Staff: Sec.-Gen. Venus Ilagan.

Address: 1 Liberty Plaza, Office 2342, New York, NY 10006.

Telephone: (212) 420-1500; **Fax:** (212) 505-0871; **Internet:** www.riglobal.org; **e-mail:** info@riglobal.org.

Relief International

Founded in 1990 to reduce suffering worldwide.

Activities: Provides humanitarian assistance in the form of emergency relief, rehabilitation, development assistance and more long-term services to communities around the world, incl. health, shelter, reconstruction, education, community development, agriculture, food, income generation and conflict resolution. The organization promotes self-reliance in developing countries and empowers communities by maximizing local resources.

Geographical Area of Activity: Afghanistan, Azerbaijan, Bangladesh, Ghana, Indonesia, Iran, Iraq, Jordan, Lebanon, Myanmar, Niger, Pakistan, the Palestinian Territories, Senegal, Somalia, Sri Lanka, Sudan (Darfur and South Sudan) and Tajikistan.

Publications: Annual Report.

Finance: Annual revenue US $26,902,671, expenditure $29,301,177 (31 Dec. 2013).

Board of Directors: Paul Levengood (Chair.).

Principal Staff: CEO Nancy Wilson.

Address: 5455 Wilshire Blvd, Suite 1280, Los Angeles, CA 90036.

Telephone: (323) 932-7888; **Fax:** (323) 932-7878; **Internet:** www.ri.org; **e-mail:** info@ri.org.

Research Corporation for Science Advancement—RCSA

Founded in 1912 by Frederick Gardner Cottrell and others to receive and acquire inventions, patent rights and letters patent, and to render the latter more available and effective in the useful arts and manufactures; to provide means for the advancement of technical and scientific investigation, research and experimentation, by contributing the net earnings of the Corporation to scientific and educational institutions and societies.

Activities: Aids research proposed by college and university faculty members. Corporation programmes include the Cottrell College Science Awards (physics, chemistry and astronomy at undergraduate institutions); Research Opportunity Awards (to assist mid-career chemists, astronomers and physicists in doctoral departments to pursue new areas of research); Research Innovation Awards (to assist highly original research by faculty members at research universities); Cottrell Scholars Awards (research and teaching in physics, chemistry and astronomy at graduate institutions); and Special Opportunities in Science Awards (to assist projects with potential for advancing science that do not fall under other programme guidelines).

Geographical Area of Activity: USA and Canada.

Publications: Newsletter; Annual Report; occasional reports; books.

Finance: Annual revenue US $22,064,521, expenditure $4,091,628 (31 Dec. 2013).

Board of Directors: G. Scott Clemons (Chair.).

Principal Staff: Pres. Dr Robert Shelton.

Address: 4703 East Camp Lowell Dr., Suite 201, Tuscon, AZ 85712.

Telephone: (520) 571-1111; **Fax:** (520) 571-1119; **Internet:** www.rescorp.org; **e-mail:** awards@rescorp.org.

Christopher Reynolds Foundation, Inc

Founded in 1952 by Libby Holman Reynolds to support initiatives in the field of international relations.

Activities: Supports projects dealing with injustice in social, economic and environmental matters; provides funds to humanitarian organizations in the USA and in Cuba; and seeks to promote improved relations between the two countries.

Geographical Area of Activity: USA and Cuba.

Restrictions: Does not support individuals, capital or endowment funds, deficit financing, scholarships or matching gifts.

Publications: Report (every 5 years); Annual Report.

Finance: Annual revenue US $1,716,830, expenditure $1,618,470 (2013).

Board of Directors: John R. Boettiger (Chair.); Suzanne Derrer (Vice-Chair.); Nicholas Jacangelo (Treas.).

Principal Staff: Exec. Dir Andrea Panaritis.

Address: 77 Summer St, 8th Floor, Boston, MA 02110.

Telephone: (617) 391-3101; **Fax:** (617) 426-7087; **Internet:** www.creynolds.org; **e-mail:** crau@gmafoundations.com.

Righteous Persons Foundation

Established in 1994 by film-maker Steven Spielberg, initially with his profits from the film *Schindler's List*.

Activities: Dedicated to supporting efforts that build a vibrant, just and inclusive Jewish community in the USA. The Foundation has invested in organizations and efforts working to: revitalize Jewish arts, culture and identity; engage the next generation; strengthen a commitment to social justice; and promote understanding between Jews and those of other faiths and backgrounds.

Geographical Area of Activity: Mainly USA.

Restrictions: No grants are made to individuals.

Publications: Application guidelines.

Finance: Annual revenue US $2,125,001, expenditure $2,189,810 (2013).

Board of Directors: Steven Spielberg (Chair.).

Principal Staff: Pres. Gerald Breslauer; Exec. Dir Rachel Levin.

Address: 400 S Beverly Dr., Suite 420, Beverly Hills, CA 90212.

Telephone: (310) 314-8393; **Fax:** (310) 314-8396; **Internet:** www.righteouspersons.org; **e-mail:** grants@righteouspersons.org.

RNRF—Renewable Natural Resources Foundation

Founded in 1972 to advance scientific and public education in renewable natural resources; to promote the application of sound scientific practices in managing and conserving renewable natural resources; and to foster co-operation among professional, scientific and educational organizations having leadership responsibilities for renewable natural resources.

Activities: Operates in the field of conservation and the environment, nationally through self-conducted programmes, and nationally and internationally by awarding prizes, organizing conferences and through publications.

Geographical Area of Activity: International.

Restrictions: Funds own activities and solicits grants from public and private entities.

Publications: *Renewable Resources Journal* (quarterly); reports include *Environmental Impacts of Emerging Contaminants; Building Capacity for Coastal Solutions; Federal Natural Resources Agencies Confront an Aging Workforce and Challenges to Their Future Roles; Assessing America's Renewable Energy Future; Sustaining Natural Resources and Conservation Science; Coastal Resilience and Risk*.

Finance: Annual revenue US $1,750,000, expenditure $646,000 (31 Dec. 2013).

Board of Directors: Richard A. Engberg (Chair.); John E. Durrant (Vice-Chair.).

Principal Staff: Exec. Dir Robert D. Day.

Address: 6010 Executive Blvd, 5th Floor, North Bethesda, MD 20852-3827.

Telephone: (301) 493-9101; **Fax:** (301) 770-9104; **Internet:** www.rnrf.org; **e-mail:** info@rnrf.org.

Robertson Foundation for Government—RFFG

Established in 2010 by the family of the late Charles and Marie Robertson.

Activities: Prepares US graduate students for careers in foreign policy, national security and international affairs. The Foundation's flagship Robertson Fellows Program offers scholarships and stipends to students at five universities.

Geographical Area of Activity: USA.

Finance: Annual revenue US $6,795,948, expenditure $1,858,875 (31 Dec. 2013).

Board of Directors: Robert Halligan (Chair.); Geoffrey Robertson (Sec.); John H. Linnartz (Treas.).

Principal Staff: Pres. Katherine Ernst; Exec. Dir Timothy 'Bo' Kemper.

Address: 1801 F Street, NW, Suite 3A, Washington, DC 20006.

Telephone: (202) 289-6700; **Fax:** (202) 289-6333; **Internet:** www.rffg.org; **e-mail:** info@rffg.org.

Rockefeller Brothers Fund

Founded in 1940 as a vehicle through which the five sons and daughter of John D. Rockefeller, Jr, could share advice and research on charitable activities and combine philanthropies to better effect. John D. Rockefeller, Jr, made a substantial gift to the Fund in 1951, and in 1960 the Fund received a major bequest from his estate. Together, these constitute the original endowment of the Fund.

Activities: Advances social change that contributes to a more just, sustainable and peaceful world. The Fund's grantmaking is organized around three themes: Democratic Practice, Peacebuilding and Sustainable Development. The Fund pursues its programmes worldwide but concentrates cross-programmatic attention on specific 'RBF pivotal places': subnational areas, nation states or cross-border regions that have special importance with regard to the Fund's substantive concerns, and whose future will have disproportionate significance for the future of a surrounding region, ecosystem or the world. The Fund currently works in three pivotal places: New York City, the southern part of the People's Republic of China and the western Balkans.

Geographical Area of Activity: Worldwide.

Publications: *Charting Our Progress*; various other publications.

Finance: Annual revenue US $145,085,287, expenditure $49,743,372 (31 Dec. 2013).

Board of Trustees: Valerie Rockefeller Wayne (Chair.); Joseph Pierson (Vice-Chair.); Stephen B. Heintz (Pres.); Nancy L. Muirhead (Sec.).

Principal Staff: Exec. Dir Judy Clark.

Address: 475 Riverside Dr., Suite 900, New York, NY 10115.

Telephone: (212) 812-4200; **Fax:** (212) 812-4299; **Internet:** www.rbf.org; **e-mail:** communications@rbf.org.

Rockefeller Foundation

Founded in 1913 by John D. Rockefeller, Sr, to promote the well-being of mankind throughout the world.

Activities: Operates nationally and internationally through offering grants. The Foundation runs a series of international conferences and residencies for artists and scholars at its Bellagio Study and Conference Center (f. 1959) on Lake Cuomo in northern Italy. It also maintains offices in Bangkok, Nairobi and San Francisco.

Geographical Area of Activity: International.

Restrictions: No grants are made for personal aid to individuals, nor for general institutional support or fund endowments, nor for building or operating funds.

Publications: Annual Report.

Finance: Annual revenue US $205,875,970, expenditure $223,652,447 (31 Dec. 2013).

Board of Trustees: David Rockefeller, Jr (Chair.).

Principal Staff: Pres. Dr Judith Rodin.

Address: 420 Fifth Ave, New York, NY 10018.

Telephone: (212) 869-8500; **Fax:** (212) 764-3468; **Internet:** www.rockefellerfoundation.org; **e-mail:** cmmocommon@rockfound.org.

The Rotary Foundation

Founded in 1917 by Rotary International to further understanding and friendly relations between peoples of different nations.

Activities: Operates internationally in financing scholarships, grants for charitable and educational projects, cultural and educational exchanges of business and professional leaders, and grants for major health, hunger relief and humanitarian projects. Foundation awards and grants are open to men and women, with no restriction on race or creed. Programmes include: PolioPlus Grants; Disaster Recovery; District Simplified Grants; Health, Hunger and Humanity Grants; Matching Grants; Volunteer Service Grants; Ambassadorial Scholarships; Group Study Exchange; Rotary Grants for University Teachers; and Rotary World Peace Fellowships.

Geographical Area of Activity: International.

Publications: Annual Report; programme brochures.

Finance: Annual revenue US $296,527,000, expenditure $198,844,000 (30 June 2013).

Board of Trustees: John Kenny (Chair.); Ray Klingsmith (Chair.-elect); Michael K. McGovern (Vice-Chair.).

Principal Staff: Gen. Sec. John Hewko.

Address: 1 Rotary Center, 1560 Sherman Ave, Evanston, IL 60201.

Telephone: (847) 866-3000; **Fax:** (847) 328-8554; **Internet:** www.rotary.org/foundation; **e-mail:** contact.center@rotary.org.

The Judith Rothschild Foundation

Founded in 1993 to promote, present and interpret the work of lesser-known American artists who had died since 12 September 1976.

Activities: Promotes lesser-known artists through support for exhibitions, the acquisition of their work by museums and the safe keeping of paintings; the cataloguing of works of art; scholarly research; and the operation of programmes for study and interpretation of works of art. The Foundation's main projects are the Masterworks Collection, Grant and Technical Assistance Programs and the Works of Judith Rothschild.

Geographical Area of Activity: USA.

Restrictions: Funds are directed mainly towards the acquisition by public galleries and museums of work by deceased contemporary American artists.

Publications: Annual Report.

Finance: Annual revenue US $941,436, expenditure $741,251 (2013).

Principal Staff: Trustee Harvey S. Shipley Miller.

Address: 7036A Sheaff Lane, Fort Washington, PA 19034; POB 233, Flourtown, PA 19031.

Telephone: (215) 540-8400; **Fax:** (215) 540-8401; **Internet:** judithrothschildfdn.org; **e-mail:** judithrothschildfoundation@gmail.com.

The Edmond de Rothschild Foundations

Founded in 1963 by Edmond de Rothschild for general charitable purposes.

Activities: Operate primarily in New York and in France, but also make grants in Israel, in the fields of Jewish social welfare, education (incl. business administration and religious education), science and medicine, and the arts and humanities, through grants to institutions.

Geographical Area of Activity: USA, France and Israel.

Restrictions: Grants made only to pre-selected organizations. Unsolicited applications are not accepted.

Finance: Annual revenue US $4,434,970, expenditure $6,954,700 (2013).

Board of Directors: Benjamin de Rothschild (Chair.); Philip M. Susswein (Sec. and Asst Treas.).

Principal Staff: Pres. Ariane de Rothschild; Exec. Vice-Pres. and Treas. Firoz Ladak.

Address: 1585 Broadway, 24th Floor, New York, NY 10036-8204.

Telephone: (212) 969-3250; **Internet:** www.edrfoundations.org; **e-mail:** info@edrfoundations.org.

Samuel Rubin Foundation

Founded in 1958 to promote peace and justice.

Activities: Operates in the fields of education, human rights and social welfare. The Foundation provides grants to organizations concerned with human rights, justice, peace and the redistribution of resources in the world; promotes social, economic, political, civil and cultural rights.

Geographical Area of Activity: Worldwide.

Restrictions: No grants to individuals, for building funds or scholarships.

Publications: Programme policy statement.

Finance: Annual revenue US $1,696,664, expenditure $875,718 (30 June 2014).

Board of Directors: Peter Weiss (Chair. and Treas.); Cora Weiss (Pres.).

Principal Staff: Grants Admin. Lauranne Jones.

Address: 50 Church St, 5th Floor, Cambridge, MA 02138.

Telephone: (617) 547-0444; **Internet:** www
.samuelrubinfoundation.org; **e-mail:** office@
samuelrubinfoundation.org.

Damon Runyon Cancer Research Foundation

Founded in 1946 to support all theoretical and experimental research relevant to the study of cancer, and the search for its causes, mechanisms, treatment and prevention.

Activities: Awards up to 60 postdoctoral research fellowships a year for basic scientists and physician scientists, allowing scientists and medical practitioners beginning full-time post-doctoral research to carry out cancer research.

Geographical Area of Activity: USA.

Restrictions: US citizens may study in any country; foreign researchers' study must be carried out in the USA.

Publications: Annual Report.

Finance: Annual revenue US $20,326,072, expenditure $16,017,503 (30 June 2013).

Board of Directors: Alan M. Leventhal (Chair.); David M. Livingston (Vice-Chair.); Leon G. Cooperman (Vice-Chair. and Treas.); Sanford W. Morhouse (Vice-Chair. and Sec.); Michael L. Gordon (Vice-Chair.); David M. Beirne (Vice-Chair.).

Principal Staff: Pres. and CEO Lorraine W. Egan; CFO Travis Carey.

Address: 1 Exchange Plaza, 55 Broadway, Suite 302, New York, NY 10006.

Telephone: (212) 455-0500; **Fax:** (212) 455-0509; **Internet:** www.damonrunyon.org; **e-mail:** info@damonrunyon.org.

Russell Sage Foundation—RSF

Founded in 1907 by Margaret Olivia Sage for the improvement of social and living conditions in the USA.

Activities: Devoted exclusively to research in the social sciences, as a means to improve social policies. The Foundation's professional staff of about 21 social scientists (Resident Scholars, Visiting Scholars, Visiting Postdoctoral Fellows and part-time advisers and consultants) conduct research on selected topics (including basic research in improvements in methodology, data and theory). The Foundation also supports the work of scholars at other academic and research institutions; sponsors special seminars; and publishes books and monographs. Research grants are made in the main programme areas of the future of work, immigration, cultural contact and social inequality. Other special projects and research initiatives include the September 11 Initiative and the Behavioral Economics Roundtable.

Geographical Area of Activity: USA.

Restrictions: No grants are made internationally; no grants for pre-doctoral study or research; no scholarships or other types of grants for support of college funding.

Publications: Biennial Report; books and monographs.

Finance: Annual revenue US $13,055,581, expenditure $12,865,501 (31 Aug. 2013).

Board of Trustees: Sara S. McLanahan (Chair.); Shelley E. Taylor (Treas.).

Principal Staff: Pres. Sheldon Danziger; CFO Christopher Brogna.

Address: 112 East 64th St, New York, NY 10065.

Telephone: (212) 750-6000; **Fax:** (212) 371-4761; **Internet:** www.russellsage.org; **e-mail:** info@rsage.org.

Rutherford Institute

Founded in 1982 by John Whitehead.

Activities: Dedicated to the defence of civil and human rights. The Institute provides lawyers to help people whose civil rights or human rights have been violated. It also provides educational opportunities to improve standards of social justice in the USA.

Geographical Area of Activity: International.

Publications: *Insider* (e-mail newsletter); various pamphlets, books and videos.

Finance: Annual revenue US $1,323,835, expenditure $1,593,983 (30 June 2014).

Board of Directors: John W. Whitehead (Pres. and Chair.); Thomas S. Neuberger (Sec. and Treas.).

Address: POB 7482, Charlottesville, VA 22906.

Telephone: (434) 978-3888; **Fax:** (434) 978-1789; **Internet:** www.rutherford.org; **e-mail:** staff@rutherford.org.

Samaritan's Purse

Founded in 1970 by Dr Robert Pierce; an international non-denominational Christian organization.

Activities: Aims to help people suffering around the world. The organization provides aid and assistance to victims of war, disasters, disease, famine and poverty, as well as promoting the Gospel worldwide. It is active in many countries, engaging in a number of programmes, including emergency health care and improving existing medical facilities, providing emergency supplies (including food and clothing), funding community development projects, and providing shelters for abandoned children. Also organizes evangelical festivals throughout the world. Has offices in Australia, Canada, Germany, Ireland, the Netherlands and the United Kingdom.

Geographical Area of Activity: International.

Publications: Newsletter; Annual Report.

Finance: Annual revenue US $460,090,492, expenditure $402,039,746 (31 Dec. 2013).

Board of Directors: Franklin Graham (Chair.); James Furman (Vice-Chair. and Asst Treas.); Sterling Carroll (Treas.); Phyllis Payne (Sec.).

Principal Staff: Pres. and CEO Franklin Graham.

Address: POB 3000, Boone, NC 28607.

Telephone: (828) 262-1980; **Fax:** (828) 266-1056; **Internet:** www.samaritanspurse.org; **e-mail:** info@samaritan.org.

San Diego Foundation

Charitable endowment, established in 1975, which aims to improve the human condition in San Diego.

Activities: Supports communities and individuals in San Diego, and increases effective philanthropy. The Foundation awards grants to individuals and organizations in areas incl. the arts and culture, economic development, education, the environment, health care and human service, and religious endeavours. It contributes to charitable causes; awards scholarships; lends organizational support to projects; and acts as a centre of communication for San Diego's communities, raising and discussing issues that effect people in the area.

Geographical Area of Activity: USA.

Finance: Annual revenue US $80,029,028, expenditure $58,940,829 (30 June 2013).

Board of Governors: Prof. Steven R. Smith (Chair.); Dr John Cambon, Benjamin Haddad (Vice-Chair.); Connie Matsui (Vice-Chair. and Sec.).

Principal Staff: Pres. and CEO Bob Kelly.

Address: 2508 Historic Decatur Rd, Suite 200, San Diego, CA 92106.

Telephone: (619) 235-2300; **Fax:** (619) 239-1710; **Internet:** www.sdfoundation.org; **e-mail:** info@sdfoundation.org.

San Francisco Foundation (The San Francisco Foundation)

Founded in 1948 for the support of philanthropic undertakings in the San Francisco Bay area, CA.

Activities: Makes grants to organizations in the San Francisco Bay area in the fields of arts, education, environment, community health and community development to mobilize resources, act as a catalyst for change, foster civic leadership, and promote philanthropy in the area. Foundation initiatives include leadership programmes, such as the Koshland Program, which makes awards to grassroots social innovators, and the Community Leadership Awards, which recognize outstanding individuals and organizations.

Geographical Area of Activity: San Francisco Bay area, USA.

Restrictions: Serves the Alameda, Contra Costa, Marin, San Francisco and San Mateo counties only.

Publications: Annual Report; *Enews*; *Koshland Connect* (annually).

Finance: Annual revenue US $137,210,111, expenditure $101,595,858 (30 June 2013).

Board of Trustees: Andy Ballard (Chair.); Kurt Organista (Vice-Chair.).

Principal Staff: CEO Fred Blackwell.

Address: One Embarcadero Center, Suite 1400, San Francisco, CA 94111.

Telephone: (415) 733-8500; **Fax:** (415) 477-2783; **Internet:** www.sff.org; **e-mail:** info@sff.org.

Scaife Family Foundation

Established in 1983 by the Scaife family.

Activities: Supports projects that strengthen families, address issues surrounding the health and welfare of women and children, promote animal welfare, demonstrate the beneficial interaction between humans and animals, and encourage private conservation. The Foundation also makes grants to organizations working in the area of early intervention and prevention efforts in the area of drug and alcohol addiction.

Geographical Area of Activity: USA (emphasis on Florida and Pennsylvania).

Restrictions: No grants for events, capital campaigns nor renovations, nor for government agencies. No grants for individuals.

Publications: Annual Report.

Finance: Annual revenue US $4,568,169, expenditure $3,463,620 (2013).

Trustees: Jennie K. Scaife (Chair.).

Principal Staff: Pres. David A. Zywiec.

Address: Phillips Point, 777 South Flagler Dr., West Tower, Suite 903, West Palm Beach, FL 33401.

Telephone: (561) 659-1188; **Internet:** www.scaifefamily.org.

Sarah Scaife Foundation, Inc

Founded in 1941 by Sarah Mellon Scaife for broad charitable purposes; present name adopted in 1974. Merged with the Carthage Foundation (f. 1966) in 2015.

Activities: Supports public policy programmes that address major domestic and international issues, in areas such as education, government, economics, international law, crime and law enforcement, international affairs, etc. Makes grants for fellowships, research, projects, conferences and publications.

Geographical Area of Activity: Worldwide.

Restrictions: No grants are made to individuals nor to nationally-organized fund-raising groups.

Publications: Annual Report.

Finance: Annual revenue US $14,107,168, expenditure $14,268,969 (2012).

Trustees: Michael W. Gleba (Pres., Chair. and Treas.).

Address: 1 Oxford Centre, 301 Grant St, Suite 3900, Pittsburgh, PA 15219-6401.

Telephone: (412) 392-2900; **Internet:** www.scaife.com/sarah.html.

Robert Schalkenbach Foundation, Inc—RSF

Founded in 1925 by Robert Schalkenbach to promote the social and economic philosophy of Henry George, especially his views concerning the single tax on land values and international free trade.

Activities: Promotes sustainable economic development, human rights, the resolution of conflicts regarding land rights, wealth redistribution, ecological use of the earth's resources and the public sharing of land values (including electromagnetic, oceanic, mineral, forest, agricultural and urban location values). The Foundation operates through research, publications, seminars and conferences, and grants to educational institutions.

Geographical Area of Activity: The USA, the People's Republic of China, Europe and the Russian Federation.

Restrictions: No grants are made to individuals; grants are made only to specific organizations.

Publications: *Progress and Poverty* (by Henry George); *Land Value Taxation Around the World* (by R.V. Andelson); *The American Journal of Economics and Sociology* (quarterly); numerous monographs.

Finance: Annual revenue US $523,240, expenditure $642,507 (30 June 2013).

Board of Directors: Francis K. Peddle (Pres.); Ted Gwartney (Vice-Pres.); Gregg Erickson (Treas.).

Principal Staff: Admin. Dir and Sec. Mark A. Sullivan.

Address: 90 John St, Suite 501, New York, NY 10038.

Telephone: (212) 683-6424; **Fax:** (212) 683-6454; **Internet:** www.schalkenbach.org; **e-mail:** info@schalkenbach.org.

Dr Scholl Foundation

Founded in 1947 by William M. Scholl for general charitable purposes. Formerly known as the William M. Scholl Foundation.

Activities: Operates in the fields of education, civil society and culture, health, social service, and the environment. The Foundation has awarded grants for private education, medical and nursing institutions; medical and scientific research; programmes for children, young people, the developmentally disabled and older people; civic, cultural, social services, environmental and religious institutions; and for conferences and seminars.

Geographical Area of Activity: Mainly the USA.

Restrictions: No grants are made to individuals, endowments or capital campaigns, political organizations, political action committees, or for operating deficit reduction, loans, general support, liquidation of a debt, event sponsorships; only one request from the same organization in the same year.

Finance: Annual revenue US $6,832,908, expenditure $9,734,812 (2013).

Board of Directors: Pamela Scholl (Chair.); Jeanne M. Scholl (Sec.); John A. Nitschke (Treas.).

Principal Staff: Pres. Pamela Scholl; Vice-Pres. Anne Moseley.

Address: 1033 Skokie Blvd, Suite 230, Northbrook, IL 60062.

Telephone: (847) 559-7430; **Internet:** www.drschollfoundation.com.

Charles and Lynn Schusterman Family Foundation—CLSFF

Established in 1987.

Activities: Committed to strengthening the Jewish people, public education in the USA and quality of life in Tulsa, OK. Rooted in Jewish values, the Foundation provides young people with high-quality education, identity development, leadership training and service opportunities that foster their growth as individuals and as leaders in their communities, the Jewish world and beyond. It empowers young people to engage in meaningful Jewish experiences, build inclusive Jewish communities, connect with Israel and repair the world. In the field of education, the Foundation invests in reform efforts within and outside of US school systems that improve educational opportunities and outcomes for all students. It provides assistance to organizations in Tulsa that are dedicated to enhancing the quality of life, especially in the areas of child advocacy, youth development and community service. Has offices in Tulsa, Washington, DC, Atlanta and Israel.

Geographical Area of Activity: USA, Israel.

Restrictions: Grants are not made to: individuals; non-sectarian groups or local Jewish programmes outside Tulsa; endowments; deficits; appropriately funded government programmes; permanent financing.

Finance: Annual revenue US $123,986,975, expenditure $73,796,140 (2013).

Board of Trustees: Lynn Schusterman, Stacy Schusterman (Co-Chair.).

Principal Staff: Pres. Sanford R. Cardin; Vice-Pres. Lisa Eisen.

Address: 110 W Seventh Street, Suite 2000, Tulsa, OK 74119.

Telephone: (918) 879-0290; **Fax:** (918) 392-9724; **Internet:** www.schusterman.org; **e-mail:** information@schusterman .org.

Seeds of Peace

Founded in 1993 by John Wallach to empower young leaders from regions of conflict with the leadership skills required to advance reconciliation and co-existence.

Activities: Seeks to develop the leadership skills of young people in regions of conflict, with a particular emphasis on the Middle East, as well as South Asia, Cyprus and the Balkans. In the Middle East, the organization focuses on training young people in conflict-resolution skills that have been used in other conflict regions, including Cyprus, Albania, Bosnia and Herzegovina, Bulgaria, Croatia, the former Yugoslav republic of Macedonia, the former Yugoslavia (including Montenegro, Serbia and Kosovo), Romania, Afghanistan, India and Pakistan. It also runs the domestic Maine Seeds programme to address ethnic and racial tensions between the diverse communities that have settled in the organization's home state of Maine; and through its Beyond Borders programme brings teenagers from additional Middle East countries, incl. Iraq, Saudi Arabia and Kuwait, to Maine to participate in a cultural exchange programme between American and Arab young people. Maintains offices in Otisfield, ME, and Washington, DC, as well as Kabul, Lahore, Mumbai, Amman, Cairo, Gaza, Jerusalem, Ramallah and Tel-Aviv.

Geographical Area of Activity: USA, Middle East, South Asia, Cyprus and the Balkans.

Publications: e-Newsletters (monthly); Annual Report.

Finance: Annual revenue US $5,554,490, expenditure $5,431,750 (31 Dec. 2013).

Board of Directors: Peggy Tanner (Chair.); Michelle Mercer (Vice-Chair.); Samuel L. Samelson (Treas.); Christine Ramsay Covey (Sec.).

Principal Staff: Exec. Dir Leslie Adelson Lewin.

Address: 370 Lexington Ave, Suite 2103, New York, NY 10017.

Telephone: (212) 573-8040; **Fax:** (212) 573-8047; **Internet:** www.seedsofpeace.org; **e-mail:** info@seedsofpeace.org.

William G. and Marie Selby Foundation

Established in 1955 to carry out philanthropic activities, especially in the area of education in the Sarasota County area.

Activities: Focuses on social welfare, education, community development, health and culture. The Foundation provides scholarships and grants for students and organizations in Florida.

Geographical Area of Activity: Florida, USA only.

Restrictions: No grants are made to individuals, nor generally for endowments, deficit financing, debt reduction, or ordinary operating expenses; conferences, seminars, workshops, travel, surveys, advertising, fund-raising costs or research; annual giving campaigns; or projects that have already been completed.

Publications: Commemorative publications.

Finance: Annual revenue US $881,480, expenditure $3,593,894 (31 May 2013).

Board of Trustees: John W. Schaub, III (Chair.); Doug Mrstik (Vice-Chair.).

Principal Staff: Pres. and CEO Dr Sarah H. Pappas; Grants Man. Evan G. Jones.

Address: 1800 Second St, Suite 954, Sarasota, FL 34236.

Telephone: (941) 957-0442; **Fax:** (941) 957-3135; **Internet:** www.selbyfdn.org; **e-mail:** ejones@selbyfdn.org.

SERRV International, Inc

Established in 1949 by the Church of the Brethren to help refugees in Europe after the Second World War. Present name adopted in 1999.

Activities: Promotes the economic and social progress of people living in developing countries and aims to alleviate poverty through fair trade. Acts as a fair trade, non-profit organization, through advancing money to low-income artisans in developing countries so they can buy raw materials to make crafts. The organization then purchases and markets the finished items, selling them through more than 3,000 churches, non-profit groups and retail outlets.

Geographical Area of Activity: Worldwide.

Publications: *SERRV Catalogue*; newsletters (quarterly).

Finance: Annual revenue US $6,279,472, expenditure $6,249,805 (31 Dec. 2013).

Board of Directors: Marsha Hoover (Chair.); Colin Crawford (Vice-Chair.); Brad J. Hamrlik (Treas.); Pushpika Freitas (Sec.).

Principal Staff: Pres. and CEO Robert Chase.

Address: 122 State St, Suite 600, Madison, WI 53701.

Telephone: (608) 251-3766; **Fax:** (608) 255-0451; **Internet:** www.serrv.org; **e-mail:** orders@serrv.org.

Seva Foundation

Established in 1978.

Activities: Aims to alleviate the suffering caused by disease and poverty. The Foundation operates internationally to promote health, incl. eye care, nutrition, education, economic development and self help, native Americans, community development and social and economic justice. It works with partner organizations in Cambodia, Guatemala, India, Mexico, Nepal, Tanzania, Tibet and the USA.

Geographical Area of Activity: USA, Asia and Africa.

Restrictions: No unsolicited grant requests accepted.

Publications: Annual Report; newsletters; special programme reports; *25th Anniversary Report; Spirit of Service* (newsletters).

Finance: Annual revenue US $5,807,007, expenditure $7,480,441 (30 June 2014).

Board of Directors: Stephen D. Miller (Chair.); Dr Leslie Louie (Vice-Chair.); Lisa M. Laird (Treas.); Laura Bird (Sec.).

Principal Staff: Exec. Dir Jack Blanks; Finance Dir Deborah Moses.

Address: 1786 Fifth St, Berkeley, CA 94710.

Telephone: (510) 845-7382; **Fax:** (510) 845-7410; **Internet:** www.seva.org; **e-mail:** admin@seva.org.

The Sierra Club Foundation

Founded in 1960 to advance the preservation and protection of the natural environment.

Activities: Works to educate, inspire and empower humanity to preserve the natural and human environment. Provides resources to the Sierra Club and other non-profit organizations for charitable programmes that protect and restore the environment. Raises funds, donated for tax-exempt charitable purposes; and preserves, enhances and administers these funds so that future generations will inherit a healthy planet with wild places left to explore.

Geographical Area of Activity: USA and international.

Restrictions: Does not accept unsolicited proposals.

Publications: Annual Report; information brochure; financial statement.

Finance: Annual revenue US $58,503,816, expenditure $57,443,349 (31 Dec. 2013).

Board of Directors: Steven Berkenfeld (Chair.); Marni McKiney (Vice-Chair.); Doug Walker (Treas.); Sanjay Ranchod (Sec.).

Principal Staff: Exec. Dir Peter Martin.

Address: 85 Second St, Suite 750, San Francisco, CA 94105.

Telephone: (415) 995-1780; **Fax:** (415) 995-1791; **Internet:** www.sierraclubfoundation.org; **e-mail:** foundation@ sierraclub.org.

Silicon Valley Community Foundation

Established to offer support within the local community and worldwide.

Geographical Area of Activity: California, USA.

Finance: Annual revenue US $1,474m., expenditure $1,129m. (31 Dec. 2013).

Board of Directors: C. S. Park (Chair.); Samuel Johnson, Jr (Vice-Chair.); David P. López (Sec./Treas.).

Principal Staff: CEO and Pres. Dr Emmett D. Carson.

Address: 2440 West El Camino Real, Suite 300, Mountain View, CA 94040-1498.

Telephone: (650) 450-5400; **Fax:** (650) 450-5401; **Internet:** www.siliconvalleycf.org; **e-mail:** grants@siliconvalleycf.org.

Skoll Foundation

Established in 1999 by Jeff Skoll and based on the belief that small investments can lead to significant social change; incorporates the Skoll Fund (f. 1999), associated with Silicon Valley Community Foundation (q.v.).

Activities: Invests in mid- to late-stage social entrepreneurs and their initiatives around the world, including supporting microfinance projects, and the development of mass-market, low-cost technologies to help create new businesses. The Foundation connects change agents through Social Edge, an online community it has created for social entrepreneurs and other members of the social sector to promote networking and resource sharing. It established the Skoll Awards for Social Entrepreneurship. Also supports conferences, and in 2003 funded the launch of the Skoll Centre for Social Entrepreneurship at the Said Business School, Oxford University, United Kingdom, with a donation of US $7.5m.

Geographical Area of Activity: USA.

Publications: Annual Report.

Finance: Annual revenue US $31,746,607, expenditure $18,047,425 (31 Dec. 2013).

Board of Directors: Jeffrey S. Skoll (Chair.).

Principal Staff: Pres. and CEO Sally Osberg; COO Richard Fahey.

Address: 250 University Ave, Suite 200, Palo Alto, CA 94301.

Telephone: (650) 331-1031; **Fax:** (650) 331-1033; **Internet:** www.skollfoundation.org; **e-mail:** info@skollfoundation.org.

Alfred P. Sloan Foundation

Established in 1934 by Alfred Pritchard Sloan Jr, then President and Chief Executive Officer of the General Motors Corporation, the Foundation makes grants in support of original research and education in science, technology, engineering, mathematics and economic performance.

Activities: Operates through self-conducted programmes and grants to institutions within six areas: basic research, science education, public understanding of science and technology, economic performance and quality of life, select national issues, and civic initiatives. The Foundation sponsors the Sloan Fellowships for Basic Research for young chemists, physicists, mathematicians, neuroscientists and economists in institutions in the USA and Canada.

Geographical Area of Activity: USA.

Restrictions: Only rarely supports activities outside the USA and does not normally support projects in areas of religion, creative or performing arts, elementary or secondary education, the humanities, medical research or health care. No grants for endowments, buildings or equipment.

Publications: Annual Report; information brochure.

Finance: Annual revenue US $102,325,479, expenditure $109,355,508 (31 Dec. 2013).

Board of Trustees: Sandra O. Moose (Chair.).

Principal Staff: Pres. Paul Joskow.

Address: 630 Fifth Ave, Suite 2550, New York, NY 10111-0242.

Telephone: (212) 649-1649; **Fax:** (212) 757-5117; **Internet:** www.sloan.org; **e-mail:** myerson@sloan.org.

Smith Richardson Foundation, Inc

Founded in 1935 by H. S. Richardson, Sr and Grace Jones Richardson to support research relating to government operations and for programmes promoting a better understanding of American society and the economy.

Activities: Aims to inform important public policy debates through supporting pragmatic, policy-relevant research, analysis and writing. The Foundation provides grants in two main programme areas: the International Security and Foreign Policy Program, which supports research and policy projects on issues central to the strategic interests of the USA; and the Domestic Public Policy Program, researching the development of US economic, social and governmental institutions.

Geographical Area of Activity: USA.

Restrictions: The majority of unsolicited applications are rejected. No grants are made for projects in the arts and humanities, physical sciences or historic restoration, nor are grants made to individuals.

Publications: Annual Report.

Finance: Annual revenue US $76,616,690, expenditure $28,668,912 (31 Dec. 2013).

Trustees: Peter L. Richardson (Pres. and Chair.); Stuart S. Richardson (Vice-Chair.); Dr Arvid R. Nelson (Sec.); Karla W. Frank (Asst Sec.).

Principal Staff: Sr Vice-Pres. Dr Marin Strmecki.

Address: 701 Green Valley Rd, Greensboro, NC 27408-7096.

Telephone: (336) 379-8600; **Internet:** www.srf.org.

Smithsonian Institution

Created in 1846 by an Act of Congress in accordance with the terms of the will of James Smithson of England, who in 1826 bequeathed his property to the USA to found at Washington, DC, under the name of the Smithsonian Institution, an establishment for the increase and diffusion of knowledge among men.

Activities: Operates nationally and internationally in the fields of education, science, the arts and humanities, and the conservation of natural resources. The Institution performs basic research; publishes results of studies, explorations and investigations; maintains study and reference collections in the sciences, culture and history; and exhibitions in the arts, American history, technology, aeronautics, space exploration and natural history. It administers various museums, art galleries and other institutions, including the Anacostia Museum and Center for African American History and Culture; Archives of American Art; Arts and Industries Building; Cooper-Hewitt, National Design Museum; Freer Gallery of Art; Hirshhorn Museum and Sculpture Garden; National Air and Space Museum, including the Steven F. Udvar-Hazy Center; National Museum of African Art; Smithsonian American Art Museum; National Museum of American History; National Museum of the American Indian; National Museum of Natural History/Museum of Man; National Portrait Gallery; National Postal Museum; National Zoological Park; Renwick Gallery; Arthur M. Sackler Gallery; Smithsonian Astrophysical Observatory; Smithsonian Environmental Research Center; Smithsonian Institution Building; and the

Smithsonian Tropical Research Institute. Fellowships are offered to students of all nationalities to study at Smithsonian Institution facilities. Through the National Museum Act, grants are made to museum professionals for museum studies. The Smithsonian Institution Travelling Exhibition Service organizes exhibitions that circulate to museums around the USA, while the Smithsonian Affiliates Program establishes links and affiliations across the country.

Geographical Area of Activity: USA.

Publications: Annual Report and financial statement; *Smithsonian Opportunities for Research and Study*; *Smithsonian Magazine*; various scholarly and popular publications; *Air and Space Magazine*; *American Art*; *Zooger*; museum publications; Research Center publications and books.

Finance: Annual revenue US $1,371,587,031, expenditure $1,162,329,865 (30 Sept. 2013).

Board of Regents: John W. McCarter, Jr (Chair.); Shirley Ann Jackson (Vice-Chair.).

Principal Staff: Sec. David J. Skorton; Chief of Staff to Sec. Patricia Bartlett.

Address: POB 37012, SI Bldg, Rm 494, MRC 035, Washington, DC 20013.

Telephone: (202) 357-1729; **Internet:** www.si.edu; **e-mail:** info@si.edu.

Sorenson Legacy Foundation

Established in 2002 by the James LeVoy Sorenson family to offer support in the areas of welfare, religion, education, the arts and science.

Activities: Operates in the USA in the fields of social welfare, education, the arts and humanities, science and religion. It was announced in 2008 that James LeVoy Sorenson had left his entire fortune, estimated at some US $4,500m., to the Foundation.

Geographical Area of Activity: USA.

Finance: Annual revenue US $19,191,784, expenditure $33,070,227 (2013).

Board of Directors: Shauna Johnson (Pres.); Greg Taylor (Sec.); Terry D. Hodder (Treas.).

Principal Staff: Contact Lisa Meiling.

Address: 2511 South West Temple, Salt Lake City, UT 84115.

Telephone: (801) 461-9700; **Internet:** sorensonlegacyfoundation.org; **e-mail:** lisa@sorensonlegacyfoundation.org.

Soros Economic Development Fund

Established in 1997; a non-profit private foundation, part of the Soros foundations network.

Activities: Aims to alleviate poverty through making investments in banks, microfinance institutions, co-operatives and other such organizations worldwide. The Fund operates mainly in Eastern and Central Europe, but also in Africa, Central and South America, the Caribbean and South Asia, offering loans, equity, guarantees and deposits to selected financial institutions.

Geographical Area of Activity: International.

Finance: Annual revenue US $602,255, expenditure $8,703,199 (31 Dec. 2013).

Board of Directors: Michel Zaleski (Chair.); Maria Santos Valentin (Sec. and Gen. Counsel); James Beaver (Treas.).

Address: 224 West 57th St, 9th Floor, New York, NY 10019.

Telephone: (212) 548-0111; **Fax:** (646) 557-2551; **Internet:** www.sedfny.org; **e-mail:** sedf@opensocietyfoundations.org.

Spencer Foundation

Founded in 1962 by Lyle M. Spencer to support research leading to the improvement of education.

Activities: Supports research into all aspects of education, in the USA and abroad. The Foundation is interested in a wide variety of disciplinary and interdisciplinary approaches, but emphasizes the behavioural sciences; it defines education broadly to include all the situations and institutions in which education proceeds, regardless of age. The Foundation is interested in a wide variety of research formats, from relatively low-cost efforts extending over a few months to more expensive collaborative efforts over several years.

Geographical Area of Activity: Worldwide.

Publications: Annual Report; conference reports; influential research; usable knowledge in education; grantee books.

Finance: Annual revenue US $21,247,686, expenditure $22,485,483 (31 March 2014).

Board of Directors: Deborah Loewenberg Ball (Chair.); Pamela Grossman (Vice-Chair.).

Principal Staff: Pres. Michael S. McPherson; Sr Vice-Pres. Diana Hess; CFO Julie Hubbard.

Address: 625 North Michigan Ave, Suite 1600, Chicago, IL 60611.

Telephone: (312) 337-7000; **Fax:** (312) 337-0282; **Internet:** www.spencer.org; **e-mail:** pres@spencer.org.

The Stanley Foundation

Founded in 1956 by C. Maxwell and Elizabeth M. Stanley to encourage study, research and education in the field of international policy that contributes to secure peace with freedom and justice. Emphasis is placed on activities related to international institutions and US foreign policy.

Activities: Operates the following initiatives: UN and Global Institutions; US and Global Security; US and Middle East Security; US and Asian Security; Rising Powers; Nonproliferation, Arms Control and Disarmament; and Community Partnerships. The Foounation also organizes off-the-record conferences for policy-makers to discuss global issues and global security. Reports from conferences and seminars are published periodically and distributed free.

Geographical Area of Activity: Worldwide.

Restrictions: Not a grantmaking organization.

Publications: *Courier* (newsletter, 3 a year); conference reports; books on global change, the UN, security and disarmament, human rights and global education; policy briefs; analytical articles; reports; and other publications.

Finance: Annual revenue US $16,562,708, expenditure $4,235,549 (31 Dec. 2012).

Board of Directors: Richard H. Stanley (Chair.); Brian T. Hanson, Sarah C. Stanley (Vice-Chair.); Betty J. Anders (Sec.); Dana W. Pittman (Treas.).

Principal Staff: Pres. and CEO P. Keith Porter.

Address: 209 Iowa Ave, Muscatine, IA 52761.

Telephone: (563) 264-1500; **Fax:** (563) 264-0864; **Internet:** www.stanleyfoundation.org; **e-mail:** info@stanleyfoundation.org.

Star of Hope International

Since 1966 Star of Hope organizations have cared for people who are suffering or in need around the world.

Activities: Operates internationally in the fields of aid to less-developed countries, through assisting local organizations in areas of greatest need, and particularly through helping children. The organization has offices in Argentina, Brazil, Finland, Ghana, Haiti, Kenya, Latvia, Norway, the Philippines, Romania, Belarus, Sweden and Trinidad.

Geographical Area of Activity: International.

Publications: Newsletters; Annual Report.

Finance: Annual revenue US $519,661, expenditure $606,096 (31 Dec. 2013).

Board of Directors: Kenneth Wayne Borror (Pres.); Henry Conner (Treas.).

Principal Staff: Pres. and CEO Barry W. Borror.

Address: POB 427, Ellinwood, KS 67526-0427.

Telephone: (866) 653-0321; **Internet:** www.starofhope.org; **e-mail:** info@starofhope.org.

The Starr Foundation

Founded in 1955 by Cornelius V. Starr.

Activities: Makes grants largely in the area of education, particularly higher education. Also active in culture, medicine and health, human needs, public policy in international relations, welfare and social services. Offers funding for scholarships, professorships, fellowships and endowment funds.

Geographical Area of Activity: USA.

Restrictions: No grants are made to individuals. Does not accept unsolicited applications for grants.

Publications: Annual report; *Biography of Cornelius Vander Starr (1892–1968)*; *Introduction: The Gentle Laopan*; *A Family Album*; *A Man for Many Seasons*; *Citizen of the World*; *The World of Business*; *The Opera*; *Fine Art*; *Places He Loved*; *A Sense of Common Humanity*; *Architecture*; *Thirst for Knowledge*; *An Interest in People*; and other books.

Finance: Annual revenue US $40,463,562, expenditure $90,160,261 (31 Dec. 2012).

Board of Directors: Maurice R. Greenberg (Chair.); Joan Katz (Sec.); Howard I. Smith (Treas.); Yelena Lukonen (Asst Treas.).

Principal Staff: Pres. Florence A. Davis; Vice-Pres Paula Lawrence, Martha Livingston.

Address: 399 Park Ave, 17th Floor, New York, NY 10022.

Telephone: (212) 909-3600; **Fax:** (212) 750-3536; **Internet:** www.starrfoundation.org.

Stewardship Foundation

Founded in 1962 by the C. Davis Weyerhaeuser Irrevocable Trust to contribute to the propagation of religious organizations.

Activities: Concerned with funding evangelical religious organizations whose ministries operate over a wide area. The Foundation's areas of involvement include education, mental health, youth development, international economic development, and peace and reconciliation. It makes grants to international development organizations, foreign missions and youth ministries.

Geographical Area of Activity: Worldwide.

Restrictions: No grants are made to individuals; grants are made only to US public non-profit organizations.

Finance: Annual revenue US $14,108,430, expenditure $2,749,604 (2013).

Board of Trustees: Dr William T. Weyerhaeuser (Chair.); Gail T. Weyerhaeuser (Vice-Chair. and Treas.).

Principal Staff: Exec. Dir Cary A. Paine; Grants Man. Amy Alva.

Address: POB 1278, Tacoma, WA 98401-1278; 1145 Broadway, Suite 1500, Tacoma, WA 98402.

Telephone: (253) 620-1340; **Fax:** (253) 572-2721; **Internet:** www.stewardshipfdn.org; **e-mail:** info@stewardshipfdn.org.

The Streisand Foundation

Founded in 1986 by Barbra Streisand to provide funding in the fields of civil rights, voter outreach, the environment, women's issues, AIDS, and programmes for the disadvantaged youth of Los Angeles, CA.

Activities: Makes grants to US-based organizations working on a national level to promote and support: environmental issues; women's issues including reproductive choice and health-related concerns; civil liberties and democratic values; civil rights and race relations; children's and youth-related issues with a focus on the economically disadvantaged; nuclear disarmament; and AIDS research, advocacy, service and litigation. Awards are in the range of US $1,000–$25,000.

Geographical Area of Activity: USA.

Restrictions: No grants are made to individuals, nor to local organizations, except for programmes for disadvantaged youth in Los Angeles.

Publications: Application guidelines.

Finance: Annual revenue US $2,253,851, expenditure $894,225 (31 Dec. 2013).

Trustees: Barbra Streisand (Pres.); Margery Tabankin (Treas./Sec.); Lester J. Knipsel (Asst Sec.).

Principal Staff: Exec. Dir Margery Tabankin.

Address: 1460 4th St 212, Santa Monica, CA 90401.

Telephone: (818) 592-2000; **Internet:** www.barbrastreisand.com.

Surdna Foundation, Inc

Founded in 1917 by John E. Andrus for general charitable purposes.

Activities: Operates in the following areas: the environment (in particular energy, transportation, urban and suburban land use, human systems, and biological and cultural diversity); community revitalization (taking a comprehensive and holistic approach to restoring communities in the USA, in particular through entrepreneurial programmes offering solutions to difficult systemic problems); building an effective citizenry (promoting a civil society through character development, ethical behaviour, social and emotional learning, and conflict resolution); and the arts, focusing on arts education and young people. Also provides funding to support the development of the non-profit sector in the US, grants for organizational capacity building, and commissions reports in its areas of interest.

Geographical Area of Activity: USA.

Restrictions: No grants are made to individuals.

Publications: Annual Report; reports; announcements; commissioned reports.

Finance: Annual revenue US $157,872,719, expenditure $43,552,855 (30 June 2013).

Board of Directors: Jocelyn Downie (Chair.); Peter B. Benedict, II (Vice-Chair.); Lawrence S. C. Griffith (Sec. and Treas.).

Principal Staff: Pres. Phillip Henderson.

Address: 330 Madison Ave, 30th Floor, New York, NY 10017-5001.

Telephone: (212) 557-0010; **Fax:** (212) 557-0003; **Internet:** www.surdna.org; **e-mail:** grants@surdna.org.

Synergos—The Synergos Institute

Established in 1986 by Peggy Dulany.

Activities: Aims to develop effective, sustainable and locally based solutions to poverty in Africa, Asia and Central and South America. The Institute strengthens the capacity of civil society in less-developed countries and of leading philanthropists from around the world to deepen the effectiveness of their social investments and to forge partnerships. Its projects—Global Philanthropy and Foundation Building, Bridging Leadership and Global Philanthropists Circle—help grassroots grantmaking organizations to provide long-term solutions and sustainable development. Maintains an online database of foundations operating in Central and South America and South-East Asia and also works through a Country Office in Brazil.

Geographical Area of Activity: Africa, Asia and Central and South America.

Publications: Annual Reports; *Foundation Building Sourcebook: A Practitioner's Guide Based upon Experience from Africa, Asia and Latin America*; *Global Giving Matters* (online newsletter, 6 a year); case studies, conference reports and other publications.

Finance: Annual revenue US $11,604,935, expenditure $12,148,110 (31 Dec. 2013).

Board of Directors: Peggy Dulany (Chair.).

Principal Staff: Pres. and CEO Robert H. Dunn.

Address: 3 East 54th St, 14th Floor, New York, NY 10022.

Telephone: (646) 963-2100; **Fax:** (646) 201-5220; **Internet:** www.synergos.org; **e-mail:** synergos@synergos.org.

TechnoServe

Founded in 1968 by American businessman Ed Bullard to connect people in the developing world to the knowledge, skills and tools they need to lift themselves out of poverty.

Activities: Works with people in the developing world to build competitive farms, businesses and industries. The organization develops business solutions to poverty by linking people to information, capital and markets. It gives advice, shares technical expertise, and provides the marketing and capital needed to create prosperity and long-term sustainable solutions to poverty. Works in more than 30 countries.

Geographical Area of Activity: Africa, Central and South America and the Caribbean, South Asia.

Restrictions: Runs own projects. No unsolicited applications for grants accepted. Not a grantmaking foundation.

Publications: Annual Report.

Finance: Annual revenue US $82,465,235, expenditure $76,996,754 (31 Dec. 2014).

Board of Directors: Paul E. Tierney, Jr (Chair.); John B. Caron, Peter A. Flaherty (Vice-Chair.); Suzanne Nora Johnson (Treas.); Jennifer Bullard Broggini (Sec.).

Principal Staff: Pres. and CEO Will Warshauer; CFO Tim McLellan.

Address: 1120 19th St NW, 8th Floor, Washington, DC 20036.

Telephone: (202) 785-4515; **Fax:** (202) 785-4544; **Internet:** www.technoserve.org; **e-mail:** info@technoserve.org.

John Templeton Foundation

Founded in 1987 by Sir John Templeton.

Activities: Encourages civil, informed dialogue among scientists, philosophers and theologians, on subjects including complexity, evolution, infinity, creativity, forgiveness, love and free will. The Foundation awards the Templeton Prize, established in 1972, to a living person who has made an exceptional contribution to affirming life's spiritual dimension.

Geographical Area of Activity: International.

Publications: *The Templeton Report* (e-newsletter, twice a month); *Big Questions Online* (magazine); books.

Finance: Annual revenue US $704,549,618, expenditure $144,645,858 (31 Dec. 2013).

Board of Trustees: Dr Jack Templeton (Chair.); Harvey M. Templeton, III (Sec.); Ann T. Cameron (Treas./Asst Sec.); Valene K. Martin (Asst Treas.).

Principal Staff: Pres. Dr Jack Templeton.

Address: 300 Conshohocken State Rd, Suite 500, West Conshohocken, PA 19428.

Telephone: (610) 941-2828; **Fax:** (610) 825-1730; **Internet:** www.templeton.org; **e-mail:** info@templeton.org.

Thiel Foundation

Established in 2006 to defend and promote freedom in all its dimensions: political, personal and economic.

Activities: Runs programmes in the areas of freedom, anti-violence and science. The Foundation offers 20 scholarships to people under the age of 20 years to pursue innovative scientific and technical projects. In 2011, it launched the Breakout Labs programme to support entrepreneurial research in science.

Geographical Area of Activity: International.

Finance: Annual revenue US $15,577,231, expenditure $9,102,901 (31 Dec. 2013).

Board of Directors: Peter Thiel (Chair.); Matthew Alexander (Treas. and Sec.).

Principal Staff: Pres. Jonathan Cain; CEO Alana Aldag Ackerson.

Address: 1 Letterman Dr., Bldg C, Suite 400, San Francisco, CA 94117.

Internet: thielfoundation.org; **e-mail:** info@thielfoundation.org.

Thrasher Research Fund

Founded in 1977 by E. W. Thrasher to support meritorious, innovative research projects that seek to improve child health and well-being.

Activities: Makes grants to institutions in any country for medical research, without restriction as to geographical location, ethnicity, gender, creed or nationality. The Fund prioritizes practical applied research with the potential to benefit large numbers of children and find sustainable solutions to major problems of child health and well-being. The main focus is currently on gaps in paediatric medical research most likely to have an impact on the treatment of children with critical illnesses and major health problems. Grants range from US $10,000 to $400,000 and generally run for one to three years.

Geographical Area of Activity: International.

Restrictions: No grants for research on human foetal tissue; behavioural science research; educational programmes; general operating expenses; construction or renovation of buildings or facilities; general donations; loans, student aid, scholarships; nor to other funding organizations.

Publications: Biennial Report and application brochure.

Finance: Annual revenue US $8,445,520, expenditure $6,665,719 (31 Dec. 2012).

Principal Staff: Pres. R. Justin Brown.

Address: 68 S. Main St, Suite 400, Salt Lake City, UT 84101.

Telephone: (801) 240-4753; **Fax:** (801) 240-1625; **Internet:** www.thrasherresearch.org; **e-mail:** brownrj@thrasherresearch.org.

Tibet Fund

Established in 1981 to assist the educational, social and economic development of Tibetans living inside and outside Tibet.

Activities: Supports community and economic development projects in Tibetan refugee communities in India and Nepal. The Fund provides emergency relief, resettles new refugees who have fled Tibet, and improves their health conditions. It also awards scholarships to Tibetan students and professionals; preserves Tibetan culture and promotes cultural exchange; and provides assistance for health, education and economic development projects in Tibet.

Geographical Area of Activity: People's Republic of China, India, Nepal, Tibet and the USA.

Publications: Brochures.

Finance: Annual revenue US $5,817,045, expenditure $5,100,167 (31 Dec. 2013).

Board of Directors: Michael Lemle (Chair.); Geoffrey Menin (Vice-Pres.); Jessica Brackman (Sec.); Susan M. Holgate (Treas.).

Principal Staff: Pres. Rinchen Dharlo; Exec. Dir Lobsang Nyandak; Vice-Pres. Bob Ankerson.

Address: 241 East 32nd St, New York, NY 10016.

Telephone: (212) 213-5011; **Fax:** (212) 213-1219; **Internet:** www.tibetfund.org; **e-mail:** info@tibetfund.org.

Tides

Founded in 1976; a grantmaking organization dedicated to positive social change.

Activities: Mediates between donors and charitable organizations in need of resources, promoting human rights, social justice and a healthy environment. The organization strengthens community non-profit organizations, and awards grants in a large number of areas, including progressive media, arts and culture; economic development; the environment; gay and lesbian issues; HIV/AIDS; Native American communities; women's empowerment; violence prevention; reproductive health; and youth. Current programmes include the Death Penalty Mobilization Fund, Bridging the Economic Divide, Rapid Response Initiative and a Democracy Fund. Offers a number of services to donors to ensure that their money makes a lasting social impact. These include flexible and personalized grantmaking programmes, expert advice and the opportunity to network.

Geographical Area of Activity: USA.

Publications: Donor guides.

Finance: Annual revenue US \$114,031,827, expenditure \$112,649,431 (31 Dec. 2013).

Board of Directors: Vincent McGee (Chair.).

Principal Staff: CEO Kriss Deiglmeier.

Address: The Presidio, 1014 Torney Ave, San Francisco, CA 94129-1755; POB 29198, San Francisco, CA 94129-0198.

Telephone: (415) 561-6400; **Fax:** (415) 561-6401; **Internet:** www.tides.org; **e-mail:** info@tides.org.

Tiffany & Co Foundation

Established in 2000.

Activities: Operates nationally and internationally in the fields of art and culture, and preservation of the environment, specifically promotion of responsible mining.

Finance: Annual revenue US \$1,464,574, expenditure \$6,204,616 (2013).

Board: Anisa Kamadoli Costa (Chair. and Pres.); Leigh M. Harlan (Sec.); Robyn Wapner (Asst. Sec.); Michael W. Connolly (Treas.).

Principal Staff: Programme Officer Samara Rudolph.

Address: 200 Fifth Ave, New York, NY 10010.

Telephone: (973) 254 7651; **Internet:** www .tiffanyandcofoundation.org; **e-mail:** foundation@tiffany .com.

Tinker Foundation, Inc

Founded in 1959 by Edward Larocque Tinker to promote better understanding between the peoples of the Americas and for the support of work in, or directly related to, Antarctica.

Activities: Works in the fields of environmental policy and social sciences, with particular emphasis on economic and political matters having strong public policy implications. The Foundation supports research projects, conferences and workshops. It also promotes collaboration between organizations in the USA and Central and South America, and Antarctica, and among institutions in those regions. Offers the Martha T. Muse Prize for Science and Policy in Antarctica, an award of US \$100,000 given to an individual for work in the area of Antarctic science or policy that will enhance understanding of the region.

Geographical Area of Activity: Central and South America, Mexico and Antarctica.

Restrictions: No grants are made to individuals.

Publications: Annual Report.

Finance: Annual revenue US \$6,437,082, expenditure \$5,247,316 (31 Oct. 2013).

Board of Directors: Renate Rennie (Chair. and Pres.); Kathleen Waldron (Treas.); Alan Stoga (Sec.).

Principal Staff: Dir of Finance and Admin. Jessica Tomb.

Address: 55 East 59th St, New York, NY 10022.

Telephone: (212) 421-6858; **Internet:** www.tinker.org; **e-mail:** tinker@tinker.org.

The Trull Foundation

Founded in 1967 for general charitable purposes.

Activities: Focuses its grants on four priority areas: Matagorda County area, Texas, where the Foundation has its roots; children and families, directing them from abuse, neglect and hunger; those dealing with substance abuse; and the coastal environment of Texas, including farming, ranching, aquaculture and birds.

Geographical Area of Activity: USA (mainly Texas).

Restrictions: Does not provide grants for long-term commitments, buildings, endowments or research.

Publications: Report (biennially).

Finance: Annual revenue US \$1,951,554, expenditure \$2,590,658 (2013).

Board of Trustees: R. Scott Trull (Chair.); Cara P. Herlin (Vice-Chair.); Craig A. Wallis (Sec. and Treas.).

Principal Staff: Exec. Dir E. Gail Purvis.

Address: 404 Fourth St, Palacios, TX 77465.

Telephone: (361) 972-5241; **Fax:** (361) 972-1109; **Internet:** www.trullfoundation.org; **e-mail:** info@trullfoundation.org.

Trust for Mutual Understanding

Founded in 1984 to provide support to American non-profit cultural and environmental organizations for professional exchanges between the USA and Central and Eastern Europe and the countries of the former USSR.

Activities: Some three-quarters of funds are directed at cultural exchanges, with the remainder allocated to environmental projects. The Trust makes grants for exchange programmes that include a significant amount of professional interaction and collaboration between the two countries involved.

Geographical Area of Activity: USA, Central Asia, Eastern and Central Europe, and the countries of the former USSR.

Restrictions: Grants only to American non-profit organizations for international travel, and related expenses of Russian, Eastern and Central European, and American exchange participants.

Publications: Annual Report.

Finance: Annual revenue US \$3,331,943, expenditure \$3,152,399 (31 Dec. 2013).

Principal Staff: Dir Barbara Lanciers.

Address: 6 West 48th St, 12th Floor, New York, NY 10036-1802.

Telephone: (212) 843-0404; **Fax:** (212) 843-0344; **Internet:** www.tmuny.org; **e-mail:** tmu@tmuny.org.

Tulsa Community Foundation

Founded in 1998 as a community-owned institution.

Activities: Promotes personal and corporate charitable giving. The Foundation provides disaster relief and medical assistance to people in emergencies and who are experiencing financial hardship. It organizes the Funders Roundtable, composed of representatives from foundations in Tulsa; the Planned Giving Partnership, which comprises 60 non-profit agencies; and the Women Impacting Tulsa giving circle. Also administers educational and scholarship programmes. Maintains financial stewardship of 913 funds.

Geographical Area of Activity: Mainly Tulsa and Eastern Oklahoma.

Finance: Annual revenue US \$111,422,650, expenditure \$59,680,951 (31 Dec. 2013).

Board of Trustees: Steadman Upham (Chair.).

Principal Staff: CEO Phil Lakin, Jr; COO Jeff Stava.

Address: 7030 South Yale Ave, Ste 600, Tulsa, OK 74136.

Telephone: (918) 494-8823; **Fax:** (918) 494-9826; **Internet:** tulsacf.org; **e-mail:** info@tulsacf.org.

Turner Foundation, Inc

Founded in 1990 to prevent damage to the environment and to support those institutions working to protect the environment and promote sustainable practices.

Activities: Focuses on the areas of conservation and protection of natural resources; preservation of the environment; protection of wildlife and population management; and supports education and activism in these areas. The primary environmental concerns of the Foundation are: protection of the atmosphere through promotion of energy efficiency and renewables; the protection of biodiversity through habitat preservation; the protection of water from toxic pollution; and the development and implementation of sound, equitable practices and policies designed to reduce population growth rates.

Geographical Area of Activity: International.

Restrictions: No funding for buildings, land acquisition, endowments, or start-up funds, nor to fund films, books, magazines, or other specific media projects. No support for individuals. Some programmes are restricted to certain states of the USA.

Publications: Annual Report.

Finance: Annual revenue US $12,275,886, expenditure $11,747,328 (2013).

Board of Trustees: R. E. (Ted) Turner, III (Chair.); J. Rutherford Seydel, II (Sec.); Mike Finley (Pres. and Treas.).

Principal Staff: Sr Program Officer Judy Adler.

Address: 133 Luckie St NW, 2nd Floor, Atlanta, GA 30303.

Telephone: (404) 681-9900; **Fax:** (404) 681-0172; **Internet:** www.turnerfoundation.org; **e-mail:** turnerfi@turnerfoundation.org.

Desmond Tutu Peace Foundation—DTPF

Established in 2000 to advance the philosophy and practices of Archbishop Desmond Tutu.

Activities: Establishes leadership academies in the USA and Africa. The academies focus on developing emerging leaders who act for peace, reconciliation and restorative justice, and human rights.

Geographical Area of Activity: South Africa and the USA.

Publications: Grant list; annual reports; news.

Finance: Annual revenue US $209,731, expenditure $248,358 (31 Dec. 2013).

Board of Directors: Robert V. Taylor (Chair.); Dr David Caitlin Pierce (Sec.); Dr Barry H. Smith (Treas.).

Address: 205 East 64th St, Suite 503, New York, NY 10066.

Telephone: (212) 750-5504; **Fax:** (212) 371-2776; **Internet:** www.tutufoundationusa.org; **e-mail:** info@tutufoundationusa.org.

G. Unger Vetlesen Foundation

Founded in 1955 by Georg Unger Vetlesen to contribute to religious, charitable, scientific, literary and educational causes worldwide. Shares an administration with the Ambrose Monell Foundation (q.v.).

Activities: Operates in New York, the USA in general and internationally in education and other fields. The Foundation makes grants mainly in the areas of oceanographies, climate studies and other earth sciences, and offers an international science award biennially for discoveries in the earth sciences. It also makes grants for biological, geophysical and environmental scientific research, higher education and cultural activities, with an emphasis on Norwegian-US relations and maritime issues; and supports public policy research and libraries.

Geographical Area of Activity: International.

Restrictions: No grants are made to individuals.

Publications: Annual Report.

Finance: Annual revenue US $8,957,263, expenditure $6,231,617 (2013).

Board of Directors: Ambrose K. Monell (Pres. and Treas.); Maurizio J. Morello (Exec. Vice-Pres. and Asst Treas.); Kristen G. Pemberton (Sec.).

Address: c/o Fulton, Rowe & Hart, 1 Rockefeller Plaza, Suite 301, New York, NY 10020.

Telephone: (212) 586-0700; **Fax:** (212) 245-1863; **Internet:** www.monellvetlesen.org/vetlesen/default.htm; **e-mail:** info@monellvetlesen.org.

Unitarian Universalist Service Committee

Established in 1940.

Activities: A human rights organization, powered by grassroots collaboration, which fosters social justice and alleviates oppression. The Committee's work is grounded in the moral belief that all people have inherent power, dignity, and rights. It works specifically with people and communities who are denied their rights because of who they are—women, people of colour, religious minorities, and others—and who are not served by mainstream human rights organizations. Promotes economic justice, bolsters environmental justice, and protects civil liberties. Also works to deliver aid with dignity and advance the rights of people left behind during humanitarian crises, including forgotten conflicts and natural disasters.

Geographical Area of Activity: International.

Publications: Newsletter; Annual Report.

Finance: Annual revenue US $7,811,460, expenditure $6,892,611 (30 June 2014).

Board of Trustees: Lucia Santini-Field (Chair.); John Buehrens (Vice-Chair.); Todd J. Hess (Treas.); Martha Easter-Wells (Sec.).

Principal Staff: Pres. and CEO Rev. Dr William F. Schulz.

Address: 689 Massachusetts Ave, Cambridge, MA 02139-3302.

Telephone: (617) 868-6600; **Fax:** (617) 868-7102; **Internet:** www.uusc.org; **e-mail:** info@uusc.org.

United Nations Foundation

Established in 1997 along with its sister organization, the Better World Fund (q.v.), following a gift of US $1,000m. to the UN by R. E. (Ted) Turner.

Activities: Supports the goals and objectives of the UN and its Charter to promote a more peaceful, prosperous and just world, with special emphasis on the work of the UN, especially on behalf of economic, social, environmental and humanitarian causes. The Foundation invests in UN-sponsored agencies and programmes. Its main campaigns and initiatives include: the Better World Campaign; the Energy Future Coalition; Friends of World Heritage; Nothing But Nets (grassroots campaign to prevent malaria); and The People Speak (international co-operation). It also funds campaigns and projects in the fields of renewable energy, education, health (AIDS, tuberculosis, malaria and polio), and land-mine clearance.

Geographical Area of Activity: International.

Restrictions: Grants are made only in support of UN programmes.

Publications: Annual Report; campaign reports; *UN Wire* (e-mail news briefing).

Finance: Annual revenue US $230,764,474, expenditure $137,838,875 (31 Dec. 2013).

Board of Directors: R. E. (Ted) Turner (Founder and Chair.); Timothy E. Wirth (Vice-Chair.).

Principal Staff: Pres. and CEO Kathy Calvin; COO Richard S. Parnell.

Address: 1800 Massachusetts Ave, NW, Suite 400, Washington, DC 20036.

Telephone: (202) 887-9040; **Fax:** (202) 887-9021; **Internet:** www.unfoundation.org; **e-mail:** unf@unfoundation.org.

United States African Development Foundation—USADF

Established in 1980 by the US Congress as an independent agency to provide economic assistance to grassroots communities in Africa.

Activities: Provides economic development assistance and capacity-building resources in the areas of: agricultural production; micro- and small enterprises; micro-credit; education and training; community grassroots empowerment; HIV prevention; natural resource management and conservation; travel grants; research; institutional strengthening; and educational outreach, through publications and electronic media. The Foundation currently funds projects in more than 19 countries in Africa. Grants are available for up to US $250,000. In 2014/15, the Foundation awarded US $24m. in grants.

Geographical Area of Activity: Sub-Saharan Africa.

Restrictions: Grants only in those Sub-Saharan African countries where the Foundation is active; grants only to registered African NGOs and community-based organizations; does not provide funding for individuals.

Publications: *USADF Messenger* (online); *USADF e-news*; *USADFApproach* (online); issue papers; project briefs; Annual Report; reports.

Finance: Annual resources US $42,115,960, expenditure $36,162,507 (30 Sept. 2014).

Board of Directors: Jack Leslie (Chair.); Dr John O. Agwunobi (Vice-Chair.).

Principal Staff: Pres. and CEO Shari Berenbach.

Address: 1400 I St NW, Suite 1000, Washington, DC 20005-2248.

Telephone: (202) 673-3916; **Fax:** (202) 673-3810; **Internet:** www.adf.gov; **e-mail:** info@adf.gov.

United States-Japan Foundation

Founded in 1980 by Ryoichi Sasakawa to strengthen co-operation and understanding between the people of the USA and Japan.

Activities: Supports grants in the areas of pre-college education, communications/public opinion, and policy in the USA and Japan.

Geographical Area of Activity: USA and Japan.

Restrictions: No grants to individuals or for-profit organizations.

Publications: Annual Report.

Finance: Annual revenue US $2,641,672, expenditure $4,634,240 (31 Dec. 2013).

Board of Trustees: James W. Lintott (Chair.); Dr Shinichi Kitaoka (Vice-Chair.); Maria Cristina Manapat-Sims (Asst Sec. and Treas.).

Principal Staff: Pres. Dr George R. Packard.

Address: 145 East 32nd St, 12th Floor, New York, NY 10016.

Telephone: (212) 481-8753; **Fax:** (212) 481-8762; **Internet:** www.us-jf.org; **e-mail:** info@us-jf.org.

United Way Worldwide

Established in 1974 as a support organization, helping to build community capacity for a better quality of life worldwide, through voluntary giving and action. Formerly known as United Way International (UWI).

Activities: Operates in the area of community development, working with corporations, foundations and other donors to assist them with their global philanthropic needs.

Geographical Area of Activity: International.

Publications: Annual Report; campaign brochure; newsletter; financial statements.

Finance: Annual revenue US $80,661,236, expenditure $89,919,027 (31 Dec. 2013).

Board of Directors: John Lechleiter (Chair.); Phillip N. Baldwin (Treas.); Peggy Conlon (Sec.).

Principal Staff: Pres. and CEO Brian A. Gallagher.

Address: 701 North Fairfax St, Alexandria, VA 22314-2045.

Telephone: (703) 836-7112; **Fax:** (703) 519-0097; **Internet:** www.unitedway.org; **e-mail:** worldwide@unitedway.org.

University of Southern California Shoah Foundation—The Institute for Visual History and Education

Established in 1994 by the film-maker Steven Spielberg to record and preserve the testimonies of Holocaust survivors and other witnesses, and to overcome prejudice, ignorance and bigotry, and the suffering they cause, through the educational use of visual history testimonies.

Activities: Has collected nearly 52,000 recorded testimonies of Holocaust survivors and other witnesses in 56 countries. The Foundation works to develop partnerships to support three main strategic goals: to use the archive to create educational projects for classrooms and broader dissemination; to build and support educational programmes; and to preserve the archive and provide access to it. Under its Witnesses for Humanity programme, the Foundation will collect and publish testimonies of other genocides.

Geographical Area of Activity: Worldwide.

Restrictions: Does not make grants.

Publications: *Past Forward* (newsletter, 2 a year); documentary films; CD-ROMs; study guides; and books.

Board of Councilors: Robert J. Katz (Chair.); Susan Crown, Harry Robinson (Vice-Chair.).

Principal Staff: Exec. Dir Dr Stephen D. Smith; Man. Dir Kim Simon.

Address: Leavey Library, 650 West 35th St, Suite 114, Los Angeles, CA 90089-2571.

Telephone: (213) 740-6001; **Fax:** (213) 740-6044; **Internet:** sfi.usc.edu; **e-mail:** vhi-web@usc.edu.

UPS Foundation

Established in 1951 by United Parcel Service founder James E. Casey to support higher education and social welfare projects and charities.

Activities: Operates nationally and internationally, making grants in areas including economic and global literacy, environmental sustainability, non-profit effectiveness, strength from diversity and community safety.

Geographical Area of Activity: USA and international.

Restrictions: Unsolicited requests for funding are not accepted.

Publications: Annual Report.

Finance: Annual revenue US $45,314,860, expenditure $42,895,775 (31 Dec. 2013).

Board of Trustees: John McDevitt (Chair.); David Abney (Sec.); Kurt Kuehn (Treas.).

Principal Staff: Pres. Eduardo Martinez.

Address: 55 Glenlake Parkway NE, Atlanta, GA 30328.

Telephone: (404) 828-7123; **Internet:** www.community.ups.com/UPS+Foundation; **e-mail:** community@ups.com.

US-Ukraine Foundation

Established in 1991 to support democracy, a free market and human rights in Ukraine.

Activities: Supports democratic development in Ukraine through its own projects, in the areas of public policy, economic development and education. The Foundation established the Pylyp Orlyk Institute for Democracy in Ukraine to carry out policy research. Activities include sponsoring workshops and seminars, providing support, training and technical resources, publishing and disseminating information; and providing emergency and development relief to certain sectors of the population in Ukraine. Maintains an office in Kyiv, Ukraine.

Geographical Area of Activity: Ukraine.

Restrictions: Does not make grants.

Finance: Annual revenue US $613,087, expenditure $624,142 (31 Aug. 2013).

Principal Staff: Pres. Nadia K. McConnell; Vice-Pres. and COO John A. Kun.

Address: 1660 L Street, NW, Suite 1000, Washington, DC 20036-5634.

Telephone: (202) 524-6555; **Fax:** (202) 280-1989; **Internet:** www.usukraine.org; **e-mail:** info@usukraine.org.

Lawson Valentine Foundation

Founded in 1989 for general charitable purposes.

Activities: Primarily concerned with the fields of sustainable agriculture and food systems, environment, human rights, race relations and community programmes.

Geographical Area of Activity: Africa, Asia and Latin America.

Restrictions: No funds granted to groups with annual budgets of several million dollars. Maximum grant US $25,000.

Publications: Application guidelines.

Finance: Annual revenue US $734,961, expenditure $809,115 (2013).

Principal Staff: Programme Officer Valentine Doyle.

Address: 1000 Farmington Ave, West Hartford, CT 06107.

Telephone: (860) 570-0728; **Fax:** (860) 570-0728; **e-mail:** valentinedoyle@sbcglobal.net.

Virtual Foundation

Founded in 1996 by ECOLOGIA (q.v.), an international non-profit organization, to support community-based projects in the areas of the environment, sustainable development and health; and to encourage philanthropy by fostering partnerships between local groups and online donors.

Activities: Works in collaboration with NGOs worldwide to fund projects in the fields of the environment; health; community building and sustainable economic activity; and increasing capacity of grassroots NGOs. Project proposals submitted to the Foundation are posted on its website for evaluation by visitors to the site, who may make a donation to the project of their choice.

Geographical Area of Activity: International.

Restrictions: No grants for emergency crisis aid or research.

Finance: Annual revenue US $105,938, expenditure $109,594 (30 June 2013).

Board of Directors: Randy Kritkausky (Pres.); Carolyn Schmidt (Sec.); Ed Shoener (Treas.).

Principal Staff: Programme Man. Carolyn Schmidt.

Address: POB 268, Middlebury, VT 05753.

Telephone: (802) 623-8075; **Fax:** (802) 623-8069; **Internet:** www.virtualfoundation.org; **e-mail:** cschmidt@ecologia.org.

Alberto Vollmer Foundation, Inc

Founded in 1965 by Alberto F. Vollmer for general charitable purposes; incorporated in 1987.

Activities: Operates in the fields of education, social welfare, medicine and the arts through grants to hospitals and institutions of higher education in Venezuela. The Foundation owns and operates the AVF Research facilities in Caracas, with extensive archives on Venezuelan art history, photography, and architecture of the 19th and 20th centuries, and the development of agriculture in Venezuela since 1826. Also supports the Catholic Church in Venezuela.

Geographical Area of Activity: South America.

Restrictions: No grants are made to individuals.

Finance: Annual revenue US $3,155,008, expenditure $3,105,412 (2013).

Board of Directors: Gustavo J. Vollmer (Pres. and Sec.); Ana Luisa Estrada Wallis (Vice-Pres. and Treas.).

Address: c/o Claudia Sanchez, Prodek, Inc, 10900 NW 21st St, Unit 190, Miami, FL 33172.

Telephone: (305) 594-4488; **Internet:** www.fundavollmer.com; **e-mail:** fundavollmer@gmail.com.

The Wallace Foundation

Established in 2003 by the merger of the DeWitt Wallace—Reader's Digest Fund, Inc and the Lila Wallace—Reader's Digest Fund, Inc, both founded in the 1950s by the founders of the Reader's Digest Association to provide support to arts and cultural organizations, and promote educational and youth development opportunities.

Activities: Seeks to enable institutions to expand learning and enrichment opportunities for all people. The Foundation aims to improve student achievement through strengthening education leadership; to improve after-school learning opportunities; and to expand participation in the arts and culture.

Geographical Area of Activity: USA only.

Restrictions: Grants are rarely made for unsolicited projects; no grants are made to individuals.

Publications: Annual Report; education reports.

Finance: Annual revenue US $131,330,403, expenditure $81,051,379 (31 Dec. 2013).

Board of Directors: Kevin W. Kennedy (Chair.).

Principal Staff: Pres. Will I. Miller; Sec. Kenneth W. Austin.

Address: 5 Penn Plaza, 7th Floor, New York, NY 10001.

Telephone: (212) 251-9700; **Fax:** (212) 679-6990; **Internet:** www.wallacefoundation.org; **e-mail:** info@wallacefoundation.org.

Miriam G. and Ira D. Wallach Foundation

Founded in 1956 to support general charitable purposes, mainly in New York.

Activities: Provides financial assistance in the fields of international affairs, education, the humanities, social welfare and Jewish organizations.

Restrictions: Grants are made to pre-selected organizations only, applications are not accepted.

Finance: Annual revenue US $17,201,387, expenditure $8,881,423 (31 Oct. 2013).

Board of Directors: Kenneth L. Wallach (Chair. and Pres.); Edgar Wachenheim, III (Vice-Pres.); Howard Herman (Sec.); Steven M. Eigen (Treas.).

Address: 3 Manhattanville Rd, Purchase, NY 10577-2110.

Telephone: (914) 696-9060; **Fax:** (914) 696-1066.

Walmart Foundation

Established in 2006.

Activities: Operates four main programmes: Hunger Relief & Healthy Eating; Sustainability; Women's Economic Empowerment; and Career Opportunity.

Geographical Area of Activity: International.

Finance: Annual revenue US $169,079,669, expenditure $169,082,841 (31 Jan. 2014).

Board of Directors: Dooug McMillon (Chair.); Tanya Farah (Treas.); Scott Hardin (Sec.); Karrie Denniston (Asst. Treas.); Kabir Kumar (Asst Sec.).

Principal Staff: Pres. Kathleen McLaughlin; Vice-Pres. Julie Gehrki.

Address: 702 SW 8th St, Bentonville, AK 72716-8611.

Internet: foundation.walmart.com.

Walton Family Foundation

Established in 1988 by the founder of the Walmart retail chain, Sam Walton, and his wife Helen.

Activities: Operates in the USA in the area of education reform and the environment; and in the USA, Central and South America and Indonesia in the area of freshwater and marine conservation.

Geographical Area of Activity: USA, Central America and South-East Asia.

Restrictions: Does not accept unsolicited proposals.

Finance: Annual revenue US $593,729,358, expenditure $336,040,265 (31 Dec. 2013).

Board of Directors: Jim C. Walton (Sec./Treas.).

Principal Staff: Exec. Dir Buddy D. Philpot.

Address: POB 1860, Bentonville, AK 72712.

Telephone: (479) 464-1570; **Fax:** (479) 464-1580; **Internet:** www.waltonfamilyfoundation.org; **e-mail:** info@wffmail.com.

The Andy Warhol Foundation for the Visual Arts, Inc

Founded in 1987 by Andy Warhol for the promotion of the visual arts.

Activities: Operates nationally and (on a limited scale) internationally in the areas of the visual arts, aspects of performing arts incorporating the plastic arts, education and historic preservation and urban development. The Foundation makes grants for curatorial programmes in museums, universities and other organizations to assist in the presentation of the visual arts in innovative ways and to support artists themselves and their work; and to organizations assisting in the preservation of historic properties and parks, and promoting public participation in urban planning.

Geographical Area of Activity: Mainly USA, but organizations elsewhere are eligible to apply.

Restrictions: Unable to make grants directly to individuals.

Publications: Annual Report.

Finance: Annual revenue US $30,954,259, expenditure $19,933,338 (1 May 2012).

Board of Directors: Joel Wachs (Pres.); Donald Warhola (Vice-Pres.); Kathleen C. Maurer (Sec. and Treas.).

Address: 65 Bleecker St, 7th Floor, New York, NY 10012.

Telephone: (212) 387-7555; **Fax:** (212) 387-7560; **Internet:** www.warholfoundation.org; **e-mail:** info@warholfoundation.org.

Water.org, Inc

Established in 2009 by the actor Matt Damon and Gary White through a merger between Water Partners and H2O Africa to help provide access to clean drinking water and sanitation.

Activities: Operates in Africa, South Asia and Central America to help provide access to safe water and sanitation. Maintains offices in India and Kenya.

Geographical Area of Activity: Africa, South Asia and Central America.

Publications: Newsletter.

Finance: Annual revenue US $15,535,339, expenditure $11,344,379 (30 Sept. 2014).

Board of Directors: Lynn Taliento (Chair.); Andy Sareyan (Vice-Chair.); Terry Trayvick (Treas.); Larry Tanz (Sec.).

Principal Staff: CEO Gary White; Pres. Jennifer Tisdel Schorsch.

Address: 920 Main St, Suite 1800, Kansas City, MO 64105.

Internet: water.org.

Water for People

Established in 1991 to support the development of sustainable drinking water resources and sanitation in less-developed countries.

Activities: Supports the development of water and sanitation infrastructure. Maintains offices in Bolivia, Guatemala, Honduras, India, Malawi, Peru, Rwanda and Uganda. A sister organization operates in Canada.

Geographical Area of Activity: Central and South America, Africa and India.

Finance: Annual revenue US $18,516,050, expenditure $16,743,517 (30 Sept. 2014).

Board of Directors: Patrick McCann (Chair.); Mary Kay Kaufmann (Vice-Chair.).

Principal Staff: CEO and Sec. Ned Breslin.

Address: 100 E. Tennessee Ave, Denver, CO 80209.

Telephone: (720) 488-4590; **Internet:** www.waterforpeople.org; **e-mail:** info@waterforpeople.org.

Weeden Foundation

Founded in 1963 by Frank Weeden to address concerns about the destruction of natural resources and the problems associated with a growing global population.

Activities: Operates nationally and internationally in the field of conservation and the environment through running programmes: Domestic Bio-diversity; International Bio-diversity (30%–40% of annual grants expenditure, with projects based in Chile and the Russian Federation); Land Acquisition (acquisition of threatened natural areas of biodiversity, with projects in Africa and Central and South America); Population; and Consumption (promoting sustainability).

Geographical Area of Activity: International.

Restrictions: No grants for individuals, nor for endowment or capital fund projects, for large organizations unless for new projects, or for general support.

Finance: Annual revenue US $4,475,765, expenditure $3,508,261 (30 June 2013).

Board of Directors: Dr Norman Weeden (Pres.); Tina Roux (Vice-Pres.); Leslie Weeden (Sec.); Bob Weeden (Treas.).

Principal Staff: Exec. Dir Don A. Weeden.

Address: 35 Adams Street, Ground Floor, Bedford Hills, NY 10507-1819.

Telephone: (914)864-1375; **Fax:** (914) 864-1377; **Internet:** www.weedenfoundation.org; **e-mail:** info@weedenfoundation.org.

Harry and Jeanette Weinberg Foundation, Inc

Established in 1959 to assist the poor.

Activities: Operates in the areas of social welfare and health, particularly in housing, nutrition and socialization, through grants to organizations located in Hawaii, Pennsylvania, New York, Israel and the countries of the former USSR. The Foundation concentrates on the elderly and the Jewish community. Has offices in Maryland and Hawaii.

Geographical Area of Activity: USA, former USSR and Israel.

Restrictions: No grants are made to individuals.

Finance: Annual revenue US $113,280,787, expenditure $117,295,250 (28 Feb. 2014).

Board of Trustees: Ellen M. Heller (Chair.); Alvin Awaya (Vice-Pres.); Barry I. Schloss (Treas.).

Principal Staff: Pres. Rachel Garbow Monroe.

Address: 7 Park Center Ct, Owings Mills, MD 21117-4200.

Telephone: (410) 654-8500; **Fax:** (410) 654-4900; **Internet:** hjweinbergfoundation.org; **e-mail:** cdemchak@hjweinberg.org.

The Welch Foundation

Founded in 1954 by Robert A. Welch for basic chemical research.

Activities: Supports a programme of basic research in chemistry with grants to faculty members at colleges and universities in Texas. The Foundation also sponsors a conference; and awards the Welch Award in Chemistry and the Norman Hackerman Award in Chemical Research.

Geographical Area of Activity: USA.

Publications: Annual Report.

Finance: Annual revenue US $37,838,695, expenditure $41,006,670 (31 Aug. 2014).

Board of Directors: Wilhelmina E. Robertson (Chair.); Charles W. Tate (Vice-Chair.); Carin Marcy Barth (Treas.); Robert C. Robbins (Sec.).

Principal Staff: Pres. Norbert Dittrich.

Address: 5555 San Felipe, Suite 1900, Houston, TX 77056.

Telephone: (713) 961-9884; **Fax:** (713) 961-5168; **Internet:** www.welch1.org; **e-mail:** dittrich@welch1.org.

Rob and Bessie Welder Wildlife Foundation

Founded in 1954 to promote graduate-level education in wildlife conservation, and to support research into wildlife and methods for increasing wildlife populations.

Activities: Operates in the field of conservation and the environment, through funding research, fellowships and internships (open to US citizens or to foreigners registered at a US university for a graduate degree); and the operation of the Welder Foundation Refuge.

Geographical Area of Activity: USA, particularly Texas.

Restrictions: No grants for work outside continental USA.

Publications: Report (biennially).

Finance: Annual revenue US $1,172,342, expenditure $1,079,523 (31 Dec. 2013).

Board of Trustees: John J. Welder, V (Pres.); H. C. Weil (Vice-Pres.); Hughes C. Thomas (Sec.).

Principal Staff: Dir Dr Terry L. Blankenship; Asst Dir Dr Selma Glasscock.

Address: POB 1400, Sinton, TX 78387.

Telephone: (361) 364-2643; **Fax:** (361) 364-2650; **Internet:** www.welderwildlife.org; **e-mail:** welderfoundation@welderwildlife.org.

Wenner-Gren Foundation for Anthropological Research, Inc.

Founded in 1941 as the Viking Fund, Inc, by Dr Axel L. Wenner-Gren to support research in all branches of anthropology, including cultural and social anthropology, ethnology, biological and physical anthropology, archaeology, anthropological linguistics, and in closely related disciplines concerned with human origins, development and variation.

Activities: Operates an individual research grants programme, awarding up to approximately US $25,000 for basic research in anthropology to holders of a doctorate degree and doctoral candidates undertaking dissertation projects; and offers a number of awards and scholarships, including: Richard Carley Hunt Postdoctoral Fellowships for applicants who have had a PhD for 10 years or less, and up to a maximum of approx. $40,000 is available to aid the writing up of research results for publication; Professional Development International Fellowships for training in anthropology at PhD level and for postdoctoral scholars and advanced students from developing countries; Conference Grants, of up to approx. $15,000, to organizers of conferences; and International Collaborative Research Grants, of up to approx. $30,000, to assist anthropological research projects undertaken jointly by two or more investigators from different countries, with priority given to projects involving at least one principal investigator from outside the countries of North America and Western Europe. Sponsors the publication of *Current Anthropology* journal.

Geographical Area of Activity: International.

Restrictions: No scholarships.

Publications: Annual Report.

Finance: Annual revenue US $9,453,639, expenditure $8,388,168 (2013).

Board of Trustees: Seth Masters (Chair.); Lorraine Sciarra (Vice-Chair.); Lauren Meserve (Treas.); Maugha Kenny (Sec.).

Principal Staff: Pres. Prof. Leslie C. Aiello; Exec. Vice-Chair. Seth Masters.

Address: 470 Park Ave S, 8th Floor, New York, NY 10001.

Telephone: (212) 683-5000; **Fax:** (212) 532-1492; **Internet:** www.wennergren.org; **e-mail:** inquiries@wennergren.org.

Weyerhaeuser Family Foundation, Inc

Founded in 1950 for the relief of the poor, the advancement of the Christian religion, education and science, including medical science, and the application of the same through hospitals, clinics and research institutions. Formerly known as the Weyerhaeuser Foundation.

Activities: Supports programmes of national and international significance that attempt to identify and correct the causes of maladjustment in society. The Foundation operates nationally and internationally in the fields of the arts and humanities (through programmes that assist the public to understand various art forms), education (opportunities for minority groups, religious training, youth development projects and private higher education), health (mental health, alcoholism, psychiatry), social welfare, international activities, religion and the environment, science and technology (environmental preservation, use of scarce resources and forestry), through grants to institutions. The Foundation supports international projects that enable people to help

themselves through population planning, agricultural improvements, self-government and peace education.

Geographical Area of Activity: International.

Restrictions: Does not normally make grants for projects with limited geographical emphasis, operating budgets, annual campaigns, building and equipment, elementary and secondary education, lobbying or propaganda. Nor does it make grants to individuals, for scholarships, fellowships or for travel.

Publications: Annual Report.

Finance: Annual revenue US $3,514,380, expenditure $1,134,664 (2013).

Board of Trustees: Frederick W. Titcomb (Pres.); John B. Driscoll (Vice-Pres.); Blaine Gaustad, Gretchen Sprafke (Secs); John W. Titcomb, Jr, Mike Slocum (Treas).

Principal Staff: Grants Admin. Gayle Roth; Programme Consultant Peter A. Konrad.

Address: 30 E Seventh St, Suite 2000, St Paul, MN 55101-4930.

Telephone: (651) 215-4408; **Internet:** www.wfamilyfoundation.org; **e-mail:** wff@fidcouns.com.

Whirlpool Foundation

Founded in 1951 by Louis and Frederick Upton, co-founders of the Whirlpool Corporation, to improve quality of life in the communities where the corporation operates.

Activities: Operates worldwide, particularly in the USA and Canada, Western and Eastern Europe, and Asia, within three programme areas—quality of family life, cultural diversity, life-long learning—principally aimed at projects likely to have an impact in communities where the company has a presence. The Foundation also runs a programme of citizenship grants within the USA, aimed at organizations supporting general education, health and human services, arts and culture, and civic and community. It also runs employee-directed programmes.

Geographical Area of Activity: International.

Restrictions: No grants are given to religious or labour organizations.

Finance: Annual revenue US $14,600,000, expenditure $14,148,612 (31 Dec. 2013).

Board of Trustees: D. Jeffrey Noel (Pres.); David Binkley (Vice-Pres.); John F. Geddes (Treas.); Laurence W. Prange (Sec.).

Principal Staff: Man. Candice Garman.

Address: 2000 North M-63, Benton Harbor, MI 49022.

Telephone: (269) 923-5580; **Fax:** (269) 925-0154; **Internet:** www.whirlpoolcorp.com/responsibility/building_communities/whirlpool_foundation.aspx.

Whitehall Foundation, Inc

Founded in 1937 to give financial aid to charitable, benevolent or educational work.

Activities: Assists scholarly work in the life sciences, through a programme of grants and grants-in-aid, primarily targeting dynamic areas of basic biological research that are not generally supported by federal agencies or other foundations with specialized missions. The Foundation is currently interested in basic research in neurobiology: invertebrate and vertebrate neurobiology, exclusive of human beings, including investigation into the neural mechanisms involved in sensory, motor and other complex functions of the whole organism as these relate to behaviour. Research grants are for up to three years, awarded to established scientists working at accredited institutions in the USA. Grants-in-aid are for one year and are designed especially for young postgraduate investigators who have not yet established themselves, as well as for senior scientists. Research grants range from US $30,000–$75,000 per year; grants-in-aid do not exceed $30,000.

Geographical Area of Activity: USA.

Restrictions: Funds are not awarded to investigators who have substantial existing or potential support, for construction projects, office expenses, nor for research focused primarily on disease(s) unless it will also provide insights into normal functioning. The Foundation does not consider grant applications from outside the USA.

Publications: Report of operations and financial statement.

Finance: Annual revenue US $4,887,560, expenditure $5,562,385 (30 Sept. 2013).

Board of Trustees: George M. Moffett, II (Pres. and Treas.); J. Wright Rombough, Jr (Vice-Pres.); Catherine M. Thomas (Sec./Asst Treas.).

Address: POB 3423, Palm Beach, FL 33480; 125 Worth Ave, Suite 220, Palm Beach, FL 33480.

Telephone: (561) 655-4474; **Fax:** (561) 655-1296; **Internet:** www.whitehall.org; **e-mail:** email@whitehall.org.

The Elie Wiesel Foundation for Humanity

Founded in 1986 by Elie Wiesel, winner of the Nobel Peace Prize, for the promotion of human rights and peace worldwide, and to combat indifference, intolerance and injustice, particularly in parts of the world where those rights are repeatedly ignored, abused or denied, to preserve memory by encouraging an understanding or appreciation of history to create a more humane and hopeful future.

Activities: Seeks to promote human rights and peace through the creation of a new forum for the discussion of the ethical and moral issues confronting the world. The Foundation holds international conferences. It established a Humanitarian Award, and the Elie Wiesel Prize in Ethics (an essay competition). Operates also in Israel, in the area of education.

Geographical Area of Activity: Worldwide.

Finance: Annual revenue US $5,499,927, expenditure $1,239,783 (31 Dec. 2013).

Board of Directors: Prof. Elie Wiesel (Pres.); Marion Wiesel (Vice-Pres.); Marc Winkelman (Sec. and Treas.).

Principal Staff: Program Co-ordinator Leslie Meyers.

Address: 555 Madison Ave, 20th Floor, New York, NY 10022.

Fax: (212) 490-6006; **Internet:** www.eliewieselfoundation .org; **e-mail:** info@eliewieselfoundation.org.

Wikimedia Foundation

Established in 2003 by Jimmy Wales, co-founder of the Wikipedia online encyclopedia, to disseminate information worldwide through the Internet, in multi-lingual format.

Activities: Operates Internet information sites, including Wikipedia, dictionaries and e-books.

Finance: Annual revenue US $39,702,445, expenditure $28,964,052 (30 June 2013).

Board of Trustees: Jan-Bart de Vreede (Chair.); Patricio Laurente (Vice-Chair.).

Principal Staff: Exec. Dir Lila Tretikov.

Address: 149 New Montgomery St, 3rd Floor, San Francisco, CA 94105.

Telephone: (415) 839-6885; **Fax:** (415) 882-0495; **Internet:** wikimediafoundation.org; **e-mail:** info@wikimedia.org.

The WILD Foundation—International Wilderness Leadership Foundation

Founded in 1974 by Ian Player, as the International Wilderness Leadership Foundation, to protect and sustain critical wild areas, wilderness values and endangered wildlife throughout the world, with a special emphasis on Southern Africa, by initiating or assisting environmental education, experiential projects and programmes.

Activities: Operates internationally in the field of conservation and the environment. The Foundation runs programmes on wilderness and wildlife, eco-tourism, and education and training; the World Wilderness Congress is its flagship programme. Promotes the wise use of wildland resources and

provides environmental education and training. Works in partnership with other organizations worldwide.

Geographical Area of Activity: International, with an emphasis on southern Africa.

Publications: include Annual Report; *The White Rhino Saga*; *Climate for Life: Meeting the Global Challenge*; *Protecting Wild Nature on Native Lands*; *When Elephants Fly*; *International Journal of Wilderness*; *A Handbook on International Wilderness Law and Policy*.

Finance: Annual revenue US $4,928,054, expenditure $4,076,494 (31 Dec. 2013).

Board of Directors: Dr Marilynn Cowgill (Chair.); Charlotte Baron (Vice-Chair.).

Principal Staff: Pres. Vance G. Martin.

Address: 717 Poplar Ave, Boulder, CO 80304 USA.

Telephone: (303) 442-8811; **Fax:** (303) 442-8877; **Internet:** www.wild.org; **e-mail:** info@wild.org.

WILPF—Women's International League for Peace and Freedom

Founded in 1915 to create an environment of political, economic, social and psychological freedom for all members of humanity.

Activities: Operates campaigns and advocacy projects worldwide on a variety of issues, including peace and disarmament, empowerment of women and racial justice. WILPF has an international office located in Geneva, Switzerland, a UN office in New York City, and sections in 37 countries worldwide.

Geographical Area of Activity: International.

Restrictions: Not a grantmaking organization.

Finance: Annual revenue US $271,211, expenditure $320,422 (31 Dec. 2013).

Board of Directors: Mary Hanson Harrison (Pres.); Mylee Livingston (Treas.); Candace Perry (Sec.).

Principal Staff: Dir (a.i.) Paula Herrington.

Address: 11 Arlington St, Boston, MA 02116.

Telephone: (617) 266-0999; **Fax:** (617) 266-1688; **Internet:** www.wilpf.org; **e-mail:** president@wilpf.org.

E. O. Wilson Biodiversity Foundation

Established in 2005 to promote understanding of the importance of biodiversity.

Activities: Fosters a 'knowing stewardship' of the planet through research and education, promoting and informing public understanding of biodiversity. The Foundation runs the National Park Service Biodiversity Youth Ambassador Program in the USA, and the Collaborative Storytelling Project; and is involved in the MEMO art-science project on biodiversity and species extinction on the Isle of Portland, United Kingdom. Has a laboratory at Gorongosa National Park, Mozambique.

Geographical Area of Activity: International.

Publications: *Life on Earth* digital textbook and online materials.

Finance: Annual revenue US $204,537, expenditure $446,665 (31 Dec. 2013).

Board of Directors: David J. Prend (Chair.); Gregory C. Carr (Treas.); Charles C. Smith (Sec.).

Principal Staff: Pres. and CEO Dr Paula J. Ehrlich.

Address: Environment Hall, 9 Circuit Dr., 5th Floor, Rm 5101, Durham, NC 27708.

Telephone: (919) 613-8722; **Internet:** www .eowilsonfoundation.org; **e-mail:** info@eowilsonfoundation .org.

Woodrow Wilson International Center for Scholars

Founded in 1968 as a memorial to President Woodrow Wilson to symbolize and strengthen the fruitful relation between the world of learning and the world of public affairs. The Center is part of the Smithsonian Institution (q.v.), but is administered by its own Board of Trustees.

Activities: Awards 20–25 annual postdoctoral fellowships for full-time research to be conducted at the Center by scholars from any country. The Center awards Fellowships within the broad themes of governance, including the key issues of the development of democratic institutions, democratic society, civil society and citizen participation; the US role in the world and issues of partnership and leadership; and key long-term future challenges confronting the USA and the world.

Geographical Area of Activity: Worldwide.

Publications: *The Wilson Quarterly* (online magazine); Woodrow Wilson Center Press (peer-reviewed books); policy briefs; research reports; conference reports.

Finance: Annual revenue US $15,037,461, expenditure $19,161,977 (30 Sept. 2013).

Trustees: Thomas R. Nides (Chair.).

Principal Staff: Dir, Pres. and CEO Jane Harman; Exec. Vice-Pres. Andrew Selee.

Address: Ronald Reagan Bldg and International Trade Center, 1 Woodrow Wilson Plaza, 1300 Pennsylvania Ave NW, Washington, DC 20004-3027.

Telephone: (202) 691-4000; **Fax:** (202) 691-4001; **Internet:** www.wilsoncenter.org; **e-mail:** wwics@wilsoncenter.org.

Woodrow Wilson National Fellowship Foundation

Founded in 1945 to respond to a shortage of college faculty at the conclusion of World War II by offering talented students the opportunity to attend doctoral programmes and begin college teaching careers.

Activities: Fellowships support the development of future leaders at a variety of career stages in several critical fields: teaching; foreign affairs; conservation; women and gender; religion and ethics; access and opportunity. The Foundation's more than 21,000 Fellows include 14 Nobel Laureates, 36 MacArthur 'genius grant' recipients, 16 Pulitzer Prize winners, two Fields Medalists in mathematics, and many other noted scholars and leaders.

Geographical Area of Activity: USA.

Publications: Annual Report; newsletter (2 a year); policy reports; news releases.

Finance: Annual revenue US $21,568,879, expenditure $17,864,858 (30 June 2014).

Board of Trustees: Walter W. Buckley, Jr (Chair.); Thomas C. Hudnut (Chair.-elect); Beverly Sanford (Sec.) Ray Clark (Treas.).

Principal Staff: Pres. Arthur Levine; Exec. Vice-Pres. and COO Stephanie Hull.

Address: POB 5281, Princeton, NJ 08543-5281; 5 Vaughn Dr., Suite 300, Princeton, NJ 08540-6313.

Telephone: (609) 452-7007; **Fax:** (609) 452-0066; **Internet:** www.woodrow.org.

Winrock International

Formed in 1985 by the merger of the Agricultural Development Council (f. 1953 by John D. Rockefeller, III), the International Agricultural Development Service (f. 1975 by the Rockefeller Foundation, q.v.) and the Winrock International Livestock Research and Training Center (f. 1975 by the bequest of Winthrop Rockefeller).

Activities: Aims to reduce poverty and hunger through sustainable agricultural and rural development. The Institute offers sustainable solutions through comprehensive, integrated programmes in more than 100 countries, responding to changing economic, environmental and social conditions. Technical assistance and development services are grouped into three programmes: Empowerment and Civic Engagement aimed at strengthening capacity of women, children, youth and civil society organizations; Enterprise and Agriculture to support establishment and growth of small and medium-sized enterprises and agricultural initiatives targeting sustainable production driven by market demand; and

Environment—Forestry, Energy and Ecosystem Services—promoting sustainable use and management of natural resources to support the food and income needs of growing populations and the health of the planet. Maintains an office in Arlington, Virginia.

Geographical Area of Activity: Asia, Africa, the Middle East, North, Central and South America, the Caribbean, Eastern Europe.

Publications: *Innovations* (e-mail newsletter); global projects and financial statement report; project fact sheets; development education series books; research papers.

Finance: Annual revenue US $82,993,591, expenditure $84,968,791 (31 Dec. 2013).

Board of Directors: Elizabeth (Betsy) Campbell (Chair.); Peter M. O'Neill (Vice-Chair.); Patty Allison (Sec.); Mike Myers (Treas.).

Principal Staff: Pres. and CEO Rodney Ferguson.

Address: 2101 Riverfront Dr., Little Rock, AR 72202.

Telephone: (501) 280-3000; **Fax:** (501) 280-3090; **Internet:** www.winrock.org; **e-mail:** information@winrock.org.

WMF—World Monuments Fund

Established in 1965 for the preservation of historic structures.

Activities: Works to preserve historic structures at sites in more than 90 countries. Headquarters in New York City and offices in Paris, London, Madrid and Lisbon. Issues World Monuments Watch, a list of 100 most endangered sites, biennially.

Geographical Area of Activity: Worldwide.

Publications: Project reports; Annual Report.

Finance: Annual revenue US $21,695,734, expenditure $19,204,725 (30 June 2013).

Board of Trustees: Christopher Ohrstrom (Chair.); James E. Jordan (Vice-Chair.); David B. Ford (Treas.); John J. Kerr, Jr (Sec.).

Principal Staff: Pres. Bonnie Burnham; Exec. Vice-Pres. and COO Lisa Ackerman.

Address: 350 Fifth Ave, Suite 2412, New York, NY 10118.

Telephone: (646) 424-9594; **Fax:** (646) 424-9593; **Internet:** www.wmf.org; **e-mail:** wmf@wmf.org.

Women's Environment and Development Organization—WEDO

Established in 1990 by Bella Abzug and Mim Kelber; an international advocacy network.

Activities: Aims to increase the power of women worldwide as policy-makers in governance and policy-making institutions. WEDO runs three programmes: Climate Change; Corporate Accountability; and Governance. Established the Women's Caucus, an advocacy organization participating at UN and other inter-governmental conferences.

Geographical Area of Activity: International.

Restrictions: Not a grantmaking organization; carries out its own projects.

Publications: Newsletters.

Finance: Annual revenue US $1,309,188, expenditure $1,263,626 (31 Dec. 2013).

Board of Directors: Marcela Tovar-Restrepo (Chair.); Carmen Chiong (Treas.).

Principal Staff: Head of Office Eleanor Blomstrom.

Address: 355 Lexington Ave, 3rd Floor, New York, NY 10017.

Telephone: (212) 973-0325; **Fax:** (212) 973-0335; **Internet:** www.wedo.org; **e-mail:** eleanor@wedo.org.

World Concern

Founded in 1955 as an international relief and development organization.

Activities: Aims to alleviate human suffering. The organization works in the field of aid to less-developed countries, through emergency relief, rehabilitation and long-term development programmes. Projects have included vocational training to equip people with the skills to support themselves; providing emergency food supplies to famine victims; training farmers in improved agricultural methods of food production; and supplying survivors of disasters with food, clothing and critical aid.

Geographical Area of Activity: Africa, Asia, and North, Central and South America.

Restrictions: Not a grantmaking organization.

Publications: Annual Report.

Finance: Annual revenue US $3,991,299, expenditure $4,500,955 (30 June 2014).

Board: Dale Cowles (Chair.); Kirsten Miller (Vice-Chair.); Kevin Gabelein (Treas.).

Principal Staff: Pres. Jacinta Tegman.

Address: 19303 Fremont Ave North, Seattle, WA 98133.

Telephone: (206) 546-7201; **Fax:** (206) 546-7269; **Internet:** www.worldconcern.org; **e-mail:** info@worldconcern.org.

World Education, Inc

Founded in 1951 to meet the needs of the educationally disadvantaged and improve the lives of the poor through economic and social development.

Activities: Provides training and technical assistance in non-formal education across a wide array of sectors. The organization works in the field of development aid, with an emphasis on education and capacity building, with projects in areas including child labour and trafficking, skills training, literacy, civil society development, support for refugees, and sustainable agriculture. It provides training and technical assistance for adults and children who are not in formal education to help generate an income for themselves and their families; provides relief and assistance to refugees and displaced people; runs an enterprise development programme; and educates people about the environment, reproductive and family health, including HIV/AIDS prevention. Projects aim to develop individual growth as well as contributing to the community and the nation.

Geographical Area of Activity: Africa, Asia, North, Central and South America, and Eastern Europe.

Restrictions: Not a grantmaking organization.

Publications: *IDR Reports*; training manuals; development resources; Annual Report; newsletter.

Finance: Annual revenue US $36,727,978, expenditure $36,804,840 (30 June 2014).

Board of Trustees: Dr Louis Kaplow (Chair.); Paul Musante (Treas.); Lisa Stockberger (Sec.).

Principal Staff: Pres. Joel H. Lamstein.

Address: 44 Farnsworth St, Boston, MA 02210.

Telephone: (617) 482-9485; **Fax:** (617) 482-0617; **Internet:** www.worlded.org; **e-mail:** wei@worlded.org.

World Emergency Relief—WER

Established in 1985; a Christian-founded, public-benefit, non-profit organization aiming to help people in need around the world, especially children and families.

Activities: Responds to aid requests from around the world, delivering emergency supplies to people in need, including food, clothing, medical care, shelter, education and emotional and spiritual support. The organization helps children in particular and has supported many orphanages and child refugees. It runs domestic programmes focusing on the needs of Native Americans, and to provide basic needs to severely wounded returning service members. Currently prefers to direct its work towards its own projects or to partner projects in the areas supported. Maintains offices in Honduras, Asia, France, the Netherlands and the United Kingdom.

Geographical Area of Activity: Africa, Asia, North, Central and South America and the Caribbean, South-Eastern Europe, the Russian Federation.

Restrictions: Does not accept unsolicited requests for support. No grants are made to individuals.

Publications: Annual Reports; financial statements.

Finance: Annual revenue US $18,951,049, expenditure $19,034,757 (31 Dec. 2013).

Board of Directors: Gary Becks (Chair.); Lawrence E. Cutting (Sec.).

Principal Staff: CEO Kristy Scott.

Address: POB 1760, Temecula, CA 92593; 27715 Jefferson Ave, Suite 205, Temecula, CA 92590.

Telephone: (951) 225-6700; **Fax:** (951) 225-6799; **Internet:** www.wer-us.org; **e-mail:** info@wer-us.org.

World Federation for Mental Health—WFMH

Founded in 1948 to advance the prevention of mental illnesses around the world, promote the cause of mental health and raise public awareness, and improve the treatment and care of mental and emotional disorders.

Activities: Works through public education programmes. The Federation holds a World Congress biennially, alternating with a smaller conference on evidence-based prevention of mental and behavioural disorders and promotion of mental health. It has nine regional vice-presidents (Africa, Eastern Mediterranean, Europe, Mexico and Central America, North America and the Caribbean, Oceania, South America, South-East Asia and Western Pacific) who promote regional and local programmes and activities. Eight academic collaborating centres at universities provide advice. Established the annual project World Mental Health Day in 1992.

Geographical Area of Activity: International.

Restrictions: Does not make grants.

Publications: Newsletter; Annual Report; World Mental Health Day campaign packet (distributed internationally); mental health/illness related educational material.

Finance: Annual revenue US $192,888, expenditure $112,405 (31 Dec. 2013).

Board of Directors: George Christodolou (Pres.); Gabriel Ivbijaro (Pres.-elect); Deborah Wan (Immediate Past Pres.); Helen Millar (Treas.); Larry Cimino (Sec.).

Principal Staff: Dir of Admin. Deborah Maguire; Dir, Programs and Government Relations Elena Berger.

Address: POB 807, Occoquan, VA 22125.

Internet: www.wfmh.org; **e-mail:** info@wfmh.com.

World Learning

Founded in 1932, as The Experiment in International Living, to improve mutual understanding and respect between cultures and countries.

Activities: Operates in the fields of education, training, international exchange and international development, through the following major programme areas: World Learning International Development and Exchange Programs; the School for International Training, including SIT Graduate Institute and SIT Study Abroad; and The Experiment in International Living. Administers social and economic projects in international development and training worldwide, under US government and international contracts and grants, specializing in developing the skills and potential of individuals and institutions. Active in five broad sectors: democracy and governance, education, training and exchange, institutional capacity building, and societies in transition.

Geographical Area of Activity: Worldwide.

Publications: Annual Reports; *SIT Occasional Papers Series*; *World Learning Odyssey*; and others.

Finance: Annual revenue US $118,454,295, expenditure $121,142,172 (30 June 2013).

Board of Trustees: Thomas Hiatt (Chair.); Virginia Loeb, Cheryl Winter Lewy, William Michaelcheck (Vice-Chair.).

Principal Staff: Pres. and CEO Donald Steinberg.

Address: 1 Kipling Rd, POB 676, Brattleboro, VT 05302-0676.

Telephone: (802) 257-7751; **Fax:** (802) 258-3248; **Internet:** www.worldlearning.org; **e-mail:** info@worldlearning.org.

World Lung Foundation

Established in 2004 with the aim of assisting communities around the world in preventing and and managing lung disease.

Activities: Projects supported include: research and scientific exchanges; pilot projects in treatment and control of tuberculosis and lung disease; training of health personnel in Sub-Saharan Africa.

Geographical Area of Activity: Worldwide.

Publications: Annual report; economic reports.

Finance: Annual revenue US $21,926,854, expenditure $29,360,640 (31 Dec. 2013).

Board of Directors: Louis James de Viel Castel (Pres.); Marc Sznajderman (Vice-Pres.); Andrew S. Rendeiro (Treas.); Eric Rosenbaum (Sec.).

Principal Staff: CEO Peter A. Baldini.

Address: 61 Broadway, Suite 2800, New York, NY 10006.

Telephone: (212) 542-8870; **Internet:** www .worldlungfoundation.org; **e-mail:** info@ worldlungfoundation.org.

World Neighbors

Founded in 1951 by Dr John L. Peters.

Activities: Aims to improve the lives of those living in rural communities in developing countries through long-term development. The organization works to improve agriculture, health care and family planning, conservation, water and sanitation, and small business development through programmes in 13 countries in Asia, Africa and Latin America and the Caribbean. Its programmes focus on helping individuals and communities determine their own solutions to poverty.

Geographical Area of Activity: Africa, Latin America and the Caribbean, Asia.

Restrictions: Not a grantmaking organization. Works directly with selected partners in the regions in which it operates.

Publications: Books; videos; papers; financial statements; Annual Report; monthly e-newsletter; *Neighbors* magazine.

Finance: Annual revenue US $3,226,795, expenditure $4,709,089 (30 June 2013).

Board of Trustees: David Bearden (Chair.); Mindy Roe Galoob (Vice-Chair.); Tommy Barrow (Treas.); Gordon Perkin (Sec.); Barbara Lee (Asst Sec.).

Principal Staff: Pres. and CEO Kate Schecter.

Address: 4127 NW 122nd St, Oklahoma City, OK 73120; POB 270058, Oklahoma City, OK 73137 0058.

Telephone: (405) 815-4200; **Fax:** (405) 752-9393; **Internet:** www.wn.org.

World Peace Foundation—WPF

Established in 1910 by Edwin Ginn, a Boston-based publisher of educational texts and an advocate for international peace. Created initially as the International School of Peace to educate a global audience about the ills of war and to promote international peace.

Activities: Concerned with peace, justice and security. The Foundation carries out activities in the areas of research, education and policy engagement. Projects under its research programme include: New Wars, New Peace; How Mass Atrocities End; Global Arms Trade and Corruption; Conflict in the Horn of Africa; Justice and Security Research Program; and the Seminar Series.

Geographical Area of Activity: International.

Restrictions: Support only for its self-initiated projects.

Publications: Seminar briefings, occasional papers, staff publications.

Finance: Annual revenue US $1,409,644, expenditure $941,831 (30 June 2014).

Board: Peter Blum (Chair.); Thomas O'Reilly (Treas.).

Principal Staff: Exec. Dir Alex de Waal; Research Dir Bridget Conley-Zilkic.

Address: 169 Holland St, Suite 209, Somerville, MA 02144.

Telephone: (617) 627-2255; **Fax:** (617) 627-3178; **Internet:** www.worldpeacefoundation.org; **e-mail:** worldpeacefoundation@tufts.edu.

World Resources Institute

Founded in 1982 with a grant from the John D. and Catherine T. MacArthur Foundation (q.v.) as a centre for policy research seeking to discover how the world's people and nations can meet their basic needs and economic requirements without at the same time undermining the earth's ability to provide the natural resources and environmental quality on which life, growth and security depend.

Activities: Carries out specific policy research in four major areas: Climate, Energy and Transport; Governance and Access; Markets and Enterprise; and People and Ecosystems. In developing countries, the Institute's Center for International Development and Environment provides policy advice, technical assistance and other supporting services to governments, NGOs and local groups charged with managing natural resources and economic development. Research is conducted by the Institute's own staff or by visiting fellows, or may be undertaken in collaboration with other institutions and affiliated groups throughout the USA and abroad. The Institute organizes conferences and seminars, issues publications and offers material for use in the media.

Geographical Area of Activity: International.

Publications: Annual Report; *WRI Digest;* books; reports; studies; papers; handbooks; videos and CD-ROMs.

Finance: Annual revenue US $84,401,990, expenditure $65,763,955 (30 Sept. 2014).

Board of Directors: James A. Harmon (Chair.); Harriet Babbitt (Vice-Chair.).

Principal Staff: Pres. and CEO Andrew Steer; Exec. Vice-Pres. and Man. Dir Manish Bapna.

Address: 10 G Street, NE, Suite 800, Washington, DC 20002.

Telephone: (202) 729-7600; **Fax:** (202) 729-7610; **Internet:** www.wri.org; **e-mail:** moko@wri.org.

World Vision Inc

Established in 1950; an international Christian organization that helps the poor through humanitarian programmes and relief.

Activities: Engages in emergency relief, providing aid for victims of disaster, including food, clothing and shelter; and long-term development and advocacy work. The organization works in the areas of community development, child sponsorship, education, health care, agriculture, micro-enterprise and clean water and sanitation; most work is child-focused.

Geographical Area of Activity: International.

Publications: Annual Report; *World Vision Magazine* (quarterly); *World Vision News* (quarterly); *World Vision eNews* (monthly); reports; research papers; books.

Finance: Annual revenue US $981,898,000, expenditure $970,899,000 (30 Sept. 2013).

Board of Directors: Dr Joan Singleton (Chair.); Sandy Grubb (Vice-Chair.); Gary T. Duim (Sec.-Treas.).

Principal Staff: Pres. Richard E. Stearns.

Address: POB 9716, Department W, Federal Way, WA 98063-9716.

Telephone: (253) 815-1000; **Internet:** www.worldvision.org; **e-mail:** info@worldvision.org.

World Wide Web Foundation

Established in 2008 by Sir Tim Berners-Lee, inventor of the Web.

Activities: Promotes the use of the World Wide Web for progress. The Foundation operates in the area of web technology, including training and tools to support content creation, community building, support of Web science and research, advancement of Web standards.

Geographical Area of Activity: International.

Publications: Newsletters.

Finance: Annual revenue US $5,010,997, expenditure $4,178,197 (31 Dec. 2013).

Board of Directors: Rick Haythornthwaite (Chair.); Tim Berners-Lee, Rosemary Leith (Founding Dirs).

Principal Staff: CEO Anne Jellema.

Address: 1110 Vermont Ave, NW, Suite 500, Washington DC 20005.

Telephone: (202) 595-2892; **Internet:** www.webfoundation .org; **e-mail:** contact@webfoundation.org.

Worldwatch Institute

Founded in 1974 as a non-profit research organization that aims to inform policy-makers and the public about emerging global problems, and the implications of links between the world economy and its environmental support systems.

Activities: Works to foster an environmentally sustainable society, through the provision of information. Disseminates the results of research regarding global environmental issues through a number of publications, thus raising public awareness of environmental threats. Focuses on issues such as: climate change; depletion of the ozone layer; pollution of the oceans; population growth; biodiversity; ecosystems; sustainable agriculture and economics; the impact of globalization on the environment; and energy.

Geographical Area of Activity: International and USA.

Restrictions: Does not make grants to individuals or organizations.

Publications: _State of the World_ (annually); _Vital Signs_ (annually); Worldwatch Reports (3–4 annually); Annual Report; books; papers.

Finance: Annual revenue US $2,396,183, expenditure $2,260,576 (31 March 2014).

Board of Directors: Ed Groark (Chair.); Robert Charles Friese (Vice-Chair.); John Robbins (Treas.).

Principal Staff: Pres. (a.i.) Ed Groark.

Address: 1400 16th Street, NW, Suite 430, Washington, DC 20036.

Telephone: (202) 745-8092; **Fax:** (202) 478-2534; **Internet:** www.worldwatch.org; **e-mail:** worldwatch@worldwatch.org.

The Helene Wurlitzer Foundation of New Mexico

Founded in 1954 by Mrs Howard E. Wurlitzer to promote the arts and humanities.

Activities: Provides artist residencies in Taos, New Mexico, to national and international artists in the literary and visual arts, and to musicians and composers.

Geographical Area of Activity: South-western USA.

Restrictions: Artist residencies offered to individuals only.

Finance: Annual revenue US $115,778, expenditure $245,103 (31 March 2013).

Board of Directors: Rena Rosequist (Pres.); Peggy Nelson (Vice-Pres.); William Ebie (Treas.); Harold Hahn (Sec.).

Principal Staff: Exec. Dir Michael A. Knight.

Address: 218 Los Pandos Rd, POB 1891, Taos, NM 87571.

Telephone: (575) 758-2413; **Fax:** (575) 758-2559; **Internet:** www.wurlitzerfoundation.org; **e-mail:** hwf@taosnet.com.

X Prize Foundation

Established in 1999 to promote innovation that will benefit humanity.

Activities: Awards prizes of US $10m. to first team to achieve a specific goal in areas that include Exploration (Space and Underwater); Life Sciences; Energy and Environment; Education; and Global Development. In 2011, the Foundation announced that it would offer the prize for the development of a medical diagnostic device similar to the 'tricorder' that appeared in television science fiction series Star Trek.

Geographical Area of Activity: Worldwide.

Finance: Annual revenue US $30,452,212, expenditure $15,827,863 (31 Dec. 2012).

Board of Trustees: Dr Peter H. Diamandis (Founder and Chair.); Robert K. Weiss (Vice-Chair.); Gregg E. Maryniak (Sec.); J. Barry Thompson (Treas.).

Principal Staff: Pres. Robert K. Weiss; CEO Dr Peter H. Diamandis.

Address: 5510 Lincoln Blvd, Suite 100, Playa Vista, CA 90094-2034.

Telephone: (310) 741-4880; **Fax:** (310) 741-4974; **Internet:** www.xprize.org.

Zonta International Foundation—ZIF

Founded in 1984; a worldwide service organization of executives in business and the professions working together to advance the status of women.

Activities: Supports the charitable and educational programmes of Zonta International through effective fund-raising, investment of funds, and the distribution of proceeds. Through its financial support of Zonta International programmes, the Foundation becomes the catalyst for greater service to women throughout the world. It has more than 30,000 members in more than 1,200 clubs in 63 countries and geographic areas, supporting women's advancement, rights, education and leadership.

Geographical Area of Activity: International.

Restrictions: No grants to individuals except for established scholarships; international development projects for women primarily through UN agencies.

Finance: Annual revenue US $3,335,178, expenditure $633,762 (31 May 2013).

Board of Directors: Maria Jose Landeira Oestergaard (Pres.); Sonja Hönig Schough (Pres.-elect); Suzanne von Bassewitz (Vice-Pres.); Bridget Masters (Treas./Sec.).

Principal Staff: Exec. Dir Allison Summers.

Address: 1211 West 22nd St, Suite 900, Oak Brook, IL 60523.

Telephone: (630) 928-1400; **Fax:** (630) 928-1559; **Internet:** www.zonta.org/ZIFoundation.aspx; **e-mail:** zontaintl@zonta .org.

Uruguay

FOUNDATION CENTRE AND CO-ORDINATING BODY

Instituto del Tercer Mundo—ITeM (Third World Institute)

Established in 1989 to promote civil society internationally, in particular with the aim of building democratic and environmentally sustainable societies.

Activities: Aims to promote the development of civil society nationally and internationally, through communication, information, research and education. Encourages networking between organizations, through the promotion of electronic information networks. Publishes books on the subject of the third sector. Has consultative status at the UN.

Geographical Area of Activity: International.

Restrictions: No grants to individuals; grants made only in specific countries or regions.

Publications: *The World Guide* (biennially); *Social Watch Report* (annual); *Revista del Sur*; *Tercer Mundo Económico*; books and magazines and CD-ROMs.

Finance: Financed by grants from international organizations, and from the sale of its own products and services.

Executive Board: Cecilia Fernández (Pres.); Carlos Abin (Sec.).

Principal Staff: Exec. Dir Roberto Bissio.

Address: Avda 18 de julio 2095/301, Montevideo 11200.

Telephone: (2) 4031424; **Internet:** www.item.org.uy; **e-mail:** item@item.org.uy.

Uzbekistan

FOUNDATIONS, TRUSTS AND NON-PROFIT ORGANIZATIONS

Sog'lom Avlod Uchun (For a Healthy Generation)

Founded in 1993 by I. A. Karimov to promote improved health for future generations.

Activities: Conducts programmes and carries out research in the following areas: medical, humanitarian, educational, cultural and sports. Operates a network of more than 180 branch offices throughout Uzbekistan for the distribution of donated medicines and humanitarian assistance, and conducts health and other programmes, including humanitarian and educational programmes. Works in co-operation with international partners. Also owns two journals and three newspapers.

Geographical Area of Activity: Uzbekistan.

Finance: Owns five commercial companies. Net assets US $70m.; annual revenue approx. $20m.

Board of Directors: Svetlana Tursunovna Inamova (Chair.); Nazimjan Ergashevich Muminov (Vice-Chair.).

Principal Staff: Sec. Durdona Ibrakhimova Akramova.

Address: Istiqbol str. 15, 100047 Tashkent.

Telephone: (71) 232-00-82; **Fax:** (71) 233-89-49; **Internet:** sau .uz; **e-mail:** fondsau@yahoo.com.

Vatican City

FOUNDATION CENTRE AND CO-ORDINATING BODY

Caritas Internationalis—CI

Established in 1950, in Rome, Italy, as International Caritas Conference (ICC) to respond to the need for a high-level global umbrella organization for the various national Catholic humanitarian assistance, social service and development organizations worldwide, many of which, but not all, used the name 'Caritas'. Incorporated the already-existing Caritas Internationalis based in Lucerne, Switzerland. Present name adopted in 1954. Full title is Caritas Internationalis—International Confederation of Catholic Organizations for Charitable and Social Action (Confédération Internationale d'Organismes Catholiques d'Action Charitable et Sociale—Confederación Internacional de Organizaciones Católicas de Acción Caritativa y Social).

Activities: As an international Catholic organization, stimulates and aids national Caritas organizations to facilitate the assistance, advancement and integral development of the most underprivileged, by means of active charity in keeping with the teaching and tradition of the Catholic Church. Studies the problems arising from poverty; investigates causes and proposes solutions conforming to justice and the dignity of the human person; encourages national Caritas organizations to undertake collaborative study and research; with the approval of the local hierarchy, fosters the foundation of national Catholic charitable organizations where none exists, and, if necessary, contributes to their development; promotes collaboration among member organizations and co-ordinates their international activities, without infringing on their autonomy; participates in efforts of all people to better their individual and collective living standards, so as to achieve full human development; encourages and co-ordinates humanitarian assistance work by member organizations in cases of disaster as and when emergency intervention is required; represents member organizations conforming to current statutes at inter-denominational and international levels; and promotes maximal co-operation with other international aid and development organizations. Caritas Internationalis has consultative status with a number of international organizations, including the UN Economic and Social Council (ECOSOC), the Office of the UN High Commissioner for Refugees (UNHCR), FAO, the World Food Programme, the World Health Organization, the UN Children's Fund (UNICEF) and ILO. Maintains offices at the UN in New York and Geneva and comprises more than 160 member organizations.

Geographical Area of Activity: International.

Publications: Blog; annual report; information sheets, reports and monographs.

Finance: Total expenditure €3,982,509 (2014).

Bureau: Cardinal Oscar Rodríguez Maradiaga (Pres.); Dr Juerg Krummenacher (Treas.).

Principal Staff: Sec.-Gen. and CEO Michel Roy.

Address: Palazzo San Calisto 16, 00120 Vatican City.

Telephone: (06) 69879799; **Fax:** (06) 69887237; **Internet:** www.caritas.org; **e-mail:** caritas.internationalis@caritas.va.

FOUNDATIONS, TRUSTS AND NON-PROFIT ORGANIZATIONS

Fondazione Centesimus Annus—Pro Pontifice

Established in 1993 to promote informed knowledge of the teachings of the Catholic Church and of the Holy See.

Activities: Operates in Germany, Italy, Malta, the Netherlands, Slovakia, Spain, Switzerland and the USA, organizing courses and conferences to promote the teachings of the Catholic Church. Holds courses and an annual conference held in the Vatican City.

Geographical Area of Activity: Western and Central Europe, and the USA.

Board of Directors: Domingo Sugranyes Bickel (Chair.); Dr Camilla Borghese Khevenhüller-Metsch (Vice-Chair.).

Principal Staff: Sec.-Gen. Massimo Gattamelata.

Address: 00120 Vatican City.

Telephone: (06) 69885752; **Fax:** (06) 69881971; **Internet:** www.centesimusannus.org; **e-mail:** info@centesimusannus.org.

Foundation 'Populorum Progressio'

Established in 1992 by Pope John Paul II to promote solidarity with the poor in the developing countries of Central and South America and the Caribbean, support the work of other charities working in the region, and contribute to the development of populations that are marginalized, especially indigenous and mixed-race peoples, in accordance with the social teachings of the Church.

Activities: Operates in the field of aid to less-developed countries through financing projects nominated by national sociopastoral institutions, and which conform to the aims of the Foundation. Maintains an Administration Council in Colombia.

Geographical Area of Activity: Central and South America and the Caribbean.

Restrictions: Grants only to projects approved by the local ecclesiastical authority.

Finance: Grants awarded US $1,995,000 (2013).

Board of Directors: Most Rev. Edmundo Luis Flavio Abastoflor Montero (Chair.); Most Rev. Antonio Arregui Yarza (Vice-Chair.).

Principal Staff: Pres. and Legal Rep. Cardinal Robert Sarah; Sec. Mons. Giampietro Dal Toso; Sub-Sec. Mons. Segundo Tejado Muñoz.

Address: Pontificio Consiglio Cor Unum, Palazzo San Pio X, 00120 Vatican City.

Telephone: (06) 69887331; **Fax:** (06) 69887301; **Internet:** www.corunum.va; **e-mail:** corunum@corunum.va.

Venezuela

FOUNDATION CENTRE AND CO-ORDINATING BODY

Sinergia—Asociación Nacional de Organizaciones de la Sociedad Civil (National Association of Civil Society Organizations)

Founded in 1996 to support the development of civil society organizations in Venezuela.

Activities: Provides and publishes information on civil society organizations in Venezuela; provides technical assistance for establishing civil society organizations; and promotes philanthropy in Venezuela.

Geographical Area of Activity: Venezuela.

Restrictions: No grants available.

Publications: *Monthly Information Bulletin*; *Las Redes y el Cambio Social (Networks and social change,* 2000); online articles on civil society and NGO development.

Finance: Income is based on projects financed by such institutions as the Konrad Adenauer Foundation (q.v.), Thalita Koum and the Govt of Canada.

Operating Committee: Déborah Van Berkel (Pres.); Diana Vegas (Vice-Pres.); Manuel Gómez (Treas.).

Principal Staff: Exec. Dir Wileyma Meneses.

Address: Centro Rental de la Universidad Metropolitana, Edificio Andrés Germán Otero, 2°, Urb. Terrazas del Ávila, Caracas 1071.

Telephone: (212) 242-0101; **Fax:** (212) 243-9133; **Internet:** www.sinergia.org.ve; **e-mail:** acsinergia@gmail.com.

FOUNDATIONS, TRUSTS AND NON-PROFIT ORGANIZATIONS

Fundación Bigott

Established in 1963 by Cigarerra Bigott, the Venezuelan subsidiary of British American Tobacco, to preserve and promote traditional cultural heritage.

Activities: Operates through educational, cultural and environmental programmes to promote and protect Venezuela's traditional cultural heritage.

Geographical Area of Activity: Venezuela.

Principal Staff: Pres. Rafael Márquez; Gen. Man. Karina Zabarce.

Address: Centro Histórico de Petare, Calle Vigía, Casa 10–11, Caracas.

Telephone: (212) 205-7111; **Internet:** www.fundacionbigott .com; **e-mail:** fundacion_bigott@bat.com.

Fundación para la Defensa de la Naturaleza— FUDENA (Foundation for the Protection of Nature)

Founded in 1975 to promote the conservation of the environment through the preservation of natural resources and sustainable development.

Activities: Conducts research; organizes the planning and management of protected areas and endangered species; runs environmental education and community participation projects; promotes co-operation between environmental groups; and disseminates information to the public.

Geographical Area of Activity: Venezuela.

Publications: Newsletters; research reports; technical reports.

Principal Staff: Exec. Dir Déborah Bigio.

Address: Edif. Centro Empresarial Senderos, 5°, Oficina 505, Avda Principal de Los Cortijos de Lourdes con 2°, Apdo 77076, Caracas 1071.

Telephone: (212) 238-2930; **Fax:** (212) 239-6547; **Internet:** www.fudena.org.ve; **e-mail:** fudena@fudena.org.ve; comunicacionesfudena@gmail.com.

Fundación Empresas Polar (Polar Companies Foundation)

Founded in 1977 by Empresas Polar to contribute to the social development of Venezuela.

Activities: Collaborates with other public and private development institutions; conducts projects in the fields of education, community development and health. Since 1983, the Foundation has awarded the Lorenzo Mendoza Fleury Prize every two years to Venezuelan scientists working in the fields of biology, physics, maths, chemistry.

Geographical Area of Activity: Venezuela.

Publications: Environmental publications; science magazine; and publications within other interest areas.

Board of Directors: Leonor Giménez de Mendoza (Chair.); Morella Pacheco Ramella (Vice-Chair.).

Principal Staff: Gen. Man. Alicia Pimentel.

Address: Segunda avenida, Los Cortijos de Lourdes, edif. Fundación Polar, 1°, Los Ruices Municipio Sucre, Caracas 1071.

Telephone: (212) 202-7530; **Fax:** (212) 202-7522; **Internet:** www.fundacionempresaspolar.org; **e-mail:** institucional@ fundacionempresaspolar.org.

Fundación La Salle de Ciencias Naturales—FLASA (La Salle Foundation for Natural Sciences)

Founded in 1957 by Pablo Mandazen Soto to develop scientific research on natural resources and technical training of the young; to disseminate the knowledge acquired by means of specialized publications, lectures, seminars and museums; and to assist the marginal population, mainly workers, peasants, tribal Indians and fishermen, by direct action such as the setting up of co-operatives and assisted projects.

Activities: Promotes national development in science and technology, education, social welfare, conservation and the environment, through self-conducted programmes, environmental and social impact services for the industry and the state, conferences, courses, publications and lectures. Maintains a Marine Research Station at Isla de Margarita, on the eastern coast, to increase knowledge of the Venezuelan sea and its resources and to help to establish an education system adapted to the needs of the fishing industry. The Foundation has also pioneered the development of technical schools whose programmes combine academic preparation with technical training—courses are of six years' duration, and embrace a wide range of subjects from mechanics and refrigeration to fishing and marine biology. The Foundation established three schools, at Isla de Margarita, Ciudad Guayana and San Carlos (Edo. Cojedes); also at Isla de Margarita the Instituto Universitario de Tecnología del Mar (IUTEMAR) was created, devoted to research on marine ecosystems and resources, emphasizing fisheries management. Other specialist institutes established by the Foundation are the La Salle Museum of Natural History, whose long-term commitment is producing an inventory of Venezuela's biodiversity, the Station of Hydrobiological research, and the Instituto Caribe de Antropología y Sociología (Caribbean Institute of Anthropology and

Sociology), which houses projects of applied anthropological research, aimed at reducing the shock of cultural transition and providing Indian communities with a basic training that will enable them to raise their standard of living. Maintains offices in Cojedes, Isla de Margarita and Trujillo, and in Guyana.

Geographical Area of Activity: Venezuela.

Publications: Report of operations and financial statement; *Antropológica* (review); *Memoria* (monographic series); *Natura;* books on science and technology.

Finance: Funded by the Ministry of Education and corporate donations.

Board of Directors: Francer Goenaga (Pres.).

Principal Staff: Exec. Vice-Pres. Elio Villalobos Manzo.

Address: Edif. Fundación La Salle, Avda Boyacá, Cota Mil, Apdo 1930, Caracas 1010-A.

Telephone: (212) 709-5811; **Internet:** www.fundacionlasalle .org.ve; **e-mail:** comunicaciones@fundacionlasalle.org.ve.

Fundación Eugenio Mendoza (Eugenio Mendoza Foundation)

Founded in 1951 by Eugenio Mendoza and Luisa R. de Mendoza to promote social development, education, agriculture and culture.

Activities: Provides microfinance for community development programmes and entrepreneurial training for low-income families. In co-operation with other organizations, the Foundation has created Bangente, the first private Venezuelan bank in microfinances, and in 2005, with Grupo Santander, it created Bancrecer development bank.

Geographical Area of Activity: Venezuela.

Restrictions: No grants are made to individuals or organizations.

Publications: Operations and financial reports, publications in the arts and regarding children.

Board of Directors: Luisa Elena Mendoza de Pulido (Pres.); Luisa Mariana Pulido de Sucre (Exec. Vice-Pres.).

Address: Avda Principal de Las Mercedes, entre Calles Nueva York y Orinoco, Edificio Ávila, PH Baruta, Caracas 1073.

Telephone: (212) 993-0438; **Internet:** www .fundacioneugeniomendoza.org.ve; **e-mail:** fem@ fundacionmendoza.org.ve.

Fundación de la Vivienda Popular (Foundation for Low-Cost Housing)

Founded in 1958 by Eugenio Mendoza, with the support and participation of 41 public figures, 59 companies and four foundations, to address housing problems among low-income sections of the community.

Activities: Operates nationally in the field of housing in two areas: Social Action; and Research and Development. The Social Action programme aims to stimulate community self-management, supporting low-income families and motivating them to take part in improving their housing and environment through the creation of a housing association (Asociación Civil de Vivienda); it also advises businesses wishing to contribute a solution to housing problems experienced by their workers, and trains public and private institutions interested in setting up housing associations. The Research and Development programme aims to carry out research in areas associated with housing, especially families with few economic resources; its support programmes seek to advance knowledge of housing and the environment, and it promotes the Eugenio Mendoza Chair in Housing at national universities, and the Eugenio Mendoza Prize for Research in Housing. The Foundation also maintains a documentation and information centre, which offers information on housing and the environment.

Geographical Area of Activity: Venezuela.

Publications: The Foundation is the main publisher of housing literature in Venezuela.

Board of Directors: Eugenio A. Mendoza (Chair.); Dr Pablo A. Pulido M., Dr Manuel Azpúrua Arreaza, Omar Feaugas Guédez (Vice-Chair.).

Principal Staff: Exec. Vice-Pres. Oswaldo Carrillo Jiménez; Gen. Man. R. Alexis Delgado Silva.

Address: Avda Diego Cisneros (Principal de Los Ruices), Edif. Centro Empresarial Autana, 1°, Urb. Los Ruices, Municipio Sucre, Estado Maranda, Caracas.

Telephone: (212) 238-4708; **Fax:** (212) 234-6513; **Internet:** www.viviendaenred.com; **e-mail:** viviendaenred@cantv.net.

Viet Nam

FOUNDATION CENTRE AND CO-ORDINATING BODY

LIN Center for Community Development

Established in 2009.

Activities: Provides training, capacity building and small grants to more than 100 non-profit organizations and volunteers at community level. Maintains a library and research room.

Geographical Area of Activity: Viet Nam.

Board of Directors: Nguyen Tran Hoang Anh (Chair.).

Principal Staff: Exec. Dir Ngo Quynh Nhu; Deputy Dir Pham Truong Son.

Address: 180/47 Nguyen Huu Canh, Ward 22, Binh Thanh Dist, Ho Chi Minh City.

Telephone: (8) 35120092; **Internet:** linvn.org; **e-mail:** info@linvn.org.

FOUNDATIONS, TRUSTS AND NON-PROFIT ORGANIZATIONS

Toyota Vietnam Foundation—TVF

Established in 2005 by Toyota Motor Vietnam Co Ltd in recognition of the company's 10th anniversary of operations in Viet Nam.

Activities: Aims to contribute to the development of Vietnamese society, supporting initiatives in traffic safety, education, sports and culture. In 2014, the Foundation awarded scholarships to 115 Vietnamese students. It also sponsors the Vietnam National Symphony Orchestra.

Geographical Area of Activity: Viet Nam.

Finance: Established with an initial donation from Toyota Motor Vietnam Co Ltd of US $4m.

Principal Staff: Chair. Yoshihisa Maruta.

Address: c/o Toyota Motor Vietnam Co Ltd, Phuc Thang Ward, Phuc Yen Town, Vinh Phuc Province.

Telephone: (3) 868100112; **Fax:** (3) 868117; **Internet:** www.toyotavn.com.vn/templates/views/38/203; **e-mail:** tmv_cs@toyotavn.com.vn.

Unilever Vietnam Foundation—UVF

Established in 2004 by Unilever Vietnam to co-ordinate the company's social and community programmes.

Activities: Funding is directed to projects providing support to children and women, especially those living in rural areas, including initiatives focusing on community health care and hygiene, education, environmental protection, and supporting people in need.

Geographical Area of Activity: Viet Nam.

Finance: Annual disbursements to social and community projects 70,000m. dong.

Principal Staff: Contact Le Thi Thu Tram.

Address: 156 Nguyen Luong Bang, District 7, Ho Chi Minh City.

Telephone: (8) 5 4135686-2403; **Fax:** (8) 5 4135626; **Internet:** www.unilever.com.vn/aboutus/foundation; **e-mail:** le-thi-thu.tram@unilever.com.

Zambia

FOUNDATIONS, TRUSTS AND NON-PROFIT ORGANIZATIONS

Mindolo Ecumenical Foundation—MEF

Founded in 1958 by Rev. Peter Mathews to promote, develop and train lay and ordained church leaders.

Activities: Serves as an ecumenical training centre, organizing courses for African churches, church-related organizations and NGOs. Programmes operated by the Foundation include: women's training; youth leadership; ecumenical church ministries; pre-school teachers and trainers; peacebuilding and conflict transformation; and community development. Awards scholarships, organizes conferences and training courses, and issues publications. Maintains a library of 30,000 books.

Geographical Area of Activity: Africa.

Publications: *Mindolo World* (two a year); *MEF Newsletter;* conference reports.

Board: Rev. Suzanne Matale (Chair.).

Principal Staff: Dir Most Rev. Dr Robert K. Aboagye-Mensah.

Address: POB 21493, Kitwe.

Telephone: (2) 966780580; **Fax:** (2) 211001; **e-mail:** mef@zamnet.zm.

Zimbabwe

FOUNDATIONS, TRUSTS AND NON-PROFIT ORGANIZATIONS

African Capacity Building Foundation—ACBF (Fondation pour le Renforcement des Capacités en Afrique)

Founded in 1991 through a collaboration between the African Development Bank, the World Bank and the UN Development Programme to help the countries and regional organizations of Africa build and strengthen indigenous capacity to reduce poverty.

Activities: Promotes and supports the improvement of human and institutional capacities in the areas of policy analysis and development management in Sub-Saharan Africa. The Fund awards fellowships to improve research and training skills and to expand in-service training for professionals. Provides direct funding for capacity-building projects. The Partnership for Capacity Building in Africa (PACT) initiative aims to provide an integrated framework for capacity building, good governance and sustainable development in Africa; to promote a partnership between African governments, the private sector, civil society and development partners to strengthen Africa's ownership, leadership and responsibility in the capacity-building process; and to provide a forum for sharing experiences and best practices, and discussing issues and problems. Maintains a library of more than 10,000 publications.

Geographical Area of Activity: Sub-Saharan Africa.

Publications: *ACBF Newsletter* (quarterly); *ACBF Working Paper Series (AWPS)*; *Challenges in the Building of Public Service Capacity in Africa*; *Beating Occupational Fraud through Awareness and Prevention*; *The Role of Agriculture in Strengthening Regional Integration in Africa*; Annual Report; books; workshop reports; occasional reports.

Finance: Total disbursements US $32.8m. (2010); resources pledged $28,150,000 (2013).

Board of Governors: Christian Magnagna (Chair.).

Principal Staff: Chair. of Exec. Board Calisto Enias Madavo; Vice-Chair. Charlotte Osei; Exec. Sec. Prof. Emmanuel Nnandozie.

Address: 2 Fairbairn Dr., Mount Pleasant, Harare.

Telephone: (4) 304663; **Internet:** www.acbf-pact.org; **e-mail:** root@acbf-pact.org.

African Forum and Network on Debt and Development—AFRODAD

Established with the aim of securing lasting solutions to Africa's mounting debt problem and to promote the continent's development.

Activities: Network of African NGOs, organizations, churches and individuals that work on debt, development aid, economic governance issues within Africa; takes part in conferences in the Northern hemisphere to promote empathy with the African position regarding debt, aid and development; main areas of research include: domestic and external loan contraction processes; debt profiles; legal and institutional frameworks of government debt systems; fair and transparent arbitration of sovereign debts; emerging lenders to Africa; development effectiveness; transparency and accountability in extractive industries; development finance and financial flows; and fiscal space in Africa, with country case studies on 33 of African countries.

Geographical Area of Activity: Africa.

Publications: Research, discussion and occasional papers; articles; policy briefs; newsletter.

Board of Trustees: Opa Kapijimpanga (Chair.).

Principal Staff: Exec. Dir Dr Fanwell K. Bokosi.

Address: 31 Atkinson Dr., Hillside, POB CY1517, Causeway, Harare.

Telephone: (4) 778531; **Fax:** (4) 747878; **Internet:** www.afrodad.org; **e-mail:** afrodad@afrodad.co.zw.

Community Foundation for the Western Region of Zimbabwe—CFWRZ

Established in 1997.

Activities: Works in Matabeleland North, Matabeleland South and Midlands Provinces to improve quality of life in economically disadvantaged communities. The Foundation operates as a grantmaker, broker and facilitator, supporting social enterprise initiatives and promoting sustainable socio-economic development. Programme areas include water and agriculture, women's economic empowerment, education, youth development and HIV/AIDS.

Geographical Area of Activity: Western Zimbabwe.

Finance: Initial funding provided by a 'Qogelela' endowment, a community savings programme to which more than 50,000 people contributed, worth approx. US $100,000.

Principal Staff: Exec. Dir Stewart Mantula.

Address: POB 1799, Bulawayo; 21 Walter Howard Road, Northend, Bulawayo.

Telephone: (0) 9200078; **Fax:** (0) 9209617; **Internet:** www.westfound.org; **e-mail:** mantula@westfound.org.

Higher Life Foundation

Established in 1996 by Strive Masiyiwa, founder and Exec. Chair. of Econet Wireless International, a telecommunications company, and his wife Tsitsi Masiyiwa.

Activities: A umbrella organization, which comprises: the Capernaum Trust (f. 1996) and Capernaum Trust International, providing for the education of orphaned and vulnerable children; Christian Community Partnership Trust (f. 2005), supporting evangelical Christian organizations; the Joshua Nkomo Scholarship Fund (f. 2005), sponsoring secondary- and tertiary-level students in Zimbabwe; and the National Healthcare Trust Zimbabwe (f. 2008), which runs six programmes (Health Information Systems; Human Resources for Health Development; Infrastructure Development; Lobbying and Advocacy; Total Wellness and Transformation; and Water, Sanitation and Waste Management), as well as providing emergency health care, refurbishing hospitals, training health workers and, providing scholarships to medical students.

Geographical Area of Activity: Burundi, Lesotho, South Africa, Swaziland, Zimbabwe.

Principal Staff: Exec. Chair. Tsitsi Masiyiwa.

Address: Westgate House East, Suite 5, David Frost Way, Westgate, Harare.

Telephone: 772222922; **Internet:** www.higherlifefoundation.com; **e-mail:** info@higherlifefoundation.com.

The J. F. Kapnek Trust Zimbabwe

Established in 1955 from the estate of James F. Kapnek.

Activities: Collaborates with government ministries, NGOs and communities to implement meaningful interventions for the prevention, management and treatment of HIV/AIDS and related disorders, and to develop programmes of support for those affected by the disease; develops child- and youth-focused programmes that address issues relevant to the lives of young Zimbabweans, including educational and psycho-social support, self-empowerment, AIDS/sexual awareness, gender issues and life skills; and supports the development of comprehensive programmes for disabled children and their caregivers. The Trust has three main programmes: Early Childhood Development, renovating and furnishng pre-school classes in state primary schools and introducing ancillary services, including nutritional support, health checks and teacher training; Childhood Disability, supporting the Children's Rehabilitation Unit at Harare Central Hospital and disabled children nationwide, and building the capacity of the Ministry of Health and Child Care's rehabilitation infrastructure at provincial and district levels through staff training, renovation of facilities and equipment supply; and Prevention of Mother to Child Transmission of HIV, supporting government programmes over the past decade through the provision of training, site support and monitoring, with a total of 431 health facilities. Through its Strengthening Science through Women programme the Trust offers scholarships to female high-school students to continue their education through to university.

Geographical Area of Activity: Zimbabwe.

Publications: Annual Report.

Finance: Annual revenue US $2.8m. (2013/14).

Board of Directors: Tsungai Chipato (Chair.).

Principal Staff: Dir Greg Powell; Admin. Man. Gail Downey.

Address: 33 Lawson Ave, Milton Park, Harare.

Telephone: (4) 792153; **Internet:** www.jfkapnektrust.org; **e-mail:** gdowney@ctazim.co.zw.

Self Help Development Foundation–Training and Development Services

Established in 1963 by Francis Waddelove for the reduction of poverty through food security.

Activities: Operates in Zimbabwe and Southern Africa in the areas of economic affairs, education and social welfare, through providing credit; education for self-survival; mobilization of savings; civic education; and social welfare in the area of food security. The Foundation makes grants and loans to groups and individual members, and carries out projects.

Geographical Area of Activity: Zimbabwe and Southern Africa.

Principal Staff: Exec. Dir Wadzanayi Vere.

Address: 17 Nirvana Rd, Hatfield, POB 4576, Harare.

Telephone: (4) 570611; **Fax:** (4) 570139; **e-mail:** shdftas@ africaonline.co.zw.

Uluntu Community Foundation

Established in 2008.

Activities: Main areas of interest are education, food security and livelihoods, research and social entrepreneurship. The Foundation works as a grantmaker, broker and facilitator, investing in community empowerment partnerships and building community-giving networks between individuals and organizations. It promotes accessibility, accountability, inclusiveness, integrity and transparency.

Geographical Area of Activity: Matabeleland South and North Provinces.

Publications: Annual Report.

Finance: Annual income US $61,654, expenditure $44,147 (31 Dec. 2013).

Board of Trustees: Busani Bafana (Chair.).

Principal Staff: Exec. Dir Inviolatta Mpuli Moyo.

Address: 1 Coghlan Ave, Kumalo, Bulawayo.

Telephone: (9) 231294; **Internet:** www.uluntu.org; **e-mail:** uluntufoundation@gmail.com.

Select Bibliography

Acs, Zoltan J. *Why Philanthropy Matters: How the Wealthy Give, and What It Means for Our Economic Well-Being.* Princeton University Press, Princeton, NJ, 2013.

Alliance Publishing Trust. *Alliance* (quarterly journal).

Anheier, H. K. *Civil Society: Measurement, Evaluation, Policy.* Earthscan, London, 2004.
Non-Profit Organizations: Theory, Management, Policy (2nd edn). Routledge, Abingdon, 2014.

Anheier, H. K. and S. Daly. *The Roles and Visions of Foundations in Europe.* London School of Economics, London, 2004.
(Eds) *The Politics of Foundations: Comparative Perspectives from Europe and Beyond.* Routledge, Abingdon, 2006.

Anheier, H. K., M. Glasius and Prof. M. H. Kaldor (Eds). *Global Civil Society Yearbook 2009: Global Civil Society and Poverty Alleviation.* Sage Publications, London, 2009.

Anheier, H. K. and David Hammack. *American Foundations: Roles and Contributions.* Brookings Institution, Washington, DC, 2010.

Anheier, H.K. and David Hammack. *A versatile American institution: the changing ideals and realities of philanthropic foundations.* Brookings Institution Press, Washington, DC, 2013

Anheier, H. K. and Jeremy Kendall. *Third Sector Policy at the Crossroads: An International Non-Profit Analysis.* Routledge, London, 2001.

Anheier, H. K. and D. Leat. *From Charity to Creativity: Philanthropic Foundations in the 21st Century: Perspectives from Britain and Beyond.* Comedia, Stroud, 2002.
Creative Philanthropy: Toward a New Philanthropy for the Twenty-First Century. Routledge, Abingdon, 2006.

Anheier, H. K. and Regina A. List. *A Dictionary of Civil Society. Philanthropy and the Non-Profit Sector.* Routledge, London, 2005.

Anheier, H. K. and S. Toepler (Eds). *Private Funds, Public Purpose: Philanthropic foundations in international perspective.* Kluwer Academic/Plenum Publishers, USA, 1999.

Armstrong, D., V. Bello, J. Gilson and D. Spini. *Civil Society and International Governance: The role of non-state actors in the EU, Africa, Asia and Middle East.* Routledge, Abingdon, 2010.

Baker, G. and D. Chandler. *Global Civil Society: Contested Futures.* Routledge, Abingdon, 2006.

Bebbington, A. J., S. Hickey and D. Mitlin (Eds). *Can NGOs Make a Difference? The Challenge of Development Alternatives.* Zed Books, London, 2007.

Bremner, Robert H. *Giving: Charity and Philanthropy in History.* Rutgers University Press, New Brunswick, NJ, 1995.

Brown, Rajeswary Ampalavanar, and Justin Pierce. *Charities in the non-western world: the development and regulation of indigenous and Islamic charities.* Routledge, Abingdon, 2013.

Bundesverband Deutscher Stiftungen e.V. (Ed.). *Verzeichnis Deutscher Stiftungen.* Verlag Deutscher Stiftungen, Berlin, 2014.

Cammett, Melani Claire. *The politics of non-state social welfare.* Cornell University Press, Ithaca, NY, 2014.

Cavatorta, F. and V. Durac. *Civil Society and Democratization in the Arab World.* Routledge, Abingdon, 2010.

Centro Porguguês de Fundações. *Guia das Fundações Portuguesas/Portuguese Foundations Guide,* 1996.

Chew, Celine. *Strategic Positioning in Voluntary and Charitable Organizations.* Routledge, Abingdon, 2009.

Christie, Ryerson. *Peacebuilding and NGOs: state-civil society interactions.* Routledge, Abingdon, 2013.

Claeyé, Frederick. *Managing Nongovernmental Organizations: Culture, Power and Resistance.* Routledge, Abingdon, 2014.

Cornforth, Chris and William A. Brown. *Nonprofit Governance: Innovative Perspectives and Approaches.* Routledge, Abingdon, 2013.

Create (Ed.). *The Irish Funding Handbook.* Dublin, 6th edn, 2007.

Cuninggim, Merrimon. *Private Money and Public Service: The Role of Foundations in American Society.* Herder & Herder, New York, 1972.

Davies, Thomas. *NGOs: A New History of Transnational Civil Society.* Oxford University Press, New York, 2014.

Directory of Social Change. *The Directory of Grant Making Trusts* (London, annually); *A Guide to the Major Trusts* (2 vols, London, annually); *The Guide to New Trusts* (London, annually).

Dogra, Nandita. *Representations of Global Poverty: Aid, Development and International NGOs.* IB Tauris, London, 2012.

Editions Ruyant. *GAFA—Guide Annuaire des Fondations et des Associations.* Cosne sur Loire, 2009.

Edwards, Michael. *Civil Society.* Polity, Cambridge, 3rd edn, 2014.

Edwards, Michael (Ed.). *The Oxford Handbook of Civil Society.* Oxford University Press USA, 2011.

Ellsworth, F. K. and J. Jumarda (Eds). *From Grantmaker to Leader: Emerging Strategies for Twenty-First Century Foundations.* John Wiley & Sons, Hoboken, NJ, 2003.

Enjolras, Bernard. *Voluntas: International Journal of Voluntary and Nonprofit Organizations* (official quarterly journal of the International Society for Third-Sector Research). Springer.

Europa Publications. *European Foundations and Grant-making NGOs.* London, 2004.

European Foundation Centre (EFC). *Selected Bibliography on Foundations and Corporate Funders in Europe* (1994); *European Foundation Fundaments* (1999); *Working With Foundations: Why and How?* (2001); *Foundations for Europe: Rethinking our Legal and Fiscal Environments* (2003); *Disaster Grantmaking: A Practical Guide for Foundations and Corporations* (2002); *Foundations in the European Union: Profiling Legal and Fiscal Environments* (2002); *Funding Vocational Training and Employment for People with Disabilities: Guidelines for Good Grantmaking Practice* (2002); *Foundation Facts and Figures across the EU* (2005); *Foundations' Legal and Fiscal Environments: Mapping the European Union of 27* (2007); *EFC Principles of Good Practice* (2007); *Comparative Map of the Foundation Sector in the EU* (2008); *Foundations in Europe Together: Be part of the bigger picture* (2011); *European Environmental Funding by European Foundations* (2011); *Comparative Highlights of Foundation Laws* (2011); *efc bookshelf* (quarterly newsletter, updating the bibliography); *EFFECT Magazine* (2 a year); other books, conference and meeting reports, and annual reports.

Fleishman, J. *The Foundation: A Great American Secret—How Private Wealth is Changing the World.* PublicAffairs, New York, 2007.

Foundation Center. Publications include: *The Foundation Directory* (annually); *Philanthropy News Digest* (weekly, by e-mail); *The Celebrity Foundation Directory; The Foundation Grants Index* (quarterly and annually); *Guide to US Foundations, their Trustees, Officers, and Donors; The Foundation 1000; Guide to Funding for International and Foreign Programs; Foundation Grants to Individuals; Foundation Giving; National Directory of Corporate Giving.*

Freeman, David F. and the Council on Foundations. *Handbook on Private Foundations.* Foundation Center, New York, 1991.

Fundación José María Aragón. *Primer Directorio de Fundaciones de la República Argentina.* Buenos Aires, 1980; *Guía de Becas de Postgraduado 1991–92.* Buenos Aires, 7th edn, 1991.

Fundación Arias para la Paz y el Progreso Humano. *Directorio de organizaciones para la promoción de la micro, pequeña y mediana empresa en Centroamérica.* San José, 2006.

Gabay, Clive. *Civil Society and Global Poverty: Hegemony, Inclusivity, Legitimacy.* Routledge, Abingdon, 2012.

Gale Cengage Learning. *Encyclopedia of Associations, International Organizations.* Detroit, MI, 54th edn, 2015.

Germain, R. and M. Kenny. *The Idea of Global Civil Society: Ethics and Politics in a Globalizing Era.* Routledge, Abingdon, 2006.

Glasius, M., D. Lewis and Hakan Seckinelgin (Eds). *Exploring Civil Society: Political and Cultural Contexts.* Routledge, Abingdon, 2004.

Hilton, Matthew. *A historical guide to NGOs in Britain: charities, civil society and the voluntary sector since 1945.* Palgrave Macmillan, Basingstoke, 2012.

Imagine Canada. *Canadian Directory to Foundations and Corporations.*

Information Today. *Annual Register of Grant Support.* Medford, NJ, 48th edn, 2015.

International Society for Third-Sector Research—ISTR. *Inside ISTR* (quarterly newsletter); *ISTR Report; Voluntas.*

James, H. (Ed.). *Civil Society, Religion and Global Governance.* Routledge, Abingdon, 2007.

Japan Foundation Center. *JFC Views* (in Japanese); *Directory of Grantmaking Foundations* (in Japanese).

Jegers, Marc. *Managerial Economics of Non-Profit Organizations.* Routledge, Abingdon, 2009.

Jobert, B. and B. Kohler-Koch (Eds). *Changing Images of Civil Society.* Routledge, Abingdon, 2008.

Joseph James A. (Ed.). *The Charitable Impulse: Wealth and Social Conscience in Communities and Cultures Outside the United States.* Foundation Center, New York, 1989.

Jung, Tobias, Susan Phillips and Jenny Harrow. *The Routledge Companion to Philanthropy.* Routledge, Abingdon, 2014.

Kaldor, Mary, Sabine Selchow and Henrietta L. Moore. (Eds). *Global Civil Society 2012: Ten Years of Critical Reflection.* Palgrave Macmillan, Basingstoke, 2012.

Kane, D., P. Bass and J. Heywood. *UK Civil Society Almanac 2012.* London, NCVO, 2014.

Keck, M. and K. Sikkink. *Activists Beyond Borders: Advocacy Networks in International Society.* University of Cornell Press, Ithaca, NY, 1998.

Kennisbank Filantropie. *Fondsenboek.* Uitgeversmaatschappij Walburg Pers, Zutphen, 2014.

Keohane, Georgia Levenson. *Social Entrepreneurship for the 21st Century: Innovation Across the Nonprofit, Private, and Public Sectors.* McGraw-Hill, 2013.

Lang, Sabine. *NGOs, civil society, and the public sphere.* Cambridge University Press, Cambridge, 2013.

Magat, Richard (Ed.). *An Agile Servant: Community Leadership by Community Foundations.* Foundation Center, New York, 1989.

Martin, Mike W. *Virtuous Giving: Philanthropy, Voluntary Service, and Caring.* Indiana University Press, Bloomington, IN, 1995.

Martin, Samuel A. *An Essential Grace: Funding Canada's Health Care, Education, Welfare, Religion and Culture.* McClelland and Stewart, Toronto, 1984.

Moran, Michael. *Private Foundations and Development Partnerships: American Philanthropy and Global Development Agendas.* Routledge, Abingdon, 2014.

Nagai, A., R. Lerner and R. Rothman (Eds). *Giving for Social Change: Foundations, Public Policy, and the American Political Agenda.* Praeger Publishers, Westport, CT, 1994.

O'Connell, Brian (Ed.). *America's Voluntary Spirit: A Book of Readings.* Foundation Center, New York, 1983.

Odendahl, Teresa, Elizabeth Boris and Arlene Daniels. *Working in Foundations: Career Patterns of Women and Men.* Foundation Center, New York, 1985.

Osborne, Stephen P. *The Third Sector in Europe: Prospects and Challenges.* Routledge, Abingdon, 2008.
The Third Sector in Europe. Routledge, Abingdon, 2011.

Palgrave Macmillan. *The Grants Register 2016: The Complete Guide to Postgraduate Funding Worldwide.* London, 34th edn, 2015.

Pétric, Boris-Mathieu. *Democracy at large: NGOs, political foundations, think tanks, and international organizations.* Palgrave Macmillan, New York, 2012.

Philanthropy Australia Inc. *Australian Philanthropy* (journal, 3 a year); *The Australian Directory of Philanthropy* (online).

Pifer, Alan. *Philanthropy in an Age of Transition.* Foundation Center, New York, 1984.

Pomey, Michel. *Traité des Fondations d'Utilité Publique.* Presse Universitaire de France, 1980.

Randel, Judith, Tony German and Deborah Ewing. *The Reality of Aid 2000* (7th edn). Routledge, Abingdon, 2013.

Roeger, Katie L., Amy S. Blackwood and Sarah L. Pettijohn. *The Nonprofit Almanac 2012.* Urban Institute Press, Washington, DC, 2012.

Routledge. *Journal of Civil Society* (journal, 3 a year). Routledge, Abingdon.

Sahoo, Sarbeswar. *Civil Society and Democratization in India: Institutions, Ideologies and Interests.* Routledge, Abingdon, 2013.

Salamon, Lester M. *Leverage for good: an introduction to the new frontiers of philanthropy and social investment.* Oxford University Press, Oxford, 2014.
New frontiers of philanthrophy: a guide to the new tools and actors reshaping global philanthropy and social investing. Oxford University Press, Oxford, 2014.
The Global Associational Revolution: The Rise of the Third Sector on the World Scene. Johns Hopkins University, Institute for Policy Studies, Baltimore, MD, 1993.

Salamon, Lester M. and Anheier, H. K. *The Emerging Nonprofit Sector: An Overview.* Manchester University Press, Manchester, 1996.

Salamon, Lester M. and H. K. Anheier. *The Emerging Sector: The Nonprofit Sector in Comparative Perspective: An Overview.* Johns Hopkins University, Institute for Policy Studies, Baltimore, MD, 1994.

Salamon, Lester M. and H. K. Anheier (Eds). *Defining the Nonprofit Sector: A Cross-National Analysis.* Manchester University Press, Manchester, 1997.

Salamon, Lester M., H. K. Anheier, S. Toepler, S. W. Sokolowski, R. List, et al. *Global Civil Society: Dimensions of the Nonprofit Sector.* Kumarian Press, 2006.

Salamon, Lester M., S. W. Sokolowski and R. List. *Global Civil Society: An Overview.* Johns Hopkins University, Institute for Policy Studies, Baltimore, MD, 2003.

Sanchez Salgado, Rosa. *Europeanizing civil society: how the EU shapes civil society organizations.* Palgrave Macmillan, Basingstoke, 2014.

Schoolhouse Partners. *Directory of Research Grants; Directory of Grants in the Humanities; Directory of Biomedical and Health Care Grants; Operating Grants for Nonprofit Organizations; Directory of Environmental Grants; Funding Sources for Faith-Based Programs.* Nashville, IN.

Schwittay, Anke. *New media and international development: representation and affect in microfinance.* Routledge, New York, 2015.

Siegel, Daniel and Jenny Yancey. *The Rebirth of Civil Society: The Development of the Nonprofit Sector in East Central Europe and the Role of Western Assistance.* Rockefeller Brothers Fund, New York, 1992.

Sievers, Bruce R. *Civil Society, Philanthropy, and the Fate of the Commons.* Tufts, 2010.

Simsa, Ruth, Michael Meyer and Christoph Badelt (Eds). *Handbuch der Nonprofit-Organisationen.* Schäffer-Poeschel Verlag, Stuttgart, 2013.

Sudetic, Chuck. *The Philanthropy of George Soros: Building Open Societies.* PublicAffairs, Perseus Books Group, New York, NY, 2011.

Sundar, Pushpa. *Business & Community: Evolution of Corporate Social Responsibility in India.* Sage Publications India, New Delhi, 2013.

Sundar, Pushpa. *Foreign Aid for Indian NGOs: Problem or Solution?* Routledge, Abingdon, 2009.

Thomas, Ralph Lingo. *Policies Underlying Corporate Giving.* Prentice-Hall, Inc, Englewood Cliffs, NJ, 1966.

Ural, Engin (Ed.). *Foundations in Turkey.* Development Foundation of Turkey, Ankara, 1978.

Weaver, Warren. *U.S. Philanthropic Foundations: Their History, Structure, Management and Record.* Harper & Row, New York, 1967.

Weiss, Thomas and Rorden Wilkinson. *International organization and global governance.* Routledge, London; New York, 2014.

PART THREE

Indexes

Index of Foundations

Index of Main Activities

FOUNDATION CENTRES AND CO-ORDINATING BODIES

Academy for the Development of Philanthropy in Poland, Poland, 310

ACRI—Associazione di Fondazioni e di Casse di Risparmio Spa, Italy, 219

ADI—Association for Democratic Initiatives, Macedonia (FYR), 263

AF—Association of Foundations, Philippines, 306

Africa Grantmakers' Affinity Group—AGAG, USA, 459

AGAG—Africa Grantmakers' Affinity Group, USA, 459

Agency for the Non-profit Sector, Czech Republic, 112

AGNES—Vzdělávací Organizace, Czech Republic, 112

Akademia Rozwoju Filantropii w Polsce, Poland, 310

AKNS—Asociácia komunitných nadácií Slovenska, Slovakia, 334

Albanian Civil Society Foundation, Albania, 25

ALIDE—Asociación Latinoamericana de Instituciones Financieras para el Desarrollo, Peru, 304

Allavida—Alliances for Voluntary Initiatives and Development, Kenya, 248

Alliances for Voluntary Initiatives and Development—Allavida, Kenya, 248

American Council for Voluntary International Action—InterAction, USA, 460

ANGOC—Asian NGO Coalition for Agrarian Reform and Rural Development, Philippines, 306

ANND—Arab NGO Network for Development, Lebanon, 257

AsiaDHRRA—Asian Partnership for the Development of Human Resources in Rural Asia, Philippines, 306

Asian NGO Coalition for Agrarian Reform and Rural Development—ANGOC, Philippines, 306

Asian Partnership for the Development of Human Resources in Rural Asia—AsiaDHRRA, Philippines, 306

Asian Philanthropy Advisory Network, USA, 460

Asociace komunitních nadací v České, Czech Republic, 112

Asociácia komunitných nadácií Slovenska—AKNS, Slovakia, 334

Asociación Española de Fundaciones, Spain, 344

Asociación Latinoamericana de Instituciones Financieras para el Desarrollo—ALIDE, Peru, 304

Asociación Latinoamericana de Organizaciones de Promoción al Desarrollo—ALOP, Mexico, 267

Asociación Nacional de Organizaciones Sociedad Civil, Venezuela, 564

Assembly of Belarusian Pro-democratic Non-governmental Organizations, Belarus, 54

Association of Charitable Foundations, UK, 401

Association for Civil Society Development—SMART, Croatia, 109

Association of Community Foundations in Bulgaria, Bulgaria, 75

Association for Democratic Initiatives—ADI, Macedonia (FYR), 263

Association des Fondations Donatrices Suisses, Switzerland, 366

Association of Foundations in the Netherlands, Netherlands, 277

Association of German Foundations, Germany, 159

Association of Grantmaking Foundations in Switzerland, Switzerland, 366

Association of Italian Foundations and Savings Banks, Italy, 219

Association of Medical Research Charities—AMRC, UK, 401

Association of Non-Governmental Organizations in The Gambia—TANGO, Gambia, 156

Association of Slovakian Community Foundations, Slovakia, 334

Association of Voluntary Agencies for Rural Development—AVARD, India, 200

Associazione di Fondazioni e di Casse di Risparmio Spa—ACRI, Italy, 219

Australian Association of Philanthropy, Australia, 34

Autonómia Alapítvány, Hungary, 197

Autonómia Foundation, Hungary, 197

Auxilia Foundation, Czech Republic, 112

AVARD—Association of Voluntary Agencies for Rural Development, India, 200

AVINA Foundation, Panama, 302

BCAF—Bulgarian Charities Aid Foundation, Bulgaria, 75

Belgian Foundation Network, Belgium, 55

Black Sea NGO Network—BSNN, Bulgaria, 75

BOCONGO—Botswana Council of NGOs, Botswana, 69

Botswana Council of Non-Governmental Organisations—BOCONGO, Botswana, 69

Bulgarian Donors' Forum, Bulgaria, 75

Bundesverband Deutscher Stiftungen eV, Germany, 159

CAF America, USA, 459

CAF—Charities Aid Foundation, UK, 401

CAF—Charities Aid Foundation Australia, Australia, 34

CAF India, India, 200

CAF Russia—Charities Aid Foundation Russia, Russian Federation, 323

CAF South-East Asia, Singapore, 333

CAF Southern Africa, South Africa, 338

Canadian Centre for Philanthropy, Canada, 80

Canadian Co-operative Association, Canada, 80

Canadian Council for International Co-operation—CCIC/Conseil Canadien pour la Coopération Internationale—CCCI, Canada, 80

Caribbean Policy Development Centre, Barbados, 53

CCCI—Conseil Canadien pour la Coopération Internationale, Canada, 80

CCIC—Canadian Council for International Co-operation, Canada, 80

CDCS—Centre for Development of Civil Society, Armenia, 33

CEAAL—Consejo de Educación Popular de América Latina y el Caribe, Panama, 302

Centar za razvoj neprofitnih organizacija—CERANEO, Croatia, 109

Centar za Razvoj Nevladinih Organizacija—CRNVO, Montenegro, 272

Center for Training and Consultancy, Georgia, 157

CENTRAS—Assistance Centre for NGOs, Romania, 321

Centre for Advancement of Philanthropy—CAP, India, 200

Centre for Civil Society, India, 200

Centre for the Development of Civil Society—CDCS, Armenia, 33

Centre for the Development of Non-governmental Organizations, Montenegro, 272

Centre for Development of Non-profit Organizations, Croatia, 109

Centre for Development of Non-Profit Sector, Serbia, 331

Centre Français des Fondations—CFF, France, 135

Centre for the Information Service, Co-operation and Development of NGOs, Slovenia, 337

Centre for Philanthropy, Ukraine, 398

Centre for Philanthropy and Social Responsibility—Ufadhili, Kenya, 248

Centre for Promotion and Development of Civil Initiatives—OPUS, Poland, 310

Centro Mexicano para la Filantropía—CEMEFI, Mexico, 267

Centro Português de Fundações—CPF, Portugal, 315

Centrul Naţional de Asistenţă şi Informare a Organizaţiilor Neguvernamentale din Republica Moldova, Moldova, 269

CERANEO—Centar za razvoj neprofitnih organizacija, Croatia, 109

CERES—Ecuadorean Consortium for Social Responsibility, Ecuador, 124

Česká rada sociálních slueb—CRSS, Czech Republic, 112

Charities Advisory Trust, UK, 401

Charities Aid Foundation of America, USA, 459

Charities Aid Foundation Bulgaria, Bulgaria, 75

Charities Aid Foundation—CAF, UK, 401

China Foundation Center, China (People's Republic), 102

Civic Initiatives, Serbia, 331

Civil Society Development Centre, Turkey, 392

Civil Society Development Foundation, Romania, 321

CIVITAS Foundation for Civil Society, Romania, 321

CLADEM—Comité de América Latina y el Caribe para la Defensa de los Derechos de la Mujer, Peru, 304

CNVOS—Zavod Center za Informiranje, Sodelovanje in Razvoj Nevladnih Organizacije, Slovenia, 337

Co-operation Committee for Cambodia, Cambodia, 79

Coalition of National Voluntary Organizations, Canada, 80

Comité de América Latina y el Caribe para la Defensa de los Derechos de la Mujer—CLADEM, Peru, 304

Community Foundation Partnership, Russian Federation, 323

Community Foundations of Canada, Canada, 80

Community Foundations of Florida, USA, 459

Community Foundations Initiative, Germany, 159

AID TO LESS-DEVELOPED COUNTRIES

ARTS AND HUMANITIES

CONSERVATION AND THE ENVIRONMENT

ECONOMIC AFFAIRS

EDUCATION

INTERNATIONAL AFFAIRS

LAW, CIVIL SOCIETY AND HUMAN RIGHTS

SCIENCE AND TECHNOLOGY

SOCIAL WELFARE

Index by Area of Activity

Note: organizations will appear either in the All Regions index or in one or more of the regions listed below. All Regions means an organization is active in every region of the world. If an organization is listed under All Regions, it will not appear under any other region heading.

ALL REGIONS

30 Million Friends Foundation, France, 150
A. S. Hornby Educational Trust, UK, 424
AAUW—American Association of University Women Educational Foundation, USA, 464
Accademia Musicale Chigiana, Italy, 219
ACDI/VOCA, USA, 461
ACLS—American Council of Learned Societies, USA, 464
Action d'Urgence Internationale—AUI, France, 136
ActionAid, South Africa, 339
Adenauer (Konrad) Stiftung eV, Germany, 160
Adessium Foundation, Netherlands, 277
ADL—Anti-Defamation League of B'nai B'rith, USA, 469
ADRA—Adventist Development and Relief Agency International, USA, 461
Adventist Development and Relief Agency International—ADRA, USA, 461
Aga Khan Development Network—AKDN, Switzerland, 366
Aga Khan Foundation (UK)—AKF, UK, 404
Aga Khan Trust for Culture—AKTC, Switzerland, 367
Agence Internationale pour le Développement Fédération—AIDE, France, 135
AIC—Association Internationale des Charités, Belgium, 57
Aid to the Church in Need—ACN, Germany, 160
Air Pollution and Climate Secretariat—AirClim, Sweden, 358
AirClim—Air Pollution and Climate Secretariat, Sweden, 358
Albert Einstein Institution, USA, 488
Alcoa Foundation, USA, 463
Alessio Pezcoller Foundation, Italy, 227
Alexander von Humboldt Foundation, Germany, 171
Alexander von Humboldt Stiftung, Germany, 171
Alexander S. Onassis Public Benefit Foundation, Greece, 189
Alfred Friendly Press Partners, USA, 495
Alfried Krupp von Bohlen und Halbach Foundation, Germany, 174
Alfried Krupp von Bohlen und Halbach-Stiftung, Germany, 174
All Saints Educational Trust, UK, 404
Alliance Israélite Universelle, France, 137
Alliance Sud—Swiss Alliance of Development Organisations, Switzerland, 365
The Ambrose Monell Foundation, USA, 526
American Association of University Women Educational Foundation—AAUW, USA, 464
American Council of Learned Societies—ACLS, USA, 464
American Express Foundation, USA, 465
American Health Assistance Foundation, USA, 474
American Jewish Joint Distribution Committee—JDC, USA, 466

American Philosophical Society—APS, USA, 467
American Refugee Committee—ARC, USA, 467
AmeriCares Foundation, Inc, USA, 468
amfAR—The Foundation for AIDS Research, USA, 468
AMI—Fundação Assistência Médica International, Portugal, 315
Amigos de la Tierra, Netherlands, 280
Les Amis de la Terre, Netherlands, 280
Amnesty International, UK, 404
Dell'Amore (Giordano) Foundation, Italy, 224
AMURT—Ananda Marga Universal Relief Team, USA, 469
Ananda Marga Universal Relief Team—AMURT, USA, 469
Andrews Charitable Trust—ACT, UK, 405
Anne Frank-Fonds, Switzerland, 372
Anne Frank Foundation, Netherlands, 280
Anne Frank Fund, Switzerland, 372
Anne Frank Stichting, Netherlands, 280
Anti-Defamation League of B'nai B'rith—ADL, USA, 469
Anti-Slavery International, UK, 405
APC—Association for Progressive Communications, South Africa, 338
ARC—American Refugee Committee, USA, 467
Arcus Foundation, USA, 469
Arthur S. DeMoss Foundation, USA, 484
Asahi Glass Foundation, Japan, 233
Asia Crime Prevention Foundation—ACPF, Japan, 234
Association International Cancer Research, UK, 457
Association Internationale des Charités—AIC, Belgium, 57
Association for Progressive Communications—APC, South Africa, 338
Association for the Study of the World Refugee Problem, Germany, 168
AT&T Foundation, USA, 472
Atlas Economic Research Foundation, USA, 471
Atlas Network, USA, 471
ATSE—Australian Academy of Technological Sciences and Engineering, Australia, 36
Australian Academy of Technological Sciences and Engineering—ATSE, Australia, 36
Australian Council for International Development, Australia, 36
Aventis Foundation, Germany, 161
Aviation Sans Frontières—ASF, France, 137
Aviation Without Borders, France, 137
Bagnoud (François-Xavier) Association, USA, 495
Balzan Fonds, Internationale Stiftung, Switzerland, 374
Baptist World Aid—BWAid, USA, 472
Beinum (Eduard Van) Stichting, Netherlands, 278
Bernadottes (Folke) Minnesfond, Sweden, 358
Bernard van Leer Foundation, Netherlands, 282
Bertrand Russell Peace Foundation—BRPF, UK, 447
Better World Campaign—BWC, USA, 473

Better World Fund, USA, 473
Big Lottery Fund, UK, 408
Bill & Melinda Gates Foundation, USA, 495
BirdLife International, UK, 408
Bischöfliches Hilfswerk Misereor eV, Germany, 162
BMW Foundation Herbert Quandt, Germany, 162
BMW Stiftung Herbert Quandt, Germany, 162
BNP Paribas Foundation, France, 140
The Body Shop Foundation, UK, 409
Boehringer Ingelheim Fonds–Stiftung für medizinische Grundlagenforschung, Germany, 162
Böll (Heinrich) Stiftung, Germany, 162
Born Free Foundation Limited, UK, 409
Brandt (Bundeskanzler Willy), Stiftung, Germany, 163
BrightFocus Foundation, USA, 474
Brigitte Bardot Foundation, France, 140
Bristol-Myers Squibb Foundation, USA, 474
British Academy, UK, 410
The British Council, UK, 410
British Institute of International and Comparative Law, UK, 411
British Red Cross, UK, 411
The Brush Foundation, USA, 475
Bundeskanzler-Willy-Brandt-Stiftung, Germany, 163
Business Institute Foundation, Spain, 350
C. G. Jung-Institut Zürich, Switzerland, 376
CAB International, UK, 411
CABI, UK, 411
CAFOD—Catholic Agency for Overseas Development, UK, 411
Calouste Gulbenkian Foundation, Portugal, 316
Cambridge Commonwealth, European and International Trust, UK, 412
Canada World Youth/Jeunesse Canada Monde, Canada, 83
Caritas de France—Secours Catholique, France, 154
Caritas Internationalis—CI, Vatican City, 563
Carnegie Endowment for International Peace, USA, 476
Carnegie Foundation, Wateler Fund, Netherlands, 278
Carnegie-Stichting, Watelerfonds, Netherlands, 278
Cassel (Sir Ernest) Educational Trust, UK, 412
Caterpillar Foundation, USA, 477
Catholic Agency for Overseas Development—CAFOD, UK, 411
Catholic Fund for Overseas Development—CAFOD, UK, 411
Catholic Help—Caritas France, France, 154
CBM, Germany, 163
CCKF—Chiang Ching-Kuo Foundation for International Scholarly Exchange, Taiwan, 385
CEDPA—Centre for Development and Population Activities, USA, 478
Center for Civic Education, USA, 481

AFRICA SOUTH OF THE SAHARA

CENTRAL AND SOUTH-EASTERN EUROPE

EAST AND SOUTH-EAST ASIA

EASTERN EUROPE AND THE REPUBLICS OF CENTRAL ASIA

MIDDLE EAST AND NORTH AFRICA

SOUTH ASIA

WESTERN EUROPE